Routledge Companion to Sports History

The field of sports history is no longer a fledgling area of study. There is a great vitality in the field and it has matured dramatically over the past decade. Reflecting changes to traditional approaches, sports historians need now to engage with contemporary debates about history, to be encouraged to position themselves and their methodologies in relation to current epistemological issues, and to promote the importance of reflecting on the literary or poetic dimensions of producing history. These contemporary developments, along with a wealth of international research from a range of theoretical perspectives, provide the backdrop to the new *Routledge Companion to Sports History*.

This book provides a comprehensive guide to the international field of sports history as it has developed as an academic area of study. Readers are guided through the development of the field across a range of thematic and geographical contexts and are introduced to the latest cutting edge approaches within the field. Including contributions from many of the world's leading sports historians, the *Routledge Companion to Sports History* is the most important single volume for researchers and students in, and entering, the sports history field. It is an essential guide to contemporary research themes, to new ways of doing sports history, and to the theoretical and methodological foundations of this most fascinating of subjects.

S.W. Pope is Adjunct Professor of the School of Recreation, Health, and Tourism in the Affiliated Faculty, Academy of International Sport, George Mason University, USA.

John Nauright is Director of the Academy of International Sport and Professor in the School of Recreation, Health, and Tourism at George Mason University, USA. He is also Visiting Professor of Cultural Studies at the University of the West Indies, Cave Hill in Barbados.

Routledge Companion to Sports History

Edited by
S.W. Pope and John Nauright

LONDON AND NEW YORK

First published 2010 by Routledge
2 Park Square, Milton Park, Abingdon, Oxon OX14 4RN

Simultaneously published in the USA and Canada
by Routledge
711 Third Avenue, New York, NY 10017

This Paperback edition published 2012 by Routledge.

Routledge is an imprint of the Taylor & Francis Group, an informa business

British Library Cataloguing in Publication Data
A catalogue record for this book is available from the British Library

Library of Congress in Publication Data
  Routledge companion to sports history / edited by John Nauright and S. W. Pope.
  p. cm.
  1. Sports–History. I. Pope, S. W., 1962- II. Nauright, John, 1962-
  GV571.R68 2012
  796–dc23
                                                    2011032317

ISBN 978-0-415-77339-3 (hbk)
ISBN 978-0-415-50194-1 (pbk)
ISBN 978-0-203-88541-3 (ebk)

Typeset in Bembo
by Taylor & Francis Books

Contributors

Daryl Adair, University of Canberra, Australia

Mahfoud Amara, Loughborough University, UK

William J. Baker, University of Maine, USA

Susan J. Bandy, Semmelweis University, Hungary

Douglas Booth, University of Waikato, New Zealand

Alan Gregor Cobley, University of the West Indies, Barbados

Mark Dyreson, Penn State University, USA

Henning Eichberg, Syddansk Universitet, Denmark

Gerald R. Gems, North Central College, USA

Matti Goksøyr, Norwegian School of Sport Science, Norway

David Hassan, University of Ulster, UK

Fan Hong, University College Cork, Ireland

Colin Howell, St Mary's University, Canada

Barbara Keys, University of Melbourne, Australia

Arnd Krüger, Georg-August-Universität Göttingen, Germany

Donald G. Kyle, University of Texas at Arlington, USA

Daryl Leeworthy, Oriel College, Oxford, UK

Richard L. Light, Univesity of Sydney, Australia

Charles Little, London Metropolitan University, UK

Malcolm MacLean, University of Gloucestershire, UK

Dominic Malcolm, University of Loughborough, UK

Louise Mansfield, Canterbury Christ Church University, UK

Richard V. McGehee, Concordia University, USA

Verner Møller, Aarhus University, Denmark

Niels Kayser Nielson, Aarhus University, Denmark

Philip O'Kane, University of Ulster, UK

Gary Osmond, University of Queensland, Australia

Murray Phillips, University of Queensland, Australia

Dilwyn Porter, De Montfort University, UK

Robert E. Rinehart, The University of Waikato, New Zealand

James Riordan, University of Surrey, UK

Ian Ritchie, Brock University, Canada

Peter N. Stearns, George Mason University, USA

Ruud Stokvis, University of Amsterdam, Netherlands

Amanda N. Schweinbenz, Laurentian University, Canada

Thierry Terret, Université Lyon 1, France

Cesar R. Torres, The State University of New York, USA

Chris Valiotis, University of New South Wales, Australia

Marek Waic, Charles University in Prague, Czech Republic

David K. Wiggins, George Mason University, USA

Stefan Zwicker, Die Johannes Gutenberg-Universität, Germany

Foreword

Peter N. Stearns

A companion in a relatively new field of inquiry – and the serious history of sports certainly qualifies here – is a major achievement. Sports history, as more than an antiquarian account of some past team or game, is forty years old at most. Clearly, and legitimately, it has inspired a major group of scholars, eager to find out what sports were like in the past and how the past informs the present. The result, among other things, is the possibility of generating a comprehensive treatment like this book, with an impressive array of specific topics and genuinely global coverage. The result is also a testimony to how much we have learned about sports and their social role, and a foundation as well for further teaching and research alike.

A companion in a relatively new field of inquiry is also, of course, an invitation to note how much we don't know, at least in any readily available way. It's no insult to the high quality of the articles in this venture, or the truly impressive range of topics that are included, to comment that there's a great deal still to be done. Indeed, to the extent that a companion not only provides current data and analysis, but also identifies (either explicitly or implicitly) further areas to explore, it does the whole field an extra service. And there's abundant inspiration here for additional effort.

A vital task in any new subject area is to establish its validity and significance. Sports history has always risked being dismissed as trivial, compared to the real stuff of life which (some historians still absurdly argue) is wars, kings and presidents. Apparently in some countries, like Australia, this baffling mood still persists, despite the obvious importance of the role sports plays in everyday life, business and politics. Modern sports history emerged from the more general rise of social history, which in turn insisted on the need to explore the experiences of various groups of people, and not just elites, and the various facets of everyday life, and not just politics or high ideas, on grounds that only through this expansion would we get a real grasp of the past and a basis for using historical analysis to better understand the present. Sports history in this sense emerges from the same important impulses that have established fields like family history, the history of crime, or the history of work.

Articles in this collection make it abundantly clear, not only that we can access a host of aspects of sports history, but that the topic must be tackled as part of an array of familiar and self-evident historical topics, from gender to business to international relations. Inclusion of connections to religion and to science is a brilliant stroke. It's clear also that the now considerable ranks of sports historians have legitimized their work in another sense, by handling a variety of theoretical issues and contributing to theory in turn, and by taking issues of source materials and analytical categories (like the familiar trilogy of race, class and gender) very seriously indeed. It's legitimate to ask sports historians why one should know their work independent of a specific interest in sports, and it's evident that they can respond quite adequately.

Of course, no one wishes to deprive an interested sports fan of opportunities to follow up a particular passion. By avoiding sport-by-sport summaries, the editors obviously seek to avoid the most purely descriptive approach to sports history, whether it is a list of boxing champions or the story of golf. But there's a great deal of relevant information about these more specific topics in the articles and also in suggestions for further reading (this last a tremendous service to students and scholars of all sorts).

But the really big point in sports history is to help us figure out why sports have become so important in so many modern societies, in serving so many different functions and rousing such obvious, and often highly entertaining, passions. Here, obviously, a host of articles in this volume provide vital explanatory cues. Sports were part of the imperialist enterprise of the 19th century. In Europe and the United States, sports connected to images of virility that also applied to empire, and of course the imperialists proudly took their sports with them to their new domains. But sports also provided channels for subtle resistance to imperialism. Colonial peoples could maintain some of their traditional sports as a means of continued identity – the discussion of Latin America offers some particularly rich cues here. Even more commonly, however, they could master sports the Westerners brought in and, surprisingly quickly, often beat the Westerners at their own game. The Indian football triumph over a British team in 1911 is an obvious case in point, a source of burgeoning national pride; so, at a lower key, was a victory of a Japanese schoolboy baseball team in the 1890s over a group of American sailors. Modern sports, in other words, have served not only varied but sometimes contradictory purposes. This is one reason, surely, that sports have become such an important part of many people's identities – national but also local – at a time when many traditional sources of loyalty and community were under challenge.

The varied services of sports go well beyond nationalism, however, and this is where sports have increasingly commanded the attention of social and cultural historians, beyond specialists in particular geographic areas. Slightly below the level of the most formal theory, for example, scholars in social and cultural history spent some time trying to figure out whether modern sports gain momentum by providing alternatives to the intensities of modern work, or whether they served rather as a support system. From the late 19th century onward, sports became part of that novel and characteristic modern insistence that waking hours of the day be divided between a work period and a period of leisure or recreation with sports playing a vital role in shaping the latter. But again, what was leisure for: to provide experiences different from work, or to support work in additional ways? On the alternative side, experts pointed to ways in which sports venues, like baseball stadiums or football fields, provided visual contrasts to factories and offices, allowing a sense of contact if not with nature at least with groomed greenery. But against this, other sports history specialists noted how the introduction of formal, regular rules resembled what was happening in the workplace – arguing that the new service of umpires or referees could be compared to what foremen did on the shop floor. Similarly, injunctions for speed and record keeping, such obvious parts of most modern sports, helped connect people to attributes sought on the job as well. The role of sports in education, formal and informal, also calls attention to ways in which governments sought to use sports to help train in qualities that would be useful to work as well as military life, including team work itself. In fact, of course, modern sports do both: they provide different experiences and outlets that contrast with normal work life, helping many people endure this life, but they also school in modern ways. Here again is a key source of the deep meanings sports have to many modern people.

Indeed, sports history sits on some crucial frontiers in the effort to understand the emergence of modern industrial societies. The inquiries continue the process of situating sports history in a set of wider topics, some of them less familiar than imperialism or business development but arguably as important. They also contribute directly to the analysis of change and continuities in sports themselves.

Connections between sports history and explorations of changing patterns of modern emotions and sexuality, for example, deserve emphasis. We already know some of the relationships involved, but there's more to be done. In Western society, at least, modern sports were initially urged as something of an alternative to rampant sexuality, a form of salutary discipline amid great concerns that youth, particularly male youth, might go astray. Older beliefs, for example that male orgasm was equivalent to the loss of 40 ounces of blood, contributed to widespread efforts by coaches to make sure that athletes restrained themselves before a match. Over time, of course, the heightened valuation of recreational sex and better knowledge of biology changed these formulas, but the process deserves further attention. In Western society also, the early 20th century saw heightened concerns about homosexuality, with important constraints placed on same-sex, particularly male, friendships and physical contact as a result. But as many observers have noted, sports provided a bit of a legitimate exception, with male embraces, for example, contrasting with acceptable patterns in virtually every other aspect of life.

Some of the same tension inhabits the role of sports in evolving emotional standards. Here too, modern sports can dramatize emotions that are increasingly reproved in normal life. Anger is the obvious case in point. Strenuous efforts were devoted to inhibiting anger at work in the United States, from the 1920s onward, with both managers and human resources authorities trained to point workers away from anger or to emphasize their immaturity if the emotion persisted; "anger management" programs were one outcome of this new emphasis. But in sports, certain amounts of anger could be directly or symbolically represented, in ways that might provide a sense of outlets not only for athletes themselves, but for many spectators. A particularly charming setting involved the baseball manager and the umpire, face to face in apparently intense rage after a bad call, a posture that ordinary people in ordinary life could not get by with but which they clearly enjoyed watching. Correspondingly, many coaches used anger and ridicule as motivators in ways that were discouraged, even banned in normal classrooms. At the same time, however, sports did not provide emotional constants, and significant shifts within sports, in terms of allowable emotions and emotionally-charged behaviors, also form an important part of the overall topic. The growth of more demonstrative celebrations in athletics, and efforts to rein them in, form an interesting subset of a larger history of exuberance and braggadocio in modern societies.

The relationship between sports and age categories is another vital topic, open to further exploration. Age-cohort history has declined a bit in social history since a great interest in youth, and some in old age, in the 1960s and 1970s. But there's a significant revival of work on childhood, on as global a basis as possible. Sports history, particularly as it attaches to school activities or to broader socializations in masculinity or femininity (or more contemporary alternatives), obviously has a great role to play here. Figuring out how children acquire sports knowledge and how this helps them relate to schools, to peers, and to adults including parents is a vital research area, under way but incomplete. It would also be good to think about other age groups including, as later age becomes more prominent demographically and economically and regains a place in historical research, to see some newer work on the role of participant and spectator sports in different phases of adulthood.

In these respects and many others, sports history figures centrally in the larger project of expanding our understanding of what the past contains and using this expansion, in turn, both to see how current patterns depart from or maintain earlier patterns and exploring the basic meanings of changes and continuities alike. History helps us see, in sports as in other topics, how many taken-for-granted aspects of our own lives – such as the tremendous amount of time and money athletics consumes, and the prestige athletes command – are actually historical products, not inevitable or divinely-appointed but caused by human agents and evolving human needs.

There are, of course, some additional challenges, beyond the basic invitation to continue to explore new aspects and connections of sports history – including the many avenues suggested by the preceding essays in this volume.

Interdisciplinary linkage is an obvious issue. Sports historians have generated fundamental findings and great excitement, but they do not always connect well with other disciplines that deal with sports. Some productive interplay has occurred, particularly with sociology, around issues such as class and race but also larger interpretations of the meanings of developments like mass spectatorship. From the historians' standpoint, given the insistence on the importance of the changing role of sports in modern society, persuading more scholars in non-historical fields of the importance of incorporating developments over time, even if the past for its own sake is not of interest, remains a key task.

The elaborate connections between sports history and the exploration of modernity form another area of challenge. On the one hand, the linkage is both justifiable and desirable. It's abundantly clear that sports have changed a lot over the past two centuries (less, in cases like China), in ways that connect intimately with all sorts of major historical developments, and that the role of sports has been transformed as well. So we need a lot of modern historical attention, and it pays off as well in helping to explain current patterns and issues through an understanding of recent historical evolution. But history, even modern history, depends as well on a grasp of where the modern has come from – where it builds on earlier patterns and where it has undergone major departures. Here, clearly, sports historians have some work cut out for them. We know the hallowed place of certain sports in the classical Mediterranean – Greece and Rome – but we're much vaguer on origins in other major regions and there are considerable gaps, even in Western history, between classical celebrations and the advent of the modern. We actually know, of course, that many of the games that would rise to ascendancy in the 19th century, like soccer football, admittedly becoming substantially transformed in the process, originated in village sports in the Middle Ages, but the overall place of sports in pre-modern settings and the connections between earlier patterns and later, modern outcroppings need a lot of work still. Even spectatorship warrants attention, as we think back on the village festival crowds, admittedly a few hundred strong at most, that would gather around village games and wonder about their contrasts and links to the more-studied modern spectator.

Perhaps the most general invitation, which would richly apply to societies in Asia, Africa and Latin America perhaps even more than to the West, involves figuring out how sports traditions worked out before the advent of modern global contacts and more recent sports developments affected the unfolding of recent patterns themselves. It's clear for example that in Latin America a concerted effort has helped preserve some traditional sports or amalgams in which they play a role; the same applies to Japan. But an active sense of how pre-modern patterns inform distinctive approaches even to globally standard sports probably involves a richer sense of the earlier history than we have yet developed. It's true of course that different societies placed sports in categories of varying prominence before modern times (indeed, the same is true today, as differential national investments in Olympic performance attest even among the various major regions of Asia); this means that records for earlier periods vary tremendously, as the coverage of China for example suggests. Still, social and cultural historians generally have found that, when a topic is defined as important, researchers can prove fairly imaginative in uncovering new sources and reexamining old ones, so the idea that there's a chronological challenge that should still be met is not unreasonable.

Finally, geographical range is a key issue in any new historical field, and sports history, though not at all uniquely, clearly shares this problem with a vengeance. In many branches of social and cultural history, relatively novel topics have first developed in Western contexts, with a focus on the United States, Britain, France and a few other settings. The history of childhood, for example, is only now opening to serious work outside the West, with really significant work on China: increasing pilot efforts on places like Latin America, but a distressing number of continuing voids. Sports history, in one sense, has moved ahead more smartly, and this project indicates how sports historians realize the global dimensions of their topics and how eager they are to bring in an appropriate variety of world regions. The fact that modern sports have important commonalities, based in part on Western influence and the colonial experience, facilitates this wider scope. There's much to build on already. Still, some areas are not as well served as is desirable.

And the next phase of a global approach needs additional attention to another category of analysis without much question, as is true for almost all branches of the newer historical inquiries: the reference here is to the challenge of comparison. As social historians have tried to move beyond Western confines with their expanded list of topics, they have had to skate between two extremes, and their levels of success have varied. The first extreme involves an assumption that each region has its own unique social experience, even in the modern era, so that efforts to point to general patterns smack of Western bias or neo-imperialism; each story is unique. The other extreme assumes that thanks to imperialism, Western-dominated globalization and the sheer intricacy of modern global contacts, a number of key patterns are in fact shared across political and cultural boundaries. Sports history, again, is relatively far along in geographical sophistication, despite the nagging gaps. But because some of the basic modern sports have roused such wide interest and participation, there may be a temptation to overemphasize commonalities, the shared modern contours. Yet, as several of the preceding articles point out, even common sports, like football or baseball, often receive distinctive regional twists, reflecting the way the sport arrived and the potential impact of earlier sports traditions as well. We need to know more about these twists, without losing sight of shared elements. As well, given the extent to which sports serve different functions, national identities as well as cosmopolitanism, resistance as well as imitation, significant if subtle differences are to be expected. Indeed a standard finding, when social history and world history combine, is to expect a syncretic response when the patterns of one society are brought to bear on another – that is, a response that combines some outright imitation with the interweaving of distinctive traditions and regional needs. Teasing out these variants must be part of the coming agenda for sports history, and this means not only more work on certain regions but a more active effort at comparison.

One of the defining features of good sports history, along with its relationship with kindred disciplines and its deep interest in linking to other historical facets, involves its commitment to high-level analysis. Precisely because sports history can drift into entertaining but frankly narrow narratives, about this athletic heroine or that set of scoring records, sports historians have taken pains to make sure they seek real social and cultural meaning in their topics. This is why, at its best, sports history illuminates so many aspects of the modern life experience, as scholars try to figure out why sports developed as they did and what place they hold in the lives of participants and spectators alike. The future for sports history invites extensions of this analytical commitment, to explore more deeply the relationship between pre-modern experiences and those of the past century or century and a half and to venture more ambitious comparisons within partially shared frameworks. Modern sports provide both a cosmopolitan outreach and some very intimate regional languages around particular teams and particular passions. Here, indeed, is another example of the significance but also the complexity of the role of sports in modern global life.

Acknowledgements

This book is dedicated to several pioneers of sports history globally, to those who have continued to expand the horizons of sports history and most especially to those whose work inspired and mentored us in the field of sports history, namely: William Baker, Richard Cashman, Richard Gruneau, Stephen Hardy, Richard Holt, Tony Mangan, Alan Metcalfe, Donald Mrozek, Roberta Park, Steven Riess, Brian Stoddart, Wray Vamplew and Patricia Vertinsky.

In addition to these pioneers within sports history we wish to acknowledge others whose scholarship inspired our work (as well as that of numerous other sports historians): Clifford Geertz, Eric Hobsbawm, C.L.R. James, E.P. Thompson, Charles van Onselen, Raymond Williams and William Appleman Williams.

Introduction

S.W. Pope and John Nauright

We are delighted to have had the opportunity to co-edit this volume of work on the 'state of play' in sports history around the world. Routledge is to be commended for adding sports history to their well-established list of 'Handbooks' (although we preferred 'Companion'), which is evidence of the vibrancy of the field and testament to the work of the numerous scholars featured in this volume (as well as the countless others whose work has expanded the international sub-discipline of sports history). In this brief, introductory essay, our discussion parallels the structure of the *Companion* – we consider some general aspects of the rise of sports history as a recognized field of academic study and prominent themes within the literature, and then reflect upon the international development of sports history.[1]

All scholarly attempts to capture the 'totality' of a given field of academic study are invariably partial and incomplete. This book is no different. While our aim in developing this book was to be as comprehensive as possible, some gaps remain due to contributors pulling out along the way, not being able to submit their commissioned pieces on time or simply not being able to adequately cover the desired topic at all. The end result of the *Companion* is, though, a broad representation of the major themes that have focused the minds of sports historians around the globe, as well as the areas where scholarship has developed rapidly in recent years. Not every theoretical or methodological issue appears here, nor does every country with a substantial history (or historiographical tradition) of sport. Again, several prominent contributors were, unfortunately, unable to deliver for this collection. Nevertheless, our purpose has been fundamentally achieved in systematically presenting the field of sports history that will be useful to students and scholars of sports history wherever they may live.

Sports history: looking backward

Sports history is no longer an academic curiosity. Historians of sport are no longer forced to advance elaborate justifications for their chosen field of study or couch their research within the history of 'popular culture' or 'leisure', or as a novel way of engaging key issues within the historical profession (as was the case 20 or 30 years ago). The *Companion* provides abundant evidence of this 'coming of age' story whereby a fledgling topical area that had been embraced by only a relative handful of scholars prior to the early 1970s, became linked to the 'new' social history and flourished during the late 20th century, and has finally achieved the long sought 'holy grail' of mainstream academic legitimacy and acclaim during the past decade or so. Practitioners are no longer forced to encounter the smirks and repressed laughs from so-called (and professed) 'mainstream' historians which the editors of this volume encountered as young historians coming into the field in the early 1990s.

The key dynamic in the development of this sub-discipline is the engagement of historians of sport with wider historiographical trends within social and cultural history along with a latent interest in critical social theory. A young generation of historians who came into the profession during the 1970s and early 1980s challenged many of the prevailing assumptions in the craft surrounding what and how best to study the past. Armed with new assumptions, questions, topics and methods, the 'new' historians fundamentally shifted their collective attention from political events and big ideas toward the processes and experiences of everyday life. In particular, the 'new' social history drew upon two prominent European intellectual trends: the notion of *histoire totale* championed by scholars connected to the French journal *Annales* (an attempt to incorporate all of the human and social sciences so as to recreate the totality of the past) and 'history from the bottom up', as advanced by various British Marxist historians (who employed an analysis of society that emphasized the role of 'human agency' and class struggle in the making of history). In addition to these two fundamentally European 'schools' of historical scholarship, the 'new' historians incorporated the work of social theorists and thereby expanded their understanding of concepts such as society, culture, community and power.[2]

Sports historians borrowed freely (albeit selectively) from anthropology and sociology and examined the complex relationships between sport and social structures. The most prominent example of this emergent trend within sports history was Allen Guttmann, whose wide interdisciplinary training and command of European languages enabled him to define a new social scientifically-based interpretive paradigm informed by Weberian sociology and modernization theory. Simultaneously, sports historians were investigating the socially constructed ideas of race, class, gender, ethnic and national identities surrounding modern sport. One can easily look back upon the flood of sports historical research produced during those feverish 1980s as a first 'golden age' in the development of the field.[3]

The bulk of assessments of the 'state' of the field published during the past 20 or so years have rarely subjected sports history's existence to a critique, but rather a gentler assessment of its steady ascendancy. Such periodic 'progress reports' have been common within the English-language historiography of North America and the United Kingdom (and supported by the organizations of the North American Society for Sport History and the British Society for Sport History in their official journals, *Journal of Sport History* and *The Sport Historian* renamed *Sport in History* in 2003).[4] The other key sports history journals are *International Journal of the History of Sport* (formerly the *British Journal of Sports History*, which began in 1984); *Sporting Traditions* (launched in 1984 by the Australian Society for Sport History), and the *Sport History Review* (formerly the *Canadian Journal of History of Sport*, established in 1973). A number of important contributions on the international history of sport were also published in the *Journal of Olympic History, Olympika, Stadion, Internationale Zeitschrift für Geschichte des Sports*, and the *Revue Internationale d'Histoire du Sport*. Although the bulk of the periodical literature has appeared in sports history journals, there have been some notable contributions published in leading mainstream historical journals as well.[5]

While the field has been driven internally by the publication of research in scholarly journals, the monograph and occasional mid-list trade book have externally elevated the stature of sports history. There was a dramatic expansion of monographic literature during the 1980s and 1990s aided by the establishment of several seminal book series and the sustained interest by university presses and commercial publishers in the USA.[6]

Clearly, the preceding has been merely a cursory synopsis of the rise of sports history. Readers of the *Companion* will be treated to the most authoritative and current analyses of sports historiography published to date in the pages that follow.

Sports history: present and future

While assessing the state of the US literature in 1997, S. W. Pope characterized the field to be in its late adolescence; yet, during that same year, Douglas Booth wondered whether sports history was in its death throes.[7] In early 1999, Booth and John Nauright organized a conference in Queenstown, New Zealand with the provocative theme 'The End of Sports History?'[8] However, despite the prodigious growth in both the volume and quality of sports historical scholarship during the past decade, the field of sports history is not without its critics. One of the most respected and prolific scholars of the field, Mike Cronin (an Oxford-trained historian) recently offered a trenchant critique:

> I would argue that the most basic problem with sports history ... is that it spends too long talking to itself. We can make long arguments about whether the media or other academics are somehow excluding us, but I would suggest that the most basic reason is this: much of what passes for sports history is bad history. For all the people who have gone out there and got work published in the mainstream history journals, many are content with recycling work in the (far too many) specialist sports history and studies journals. The work is not up to speed with current historical practice, it is theoretically vague, and the focus far too tight. In the three decades or so since sports history first pushed its boat out into the waters, we are still dominated by too many fans with typewriters. That's not necessarily a bad thing if the fans are engaged with contemporary developments in history, but most of them aren't.
>
> I believe that we have probably taken sports history as far as we can, and to a level that suits it. It will have its societies where the like minded can gather in private for their own pleasure, while a few brave souls will take the option of exposing themselves to the wider world. I think that we are well past the bad old days when various history departments would rule sports out of order, and our collective efforts (plus the advent of searchable electronic journals that are widely available) means that our outputs and the archival resources are well understood.
>
> In conclusion, sports history is a minor backwater (like most historical sub-disciplines these days). Quality will always shine out, no matter what the topic, and good sports history will always be accepted into key journals and by major publishers. Sports history is taught around the world in a variety of institutions ... and will be popular for those who are interested when faced with a multitude of topics to choose from. Unless we are going to have some root and branch clearance of antiquarian approaches much beloved by many sports historians [which] is never going to happen because the field is too institutionally cozy in its various national societies ... [therefore we're forced to] accept sports history for what it is: a sub-discipline chosen by many of its adherents precisely because they are fans, collectors, ex- and failed athletes (delete as appropriate). It is not a sub-discipline where rigorous standards are always demanded and the routes of entry to the sub-discipline (i.e. long term professional training) are not common.[9]

To be sure, Cronin's view of sports history (however discerning and provocative) exists on the margins, rather than the mainstream, of the field.[10] In developing the

Companion, the Editors have attempted to identify the major thematic and methodological trends that currently define the field of sports history. There is no exact science to such an endeavour. Any two other historians would have invariably produced a different list of key topics which merely emphasizes the inherently selective and subjective nature of historical enquiry. Nevertheless, we are satisfied with the resulting range of essays for providing a substantially comprehensive overview of academic sports historiography. Like any collection, this volume is incomplete. The Editors had originally commissioned thematic contributions on amateurism, biography, globalization, institutionalization of modern sport, modern Olympics, physical education, politics, post-colonialism, traditional sports and women's sport from the leading scholars in these topical areas, who were ultimately unable to deliver these essays. In certain cases, we approached other prospective authors; in others, late withdrawals did not afford us the luxury of seeking replacements. As it turned out, several of these original, 'pet' topics have been capably addressed within multiple chapters by various other contributors.

The global development of sports history

While the first half of the book deals with theoretical and methodological issues around broad themes that have been of concern to historians of sport, the second half of the book is more traditionally organized. Even though one of the authors criticizes the national/regional approach that serves to compartmentalize analysis, it is clear from the work of many of these authors that much sporting historiography remains nationally focused, as many doctoral students working on sport focus on research dealing with the geographical spaces of their own country. Some authors here even go so far as to focus almost exclusively on scholars within a particular country and their work on sport there. Yet it is clear that there is a process of change underway in the study of sport in national and regional settings to take greater note of 'global' influences. International sporting competition is nearly as old as domestic competition within modern sporting forms and it is virtually impossible to discuss sport within one nation without reference to international sport.

Our organizational structure is no more 'balanced' than the field of sports history in general. Western European, North American and Australasian societies have been well covered by historians of sport, while China, Japan, Eastern Europe and South Africa have vibrant sports history communities. Even in the well-established national historiographies of countries like Australia, our understanding remains partial, as much academic writing concentrates on the major cities, particularly the two largest of Sydney and Melbourne. As Editors, we are both English speakers and, therefore, the collection is biased towards sports history written in the English language and coverage of sporting cultures in countries where English is the first language. Thus, some countries with significant sporting cultures and international success, most notably Italy and Spain, are missing from this volume. Part of the difficulty lies in finding scholars with the time frame to write a detailed piece in a second or third language. As a result, we are not comprehensive, nor could we be for that matter in a single volume covering sports history around the world. We do argue, though, that despite these limitations, we have provided a solid guide to the 'state of play' in sports history in most regions of the world.

As we mentioned earlier, the history of sports in a number of countries is well developed and sophisticated in terms of analysis. Notably English-speaking countries, Germany, France and the Nordic countries. Critical mass helps. In the United Kingdom and the USA with many universities and independent scholars, for example, far greater numbers of historians have delved into a vast array of topics that it is not possible to cover in much smaller nations. A number of convergences that we have outlined took place by the 1970s to launch the current academic field of sports history. While sport was discussed in ancient texts, appears in Castiglione's *Book of the Courtier*, was famously discussed by Joseph Strutt in 1801 and so on,[11] it was only after the emergence of social histories and labour histories that concentrated on 'history from below' that made the development of other formerly marginalized topics worthy of study. In many countries, early histories of sport emerged out of physical education disciplines. Within social and cultural histories, though, national level studies began to appear in the 1960s and 1970s, which led to an explosion of studies from the 1980s onward and this was a global trend.

A couple of key turning points can be mentioned, though. Harold Seymour published a three-volume history of American baseball, beginning with the first volume in 1960, which emerged out of his 1956 doctoral dissertation at Cornell University.[12] Three years earlier, he was unanimously voted down by colleagues when he proposed a course on the history of baseball. As Johnes notes in his chapter on the United Kingdom in this volume, Peter McIntosh effectively launched British academic studies of sports history with his 1952 history of physical education[13] (and further delineated the new field with the publication of his book *Sport in Society* in 1963). While not referenced, these works started the ball rolling, though key texts began to appear only around the 1970s and 1980s. In 1973 Robert Malcolmson, a student of the giant of English social history, E.P. Thompson, published *Popular Recreations in English Society 1700–1850*, which is still a standard for early modern popular recreational and sporting pastimes.[14] Tony Mason followed in 1980 with his ground-breaking work *Association Football and English Society 1860–1915*.[15] This was followed by Tony Mangan's (J.A. Mangan) *Athleticism in the Victorian and Edwardian Public School* (1981), which sparked an array of international studies on the role of educational institutions in the development of modern sport, further enhanced by Mangan's follow-up volume *The Games Ethic and Imperialism* (1987).[16] During this same period Richard Holt's doctoral study at the University of Oxford on the history of sport in France was later published in 1981 as *Sport and Society in Modern France*. At the end of the 1980s, enough work had appeared for broad syntheses of sport at national level to appear most successfully in Holt's magisterial *Sport and the British* (1989), which, at least in our humble opinion, remains the single most impressive national level history of sport (notwithstanding debates about the United Kingdom or even Great Britain as 'one' nation). Early contributions to sports history appeared in other countries as well. The first PhD thesis on sports history in the Netherlands was completed in 1955, for example.[17] Yet these remained largely isolated projects that merely opened the door to future possibilities.

As these developments were appearing, particularly in the USA and the United Kingdom, an Australian named Maxwell Howell set about starting the first doctoral programme devoted to sports history at the University of Alberta in Canada during the 1960s. Howell took the history of Canadian sport and assigned periods to several of his students to create a chronology of sport in Canada, which he and his first wife Nancy Howell summarized in their 1969 history of Canadian sport. That same year Frank Cosentino published a descriptive history of Canadian football. These studies remained largely descriptive, but provided a foundation, as did McIntosh in the United Kingdom, for critical histories and historical sociologies of sport that emerged by the 1980s, most famously in Richard Gruneau's *Class, Sport and Social Development* (1982) and Alan Metcalfe's *Canada Learns to Play* (1987). Back in Howell's homeland, a group of young historians, both locals and expatriates, began to examine the history of sport there as well and pioneering studies of sport in other countries. This group of scholars, notably Richard Cashman, Bill Murray, Brian Stoddart and Wray Vamplew among others, formed a core of historians, most of whom were based in history departments,[18] unlike in other countries, who did much to transform the critical history of sport that inspired a second and third generation of scholars with ties 'down under', some of whom are featured in this volume (Douglas Booth, Murray Phillips, Daryl Adair, Barbara Keys, Malcolm MacLean, John Nauright, Richard Light, Gary Osmond, Charles Little and Chris Valiotis from this volume alone – fully one-quarter of the total authors whose work is presented here). Vibrant national societies of sports history emerged in Australia and the United Kingdom, and the Americans and Canadians combined in the North American Society of Sport History. European national and continent-wide associations have also been formed to provide professional associations as we have outlined. The key here is that most of the studies that appeared prior to 1990 focused on sport at the national and regional level; Guttmann's pioneering 'big picture' approach to the trans-historical, transnational context represented the greatest exception to these.

Outside the English-speaking world of North America, the British Isles and Australasia, vibrant sports histories have emerged across Europe and have begun to appear across Asia, Latin America and Africa, though the literature in Europe is much more widely developed, particularly in Germany, France, the Netherlands and the Nordic countries, with a number of scholars publishing works regularly in English as well as in their native languages.[19] Within other English-speaking countries as well as these, it is easy to count the number of scholars making a sustained impact on the field on one or two hands at most.[20] Much remains to be done.

As we can see from the chapters dealing with France, Belgium and the Netherlands, Central and Eastern Europe, Germany, and the Nordic countries, much of the focus remains on domestically generated literatures derived from a small number of programmes in which students of sports history have been trained primarily within departments or schools of sports science.

Once sports histories within particular nations have been established, are there themes that can been highlighted? Can we see commonalities? What differences exist? How important are these? These are all crucial questions. Several contributors point to the fact that within certain countries there is a concept that the people there are particularly, perhaps uniquely 'sporting' (or even 'sporty') as a national characteristic. One can see explicit or implicit references to this in chapters or sections on Australia, Ireland, New Zealand/Aotearoa, or the USA, for example. In discussing the writing of sports history in New Zealand, MacLean suggests that: 'scholars have accentuated three interwoven themes. In the first, there is a propensity to construct a history that is nationally distinctive. In the second, paradoxical given the first, there is a lack of comparative historical analysis. The third principle tendency is a focus on masculinist games – especially rugby union'. Substitute another sport (usually association football, another football code or ice-hockey) for rugby union and one would be referring to the writing of sports history in most of the countries discussed in this volume. Yet as MacLean, Adair and others have argued, how we measure national distinctiveness or whether one nation is more 'sporty' than another has not been subjected to critical scrutiny or theorized in any sophisticated way. Are the Danes or the Norwegians more sporty because of their high adult participation rates, or are Americans with their 80,000–110,000-seat university American football stadiums that dwarf many countries' national stadiums? Or, as some have argued, are *idrett* (sports) and commercialized sports two different things altogether that may even defy comparison? Abundant material for future research exists in this area of enquiry alone.

Taken individually or as a whole, the chapters contained in this book provide a snapshot of sports history internationally at the present time, but more than that they provide a guide for areas and approaches to future research in the field that will remain relevant for quite some time to come. As sport becomes more and more globalized, it is timely to have a global overview of sports history, which has too often been artificially constrained by national borders. Sports historians of the 21st century need to understand the concerns of their colleagues in other parts of the world in order to advance the field into new areas of enquiry, analysis and conceptualization. We hope this volume will be merely the starting point for a new sports history that builds upon the solid foundations that have been laid by the pioneers of our academic field.

Notes

1 The Editors are well aware of the distinctions made by various historians (see for example Mark Dyreson's chapter in this book) between 'the history of sport' (the province of the professionally trained historian attempting to contextualize sport within broader historical currents) and 'sports history' (a genre fundamentally focused on the sporting past). Both of us (like most historians in our field) have consistently referred to our work as 'sport history' which somehow seemed a bit more serious than 'sports history'. Routledge preferred 'sports history' and as a couple of mid-career historians working within a less snobbish academic culture than even 10 or 15 years ago, we were content to go along with this descriptor (which is actually easier to pronounce and is more accessible to the non-specialist readers and audiences who are likely to encounter this book).

2 For an overview of this within sport studies, see R. Giulianotti, ed., *Sport and Modern Social Theorists* (Harlow: Palgrave, 2004).

3 For a brief review of this within (primarily) the US historiography, see S.W. Pope, ed., *The New American Sport History: Recent Approaches and Perspectives* (Urbana: University of Illinois Press, 1997), 1–30. The most comprehensive and authoritative study of sports historiography is Douglas Booth, *The Field: Truth and Fiction in Sport History* (London: Routledge, 2005).

4 Such representative historiographical assessments include Roberta J. Park, 'Research and Scholarship in the History of Physical Education and Sport: The Current State of Affairs', *Research Quarterly of Exercise and Sport Science* 54 (June 1983), 93–103; Melvin Adelman, 'Academicians and American Athletics: A Decade of Progress', *Journal of Sport History* 10 (Spring 1983), 80–106; William J. Baker, 'The State of British Sport History', *Journal of Sport History* 10 (Spring 1983), 53–66; Steven A. Riess, 'The New Sport History', *Reviews in American History* 18 (September 1990), 311–25; and Nancy Struna, 'Sport History', in *The History of Exercise and Sport Science*, John D. Massengale and Richard A. Swanson, eds (Champaign: Human Kinetics, 1997), 143–79.

5 Sports historians have published in such prominent journals as the *American Historical Review, Journal of American History, Journal of Social History, Journal of Modern History, Journal of Southern History,* and the *Canadian Historical Review.*

6 Larry Malley and Richard Wentworth were responsible for establishing the 'Sport in Society' book series at the University of Illinois Press in the mid-1980s. Other academic publishers followed suit, including Routledge, University of Nebraska Press, Oxford University Press, Syracuse University Press, State University of New York Press and the University of Tennessee Press. Most major US university presses have and continue to publish occasional volumes of sports history, including North Carolina University Press, Johns Hopkins University Press, Columbia University Press, New York University Press, Harvard University Press, Cornell University Press and Yale University Press.

7 S.W. Pope, *The New American Sport History*, 20; D. Booth, 'Sports History: What Can Be Done?', *Sport, Education and Society* 2 (1997), 191–204.

8 The Australian Society for Sport History conference programme can be accessed at: www. la84foundation.org/SportsLibrary/SportingTraditions/1998/st1501/st1501r.pdf. For a birds-eye perspective, see John Nauright, '"The End of Sports History?": From Sports History to Sports Studies', *Sporting Traditions* 16 (November 1999), 5–13.

9 Mike Cronin's comments on the field appeared on the SPORTHIST internet list, 23 October 2007.

10 For a complementary, albeit less strident critique of the lack of active engagement of American sports historians with central theoretical and conceptual developments within the historical profession, see S.W. Pope, 'Rethinking Sport, Empire and "American Exceptionalism"', *Sport History Review* 38 (November 2007), 92–120. Pope writes: 'American sports history flourishes and yet, simultaneously, the field is increasingly estranged from the mainstreams within social, cultural, and political history. After its rise to become a promising subfield of social history during the 1970s and 1980s, American sports history came to be recognized, albeit grudgingly in some staid circles, as a serious area of inquiry during the 1990s. However, after achieving its status as a recognized area of research, it has become seemingly less visible and relevant within mainstream history. Seldom are the revered sports history monographs cited in the footnotes and bibliographies of key works in American history, and even more seldom do sports historians publish their research in the leading American history and American Studies journals. Even though there is a new generation of scholars who are transforming the field of sports history in the USA, many sports historians have been less reflexive about the wider implications of their research at precisely the moment when their peers in social, cultural, and political history have become more actively engaged in debates about method and epistemology' (pp. 93–94).

    With regard to Cronin's charge that the field has been less than self-reflexive, see Pope's supporting 1998 statement that while 'both American history and sport sociology (to say nothing about the Modern Language Association) are contentious. So why isn't sport history? Most people I know come away from the annual North American Society for Sport History (NASSH) conference with warm, supportive experiences and memories. I rarely read of any substantive debate in our journals or Internet listserv [sic]. Does such collegiality imply disciplinary consensus? Does the lack of explicit, sustained debate suggest that sports history is [indeed] in its death throes?', S. W. Pope, 'Sport History: Into the 21st Century', *Journal of Sport History* 25 (1998), iii. The definitive work on this debate is D. Booth, *The Field: Truth and Fiction in Sport History* (London: Routledge, 2005).

11 B. Castiglione, *Il Libro del Courtegiano* (Venice: Aldine Press, 1528); J. Strutt, *The Sports and Pastimes of the People of England: Including the Rural and Domestic Recreations … From the Earliest Period to the Present Time* (London, 1801).

12 H. Seymour, *Baseball: The Early Years* (New York: Oxford University Press, 1960).

13 P.C. McIntosh, *Physical Education in England since 1800* (London: Bell, 1952).

14 R.W. Malcolmson, *Popular Recreations in English Society 1700–1850* (Cambridge: Cambridge University Press, 1973).

15 Mason's book did much to shape subsequent exploration of sport in society. [Editor's note: This was by coincidence the first book on sports history that I (Nauright) read while studying history at the University of Warwick in the early 1980s and Malcolmson's was the second. Coincidentially, both Malcolmson and Mason were at Warwick early in their careers and Malcolmson chaired the history deparment at Queen's when Nauright was there studying for his PhD in history. Perhaps it is a small world after all.]

16 J.A. Mangan stands as a colossus in international sports history through his early works, long-time editorship of the *International Journal of the History of Sport*, his book series with Frank Cass Press, now with Routledge, and his supervision of numerous post-graduate students working on topics in sports history around the world. His two primary and early works have shaped much subsequent research on imperial and colonial sporting histories as well as national level studies in former colonial societies, see *Athleticism in the Victorian and Edwardian Public School: The Emergence and Consolidation of an Educational Ideology* (Cambridge: Cambridge University Press, 1981); and *The Games Ethic and Imperialism: Aspects of Diffusion of an Ideal* (Harmondsworth: Viking, 1987).

17 C. Miermans, *Voetbal in Nederland: Een onderzoek naar de maatschappelijke en sportieve aspecten* (Assen: Van Gorcum, 1955). The next PhD thesis, which Stokvis refers to in this volume, did not appear until 1979, however.

18 Key texts from this group include: W. Vamplew, *The Turf* (1976), *Pay Up and Play the Game* (Cambridge: Cambridge University Press, 1988); B. Stoddart, *Saturday Afternoon Fever: Sport in the*

Australian Culture (North Ryde, NSW: Angus & Robertson, 1986); R. Cashman, *Patrons, Players and the Crowd: The Phenomenon of Indian Cricket* (New Delhi: Orient Longman, 1980), *'Ave a Go Yer Mug* (Sydney: Collins, 1984), *Paradise of Sport: The Rise of Organised Sport in Australia* (Melbourne: Oxford University Press, 1995); R. Cashman and M. McKernan (eds), *Sport in History: The Making of Modern Sporting History* (St Lucia, Qld: University of Queensland Press, 1979); W.A. Murray, *The Old Firm: Sectarianism, Sport and Society in Scotland* (Edinburgh: John Donald Publishers, 1984).

19 Notably Arnd Krüger, Joachim Rühl, Gertrud Pfister (Germany); Thierry Terret, Pierre Lanfranchi (France/Italy); Henning Eichberg, Verner Møller (Denmark); Roland Renson (Belgium); Maarten van Bottenburg, Paul de Knop (Netherlands); Matti Gøksoyr, Gerd van der Lippe (Norway); Hendrik Meinander (Finland); though there are others who have also made valuable contributions to sports history, particularly in their own language.

20 For example, South Africa (Alegi, Booth, Grundlingh, Merrett, Nauright, Odendaal); Ireland (Bairner, Cronin, Darby, Hassan). The number of scholars whose work has concentrated on more than two different societies in some detail still remains surprisingly low (notably Bale, Booth, Guttmann, Hoberman, Jarvie, Mangan, Nauright, Stoddart, van Bottenburg, Vertinsky).

1 Theory

Douglas Booth

Theory is a contentious subject for historians. Many practitioners conceptualize history as an a-theoretical discipline in which historical phenomena are unique configurations and one-off occurrences; history consists of 'stories of ... individual lives or happenings, all seemingly [unique] and unrepeatable'.[1] Among these historians, theory distorts the study of the past by 'infus[ing] predestined meaning' and casting the discipline into the realm of speculation.[2] However, few historians consider the investigation of unique events as the 'litmus test' of historical knowledge. Most practitioners generalize and categorize different human behaviours across time and space. Such abstractions, which in sports history include a range of collective identities (e.g., nationalities, genders, occupations, social classes, sub-cultures), are the building blocks of theory and integral to historical analysis.[3] Although few historians employ the historical record to construct formal theories or set out to apply, test or confirm theories, many sports historians incorporate theory into their work as 'frameworks of interpretation'. In other words theory helps frame the questions practitioners ask, directs them to particular sources, organizes their evidence, and shapes their explanations.[4]

Sports historians have embraced many theoretical frameworks such as modernization, materialism, hegemony, structuration, feminism, discourse and textualism.[5] In this chapter, I investigate several theoretical frameworks found in sports history across two distinct paradigms: social history and cultural history.[6] Each investigation includes an outline of the theory, examples of specific applications in sports history, and a critical appraisal. Working in the social history paradigm, historians of sport employed grand sociological theories as tools to incorporate sport into holistic notions of society and to explain changes in the nature of sport. In this manner, sports historians broadly followed a model for the study of society developed by the natural sciences. The more recent shift to cultural analysis, which resides in the hermeneutic tradition, has seen historians of sport engage new theories such as discourse, textualism and narrative as ways to understand how people interpret their worlds and represent their experiences. However, it must be stressed that sports historians still privilege the authority of material evidence as the fount of historical knowledge and that few explicitly engage theory.

Sport, society, theory

Aligning themselves with the broader discipline of social history and its emphasis on the lives of ordinary people, and determined to demonstrate their academic credibility (and in some cases counter charges that the history of sport amounted to a trivial intellectual pursuit), many sports historians in the 1970s and 80s conceptualized sport as an integral element in the social totality.[7] Often this meant simply putting sport into broader social, economic and political contexts. Some sports historians, though, incorporated sociological theories of structural-functionalism and structuralism to buttress their conceptualizations of the relationship between sport and society. Logically, these theories spilled into explanations of the changing nature of sport especially with respect to power relationships across class, gender and race. In the first part of this chapter, I examine the influences of structural-functionalism and structuralism in sports history; I also look at the search for a non-determinist approach to the role of sport in society in an effort to overcome the limitations of these theories.

Structural-functionalism and holistic notions of society

Using metaphors of the physical world to visualize human societies as wholes or totalities, structural-functionalist theories liken societies to organisms whose component parts – structures – function to maintain relative stability or equilibrium, and ensure their survival.[8] Structural-functionalism guided several early historians of sport in North America. They conceptualized sport as a social-cement that functioned to maintain stability in nineteenth-century cities. The sporting structure inculcated spirits of responsibility and loyalty to, and solidarity within, local communities and redirected 'surplus energies and natural aggressions' that in congested, crime-plagued, stultifying urban environments might otherwise have fuelled crime and public disorder.[9] Yet, notwithstanding the subsequent widespread appearance of structural-functionalist thinking in sports history, few practitioners offered precise theoretical explanations.[10]

Robert Malcolmson employed structural-functionalism to explain the recreational and sporting habits of the labouring classes in eighteenth- and early nineteenth-century England. Sport 'foster[ed] social cohesiveness and group unity' and 'functioned as outlets' for licentious and socially confrontational behaviours that in the course of normal day-to-day life were 'repressed'. Football, cricket, boxing, running, wrestling and cudgelling afforded labouring men rare opportunities to 'perform publicly for the esteem of their peers' and they also 'left in their wake a reservoir of incidents which could be retrospectively enjoyed and discussed' and thus 'incorporated into the [group's] changing assessments of its own members'. According to Malcolmson, smock races – common at wakes and other rural gatherings – and Shrovetide football in Derby were outlets for socially sanctioned aberrant behaviour. Conventional sexual proprieties evaporated at smock races with female competitors encouraged to attend 'lightly clad'; at Derby locals 'dusted' well-to-do spectators with bags of soot or powder.[11]

Critics consider structural-functionalism 'too abstract to account for the detail of history's vast panorama', teleological (i.e., actions, phenomena, events and the like occur for the sake of their own goals), and tautological (i.e., vacuous propositions that conflate causes and effects). Structural-functionalist explanations of sport typically gloss over disparities in sporting interests between different social and economic groups, exaggerate social stability and harmony, and ignore the inevitable losers and outsiders in consensus-building initiatives whether at the community, regional or national levels.[12] Scarce on facts and frugal with context, Malcolmson's functionalist account of sport 'challenging conventional proprieties' raises many questions. Were the 'dusted' selected at random or carefully chosen? Who received 'dustings' – magistrates, employers, merchants, elites, publicans, parsons, squires? Were the architects and perpetrators of 'dustings' one and the same? Did multiple 'dustings' occur at single events? How might historians assess the popularity of such non-verbal acts?

Distinguishing between strong and weak functionalism, Christopher Lloyd claims that the former avoids the problem of teleology by incorporating causal mechanisms.[13] Malcolmson's work meets this criterion of strong functionalism. The English class system in the eighteenth and early nineteenth centuries reproduced itself, in part, through the different sports pursued by each class. Playing strictly among themselves allowed the classes to distinguish themselves and to coalesce as distinct entities. Why did this system preserve labouring-class sports? This question is the key to finding the causal mechanisms by which the system functioned. Acts of defiance against authority figures, such as 'dusting' men-of-rank during Shrovetide football, provide important clues. Malcolmson suggests that expressions of hostility against the well-to-do articulated ordinary people's frustration with prevailing norms and constraints. For their part, the ruling classes sanctioned these acts as a relatively harmless safety valve for ordinary folk. Spatially and temporally delineated 'dustings' and like acts posed no threat to an established order that remained remarkably secure. Hence, hostilities and safety valves helped maintain the class system and its respective sports.[14]

Most structural-functionalist explanations in sports history, however, fall into the weak category with practitioners imputing abstractions (e.g., sport, society) with agency and then assigning those abstractions functions and needs. In his history of American sport Benjamin Rader emphasizes the maintenance and equilibrium of society and insinuates that the latter is itself a goal. As he puts it, spectator sport constitutes one of the 'major pillars' of the twentieth-century 'social order'. It has 'replaced or supplemented the church, the family, the local community, subcommunities based upon status or ethnicity, and the older system of mutual class obligations as one of the sinews which held modern society together'.[15] Rader supplies no causal mechanism and implies that spectator sport is the product of processes operating according to a predetermined schedule. While his discussions of key components of spectator sport, notably television and its role in transforming sport into a popular pastime, contain empirically based assessments of intentional subjects, he implies that American society, an abstract concept, has needs and agency.

Although few sports historians explicitly expounded their versions of structural-functionalism, this theoretical perspective gained a foothold in the field through the highly influential modernization school's approach to social change. Conceiving societies and cultures as 'organic holistic systems' that progressively evolve, becoming increasingly differentiated and complex,[16] the modernization school focused on the transformation of tradition-bound pre-modern rural and agrarian societies into modern urban and industrial forms. Stability, localism, unspecialized social roles and paternal social hierarchies characterized traditional societies. Modern societies, by contrast, are dynamic, cosmopolitan, technological, mobile, industrial and constantly modified by rational thought, these scholars argued. Both societies support different sporting structures.[17] Pre-modern societies tied sport to religious customs and interwove it with agrarian rhythms; modern sport is secular, democratic, bureaucratized, specialized, rationalized, quantified and grounded in an obsession with records.[18]

Yet, while notions of traditional and modern sport litter sports history, surprisingly few practitioners theorize the changes from traditional to modern sport. The first sports historian to systematically compare traditional and modern sports, and the first to provide a typology – that still endures – of the formal structural properties of each, Allen Guttmann also identified the processes by which sport passed from the traditional to its modern structural form.[19] Prior to Guttmann (and in numerous cases since), sports historians

simply attributed the transformation to the 'end products' of urbanization and industrialization, notably improved standards of living, communications and transport, reduced
working hours and technological innovations.[20] Missing from these explanations were
accounts of the processes that predispose and precipitate change and details of the conditions under which 'social, ideological, and cultural contexts' change.[21] Guttmann
located the basic mechanism of structural change in human desire and the quest for
achievement and status that underpinned the scientific revolution. He identified modern
sport as a cultural expression of the scientific world. 'The emergence of modern sports',
he said, 'represents ... the slow development of an empirical, experimental, mathematical
Weltanschauung'. This 'intellectual revolution ... symbolized by the names of Isaac
Newton and John Locke and institutionalized in the Royal Society', explains the likes of
'athletic achievement' in Eastern Europe after World War II. There the 'vestiges of
premodern social organization and ideology were suddenly, even ruthlessly, challenged
by a relentlessly modern attitude'.[22]

At first glance, Guttmann's account of social change rests on an historically grounded
notion of culture in the tradition of the German sociologist Max Weber. Indeed,
Guttmann labels his interpretation Weberian.[23] However, whereas dialectical interactions
between the individual and society, the material and cultural, and the subjective and the
objective underpinned Weber's theory, Guttmann locates the origins of the 'impulse to
quantification' and the 'desire to win, to excel, to be the best' in the scientific culture of
seventeenth-century England. Moreover, he is scant on detail, silent about the international diffusion of this scientific *Weltanschauung*, and paints the mania for records as the
telos of Western society and modern sport.[24]

Structuralism and holistic notions of society

Typically incomplete and unsatisfying, structural-functionalist explanations waned
quickly in sports history. In contradistinction, structuralist explanations proved more
enduring – and more controversial. In the 1960s and 70s social theorists typically
approached structures in one of two ways. The so-called essentialist approach conceptualized
a structure as a determining factor underlying surface appearances. According to this
conceptualization, expounded here by Malcolm Waters, 'everyday social experience ...
masks a ... hidden reality which lies beneath the level of consciousness'. The hidden
reality constitutes a structure that typically endures, usually over long periods, and
determines action independent of the will of human agents. By contrast, the so-called
constructionist approach views structures as patterns arising from human actions. Here
conscious actors 'create structural arrangements' including 'the constraints which adhere
in them'. These structures, Waters elaborates, 'impinge upon and constrain each human
individual and have the force of concrete reality, but their source and origin are within
the sphere of human action – the whole structure has no greater reality than the sum of
its constituent action components'.[25]

Under the banner of structural Marxism and the influences of prominent European
sociologists of sport including Jean-Marie Brohm, Bero Rigauer and Gerhard Vinnai,
essentialist approaches to abstract structures constituted a theoretical strand of sport
sociology in the 1970s.[26] However, structural Marxism raised the hackles of sports historians for whom the removal of free-thinking and -acting agents violated a tenet of their
discipline. In the eyes of sports historians, structural Marxists appeared more concerned
with proving their theory than with identifying the facts.[27] Moreover, structural

Marxism's view of sport as a 'completely determined product' repeatedly faltered under the weight of historical evidence. The notion that sport socializes participants into 'reactionary political views' or that it '*necessarily* ... discourages the development of an oppositional class consciousness within capitalism', appeared ludicrous to historians conversant with the workers' sports movement (founded as 'a socialist alternative to bourgeois competitive sport') or the athletic revolution of the 1960s. It could not explain, for example, the experiences of heavyweight boxer Muhammed Ali who 'thumbed his nose' at the American 'government, military, and the capitalist economy that supported them both'.[28] Structural Marxist conceptualizations of the working class stereotyped a group that embraced 'a range of lived cultures'. Notwithstanding workers' subordinate relationship to capital, historical investigations repeatedly showed that family, church, neighbourhood, locality and specific worker–employer relations also structured working class experiences.[29]

Sports historians found that rather than using sport as capitalist vehicle to accumulate wealth, those who organized sport typically sought to 'break even, or to operate at least cost in order to remain financially viable'. Similarly, business interests mostly 'invest in sport for non-economic reasons: to gain prestige from being associated with a popular cultural activity, ... [as a] commitment to life-style, and to exert social and cultural influence'.[30] Thus sports historians rebuffed essentialist approaches to structure that raised seemingly unanswerable questions for an evidence-based discipline. What constitutes evidence for the effects of structures? Could victims of structures provide valid accounts of their positions? How do historians distinguish the effects of overlapping structures? How, for example, do historians separate the effects of capitalism and patriarchy on women's participation in sport?[31]

While structural Marxism alerted at least some practitioners to the relations of power in sport, especially within capitalist structures, and to new areas of research around social class, gender and race, it offered few insights into social change. Structural Marxists assigned primacy to the economy that they held determined the composition and power of social classes.[32] In this theory, culture serves an ideological function, persuading individuals to accept situations that belie their class (that is, their natural) interests, and is reducible to class structures in which individuals are cultural dupes unable to fathom their situations. According to this theory, change derives from the 'transformation of consciousness' under conditions where ideological statements about the social relations of capitalism appear increasingly contradictory and workers' organizations, trade unions and left-leaning political parties unite the masses who transform society.[33] However, the perseverance of capitalist structures of domination belied all notions of transformed consciousness; many sports historians responded by embracing the Italian Marxist Antonio Gramsci's theory of hegemony to explain the stability of capitalist societies and the persistence of sporting structures that subordinate the underclasses.

A coterie of scholars that included John Hargreaves and Stephen Hardy, introduced the theory of hegemony into sports history. Rather than following Gramsci's notion of hegemony as a 'mechanism of bourgeois rule over the working class',[34] they subscribed to Raymond Williams' concept as an ongoing political process 'characterized by conflict and consent [and] coercion and struggle'.[35] Hegemony theory enabled this group to ameliorate the determinism of structural Marxism and introduce agency into their analyses. However, few historians of sport picked up on the subtleties of the Williams approach;[36] most simply conflated hegemony with ideology (as a set of false ideas) and viewed it as a force that 'persuades the general public to consider their society and its norms and values to be natural, good, and just, [and thereby] concealing the inherent system of domination'.[37] Sports historians used hegemony theory primarily to explain impediments to social change and the staying power of structures of domination. Hegemony theory, in short, never freed sports historians from the shackles of an essentialist conceptualization of structure.[38]

Before examining the constructionist approach to structure in sports history, it is worth digressing to reflect on theory as an ideological discourse shaped by politics and material conditions.[39] According to Jeffrey Alexander, the popularity of functionalism in postwar America derived from the 'distinctive social characteristics' of prosperity and suburban growth that nurtured functionalist assumptions about social stability, social uniformity and peaceful, incremental social change. Similarly, Alexander attributes the death of functionalism to 'the destruction of its ideological ... core' from the 'new social movements that ... espous[ed] collective emancipation ... , black and Chicano national movements, indigenous people's rebellions, youth culture, hippies, rock music, and women's liberation'.[40] Political activism in sport in the 1960s similarly influenced the emerging generation of sports historians.[41]

Political activism in sport undoubtedly helps explain the early appeal of structural Marxism. Marxist historian Eric Hobsbawm described the insights as 'concentrated charges of intellectual explosive, designed to blow up crucial parts of the fortification of traditional history'. Ironically, the power of these insights lay in their simplicity. 'Those of us who recall our first encounters with [Marxism] may still bear witness to the immense liberating force of such simple discoveries', he observed.[42] Sport sociologist Richard Gruneau conceded that for all its overstatements and exaggerations, structural Marxism provided 'powerful' and 'penetrating' insights, especially into the ways sport reproduces many of the 'repressive constraints inherent in capitalism'.[43]

Raymond Williams' approach to hegemony provided left-leaning sports historians with the tool to escape the reductionism and determinism of structural Marxism and include expressions of agency *while* accounting for the ongoing dominance of capitalist structures. Arguably the appeal of hegemony owed just as much to the politics of disappointment in the face of growing conservatism in the 1980s.[44] A tone of pessimism appears in many historical analyses of sport where the authors blame the co-opting of oppositional or alternative sporting values on the objective structures of hegemonic capitalism or patriarchy. John Hargreaves, for example, observed that 'hegemony over the working class' may have allowed them to indulge in popular sports but 'this development' also contributed to the depoliticization of the working classes which commercial interests exploited.[45] Similarly, Jan Cameron noted the failure of government policy initiatives and sports controlling agencies to improve women's participation in sport in the face of 'the hegemonic apparatus' that continued to keep women 'in their place' and 'away from the locus of control and ... the applause of the crowd'.[46]

As well as introducing hegemony theory to sports historians, Hardy led the constructionist approach to structures. Like Williams' approach to hegemony, constructionism afforded agents key roles in the production and reproduction of structures. Borrowing from the sociologist Anthony Giddens, Hardy and the sport sociologist Alan Ingham defined structures as 'regularized relations of interdependence that contour and generate social practices'. In this conceptualization, structures are 'constituted and transformed over time through social practices' and, critically, agency 'works in and through social structures. In Giddens' words, "social structures are both constituted by human agency, and yet at the same time are the very medium of this constitution."'[47] Hardy later applied this definition to an examination of four entrepreneurs (Henry Chadwick, Albert Spalding, James Sullivan and Senda Berenson) who profoundly influenced American sport in the late nineteenth and early twentieth centuries. Here he showed how agency works in and through social structures. Attempting to 'harness ... personal visions of the Sportgeist' (the spirit of sport), these entrepreneurs cemented a new sport structure based on commercialized sports. On the one hand, the Sportgeist allows individuals to 'invigorate' sport with their own meanings: 'players, fans, and coaches constantly make their own decisions on physicality, achievement, competition and creativity'. On the other, while 'every participant has ... a measure of agency in making sport history', individuals can only make history within external constraints that they cannot change, such as the sport structure (rules, tactics, organizations, facilities, records, equipment) and the general structure (climate, topography, economic systems, class, gender and race relations).[48]

Hardy's incorporation of the Sportgeist and the sport structure into his examination of Spalding and other sport entrepreneurs is a brilliant example of a concept of structure contributing to historical analysis. Had Hardy simply treated Spalding and his colleagues as individuals, or even had he compared them, our understanding of entrepreneurship in late nineteenth-century American sport would be far shallower; the Sportgeist and sport structure reveal the ways in which entrepreneurs shaped and ordered sport, and in turn, the limitations and constraints they faced.

By incorporating the concept of agency into a structural analysis and 'attach[ing] great importance to the relative autonomy of evidence', Hardy laid the ground work for a non-determinist methodological approach to social change (as distinct from a general theory of social change). Following Giddens, Hardy ultimately located the 'forces for change in the relations between action, consciousness, institutions and structures'.[49] However, the application of this approach would have to wait until Pamela Grundy's *Learning to Win*.

Non-determinist theories of sport and society

Seeking to understand how sport became 'a model for a conservative view of the American social and economic order', Grundy found the answer in a new ideology that emerged in the nineteenth century and portrayed competition as inevitable and generally admirable. Such was the power of this ideology that it obscured the dark side of sporting competition (e.g., violence, bribery, corruption) and shrouded it in a 'celebratory rhetoric'.[50] In developing this thesis, Grundy explored six sets of theoretical relationships: action and consciousness, action and institutions, action and structures, consciousness and institutions, consciousness and structures, and institutions and structures. For example, Grundy acknowledged both the determining effects of structure and the power of agents to transform structures. 'Residents from every walk of life', she noted, 'refashion[ed their] lives and identities' under the 'demands of industrial labor, urban life, and the ideas and images of national mass culture'. Grundy referred to 'athletic fields' as sites where minority groups could, on occasion, 'effectively challenge the assumptions that cast them as unworthy of full participation in US society'. Similarly, she observed conscious actors interrelating with the broader structures of society in complex ways. Grundy described a cross section of citizens using sport for their own ends amid widespread social changes in North Carolina in the first few decades of the twentieth century. Sport, she said, enabled 'North Carolinians to engage this new society'; it became 'an arena where residents could school themselves in the discipline and coordinated effort that were becoming hallmarks of American achievement, experiment with the pleasures of self-expression and public performance, and negotiate the boundaries between local cultures and national ideals'.[51]

In *Learning to Win* Grundy offered an unsurpassed non-determinist methodological approach to understanding the place of sport in a capitalist society and to interpreting social change – and the lack of change – in sport. Like most sports historians, however, Grundy does not make explicit her assumptions, methodology or theories and, unlike Hardy, she offers no definitional or theoretical clarity with respect to structure or structural analysis. Over the last decade, sports historians have shown less interest in the place of sport in holistic notions of society. The intellectual traditions of social theory appear to be fading from sports history as practitioners, under the sway of the cultural paradigm, focus more on cultural meanings, representations and interpretations. John Tosh defines culture as the 'web of meanings which characterizes a society and holds its members together', and its analysis introduced a new set of theories to the field.[52]

Theory, sport, culture

It is impossible to give a precise date for the turn from social to cultural history. Victoria Bonnell and Lynn Hunt refer to the 'cultural turn' running across the 1980s and 90s. Nor is it possible to isolate a single explanation. Bonnell and Hunt identify a raft of contributing factors including 'questions about the status of "the social," seemingly inevitable methodological and epistemological dilemmas, a resulting or perhaps precipitating collapse of explanatory paradigms, and a consequent realignment of the disciplines (including the rise of cultural studies)'.[53]

Cultural themes and topics became conspicuous in sports history in the second half of the 1980s.[54] This visibly increased in the following decade as historians identified sport as a medium of identity for all kinds of groups (e.g., local communities, genders, nations and so forth).[55] By the turn of the century, however, the range of cultural themes in sports history had diversified further.[56] Walter Licht emphasizes that cultural history comprises 'varying and vying projects', although he usefully categorizes these into 'social constructionism' and two forms of deconstructionism, 'pure and 'less nihilistic'.[57] In this section, I examine the theoretical content of social constructionism and less nihilistic deconstructionism. The latter includes discourse theory, textualism and narrative theory. Historians of sport have not embraced pure deconstructionism. Promoted by the likes of Jacques Derrida and Dominick LaCapra, pure deconstructionism is 'truly poststructuralist: nothing can be known. Texts or subjects of analysis are filled with contradictions and voids, and there is no need even to consider the author and his or her intentions'.[58]

The social construction of sporting culture

Social constructionists conceptualize culture as a 'deliberate product, a social construction … produced out of existing social tensions'.[59] This conceptualization underpins most cultural approaches in sports history. Social constructionists argue that cultural formations arise under any number of conditions: from on high 'as an instrument of social control', as a result of 'dialogue' between dominant and subordinate groups, stemming from 'conflict and negotiation' between dominant and subordinate groups, or simply among different groups who seek to 'distinguish themselves and sanctify their authority or to eke out separate, autonomous places'.[60] As with the constructionist approach to structure and some strands of hegemony theory, process is a common theme in social constructionism that views culture as always 'porous, subject to constant change, and forever being remade'.[61]

Examinations of racially based sporting cultures offer good examples of the social constructionist approach in sports history. These are particularly pertinent because 'commonsense' frequently portrays race as a natural or essential entity. Underpinning the constructionist concept of race is the enforced separation of people of colour – in Australia, South Africa, the USA and elsewhere – which predisposed the formation of distinct cultures. Even in northern cities such as New York, Chicago and Detroit, where approximately 1.75 million African Americans fled between 1910 and 1940 to escape the rigid segregation of the south, the colour line remained essentially in place and African Americans formed their own institutions, including churches, media and sporting clubs, and ultimately distinct cultures.[62] In the case of sport, the organizers of black sporting leagues in the USA may have 'crafted organizational plans and operational procedures that mirrored the efforts of their white counterparts', but African American baseball and basketball teams such as the Harlem Renaissance Five (the 'Rens') and Cumberland Posey's 'Big Five' from Pittsburgh still 'fashioned distinctive patterns of play'.[63] Drawing the link between early black professional basketball games and post-match dances, Steven Pope argues that:

> ... guys and gals watched the 'Rens' [and the 'Big Five'] and afterward danced to the music of leading jazz bands (e.g., Count Basie, Duke Ellington, Chick Webb) at the most popular dance halls. [At] the thirty-five hundred seat capacity Renaissance Casino and Ballroom ... [the 'Rens'] provide[d] basketball exhibitions for the throngs of people waiting to dance the night away. ... Ballplayers were probably among those who danced after games so that the diffusion of taste flowed from musicians to dancers to basketball players or from players to the dancers and musicians.[64]

The distinguishing style of African American basketball, says Pope, centres on 'fast breaks, explosive speed, innovative ball handling, and varied shot selection'. By appropriating this style black people 'transformed an *American* ludic endeavour into an *African American* cultural expression thereby redefining the meaning of being American in their own terms through the game'. In other words, African Americans took a cultural rather than a racial trait and 'adapted it as a ritualized style, as a performance ... [so as] to distinguish themselves from whites'.[65]

In his history of African American basketball, Pope engages interpretations that exceed the material evidence and thus highlights a key methodological issue associated with social constructionism. Culture, Pope reminds us, 'is always a vexing process ... to document through traditional sources and methods'. This is all the more so when the culture under consideration is a 'stylized physical ... primarily non-verbal ... performance'. Here Pope cites historian Stephen Fox who argues basketball developed 'spontaneous[ly] ... in thousands of isolated pockets around the country' and 'bounc[ed] forward in the hands of numberless innovators, most of them now unknown and unknowable'. Thus, Pope concludes, 'if it is difficult to substantiate the timing of the sport itself, we must also confess that any documentation on the development of a distinctly *black* style of play is even more elusive and thus open to speculation and historical conjecture'.[66]

How do historians deal with the problem of elusive sources? Social historians typically appeal to theory and cultural historians to epistemology. Pope advocates a 'postmodern sensibility' that 'allows us "to know something without claiming to know everything"'. He also urges historians to move beyond seeking objective facts and instead ask questions about the origins of facts and their operation '*in* history, especially insofar as they cultivate the subjects *of* history'.[67] Yet, notwithstanding Pope's deconstructionist sentiments, he remains committed to a knowledge-based, causally orientated social constructionism including investigating 'the structure and function of cultural production' and 'why social groups develop distinctive styles of performance'.[68]

Deconstructing sporting culture

Sports historians may have shied away from pure deconstructionism, but they have been receptive to less nihilistic versions. Although less nihilistic deconstructionists too deny all 'truths or essences', they admit 'the past can be studied and known'. In their view 'all knowledge is constructed', whether it be a source, archive, text, narrative or even a language, and the reader must 'discern the premises' of its existence.[69] Thus instead of conceptualizing history as a set of 'concrete phenomenological objects with a fixed meaning', historians with a deconstructionist bent regard it as a 'system or structure of meaning flowing from semiotic, social and cultural processes' which they subject to 'diverse readings and various interpretations'.[70] While the approach paradoxically contains structuralist elements, structural formations in less nihilistic deconstructionism are not responses to social determinants or external reality.[71] Linguistic structures in less nihilistic deconstructionist theories, for example, shape social structures and cultural practices, such as sport, and therefore *constitute* history, by virtue of facilitating or excluding from consideration certain ways of thinking about experiences and influencing behaviour. Such a concept stands in marked contrast to earlier theories that viewed language as a faithful replication, or at least an unproblematic representation, of reality.[72] Following Michel Foucault, this conceptualization of language is termed discourse.[73] Discourse theory, along with textualism and narrative theory support less nihilistic versions of deconstructionism in sports history. I discuss these in turn below.

At the heart of Foucauldian discourse theory are variable and contested meanings and notions of truth and knowledge embroiled in struggles for power. In his later historical projects, Foucault connected the deployment of power to the body.[74] Here he focused on the body as a product of discourse and as '*the* link between daily practices on the one hand and the large scale organisation of power on the other'.[75] Foucault argued that scientific, rational and implicitly modern discourses of the human body, especially medicine, psychiatry and psychology, provided both the philosophical and organizational power to repress bodies. Foucault's interest in the body as the link between practice and power derived from his study of different technologies of discipline and in particular the emergence of public surveillance as a prominent technology. Initially encouraging and stimulating convicted criminals to monitor and exert self-control over their behaviour,[76] the gaze of surveillance quickly diffused from prisons into other state institutions such as army barracks, hospitals and schools, and then into everyday life – in the street, at the shopping mall, in the open-plan office. At these sites, individuals constitute themselves as 'normal' through the visibility of acceptable appearance and behaviour.[77] Critical to the successful operation of surveillance as a technology of discipline in everyday life is the stimulation of desire by a consumer culture that compels individuals to address the presentation of their bodies in public. Foucault found in consumer culture a new mode of control that proceeds not through institutional repression but by individual investment in, and stimulation of, the body. In his words, 'Get undressed – but be slim, good looking, tanned!'[78]

Foucauldian theories of, and insights into the knowledge–body–power trilogy attracted the attention of sports historians interested in the corporeal dimensions of sport and physical activity, and issues related to power. Patricia Vertinsky brought discourse to the fore in *The Eternally Wounded Woman*. Referring to the controlling power of discourse and its ability to subordinate women, Vertinsky observed that by 'speaking as experts', medical practitioners in the late nineteenth and early twentieth centuries 'constituted women in particular ways'.

> Medicine took on the authority to label female complaints, or to declare women potentially sick even if they did not complain. The labelling of normal female functions such as menstruation and menopause as signs of illness requiring rest and medical observation did not, in itself, *make* women sick or incapable of vigorous activity. It did, however, provide a powerful rationale to persuade them from acting in any other way.[79]

Thus, from a Foucauldian perspective, discourse became the material reality of female subordination by defining women's problems (of the body) and the solutions.

Discourse as a means of policing women's bodies and female physicality and sexuality became orthodox in sports history during the 1990s. Susan Cahn, for example, analysed women's sport in *Coming on Strong: Gender and Sexuality in Twentieth-Century Women's Sport* as a cultural product in which popular discourses about the meaning of gender and sexuality competed against each other. In the struggle over women's participation in sport, she notes that 'matters went far beyond the issue of decorum' and the 'kinds of behaviour … deemed appropriate for the female sex'. They in fact 'broached fundamental questions about the content and definition of American woman- and man-hood'. These included, 'would women engaging in traditionally male activity become more manlike? [and] What exactly were "manly" and "womanly" qualities?'[80] The discourse of lesbianism emerged as a powerful weapon to police female coaches, athletes and administrators in the twentieth century. Unease with lesbianism, Cahn wrote, effects decisions around hiring coaches, recruiting players and publicizing clubs. In short, Cahn maintained that the discourse of female heterosexuality and homosexuality has a material reality in the distribution and allocation of opportunities and rewards in the sporting world.

Sports historians have been less receptive to Foucauldian theories of the relationships between sport, consumer culture, the stimulation of desire and the subordination of bodies. Most sports historians merely touch on the debate as to whether sport liberates or represses women. Discussions typically conclude on the claim that media images of activities such as aerobics seduce women to strive for unattainable ideal body types and thus 'reproduce inequalities and inadequacies among participants'.[81] The lack of attention given to these interrelationships is surprising in light of the directions John Hargreaves provided in *Sport, Power and Culture*.

Hargreaves rejected the view that the 'economic power' of cultural producers and brokers can fully explain the 'power-generating capacity of consumer culture'. Rather, consumer culture derives its 'coherence and power' from the articulation of key discourses and practices. The 'dominant discourses/practices' of contemporary social life, according to Hargreaves, are 'organised around consumer culture'; they include 'youth, beauty, romance, sexual attraction, energy, fitness and health, movement, excitement, adventure, freedom, exotica, luxury, enjoyment, entertainment, fun'. Hargreaves explored the relationship between physical practices and the organization of power through the workings of consumer culture which manipulates the public representation of bodies.[82]

Hargreaves influenced my work on the history of the beach and my examination of different methods used to discipline Australian beachgoers in the early twentieth century. For example, although briefer bathing costumes introduced onto Australian beaches after World War I 'gave women new freedoms, … they also enticed them to reveal more of their bodies which were then subjected to new disciplinary methods – exercise, dieting, toiletries, cosmetics, accessories – to ensure that they conformed to the correct shape, colour, smell and demeanour'.[83] In his history of Canadian sport, Colin Howell premises his discussion of sporting bodies on Foucauldian theories of mass consumer culture disciplining the modern body. Although 'liberated from Victorian prudery', Howell writes, the body is now 'subjected to the cultural technologies of consumer capitalism, which through advertising presents the body as a commodity for consumption'.[84]

Textualism constitutes a second body of theory in less nihilistic versions of deconstructionist sports history. Deconstructionists expanded the notion of texts to include non-literary forms such as paintings, films, television programmes, clothing styles, sports spectacles, political rallies and even societies and cultures. Elaborating on the idea of life as a text, Robert Berkhofer explains that:

> … not only do human behaviour and social interaction produce texts, but humans and their societies understand themselves through and as interpretative textualizations. It is only through such textualizations that humans can reproduce their cultures and social institutions. All behaviour can be interpreted like texts because it was produced in the first place through a process of textualization broadly conceived.[85]

Interestingly, the cultural anthropologist Clifford Geertz introduced the idea of sport as an interpretative text in his seminal essay on Balinese cockfighting. 'To treat the cockfight as a text', Geertz said, 'is to bring out … the central feature of it that treating it as a rite or a pastime, the two most obvious alternatives, would tend to obscure – its use of emotion for cognitive ends':

> What the cockfight says it says in a vocabulary of sentiment – the thrill of risk, the despair of loss, the pleasure of triumph. Yet what is says is not merely that risk is exciting, loss depressing, or triumph gratifying, banal tautologies of effect, but that it is of these emotions, thus exampled, that society is built and individuals put together. Attending cockfights and participating in them is, for the Balinese, a kind of sentimental education. What he learns there is what his culture's ethos and his private sensibility (or, anyway, certain aspects of them) look like when spelled out externally in a collective text.[86]

Thus, the cockfight 'provides a metasocial commentary' upon Balinese life, especially its hierarchical structure; and 'its function … is interpretative: it is a Balinese reading of Balinese experience; a story they tell themselves about themselves'.[87] Yet, if Geertz teaches historians to interpret what participants in cultural events already know, he also issues a caution: 'the cockfight is not the master key to Balinese life, any more than bullfighting is to Spanish. What it says about life is not unqualified nor even unchallenged by what other equally eloquent cultural statements say about it'. 'The culture of a people', he continues, 'is an ensemble of texts, themselves ensembles'. Hence the scholar's task is to 'read over the shoulders of those to whom [the texts] properly belong'.[88]

Surprisingly, sports historians have ignored Geertz's work, even though he referred to America revealing itself in the ball park, on the golf links, at the race track and around the poker table, just as 'Bali surfaces in a cock ring'.[89] In fact textual analysis only emerged in sports history in the early 1990s, at which point it had benefited from two decades of theoretical advances in cultural interpretation. One crucial advance was the shift from ideological readings of texts to reader-orientated readings. Whereas the former tended to present popular or mass culture as monolithic, the latter recognized that no single reading could represent the diversity of responses that readers assign texts; the breadth of readers' personal and social experiences is just too great. Sports historians including H.F. Moorehouse, Richard Holt, Jeffrey Hill and Michael Oriard applied this concept of textualism,[90] although the most theoretically explicit accounts reside in Oriard's *Reading Football* and Hill's *Sport and the Literary Imagination*.

Analysing the development of American football as a mass spectacle, Oriard captured the limitless possibilities for spectators interpreting a sporting text when he identified a range of possible responses (readings) to a violent collision in American football between a receiver and defender:

> While fans probably choose teams most often for reasons of personal connection or regional rootedness, several other factors come easily to mind. Imagine our receiver as black, the defender white. Or one of them from Notre Dame, the other from Brigham Young; one from the Big Ten, the other from the Southeast Conference; one a candidate for a Rhodes Scholarship, the other a known drug-user or sex-offender; one a street kid from the inner city, the other the son of a wealthy cardiologist; one a well-known volunteer for the Special Olympics, the other a arrogant publicist of his own athletic brilliance. Certain teams have their own distinctive images: think of the Cowboys, the Bears, the Raiders, the 49ers in the National Football League; or, of Penn State, Miami, Oklahoma, Southern California among the colleges. Imagine the fans watching these players and teams not as a 'mass' audience but as actual people: European-, African-, Hispanic-, and Asian-American; Catholic, Protestant, Jew, and non-believer; WASP and redneck; college graduate and high-school dropout; conservative and liberal; racist and humanitarian; male and female, rich and poor, urban and rural, sick and well; ones just fired from jobs and ones just promoted; ones just fallen in love and ones just separated from a spouse; some pissed off at the world and some blissfully content.[91]

Acknowledging that any reading of American football will confront a plurality of meanings, Oriard sets out to highlight the diversity of audiences and to explain the power of texts to create meaning. According to Oriard, textual analysis focuses on people's actual experiences; it challenges historians to break free from master narratives that impose predetermined meanings grounded in the economic and social conditions that supposedly frame all experiences.[92] As Hill puts it, 'the text has the capacity to *create* meaning as much as to *reflect* meanings construed elsewhere'.[93]

In his foreword to *Reading Football*, Alan Trachtenberg describes Oriard's work as one that 'tells the story of how stories are told'. In Trachtenberg's words, 'the story told in *Reading Football* is that the game emerged as narrative through a process of reading, of mediated interpretation on the part of several cohorts of historical actors'.[94] *Reading Football* has not launched a plethora of imitations but at least two sports historians employ narrative in a similar manner. Whereas Geertz and Oriard conceptualized Balinese cockfighting and early American football as texts, Catriona Parratt and Peter Mewett approached the Haxey Hood (a folk-football-type game played at Haxey village in north-west Lincolnshire) and the dying Australian sport of professional running respectively as narratives.

Seeking to understand the different 'meanings that can be read in the Hood, and specifically with what it has to say about the people and the place of Haxey and about their connections with the game and with each other', Parratt viewed the Hood as 'a set of narratives'. Many narratives constitute the Hood; there are narratives relating to the actual game, narratives of the rituals and practices that precede the game and narratives about its origins. Of particular interest to Parratt are those narratives that assign crucial roles to women.[95]

Mewett approached professional running as a network of narratives that the runners and their coaches employed as 'models of how to win and strategies to combat threats to winning'. Illustrating the latter, Mewett offered a story told by one runner, 'Tony Holborn', who described the tactics used by his coach, 'Charlie Davis', during trials (full-speed runs over race distances), and 'the consequences that could befall snoopers' – spies working for competing stables or for bookmakers.[96] Narratives such as these, Mewett suggested, make professional running in the sense that they guide the actions of runners and coaches in a range of circumstances.

Parratt and Oriard concur. Narratives, says Parratt, 'help to define Haxey as a distinctive place and Haxonians as a distinctive people, to produce a sense of community and attachment within and across generations, even across centuries, and to evoke feelings of belonging to the land and locale'.[97] Similarly, Oriard argued, 'the very experience of playing [football] is determined to a considerable degree by the narratives through which boys and young men consciously and unconsciously learn to read its meanings'.[98]

Critics remain unconvinced. Edward Said sums up the position of the detractors. While Said agreed that under certain conditions some texts may have a material reality, he maintained that 'the realities of power and authority – as well as the resistances offered by men, women and social movements to institutions, authorities, and orthodoxies – are the realities that make texts possible, that deliver them to their readers'.[99] Bryan Palmer applied Said's logic to the entire deconstructionist project and questioned whether it can 'transcend its limitation' of forever turning inward towards interpretation and denying that understanding of the past can exist outside of texts, discourses, languages and signification.[100] Palmer's criticism resonates with Vertinsky and Hargreaves, both of whom treated language as a supplementary analytical tool; language assisted in shaping and understanding lived experiences rather than constituting them.[101] Vertinsky, for example, saw 'networks of discursive practices' as 'moulded and influenced by social institutions' while Hargreaves linked discourse to the 'production system'.[102] Indeed, its broad acceptance can probably be explained by the fact that discourse approaches in sports history typically run in tandem with the traditional focus on institutions and practices associated with social history.[103] Narrative theory has also surfaced in sports history, albeit in a very minor way, through the issue of representation.

Representations of sports history

Several years before sports historians turned their attention to cultural analysis Lynn Hunt predicted that it would sharpen the methods and goals of history. In her words, 'as historians learn to analyze their subjects' representations of their worlds, they inevitably begin to reflect on the nature of their own efforts to represent history; the practice of history is, after all, a process of text creating and of "seeing," that is, giving form to subjects'.[104] Indeed, following on this issue, Steve Pope recently commented, 'history is not something … waiting to be discovered in "primary" sources … but an activity embodied in "performance," in the sense of action enfolded in the resources of representation and of representation as itself a form of action'.[105] Synthia Sydnor raised the issue of representation in the field with her history of synchronized swimming. Presented as series of evocatively titled tableaux (e.g., 'Proem', 'Also Known As', 'Fin de Millennium Synchronized Swimming'), Sydnor's history contains lists of words, each of which amounts to a 'show' of images and ideas about synchronized swimming. Sydnor classified her text as Benjaminian, after the German Marxist and cultural critic Walter Benjamin. He conceptualized history as a series of snapshots, a model that derived from his interest in the montage production techniques used in photography and film, and which he translated into 'showing' history. In this sense Benjamin likened the production of history to an act of aesthetics and ethics rather than science. Sydnor followed Benjamin, describing her essay on the history of synchronized swimming as 'a hybrid'.[106]

However, Murray Phillips was the first historian of sport to delve into the theory of narrative representation in any substantial way. Phillips employed Hayden White's theory of historical narratives to compare those produced by Ed Jaggard and I pertaining to the Australian surf lifesaving movement. Drawing essentially on the same evidence, Jaggard and I frame remarkably different narratives, which Phillips, following White, attributed to our respective tropes, emplotments and arguments. According to Phillips, my account of female surf lifesavers unfolded as a tragedy whereas Jaggard's history of women's involvement in surf lifesaving followed a romantic plot. In my narrative, women fought for, and gained, access to the masculine domain of surf lifesaving, although full admission did not alleviate their 'suffering' and 'agony'. My story line was one of enduring tragedy exemplified by frequent 'buts' which served as a literary device to amplify women's pain. 'Women were admitted as full members *but* …; women gained administrative positions *but* …; and discrimination has been tempered *but* … ' Unlike my 'tortured souls', Jaggard's women were 'heroes'. Female triumphs and achievements shaped Jaggard's story. In the face of 'barriers, discrimination and abuse', women 'persisted with dogged determination' to become 'accepted' in surf lifesaving.[107]

Phillips claimed that the different emplotments (and tropes and arguments) in our works fuse with our respective ideologies. Our histories reveal liberal and radical ideologies in discussions about social changes within surf lifesaving and in particular the pace and desirability of change. Jaggard agreed that surf lifesaving is a 'conservative, masculine institution'. Yet, notwithstanding these 'warts', he believed surf lifesaving 'deserves' its place on the beach and that its governing council needs merely to fine tune its policies to preserve what is ultimately a well-earned iconic status in Australia. By contrast, I demanded 'structural transformations' to 'reconstitute' the movement.[108]

Phillips' application of White's model to the interrogation and analysis of a specific historical debate lends powerful support to White's contention that historians invent and imagine their narratives rather than discover them in their sources.[109] At the very least, Phillips showed that sports historians are no different to other scholars who impose themselves on their narratives. Of course, White's work has been subject to numerous criticisms,[110] including the precise relationship between ideology and trope. Keith Jenkins argued that White mistakenly inverts the relationship between trope and ideology and that rather than tropes prefiguring the modes of ideology, the ideological mode prefigures which trope historians use to 'metaphorically "figure things out"'. Notwithstanding his criticism, Jenkins believed that White provides a serious model for 'constructing histories' and he urged his colleagues to acknowledge the 'constituted rather than the found nature of ... "the historicised past"'.[111]

Whether couched in Jenkins' terms of acknowledging the constituted nature of history or in Hunt's language of giving form to subjects, deconstructionist notions of representation underscore reflexivity. Historians of sport have shown reflexivity under specific conditions, such as when they write historiography, reviews and rejoinders, and in prefaces and footnotes. Deconstructionist reflexivity, however, is a heightened form of reflexivity in which historians reveal their ontological, epistemological, theoretical, ethical, moral and political positions throughout their texts.[112] This heightened reflexivity also includes what Robert Berkhofer calls reflexive contextualization; here historians explain their choices about different levels of context, including the relationship between the personal context and more traditional contextualized versions of the past.[113]

Patricia Vertinsky and her colleagues embrace reflexive contextualization in *Disciplining Bodies in the Gymnasium*. As faculty at the University of British Columbia, these researchers have an intimate knowledge of the War Memorial Gymnasium and the past that they choose to record resonates with their experiences.[114] For example, in their essay 'No Body/ies in the Gym', Vertinsky, McKay and Petrina report that women occupying offices in the War Memorial Gymnasium as faculty in the School of Human Kinetics call the building 'the bastion of "the basement boys," the male scientists who [take] up most of the working space there'. They cite a female faculty member who registers her 'disappointment' at men who refuse 'to play ball with us' and who exclude women from the team. This example is clearly one with which the authors personally identify and in this sense is part of their context. They also put this personal context into a broader context of civil rights for women and the movement towards affirmative action and gender sensitive policies in the 1990s. These trends encouraged administrators at the University of British Columbia to hire female faculty in the School of Human Kinetics. Importantly, they also extend the broader context into a commentary on change and continuity in gender attitudes and policies. On the one hand, women and men now 'share playing space and practice times in the War Memorial Gymnasium and it is widely accepted that games such as basketball are good for developing physical mastery and group coordination for women, just as they are for men'. On the other hand, officials continue to schedule women's intercollegiate basketball games as preludes to men's games, the Department of Athletics and Sports Services employs only one female coach compared to twenty-one male coaches, and 'the lion's share of the athletic budget still flows to the men's sports'.[115]

Representation and reflexivity perhaps provide the best indication of the theoretical chasm between social and cultural history. Whereas sociological theories in social history framed the search for unified and unambiguous interpretations of the past, cultural theories conceptualize history as a more creative, self-conscious and critical enterprise.[116] As I shall discuss in the conclusion, this has major epistemological consequences for historians.

Conclusion

Historians of sport privilege the authority of evidence and remain ever vigilant over what they regard as the distorting effects of theory on historical analysis. Nonetheless, theory holds a prominent place in the field. Sports historians may not have written many explicitly theoretical pieces, but the assumptions that underpin their work, as well as the abstractions they freely embrace, are all richly theoretical. Over the last decade, the theoretical content of sports history has crossed from the social to the cultural paradigm. In the former, sports historians used social theories based on analogies with the physical world and concepts of structure to explain the place of sport in society; these same theories also offered insights into social change – and its absence. In the latter, historians of sport engage different theories to tackle problems associated with meaning and representation. While interpretation of meaning and issues of representation have always been integral to history, sports historians typically considered them in the context of factually accurate and verifiable sources that produced reality. Under the sway of cultural history, however, historians of sport have increasingly approached meaning and representation through a range of new theoretical lenses such as social constructionism, discourse, texualism and narrative; these theories approach sources as artefacts, the meaning of which exists in their reading / telling rather than their connection to a past reality.[117]

Reflecting on these developments, Catriona Parratt believes that most sports historians have developed a certain degree of comfort with the current incorporation of different cultural theories which she suggests have helped sharpen and enrich the field.[118] Cahn's *Coming on Strong*, Oriard's *Reading Football* and Vertinsky's *Eternally Wounded Woman* are classic cases in point. However, sports historians have not yet confronted the full epistemological implications of the newer cultural theories. It remains to be seen how they will respond to Steve Pope's call for a postmodern sensibility when dealing with elusive sources, to John Bale's scepticism towards facts (he labels them 'beliefs') and language (which he insists is 'complex', 'multifaceted' and 'slippery'),[119] to Jeff Hill's interpretation of the sports novel as reformulating 'the idea of "sport" through a fluid, shifting, and complex process of negotiated meaning',[120] or to Patricia Vertinsky and her colleagues' reflexive contextualization. Despite the angst directed at traditional sociological theories, which sports historians accused of distorting evidence,[121] those theories never disturbed the epistemological foundations of the field. By contrast, the new cultural theories expose what Murray Phillips calls the fragile epistemology of sports history[122] and in so doing question history's status as an objective project.

Notes

1 Michael Postan, *Fact and Relevance: Essays on Historical Method* (Cambridge: Cambridge University Press, 1971), 62.
2 Geoffrey Elton, *Return to Essentials* (Cambridge: Cambridge University Press, 1991), 15, 19.
3 Alun Munslow, *Deconstructing History* (London: Routledge, 1997), 22–23. See also John Tosh, *The Pursuit of History: Aims, Methods and New Directions in the Study of Modern History*, second edn (London: Longman, 1991), 154–55; and Richard Evans, *In Defence of History* (London: Granta, 1997), 83.
4 John Tosh, *The Pursuit of History: Aims, Methods and New Directions in the Study of Modern History*, third edn (Harlow: Pearson, 2000), 134.
5 Nancy Struna, 'Social History and Sport', in Jay Coakley and Eric Dunning, eds, *Handbook of Sports Studies* (London: Sage, 2000), 189. See also Jeffrey Hill, 'British Sports History: A Post-modern Future?', *Journal of Sport History* 23, 1 (1996): 14.
6 Victoria Bonnell and Lynn Hunt, eds, *Beyond the Cultural Turn: New Directions in the Study of Society and Culture* (Berkeley: University of California Press, 1999), 1; Allan Megill, *Historical Knowledge, Historical Error: A Contemporary Guide to Practice* (Chicago: University of Chicago Press, 2007), 204–5.
7 See for example William Baker, 'The State of British Sport History', *Journal of Sport History* 10, 1 (1983): 53–66; James Walvin, 'Sport, Social History and the Historian', *British Journal of Sports*

History 1, 1 (1984): 5–13; Bruce Kidd, *The Struggle for Canadian Sport* (Toronto: University of Toronto Press, 1996), 8; and Jeff Hill, *Sport and the Literary Imagination: Essays in History, Literature, and Sport* (New York: Peter Lang, 2007), 13.

8 Christopher Lloyd, *Explanations in Social History* (Oxford: Basil Blackwell, 1988), 149, 154.

9 Keith Sandiford, 'The Victorians at Play: Problems in Historiographical Methodology', *Journal of Social History* 15, 2 (1981): 272. Commonly cited examples include: Frederick Paxson, 'The Rise of Sport', *Mississippi Valley Historical Review* 4 (1917), 143–68, reprinted in George Sage, ed., *Sport and American Society: Selected Readings* (Reading: Addison-Wesley, 1974), 80–103; and Foster Rhea Dulles, *A History of Recreation: America Learns to Play* (New York: Appleton-Century-Crofts, 1965).

10 Peter McIntosh, 'An Historical View of Sport and Social Control', *International Review of Sport Sociology* 6 (1971): 6, 10–11.

11 Robert Malcolmson, *Popular Recreations in English Society, 1700–1850* (Cambridge: Cambridge University Press, 1973), 76–79, 84–86. See also John Daly, *Elysian Fields: Sport, Class and Community in Colonial South Australia 1836–1890* (Adelaide: John Daly, 1982).

12 Quotation from Allen Guttmann, 'From Ritual to Record: A Retrospective Critique', *Sport History Review* 32, 1 (2001): 5. See also Gareth Stedman Jones, 'Class Expression Versus Social Control: A Critique of Recent Trends in the Social History of "Leisure"', *History Workshop* 4 (1977): 163–64; Melvin Adelman, 'Academicians and American Athletics: A Decade of Progress', *Journal of Sport History* 10, 1 (1983): 86–87; Richard Gruneau, 'Modernization or Hegemony: Two Views of Sport and Social Development', in Jean Harvey and Hart Cantelon, eds, *Not Just a Game: Essays in Canadian Sport Sociology* (Ottawa: University of Ottawa Press, 1988), 15–16; Richard Holt, *Sport and the British: A Modern History* (Oxford: Clarendon Press, 1989), 359–60; Tony Mason, 'Afterword', in Tony Mason, ed., *Sport in Britain: A Social History* (Cambridge: Cambridge University Press, 1989), 345; and Kidd, *Canadian Sport*, 9.

13 Lloyd, *Explanations*, 155–56.

14 Malcolmson, *Popular Recreations* (CUP Archive, 1979), 75–76.

15 Benjamin Rader, *American Sports: From the Age of Folk Games to the Age of Television* (Englewood Cliffs: Prentice Hall, 1983), 360.

16 Lloyd, *Explanations*, 200–1, also 176.

17 Describing patterns of institutionalized or constrained behaviour, structuralism emphasizes 'ruled, shaped, ordered, limited and determined' human behaviour. E.P. Thompson, *The Poverty of Theory: Or an Orrery of Errors* (London: Merlin, 1995), 198. Unlike institutions such as the International Olympic Committee and the World Anti-Doping Association, which are endowed with agency (i.e. decision-making capabilities) and which pursue goals, structures are conceptualized as existing beyond the interaction of individuals. The weight of a crowd is a good example: 'The great movements of enthusiasm, indignation, and pity in a crowd do not originate in any one of the particular individual consciousness. They come to each one of us from without and can carry us away in spite of ourselves. Of course, it may happen that, in abandoning myself to them unreservedly, I do not feel the pressure they exert upon me. But it is revealed as soon as I try to resist them. Let an individual attempt to oppose one of these collective manifestations, and the emotions that he denies will turn against him. Now, if this power of external coercion asserts itself so clearly in cases of resistance, it must exist also in the first-mentioned cases, although we are unconscious of it' (Emile Durkheim, *The Rules of Sociological Method*, eighth edn (Glencoe: Free Press, 1964), 4–5).

The critical point is that structures such as crowds, societies and sport are objects of knowledge even though historians cannot attribute their properties to constituent individuals.

18 Allen Guttmann, *From Ritual to Record: The Nature of Modern Sports* (New York: Columbia University Press, 1978), 15–55.

19 See also Mel Adelman, *A Sporting Time: New York City and the Rise of Modern Athletics, 1820–1870* (Urbana: University of Illinois Press, 1986). Sport sociologist Eric Dunning is another leading theorist of the change from traditional to modern sport. His figurational approach has been the subject of much debate with critics pointing to its functionalist tendencies, a charge vigorously denied by Dunning. Eric Dunning and Kenneth Sheard, *Barbarians, Gentlemen and Players: A Sociological Study of the Development of Rugby Football*, second edn (London: Routledge, 2005).

20 See for example John Lucas and Ronald Smith, *Saga of American Sport* (Philadelphia: Lea and Febiger, 1978), 125–33; and Wray Vamplew, 'Sport and Industrialization: An Economic Interpretation of the Changes in Popular Sport in Nineteenth-Century England', in J.A. Mangan, ed.,

Pleasure, Profit, Proselytism: British Culture and Sport at Home and Abroad, 1700–1914 (London: Frank Cass, 1988), 7–20.

21 Lloyd, *Explanations*, 208.

22 Guttmann, *From Ritual to Record* (Irvington: Columbia University Press, 1979), 80–82, 85–86.

23 Guttmann, *From Ritual to Record* (Irvington: Columbia University Press, 1979), 80.

24 Guttmann, *From Ritual to Record* (Irvington: Columbia University Press, 1979), 47, 48, 50–51, 51, 52, 54, 55.

25 See note 17 above for the crowd as an example of an essentialist structure. Malcolm Waters, *Modern Sociological Theory* (London: Sage, 1994), 92–93.

26 Jean-Marie Brohm, *Sport – A Prison of Measured Time* (London: Ink Links, 1978); Bero Rigauer, *Sport and Work* (New York: Columbia University Press, 1981); and Gerhard Vinnai, *Football Mania* (London: Ocean Books, 1973). See also Paul Hoch, *Rip Off the Big Game* (New York: Doubleday, 1972).

27 Tony Mason, *Sport in Britain* (London: Faber and Faber, 1988), 75; Adelman, 'Academicians', 94; and Benjamin Rader, 'Modern Sports: In Search of Interpretations', *Journal of Social History* 13, 2 (1979): 312–13.

28 Richard Gruneau, *Class, Sports, and Social Development* (Amherst: University of Massachusetts Press, 1983), 37. On these topics see: Arnd Krüger and James Riordan, *The Story of Worker Sport* (Champaign: Human Kinetics, 1996); and Harry Edwards, *The Revolt of the Black Athlete* (New York: Free Press, 1969). The reference to Muhammed Ali comes from David Zang, *SportsWars: Sport in the Age of Aquarius* (Fayetteville: The University of Arkansas Press, 2001), 112.

29 Alan Tomlinson, 'Good Times, Bad Times and the Politics of Leisure: Working-Class Culture in the 1930s in a Small Northern English Working-Class Community', in Hart Cantelon and Robert Hollands, eds, *Leisure, Sport and Working-Class Cultures: Theory and History* (Toronto: Garamond Press, 1988), 48.

30 John Hargreaves, *Sport, Power and Culture: A Social and Historical Analysis of Popular Sports in Britain* (Cambridge: Polity Press, 1986), 114–15.

31 Jennifer Hargreaves, *Sporting Females: Critical Issues in the History and Sociology of Women's Sports* (London: Routledge, 1994).

32 Tom Bottomore, 'Structure and History', in Peter Blau, ed., *Approaches to the Study of Social Structure* (New York: The Free Press, 1975), 165.

33 Waters, *Modern Sociological Theory* (Thousand Oaks: SAGE Publications, 1994), 177–78.

34 Perry Anderson, 'The Antinomies of Antonio Gramsci', *New Left Review* 100 (1976/77): 20. According to Gramsci: 'hegemony works through ideology but it does not consist of false ideas, perceptions, definitions. It works *primarily* by inserting the subordinate class into key institutions and structures which support the power and social authority of the dominant order. It is above all, in these structures and relations that a subordinate class *lives its subordination*' (Quintin Hoare and Geoffrey Nowell Smith, eds, *Selections from the Prison Notebooks of Antonio Gramsci* (London: Lawrence and Wishart, 1971), 164).

35 John Hargreaves, 'Sport and Hegemony: Some Theoretical Problems', in Hart Cantelon and Richard Gruneau, eds, *Sport, Culture, and the Modern State* (Toronto: University of Toronto Press, 1982), 134–35. See also Stephen Hardy and Alan Ingham, 'Games, Structure, and Agency: Historians on the American Play Movement', *Journal of Social History* 17 (1983): 285–301; Gruneau, *Class, Sports, and Social Development* (Champaign: Human Kinetics, 1999); Raymond Williams, *Marxism and Literature* (Oxford: Oxford University Press, 1977), 112; and Alan Ingham and Stephen Hardy, 'Introduction: Sport Studies Through the Lens of Raymond Williams', in Alan Ingham and John Loy, eds, *Sport in Social Development: Traditions, Transitions and Transformations* (Champaign: Human Kinetics, 1993), 1–19.

36 For important exceptions see Stephen Jones, *Sport, Politics and the Working Class: Organised Labour and Sport in Inter-War Britain* (Manchester: Manchester University Press, 1988); and Kevin Wamsley, 'Cultural Signification and National Ideologies: Rifle-shooting in Late Nineteenth-century Canada', *Social History* 20, 1 (1995): 63–72.

37 George Sage, *Power and Ideology in American Sport: A Critical Perspective* (Champaign: Human Kinetics, 1990), 19.

38 This is particularly pronounced in historical investigations dealing with gender relations and masculine hegemony. See Mike Donaldson, 'What is Hegemonic Masculinity?', *Theory and Society* 22 (1993): 643–57. For critiques of hegemony theory by sports historians see Holt, *Sport and the British*, 364;

and Tony Collins, *Rugby's Great Split: Class, Culture and the Origins of Rugby League Football* (London: Frank Cass, 1998), 232.

39 Jeffrey Alexander, 'Modern, Anti, Post and Neo', *New Left Review* 210 (1995): 75–76.

40 Alexander, 'Modern, Anti, Post, Neo', 69, 71, 73, 75–76, 77, 78.

41 Zang, *SportsWars*, xii.

42 Eric Hobsbawm, *On History* (London: Abacus, 1998), 193–94.

43 Gruneau, *Class, Sports, and Social Development* (Champaign: Human Kinetics, 1999), 36.

44 Alexander, 'Modern, Anti, Post, Neo', 80–82.

45 Hargreaves, *Sport, Power and Culture*, 82–83.

46 Jan Cameron, 'The Issue of Gender in Sport: "No Bloody Room for Sheilas ... "', in Chris Collins, ed., *Sport in New Zealand Society* (Palmerston North: Dunmore Press, 2000), 178–79.

47 Hardy and Ingham, 'Games, Structure, and Agency', 286. See also Alan Ingham and Stephen Hardy, 'Sport: Structuration, Subjugation and Hegemony', *Theory, Culture and Society* 2, 2 (1984): 100, notes 1 and 2.

48 Stephen Hardy, 'Entrepreneurs, Structures, and the Sportgeist: Old Tensions in a Modern Industry', in Donald Kyle and Gary Stark, eds, *Essays on Sport History and Sport Mythology* (College Station: Texas A & M Press, 1990), 45–82.

49 Lloyd, *Explanations*, 288, 310. See also Christopher Lloyd, *The Structures of History* (Oxford: Basil Blackwell, 1993), 186, 285.

50 Pamela Grundy, *Learning to Win: Sports, Education, and Social Change in Twentieth-Century North Carolina* (Chapel Hill: The University of North Carolina Press, 2001), 299.

51 Grundy, *Learning to Win*, 180, 296–97.

52 Tosh, *The Pursuit of History*, third edn (White Plains: Longman, 2002), 177.

53 Bonnell and Hunt, *Beyond the Cultural Turn*, 6. Allan Megill claims that the new cultural history 'arose in the 1980s as both an extension of and a rebellion against the dominance of social history' (*Historical Knowledge, Historical Error*, 188, 199–204).

54 Early pieces include Brian Stoddart, *Saturday Afternoon Fever: Sport in Australian Culture* (Sydney: Angus & Robertson, 1986); Elliot Gorn, *The Manly Art: Bare-Knuckle Prize Fighting in America* (Ithaca: Cornell University Press, 1986); J.A. Mangan, *The Games Ethic and Imperialism* (Harmondsworth: Viking, 1986); J.A. Mangan and Roberta Park, eds, *From Fair Sex to Feminism: Sport and the Socialization of Women in the Industrial and Post-Industrial Eras* (London: Frank Cass, 1987); Mangan, *Pleasure, Profit, Proselytism*; and Richard Holt, ed., *Sport and the Working Class in Modern Britain* (Manchester: Manchester University Press, 1990).

55 Three key texts in this regard were Lincoln Allison, ed., *The Changing Politics of Sport* (Manchester: Manchester University Press, 1993); Grant Jarvie and Graham Walker, eds, *Scottish Sport in the Making of the Nation* (Leicester: Leicester University Press, 1994); and John Nauright and Tim Chandler, eds, *Making Men: Rugby and Masculine Identity* (London: Frank Cass, 1996).

56 For a nice explication see Hill, *Sport and the Literary Imagination* (New York, Peter Lang, 2007), 13.

57 Walter Licht, 'Cultural History / Social History: A Review Essay', Historical Methods 25, 1 (1992): 41. Historians of sports tend to discuss the two strands of deconstructionism under the heading postmodernism. See Hill, 'British Sports History' 15–16; and Murray Phillips, 'Deconstructing Sport History: The Postmodern Challenge', *Journal of Sport History* 28, 3 (2001): 327–43. Sports historians have generally shied from postmodernism as a theory of change. For fuller discussions of postmodernism in sports history see Douglas Booth, *The Field: Truth and Fiction in Sport History* (London: Routledge, 2005), 168–72; and Murray Phillips, ed., *Deconstructing Sport History: A Postmodern Analysis* (Albany: SUNY Press, 2006), 6–8.

58 Licht, 'Cultural History / Social History', 41. See Jacques Derrida, *Writing and Difference*, translated by A. Bass (Chicago: University of Chicago Press, 1978); and Dominick LaCapra, *History and Criticism* (Ithaca: Cornell University Press, 1987).

59 Licht, 'Cultural History / Social History', 41.

60 Licht, 'Cultural History / Social History', 41. See also Laurie Nussdorfer, 'The New Cultural History', History and Theory 32, 1 (1993): 79.

61 Ben Carrington and Ian McDonald, 'Introduction: "Race," Sport and British Society', in *"Race," Sport and British Society* (London: Routledge, 2004), 4.

62 David Wiggins and Patrick Miller, *The Unlevel Playing Field: A Documentary History of the African American Experience in Sport* (Urbana: University of Illinois Press), 85.

63 Wiggins and Miller, *The Unlevel Playing Field*, 87.

64 Steven Pope, 'Decentering "Race" and (Re)presenting "Black" Performance in Sport History: Basketball and Jazz in American Culture, 1920–50', in Phillips, *Deconstructing Sport History*, 155.

65 Pope, 'Decentering "Race"', 148. Here Pope cites Gerald Early. For additional examples of racially based sporting cultures see Grant Farred, '"Theatre of Dreams": Mimicry and Difference in Cape Flats Township Football', in John Bale and Mike Cronin, eds, *Sport and Postcolonialism* (Oxford: Berg, 2003), 123–45; and John Nauright, 'Rugby, Carnival, Masculinity and Identities in "Coloured" Cape Town', in Timothy Chandler and John Nauright, eds, *Making the Rugby World: Race, Gender, Commerce* (London: Frank Cass, 1999), 27–42.

66 Pope, 'Decentering "Race"', 148.

67 Pope, 'Decentering "Race"', 163–64.

68 Pope, 'Decentering "Race"', 164.

69 Licht, 'Cultural History / Social History', 41.

70 Robert Berkhofer, *Beyond the Great Story: History as Text and Discourse* (Cambridge, MA: Harvard University Press, 1995), 21.

71 Licht, 'Cultural History / Social History', 41.

72 Tosh, *Pursuit of History*, second edn (Cambridge, Longman, 1991), 87, 89; and Munslow, *Deconstructing History*, 122.

73 John Toews, 'Intellectual History After the Linguistic Turn: The Autonomy of Meaning and the Irreducibility of Experience', *American Historical Review* 92 (1987): 889–93.

74 For example Michel Foucault, *The History of Sexuality: An Introduction*, translated by Robert Hurley (Harmondsworth: Penguin, 1981), 151–52.

75 Chris Shilling, *The Body and Social Theory* (London: Sage, 1993), 75.

76 Michel Foucault, *Discipline and Punish: The Birth of the Prison*, translated by Alan Sheridan (Harmondsworth: Penguin, 1977), 202–3.

77 Michel Foucault, *Discipline and Punish* (New York, Vintage, 1995), 3–6, 211, 223.

78 Colin Gordon, ed., *Michel Foucault: Power/Knowledge, Selected Interviews and Other Writings 1972–1977* (Brighton: Harvester Press, 1980), 78.

79 Patricia Vertinsky, *The Eternally Wounded Woman: Women, Doctors, and Exercise in the Late Nineteenth Century* (Urbana: University of Illinois Press, 1994), 10, 11–12.

80 Susan Cahn, *Coming on Strong: Gender and Sexuality in Twentieth-Century Women's Sport* (Cambridge, MA: Harvard University Press, 1995), 3.

81 Martin Polley, *Moving the Goalposts: A History of Sport and Society Since 1945* (London: Routledge, 1998), 94. See also Douglas Booth and Colin Tatz, *One-Eyed: A View of Australian Sport* (Sydney: Allen & Unwin, 2000), 204–6; Richard Cashman, *Paradise of Sport: The Rise of Organised Sport in Australia* (Melbourne: Oxford University Press, 1995), 79–82; and Allen Guttmann, *Women's Sports: A History* (New York: Columbia University Press, 1991), 261–63.

82 Hargreaves, *Sport, Power and Culture*, 132–35. Although he makes numerous references to Foucault's work, Hargreaves' perspective derives more directly from Bryan Turner, *The Body and Society* (Cambridge: Blackwell, 1984) and Mike Featherstone, 'The Body in Consumer Culture', *Theory, Culture and Society* 1, 2 (1982): 18–33.

83 Douglas Booth, *Australian Beach Cultures: The History of Sun, Sand and Surf* (London: Frank Cass, 2001), 46.

84 Colin Howell, *Blood, Sweat, and Cheers: Sport and the Making of Modern Canada* (Toronto: University of Toronto Press, 2001), 108.

85 Robert Berkhofer, *Beyond the Great Story* (Cambridge, MA: Harvard University Press, 1995), 11, 21.

86 Clifford Geertz, 'Deep Play: Notes on the Balinese Cockfight', *Dædalus* 101 (1972): 27.

87 Geertz, 'Deep Play', 26.

88 Geertz, 'Deep Play', 29.

89 Geertz, 'Deep Play', 5.

90 H.F. Moorehouse, 'Shooting Stars: Footballers and Working-Class Culture in Twentieth Century Scotland', in Holt, *Sport and the Working Class*, 179–97; Richard Holt, 'King Across the Border: Denis Law and Scottish Football', in Jarvie and Walker, *Scottish Sport*, 58–74; Jeffrey Hill, 'Reading the Stars: A Post-Modernist Approach to Sports History', *The Sports Historian* 14 (1994): 45–55, and *Sport and the Literary Imagination*; and Michael Oriard, *Reading Football: How the Popular Press Created an American Spectacle* (Chapel Hill: University of North Carolina Press, 1993).

91 Oriard, *Reading Football*, 2–3.

92 Oriard, *Reading Football*, 15.

93 Hill, *Sport and the Literary Imagination*, 22, 24–25.

94 Alan Trachtenberg, 'Foreword', in Oriard, *Reading Football*, xiv–xv.

95 Catriona Parratt, 'Of Place and Men and Women: Gender and Topophilia in the "Haxey Hood"', *Journal of Sport History* 27, 2 (2000): 229–30, 239.

96 Peter Mewett, 'History in the Making and the Making of History: Stories and the Social Construction of Sport', *Sporting Traditions* 17, 1 (2000): 2, 5, 14–15.

97 Parratt, 'Of Place and Men and Women', 229.

98 Oriard, *Reading Football*, xxii.

99 Cited in Bryan Palmer, *The Descent into Discourse: The Reification of Language and the Writing of Social History* (Philadelphia: Temple University Press, 1990), 42. See also John Murphy, 'The Voice of Memory: History, Autobiography and Oral Memory', *Historical Studies* 22, 87 (1986): 170.

100 Palmer, *Descent into Discourse*, 197.

101 Toews, 'Intellectual History', 882.

102 Vertinsky, *The Eternally Wounded Woman*, 10; and Hargreaves, *Sport, Power and Culture*.

103 See for example John Bloom, *To Show What an Indian Can Do: Sports at Native American Boarding Schools* (Minneapolis: University of Minnesota Press, 2000) and my analysis of Bloom's approach in Booth, *The Field*, 203–5.

104 Lynn Hunt, ed., *The New Cultural History* (Berkeley: University of California Press, 1989), 20.

105 Pope, 'Decentering "Race"', 164.

106 Synthia Sydnor, 'A History of Synchronized Swimming', *Journal of Sport History* 25, 2 (1998): 259. Open hostility greeted Sydnor when she presented her work to the North American Society for Sport History conference in 1997. Sydnor's history is, in fact, more substantial than a pastiche of images; she affirms her role as a narrator and organizer of text, declares herself 'loyal to the canon of historical methodology and theory', 'faithful to observing continuity and change', and 'conscious of the complex problems concerning truth, relativism, and representation'. With respect to her use of sources, the meticulously referenced 105 notes confirm Sydnor's claim that she is 'true [to her] grounding in classical source use' (254, 260). In the words of Phillipe Carrard, Sydnor 'play[s] the game by the rules'. Philippe Carrard, *Poetics of the New History: French Historical Discourse from Braudel to Chartier* (Baltimore: The Johns Hopkins University Press, 1992), 160.

107 Murray Phillips, 'A Critical Appraisal of Narrative in Sport History: Reading the Surf Lifesaving Debate', *Journal of Sport History* 29, 1 (2002): 30–32.

108 Phillips, 'A Critical Appraisal of Narrative', 33–34.

109 Hayden White, *Metahistory: The Historical Imagination in Nineteenth-century Europe* (Baltimore: The Johns Hopkins University Press, 1973), ix.

110 *History and Theory* devoted an entire edition of the journal to a critical assessment of *Metahistory*. See *History and Theory* 19, 4 (1980).

111 Keith Jenkins, *On 'What is History?' From Carr and Elton to Rorty and White* (London: Routledge, 1995), 10, 171, 176

112 Berkhofer, *Beyond the Great Story*, 243–83.

113 Berkhofer, *Beyond the Great Story*, 244, 249.

114 Patricia Vertinsky and Sherry McKay, eds, *Disciplining Bodies in the Gymnasium* (London: Routledge, 2004), xii.

115 Patricia Vertinsky, Sherry McKay and Stephen Petrina, 'No Body/ies in the Gym', in Vertinsky and McKay, eds, *Disciplining Bodies*, 163–64.

116 Evans, *In Defence of History*, 126.

117 Hill, *Sport and the Literary Imagination*, 23–27.

118 Catriona Parratt, 'Reflecting on Sport History in the 1990s', *Sport History Review* 29, 1 (1998): 13.

119 John Bale, *Roger Bannister and the Four-Minute Mile: Sports Myth and Sports History* (Routledge: London, 2004), 9–11.

120 Hill, *Sport and the Literary Imagination*, 197.

121 More often the angst surfaces at conferences rather than in print. Heated discussions about theory and sports history occurred at the Australian Society for Sport History conference at the University of Queensland in 1995. The *Victorian Bulletin of Sport and Culture* (a newsletter published by Victoria University of Technology) kept the debate running for a few issues. See numbers 4 (September 1995), 5 (December 1995), 6 (March 1996) and 7 (June 1996).

122 Phillips, *Deconstructing Sport History*, 14.

2 Sources

Gary Osmond and Murray Phillips

Sources matter to historians. This statement may appear banal and self-evident, but it is only when we examine what historians do and how they do it – particularly the intricate, often dense and unique system of footnoting,[1] or the collection of documents that are published in multi-volume editions,[2] or if we compare historians with other allied fields – that the emphasis on sources become apparent. A comparison between two sport sociology and sports history books aimed to acculturate young scholars into their respective fields makes the point. Grant Jarvie and Joseph Maguire's *Sport and Leisure in Social Thought* (1994), written for aspiring sport sociologists, concentrates on the relationship of different forms of social theory – feminist, figurational, functionalist, globalization, hegemonic, Marxist, modernist and postmodernist – to sport studies.[3] Alternatively, Martin Polley's *Sports History: A Practical Guide* (2007), targeted toward undergraduate and postgraduate history students, has very little on theory but devotes three of its eight chapters to sources.[4] The fact that over one-third of Polley's book is devoted to the variety of sources, the ways in which sources are used by historians as well as their strengths and weaknesses, rather than some other facet of the production of history, indicates the perceived importance given to this part of the history-making process. This situation raises a number of issues. Why is there so much emphasis on sources in sports history? Given this interest, what are the popular sources and how do sports historians use the evidence derived to create their histories? What are the epistemological and ontological bases for the types of sources preferred and their usage by sports historians? What are the challenges to the philosophical premises that underpin the use of sources by sports historians raised by the aesthetic, literary or cultural turns? Finally, what have been the responses from sports historians to changing perceptions of the types and roles of sources used in the production of history, and what new directions are possible? In the course of this chapter we will sketch some brief responses to these questions.

Before these questions are answered, it is necessary to qualify what is meant by several key and related terms: sources, evidence and facts. Sources constitute the full range of materials from which historians might draw their understanding and 'encompass every kind of evidence which human beings have left of their past activities – the written word and the spoken word, the shape of the landscape and the material artefact, the fine arts as well as photography and film'.[5] They are metaphoric quarries, forests and oceans, in which historians speak of 'mining' for evidence, 'gathering facts like nuts and berries', and casting nets.[6] Sources are usually categorized as either primary or secondary, with the former meaning those materials created close to or at the time in question. Primary sources are those 'with a direct link, in time and place, to the person, event, situation or culture under study'.[7] They contrast with secondary sources, which are those that 'provide commentary on, or interpretations of, past events'.[8] The distinction between the two categories sometimes blurs or, as we will demonstrate, collapses as historians are influenced by other disciplines.[9]

By evidence we mean those materials gathered from the sources and adduced to support an argument. If the sources are the 'the detritus of past living', then evidence is what is extracted from that rubble.[10] The discovery of draft constitutions for sporting clubs, lists of competitors or eye-witness descriptions of particular athletic events, for instance, illuminate the distant past and are marshalled to produce histories.[11] Epistemologically, evidence is central to the empirical history-making process, and is seen to separate history from fiction. As Alun Munslow argues, the 'way in which the sources of the past are mined as evidence for the nature of change over time' is what distinguishes the historian's training from that of other intellectuals.[12]

Facts are conceived as raw details arising largely from the source material that has been garnered as evidence. They may include names, dates and scores, details that may seem straightforward, transparent and irrefutable and the 'converse of opinion, supposition and conjecture'.[13] Yet facts are not unproblematic. At a basic level, core factual material may be simply incorrect, and require corroboration and close interrogation. At a more fundamental level, facts, like the sources from which they are derived, are often culturally determined, definitionally relational and interlaced with opinion.[14] Douglas Booth deconstructs eleven statements about the legendary English cricketer, W.G. Grace, all taken from factual histories, to illustrate the constructed and contentious nature of facts.[15]

Sources, then, as used in this chapter, will refer to the broad gamut of materials available to the historian and which yield evidence and facts. This generative dimension is central to their importance to historians: 'Sources are useful only when they are processed like raw materials into the evidence from which historical facts are created'.[16] Such a neat distinction between the terms sources, evidence and facts is problematic because they are often used interchangeably. Nonetheless, these characteristics of sources, evidence and facts serve to define the extensive if not limitless palette from which historians can choose in focusing their research attention and creating their histories.

Examining the state of the field in sports history

How historians use sources depends on the philosophical premises underpinning the history-making process. Munslow has posited a three-fold typology – reconstructionism, constructionism and deconstructionism – to explore how historians create their histories.[17] Booth, applying this lens to sports history, summarizes the differences in each approach to sources:

> Reconstructionists treat historical materials as concrete artifacts and interrogate them to ascertain their truthfulness … ; constructionists contextualise historical materials within theoretical frameworks that they hold as the primary means by which historians reveal reality … ; deconstructionists conceptualise historical materials as discourses and texts, and search these linguistic forms for their inherent power relations.[18]

These distinctions accurately capture the different ways historians work with sources, but for the purposes of this chapter we will collapse the first two categories – reconstructionism and constructionism – under the umbrella of the empirical-analytical model of history as distinct from deconstructionist history. This conflation is based on the centrality placed on sources in both the reconstructionist and constructionist modes of history production, as distinct from deconstructionism which balances the importance of sources with other dimensions of the history-making process.

In practice, the majority of sports historians are reconstructionist or constructionist and their work falls squarely within the boundaries of the empirical-analytical model of history.[19] The foundation stone of the empirical-analytical model is the evidence of the past used by historians to create their story.[20] One key assumption is that historians, through their craft-like training, carefully and critically work with the sources to produce historical accounts. Arthur Marwick, for example, mandates the value of a wide range of sources and offers a 'catechism', or step-by-step guide, for the analysis, evaluation and implementation of primary sources.[21] This evidence-based model is constructed around the belief that the past is knowable through the sources and the more the evidence, which is often partial, fragmented and even misleading, is critically analysed by impartial, objective and disinterested historians, the closer we get to the truth.[22] Answers to questions like: who created the sources, for what purposes and how did they create it, enable historians to ascertain the intention of the author/s of the source/s. Through this process historians gain insights into decisions by purposeful historical agents under specific circumstances, and, by laying out the evidence against pieces of other evidence through a process of contextualization, historians create historical accounts. Attaining the truth is certainly not guaranteed, but forensic analysis of the evidence and the process of contextualization enables historians to get as close as possible to the most likely explanation.

How historians work within the empirical-analytical model, however, is not universally appreciated or practised. Some sports historians advocate the mantra espoused in Geoffrey Elton's *Return to Essentials*, and more recently in Arthur Marwick's *The New Nature of History*, which suggests that historians work inductively with the evidence and, importantly, they argue that the stories emerge from the evidence free from a priori assumptions, ideology and bias.[23] An increasing number of sports historians, though, contend that drawing inferences from the evidence is a much more complicated process. This process consists of a complex deductive/inductive inferential loop representing a continuous dialogue between the historian, who employs working hypotheses, conceptual frameworks or fully fledged theories, and the sources. While the pure inductive (reconstructionist) and deductive/inductive (constructionist) positions adopted by historians point to different versions of the empirical-analytical model of history, there is a consistent belief that it is possible for historians to mitigate the limitations created by the partial, misleading and contrived nature of the archive. Additional challenges associated with representation and referentiality are acknowledged as requiring new sensitivities and strategies in relation to the evidence, but they are not fatal to the cause of producing history. Neither problems associated with the nature of the archive nor textuality are sufficient enough to destabilize the centrality of evidence to the empirical-analytical model of history.[24]

The empirical-analytical model of history has several additional key features. It privileges primary over secondary sources; advocates an expansive range of primary sources; and heavily favours written over non-written sources. Polley captures the significance of primary sources to producing historical accounts: 'Primary evidence is the foundation of all historical research. Unless we have evidence from the time that we are studying, we cannot conduct historical research'.[25] Primary sources come in myriad forms including written documents (literature, newspapers, magazines, official records and private papers), visual representations (artwork, cartoons, maps, photographs), material culture (artefacts, ephemera, fine art), oral information (testimonies and interviews) and audiovisual material (documentaries, films, newsreels, radio, television). Historians prioritize primary sources – over secondary sources – as these are deemed to be the most original, authentic and reliable in order to seek 'truths' about the past. As Polley stresses:

> We need primary evidence so that we know what happened in the past, and so that we can get an insight to what people thought was happening. Primary evidence not only takes us into the events of the past, but can also give us a sense of the feelings, perceptions, and ideas of the people who lived in the past, and how they interpreted and perceived events.[26]

In these ways, sources are perceived to be metaphorically akin to flowing water whose origins can be traced back to an original, pure and true wellspring. Historians, as Peter Burke argues, refer to 'their documents as "sources", as if they were filling their buckets from the stream of Truth, their stories becoming increasingly pure as they move closer to the origins'.[27] Many historians believe the maxim: 'know the archive, know the past'.[28]

How sports historians work with primary sources in practice varies considerably. Historians of pre-modern sport are adept at interpreting many types of sources and are pragmatic when faced with limited options. For instance in pre-literate cultures, or in civilizations such as Ancient Egypt where the literary evidence is scant, or in Minoan, Mycenaean and Etruscan societies where language is not completely deciphered, sports historians embrace a wide range of archaeological evidence. Relief carvings, friezes and paintings have been important in understanding physical activities in Ancient Egypt; Minoan and Mycenaean frescos have provided detail about their bull-leaping activities; and sporting activities of the Etruscans have been determined from their elaborate tombs.[29] In other ancient societies from which both documentary and non-documentary sources are available, sports historians employ a cross-section of evidence to create their histories. With the Ancient Greeks, for example, literary sources from Aristotle, Homer, Pausanias, Plato, Plutarch and Xenaphon are complemented with evidence from black-and-red-figured vases, statues, coins and other forms of material culture as well as evidence from the archaeological sites where athletic festivals were held.[30] As Zahra Newby's *Greek Athletes in the Roman World* states: 'The overarching programme is to integrate images, monuments, texts, performances, and rituals with the places, participants, and broader historical environment that gave them meaning'.[31] Similarly, European sport in the Middle Ages has been understood from a range of written sources including regulations, statutes, prose and poetry, as well as engravings, illuminated manuscripts, paintings, sketches and material culture including the Bayeux Tapestry and the Great Tournament Roll of Westminster.[32]

These historians epitomize the advice of Martin Polley, who advocates all forms of primary sources. He argues that 'historians use many different types of evidence, ranging from minute books to newspapers, from films to artefacts, and from interviews to novels', and he spends considerable space (some three chapters in his book) detailing the virtues and pitfalls of nearly twenty categories of primary sources.[33] What is noticeable, however, with sports historians working with events in the late 19th and 20th centuries, is their heavy reliance on written sources and their tendency to avoid or marginalize non-written sources. To explore this, we informally surveyed the major, English-language, sports history journals over the past two years in order to gauge types, and uses, of sources.[34] Some 116 of the 130 articles surveyed, or fully 90 percent, relied overwhelmingly on written documents. This is not to say that they eschewed non-written sources entirely, but typically these are employed in an illustrative sense and not conceptualized in any significant way. The remaining 14 articles also used written sources, often extensively and meticulously, but their primary focus of enquiry is on non-written items as historical representations. The authors of these examples typically employ written sources to provide context, however they tend to be less concerned with what actually happened in the past than with present-focused narratives and meanings of the past. Jaime Schultz, for instance, considers the 'Floyd of Rosedale' football trophy in American college football as an example of narrativization or form of social memory.[35] We will return to these examples, however the point for now is that the survey highlights the continuing dominant emphasis on written sources in contemporary sports history.

The ways that written sources are skilfully used by sports historians working within an empirical-analytical mode are demonstrated by many excellent works. Three sports history books can be used to exemplify this. Melvin L. Adelman, in *A Sporting Time: New York City and the Rise of Modern Athletics, 1820–70* (1990), draws widely from mid-19th-century daily newspapers and sporting journals, diaries, scrapbook and club records to examine the rise of modern sport in New York City. The formalization and professionalization of sport in the shift from the pre-modern to modern eras generated the type of 'sport information and statistics and records' that he researches.[36] In his focus on class and ethnicity of sporting participants, Adelman creates an occupational profile of ball players by researching myriad sources, including city directories, 'club records, guidebooks, newspaper accounts, and published box scores'.[37] As with most empirical-analytical historians, Adelman contextualizes his discussion within a range of secondary source material.

Ronald A. Smith, in his book exploring the relationship between big-time college athletics and radio and TV broadcasters, *Play-by-Play: Radio, Television, and Big-Time College Sport* (2001), also draws extensively on primary sources, most notably the holdings of around fifty archives throughout the USA, including colleges, athletic conferences and the National Collegiate Athletic Association (NCAA). Like Adelman, Smith acknowledges a debt to a significant range of secondary sources, but sees archival sources as the 'most important material' used in the writing.[38] These include institutional presidential papers, and 'faculty athletic committee minutes, athletic directors' papers, athletic association records, coaches' documents, conference commissioners' correspondence and reports, alumni records, and student diaries and reminiscences'.[39] His meticulous research enables him to piece together the little-known, back-room story of the commercialization of college sport.

More recently, Barbara J. Keys also demonstrates the potential of archival research in her book, *Globalizing Sport: National Rivalry and International Community in the 1930s* (2006).[40] Keys extracts primary evidence from both newspapers and international government and sport archives to map the growth of global sport in the 1930s. To trace the role of international sport organizations and governments in the consolidation of international sport in this era, she trawls the archives of the International Olympic Committee, US Olympic Committee, Avery Brundage Collection, FIFA, and those of the USA, Soviet and German national authorities. Her combination of primary, archival and newspaper sources with secondary literature offers insight into decisions, debates and politics of the era.

Several points about the importance of written sources to sports historians emerge from these examples. First, they reveal the type and range of sources available at local, national and international levels, from newspapers, minute books and official records to diaries, letters and scrapbooks. Second, they confirm the importance placed on primary sources, especially those located in the archive. Despite awareness of their 'gaps and omissions', empirical-analytical historians tend to view archives as 'neutral sites of knowledge' that are indispensable to the history-making process.[41] Third, secondary sources are valued to help contextualize primary evidence, and all sources are carefully recorded through standard footnote and bibliographic procedure. Both Adelman and Smith go an additional step in offering comprehensive bibliographical essays aimed at summarizing the relative importance of sources used and offering direction to future researchers.[42] Finally, while all three authors either implicitly or explicitly privilege written sources, particularly primary documents, Adelman reflects on the limitations of the archive. In an appendix called 'Collecting and Collating Occupational Data', he admits the shortcomings of some source materials, especially city directories, in terms of thoroughness, accuracy and reliability, and acknowledges that he was required to make certain assumptions.[43] He also critiques primary sources as 'impressionistic and often inaccurate', and cautions sports historians to be 'sensitive' to the limitations of 19th-century journalism and 'examine and interpret such sources judiciously'.[44] His reflexivity typifies those sports historians operating in the empirical-analytical mode who acknowledge the limitations of the archive but who argue that these are not insurmountable in producing history.

The emphasis on written documents, as illustrated by these examples, may in some cases be a necessity, but in many instances it is a preference. There are, moreover, several important exceptions to the reliance on written documents. John Bale focuses on photographs to analyse a Rwandan 'jumper' participating in the body cultural activity of *gusimbuka-urukiramentde*.[45] Tony Mangan investigates the artistic visual artefacts of Nazi Germany to reveal how public sculpture was co-opted to represent the masculine, athletic body as the aspirational ideal of Nazi eugenic ideology.[46] Also examining the intersection between the Third Reich and sport, Richard Mandell openly acknowledges his reliance on film in his book, *The Nazi Olympics* (1972): 'The impression dominant among us as to what took place at the 1936 Games has been largely due to Leni Riefenstahl's *Olympia*'.[47] In another context, Michael Oriard understands the emergence of American football from the middle of the 19th century by reading cartoons, illustrations and sketches, as well as written material, contained in newspapers, magazines and journals.[48] Oral testimony, including over sixty interviews, is integral to Pamela Grundy's history of sport in twentieth-century North Carolina.[49] The built environment and natural landscape are the focus of Patricia Vertinsky and John Bale's edited book, *Sites of Sport* (2004), that examines gymnasia, swimming pools, ice skating rings, marching formations, the beach and mountaineering.[50] Vertinsky has extended her work on gymnasia into a co-authored book on the War Memorial Gym at the University of British Columbia.[51] These works are not exhaustive, but they are indicative of historians who are prepared to examine non-written remnants of the past, created in the time-frame under investigation, to create their histories.

It would be misleading to imply that an absolute demarcation can be made between histories that focus on non-written sources and those that do not. Sports historians, at various times and to various degrees, do refer to non-written materials, but overall these sources are not the main focus of inquiry, or conceptualized in any significant way.[52] Photographs are a case in point. Sports historians, like many other historians, have 'tended to use photographic images simply as appendages to text, confirming the truth of the narrative and adding to its emotional force'.[53] This can be seen in the way photographs are used as cover adornments in sports history journals. For instance, the *Journal of Sport History* and *Sporting Traditions* both use photographs as large-scale, eye-catching decorations that aesthetically improve the journals but usually do not engage critically with the presented images. Photographs are also regularly included in published histories without significant discussion or analysis, at best chronologically denoting events and at worst appearing 'almost gratuitously, apparently bearing no relation to the written word and bundled together at the centre of a book for what seems to be purposes of light relief'.[54] Meanings in photographs are often assumed to be self-evident and are rarely critically analysed or exposed to potential understandings through methodologies such as semiotics, iconography or psychoanalysis.[55]

In these ways, sports historians do not appear to be vastly different from the larger body of historians who rely heavily on written evidence and regard non-written material as 'extras, peripheral to the discipline'.[56] Tosh, discussing trends in historical practice more generally, contends that written sources are 'the most rewarding and (in most cases) the most plentiful'. He adds: 'Small wonder, then, that historians seldom look elsewhere'.[57] There are certainly many forms of written documents that are available for sports historians and, in many cases, Tosh's plentiful argument is accurate. Newspapers are a good example. Sports historians working on 19th- and 20th-century sport have extensively used newspapers. As Hill argues: 'Press reports have become a staple – perhaps *the* staple – source in the task of reconstructing the history of sport and games'.[58] Co-existing with these abundant written sources is an increasing array of non-written sources – art, cartoons, films, geography, landscape, material culture, photographs and structural forms – available to sports historians, but they are either used peripherally or avoided altogether. It may be that written sources are the most rewarding, as Tosh points out, because these sources are the most comfortable for sports historians to engage with and non-written sources are less rewarding because they require expertise in fields as diverse as anthropology, art history, cartography, cultural studies, film studies, material culture, semiotics and sociology. Sports historians may feel they lack the appropriate training, or are ill-equipped, for utilizing the wide range of available non-written sources.

Challenging the empirical-analytical model

The emphasis on primary written evidence as part of the empirical-analytical model has been seriously questioned from the 1970s onward. Doubts are raised at the epistemological and ontological levels of the empirical-analytical model. Serious questions have been posed about historians' capacity to reveal 'the' past through forensic analyses of the sources. The historians' ability to ascertain the authorial intent in the sources, it is argued, is undermined by the critique of the Enlightenment-inspired, universally centred, knowing subject. Authors of the sources are more indicative of further texts and ideological positions rather than being the originator of meaning. This textualization is compounded by the structuralist/poststructuralist-inspired crisis in referentiality and representation. Language is seen as an inadequate medium of representation that fails to describe reality, diminishing the ability of the historian to get at the meaning behind the evidence. What historians face is the unreliable signifier–signified–sign equation and, rather than uncovering primal meaning, the best on offer are chains of interpretative signification. In other words, there is an irresolvable textualization in the sources as the historian tries to read complex codes of metaphorical meanings and understandings. In all, these issues culminate in the view that many historians place too much faith in their ability to understand meaning behind the sources at the expense of recognizing the limitations of processing evidence within the analytical-empirical model.

Beyond the issues of textualization, referentiality and representation, there is an inevitable impositionalist role of the historian in regard to the selection and interpretation of the evidence. Historians have no choice in taking an impositionalist role when they decide which evidence is foundational to the history, which is peripheral and which to discard, and when they try to explain what the authors' intentions were, what the sources really say and what the past really means. When the impositionalist role of the historian is appreciated, the pendulum swings away from the centrality accorded to the evidence in the empirical-analytical model. The emphasis shifts to what historians take to the task of history, particularly their methodological, epistemological and ontological positions that organize, configure and determine not only the appropriate historical evidence but also generate meaning from this evidence. In essence, history only exists because a narrative or story structure has been created, not discovered, by the historian.[59]

A seminal figure who has critiqued the empirical-analytical model and the importance placed on evidence is Hayden White. In essence, he contends that history is a product of the historical imagination as much as it is a product of the evidence. A narrative or story-line is not intrinsically found in the past but imposed by the historians who themselves are the products of a number of cultural, professional and ideological discourses. It is the prefigured emplotment of the historian that determines the evidence to be consulted, the way it is described, its interpretation and the creation of the historical narrative. White argues that this process of history-making is best comprehended as a form of literature in which historians employ the same formal narrative structures as those used in realist literature. In White's model of historical explanation there are three surface tiers – emplotment, argument and ideological implication – and a single deep structure of tropes. We will not explore White's model in any depth, or detail its many critics, except to note that White recognizes the role of evidence in the historical endeavour but his model stresses the literary or poetic dimension of history as the central feature of history-making.[60]

What is interesting in sports history is that there are few examples of White's critique of the empirical-analytical model of history or broader debates about the aesthetic, linguistic or cultural turns having greatly influenced the centrality of sources, evidence and facts. Sports history, nevertheless, is not a stagnant field. The relationship between sports historians and the evidence has been continually shifting. Contemporary sports historians are considering a broader range of sources, not necessarily written in many cases, and not necessarily from the time-frame under examination but also from subsequent periods. The genesis for change, in all probability, has not been the philosophical debate about sources in history, but rather the influence from allied disciplines on sports history. Of the 14 journal articles identified in our survey as focusing on non-written source material, direct influences can be discerned from disciplines including media studies, cultural studies, anthropology, geography and sociology. Sine Agergaard, for instance, combines the work of human geographers with an ethnographic perspective on sporting spaces as historical landscapes; Douglas A. Brown applies modernist aesthetics as an analytical framework for the study of photographs of Canadian mountaineers; and Nissim Mannathukkaren employs a postcolonial perspective to assess the representation of cricket in the Bollywood movie *Lagaan*.[61] An increasing number of sports historians are consulting sources such as comic books, documentaries, films, halls of fame, Internet sites, museums, stadiums, statues, trophies and sporting venues. In effect, the demarcation between primary and secondary sources, so important to the empirical-analytical model, is becoming increasingly blurred.

The extension of sources beyond the written, the melding of epistemological distinctions between primary and secondary sources, and the influence of allied disciplines illustrated in this survey of journal articles, is further demonstrated by three recent and influential sports history books. Their authors, while not eschewing written, archival sources, are more concerned with present-focused narratives about the past and their meanings than with what actually happened in the past. They represent those sports historians who seek to understand how non-written and 'secondary' sources can 'play central roles in the creation and maintenance of cultural memories'.[62] David McGimpsey, in *Imagining Baseball: America's Pastime and Popular Culture* (2000), addresses baseball as a cultural product with common, recurring, idealistic themes.[63] He examines baseball's perfect, timeless, mythical qualities, its pastoral associations, opportunity myths and generational appeal, along with its 'fixes', not via an empirical-analytical model, but instead as cultural discourses through fiction, film, television and other representations. These range from W.P. Kinsella's novel *Shoeless Joe* (1982), to the Hollywood movie *A League of Their Own* (1992), to an episode of the television series *Northern Exposure* (1995), and to the Cleveland Indians' team mascot. In addition, McGimpsey explores how editors and producers of these 'baseball fictions' mediate between the sport and its audiences.[64] These myriad representations, which are effectively secondary sources in the empirical-analytical vernacular, are valued because they constitute a 'material product … not remarkably different from other souvenir products' that asserts the sport's cultural ascendancy.[65]

Daniel A. Nathan, in *Saying It's So: A Cultural History of the Black Sox Scandal* (2003), also uses a range of 'secondary' sources to consider baseball in an interdisciplinary approach to examine memories and cultural meanings of the Black Sox scandal in which the Chicago White Sox fixed their 1919 World Series loss.[66] His book is significant in the context of this chapter because of his epistemological and ontological positions on evidence and narrative and for the types of source materials consulted. Nathan is less concerned with the 'truth' of the event, which he argues 'was inevitably left behind in the shadowy hotel rooms, bars, and pool halls' frequented by the offending players, and more interested in exploring its entrenched hold on collective memory through a variety of representations and texts.[67] In other words, he is less concerned with the event than with the tale, and in understanding why the tale persists. He reflexively offers a cultural history that reveals his 'handiwork, seams and all', and not a seamless narrative that obscures the storyteller and makes the past seem neater and more straightforward than it was.[68] His sources and evidence base, plumbed to extract changing values and meanings over time, range from initial press reportage to popular histories such as Eliot Asinof's book *Eight Men Out* (1963), novels such as Bernard Malamud's *The Natural* (1952), movies such as Phil Alden Robinson's *Field of Dreams* (1989), television documentaries such as Ken Burns' *Baseball* (1994), and fan pilgrimages to the Dyersville, Iowa ball field where *Field of Dreams* was filmed.

Sport media, including 'journalism, blogs, advertising, film, television, popular music, websites, pop literature and photography' are the 'representational fodder' of Tara Brabazon's *Playing on the Periphery: Sport, Identity, and Memory* (2006) which examines sport within popular culture.[69] The 'vision of history', as represented through these media, aims to provide 'new dimensions to our understanding of the past through a juxtaposition of sound, landscape and dialogue'.[70] Brabazon's overall focus on sport representations, memories and peripheries demonstrates the possibilities of combining history with cultural studies. Arguing that sports history is replete with non-written source material, she suggests new opportunities for research. One case study in particular stands out. The 1966 soccer (football) World Cup final ball, now housed in the Preston National Football Museum in England, is considered variously as a relic of material culture, a venerated object, a record of one game, a unique signifier of the particular match and a retrieved memory.[71] The ball example is valuable not only because it is used to free such objects from normal interpretive confines imposed by their positioning in museum displays, but also because it exemplifies the vast range of source material available to sports historians and points to possible new directions for research.

Sourcing new directions

The willingness of some sports historians to embrace a broad range of sources, as indicted by the works of McGimpsey, Nathan and Brabazon, refocuses attention onto epistemological issues that have been raised previously about the empirical-analytical model. These include the veracity, transparency and reliability of primary source material, the ability to draw meaningful distinctions between primary and secondary sources, and the wisdom of giving preference to primary sources over others that are available for examination, critique and analysis. These epistemological challenges to traditional history effectively decentre primary sources. Decentring does not devalue or denigrate primary sources, but rearranges traditional hierarchies of importance to elevate a wider range of other types of source materials and methods of assessing these. All sources, whether traditionally viewed as either primary or secondary, become representations of the past.

When sources are redefined as representations of the past rather than as evidence to be mined for factual information, the range of possible sources and ways of viewing them expands exponentially. This encompasses under-explored textual and material artefacts, from the obvious – statues, films, photographs, landscapes, museums – to less obvious examples such as the soccer ball from the 1966 soccer World Cup final and other such culturally laden items. Understanding these sources as representations of the past requires new levels of conceptualization and theorization, and in many instances may require improving the literacy and skills needed to fully engage with meanings.[72] This will involve drawing on methodological approaches developed in other disciplines to expand assessment of sources beyond content veracity to include a range of additional approaches – cultural text analysis, discourse analysis, material culture analysis, materiality, pedagogical theory, memory practices and semiotics – in ways that recognize the present in the past and the processes of remembering and forgetting involved in any representation of the past. The engagement of some sports historians with such detailed, theoretically rigorous and interdisciplinary approaches demonstrates the potential to further exploit sources in new and intellectually creative ways. Consideration in the following section of how new approaches have been and might be applied to a select range of sources points to the possibilities. Our choice of visual images, museums, films and monuments is indicative only, based on our recent work, and is certainly not exhaustive of the range of sources available to sports historians.

Visual images

Visual images are rarely vigorously examined as credible sources by historians.[73] This is especially true in sports history, where images 'have not been seen as a source in their own right, which can be read, interpreted and understood'.[74] While there are several notable examples, photographs, to take one visual medium, are seldom utilized beyond content analysis and as illustrative fodder for articles, journal covers and books.[75] While photographs are attractive because of their 'beguiling realism' and as de facto representations of reality, there is also an awareness of potential for photographer bias and tampering.[76] Traditionally then, we look for evidence of content as true or false, and photographs are only considered useful if they are considered to veraciously capture an individual, action or event. Posters, cartoons, paintings and postage stamps, because of additional levels of mediation, have had even less exposure as sources in their own right, particularly in sports history.

In contemplating interdisciplinary approaches taken to visual sources, several methodological possibilities emerge that may assist sports historians in approaching anew the wide gamut of sporting images. These include, but are not limited to, semiotics, materiality and affect. Semiotics involves examining images as signs capable of conveying dominant, subordinate and competing meanings. The application of semiotics to photographs suggests its potential to other forms of visual images such as stamps.[77] Materiality, an approach honed by anthropologists in particular, involves seeing visual images as objects, with meanings conferred by the uses to which they are put and the contexts in which they are encountered.[78] The widespread promulgation, for instance, of the famous photograph of Tommie Smith and John Carlos on the medal dais at the 1968 Mexico City Olympics, has led to it becoming a powerful 'object of meaning and collective memory'.[79] Affect, describing bodily emotions and feelings, closely relates to materiality and has been used by Douglas Booth to explore how images, stories and voices connect a surfing magazine with its readership.[80] Together, these three approaches – semiotics, materiality and affect – suggest powerful yet under-utilized possibilities for critically evaluating visual images as sources and as histories unto themselves that shape representations of the past.

Museums

Museums are widely acknowledged as both highly trustworthy and powerful cultural institutions.[81] Sport museums, sport halls of fame and sport-focused exhibits are manifold, and play important cultural, educative and social roles. As Wray Vamplew has noted, however, few researchers of sport avail themselves museum collections beyond their library and archival document and picture holdings.[82] This reflects the traditional epistemological reliance of sports historians on the written word and conventional approaches to photographs, but also indicates several specific concerns held about museums. These include their tendency to cater to the nostalgia market, perpetuate myths, and provide simplistic and insufficient information without full and proper contextualization.[83] While many of these concerns are valid, sport museums do continue to attract enthusiastic public audiences whose perceptions of the past are shaped by what they witness and experience. To ignore museums as sources and to focus mainly on their documentary collections risks missing opportunities to understand how museums manufacture knowledge about the past and to bridge the chasm between 'what sports scholars do and what the larger public consumes and conceives of as sports history'.[84]

Consideration of pedagogical and memory practices utilized by and in museums can enable sports historians to investigate how the organization, demarcation and structural forms of museum displays, both physical and virtual, shape understandings of the past.

Key questions concern how objects, labels, audio–visual material, interactive components as well as lighting, sound and spacing are combined in a pedagogical environment to create memories and meanings.[85] One of the missions of museums is to educate the public through specific technologies and techniques and, in this capacity, they are important agents in generating social memory.[86] With the invention of the Internet, the limited reach of museums has extended from personal visits to virtual tours which has increased their potency as a form of social memory. In their traditional and digital versions, museums not only collect and store memories but also create memories.[87] A social memory approach to museums would ask what artefacts are displayed, what is omitted or forgotten and why, and what version/s of the past is privileged. Such an approach does not dispute that meanings are created in the eyes of the beholder, and that no single meaning can therefore be isolated, but accepts that dominant messages are intended, presented and transmitted through codes, conventions and practices that are particular to representations of the past in museums.

Films

Films, including dramatic films, documentaries and newsreels, have received limited critical attention from sports historians relative to written documents. Dramatic films in particular are not taken seriously as historical representations because of their fictional basis and the commercial imperative which is closely related to providing entertainment for audiences. Documentaries are generally more valued by historians because of their utilization of primary source material, including archival material, and their attempts to adhere to the accuracy of the stories depicted. Traditional critiques of films, particularly documentaries, measure factual accuracy to assess validity, using the standards of written histories as a yardstick. Judged against the criterion of the fully referenced, written artefacts of books, articles and theses, films – documentary and especially dramatic – rarely measure up.

An alternative approach might involve evaluating films as cultural texts that contribute to memories and representations of the past using codes, conventions and practices that are different from those underlying written works but valid on their own terms. This involves understanding the importance of the visual and aural experience of films and appreciating the broad creative palette available to filmmakers via props, actors, costumes, settings, dissolves, effects, colour, sound, slow and fast motion together with combinations of archival material, still and moving images, read documents, and oral testimony as well as fictive elements.[88] In a cultural-text analysis, less attention is paid to the fidelity of events portrayed than to the creation of meanings and the forces that lie behind choices made in the creative process. Questions in this analysis may include: How do films create memories through visual, aural and aesthetic mediums? What discourses are privileged, marginalized or excluded? How is the privileging, marginalizing and exclusion of these discourses understood?[89] While recognizing the differences between various filmic genres, cultural text analysis offers one approach to expanding the ways in which sports historians engage with films.

Monuments

Sporting monuments, including memorials, statues and the built environment, offer a range of possibilities as sources. John Bale's concept of 'sportscapes', or landscapes of sport, highlights the spatiality of sporting experiences created through geographic and architectural configurations.[90] Works edited by Vertinsky and Bale (2004) and Vertinsky and McKay (2004) on various sporting sites, as previously noted, offer excellent examples of the possibilities for studying these various forms.[91] Less attention has been given to sport statues and memorial monuments, which proliferate in cities and towns across the globe. One notable exception is Synthia Sydnor's journal article about the aesthetic and voyeuristic connotations of the Michael Jordan statue in Chicago.[92]

As artefacts of material culture, statues and other monuments can be assessed to understand their reflection, mediation or rejection of 'culturally shared beliefs and values'.[93] Campaigns to initiate statues dedicated to sportspeople, as well as the changing and competing cultural discourses surrounding these monuments, offer insight into the cultures and times in which they were created, unveiled and situated. Analyses of artistic form, expression and semiotics offer additional methodological approaches to interpreting broader socio-cultural contexts. Another potentially fruitful but under-utilized approach involves studying statues in particular as 'hollow icons', or 'empty vessels' that stand 'ready to be charged with fresh interpretation'.[94] The 'hollow icon' concept allows for assessment of statues as cultural artefacts capable of multiple, competing and changing meanings. For example, research on the prominent statue of Duke Kahanamoku at Waikīkī Beach in Honolulu has revealed that the monument has been read not only as typifying Western stereotypes of Pacific Islander aquatic prowess, but that indigenous Hawaiians understand this statue more in terms of localism, racial identity and reconciliation.[95] The 'hollow icon' approach used in this example, which emphasizes the capacity of solid form to assume fluidity of meaning, is applicable to all sport statues and offers a worthwhile way of engaging with monuments.

The focus here on visual images, museums, films and monuments is representative only, intended to indicate the expanse of possible source types and range of possible approaches to these. While we have examined each example separately, we do not wish to create the impression that studies based on non-traditional sources need to be done in isolation from one another. This has been the habit in mainstream history, and many of the works cited here confirm that this also occurs in sports history.[96] If the point of expanding sources is to embrace multiple voices on past events in order to enhance understandings of the meanings of those events, then combining varied sources and media, as in the works of Nathan, McGimpsey and Brabazon, is perhaps most valuable.

Conclusion

The centrality of primary, written sources, long the mainstay of sports history, is sweating under the spotlight of critical re-evaluations of the traditional empirical-analytical model of history production. Debates in the philosophy of history have caused historians to question many assumptions underlying the empirical-analytical model, including the objectivity of historians, the relativity of truth, the neutrality of the archive and, most pertinently for this chapter, the centrality accorded to primary sources. While the majority of sports historians have responded in limited ways to these challenges, there are several examples, some of which are detailed above, that use sources in ways that are different from the empirical-analytical model.

What the philosophical challenges and the examples in sports history illustrate is the potential for historians when sources are considered much more broadly than is the practice under the empirical-analytical model. We argue that sports history will be richer, closely connected with other academic disciplines, and more engaging for a larger readership by embracing written documents, visual representations, material culture, oral information and audiovisual material. In effect this approach will collapse the arbitrary and artificial hierarchy that exists between primary and secondary sources and will enable a much larger transition from sources, as defined earlier as every kind of material related to the past, to what historians believe is appropriate to be used as evidence for their historical accounts. The larger range of sources that make the transition to evidence for sports historians will be challenging because it necessitates the acquisition of knowledge, techniques and skills from other disciplines to help make sense of these sources. For some sports historians, this approach will seem reasonable, worthwhile and productive but for others it will threaten the ontological, epistemological and methodological basis of history-making and be akin to the medieval witchcraft practice of 'sorcery'.

Notes

1 Anthony Grafton, *The Footnote: A Curious History* (London: Faber and Faber, 1997).
2 See, for instance: Martin Polley, *The History of Sport in Britain, 1880–1914* (London: Routledge, 2004); Larry K. Menna et al., eds, *Sports in North America: A Documentary History* (Gulf Breeze, FL: Academic International Press, 1992).
3 Grant Jarvie and Joseph A. Maguire, *Sport and Leisure in Social Thought* (London: Routledge, 1994).
4 Martin Polley, *Sports History: A Practical Guide* (Basingstoke: Palgrave, 2007).
5 John Tosh, *The Pursuit of History: Aims, Methods and New Directions in the Study of Modern History*, second edn (London: Longman, 1991), 30.
6 Alun Munslow, *The Routledge Companion to Historical Studies*, second edn (London: Routledge, 2006), 100; David Hackett Fischer, *Historians' Fallacies: Toward a Logic of Historical Thought* (New York: Harper & Row, 1970), 4; Andy Carr, 'After the Siren: Sources for Rugby League History Research in Australia', *Sport in History* 27, 3 (September 2007), 448.
7 Douglas Booth, *The Field: Truth and Fiction in Sport History* (London: Routledge, 2005), 27.
8 Ibid.
9 Ibid., 229, note 11; Polley, *Sports History*, 125.
10 Joyce Appleby, Lynn Hunt and Margaret Jacob, *Telling the Truth About History* (New York: Norton, 1994), 259.
11 Munslow, *The Routledge Companion to Historical Studies*, 100–3.
12 Ibid., 100.
13 Booth, *The Field*, 25.
14 Ibid., 25–31; Munslow, *The Routledge Companion to Historical Studies*, 107–9.
15 Booth, *The Field*, 29–31.
16 Alun Munslow, *Deconstructing History* (London: Routledge, 1997), 85.
17 Ibid., 18–26; Munslow, *The Routledge Companion to Historical Studies*, 228.
18 Booth, *The Field*, 82.
19 Ibid., 7.
20 Munslow, *The Routledge Companion to Historical Studies*, 228–29.
21 Arthur Marwick, *The New Nature of History: Knowledge, Evidence, Language*, fourth edn (Basingstoke, UK: Palgrave, 2001), 168, 172, 179, 185.
22 Munslow, *The Routledge Companion to Historical Studies*, 100–3.
23 Marwick, *The New Nature of History*; G.R. Elton, *Return to Essentials: Some Reflections on the Present State of Historical Study* (Cambridge: Cambridge University Press, 1991).
24 For a synopsis, see Munslow, *Deconstructing History*, Chapter 3; for a strident advocate, see Marwick, *The New Nature of History*; for application to sports history, see Polley, *Sports History*.
25 Polley, *Sports History*, 76.
26 Ibid., 78.
27 Peter Burke, *Eyewitnessing: The Uses of Images as Historical Evidence* (Ithaca, NY: Cornell University Press, 2001), 13.
28 Munslow, *The Routledge Companion to Historical Studies*, 108.
29 See, for example: Wolfgang Decker, *Sports and Games of Ancient Egypt* (New York: Yale University Press, 1992); E. Norman Gardiner, *Athletics of the Ancient World* (London: Oxford University Press,

1967); Mark Golden, *Sport in the Ancient World from A to Z* (London: Routledge, 2004); Donald G. Kyle, *Sport and Spectacle in the Ancient World* (Malden, MA: Blackwell, 2007); Zahra Newby, *Athletics in the Ancient World* (Bristol: Bristol Classical Press, 2006); Vera Olivova, *Sports and Games in the Ancient World* (London: Bloomsbury, 1984).

30 See for example: Golden, *Sport in the Ancient World from A to Z*; H.A. Harris, *Greek Athletes and Athletics* (London: Hutchinson, 1964); Jason König, *Athletics and Literature in the Roman Empire* (Cambridge: Cambridge University Press, 2005); Kyle, *Sport and Spectacle in the Ancient World*; Zahra Newby, *Greek Athletics in the Roman World: Victory and Virtue* (Oxford: Oxford University Press, 2005); Olivova, *Sports and Games in the Ancient World*; David Phillips and David Pritchard, *Sport and Festival in the Ancient Greek World* (London: Classical Press of Wales, 2003).

31 Newby, *Greek Athletics in the Roman World*, Series Prelude, inside cover.

32 John Marshall Carter, *Sports and Pastimes of the Middle Ages* (Lanham, MD: University Press of America, 1988); Allen Guttmann, *Sports: The First Five Millennia* (Amherst: University of Massachusetts Press, 2004).

33 Polley, *Sports History*, 90.

34 Journals surveyed were: *Sporting Traditions* 23, 1–23, 2; *Journal of Sport History* 32, 1, 1–33; *International Journal of the History of Sport* 24, 9, 1–24; *Sport History Review* 37, 2, 1–37; *Sport in History* 26, 3, 2–27. The survey is limited due to the exclusion of non-English language journals; however, it offers a 'slice' of the field internationally.

35 Jaime Schultz, '"A Wager Concerning a Diplomatic Pig": A Crooked Reading of the Floyd of Rosedale Narrative', *Journal of Sport History* 32, 1 (2005).

36 Melvin L. Adelman, *A Sporting Time: New York City and the Rise of Modern Athletics, 1820–70* (Urbana: University of Illinois Press, 1990), 9.

37 Ibid., 287.

38 Ronald A. Smith, *Play-by-Play: Radio, Television, and Big-Time College Sport* (Baltimore, MD: The Johns Hopkins University Press, 2001), 283.

39 Ibid.

40 Barbara J. Keys, *Globalizing Sport: National Rivalry and International Community in the 1930s* (Cambridge, MA: Harvard University Press, 2006).

41 Booth, *The Field*, 85–86.

42 Adelman, *A Sporting Time*, 369–79; Smith, *Play-by-Play*, 283–94.

43 Adelman, *A Sporting Time*, 287–89.

44 Ibid., 10, 369.

45 John Bale, 'Partial Knowledge: Photographic Mystifications and Constructions of "the African Athlete"', in Murray G. Phillips, ed., *Deconstructing Sport History: A Postmodern Analysis* (Albany: State University of New York Press, 2006). For another example, see Cheryl L. Cole, 'One Chromosome Too Many?', in Kay Schaffer and Sidonie Smith, eds, *The Olympics at the Millennium: Power, Politics, and the Games* (New Brunswick, NJ: Rutgers University Press, 2000).

46 J.A. Mangan, 'Icon of Monumental Brutality: Art and the Aryan Man', in J.A. Mangan, ed., *Shaping the Superman: Fascist Body as Political Icon – Aryan Fascism* (London: Frank Cass, 1999).

47 Richard D. Mandell, *The Nazi Olympics* (New York: Ballantine, 1972), xiv.

48 Michael Oriard, *Reading Football: How the Popular Press Created an American Spectacle* (Chapel Hill: University of North Carolina Press, 1993).

49 Pamela Grundy, *Learning to Win: Sports, Education and Social Change in Twentieth-Century North Carolina* (Chapel Hill: University of North Carolina Press, 2001).

50 Patricia Vertinsky and John Bale, eds, *Sites of Sport: Space, Place, Experience* (London: Routledge, 2004).

51 Patricia Vertinsky and Sherry McKay, *Disciplining Bodies in the Gymnasium: Memory, Monument, Modernism* (London: Routledge, 2004).

52 Booth, *The Field*.

53 Tessa Morris-Suzuki, *The Past Within Us: Media, Memory, History* (New York: Verso, 2005), 118.

54 John Bale, 'Capturing "The African" Body? Visual Images and "Imaginative Sports"', *Journal of Sport History* 25, 2 (1998), 234.

55 Murray G. Phillips, Mark E. O'Neill and Gary Osmond, 'Broadening Horizons in Sport History: Films, Photographs and Monuments', *Journal of Sport History* 34:2 (2007), 401–21.

56 Tosh, *The Pursuit of History*, 31.

57 Ibid., 32.

58 Jeffrey Hill, 'Anecdotal Evidence: Sport, the Newspaper Press, and History', in Murray G. Phillips, ed., *Deconstructing Sport History: A Postmodern Analysis* (Albany: State University of New York Press, 2006), 118. Emphasis in the original.

59 Munslow, *Deconstructing History*, chapters 4 and 6.

60 For an example of White's ideas in sports history, see Hayden V. White, *Metahistory: The Historical Imagination in Nineteenth-Century Europe* (Baltimore, MD: The Johns Hopkins University Press, 1973); Murray G. Phillips, 'A Critical Appraisal of Narrative in Sport History: Reading the Surf Lifesaving Debate', *Journal of Sport History* 29, 1 (2002).

61 Sine Agergaard, 'Dualities of Space in Danish Sports History', *Sport in History* 27, 2 (2007); Douglas A. Brown, 'The Modern Romance of Mountaineering: Photography, Aesthetics and Embodiment', *International Journal of the History of Sport* 24, 1 (2007); Nissim Mannathukkaren, 'Reading Cricket Fiction in the Times of Hindu Nationalism and Farmer Suicides: Fallacies of Textual Interpretation', *International Journal of the History of Sport* 24, 9 (2007).

62 Jaime Schultz, '"Stuff From Which Legends Are Made": Jack Trice Stadium and the Politics of Memory', *The International Journal of the History of Sport* 24, 6 (2007), 717.

63 David McGimpsey, *Imagining Baseball: America's Pastime and Popular Culture* (Bloomington: Indiana University Press, 2000).

64 Ibid., 2.

65 Ibid., 2–3.

66 Daniel A. Nathan, *Saying It's So: A Cultural History of the Black Sox Scandal* (Urbana: University of Illinois Press, 2003).

67 Ibid., 8.

68 Ibid., 9.

69 Tara Brabazon, *Playing on the Periphery: Sport, Identity, and Memory* (New York: Routledge, 2006), 2.

70 Ibid., 76–77.

71 Ibid., 82–87.

72 Douglas Booth, 'Evidence Revisited: Interpreting Historical Materials in Sport History', *Rethinking History* 9, 4 (2005), 477; Booth, *The Field*, 105; Brabazon, *Playing on the Periphery*, 83.

73 Burke, *Eyewitnessing*, 10.

74 Richard Cashman, *Paradise of Sport: The Rise of Organised Sport in Australia* (Melbourne: Oxford University Press, 1995), 171.

75 Exceptions include Bale, 'Partial Knowledge'; Thierry Terret, 'Race and Gender in the French Sporting Press at the End of the 1950s: The Example of Sport & Vie', *Sporting Traditions* 23, 1 (2006).

76 Elizabeth Edwards, *Raw Histories: Photographs, Anthropology and Museums* (Oxford: Berg, 2001), 9.

77 Roland Barthes, *Mythologies*, translated by Annette Lavers (London: Paladin, 1972; reprint 1986); Gary Osmond, '"Modest Monuments"? Postage Stamps, Duke Kahanamoku and Hierarchies of Social Memory', *Journal of Pacific History* 43, 3 (2008), 313–29.

78 Elizabeth Edwards and Janice Hart, eds, *Photographs Objects Histories: On the Materiality of Images* (London: Routledge, 2004).

79 Douglas Hartmann, *Race, Culture, and the Revolt of the Black Athlete: The 1968 Olympic Protests and Their Aftermath* (Chicago: University of Chicago Press, 2003), 8, 169.

80 Douglas Booth, '(Re)Reading the Surfers' Bible: The Affects of Tracks', *Journal of Media & Cultural Studies* 22, 1 (2008).

81 Paula Hamilton and Paul Ashton, 'At Home with the Past: Initial Findings from the Survey', *Australian Cultural History* 23 (2003); Roy Rosenzweig and David Thelen, *The Presence of the Past: Popular Uses of History in American Life* (New York: Columbia University Press, 1988).

82 Wray Vamplew, 'Facts and Artefacts: Sports Historians and Sports Museums', *Journal of Sport History* 25, 2 (1998), 268.

83 Ibid., 270–72.

84 S.W. Pope, ed., *The New American History: Recent Approaches and Perspectives* (Urbana: University of Illinois Press, 1997), 21.

85 Brian Goldfarb, *Visual Pedagogy: Media Cultures in and Beyond the Classroom* (Durham, NC: Duke University Press, 2002).

86 Chris Healy, *From the Ruins of Colonialism: History as Social Memory* (Melbourne: Cambridge University Press, 1997).

87 Susan A. Crane, *Museums and Memory* (Stanford, CA: Stanford University Press, 2000).

88 Robert A. Rosenstone, ed., *Revisioning History: Film and the Construction of a New Past* (Princeton, NJ: Princeton University Press, 1995); Murray G. Phillips, 'An Athletic Clio: Sport History and Television History', *Rethinking History* 12, 3 (2008), 399–416.

89 Aaron Baker, *Contesting Identities: Sports in American Film* (Urbana: University of Illinois Press, 2003).

90 John Bale, *Landscapes of Modern Sport* (London: Leicester University Press, 1994).

91 Vertinsky and Bale, eds, *Sites of Sport*; Vertinsky and McKay, *Disciplining Bodies in the Gymnasium*.

92 Synthia Sydnor, 'Sport, Celebrity and Liminality', in Noel Dyck, ed., *Games, Sports and Cultures* (Oxford: Berg, 2000).

93 Jackson B. Miller, '"Indians", "Braves", and "Redskins": A Performative Struggle for Control of an Image', *Quarterly Journal of Speech* 85, 2 (1999), 189.

94 Albert Boime, *Hollow Icons: The Politics of Sculpture in Nineteenth-Century France* (Kent, OH: Kent State University Press, 1987), 113.

95 Gary Osmond, Murray G. Phillips and Mark O'Neill, '"Putting up Your Dukes": Statues, Social Memory and Duke Paoa Kahanamoku', *International Journal of the History of Sport* 23, 1 (2006).

96 Morris-Suzuki, *The Past Within Us*, 16.

3   The city

Gerald R. Gems

The evolution of sports historiography and the city

The relationship of sport and the city can be traced back to ancient times. Historians initiated such studies with descriptions of sport in the Greek city-states, though many focused more intently on the Olympic Games, which tied religion to sport. As early as 1910 E. Norman Gardiner published *Greek Athletic Sports and Festivals*, followed by the works of H.A. Harris, which covered both Greece and Rome. Such idealistic descriptive narratives, though valuable in establishing a small foothold for sports history, paled in comparison to the more erudite academic examinations of the latter 20th century, especially in the works of Donald Kyle, David Sansone, David Young, Hugh Lee, Thomas Scanlon, and Stephen Miller. The latter scholars, influenced by the new social history and its interdisciplinary approaches, affected more nuanced analyses of the relationships between sport, religion, gender, politics, and community. Michael Poliakoff's *Combat Sports in the Ancient World* compared developments throughout the Mediterranean region, and Jean-Paul Thuillier's *Sport im antiken Rom* briefly examines urban stadiums. German historians, such as Wolfgang Decker, have expanded the study of ancient sport to Egypt. Decker has also served as editor of *Nikephoros*, an annual journal of ancient sport. Karl Lennartz has also painstakingly detailed the modern version of the Games and their civic locations have added much to the historical knowledge base and corrected the factual errors of the early works.[1]

The feudal nature of European societies during the medieval era allowed for folk games, but few studies exist of urban sporting life in Europe or Asia. John McClelland has done considerable work in the period though he has not focused specifically on urban locales. The flowering of the Renaissance attracted great scholarly attention, with a multitude of studies on the Italian city-states of the era, but little in the way of sport. Many studies assumed the Marxist approach in vogue during the 1970s and 1980s, and drew upon the new social history to dissect social class arrangements. Those that most clearly, but not explicitly, approached sport studies dealt with politics or the violent nature of society and ritualized violence. Dundas and Falassi's *La Terra in Piazza* presented the varied inter-relationships and neighbourhood rivalries that comprised the palio, the horse-race for local pride in Siena. Gigliola Gori has examined a village folk game as a precursor to the sport of basketball, and Robert Davis's *The War of the Fists: Popular Culture and Public Violence in Late Renaissance Venice* analysed neighbourhood and clan tensions celebrated in regular and eventually scheduled melees for control of the Venetian bridges. Pugilistic champions won honour and might retire to become organizers, strategists, promoters and referees of the ritual battles, witnessed by as many as

30,000 spectators. Such activities presaged modern sports (as identified below) and continued into the 18th century before replacement by more 'civilized' regatta competitions. Werner Korbs, a German scholar, published an early study of sports during the Renaissance. Kazuhiko Kusudo provided a study of shooting festivals involving crossbow and musket competitions, as well as races among women in 15th-century German cities. Similarly, Joachim Ruhl published a study of German jousting tournaments during the 15th century, which included regions and cities, but focused on rules rather than the community.[2]

The initial study of sport in the modern city was largely the result of developments in the USA. The most famous, and perhaps enduring early historical theory (frontier theory) was postulated by Frederick Jackson Turner at the 1893 World's Fair in Chicago. There Jackson lamented the loss of the American frontier, that expanse of free land that drew migrants ever westward, forced the Native Americans on to reservations, and in Jackson's estimation, created a distinct American character. Historians still debate such a notion of American exceptionalism.[3]

As Turner spoke, American civilization was undergoing a rapid transformation from the independent farmers of the early republic to an industrial economy centred in the cities and fuelled by a largely immigrant labour force. The 1920 census indicated that the USA had become an urban nation, as city dwellers surpassed farmers. One of Turner's students at the University of Wisconsin, Frederick Paxson, the recently crowned president of the Organization of American Historians, declared in a 1917 essay that sport had become the new frontier. Paxson asserted that sport provided a social safety valve for the tensions of the teeming, unhealthy cities. In 1938 the prominent historian Arthur M. Schlesinger, Sr concurred that sport provided the means for the vicarious return to the rural pleasures of the past, particularly in the open air stadiums of the cities. Similar to such compensation theorists Foster Rhea Dulles, in his *America Learns to Play*, published in 1940, saw sport as the culmination of American democracy. John R. Betts, in his 1951 dissertation, 'The Rise of Organized Sport in America' argued that modern sport had evolved as a result of the industrial and urban processes in the USA. While Betts produced a more thorough and complex analysis of the evolution of sporting practices, he, like his predecessors, assumed an idealistic perspective based on the experiences of the middle class mainstream population. In 1972 Dale Somers followed the idealist approach in *The Rise of Sports in New Orleans*, the first case study of the evolution of sport in an American city. A year later Robert Malcolmson exhibited the influence of E.P. Thompson as his *Popular Recreations of English Society, 1700–1850* showed some departure from the established framework.[4]

The functionalist approach, also prevalent in early sociological studies, assumed sport to be a good and beneficial activity; one that socialized and acculturated the immigrants in an American melting pot and served a character building process that culminated in a homogeneous democratic citizenry. The structuralist approach assumed greater sophistication with the advent of modernization theory, which drew from the sociological insights of Max Weber, Norbert Elias and Eric Dunning, among others. Allen Guttmann, in his seminal work *From Ritual to Record* (1978), provided the framework and the characteristics of modern sport. Guttmann identified rationalization, secularization, bureaucratization, quantification and specialization as hallmarks of modern sport, causing sports historians to measure their analyses against his criteria. Melvin Adelman, in his case study of New York City, further extended the modernization theory by stipulating the urban, commercial and industrial nature of the process. Modernization theory ethnocentrically assumed that process to be a linear one modelled on Western notions of progress in which societies might be measured on the evolutionary continuum.[5]

The social turmoil that wracked American society during the 1960s and 1970s brought alternative visions of society and historiography. The Cold War, the civil rights movement, feminism and a rebellious youth culture spawned numerous critiques of the idealistic functionalist paradigm. Robert Wiebe's *The Search for Order*, published in 1967, adhered to the modernization paradigm, but spawned a host of studies that examined the forces of order and social control. Benjamin Rader incorporated a modernization approach and the role of sport in community building in several cities in a larger national study.[6] Other case studies took a more critical approach. As functionalists claimed the benevolence and assimilative aims of the social reformers in the cities, Dominick Cavallo, in his *Muscles and Morals: Organized Playgrounds and Urban Reform* (1981), and Paul Boyer, in *Urban Masses and Moral Order in America* (1978) examined the ideological foundations of the play movement in America. Gary Ross Mormino found sport to be both integrative and exclusionary in his study of Italians in St Louis. Cary Goodman's case study of New York, *Choosing Sides: Playground and Street Life on the Lower East Side* (1979), was a strong departure from the consensus historians in its Marxist approach.[7]

Marxist theory gained ascendance with the publication of two pioneering texts in the 1960s, E.P. Thompson's *The Making of the English Working Class* and C.L.R. James' *Beyond a Boundary*. Thompson's use of contextualization, that is, 'the networking of facts in an ensemble of other meanings' produced an alternative vision of class formation via human agency rather than a sequential and deterministic narrative. James' study of West Indian cricket invoked memory, personal insight and history as it presaged the post-modern analyses and the postcolonial and imperialist studies of the latter 20th century.[8] French historians, particularly Fernand Braudel of the Annales School of history, also emphasized the *longue durée*, or the evolution of events over a protracted period of time to discern the true meaning of the past. The Annales historians pursued interdisciplinary study through the use of geography, anthropology and economics, implementing the quantification of their data.

Quantification and statistical analysis enjoyed a burst of popularity as historians sought to convince their readers through hard science. In 1964 Stephan Thernstrom quantified his findings in *The Other Bostonians: Poverty and Progress*, followed by Sam Bass Warner's social history of Philadelphia, *The Private City* (1968). Among sports historians Steven Riess adopted quantification techniques in *City Games* (1989) to investigate demographic changes and the relationships between sport and urban structures, organizations and ideologies. Riess extended the new social history to include residential patterns, transport networks, economic and political systems, as well as gender, class, ethnicity and race.[9]

The Marxists proposed a conflict theory at odds with the functionalists. Conflict theory presupposed the power and intention of the social and economic elite to act in their own best interests. Sport depended upon the capitalist needs and wants, with workers and their pastimes subordinated to the upper classes. Within such a framework labour historians gained increasing prominence as Herbert Gutman, David Montgomery, Alan Dawley and Eric Foner tracked the (mis)fortunes of the working classes. Sports historians who followed their lead surmised that sport generated alienation, aggression, violence, nationalism, sexism and materialism. The capitalists used it as a means to socially control workers, induce ideological conformity, and it further served as a commercial marketing tool. British Marxist historians Eric Hobsbawm and Terence Ranger even claimed that the elites 'invented traditions' to achieve the desired outcomes.[10]

Critics of the Marxist approach found it to be deterministic, tied to the economic system and one's role in that system. Social class became assigned, without consideration for the mitigating factors of ethnicity, race, religion, gender and so on. The theoretical debate spawned Neo-Marxism, which merged Freudian psychology with the Marxist economic outlook to explain motives of 'the capitalistically distorted form of play' to produce greater achievement (as in capitalistic production) and bring relief to pent up aggressions.[11] The Italian Marxist, Antonio Gramsci, provided greater analytical power with his hegemony theory, refined by British sociologist Raymond Williams. Hegemony theory claimed that a dominant group within any society would be able to set the norms, standards and values, while members of the subordinate group(s), having free will or human agency, had the choice to accept, reject, adopt, or adapt such impositions. The contest of differences would result in a continual power struggle in which sport might be used to reinforce the position of the dominant group or as a means of opposition or protest by the less powerful. This more complex theoretical framework allowed for a multitude of groups based on race, ethnicity, class, gender, religion, age, sexuality and so on with competing interests, as well as the organic intellectual who might bridge the factions. Chronology also mattered, as conditions in a particular time period allowed for the unfolding of events that might not be replicable. For example, the historical conditions inherent after World War I enabled Adolf Hitler to gain control of the German state, an occurrence that would be inconceivable today.[12]

Adding to the melange of intellectual perspectives, anthropologists, such as Clifford Geertz and John MacAloon, offered new insights. Geertz's classic ethnographic study of the Balinese cockfight and its revelatory meanings allowed sport to be read as a text, whereas MacAloon's study of the Olympic Games and his conception of frames, influenced by the earlier work of Victor Turner, likened sport to a symbolic cultural performance. German scholar Henning Eichberg also introduced innovative insights into sport as a ritual performance. Such perceptions only grew in importance as sport moved closer to entertainment throughout the 20th century. Anthropologists have gained an increasing interest in sport and taken the analysis in new directions. For example, George Gmelch and J.J. Weiner have provided insightful analysis of the workers (non-athletes) who labour in urban baseball parks in the USA.[13]

With the surge of ideas and a growing interest in and investigation of community studies, popular culture and sport in particular slowly gained academic credibility. Reflecting this transition, Eastern European scholars founded the International Committee for the History of Sport and Physical Education in Prague in 1967. The Canadian Journal of the History of Sport and Physical Education appeared in 1970, but more than 12 years later Don Morrow determined that Canadian studies still consisted of narrative descriptive works, with the exception of the Marxist analyses of Alan Metcalfe. The North American Society for Sport History formed in 1972, followed by the International Association for Sport History in Zurich a year later. A British History of Sport Association was organized in 1978 and national sports history organizations followed in Australia, Brazil, the Netherlands, Finland, Japan, Norway and France. The transnational European Committee for Sport History came about in 1995. Annual conferences brought scholars from different disciplines together with a fruitful exchange of ideas relative to the new social history and the topic of sport. By 1983 Europeans, German scholars in particular, had produced a wealth of works, but most centred on national rather than urban histories. In Germany there was a long history of the turner movement and physical education, but by the 1960s East German historians presented Marxist interpretations of sport. In the ensuing decades workers' sport received increasing attention, as did biographical studies. By the 1980s a number of studies chronicled club sports, especially soccer (football) teams in urban locales.[14]

The interdisciplinary contact became evident in the works of Stephen Hardy and Alan Ingham. Hardy's case study, *How Boston Played* (1982), merged social history with labour history in his analysis of community building. Roy Rosenzweig's *Eight Hours for What We Will* (1983) expanded the scope of leisure studies, which included amusement parks, saloons and feminist investigations of the recreational practices of urban women. The expanded interest in ethnicity, race, gender and social class brought a multicultural hue to sports studies.[15]

Historians periodically assessed the state of sports history and by 1985 Nancy Struna had determined that the sub-discipline had reached a stage of 'glorious disarray', a judgement that was both critical yet promising. The field had broadened its scope considerably with new questions, new forms of evidence and greater contextualization, but it lacked a coherent paradigm and any systematic analysis. A sampling of articles indicated the growth of urban sports, the role of particular sports and social relations within sporting enterprises; however, the deeper meanings of sport and comparative studies remained unresolved.[16]

By the 1980s French intellectuals had introduced postmodern concepts and analytical frameworks that sharply diverged from and questioned previous knowledge. The postmodernists' contention that knowledge was constructed via power relationships raised questions about the nature of history, truth and objectivity. Michel Foucault's emphasis on discourse and the repression of bodies had ramifications for the study of sport and the fitness movement. Patricia Vertinsky's *The Eternally Wounded Woman* (1990) demonstrated female subordination imposed by the power of the largely male medical establishment. Pierre Bourdieu injected the concepts of fields, habitus, social capital and cultural capital based on class and the power of language, while Jacques Derrida claimed that there was no reality, all history is subjective, therefore all texts have to be deconstructed. In such a view the historian, as narrator, is only one of many possible interpreters in the historical process. Texts were broadly construed as any form of media or performance, including sport. Patricia Vertinsky deconstructed the design, scheduling and use of the gymnasium space at the University of British Columbia to analyse its gendered nature. Catriona Parratt deconstructed Haxey Hood, a village in Lincolnshire, as a set of multiple narratives that revolved around a local game; Michael Oriard analysed the narratives of American football in the print media to explicate its cultural meanings. By the late 1990s the contentious struggle over theoretical frameworks had so divided American historians that the prestigious American Historical Association and the Organization of American Historians faced defections to the newly formed Historical Society, which favoured a more radical perspective. Similar developments occurred within the field of sports studies, though with less rancour. The establishment of a new journal, *Rethinking History*, in 1997 gave voice to the adherents of postmodernism. Sports historians from Australia and New Zealand have conducted several urban studies of the lifesaving culture in Australia that mark the departure from traditional social history to the postmodern literary paradigm. Both Sean Brawley and Ed Jaggard have employed traditional empirical techniques, while Doug Booth and Murray Phillips have pursued the 'cultural turn'. A special issue of the *Journal of Sport History* (Spring 2002) was devoted to the debate without resolution. Sport sociologists have been more amenable than sports historians to adapting the postmodern framework, which has engendered strong debate within the latter community.[17]

British sports history has undergone a similar evolution, from a multitude of antiquarian studies to an acknowledged position in academia. It emerged in the 1970s and clearly arrived with the publication of Tony Mason's *Association Football and English Society, 1863–1915* in 1980. A British History of Sport Association had formed by 1978. Urban studies proliferated, influenced by labour history with a strong emphasis on social class, community building and particular sports, especially soccer and cricket. Jeffrey Hill's assessment of the field in 1996 noted its growing scope, but lamented the continued absence of media, military, consumption and gender studies, with notable exceptions to the latter by Kathleen McCrone and Jennifer Hargreaves. Hargreaves provided a new feminist theoretical perspective but, like the Marxists, feminism fragmented into various factions. J.A. Mangan also advanced the level and scope of British sports history with his investigation of school sports and colonialism. The latter extended the study of sport to locations (urban and otherwise) throughout the British empire. Hill called for a greater attention to theory and a recognition and incorporation of the postmodern influences to derive insights into identity and meaning. By that time the same debates over the values of empiricism versus literary theory affected British sports historians and their sociological counterparts.[18]

In 2004 Martin Johnes made a further assessment of the state of sports history in Great Britain. By that time urban, local and nationalistic studies had moved beyond England to include Scotland, Wales and Ireland. Johnes concluded that sports history had reached the level of a sub-discipline, with no fewer than 12 journals and a host of published monographs, its own academic society, research centres and academic courses in the universities. A continued lack of respect in academic circles and charges of irrelevance, though, elicited a call for a move to the more multidisciplinary approach of sports studies, already evident in Australia. Johnes found British sports history to be still deficient in comparative studies, and in the use of oral history and ethnography, methodologies championed by the postmodernists. A sharp divide existed between the sports historians and the sports sociologists, who had wholeheartedly adopted more theoretical approaches. On both sides of the Atlantic the debate over postmodernism continued.[19]

The interdisciplinary flow of sports history

The new social history spawned new questions, new methodologies and new theories that greatly broadened the scope of sports history. Scholars investigated such varied topics as geography, economics, politics, education, parks and playgrounds, race, ethnicity, religion and gender in the evolution toward cultural studies. Those engaged in the urban paradigm built upon the early social studies of Louis Wirth and the early sociologists of the Chicago School (at the University of Chicago). Wirth perceived the city as a physical structure, a social organization and a state of mind.[20] Historians took note of the growing interest in urban studies, marked by a joint conference sponsored by Harvard University and the Massachusetts Institute of Technology in 1961 that addressed technology and economic development, the concept of the city, urban growth, urban forms and urban planning.[21] More recent works on urban studies adhere to a similar categorization: the evolution of cities, urban culture and society, urban space, politics, governance, economics and urban planning.[22]

The study of cities within the discipline of history spans the ancient to the modern to the speculations of futurists, with particular emphases on politics, economics, social relations and power. Sports historians are also concerned with such factors, but few have pursued the *longue durée* in such developments. However, rapid globalization has expanded the international scope of both historians and sociologists, who have examined the reach of multinational corporations, such as Nike, and international governing bodies such as the IOC and FIFA, or those intent on reaching international markets, such as the American NFL, NBA and MLB.[23]

The work on urban culture is extensive and has included a wide range of topics including race, ethnicity, gender, religion, social class and communities of sports fans. The vast literature on African Americans in the USA ranges from early case studies, such as Kenneth Kusmer's *A Ghetto Takes Shape: Black Cleveland, 1870–1930* (1976), to more specific investigations of sporting life, such as black entrepreneurship and distinct playing styles in basketball. The interdisciplinary approach is evident in Reuben May's recent *Living through the Hoop* (2008), a seven-year ethnographic study of a community high school basketball team that provides sociological insight into race, an alternative culture and perceptions of masculinity. Davarian Baldwin's *Chicago's New Negroes: Modernity, The Great Migration, and Black Urban Life* (2007) also exemplifies the new scholarship which transcends the traditional disciplinary boundaries as he weaves through a variety of factors such as race, sexuality, geography, music, film and sport to derive meanings for an urban subculture. A growing literature has also addressed the plight of Hispanic athletes and women's experiences. Some of my own work has examined ethnic, religious and working class communities within the city of Chicago. In Europe Gertrud Pfister has explored the role of sport in the assimilation of immigrant Muslim women in both Germany and Denmark, and there is an ongoing and fervent movement among urban female scholars in Islamic countries to gain greater freedom through sport. Other scholars have produced case studies of sport in German cities. A host of sporting biographies take place within the urban setting, though few authors have explored the relationships between sport, place and life other than in novels. In the United Kingdom, South America and the USA fan culture has been an absorbing interest, and recent studies involving ethnographic research have provided new insights into the interrelationships within and the complexity of fan communities.[24]

Traditional urban historians have begun to incorporate or at least acknowledge the broader aspects of sport in their work. Urban planners have taken a renewed interest in the work of park designers Frederick Law Olmsted and Jens Jensen, as well as architect Daniel Burnham, who designed not only American cities, but the reconstruction of the Philippines under American rule. Company towns, their workers' sporting lives and health resorts have all become the subjects of urban sports historians. Henning Eichberg was among the first to explore the relationships of space, the environment and body culture. There is an extensive body of work on urban playgrounds (previously cited), and sports historians have adopted the approaches of the social historians, as well as the postmodernists in their economic and political analyses of the construction of urban stadiums. The nexus of sport, recreation, economics, politics and commercialization has resulted in athletic arenas being constructed, often as the centrepiece of urban entertainment zones including restaurants, theatres, amusement parks and museums or halls of fame, all directed at obtaining the tourist trade. Such entertainment zones have spawned a remarkable global urban homogeneity from the USA to Australia. Sports tourism has become a subsystem of its own, with loyal fans making pilgrimages to athletic shrines and nostalgic places of remembrance, giving impetus to the *Journal of Sport and Tourism*.[25]

The city of Indianapolis has attempted to reconstruct its image as 'the amateur sports capital of the world' by building its economy around sport and tourism. *ESPN The*

Magazine named it the top professional sports city in 2003. Sport sociologists Kimberley Schimmel, Alan Ingham and Jeremy Howell analysed the political manipulations in Indianapolis that enabled the local government to not only construct new facilities to attract professional sports teams, but to provide headquarters for the NCAA and several sport federations: gymnastics, track and field, diving, synchronized swimming, as well as the Indy Racing League, the Black Coaches Association, the American College of Sports Medicine, and the National Federation of State High School Associations. The city also serves as the site of two major auto races, but little of the revenue from such ventures has trickled down to the poor families displaced by all of the construction.[26]

Other scholars have also invoked interdisciplinary methods in their investigations of urban stadium construction. Andrew Zimbalist's economic studies are at odds with team owners' contentions of financial benefit to the community, as the jobs created are seasonal rather than permanent and most benefit seems to be derived by the team owners in the way of civic subsidies. Kevin Delaney and Rick Eckstein (see note 24) used journalistic methods, such as interviews, to track the stadium-building surge in the USA over a 20-year period, identifying the role of several parties, such as team owners, politicians, the media and corporate interests in the process. In Phoenix and Pittsburgh political manipulations enabled stadiums to be built despite the objections of the populace. Their study covers not only the historical, but the political, sociological, economic and even architectural factors that bear upon the matter. Daniel Rosensweig's *Retro Ball Parks: Instant History, Baseball, and the New American City* invokes postmodern analyses from the viewpoint of a fan who is also an historian. His study covers alienation, social stratification and nostalgia in Baltimore and Cleveland, which also allows for some comparison. He ruminates on the past history of the sport of baseball, its former stadiums and the racial composition of fans, mixed with ethnographic study and interviews of those involved in the present in an attempt to decipher conflicted meanings.[27]

The nature of memory and the uses of nostalgia have become an area of interest for both social historians and, more recently, sports historians as well. New stadiums inevitably include remembrances of the past in their construction, symbols, memorials and imagery. Past players are honoured with adjacent statuary, walls, or walks of fame, public imagery that adorns the site, or in public ceremonies. Athletic contests are presented in conjunction with nationalistic displays, clearly intended to promote a sense of patriotism and a particular political agenda.[28]

Sports history has become a popular form of public history in Europe, Australia and North America as urban museums increasingly mount sport-related exhibitions. The Australian National Museum recently offered an exhibit on the history of lifesaving and the National Portrait Gallery at the Smithsonian Institute in Washington, DC presented a display on a variety of athletes. The USA has two museums for sporting art, and all major sports and many minor ones in America have museums dubbed as 'international', 'national', or local repositories of sporting heritage. The Roman Colosseum has long been a tourist site, but even small villages now attempt to attract visitors with sport artefacts, photos, documents and local guides who act as interpreters and keepers of past knowledge.[29]

Such developments attest to the success of sports historians in the development of interest in and the dissemination of knowledge about sport. The general public is much more aware of sporting heritage, professional teams and leagues market sport nostalgia to fill their coffers, and even the top universities offer sports history courses within their history departments or other academic programmes. A surfeit of publications purport to offer sports history to their readers. Still, much work remains. While the *Journal of Sport History* concentrates largely on North American sporting culture, the *International Journal of the History of Sport*, aptly named, has taken a more global perspective, covering not only North America and Europe, but Latin America, Asia and Africa as well.[30]

However, the success of sports history has also been its bane. The acceptance of sports history within social history has caused a unidirectional flow as the sub-discipline is increasingly absorbed within departments of history, American Studies, or cultural studies, to the chagrin of many practitioners still housed in physical education departments, where graduate programmes in sports history have faced contraction. Both Nancy Struna, in her assessment of the field in 1997 and Martin Johnes' 2004 review anticipated such developments. Regardless of the academic ownership, and despite several decades of research, sports historians have hardly scratched the surface of possibilities for urban history.[31]

The future of sports history

While sports history has made substantial strides, sports historians (at least those who emanated from physical education departments) have not fared as well. Sports history within the domain of physical education is in a precarious state. Such positions have dwindled in the USA, the United Kingdom and Germany, as sports history has become more acceptable within history departments, American studies and cultural studies programmes. Within departments of kinesiology, sports history is increasingly absorbed within emerging programmes of the more generic nomenclature of sport studies. As an area of study, though, sports history continues to grow and the scope of research is seemingly endless.

Theoretically, sports historians continue to wrestle with the influences of postmodernism, with three apparent factions. More traditional sports historians continue to reject the emphasis on linguistic analysis and retain empirical evidence as the basis for their interpretations and explanations. Postmodernists continue to argue the inability of any truth or generalization based on the multiple interpretations and possible meanings of past events. Practitioners of the two extremes can agree on basic historical facts, such as who did what, when and where, which allows for some middle ground for sports historians who accept some of the insights offered by postmodernists as they explore new methodologies and (re)presentations. Battles over reconstruction, analytical history, deconstruction and the nature of knowledge have brought a great vitality to intellectual debate within the humanities and, to a lesser extent, sports history.[32]

Much could be gained from a Foucauldian analysis of urban sport, such as playground games, interscholastic teams, communities of fans, or particular sport forms. Emergent sports, such as skateboarding, snowboarding, windsurfing, adventure racing, extreme sports, or those with a long history, such as dragon boat racing or that of outrigger canoes, still beg for contextualization and a fuller history. Interdisciplinary research, such as that undertaken in cultural studies approaches, offers a more nuanced view of sport in the urban environment.[33]

There is still a great need for the understudied sports histories of villages, towns and cities, but especially in Africa, Asia and Latin America.[34] While the Australian scholar, Peter Horton, has offered several studies of sport in Singapore, we still know too little about indigenous sports such as sepak takraw, kickboxing, the urban New Year festivals, or kite flying conducted in Asian cities. What is the legacy of imperialism and colonialism, and how have the indigenous peoples of Asia, Africa and the Caribbean reacted to such incursions? The colonial administrators' introduction of Western sport forms in China, Japan, India and the Philippines brought Christianity as well as sport. The organization of the Far East Olympics by the American YMCA in 1913 and hosted quadrennially thereafter in Asian cities brought racial, religious, social, gender, cultural and nationalistic ramifications for the populations of Asia.[35]

Even within the more studied regions of the world, such as North America, the United Kingdom and Europe, there are considerable lacunae. There is a relative dearth of research or a limited knowledge base in particular periods of ancient sport, the medieval era (an ethnocentric European designation not applicable to Asian cultures), and the Renaissance. For instance, we know something about gladiatorial contests, but what influence did the charioteers and their neighbourhood fans have on the civic welfare of ancient Rome? Did they serve as a means of social control of a potentially rebellious populace? We know little of the role of sport in the contentious rivalries of aristocratic families, their sponsorship of sporting festivals and the role of sport in effecting a civic identity. The palio horse-race in Siena is one notable exception.

Despite the numerous urban studies of modern sport there is still much ground (literally and figuratively) to be covered. How has gentrification affected sport? What does it mean to urban aesthetics? How has it reordered urban space with all the ramifications for social groups and power relationships? In what ways are such urban spaces gendered, racialized and contested? Has the restructuring of the city brought a greater sense of community or a disintegration of neighbourhood cultures? What do the choices of policy-makers mean to the health and welfare of city residents? Recent histories of stadium construction (previously stated) have only begun to examine such relationships. Stadiums and athletic arenas are symbols of power; they make statements about the architecture of cities and their sporting cultures. Grant Jarvie has recently called for sport scholars to assume a greater role as public intellectuals. What is the role of sport and its interpreters in the nostalgic movement of public history, such as memorializing the past in the new stadiums, museums, halls of fame, statuary and other invented traditions? Steve Hardy has long called for an investigation of the urban entrepreneurs at the root of the many developments in modern sporting practices, the marketing of sport in consumer culture, its economic and political ties. Who are the sponsors of urban sport and what are their motives? Steve Riess has even analysed the relationship of sport to urban transport networks in a few American cities, but we do not know if conditions and results differed elsewhere.[36]

While a number of urban case studies have illuminated the past, there is still much to be gleaned about class, religious, ethnic and racial enclaves, immigration and assimilation, and the cultural flow of sport. In the USA there is still too little known about the sporting lives of Hispanics, Asians and other communities. What do we know of the sporting lives of transient peoples who migrate in search of opportunities in a globalized economy? Is sport an assimilative factor or a divisive one? Does sport change ideologies, forms and meanings in the cultural flow? For example, there is evidence that styles of play in American football changed as they spread from the East Coast westward, but what happened to the German turner movement as it migrated to American cities? Is American baseball, basketball, or football played differently in its European, Mexican, or Asian contexts? Do South American soccer fans or players differ from Europeans in their ties to the game, its teams and its locations? Ethnographic studies could shed new light on such developments.[37]

City politicians use sports to market, promote and bring a particular identity to their cities by staging mega-events such as the Olympics, the World Cup, national championships, or marathons, triathlons and ultra-endurance events; however, there are few accounts beyond the promotional literature and some popular histories for the latter occurrences. Suburbanization has blurred the lines between distinct cities and their larger metropolitan areas, perhaps calling for a definition of terms. Suburbs have invoked sport, sport teams and sports facilities to transform their identity and economy in attempts to dissociate themselves from the shadow of larger cities. Although such developments have been occurring for over a century the effects of urban sprawl on people's sporting lives await thorough documentation.[38]

As sport forms, agents and cultures transcend municipalities in the globalization process, studies encompassing international workforces, markets and economies are being conducted, but the questions are ever evolving. Will globalization bring greater homogeneity to sporting cultures? What are the ramifications for local cultures and traditional sports and pastimes? How has the large influx of foreign players changed American baseball or basketball, and European soccer? Will sumo wrestling lose its cultural meanings as non-Japanese integrate the sport? Can bushkazi survive the American presence in Afghanistan? Will hybrid sports evolve? What are the consequences for dominant and subordinate economic regions?[39]

Globalization is not a new concept. Alexander the Great spread Greek culture throughout much of the known world and was greatly changed by the cultural relationships in the process. British studies of imperialism have shown the imposition of British culture, including sport, on colonial subjects, but there is much to be learned in the voices of the subordinate groups. The investigations into the role of sport in American imperialistic efforts have only just begun. Early examinations suggest that even within the military units that spread particular sport forms, the games had different meanings; for example, African American baseball players in segregated army units, who also played with Japanese, Chinese, and Filipino teams in Hawaii and the Philippines often felt greater affinity with their non-white competitors. Plantation teams in the Pacific and Caribbean eschewed the social control intentions of their managers and used games and practices to foment rebellion and class unity.[40] The similarities and differences point to the need for more comparative studies.

Body culture, sexuality and gendered bodies still represent something of a frontier in the sports history landscape. Women have integrated the highly masculine environment of the gym and urban health clubs, yet some women prefer segregated facilities in female-only clubs. Hospitals, therapy and rehabilitation clinics, homes for the elderly, health spas and luxurious resorts represent still other elements in the diverse locales and populations of the fitness and body sculpting movements. In such spaces and under differing conditions, in a variety of historical periods, multiple versions of masculinity and femininity emerge.[41]

The internet has added yet another dimension to the multiple discourses that comprise society, culture and inquiry. It provides ready access to information, but confounds the issues of veracity, sources and truth as people write their own histories in daily blogs and produce pieces of knowledge in Wikipedia, including sports history. The new technologies have already transformed cities and economies, as global communities are networked and labour is outsourced. Not only civic but national identities become blurred as social classes, governments and power relationships are reorganized around information technologies. That ever-changing environment holds some promise for sports historians who can hold video conferences, exchange ideas and texts via email, and continue to search for answers to both the new and the old questions within the field.[42]

Notes

1 E.N. Gardiner, *Greek Athletic Sports and Festivals* (London: Macmillan, 1910); H.A. Harris, *Greek Athletes and Athletics* (London: Hutchison, 1964), and *Sport in Greece and Rome* (London: Thames and Hudson, 1972); Donald G. Kyle, *Athletics in Ancient Athens* (Leiden: Brill, 1987), and *Spectacles of Death in Ancient Rome* (London: Routledge, 1998); David Sansone, *Greek Athletics and the Genesis of Sport* (Berkeley: University of California Press, 1988); David C. Young, *The Olympic Myth of Greek Amateur Athletics* (Chicago, IL: Ares, 1984); Thomas F. Scanlon, *Eros and Greek Athletics* (Oxford: Oxford University Press, 2002); Stephen G. Miller, *Ancient Greek Athletics* (New Haven, CT: Yale University Press, 2004); Michael B. Poliakoff, *Combat Sports in the Ancient World* (New Haven, CT: Yale University Press, 1987); Wolfgang Decker, *Sports and Games of Ancient Egypt* translated by Allen Guttmann (New Haven, CT: Yale University Press, 1992). See Guttmann's review of the work of Decker and Thuillier in the *Journal of Sport History* 27, 1 (Spring 2000), 151–52. Among Lennartz's contributions, see *Die Beteiligung Deutschlands an den Olympischen Spielen 1896 in Athen* (Bonn: Wegener, 1981), *Die Beteiligung Deutschlands an den Olympischen Spielen 1900 in Paris und 1904 in St Louis* (Bonn: Wegener, 1983), and *Die Beteiligung Deutschlands an den Olympischen Spielen 1906 in Athen und 1908 in London* (Bonn: Wegener, 1985).

2 See John McClelland, *Body and Soul: Sport in Europe from the Roman Empire to the Renaissance* (London: Routledge, 2007). Other period studies include John Marshall Carter, *Sports and Pastimes of the Middle Ages* (Lanham, MD: University Press of America, 1988); and Richard Barber and Juliet Barker, *Tournaments* (Woodbridge: Boydell Press, 1989). Among a wealth of urban Renaissance studies, see Samuel Kline Cohn, Jr, *The Laboring Classes in Renaissance Florence* (New York: Academic Press, 1980); Dale Kent, *The Rise of the Medici* (Oxford: Oxford University Press, 1978); Gene Brucker, *The Civic World of Early Renaissance Florence* (Princeton, NJ: Princeton University Press, 1977); Guido Ruggiero, *Violence in Early Renaissance Venice* (New Brunswick, NJ: Rutgers University Press, 1980); Robert Brentano, *Rome Before Avignon* (New York: Basic Books, 1974); Richard C. Trexler, *Public Life in Renaissance Florence* (New York: Academic Press, 1980); and Lauro Martines, *Power and Imagination: City-States in Renaissance Italy* (New York: Alfred A. Knopf, 1979) on the theme of violence. Alan Dundas and Alesandro Fallassi, *La Terra in Piazza* (Berkeley: University of California Press, 1975), reviewed in Allen Guttmann, 'Recent Work in European Sport History', *Journal of Sport History* 10, 1 (Spring 1983), 40–41; Gigliola Gori, 'In Search of the Origins of Basketball', in G. Pfister, G. Niewerth and T. Steins, eds, *Spiele der Welt im Spannungsfeld von Tradition und Moderne* (St Augustin: Academia Verlag, 1996), 76–83; Robert C. Davis, *War of the Fists: Popular Culture and Public Violence in Late Renaissance Venice* (New York: Oxford University Press, 1998) for a more recent and nuanced study of the phenomenon. Werner Korbs, *Vom Sinn Der Leibesubungen zur Zeit der italieneschen Renaissance* (Berlin: Wiedmann, 1938); Kazuhiko Kusudo, 'Open Shooting Festivals (Freischiessen) in German Cities, 1,455–501', *International Journal of the History of Sport* 16, 1 (March 1999), 65–86. Joachim K. Ruhl, 'German Tournament Regulations of the 15th Century', *Journal of Sport History* 17, 2 (Summer 1990), 163–82.

3 Allan G. Bogue, *Frederick Jackson Turner, Strange Roads Going Down* (Norman: University of Oklahoma Press, 1998) on the life and influence of Turner.

4 Steven A. Riess, ed., *Major Problems in American Sport History* (Boston: Houghton Mifflin, 1997), 2; S.W. Pope, ed., *The New American Sport History: Recent Approaches and Perspectives* (Urbana: University of Illinois Press, 1997), 2; Nancy Struna, 'Sport History', in John D. Massengale and Richard A. Swanson, eds, *The History of Exercise and Sport Science* (Champaign: Human Kinetics, 1997), 153–54. Dale Somers, *The Rise of Sports in New Orleans* (Baton Rouge: Louisiana State University Press, 1972); Robert W. Malcolmson, *Popular Recreations of English Society, 1700–1850* (Cambridge: Cambridge University Press, 1973). See Catriona Parratt, 'Robert W. Malcolmson's Popular Recreations in English Society, 1700–1850: An Appreciation', *Journal of Sport History* 29, 2 (Summer 2002), 313–23, as a harbinger of the new social history.

5 Allen Guttmann, *From Ritual to Record: The Nature of Modern Sports* (New York: Columbia University Press, 1978); Melvin L. Adelman, *A Sporting Time: New York City and the Rise of Modern Athletics, 1820–1870* (Urbana: University of Illinois Press, 1986). See Jeffrey Hill's review of *From*

Ritual to Record, in the *Journal of Sport History* 32, 1 (Spring 2005), 91–94, on Guttman's lasting influence. For further discussions of modernization theory see Joyce Appleby, 'Modernization Theory and the Formation of Modern Social Theories in England and America', *Comparative Studies in Society and History* 20, 2 (1978), 259–85; Peter Stearns, 'Modernization and Social History: Some Suggestions and a Muted Cheer', *Journal of Social History* 14 (1980), 189–209; and Richard S. Gruneau, 'Modernization or Hegemony: Two Views on Sport and Social Development', in Jean Harvey and Hart Cantelon, eds, *Not Just a Game* (Ottawa: University of Ottawa Press, 1988), 9–32.

6 Robert Wiebe, *The Search for Order, 1877–1920* (New York: Hill and Wang, 1967); Benjamin Rader, 'The Quest for Subcommunities and the Rise of American Sport', *American Quarterly* 29: 355–69, and *American Sports: From the Age of Folk Games to the Age of Television* (Englewood Cliffs, NJ: Prentice Hall, 1983).

7 Dominick Cavallo, *Muscles and Morals: Organized Playgrounds and Urban Reform, 1880–1920* (Philadelphia: University of Pennsylvania Press, 1981); Paul Boyer, *Urban Masses and Moral Order in America, 1820–1920* (Cambridge, MA: Harvard University Press, 1978); Gary Ross Mormino, 'The Playing Fields of St. Louis: Italian Immigrants and Sport, 1925–1941', *Journal of Sport History* 9 (Summer 1982), 5–16; Cary Goodman, *Choosing Sides: Playground and Street Life on the Lower East Side* (New York: Schocken Books, 1979).

8 E.P Thompson, *The Making of the English Working Class* (New York: Vantage Books, 1966 [1963]); C.L.R. James, *Beyond a Boundary* (London: Stanley Paul, 1963); Nancy Struna, 'E. P. Thompson's Notion of "Context" and the Writing of Physical Education and Sport History', *Quest* 38 (1986), 22–32, (quote 27).

9 Stephan Thernstrom, *The Other Bostonians: Poverty and Progress in the American Metropolis, 1880–1970* (Cambridge, MA: Harvard University Press, 1964); Sam Bass Warner, *The Private City: Philadelphia in Three Periods of Its Growth* (Philadelphia: University of Pennsylvania Press, 1968); Steven A. Riess, *City Games: The Evolution of American Urban Society and the Rise of Sports* (Urbana: University of Illinois Press, 1989).

10 Among the numerous works of the labour historians, see Herbert Gutman, *Work, Culture, and Society in Industrializing America* (New York: 1976); David Montgomery, *Beyond Equality: Labor and the radical republicans, 1862–1872* (Urbana: University of Illinois Press, 1967); Alan Dawley, *Class and Community: The Industrial Revolution in Lynn* (Cambridge, MA; Harvard University Press, 1976); Eric Foner, *Free Soil, Free Labor, Free Men: The Ideology of the Republican Party Before the Civil War* (London: Oxford University Press, 1970); Eric Hobsbawm and Terence Ranger, eds, *The Invention of Tradition* (Cambridge: Cambridge University Press, 1983). For significant works on Canada, see Alan Metcalfe, *Canada Learns to Play: The Emergence of Organized Sport, 1807–1914* (Toronto: McClelland and Stewart, 1987); and Bruce Kidd, *The Struggle for Canadian Sport* (Toronto: University of Toronto Press, 1996). There is a relative dearth on Francophone Canada; but Gilles Janson, *Emparons-nous du Sport: Les Canadiens francais et le sport au XIX siècle* (Montreal: Guerin, 1995), covers Montreal; while Donald Guay, *La Conquete du Sport: Le sport et la societe quebecoise au XIXe siècle* (Outremont: Lanctot, 1997), provides an account of developments in Quebec.

11 Riess, *Major Problems in American Sport History*, 8, indicates that French and German intellectuals developed the Neo-Marxist framework by the 1920s; but its application to sport appeared somewhat later (quote, 9).

12 Quintin Hoare and Geoffrey N. Smith, eds, *Selections from the Prison Notebooks of Antonio Gramsci* (New York: International Publishers, 1971); Raymond Williams, *The Sociology of Culture* (New York: Schocken Books, 1981). See T.J. Jackson Lears, 'The Concept of Cultural Hegemony: Problems and Possibilities', *American Historical Review* 90 (June 1985), 567–83 for a more detailed discussion.

13 Clifford Geertz, 'Deep Play: Notes on the Balinese Cockfight', *Daedalus* (Winter 1972), 1–38; John MacAloon, *This Great Symbol: Pierre De Coubertin and the Origins of the Modern Olympic Games* (Chicago, IL: University of Chicago Press, 1981); Henning Eichberg, *die Veranderung des Sports ist gesellschaftlich* (Munster: lit, 1986); George Gmelch and J.J. Weiner, *In the Ballpark: the Working Lives of Baseball People* (Washington, DC: Smithsonian Institute, 1999). Other anthropological works are contained in Robert Sands, ed., *Anthropology, Sport, and Culture* (Westport, CT: Bergin & Garvey, 1999).

14 Don Morrow, 'Canadian Sport History: A Critical Essay', *Journal of Sport History* 10, 1 (Spring 1983), 67–79; Alan Metcalfe, 'The Evolution of Organized Physical Recreation in Montreal, 1840–1895', *Histoire Social – Social History* 11, 2 (May 1978), 144–66, and 'Organized Sport and Social Stratification in Montreal', in R.S. Gruneau and J.G. Albinson, eds, *Canadian Sport:*

Sociological Perspectives (Don Mills: Addison-Wesley, 1976), 77–101. Since that time Canadian sports historians have produced some substantial urban histories; see Colin Howell, *Northern Sandlots: A Social History of Maritime Baseball* (Toronto: Univesity of Toronto Press, 1995); Nancy B. Bouchier, *For the Love of the Game and the Honour of the Town: Amateur Sport and Middle Class Culture in Nineteenth Century Ontario Towns, 1838–1895* (Montreal: McGill-Queen's University Press, 2003); Nancy B. Bouchier and Ken Cruikshank, 'The War on the Squatters, 1920–1940: Hamilton's Boathouse Community and the Re-Creation of Recreation on Burlington Bay', *Labour/Le Travail* 51 (Spring, 2003), 9–46. William T. Boyd, *Hockey Towns: Stories of Small Town Hockey in Canada* (Toronto: Doubleday, 1998) details smaller urban communities; and Lynne Marks exemplifies the new social history in the interdisciplinary *Revivals and Roller Rinks: Religion, Leisure, and Identity in Late-Nineteenth-Century Small-Town Ontario* (Toronto: University of Toronto Press, 1996).

See Guttmann, 'Recent Work in European Sport History', 35–52, on European works; as well as more recent efforts by Arnd Kruger and James Riordan, eds, *The Story of Worker Sport* (Champaign, IL: Human Kinetics, 1996), which covers North America, Europe and Israel; and Peter A. Frykholm, 'Soccer and Social Identity in Pre-Revolutionary Moscow', *Journal of Sport History* 24, 2 (Summer 1997), 143–54.

See Arnd Kruger, 'Puzzle Solving: German Sport Historiography of the Eighties', *Journal of Sport History* 17, 2 (Summer 1990), 261–77, which lists Siegfried Gehrmann, *Fussball-Vereine-Politik: Zur Sportgeschicte des Reviers, 1900–1940* (Essen: Hobbing, 1988); Hans Dieter Baroth, *'Jungens, Euch gehort der Himmel!' Die Geschicte der Oberliga West, 1947–1963* (Essen: Klartext, 1988); and Karl Mintenbeck, *Es began 1848, Der Ruhrgebietssport im Spiegel der Presse* (Essen: P. Pom, 1988) among the histories of soccer clubs.

15 See Stephen Hardy and Alan Ingham, 'Games, Structures, and Agency: Historians on the American Play Movement', *Journal of Social History* 17 (1983), 285–302, and 'Sport, Structuration, Subjugation, and Hegemony', *Theory, Culture, and Society* 2 (1984), 85–103; Stephen Hardy, *How Boston Played: Sport, Recreation, and Community, 1865–1915* (Boston: Northeastern University Press, 1982); Roy Rosenzweig, *Eight Hours for What We Will: Workers and Leisure in an Industrial City, 1870–1920* (New York: Cambridge University Press, 1983); John F. Kasson, *Amusing the Million: Coney Island at the Turn of the Century* (New York: Hill and Wang, 1978); David Nasaw, *Going Out: The Rise and Fall of Public Amusements* (New York: Basic Books, 1993); Perry R. Duis, *The Saloon: Public Drinking in Chicago and Boston, 1880–1920* (Urbana: University of Illinois Press, 1983); Madelon Powers, *Faces Along the Bar: Lore and Order in the Workingman's Saloon, 1870–1920* (Chicago, IL: University of Chicago Press, 1998); Kathy Piess, *Cheap Amusements: Working Women and Leisure in Turn-of-the-Century New York* (Philadelphia: Temple University Press, 1986).

16 Nancy L. Struna, 'In Glorious Disarray: The Literature of American Sport History', *Research Quarterly for Exercise and Sport* 56, 2 (June 1985), 151–60. Among the studies cited were Jack W. Berryman, 'Sport, Health, and the Rural–Urban Conflict: Baltimore and John Stuart Skinner's American Farmer, 1819–1829', *Conspectus of History* 1, 8 (1982), 43–61; Stephen Freedman, 'The Baseball Fad in Chicago, 1865–1870: An Exploration of the Role of Sport in the Nineteenth-Century City', *Journal of Sport History* 5 (Summer 1978), 42–64; William Gudelunas and Stephen Couch, 'The Stolen Championship of the Pottsville Maroons: A Case Study in the Emergence of Modern Professional Football', *Journal of Sport History* 9 (Spring 1982), 53–64; and Joe D. Willis and Richard G. Wettan, 'Social Stratification in New York City Athletic Clubs, 1865–1915', *Journal of Sport History* 3 (Spring 1975), 45–76.

Other reviews have included more topical assessments, such as Roberta J. Park, 'Research and Scholarship in the History of Physical Education and Sport: The Current State of Affairs', *Research Quarterly for Exercise and Sport* 54, 2 (1983), 93–103; Melvin L. Adelman, 'Academicians and American Athletics: A decade of Progress', *Journal of Sport History* 10, 1 (Spring 1983), 80–106; Patricia A. Vertinsky, 'Gender Relations, Women's History and Sport History: A decade of Changing Enquiry, 1983–1993', *Journal of Sport History* 21, 1 (Spring 1994), 1–24; Stephen Hardy, 'Sport in Urbanizing America: A Historical Review', *Journal of Urban History* 23, 6 (September 1997), 675–708; and Nancy L. Struna, 'Social History and Sport', in Jay Coakley and Eric Dunning, eds, *Handbook of Sports Studies* (London: Sage, 2000), 187–203.

17 Michel Foucault, *Discipline and Punish: The Birth of the Prison* (New York: Random House, 1995); Patricia Vertinsky, *The Eternally Wounded Woman: Women, Doctors, and Exercise in the Nineteenth Century* (Manchester: Manchester University Press, 1990); Pierre Bourdieu, *Outline of a Theory of Practice* (Cambridge: Cambridge University Press, 1977), and *Distinction: A Social Critique of the*

Judgment of Taste (Cambridge, MA: Harvard University Press, 1984); Patricia Vertinsky and Sherry McKay, eds, *Disciplining the Body in the Gymnasium: Memory, Monument and Modernism* (London: Routledge, 2004); Catriona Parratt, 'Of Place and Men and Women: Gender and Toxophilia in the "Haxey Hood"', *Journal of Sport History* 27, 2 (Summer 2000), 229–45; Michael Oriard, *Reading Football: How the Popular Press Created an American Spectacle* (Chapel Hill: University of North Carolina Press, 1993).

On the debate over postmodernism, see Catriona Parratt, 'About Turns: Reflecting on Sport History in the 1990s', *Sport History Review* 29 (1990), 4–17; S.W. Pope, 'Sport History: Into the 21st Century', *Journal of Sport History* 25, 2 (Summer 1998), i–x; Murray G. Phillips, 'Deconstructing Sport History: The Postmodern Challenge', *Journal of Sport History* 28 (2001), 327–43; Douglas Booth, *The Field: Truth and Fiction in Sport History* (London: Routledge, 2005); Murray Phillips, ed., *Deconstructing Sport History: A Postmodern Analysis* (Albany: State University of New York Press, 2006); Allen Guttman, 'Straw Men in Imaginary Boxes', *Journal of Sport History* 32, 3 (Fall 2005), 395–400.

On Australian urban studies of the lifesaving culture, see Sean Brawley, *Vigilant and Victorious: A Community History of the Collaroy Surf Lifesaving Club 1911–1995* (Collaroy Beach, Sidney: Collaroy Surf Life Saving Club, 1995), and *Beach Beyond: History of the Palm Beach Surf Club 1921–1996* (Sydney: University of New South Wales Press, 1996); Ed Jaggard, 'Writing Australian Surf Lifesaving's History', *Journal of Sport History* 29, 1 (Spring 2002), 15–23; Doug Booth, *Australian Beach Cultures: The History of Sun, Sand, and Surf* (London: Frank Cass, 2001); Phillips, *Deconstructing Sport History*, 245–53. The *Journal of Sport History* 29, 1 (Spring 2002), 1–46 carries the debate between empirical evidence versus postmodernism.

See Peter A. Horton, 'Football, Identity, Place: The Emergence of Rugby football in Brisbane', *The International Journal of the History of Sport* 23, 8 (December, 2006), 1,341–68, on rugby culture in Australia.

18 On British sports history, see William Baker, 'The State of British Sport History', *Journal of Sport History* 10, 1 (Spring 1983), 53–66; and Jeffrey Hill, 'British Sport History: A Postmodern Future?', *Journal of Sport History* 23, 1 (Spring 1996), 1–19. On working class case studies, see Richard Holt, ed., *Sport and the Working Class in Modern Britain* (Manchester: Manchester University Press, 1990). Kathleen E. McCrone, *Sport and the Physical Emancipation of Women, 1870–1914* (London: Routledge, 1988); Jennifer Hargreaves, *Sporting Females: Critical Issues in the History and Sociology of Women's Sports* (London: Routledge, 1994). J.A. Mangan, *Athleticism in the Victorian and Edwardian Public School* (Cambridge: Cambridge University Press, 1981), and *The Games Ethic and Imperialism: Aspects of the Diffusion of an Ideal* (London: Allen Lane, 1986).

19 Martin Johnes, 'Putting History into Sport: On Sport History and Sport Studies in the U.K.', *Journal of Sport History* 31, 2 (Summer 2004), 145–60; the same issue includes Neal Garnham, 'Sport History: The Cases of Britain and Ireland Stated', 139–44; and Grant Jarvie, 'Lonach, Highland Games, and Scottish Sports History', 161–75. See Grant Jarvie, 'Sport, Parish, and the Émigré', *Journal of Sport History* 25, 3 (Fall 1998), 381–97, for an overview of sport in numerous Scottish communities.

20 John Bale has been particularly prominent in the pursuit of geographical scholarship. His *Sports Geography* (London: Routledge, 2003) covers developments in Europe, North America, Australia and New Zealand. For other geographical works, see John Bale, *The Landscape of Modern Sport* (Leicester: University of Leicester Press, 1994); and Karl Raitz, ed., *The Theater of Sport* (Baltimore, MD: Johns Hopkins University Press, 1995).

Wirth is cited in Hardy, *How Boston Played*, 17–18. Immigration studies in Chicago started as early as 1895 with Richard T. Ely, ed., *Hull House Maps and Papers* (New York: Crowell, 1895); and continued with Louis Wirth, *The Ghetto* (Chicago, IL: University of Chicago Press, 1928); Harvey W. Zorbaugh, *The Gold Coast and the Slum* (Chicago, IL: University of Chicago Press, 1929); Robert E. Park, Ernest Burgess and Roderick McKenzie, *The City* (Chicago, IL: University of Chicago Press, 1925); Ernest Burgess, ed., *The Urban Community* (Chicago, IL: University of Chicago Press, 1926); Frederic Thrasher, *The Gang* (Chicago, IL: University of Chicago Press, 1927); Paul G. Cressey, *The Taxi Dance Hall: A Sociological Study in Commercialized Recreation and City Life* (Chicago, IL: University of Chicago Press, 1932); Allen H. Spear, *Black Chicago: The Making of a Negro Ghetto, 1890–1920* (Chicago, IL: University of Chicago Press, 1967); and Gerald D. Suttles, *The Social Order of the Slum: Ethnicity and Territory in the Inner City* (Chicago, IL: University of Chicago Press, 1968).

21 Oscar Handlin and John Burchard, eds, *The Historian and the City* (Cambridge, MA: MIT Press, 1963).
22 Richard T. LeGates and Frederic Stout, *The City Reader* (New York: Routledge, 2000).
23 Christopher Hibbert, *Cities and Civilizations* (New York: Welcome Rain, 1996); Saskia Sassen, *Cities in a World Economy* (Thousand Oaks, CA: Pine Forge Press, 2000); Janet L. Abu-Lughod, *New York, Chicago, Los Angeles: America's Global Cities* (Minneapolis: University of Minnesota Press, 1999), LeGates and Stout, eds, *The City Reader*, 531–89. On sport and globalization, see Joseph Maguire, *Global Sport: Identities, Societies, Civilizations* (Cambridge: Polity Press, 1999); J.A. Mangan, ed., *Europe, Sport, World: Shaping Global Societies* (London: Frank Cass, 2001); and Toby Miller, Geoffrey Lawrence, Jim McKay and David Rowe, *Globalization and Sport: Playing the World* (London: Sage, 2001).
24 Kenneth Kusmer, *A Ghetto Takes Shape: Black Cleveland, 1870–1930* (Urbana: University of Illinois Press, 1976); Reuben A. Buford May, *Living through the Hoop: High School Basketball, Race, and the American Dream* (New York: New York University Press, 2008); Davarian L. Baldwin, *Chicago's New Negroes: Modernity, The Great Migration, and Black Urban Life* (Chapel Hill: University of North Carolina Press, 2007).

On entrepreneurs, see Bob Kuska, *Hot Potato: How Washington and New York Gave Birth to Black Basketball and Changed America's Game Forever* (Charlottesville: University of Virginia Press, 2004); Michael Lomax, *Black Baseball Entrepreneurs: Operating by Any Means Necessary, 1860–1901* (Syracuse, NY: Syracuse University Press, 2003); Rob Ruck, *Sandlot Seasons: Sport in Black Pittsburgh* (Urbana: University of Illinois Press, 1987); James Overmyer, *Queen of the Negro Leagues: Effa Manley and the Newark Eagles* (Lanham, MD: Scarecrow Press, 1993).

On black improvisational style, see Nelson George, *Elevating the Game* (New York: Harper Collins, 1992), Gerald R. Gems, 'Blocked Shot: The Development of Basketball in the African-American Community of Chicago', *Journal of Sport History* 22, 2 (Summer 1995), 135–48; and Steven Pope, 'Decentering "Race" and (Re)presenting "Black" Performance in Sport History: Basketball and Jazz in American Culture, 1920-1950', in Murray Phillips, ed., *Deconstructing Sport History*, 147–77. For other black cultures, see John Bale and Mike Cronin, eds, *Sport and Post-coloniality* (Oxford: Berg, 2003); and Timothy Chandler and John Nauright, eds, *Making the Rugby World* (London: Frank Cass, 1999).

On Hispanics, see Samuel O. Regalado, *Viva Baseball: Latin Major Leaguers and their Special Hunger* (Urbana: University of Illinois Press, 1998); and Adrian Burgos, *Playing America's Game: Baseball, Latinos, and the Color Line* (Berkeley: University of California Press, 2007).

Gerald R. Gems, *Windy City Wars: Labor, Leisure, and Sport in the Making of Chicago* (Metuchen, NJ: Scarecrow Press, 1997), and 'The Chicago Turners: Sport and the Demise of a Radical Past', in *Adolf Cluss und die Turnbewegung* (Heilbronn, Germany: Heilbronn Stadt Archiv, 2007), 85–95, and 'Sport and the Forging of a Jewish-American Culture: The Chicago Hebrew Institute', *Journal of American Jewish History* 83 (March 1995), 15–26, and 'Sport, Religion, and Americanization: Bishop Sheil and the Catholic Youth Organization', *International Journal of the History of Sport* (August 1993), 233–41, and 'The Prep Bowl: Sport, Religion, and Americanization in Chicago', *Journal of Sport History* (Fall 1996), 284–302, and 'The Politics of Boxing: Resistance, Religion, and Working Class Assimilation', *International Sports Journal* 8, 1 (Winter 2004), 89–103.

Gertrud Pfister and Gerd Steins, eds, *Vom Rittertunier zum Stadtmarathon: Sport in Berlin* (Berlin: Forum für Sportgeschichte, 1987); Gertrud Pfister, 'Doing Sport in a Headscarf? German Sport and Turkish Females', *Journal of Sport History*, Special Issue: Ethnicity, Gender, and Sport in Diverse Historical Contexts, 27, 3 (Fall 2000), 497–525, and 'Health, Fitness, Leisure and Sport among Girls of Ethnic Minorities', in Aland Islands Peace Institute, ed., *Girl Power* (Mariehamn: Aland Islands Peace Institute, 1999), 35–65; Hans Bonde, Gertrud Pfister, Laila Ottesen, Birger Peitersen and Stehen Ankerdal, 'Integration, sundhed og idræt – med fokus på piger og kvinder', in *Humanistisk og samfundsvidenskabelig idrætstheori* (Copenhagen: Frydenlund, 2007)

On other German urban studies see, Marie-Luise Klein and Wiebke Lamprecht, *Paderborner Sportgeschichte* (Paderborn: Schöningh, 2000); Hans Langenfeld, *Münster – die Stadt und ihr Sport* (Münster: Aschendorff, 2002); and Arnd Kruger and Hans Langenfeld, *Sport in Hannover: von der Stadtgrundung bis Heute* (Gottingen: Verlag die Werkstatt, 1991).

On the multitude of sports biographies, see David Maraniss, *When Pride Still Mattered: A Life of Vince Lombardi* (New York: Touchstone, 2000), which considers the city culture and its relationship to team and fans. On the use of sports fiction, see Martin Johnes, 'Texts, Audiences, and

Postmodernism: The Novel as Source in Sport History', *Journal of Sport History* 34, 1 (Spring 2007), 121–33.

On fan culture, see an ethnographic study by Holly Swyers, 'Who Owns Wrigley Field? Sport in American Society – Past and Present', *International Journal of the History of Sport* 22, 6 (2005); Jaye Kemp Bilyeu and Daniel L. Wann, 'An Investigation of Racial Differences in Sport Fan Motivation', *International Sports Journal* (Summer 2002), 93–106; and Merrill J. Melnick and Daniel L. Wann, 'Sport Fandom Influences, Interests, and Behaviors among Norwegian University Students', *International Sports Journal* 8, 1 (Winter 2004), 1–13. Other ethnographic studies include Loic Wacquant, *Body and Soul: Ethnographic Notebooks of an Apprentice Boxer* (Oxford: Oxford University Press, 2000); Benita Heiskanen, 'The Latinization of Boxing: A Texas Case Study', *Journal of Sport History* 32 (2005), 45–66; and Gerald R. Gems, 'The Neighborhood Athletic Club: An Ethnographic Study of the Working Class Athletic Fraternity', *Colby Quarterly* (March 1996), 36–44. Daniel L.Wann, Merrill J. Melnick, Gordon W. Russell and Dale G. Pease, *Sport Fans: The Psychology and Social Impact of Spectators* (New York: Routledge, 2001) offers some historical background.

25 Hibbert, *Cities and Civilizations*, 201, 203–4, 214 on developments in Tokyo and Berlin; LeGates and Stout, eds, *The City Reader*, 314–20, on Olmsted, as well as several biographies; Galen Cranz, *The Politics of Park Design: A History of Urban Parks in America* (Cambridge, MA: MIT Press, 1982); A.J. Arnold, '"Not playing the game"?: Leeds city in the great war', *International Journal of the History of Sport* 7, 1 (1990), 111–19; Richard Holt, 'Working class football and the city: the problem of continuity', *International Journal of the History of Sport* 3, 1 (1986), 5–17; Robert M. Lewis, 'Cricket and the beginnings of organized baseball in New York city', *International Journal of the History of Sport* 4, 3 (1987), 315–32.

Henning Eichberg, 'Race-Track and Labyrinth: The Space of Physical Culture in Berlin', *Journal of Sport History* 17, 2 (Summer 1990), 245–60. More recent scholarship includes John Bale, *Sport, Space, and the City* (London: Routledge, 1993); D. Rowe, and P. McGuirk, 'Drunk for Three Weeks: Sporting Success and City Image', *International Review for the Sociology of Sport* 34, 2 (1999), 125–41; Hanwen Liao and Adrian Pitts, 'A brief historical review of Olympic urbanization', *International Journal of the History of Sport* 23, 7 (2006), 1,232–52; A. Smith, 'Cars, Cricket, and Alf Smith: The Place of Works-based Sports and Social Clubs in the Life of Mid-Twentieth-Century Coventry', *International Journal of the History of Sport* 19, 1 (2002), 137–50; Adrian Smith, 'Oval Ball and a Broken City: Coventry, its People and its Rugby Team, 1995–98', *International Journal of the History of Sport* 16, 3 (1999), 147–57; Iain Borden, *Skateboarding, Space and the City: Architecture and the Body* (Oxford: Berg, 2001).

Among the growing literature on stadia, see Robin Bachin, *Building the South Side: Urban Space and Civic Culture in Chicago, 1890–1919* (Chicago, IL: University of Chicago Press, 2004); Costas Spirou and Larry Bennett, *It's Hardly Sportin': Stadiums, Neighborhoods, and the New Chicago* (DeKalb: Northern Illinois University Press, 2003); Kevin J. Delaney and Rick Eckstein, *Public Dollars, Private Stadiums: The Battle Over Building Sports Stadiums* (New Brunswick, NJ: Rutgers University Press, 2003); and Daniel Rosensweig, *Retro Ball Parks: Instant History, Baseball, and the New American City* (Knoxville: University of Tennessee Press, 2005).

On the numerous sport museums and halls of fame, see Wray Vamplew, 'Facts and Artefacts: Sports Historians and Sports Museums', *Journal of Sport History* 25, 2 (Summer 1998), 268–82; Ellen J. Staurowsky, 'The National Collegiate Athletic Association Hall of Champions', *Journal of Sport History* 29, 2 (Summer 2002), 364–68; John J. Cahill, 'The Babe Ruth Museum and Birthplace', *Journal of Sport History* 24, 2 (Summer 1997), 203–5. The *Journal of Sport History* 25, 1 (Spring 1998) carries the following reviews of some other sports museums: Rick Knott and C. Keith Harrison, 'The College Football Hall of Fame', 152–56; Daniel A. Nathan, 'The International Boxing Hall of Fame Museum', 157–59; Scott A.G.M. Crawford, 'The Wimbledon Lawn Tennis Museum', 160–62; Scott A.G.M. Crawford, 'The Indianapolis Motor Speedway Hall of Fame', 163–67. See Charles Fruehling Springwood, *Cooperstown to Dyersville: A Geography of Baseball Nostalgia* (Boulder, CO: Westview Press, 1996) for an ethnographic account of an athletic pilgrimage.

26 Kimberley S. Schimmel, Alan G. Ingham and Jeremy W. Howell, *Professional Team Sport and the American City: Urban Politics and Franchise Relocation* (Champaign, IL: Human Kinetics, 1993). See Terry Reed, *Indy: The Race and Ritual of the Indianapolis 500* (Washington, DC: Potomac Books, 2005) for an historical account of the oldest and most prestigious race in American auto racing.

27 Roger G. Noll and Andrew Zimbalist, *Sports, Jobs & Taxes: The Economic Impact of Sports Teams and Stadiums* (Washington, DC: Brookings Institute Press, 1997); Bob Trumpbour, review of Delaney

and Eckstein, *Public Dollars: Private Stadiums, Journal of Sport History* 34, 2 (Summer 2007), and review of Rosensweig, *Retro Ball Parks, Journal of Sport History* 34, 2 (Summer 2007).

28 Michael Kammen, *Mystic Chords of Memory: The Transformation of Tradition in American Culture* (New York: Alfred A. Knopf, 1991); Paul Connerton, *How Societies Remember* (Cambridge: Cambridge University Press, 1989); see my 'Stadiums, Nostalgia, and Urban Identity', *Chicago History* (Summer 2008) for a recent analysis. See Horst Ueberhorst, 'The Importance of the Historians' Quarrel and the Problem of Continuity for the German History of Sport', *Journal of Sport History* 17, 2 (Summer 1990), 232–44 on the German debate over nationalism, museum exhibitions and the role of sport.

   Murray Phillips, '"Not Just a Book on a Wall": Representing the History of Surf Lifesaving through the Australian National Museum', presentation delivered at the North American Society for Sport History Convention, Lake Placid, NY, 26 May 2008; and Jennifer Sterling, 'Halls of Fame: Exhibiting Champions at the Smithsonian National Portrait Gallery', presentation delivered at the North American Society for Sport History Convention at Lake Placid, NY, 24 May 2008.

29 Nancy B. Bouchier and Ken Cruikshank, 'Reflections on Creating Critical Sport History for a Popular Audience: The People and the Bay', *Journal of Sport History* 25, 2 (Summer 1998), 309–16.

30 A small sample of articles, by no means complete, provides an example of the broad scope of coverage in *IJHS*: Tony Joyce, 'Canadian Sport and State Control: Toronto, 1845–86', *International Journal of the History of Sport* 16, 1 (March 1999), 22–37, on the social control of the working class; William J. Baker, 'Muscular Marxism and the Chicago Counter-Olympics of 1932', *International Journal of the History of Sport* 9, 3 (December 1992), 397–410, on urban workers' radical sport culture; Hilary A. Braysmith, 'Constructing Athletic Agents in the Chicano/a Culture in Los Angeles', *International Journal of the History of Sport* 22 (March 2005), 177–95, on urban art, wall murals and the agency of female athletes; Roman Horak and Wolfgang Maderthaner, 'A Culture of Urban Cosmopolitanism: Uridil and Sindelar as Viennese Coffee-House Heroes', *International Journal of the History of Sport* 13:1 (March 1996), 139–55, a study of 1920s soccer heroes; Greg Downey, 'Domesticating an Urban Menace: Reforming Capoeira as a Brazilian National Sport', *International Journal of the History of Sport* 19 (2002), 1–32, on the mainstreaming of an outlaw sport; Alan Gregor Cobley, 'A Political History of Playing Fields: The Provision of Sporting Facilities for Africans in the Johannesburg Area to 1948', *International Journal of the History of Sport* 11, 2 (August 1994), 212–30; Tony Mason, 'Football on the Maidan: Cultural Imperialism in Calcutta', *International Journal of the History of Sport* 7, 1 (May 1990), 85–96; N.G. Aplin and Quek Jin Jong, 'Celestials in Touch: Sport and the Chinese in Colonial Singapore', *International Journal of the History of Sport* 19 (June–September 2002), 67–98; Janice N. Brownfoot, '"Healthy Bodies, Healthy Minds": Sport and Society in Colonial Malaya', *International Journal of the History of Sport* 19 (June–September 2002), 129–56; Boria Majumdar, 'Cricket in Colonial India: The Bombay Pentangular, 1892–1946', *International Journal of the History of Sport* 19 (June–September 2002), 157–88; Peter A. Horton, 'Shackling the Lion: Sport in Independent Singapore', *International Journal of the History of Sport* 19 (June–September 2002), 243–74; Iain Adams, 'Pancasila: Sport and the Building of Indonesia – Ambitions and Obstacles', *International Journal of the History of Sport* 19 (June–September 2002), 295–318; Trevor Slack, Hsu Yuan-min, Tsai Chiung-tzu and Fan Hong, 'The Road to Modernization: Sport in Taiwan', *International Journal of the History of Sport* 19 (June–September 2002), 343–65; Shamya Dasgupta, 'An Inheritance from the British: The Indian Boxing Story', *International Journal of the History of Sport* 21 (2004), 433–51, with a focus on Calcutta, and Muslim and women boxers.

   On other international studies, see Rob Ruck, 'Three Kings Day in Consuelo: Cricket, Baseball, and the Cocolos in San Pedro de Macoris', *Studies in Latin American Culture* 13 (1994), 129–42, on sport and festival; Matthew B. Karush, 'National Identity in the Sports Pages: Football and the Mass Media in 1920s Buenos Aires', *The Americas* 60 (July 2002), 11–32; and Mike McNeill, John Sproule and Peter Horton, 'The Changing Face of Sport and Physical Education in Post-Colonial Singapore', *Sport, Education, and Society* 8 (2003), 33–56.

31 Struna, 'Sport History', 169; Johnes, 'Putting History into Sport'.

32 Phillips, *Deconstructing Sport History*, and 'Introduction: Sport History and Postmodernism', in Phillips, *Deconstructing Sport History*, 1–24, for the current state and history of such debates.

33 Traditional histories continue to add the knowledge base of urban areas, as in Edward Hotaling, *They're Off!: Horse Racing at Saratoga* (Syracuse, NY: Syracuse University Press, 1995); and George

B. Kirsch, 'Municipal Golf Courses in the United States: 1895–1930', *Journal of Sport History* 32, 1 (Spring 2005), 23–44.

Holly Thorpe, 'Embodied Boarders: Snowboarding, Status and Style', *Waikato Journal of Education*, 10 (2004), 181–202, and 'Beyond "Decorative Sociology": Contextualizing Female Surf, Skate, and Snow Boarding, *Sociology of Sport Journal* 22, 3 (September 2006), 205–28; and Belinda Wheaton, ed., *Understanding Lifestyle Sports: Consumption, Identity and Difference* (London: Routledge, 2004) provide sociological and historical initiatives in the area of lifestyle sports.

34 Charles Little, 'Towards a History of Sport in South East Asia', a presentation delivered at the North American Society for the History of Sport Convention in Lake Placid, NY, 24 May 2008, indicated that the *Journal of Sport History* had never published an article on the region; while the *International Journal of the History of Sport* had published 12 on Southeast Asia. Huan Xiong, 'The Evolution of Urban Society and Social Changes in Sports Participation at the Grassroots in China', *International Review for the Sociology of Sport* 42, 4 (December 2007), 441–71, presents an interdisciplinary study that encompasses history, sociology, economics and politics.

35 M.C. McNeill, J. Sproule and P.A. Horton, 'The Changing Face of Sport and Physical Education in Post-Colonial Singapore', *Journal of Sport, Education & Society* 8, 1 (2003), 35–56; P.A. Horton, 'Shackling the Lion, Sport in Independent Singapore', *The International Journal of the History of Sport* (Frank Cass: London, September/October 2002), and 'Complex Creolization: The Evolution of Modern Sport in Singapore', *European Sport History Review* 3, (London: Frank Cass, 2001); Gerald R. Gems, *The Athletic Crusade: Sport and American Cultural Imperialism* (Lincoln: University of Nebraska Press, 2006), 1–66.

36 Grant Jarvie, 'Sport, Social Change and the Public Intellectual', *International Review for the Sociology of Sport* 42, 4 (December 2004), 411–24. See Daniel Nathan, *Saying It's So: A Cultural History of the Black Sox Scandal* (Urbana: University of Illinois Press, 2003) on new approaches to the incorporation of nostalgia in sports history. Hardy, *How Boston Played*, xx–xxii, xviii; Hardy and Ingham, 'Games, Structures, and Agency'; Stephen H. Hardy, 'Entrepreneurs, Organizations, and the Sports Marketplace', in Pope, ed., *The New American Sport History*, 341–65; Steven Riess, *Touching Base: Professional Baseball and American Culture in the Progressive Era* (Westport, CT: Greenwood, 1980).

37 Hibbert, *Cities and Civilizations*; Gunther Barth, *City People: The Rise of Modern City Culture in Nineteenth-Century America* (New York: Oxford University Press, 1980); Struna, 'Social History and Sport', 197; see the *Journal of Sport History* 26, 1 (Spring 1999) and the special issue 'Ethnicity, Gender and Sport in Diverse Historical Contexts', *Journal of Sport History* 27, 3 (Fall 2000), as well as Susan G. Zieff, 'From Badminton to the Bolero: Sport and Recreation in San Francisco's Chinatown, 1895–1950', *Journal of Sport History* 27, 1 (Spring 2000), 1–29, as attempts to address some of the questions. Annette Hofmann, ed., *Turnen and Sport: Transatlantic Transfers* (Munster: Waxmann, n.d.) examines the transitions in the turner movement in selected American cities. Baseball differences are noted in Joseph A. Reaves, *Taking in a Game: A History of Baseball in Asia* (Lincoln: University of Nebraska Press, 2002); Roberto Gonzalez Echevarria, *The Pride of Havana: A History of Cuban Baseball* (New York: Oxford University Press, 1999); Alan M. Klein, *Sugarball: The American Game, the Dominican Dream* (New Haven, CT: Yale University Press, 1991).

38 Andrew G. Suozzo, *The Chicago Marathon* (Urbana: University of Illinois Press, 2006), offers a recent study of a mega-event that attracts tens of thousands, but dismisses particular segments of the culture. See the review by Laura Frances Chase, *Journal of Sport History* 34, 1 (Spring 2007), 162–63.

39 Abu-Lughod, *New York, Chicago, Los Angeles*, 399–426; Maguire, *Global Sport*; Walter LaFeber, *Michael Jordan and the New Global Capitalism* (New York: Norton, 1999); J.A. Mangan, ed., *Europe, Sport, World: Shaping Global Societies* (London: Frank Cass, 2001).

40 Among the many British imperial studies, see J.A. Mangan, ed., *The Cultural Bond: Sport, Empire, Society* (London: Frank Cass, 1992), and *The Imperial Curriculum: Racial Images and Education in the British Colonial Experience* (London: Routledge, 1993), and *Making Imperial Mentalities: Socialisation and British Imperialism* (Manchester: Manchester University Press, 1990); H.E. Chehabi and Allen Guttmann, 'From Iran to All of Asia: The Origin and Diffusion of Polo', *International Journal of the History of Sport* 19 (June–September 2002), 384–400. Allen Guttmann, *Games and Empires: Modern Sports and Cultural Imperialism* (New York: Columbia University Press, 1994), takes a broad approach; while Gems, *The Athletic Crusade*, focuses on US colonies.

41 The growing emphasis on the body can be seen in Susan Brownell, *Training the Body for China: Sports in the Moral Order of the People's Republic* (Chicago, IL: University of Chicago Press, 1995);

4 Borderlands

Colin Howell and Daryl Leeworthy

In his 1932 presidential address to the American Historical Association entitled 'The Epic of Greater America', Herbert Eugene Bolton called for 'a broader treatment of American history, to supplement the purely nationalist presentation to which we are accustomed … and [which] helped to raise up a nation of chauvinists'.[1] Earlier in his career Bolton had fashioned his Spanish 'borderlands model' as an alternative to Frederick Jackson Turner's argument that the frontier was the crucible of America's democratic exceptionalism.[2] Bolton challenged the nationalist presumptions of most American historians, suggesting that much of what they wrote was connected to broader processes affecting both Europe and the Americas. He called as well for a grand synthesis based upon a transnational and comparative approach to the past. 'It is my purpose, by a few bold strokes', he wrote, 'to suggest that … [the seemingly different experiences of the southwestern frontier and borderlands and America's seaboard colonies] are but phases common to most portions of the Western Hemisphere; that each local story will have a clearer meaning when studied in the light of others: and that much of what has been written of each national history is but a thread of a larger strand'.[3]

Bolton had come to this conclusion after working on the Spanish borderlands. His work influenced generations of scholars, culminating in the formation of the Association of Borderlands Scholars in 1976.[4] Canadian scholars fashioned their own alternative narratives presenting the frontier less as the dynamic force that Turner suggested, emphasizing instead the continuing influence of the Old World in the New. For Harold Innis, a political economist writing in the interwar years and whose influence in Canada rivalled that of Turner in the USA, the frontier was a passive hinterland where staples commodities could be exploited to serve metropolitan communities not only in Canada but overseas as well.[5] J.M.S. Careless reinforced this idea of the frontier as a subservient hinterland dependent upon a dynamic and culturally productive metropolitan core. The influence of the metropolis, Careless argued, could be felt in all spheres; it 'might be displayed not only in economic structures, political fabrics, or social networks, but also in attitudes of regard, modes of opinion, or popular images and traditions – all in turn, to affect identity'.[6]

Metropolitanism inadvertently remains at the very heart of modern history. Reminiscent of the modernization model, in which local and regional communities and their cultural practices (including sport) are absorbed into more highly organized national systems and civic practices, metropolitanism was an ideology connected to the imagining and legitimizing of the nation-state.[7] Many sports historians have shared this preoccupation with modernization, assuming that it was in metropolitan centres that sporting culture was forged and diffused, spawning national identities in turn.[8] Although Frederick Paxson, writing in 1917, argued that 20th-century American sport was a product of 'restless spirits' who turned to sport in order to compensate for the closing of the frontier, the implicit assumption was that modern sport as a surrogate frontier would flourish in urban America.[9] It was not a great leap, therefore, to argue, as did one American historian, that the metropolis established models for smaller centres to emulate, and that in 'cities of all sizes organized sports are structured pretty much the same way, with the same latent and manifest functions'.[10]

Contemporary historians, especially those enamoured of the postmodern impulse, are suspicious of grand narratives of national development or the larger epic that Bolton envisaged.[11] In their insistence on the multiple meanings inherent in historical evidence, moreover, postmodernists have subjected older categories of understanding to rigorous deconstruction, blurring the boundaries associated with the nation, and leading some even to lament the dissolution of history itself.[12] With globalization and the associated mobility of capital, populations and ideas, moreover, there is a concomitant interest in borderlands as sites of contested meanings and malleable identities. Rejecting uni-directional analyses of power, social conflict and identity-construction, borderlands scholars are now more sensitive to the dialectical and ambiguous relationship between metropolitan centres and hinterland regions. Borders and frontiers are presented as conduits for remarkable cultural and social exchange, just as the Atlantic Ocean has been imagined as a highway of cultural transmission rather than as a barrier to comparative understanding.[13]

That said, it is equally the case that the nation remains the focus of much that is written about in sport studies.[14] Like sport itself, sports history is routinely placed in service of the nation and the metropolis. Big-time professional sport, international competitions such as the Olympic Games, the national rivalries that they engender, and histories of sport at the national level all continue to dominate the publication lists of major publishing houses interested in the sporting past. This leads us to raise a number of questions. What if we were to detach ourselves from the nationalist agenda and approach the history of sport from what is often dismissed as the 'periphery'? What if we heeded Bolton's call for a history more attentive to local stories, to the ambiguous meanings associated with borderland regions and to transnational comparative analysis? What if we tempered our nationalist conceits with an approach that focuses more on 'limited identities'?[15] What would sports history look like if we wrote it from the vantage point of those on the social margins or those who challenged sport's hegemonic influences?

Our objective here is to investigate how reconstituted metaphors of borderlands and frontiers might allow us to uncover the possibilities of comparative sports history and confront the metropolitan fallacy. By focusing on two regions often regarded as 'peripheral' to the nation-building epic – one in the British Isles and another in north-eastern North America – we probe the connections between working-class consciousness, community identities and sporting culture in the early stages of industrial capitalist development on both sides of the Atlantic. In Britain our focus will be upon the sporting culture of the South Wales coalfields (in particular Glamorgan), while in North America we turn our attention to the colliery towns of industrial Cape Breton at the turn of the century. Both regions shared a population of Celtic origin, confronted language insecurity, experienced the wrenching impact of industrial capitalist development and hegemony, and among other things evinced a love of Rugby Football. In a sense they were frontier communities – industrial frontiers shaped by the influx of migrants who crossed both regional and national boundaries – and borderland regions that fashioned identities out of imported sporting traditions such as rugby and baseball that they put to their own purposes.

Neither region perceived their lot simply in relation to metropolitan centres, nor did they consider themselves cultural backwaters or genuflect to the modernist hope. Instead, the formation of local identities and local rivalries were key to the dynamic relations of both coalfields.[16] As we shall see, sports such as rugby and baseball developed there in ways quite different from those envisaged by proponents of the metropolitan model or by those who approach sport in hinterland regions as a product of a top-down process of cultural diffusion.

'The fight for manod': confronting the metropolitan on the industrial frontier

The intimate connections between South Wales and the South-west of England stretch back far into the annals of the British Isles. The persistent belief among some archaeologists that part of the stone used to construct Stonehenge came from South Wales is but one indication of the long cultural connections between the two regions. In addition, the early metropolitan influence exerted by Bristol should not be understated. At least one historian of modern Wales has spoken of the 'hegemony of Bristol'. 'Bristol, an intellectually lively city', argued Gwyn Alf Williams, 'was the region's capital'.[17] The largest city in the West Country and for half a millennium the third largest city in England, save for London and York, Bristol certainly dominated the entire region; providing reasonable grounds for seeing the rest of the South-west of England down to Exeter and South Wales as the hinterland of the city. Not before the remarkable transformations of the 19th century and Wales' industrial revolution was Bristol displaced by the maritime emporia of Cardiff, Swansea and Newport. However, the region was not a hinterland of the sort described by Careless, offering up few alternatives to the dominance of Bristolian, metropolitan culture. In many ways Bristol was to the sporting region of South Wales–South-west England what Boston was to the North-east-Maritimes borderland. For the latter Boston was a cultural Mecca whose metropolitan influence seemed far more benign than that of either Montreal or Toronto, and part of a larger imagined trans-border sporting community.

Yet, the legacy of industrial transformation in South Wales and Cape Breton stands not merely in coal towns but rather in the development of a separate sphere of culture, identity and society that reflected the industrial character of the communities as well as their separation from the metropolis. To understand fully the role of sport in these industrial communities we must first understand the 'industrial frontier'. As has been shown of Careless and Turner's visions of the frontier, there is a finite amount of autonomy and dynamism allotted to the communities of the frontier (or hinterland). They are, in a sense, incomplete scale-models of the metropolitan centre. Of course as soon as we begin to recognize the dynamic character of these industrial communities – their self-determination, self-awareness, indeed even class-consciousness – we are required to consider the organic nature of many of the institutions present on the industrial frontier. Thus, we need to redefine our understanding of the frontier because that dynamism is entirely lost along with the dialectical nature of identity and class formation.

The industrial frontier, then, is neither a rural haven nor a subservient realm for it creates its own institutions and cultural forms. In doing so, it becomes a source for anti-hegemonic culture, albeit within the dialectical context of industrial capitalism. The industrial frontier returns agency to the population of the coalfields of South Wales and Cape Breton but requires us to always keep an eye on the external context, for the coalfields did not develop in an airlock. As Raymond Williams wrote in his *Keywords*, hegemony:

> ... is not limited to matters of direct political control but seeks to describe a more general predominance which includes, as one of its key features, a particular way of seeing the world and human nature and relationships ... not just intellectual but political facts, expressed over a range from institutions to relationships and consciousness ... The idea of hegemony, in its wide sense, is then especially important in societies ... in which social practice is seen to depend on consent to certain dominant ideas which in fact express the needs of a dominant class.[18]

In confronting the metropolitan fallacy, historians shall find those sources (dynamic, alive, exciting) upon which people drew to combat industrial capitalism. It is a comparative mode of history that allows us to see the contested realm of relations between the working class and industrial capital. Given the prominence of sport in working-class culture, it seems apparent that sports history, alongside labour history, shall be able to trace these anti-hegemonic forces.

The pre-eminent sports of South-western England and South Wales adhere to some form of football code, either Rugby Football or Association Football (soccer).[19] The historiography, in a strange melding with cultural nationalism, has tended to throw forward the accusation that soccer was an English game and that rugby was inherently Welsh.[20] Yet, despite this 'academic' nationalism, historians of sport in the region are almost entirely in agreement that 'in their modern refined forms', both rugby and soccer, 'were imported from over the border – soccer into north and mid-Wales from Cheshire and south Lancashire, especially Merseyside, and rugby into the southern industrial belt via Bristol and the West Country',[21] particularly Somerset, a county that 'is essentially a football county, one of the best in England'.[22] The migrants from that region of the country bringing with them a love of the game helped speed up the process of the game's proletarianization. By 1889, the Bristol-based *Amateur Sport* journal was able to note that 'in South Wales the Rugby game commands the popular attention and Association has had to "take a back seat"'.[23] Absorption of an imported game into the popular consciousness, even the national consciousness, tells us much about the nature of settlement in these regions and provides us with further parallels in the North American context. Rugby, as with baseball, can be understood as an aspect of cultural production which ultimately derives from the inequalities in power relations within a hierarchical, class-based, capitalist system.[24]

Moreover, the story of Rugby Football in South Wales provides a window onto the social forces that transformed the county of Glamorgan (in particular) in the last quarter of the 19th century. From the 1880s onwards thousands of people migrated from the largely rural areas of the West Country – Somerset, Devon, Gloucestershire and Herefordshire – to settle and work in the new coalmining communities of the burgeoning South Wales Coalfield. In that decade alone the population of Glamorgan rose from 405,798 to 518,383 or some 27 percent. The most marked increases came in the maritime centres of Cardiff and Swansea as well as the Pontypridd registration district that included the Rhondda valleys, which were fast becoming the heartland of the coalfield.[25] The population did not all come from Wales itself, which harnessed a population of only 1.5 million. As the twin concepts of Wales and Welshness were becoming increasingly focused in the years after 1880 historians have been careful to place these developments in the context of Anglophone migration, particularly from the West Country. Yet this migration merely underlines the historic connections between the two regions and emphasizes the applicability of the borderlands approach, for not only did modern-day historians understand the power of the east–west link, so too (and more importantly perhaps) did contemporary sports patrons. As Smith and Williams note, 'in September 1875 the South Wales Football Club was formed "with the intention of playing matches with the principal clubs in the West of England and the neighbourhood. The rugby rules will be the code adopted"'.[26]

The proximity of opposition, the promise of greater wealth, and the new culture being formed by the in-migration of people from the West Country into the South Wales Valleys fostered a borderland sporting community. That is not to say, however, that the migration to the coalfield and the cultural interaction between the English and the Welsh produced a harmonious marriage:

> *Mae y dyglif Saxonaidd yng Nghymru wedi dwyn difyrion y byddau yn well i'n gwlad beidio byth eu gweled. Carem i'r Saeson gadw eu rhedegfeydd, eu saethu a chigyddio colemenod, eu dawnsfeyudd nosawl a'r gwelyth llygredig. /* The English deluge into Wales has brought amusements it would have been better for our country not to have seen. We would like to see the English keep their races, their shooting and butchering of pigeons, their night-time dancing, and their polluted lineage to themselves.[27]

Such attitudes are not entirely surprising given the fear among the native Welsh (particularly the Welsh-speaking population) that their culture would be lost;[28] yet, the precocious marriage of the two cultures into an industrial, Anglo-Welsh identity is one of the principal features of this borderland region and sport, as much or even more than religion, played a large role in the making and remaking of identities in this region. Welsh-medium chapels, driven by a puritanical sense of Calvinist theology, refused to adopt a rounded and balanced doctrine that would enable them to adapt to the cultural demands of the new industrial working class just as the Roman Catholic Church or the English Nonconformist chapels had been able to do. Some ministers suggested that they 'would prefer to see the young people in the Church under [their] care pursuing sports in the most godforsaken places, than see sports being linked with the house of God'.[29] Others suggested that 'many current sports are innocent in themselves, though they had been undertaken in an evil manner. This is true, for instance of [rugby] football'.[30] More often than not though, the total hostility of the native Welsh churches was directed towards rugby, as this lecture by Reverend John Rees suggests:

> Were churches what they professed to be why should their young men seek their pleasures in play-houses and on football fields? Football he declared to be the dullest and most senseless game the world had ever seen (laughter). Even an ape … would not disgrace itself by seeking pleasures in kicking a football. Why, if they and middle aged men found any pleasure in going to the pubs, theatres and football field then let them, in the name of God and for the honour, success and influence of the Church upon the world remain outside her pale (applause).[31]

Of course the mapping of identity and religious affiliation in this period is particularly complex and we find that the making of Anglo-Welsh identity among the workers of the coalfield is not only fostered by in-migration of people but religious allegiances as well. Crucial here is the different attitude to sport among different denominations. The Catholic Church did not protest against sporting activities, they were merely seen as another aspect of the expanding parochial network and the Catholic Church's presence can be felt with the sporting culture of the coalfield. In Cardiff, St Peter's Church was proud of the long-standing tradition of (Irish) Catholic rugby clubs in the city, 'the old Catholic Clubs in the town have played their part in building up the City Club'.[32] In Merthyr Tydfil similarly the growth of rugby was sponsored by the Roman Catholic St Illtyd's Church. Photographs show a large Irish contingent involved in the side but Irish Catholics were not the only ones to involve themselves in local sports. The Dowlais International Colliery produced several Spanish Association Football teams.[33] Likewise, the English chapels of the coalfield seem to have made the same connection between religion and sport that the Irish and Spanish Catholics did, with the philosophy of muscular Christianity prominent among both Dissenters and Anglicans. For Welsh Dissent, however, football – either the Rugby or Association codes – was something of an anathema; angry at its associations with drink and gambling, and (as we have seen) its breaking down of the purity of Welsh culture in the form of distracting people away from religious services, Welsh ministers seemed determined to undermine these new leisure pursuits. Gradually though they grew to tolerate sport and its place in society, though scorn remained for professional sport.[34] The reaction of the Welsh ministers makes plain the interactions between South Wales and the West Country, for if these interactions were not omnipresent they probably would not have worried in quite the same xenophobic terms as they did.

If we now turn our attention to the structure of both Rugby and Association football leagues and the interactions between South Wales and the West Country in terms of matches played we continue to see evidence of a large sporting region. As Martin Johnes has written, 'participation in English leagues was … to prove critical to the development of soccer in south Wales'.[35] By 1908 four teams, Treharris, Newport, Aberdare Town and Barry District, were all playing in the Western League, a competition made up of teams from the South-west of England. Matches against English opposition were attractive because of the higher level of competition compared with that of local leagues; it was hampered, though, by the expense of travelling across the Severn on a regular basis.[36] It is not, therefore, a surprise that the biggest soccer clubs in South Wales emerged in the maritime centres of Cardiff and Swansea with their superior transport connections. Welsh teams participating in English competitions were not simply limited to soccer either; the other 'rebellious' sport of the Welsh sporting palate, Rugby League Football, incorporated a handful of Welsh sides in the early 20th century. Professionalism and English competition it seems became a particular feature of Edwardian sport.

Jumping forward to the 1930s this sporting community can be seen to have extended its reach both in Rugby Football and in Association Football (or soccer). Bristol City, Cardiff City, Swansea Town, Aberdare Athletic, Merthyr Town, all fielded sides that regularly competed against each other across the national divide.[37] Technically the Welsh teams were part of their own association, the Football Association of Wales (FAW) and the English sides came under the umbrella of the Football Association (FA). Yet as Cardiff City's victory in the 1927 FA Cup against Arsenal indicates, there was much cross-border interaction.[38] In rugby the long-standing tradition of seeking English opposition remained but the strength of internal competition, the growing out-migration from the economically deprived coalfield, and the emergence of professional Rugby League in Northern England as a legitimate route for good footballers to escape the poverty of the coalfield meant that it was the professional rather than amateur sides that found comfort in the borderland connections.[39] Indeed it seemed for a time that a new borderland might open up with the attentions of the valleys shifting north to the industrial belt of Lancashire and Yorkshire. Wigan, Saint Helens, Bradford and Leeds might replace Bristol, Bath, Weston-super-Mare and Gloucester.[40] Unlike the cross-border matches between the amateur rugby clubs of the West Country, the move North and to professional sport meant that a player could never return to the amateur (more properly shamateur) game of his native land. 'In short', Collins rightly records, 'rugby league gave working-class Welsh rugby players the chance to escape from a life spent down the pit, in the steelworks or on the dole'.[41]

The weaknesses of Northern Union (Rugby League) in South Wales is one of the simpler sporting conundrums to solve and relates very much to the historically absent North–South axis of communications in Welsh history. The difficulties of travelling north to Manchester or deeper into Yorkshire and returning within the period of leisure time afforded to working families was difficult and the prospect of being soundly beaten was not in the least attractive.[42] The Secretary of the Welsh Rugby Union, Walter Rees, railing against the onset of professional rugby, proved prophetic. 'We are confident', he claimed, 'that the Northern Union cannot live in Wales under any circumstances for long, and we are determined to kill it and its insidious influence without delay'.[43] Conditions of geography and widespread public disinterest helped in that mission. Moreover the rising fortunes of the round-ball game were transforming the sporting landscape. Where the Northern Union clubs had failed, soccer clubs rose, phoenix-like, out of their collapse. In Tonypandy, the collapse of the Mid-Rhondda Northern Union side meant that their ground became available for the soccer club to use. One of the more painful problems faced by clubs in this period, after all, was the lack of sporting space.[44] The professional sports helped each other and often used the same grounds; in the case of soccer, rugby union's reluctance to help only helped to foster professional soccer.[45]

Yet, as with rugby union, the true saviour of soccer in South Wales was the east–west communications route and the growing strength of the Association game in the West Country.[46] Participation in English leagues and English competitions had an element of international competition, a fact which proved popular with spectators; they were, crucially, lucrative. Treharris and Newport FC joined the Western League in 1906, the first of the South Wales teams to do so; by the end of the decade they had been joined by Merthyr Town, Ton Pentre, Barry District and Aberdare. Disputes in the summer of 1910 resulted in the withdrawal of every Welsh side save Newport and Barry.[47]

The failure of the Western League experiment, however, merely paved the way for a much more successful venture. The Southern League, a rival to the richer Football League, became focused upon the South Wales clubs as a means of salvaging its own fortunes. This followed a second rejection by the Football League for a merger between the two competitions. Instead, the Southern League's expansion into South Wales proved decisive in the development of professional football in the southern half of the principality; yet the expansion might well have proved its downfall had generous travel expenses not been granted to placate the hostile English sides.[48]

In both of South Wales' pre-eminent sports, Rugby Football and Association Football, underlying social forces proved crucial in the development of the games. Migration from the West of England had brought enthusiasm and working-class knowledge of the sports to Wales, and greater wealth and international competition had prompted the Welsh clubs to seek out the English sides. In human terms, the upheaval of the second Industrial Revolution at the end of the 19th century with the rapid expansion of the South Wales coalfield had helped to create new communities and to refashion Welsh identity. Sport helped ease the human pains of that new world and helped bring a shared experience that brought people together and was a bastion of a newly developed self-expression, a national identity. It is clear, and has long been clear to historians of South Wales, that the to-ing and fro-ing of people and material goods across the Welsh border was part and parcel of the 'borderland' society that existed in that part of the British Isles.

Navigating the Atlantic highway: Cape Breton as 'industrial frontier' and sporting borderland

There are other borderlands within the British Isles that deserve attention, of course, but they will not be pursued here as we turn our attention instead to the industrial sporting frontier of Cape Breton in Nova Scotia.[49] That said, sporting interactions and rivalries involving Scotland and Ireland nonetheless prompt us to think more about the nature of what a sporting borderland or frontier might be in the absence of a land boundary or in a transatlantic context. Given the widespread migrations from Scotland to Nova Scotia that followed the Highland clearances, moreover, and the fact that by the 1920s over a quarter of Nova Scotia's population was Scottish in origin, the transatlantic comparison is more than just an exercise in academic theorizing. Instead it grows out of the patterns of economic, social and cultural interconnections between the Old World and the New, and the shared experience of the capitalist transformation of coalfields in South Wales and Cape Breton.[50]

Like South Wales, Cape Breton can be understood as an 'industrial frontier' region operating within a larger transnational borderland community involving the Maritimes and New England. Although much of Cape Breton Island remains rural even to the present, those parts of the island connected to coalmining, and eventually to steel production, expanded rapidly during the last half of the 19th century, drawing workers (many of them of Scottish origin) from the surrounding countryside and from across the Atlantic. By the turn of the century a highly internationalized and class-conscious workforce had gravitated to this volatile 'industrial frontier' region, which by the end of World War I had declared war on the absentee owners of the mines and the Sydney steel plant. The process of radicalization had begun much earlier, of course, evident in the bitter miners' strikes of 1890 and 1909,[51] and culminated with the declaration of UMWA District 26 that it stood for the overthrow of the capitalist system, 'peaceably if we may, forcibly if we must'. For workers in industrial Cape Breton, sport – particularly rugby and baseball – also contributed to what David Frank calls 'the cohesion of life in the coal mining communities and the strength of working-class solidarity among the coal miners' during the 1920s.[52] Despite the attempt of middle-class cultural producers to present a romanticized story of the region's Highland origins as part of an interwar 'quest of the folk', class identities remained as important – often more important – than identities rooted in ethnic origin.[53]

It is instructive to reflect upon the popularity of rugby and baseball, sports that came to Cape Breton from two different directions, one transatlantic the other continental. According to Dan Macdonald the allegiance of the Island's working class to rugby was unique. While the rest of Canada began to incorporate the influences of American football into existing rugby codes, eventually creating Canadian football, Cape Breton doggedly resisted any change to rugby codes. (Canadian football did not come to Nova

Scotia until the 1950s.)[54] Rather than an expression of the region's anti-modern sensibilities, moreover, the refusal to adopt Canadian rugby codes was connected to the miners' resistance to Central Canadian capitalist control of the coalfields and represents their appreciation of the game as a working-class pastime.[55] Ironically rugby had been introduced into Cape Breton in 1899 by a group of university students hired to work at the Dominion Iron and Steel Corporation, including a man from the old country named Jones who may have been Welsh. By 1901 teams from Sydney, Glace Bay, Port Morien and Louisbourg were competing under the banner of the Cape Breton Rugby Association, and were later joined by teams from New Waterford, Dominion and Reserve Mines.[56]

What had come to the Island as a middle-class sporting pursuit was quickly captured by workers – many of them of Scottish origin. Of all the rugby clubs emerging in Cape Breton at the time, none was more prominent than the Caledonia Rugby Club. The club's name indicated its Scottish allegiances, and a glance at the team roster in 1911 includes surnames such as McIntyre, McKenzie, McDonald, Weir and McLean. By the 1920s surnames such as MacKenzie, Burns, MacKay, MacDonald, MacVicar and Cameron often dotted the club roster, but Joseph Boutillier's appearance suggest that workers of Acadian ancestry were welcome participants, as were players such as Driscoll and Lawley, names that are Irish and English respectively. By the 1930s the Caledonians had recruited their first black player. According to Melvin Shephard, a star fullback in rugby who played baseball in the summer as a catcher, what was most important to the club was that all its players were miners who were fiercely antagonistic towards the mine-owners and bosses in the pits and to non-resident capitalists residing in metropolitan centres outside the region.[57]

Formed in 1906 as an intermediate league team, and advancing to senior level competition in 1911, the Caledonians emerged as the finest rugby club in Nova Scotia during the interwar period, at one point winning ten consecutive Eastern Canadian rugby championships under coach John McCarthy. (Since there was no Canadian rugby championship at the time, the Caledonians might arguably be considered the top rugby side in the country.) In the years immediately after World War I, moreover, the Caledonians had been excluded from competing for the Maritime Rugby championship trophy, the McCurdy Cup, which had instead been contested by university-based teams. An oft-told story concerning the Caledonians' first trip to Eastern Championships suggests the working-class sensibilities of the team and their refusal to defer to those who represented the sophistication of the metropolis. On the night prior to the big match, railway magnate W.S. McTier hosted a dinner in honour of the two teams. Seated between the two team captains, McTier turned to the young Cape Bretoner and asked: 'And what college are you attending, young man?' 'Why sir', the Caledonian captain replied, 'I am at Dinn's College', a reference to mine-manager Dinn at the Caledonia mine in Glace Bay. 'Dinn's College', said McTier, 'I don't think I know it'. 'Oh yes sir, Dinn's College', was the reply. 'I'm taking my degree in pan-shoveling coal'. Although this is a story likely to have altered with its many tellings, it nonetheless reflects the intermingling of class and sporting identities.[58] It provides an indication of the confidence colliers had in their own self-worth, and their willingness to assert themselves in their relations with their self-styled social betters.

If rugby, as was true in South Wales, was one of the great pastimes of the working class, the same can be said of baseball. Baseball came to industrial Cape Breton later than it did to most other parts of Nova Scotia, reflecting both the gradual continental diffusion of the sport and the emergence of an imagined borderland sporting community in the north-east. The invention of this regional sporting universe included such things as long-distance and marathon racing, sailing, boxing and recreational hunting, but baseball was most prominent. Indeed, while rugby revealed transatlantic influences, reinforced traditions of Celtic and Gaelic history, and connected with working-class culture and labour radicalism, baseball symbolized the metropolitan cultural reach of Boston. Touring baseball teams from New England were regular visitors to the province and to Cape Breton each summer. Massachusetts teams from Arlington, Malden, Taunton, Salem, Attleboro, Dorchester, Quincy, Newburyport and Somerville, joined Bob Bigney's South Boston All Stars, and the Boston Travellers, often spending up to a month barnstorming the province and crowding the local teams' summer schedules. Then there were Black barnstorming teams such as the Cleveland Giants, Philadelphia Stars and the Boston Royal Giants whose rosters were filled with stars of the so-called Negro leagues in the USA. While American teams looked upon the Maritimes as a northern extension of New England, and revealed the continuing influence of Boston on the sporting life of Cape Breton, Canadian teams flatly ignored the region. In the entire interwar period not a single team ventured onto Cape Breton Island from anywhere in Canada outside the Maritimes.

Similar to Bristol's relationship with South Wales, Boston's metropolitan influence over Nova Scotia was more culturally enriching than it was dominating. Most Cape Bretoners considered Boston's influence far more benign than that exerted by Canadian centres such as Montreal and Toronto. More than rugby, moreover, baseball offered the more accomplished athlete the possibility of remuneration both in semi-pro leagues at home and in some cases in the larger network of professional baseball across the border. By 1905 professional baseball had developed on the Island with teams in Sydney, Sydney Mines, Reserve Mines and Glace Bay importing players from elsewhere in the Maritimes and New England to supplement local players, most of whom were from working-class backgrounds. The Dominion No. 1 team was the only one not to import professionals, and relied completely on players who worked the mines but turned to baseball as a way to supplement their income.[59] Operators of the Dominion Coal Company bitterly opposed the introduction of professional baseball, arguing that the scheduling of games during the week resulted in a considerable number of its employees leaving work early in the day and a lessening of worker productivity. Echoing the position of the mine-owners, the *Sydney Record* lamented that 'this taking a day or a half day off at frequent intervals disorganizes the working man. England today is suffering from an excess of the sporting and holidaying spirit and … is feeling the competition of the steadier and more industrious continental nations'.[60] These claims had little influence on workers, however, and their continuing support for and involvement in baseball helped it flourish for decades. It is perhaps not surprising, therefore, that the professional Cape Breton Colliery League which operated from 1936 to 1939, represents until now the only professional baseball league east of Quebec ever to be affiliated with Organized Baseball's minor league system.[61] Sustained by its roots in working-class culture, baseball's centrality in the life of this 'industrial frontier' region was an important component of a broader north-eastern borderland community nourished by social, cultural, demographic and sporting connections from the late 19th century until World War II.

Conclusion

In this chapter, meant to be provocative rather than exhaustive, we have argued that the notions of frontier and borderlands can be imagined in ways that contribute to an understanding of transnational sporting linkages and provide ways of approaching sports history in comparative fashion. Revisiting the ideas of frontier and borderlands, moreover, allows us to confront assumptions about how the metropolis creates broad patterns of sporting culture that hinterland regions passively emulate, and turns our attention away from sport's contribution to the making of the nation-state. Our objective is to understand the agency of those who fashioned sporting practice in regions that are often considered 'peripheral' or on the margins, and to demonstrate the social significance of what people – in this case working people – created from the ground up. This is not to deny the significance of sportive nation building, and undoubtedly there is considerable value in studies such as Thomas Zeiler's *Ambassadors in Pinstripes; The Spalding World Tour and the Birth of American Empire*, that focuses on how the Spalding 1888 baseball world tour encouraged the diffusion not only of American sport but of principles of free market capitalism inherent in the 'open door' diplomacy of the USA.[62] Our intent is not to impeach such work, but to reflect upon its limitations, and to suggest that to ignore how history is made in so-called hinterland communities is to succumb to the 'metropolitan fallacy'. For us, the validation of history from the margins is part of the larger enterprise of writing history 'from the bottom up' and explains our interest in the construction of working-class sporting culture. In addition, growing up as we have in South Wales and Nova Scotia respectively, has left us acutely sensitive to the denial of the importance of these regions in larger narratives about the nation. For us place matters! Paraphrasing E.P. Thompson, we find that revamped metaphors of both frontier and borderland allow us to avoid the 'condescension of the metropole'.

Notes

1 Herbert E. Bolton, 'The Epic of Greater America', Presidential address to the American Historical Association, 1932. *American Historical Review* 38, 3 (April, 1933), 448–74, (quotation 448).

2 David J. Weber, 'Turner, the Boltonians, and the Borderlands', *American Historical Review* 91 (1986), 66–81. For an insightful discussion of the idea of American exceptionalism and what it means for the writing of sports history see Steven W. Pope, 'Rethinking Sport, Empire and American Exceptionalism', *Sport History Review* 38, 2 (November, 2007), 92–120. In addition to providing a comprehensive historiographical survey of the notions of exceptionalism and empire, Pope urges 'American sport historians to engage more actively with debates within the "parent" discipline and to better situate their research within the global history of sport. If historians follow along this path, I suspect that the history of American sport will not appear to be so "exceptional" after all' (109).

3 Bolton, 'Epic of Greater America', 449.

4 Ellwyn R. Stoddard, Richard Nostrand and Jonathan P. West, *Borderlands Sourcebook: A Guide to the Literature on Northern Mexico and the American Southwest* (Norman: University of Oklahoma Press, 1983).

5 Innis developed his 'staples thesis' in a number of seminal works on the exploitation of resources in British North America and the 'backward linkages' to metropolitan centres overseas. See, for example, Harold Innis, *The Fur Trade in Canada* (New Haven, CT: Yale University Press, 1930) and *The Cod Fisheries* (Toronto: University of Toronto Press, 1940).

6 J.M.S. Careless, *Frontiers and Metropolis: Regions, Cities, and Identities in Canada before 1914* (Toronto: University of Toronto Press, 1989), 7.

7 Cecelia Applegate, 'A Europe of Regions: Reflections on the Historiography of Sub-National Places in Modern Times', *American Historical Review* 104, 4 (October, 1999), 1,157–82. According to Applegate the modernization model since 1945 'did more to obscure our view of Europe's regions than any other conceptual model' (1,158).

8 See, for example, Melvin Adleman, *A Sporting Time: New York City and The Rise of Modern Athletics, 1820–1870* (Urbana and Chicago: University of Illinois Press, 1986).

9 Fredrick Paxson, 'The Rise of Sport', *Mississippi Valley Historical Review* 4 (September 1917), 143–68.

10 Steven A. Riess, *City Games: The Evolution of American Urban Society and the Rise of Sports* (Urbana and Chicago: University of Illinois Press, 1989), 9.

11 In 1999, for example, a special issue, 'The Nation and Beyond: International Perspectives on United States History', *Journal of American History* 86, 3 (December 1999), challenged older assumptions that nations are the self-evident focus of historical inquiry. The thrust of the issue was to interrogate rather than to assume the centrality of the nation state and to look more closely at transnationalism and the prospect of comparative inquiry. See the essays in this issue by David Thelen, Bruno Ramirez, Ian Tyrrell and Robin Kelly. See also George M.Frederickson, 'From Exceptionalism to Variability: Recent Developments in Cross-National Comparative History', *Journal of American History* 82, 3 (September 1995), 587–604.

12 For a cogent discussion of postmodernism and sports history see Martin Johnes, 'Texts, Audiences, and Postmodernism: The Novel as Source in Sport History', *Journal of Sport History* 34, 1 (Spring, 2007), 121–33.

13 Ian K. Steele, *The English Atlantic 1546–1740: An Exploration of Communication and Community* (New York: Oxford University Press, 1986); Paul Jay, 'The Myth of "America" and the Politics of Location: Modernity, Border Studies, and the Literature of the Americas', *Arizona Quarterly* 54, 2 (Summer 1998), 165–92; Stephen Hornsby, Victor A. Konrad and James J. Herland, eds, *The Northeastern Borderlands: Four Centuries of Interaction* (Orono, ME and Fredericton, NB: Canadian-American Center, University of Maine and Acadiensis Press, 1989). On the sporting borderlands see Colin D. Howell, 'Borderlands, Baseball, and Big Game: Conceptualizing the Northeast as a Sporting Region', in Stephen J. Hornsby and John G. Reid, eds, *New England and the Maritime Provinces: Connections and Comparisons* (Montreal & Kingston: McGill-Queens University Press, 2006); and 'Baseball and Borders: The Diffusion of Baseball into Mexican and Canadian-American Borderland Regions, 1885–1911', *Nine: A Journal of Baseball History and Culture* 11, 2 (Spring 2003), 16–26; Alan Klein, *Baseball on the Border: A Tale of Two Laredos* (Princeton, NJ: Princeton University Press, 1997).

14 There are, of course, many fine studies of the place of sport in the development of national culture. For the USA see S.W. Pope, *Patriotic Games: Sporting Traditions in the American Imagination 1876–1926* (New York: Oxford University Press, 1997); Mark Dyreson, *Making the American Team: Sport, Culture and the Olympic Experience* (Urbana: University of Illinois Press, 1998). For Canada see Bruce Kidd, *The Struggle for Canadian Sport* (Toronto: University of Toronto Press, 1996); Colin Howell, *Blood, Sweat and Cheers: Sport and the Making of Modern Canada* (Toronto: University of Toronto Press, 2001). For the United Kingdom see Richard Holt, *Sport and the British: A Modern History* (Oxford: Clarendon Press, 1989); and Grant Jarvie and Graham Walker, eds *Scottish Sport in the Making of the Nation: Ninety-Minute Patriots?* (Leicester: Leicester University Press, 1994).

15 Ramsay Cook, 'Limited Identities in Canada', *Canadian Historical Review* L, 1 (March 1969), 1–10, suggested that Canadian historians should focus less on the issue of a national identity and more upon regional, ethnic, linguistic and class identities. J.M.S Careless, 'Limited Identities – Ten Years Later', *Manitoba History* 1 (1981) subsequently warned that 'limited identities threaten to take over and settle the matter of a Canadian national identity by ending it outright, leaving perhaps a loose league of survivor states essentially existing on American outdoor relief'. Few Canadian historians today would take such a pessimistic view.

16 Such an argument reminds us of the geographic isolation of many of the towns of the industrial frontier. See for example: Peter Stead, 'Working-Class Leadership in South Wales, 1900–1922', *Welsh History Review* 6, 3 (1973), 329–53, who suggests that the nature of settlement had a great deal of impact upon the development of identity. See also Hywel Francis' analysis of proletarian internationalism in the coalfield and the responses to the Spanish Civil War: *Miners Against Fascism: Wales and the Spanish Civil War* (London: Lawrence & Wishart, 1984); note the absence of this sort of analysis in Michael Petrou's recent work on Canadian International Brigadiers: *Renegades: Canadians in the Spanish Civil War* (Vancouver: University of British Columbia Press, 2008).

17 Gwyn Alf Williams, *When Was Wales? A History of the Welsh* (London: Penguin, 1985), 166. Other important studies that provide insights into metropolitan centres in the region include M.J. Daunton, *Coal Metropolis: Cardiff, 1870–1914* (Cardiff: University of Wales Press, 1981); John Davies, *Cardiff and the Marquesses of Bute* (Cardiff: University of Wales Press, 1981) and *Cardiff: A Pocket Guide* (Cardiff: University of Wales Press, 2002); Louise Miskell, *Intelligent Town: An Urban*

History of Swansea, 1780–1855 (Cardiff: University of Wales Press, 2006) and 'The Making of a new "Welsh Metropolis": Science, Leisure and Industry in early Nineteenth-Century Swansea', *History* 88, 1 (2003), 32–52; and W. Minchinton, 'Bristol – Metropolis of the West in the Eighteenth Century', *Transactions of the Royal Historical Society* 5th Series, 4 (1954), 69–89.

18 Raymond Williams, *Keywords: A Vocabulary of Culture and Society* (London: Croom Helm, 1976), 117–18.

19 Gareth Williams, *1905 And All That: Essays on Rugby Football, Sport and Welsh Society* (Llandysul: Gomer Press, 1991), 132. As he notes, 'It is likely soccer evoked much of the same spectator appeal as rugby … they were complementary rather than alternative to each other' (132).

20 As Kenneth Morgan notes, football is 'not really a Welsh institution' and 'rugby continued to capture far more support amongst the sporting population of south Wales', Kenneth O. Morgan, *Rebirth of a Nation: A History of Modern Wales* (Oxford: Oxford University Press, 1981), 237.

21 Brian Lile and David Farmer, 'The Early Development of Association Football in South Wales, 1890–1906', *Transactions of the Honourable Society of Cymmrodorion* (1984), 194; cf. Grant Jarvie, 'Sport in the Making of Celtic Cultures', in idem (ed.), *Sport in the Making of Celtic Cultures* (Leicester: Leicester University Press, 1999), 2.

22 *Amateur Sport*, 25 September 1889.

23 *Amateur Sport*, 11 September 1889.

24 Colin D. Howell, *Northern Sandlots: A Social History of Maritime Baseball* (Toronto: University of Toronto Press, 1995), 5.

25 *Census of England and Wales, Vol. IV. General Report,* Parl. Papers 1883, ixxx (C.3797), 583 ff.

26 David Smith and Gareth Williams, *Fields of Praise: The Official History of the Welsh Rugby Union, 1881–1981* (Cardiff: University of Wales Press, 1980), 31.

27 *Glamorgan Free Press*, 5 September 1891.

28 As one correspondent of the *Glamorgan Free Press* noted: 'Sir, a good number of our Welsh parents cannot prevail upon their own children to learn the Welsh language upon their own hearths and among their own family and I admit that it is a most difficult matter in many instances in a town like Pontypridd where the English tongue is so predominant among all classes. Even in the Welsh chapel after a Welsh service we find as soon as the service is over that most of the conversation takes place in English' (*Glamorgan Free Press*, 26 April 1902).

29 *Tyst* (18 October 1889), 3–4.

30 *Report of the Union of Welsh Independents* (Bridgend, 1896), 123–27.

31 Reverend John Rees, *South Wales Daily News*, 5 May 1894.

32 *St Peter's Magazine*, February 1925, 43.

33 Cf. Photograph printed *Merthyr Express*, 28 May 1987; several photographs held by Merthyr Tydfil Library.

34 See Gareth Williams, *1905 And All That*, 76–78; Andy Croll, *Civilizing the Urban: Popular Culture and Public Space in Merthyr, c.1870–1914* (Cardiff: University of Wales Press, 2000), chapter 6; Martin Johnes, *Soccer and Society: South Wales, 1900–1939* (Cardiff: University of Wales Press, 2002), 30–35.

35 Johnes, *Soccer*, 35–36.

36 *South Wales Daily News*, 20 June, 1 July 1910. English teams were not immune either to the costs of travelling across the sporting region.

37 David M. Woods and Andrew Crabtree, *Bristol City: A Complete Record, 1894–1987* (Derby: Breedon Books, 1987).

38 The Arsenal goalkeeper that day, Dan Lewis, hailed from the Rhondda. For more on the 'British' nature of English football competitions see: Matthew Taylor, The Leaguers: The Making of Professional Football in England, 1900–1939 (Liverpool: Liverpool University Press, 2005), and The Association Game: A History of British Football, 1863–2000 (London: Longman, 2007); also Martin Johnes, Soccer and Society. South Wales, 1900–1939 (Cardiff: University of Wales Press, 2002), and 'Irredeemably English? Association Football and Wales', Planet: The Welsh Internationalist 133 (1999), 72–79; Martin Johnes and Ian Garland, '"The New Craze": Football and Society in North-East Wales, c.1870–1890', Welsh History Review 22, 2 (2004), 278–304; Brian Lile and David Farmer, 'The Early Development of Association Football in South Wales, 1890–1916', Transactions of the Honourable Society of Cymmrodorion (1984), 193–215.

39 On the history of Rugby League see: Tony Collins, *Rugby's Great Split: Class, Culture and the Origins of Rugby League Football* (London: Routledge, 2006), and *Rugby League in Twentieth Century*

Britain: A Social and Cultural History (London: Routledge, 2006); Peter Lush and Dave Farrar, eds, *Tries in the Valleys: A History of Rugby League in Wales* (London: London League Publications, 1998).

40 This was a 'borderland' that was specifically focused upon Rugby League, as Tony Collins notes: 'Those without rugby skills to trade did not go to the north of England but to the new engineering and services industries of the Midlands and South East', *Rugby League in Twentieth Century Britain*, 53.

41 Collins, *Rugby League in Twentieth Century Britain*, 54.

42 Of the six Northern Union clubs formed in Wales in the first decade of the 20th century only Ebbw Vale and Merthyr Tydfil had any sort of success, winning around one-third of their matches. Aberdare won just under six percent. Wray Vamplew, *Pay Up and Play the Game: Professional Sport in Britain, 1875–1914* (Cambridge: Cambridge University Press, 1988), 147.

43 *Merthyr Express*, 5 October 1907.

44 Andy Croll, *Civilizing the Urban: Popular Culture and Public Space in Merthyr, c.1870–1914* (Cardiff: University of Wales Press, 2000), 137–75 passim. For the Bristol context, see H.E. Meller, *Leisure and the Changing City, 1870–1914* (London: Routledge & Kegan Paul, 1976). Also, John Bale, *Sports Geography*, second edn (London: Routledge, 2002).

45 Martin Johnes, *Soccer and Society: South Wales, 1900–1939* (Cardiff: University of Wales Press, 2002), 29.

46 The short-lived, Bristol-based sports newspaper, *Amateur Sport* had noted in 1889 that in the 1870s, 'the [Association] game was almost unknown in these parts', yet by the close of the 1880s, 'We predict that this season Association will slightly preponderate, so Rugby must look to its laurels'. *Amateur Sport*, 11 September 1889.

47 *South Wales Daily News*, 20 June, 1 July 1910. As with the failure of Northern Union sides in their ventures north, finance and the cost of east–west travel proved decisive.

48 Martin Johnes, *Soccer and Society*, 39, note 71.

49 On sporting interactions involving England and Scotland see, for example Neil Blain and Raymond Boyle, 'Battling along the Boundaries: The Marking of Scottish Identity in Sports Journalism', in Jarvie and Walker, eds, *Scottish Sport in the Making of the Nation*, 125–41; and Richard Holt, 'King Across the Border: Denis Law and Scottish Football', ibid., 58–74.

50 Marjorie Harper and Michael E. Vance, eds, *Myth, Migration and the Making of Memory: Scotia and Nova Scotia c. 1700–1990*, published for the Gorsebrook Research Institute for Atlantic Canada Studies (Halifax and Edinburgh: Fernwood Publishing and John Donald Publishers, 1999) provides the most exhaustive study of this interaction to date.

51 Ian Mckay, '"By Wisdom, Wile or War": The Provincial Workmen's Association and the struggle for Working-Class Independence in Nova Scotia, 1879–97', *Labour/Le Travail* 18 (Fall 1986), 13–62.

52 David Frank, 'Class Conflict in the Coal Industry: Cape Breton, 1922', in Gregory S. Kealey and Peter Warrian, eds, *Essays in Canadian Working-Class History* (Toronto: McClelland and Stewart, 1976).

53 Ian McKay, *The Quest of the Folk. Antimodernism and the Politics of Cultural Selection in Nova Scotia* (Toronto: University of Toronto Press, 1994), and 'Tartanism Triumphant: The Construction of Scottishness in Nova Scotia, 1933–1954', *Acadiensis* XXI, 2, 8.

54 D.W. Brown, *The History and Development of Organized Canadian Football in Nova Scotia* (unpublished MSc Thesis, Halifax: Dalhousie University, 1980).

55 D.A. MacDonald, *Gridiron and Coal: The Making of Rugby Football in Industrial Cape Breton, 1900–1960* (unpublished MA Thesis, Halifax: Saint Mary's University, 2001).

56 Daryl Shane Leeworthy, 'The One Great Pastime of the People': Rugby, Religion and the Making of Working-Class Culture on the Industrial Frontier: Cape Breton and South Wales, 1850–1914 (unpublished MA Thesis, Halifax: Saint Marys University, 2008).

57 Colin Howell interview with Melvin Sheppard, Glace Bay, Nova Scotia, November 1990.

58 Neil Hooper, *The History of the Caledonia Amateur Athletic Club of Glace Bay, Nova Scotia* (unpublished MPhysEd Thesis, Fredericton: University of New Brunswick, 1988).

59 For a more comprehensive treatment of baseball in Cape Breton see Howell, *Northern Sandlots*, 133–36, 168–70.

60 *Sydney Record*, 2 August 1906.

61 D.J. Myers, *Hard Times – Hard Ball: The Cape Breton Colliery League, 1936–1939* (unpublished MA Thesis, Halifax: Saint Mary's University, 1997).

62 Thomas Zeiler, *Ambassadors in Pinstripes: The Spalding World Baseball Tour and the Birth of the American Empire* (Lanham, MD: Rowman & Littlefield, 2006).

5 Marxism

Ian Ritchie

Douglas Booth suggests quite correctly in the initial chapter of this volume that theory in general is a contentious subject for sports historians. It may in fact be the case that the theoretical insights of Karl Marx and the various Marxist interpretations of sports history are among the most contentious of all. As Booth says, the issue that raises the 'hackles' of sports historians perhaps more than any other is that of *agency*. In other words, based on Marx's particular understanding of the capitalist mode of production, people's free actions and volition – their agency – seem to disappear in favour of social structures, in particular Marx's emphasis on the basic economic foundation of capitalist society, its attendant class structure, and the over-arching influence these have on individuals' lives. This criticism of Marx's theory of capitalist society may seem judicious given the countless examples of historical figures and groups who demonstrate their ability to 'see through' the ideological false consciousness of capitalist class structure. Not the least of which, the working-class based workers' sports movement during the 1920s and 1930s, used sport to fight for workers' rights and, in the process, organized into vibrant national and international movements, including the Workers' Olympics, which at one point in time stood as a viable alternative to Coubertin's Olympic movement. Apparently the *camera obscura* to which Marx famously referred in *The German Ideology* may not be so all pervasive after all.[1]

At the same time, Booth's introduction also points out that critical Marxist accounts in both sport sociology and sports history correctly draw attention to some glaring lacunae in sports studies, specifically and most obviously the important role played by class in the development of sport, but also the role sport plays ideologically in reinforcing other inequitable social structures. Also, extensions of Marx's oeuvre – most notable hegemony theory – have given us a greater and more nuanced understanding of many aspects of sport in society, past or present. Indeed, the recent publication of a major sociological work – Ben Carrington and Ian McDonald's edited volume *Marxism, Cultural Studies and Sport*[2] – attests to the ongoing discussion with Marx in sports studies, some 125 years after his death.

The purpose of this chapter is to introduce the essential elements of Marx's theory of capitalist society and then to present some of the ways Marx's work both has been valuable, and potentially can continue to aid in a greater understanding of the history of sport. The two major sections in this chapter reflect those two goals. The first section presents Marx's original theories in what is hopefully a simple, straightforward way. It is prepared based on the assumption that the reader has little or no experience with Marx's theories, or debates within Marxist scholarship, either within sports studies or in the more general sociological literature. The purpose of presenting the material in this way is twofold. First, this introduction will provide tools for students of sports history to be able to make independent objective assessments of research in sports history that make use of Marx's original work and, by extension, those that refer to second-hand literature as well. Second, and more importantly, few historians use the work of Marx directly. Instead, secondary sources are often employed and as a result grand assumptions and generalizations are often made. As we will see in the assessment of the literature that follows, debates about many of Marx's most fundamental concepts continue still today, well over a century after his death. Part of the reason for this is the complexity and scope of his work but another important part of the reason is that many changes and nuances can be seen in Marx's ideas, changes that were based on a number of factors (discussed in the next section) that influenced his theories during his lifetime. In short, students of sports history, scholars in the field and general readers should always keep in mind that there is no substitute for serious critical engagement with *original* theoretical work, whether Marx's or, for that matter, any of the other important theorists presented in this volume.

Marx and capitalist society

Karl Marx (1818–1883) was born and raised in Trier, in the Rhineland in what is now Germany. In the early days of his higher education, he followed the footsteps of his father and studied law at the University of Bonn and University of Berlin. His interests shifted, however, in the late 1830s, as he became involved in radical student politics, especially at the University of Berlin. His academic interests also shifted from law, to philosophy of law and then finally to philosophy in general and he completed his doctorate in philosophy at the University of Jena in 1841. After teaching for a brief period of time, he began work in journalism, critical writing and publishing, and political activism, all activities that would come to dominate his working life for the remainder of his days.[3] His radical politics and activism in various workers' organizations played a significant role in his sometimes-forced movement from Germany to France and finally to England.[4]

In considering summaries of Marx's work, such as the one to follow, it is important to realize its incredible breadth, but perhaps more importantly, the complexity of his work. Summaries, it should always be kept in mind, are heuristic devices used to provide a general sense of a body of research by reducing complex theories and ideas into convenient and practical categories. However, they belie the immensity of Marx's oeuvre in addition to the many theoretical twists and turns he took during his lifetime as he worked towards a critique of the political and economic developments of his day. Marx first of all drew upon an immense knowledge base – throughout his life he read widely in philosophy, history, law, economics and several other disciplines, and he combined that knowledge with careful observations of the world around him. Also, Marx worked and reworked many of his central theories and concepts throughout his working life. Marx's thinking on such important concepts as the nature of the capitalist mode of production itself, the role of the individual in society, labour, alienation, class relations, the general nature of social relations in the capitalist economy, in addition to many others, shifted and changed throughout his career. These shifts of focus and reworking of ideas and theories were based on countless, complex factors: the nature of the evidence accumulated, Marx's reading and interpretations of other authors, real historical transformations taking place in the 19th century and his interpretation of those events, the motivation and political commitments of those who agreed to publish his work, and so forth. These factors should be kept in mind. Debates continue still today not only because of the complexity of interpretation of those that followed in Marx's footsteps but, perhaps more importantly, because of the complexity of Marx's original work itself. Marx's theoretical oeuvre is still an ongoing 'project' of interpretation and there still remains an intense and important scholarship based on his original writing and publication.[5]

Marx's theory of capitalist society must be understood in the particular context of radical workers' movements, of which he was a part, and in the more general context of emerging industrial-capitalism in European society. So important was the development of industrial society to the emergence of the discipline that would later claim Marx as one if its central 'fathers' that in its earliest days sociology was more or less defined as the study of the industrial revolution's causes and consequences. The most important aspects of the revolution that would impact Marx's work were the dramatic changes and problems it brought to a vast majority of people in Europe: mass exoduses of people from rural areas to cities, miserable living and quite often dangerous working conditions, new forms of urban crime, increasing inequalities between the rich and the poor, and a general sense of alienation or disaffection caused by the dramatic changes in people's lives. In light of the hardships wrought by the industrial revolution, the earliest social thinkers were concerned with how to create a social order that could resolve some of the fundamental problems: food production and distribution, the availability of clean water, poor hygienic living conditions, the physical hardships from long hours of strenuous work in factories, child labour, and tensions created by the vast inequalities between the rich and poor. Marx's attempt to develop a body of work that both understood the world around him and attempted to actively change that world and make it a more egalitarian and democratic one is perhaps no better encapsulated in his famous statement written in the spring of 1845: 'The philosophers have only *interpreted* the world, in various ways; the point, however is to *change* it'.[6]

What set Marx's analysis and critique of capitalist society apart from others was the unique blend of elements. Marx first of all recognized that economic conditions formed the foundation of social life more generally. Second, Marx expanded his observations regarding the economic conditions into a more general theory of social life and social relations, one that included elements of culture and even individual everyday life. Finally, Marx recognized the unique role social conflict played in the history of societies. Each of these elements warrants careful attention, as does the manner in which Marx combined the elements.

At the core of Marx's theory is the idea that economic conditions lay the foundation of social life. Marx based this on observations of the emerging capitalist society in which he lived in the 19th century but also on observations of the economic foundation of several other societies in human history, including primitive communalism, the feudal system, and other societies. He referred to the economic form that shaped societies in various historical epochs as the *mode of production*. What lay at the core of each mode of production was the *material* conditions upon which humans labour to create the essentials of life. *Labour* here is an important concept that Marx studied extensively in his lifetime, and we will return to it later because of its implications for the study of sport. However, for now, it is important to realize that for Marx labour should not be confused with common-sense notions of 'work'. Labour for Marx was a much more fundamental concept. In the most general of terms, labour is, in the words of Marxist scholar Rob Beamish, 'the way humans externalize their unique capacities and actualize human potential'.[7] In interacting with the natural world, that world is transformed into a form adapted for the person's needs or desires. Labour is both ubiquitous – 'a condition of human existence which is independent of all forms of human society'[8] – and a fundamental human practice through which human potential and development – for both instrumental and non-instrumental purposes[9] – is ultimately realized. Labour is:

> ... a condition by which man, through his own actions, mediates, regulates and controls the metabolism between himself and nature. ... He sets in motion the natural forces which belong to his own body, his arms, legs, head and hands, in order to appropriate the materials of nature in a form adapted to his own needs. Through this movement he acts upon external nature and changes it, and in this way he simultaneously changes his own nature. ... Man not only effects a change of form in the materials of nature; he also realizes his own purpose in those materials.[10]

Marx's notion of labour ultimately had – and continues to have – revolutionary implications. First, the idea that any social analysis should start with labour was contrary to most religious, philosophical, political, and economic thought in Marx's day. More importantly, it set the foundation for Marx's assessment of the specific experience of labour – as alienated and exploited – in the capitalist economy.

Marx expanded his central observations regarding human labour and the material conditions of life into a general theory of society. Human beings, of course, do not labour in a social vacuum; they relate to one another and form social relations:

> In the social production of their life, men enter into definite relations that are indispensable and independent of their will, relations of production which correspond to a definite stage of development of their material productive forces. The sum total of these relations of production constitutes the economic structure of society, the real foundations, on which rises a legal and political superstructure and to which correspond definite forms of social consciousness. The mode of production of material life conditions the social, political and intellectual life process in general. It is not the consciousness of men that determines their being, but, on the contrary, their social being that determines their consciousness.[11]

Here, in one quotation, we see the essential elements of Marx's thought regarding the material foundation of social life, human labour, the specific social relations that emerge out of the economic foundation, culture and human thought itself. In a letter written in 1846, Marx described the process in these words:

> What is society, whatever its form may be? The product of men's reciprocal action. Are men free to choose this or that form of society? By no means. Assume a particular state of development in the productive faculties of man and you will get a particular form of commerce and consumption. Assume particular stages of development in production, commerce and consumption and you will have a corresponding social constitution, a corresponding organisation of the family, or orders or of classes, in a word, a corresponding civil society.[12]

We find in these words not only a hint at the eventual motivation for sociology to adopt Marx as one of its 'fathers' – Marx provided a robust and scientific explanation of social life as a reflection of economic conditions – but also an explanation of history and historical transformation. Society transformed itself from one stage to another depending on the relative progression or development of the mode of production and its concomitant social relations.[13]

While the all-important social relations to which Marx refers in his lines above are discussed in only vague terms, he spent considerable time studying the specific construction of those relations, and in particular the class relations that emerge out of the basic economic foundation of society. Marx also observed that within each mode of production he studied, classes emerged based on their ability to wrest control over economic resources and the means of producing goods essential for human life. He also observed that this led to a state of conflict between respective groups in each case, as he and Frederick Engels make clear in the famous opening lines of *Manifesto of the Communist Party*:

> The history of all hitherto existing society is the history of class struggles. Freeman and slave, patrician and plebeian, lord and serf, guildmaster and journeyman, in a word, oppressor and oppressed, stood in constant opposition to one another, carried on an uninterrupted, now hidden, now open fight, a fight that each time ended, either in a revolutionary reconstitution of society at large, or in the common ruin of the contending classes.[14]

As the words above suggest, Marx was interested in various modes of production throughout history and the class conflicts that emerged from them; however, the *capitalist* mode of production drew the lion's share of his attention. In his most important work, *Capital*, published in 1867, Marx attempted to explain in scientific terms the manner in which the capitalist mode of production worked.

Capitalism was for Marx a mode of production developed in the 17th and 18th centuries based on gradual economic, political, and social changes. The growth of urban centres, the eradication of the feudal landholding system, and the emergence of national economies and concomitant national currencies were some of the central preconditions for the growth of capital markets and practices. The essential components of capitalism for Marx were: private ownership of wealth and property; the use of wealth to create greater wealth through trade and investment; wage-labour, or the sale of work in exchange for wages; and perhaps most importantly, capitalists' realization of profit – a sum above and beyond that invested in the resources necessary for the production of commodities in addition to the cost of wages.[15]

Capitalism, though, in its unyielding drive to create profit, produces two separate classes – capitalists (the *bourgeoisie*) who realize the profits and surpluses from the system, and workers (the *proletariat*) who do not. However, the strength of the capitalist mode of production – one unlike other modes of production – is that workers *appear* to be acting freely and of their own choice. However, workers do not realize their full potential because their labour is *alienated* labour; that is, labour that ultimately benefits only those who profit from it. As Marx stated clearly: 'work is *external* to the worker ... consequently, he does not fulfil himself in his work but denies himself. ... His work is not voluntary but imposed, *forced labour*. It is not the satisfaction of a need, but only a *means* for satisfying other needs'.[16] Indeed, Marx's dual insights regarding the production of the class system within the capitalist mode of production and the alienation of the worker would many years later be central to both Marxist thought and debates, and also sociological and historical accounts of sport.

For Marx, capitalism and its essential class structure would ultimately create the conditions for its own destruction, for two central reasons. First, in their drive for profitability, capitalists require the production and sale of as many commodities as possible while at the same time attempting to keep workers' wages low. This, Marx believed, would ultimately lead to a series of crises of *overproduction*, during which the potential market for the sale of commodities – of which workers themselves comprise the vast majority – cannot keep pace with the production of commodities.[17] Second, the capitalist market tended, Marx believed, towards greater and great centralization and concentration of capital. This would inevitably throw together an increasing number of deprived workers, sowing the seeds for revolution and historical transformation. In Marx's words:

> Along with the constant decrease in the number of capitalist magnates, who usurp and monopolize all the advantages of this process of transformation, the mass of misery, oppression, slavery, degradation and exploitation grows; but with this there also grows the revolt of the working class, a class constantly increasing in numbers, and trained, united and organized by the very mechanism of the capitalist process of production. The monopoly of capital becomes a fetter upon the mode of production which has flourished alongside and under it. The centralization of the means of production and the socialization of labour reach a point at which they become incompatible with their capitalist integument. This integument is burst asunder. The knell of capitalist private property sounds. The expropriators are expropriated.[18]

In short, the combined forces of the inevitable crises of overproduction alongside the misery of the working class would, for Marx, spell the end of capitalism and the collapse of the system.

Well over a century since his death, the basic tenets of Marx's ideas are still widely debated. He provided nothing less than one of the most robust sociological theories in that discipline's long history. Among the social forces at large still analysed and under-stood using Marx's insights: social structure and the relationship of major institutions in society to the economic foundation; labour, workers' rights and workers' movements; the division of labour and class divisions; alienation; ideology; the manner in which the capitalist economy adapts to changes and challenges, and historical transformation; the relationship of the economy to cultural and personal life; state welfare policies; and many other topics as well.

Marx, history and sport

In the big historical picture, the application of Marx's theoretical insights to sport has occurred only relatively recently. The production of the first and some of the most seminal texts followed a wave of renewed interest in Marx in largely – although not completely – academic circles in the 1960s and 1970s. This interest grew in part out of the political radicalism of the late-1950s and 1960s, and the emergence of significant social movements, including anti-colonial, civil rights, anti-war, student and workers' movements. This section will present a sample of certain significant works only, as a summary of the entire oeuvre is clearly impossible. Also, certain thematic issues are highlighted, ones that have been the most important in the literature and, not coincidently, were emphasized by Marx as well: *class*, *labour* and *alienation*. In their new edited volume *Marxism, Cultural Studies and Sport*, which itself is destined to become an important piece of literature in the area, and which represents a renewed interest in Marx in the sports studies discipline, editors Ben Carrington and Ian McDonald summarize Marxist scholarship into three distinct phases, in terms of both time period and shifts in theoretical emphasis. I follow their lead here because their period summary is a useful and clear one.

The first phase of Marxist scholarship took place, roughly, in the late-1960s and 1970s. There certainly was not a co-ordinated effort during this phase, but instead there arose somewhat sporadically common themes, despite that fact that the work came from different countries and from varied perspectives within the Marxist literature. The phase was a reflection of the radical social movements mentioned above but also a reaction to a conservative structural-functionalist trend in sociology that had dominated the discipline since just before the start of World War II.[19] The work as a whole attempted to counter the naive structural-functionalist interpretation that sport simply positively reinforced other major institutions in society; it revealed the many potential and existing ways – both in the present and historically – that sport served to reproduce class divisions; and it demonstrated the ways in which sport – especially at the highest ranks of organized national and international competition, both professional and amateur – could be an alienating experience, especially in as much as the athlete's body was trained like a machine comparable to workers bodies in the capitalist system of production. In short, the newly emerging Marxist scholarship attempted to reveal the many problems in sport, reflecting the 'muckraking' role that the discipline of sociology saw itself playing during this period.[20]

Some of the most important Marxist accounts from this period include: Bero Rigauer, *Sport and Work* (translated from the original *Sport und Arbeit*); Gerhard Vinnai, *Football Mania* (translated from the original *Fußballsport als Ideologie*); Jack Scott, *The Athletic Revolution*; Paul Hoch, *Rip Off the Big Game: The Exploitation of Sport by the Power Elite*; and Jean-Marie Brohm, *Sport: A Prison of Measured Time* (translated from the original *Critiques du Sport*).[21] The texts did not have one unified voice in terms of the theoretical approaches. They varied from using the theoretical insights of the Frankfurt Institute for Social Research (the 'Frankfurt School'), as was the case in Rigauer's *Sport and Work*; to Hoch's Marxist-Leninist approach in *Rip Off the Big Game*; to the influence of French Marxism and, in particular, Louis Althusser's theories of the State and 'Ideological State Apparatuses' on Brohm in *Sport: A Prison of Measured Time*.[22]

Brohm's text warrants some attention because it continues today to be one of the more well-known works produced during this period, and because his account is a far-reaching one that covers several major themes in Marx's, and Marxist, scholarship. Two themes stand out in *Sport: A Prison of Measured Time*. First, again, following the French Marxist theorist Louis Althusser, Brohm claimed that by instilling people with values and reinforcing practices supportive of capitalist relations, sport, under the direction of the State in particular, constrains and controls the populace. Ideologically, for example, sport:

> … *veils* the real structure of production relations which it assumes as 'natural'. This ideology *masks* class relations by turning the relations between the individuals within the sporting institution into material relations between things: scores, machines, records, human bodies treated as commodities and so on.[23]

Also, following Marx's discussion of labour under the capitalist mode of production and, in particular, his ideas regarding alienated labour (both discussed earlier), Brohm's text is full of examples of athletic endeavours bordering on the insane: the masochistic celebration of pain during training and competition; the treatment of the body as a machine at the expense of free, liberating physical movement; and, as the title of Brohm's book suggests, the reduction of the human body's ability to freely express itself to carefully timed and spatially restricted movement.[24]

If the first phase of research served sociology's muckraking role by exposing the more exploitative aspects of sport, the second phase, as Carrington and McDonald summarize, was concerned with the 'limits and possibilities of resistance and transformation of these exploitative and ideological structures'.[25] Having said that, the second phase also continued to follow in the footsteps of the first in terms of its critique of the exploitative and restrictive elements in sport. This second phase in fact saw two distinct sub-phases. Taking the second one first, Carrington and McDonald summarize work that was completed from approximately the mid-1980s into the 1990s, involving mainly British and Australian scholars. The major texts from this phase included: John Hargreaves, *Sport, Power and Culture*; Jennifer Hargreaves, *Sporting Females*; Alan Tomlinson, *The Game's Up: Essays in the Cultural Analysis of Sport, Leisure and Popular Culture*; Garry Whannel, *Blowing the Whistle: The Politics of Sport* and *Fields in Vision*; and David Rowe, *Popular Cultures: Rock Music, Sport and the Politics of Pleasure*.[26] As is perhaps obvious from the titles in this list, this second phase is, strictly speaking, less Marxist or 'orthodox' Marxist in approach. We find in this phase the various authors moving beyond the traditional aspects of capitalist society as outlined by Marx and more towards aspects of everyday life, culture, popular entertainment, the mass media, gender and other major emerging issues. An overriding theme is *agency* and the ability of individuals and groups to both 'see through' the controlling and exploitative aspects of capitalist sporting culture and also, at times, resist it. In short, this work generally did not accept that people are as 'duped' by the 'veils' of capitalist social relations as those such as Brohm had claimed. In fact, sport as a 'contested terrain' became a common moniker in sports studies during this phase.[27]

The works in the first sub-phase, however, took more traditionally Marxist approaches. Concentrated in Canada, a series of essays by authors Alan Ingham, Richard Gruneau, Hart Cantelon and Rob Beamish continued the critical approach begun in the major works of the first phase cited earlier, concentrating at times on more specific elements of Marx's theory and the politics of class development and reproduction. One major text – Gruneau's *Class, Sports, and Social Development* – stands out and this text has recently been republished and updated.[28]

For the history of sport, this first part of the second phase was an important one. In his classic essay on the topic – 'Modernization or Hegemony: Two Views on Sport and Social Development' – Canadian sports studies scholar Richard Gruneau – again, one of the central theorists of phase two – makes a strong claim for considering class and power in sports history.[29] The article is an important part of historiographical debates regarding sports history, and a classic account of the transition in social-historical accounts of sport as they made the shift, described by Booth in the introduction to this volume, from structural-functionalist to Marxist and other critical 'structural' approaches. Gruneau pits functionalist-inspired accounts, or what he refers to as accounts that fall under the umbrella of the 'theory of industrial society', against newer critical accounts inspired by the works of Marx and other progressive scholars, ones that fall under, in Gruneau's terms, the 'theory of capitalist society'. Both 'theories' are in fact not really theories per se but a set of assumptions and guideposts that have led historical accounts of sport in particular directions.

Those accounts of sports history that fall under the umbrella of the theory of industrial society are ones that have tended to emphasize the shift from agrarian to industrial societies, within which are included improvements in technology, mass communications and transportation, urbanization and the demographic shift away from rural settings, and the emergence of bureaucracies and attendant specialization, most notably in the division of labour itself but also in other more general social and cultural roles. The industrial society shift also involved the process of rationalization and the concomitant secularization of society, or in Gruneau's words, the shift towards 'the idea that social order was made by humans rather than being something natural and inevitable'.[30] Finally, the development of nations and the important process of nation-building – the idea that common bonds have to be created through mass communications, national propaganda and myth construction[31] – was also an important part of the process, and of course this factor would continue to play a vital role in the transformation of sport in the 20th century as well.[32] In terms of the development of modern sport, the theory of industrial society has tended to emphasize its bureaucratic organization; the codification of rules; specialization, both in the sense of separate unique positions on a team but also specialization in training; and finally, sport as a reflection of industrial society's values, in particular merit, individual achievement, and the resulting emphasis on record breaking and the performance imperative.[33]

The problem, Gruneau points out, is not with the inaccuracy of historical detail in the accounts that fall under the rubric of the theory of industrial society, but rather in terms of their underlying theoretical assumptions and, as a result, the particular spin that gets put on the history that is told as well as the explanatory details of history that go untold. The central problems as Gruneau demonstrates are, first, the evolutionary tendency in the theory of industrial society, or in other words the largely unquestioned assumption that history is progressing towards something better; second, the tendency to privilege description over explanation; and finally, and most importantly, the fact that power, class, and other inequalities are largely ignored.[34]

The accounts of sports history that fall under the umbrella of the theory of capitalist society, on the other hand, consider capitalism as an economic system but also as a social system – as a system of social relations. Based on Marx's insights into the nature of capitalist society discussed earlier, this theory accounts for class divisions as an important factor in the development of sport, but also the manner in which sport reproduces class through such means as reinforcing values appropriate for work under capitalism's system of production, and the alienation experienced by athletes and participants.[35]

One important example of an historical account of sports history that takes into consideration the issues of power and class is Bruce Kidd's *The Struggle for Canadian Sport*.[36] While not explicitly a Marxist approach, it certainly does take into account the power struggles of organizations during the period between the two world wars as they attempted to wrest control over sport in Canada, and class played a crucial role in all of the groups' struggles, albeit in different ways. The result of these struggles, Kidd demonstrates, very much dictated the landscape of sport in Canada for the years to come. The male middle- and upper-middle-class leaders of the Canadian Amateur Athletic Union, the middle-class women who attempted to promote girls' and women's sport through the Women's Amateur Athletic Federation, the workers who attempted to create sport for themselves and to enhance working-class interests through the Workers' Sports Association of Canada, and finally the profiteering businessmen of the National Hockey League all fought for the control of sport, for the attention and commitment of Canadian people, and ultimately to control the *meaning* of sport in the country. However, it was the businessmen of the NHL – the interests of a very small handful of capitalists –

that eventually won out and set the agenda for Canadian sport at the expense of other vibrant traditions.

Finally, the third phase as Carrington and McDonald see it began in the mid-to-late 1990s and continues today. It is characterized by the attempt to bring together traditional Marxist scholarship and many of the radical features of Marx's work, with non-Marxist approaches in social theory, especially post-structuralist theories and many perspectives in cultural studies. This phase undoubtedly represents a return to some of the traditional concepts of Marx and in particular the Marxist commitment to political action, alongside newer perspectives. Carrington and McDonald's volume itself will no doubt be seen as an important contribution to this phase. The various authors featured in this volume address topics as diverse as media, the Olympic Games, race and ethnicity, sports celebrity and the urban sports spectacle, and they do so from diverse Marxist and non-Marxist perspectives.

Rob Beamish's chapter 'Marxism, Alienation and Coubertin's Project'[37] is important for three reasons. First, Beamish accomplishes what unfortunately a vast majority of scholarship does not – the direct application of Marx's theory using primary sources from his original work. Too many 'theoretical' applications are based on secondary sources and their attendant generalizations and assumptions. The second, and related, reason that this article is important is that, being completely fluent in German in addition to being very well-versed in the original production of Marx's ideas in the 19th century, Beamish brings that original work in its first form to an English-speaking sports studies audience. Finally, while not a full manuscript-length account of the historical topic at hand – the Olympic Games, Coubertin's vision for the Games, and historical and social factors contributing to the deterioration of Coubertin's vision – and therefore not what can be considered a 'traditional' sports history text, the piece does at the same time relate very specific elements of Marx's theory to important events in sports history; the chapter represents, in other words, a clear example of theory and history unified.

Beamish applies one of Marx's most important concepts (also introduced earlier) to the history of the Olympic Games: alienation. Keeping in mind first of all that Marx's life-long commitment to the study of the nature and development of capitalist society led him to an immense breadth of work but also to a very complex oeuvre that realized many changes and alterations, especially as the latter part of his career wore on, Beamish summarizes several stages in the production of *Capital* in particular and points out that much effort in the latter part of his career was focused on specific details of that work. As such, it is in Marx's earlier works that can be found a much broader outline of his general vision for both his future research but also the general relationships between the development of capitalism and other fundamental aspects of human social life.[38] In that earlier work, and in particular in his careful reading of early political economists in addition to the specific philosophy of Hegel, Marx demonstrated both the State (in the case of Hegel) and the production process under conditions of capitalist relations and private ownership (in the case of traditional political economists) took precedence as determining factors over human labour.[39] The order, in Marx's mind, was reversed. Under conditions of work in capitalism, 'labour, which should actualize human potential does the opposite – it diminishes workers and progressively estranges them from their full human potential, their "Being" as humans'.[40] Labour, in other words, is alienated, and it is so, first, because workers are separated from the full value of the products they produce; second, because they have no control over the process of production; third, because under the conditions of work in capitalist society labour does not provide the potential for free, creative activity, not just in terms of the realization of the full material value of the product produced (i.e. the first point), but perhaps more importantly, in terms of the general realization of free activity, whether for necessary or 'unnecessary' ends; and finally, labour under the conditions of capitalism perpetuates and 'naturalizes' the social relations that reinforce the system in the first place, in particular the class antagonisms that permeate capitalist relations.[41]

Beamish points out that for historical and sociological considerations of sport, Marx's theory of alienation can provide a useful framework for understanding the conditions under which sport is practised in modern societies. As he says, sport, as a human practice:

> ... is continually raised as one that permits individuals and groups to explore their physical potential, to develop strong team and social bonds, and to aid in the fulfillment of their individual potential needs. ... [I]t is against a framework like Marx's conception of alienation that one may assess the extent to which sport in contemporary society meets those high aspirations. Moreover, if contemporary sport forms do not help people realize their full human potential ... then the alienation theme also allows one to focus upon those aspects of sport which must be changed if it is ever to deliver upon its implicit promise.[42]

The Olympic Games, Baron Pierre de Coubertin's vision for the Games, and finally the social and political forces in the 20th century that came to play the most important roles in holding back Coubertin's vision, combined serve as an important historical example to face the 'litmus test' of Marx's theory of alienation. One would not think that two figures as radically different as Marx and Coubertin could potentially be recognized as having similar views on the development of society in the 19th century; however, both shared a concern for the fact that capitalism and the culture of materialism it promoted was misdirecting humanity in important ways. For Coubertin, this meant that his Olympic project – the grand vision he had for the development of the Olympic Games as a *social movement*[43] – would potentially overcome the crass materialism he saw as leading to moral decline in European society and, in particular, in the lives of French youth. The celebration of mind and body combined together, the development of character and courage through sport, camaraderie generated through competition, the celebrations of arts and culture, and the joy of effort without any financial compensation or other 'external' inducements are just some of the most important goals Coubertin envisioned for the Olympic movement.

The dilemma facing Coubertin, then, was how to protect the Games from the crass materialism of European society and increasingly the rest of the world, and it was for this reason that the amateur rule, adopted by the International Olympic Committee in 1894 two years before the first Games were held in Athens, and enshrined in the Olympic Charter, became the central philosophical cornerstone of the movement – it was *the ethos* of the Games.[44] For Coubertin amateurism was not perfect because it did not embody the totality of values and goals in his vision for the Games, but it was the best rule in existence in late 19th-century sport and would become the overriding imperative for the Olympic movement as a result.

However, over the ensuing half century and beyond, three forces shifted the Olympic movement away from Coubertin's lofty vision: nationalism, the gradual but systematic support of instrumental rationality in the pursuit of records and physical performance, and creeping commercialism and professionalism. Gradually national aggrandizement would replace athletes competing as comrades and 'brothers in arms' as Coubertin wished,[45] with the 1936 'Nazi' Olympics serving as the turning point in the Games in that regard. Also, the emerging ideological conflicts of the cold war drove athletic competition towards the ever-more scientifically and technologically supported pursuit of physical limits.[46] Finally, seizing upon the increasingly international celebrity status of Olympic athletes, private, commercial interests combined with the widespread visibility of Olympic athletes made possible by commercial television to put pressures on the IOC to abandon its central principle in favour of an open, fully commercialized, professionalized, and corporatized Games. The combined forces won out and the IOC did finally abandon its central principle in 1974 when the amateur clause was revoked from the Charter. What once had the potential for an unalienated sports movement had gradually succumbed to the very forces Coubertin and Marx both decried; today the Olympic athlete embodies the forces of instrumental rationality in the pursuit of the limits of human performance, with the IOC and the Olympic movement as a whole fully embracing commercial and corporate interests. Marx's concept of alienation provides a framework to understand these changes:

> From 1896 onwards, on a growing scale, the athletes of the Games created a product – the Olympic spectacle – that they did not and could not control, under conditions they did not determine, within a system that prevented them from exploring and fulfilling their full human potential through their athletic endeavours.[47]

Conclusion

The careful reader will notice that much of the scholarship summarized here is, strictly speaking, from the discipline of sociology and not history. While it is in fact the case that Marx has been used to a much more significant degree in the discipline of sociology than sports history, and while that fact is certainly not surprising given Marx's iconic status in sociology, part of the goal of this chapter is to propose that Marx's original work and Marxist scholarship as a whole can provide a fertile base upon which to advance scholarship in sports history. The renewed interest in Marx's work in very recent times in particular, but more generally in the last few decades, signals a hopeful rapprochement between sociology and history – the two disciplines can only benefit from one another's attention. The purpose of this chapter has been, first, to introduce Marx's unique theory on the development of capitalist society, and second, to present a summary of important work in sports history and sport sociology that has attempted to understand sport through Marx's unique 'lens'.

In concluding the postscript to the second edition of his important *Class, Sports, and Social Development*, Richard Gruneau makes a challenge for sociologists and historians alike to 'write theoretically-informed histories that are sensitive to multiple and uneven paths of change, histories where the structuring principles of the field of sporting practice at any given time are recognized to involve complex sets of dominant, residual, and emergent tendencies'.[48] While theoretical frameworks that attempt to understand the role of sport in society and history will undoubtedly continue to become more complex and diverse, Marx's original insights will continue to play an important – hopefully *increasingly* important – role in the development of those frameworks.

Notes

1 Karl, Marx, 'The German Ideology', in Robert C. Tucker, ed., *The Marx-Engels Reader* (New York: W.W. Norton & Company, 1972), 118. The full text reads: 'If in all ideology men and their circumstances appear upside-down as in a *camera obscura*, this phenomenon arises just as much from their historical life-process as the inversion of objects on the retina does from their physical life-process'.

2 Ben Carrington and Ian McDonald, eds, *Marxism, Cultural Studies and Sport* (London and New York: Routledge, 2009).

3 See Rob Beamish, 'Karl Marx's Enduring Legacy for the Sociology of Sport', in Joseph Maguire and Kevin Young, eds, *Theory, Sport & Society* (Amsterdam: JAI, 2002), 25–26.

4 Beamish, 'Karl Marx's Enduring Legacy', 25–39.

5 Beamish, 'Karl Marx's Enduring Legacy'; see also Rob Beamish, 'The Making of the Manifesto', *Socialist Register* (1998), 218–39.

6 Karl Marx, 'Thesis on Feuerbach', in Tucker, ed., *The Marx-Engels Reader*, 109.

7 Rob Beamish, 'Understanding Labor as a Concept for the Study of Sport', *Sociology of Sport Journal* 2, (1985), 359.

8 Karl Marx, *Capital, Vol I* (New York: Vintage Books, 1977), 133.

9 Beamish, 'Understanding Labour'.

10 Marx, *Capital*, 283–84.

11 Karl Marx, Preface to *A Contribution to the Critique of Political Economy*, in Tucker, *The Marx-Engels Reader*, 4.

12 Karl Marx, 'Letters: Marx to P.V. Annenkov in Paris', in *Karl Marx and Frederick Engels: Selected Works (Vol. 1)* (Moscow: Progress Publishers, 1977), 518.

13 On Marx's theory of history, see G.A. Cohen, *Karl Marx's Theory of History: A Defence* (Princeton, NJ: Princeton University Press, 1978).

14 Karl Marx and Frederick Engels, *Manifesto of the Communist Party* (New York: International Publishers, 1948), 9.

15 See the Introduction by Ernest Mandel to Marx, *Capital*, 11–86. See also Donald McQuarie, 'Marxism and Neo-Marxism', in Donald McQuarie, ed., *Readings in Contemporary Sociological Theory: From Modernity to Post-Modernity* (Englewood Cliffs, NJ: Prentice Hall, 1995), 114–23 for a clear introduction.

16 Karl Marx, 'Economic and Philosophical Manuscripts', in T.B. Bottomore, ed., *Karl Marx: Early Writings* (New York: McGraw Hill, 1963), 124–25.

17 Marx and Engels, *Manifesto*, 14–15; Frederick Engels, 'Ludwig Feuerbach and the End of Classical German Philosophy', in *Karl Marx and Frederick Engels: Selected Works (Vol. 3)* (Moscow: Progress Publishers, 1977), 369.

18 Marx, *Capital*, 929.

19 In addition to Carrington and McDonald, *Marxism*, 2, see McQuarie, *Readings*, 3–5.

20 Carrington and McDonald, *Marxism*, 2.

21 Bero Rigauer, *Sport and Work* (New York: Columbia University Press, 1981); Gerhard Vinnai, *Football Mania* (London: Ocean Books, 1973); Jack Scott, *The Athletic Revolution* (New York: The Free Press, 1971); Paul Hoch, *Rip Off the Big Game: The Exploitation of Sport by the Power Elite* (New York: Doubleday & Company Anchor Books, 1972); Jean-Marie Brohm, *Sport: A Prison of Measured Time* (London: Ink Links, 1978). There are a few other texts that should rightly fall within this first phase, but they are ones never translated into English and I have not included them for this reason. For a full list and summary, see Beamish, 'Karl Marx's Enduring Legacy', 27–33. See also Bero Rigauer, 'Marxist Theories', in Jay Coakley and Eric Dunning, eds, *Handbook of Sports Studies* (London: Sage, 2000), 28–47.

22 Beamish, 'Karl Marx's Enduring Legacy', 27–33.

23 Brohm, *Sport: A Prison*, 55.

24 See, for example, Brohm, *Sport: A Prison*, 18–29, 56–57, 59–64, 66–76, and passim.

25 Carrington and McDonald, *Marxism*, 3.

26 John Hargreaves, *Sport, Power and Culture* (Cambridge: Polity Press, 1986); Jennifer Hargreaves, *Sporting Females* (London: Routledge, 1994); Alan Tomlinson, *The Game's Up: Essays in the Cultural Analysis of Sport, Leisure and Popular Culture* (Aldershot: Arena, 1999); Garry Whannel, *Blowing the Whistle: The Politics of Sport* (London: Pluto Press, 1983) and *Fields in Vision* (London:

Routledge, 1992); David Rowe, *Popular Cultures: Rock Music, Sport and the Politics of Pleasure* (London: Sage, 1995).

27 Carrington and McDonald, *Marxism*, 4.

28 Richard Gruneau, *Class, Sports, and Social Development* (Amherst: The University of Massachusetts Press, 1983) and *Class, Sports, and Social Development* (Champaign, IL: Human Kinetics, 1999). Other essays mentioned by Carrington and McDonald are Rob Beamish, 'Central Issues in the Materialist Study of Sport as Cultural Practice', in Susan Greendorfer and Andrew Yiannakis, eds, *Sociology of Sport: Diverse Perspectives* (New York: Leisure Press, 1981), 38–55; 'Sport and the Logic of Capitalism', in Hart Cantelon and Richard Gruneau, eds, *Sport, Culture and the Modern State* (Toronto: University of Toronto Press, 1982), 141–97; and 'Understanding Labor'; Cantelon and Gruneau, *Sport, Culture*; and Alan Ingham, 'Sport, Hegemony and the Logic of Capitalism: Response to Hargreaves and Beamish', in Cantelon and Gruneau, *Sport, Culture*, 198–208. Alan Ingham's 'From Public Issue to Personal Trouble: Well-Being and the Fiscal Crisis of the State', *Sociology of Sport Journal* 2, (1985): 43–55 should also be included in this list. The latter article has been widely cited in the sociology literature since it was published.

29 Richard S. Gruneau, 'Modernization or Hegemony: Two Views on Sport and Social Development', in Jean Harvey and Hart Cantelon, eds, *Not Just a Game: Essays in Canadian Sport Sociology* (Ottawa: University of Ottawa Press, 1988), 9–32.

30 Gruneau, 'Modernization or Hegemony', 11.

31 Benedict Anderson's *Imagined Communities: Reflections on the Origins and Spread of Nationalism* (London: Verso, 1995) is a widely cited source in terms of the development and spread of nationalism as both a geo-political and interpersonal entity.

32 Gruneau, 'Modernization or Hegemony', 10–12.

33 Gruneau, 'Modernization or Hegemony', 12–14.

34 Gruneau, 'Modernization or Hegemony', 16–18. On the important Marxist and conflict theoretical critique of structural-functionalist accounts in sociology, see Ian Ritchie, 'Sociological Theories of Sport', in Jane Crossman, ed., *Canadian Sport Sociology*, second edn (Toronto: Thomson/Nelson, 2008), 21–39 and McQuarie, *Readings*, 5.

35 It should also be noted that Gruneau goes on to critique the Marxist approach to sports history as well, for some of its own limitations and, in particular, to favour the concept of hegemony. However, this concept, as well as critiques of Marxism, are discussed elsewhere in this volume, including in Booth's first chapter, so I will not discuss these issues here.

36 Bruce Kidd, *The Struggle for Canadian Sport* (Toronto: University of Toronto Press, 1996).

37 Rob Beamish, 'Marxism, Alienation and Coubertin's Olympic Project', in Carrington and McDonald, *Marxism*, 88–105.

38 Beamish, 'Marxism, Alienation', 88–91.

39 Beamish, 'Marxism, Alienation', 91–3. See the discussion earlier in this chapter about the importance of labour as a condition of human existence and potential for Marx.

40 Beamish, 'Marxism, Alienation', 93.

41 Beamish, 'Marxism, Alienation', 93–5.

42 Beamish, 'Marxism, Alienation', 95.

43 See Coubertin's extensive writings in Pierre de Coubertin, *Olympism: Selected Writings* (Lausanne: International Olympic Committee, 2000).

44 Beamish, 'Marxism, Alienation'. See also Rob Beamish and Ian Ritchie, 'From Chivalrous "Brothers-in-Arms" to the Eligible Athlete: Changed Principles and the IOC's Banned Substance List', *International Review for the Sociology of Sport* 39, 4 (2004), 355–71; and Rob Beamish and Ian Ritchie, *Fastest, Highest, Strongest: A Critique of High-performance Sport* (London: Routledge, 2006), 11–30.

45 Coubertin, *Olympism*, 581.

46 See Beamish and Ritchie, *Fastest, Highest, Strongest*.

47 Beamish, 'Marxism, Alienation', 98.

48 Gruneau, *Class, Sports, and Social Development* (1999), 127.

6 Sociology

Louise Mansfield and Dominic Malcolm

History, sociology and historical sociology

If the common sense definition of history is 'the study of past events', the equivalent definition of sociology might be 'the study of the development, structure and functioning of human society'. Adding the word 'sport' at an appropriate place serves to define the respective sub-disciplines. These definitions imply that the major distinction between history and sociology is temporal; the former encompassing the actions and experiences of our ancestors, the latter focused on contemporary experiences or, at most, how the social world came to take its contemporary form.

Of course, there probably isn't a single mainstream historian or sociologist who would want to have these dictionary-like definitions rigidly applied, let alone those historians or sociologists whose common interest in sport draws them together into interdisciplinary sports studies. We would argue that every snapshot in time captured in empirical research, be it last week or last century, can only be understood as the abstraction of broader social processes. Yet within the field of sports studies the time-orientated distinction between history and sociology has been increasingly blurred by a number of texts, edited collections and journals (i.e. *Football Studies*, *Olympika*, *Soccer and Society*, *Sport in Society*) which are explicitly interdisciplinary, as well as the increasing propensity of sports history journals such as *Sporting Traditions* and *Journal of Sport History* to publish sociologically informed analyses of sport. More recent debates about the nature and state of sports history, the consequences of the 'cultural turn' for history scholars and sociologists of sport and specifically the impact of postmodernism on sports history have also led to critical dialogues about the relationship between time and the interpretation and explanation of sport in social life.[1]

The central similarity between the sociology of sport and sports history relates to the importance of context. Douglas Booth argues that sports historians can broadly be categorized as re-constructionists (who believe we can examine the past as it actually was), constructionists (who believe evidence needs to be interpreted using questions like how and why), and deconstructionists (poststructuralist and postmodern scholars who see historical data as fragmented and partial).[2] Martin Polley similarly proposes a *past-narrative-analysis* framework for categorizing sports historiography in which *past* refers to the evidence of events involving people in previous time frames; *narrative* concerns the use of that evidence to tell a story; and *analysis* examines sport in its 'full cultural context' relative to the society in which it took place (constructionists in Booth's schema).[3] Within the sociology of sport, Coakley alludes to the importance of examining social life '*in context*', while in *Sport, Culture and Society*, Jarvie similarly argues that 'sport must be properly located within the social, cultural and historical context in which it moves or is located'.[4] The parallels between these sociological approaches and the analysis/constructionist historians illustrate how indistinct are the aims of sports history and the sociology of sport.

Thus the divide between sociology and history can be too sharply drawn. Each discipline seeks to avoid present-centred understandings of sport, both in the temporal and spatial sense. Each discipline critically examines 'common sense' understandings of sport and seeks to understand social life in terms of complex relations of power marked by nuances of competing and overlapping social processes. Consequently, 'there can be no relationship between [sociology and history] because in terms of their fundamental preoccupations, history and sociology are and always have been the same thing'.[5] As Goudsblom observes, 'the divorce of history and sociology is detrimental to both: It makes historians needlessly allergic to the very idea of structures, and sociologists afraid of dealing with single events'.[6] Moreover, in sport science and kinesiology departments all over the world, sports history and the sociology of sport have shared a marginalization in relation to the natural science disciplines as a consequence of economic and political developments and paradigmatic conflict.[7]

Having introduced the case for an interdisciplinary approach, or socio-historical studies, it is important to reiterate the opening point of this chapter; that in academic and everyday thinking history and sociology are distinct disciplines. History and sociology invariably exist as separate university departments. Even within multi-disciplinary sports science departments, where historians often teach sociological aspects of sport and sociologists deliver history modules, there are no more than a handful of scholars who would *not* see themselves as primarily belonging to one school. Moreover, within existing debates about interdisciplinary relations there is a strong element of advocacy for the way individuals would *like* the two disciplines to be orientated, as opposed to accurate descriptions of the way they are. While cultural studies and Eliasian scholars have been at the forefront of attempts to 'blend the sociological with the historical',[8] some sociologists influenced by Bourdieu, symbolic interactionism, poststructuralism and postmodernism (discussed in the conclusion) have been at best dismissive of, and at worst antithetical to, a diachronic approach. Debates within both sociology and history can often, although not always, reinforce distinct disciplinary identities and reflect power struggles within the broader intellectual sphere.[9]

Indeed, on a 'practical' level the traditional and most clearly expressed division between sports historians and sociologists of sport relates to the role of theory. Holt neatly summarizes this point:

> Sociologists frequently complain that historians lack a conceptual framework for their research, while historians tend to feel social theorists require them to compress the diversity of the past into artificially rigid categories and dispense with empirical verification of their theories.[10]

While an accurate assessment of the field in the late 1980s, more recent developments, particularly in sports history, have made the divisions between the two sub-disciplines less marked in recent years. These processes of convergence (and divergence) will form the central theme of this chapter. In order to do this we first chart some of the major historically orientated works conducted within the sociology of sport field, before identifying some of the more theoretically informed and critical sports histories produced in recent years which offer theoretical and methodological possibilities for the future direction of historical studies of sport. We then investigate the relations between the two disciplines by examining the substance of the critical debates between sports historians and sociologists of sport before concluding by turning our attention to the future prospects of these increasingly interdependent areas.

Sociological perspectives on the history of sport

Sociologists using a variety or combination of Eliasian, Marxist, hegemony, modernization, Weberian, feminist, cultural studies and postmodern theories, and exploring a range of topics including social class, race/ethnicity, gender, imperialism, nationalism and commercialism, have made significant contributions to the historical analysis of sport. Not all sociologists agree about either the desirability of an historical approach or what counts as a good sports history. Debates have centred on the role of theory, the relative merits of interdisciplinary sports histories versus sports history as a distinct academic discipline, and epistemological self-reflection emerging in the context of postmodernist critiques and deconstructionist approaches to history. Before considering these debates we provide a selective overview of what we take to be some of the most significant historically orientated texts produced by sociologists of sport.

Eric Dunning's work began in the 1960s and was the first to emphasize the importance of examining sport from an historical sociological, or developmental, perspective. Dunning and Sheard's *Barbarians, Gentlemen and Players* is one of the most significant sociological texts on the historical development of sport and uses an Eliasian perspective to illustrate how rugby emerged from a tradition of violent, local, informal folk games in pre-industrial Britain. Rugby developed in contradistinction to football, driven by class differences and conflict and refined in public schools in the 19th century. The sport's development into a unified national game was marked by the emergence of the Rugby Football Union (RFU), and the subsequent bifurcation into union and league codes as class and regional tensions re-emerged.[11]

Other research variously employing aspects of Elias's work has contributed to historical understandings of sport. Some are explicitly historical in the sense of locating studies 'in the past' and/or interrogating primary and secondary historical material,[12] while others have attempted to provide a sociology imbued with *developmental thinking*, involving consideration of the character of structured processes over time and space.[13] Dunning et al.'s *The Sports Process* is particularly notable for its advocacy of historical/developmental and cross-cultural analysis and its combination of sociologists' and historians' work.[14] Grant Jarvie is also worthy of mention here in that his career illustrates the liminal qualities of the two sub-disciplines. Jarvie completed a PhD under Dunning, having previously studied for a sociology masters in Canada. His *Highland Games*, and *Scottish Sport and the Making of the Nation* (co-edited with political historian Graham Walker), have received considerable critical acclaim within sports history.[15] His election as Chair of the British Society of Sports History (BSSH) illustrates his general acceptance in both sub-disciplines.

There have, however, been many sociological histories of sport that have drawn on social theory other than figurational sociology. Advancing the cause of an historical agenda for the sociology of sport have been scholars emphasizing the importance of cultural studies perspectives for understanding sport as a cultural phenomenon marked by processes of social development. While Richard Gruneau might not strictly define his work as cultural studies, rather arguing for a reformulated Marxist approach, he never-theless challenges sociologists of sport to understand the ways in which the personal issues of people involved in sport in any particular time frame are connected to changes in wider social formations (cf. Wright-Mills). Two editions of *Sport, Class and Social Development* provide a theoretical analysis of the historical development of sport in Canada and the synthesis between the historical and theoretical, interpretive cultural analysis and political economy, and also provided the framework for his co-authored *Hockey Night in Canada*.[16]

Before and since then several scholars have linked sport to historical context and the broader cultural studies paradigm. Alan Ingham and John Loy's *Sport in Social Development* provided a collection of work that emphasized the importance of historically orientated studies of social, political and cultural analyses of sport.[17] Both John Hargreaves' *Sport, Power and Culture* and Jennifer Hargreaves' *Sporting Females* illustrate the significance of combining cultural studies and hegemony theory with historical approaches in under-standing sport as a social phenomenon.[18] John Hargreaves examines sport as a site for the expression of class, gender and ethnic relations, shedding light on the sport–education dynamic and commercialization of sport. Combining the concept of hegemony with a feminist sensibility, Jennifer Hargreaves analyses the connections between sport, gender relations and capitalist social relations, exploring changes in the sport–gender dynamic since the 19th century and the wider social conditions under which ambiguous and contradictory developments in women's sports have been made.

John Sugden emphasizes that his *Boxing and Society* is not a social history of the sport, and it would also be inaccurate to locate his work solely within cultural studies, but his combination of ethnographic research with a discussion of boxing in ancient and medieval societies and the popularization of bare-knuckle prize fighting in Regency Britain, illustrates an historical sensibility and allows for a comparison of traditions of dispute resolution via violent physical means and boxing's role in the development of physical skill for attack and self-defence.[19] Sugden's historical orientation is underscored in his work with Alan Bairner on sport in divided Ireland,[20] and with Alan Tomlinson on the global politics of world football. In *FIFA and the Contest for World Football* Sugden and Tomlinson identify and connect social development with the emergence and develop-ment of football to explain the ways that key personnel in the Fédération Internationale de Football Association (FIFA), the international governing body of football, have enabled the emergence of a global political economy of football dominated by corporate sponsorship, market forces and media relations.[21]

While different in their particular theoretical orientations, those singled out so far share a commitment to understanding sport and society through an historical approach. As sociologists what distinguishes these authors is their call for the importance of historical analysis. More or less explicitly these authors also share a critique of 'traditional', more descriptive, past or re-constructionist forms of sports history. Some use secondary sources as the point of departure for their own primary historical data gathering, while others essentially construct their arguments through the theorization of historiographical work.

Of course, a significant number of sports historians have also been critical of what Vamplew has described as the 'chronicle and numbers' approach to sports history,[22] and have produced analyses which sociologists have commended for their more explicitly theory-driven focus. Here we have in mind the work of, among others, Allen Guttmann, Richard Holt, Stephen Jones, Kathleen McCrone and Patricia Vertinsky.[23] More recent critiques of a-theoretical and anti-intellectual sports history have come from those influenced by debates in mainstream history regarding the impact of postmodernism and the cultural turn on the methodological and theoretical state of sports history. Such work calls for understandings of sport and society that are, simultaneously, historically orientated, theoretically informed and sensitive to the complex intersections of a range of social structures, processes and centres of power. Steve Pope's *The New American Sport History* emphasizes the importance of critical analyses of the development of sport in relation to broader social and cultural issues.[24] Indeed, Pope's approach to sports history is defined by a critical perspective of where sport has come from, the meanings of sport in contemporary society and considerations of the future of sport in society. His deconstructionist approach is central, for example, in his comparative analysis of stylized performances of jazz musicians and black basketball players in American culture in the early 20th century in which he rejects the notion of 'race' for its essentialist implications and focuses on the production and reproduction of the complex histories of basketball and jazz.[25] In a similar vein, David Andrews' work signals the centrality of the connection between past, present and future events, products and services in understanding the consequences of late capitalism for contemporary sport.[26] His varied work emphasizes that sports history is, perhaps, one of the few areas of scholarly activity that can help us understand the so-called cultural banality of 'postmodern' sport, which is marked by the dominance of commercial motivation and political and historical amputation. The publication of Murray Phillips' *Deconstructing Sport History* provides one of the most recent collections to address the postmodern challenge to sports history, arguing for a deconstructionist perspective which frees the researcher from the belief that the past is unchanging and set in stone, and embraces a critical reflexive approach to the relationship between interpretation and explanation.[27] Jeff Hill has perhaps been the most prominent British sports historian to call for sports historians to embrace these theoretical developments. While by no means a postmodernist himself, his recent empirical work has clearly been influenced by the epistemological critique of Derrida, Baudrillard and others.[28]

There are, of course, many other sociologists writing sports history and theoretically orientated sports historians who we could have mentioned. Suffice to say, sociologists of sport and sports historians have both produced some important research that has, at times, been well received in the other sub-discipline. However, at times the reception of each others' work has been more critical. In the following section we address the debates and critiques that have been aired.

Sports history and sociology of sport: critiques, counter-critiques and points of debate

While the traditional division between sports historians and sociologists of sport has related to the role of theory, tensions between the two sub-disciplines have not been static. This section attempts to chart the development of interdisciplinary relations over the last 20 years. Though not wishing to portray them as temporally discrete, we suggest that the way sports historians approach sociological work can be categorized in three ways: an initial approach which stressed the distinctiveness of the disciplines; a subsequent recognition of convergence; and a more recent resumption of hostilities which, while appearing to re-draw discipline boundaries, actually belies some of the significant developments in sports history in recent years which we charted in the previous section.

Sports history and the sociology of sport developed somewhat in tandem. The publication of the first sociology of sport monographs coincided with such landmark sports history texts as Guttmann's *From Ritual to Record*, Mason's *Association Football and English Society, 1863–1915* and Mangan's *Athleticism in the Victorian and Edwardian Public Schools*.[29] At this early stage relations were relatively harmonious (in print at least), with researchers developing a sense of solidarity from the shared experience of attempting to convince their parent discipline of the legitimacy of their focus on sport.

As noted, the historically orientated texts produced by sociologists contained more or less explicit critiques of existing, largely a-theoretical, historical research. Sociologists, coming from a discipline with a longer and more marked tradition of paradigmatic conflict saw little out of the ordinary in overtly critical engagement, but by the late 1980s sports historians began to fight back and the divergence of the sub-disciplines became more pronounced. It may be that this development stemmed from the relative maturing of sports history in Britain (the BSSH and the *British Journal of Sports History* were established in 1981 and 1984 respectively), or from the increased significance of sports studies in the United Kingdom in lieu of the political crisis over football hooliganism, but it was certainly the case that these debates were initially raised in texts written by UK historians which included the analysis of the contemporary sporting scene. The movement into territory traditionally seen as the sociologist's preserve behove historians to address competing explanations and thus the theories which underpinned them. It also provided an opportunity for retaliation against sociologist's criticisms of history and an evaluation of the two discipline's relative contributions to knowledge. While Mason (implicitly) and Holt (explicitly) both acknowledged the interdependence of history and sociology and the desirability of a cross-fertilization, they took positions which effectively asserted the distinctiveness, if not the superiority, of sports history.[30]

Mason's critique addressed two sociological works, Thorstein Veblen's *The Theory of the Leisure Class* and Bero Rigauer's *Sport und Arbeit* (translated as *Sport and Work*).[31] Mason provides only a tacit critique of Veblen, citing the pre-1914 workers' sports movement as a counter to Veblen's bias towards the elite, but he treats Rigauer more harshly, arguing that Rigauer fails to capture the complexities of the real world. Mason's underlying view is exposed in his dismissal of sociological theorizing as, 'a worthwhile exercise if for no other reason than that it compels at least some of those heavily involved in sport to look closely at the assumptions which they make about it'. He then proceeds to a 'much more concrete', and thus in his view, more adequate level of analysis.[32]

Horne et al. share our critical reading of Mason. They argue that elsewhere Mason has 'referred somewhat condescendingly' to sociological theorization, has reduced the sociologist to 'a figure of fun, a naïve gossip' and, in failing to acknowledge his own reliance on such theories, produces a 'bogus' and 'disingenuous' critique.[33] The intent to separate rather than integrate the sub-disciplines is further apparent in Mason's selection of theories to review. Mason is highly selective in his evidence, overlooking the aforementioned sociology texts which have had the greatest impact on sports history. In a book titled *Sport in Britain* Mason's focus on Veblen's analysis of late 19th-century American society seems obtuse. By failing also to acknowledge the (then) recent publication of critiques by leading British sociologists of sport that highlight similar deficiencies in Rigauer's work,[34] Mason effectively critiques a sociological 'straw man'.

Holt's discussion of sociological theory has similarly been counter-critiqued but perhaps with less justification. Horne et al. summarize Holt's position vis-à-vis sociology as follows: 'The charge is obscurantism, then, plus finding the facts to fit the theory' but this time it is Horne et al. who (partly) misrepresent and lampoon the argument of their opponent through selective reading and misrepresentation.[35] Holt's central point – that complex and esoteric language limits the impact of sociological work – is, after all, a critique which sociologists of sport level at each other. Conversely Maguire merely regrets that Holt's 'laudable' call for dialogue is 'tucked away in an appendix'.[36] While critical in parts, Holt's call for sports history to embrace social theory illustrates a qualitative difference from Mason.

Unlike Mason, Holt embraces various sociological analyses of sport, and especially those which are historically orientated. Holt's discussion also differs in the extent of its praise of sociology, identifying in particular how sociological theory has clarified historians' understanding of concepts such as class. He argues that Dunning and Sheard have produced 'probably the most detailed and important contribution to the discussion of British Amateurism',[37] compliments Gruneau's synthesis of theory and historical research, and identifies a 'convergence' between his own work and the classic problems in the sociology of the city.[38] He further stresses that historians should recognize that their selection of research themes rests on subjective assumptions and 'hard to pin down' 'hunches'. He may even have Mason in mind when he criticizes some historians for their cursory and dismissive treatment of sociological theories.[39]

Despite such positive comments, Holt remains critical of sociology, in particular *Barbarians, Gentlemen and Players* which he sees as overly 'schematic' and John Hargreaves' *Sport, Power and Culture* which he describes as too theoretically 'neat'. While not wishing to embrace Holt's critique in its entirety it is interesting to note that the sociology of sport has since embraced many of the areas which Holt identified as lacking. In retrospect, Holt's comments regarding the importance of sexual identity (and masculinity in particular), local and regional identities, and the role of sport as a source of sociability (cf. Bourdieu) seem particularly prescient, for such themes have become increasingly prominent in the sociology of sport. While Holt remains committed to a position which extols the merits of history relative to sociology, his call is for historians to show healthy respect for the concepts and methods of sociology. Centrally he contends that sports historians will find dialogue productive.

The cross-fertilization of history and sociology of sport has become more prominent since the 1990s. All the major sociology of sport textbooks now devote chapters to the historical contextualization of contemporary sport. Sports historians, as we have seen, also pay greater heed to social theory, and acknowledge the contribution of sociology to historical thinking. Nancy Struna cites the work of John Hargreaves alongside Richard Holt, Stephen Jones, Wray Vamplew and Brian Stoddart, without making any distinction between the quality of, or the premises underlying, their work. She also acknowledges historians' debt to feminist sociologists (Jennifer Hargreaves, Ann Hall and Nancy Theberge), and praises C.L.R. James, for stimulating research on the structure and meanings of sport in the Caribbean, and Victoria Paraschak for work highlighting how native peoples have negotiated the imposition of (Western) modern sport.[40] Martin Polley similarly singles out Jennifer Hargreaves and Dunning and Sheard for praise, cites the influence of 'concepts and models' from figurational sociology, and credits sociology more generally with fostering the development of oral history research.[41] Martin Johnes acknowledges his own debt to postmodernism and the influence of Gramscian cultural studies in sports history more generally.[42]

Some sociologists, notably Maguire and Jarvie, have gone as far as to make the case that the sub-disciplines (and indeed sport geography) should be more co-ordinated in their efforts, if not actually fused as one. To underscore their position, Maguire and Jarvie demonstrate that just as good history should be judged according to '[a] sophisticated grasp of theory … intertwined with substantive research', so good sociology exhibits 'the mutual contamination of theory and evidence'.[43] Writing on his own, however, Maguire has been critical of historians' research on football spectator disorder, citing limited sources, a failure to question media sources, and the lack of a theoretical model by which evidence can be evaluated. The thrust of Maguire's argument, however, is that there are areas within the sub-disciplines where research is barely distinguishable and thus disciplinary convergence is desirable *and* logically possible.[44]

More recently, however, a new wave of debates between the sub-disciplines has arisen, containing elements of increasing antagonism. These debates have focused upon more detailed examinations of empirical 'fact' and their interpretation in light of the broader historical context. Though the first of these appeared in the late 1980s, the majority have appeared in the early 21st century. Interestingly all of these critiques come from British historians and relate to the work of figurational sociologists rather than sociologists per se.

In the first critique of this type, Douglas Reid argued that there is little evidence to support Dunning and Sheard's contention that the aristocracy withdrew from folk football and became more status exclusive in the late 18th and early 19th centuries, thus precipitating the emergence of 'new' sport forms.[45] Robert Lewis subsequently argued that gambling-related football crowd disorder was far more significant than previously imagined, and that differences between 19th-century and contemporary forms of football hooliganism indicate that Dunning et al. were wrong to present a 'continuity thesis' of spectator violence.[46] John Goulstone later argued that Dunning and Sheard's 'public school status-rivalry' thesis was undermined by new historical evidence which showed that a) modern notions of equality in football stemmed from working class forms of the game, and b) the bifurcation of football codes predates codification in the public school.[47] Adrian Harvey similarly critiques the 'public school status-rivalry' thesis, arguing that evidence of football in Sheffield indicates that 'modern forms' of the sport did not necessarily stem directly from the public schools or their former pupils.[48] More recently Tony Collins has suggested that civic rivalries rather than public school rivalries drove the bifurcation of football and rugby and that figurational sociologists' use of the theory of civilizing processes leads to teleological historical analyses.[49] Finally Vamplew argued that Malcolm's work is flawed by factual error and misinterpreted evidence stemming from unchecked secondary sources.[50]

Each of these critiques evoked a response.[51] There is not space here to provide an assessment of these debates; suffice to say, there is little by way of consensus. Their common themes are, however, revealing. Goulstone, Harvey, Collins and Vamplew all argue that (figurational) sociologists lack empirical evidence, Collins, Harvey and Vamplew question the sources used and the accuracy of the representation of evidence, and Collins and Vamplew suggest a failure to contextualize data and historical events. The counter-critiques are similarly characterized by persistent themes. All accuse their historian critics of misrepresenting their arguments, Lewis, Harvey, Collins and Vamplew are all accused of factual inaccuracies, and of using limited or problematic sources and, perhaps most crucially, Lewis, Harvey and Collins are all accused of failing to understand and take account of the context in which primary evidence was generated.

In contrast to the late 1980s therefore, when sports historians and sociologists of sport essentially argued from divergent positions, much of the debate today centres upon commonly accepted premise; *pace* Polley and Jarvie, the need to analyse sport in its wider cultural context. The key difference between historians' critiques of sociological work and sociologists' counter-critiques is that the latter complain that their adversaries have failed to fully understand the underlying theoretical perspective. As important as these concerns are, the existence of so much common terrain is a notable development. Recent debates constitute something of a re-drawing of battle lines between the two sub-disciplines and thus illustrate the legacy of the previous period of convergence during which more established social theories such as Marxism and feminism, if not sociological theories per se, became increasingly, if somewhat implicitly, accepted.

Deconstructing sports history?

We have focused so far on debates between sports historians and sociologists of sport that have been founded on disagreements about the role of theory and interpretation of specific evidence. To an extent, these discussions have centred on the relative merits of re-constructionist and constructionist approaches to history. There is, however, an emerging deconstructionist lens through which histories of sport are being produced. Deconstructionist sports history involves a set of polemics surrounding the state and character of sports history that, as noted previously, is connected to wider debates in the history profession about the postmodern critique of historical practices emerging since the so-called 'cultural turn' in the humanities and social sciences of the late 1960s. This theoretical and methodological moment absorbed and extended an ongoing disillusionment with a view of the important, fixed and transparent nature of historical archives and the quest for objective empiricism in history. The 'turn' saw a shift towards the idea that the historic meaning of any form of representation is partial, dynamic and produced and reproduced in complex social relations that involve the interpretive efforts of the historian.[52]

While contributions might be relatively few in number, debates about the consequences of the cultural turn for sports history began in the 1990s and are significant in understanding the postmodern challenge to re-constructionist and constructionist history. Central to discussions about the 'state' of sports history are questions about the fundamental practices of producing histories of sport. In Phillips' *Deconstructing Sport History* E. H.Carr's seminal question *What is History?* is re-posed as 'what is sports history?' and contributions engage with the kind of epistemological, ontological and methodological reflection already witnessed in the mainstream discipline. The result is a text that challenges a re-constructionist promotion of objective explanations of a fixed past, and critiques constructionist claims for the fundamental importance of theory in understanding the history of sport. It embraces a deconstructionist vision for sports history (and therefore implicitly also sociology) that abandons the idea of objectivity and reflects a consciousness about the multiple cultural causes and consequences in which historical events are produced and reproduced.

A 'deconstructionist consciousness' recognizes that interpretation by both the producers and consumers of ideas are themselves linguistic creations.[53] Historical records can be interpreted in a number of ways and may be read differently by different audiences. Sports histories are, then, a matter of historical production and reproduction and there is a complex web of meaning connected to the culture of sport. In saying this, a cautionary note should be sounded. Particularly problematic is a postmodern view that the world is experienced in fragments of disconnected difference. Such a position tends to drift towards a position of cultural relativism implying that all accounts and claims to knowledge are equally valid; a standpoint that effectively removes the interpretive role of the sociologist or historian leaving no space to critically explore power relations in terms of political and ideological frameworks of analysis. A postmodern perspective that purports the idea that mediated images of sport 'the copy, the "similacrum", the "hyperreality" – is all there is', that sport is simply discourse, denies the involvement of active consumers and producers of sport culture.[54] Having said that, the cultural turn ultimately forces us to revisit the classical sociological debate concerning the role of values and evaluation in understanding sport and society.[55]

The twin challenges of a deconstructionist history are epistemological and ontological. Epistemological doubts are cast upon the methods and theoretical foundation of historical knowledge and ontological questions are raised about the assumptions of historians who claim certain knowledge about the reality of the past. Deconstructionist sports history emphasizes the unstable and partial character of understanding what happened in previous times and the complexity of historical interpretations of socio-cultural life. If the task of the deconstructionist historian is the discovery of a past founded on the assumptions that historical knowledge is always relative and partial, and interpretation is marked by epistemological limitations, there is a degree of dovetailing with the works reviewed in previous sections of this chapter, some of which can be defined in the deconstructionist mode and some which can not. Having said this, it should be noted that the works of Dunning, Jarvie, Gruneau, Sugden, and Jennifer and John Hargreaves cited in this chapter, are closer to the constructionist approach to history than they are to the works of deconstructionist sports historians such as Pope and Phillips. Ontologically the figurational sociologists such as Dunning, Maguire, Malcolm and Sheard, have much more in common with their critics Wray Vamplew and Tony Collins than they do with Philips et al. While arguably the most interesting recent developments in sports history have stemmed from an approach which rests upon understanding the production and reproduction of complex socio-cultural relations through the employment of a 'self-reflexive historical imagination' and which emphasizes a critical analysis of the construction and reconstruction of historical knowledge,[56] these works not only pose challenges to sports history, but to the existing body of historical sociological work.

Sports history and the sociology of sport: the future

While sports history and the sociology of sport have both changed radically since their respective inceptions, and while there is evidence of increasing interdependence and co-operation between the two scholarly communities (e.g. ISHPES and ISSA's co-hosting of an international conference in Copenhagen in 2007), they remain distinct and, at times, competitive sub-disciplines with their internal interests and tensions. As a consequence of remaining somewhat peripheral to their respective mainstreams, elements of both subject communities have promoted interdisciplinary studies based upon their shared empirical focus on sport. In part this cross-fertilization of ideas might result from the fact that historians and sociologists of sport tend to work alongside each other in sports science departments. In part it might also stem from the perceived weaknesses within the each field which lead scholars to look 'sideways' into parallel sub-disciplines for empirical evidence and theoretical inspiration. Some, though on the basis of our overview we would argue a very small minority, advocate a sports studies approach because they are convinced of the inherent value of an interdisciplinarity. However, regardless of motive, it is undoubtedly true that sports historians and sociologists of sport have increasingly become convinced of the value of understanding each other's literature and debates. There has also been a clear convergence over the importance and use of theory, with the developments in sports history discussed above paralleled by the relative decline of largely empirical, quantitative and descriptive studies in the sociology of sport. Finally we might also point to a convergence in the willingness to engage in cross-disciplinary critical debates, and indeed in the style in which those debates are conducted.

Yet sports history and the sociology of sport remain divided in many crucial respects. The majority of historians and sociologists of sport still crave recognition from their parent discipline, value publication in their respective 'mainstream' journals more highly than they do publication in the journals of their own associations, and covet employment in history or sociology departments above sports science departments. These factors both underscore and fuel sub-disciplinary divergence. One significant conclusion that can be drawn from this review is that in sharp contrast to the impressive developments in sports history, many inspired by sociology and social theory more generally, the historical sociology of sport is, itself, fast becoming history. For all that an historical sensibility has become part of the habitus of the sociologist of sport in the 21st century, the number of sociologists of sport who now unquestioningly accept the value of an historical contextualization seems inversely proportional to the number actually engaged in historically orientated research. For instance, one rarely hears an historical sociological paper at an international sociology of sport conference. Our selection of the most significant historically orientated texts produced by sociologists of sport contains nothing published in the third millennium and, if ordered chronologically, would probably also chart sociologists' increasing reliance on secondary rather than primary historical data and a shift from historical analysis as central to merely contextual.

Indeed it is particularly ironic that the very epistemological and ontological debates which have re-invigorated sports history could be said to have been partly responsible for the decline of the historical sociology of sport. In concentrating on fragmented and fluid identities, postmodernist sociologists of sport argue that individualized, commercialized and mediatized sports forms are emerging and have focused on the transgression of boundaries in sport, between male and female, homosexual and heterosexual, the 'natural' body and the cyborg. Work has also examined the excesses of postmodern society, such as exercise addiction, and on the concomitant decline of the 'sport for health' paradigm and rise of notions of 'sport for pleasure'. Postmodernist sociologists of sport might respectfully nod in the direction of their colleagues in sports history who share their theoretical orientation, but show no inclination to contribute empirically. In this respect the two sub-disciplines seem to be embarking on a process of divergence.

What kind of relationship might exist between sports history and the sociology of sport in future? Logically there seem to be three possibilities: an antagonistic relationship in which the sub-disciplines work largely autonomously and dismiss each other's intellectual advances; a collaborative relationship where scholars embrace the research produced in both their own and the other sub-discipline; or the possibility suggested by Maguire in which the two fuse, and essentially become one disciplinary paradigm.

For us, the first possibility would be both the least likely and least desirable. Where historians have engaged with social theory, considerable and irreversible knowledge gains have been made. Perhaps due to the overarching political goal of female advancement, the cross-fertilization of the disciplines is most complete among feminist historians and sociologists. Hargreaves and Vertinsky's recent collaboration is in some ways remarkable; one of the first texts co-edited by a leading sociologist of sport and a leading sports historian.[57] The collaboration of Beckles and Stoddart similarly shows a shared commitment among sociologists and historians to what might broadly be termed a cultural studies approach.[58] It is inconceivable that that clock will be turned back, either in terms of historians' appreciation of theory or sociologists' historical sensibilities.

The likelihood of the third scenario being realized is also, as Maguire himself admits, 'relatively slight'.[59] In part this stems from philosophical differences. For the kind of fusion Maguire advocates to come into being, significant traditions within sociology of sport and sports history would need to disappear, or at least be significantly marginalized. Moreover, while one could envisage sports history increasingly drifting in a more theoretical (and therefore sociological) direction, given the current ascendancy of the natural sciences within academia and the funding implications this entails, it seems unlikely that the sociology of sport will move closer to the humanities model and history in particular. There are many pressures for sociologists of sport to become more applied and the greater penetration of management and policy perspectives in the sociology of sport is further evidence of a momentum which is likely to keep historians and sociologists of sport apart.

This leaves the middle possibility – a growing interdependence of sports history and the sociology of sport – as both the most likely and the most desirable future. If the sub-disciplines are to learn from each other, it behoves both sets of academics not only to use conciliatory rather than divisive language in their critical debates, but also to embrace the 'best' work within the other discipline (as opposed to Mason's attack on straw men). More particularly, each needs to recognize that that is what they are doing. Sociologists should welcome instances of historians engaging with social theory not only because this is what sociologists advocate they should do, but also because there are many historians who still do not engage with theory. Historians should similarly commend sociologists who undertake developmental analyses for this similarly shows the influence of their discipline upon another. Most historians simply ignore much sociological work which is not historically orientated, and most sociologists simply ignore historical work which, *pace* Polley, concentrates on a narrative of past events rather than an analysis of broader cultural context. Paradoxically, it is the areas on which historians and sociologists are silent that are the areas which historical sociologists and theory-sensitive historians find least productive. Most of the sub-disciplinary conflict occurs in those areas where historians and sociologists attempt similar kinds of analysis.

If our overriding goal is the development of more adequate understanding of the past (and present), a fundamental principle of future relations between sports history and the sociology of sport, we would suggest, should be an outward looking, open and genuine attempt to understand and empathize with our proponents in the competing disciplines. If our overriding goal is the more prosaic desire simply to survive in the face of the considerable challenges posed by both our parent disciplines and within sports science, then the recognition of our interdependence and common interests may also be tactically astute.

Notes

1 J. Nauright, '"The End of Sports History"? From Sports History to Sports Studies', *Sporting Traditions* 16, 1 (1999), 5–13; S. Pope, ed., *The New American Sport History: Recent Approaches and Perspectives* (Urbana: University of Illinois Press, 1997); M. Phillips, ed., *Deconstructing Sport History: A Postmodern Analysis* (New York: SUNY Press, 2005).

2 D. Booth, *The Field: Truth and Fiction in Sport History* (London: Routledge, 2005).

3 M. Polley, *Sports History: A Practical Guide* (Basingstoke: Palgrave Macmillan, 2007), 8–9.

4 J. Coakley, *Sport in Society: Issues and Controversies* (Boston, MA: McGraw-Hill, 2006), 4; G. Jarvie, *Sport, Culture and Society* (London: Routledge, 2006), 61.

5 P. Abrams, *Historical Sociology* (Wells, UK: Open Books, 1982), x.

6 J. Goudsblom, *Sociology in the Balance* (Oxford: Blackwell, 1977), 136.

7 D. Booth, 'Sport History: What can be Done?', *Sport, Education and Society* 2, 2 (1997), 191–204; S. Pope, 'Sport History: Into the 21st Century', *Journal of Sport History* 25, 2 (1998), i–ix.

8 J. Horne, A. Tomlinson and G. Whannel, 'Interpreting the Growth of Sports: Debates in History and Theory', in J. Horne, A. Tomlinson and G. Whannel, eds, *Understanding Sport: An Introduction to the Sociological and Cultural Analysis of Sport* (London: Routledge, 1999), 73.

9 J. Maguire, 'Common Ground? Links Between Sports History, Sports Geography and the Sociology of Sport', *Sporting Traditions* 12, 1 (1995), 3–25.

10 R. Holt, *Sport and the British* (Oxford: Oxford University Press, 1989) 357.

11 E. Dunning and K. Sheard, *Barbarians, Gentlemen and Players: A Sociological Study of the Development of Rugby Football* (Oxford: Martin Robertson, 1979 / London: Routledge, 2005).

12 For example, C. Brookes, *English Cricket: The Game and its Players through the Ages* (London: Weidenfeld and Nicolson, 1978); E. Dunning, P. Murphy and J. Williams, *The Roots of Football Hooliganism: An Historical and Sociological Study* (London: Routledge, 1988); J. Maguire, 'Images of Manliness and Competing Ways of Living in Late Victorian and Edwardian Britain', *British Journal of Sport History* 3, 3 (1986), 265–87; D. Malcolm, 'Cricket and Civilizing Processes: A Response to Stokvis', *International Review for the Sociology of Sport* 37, 1 (2002), 37–57; K. Sheard, 'Aspects of Boxing in the Western "Civilizing Process"', *International Review for the Sociology of Sport* 32, 1 (1997), 31–57.

13 For example, K. Green, 'Philosophies, Ideologies and the Practice of Physical Education', *Sport, Education and Society* 3, 2 (1998), 125–43; J. Maguire, *Global Sport: Identities, Societies, Civilizations* (Cambridge: Polity Press, 1999); L. Mansfield, 'Reconsidering Feminisms and the Work of Norbert Elias for understanding Gender, Sport and Sport-related Activities', *European Physical Education Review* 14, 1 (2008), 93–123; M. Van Bottenburg, *Global Games* (Urbana: University of Illinois Press, 2001); I. Waddington, *Sport, Health and Drugs* (London: E & FN Spon, 2000).

14 E. Dunning, J. Maguire and R. Pearton, eds, *The Sports Process: A Comparative and Developmental Approach* (Champaign, IL: Human Kinetics, 1993).

15 G. Jarvie, *Highland Games: The Making of the Myth* (Edinburgh: Edinburgh University Press, 1991); G. Jarvie and G. Walker, eds, *Scottish Sport and the Making of the Nation* (Leicester: Leicester University Press, 1994).

16 R. Gruneau, *Class, Sports and Social Development* (Amherst: University of Massachusetts Press, 1983 / Champaign, IL: Human Kinetics, 1999); R. Gruneau and D. Whitson, *Hockey Night in Canada: Sport, Identities and Cultural Politics* (Toronto: Garamond, 1993).

17 A. Ingham and J. Loy, eds, *Sport in Social Development: Traditions, Transitions and Transformations* (Champaign, IL: Human Kinetics, 1993).

18 J.E. Hargreaves, *Sport, Power and Culture* (Cambridge: Polity Press, 1986); J.A. Hargreaves, *Sporting Females: Critical Issues in the History and Sociology of Women's Sport* (London: Routledge, 1994).

19 J. Sugden, *Boxing and Society: An International Analysis* (Manchester: Manchester University Press, 1996).

20 J. Sugden and A. Bairner, *Sport, Sectarianism and Society in a Divided Ireland* (Leicester: Leicester University Press, 1993).

21 J. Sugden and A. Tomlinson, *FIFA and the Contest for World Football: Who Rules the People's Game?* (Cambridge: Polity, 1998).

22 W. Vamplew, 'History', in R. Cox, G. Jarvie and W. Vamplew, eds, *Encyclopedia of British Sport* (Oxford: ABC-Clio, 2000), 178–80.

23 A. Guttmann, *From Ritual to Record: The Nature of Modern Sport* (New York: Columbia University Press, 1978); Holt, *Sport and the British*; S.G. Jones, *Workers at Play: A Social and Economic History of Leisure, 1918–1939* (London: Routledge, 1986); S.G. Jones, *Sport, Politics and the Working Class* (Manchester: Manchester University Press, 1988); K. McCrone, *Sport and the Physical Emancipation of English Women* (London: Routledge, 1988); P. Vertinsky, *The Eternally Wounded Woman: Women, Doctors and Exercise in the Late Nineteenth Century* (Manchester: Manchester University Press, 1990).

24 S. Pope, ed., *The New American Sport History: Recent Approaches and Perspectives* (Urbana: University of Illinois Press, 1997).

25 S. Pope, 'Decentring "Race" and (Re)presenting "Black" Performance in Sport History: Basketball and Jazz in American Culture 1920–1950', in M. Phillips, ed., *Deconstructing Sport History: A Postmodern Analysis* (New York: SUNY Press, 2006), 147–181.

26 D. Andrews, 'Sport and the Masculine Hegemony of the Modern Nation: Welsh Rugby Culture and Society 1890–1914', in J. Nauright and T. Chandler, eds, *Making Men: Rugby and Masculine Identity* (London: Frank Cass, 1996), 50–70; D. Andrews, ed., *Michael Jordan Inc.: Corporate Sport, Media Culture and Late Modern America* (New York: SUNY Press, 2001); D. Andrews, 'Feminizing Olympic Reality: Preliminary Dispatches from Baudrillard's Atlanta', *International Review for the Sociology of Sport* 33, 1 (1998), 5–19; D. Andrews, 'Dead and Alive? Sports History in the Late Capitalist Moment', *Sporting Traditions* 16, 1 (1999), 73–83; D. Andrews, and S. Jackson, *Sport Stars: The Cultural Politics of Sporting Celebrities* (London: Routledge, 2001).

27 M. Phillips, ed., *Deconstructing Sport history: A Postmodern Analysis* (New York: SUNY Press, 2005).

28 J. Hill, 'British Sports History: A Post-modern Future', *Journal of Sport History* 23, 1 (1996), 1–19; J. Hill, *Sport, Leisure and Culture in Twentieth-Century Britain* (Basingstoke: Palgrave Macmillan, 2002); J. Hill, *Sport and the Literary Imagination: Essays in History, Literature and Sport* (Bern: Peter Lang, 2006).

29 A. Guttmann, *From Ritual to Record: The Nature of Modern Sport* (New York: Columbia University Press 1977); A. Mason, *Association Football and English Society, 1863–1915* (Brighton: Harvester, 1980); A.J. Mangan, *Athleticism in the Victorian and Edwardian Public Schools* (Cambridge: Cambridge University Press, 1981). See also, P. Bailey, *Leisure and Class in Victorian England* (London: RKP, 1978); W.J. Baker, *Sport in the Western World* (Totowa, NJ: Rowman and Littlefield, 1982); H. Cunningham, *Leisure in the Industrial Revolution c.1780–1880* (London: Croom Helm, 1980); W. Vamplew, *The Turf: A Social and Economic History of Horse Racing* (London: Allen Lane, 1976); J. Walvin, *The People's Game: A Social History of British Football* (London: Allen Lane, 1975).

30 Holt, *Sport and the British*; A. Mason, *Sport in Britain* (London: Faber and Faber, 1988).

31 T. Veblen, *The Theory of the Leisure Class: An Economic Study of Institutions* (New York: Mentor, 1953); B. Rigauer, *Sport and Work* (New York: Columbia University Press, 1969).

32 Mason, *Sport in Britain*, 77.

33 Horne et al., *Understanding Sport*, 75.

34 J.E. Hargreaves, *Sport, Power and Culture*; E. Dunning, 'The Dynamics of Modern Sport: Notes on Achievement-Striving and the Social Significance of Sport', in N. Elias and E. Dunning, eds, *Quest for Excitement: Sport and Leisure in the Civilizing Process* (Oxford: Blackwell, 1986), 205–23.

35 Horne et al., *Understanding Sport*, 76–77.

36 Maguire, 'Common Ground?', 6.

37 R. Holt, 'Amateurism and its interpretation: the social origins of British Sport', *Innovation* 5, 4 (1992), 19–31; updated and reprinted as 'The Historical Meaning of Amateurism', in E. Dunning and D. Malcolm, eds, *Sport: Critical Concepts in Sociology, Vol 3* (London: Routledge, 2003), 270–85.

38 Holt, *Sport and the British*, 363.

39 Ibid., 358.

40 N. Struna, 'Social History and Sport', in J. Coakley and E. Dunning, eds, *Handbook of Sport Studies* (London: Sage, 2000), 187–203.

41 Polley, *Sports History*, 47–48, 55–56.

42 M. Johnes, 'Putting the History into Sport: On sports history and sport studies in the UK', *Journal of Sport History* 31, 2 (2004), 145–60.

43 J. Maguire, and G. Jarvie, 'Historical Sociology and Sport: A Review and Critique' (unpublished paper, 1992), 38.

44 Maguire, 'Common Ground?', 19.

45 D. Reid, 'Folk Football, the Aristocracy, and Cultural Change', *International Journal of the History of Sport* 5, 2 (1988), 224–38.

46 R.W. Lewis, 'Football Hooliganism in England before 1914: A Critique of the Dunning thesis', *International Journal of the History of Sport* 13, 3 (1996), 310–39.

47 J. Goulstone, 'The Working Class Origins of Modern Football', *International Journal of the History of Sport* 17, 1 (2000), 135–43.

48 A. Harvey, 'The Curate's Egg put Back Together: Comments on Eric Dunning's response to "An Epoch in the Annals of National Sport"', *International Journal of the History of Sport* 19, 4 (2002), 192–99; A. Harvey, 'Curate's Egg Pursued by Red Herrings: A reply to Eric Dunning and Graham Curry', *International Journal of the History of Sport* 21, 1 (2004), 127–31.

49 T. Collins, 'History, Theory and the "Civilizing Process"', *Sport in History* 25, 2 (2005), 289–306.

50 W. Vamplew, 'Empiricist Versus Sociological History: Some comments on the "Civilizing Process"', *Sport in History* 27, 2 (2007), 161–71.

51 G. Curry, E. Dunning and K. Sheard, 'Sociological Versus Empiricist History: Some comments on Tony Collins's "History, Theory and the 'Civilizing Process'"', *Sport in History* 26, 1 (2006), 110–23; E. Dunning, 'Something of a Curate's Egg: Comments on Adrian Harvey's "An Epoch in the Annals of National Sport"', *International Journal of the History of Sport* 18, 4 (2001), 88–94; E. Dunning and G. Curry, 'The Curate's Egg Scrambled Again: Comments on "The Curate's Egg Put Back Together"', *International Journal of the History of Sport* 19, 4 (2002), 200–4; D. Malcolm, 'A Response to Vamplew and Some Comments on the Relationship Between Sports Historians and Sociologists of Sport', *Sport in History* (2008), 259–79; P. Murphy, E. Dunning and J. Maguire, 'Football Spectator Violence and Disorder before the First World War: A Reply to R.W. Lewis', *International Journal of the History of Sport* 15, 1 (1998), 141–62.

52 A. Munslow, *Deconstructing History* (London: Routledge, 2006).

53 Ibid., 3.

54 M. Oriard, 'A Linguistic Turn into Sport History', in M. Phillips, ed., *Deconstructing Sport History* (New York: SUNY, 2006), 75.

55 For example, C. Brackenridge 'Managing Myself: Investigator Survival in Sensitive Research', *International Review for the Sociology of Sport* 34, 4 (1999), 115–130; E. Dunning, 'Figurational Sociology and the Sociology of Sport: Some Concluding Remarks', in E. Dunning and C. Rojek, eds, *Sport and Leisure in the Civilizing Process* (London: Macmillan, 1992), 221–85; L. Mansfield, 'Involved-Detachment: A Balance of Passion and Reason in Feminisms and Gender-related Research in Sport, Tourism and Sports Tourism', *Journal of Sport and Tourism* 12, 2 (2007), 115–43; J. Sugden and A. Tomlinson, 'Digging the Dirt and Staying Clean: Retrieving the Investigative Tradition for a Critical Sociology of Sport', *International Review for the Sociology of Sport* 34, 4 (1999), 385–87; J. Sugden and A. Tomlinson, eds, *Power Games: A Critical Sociology of Sport* (London: Routledge, 2002).

56 Pope, 'Decentring "Race" and (Re)presenting "Black" Performance in Sport History', 162.

57 J. Hargreaves and P. Vertinsky, *Physical Culture, Power and the Body* (London: Routledge, 2006).

58 H. Beckles and B. Stoddart, eds, *Liberation Cricket: West Indies Cricket Culture* (Manchester: Manchester University Press, 1995).

59 Maguire, 'Common Ground?', 3.

7 Origins

Donald G. Kyle

Long a venerable but lesser part of the study of sports history, ancient sports history has matured into a thriving sub-discipline in Ancient History and Classics. Highlighting selected recent works in English but noting some major non-English scholarship, this chapter outlines the development and approaches of ancient sports history, and it surveys ages and issues from early to Greek and Roman times. I follow the usual emphasis on Greek athletics, but, consistent with recent trends and my own arguments for sport and spectacle as overlapping phenomena, I also discuss Roman physical contests and spectacles.[1]

As detailed below, the study of ancient sport used to be rather circumscribed and conceptually unambitious, but it can no longer be dismissed as the esoteric pursuit of hidebound antiquarians. Focusing on the rules and techniques of events, early works discussed practices and muscles more than processes and meanings. Retelling sporting myths and tall tales of the feats and defeats of famous athletes, sport enthusiasts mined and reconstructed the past to offer lessons for the present. Today, however, ancient sport studies are professional and disciplined, broader in scope, deeper in analysis, more international and interdisciplinary, and more innovative and sophisticated in approaches and interpretation. We have advanced the study of ancient sport – the acts, actors, audiences and arenas – by assessing new archaeological evidence, re-examining existing texts and artefacts, and applying approaches from sociology and social history, political and symbolic anthropology, and cultural studies. Overall, the trend is revisionist and demythologizing, a questioning of traditional assumptions, periodization and parochialism.[2]

Interested in both change and continuity, in interactions and adaptations over broad spans of time and space, we have expanded the chronological and geographical scope of ancient sport. Going beyond the traditional concentrations on the Greek Olympics and the Roman arena, we now examine the sporting activities of earlier Near Eastern peoples and the Bronze Age Aegean, local Greek games with their intriguing contests, social issues of class and gender, the transitional Hellenistic era, the emergence of Etruscan and Roman spectacles, the stagecraft of both sports and spectacles, and the persistence of Greek sport under Rome.

Scholars and students

Since the 1970s scholars have promoted the study of ancient sport as an academically respectable and promising subfield of research and teaching. European scholars, including Ingomar Weiler, Wolfgang Decker, H.W. Pleket and Joachim Ebert, led the way, soon to be assisted by Americans, including Stephen G. Miller, Michael B. Poliakoff and Thomas F. Scanlon. A new sports history journal, *Stadion: Internationale Zeitschrift für*

Geschichte des Sports, appeared in 1975 and welcomed articles on antiquity. Introduced in 1988, *Nikephoros: Zeitschrift für Sport und Kultur im Altertum* has become a prestigious forum for international scholarship on ancient sport. Other periodicals, such as the *Journal of Sport History* (11 (1984); 30 (2003)), have put out special issues and colloquia, conferences and museum exhibitions have produced valuable anthologies, catalogues and illustrated works.[3]

As educators realized sports history's potential for enriching our understanding of ancient life, courses, textbooks and sourcebooks proliferated. A highpoint came in 2004 when Stephen G. Miller, an internationally respected authority, published both his masterful textbook, *Ancient Greek Athletics* (New Haven: Yale University), with illustrations and coverage of all aspects of Greek sport, and the third and expanded edition of his excellent sourcebook, *Arete: Greek Sports from Ancient Sources* (Berkeley: University of California).[4] Two broader syntheses appeared in 2007. Nigel B. Crowther, a leading scholar whose numerous articles are collected in his *Athletika: Studies on the Olympic Games and Greek Athletics* (Hildesheim: Weidmann, 2004), surveys sport in the Ancient Near East, the Far East and the Classical World, as well as Byzantium and Mesoamerica, in *Sport in Ancient Times* (Westport: Praeger, 2007). Without notes but with helpful timelines and recommended readings, it covers athletes, gladiators, women, team sports, and board and ball games. My own *Sport and Spectacle in the Ancient World* (Oxford: Blackwell, 2007) examines the history of competitive physical performances in the Ancient Near East, Greece and Rome. It argues that ancient sport and spectacle were not incompatible but rather formed a spectrum of physical public performance. Intense athletic competitions became spectacles, and ancient spectacles often incorporated competitive physical activities.[5]

Evidence

From Herodotus to Suetonius, from Greek vases to Roman reliefs, from ruins to epitaphs, an abundance and variety of literary and archaeological evidence exists for ancient sport, but there are no ancient box scores or record books, no interviews or diaries and no tell-all biographies. Classical literature abounds with sporting images and references, and funeral games remained a stock element of epic from Homer to late antiquity, but few works in the classical canon focus on sport.[6] Scholars cherish the fifth-century victory odes of Pindar but his artistic efforts to please victors mixed mythology and genealogy with idealistic characterizations. We must always consider the contexts, motives and reliability of those ancient authors who overly criticize or praise Greek athletics or Roman spectacles. Ironically, some heavily used sources on early athletics, such as Lucian, Philostratus and Pausanias, are from Roman imperial times.

Contributions from archaeology are fundamental as exciting discoveries of works of art and remnants of structures attest the energy and resources committed to sport and performances in the Mediterranean world. From simple natural sites, ancient sport facilities became architecturally monumental and sophisticated, and performers, patrons and states commemorated games and victories with dedications and statues. While traditional archaeological excavations focused on major sites and sanctuaries and sought to validate literary sources, contemporary archaeology goes beyond excavation and no longer sees literary accounts as inviolable. Using surface surveys and new technologies, and looking beyond centres and elites, archaeologists now seek to reveal the total material culture of societies, which usually entails some evidence of sport. Finally, from proclamations to victor lists, the study of agonistic inscriptions (and papyri) is fruitful and essential.[7]

Ancient sports historiography

Ancient sport has attracted attention since the Renaissance and 19th-century scholars produced important works,[8] but for much of the 20th century the study and teaching of ancient sport followed the conventional approach and ill-founded idealism of E.N. Gardiner (1864–1930) and his ideological heir, H.A. Harris (1902–1974).[9] Their books remain valuable compendia of information but their overarching schema of ancient athletics was a tragic tale of early athletic glory, decline and fall – a morality play for modern sport. Supposedly deriving from spontaneous, aristocratic Homeric games, Greek sport reached a brief golden age in the amateur Panhellenic Games of the sixth century. Soon falling victim to its own popularity, sport entered a long, regrettable process of decline. Rewards, training and specialization led to lower class professionalism, which debased sport socially and morally until fourth-century sport was mere 'spectacle'. The Hellenistic era saw further decline and Rome soon spread a pall over ancient sport. Despite evidence of expansion and vitality, Hellenistic and Roman athletics at times were dismissed as 'entertainments' dominated by guilds of professionals and barely tolerated by Romans, who 'lusted for blood' and could only appreciate the arena and circus. Later, Christianity admirably condemned Roman spectacles, but unfortunately the Church also ended ancient sport as a pagan practice. Methodologically archaic and espousing modern ideologies including Hellenism, amateurism and Olympism, this model, which merely fitted sport into traditional political eras, has not fared well under scrutiny.

In the 1970s and 1980s, as Modern Olympic crises, scandals and tragedies undermined idealism, and as sports history studied texts and society in sophisticated new ways, revisionist scholars viewed ancient sport more critically. In 1975 H.W. Pleket's watershed article, 'Games, Prizes, Athletes and Ideology: Some Aspects of the History of Sport in the Greco-Roman World', *Stadion*, 1 (1975): 49–89, insightfully noted that ancient sports studies were hindered by an excess of antiquarianism, a classicist preference for rise and fall patterns, and an anachronistic amateurish bias against professionalism. He argues that members of the upper class stayed active in sport and that the aristocratic ethos of sport, stressing glory, toil and endurance, continued into post-classical times. Getting the word out, Pleket and M.I. Finley co-authored a popular but demythologizing book, *The Olympic Games: The First Thousand Years* (New York: Viking, 1976), which describes realistic Ancient Olympics replete with violence, profits and political abuses.

Traditional and popular works continue to appear but in the 1990s and the 21st century discussions of theory, epistemology and rhetoric intellectualized sports historiography. Ancient sports historians quickly and ably embraced new interpretive approaches by applying anthropological and sociological models and the theoretical insights of new literary criticism and cultural historical studies. Postmodernist sports historians, adamant that knowledge is constructed, approach history and sport as contested realms of power. Indeed, historical discourses are dynamic; they involve conflicts and negotiation as ideologies, desires and needs affect the representation of the past. More aware of problems of perception and reception, of representation and construction, of the impossibility of objectively writing history 'as it actually was', recent studies have a more reflexive and ideologically self-conscious approach, one wary of classicist biases that tend to see Greece as an ideal and Rome as a warning. We realize that we too are reinventing antiquity, but we no longer put ancient sport in service to elitist, evolutionist, Eurocentric historiography.

We also understand that we cannot just 'let the sources speak for themselves'. Ancient literature was highly rhetorical, and artefacts (e.g. monuments, statues, prizes, coins) involve self-representation and social memory. Avoiding antiquarian disciplinary compartmentalization, the holistic or interdisciplinary approach of New Historicism helps us contextualize ancient evidence by appreciating the cultural discourses and social, individual and political agendas that inspired and fashioned commemorations and representations of sport in art and texts.

This new cultural turn will continue and one promising approach is to study sports and spectacles as cultural performances. Modern cultural and symbolic anthropology regards cultural performances, such as sports, dance and drama, not as mere entertainment but as distinct systems of meaning by which cultural orders (i.e. values, norms, status relationships) are formulated, communicated and reformulated. Public performances both make (encode, contest) and are made by (they reflect) culture.[10] Human action, especially ritualized, public, social action, is communicative, and intensely physical games were forms of symbolic communication and means of cultural (re)formation.

Origins and early sport

Scholars debate whether ancient sport and modern sport are fundamentally different, and whether sport in origin and essence is practical, autotelic (an end in itself), ludic (playful), or symbolic.[11] Challenging earlier theories about cults or funeral games, and applying sociobiology and ethology (on instinctive impulses in human nature), David Sansone, *Greek Athletics and the Genesis of Sport* (Berkeley: University of California, 1988), asserts a single nature and origin for both ancient and modern sport in the 'ritual sacrifice of physical energy'. By a process of ritualization, once productive Paleolithic hunting practices continued, became stylized and took on new communicative functions as sport. Sansone's explanations of some features of Greek sport (e.g. nudity, oil, crowns) may not persuade all, but his thesis remains stimulating. Ultimately, the true origins of sport must remain speculative because the phenomenon predates substantial evidence for itself.

Traditional works claimed that earlier Near Eastern societies lacked physical competitions and that the Greeks had a unique and pervasive spirit of agonism or competitiveness, which led them to invent sport and raise it to the level of great athletic games. Most sports historians, however, now agree that agonism is fundamental to human survival and socialization, that sport in some form is a universal human phenomenon and that sport exhibits significant local adaptations and variations as different classes, cultures and societies practice and view sport in revealing and characteristic ways.

More scholars are taking a broader and more Mediterranean approach that includes sport and spectacles in Bronze Age Egypt and the Near East.[12] The dean of Egyptian sport studies, Wolfgang Decker, has published major studies of the available evidence and relevant scholarship, including *Sports and Games of Ancient Egypt*, trans. A. Guttmann (New Haven: Yale University, 1987). Although without specialized athletic facilities or open contests, Egyptian civilization had many sporting and recreational activities, often with the pharaohs playing a central role consistent with their ideology of kingship.[13] Admirably broad, Michael B. Poliakoff, *Combat Sports in the Ancient World: Competition, Violence and Culture* (New Haven: Yale University, 1987), offers an authoritative clarification of terms, rules and techniques as he compares Greek combat sports with precursors throughout the Mediterranean. He also discusses of the origins of sport, the tolerance of violence in ancient games and the symbolism of violent victory for leadership and ethnic pride.

Studies now challenge Greek exceptionalism by showing that Mediterranean peoples had physical performances and recreational games long before the Greeks, but, admittedly, the evidence suggests state or court-sponsored activities – strongmen and acrobats in festivals, military exercises and staged or ritualized performances by monarchs. Bronze Age Mycenaean Greeks had funeral games and chariot races, the memory of which seems to have endured down to Homer, but it is likely that sporting discourse with earlier civilizations, including Egypt and Minoan Crete, was influential, especially in spectacular aspects of performances such as bull leaping and boxing.[14] The Greeks nevertheless remain distinctive for the degree to which they institutionalized athletics in festivals that included public, physical, intense competitions for prizes, which Greek citizens entered on a voluntary basis, and for the development of purpose-built athletic facilities.

Olympia and Greek athletics

The showplace if perhaps not the birthplace of ancient sport, Ancient Olympia and its games cultivate quadrennial bumper-crops of books, some with considerable redundancy but some with new insights and controversies.[15] An essential step for anyone studying Ancient Olympia is to separate the ancient phenomenon from the Modern Olympics. Revealing misperceptions about ancient amateurism and the modern revival of the games, David C. Young argues forcefully that our Olympics were not true to ancient times and ideals even in 1896, when revived at Athens by modern Greeks and Pierre de Coubertin.[16] That the Modern Olympics still bolster popular illusions about the ancient games, despite evidence for ancient professionalism, corruption and commercialism, shows us much about modern notions of nostalgia, early purity and decline.

Thanks to the German Archaeological Institute, Olympia was the first centre of athletics to be thoroughly excavated.[17] Ongoing archaeology has raised questions about the earliest Ancient Olympics, the politicization of the games by Elis and Macedon in the Classical and Hellenistic ages, the supposedly corruptive influence of Rome, and the *nachleben* of the games and site. A distinguished archaeologist, Ulrich Sinn, in *Olympia: Cult, Sport and Ancient Festival*, translated by T. Thornton (Princeton: Marcus Wiener, 2000), offers a concise survey of the origins, site, buildings, cults and games at Olympia over its entire history. Studies now doubt legends about very early games at Olympia and even wonder about significant games in 776 BC: Elis and Pisa clearly fostered mythologies of early founders to legitimize their claims to operate the games, some archaeologists reject an early shrine to Pelops, and the evidence of early wells and dedications supports down dating major games to around 700.[18] We now see the Olympic Victor List (of names of eponymous men's *stadion* (sprint) victors for each Olympiad) of the late fifth-century sophist, Hippias of Elis, as unreliable for items prior to the early sixth century.[19] Apparently the Ancient Olympics did not begin as early or as gloriously, decline as tragically, or end as soon as we had assumed.

Scholars have done impressive work on traditional Ancient Olympic topics, including the schedule of the festival, the programme of contests and related questions (e.g., defining a fall in wrestling, the rules in the *pankration* (a combination of wrestling and boxing), scoring the pentathlon, lanes and turns in footraces, and the operation of chariot races).[20] Recently, more attention is being paid to demythologizing the games and recognizing the significance of status display, politics, commerce and spectatorship. Rooted in an elitist reception of the Classical Tradition, earlier historians like Gardiner credited Olympia with ideals that they themselves wanted to find: competitiveness, victory, effort, piety – fair enough, but also anachronistic amateurism, internationalism, inclusive brotherhood, participation and magnanimous sportsmanship. Simply put, the main ideal at Olympia, with its first place only wins and decorated with monuments to triumphs in both wars and games, was victory. Involvement with Panhellenic games need not have been apolitical or altruistic and the spectacular dimension of the games went far beyond sport for the sake of sport.[21] With its games, nudity and wreath prizes, Olympia remained central to the Greeks' perception of their ethnicity,[22] but the Olympic truce and Panhellenic unity were not fully effective and Olympia was often used and abused for political ends.

The *periodos* and local games

In the first half of the sixth century a 'circuit' (*periodos*) of four Panhellenic crown games arose at interstate sanctuaries at Delphi, Isthmia, Nemea and Olympia, and archaeology at these sites has revealed the significance of settings and spectatorship in ancient sport.[23] Ongoing excavations directed by S.G. Miller at Nemea, the least prestigious of the four, is providing exciting new information. Built at a considerable distance from the sanctuary and temple of Zeus, a later fourth-century stadium, with seating arrangements for some 40,000 people, it has a vaulted entrance tunnel (complete with graffiti) leading from a 'locker room' (*apodyterion*) to the track with its starting line and mechanism (*hysplex*).[24]

Since Greek sport was intimately associated with religion, the study of early sanctuaries and Panhellenic festivals has great value, but sport also was central to civic life and education. Most Greeks experienced sport in their own city-states, so scholarship has expanded to study sport in urban and local settings. At Athens and even at less urbanized Sparta, earlier contests, cults and rites of passage of clans and sub-communities were incorporated or 'nationalized' in local athletic systems supported and supervised by the city-state. My *Athletics in Ancient Athens* (Leiden: Brill, 1987) studied the historical development, facilities, festivals, prosopography and political dimensions of athletics in relationship to Athenian community life and civic identity. Jenifer Neils went further with an exhibition and publications on the contests, prizes, procession and other aspects of the Panathenaic festival.[25] Turning to Sparta and mastering the limited physical and problematic literary evidence, Nigel M. Kennell, *The Gymnasium of Virtue: Education and Culture in Ancient Sparta* (Chapel Hill: University of North Carolina, 1995), reconstructs early forms of Spartan physical training but down dates many excessive and notorious practices to later eras; and Stephen Hodkinson persuasively situates chariot racing and athletics within the agonistic dimensions of Spartan social history.[26]

Athletes and society

Ancient sports historians show a refreshing willingness to read sport as a rich text in social and cultural history, and to suggest social and political conflicts between privileged athletes and common citizens. Championing such an approach, Mark Golden, *Sport and Society in Ancient Greece* (Cambridge: Cambridge University, 1988), applies the theme of sport and social difference to categories of class, age and gender. Also investigating the social dynamics of athletics, Leslie Kurke, *The Traffic in Praise: Pindar and the Poetics of Social Economy* (Ithaca: Cornell University, 1991), argues that Pindar's 'sociological poetics' sought to mediate and to diffuse tensions, to help reintegrate the athletic victor, isolated by his achievement, into his social and political communities.[27] With similar assumptions from New Historicism, Nigel J. Nicholson, *Aristocracy and Athletics in Archaic and Classical*

Greece (Cambridge: Cambridge University, 2005), argues that challenges by non-elite citizens in late archaic and early classical Greece moved anxious aristocracies to minimize the contributions of hired charioteers and jockeys, and paid professional trainers, in their victory commemorations (victory odes, dedications, vases).

Controversies about amateurism and professionalism in modern sport have fed an ongoing debate about the origins, social status and social mobility of Greek athletes. Old claims that lower class professionals drove noble amateurs out of competition have been refuted. The great games perhaps began as casual contests won by natural ability, but by the sixth century competitive athletes were specialized and intensively trained by coaches, and states honoured their Panhellenic victors with material rewards and symbolic honours, sometimes establishing hero cults to them after their deaths. Local games offered valuable material prizes as well as team and tribal events, but assessing the influence of rewards and prizes on social mobility is difficult. While Young claims that non-aristocratic professionals were present in significant numbers from the beginning, Pleket argues that lower class professionalism arose only after Pindar and that the upper classes continued to compete, even in combat sports, into Roman imperial times. My work suggests that athletics in classical Athens remained elitist as wealthier families predominated but did not monopolize high-level competition.[28] We simply cannot know as much as we want to know about ancient athletes. History privileges the privileged and those with status and resources can best insert their victories and values into the historical record.

Studies of the nude body, physical culture and gender are now definitely in vogue. Thomas F. Scanlon, *Eros and Greek Athletics* (Oxford: Oxford University, 2002), examines the role of eros in Greek sport, religion, education and gender formation. He explains that nude physical education (*gymnike paideia*) constructively incorporated erotically charged (pederastic) relationships in which teenage youths followed the cultural example of mature males. Most scholars now agree that nude exercise and reviews in Sparta spread nudity to Olympia and throughout Greece. Gymnastic nudity was a costume, a social marker of freedom, male status and Greekness.[29] Miller adds the intriguing suggestion that, along with objective standards of judging at Olympia, nudity precluded signs of status, supported *isonomia* – a general notion of equality – and fostered the spread of democracy.[30]

Despite the profoundly male-dominated evidence, recent work on females and sport has been instructive. Girls' initiation rites with dances or running seem widespread, but Spartan female physical education was eugenic and exceptional, and female involvement at Olympia has been exaggerated. Except for one priestess, all women were prohibited from attending the Olympics. Pausanias' tale about a mother sneaking in to watch her son compete may be unreliable, and the suggestion that virgin girls (*parthenoi*) were allowed to watch the games also seems ill founded. Young maidens did run races at Olympia in the festival of Hera but as a form of initiation, not as an Olympic competition. Women could enter chariots and be proclaimed Olympic victors *in absentia*, as Kyniska of Sparta did in 396 BC, but she may have entered under pressure from her brother, King Agesilaus. Realistically, it seems that female sport expanded and became fully athletic only after Classical Greece.[31]

The Hellenistic age

Once taken as an age of decline, athletic withdrawal, debased professionalism and idle spectatorship, the Hellenistic age is now seen as a transitional age of sporting discourse among Greece, the Near East and Rome. Philip, Alexander and other Macedonians appreciated the political value of Olympic wins and of Olympia as a forum; but Macedonian and Hellenistic rulers also patronized the great games and Alexander's conquests spread cities with games and facilities over a vast territory. Mainland Greece was less powerful but sporting traditions remained strong and interaction between Hellenistic Greeks and Romans brought a wider world of sport and spectacle.[32]

Roman sport and spectacle

With Hellenist and elitist biases, traditional studies applaud Greek sports as pure, participatory, noble and inspirational, and they denounce Roman spectacles as vulgar, spectatory, brutal and debasing – an unfortunate defect in a society that achieved so much in engineering, law and other areas. Again, renewed and revisionist scholarship, especially since the 1990s, has re-evaluated Roman customs and values.

Studies have examined the history, operation and settings of Roman spectacles in detail. Jean-Paul Thuillier has shown that the Etruscans' distinctive system of sport influenced early developments at Rome, especially in chariot racing, which was the earliest and longest enduring Roman spectacle.[33] John H. Humphrey's monumental and authoritative synthesis of archaeological evidence for circuses all over the Empire, *Roman Circuses: Arenas for Chariot Racing* (Berkeley: University of California, 1986) explains the history and organization of the races as well as the evolution, design and operation of the circuses. Alan Cameron's *Circus Factions: Blues and Greens at Rome and Byzantium* (Oxford: Clarendon, 1976) remains essential in the ongoing debate on the evolution and significance of the circus factions or colours (both the commercial enterprises and the groupings of spectators) in Roman and Byzantine history. Turning to the arena, George Ville's masterful *La gladiature en occident des origines à la mort de Domitien* (Rome: École française de Rome, 1981), clarifies the actual operation – the who, where and how – of Roman blood sports (*munera*); and recent studies of amphitheatres in Italy and beyond have shown the spread of the phenomenon.[34] As well as detailing how spectacles were organized, financed and housed, scholarship moved on to rethink the meaning of Roman violence, spectatorship and mass entertainment.

Sophisticated and more dispassionate studies, such as J.P. Toner, *Leisure and Ancient Rome* (Cambridge: Polity, 1995), approach Roman spectacles not as unfathomable decadence but as elements of Roman sport and leisure, as means whereby Romans recreated or entertained themselves. Toner showed that, from baths to taverns, Roman pastimes could be humble and playful as well as grandiose and dangerous. In a similarly inclusive exhibition and catalogue, Eckart Köhne and Cornelia Ewigleben, eds, *Gladiators and Caesars: The Power of Spectacle in Ancient Rome* (Berkeley: University of California, 2000), discuss theatrical and athletic performances as well as circus and arena games; and David Potter's detailed and balanced survey of Rome's entertainment industry brings that approach to the classroom.[35] Scholars now look at the status and symbolism of all performers, from charioteers and gladiators to athletes and beasts, and they explain the social and political dynamics and cultural significance of all types of performance – competitive and violent, cultured and coarse, native and imported.

Spectacles as communication

Sociologically informed recent works explain how Rome's spectacles communicated social order and values, reinforced political dominance and assisted cultural imperialism.

In a seminal article for interpretive approaches to the arena, 'Fatal Charades: Roman Executions Staged as Mythological Enactments', *Journal of Roman Studies*, 130 (1990): 44–73, Kathleen M. Coleman discusses the punitive and deterrent aims of mythologized violence in 'fatal charades' in the early Empire, explaining that increasingly autocratic emperors demonstrated their power of life and death by turning myths into reality. As well as profound articles on mass spectatorship, female gladiators and more,[36] Coleman has produced an important translation and commentary on Martial's poems on the inauguration of the Colosseum: *Martial: Liber Spectaculorum* (Oxford: Oxford University, 2006). Essays in B. Bergmann and C. Kondoleon, eds, *The Art of Ancient Spectacle* (New Haven: Yale University, 1999) present varied activities and multiple contexts as all part of a common visual, symbolic, performative art or language of spectacle, one as articulate as (and faster than) the spoken word, from Etruscan and Hellenistic through to Roman times. Similarly, Richard C. Beacham's *Spectacle Entertainments of Early Imperial Rome* (New Haven: Yale University, 1999) argues that spectacles expressed Roman power and ideology, that Augustus was profoundly aware of the political capital of shows, and that Rome experienced a 'stage-craft of state craft' – an 'aestheticization' of politics and a 'theatricalization' of public life.

Certainly the relationship of emperors to the Roman people, especially crowds at spectacles, was far more complex than Juvenal's famous 'bread and circuses' or the conventional notion of politically impotent, apathetic masses being manipulated by self-indulgent megalomaniacs. Interaction between the emperor and his people at the games entailed communication and co-operation as well as sublimation and dominance. Seating arrangements reflected the hierarchy of Rome but the stands also functioned as surrogate assemblies. The ideology of spectacles included the expectations and influence of the crowds and the obligations – from generosity to decorum – on the emperors who sustained a system of urban relief and mass diversion.[37]

Gladiators, beasts and arenas

Controversy about violence in society and the media in the 1990s prompted scholars to investigate the paradoxical significance of the arena for Rome. Were cruel spectacles inconsistent with – or central to – Roman civilization? Why did Romans have such ambivalent attitudes to gladiators, stigmatizing them in society, literature and legislation and yet attending, glorifying and sometimes even volunteering for their combats? No longer just condemning arena shows as perversions for the plebs, innovative scholarship uses interpretive, theoretical approaches to present the amphitheatre as a highly ritualized and symbolic realm. The deaths of exotic beasts represented Rome's control over distant lands and gladiatorial combats were not senseless, sadistic mass slaughters 'to the death' but rather orchestrated duels of trained, well-equipped professionals with referees, rules and rewards.[38]

In *Emperors and Gladiators* (London: Routledge, 1992), Thomas Wiedemann reads the arena as a liminal site where Romans confronted the limits of the human versus the natural world in beast fights, the limits of morality, law and social order in executions of criminals, and the limits of human mortality in gladiatorial combats. Relating the arena as a symbol of Rome's cultural identity (*Romanitas*) to the socio-political dynamics of emperorship and imperial rule, he also suggests that elitist literary criticisms of the arena lacked humanitarianism,[39] and that the end of the combats was not a simple matter of abolition due to Christian values. In *Sorrows of the Ancient Romans: The Gladiator and the Monster* (Princeton: Princeton University, 1993), Carlin A. Barton uses interpretive and cultural theories (e.g., Foucault, Derrida, Goffman) to examine the Romans' collective psychology concerning pervasive images of gladiators and monsters (abnormal or deformed creatures), and she relates the arena's appeal to a 'physics' of desire, despair, envy and fascination arising from the crises of the Late Republic. As the arena became the new battlefield for demonstrating military virtue, gladiatorial combats became a form of simplified, purified soldiering. By their self-sacrifice (*devotio*), gladiators achieved an 'inverse elevation' above their vile origins, an escape from the humiliation of compulsion through enthusiastic complicity. Applying studies of rhetoric, cognitive dissonance and cultural anthropology, Paul Plass, *The Game of Death in Ancient Rome: Arena Sport and Political Suicide* (Madison: University of Wisconsin, 1995), suggests parallels between the violence of the arena and the dynamics of political suicide at Rome. As socially sanctioned violence and controlled disorder, both had a social purpose in dealing with problems of security and survival. Both addressed social anomaly by incorporating disorder into order, restoring social routine and (re)affirming security.

   Alison Futrell, *Blood in the Arena: The Spectacle of Roman Power* (Austin: University of Texas, 1997), interprets gladiatorial combats as human sacrifices and she traces the spread and adaptation of amphitheatral architecture in the northern Empire as extensions of imperial power and cultural Romanization. My *Spectacles of Death in Ancient Rome* (London: Routledge, 1998) investigates the procurement, treatment, combats, death and disposal of human and animal arena victims to establish the spectacular symbolism of living and dead bodies. To better understand violent spectacles Futrell and I both considered comparative phenomena ranging from Aztec rituals to Spanish bullfights.

Greek sport at Rome and in the Greek East

In a refreshing development, scholars are showing that Greek and Roman discourse on athletics and arena spectacles was not one-dimensional, mutual disdain and rejection. Patterns of initial resistance but later accommodation and patronage apply to both Roman reactions to Greek athletics and Greek reactions to Roman spectacles. As Louis Robert demonstrated decades ago in *Les Gladiateurs dans l'Orient grec* (Paris: L'École des Hautes Études, 1940), the Greek East under the Empire came to accept gladiatorial combat by attaching to it the iconography and values of Greek athletics. For its part, Rome included athletics in spectacles as Romans came to appreciate the skills and sus-pense of athletic contests.[40] Augustus' harmonizing of Greek and Roman traditions included an eclectic, cosmopolitan imperial system of public entertainments with Greek athletics as well as Roman arena and circus spectacles.

   Again building on Robert's epigraphic work, scholars now emphasize the acceptance and institutionalization of Greek sport at Rome and the expansion and significance of agonistic festivals in the Greek East.[41] Two important recent works, Zahra Newby's art historical study, *Greek Athletics in the Roman World* (Oxford: Oxford University, 2005), and Jason König's literary study, *Athletics and Literature in the Roman Empire* (Cambridge: Cambridge University, 2005), investigate the experiences, identifications, self-representations and cultural importance of athletics under the Empire. They explain that old notions of Rome's hostility to Greek sport and of the decline of Greek sport under Rome were based on the facile acceptance of literary criticisms of athletics (e.g., in Juvenal and Tacitus), which actually suggest popularity rather than strong opposition, on insufficient attention to the physical evidence of classicizing art and architecture, and on casual, piecemeal use of literature from the imperial era.

Newby details the introduction, growth and acceptance of athletics, from Augustus to the Severans, as part of the Empire's 'spectacle culture'. Emperors (e.g., Nero, Domitian) fostered Greek sport with athletic festivals and a stadium at Rome, the headquarters of the international guild of star athletes moved to Rome and public facilities, especially the imperial baths, made Greek-style exercise more appealing and convenient for Romans. Athletic mosaics and idealizing copies of Greek sculptures in baths, villas and public spaces indicate that athletics were prominent in Roman life and recreation. Turning to the Greek East, Newby shows that athletic art, facilities and festivals were popular in the self-representation of cities, competitors, patrons and intellectuals. While celebrating contemporary accomplishments, later Greeks, especially elite patrons and fathers of ephebes (cadets), asserted their Hellenic identity as worthy heirs of classical Greece. Athletics also contributed to positive interactions between Greek and Roman culture and between Eastern Greeks and the imperial administration.

Köhne agrees that institutionalized agonistic festivals, ephebic education and athletic victories and patronage were central to the identity and self-representation of Eastern Greeks but, like New Historicists, he sees identities, cultures and texts as contested, unstable and ambiguous. Applying recent theoretical studies of rhetoric, representation and bodily display to athletics, he reads claims, valuations, or assertions about athletics in inscriptions and literary works as contestations, as indications of alternative opinions or rival claims to identity and status. He analyses previously misused or underappreciated texts (e.g., Lucian, Galen, Philostratus) that reveal athletics as a high-status activity in civic life and festival culture and as a locus of conflicted elite self-identification, self-perception and broader cultural controversies about education, bodies, civic virtue and the Hellenic tradition. He shows that constructions of the history and sport of Classical Greece in literature of the imperial era were fashioned by the authors' concerns about nostalgia, (Pan)Hellenic traditions, self-representation, or professional rivalries. For example, following recent re-evaluations of Pausanias, König argues that Pausanias' selection and emphasis of athletic commemorations from earlier Greece reflects contemporary tensions between attempts to recapture or distance a Panhellenic past.

König and Newby effectively demonstrate the significance of athletics for elite identity, education and masculine self-display for the urban elites of the Greek East. Athletic festivals multiplied and athletic art and facilities (gymnasia, stadia, baths) flourished in Asia Minor because agonistic festivals and ephebic education remained central to the self-representation of cities and individuals as Greeks, victors and patrons.[42] Also, by sanctioning numerous festivals and supervising athletic pensions and guilds, Rome's imperial administration and the emperor cult provided institutionalization and regularity for spectacular Greek as well as Roman games in the eclectic Greco-Roman entertainment system of the Empire.

Olympia and Rome

Such insights confirm a positive reinterpretation of the later Olympic Games within the Roman Empire. Old notions that Olympia suffered oppression, neglect and corruption under Rome derived from the scenario of decline and from uncritical use of literary texts. Indictments of Nero's tour of Greece in hostile ancient and modern works have also been challenged as unreliable proof of corruption and debasement.[43] Scanlon and others write not of decadent and feeble later Olympics but of 'ecumenical Olympics' that adapted constructively to Roman rule. An Olympic victory remained supremely honorific and Olympia drew competitors and spectators from a wider Greco-Roman world. Moreover, recent archaeology on later Olympia shows that Rome brought welcome patronage and prosperity, which assisted Olympia's vigour and longevity. A first-century facility identified as a clubhouse of Olympic victors is credited to Nero and the Flavians and further benefactions brought Olympia to its architectural height in the second century AD. A bronze plaque found in a gutter of the clubhouse has revealed the names of 14 additional Olympic victors, extending the names of known victors from AD 369 to 385, and archaeologists suggest that Olympia survived into very late antiquity.[44]

Looking back and forward

Ancient sport and modern sport have different institutions, ideologies and technologies but ancient sports history helps us ponder both our modernity and our cultural heritages. Providing perspective on our contemporary mania for sporting violence and victory, ancient sports history shows that human nature has changed little over the millennia. As embodied, emotional, instinctual beings, we have always been – and will always be – impressed by fit, powerful and talented bodies in motion and especially in competition.

In future ancient sport studies Olympia and Rome will remain alluring but more original and exciting work will turn to less famous sites and understudied ages. Much work remains to be done on pre-classical times, the Hellenistic world and the provinces of the Roman Empire. Cultural studies and interests in identity, ethnicity and cultural imperialism will lead scholars to delve further into cultural discourses on sport: between the ancient Near East and Greece, between Greece and Rome, and between pagans, Christians and Jews. The sociology of sport will inspire more work on gendered bodies, age groups and initiation, class and leisure. Comparative history and anthropology will offer more insights from Meso-American and Amerindian games, Asian martial arts and beast sports from hunting to rodeo.

Scholars have illuminated the rich history of ancient sport but some flirt with approaching history itself as a sport. Conceptual and theoretical models can suggest possible parallels but they should not be imposed as certainties that overlook changes over time and culture. The desire to recover distant voices cannot produce lost or perhaps never existent evidence, nor does a dearth of evidence prove that a phenomenon must have existed. Applications of sophisticated interpretive approaches from cultural and social history are stimulating but more therapeutic and enduring for ancient sport will be the discovery and integration of new evidence, mainly from archaeology and epigraphy. Old wine in new bottles and new wine in old bottles both can grace our table.

Notes

1 'Sport' is not an ancient word but the ancients had words (e.g. *agones*, *ludi*) for their various physical activities, contests and public spectacles. This chapter expands upon my 'Games, Prizes and Athletes in Greek Sport: Patterns and Perspectives (1975–1997)', *Classical Bulletin* 74, 2 (1998), 103–27; and *Sport and Spectacle in the Ancient World* (Oxford: Blackwell, 2007), 1–22.

2 Bibliographical surveys include Ingomar Weiler, *Der Sport bei den Völkern der alten Welt* (Darmstadt: Wissenschaftliche Buchgesellschaft, 1981, 2nd edn 1988); Nigel B. Crowther, 'Studies in Greek Athletics', Parts I and II, Special Survey Issues, *Classical World* 78: 5; 79: 2 (both 1985); Thomas F. Scanlon, *Greek and Roman Athletics: A Bibliography* (Chicago: Ares, 1984); but now consult the annual bibliographies in *Nikephoros*. Mark Golden, *Sport in the Ancient World from A to Z* (London: Routledge, 2004), is a helpful reference work.

3 For example, David J. Phillips and David Pritchard, eds, *Sport and Festival in the Ancient Greek World* (Swansea: Classical Press of Wales, 2003); Sinclair Bell and Glenys Davies, eds, *Games and Festivals in Classical Antiquity* (Oxford: Archaeopress, 2004); Gerald P. Schaus and Steven R. Wenn, eds, *Onward to the Olympics: Historical Perspectives on the Olympic Games* (Waterloo: Wilfred Laurier University, 2007); Olga Tzachou-Alexandri, ed., *Mind and Body: Athletic Contests in Ancient Greece* (Athens: Hellenic Ministry of Culture, 1989); John J. Herrmann, Jr and Christine Kondoleon, *Games for the Gods: The Greek Athlete and the Olympic Spirit* (Boston: Museum of Fine Arts, 2004).

4 Waldo E. Sweet, *Sport and Recreation in Ancient Greece* (Oxford: Oxford University, 1987) remains useful but Rachel S. Robinson, *Sources for the History of Greek Athletics* (Cincinnati: privately published, 1955) less so. Zahra Newby, *Athletics in the Ancient World* (London: Bristol Classical Press, 2006) is a good but very brief text. Wolfgang Decker, *Sport in der griechischen Antike* (Munich: Beck, 1995) is detailed and dependable.

5 For courses on Rome, Alison Futrell, *The Roman Games: A Sourcebook* (Oxford: Blackwell, 2006), has surpassed Anne Mahoney, *Roman Sports and Spectacles: A Sourcebook* (Newburyport: Focus, 2001). David S. Potter and D.J. Mattingly, eds, *Life, Death, and Entertainment in the Roman Empire* (Ann Arbor: University of Michigan, 1999) has excellent chapters on entertainment.

6 For example, see David H.J. Larmour, *Stage and Stadium: Drama and Athletics in Ancient Greece* (Hildesheim: Weidmann, 1999). On epic now see Helen Lovatt, *Statius and Epic Games: Sport, Politics and Poetics in the Thebaid* (Cambridge: Cambridge University, 2005).

7 For example, Joachim Ebert, *Griechische Epigramme auf Sieger an gymnischen und hippischen Agonen* (Berlin: Akademie Verlag, 1972), and *Agonismata: Kleine philologische Schriften zur Literatur, Geschichte und Kultur der Antike* (Stuttgart and Leipzig: Teubner, 1997). On H.W. Pleket, see below.

8 See Hugh M. Lee, 'Galen, Johann Heinrich Krause, and the Olympic Myth of Greek Amateur Athletics', *Stadion* 29 (2003), 11–20.

9 E.N. Gardiner, *Greek Athletic Sports and Festivals* (London: Macmillan, 1910), and *Athletics of the Ancient World* (Oxford: Clarendon, 1930); H.A. Harris, *Greek Athletes and Athletics* (London: Hutchinson, 1964), and *Sport in Greece and Rome* (London: Thames and Hudson, 1972).

10 For example, see Simon Goldhill and Robin Osborne, eds, *Performance Culture and Athenian Democracy* (Cambridge: Cambridge University, 1999).

11 See Allen Guttmann, *From Ritual to Record: The Nature of Modern Sports* (New York: Columbia University, 1978) and the modernist debate infra in this *Companion*.

12 For example, W. Decker and Jean-Paul Thuillier, *Le sport dans l'Antiquité: Égypte, Grèce et Rome* (Paris: Picard, 2004). Vera Olivová's broad, illustrated *Sports and Games in the Ancient World* (New York: St Martins, 1984), was innovative in its ethnological approach. On pre-Greek sport, now see W. Decker, 'Vorformen griechischer Agone in der Alten Welt', *Nikephoros* 17 (2004), 9–25; Kyle, *Sport*, 23–37; Crowther, *Sport*, 15–39.

13 Now see Decker, *Pharao und Sport* (Mainz: Philipp von Zabern, 2006).

14 See H.D. Evjen, 'The Origins and Functions of Formal Athletic Competition in the Ancient World', in W. Coulson and H. Kyrieleis, eds, *Proceedings of an International Symposium on the Olympic Games* (Athens: Deutsches Archäologisches Institut Athens, 1992), 95–104; Senta German, *Performance, Power and the Art of the Aegean Bronze Age* (Oxford: Archaeopress, 2005); T.F. Scanlon, 'Women, Bull Sports, Cults and Initiation in Minoan Crete', *Nikephoros* 12 (1999), 33–70.

15 For example, Judith Swaddling, *The Ancient Olympic Games*, 3rd edn (London: British Museum, 2004); David C. Young, *A Brief History of the Olympic Games*, 3rd edn (Oxford: Blackwell, 2004); Nigel Spivey, *The Ancient Olympics* (Oxford: Oxford University, 2004); W.B. Tyrrell, *The Smell of Sweat: Greek Athletics, Olympics and Culture* (Wauconda: Bolchazy-Carducci, 2004). As a coffee-table book, Panos Valavanis, *Games and Sanctuaries in Ancient Greece: Olympia, Delphi, Isthmia, Nemea, Athens* (Los Angeles: Getty Museum, 2004), has outdone N. Yalouris, *The Eternal Olympics. The Art and History of Sport* (New Rochelle: Caratzas, 1979).

16 David C. Young, *The Olympic Myth of Greek Amateur Athletics* (Chicago: Ares, 1984), and *The Modern Olympics: A Struggle for Revival* (Baltimore: Johns Hopkins University, 1996).

17 See Helmut Kyrieleis, 'The German Excavations at Olympia: An Introduction', in Phillips and Pritchard, eds, *Sport*, 41–60. Wendy J. Raschke, ed., *The Archaeology of the Olympics: The Olympics and Other Festivals in Antiquity* (Madison: University of Wisconsin, 1988) and Coulson and Kyrieleis, *Proceedings*, collect valuable essays on early games.

18 Alfred Mallwitz, 'Cult and Competition Locations at Olympia', in Raschke, ed., *Archaeology*, 79–109; Catharine Morgan, *Athletes and Oracles: The Transformation of Olympia and Delphi in the Eighth*

Century BC (Cambridge: Cambridge University, 1990), 26–56. On the Pelopeion, now see S.G. Miller, 'The Shrine of Opheltes and the Earliest Stadium of Nemea', in H. Kyrieleis, ed., *Akten des Internationalen Symposions Olympia 1875–2000* (Mainz: Philipp von Zabern, 2002), 239–50.

19 See Paul Christesen, *Olympic Victor Lists and Ancient Greek History* (Cambridge: Cambridge University, 2007).

20 Miller, *Athletics*, and Crowther, *Athletika*, discuss events, athletes, judging and spectators. Hugh M. Lee's important contributions include *The Program and Schedule of the Ancient Olympic Games* (Hildesheim: Weidmann, 2001), and articles on females, historiography, sources, technical questions and boxing gloves.

21 See Young, *Myth*; Crowther, 'The Ancient Olympics and their Ideals', in Schaus and Wenn, eds, *Onward*, 69–80 (also *Athletika*, 11–22), and 'Power and Politics at the Ancient Olympics: Pisa and the Games of 364 BC', *Stadion* 29 (2003), 1–10, and 'Elis and Olympia: City, Sanctuary and Politics', in Phillips and Pritchard, eds, *Sport*, 61–73 (also *Athletika*, 53–64).

22 Thomas H. Nielsen, *Olympia and the Classical Hellenic City-State Culture* (Copenhagen: Danish Academy of Sciences and Letters, 2007).

23 For example, Miller, *Athletics*; Raschke, *Archaeology*; Valavanis, *Games*; Morgan, *Athletes*; D.G. Romano, *Athletics and Mathematics in Archaic Corinth: The Origins of the Greek Stadion* (Philadelphia: American Philosophical Society, 1993). On later Delphi, see Robert Weir, *Roman Delphi and its Pythian Games* (Oxford: Archaeopress, 2004).

24 See Miller, *Nemea: A Guide to the Site and Museum* (Athens: Hellenic Ministry of Culture, 2004), and *Excavations at Nemea II: The Early Hellenistic Stadium* (Berkeley: University of California, 2001).

25 Jenifer Neils, ed., *Goddess and Polis: The Panathenaic Festival in Ancient Athens* (Hanover: Hood Museum, 1992), and ed., *Worshipping Athena: Panathenaia and Parthenon* (Madison: University of Wisconsin, 1996), and 'The Panathenaia and Kleisthenic Ideology', in W.D.E. Coulson et al., eds, *The Archaeology of Athens and Attica under the Democracy* (Oxford: Oxbow, 1994), 151–60. Now see O. Palagia and A. Choremi-Spetsieri, *The Panathenaic Games: Proceedings of an International Conference held at the University of Athens* (Oxford: Oxbow, 2006).

26 Stephen Hodkinson, 'Inheritance, Marriage and Demography', in Anton Powell, ed., *Classical Sparta: Techniques Behind her Success* (Norman: University of Oklahoma, 1988), 79–121, and 'An Agonistic Culture? Athletic Competition in Archaic and Classical Spartan Society', in S. Hodkinson and A. Powell, eds, *Sparta: New Perspectives* (London: Duckworth, 1999), 147–87.

27 C. Mann, *Athlet und Polis im archaischen und frühklassischen Griechenland* (Göttingen: Vandenhoeck & Ruprecht, 2001) looks at tensions in several states.

28 See M.I. Finley and H.W. Pleket, *The Olympic Games: The First Thousand Years* (London: Chatto & Windus, 1976); H.W. Pleket, 'Zur Soziologie des antiken Sports', *Mededelingen Nederlands Historisch Instituut te Rome* 36 (1976), 57–87, revised in *Nikephoros* 14 (2001), 157–212, and 'The Participants in the Ancient Olympic Games: Social Background and Mentality', in Coulson and Kyrieleis, eds, *Proceedings*, 147–52; Young, *Myth*, 147–70; Kyle, *Athletics*, 102–23, and *Sport*, 198–216; D. Pritchard, 'Athletics, Education and Participation in Classical Athens', in Phillips and Pritchard, eds, *Sport*, 293–349.

29 Paul Christesen, 'The Meaning of *gymnazō*', *Nikephoros* 15 (2002), 7–37, and 'The Transformation of Athletics in Sixth-Century Greece', in Schaus and Wenn, eds, *Onward*, 59–68.

30 S.G. Miller 'Nude Democracy', in P. Flensted-Jensen et al., eds, *Polis and Politics* (Copenhagen: Museum Tusculum, 2000), 77–96; but cf. Kyle, *Sport*, 85–90.

31 See Scanlon, *Eros*, 98–174; Kyle, *Sport*, 217–28. On later female sport, see H.M. Lee, 'SIG³ 802: Did Women Compete against Men in Greek Athletic Festivals?', *Nikephoros* 1 (1988), 103–17, and 'Athletics and the Bikini Girls from Piazza Armerina', *Stadion* 10 (1984), 45–76.

32 W.L. Adams, 'Other People's Games: The Olympics, Macedonia and Greek Athletics', *Journal of Sport History* 30 (2003), 205–17; Kyle, *Sport*, 229–50.

33 J.-P. Thuillier, *Les Jeux athlétique dans la civilization Étrusque* (Rome: École française de Rome, 1985), and *Le sport dans la Rome antique* (Paris: Errance, 1996). Harris, *Sport*, 151–243, remains useful on Greek antecedents and Roman and Byzantine chariot racing.

34 For example, David L. Bomgardner, *The Story of the Roman Amphitheatre* (London: Routledge, 2000); A. Gabucci, ed., *Colosseum*, translated by M. Becker (Los Angeles: Getty Museum, 2001).

35 D.S. Potter, 'Entertainers in the Roman Empire', in Potter and Mattingly, eds, *Life*, 256–325.

36 For example, 'The Contagion of the Throng: Absorbing Violence in the Roman World', *Hermathena* 164 (1998), 65–88; '*Missio* at Halicarnassus', *Harvard Studies in Classical Philology* 100 (2000), 487–500.

37 Paul Veyne, *Bread and Circuses: Historical Sociology and Political Pluralism*, translated by B. Pearce (London: Penguin, 1990); A. Cameron, *Bread and Circuses: The Roman Emperor and his People* (Oxford: Clarendon, 1974).

38 Marcus Junkelmann, '*Familia Gladiatoria*: The Heroes of the Amphtheatre', in Köhne and Ewigleben, eds, *Gladiators*, 31–74, and *Das Spiel mit dem Tod* (Mainz: Philipp von Zabern, 2000), 31–74, details the types and techniques of gladiators. Also see L. Jacobelli, *Gladiators at Pompeii* (Los Angeles: Getty Museum, 2003); M.J. Carter, 'Gladiatorial Combat: The Rules of Engagement', *Classical Journal* 102 (2006), 97–114.

39 Stoics criticized the emotionalism of spectators but praised the gladiator's discipline and acceptance of death. See M. Wistrand, *Entertainment and Violence in Ancient Rome: the Attitudes of Roman Writers of the First Century AD* (Göteborg: Acta Universitatis Gothoburgensis, 1992).

40 See Crowther's articles in 'Roman Attitudes to Greek Athletics', *Athletika* 376–422; M. Lämmer, ed., 'Agonistik in der römischen Kaiserzeit', *Stadion* 24 (1998), 1–183.

41 See agonistic articles in Robert's *Opera Minora Selecta*, vols I–VI (Amsterdam: Hakkert, 1969–84).

42 See H.W. Pleket, 'Mass-Sport and Local Infrastructure in the Greek Cities of Asia Minor', *Stadion* 24 (1998), 151–72; Onno Van Nijf, 'Local Heroes: Athletics, Festivals, and Elite Self-Fashioning in the Roman East', in Simon Goldhill, ed., *Being Greek under Rome: Cultural Identity, the Second Sophistic and the Development of Empire* (Cambridge: Cambridge University, 2001), 306–34.

43 For example, Beacham, *Spectacle*, 197–234.

44 See Scanlon, *Eros*, 40–63; A. Farrington, 'Olympic Victors and the Popularity of the Olympic Games in the Imperial Period', *Tyche* 12 (1997), 15–46; Sinn, *Olympia*, 111–29.

8   Gender

Susan J. Bandy

Gender. n. a grammatical term only. To talk of persons or creatures of the masculine or feminine gender, meaning of the male or female sex, is either a jocularity (permissible or not according to context) or a blunder.

H.W. Fowler, *Dictionary of Modern English Usage*[1]

Introduction

In 1978, Canadian sports sociologist Ann Hall formally introduced the concept of 'gender' in sport studies[2] in a monograph entitled *Sport and Gender: A Feminist Perspective on the Sociology of Sport*, in which she reviewed the sociological research and literature as it related to the female experience in sport and offered a critique of this material from a feminist perspective. Hall's use of the term 'gender' was, to the best of my knowledge, without precedent in sports studies and, in retrospect, her early work seems crucial to the development of sports studies because it brought the concept into the discourse and called for a feminist perspective, which would begin to significantly alter research in sports studies. With the work of Hall and others, who began to use the concept 'gender' rather than 'sex', the focus of research began to shift away from the female athlete toward the concept of 'gender' and later to a critique of sport and physical culture, as I have argued elsewhere.[3] As I will attempt to show in this chapter, the concept of 'gender' would be further expanded beyond that of a distinct category and redefined as a dynamic, relational process that introduced new directions, theories and paradigms for research in the discipline of sports studies. Moreover, the inclusion of the concept of 'gender' – along with such concepts as race, social class and ethnicity, as well as a turn toward postmodernism and deconstruction (and the introduction of theories of hegemony and power) – further encouraged the study of such topics as globalization, post-colonialism, space and the media, which moved the development of the discipline of sports studies from a disciplinary to an interdisciplinary focus. Most recently 'gender' seems to have been viewed as an interrelational concept by scholars, and this perspective has paralleled and contributed to the inclusion of such concepts and topics as power, representation, narrativity and language with a more recent transdisciplinary and transnational perspective in the study of sport.[4]

The focus of this chapter is principally on scholarship in North America and the United Kingdom, not only because I am most familiar with this scholarship but also because it includes the largest volume, the most varied examples and interpretation of the subject, and the fullest elaboration of the theoretical debates concerning gender and sport.

The introduction of gender into the discourse in sports studies

The introduction of 'gender' into the discourse in sports studies in the 1970s reflected and depended on the convergence of a number of interrelated factors: the introduction of 'gender' into the discourse of the academy by female scholars, especially in women's studies and women's history; the development of disciplines generally and the academic development of sports studies specifically, which included an emphasis placed upon theory (as opposed to practice); second wave feminism and the contemporaneous increase in the participation of women in sport and an increase in the number of female scholars in sports studies; the influence of postmodernism and deconstructionism on the development of theory in sports studies (most notably Marxist theory as well as the work of Communist theorist Antonio Gramsci and the French theorist Michel Foucault); and, lastly, a general interest in the human body in the academy at large.

Following the distinctions made between 'sex'[5] and 'gender' by Robert J. Stoller[6] in 1968 and the influence of an emerging feminist scholarship in which the distinctions between male and female, nature and culture, and sex and gender were being questioned – and dualistic, hierarchical forms of knowledge challenged – scholars in women's studies incorporated 'gender' in the 1970s.[7] According to historian Gisela Bock, the concept of 'gender' was introduced 'as a social, cultural, political, and historical category, in order to express the insight that women's subordination, inferiority and powerlessness are not dictated by nature, but are social, cultural, political and historical constructions'.[8] As another historian, Joan Wallach Scott, explains, feminists began to use 'gender' as a way of referring to the social organization of the relationship between the sexes. Further, Scott argues that the word denoted a rejection of the biological determinism implicit in the use of such terms as 'sex' or 'sexual difference' and that perhaps most importantly, with the use of 'gender', feminist scholarship 'would fundamentally transform disciplinary paradigms'.[9]

Disciplines are dynamic structures that undergo continuous change,[10] and around the middle of the 20th century, disciplinary boundaries (at least those in educational institutions in the USA) began to blur. Methods, approaches, or frameworks known as interdisciplinarity and multidisciplinarity soon began to emerge. At approximately the same time, the discipline of women's studies (and sports studies) began to develop. According to Aino Saarinen, feminist researchers were inspired by Thomas S. Kuhn's theories in *The Structure of Scientific Revolutions*, in which crises in prevailing paradigms were resolved by the emergence of a new research frame.[11] Such a context provided fertile ground for the acceptance of the use of 'gender', and its use slowly began to transform disciplines of knowledge. At the same time, rather dramatic changes in the discipline of sports studies began to appear as American scholars called for a transformation of their own discipline.[12] According to these scholars, it was imperative that sports studies (then known as physical education) become an 'academic discipline' (rather than an applied field or pedagogical discipline) and to do so, theoretical work was necessary. In the context of this development, the various sub-disciplines emerged, and the need for more theoretical work opened the way for importing theories from other 'parent' disciplines such as history, sociology and so on. Women's issues and the concept of 'gender' were then embraced by feminists in a dramatically changing discipline of sports studies.

In the 1960s, 'second wave feminism' emerged and brought with it political activism that focused on gaining full social and economic equality in Western nations where women had already gained many legal rights. Second wave feminism produced the context for the emergence of the women's sports movement in North America and Western Europe, and produced a steady growth in women's sport at both the national and international levels. While more and more women were entering the sporting arena, the feminist analysis of sport 'was growing due to the emergence of a small but critical mass of women scholars trained in academic disciplines and excited by the potential of feminist theory', as Susan Birrell notes.[13] By the early 1980s, it was apparent that feminist researchers were engaged in forging connections between feminist theory, sports institutions and the social practice of sport, or as Ann Hall writes about her own experiences: 'As feminists, our theory, politics, and practices are inextricably linked'.[14] Hall and Patricia Vertinsky[15] attest to the importance of the convergence of developments in feminist thought, postmodern theory and critical theory in sports studies, particularly with regard to sociology and history, respectively. According to the extensive analysis of Alan Ingham and Peter Donnelly, the simultaneous convergence of three currents of thought – the Gramscian, the poststructuralist and the Foucauldian within sport sociological discourse – became the theoretical tools of sports feminists. The work of Gramsci was useful concerning arguments pertaining to patriarchy and enabled a focus on hegemonic masculinity and sport; poststructuralism provided an analysis of the social construction of gender and sexuality and its representation in the media; and Foucault's work concerning power – as hierarchically ordered, possessed by persons and enmeshed in networks variously asserted through modern institutions and manifested most concretely at the level of the body – informed the discourse and engaged sports feminists.[16]

Developments concerning the inclusion of 'gender' in the discourse were also furthered by an academic interest in the body that became apparent in the 1960s. By the 1970s, there was an expanding interest in the body as a topic of teaching and research as noted by Mike Featherstone and Bryan S. Turner in the introduction of the first issue of *Body and Society*.[17] 'Bodies are in', wrote Arthur W. Frank in a review article in *Theory, Culture & Society* in 1990.[18] Although this interest was the result of a diverse range of theoretical traditions, many scholars attribute it to the influence of the work of French historian and social critic Michel Foucault, the contradictory impulses of modernity, and to feminism. Further, given the emphasis upon theory in the discipline of sports studies, as well as the influence of postmodern theories, Foucault and feminism, a wide-ranging interest in the body was shared by many scholars in sport studies.[19] As Hall noted, the work of Foucault was useful because it regarded the body as an historical and culturally specific entity and allowed the conception of the sexualized body without 'positing an original sexual difference or fixed biological essence'.[20] Foucault's work concerning the social construction of bodies through discourse appealed to feminist scholars in sports studies as they sought to understand the construction of the sporting body through modern sport. With the introduction of the concept of 'gender', sports scholars, largely using constructivist theories, came to understand the sporting body as a 'gendered' body.

I propose in the following that much of the research that has been done concerning gender and sport has been done in the context of three conceptual or theoretical frameworks that have been used by many feminists, especially sports sociologists and sports historians, in the past 25 years. These are discussed in the following sections, in which the emphasis is placed on the assumptions, theories, concepts and methods used rather than the conclusions that have been drawn.

The female athlete as subject: disciplinary perspectives

As Joan Wallach Scott claims,[21] the first approach to a rewriting of women's history was based on the assumption that women are indeed different from men and have different experiences than men, which leads to a writing of 'her story'.[22] The work of the first female scholars in sports studies similarly noted that the focus of the research had been on sports*men* and *men's* sport, and they then began to study sportswomen and women's sport.[23] What underpinned such an approach was the basic assumption that the female athlete was indeed different and her experiences in sport were different as well.

By the 1970s interest in women and sport was evident in the newly emerging sub-disciplines of sports studies. Following the demand for theoretical work, female scholars in the discipline opened the way for a more scholarly approach to the study of women in sport. Some of the most influential, pioneering work was done by sport philosopher Eleanor Metheny and sport psychologist Dorothy V. Harris. Metheny exposed the ideological, symbolic and mythic nature of sport; Harris focused on the distinctive nature of the female athlete and incorporated a variety of psychological concepts in the study of female athletes.[24] Harris's work provided the foundation for the beginnings of theoretical work within the sub-discipline of sport psychology with the adaptation of the female apologetic and the notion of psychological androgyny to the sporting context. In particular, the concept of androgyny, in retrospect, can be seen as a transitional concept that would enable 'gender' to be incorporated into sports studies. In 1972, Harris hosted the first conference devoted to women in sport in the USA, and the research presented at this conference revealed an expanding interest concerning the psychological, sociological, physiological and biomechanical considerations of women in sport.[25]

With the publication of Ellen Gerber et al.'s *The American Woman in Sport* in 1974,[26] scholars introduced additional perspectives from history, sociology and biophysiology to the fledgling literature on the female athlete. This book was of particular significance in that it offered the first feminist perspectives of sport by examining the social construction of woman and femininity, as well as the symbolic aspect of sport, years before ideas concerning the social construction of women and sport entered the scholarly discourse. A few years after the publication of Gerber's book, Carole Oglesby's collection of essays, *Women and Sport: From Myth to Reality* and Hall's previously mentioned monograph also brought a feminist critique to sport research and, as a result, 'gender' entered the discourse and began to destabilize concepts such as sex and sex roles.[27]

Sports historians from the USA, Canada and the United Kingdom provided additional feminist critiques of sport and frameworks of an inclusive, relational nature rather than frameworks based on the notion of sexual difference. Nancy Struna called for the inclusion of gender as a 'fundamental historical variable' that should lie 'at the center of theoretical debates and methodological innovations' in sports history.[28] Patricia Vertinsky's work concerning exercise, the physical capabilities of women, and the medical profession further placed gender at the centre of historical research and opened the way for research concerning the ideological basis of women's exclusion from sport and the social construction of the female body.[29] Jennifer Hargreaves also forged ideas concerning the social production of gender *in* and *through* sport, linking social constructivist theories to the patriarchal character of modern sport.[30]

The historical work of this early period also reflected international perspectives as well as interest in various historical periods, as evidenced by the publication of two collections of papers that were presented at the *International Congress on Women and Sport* held in Rome, Italy in 1980. Of vital importance were those devoted to the historical aspects of women and sport, in which scholars from several countries (Australia, Canada, Egypt, England, Germany, Israel and Japan) explored the participation of women in sport in various historical periods including ancient Greece, the Renaissance, and 19th- and

20th-century Egypt and Germany.[31] The work of international scholars such as Reet Howell, Max Howell and Jennifer Hargreaves, as well as American scholar Betty Spears, fostered an interest in women and sport in classical Greece.[32] More recently, classical scholar Bettina Kratzmüller of Austria has continued to refine the scholarship concerning women and sport in classical Greece.[33] In other countries of Continental Europe, Gertrud Pfister's *Frau und Sport* was published in 1980[34] and was among the earliest books devoted to women and sport, soon to be followed by Norwegian Gerd von der Lippe's *Kvinner og Idrett: Fra Myte til Realitet* in 1982 and Leena Liane's *Kropp, idrott och kvinnohistoria* in 1991 in Finland.[35] The work of these and other European scholars placed the female athlete at the centre of the developing work in sports history and lay the foundation for comparative and more synoptic work concerning the history of women and sport, such as Uriel Simri's *A Concise World's History of Women's Sports* (1983) and Allen Guttman's *Women and Sports: A History* (1991), which also appeared in these early years.

A more expansive, international view of the female athlete was also offered by Roberta J. Park, who provided a model for other scholars to follow when examining 'gender' more closely from a transatlantic perspective in order to understand how sport is depicted as the 'natural' arena for males.[36] Her later work with J.A. Mangan, *From Fair Sex to Feminism: Sport and the Socialization of Women in the Industrial and Post-industrial Eras* (1987) indicated a turning point concerning research on women's sports history, as Vertinsky suggests, marking the trend toward the use of feminist analysis of sport and examining the crucial period of the formation of attitudes and practices concerning sport that were predominant in the 20th century.[37]

The research of these and other scholars brought the female athlete and her sporting experiences into the discourse and then called for feminist analyses of sport. Moreover, the questions that this research raised required more complex analyses concerning the gendered nature of modern sport. Thus 'gender' entered the discourse and began to destabilize concepts such as sex and sex roles.

The assumption of difference, upon which this early research was based, was problematic yet fruitful for future research. On the one hand, it presented the notion of sexual difference and reinforced essentialist ideas concerning females, which had prevented their entry into sport and would later be addressed as a political issue concerning equality in sport.[38] It also raised the age-old question of dualistic views that both feminism and postmodernism sought to address. For feminists, engagement with such oppositions as nature versus culture, body versus mind and private versus public, in which women were identified with the former, was critical in understanding the exclusion of women from sport. As the research of this and later periods revealed, arguments for the exclusion of women and sport were supported by such dominant dualistic views. On the other hand, such reigning assumptions and enduring dualisms evoked important questions that could only be addressed through the incorporation of a revised conception of 'gender' into the scholarly discourse. Accompanying this revision was a cultural studies approach, a concern with sociological and historical issues that brought a critique of modern sport and society, and the introduction of postmodern, feminist and deconstructionist theories.

From the female athlete to cultural critique: interdisciplinary and relational perspectives

The study of gender brought an examination of women and men in relation to one another in sport and began to destabilize the discourse, moving it away from a focus on sex and binary modes of thought toward an interdisciplinary focus in the various sub-disciplines.[39] In what Hall refers to as a turn from 'categoric' to 'relational' research, feminist research turned away from a focus on the female athlete toward sport and sporting culture and thus introduced an interdisciplinary and cultural studies approach incorporating a variety of disciplines in its analyses. As Scott suggests, gender, when understood in relational terms, requires scholars to ask about the implications of definitions and laws that apply to one group for another group, what the comparative location and activities of men and women reveal about each other, and what representations of sexual difference suggest about the structure of social, economic and political authority.[40] Using the work of Foucault, Gramsci, and postmodern and feminist theories, sports scholars began to deconstruct modern sport, arguing that 'sporting practices are historically produced, socially constructed, and culturally defined to serve the interests and needs of powerful groups in society', as Hall noted.[41] In a most fertile time of sports studies research, scholars embraced concepts such as globalization, post-colonialism, power, hegemony, masculinity, the socially constructed body, space and the media, which began to dominate the discourse. It was within the sub-disciplines of sport sociology and sports history, though, that one finds the use of 'gender' as a process most fruitful for research during the 1980s and 1990s.

Feminist scholars in sport, as was the case with postmodernists, began to challenge the androcentric definition of knowledge and to critique the epistemology of modernity, specifically its rationalism and dualism as masculine modes of thought that serve to legitimate a patriarchal society.[42] Researchers also began to formulate clear and coherent challenges to the conceptual frameworks in the various sub-disciplines. Using new approaches to research, scholars began to recognize the autonomy of sport in society and, therefore, its power of legitimation. The use of analytic cultural criticism, in particular, enabled scholars to examine the ideological processes concerning gender differences in sport and, as Paul Willis argued, 'achievement in sport strengthens male identity, assumes that sports success is success at being masculine, and that physical achievement and masculine activity are taken to be the same'. Willis's work further clarified the legit-imative power of sport in terms of an ideology of difference and female inferiority, and was among the first to portray sport as having been socially constructed and mediated to show that the patriarchal nature of sport is natural.[43]

In addition to analytic cultural criticism, Mary A. Boutilier and Lucinda San Giovanni's *The Sporting Woman* introduced the first analysis of alternative feminist frameworks – liberal feminism, Marxist feminism, radical feminism and socialist feminism – into the discourse. Boutilier and San Giovanni questioned the institution of male sports and called for a radical transformation of sports, an approach taken by several other scholars.[44] Sport psychologist Dianne Gill noted the importance of a feminist perspective and advocated that research in sport psychology should be placed in a broader cultural context. In 1992, Gill wrote that 'sound sport psychological research on gender beliefs and processes within the social context of sport and exercise could advance our overall understanding of gender and sport'.[45]

In 1984 Nancy Struna called for the need to understand the history of American sporting women, noting the limitations within women's sports history that employed paradigms that had been used to examine men's modern sport. Further, Struna argued, '[t]he history of sportswomen in the twentieth century also raises innumerable questions about relationships between sport and society and why people became involved, in varying degrees in sport'.[46] As Vertinsky notes in her review of women's sports history,

Struna advocated the exploration of such themes as conflict, identity and the relativity of equality.[47] In 'Gender and Sporting Practice in Early America', Struna focused on both sport and other recreational forms according to consumption and production, which 'permits one to examine more fully the dimensions of gender relations'.[48] Later, in *People of Prowess: Sport, Leisure, and Labor in Early Anglo-America*, she continued to integrate gender relations into the 'broader context of and relationships between labor and leisure'. In so doing, she framed sport more broadly and thereby more thoughtfully explored the physically recreative and sporting practices of women of the 17th and 18th centuries, and revealed the relational nature of gender and sport to the broader historical context. Following the work of Teresa de Lauretis,[49] Catriona M. Parratt similarly called for an expanded focus of sports history beyond that of the hierarchical, contemporary under-standing of sports as 'male, modern, and athletic' to encompass a more diverse range of activities and the writing of women's sports history rather than the history of women in sports.[50]

A focus on power and the processes of domination and subordination, as these relate to gender relations in sport, as well as critiques of the place of sport in cultural production, brought the body into the discourse.[51] Following the early work of Metheny concerning the symbolic nature of sport, Jennifer Hargreaves more explicitly linked the symbolic nature of the female body with the patriarchal character of modern sport.[52] The inclusion of the body in the discourse also revealed two additional areas of research that were related to an interest in the gendered body: sexuality and masculinity. In 1981, Ann Hall introduced the idea of sexual identity in sport, which would later be understood as a barrier to the participation of women in sport. Helen Lenskyj's research further elaborated the importance of male control of female sexuality and its relationship to the exclusion of women from sport.[53] Lenskyj was among the first to draw attention to the relationships among ideology, female sexuality and sports participation by linking the anatomical, physiological, social and expressive dimensions of female sexuality.[54] Of critical importance to the discussion of gender and sexuality is also the work of Susan K. Cahn's *Coming on Strong: Gender and Sexuality in Twentieth-Century Women's Sport* (1994), which extended the critique beyond that of sport to American culture at large to show that women's efforts for over a century in sport revealed the history of gender relations in American culture.[55] Equally important is that Cahn's book brought the subject of homophobia and the inclusion (perhaps for the first time) of the question of the De Beauvoirian 'other' in women's sport – black women and lesbians – into the discourse. Moreover, Cahn further clarified the notion of sport as contested terrain noting, as few feminist works have, that sport, in addition to being a site of female oppression, is also a site of female liberation.[56]

Feminist critiques concerning sex roles, sexuality, and the patriarchal and sexist character of modern sport also brought a focus on masculinity, and thus male scholars began to critique modern sport as an activity formed as a consequence of a crisis in 19th-century masculinity. The early work of D.F. Sabo and R. Runfola, *Jock: Sports and Male Identity* in 1980 was followed by critical analyses that used gender as a fundamental category of analysis.[57] Much of this work addressed the nature of the relationship among sport, men and the gender order, and the way in which sport has been used in the construction of masculinity as oppressive of women and repressive of men.[58] The research concerning sexuality also brought discussions of the marginalization of women of colour and gay men in sport as well as an exploration of homophobia in sport. Of considerable note in understanding the relationship between gender and sex and with a focus on the experience of non-elite level athletes – instead of elite level sport – is Brian

Pronger's *The Arena of Masculinity: Sports, Homosexuality, and the Meaning of Sex.*
Extending the exploration of homosexuality to a broader understanding of the relationship between sex and gender, Pronger's work foreshadowed the work that would begin
somewhat later as scholars sought to deconstruct gender in an attempt to understand the
relationships among sexuality, sex and gender, using a new feminist paradigm expressed
as intersexuality.

Viewing 'gender' as a process and with a critique turned toward the contributions of
sport and other institutions to the on-going domination and subordination of women,
scholars began to examine the history of the institutionalization of discrimination in
modern sport. It is important to recognize the socio-historical analysis of Jennifer Hargreaves
whose research noted the lack of use of gender theories in sport and offered a most
comprehensive analysis of the gendered nature of modern sport and the institutionalization of discrimination in modern sport.[59] Scholars became interested as well in the ways
in which institutions promoted sexual difference in sport, and researchers soon took up
an interest in the media and the 'importance of discourses, representations, and ideologies
in naturalizing masculine dominance in sporting practices'.[60]

Research concerning 'gender' of the 1980s and 1990s, most particularly in sports
history and sport sociology, was important for the academic development of the discipline
of sports studies for many reasons. Through a gendered analysis, scholars embraced
postmodernism and feminism and brought a much-needed critique of modern sport. The
feminist, interdisciplinary and cultural studies approaches of this period also challenged
the hegemonic nature of knowledge in the discipline (of its theories and paradigms of
analysis as well as the relation between the various knowledges and methodologies in
sub-disciplines such as sports history and sport sociology). Such research 'decentered the
center', encouraged a movement across the borders of traditional disciplinary configurations
and transformed the methodological approaches as well as the concerns of the discipline.
Issues pertaining to 'gender' also contributed to the need for an alternative view of
gender – the interrelational. Such a view required new paradigms, methodologies and
approaches to further explore the complexity of 'gender'.

It was again the work of Roberta J. Park that reflected changing perspectives and the
search for new paradigms and methodologies concerning gender and sport. In 1991, as
the guest editor of a special issue of the *Journal of Sport History* that was devoted to
gender, Park argues that conceptions of it, '[f]ar from being monolithic ... may be
influenced by race, ethnicity, chronological age, social class, political status and much
more'. Further she avers: 'For many ... 'gender' can best – and probably only – be
understood from comparative perspectives'.[61] The interconnectedness and interrelational
nature of understandings concerning gender and sport had thus become apparent and
became the basis for changing views of gender that informed the scholarly discourse in
sport as well as requiring different methodological approaches.

Gender as interrelational and intersubjective: transdisciplinary perspectives

In the 1970s women of colour, lesbians and working-class feminists began to challenge the
feminism of difference – that is difference from men – arguing that the perspective was
universalizing, creating a feminism of uniformity. The challenge stemmed from the assumption
that all women have something in common and that this commonality creates a particular
kind of common experience and, therefore, a uniform understanding of feminism.

A healthy debate that focused on the diversity among women as well as the implications of this diversity for conceptualizations of gender emerged in the literature. The claim was that white middle-class feminists did not speak for all women. According to Spelman, white feminism saw itself as a universal feminism, a feminism that could not reconstruct an inclusive foundation.[62] Second wave feminists had claimed that feminists had used the term 'gender' to destabilize biology. As feminists came to understand, female gender was not simply understood as a cultural and psychological effect of being biologically female, but rather as a cultural effect of male dominance and patriarchy. Women of colour insisted that other cultural forces such as racism and classism were also determinants of female gender, and they determined it differently for white middle-class women, women of colour and poor women.

Feminists responded with an analytical tool or a new paradigm known as 'intersectionality', which Jennifer C. Nash recently defined as the feminist paradigm for theorizing identity and oppression and combating hierarchy, hegemony and exclusivity (within feminism also). Noting that categories – including race and gender – are too simplistic to capture the complexity of lived experience, she proposed that gender be understood as the different ways in which women act, think and feel, given their historical circumstances as well as the variety of roles, expectations and limitations imposed on them. Moreover, gender always has specific, contextualized meanings; it is not something that all women share in the same way. According to Nash, intersectionality serves a few theoretical and political purposes that enable scholars to create new paradigms for a revisioning of gender. First, it simultaneously subverts binaries concerning race and gender when theorizing identity. Second, racial variations within gender and gendered variations within race can be more easily understood through an intersectional view. Last, intersectionality enables scholars to understand the legacy of exclusions of multiple marginalized subjects from feminist and anti-racist work and the impact of those absences on both theory and practice.[63]

According to this view, intersectionality allows scholars to avoid essentialism precisely because it allows for the recognition of different female genders and does not posit a sameness about women that is derived from theories based only on the experiences of middle-class women. Further, intersectionality refers to multiple oppressions experienced by non-white and poor women in particular and requires a de-gendering of our perspectives.

A number of important critiques of gender that pointed toward a need for an intersectional analysis appeared in feminist literature. In her book *Breaking the Bowls: Degendering and Feminist Change*, published in 2005, Judith Lorber argues that 'gender is a binary system of social organization that creates inequality'. To degender means 'to recognize that the two genders are not at all homogenous categories since they are intersected by other major social statuses – racial ethnic group, social class, national identity, religious affiliation – and by individual variations such as age, sexual orientation, relational and parental statuses, and physical status'.[64] In other words, multiplicities of genders – gender diversity and gender freedom – suggests a living outside of the binary sex/gender system. Further, Lorber advocates that we should be open to intersexuality, transgender queering and sexual fluidity, and deliberately ambiguous, non-gendered presentations of self. According to Patricia Collins, the construct of intersectionality references two types of relationships: 'the interconnectedness of ideas and the social structure in which they occur, and the intersecting of hierarchies of gender, race, economic class, sexuality, and ethnicity'. Collins maintains that viewing gender within the logic of intesectionality redefines it as a 'constellation of ideas and social practices that are historically situated within mutually construct multiple systems of oppression'.[65]

In support of the new paradigm of intersectionality, third wave feminists, according to Leslie Heywood and Jennifer Drake, 'take cultural production and sexual politics as key sites of struggle, seeking to use desire and pleasure, as well as anger to fuel struggles for justice'.[66] Further, third wave feminists seek a new subjectivity and languages and images that account for both multiplicity and difference, that negotiate contradiction in affirmative ways, and that give voice to a politics and coalition.

Questions concerning the methodologies of intersectionality soon appeared in order to conduct research that is not based on universalizing and essentializing ideas, research that 'lives outside of the binary sex/gender system'.[67] According to Lorber, most research designs (in sociology) assume that each person has one sex, one sexuality and one gender. In her later work, she argues we should recognize the multiplicity of genders, sexes and sexualities, but the difficulty lies in needing categories for analysis while at the same time deconstructing them. In other words, how do scholars conduct research without reifying and contributing to the existence of such categories? Further Lorber posits that scholars should split that which has been conflated or joined: sex (biology and physiology); sexuality (desire, sexual preference and sexual orientation); and gender (a social status, sometimes with sexual identity). Additionally scholars argue that there is a need to create research paradigms that examine the social constructions and means of sex, sexuality and gender as has been done for race, ethnicity and social class.

This paradigmatic shift toward intersectionality in feminist research also appeared in sport studies research concerned with gender. As early as 1990, sports studies scholars embraced the work of feminist scholars such as Judith Butler, Elizabeth Grosz and Judith Lorber. As noted previously, following the work of Roberta Park, in the early 1990s, sports historians began to recognize that gender was not monolithic; rather it intersects with a number of other dimensions of human experience and identity in sport such as race, ethnicity, age, social class and political status. Reflecting a trend toward inter-sectionality, sports scholars began to approach the study of gender in new ways, including the use of concepts or themes (rather than theories) and an admixture of methodologies and sources of knowledge, most particularly the use of narratives.[68] Moreover, scholars began to adopt transdisciplinary and transnational perspectives as they sought to deconstruct gender, viewing gender (and race, social class and ethnicity) from an interrelational and intersectional point of view.[69] Of particular note here is the appearance of a journal explicitly devoted to the use of themes as a means of approaching interdisciplinary perspectives that incorporated ideas that have often been used in scholarly analyses of sport. Structured around specific topics rather than around specific disciplines, *Junctures: The Journal of Thematic Dialogue* first appeared in December of 2003 and was created to push the boundaries of interdisciplinarity by including the work of several scholars from a variety of disciplines, who examine a particular theme such as the body, play, space, language – subjects that can easily be linked to sport.

As scholars continued their work, the interrelational and the multiplicities of gender – intersections between gender, colour, ethnicity, race and sexuality – brought forth an interest in 'other' women: women of colour, lesbians and those outside the margins of mainstream sport theory and practice entered the discourse. Susan Cahn's work concerning the 'Cinderellas' of sport, for example, included histories of women of colour as well as lesbians in sport.[70] Jennifer Hargreaves' *Heroines of Sport: The Politics of Difference and Identity* (2000) similarly recognized the 'others' in sport in a study of aboriginal, Muslim, lesbian and disabled women from a transnational perspective. Rather than an interest in the globalizing process and its impact upon contemporary sport, Hargreaves looks from a transnational point of view and uses an admixture of methods and sources to examine the relationship between the sporting experiences and identity of 'others' from different parts of the world.[71] Using Foucault's notions of power, she examines power relations among women, using concepts of inclusion and exclusion, power and privilege, and the relationship between the local and the global. In this context, gender is seen as a shared and universal experience, while at the same time is an experience of difference (according to nationality, sexuality, physical ability, religion and social class) and individual identity in sport. With an interest in the transnational – as that which exists between nations or perhaps between people – Hargreaves' work examines both the simultaneity of multiple oppressions and the complexity of identity.

In an attempt to further deconstruct gender within the context of sport, inter-sectionality surfaced as a methodology or approach to understanding the multiplicity and fluidity of gender.[72] In *Built to Win: The Female Athlete as Cultural Icon*, Leslie Heywood and Shari L. Dworkin study the female athlete as a cultural icon through a variety of approaches: representation, poetry, film, interviews and feminist theory.[73] Their work also focuses on the body in sport, including both the female and male body in sport, attempting to further explore the fluidity of gender. In a similar way, Barbara Cos and Shona Thompson connect 'multiple bodies' in sport with matters concerning the experiences of sexuality in sport and the multiple discourses that suggest the liberating bodily experiences of female soccer (football) players.[74]

Historians also turned to less traditional sources in writing scholarly analyses of sports history with the intention of more fully examining their subject. According to Jeff Segrave's analysis, Elliot Gorn's book, *The Manly Art*, is not just the history of boxing itself. Rather it includes gender history, social history and labour history in an analysis of the sport.[75] In this integrative approach, Gorn used newspapers and popular pamphlets, fiction and poetry, and even doggerel verse and ballads.[76]

It can be argued that Löic Wacquant, former student of Pierre Bourdieu with whom he wrote *An Introduction to Reflexive Sociology*, more consciously mixes sources, theories and methodologies, while embracing intersectionality as a method of studying sport by viewing race, gender and sport as social processes that inform each other while at the same time operate in specific ways. In analysing race, Wacquant advocated that social scientists should 'skirt the issues of origins and abandon a search for a single overarching concept to develop an analysis of racial domination'.[77] In his work, he dismisses a search for 'origins' and examines the way in which various processes of subordination and experience coalesce during particular social moments. In his masterful analysis of boxing in *Body and Soul: Notebooks of an Apprentice Boxer*, Wacquant not only embraces inter-sectionality, he utilizes a transdisciplinary approach, including the perspectives of sociology, ethnology, literature and sport, to provide a social critique from the perspective of the nexus of race, social class, gender and sport. Educated as a sociologist and engaged as an amateur boxer, Wacquant brings to his analysis sociological theory, ethnographic 'data' and literary insights, while at the same time validating experiential, gendered and bodily ways of knowing from the sport experience. Such an examination searches for knowledge that exists on different levels of reality and is revealed in multiple ways of knowing, thus pointing to the importance of transdisciplinary approaches to the study of sport. Wacquant describes the purpose of his book as follows:

> Breaking with the moralizing discourse – that indifferently feeds both celebration and denigration – produced by the 'gaze from afar' of an outside observer standing at

a distance from or above the specific universe, this book seeks to suggest how boxing 'makes sense' as soon as one takes pains to get close enough to it to grasp it *with one's body*, in a quasi experimental situation. It is for this reason composed of three texts of deliberately disparate statuses and styles, which juxtapose sociological analysis, ethnographic description, and literary evocation in order to convey at once percept and concept, the hidden determinations and the lived experiences, the external factors and the internal sensations that intermingle to make the boxer's world. In short, the book aims to *display and demonstrate* in the same move the social and sensual logic that informs boxing as a bodily craft in the contemporary black American ghetto.[78]

Scholars of sport can draw from Wacquant's work in a number of important ways: examining the way in which race and social categories utilize differing technologies of categorization, observing the disciplining of the body in distinctive ways, and reflecting upon the coalescing of certain social, historical, representational, bodily and sporting experiences.[79]

The introduction of 'queer theory' would also supply a theoretical framework that could be used to advance intersectional and transdisciplinary investigations of gender and sport. Introduced in 1991 by Teresa de Lauretis 'queer theory' provoked a critique of sexual identity and postmodernism's suspicion of fundamental truths and categories and altered the way we think about gender, sexuality, desire and the body in sports studies.[80] On a theoretical level, scholars have noted the absence of queer theory in sport – as is the case of the academy in general – revealing that this absence has worked against a more expansive and comprehensive, interrelational and intersectional analysis in sport. As queer theorists have discovered, multiple categories disturb the comfortable polity of the familiar opposites that assume one dominant and one subordinate group, one normal and one deviant identity, one hegemonic status and one 'other'.

Influenced by expanding notions of gender and the influence of queer theory, researchers have recently focused on the control or containment of female sexuality and the expression of sexuality in women's sports, turning their attention to sex testing and gender verification by sports organizations and to transsexual and transgender policies in sport. In 'Sex Tested, Gender Verified: Controlling Female Sexuality in the Age of Containment', Ian Ritchie argues that beneath the surface of these tests that defined what is 'natural' lay sport's gendered practices and institutions – through which athletes became markers of normalcy and deviancy, representing the biological imperative of modern sport's patriarchal ideology: that sex differences are inherent, natural, unchangeable and, therefore, unchallengeable.[81]

The collaborative research of Sheila Cavanaugh and Heather Sykes and Sykes' individual work concerning transsexual and transgender policies of the IOC suggest, as in the case of sex testing, that these policies do not reflect an acceptance of gender variance in the world of sport – rather there has been an ongoing resistance to inclusive gender policies in mainstream sport organizations.[82] Sykes argues in 'Transsexual and Transgender Policies in Sport' that 'this resistance is based on anxieties about the instability of the male/female gender binary and the emergence of queer gender subjectivities within women's, gay, and mainstream sporting communities'.[83]

In *Sport, Sexualities and Queer Theory*, Jayne Caudwell similarly argues that there is an absence of a theoretical critique of the sex/gender distinction in sport studies and an incomplete understanding of the way in which sex is understood as a pre-given and the fact sport was created on the basis of sexual differentiation. Such work is a departure from lesbian and gay politics of identity to politics of difference, resistance and challenge in that it attempts to expose the constructedness of sexuality and the fiction of sexual identity, to dismantle binary gender relations, resist normalizing regimes of sex/gender relations and undermine heteronormative hegemonic discourses.[84] Using feminist and queer theory, Caudwell's work concerning women's footballing bodies 'attempts to move beyond sex as pre-given and the sex/gender distinction' in order to further explore the way in which sport is a site/sight where sex, gender, and desire are regulated for the purposes of controlling social relations of power.[85]

The future of gender in sports studies

The inclusion of gender in sports studies research has made important contributions to the academic development of the discipline by continually challenging its boundaries and moving it from disciplinary to interdisciplinary to transdisciplinary perspectives as it replaced the focus of scholars, revealing the inadequacy of the female athlete and sex as the focus. Thinking about gender has furthered our understanding of modern sport and the theories, concepts, paradigms and research methodologies that we use to understand sport. As we have seen, it was within the sub-disciplines of sports history and sport sociology, and to a lesser extent sport psychology, that gender has been embraced by scholars.

The recent use of approaches such as intersectionality and transdisciplinarity have indicated that scholars in sport are in the process of deconstructing, perhaps even dismantling gender, as we have understood it. Such a process may in fact render gender somewhat obsolete.

Notes

1. Quoted in J.W. Scott, *Feminism and History* (Oxford: Oxford University Press, 1997), 152.
2. I am using the term sports studies to include the various names that are and have been used by departments that are devoted to the study of sport and physical culture. Among the more common of these are: exercise science, *idræt*, human movement studies, kinesiology, physical education and sport science.
3. See S.J. Bandy, 'Fra "sex" til "gender", fra kvinder og sport til kulturkritik og fra det nationale til det transnationale: En oversight over amerikansk, canadisk og britisk forskning I sport og køn', *Dansk Sociologi* 2/15 (2004), 125–35. For a more detailed analysis of this transition from 'sex' to 'gender' refer to S. J. Birrell, 'Discourses on the Gender/Sport Relationship: From Women in Sport to Gender Relations', *Exercise and Sport Sciences Reviews* 16 (1988), 459–502; and M.A. Hall, 'The Discourse of Gender and Sport: From Femininity to Feminism', *Sociology of Sport Journal* 5 (1988), 330–40. Also see P.A. Vertinsky, 'Sport History and Gender Relations, 1983–1993: Bibliography', *Journal of Sport History* 21 (1994), 25–58.
4. For a discussion of transdisciplinary perspectives of sport and physical culture, see S.J. Bandy, 'Transdisciplinarity, Sport, and Physical Culture: An Introduction', in S.J. Bandy, ed., *Nordic Narratives in Sport and Physical Culture: Transdisciplinary Perspectives* (Skriftserien LUDUS 2, Faculty of Natural Sciences, Århus University, 2004), 17–39.
5. As Gisela Bock suggests, the dichotomous distinction between sex and gender is largely specific to the English language. See 'Challenging Dichotomies: Perspectives on Women's History', in K. Offen et al., eds, *Writing Women's History: International Perspectives* (London: Macmillan, 1991), 7. As is the case with the German, Italian and Turkish languages, there is no term to designate sex and make the distinction between sex and gender in the Danish language. Therefore, the term sex, when used in this chapter, will be kept in its English form and will be used to designate the biological, with gender to be understood as the social and cultural.

6 See R.J. Stoller, *Sex and Gender: The Development of Masculinity and Femininity* (London: Karnac Books, 1968).

7 See the following books that were among the more influential during this early period: A. Oakley, *Sex, Gender and Society* (London: Temple Smith, 1972); S. Firestone, *The Dialectic of Sex* (New York: Bantam Books, 1970); N. Chodorow, *The Reproduction of Mothering: Psychoanalysis and the Sociology of Gender* (Berkeley: University of California Press, 1978); and C. Gilligan, *In a Different Voice: Psychological Theory and Women's Development* (Cambridge, MA: Harvard University Press, 1982).

8 Bock, op. cit., 7.

9 Scott, *Feminism and History*, 153.

10 See A. Koestler, *The Act of Creation* (New York: Macmillan, 1964); and A.R. King and J.A. Brownell, *The Curriculum and the Disciplines of Knowledge* (New York: John Wiley and Sons, 1966).

11 A. Saarinen, *Feminist Research – An Intellectual Adventure?* (Tampere: University of Tampere Research Institute for Social Sciences, 1992), 4.

12 See F. Henry, 'Physical Education: An Academic Discipline', *Journal of Health, Physical Education, and Recreation* 35 (1964), 32–33, 69; J.E. Nixon, 'The Criteria of a Discipline', *Quest* IX (1967), 42–48; G.L. Rarick, 'The Domain of Physical Education as a Discipline', *Quest* IX (1967), 49–52; G.S. Kenyon, 'On the Conceptualization of Sub-Disciplines Within an Academic Discipline Dealing with Human Movement', *Proceedings of the NCPEAM National Conference* (1968), 34–45; J. Loy, 'The Nature of Sport: A Definitional Effort', *Quest* 10 (1968), 1–15; and G.A. Brooks, ed., *Perspectives on the Academic Discipline of Physical Education* (Champaign, IL: Human Kinetics Publishers, 1981).

13 See Birrell, op. cit., 477 in which she traces the 'intellectual bloodlines and colleague relationships' of these women for three generations.

14 M.A. Hall, *Feminism and Sporting Bodies: Essays on Theory and Practice* (Champaign, IL: Human Kinetics, 1996), 5.

15 P. Vertinsky, 'Gender Relations, Physical Education and Sport History: Is It Time for a Collaborative Research Agenda?', in E. Trangbæk and A. Krüger, eds, *Gender & Sport from European Perspectives* (Copenhagen: Institute of Exercise and Sport Sciences, University of Copenhagen, 1999), 13–27.

16 A.G. Ingham and P. Donnelly, 'A Sociology of North American Sociology of Sport: Disunity in Unity, 1965 to 1996', *Sociology of Sport Journal* 14 (1997), 363–418.

17 M. Featherstone and B.S. Turner, 'Body and Society an Introduction', *Body and Society* I (1995), 1–12.

18 See A.W. Frank, 'Bringing Bodies Back in: A Decade Review', *Theory, Culture & Society* 7 (1990), 131–62.

19 A few examples that show the diverse and ongoing interest in the body include: J. Hovden, 'The Female Top Athlete's Body as a Symbol of Modern Femininity', in L. Laine, ed., *On the Fringes of Sport* (Sankt Augustin, Germany: Academia Verlag, 1983), 84–91; R. Greneau, 'The Critique of Sport in Modernity: Theorising Power, Culture, and the Politics of the Body', in E.A. Dunning et al., *The Sports Process: A Comparative and Developmental Approach* (London: Human Kinetics, 1993), 85–109; R.J. Park, 'A Decade of the Body: Researching and Writing About the History of Health, Fitness, Exercise and Sport, 1983–1993', *Journal of Sport History* 21 (1994), 59–82; M.A. Hall. *Feminism and Sporting Bodies: Essays on Theory and Practice* (Champaign, IL: Human Kinetics, 1994); and J. Bale and C. Philo, eds, *Body Cultures: Essays on Sport, Space and Identity* (London: Routledge, 1997).

20 Hall, *Feminism and Sporting Bodies*, 53.

21 J.W. Scott, 'Women's History and the Rewriting of History', in C. Farnham, ed., *The Impact of Feminist Research in the Academy* (Bloomington: Indiana University Press, 1987), 34–50.

22 See R. Howell, ed., *Her Story in Sport: A Historical Anthology of Women in Sports* (West Point, NY: Leisure Press, 1982).

23 E.W. Gerber et al., eds, *The American Woman in Sport* (London: Addison-Wesley, 1974), and C.A. Oglesby, ed., *Women and Sport: From Myth to Reality* (Philadelphia: Lea & Febiger, 1978).

24 Important work before Metheny and Harris was also done. For a discussion of this work see Birrell, op cit.

25 In August of 1972, Dorothy Harris hosted a conference at The Pennsylvania State University. See D.V. Harris, ed., *Women and Sport: A National Research Conference* (State College: Pennsylvania

State University, 1972). Somewhat later, physiologists became interested in the female athlete. Of particular importance are C.L. Wells, *Women, Sport and Performance* (Champaign, IL: Human Kinetics Publishers, 1985), and B.L. Drinkwater, ed., *Female Endurance Athletes* (Champaign, IL: Human Kinetics Publishers, 1986).

26 E.W. Gerber, et al., eds, *The American Woman in Sport* (Reading, MA: Addison-Wesley, 1974).
27 See N. Theberge, 'Toward a Feminist Alternative to Sport as a Male Preserve', *Quest* 17, 2 (1985), 193–202.
28 N. Struna, 'Beyond Mapping Experience: The Need for Understanding the History of American Sporting Women', *Journal of Sport History* 11 (1984), 120–33.
29 See P. Vertinsky, 'Exercise, Physical Capability and the Eternally Wounded Woman in Late Nineteenth Century North America', *Journal of Sport History* 14 (1987), 7–27 and P.A. Vertinsky, *The Eternally Wounded Woman: Women, Doctors, and Exercise in the Late Nineteenth Century* (New York: Manchester University Press, 1990).
30 J.A. Hargreaves, 'Where's the Virtue? Where's the Grace? A Discussion of the Social Production of Gender Relations In and Through Sport', *Theory, Culture and Society* 3 (1986), 109–21.
31 See J. Borms et al., *The Female Athlete: A Socio-Psychological and Kinanthropometric Approach* (New York: S. Karger, 1980) and J. Borms et al., *Women and Sport: An Historical, Biological, Physiological and Sportmedical Approach* (New York: S. Karger, 1980).
32 See J.A. Hargreaves, 'The Early History of Women's Sport', *Bulletin for the Society of the Study of Labour History* (1985), 5–6 and J.A Hargreaves, 'Playing Like Gentleman While Behaving Like Ladies: Contradictory Features of the Formative Years of Women's Sports', *British Journal of Sport History* 2 (1985), 40–52. See the following concerning women and sport in the classical world: R. Howell, 'Women in Sport in the Ancient World', in F. Landry and W.A.R. Orban, eds, *Philosophy, Theology and History of Sport and Physical Activity* (Miami: Symposia Specialists, 1978), 308; J. Mouratidis, 'Heracles at Olympia and the Exclusion of Women from the Ancient Olympic Games', *Journal of Sport History* 11 (1984), 41–55; B. Spears, 'Tryphosa, Melpomene, Nadia, and Joan: The IOC and Women's Sport', in Jeffrey O. Segrave and Donald Chu, eds, *Olympism* (Champaign, IL: Human Kinetics, 1981), 81–88; T. Scanlon, 'The Footrace at the Heraia at Olympia', *Ancient World* 9 (1984), 77–90; H.M. Lee, 'Athletics and the Bikini Girls from Piazza Armerina', *Stadion* 10 (1984), 45–76; D.M. Miller, 'Images of Ancient Greek Sportswomen in the Novels of Mary Renault', *Arete: The Journal of Sport Literature* 3 (1985), 11–16; R. Howell, 'The Atalanta Legend in Art and Literature', *Journal of Sport History* 16 (1989), 127–39; B. Spears, 'A Perspective of the History of Women's Sport in Ancient Greece', *Journal of Sport History* 11 (1984), 32–47.
33 See B. Kratzmüller's, '"Frauensport" im antiken Athen? Die Darstellungen sich körperlich betätigender Frauen als Abbild der Einstellung einer patriarchalisch geprägten Gesellschaft zum weiblichen Geschlecht', in A. Krueger-W. Buss, ed., *Transformationen: Kontinuitäten und Veränderungen in der Sportgeschichte I* (Schriftenreihe des Niedersächsischen Instituts für Sportgeschichte Hoya 16, 2001), 171–81 and 'Girls Running a Race in the Ancient *gymnasion* of Brauron? – Ancient *arkteia* and *Brauronia Reconsidered*', in G. Gori, ed., *Sport and Gender Matters in Western Countries: Old Borders and New Challenges* (Sankt Augustin: Academia Verlag, 2008), 15–31.
34 See also G. Pfister and C. Peyton, eds, *Fruen-sport in Europa* (Ahrensburg: Czwalina, 1989).
35 Considerable work concerning gender and sport has been done by scholars in a number of other countries. For example, see E. Trangbæk and A. Krüger, eds, *Gender & Sport from European Perspectives* (Copenhagen: Institute of Exercise and Sport Sciences, 1999); G. Pfister, 'Doing gender – die Inszenierung des Geschlechts im Eiskunstlauf und im Kunstturnen', in J.R. Norberg, ed., *Studier i idrott, historia och samhälle. Tillägnade professor Jan Lindroth pa has 60-arsdag* (Stockholm: HLA Förlag, 2000), 170–201; I. Harmann-Tews and G. Pfister, eds, *Sport and Women: Social Issues in International Perspective* (London: Routledge and ISCPES, 2003); and the themed edn on sports and sex, Idræt og køn, *Dansk Sociologi* 2/15 (July 2004). For additional international perspectives, see the following. Argentina: L. Morelli, *Mujeres Deportistas* (Buenos Aires: El Planeta, 1990); Australia: J. Daly, *Feminae Ludens* (Adelaide: Openbook Publishers, 1994); Canada: J. Cochrane, et al., *Women in Canadian Sports* (Toronto: Fitzhenry and Whiteside, 1977); M.A. Hall and D. Richardson, *Fair Ball: Towards Sex Equality in Canadian Sport* (Ottawa: The Canadian Advisory Council on the Status of Women, 1982); L. Robinson, *She Shouts She Scores: Canadian Perspectives on Women and Sport* (Toronto: Thompson Educational Publishers, 1997); P. White and K. Young, eds, *Sport and Gender in Canada* (Oxford: Oxford University Press, 1999); and M.A. Hall, *The Girl and the Game:*

A History of Women's Sport in Canada (Peterborough, Ontario: Broadview Press, 2002); China: F. Hong, *Footbinding, Feminism and Freedom: The Liberation of Women's Bodies in Modern China* (London: Frank Cass, 1997); and J. Dong, *Women, Sport and Society in Modern China: Holding Up More than Half the Sky* (London: Frank Cass, 2003); Denmark: I.K. Pedersen, *Den excellente præstation: Elitesport, kvinder og Karriere* (Copenhagen: Sociologisk Institut, Københavns Universitet, 1998); L.F. Thing, *Sport – en emotional affære: Kvinder, holdsport og aggression* (Copenhagen: Sociologisk Institut, Københavns Universitet, 1999); and A.R. Bach, *Kvinder på banen: sport, køn og medier* (Copenhagen: Narayana Press, 2002); France: F. Laget et al., *Le Grand Livre du Sport* (Bellville-s-Saone: SIGEFA, 1982); and P. Arnaud and T. Terret, *Histoire du sport féminin* (Paris: L'Harmattan, 1996); Germany: M.-L. Klein, *Frauensport in der Tagespress* (Bochum: Studienverl Brockmeyer, 1986); B. Palzkill, *Die Entwicklung lesbischer Identität im Sport* (Bielefeld: Frauenoffensive, 1990); and G. Pfister, *Frauensport in der DDR* (Cologne: Strauss, 2002); Hungary: R.M. Levelekiné, ed., *A Nö és a Sport* (Budapest: TTT, 1963); Italy: G.M. Madella, *Atleta al femminile: la donna e lo sport: storia di un' emancipazione difficile* (Como: Editnova, 1979); A. Salvinni, *Identita Femminile e Sport* (La Nuova Italia, n.a.); A. Teja, *Educazione fisica al femminile* (Rome: SSS Ed., 1995); and G. Gori, *Female Bodies, Sport, Italian Fascism: Submissive Women and Strong Mothers* (London: Frank Cass, 2004); Norway: G. von der Lippe, ed., *Kvinner og Idrett: Fra Myte til Realitet* (Oslo: Gyldendal Norsk Forlag, 1982); Spain: *Mujer y Deporte* (Madrid: Ministerio de Cultura, 1986); United Kingdom: K. E. McCrone, *Playing the Game: Sport and the Physical Emancipation of English Women, 1870 –1941* (Lexington: University Press of Kentucky, 1988).

36 See R.J. Park, 'Sport, Gender and Society in a Transatlantic Victorian Perspective', *British Journal of Sports History* 2 (1985), 5–28.

37 P. Vertinsky, 'Gender Relations', 1994, op. cit., 13.

38 See the following: J. English, 'Sex Equality in Sports', *Philosophy and Public Affairs* 7 (1978), 269–77; I.M. Young, 'The Exclusion of Women from Sport: Conceptual and Existential Dimensions', *Philosophy in Context* 9 (1979), 44–53; B.C. Postow, 'Women and Masculine Sports', *Journal of the Philosophy of Sport* 7 (1980), 51–58; P. Wenz, 'Human Equality in Sports', *The Philosophical Forum* 12 (Spring 1981), 238–50; and B.C. Postow, ed. *Women, Philosophy, and Sport: A Collection of New Essays* (Metuchen, NJ: Scarecrow Press, 1983).

39 Of particular importance here is D.M. Costa and S.R. Guthrie, eds, *Women and Sport: Interdisciplinary Perspectives* (Champaign, IL: Human Kinetics, 1994).

40 Scott, 'Women's History and the Rewriting of History', 41.

41 Hall, *Feminism and Sporting Bodies*, 11.

42 For a more detailed discussion of the relationship between feminism and postmodernism, see S.J. Hekman, *Gender and Knowledge: Elements of a Postmodern Feminism* (Cambridge: Polity Press, 1990).

43 P. Willis, 'Women in sport in ideology', in J. Hargreaves, ed., *Sport, Culture and Ideology* (Boston: Routledge & Kegan Paul, 1982), 117–35.

44 P. Vertinsky, 'Gender Relations', 1994, op. cit., 10. See also N. Theberge, 'Sport and Women's Empowerment', *Women's Studies International Forum* 10 (1987), 387–93; S. Birrell and D.M. Richter, 'Is a Diamond Forever? Feminist Transformations of Sport', *Women's Studies International Forum* 10 (1987), 395–409; L. Bryson, 'Sport and the Maintenance of Masculine Hegemony', *Women's Studies International Forum* 10 (1987), 349–60; and K. Fasting, 'Sport and Women's Culture', *Women's Studies International Forum* 10 (1987), 361–68.

45 D. Gill, 'Gender and Sport Behavior', in T.S. Horn, ed., *Advances in Sport Psychology* (Champaign, IL: Human Kinetics, 1992), 156.

46 N. Struna, 'Beyond Mapping Experience: The Need for Understanding in the History of American Sporting Women', *Journal of Sport History* 11 (1984), 120–33.

47 P. Vertinsky, 'Gender Relations', 1994, 9.

48 N. Struna, 'Gender and Sporting Practice in Early America', *Journal of Sport History* 18 (1991), 10–30; Nancy L. Struna, *People of Prowess: Sport, Leisure and Labor in Early Anglo-America* (Urbana: University Press, 1996), 1.

49 See T. de Lauretis, ed., *Feminist Studies/Critical Studies* (Bloomington: Indiana University Press, 1988).

50 C.M. Parratt, 'From the History of Women in Sport to Women's Sport History', in Costa and Guthrie, op. cit., 9. Also see C.M. Parratt, 'Little Means or Time: Working-Class Women and Leisure in Late Victorian and Edwardian England', *The International Journal of the History of Sport* 15 (1998), 22–53.

51 See C.L. Cole, 'Resisting the Canon: Feminist Cultural Studies, Sport, and Technologies of the Body', *Journal of Sport and Social Issues* 17 (1993), 79–97.

52 J. Hargreaves, 'A Historical Look at the Changing Symbolic Meanings of the Female Body in Western Sport', in F. van der Merwe, ed., *Sport as Symbol, Symbols in Sport* (ISHPES Studies, 4, Sankt Augustin: Academia Verlag, 1985), 249–59.

53 In 1981, M.A. Hall published *Sport, Sex Roles, and Sex Identity* (Ottawa, ON: Canadian Research Institute for the Advancement of Women), which is perhaps the first text to address issues of sexual identity in the discourse on sport. See H. Lenskyj, 'Female Sexuality and Women's Sport', *Women's Studies International Forum* 10 (1987), 381–86, and H. Lenskyj, 'Power and Play: Gender and Sexuality Issues in Sport and Physical Activity', *International Review for the Sociology of Sport* 25 (1990), 235–43. Lenskyj continued work with sport and sexuality in her recent book *Out on the Field: Gender, Sport, and Sexualities* (Toronto, ON: Women's Press, 2003).

54 P. Vertinsky's *The Eternally Wounded Woman: Women, Doctors, and Exercise in the Late Nineteenth Century* (Chicago: University of Illinois Press, 1994), is also an important work in revealing the power of the relationship between discourse, societal views of women, and their participation in sport. The essays in J.A. Mangan and R.J. Park's *From 'Fair Sex' to Feminism: Sport and the Socialization of Women in the Industrial and Post-Industrial Eras* (London: Frank Cass, 1987), added to the literature concerning the social construction of femininity and its relation to the exclusion of women from sport. In addition, the book offers the first comparative and transatlantic perspectives concerning women in sport, with essays devoted to UK, Commonwealth and American perspectives.

55 S.K. Cahn, *Coming on Strong: Gender and Sexuality in Twentieth Century Women's Sport* (London: Harvard University Press, 1994).

56 See Michael Messner, 'Sports as Male Domination: The Female Athlete as Contested Terrain', *Sociology of Sport Journal* 5 (1988), 197–211. After Birrell and Cole's works introduced homophobia, Pat Griffin published *Strong Women, Deep Closets: Lesbians and Homophobia in Sport* (Champaign, IL: Human Kinetics, 1998). The work of Cahn and others concerning sexuality has been continued in S. Scraton and A. Flintoff, eds, *Gender, Sport and Sexuality* (London: Routledge, 2002).

57 D.F. Sabo and R. Runfola, *Jock: Sports and Male Identity* (Englewood Cliffs, NJ: Prentice-Hall, 1980).

58 Several critical essays concerning masculinity in sport appeared in the 1980s, including: E. Dunning, 'Sport as a Male Preserve: Notes on the Social Sources of Masculine Identity and Its Transformations', *Theory, Culture and Society* 1 (1986), 79–90; J.A. Hargreaves, 'Where's the Virtue? Where's the Grace? A discussion of the Social Production of Gender Relations In and Through Sport', *Theory, Culture and Society* 3 (1986), 109–21; B. Kidd, 'Sports and Masculinity', *Queen's Quarterly* 94 (1987), 116–31; and S.A. Riess, 'Sport and the Redefinition of American Middle-Class Masculinity', *International Journal of Sport History* 8 (1991), 5–27. These pioneering works were followed by several others, among the more influential of which are: M. Messner and D. Sabo, *Sport, Men, and the Gender Order: Critical Feminist Perspectives* (Champaign, IL: Human Kinetics, 1990); B. Pronger, *The Arena of Masculinity: Sports, Homosexuality, and the Meaning of Sex* (New York: St Martin's Press, 1990); H. Bonde, *Mandighed og Sport* (Odense: Universitetsforlag, 1991); M.A. Messner, *Power at Play: Sports and the Problem of Masculinity* (Boston: Beacon Press, 1992); and M.A. Messner and D.F. Sabo, *Sex, Violence and Power in Sports: Rethinking Masculinity* (Freedom, CA: Crossing Press, 1994). More recently J. McKay et al., eds, *Masculinities, Gender Relations, and Sport* (Thousand Oaks, CA: Sage Publications, 2000) and P.F. McDevitt, *May the Best Man Win: Sport, Masculinity, and Nationalism in Great Britain and the Empire, 1880–1935* (New York: Palgrave Macmillan, 2004), offer perspectives of scholars from Canada, Australia, the USA and United Kingdom. Refer to R.W. Connell, *Gender and Power: Society, the Person, and Sexual Politics* (Stanford, CA: Stanford University Press, 1987) and R.W. Connell, 'Making Gendered People: Bodies, Identities, Sexualities', in M.M. Ferree et al., eds, *Revisioning Gender* (Thousand Oaks, CA: Sage Publications, 1999), 449–71.

59 J. Hargreaves, *Sporting Females: Critical Issues in the History and Sociology of Women's Sport* (New York: Routledge, 1994).

60 J. McKay and D. Huber, 'Anchoring Media Images of Technology and Sport', *Women's Studies International Forum* 15 (1992), 207. P.J. Creedon, ed., *Women, Media and Sport: Challenging Gender Values* (London: Sage Publications, 1994), was the first book devoted exclusively to women, sport and the media.

61 R.J. Park, 'Guest Editor's Introduction', *Journal of Sport History* 18 (1991), 5–6.

62 E. Spelman, *Inessential Woman* (Boston: Beacon Press, 1988).

63 J.C. Nash, 'Re-thinking Intersectionality', *Feminist Review* 89 (2008), 1–15.

64 J. Lorber, *Breaking the Bowls: Degendering and Feminist Change* (New York: W.W. Norton, 2005), 7.

65 P.H. Collins, 'Moving Beyond Gender: Intersectionality and Scientific Knowledge', in M.M. Ferree, et al., op. cit., 263.

66 L. Heywood and J. Drake, eds, *Third Wave Agenda: Being Feminist, Doing Feminism* (Minneapolis: University of Minnesota Press, 1997), 4.

67 J. Lorber, 'Beyond Binaries: Depolarizing the Categories of Sex, Sexuality, and Gender', *Sociological Inquiry* 66 (1996), 143–59.

68 See M. Bal, *Traveling Concepts in the Humanities: A Rough Guide* (London: University of Toronto Press, 2002), for a more detailed examination of the use of concepts in research and teaching. For the use of the narrative approach see: A.C. Sparkes and M. Silvennoinen, eds, *Talking Bodies* (Jyväskylä, Finland: University of Jyväskylä, 1999); J. Denison and P. Markula, eds, *Moving Writing: Crafting Movement in Sport Research* (New York: Peter Lang, 2003); S.J. Bandy, ed. *Nordic Narratives in Sport and Physical Culture: Transdisciplinary Perspectives* (Aarhus, Denmark: Center for Idræt, 2004); and P. Markula, ed., *Feminist Sport Studies: Sharing Experiences of Joy and Pain* (Albany: State University of New York Press, 2005).

69 See B. Nicolescu, *Manifesto of Transdisciplinarity*, translated by Karen-Claire Voss (Albany: State University of New York Press, 2002), for an introduction to transdisciplinarity. Feminists have often rejected the concept of the 'global' because of its exploitative and Western connotations and have, therefore, substituted the concept of the transnational into their research.

70 S. Cahn, op. cit.

71 Hargreaves used archival materials, newspapers and magazines, personal correspondence, films and videos, material from the internet and interviews using the internet.

72 For a discussion of the concept of circularity and a rejection of linearity in women's language and the hierarchical ordering of knowledge see A.S. Ostriker, *Stealing the Language: The Emergence of Women's Poetry in America* (Boston: Beacon Press, 1986).

73 L. Heywood and S.L. Dworkin, *Built to Win: The Female Athlete as Cultural Icon* (Minneapolis: University of Minnesota Press, 2003).

74 B. Cox and S. Thompson, 'Multiple Bodies: Sportswomen, Soccer and Sexuality', *International Review for the Sociology of Sport* 35 (2000), 5–20. It can be argued that Henning Eichberg's 'third way', with which he advocated several approaches to the development of a Scandinavian sociology of the body – biographical, autobiographical, situational, scenical, social ecological – suggests new methodological ways of understanding the body, and such an approach foreshadowed the work that would come after the publication of 'The Narrative, The Situational, The Biographical: Scandinavian Sociology of Body Culture Trying a Third Way', *International Review for the Sociology of Sport* 29 (1994), 99–113. In support of new directions for the integration of gender relations, physical education and sports history, Patricia Vertinsky advocates, like Eichberg, the importance of comparative studies using intercultural and inter-lingual perspectives.

75 J.O. Segrave, 'Perspectives on the Development of Sport Literature and Narrativity: From Modernism to Postmodernism', in S.J. Bandy and V. Bjerre, eds, *Fortællinger om idræt i Norden: Helte, erindringer og identitet* (Aarhus, Denmark: Aarhus University Press, forthcoming).

76 E.J. Gorn, *The Manly Art: Bare-Knuckle Prize Fighting in America* (Ithaca: Cornell University Press, 1986).

77 L. Wacquant, 'For An Analytic of Racial Domination', in D.E. Davis, ed., *Political Power and Social Theory II* (Greenwich, CT: Jai Press, 1997), 230.

78 Löic Wacquant, *Body & Soul: Notebooks of an Apprentice Boxer* (New York: Oxford University Press, 2004), 7.

79 For another interesting transdisciplinary approach to sport, see Swedish author Sven Lindqvist, *Bench Press*, translated by Sarah Death (New York: Granta, 2003).

80 T. de Lauretis, 'Queer Theory: Lesbian and Gay Sexualities', *Differences: A Journal of Feminist Cultural Studies* 3 (1991), iii–xviii.

81 I. Ritchie, 'Sex Tested, Gender Verified: Controlling Female Sexuality in the Age of Containment', *Sport History Review* 34 (2003), 80–98. Also see: S. Teetzel, 'Equality, Equity, and Inclusion: Issues in Women and Transgendered Athletes' Participation at the Olympics', *Cultural Imperialism in Action: Critiques in the Global Olympic Trust* (2006), 331–38, at www.la84foundation.org/SportsLibrary/ISOR/ISOR2006ae.pdf (retrieved 4 January 2009); and L. Wackwitz, 'Verifying the Myth:

9   Race

John Nauright and David K. Wiggins

Introduction

Few issues have consumed historians of sport in the English speaking world more than that of race. Race has also been central to analyses of sport in colonial contexts, particularly in Africa and the Caribbean, while more recently the literature on race in Asia and Latin America has expanded. Within sports history research in the USA, race plays a prominent role, exceeding almost any other area of focus. In Europe examinations of race have largely taken place in the postcolonial context, though historians realize that race has a complex relationship to the expansion of European empires and the colonial and postcolonial contexts that emerged as a result. Colonial ties still remain as it is common to find that the best soccer (football) players from Algeria or Morocco often wind up in France, Argentinan players are likely to develop careers in Spain or Italy while West Indians appear abroad frequently in England. As a result, old conceptions – and stereotypes – developed during the eras of colonialism and imperialism have been hard to break down.

In 'settler' and plantation societies such as the USA, Australia, South Africa and the British West Indies race and class were closely intertwined, which led to the development of a black underclass that took many decades to achieve equality of opportunity on the playing field. Barriers to participation in white-dominated competitions hardened in the imperial era of the late 19th and early 20th centuries such that whether in the USA, Barbados or South Africa, blacks were forced to participate in their own competitions segregated from white ones.

After World War II, though, these barriers to participation began to fall with Jackie Robinson beginning the process of integrating white professional baseball in the USA in 1945 and the first black captain of the West Indies cricket team appearing in 1960 in the person of Frank Worrell. The Olympic Games opened increasingly to include athletes from all countries particularly as colonialism gave way to independence in Asia and then Africa in the 1950s and 1960s. Black African runners began to achieve success beginning with Kenyan middle distance runners at the 1954 Empire Games.[1] While South Africa was slower to integrate, by the 1990s competitions were open to all regardless of racial background.[2]

The role of race in sport has been a complex one and one that has been examined from many angles by historians, sociologists and biological scientists. In this chapter we outline the progression of black achievement in sport and the reactions by analysts and historians, most of whom have been white, conceding that the literature on race and sport has been focused almost exclusively on the black/white divide.[3] We discuss the need to continue expanding this focus further in the conclusion, but here concentrate primarily on the black/white divide in sport as this has been most central to the work of many sports historians internationally.[4]

The literature and experience of black athletes in the USA is most well developed and will provide the majority of examples, but we want to begin to break down the tradition of purely national-level analyses and see race and sport from a more global perspective. Indeed an American myopia on race and sport has begun to be challenged by scholars working on race and sport issues outside of the USA.[5] A few key examples of why this is important will be given here. The famous late 19th century black boxer Peter Jackson was born in the Danish Virgin Islands, participated in famous bouts in the USA and Australia, the latter being where he died and is buried. American cyclist Marshall 'Major' Taylor achieved acclaim in Europe, the USA and Australia. American boxer Jack Johnson's best known fight was held in Sydney, Australia and top West Indian cricketers by the 1920s and 1930s were playing league cricket in the north of England, most famous of whom was the great Learie Constantine.[6]

Furthermore, Victorian era 'scientists' categorized humans on a continuum based on the 'Great Chain of Being' which placed Africans at one end of the spectrum and northern Europeans at the other with other 'races' in between, thus creating a dichotomy between black and white that has been hard to break down. In addition, many scholars such as K. Mercer, have argued that black people have been viewed in primarily in physical terms at the expense of mental acuity going back to the era of slavery: 'Classical racism involved a logic of dehumanization, in which African peoples were defined as having bodies but not minds: in this way the superexploitation of the black body as muscle-machine could be justified. Vestiges of this are active today'.[7]

With the closer integration of ideas and better communication and transport in the world by the early 1900s, it was impossible for events in the USA, for example, not to appear in South African newspapers. Great black leaders such as Marcus Garvey had a significant impact in the West Indies, Africa, the USA and beyond, and the sporting exploits of American boxer Joe Louis could be lauded in Johannesburg or Bridgetown as much as in Detroit. Where white-controlled newspapers that targeted white audiences rarely mentioned black sport, newspapers focused on black readers, such as the *Pittsburgh Courier* or the *Baltimore Afro-American* in the USA or the *Bantu World* and *Umteteli wa Bantu* in South Africa, reported widely on black sporting activities. These sources have provided historians with a wealth of information that has aided in the recovery and wider presentation of histories of blacks in sport.[8] Without these resources, much of what we have learned has had to be unearthed via oral histories and the piecing together of a wide array of official and unofficial sources.

The history of black involvement in sport has been a difficult one. First, black athletes faced segregation until the latter decades of the 20th century. When competitions operated in an integrated fashion, discrimination frequently occurred. In recent years there has been a more level playing field with many athletes of colour in the West obtaining equal opportunities in sport, at least on the field. Finally, we have seen the emergence of what some scholars have suggested are post-racial athletes such as Michael Jordan and Tiger Woods, though this has certainly not applied universally to black athletes.[9] Opportunities for black athletes beyond the playing field have begun to increase in recent years as well, though not as equally as on the playing fields and courts. As African-American activist and scholar Harry Edwards noted in 1999, 'Michael Jordan doesn't just want to be on the team – he wants to own the team'.[10] And while opportunites for black leaders and owners in sport has been limited, aspirations in all areas of sport are not completely unrealistic for black athletes and former athletes internationally.

Contemporary analyses during the past century have tended to place black athletes in the category of Nature as either the 'primitive', unable to compete with intellectually superior whites, or as 'beast', linked to superior physicality.[11] Even in recent studies these concepts about race and physicality and mental abilities have been central in debates about blacks and sport.[12]

These tensions in the examination of race in sport will be explored with reference to specific periods in the history of sport along with approaches to the examination of race as a problematic in sports history. In particular, recent work in sports history has begun to move beyond the 'recovery' phase of telling the his- and her-stories of forgotten sportsmen and women, or to paraphrase the title of one of our books, to move beyond merely bringing black sports *Out of the Shadows*, to a more sophisticated interrogation of the ways in which 'race' has been used in sport and wider society in the practice of sport, the telling of sports stories and the memoralizing of the sporting past and sporting heroes and heroines. Or to use Douglas Booth's taxonomy, much of the writing on race and sports history prior to 2000 involved 'reconstruction' of previously hidden pasts.[13] Recent scholarship has sought to understand more fully the historical operation of systems of power, interpretations of race and how athletes have been constructed as racial beings.

Racial segregation in sport

In colonial societies blacks were initially exposed to different sports on plantations or in larger cities. In limited cases some blacks appeared in competitions in the metropole as well. Before the 1860s, though, there were only a handful of recognized successes by black sportsmen (all women were largely excluded from sports), though a more complex picture of racial mixing in sporting activities before the mid-19th century is beginning to emerge.[14] Tom Molineaux was perhaps the most famous international black athlete in the period before 1860 and the era of 'modern' sports. In 1810 he famously fought Tom Cribb in England for the 'world' boxing championship. Cribb was a rare exception though it appears that racial barriers in sport in many places were less rigid in 1860 than they became by the end of the 1890s.

A number of outstanding African-American athletes distinguished themselves in highly organized sport at both the amateur and professional levels of competition in the years immediately following the Civil War of 1861–65. Similarly black athletes achieved success in South Africa in the sport of cricket.[15] Aborginal Australians began to achieve in the same sport, and, though marketed as a novelty that was full of racial overtones, they toured England in the late 1860s.[16] In New Zealand, Maori rugby players began to succeed and a New Zealand 'natives' tour of the Britain took place in 1888–89.[17] Both of these tours preceded the first official national tours by Australia and New Zealand by many years. In England, the West African athlete Arthur Wharton excelled in association football and athletics in the 1880s and 1890s, including establishing the initial record for the 100 yards dash.[18] Yet, in many cases black athletes were presented to the public as novelties much in the same way that African bodies were put on display in zoos and anthropological displays or as artifacts of Empire to be consumed by a curious public at 'home'.

By the latter years of the 19th century and certainly by the early 1900s, the large majority of black athletes were excluded from participating in most highly organized sports internationally and forced to establish their own teams and leagues that operated without white support or interference. This was due to several factors. First, elites in Western society set themselves apart from the masses by forming exclusive clubs and competitions and defining what a 'sportsman' was by creating 'amateur' as opposed to 'professional' sport. As social divisions included race, blacks were excluded from these competitions such as the early modern Olympic Games. Some well-to-do blacks, though, who were deemed on the path to full 'civilization' were incorporated into sport via their participation at elite universities in the USA and England during the first few decades of the 1900s. Second, racial attitudes hardened as Western societies embarked fully on the Age of Imperialism from 1885 onward, which included the dividing up of much of the rest of the world into formal colonies controlled by Western metropoles. This division of the world was justified on the basis of Western 'scientific' beliefs in European/white superiority over 'Others' as well as the 'white man's burden' of bringing civilization to the 'darker' races. Third, legal decisions reinforced racial exclusion such as the US Supreme Court's 1896 decision in *Plessey v. Ferguson* which stated that the provision of 'separate but equal' amenities for blacks and whites did not violate the US Constitution, thus ushering in an era of racist laws particularly in the American South referred to as the Jim Crow era. In South Africa, the 1913 Group Areas Act defined land ownership and use that led to further segregation and separate areas for all activities of life among different racial communities. Fourth, distinct physical characteristics were written on to the body as racial characteristics were linked to perceived differences in physicality between races in the Nature/Culture debates that continued well into the 20th century. Yet, despite this, the historical literature on race and sport has not until recently focused primarily on racial embodiment and sport which is fundamental to the understanding of the operation of racial codes and racial discrimination in sport.[19]

With the notable exceptions of boxing and international athletic contests, African-Americans, blacks in the Caribbean and in southern Africa, for example, established their own organizations behind segregated walls in such sports as football, basketball, baseball, cricket and rugby union. These separate institutions were a source of great pride to black communities and served as visible examples of black organizational skill and entrepreneurship during the oppressive years of the first half of the 20th century. Cricket clubs in Trinidad and Barbados were segregated according to race and within racial categories by class as well, as social convention prohibited playing beyond one's 'station'.[20] In South Africa, racial distinctions mixed with class and religion such that in Cape Town mixed race or 'coloured' rugby competitions were divided between a league that allowed Muslim players and one that was exclusively non-Muslim while African rugby players had yet another competition.[21] As Booth and Nauright show, though, the lure of 'Civilization' for an emerging group of middle class and Western educated elites in South Africa led them to utilize the sport of cricket as 'a form of finishing school for the body, a place to learn correct posture, dress, deportment and speech, and how to position one's body in space (respect the private space of social betters) and time (adopt a measured, self-assured tempo).[22] Odendaal refers to this group as South Africa's 'black Victorians' for adopting the vestiges of British Victorian elite culture.[23] Sandiford confirms that the lure of British social norms conveyed via cricket were powerful in colonial Barbados: 'The blacks themselves bought enthusiastically into the Anglo-Saxon ideology and placed great store not only on cricketing prowess but on cricketing forms and formalities'.[24]

The academic literature examining this period of segregation in sport has tended to laud black achievement despite great obstacles and quite rightly celebrates the achievements of black athletes and entrepreneurs in an era of often virulent racism among white elites globally.[25] In South Africa and the West Indies, though, historians discussing the role of sport have painted a complex picture of the tensions in black society between those who aspired to 'Civilization' on European terms, those who clung to African traditions and those caught in the middle, though Runstedtler's work on boxer Joe Louis discussed below demonstrates that blacks in the USA faced similar tensions. It is clear that the interwar period of the 1920s and 1930s was an era of great black achievement in education, theatre, literature, music and indeed sport, but awareness of this was limited in white communities. An increasing number of liberal whites, though, began to promote the inclusion of black elites into mainstream society; however, the majority of whites, particularly poorer whites internationally, were resistant and viewed black achievement as a threat to their own social standing. These prejudicial thoughts were supported in part by a racial sports science that sought to isolate physical explanations for black achievement in sport. Initially, though, 'scientific' research that sought to determine the existence of race, carried out most famously at Harvard University, used this research to prove the 'natural superiority' of whites.[26] This physical racial science has been debunked within the wider scientific world; however, in sports science, it has taken much longer to dissipate.[27] Fleming has highlighted how much public sway these discredited theories have had and the social impact and beliefs that have been created as a result.[28] At the end of the day, these studies have proven to be flawed in that there is no accepted method for controlling for 'race' and many times the only control has been skin colour. While the social scientific critiques of racial sports science have been persuasive, there is still a public perception of black athletic superiority. Thus, internationally, there emerged clear tensions between those who wanted to protect whiteness and those who sought a more inclusive and somewhat colour blind system based on culture and class. This battle has yet to be concluded. Black sportspeople were often caught in the middle as the old British notion of *mens sana in corpore sano* gave way to the brain versus brawn debate which became an obsession in the USA and the United Kingdom in particular, especially after World War II. As a result, a racial sports science set out to examine whether blacks had innate physical characteristics that predisposed them to sporting success. Wiggins shows that this work was being done as early as the 1930s. W. Montague Cobb, who did numerous experiments on Jesse Owens, determined that there was no scientific basis to explaining Owens's success on the basis of race and indeed that Owens possessed some physical characteristics more common to whites than blacks.[29] Cobb's findings did not end debate, though, but merely presaged research to come after World War II. In the meantime, black athletes began to emerge from the shadows and into the mainstream within Western societies, though the process has been ongoing for several decades.

Black athletes and an emerging global public

While black athletes in the USA, England, South Africa, Australia and New Zealand made an impact on sport in the late 19th century, it was the emergence of a globalizing sporting culture centred on increasing international competition that led many in the white-dominated Western world to 'discover' black sporting talent. Beginning with international football and followed by the first Modern Olympics in 1896, the trend towards international sport as the pinnacle of competition began to emerge. In the few sports where blacks were not completely segregated at this time, such as cycling and boxing, internationally recognized black sports figures began to appear.

Involvement of African-Americans in boxing has a long tradition, extending back to the early years of the 19th century when Molineaux fought Crib. Though widely covered in England, this feat was ignored by the American press.[30] Peter Jackson was a leading boxer during the 1890s having won the Australian championship in 1886 and fighting several major bouts in Australia, the USA and England. World champion John L. Sullivan refused to fight Jackson. Scholars have argued that Sullivan's refusal was due to racial prejudice. Gorn, the leading historian of the bare-knuckle era, claims that Sullivan's refusal to fight Jackson in 1892 was due to the hardening of racial lines and his fear of losing white supporters. Yet, only a few years earlier, Sullivan had participated in a barnstorming tour during 1883–84 with the New Zealand Maori boxer Herbert A. 'Maori' Slade. Sullivan seems to have become more careful in his selection of opponents as he aged, and Wiggins points out that Sullivan's manager wanted to spare him the 'humiliation of being defeated by a Negro'.[31] Sullivan's distinction between the 'Maori' Slade and the 'black or negro' Jackson also illustrates a difference that was emerging between blacks and Latinos and native peoples within sporting worlds. A black Cuban could participate in professional baseball if defined primarily as a Cuban, but a 'negro' or black American player would be excluded.

George Dixon became the first black world boxing champion, winning the bantam-weight title in 1890 and the featherweight title in 1891, so by 1892, the race line was not yet hardening, though Sullivan's obviously was. Avoidance of competition with blacks was often used as an excuse for white athletes prior to full integration of sports though this phenomenon needs further exploration. While the 'recovery' phase of sports history research on race has yielded much, there are still many gaps to fill in the literature and many worthwhile research projects yet to be done particularly on these variations and multi-ethnic distinctions that emerged between 1890 and the 1930s.

It was the success of two African-American boxers in the first decades of the 20th century, along with the performance of Jesse Owens at the 1936 Olympics, however, that finally generated significant international attention for black athletes across all forms of media in both black and white communities and that would ultimately break down the racial barriers in sport.

Jack Johnson became the first African-American to capture the world's heavyweight championship, holding on to the title for some seven years before losing to white American Jess Willard in 1915. As great as Johnson's exploits were in boxing, it was outside the ring that Johnson gained the most attention and caused the greatest controversy. He has often been referred to as a 'Bad Nigger', a man who played on the worst fears of the dominant culture by marrying three white women and having illicit affairs with a number of others, often prostitutes whom he treated with an odd mixture of affection and disdain. He was absolutely fearless and attracted to dangerous escapades that challenged white conventions and mores. Although a hero for many members of his race, Johnson drew the wrath of segments of both the African-American and white communities because of his unwillingness to assume a subservient position and play the role of the grateful black. He was eventually convicted in the USA of violating the Mann Act for transporting a white woman across state lines for illicit purposes and was forced to leave the country for a short time before returning home to serve a jail sentence at the federal prison in Leavenworth, Kansas.[32]

The reaction to Johnson's public persona was emblematic of a country built upon the exploitation of the Other. Racism was widespread in the USA and became more violent in the early 20th century particularly in the South where lynchings were common and where the Ku Klux Klan fuelled the flames of race hatred. The Klan's view was celebrated in the most famous American movie of the era, *Birth of a Nation* where fear of the black male body and its threat to the white female body were vividly displayed. It was against this context that black athletes like Johnson were judged.[33]

The bitter aftertaste from Johnson's career, combined with continuing racial discrimination in American society, made it virtually impossible for African-American boxers to secure championship fights over the next two decades. That all changed in 1937, though, when Joe Louis, the superbly talented boxer from Detroit, became the second African-American heavyweight champion by defeating James Braddock. Louis was a decidedly different champion than Johnson. Possessing enormous strength and boxing skills, Louis was a quiet, dignified man who assumed the more subservient role whites expected from members of his race, but he became a hero of almost mythical proportions in the African-American (and global black) community by demolishing white fighters with remarkable regularity and serving as a symbol of possibility for those subjugated by continuing racial discrimination, becoming what was known at the time as a 'Race Man'.[34] The coverage of Louis and his rise to stardom was not uniform, however. Praised in the black press as emblematic of racial advancement and discipline, Louis was disparaged by some in the white press for being 'lazy'. Louis's differential treatment was particularly striking in the lead up to his 1935 fight against Italian Primo Carnera, which was held against the backdrop of Italy's looming invasion of Ethiopia. Indeed fears of racial unrest nearly led to the cancellation of the fight, though the black press saw this as a diversionary tactic on the part of the white establishment that might be used to limit Louis's chances at top fights, echoing problems that went back to at least the time of John L. Sullivan and Peter Jackson. Indeed NBC and CBS radio networks refused to broadcast the fight for fears of widespread racial unrest. There had never before been more security around a fight.[35] Runstedtler, in her account of Louis, examines the black and white press coverage alongside each other and focuses on competing discourses in each that placed Louis in differing contexts of racial advancement and pride on the one hand and of white prejudice and racial embodiment of the black athlete on the other. She thus advances the analysis of Louis as much more than an improvement on Jack Johnson or a major step forward in race relations, but uncovers the complexity of competing racial discourses surrounding the black male sporting body represented by Joe Louis. Indeed, after the Carnera fight, there was debate in the black press as to how to cover Louis's success. Some argued it represented racial advancement while others argued that it took away from intellectual gains being made. Several decades later, the urban black seeming 'obsession' with sporting success, which Hoberman argued in his 1997 book *Darwin's Athletes* and which was depicted in the 1994 documentary film *Hoop Dreams*, and the white-dominated media's equal 'obsession' with black physicality, demonstrated that those concerns were certainly legitimate and have remained so.[36]

Meanwhile advances were nevertheless being made as white-dominated high schools and universities in the northeast and upper midwest regions of the USA began to have small numbers of black athletes on their sports teams, particularly in football and track and field. John Baxter Taylor, the great track star, was an example. He attended racially mixed Central High School and Brown Preparatory before enrolling in the University of Pennsylvania. Winner of the 440 yard dash in the 1904, 1907 and 1908 championships of the Intercollegiate Amateur Athletic Association, Taylor was a member of the gold medal winning 400 metre relay team in the 1908 Olympic Games in London. Paul Robeson, the great singer, actor, athlete and civil rights activist, was one of three African-Americans among the 250 students at New Jersey's Somerville High School where he starred in football, basketball, baseball, and track and field. After Somerville, Robeson enrolled at Rutgers University where he was a member of Walter Camp's All-American football team in 1917 and 1918. Fritz Pollard starred in several sports at integrated Lane Technical High School in Chicago before becoming a student at Brown University where he was selected to Walter Camp's All-American football team in 1916. He would eventually become a player with the Akron Pros in a league that evolved into the NFL and later achieved distinction as the first African-American head coach in a major team sport when he was hired to lead the Pros in 1921. Yet, as recent work is showing, there are stories of numerous African-American athletes to be recovered before we have a full picture of sport and race in the USA during the first half of the 20th century, and this picture is true in other Western and colonial societies as well.[37]

Women, race and sport

Ironically, African-American female athletes who participated in the Olympic Games often came from black colleges rather than predominantly white universities. The first wave of African-American women Olympians, including high jumper Alice Coachman, the first African-American woman to capture an Olympic gold medal, had been members at various times of Cleveland Abbott's great track teams at Tuskegee Institute. The next outstanding group of African-American women Olympians, including such great athletes as Wilma Rudolph, Barbara Jones, Martha Hudson and Lucinda Williams, were products of Ed Temple's famous Tigerbelles track teams from Tennessee State University.[38] The large number of women Olympians from historically black colleges perhaps resulted, as Cahn has suggested, from the fact that African-American women athletes were seemingly more accepted in their community than white women athletes were in their own. Although 'middle-class white women' avoided track and field because of its reputation as a 'masculine endeavor', African-American women athletes were training and honing their talents under the watchful eyes of African-American male coaches like Cleveland Abbott and Ed Temple. Unfortunately, the acceptance of African-American women in a sport such as track and field 'also reinforced disparaging stereotypes of black women as less womanly or feminine than White women'.[39] In other countries the literature on women, race and sport is less well developed, though a recent pathbreaking study by Jennifer Hargreaves demonstrates the many hurdles that Afro-Caribbean and Asian women have had to navigate in Britain as well as the challenges black women in South Africa have faced in obtaining opportunities in sport.[40]

Segregated 'opportunities'

Holding out as much interest to the African-American community as college sports were the all-black professional teams and leagues that were organized in the USA in the early 20th century. A legacy from the late 19th century, a number of all-black teams and leagues were established in the three major sports of football, basketball and baseball. Of these three, baseball was the most highly organized and popular among members of the African-American community; the sport enthralled thousands of fans, who found the game a meaningful experience and pleasurable counterpoint to the drudgery of everyday life.[41]

Black baseball's first successful league was formed in 1920 by Rube Foster, the once-great pitcher and manager of the Chicago American Giants. Foster organized that year the National Negro Baseball League (NNL), an organization patterned along the lines of Major League Baseball and composed of teams from Chicago, Detroit, St. Louis, Kansas City and Indianapolis. The NNL collapsed under the weight of financial instability and a host of other problems in 1931, just three years after the rival Eastern Negro League (ENL) ceased operation. In 1933, a second NNL was organized and four years later was in competition with the newly created Negro American League (NAL).[42] These two leagues were the cornerstone of black baseball over the next two decades, representing at once some of the worst features of American racism and the best creative energy of the African-American community. The NNL and NAL, although quite stable through much of the 1930s and 1940s, were never able to realize their financial potential, because clubs lacked ownership of baseball parks and were forced to engage in bidding wars for the services of outstanding players. Clark Griffith and other moguls in Major League Baseball never allowed black teams to establish significant profit margins because of the high rent they charged for the use of their ballparks. This situation caused myriad other problems, including inadequate working and living conditions for the league's African-American players, who already suffered the indignities associated with being members of one of this country's least esteemed minority groups. The players were forced to make long, confined road trips in buses and beat-up old cars, stay in segregated and sometimes dilapidated hotels, and survive on limited meal money. They also had to cope with the frustrations that resulted from being denied service at restaurants, hotels and other public accomodations.[43]

The more talented African-American players participated in the greatest spectacle in black baseball, the annual East-West All-Star Game. Played in Chicago's Comiskey Park, the East-West All-Star Game was a grand social event in the African-American community that drew literally thousands of fans each year from all across the country. The large attendance for the East-West All-Star Game, with estimates as high as 50,000 spectators for some of the contests, resulted in much needed profits for Greenlee and other entrepreneurs in black baseball. By 1935 half of the profits were placed into an emergency fund that would assist players who were not payed by financially strapped owners while at the same time protecting owners against extended rainouts.

In South Africa segregated competitions were the norm until the 1990s. Even in disadvantaged communities differences between groups manifested themselves on the sporting field. In Cape Town there was a rugby competition for whites, one for Africans and two for 'coloureds' (or mixed-race South Africans). Among coloureds one competition banned Muslims while the other was not exclusionary but primarily Muslim in composition.[44] Local businessmen and gangs (protection rackets) in Cape Town and in other South African urban centres sponsored sports teams as a way to promote themselves and other businesses in the community.[45]

International moves to integrate white-dominated sport

Coinciding with the creation of all-black sporting organizations were bitter campaigns waged by various individuals and groups against the colour line in white organized sport. Of all the groups that hammered away at organized sport for its exclusionary policies, perhaps none were more significant than sportswriters from such well-known African-American weeklies as the *Baltimore Afro-American*, *Chicago Defender*, *New York Amsterdam News* and *Pittsburgh Courier Journal*. Clamouring loudly for an end to discrimination in baseball that symbolically, and in actual practice, was most important to the African-American community, they led the battle against racism in white organized sport.[46]

The historic signing of Jackie Robinson by the Brooklyn Dodgers in 1945 was the beginning of the end for the separate sporting organizations in the USA and had a great symbolic effect internationally. It also helped usher in the reintegration of sport in the USA. The NFL followed baseball by beginning to integrate again in 1946. The NFL had a much shorter history of outright segregation with no black players appearing between the late 1920s and mid-1940s, though never more than two or three in a team at any one time.[47] By 1959, with the integration of the Boston Red Sox, all Major League Baseball teams had black players on their rosters. This was not an easy process, however, and in some sports, such as basketball, coaches and officials attempted to ensure that the majority of players on the court or field at any one time were white. By the early 1970s this largely disappeared as the last major sports league in the USA, the Southeastern Conference in NCAA football integrated.[48]

In other countries desegregation of sports or the opening up of opportunities for new migrants gathered pace after World War II. The exceptions to this rule were the racially based regimes in southern Africa, most notably in South Africa and Rhodesia (now Zimbabwe). Indeed, international focus on these two countries led to isolation in the Olympics by the end of the 1960s and in other sports soon thereafter. As early as 1967, though, the South African Government realized that racial exclusion in sport was a problem particularly when New Zealand postponed a planned visit to South Africa due to exclusion of its Maori players. The South African Government relented and allowed Maoris to tour in 1970 generating the first crack in a solid racist sporting policy. After piecemeal changes were rejected internationally, sport moved to integrate by the early 1990s.[49]

In the USA, toward the latter part of the 1960s, African-American athletes became involved in the Civil Rights movement by actively protesting against racial discrimination in sport and the larger society both at home and internationally. The two major forums for protest were the Olympic Games and predominantly white university campuses, where African-American athletes staged boycotts and spoke out against the racial discrimination experienced by them and other members of the African-American community. Protests of athletes contributed to South Africa's exclusion from the 1968 Olympics, its expulsion from the Olympic movement and a boycott of the 1976 Olympics in Montreal due to the participation of New Zealand, which maintained sporting ties with South Africa in rugby union. This activism sparked a rise in academic research on race and sport in the 1970s and 1980s with much of international work focused on the anti-aparthied issue and isolating white South Africa,[50] while in the USA a project of recovering black contribution to sport gathered force.

Rebellious African-American athletes publicized their fight for racial equality. Certainly the most celebrated protest of this type was the proposed boycott of the 1968 Olympic Games in Mexico City led by Harry Edwards, then an instructor at San Jose State College, who assembled a group of outstanding African-American athletes who threatened to withdraw from the Games in Mexico City unless certain demands were met. The demands included the removal of Avery Brundage as president of the International Olympic Committee, restoration of Muhammad Ali's heavyweight boxing title, exclusion of Rhodesia and South Africa from Olympic competition, appointment of at least two African-Americans to the US Olympic Committee, complete desegregation of the New York Athletic Club (NYAC), and addition of at least two African-American coaches to the men's Olympic track and field team.

By the latter part of the 1960s, African-American athletes were creating chaos on college campuses by becoming active participants in the Civil Rights movement and protesting against racial discrimination in sport and society at large. Inspired by the examples set by such outspoken individuals as Jim Brown, Bill Russell and Muhammad Ali, African-American college athletes shed their traditional conservative approach to racial matters and vehemently protested against everything from the lack of African-American studies in the curriculum to the dearth of African-American coaches and athletic administrators. This path was sometimes paved with dire consequences, many African-American athletes enduring the wrath of university administrations and jeopardizing their careers for speaking out on behalf of themselves and other members of their race.[51]

One of the targets of black protests was the apartheid system in South Africa that kept black South Africans from competing internationally. During the 1970s and 1980s blacks and whites internationally worked tirelessly to bring about an end to racial discrimination in sport there.[52] By the 1990s official segregation in sport was abolished nearly everywhere in the world though the issue of race in sport was nowhere near the 'end of its history'.

Beyond black and white: analysing race and sport into the 21st century

In North American professional sport, players now come from many parts of the world. NBA teams boast of players from Argentina, Brazil, Canada, China, Croatia, Serbia, Spain, Greece, Lithuania and a host of others. Professional baseball has had players from all over Central America, Veneuzela, the Caribbean, Japan, the Netherlands, Australia, South Africa and many more. The National Hockey League staffs its teams with players from all over Europe as well as from Canada and the USA, though it remains largely a white, non-Hispanic league. In Europe, most leagues and major teams are populated with players from other countries as well as other continents. It is common to find South Americans playing in Spain and Italy, Africans in England and the Netherlands. In *How Soccer Explains the World*, Frank Foer covers many cases of the globalization of soccer including one about a Nigerian playing in the Ukraine.[53] As sport has globalized athletes have moved with opportunities. While on the one hand this has had a deleterious impact on local competitions in places like Brazil, Argentina and Nigeria, it has brought Empires home to play so to speak. As a result, there has been more direct exposure to players from different cultures. Fans, media, administrators and analysts all have had to alter their perceptions and understandings as a result, not always to positive effect. This process has accelerated since the 1990s with the post-*Bosman* ruling era in European soccer, the fall of the Berlin Wall and migration of Eastern Europeans to North American and Western European leagues and the global search for talent among universities in the USA.

Historians of sport internationally have made a number of advances in this period as well, developing more sophisticated analyses utilizing a wider array of sources including oral histories, previously untapped media and club records, literary texts, and through the development of broader techniques of analysis drawing on post-colonialism and post-modernism. The history of race and sport has effectively moved from the discovery and recovery phases to one in which the meanings of race as a category for discussion in sport are explored through an examination of embodiment, discourse and political economy to understand the stubborn persistence of race. While great strides have been made in the recovery of the sporting histories of peoples of colour throughout the world, there remains much to be uncovered. Race also remains a powerful issue in contemporary sport and often perceptions of the past invade the present.

Notes

1 J.Bale and J. Sang, *Kenyan Running* (London: Frank Cass, 1996).

2 J. Nauright, *Sport, Cultures and Identities in South Africa* (London: Leicester University Press, 1997); D. Booth, *The Race Game* (London: Frank Cass, 1998).

3 In many former imperialist societies social divisions have diversified. In the USA, for example, there are now more people classified as Latino than African-American, and a sizable Asian minority also exists. In the United Kingdom racial divisions occur primarily between whites, African-descended people (Afro-Caribbean) and South Asians (most of whose families originated in India and Pakistan).

4 Much of this literature is discussed further in specific national and regional chapters in the second half of this volume.

5 See, for example, A. Saeed, 'What's in a Name: Muhammad Ali and the Politics of Cultural Identity', *Sport in Society* 5:3 (2002), 52–72; K. Sandiford, 'Shooting Hoops Against Darwin's Athletes: A Barbadian Response to John Hoberman', *The Sports Historian* 19, 2 (1999), 112–27.

6 A. Calder, 'A Man For All Cultures: The Careers of Learie Constantine', *Culture, Sport, Society* 6, 1 (2003), 19–42.

7 K. Mercer, *Welcome to the Jungle: New Positions in Black Cultural Studies* (London: Routledge, 1994), 138.

8 As a result, though, we know much more detail about black sport in these areas; see, for example R. Ruck, *Sandlot Seasons: Sport in Black Pittsburgh* (Urbana and Chicago: University of Illinois Press, 1993).

9 D. Andrews, ed., *Michael Jordan Inc.: Corporate Sport, Media Culture, and Late Modern America* (Albany: SUNY Press, 2001); C.L. Cole, 'The Place of Golf in U.S. Imperialism', *Journal of Sport and Social Issues* 26, 4 (2002), 331–36.

10 Cited by C.K. Harrison in his Foreword to D. Andrews, ed., *Michael Jordan Inc*, ix.

11 This is discussed in J. Nauright and T. Magdalinski, '"A Hapless Attempt at Swimming": Representations of Eric Moussambani', *Critical Arts* 17, 1&2 (2003), 106–22.

12 See J. Hoberman, *Darwin's Athletes: How Sport Has Damaged Black America and Preserved the Myth of Race* (New York: Mariner Books, 1997); and the many reviews and debates this text evoked. More controversial is J. Entine, *Taboo: Why Black Athletes Dominate Sports and Why We're Afraid to Talk about It* (New York: PublicAffairs, 2001).

13 See D. Booth, *The Field* (London: Routledge, 2006) and his chapter in this collection.

14 For example, W.H. Boulware, 'Black Urban Leisure Pursuits and Cultural Identity in Eighteenth Century South Carolina and Georgia', *International Journal of Regional and Local Studies* Series 2, 1, 1 (2005).

15 Nauright, *Sport, Cultures, and Identities in South Africa*; A. Odendaal, *Cricket in Isolation: The Politics of Race and Cricket in South Africa* (Cape Town: The Author, 1977); C. Merrett and J. Nauright, 'South Africa', in B. Stoddart and K. Sandiford, eds, *The Imperial Game: Cricket and Cultural Power* (Manchester: Manchester University Press, 1998), 55–78.

16 J. Mulvaney and R. Harcourt, *Cricket Walkabout: The Australian Aborigines in England* (Melbourne: Macmillan, 1988).

17 G. Ryan, *Forerunners of the All Blacks: The 1888–89 New Zealand Native Football Team in Britain, Australia and New Zealand* (Christchurch: Canterbury University Press, 1993).

18 P. Vasili, *The First Black Footballer, Arthur Wharton 1865–1930: An Absence of Memory* (London: Routledge, 1998).

19 See J. Bale, *Imagined Olympians* (Minneapolis: University of Minnesota Press, 2002); D. Booth and J. Nauright, 'Embodied Identities: Sport and Race in South Africa', *Contours: A Journal of the African Diaspora* 1, 1 (2003), 16–36; Nauright and Magdalinski, 'Hapless Attempt at Swimming'. Excellent historical context on embodiment, race and sport appears in D.L. Andrews, 'The Fact(s) of Michael Jordan's Blackness: Excavating a Floating Racial Signifier', in D.L. Andrews, ed., *Michael Jordan, Inc.*, 107–52; and J. Schultz, 'Reading the Catsuit: Serena Williams and the Production of Blackness at the 2002 U.S. Open', *Journal of Sport and Social Issues* 29, 3 (2005), 338–57.

20 See C.L.R. James' novel, *Beyond a Boundary* (1963); K. Sandiford, *The Cricket Nurseries of Colonial Barbados: The Elite Schools 1865–1966* (Kingstson: University Press of the West Indies, 1998).

21 J. Nauright, 'Race, Rugby and Popular Culture: "Coloured" rugby in Cape Town, South Africa', in T. Chandler and J. Nauright, *Making the Rugby World: Race, Gender, Commerce* (London: Routledge, 1999), 27–42.

22 Booth and Nauright, 'Embodied Identities', 19.
23 A. Odendaal, 'South Africa's Black Victorians: Sport and Society in South Africa in the Nineteenth Century', in J.A. Mangan, ed., *Pleasure, Profit, Proselytism: British Culture and Sport at Home and Abroad 1700–1914* (London: Frank Cass, 1988), 193–214.
24 K. Sandiford, *Cricket Nurseries of Colonial Barbados*, 147.
25 M. Lomax, *Black Baseball Entrepreneurs, 1860–1901: Operating by Any Means Necessary* (Syracuse: Syracuse University Press, 2001); D. Wiggins, *Glory Bound: Black Athletes in a White World* (Syracuse: Syracuse University Press, 1997).
26 J. Coakley, *Sports in Society: Issues and Controversies*, 10th edn (Boston: McGraw-Hill, 2009), 278.
27 B. Carrington and I. McDonald, 'Introduction', in B. Carrington and I. McDonald, eds, *'Race', Sport and British Society* (London: Routledge, 2001), 4–10.
28 See, L. Davis, 'The Articulation of Difference: White Preoccupation with the Question of Racially Linked Genetic Differences Among Athletes', *Sociology of Sport Journal* 7 (1990), 179–87; D. Wiggins, 'Great speed but little stamina: The historical debate over Black athletic Superiority', *Journal of Sport History* 16 (1989), 158–85; S. Fleming, 'Racial Science and South Asia and Black Physicality', in Carrington and McDonald, *'Race', Sport and British Society* 105–20. Fleming cites several 'scientific' studies of race and sport including M.J. Berry, T.J. Zehnder, C.B. Berry, S.E. Davis and S.K. Anderson, 'Cardiovascular Responses in Black and White Males During Exercise', *Journal of Applied Physiology* 74, 2 (1993), 755–60; J. Samson and M. Yerles, 'Racial Differences in Sports Performance', *Canadian Journal of Sports Science* 13, 2 (1988), 109–16; as well as the popular reaction: M. Gladwell, 'Why are Blacks So Good at Sport?', *The Sunday Telegraph Review*, 20 July 1997, 1–2; S. Conner, 'Bannister Says Blacks Were Born to Run', *The Independent*, 14 September 1995, 3; and S.L. Price, 'Is it in the Genes?', *Sports Illustrated* 87, 23 (1997), 53–55.
29 Wiggins, 'Great Speed but Little Stamina', 161, citing W.M. Cobb, 'Race and Runners', *Journal of Health and Physical Education* (January 1936), 3–7, 52–56.
30 E. Gorn, *The Manly Art: The Lives and Times of the Great Bare-Knuckle Champions* (London: Robson Books, 1986), 35–36.
31 D. Wiggins, 'Peter Jackson and the Elusive Heavyweight Championship: A Black Athlete's Struggle Against the Late Nineteenth Century Color-line', *Journal of Sport History* 12 (1985), 155; E. Gorn, *The Manly Art*, 227, 238.
32 R. Roberts, *Papa Jack: Jack Johnson and the Era of White Hopes* (New York: The Free Press, 1985); G. Ward, *Unforgiveable Blackness: The Rise and Fall of Jack Johnson* (New York: Vintage Press, 2006).
33 See, M. Stokes, *D.W. Griffith's the Birth of a Nation: A History of the Most Controversial Motion Picture of All Time* (New York: Oxford University Press, 2008).
34 T. Runstedtler, 'In Sports the Best Man Wins: How Joe Louis Whupped Jim Crow', in A. Bass, ed., *In the Game: Race, Identity, and Sports in the Twentieth Century* (New York: Palgrave Macmillan, 2005), 48.
35 Runstedtler, 'In Sports the Best Man Wins', 64–67.
36 John Hoberman, *Darwin's Athletes*.
37 C. Martin, 'The Color Line in Midwestern College Sports, 1890–1960', *Indiana Magazine of History* 98 (2002), 85–112; J. Nauright, 'The First African-American football captain: Theatrece Gibbs and Iowa football in the 1930s', *Gridiron Greats: Magazine of Football History* 3:6 (2004), 20–23; D. McMahon, 'Remembering the Black and Gold: African-Americans, Sport Memory, and the University of Iowa', in S.G. Whiting, ed., *Sport and Memory in North America* (London: Frank Cass, 2001), 63–98.
38 S. Cahn, *Coming on Strong: Gender and Sexuality in Twentieth-Century Women's Sport* (Cambridge, MA: Harvard University Press, 1994).
39 Cahn, *Coming on Strong*, 112.
40 J. Hargreaves, *Heroines of Sport: The Poltics of Difference and Identity* (London: Routledge, 2000).
41 N. Lanctot, *Negro League Baseball: The Rise and Ruin of a Black Institution* (Philadelphia: University of Pennsylvania Press, 2004); Lomax, *Black Baseball Entrepreneurs*; Ruck, *Sandlots*; R. Peterson, *Only the Ball Was White* (New York: Oxford University Press, 1992).
42 Lomax, *Black Baseball Entrepreneurs*; Peterson, *Only the Ball Was White*.
43 Lanctot, *Negro League Baseball*; Peterson, *Only the Ball Was White*.
44 See Nauright, *Sport, Cultures and Identities in South Africa*.
45 See discussion on sub-Saharan Africa by Nauright in this volume.
46 J. Tygiel, *Baseball's Great Experiment: Jackie Robinson and His Legacy* (New York: Oxford University Press, 1983 and 25th anniversary edn, 2008).

47 M. Lomax, 'The African-American Experience in Professional Football', *Journal of Social History* 33, 1 (1999), 163–75; T.G. Smith, 'Outside the Pale: The Exclusion of Blacks from the National Football League, 1934–1946', *Journal of Social History* 15 (1988), 255–81.

48 For an interesting discussion of the role of students and student athletes in the ending of segregation in NCAA football, see L. Demas, 'Beyond Jackie Robinson: Racial Integration in American College Football and New Directions in Sport History', *History Compass* 5, 2 (2007), 675–90.

49 For more on this see, J. Nauright, '"Like Fleas on a Dog": New Zealand and Emerging Protest against South African Sport, 1965–74', *Sporting Traditions* 10, 1 (1993), 54–77.

50 For example: C. de Broglio, *South Africa: Racism in Sport* (London: International Defense Aid Fund, 1970); R. Lapchick, *The Politics of Race and International Sport: The Case of South Africa* (Westport, CT: Greenwood Press, 1975); R. Thompson, *Retreat from Apartheid: New Zealand's Sporting Contacts with South Africa* (Oxford: Oxford University Press, 1975); R. Archer and A. Bouillon, *The South African Game: Sport and Racism* (London: Zed Press, 1982). For more discussion of the literature on South Africa see chapter 17 in this volume.

51 See H. Edwards, *The Revolt of the Black Athlete* (New York: Macmillan, 1969); D. Hartmann, *Race, Culture and the Revolt of the Black Athlete: The 1968 Olympic Protests and their Aftermath* (Chicago: University of Chicago Press, 2004).

52 For more detailed discussion of these campaigns and their role in sports history, see chapter 17 in this collection and the studies by Booth, *The Race Game*; Nauright, *Sport, Cultures, and Identities in South Africa*.

53 F. Foer, *How Soccer Explains the World: An Unlikely Theory of Globalization* (London: HarperCollins, 2005).

10 Body culture

Henning Eichberg

Body cultures meeting – a colonial case

Body culture consists of body cultures, and body cultures meet in history.

An introductory case shows such an encounter – and its problems. In the beginning of the 20th century, people of the Mentawai islands at the west coast of Sumatra (Indonesia) entered for first time into contact with the Dutch colonial power, which was dominating Indonesia at that time. Living in longhouses and clans along the rivers in the equatorial rain forest, the Mentawaians had kept to their so-called 'Stone-Age' culture. The 'mild savages', as they were also called by Westerners, lived in an 'original affluent society', without villages, without chieftains, but rich in festivities and shamanic rituals. When the Mentawaians met with colonial authorities, this isolation was broken and led to processes of cultural learning and astonishment. An old Mentawaian told about an episode with a Dutch military officer:

> But once we were not content with him. He said that we should come down to the coast and take bow and arrows with us. There they had prepared all very beautiful and waited for us on a large place. We got meal and drinking, and then they took a coconut and asked us to shoot after it. We did so, and when one of us hit the nut they cheered and screamed, as if we had hit an ape and not a coconut. At the end we received our reward and could go home again. But what was not correct after our opinion was that we did not receive equally. Some received a lot, and others did not receive anything at all. We all became a little bit angry in our hearts. But what should we do? They are as they are …

When asked who those had been who received more, he answered:

> Yes, this is exactly what we did not understand. It was purely coincidental. It was quite independent from which clan they came.[1]

The story is about a misunderstanding. The Dutch had the idea to integrate the Mentawaians who were famous for their art of shooting, into a festivity to the honour of the Dutch monarchy. By bodily activity bridges should be built between the cultures. (In a similar way, it is often said today that sport expresses an elementary, objective and universal body language, which – being far from linguistic troubles – may serve as an ideal medium of understanding across borders and of bridging between people.)

In real life, however, the encounter developed in another way, and this is what the old Mentawaian remembered. The well-intentioned meeting began in a friendly fashion with festive decoration and a meal. It turned into a ridiculous event as the Dutch cheered in a – for the indigenous guests – incomprehensible way about the arrow hitting a coconut. It ended in an insult when the Dutch officer distributed the sports rewards. The prizes were given according to the principle of achievement, and this conflicted with the artificial balance between the clans, which was basic for Mentawaian social relations. To give one person more and another less, according to their shooting results, corresponded neither to the egalitarian pattern of this stateless society nor to the complex relations between the different longhouse clans. Bow-and-arrow shooting as a Mentawaian art of chase and bow-and-arrow shooting as a Western sport were two fundamentally different activities.

The case casts light on the complexity of bodily activity, body language and body culture. It reveals how relevant body culture is for the understanding of society and cultural diversity. Furthermore it shows the entwinement between Western history of sport and non-Western history. History is not only the genesis and change of the one mainstream, which we call 'sport'.[2] It is also the history of 'non-sports' in thousands of Asian, African, Indigenous American and Pacific cultures. Their particular ways (in German: *Sonderwege*) throw light on what, there, has been the *sonderweg* of Western sports. By body culture – and in this case especially by the clash between body cultures – cultural diversity becomes visible.

Work on the history of body culture so far

The attention of cultural and social studies to 'the body' started in the 1970s in a nearly explosive process. Sociologists, historians, philosophers and anthropologists, scholars from sport studies and from medical studies suddenly met in talking about 'the return of the body' or its 'reappearance'.[3] The new interest directed towards the body was soon followed up by the term 'body culture'.

If trying to describe the history of this term and the related field of knowledge, however, one has to distinguish between three different lines of development: the line of 'classical' theories about the culture of the body, the history of the term 'body culture' itself, and the recent profile of discourse as well as the changes of social practice, which produced or promoted the new focus. These three lines lead to different historical periodizations.

Grand theories on body and culture

When the attention to 'the body' and to body culture had found its language, scholarly attention turned back to sociologists and philosophers who had earlier made studies in this field. These were – since the 1920s/30s – especially, Norbert Elias, the Frankfurt School and some phenomenologists. Michel Foucault and Pierre Bourdieu built bridges towards the new studies of body culture.

The German-Jewish sociologist Norbert Elias unfolded the first sociology which placed the body and bodily practice in its centre.[4] He started by a sociological analysis of table manners from the Middle Ages to French court society in Early Modernity. Elias described how people used knife, spoon, fork and plate in a more and more formalized way. He directed sociological attention towards practices around handkerchief and disgust, night gown and nakedness, bathroom and toilet as well as palace and garden architecture. On the basis of this material, Elias built the theory about an over-all 'process of civilization', which was linked to Western state formation, the centralization of power and the strengthening of social entwinement. Later, Elias incorporated sport into this theory of civilization and postulated a progressive, though sometimes irregular process of civilizing manners from ancient practices of chase to modern competitive sports.[5] Further-more, he studied the culture of duel in Wilhelminian Prussia in order to throw light on certain particular traits of the German *sonderweg*.[6] By all these studies in body-cultural change and difference, Elias aimed at a *Menschenwissenschaft*, which combined socio-genesis with psycho-genesis and explicated particular figurations between human beings. Though the radicalism of his approach was rarely fully realized among his disciples, who gave it some structural-functionalist and evolutionist undertones, the figurational sociology became productive especially in the field of sport studies.[7] Elias' concept of process of civilization also received, though, a harsh critique from the side of a comparative anthropology of bodily practices.[8]

The Frankfurt School, also known as Critical Theory, started in the 1920s as a co-operation of German-Jewish sociologists who combined Marxist and Freudian approa-ches. Bodily practice came soon into focus, when for instance Siegfried Kracauer compared the dancing of the Tiller girls with the capitalist rationalization of industrial work. Mass ornaments of the commercialized bodies and mass production were related to each other. Walter Benjamin followed up by reflecting on the aesthetization of bodily display in Fascist politics. In what is regarded as the main work of the Frankfurt School, Max Horkheimer and Theodor W. Adorno described the Western 'dialectics of enlightenment' as including a sort of underground history of the body.[9] The living body (in German: *Leib*), which had importance for the lord–servant relation in societies of slavery and feudalism, lost its living quality under capitalism and became a dead body. Now the corpus (in German: *Körper*) functioned as a commodity and private property on the market. Against conservative cultural criticism, which dreamt of a return to the living body, against the aesthetic illusions of modern advertisements and against Nazism, which combined body aesthetization with violence, Horkheimer and Adorno underlined that there was no way back to the non-alienated *Leib*. Furthermore the *Dialectic of Enlight-enment* pointed to the Jewish tradition, which avoided measuring the human body, because this measurement was applied to the dead corpse for the coffin. This critique could be read as a critical comment on sport and its craze of quantification. Later on, a younger generation of the Frankfurt School followed in the tracks of Adorno, giving birth to the Neo-Marxist sports critique[10] and developing alternative historical approaches to movement culture.[11] Also historical studies about the body in industrial work, in transportation and in Fascist aesthetics, as well as a philosophy of body and space in history had their roots in this critical approach.[12]

At the same time, philosophical phenomenology began to pay attention to the body. The German philosopher Helmuth Plessner studied laughter and weeping as fundamental human expressions. The French philosopher Maurice Merleau-Ponty placed the body in the centre of human existence: it is by bodily existence that the human being is in the world and experiences the world. By his focus on the body as source of understanding, love and identity, Merleau-Ponty conflicted with Jean Paul Sartre, who saw the body as object of disgust, shame and alienation. More influential became the conflict which Merleau-Ponty displayed between the body-fundamentalist position of phenomenology and the traditional body–mind dualism of René Descartes. In another way, the philosopher Gaston Bachelard approached bodily existence via a phenomenology of the four elements – fire, water, air, earth – and of space, starting with studies about the 'psycho-analysis of fire' (1938). Most of the phenomenological studies had their intellectual origin in the scientific studies of the German poet Johann Wolfgang Goethe, whose work *Zur*

Farbenlehre (1810) can be regarded as the first phenomenological research. Goethe's phenomenology of colours was built up against the mathematical-reductionist approach of Newtonian science – and it included historical studies on the production of colours.[13]

Based on phenomenological traditions, the French philosopher Michel Foucault undertook deep studies in the configurations of knowledge during the Renaissance and the 'classical age' of Baroque in order to approach the post-1800 society of modern 'development' and panoptical control. His studies approached the body by analysing the history of military discipline and the panopticon as a mechanism of control. The modern body moves in an 'archipelago of prisons' and is subjected to what Foucault called the bio-politics of power. This approach became especially influential for sport studies in body, space and architecture. It also inspired critical studies in the disciplined body of gymnastics and sport.[14]

While Foucault's studies in bodily discipline tended to focus on top-down strategies of power, the French Sociologist Pierre Bourdieu directed his attention more towards bottom-up processes of social-bodily practice. He started by studying the Kabyl Berber people in Algeria, their houses and life practices, before entering into studies among different social classes in France. From this, Bourdieu developed the influential concept of habitus.[15] Habitus is a sort of incorporated pattern, which becomes social practice by diverse forms of taste and distinction, by the display of the body – and by sports. Side by side with economic capital, the social habitus could be understood as a sort of 'cultural capital'. Some of Bourdieu's disciples, such as Jacques Defrance, applied these concepts to the history of sports and gymnastics.[16]

In the works of other 'fathers' of modern social thinking, too, 'the body' was recently discovered as being at least an underground category – in Karl Marx's reflections of the 'basis' of human practice and social relations, in Max Weber's analysis of the Protestant and capitalist 'secular asceticism', and in Marcel Mauss' observation of 'body techniques'.

'Body culture': the term and concept

Though the named 'classical' theories were centred about body and culture, they normally did not use the term 'body culture' itself. This concept had another terminological origin, which was derived from movement practices at the beginning of the 20th century. Between 1900 and World War I, new bodily practices suddenly spread in Europe and America, which took the collective name of 'life reform' (German *Lebensreform*). This referred to the reform of clothing and of nurture. Life reform expressed itself especially by new bodily activities, which constituted a sort of third sector side by side with gymnastics and sport, the established practices of the 19th century. The main fields of the 'third way' of movement culture were nudism, rhythmic-expressive gymnastics, yoga and body building, as well as a new type of youth walking.[17] Though these practices were very diverse, they found a comprehensive term in the German *Körperkultur*, in English 'physical culture', in French *culture physique* and in Danish *kropskultur* or *legemskultur*. This concept of body culture contained – besides health and functionality – strong elements of aesthetical display of the body, which shifted according to the tendencies of Art Deco, Expressionism, New Objectivity and New Classicism.[18] Furthermore, body culture and life reform gave birth to an early and for a long time singular study in the history of bodily positions and movements, a history of foot posture written by the Austrian reform gymnast Karl Gaulhofer. The classical article of the French anthropologist Marcel Mauss (1934) about the 'techniques of the body' may be seen in this context, too.[19]

German Socialist workers' sport gave a prominent place to the concept of *Körperkultur*, while Nazi sport gave priority to *Leib* and *Leibesübungen* and detested *Körperkultur* as being materialistic, decadent and Jewish. It was probably by way of German Socialist 'body culture' that the concept entered into the theory and practice of Russian Socialists under the name of *fiskultura*. After the revolution of 1917, *fiskultura* became an alternative to bourgeois sport, uniting the revolutionary factions of more aesthetically orientated *Proletkult* and more health-orientated hygienists. Under the dominance of Stalinism, however, the contradictory terms were united under the formula 'sport and body culture'. This continued in the Soviet bloc after 1945. *Körperkultur* was at that time re-imported into the German Democratic Republic, where the official review of sport sciences had the title *Theorie und Praxis der Körperkultur*, and the sports university in Leipzig was called 'German High School of Body Culture' (DHfK).

During all these transformations, the concept of body culture was generally used in the singular. Though at a closer view both historical change and cultural diversity became visible, one did not yet talk about body cultures in the plural.

When the 1968 students' movement revived Marxism in Neo-Marxist forms, the concept of 'body culture' – *Körperkultur* in West Germany, 'somatic culture' in America – re-entered the sports-critical discourse, and its alternative accents were sharpened again. This is how the Danish term *kropskultur* obtained a new actuality during the 1970/80s, used by the sports-critical school of Gerlev Sports Academy. In Finland, the concept *ruumiinkulttuuri* found similar attention. *Quel corps?* was the title of a critical review of sports, edited by the French Marxist educationalist Jean-Marie Brohm in 1975–97.[20]

Among some European scholars, the equivalent term was 'body anthropology', as in the framework of the French-Danish-German *Institut International d'Anthropologie Corporelle*.[21] The review *Stadion, Journal of the History of Sport and Physical Education* (Cologne, 1975 ff) chose for its title the terms *Sport und Körperkultur* in German, and *sport et culture physique* in French. In Japan, the sociologist Satoshi Shimizu established a *Centre for the Study of Body Culture* at the University of Tsukuba.

Innovation in studies of body culture

The concept of body culture joined a new scholarly interest in the human body since the 1970s. This innovation happened as a cross-disciplinary process. From the side of philosophy, one began to talk about 'the return of the body' with some 'post-modern' undertones. The body in sport and Fascist aesthetics found philosophical-historical interest, while an Aristotelian philosophy, critically directed against Kantian rationalism, paid attention to bodily feelings and emotions in sport such as pain, hubris and *schadenfreude*.[22]

In anthropology, Clifford Geertz's classical article about Balinese cockfighting received worldwide attention, and during the 1970s an anthropology of the body was drafted. Susan Brownell delivered important body-cultural studies of sport in China, and G. Whitney Azoy showed, by analysis of the Afghan game of Buzkashi, how power and violence were embodied in the situation of playing.[23]

In ethnology, the Tübingen School in Germany around Hermann Bausinger contributed with studies among others about the upright posture. Danish ethnologists launched the body-near concept of life-form analysis, and the Swedish 'cultural analysis' approached modernity as a transformation of bodily practice. The Birmingham school of the *Centre for Contemporary Cultural Studies* (CCCS, 1964–2002) obtained broad international attention by its studies in youth cultures, sport and rock music.[24]

Though sociology was traditionally focused on institutions and abstract societal processes, several sociologists have followed in the tracks of Elias, Adorno, Foucault and Bourdieu. Brian S. Turner and Chris Shilling presented overviews of the body in society, and the Department of Cultural Sociology in Copenhagen gave birth to several body-near studies.[25]

Psychology had some problems extending its perspective from the bodiless soul or psyche towards the body. The German Communist psychiatrist Wilhelm Reich was the first, during the 1920/30s, to give the body a central place in therapeutic practice and in psychoanalytical theory, especially 'body armour' and orgasm. He used this approach for a body-political critique of Fascism. His work was rediscovered after 1968 and led to new forms of therapy, especially in California, at the Esalen Institute and in the new field of Somatics. In Finland and the United Kingdom, the body, its subjectivity and its culture were approached by narrative and autobiographic methods. David B. Morris presented an important study in the 'culture of pain'.[26]

All this influenced the field of education. Under the heading of 'body anthropology', educationalists from France, Germany and Denmark co-operated (IIAC, founded in 1987) and undertook case studies in traditional games as well as in 'scenes' of new urban body cultures. 'Movement culture' became a pedagogical keyword in German pedagogical thinking (Moegling, 2001/02). The 'non-sportive sport', play and games, and diverse forms of sport for all were regarded as an educational challenge for the sport-dominated culture of the body.[27]

In linguistics, George Lakoff and Mark Johnson discovered the bodily basis of language, expressing a rich world of body metaphors. The linguistic dualism between German *Körper* and *Leib*, between having a body and being a body, which had already been the basis of Plessner's findings, was revisited and reconstructed in English by the word-pair 'body' and 'soma'.[28]

Even theology contributed. The French Jesuit Marcel Jousse tried to re-theorize the Christian message by pointing, in an original way, to the bodily narrative, the 'living word' as the core of Jesus' message. The central point of Christianity was not the book, but the bodily gesture, *la geste*.[29]

Among these diverse approaches, historiography found rich inspirations for hitherto neglected studies. Whether approaching from a more phenomenological historiography or from an historical-statistical background, the culture of the body became central. The posture of the body and bodily display as well as the bodily movements of transportation, automobilization and racing found their historians. Links between body history and political history became visible on the levels of ideas, literary imaginations and gymnastic practice.[30]

Opposition, resource, recognition: the body discourse and societal practice

It is not yet clear which change in the societal basis of bodily practice may have produced or promoted the new superstructure of research interests centred around body culture. At a closer view, different phases and sub-discourses can be distinguished.

The early 'return of the body' during the 1970s showed traits from alternative culture and the hippie movement. New games of Californian type spread, and so-called Somatics tried to create a theoretical superstructure in the spirit of New Age (the magazine *Somatics* was published by Thomas Hanna from 1976 onward). In the context of the counter-culture, the French critique of sports as a 'prison of measured time' developed and was enlarged towards a discourse of body culture.[31]

A further body discourse was about sexuality and gender, which had its basis in the feminist movement. This opened up awareness of another type of societal contradiction, contesting the industrial patriarchy. In other words, the new approach to body culture saw the body as oppositional – and as a field of contradictions. 'Body culture' was a term of resistance.

Soon however, so-called postmodernism entered the field. Sharing the critique of system thinking and functionalism, proponents of 'postmodernism' joined the discourse of body culture and contributed by giving increased attention to the multiplicity and diversity of body cultures in the plural. Postulating the death of the great narratives, however, postmodernism itself produced a new ideology, now under the heading of that all was fragmented, coincidental and erratic – just bricolage. Bodily existence was seen as a world of tastes, group differentiations and individual dispositions where anything goes. The body became a matter of choice and construction.

This superstructure – the 'constructed body' – expressed how market and health systems had occupied the terrain. On one hand, the fashionable body discourse was mainly about body shape and body image, about decoration and dressing, about tattoos and beauty surgery – the body, which we can buy. This corresponded to the current state of consumerism and merchandise, revealing the commoditization of the body.

On the other hand, body discourse became largely colonized by questions of health and illness, curing and hygiene. Recently, obesity and upbringing have alarmed the political world. This mirrored profound changes in the world of capitalist production, reproduction and everyday alienation. In other words, the postmodern and constructionist approach to body culture referred to the body as resource. Body culture was a world of normalization – and at the same time a supermarket where the human being chooses according to its individual inclinations.

This profile of 'the social body' was illustrative, but too narrow. It was a static body – shape and health – that attracted one-sided attention, while the dynamic body in motion was neglected. The discourse about the body as a certain 'being' showed marks of reification forced upon it by the powers of production, consumption and reproduction. What was neglected was the body as a field of dynamic human interaction, of movement – and movement cultures in the plural. In movement, human subjectivity develops through bodily dialogue with others. This is where sport, dance and games have their special place. Body culture, thus, emerges as a field of movement practice where recognition and non-recognition conflict.

How studies in body culture contribute to wider historical debates

The study of body culture has enabled the study of sport to enter into broader historical and sociological fields of discussion, concerning, among others, modernization, civilization, industrialization and colonization.

Civilization, modernization, discipline

Studies of body culture enriched the analysis of historical change – but in conflicting terms. Norbert Elias studied sport in order to throw light on the civilizing process. In sport, he saw a line going from original violence to civilized entwinement. Though there were undertones of hope, Elias tried to avoid evolutionism, which since the 19th century postulated a 'progressive' development from 'primitive' to 'civilized' patterns.[32]

Nevertheless, there remained a contrast between the concept of civilization, which had hopeful undertones, on one hand, and discipline, which had more critical undertones, on the other. The concept of discipline could – following Foucault and the Frankfurt School – be based on the study of sport and body culture, among others studies of Baroque dance, aristocratic and bourgeois pedagogy of the spinal column in the 18th–19th centuries, and hygienic strategies, school sanitation and school gymnastics in the 20th century. Military exercise in Early Modern times was a productive field for the body-cultural analysis of discipline, too.[33]

In the field of sports, a central point of dispute has been the question of whether sport had its roots in Ancient Greek competitions of the Olympic type or whether it was fundamentally modern. While the first was the hypothesis of the 19th century's Neo-Humanism, Classicism and Olympism, body-cultural studies claimed that the patterns central to modern sports – quantification, rationalization, principle of achievement – could not be dated before the early industrial culture of the 18th–19th centuries. What could be found before modern industrial culture were popular games, noble exercises, festivities of different sorts, children's games and competitions, but not sport in the modern sense. The so-called Eichberg-Mandell-Guttmann theory about the uniqueness of modern sport became a matter of controversy and was opposed by several historians. An open problem remains to analyse the body culture of the competitive festivities in Olympia, Delphi, Nemea, Isthmia and other places of Ancient Greece in contrast to modern sports. Anyway, the emergence of modern sport was an eruptive innovation rather than a logical prolongation of earlier practices – a revolution of body culture. This transformation contributed to a deeper understanding of the Industrial Revolution.[34]

What came out of the controversies among the concepts of modernization, evolution, civilization, discipline, revolution and so on was that 'modernization' – if at all – can only be thought of as a non-lineal change with nuances and full of contradictions. This is how the history of sport and of gymnastics as well as the history of running have been described in body-cultural terms.[35]

One of the visible and at the same time deeper changes in relation to the modern body concerns the reform of clothing in sport and society and the appearance of the naked body, especially in the years between 1900 and the 1920s. The change from distinguished pale skin to suntanned skin as a 'sportive' distinction was not only linked to sport, but had a strong impact on society as a whole. The change of appreciated body colour reversed the social-bodily distinctions between people and classes. Organized nudism as 'naked sport' was an especially visible and radical, sometimes even sectarian expression of this body-cultural change.[36]

The history of social and political movements appeared in a new light as soon as these were analysed under the aspect of body culture. Studies in the literature of Pre-Fascist German 'free-corps' have shown how important body and gender were in the formation of Nazi violence. Differences between the right-wing and the left-wing view of the body have been subjected to detailed studies, which pointed towards a deeper level of politics than just ideology and interest. The right and the left wing differ not only in their relation to ideas such as liberty and equality, but also and fundamentally to body-cultural practice and body display. Most of these studies have so far mainly used literary sources, while practices such as mass festivities, uniforms and dressing, styles of movement, sport and music still have to be analysed in connection if light is to be thrown on the dynamics of political and social movements.[37]

Social time

Modern society is characterized by the significance of speed and acceleration. Sport, giving priority to competitive running and racing, is central among the phenomena illustrating the specifically modern velocity. The historical change from the circulating stroll in aristocratic and early bourgeois culture to modern jogging as well as the changes from coach traffic via the railway to motor sports produced new body-cultural insights into modern social time. On the basis of transportation and urbanism, blitzkrieg and sports, the French architect and cultural theorist Paul Virilio developed the provocative terms 'dromology' (science of racing) and 'dromocracy' (power or dominance of velocity) to describe the knowledge and the politics of modern social acceleration. However, the concept of social time embraces many more facets, which can be explored by comparing the time-dynamic movements of different ethnic cultures.[38]

Social space

Bodily display and movement always created space – socio-psychical space. Bodily activities have during history changed between indoor or outdoor milieus, between a non-specialized environment, specialized facilities and bodily opposition against existing standardized facilities or what was called 'sportscape'. In movement, straight lines and the culture of the streamline were confronted by mazes and labyrinthine structures, by patterns of fractal geometry. All these patterns are not just spatial-practical arrangements, they also play together with societal orientations. From this perspective comes the history of panoptical control, of the parcellation of the sportive space, and of the hygienic purification of spaces. Proxemics – the study of bodily space – has an historical dimension.[39]

This is also true for the understanding of 'nature'. The 'nature' of body culture – of outdoor life, naturism and the green movement – could in the course of history be a world of liberation and opposition, as in the periods around 1800 and after 1900. It could also turn into ways of colonization and simulation, forming a 'second nature'. It can even be a virtual world, which simulates people's senses, a 'third nature'. Anyway, the study of body culture contributed to a history of cultural ecology.

Body-cultural studies also contributed to a differentiation between what in everyday language is often confused as 'space' and 'place' whose dialectics were clarified by the Chinese-American philosopher Yi Fu Tuan.[40] Space can be described by co-ordinates and by certain choreographies. Spatial structures can be standardized and transferred from place to place. This is the case with the standardized spatial facilities of sports. The place, in contrast, is unique – it is only here or there. Locality is related to identity. People play in a certain place – and create the place by play and games. People play the place, and the place plays with the people.

Industrialization and production

When inquiring deeper into the origins and conditions of the Industrial Revolution, which in the 18th–19th centuries transformed people's everyday life in a fundamental way, the traditional common-sense explanations of industrialization by technology and economy as 'driving forces' are shown to be insufficient. Both economic interests and technological change had their basic conditions in human social-bodily practice. The history of sport and games in body-cultural perspective showed that this practice changed over one or two generations, before the Industrial Revolution as a technological and economic transformation took place. What had been carnival-like festivities, tournaments and popular games before, became modern sport with a new focus on results, measuring and quantifying records.[41] Based on this principle of achievement, there was no sport in ancient Egypt, in ancient Greece, among the Aztecs or Vikings, and in European Middle Ages, though there were games, competitions and festivities. Sport as a new type of body culture resulted from societal changes in the 18th–19th centuries.

The genesis of sport in connection with industrial productivity called to attention the historical-cultural relativity of 'production' itself. Studies in the history of 'the human motor' and the 'mortal engines' of sport showed reification and technology as lines of historical dynamics.[42] Production became apparent not as a universal concept, but as something historically specific – and sport was its body-cultural ritual.

That societies could also develop in diverse ways was shown by the Japanese relationship to the (Western) gun. From the 17th to the 19th centuries and on the basis of other body-cultural prioritizations inside the ruling samurai class, Japan dropped the gun and returned to the sword.[43] The social body culture was revealed as being stronger than the logic of military weapon technology.

State, market and civil society – and the trialectics of body culture

Body culture is a field of contradictions. Analysis of body culture has shown that these contradictions are not necessarily dualistic in character.[44] Under the aspect of reification, state logic subjects the body to power, control, 'evaluation' and training of 'competences'. This is the reification of bureaucratic control and 'management', as it is reproduced in state sports and state gymnastics.

Market logic, in contrast, subjects the body to instrumental use – the body being a means of production. By bodily practice, human beings produce results in centimetres, grams and seconds, or points, as is the case in sport. On the other hand, commercial logic makes the body a target for the appeal of consumption – it implies the reification of the body as commodity. The body is decorated, dressed, beautified, surgically transformed, 'bettered' by prosthetic devices and chemical means. These tendencies can be observed both on the market of professional sport and on the market of fitness.

A third logic side by side with public and commercial rationality can be found in civil society with its alternative body cultures as well as traditional movement cultures and popular games. Here, it is not so much the result as the process that counts. In civil logic, the body is a medium to confirm or contest one's identity – inside and between self-organized and voluntary groups.

The spatial organization of body culture points in these three directions, too. The public space of body cultures is marked by borders. Inside certain delineations of state borders, body culture is organized both in an inward-directed unifying way and in an outward-directed competitive way, in relation to other body cultures beyond the border. The market does not know this type of border and does not recognize it. Under commercial logic, body models are rather organized and offered in series, differentiated according to different target groups. This is the order of the supermarket. In civil society, the order of body cultures is more 'confused', as body-cultural practices follow the principles of self-organization and distinction. Rationalist philosophers, such as Jurgan Habermas, have characterized this 'new non-transparence' as *Neue Unubersichtlichkeit* (the title of his 1985 work). The space of sport in its historical development shows different combinations and nuances of these conflicting patterns.

This makes evident that the differentiation between public-political, commercial and civil logics is in some way connected with trialectical relations inside the world of sports.[45] The hegemonic model of Western modern body culture is achievement sport, translating movement into records. Sportive competition follows the logic of productivity by bodily strain and forms a ranking pyramid with elite sports placed at the top and the 'losers' at the bottom. Through sportive movement, people display a theatre of production.

A contrasting model within modern body culture is delivered by mass sport. In gymnastics and fitness sport, the body is disciplined by subjecting it to certain rules of 'scientific', social geometrical or aesthetic order.[46] By rhythmic repetition and formal homogenization, the individual bodies are integrated into a larger whole, which is recommended in terms of reproduction as being healthy and educative. Through fitness and sport, people undertake a ritual of reproductive correctness and integration.

A third model is present in festivity, dance and play – it is popular assemblage. In carnival and folk sport, people meet people by festive movement. It is true that this dimension of gathering may give life to the top-down arrangements of both productive achievement sport and reproductive fitness sport. However, the body experience of popular festivity, dance, play and games is a-productive in itself – it celebrates relation in movement.

Practices of sport in both their diversity and their historical change, thus, clarify inner contradictions inside social life more generally. The trialectics of body culture throw light on the complexity of societal relations.

The body and the people

Body-cultural studies have shown a certain relation between the body and what is called the people or the folk. Play and game, dance and festivity, competition and fight are fundamental for popular culture. By mock fight, carnival and laughter, people challenged the elites.[47] In and by movement culture, people develop identity: Who are we? The body in movement is an identity marker.[48] Like one's name and one's life history, the body tells 'who we are'. As habitus, bodily display and practice marks class identity.[49]

All this questions some dominating assumptions about who 'the people' are, the folk. Like the concept of 'the body', the term 'the people' has become colonized by hegemonic theories, mainly by substantialism and constructivism.

Traditionally, one has tried to define a given people by a certain substance, treating it like a material object. The 'substantial people' was objectified by criteria of 'blood', language, historical origin, territory, religion, customs, 'national character' and inner psychic disposition, state and constitution, common economy, community of communication or whatever.

The substantial view of the folk was opposed by interpretations of folk as an idea. The 'people' was said to be nothing but a construction, created by the propagandistic actions of leaders or intellectuals, typically nationalist ideologists. The assumption about the 'constructed people' was dominated by elitist connotations: The 'people' does not exist in itself, nor does it find itself – it is made from above, as an 'imagined community' or an 'invented tradition'.

Studies of body and movement culture question this dual pattern.[50] 'We are the people!' has been a basic saying of democracy since the time of the French Revolution. The call

'We are the people!' meant 'We are in motion!' By reclaiming the street and by festivity, people reclaimed their individual and interacting bodies against ruling power elites.

The so-called 'individual' body

Studies in body culture have again and again shown that bodily existence is more than just 'the body' as an individual skin bag, which is under the control of an individual mind. Bodily practice is going on *between* different bodies. This questions two current types of thinking 'the individual' – epistemological individualism and the thesis of 'late-modern individualization'.

The methodological habit of counter-posing 'the individual' and 'the society' is largely disseminated in sociology. It was fundamentally criticized by Norbert Elias who under-lined that there is no meaning in the separation between the individual as a sort of core of human existence and the society as a secondary environment around this core. No, society is inside the body. Elias used the paradigm of the waltz in order to demonstrate that an understanding of the dance could not be based on an intellectual strategy starting from the isolated individual. There is a wholeness in space and time, couple formation and social relations that makes the waltzing human being co-act with others. In contrast, epistemological solipsism treats human existence as if the human being was alone in the world – and was only in a secondary process 'socialized'.[51]

Another current assumption is of historical character. It says that individualization during 'high' or 'late modernity' has replaced all earlier traditions – religion, nation, class – and leaves 'the individual' alone with its body. The body, thus, gets a central position as the only fix-point of 'self-identity' left after the dissolution of the traditional norms. The individual chooses and makes its own body as a sort of 'gesamtkunstwerk Ego'.[52]

Body-cultural studies can also test – and challenge – this assumption. They throw light on inter-bodily relations, within which human individuality has a much more complex position.

Basis and superstructure

The body is the material basis of human existence. Studies of body culture contribute to fundamental philosophical orientation. On one hand, the body is a part of human life, which the individual cannot choose freely. On the other hand, the body is not deter-mined from the very beginning. Between the given body on one hand and intentional body management on the other, body culture develops in a process, which is historical and collective. The study of body culture throws light on this process and its contra-dictions between 'just doing' and trying to steer and control. People 'make' their own body, but they do not make it of their own individual will. People say one thing, mean something other – and do something else again.

Studies of body culture have shown the different levels of what is called 'culture' in human life. *Body culture* can be understood side by side with *symbolic culture*, which consists of the ideas, expressions and meanings of societal life, and with *material culture*, which is the world of human-made things, instruments and technology.

However, symbolic culture, material culture and body culture do not just range on the same level. Bodily practice is the origin of material constructions as well as the basic reference of symbols and language. 'Understanding' as under-standing refers to the upright position of the human being. The 'standing' body tells also about the 'state' of things and about the political state, and the discourse about social 'movements' is based on an understanding of human bodily movement.

In this perspective, the study of body culture throws light on the history of philosophical materialism. In the origin of modern materialist thinking, among 18th-century encyclopaedists and philosophers of nature, physical matter (*materia*) was seen as determining the world of ideas. The result was a *physical materialism*. In 19th-century political philosophy, certain modes of production, technological change and resulting conflicts of interests determined the history of institutions and ideologies. This gave birth to an *economic materialism*. If bodily practice is regarded as the basis of social identities, of conscience and historical change, a third, *body-cultural materialism* can be considered.

In this connection, the study of sport, dance and games, of bodily discipline and bodily production contributes with basic research to the history of human society and human philosophy.

Body cultures in the plural

'Culture' in the singular is an abstraction. The study of body culture is always a study of body cultures in the plural. Body cultures show human life in its variety and differences, assimilation and distinction, conflicts and contradictions. This demands a comparative approach to otherness, and this is the way several studies in body culture have gone.

The study of culture as cultures already existed in the 1930s in the approach of the school of Cultural Relativism in American anthropology (e.g. Ruth Benedict). Post-colonial studies have taken this pluralistic perspective up again.[53] The fashionable discourse in the singular about 'the body in our society' became problematic when confronted with body cultures in conflict and tension.

The plurality and diversity of body cultures is, however, not only a matter of outward relations. There are also plural body cultures inside a given society. The study of different class habitus, youth cultures, gender cultures and so on opens up deeper insights into the differentiation of civil society. Side by side with the terms of symbolic culture (ideas, meanings, arts) and material culture (things, instruments, technologies), body culture raises the question: What are cultures?

Three dimensions of movement

The body is not only a certain substance or materiality, as it was and is often treated in the natural sciences. Nor is the body just a sign or construction, as recent theories of constructivism claim. By reducing the body to discourse, meaning, interpretation, symbolic expression and semiotic patterns, constructionist thinking treats the body as a text which can be 'read'. Body culture, however, refers to a third category: practice in movement.

Bodies in movement practice, is what the study of movement culture is about. However, the concept of 'movement' touches upon at least three very different dimensions of human life: bodily movement, emotional movement and social movement.

In the first dimension, people move in concrete bodily activities such as sports and dance, games and meditation, outdoor activities and festivals. To understand bodily movement, the study of body culture touches the theory of practice, praxeology, which casts light on the culture of inter-bodily situations and relations. Many of the existing body-cultural studies have this main focus, both the history of sport[54] and of gymnastics,[55] which constitute two main fields of modern body culture – but are not the only ones. On the limits between sports and non-sports, one finds fight, struggle, and martial arts,[56] running,[57] and practices of fitness.[58] Outside the hitherto defined field of sport, outdoor activities as well as play and games,[59] dance[60] and meditative practices have found historical interest.

In the second dimension, people are moved by feelings, emotions and humour. Emotions (i.e. e-motions), motives and motivations demonstrate that there is emotional movement – fascination and euphoria, anger and fear, pain and laughter.[61] This is what the psychology of social interactions and social relations is about.

In the third dimension, people unite in social movements. They meet in associations and peer groups, informal networks and formal organizations. This is what the history of popular life is interested in, but also the history of Fascism.[62] In this way, the study of body culture contributes to the discovery of civil society and its inner contradictions.

The three dimensions of movement are connected with each other. Several studies have been written in the specific fields of body movement, emotional movement and social movement. What is needed, however, is a new type of comparative synthesis between the three. It is hardly by chance that different languages use the same term for these different levels: movement – *bevægelse* (Danish), *bevegelse* (Norwegian), *rörelse* (Swedish), *Bewegung* (German), *mouvement* (French), *movimiento* (Spanish) and *movimento* (Italian).

Future perspectives of body-culture studies

Thick description

The study of body culture begins by empirical description derived from historical sources and/or field observation. Rich in details, sensual, multi-faceted and multi-dimensional, this living narrative can draw on anthropological traditions, which the American anthropologist Clifford Geertz (1973) called 'thick description'. As any possible concept is culturally relative, a general definition cannot be the starting point, but analysis starts by a certain phenomenon in its complexity and historicity. The initial case is what in Danish is called 'the good story', that is a narrative including the research interest of the researcher and his or her amazement: Wow, isn't this interesting?!

Comparison and contradictions

The study of body culture always includes an element of comparison. One case of bodily practice will always contrast with others, for instance 'traditional' versus 'modern'. Serious research raises this spontaneous and unreflected comparison to culturally reflected understanding.

The comparison of diverse practices is supported by the construction of a terminology of contradictions. This is what the philosophical tradition has called dialectical thinking. The trialectical analysis, as sketched above – between state, market and civil society, between achievement sport, disciplining exercise and popular festivity – is a non-dualistic version of this dialectical approach. How body cultures can be understood out of conflict became visible in the introductory case from Mentawai in Indonesia.

Configurational analysis

Though bodily movement may be experienced as a whole, it is the pattern which reveals the inner tensions and contradictions of a given society. That is why the study of body culture has to focus on the configurations of movement in time and space, the energy of movement, its interpersonal relations and objectification. Above this basis, people build a superstructure of institutions and ideas, organizing and reflecting body culture in relation to collective actions and interests.[63]

The *time* of bodily movement is marked – among others – by contradictions between acceleration and slowness, between living rhythm and mechanical pace, between linear-abstract and irreversible time, between cyclical, progressing and situational time. This clarifies specific tendencies of historical change as for instance the transformation from the noble exercises of the 17th and 18th centuries with their circulating and formally measured patterns to modern gymnastics and sports with their new patterns of speed, acceleration and flow.

The *space* of bodily movement is characterized by contradictory elements, too – contradictions between the straight line and the labyrinth, between connection and parcellation of spaces, between geometrical space, place of identity and intermediary space. The Foucaultian study of the panopticon as a specific modern way of organizing the space of movement and bodily visibility around 1800 has shown the societal depth of this analysis, which deserves to be followed up for other periods and societies.

The *energy* of bodily movement can be described by a multiplicity of different atmospheres, radiations, moods and modes of adjustment. These have a right of their own in the study of body culture and cannot be reduced to the categories of space and time. For instance modern *Spannung* (tension, thrill, excitement) emerged in 18th and 19th century boxing at the same time as it appeared in criminal literature. This coincidence is illustrative of the configurational change towards industrial society. The same is true for the significance of laughter in Mikhail Bakhtin's analysis of social tensions in Renaissance society.

The *interpersonal relations* in bodily movement tell about power and gender, about winners and losers, about the You and the We in motion. History of sports has especially been enriched by the attention to gender unbalances in body culture – this has to be followed up in nuanced and non-dualistic ways.

The *objectification* of bodily movement develops in the tension between process and result, between production, reproduction and a-productive encounters in bodily activity. The production of records by modern sports has been a central criterion for the understanding of modern industrial behaviour.

As well as these basic body-cultural processes, the *organizations and institutions* of body culture deserve attention. Traditional sports history has, however, often focused one-sidedly on the level of this superstructure. The same is true for the level of *meanings and ideas*, which were ascribed to bodily practices. The complex interplay between body-cultural practice and the superstructures of cultural ideas and conscience have to be elaborated in more depth. This may be the main challenge of the concept of body culture to established sports history.

Body politics and bodily democracy

The study of body culture has political dimensions. On one hand, Fascist and other undemocratic body cultures have been built on the basis of sport, gymnastics, military exercise and violence. On the other hand, democracy can be understood as bodily self-determination and recognition, to which gymnastics and sports contributed in many ways. There are complex relations between the people of movement and the people of democracy.

This democratic relation of body studies to people's democracy has at certain times made the study of body culture politically controversial. Power could regard body-cultural research as dangerous or subversive. In 1933 the Frankfurt School was purged in Nazi Germany and, after the youth unrest of 1968, the Critical School – being productive among others of the new sports critique – was again seen as 'the enemy'. In the Soviet Union, Stalinism ended the *proletkult* project of *fiskultura* and subordinated the critical concept of 'body culture' under the practice of state sport. Some research institutes particularly active in critical studies of body culture were in recent times closed down or had further funding rejected by right-wing authorities, as was the case with the Department of Cultural Sociology at the University of Copenhagen in the late 1980s, the famous Birmingham School (CCCS) in 2002 and the Danish Institute of Sport Research (IFO) in 2003.

It is unlikely that the controversial character of body-cultural studies will disappear in future, but it may very well develop into new and unexpected directions. On the global level, the post-colonial meeting between cultures and their demands for recognition tends to result in clashes of body-cultural practices. More than on religious ideas, some forms of Islam focus on body-cultural regulations, from the veil of the female to the beard of the male, from the circumcision of children to the suppression of games, sport, dance and music.[64] Moreover, interest in 'old popular games' have arisen in the Arab world as well as in East Asia and have led to a quest for body-cultural studies. Afro-American successes in certain sports have produced controversial bodily identifications with the 'Black athlete'.[65] Practices such as Indian yoga, African dances and Afro-Brazilian capoeira have contributed to what has been called an 'exotization of Western body cultures'.[66] The renaissance of the particular in body culture gave rise to critical questions about the Western-colonial ethnocentrism of Olympic sport.[67]

The questions arising from these political tensions and post-colonial innovations challenge the established knowledge of sports history. The question is no longer only about 'sport' as it had been established and taken for granted during Western industrial modernity and as it was projected back into its prehistory. The question is about the relation between sport and non-sports – dances, games, festivities, fighting arts, running techniques, outdoor activities, bodily meditation – that is about the broader field of body cultures. The colonial meeting of Mentawaian bow-and-arrow shooting, with its resultant misunderstanding, has not lost its relevance.

Notes

1 Personal communication with Reimar Schefold, 1989.
2 A standard work on this perspective is Allen Guttmann, *Sports: The First Five Millennia* (Amherst: University of Massachusetts Press, 2004).
3 Dietmar Kamper and Christoph Wulf, eds, *Die Wiederkehr des Körpers* (Frankfurt/M.: Suhrkamp, 1982).
4 Norbert Elias, *Über den Prozess der Zivilisation: Soziogenetische und psychogenetische Untersuchungen*, 17th edn (Frankfurt/M.: Suhrkamp, 1992, vols 1–2, 1939), English edn, *The Civilizing Process* (Oxford: Blackwell, 1982).
5 Norbert Elias and Eric Dunning, *Quest for Excitement: Sport and Leisure in the Civilizing Process* (Oxford: Blackwell, 1986).
6 Elias and Dunning, *Studien über die Deutschen: Machtkämpfe und Habitusentwicklung im 19. und 20. Jahrhundert* (Frankfurt/M.: Suhrkamp, 1989), English edn, *The Germans. Power Struggles and the Development of Habitus in the 19th and 20th Centuries* (Cambridge: Polity, 1996).
7 Eric Dunning, Dominic Malcolm and Ivan Waddington, eds, *Sport Histories: Figurational Studies of the Development of Modern Sports* (London: Routledge, 2004).

8 Hans Peter Duerr, *Der Mythos vom Zivilisationsprozess*. Vols 1–5: *Nacktheit und Scham, Intimität, Obszönität und Gewalt, Der erotische Leib, Die Tatsachen des Lebens* (Frankfurt/M.: Suhrkamp, 1988–2005).

9 Max Horkheimer and Theodor W. Adorno, *Dialektik der Aufklärung: Philosophische Fragmente* (Frankfurt/M.: Fischer, 1971, 1947), English edn, *Dialectic of Enlightenment* (London: Verso, 1997).

10 Bero Rigauer, *Sport und Arbeit* (Frankfurt/M.: Suhrkamp, 1969), English edn, *Sport and Work* (New York: Columbia University Press, 1981).

11 Rudolf zur Lippe, *Naturbeherrschung am Menschen* (Frankfurt/M.: Suhrkamp, Vols 1–2, 1974).

12 Anson Rabinbach, *The Human Motor: Energy, Fatigue and the Origins of Modernity* (Los Angeles: University of California Press, 1992); Wolfgang Schivelbusch, *Geschichte der Eisenbahnreise: Zur Industrialisierung von Raum und Zeit im 19. Jahrhundert* (München: Hanser, 1977), English edn, *The Railway Journey: The Industrialization and Perception of Time and Space* (Berkeley: University of California Press, 1986); Klaus Theweleit, *Männerphantasien* (Frankfurt/M.: Roter Stern, 1977), English edn, *Male Fantasies* (Minneapolis: University of Minnesota Press, 1996); Peter Sloterdijk, *Sphären: Plurale Sphärologie*. Vols 1–3 (Frankfurt/M.: Suhrkamp, 1998/2004).

13 Helmuth Plessner, *Lachen und Weinen: Eine Untersuchung der Grenzen menschlichen Verhaltens* (Bern, 1941), new edn in *Gesammelte Schriften* (Frankfurt/M.: Suhrkamp 1982), Vol. 7: 201–387; Maurice Merleau-Ponty, *Phénoménologie de la perception* (Paris: Gallimard, 1945), English edn, *Phenomenology of Perception* (London: Routledge and Kegan Paul, 1962). Gaston Bachelard, *La psychanalyse du feu*, in English as *Psychoanalysis of Fire* (Boston: Beacon, 1964 [1938]).

14 Michel Foucault, *Surveiller et punir: La naissance de la prison* (Paris: Gallimard, 1975), English edn, *Discipline and Punish* (Harmondsworth: Penguin, 1975); Patricia Vertinsky and John Bale, eds, *Sites of Sport: Space, Place and Experience* (London: Routledge, 2004); Georges Vigarello, *Le corps redressé: Historire d'un pouvoir pédagogique* (Paris: Pierre Delarge, 1978); Jean-Jacques Barreau and Jean-Jacques Morne, *Sport, expérience corporelle et science de l'homme: Éléments d'épistémologie et anthropologie des activités physiques et sportives* (Paris: Vigot, 1984); Patricia Vertinsky and Sherry McKay, eds, *Disciplining Bodies in the Gymnasium. Memory, Monument, Modernism* (London: Routledge, 2004).

15 Pierre Bourdieu, 'Champs intellectuel et projet créateur', *Temps modernes*, 22 (1966/67), 865–906.

16 Jacques Defrance, *L'excellence corporelle: La formation des activités physiques et sportives modernes* (Rennes: Presses Universitaires de Rennes, 1987).

17 Bernd Wedemeyer-Kolwe, *'Der neue Mensch'. Körperkultur im Kaiserreich und in der Weimarer Republik* (Würzburg: Königshausen & Neumann, 2004); Marion E.P. Ras, *Body, Femininity and Nationalism: Girls in the German Youth Movement 1900–1934* (New York: Routledge, 2008).

18 Visible in the illustrations of Hans W. Fischer, *Körperschönheit und Körperkultur* (Berlin, 1928).

19 Karl Gaulhofer, *Die Fußhaltung: Ein Beitrag zur Stilgeschichte der menschlichen Bewegung* (Kassel: Rudolph, 1930), reprint (Netherlands: Jan-Luiting-Stiftung, 1969); Marcel Mauss, 'Les techniques du corps' (1934), in English as 'Techniques of the Body', *Economy and Society* 2 (1973), 70–88.

20 Ove Korsgaard, *Kampen om kroppen: Dansk idræts historie gennem 200 år* [Struggling with the body. Danish sport history over 200 years] (Copenhagen: Gyldendal, 1982); Bo Vestergård Madsen, *Oplysning i bevægelse: Kultur, krop og demokrati i den folkelige gymnastik* [Enlightenment in movement. Culture, body and democracy in popular gymnastics] (Århus: Klim, 2003); Esa Sironen, *Urheilun aika ja paikka* [The time and space of sport] (Jyväskylä: LIKES, 1995); Andrew Sparkes and Martti Silvennoinen, eds, *Talking Bodies. Men's Narratives of the Body and Sport* (Jyväskylä: SoPhi, University of Jyväskylä, 1999).

21 Jean-Jacques Barreau and Jean-Jacques Morne, *Sport, expérience corporelle et science de l'homme: Éléments d'épistémologie et anthropologie des activités physiques et sportives* (Paris: Vigot, 1984); Knut Dietrich, ed., *How Societies Create Movement Culture and Sport* (Copenhagen: Institute of Exercise and Sport Sciences, University of Copenhagen, 2001), and *Socialisation and the Social Change in Movement Culture and Sport* (Copenhagen: Institute of Exercise and Sport Sciences, University of Copenhagen, 2002).

22 Dietmar Kamper and Christoph Wulf, eds, *Die Wiederkehr des Körpers* (Frankfurt/M.: Suhrkamp, 1982); Gunter Gebauer, ed.: *Körper-und Einbildungskraft: Inszenierungen des Helden im Sport* (Berlin: Reimer, 1988)

23 John Blacking, ed., *The Anthropology of the Body* (London: Academic, 1977); Susan Brownell, *Training the Body for China: Sports in the Moral Order of the People's Republic* (Chicago: University of Chicago Press, 1995); G. Whitney Azoy, *Buzkashi: Game and Power in Afghanistan* (Long Grove, IL: Waveland, 2nd edn, 2003 [1982]); Clifford Geertz, 'Deep Play: Notes on the Balinese cockfight', *Daedalus* 101 (1972), 1–37.

24 Bernd Jürgen Warneken, ed., *Der aufrechte Gang: Zur Symbolik einer Körperhaltung* (Tübingen: Tübinger Vereinigung für Volkkskunde, 1990).

25 Bryan S. Turner, *The Body and Society* (Oxford: Blackwell, 1984); Chris Shilling, *The Body and Social Theory* (London: Sage, 1993).

26 Andrew Sparkes and Martti Silvennoinen, eds, *Talking Bodies: Men's Narratives of the Body and Sport* (Jyväskylä: SoPhi, University of Jyväskylä, 1999); David B. Morris, *The Culture of Pain* (Berkeley: University of California Press, 1991).

27 Jean-Jacques Barreau and Guy Jaouen, eds, *Éclipse et renaissance des jeux populaires: Des traditions aux régions de l'Europe de demain* (Karaez: FALSAB, 1998 [1991]); Knut Dietrich, ed., *How Societies Create Movement Culture and Sport* (Copenhagen: Institute of Exercise and Sport Sciences, University of Copenhagen, 2001), and *Socialisation and the Social Change in Movement Culture and Sport* (Copenhagen: Institute of Exercise and Sport Sciences, University of Copenhagen, 2002); Klaus Moegling, ed., *Integrative Bewegungslehre*, parts 1–3 (Immenhausen/Kassel: Prolog, 2001/02).

28 George Lakoff and Mark Johnson, *Metaphors We Live By* (Chicago: University of Chicago Press, 1980); Mark Johnson, *The Body in the Mind: The Bodily Basis of Meaning, Imagination and Reason* (Chicago: University of Chicago Press, 1987); Helmuth Plessner, *Lachen und Weinen. Eine Untersuchung der Grenzen menschlichen Verhaltens* (Bern, 1941), new edn in *Gesammelte Schriften* (Frankfurt/M.: Suhrkamp 1982), Vol. 7, 201–387.

29 Marcel Jousse, *L'Anthropologie du geste* (Paris: Gallimard, 1974).

30 August Nitschke and Hans Wieland, *Körper in Bewegung: Gesten, Tänze und Räume im Wandel der Geschichte* (Stuttgart: Kreuz, 1989); Richard van Dülmen, ed., *Erfindung des Menschen: Schöpfungsträume und Körperbilder 1500 – 2000* (Vienna: Böhlau, 1998); Arthur E. Imhof, *Der Mensch und sein Körper. Von der Antike bis heute* (München: Beck, 1983); Georges Vigarello, *Le corps redressé: Histoire d'un pouvoir pédagogique* (Paris: Pierre Delarge, 1978). About tattoo: Stephan Oettermann, *Zeichen auf der Haut: Die Geschichte der Tätowierung in Europa* (Frankfurt/M.: Syndikat, 1979); Wolfgang Schivelbusch, *Geschichte der Eisenbahnreise: Zur Industrialisierung von Raum und Zeit im 19. Jahrhundert* (München: Hanser, 1977), English edn, *The Railway Journey. The Industrialization and Perception of Time and Space* (Berkeley: University of California Press, 1986); Wolfgang Sachs, *Die Liebe zum Automobil: In Rückblick in die Geschichte unserer Wünsche* (Reinbek: Rowohlt, 1984); Peter Borscheid, *Das Tempo-Virus. Eine Kulturgeschichte der Beschleunigung* (Frankfurt: Campus, 2004). About right-wing and left-wing body politics: John M. Hoberman, *Sport and Political Ideology* (Austin: University of Texas Press, 1984); Klaus Theweleit, *Männerphantasien* (Frankfurt/M.: Roter Stern, 1977), English edn, *Male Fantasies* (Minneapolis: University of Minnesota Press, 1996); Bo Vestergård Madsen, *Oplysning i bevægelse. Kultur, krop og demokrati i den folkelige gymnastik* [Enlightenment in Movement: Culture, Body and Democracy in Popular Gymnastics] (Århus: Klim, 2003).

31 Jean-Marie Brohm, ed., *Quel corps? Textes rassemblés* (Paris: Éditions de la passion, 2001).

32 Norbert Elias and Eric Dunning, *Quest for Excitement: Sport and Leisure in the Civilizing Process* (Oxford: Blackwell, 1986).

33 Rudolf zur Lippe, *Naturbeherrschung am Menschen* (Frankfurt/M.: Suhrkamp, Vols 1–2, 1974); Georges Vigarello, *Le corps redressé: Histoire d'un pouvoir pédagogique* (Paris: Pierre Delarge, 1978); Pål Augestad, *Skolering af kroppen: Om kunnskap og makt i kroppsøvningsfaget* [School of the body: About Knowledge and Power in the School Subject Physical Education] (Bø: Høgskolen i Telemark, 2003); Karl Gaulhofer, *Die Fußhaltung: Ein Beitrag zur Stilgeschichte der menschlichen Bewegung* (Kassel: Rudolph, 1930), reprint (Netherlands: Jan-Luiting-Stiftung, 1969); Harald Kleinschmidt, *Tyrocinium militare: Militärische Körperhaltungen und-bewegungen im Wandel zwischen dem 14. und dem 18. Jahrhundert* (Stuttgart: Autorenverlag, 1989).

34 Henning Eichberg, *Leistung, Spannung, Geschwindigkeit: Sport und Tanz im gesellschaftlichen Wandel des 18./19. Jahrhunderts* (Stuttgart: Klett-Cotta, 1978); Allen Guttmann, *From Ritual to Record* (New York: Columbia University Press, 1978); John Marshall Carter and Arnd Krüger, eds, *Ritual and Record: Sports Records and Quantification in Pre-Modern Societies* (New York: Greenwood, 1990).

35 Niels Kayser Nielsen, *Krop og oplysning: Om kropskultur i Danmark 1780–1900* [Body and enlightenment. About body culture in Denmark 1780–1900] (Odense: Odense Universitetsforlag, 1993); Niels Kayser Nielsen, *Body, Sport and Society in Norden – Essays in Cultural History* (Århus: Århus University Press, 2005); Jacques Defrance, *L'excellence corporelle: La formation des activités physiques et sportives modernes* (Rennes: Presses Universitaires de Rennes, 1987); Bo Vestergård Madsen, *Oplysning i bevægelse: Kultur, krop og demokrati i den folkelige gymnastik* [Enlightenment in Movement:

Culture, Body and Democracy in Popular Gymnastics] (Århus: Klim, 2003); John Bale, *Running Cultures. Racing in Time and Space* (London: Routledge, 2004).

36 Bernd Wedemeyer-Kolwe, *'Der neue Mensch': Körperkultur im Kaiserreich und in der Weimarer Republik* (Würzburg: Königshausen & Neumann, 2004); Marion E.P. Ras, *Body, Femininity and Nationalism: Girls in the German Youth Movement 1900–1934* (New York: Routledge, 2008).

37 Klaus Theweleit, *Männerphantasien* (Frankfurt/M.: Roter Stern, 1977), English edn, *Male Fantasies* (Minneapolis: University of Minnesota Press, 1996); John M. Hoberman, *Sport and Political Ideology* (Austin: University of Texas Press, 1984).

38 Henning Eichberg, *Leistung, Spannung, Geschwindigkeit: Sport und Tanz im gesellschaftlichen Wandel des 18./19. Jahrhunderts* (Stuttgart: Klett-Cotta, 1978); Peter Borscheid, *Das Tempo-Virus: Eine Kulturgeschichte der Beschleunigung* (Frankfurt: Campus, 2004); John Bale, *Running Cultures: Racing in Time and Space* (London: Routledge, 2004); Gudrun M. König, *Eine Kulturgeschichte des Spazierganges: Spuren einer bürgerlichen Praktik 1780–1850* (Vienna: Böhlau, 1996); Wolfgang Schivelbusch, *Geschichte der Eisenbahnreise: Zur Industrialisierung von Raum und Zeit im 19. Jahrhundert* (München: Hanser, 1977), English edn, *The Railway Journey: The Industrialization and Perception of Time and Space* (Berkeley: University of California Press, 1986); Wolfgang Sachs, *Die Liebe zum Automobil. In Rückblick in die Geschichte unserer Wünsche* (Reinbek: Rowohlt, 1984); Paul Virilio, *Vitesse et politique* (Paris: Galilée, 1977), English edn, *Speed and Politics: An Essay on Dromology* (New York: Semiotext (e), 1986); Edward T. Hall, *The Dance of Life: The Other Dimension of Time* (Garden City/New York: Anchor/Doubleday, 2nd edn, 1984).

39 Michel Foucault, *Surveiller et punir: La naissance de la prison* (Paris: Gallimard, 1975), English edn, *Discipline and Punish* (Harmondsworth: Penguin, 1975); Patricia Vertinsky and John Bale, eds, *Sites of Sport: Space, Place and Experience* (London: Routledge, 2004); Pål Augestad, *Skolering af kroppen. Om kunnskap og makt i kroppsøvningsfaget* [School of the Body: About Knowledge and Power in the School Subject Physical Education] (Bø: Høgskolen i Telemark, 2003); Edward T. Hall, *The Hidden Dimension* (New York: Anchor, 1966).

40 John Bale, *Running Cultures: Racing in Time and Space* (London: Routledge, 2004).

41 Henning Eichberg, *Leistung, Spannung, Geschwindigkeit: Sport und Tanz im gesellschaftlichen Wandel des 18./19. Jahrhunderts* (Stuttgart: Klett-Cotta, 1978); Allen Guttmann, *From Ritual to Record* (New York: Columbia University Press, 1978).

42 Bero Rigauer, *Sport und Arbeit* (Frankfurt/M.: Suhrkamp, 1969), English edn, *Sport and Work* (New York: Columbia University Press, 1981); Georges Vigarello, *Une histoire culturelle du sport: Techniques d'hier et aujourd'hui* (Paris: R. Lafont & Revue EPS, 1988); Anson Rabinbach, *The Human Motor: Energy, Fatigue and the Origins of Modernity* (Los Angeles: University of California Press, 1992); John M. Hoberman, *Mortal Engines: The Science of Performance and the Dehumanization of Sport* (New York: The Free Press, 1992).

43 Noel Perrin, *Giving Up the Gun: Japan's Reversion to the Sword, 1543–1879* (Boston: Godine, 1979).

44 Henning Eichberg, *The People of Democracy: Understanding Self-Determination on the Basis of Body and Movement* (Århus: Klim, 2004).

45 Jürgen Habermas, *Die Neue Unübersichtlichkeit* (Frankfurt/Main: Suhrkamp, 1985); Henning Eichberg, *Body Cultures: Essays on Sport, Space and Identity* (London: Routledge, 1998); John Bale and Joe Sang, *Kenyan Running: Movement Culture, Geography and Global Change* (London: Frank Cass, 1996); John Bale, *Imagined Olympians: Body Culture and Colonial Representation in Rwanda* (Minneapolis: University of Minnesota Press, 2002); John Bale, *Running Cultures: Racing in Time and Space* (London: Routledge, 2004).

46 Petr Roubal, *Embodying Communism: Politics of Mass Gymnastics in Post-War Eastern Europe* (Budapest: Central European University, 2007), dissertation in history.

47 Mikhail Bakhtin, *Rabelais and his World* (Cambridge: MIT Press, 1968); Peter Burke, *Popular Culture in Early Modern Europe* (London: Temple Smith, 1978); Robert C. Davis, *The War of the Fists: Popular Culture and Public Violence in Late Renaissance Venice* (New York: Oxford University Press, 1994).

48 John M. Hoberman, *Darwin's Athletes: How Sport has Damaged Black America and Preserved the Myth of Race* (Boston: Mariner, 1997); Bo Vestergård Madsen, *Oplysning i bevægelse: Kultur, krop og demokrati i den folkelige gymnastik* [Enlightenment in Movement: Culture, Body and Democracy in Popular Gymnastics] (Århus: Klim, 2003).

49 Pierre Bourdieu, 'Champs intellectuel et projet créateur', *Temps modernes*, 22 (1966/67), 865–906.

50 Henning Eichberg, *The People of Democracy: Understanding Self-Determination on the Basis of Body and Movement* (Århus: Klim, 2004).

51 Peter Sloterdijk, *Sphären: Plurale Sphärologie*. Vol. 1–3 (Frankfurt/M.: Suhrkamp, 1998/2004).
52 Ulrich Beck, in Richard van Dülmen, ed., *Erfindung des Menschen: Schöpfungsträume und Körperbilder 1500 – 2000* (Vienna: Böhlau, 1998); Chris Shilling, *The Body and Social Theory* (London: Sage, 1993) with reference to Anthony Giddens.
53 John Bale and Joe Sang, *Kenyan Running: Movement Culture, Geography and Global Change* (London: Frank Cass, 1996); John Bale, *Running Cultures: Racing in Time and Space* (London: Routledge, 2004); Susan Brownell, *Training the Body for China: Sports in the Moral Order of the People's Republic* (Chicago: University of Chicago Press, 1995); G. Whitney Azoy, *Buzkashi: Game and Power in Afghanistan* (Long Grove, IL: Waveland, 2nd edn, 2003 (1st edn, 1982)); Anne Birgitte Leseth, *Culture of Movement: Walkers, Workers and Fitness Performers in Dar Es Salaam* (Oslo: Norwegian University of Sport and Physical Education, 2004).
54 Allen Guttmann, *From Ritual to Record* (New York: Columbia University Press, 1978), and *Sports: The First Five Millennia* (Amherst: University of Massachusetts Press, 2004); Niels Kayser Nielsen, *Krop og oplysning: Om kropskultur i Danmark 1780–1900* [Body and Enlightenment: About Body Culture in Denmark 1780–1900] (Odense: Odense Universitetsforlag, 1993); Niels Kayser Nielsen, *Body, Sport and Society in Norden – Essays in Cultural History* (Århus: Århus University Press, 2005).
55 Jacques Defrance, *L'excellence corporelle: La formation des activités physiques et sportives modernes* (Rennes: Presses Universitaires de Rennes, 1987); Bo Vestergård Madsen, *Oplysning i bevægelse: Kultur, krop og demokrati i den folkelige gymnastik* [Enlightenment in Movement: Culture, Body and Democracy in Popular Gymnastics] (Århus: Klim, 2003); Pål Augestad, *Skolering af kroppen: Om kunnskap og makt i kroppsøvningsfaget* [School of the Body: About Knowledge and Power in the School Subject Physical Education] (Bø: Høgskolen i Telemark, 2003); Petr Roubal, *Embodying Communism: Politics of Mass Gymnastics in Post-War Eastern Europe* (Budapest: Central European University, 2007), dissertation in history.
56 About the duel: Norbert Elias and Eric Dunning, *Studien über die Deutschen: Machtkämpfe und Habitusentwicklung im 19. und 20. Jahrhundert* (Frankfurt/M.: Suhrkamp, 1989), English edn, *The Germans: Power Struggles and the Development of Habitus in the 19th and 20th Centuries* (Cambridge: Polity, 1996). About festivals of popular boxing: Robert C. Davis, *The War of the Fists: Popular Culture and Public Violence in Late Renaissance Venice* (New York: Oxford University Press, 1994). About Afghan equestrian games: G. Whitney Azoy, *Buzkashi. Game and Power in Afghanistan* (Long Grove, IL: Waveland, 2nd edn, 2003 (1st edn, 1982)).
57 John Bale, *Running Cultures: Racing in Time and Space* (London: Routledge, 2004).
58 Bernd Wedemeyer-Kolwe, *'Der neue Mensch': Körperkultur im Kaiserreich und in der Weimarer Republik* (Würzburg: Königshausen & Neumann, 2004).
59 Roger Caillois, *Les jeux et les hommes: Le masque et le vertige* (Paris: Gallimard, 1958); Jean-Jacques Barreau and Guy Jaouen, eds, *Éclipse et renaissance des jeux populaires: Des traditions aux régions de l'Europe de demain* (Karaez: FALSAB, 1998 (first edn, 1991)).
60 Rudolf zur Lippe, *Naturbeherrschung am Menschen* (Frankfurt/M.: Suhrkamp, Vols 1–2, 1974); Nancy Midol, *Démiurgie dans le sport et la danse: Consciences traditionnelle, moderne et postmoderne* (Paris: L'Harmattan, 1995); Noel Dyck and Eduardo P. Archetti, eds, *Sport, Dance and Embodied Identities* (Oxford: Berg, 2003).
61 Mikhail Bakhtin, *Rabelais and his World* (Cambridge: MIT Press, 1968); David B. Morris, *The Culture of Pain* (Berkeley: University of California Press, 1991).
62 Peter Burke, *Popular Culture in Early Modern Europe* (London: Temple Smith, 1978); Klaus Theweleit, *Männerphantasien* (Frankfurt/M.: Roter Stern, 1977), English edn, *Male Fantasies* (Minneapolis: University of Minnesota Press, 1996).
63 Henning Eichberg, *Leistung, Spannung, Geschwindigkeit: Sport und Tanz im gesellschaftlichen Wandel des 18./19. Jahrhunderts* (Stuttgart: Klett-Cotta, 1978); Knut Dietrich, ed., *How Societies Create Movement Culture and Sport* (Copenhagen: Institute of Exercise and Sport Sciences, University of Copenhagen, 2001), 10–32.
64 Fuad I. Khuri, *The Body in Islamic Culture* (London: Saqi, 2001).
65 John M. Hoberman, *Darwin's Athletes: How Sport has Damaged Black America and Preserved the Myth of Race* (Boston: Mariner, 1997).
66 August Nitschke and Hans Wieland, eds, *Die Faszination und Wirkung aussereuropäischer Tanz-und Sportformen* (Ahrensburg: Czwalina, 1981).
67 Susan Brownell, ed., *The 1904 Anthropology Days and Olympic Games: Sport, Race and American Imperialism* (University of Nebraska Press, 2008).

11   Science and technology

Verner Møller

The link between sport, technology and science is a close one, and in recent years increasing interest has been taken in the significance of that connection, particularly in the Anglo-Saxon world. A wide-ranging introduction to the issue can be found in Andy Miah and Simon B. Eassom (eds), *Sport Technology: History, Philosophy and Policy* (2002). *Materials in Sports Equipment* vols 1 and 2 (2003, 2007), edited by Mike Jenkins and Aleksandar Subic respectively, provides an important scientifically orientated grounding in the technology and design of sports equipment in a wide variety of sports disciplines. The technological development of sports clothing, which is a rapid growth area, is treated in Roshan Shishoo's *Textiles in Sport* (2005). The sporting arena has also become an area for technological innovation, and significant critical analysis of the influence of technology on sports space is undertaken by John Bale, for example in books such as *Sport, Space and the City* (1993), *Landscapes of Modern Sport* (1994) and *Sport Geography* (2003).

Scientific and technological developments have also had an influence on the very body of sport. Consequences of this have been exposed and criticized by John Hoberman in *Mortal Engines: The Science of Performance and the Dehumanization of Sport* (1992) and *Testosterone Dreams: Rejuvenation, Aphrodisia, Doping* (2005). Prior to the publication of these two comprehensive studies, Hoberman formulated his thought-provoking hypothesis about the wider significance of the link between technology and sport. According to Hoberman, modern sport is 'a global monoculture whose values derive in large measure from the sphere of technology',[1] and technologization is accepted and promoted on the basis of a specific agenda: 'the comprehensive technologizing of high-performance sport contains, and in some ways conceals, an agenda for human development for which high-performance athletes serve as ideal models'.[2] Hoberman's view is that this 'anthropological agenda is a sinister one that transcends, even as it includes, the cultivation of certain body-types for sportive purposes'.[3] As an extension of this he conceives the hypothesis that '[h]igh-performance sport has become an exercise in human engineering that aims at producing not simply an athletic type, but a human type as well'.[4] With the benefit of hindsight we have to concede that the idea of sport's role as causing a wildly applauded breakthrough to a general optimization of the human organism has not become a reality. It is true that the pharmaceutical industry has invested heavily in recent years on the development of lifestyle medicines, but that has happened in spite of not because of developments in the area of sport, where the fight against performance-enhancing medication has, in fact, intensified. This example shows that, although there are common features, developments in sport and in surrounding society are not identical. Although the history of sport has focused to a large extent on parallels between the two and has taken sport on board as a phenomenon that mirrors society, it is particularly in its points of difference from society that sport is interesting as a basis for understanding social development, and vice versa. In line with European sports criticism that established itself in the 1970s with works such as Jean-Marie Brohm's *Sport – A Prison of Measured Time* (1975) and Bero Rigauer's *Sport and Work* (1980, orig. 1969), Hoberman allowed his work to be influenced by the apparent coincidence in tendencies between the development of sport and of society. Today, however, we can see that those tendencies were not unambiguous. Irrefutable inconsistencies have come to light that force us to reconsider the relationship between sport, science and technology.

As has been said, interest in the area has been most marked in the Anglo-Saxon world. In Scandinavia, for example, it has been significantly less evident. The subject was taken up by the Danish state-financed Teknologinævnet (The Danish Board of Technology) with the launch of the anthology *Sport og teknologi* (Sport and Technology) (1994). The anthology took the form of an introduction to the research area and gave a brief description of developments in five branches of sport – athletics, sailing, cycle sport, tennis and windsurfing. In addition a couple of chapters dealt with the doping issue. The declared aim of the Board of Technology was to raise questions about the degree to which technological development in sport leads to a qualitative change in elite sport, and about ways in which technological innovations would influence sport as a whole. The initiative presented, therefore, a challenge to research into the links between sport and technology – but one that was never accompanied by significant investment in research. In Scandinavia the link has primarily been discussed in relation to the doping issue, which is reflected in Claudio Tamburrini and Torbjörn Tännsjö's anthologies, *Values in Sport: Elitism, Nationalism, Gender Equality and the Scientific Manufacture of Winners* (2000) and *Genetic Technology and Sport: Ethical Questions* (2005). The same tendency is to be seen in Germany. Here, too, recent years have seen the publication of a long list of works whose emphasis is on medical and technological opportunities for optimizing the body's capacity. This tendency is highlighted, for example, by the fact that Volker Caysa, the German whose account of the history of body culture entitled *Körperutopien – Eine Philosophische Anthropologie des Sport* (Body Utopias: A Philosophical Anthropology of Sport) (2003) is otherwise distinguished for the breadth of its treatment, also devotes special attention to the technologization and industrialization of the body through doping. The only general introduction to the subject that I am familiar with in German is Klaus Heinemann's *Die Technologisierung des Sports* (2001), which came into being as a commission in much the same way as the aforementioned Danish book, *Sport og teknologi*. If we look towards France, we find a similar picture. While whole shelves of books could be filled with literature written about science and technology in relation to doping – the most interesting of which in this context is Patrick Lauré's *Historie du dopage et des conduites dopantes: les alchimistes de la performance* (A History of Doping and Those Who Dope: The Performance Alchemists) (2004) – to my knowledge only one work exists that covers the area in general, namely Georges Vigarello's richly illustrated *Une histoire culturelle du sport – Techniques d'hier ... et d'aujourd'hui* (A Cultural History of Sport: Techniques of Yesterday ... and Today) (1988).

The works mentioned above are central in the context of their own domain, and they provide a basis for the reflections of the present chapter. The breadth and diversity of the subject, however, make it impossible for a chapter on its history to paint the complete picture. Instead, this presentation will take a particular perspective. The chapter deals only with a small number of sporting disciplines. It is introduced by a short section providing a context and pointing up the relation between sport and war. There follow examples from history of the effects of science and technology with an emphasis on improvements in materials and in the body, and the chapter concludes with a brief sketch of a scenario for the future.

War and sport

When the ancient roots of modern sport are presented, stress is generally placed on the religious and ritual functions of sport.[5] The same goes for its significance as an element in the harmonious development and upbringing of youth. A number of sources support the importance of this aspect. Aristotle, for example, emphasizes physical training as one of the areas essential to the schooling of youth on a par with music and reading and writing. His justification for physical training belonging to normal schooling is that '[p]hysical education is important because it contributes to manliness'.[6] Shortly after this, he formulates it in another way: 'physical education helps with health and strength'.[7] The accentuation of qualities of manliness, health and strength suggest that physical activity is important not least because it contributes to the development of a population that is capable of defending itself. The close affinity between the art of war and sport is also reflected in the register of activities from ancient times, such as *hoplites* (a race in armour), *pentathlon* (consisting of jumping, running, discus throwing, javelin throwing and wrestling) and the Roman chariot races. In the Greek city state of Athens, the ideal was to create harmonious people, and for that purpose physical training was a natural part of their schooling. In Sparta on the other hand schooling was predominantly a matter of arming the body. The primary aim of upbringing was to secure a powerful army.

Although there are differences between the emphases placed on physical training in different societies, the link between military training, war and sport can be traced down through history. 'Physical training is, in a general sense, as old as human society', claims the historian R.F. Willets. He believes that the connection is universal and links it to an apparent human propensity to warfare:

> Primitive warfare among tribes has often demanded systems of training the body to extremes of physical endurance. In the same way, tribal dances are not so much ends in themselves as social activities designed to adapt the group to the labour of the harvest or the movements of actual warfare.[8]

After the fall of the ancient city states, we pick up the connection once again in the tournaments of the Middle Ages. We find it, too, in the educational theory of the Renaissance. It is true that there was a change of emphasis from 'strengthening to straightening',[9] but riding, fencing and dance were retained as means to achieve an end.

Although it can only be a minute fraction of practitioners and spectators involved in sport nowadays who spare a thought for its historic links to the art of war, history is clearly in evidence in a series of sporting disciplines. Fencing, wrestling, cross-country running, athletics, shooting and biathlon quite clearly promote military qualities. Pierre de Coubertin's construction, the 'modern pentathlon', which is a combination of the disciplines of shooting, fencing, swimming, riding and cross-country running, looks as though it were modelled with a view to creating a complete all-round soldier. All in all there is much to suggest that David G. McComb is right in his claim that, 'of all the secondary influences on the shape and style of traditional sports ... probably warfare is the most important'.[10] Bearing this in mind, it should hardly surprise us that there is a connection between sport, science and technology, since military ambition has been a significant driving force behind scientific and technological progress. In the Danish historian Troels Lund we find an early example. In the middle ages physical exercise was pursued in great earnest, not least with a view to perfecting the use of weapons. 'At a time in which everyone carried either a sword or a spear, it was self-evident that people made a point of using them'.[11] In accordance with this, the new weapon carried about the person, the 'pistol', was included as an object for competitive sport. A foreigner, visiting Denmark in the year 1634, gives the following account of his visit to the riding arena near Copenhagen's castle:

> When we entered, a number of riders were in the process of 'running at heads'. This is a very fine and eye-catching exercise. Three heads of card or straw are brought in, the first with a complete human figure on a pole at one end of the arena, the second at the start of the arena, and the third lies on the ground. At full gallop and without making the slightest interruption, the rider now has to unleash his attack upon them. Against the first, the one on the pole, he rides with a lance. Once he has reached the end of the arena, he turns the horse about, whips a pistol out of a holster and in full gallop shoots at the head standing at the other end of the arena. The third time he finally turns about and thrusts with drawn sword at the head lying on the ground.[12]

Lund uses the example to show how the lance and the sword lost the significance they had previously had, since the invention of the pistol made it possible to dispose of imaginary opponents even as far away as the other end of the arena. On the battlefield it is clear that the lance and sword became meaningless in the face of the development of more powerful weapons. From the point of view of sport, however, it is irrelevant that one instrument is more effective than the other, as long as the competition takes place using the same means. However, the pistol represented new weapon technology that became integrated into the competition – not least in order to develop skills in using this weapon too.

It is, however, only when sport begins to take on a significance of its own, that is with the advent of modernity, that technology and science start to acquire *decisive* influence on competitions. Where previously competition had been about being best at using available military means, whether that was horse, bow, spear, lance, pistol or simply the human physique, in modernity a process gets underway in which the optimizing of means increasingly becomes incorporated as a parameter for competition. This was, furthermore, a process that coincided with the growing recognition during the second half of the 19th century that, 'political and military power now came to be increasingly based on industrial potential, technological capacity and know-how [and that] no state could maintain its place in the club of "great powers" without it'.[13] That recognition led to an acceleration in scientific and technological development, which left its mark across a broad front – including in sport.

Equipment

There are, without doubt, considerable differences in the degree to which individual sports have been influenced by technology.[14] There is, however, scarcely a single sporting discipline that has not been facilitated, altered or improved with its assistance. Both safety and comfort have been improved. It is, for example, now possible to get sports kit with built-in protection for sports such as rugby and ice-hockey. In areas that are particularly subject to damage, flexible, gel-filled protection is sewn in, which does not impede mobility but is designed to become as hard as a shield the moment it receives a violent impact. In collaboration with NASA a company called Outlast has developed clothing that is temperature-regulated, with built-in micro-capsules that absorb the body's excess heat and release it again if the user begins to get cold.[15]

Even a primitive sport such as running has been made more comfortable and kinder on the physique. Companies such as Nike, Asics and adidas have developed a range of shock-absorbent systems that reduce wear and tear on joints and backs. It was an eye-opener, therefore, in the 1980s to see that phenomenal runner, Zola Budd, competing at the highest levels in bare feet, and, despite the fact that in 1985 she even managed to set a new world record for the 5,000 metres, no top class runners have since followed her example. On the other hand companies have invested huge sums in research with a view to developing materials that have improved the comfort of running shoes and made them so light that in practice they weigh virtually nothing.[16] Developments such as these have not, however, brought about any essential change to sport.

It is a different story with other branches of sport. Some of them, cycle sport for example, have even emerged as a consequence of enthusiasm for new inventions. Cycling is genuinely modern, a fact highlighted by its also being historically one of the sports that has most avidly sought development and progress. It is true that the originator of the Tour de France, Henri Desgranges, prohibited the use of the derailleur gear, and that it was only permitted once he had retired as manager of the race in 1936. He believed on the one hand that it made the race easier for the riders and on the other that it was a break with the fundamental idea of the race itself, namely that every man should conduct the race from start to finish on the same bicycle. If you could 'sit there and change gear, you could just as well change bicycle'.[17] Desgranges' opposition to technical improvements of the bicycle, however, ended up being irrelevant in the long run. Although there have at all times been specific requirements that bicycles have had to meet, the racing bike was continually improved in a whole host of ways as manufacturers hit upon improvements to it. In addition cycle sport has derived advantages from a series of external technologies. Riders, for example, ride with pulse watches so they can monitor their physical condition, and they are in constant radio contact with their sports director, which allows them to discuss how the race is developing and to receive tactical tips out on the route.

Branches of sport with longer roots back in time seem typically to be more con-servative, but even here the transformative power of modernity has in many cases made itself felt. Tennis, which has its roots in the medieval games 'La Soule' and 'Jeu de Pomme', can serve as an example. Without the invention of the lawn mower at the beginning of the 19th century and Charles Goodyear's slightly later discovery that by heating up natural rubber with sulphur you could produce a more serviceable rubber material, tennis would not have developed into the game we know today. Its predecessors were played indoors in monasteries and galleries by monks and nobles. The balls they used were solid. They might, for example, be made of wood or of leather filled with hair or sawdust. Such balls could only bounce on hard surfaces. Using Goodyear's vulcanized rubber, it became possible to make balls that inflicted minimum damage and were elastic, enabling them to be used outdoors on soft surfaces – even protecting the close-cut grass from being damaged.

The development of materials has affected the sport in other ways. The tennis racquet made of a wooden frame and gut strings – which was already in use before lawn tennis was developed in the 1870s – kept going with astonishingly few alterations until the 1960s, when interest in artificial materials accelerated. In the 1930s there had been a brief flirtation with steel frames and steel strings, but since their durability was too poor and their weight too great, makers quickly chose to return to using laminates of various wood types.[18] The introduction in the 1970s of carbon fibre materials that were light, flexible and strong – and that started by being used in the military, aviation and space industries – finally spelled the end for the wooden racquet.

Tennis racquets made from carbon fibre have made tennis generally easier to play. At the elite level, however, it has meant that the game has become faster and the significance of the serve greater, which is a debatable advance. At all events, even though tennis cannot be said to derive directly from modernity, the game has been revolutionized by it.

Another sport in which the advantage of the use of carbon fibre has been open to question is golf. Since the first registered golf matches were played in Scotland in the 15th century clubs have been made from a variety of woods. In this sport, too, people have experimented with shapes and materials with a view to acquiring more feeling for the ball and greater distance in their shots, and this has made the game easier at all levels. With the development of clubs manufactured from carbon fibre and hollow titanium alloy heads, it has become possible for golfers to hit the ball much further than the architects who designed old courses steeped in tradition could have predicted. Bunkers and lakes – originally found naturally sited in the landscape – no longer present the challenges they were designed for. New golf courses, therefore, occupy larger areas.[19]

Since sport is basically about combating and overcoming opposition, it is natural that there should be an interest in improving the materials used. To enter the contest with a better 'weapon' than your opponent gives you a greater chance of winning. In certain sports such as sailing and Formula 1 racing the preparatory optimization of equipment is almost an integral part of the sport. Since in the various branches of sport there are rules governing the equipment that can be used, the chances for manufacturing a competitive advantage in that way is extremely limited in most sports. The same goes for the chances of cheating with the equipment.

A classic example was when the Russian pentathlete, Boris Onishchenko, appeared at the Olympic games in Montreal in 1976 in the team pentathlon fencing event with a weapon (épée) that had been 'improved' with the addition of a technical device that allowed him to activate the signal for a hit himself. Unfortunately for them the Russians had no defence against their opponents' sense of whether there had been a hit, which led to Onishchenko's fall. When the previous medallist in Mexico in 1968 and Munich in 1972 activated the hit signal against Jim Fox, the Briton was sure that Onishchenko had not delivered a hit and demanded that his épée be examined, which resulted in the ignominious discovery.

Although the exposure of the Russian pentathlete might give grounds for speculation about the extent to which the same device had paved the way for his medals in previous Olympic games (in 1968 he won the silver medal in the individual event, and he did the same in 1972, when he was also a member of the Soviet team that won the gold), it shows at the same time how difficult it is to acquire – through cheating – an advantage through improvements in equipment. The chances for improving the chances of victory by means of legal or illegal optimization of the body's capacity are substantially greater and for that reason all the more tempting. It is also in this area that the problem of cheating in sport has been at its most insistent.

The body

For as long as people have competed, they have tried to strengthen their bodies through the intake of fortifying substances. There is nothing new under the sun, 'even in the olden days it was well-known that certain substances gave fighters special strength',[20] wrote one of the pioneers of sports physiology, the internationally recognized Danish sports doctor, Ove Bøje, in his book *Idrætsteori* (Sport Theory) (1945). In that book he gives an account of his insights into sports physiology and in one chapter takes up the theme of the use of performance-enhancing stimulants. What emerges clearly from it is that things *have* changed. *Scientific* interest in the area has started to grow:

> It is not always easy to determine whether a medical preparation can boost a sporting performance, as many drugs that have been used for that purpose have in all likelihood worked through suggestion; in addition very careful examination is required to find out the extent to which some substance or other has any real effect as a means of doping. Despite many studies into this subject, our knowledge remains insufficient.[21]

Bøje's interest in the potential performance-enhancing effect of drugs reflects a basic scientific approach. He wishes to know how the human organism functions in order to optimize and protect it. His concern is primarily for the athlete's health, but he is not opposed to the use of performance-enhancing substances in sport as long as they are not detrimental to health. The problem with the insufficiency of knowledge is that, when an apparently harmless substance is used to enhance performance, it is not possible to say whether or not it is detrimental to health:

> … for it is not sufficient to show that the substance is poisonous in itself, since the simple fact that through an otherwise non-poisonous substance an organism is enabled to perform more than it can cope with, for example by causing a reduction in the natural safety valve of fatigue, can present a danger for health.[22]

Today it sounds quaint when Bøje mentions extra oxygen and irradiation with mercury vapour lamps – the precursors of modern solariums – among the things they were experimenting with in his day with a view to enhancing performance. Other more effective methods were, however, also experimented with:

> Now and again sensational reports appear in the press that certain foreign football team's phenomenal performance are attributable to players being 'gland treated', and we see pictures of a doctor in white coat in the process of giving an injection.[23]

Bøje has himself evidently no experience of that kind of treatment. He will not rule out the theoretical possibility of boosting an athlete's strength using hormone treatment, but he does not conceal the fact that he regards the media's coverage as touting myths. He therefore writes ironically: 'We are not told which hormones football players use to score their goals, though, when all is said, this is also irrelevant, since it is probably a matter of the effect of suggestion'.[24] Experience has since shown that Bøje was wrong. Treatment with hormones is an extremely effective means to enhance performance, which was something that researchers had already become aware of in the inter-war years. Human trials showed that synthetic testosterone not only gave individuals in the trial more energy but also increased their muscle mass:

> Much of the research involving testosterone and human subjects was done in Germany, before World War II. Heinz Arandt recorded 17 case studies of testosterone use, all of which showed positive results. There is also evidence that the Germans continued their experimentation during the war, and even administered testosterone to some storm troopers to increase their aggressiveness.[25]

This research would soon find a use on another field of combat, for with the Cold War scientific interest in the rearmament of the body accelerated further. The Soviet Union gave up its opposition to the Olympic idea and chose to take part in the games in Helsinki in 1952. Sport thereby became the arena for a struggle for prestige between the communist and capitalist countries. Due to its agonal nature, sport was well placed for use as propaganda material. The development of media transmitted across the ether – yet another example of the transformative power of technology – made it possible to communicate victory and defeat in these symbolic battles on the spot to radio listeners and television viewers all over the world. The Soviet athletes came visibly well prepared. In weight-lifting they won seven medals: three gold, three silver and one bronze. The basis for their success, according to the trainer for the American team, Bob Hoffman, was that the Soviet weight-lifters took hormones.[26]

With the collapse of communism and the reunification of Germany, documentary evidence emerged for the fact that there had been a political strategy in Eastern Europe to mobilize thousands of people with a view to making them productive in a sporting – and thereby a political – arena. A factor that contributed powerfully to East Germany becoming the nation that won by far the most medals in relation to population size was the unscrupulous single-mindedness shown by the state. Sports doctors who were unwilling to take part in the realization of the sports programme were excluded from the sporting organizations and councils they sat on. When doctors from the university in Leipzig publicly protested against this special state-sponsored medication of sport, the head of the Research Institute for Fitness and Sport in Leipzig, Hans Schuster, proclaimed that trainers and sports people should not take such protests seriously but on the contrary overcome every obstacle to a proper assessment of the political importance of elite sport.[27]

In the 1960s East Germany further escalated its sports programme. This included research into a range of sports with a view to developing advanced equipment, methods and techniques for training as well as methods for assessing how efficient various training initiatives were, such as the now commonly applied muscle biopsy. Among the most surprising things to have been developed was an underground chamber. In this room it was possible to simulate altitude training through training in air with low levels of oxygen and thereby produce a competitive advantage without the use of doping. The chamber was a legal supplement to their comprehensive doping programme, which for its part provoked no great surprise when it was exposed, since the doping regime produced winners with side-effects. The virilized female swimmers and shot-putters who represented the nation at the Olympics in Munich in 1972, had their bodies and their health ruined in the cause of the propaganda war. Medication was part and parcel of the programme for talent development. It was put into effect with no concern for potential damaging side-effects and without the athletes or their parents being informed about it.[28]

Seen in this light it is scarcely an exaggeration to claim that the Cold War is history's most shining example of the direct exploitation of athletes as though they were soldiers.

Although doping in the West cannot be said to have been administered and systematized as has been documented in East Germany, these synthetic sporting performances did not go unanswered. It was not necessary to force athletes into a regime of doping. Sporting ambition could on its own count provide sufficient motivation, as is witnessed by the attitude of Harold Connally, the gold medallist in throwing the hammer at the Olympics in 1954: 'I think that any athlete should take any steps necessary, short of killing himself, to maximize his performance'.[29] Athletes with that attitude will be inclined to follow trainers and sports doctors they trust, and will do so even though the advice of the experts runs counter to the rules of the sport and has health risks associated with it. There was, therefore, sympathy among American athletes when John Ziegler came out with his answer to the Soviet testosterone: Dianabol. During the world championships in weight-lifting in 1954, Ziegler had been present as team doctor. He observed the Russian team carefully and reached the same conclusion as Hoffman. The Soviet weight-lifters were using testosterone. By talking to his Soviet colleagues, he had his suspicions confirmed. When he returned home, therefore, he started to experiment with testosterone. He himself, Hoffmann and a series of weight-lifters were involved in the trials. Ziegler's aim was to develop a synthetic testosterone that had the positive effects but was free of the side-effects that took the form of increased libido and growth of the prostate. This he succeeded in doing in collaboration with the pharmaceutical company Ciba. In 1958 the drug Dianabol was launched for use in geriatric and post-operative treatments and to assist the healing of burns. However, Ziegler also had another purpose for the drug, which has given him the dubious honour of leaving behind him a reputation for being the doctor who caused the acceleration of hormone doping.[30]

It would, however, be wrong to condemn him using present day standards, since at the time there existed no ban on doping. It is true that his initiative set a process in motion that in time would make doping rules and controls necessary. Since his intention was only to secure parity for his countrymen in competition against Soviet athletes – and, what was more, ensuring that they did not suffer side-effects – he can scarcely be pilloried. In the 1950s enthusiasm for medical progress was less restrained than it is today. People had yet to experience the Thalidomide catastrophe that revealed how monstrous side-effects can be attached to apparently harmless medication, and in sport there were to date no known examples of doping-related deaths. It was impossible at that time to foresee the massive condemnation to which the use of performance-enhancing medication would later be subjected. The fact that this has happened appears fortuitous. At any event other forms of scientific and technological progress can be found that have been received and accepted in sport without being questioned, in spite of the fact that they enhance performance and that they also affect the body. Improvements in eyesight are one example.

Between equipment and bodily performance enhancement

Since their invention at the beginning of the 13th century, spectacles have been an incalculable aid for countless numbers of people. It is, therefore, not surprising that they are constantly being developed further, so that today we have glasses that are so light and comfortable that they can 'get lost' on your nose. They have also been useful in sport.

The development of plastic lenses has eliminated the risk of splintering glass and damaged sight. Frames of flexible material that can be fastened round the ears are reasonably effective in keeping the glasses in position through the abrupt movements of a sporting contest. Nevertheless glasses are a disadvantage. In the event of a hard tackle, they can fall off, they get wet in the rain and during hard physical exertion they mist up. That is why in the past near-sighted sportspeople often chose to compete without glasses and accept near-sightedness as a handicap. They played sport with the weaknesses and strengths that nature had equipped them with. In 1959 the Czech chemist, Otto Wichterle, launched his invention, the soft contact lens, which paved the way for the commercial break-through in contact lenses in the 1970s. At the beginning these lenses could not correct astigmatism, and some users found they had problems with dry or irritated eyes. As the lenses have been improved, however, it has become more and more unusual to see sportspeople with glasses, even in sports where they present fewest problems.

Contact lenses have contributed to balancing out the differences between athletes with normal vision and those with a visual handicap such as near-sightedness. No one has ever suggested that they should be banned from sport in spite of the fact that they are an artificial aid that deprives athletes with normal vision of the advantage with which nature has favoured them. Not even high-powered contact lenses that provide supernormal vision are banned. Nor have sports organizations made an issue out of optimization of vision through the use of laser surgery. In spite of the fact that such an alternative to glasses and contact lenses represents an irreversible intervention in the anatomy of the eye (layers of the cornea are peeled off making it thinner and more vulnerable), it has never been regarded as cheating others who cannot afford the technique or who do not dare to use it because its long-term side-effects are, for good reason, unknown. Sharp vision – whatever the technology used to achieve it – is regarded apparently as of undisputable value.

For reasons that are unclear, surgical intervention into the body is generally far less controversial than medical intervention. No one queries whether it is reasonable for sportspeople who have destroyed a cruciate knee ligament to be operated on to have a new synthetic replacement, after which they can resume their career more or less 'fit for fight'. Performance enhancement and health risks are topics that carry no meaning in this context.

The degree to which surgery will remain uncontroversial as technology develops further is something only time will tell. A challenging example is offered by the South African runner Oscar Pistorius, who was born with defects of the lower leg that led to him having his legs amputated just above the knees when he was 11 months old. With the help of specially manufactured carbon fibre prostheses, he has reached the point where he can compete at the elite level against normal contestants. The impetus behind this constant improvement in prosthetics is provided not least by the wish to give military invalids as normal an existence as possible. It is, however, impossible to determine precisely when a prosthesis becomes so good that it corresponds to normal function. This is precisely what has for the present put an end to Pistorius' hopes of competing against non-handicapped athletes within the framework of the International Association of Athletics Federations (IAAF). When the question was raised, IAAF commissioned an independent biomechanical analysis with a view to examining whether the prostheses gave Pistorius an advantage. The analysis was conducted by Professor Peter Bruggemann, who found that the prostheses reduce energy use by 25 percent and that 'returned energy, from the prosthetic blade is close to three times higher than with the human ankle joint in maximum sprinting'. On the basis of his calculations Bruggemann concluded that 'the mechanical advantage of the blade in relation to the healthy ankle joint of an able-bodied athlete is higher than 30%'.[31] Prosthetic technology has, therefore, developed to the point that from a sporting point of view it can now be regarded as an advantage to be handicapped.

The future

It is tempting to dismiss the Pistorius example as a curiosity, but it is probably more realistic to see it as a premonition of a new catalogue of challenges to sport. The present account would hope to have shown that sport is not static but a phenomenon that is influenced and formed by scientific and technological development. Its defining character-istic, the will to win, impels it forward to ever greater performances. Built into it is a logic of growth, one of whose effects is to whet the appetite of the best practitioners for things that can deliver progress as far as results are concerned. This goes a long way towards explaining why product development in sports equipment is a lucrative business. There are, however, also things created for entirely different purposes that have been incorporated in the hunt for improved performance. Ball players use video recordings to analyse systems of play used by themselves and others; cyclists use wind tunnels to develop the most aerodynamic cycling style; athletes benefit from computer technology to make biomechanical analyses that can help them to optimize their patterns of movement. In 1999 Tiger Woods had his eyesight improved with the aid of laser surgery to make it 20/15 compared to the norm of 20/20. This means that at a distance of 20 metres he can now see what a normally sighted person can see at 15 metres, which, in contrast to Pistorius' prostheses, has not been questioned as giving him an unfair advantage. Examples are legion. Taking the logic of sport into consideration, it is not surprising that medical advances with potential performance-enhancing effects have had an appeal.

Amphetamine was originally introduced as an inhalant marketed as a means of opening blocked air passages. Its invigorating effect was soon discovered, and use of the substance grew rapidly, which in the 1930s caused many countries to make it available on pre-scription only. With World War II the military found a use for this potent substance. German treadmill tests showed that injections with methamphetamine considerably increased the subject's endurance. Other tests showed that soldiers on amphetamine could not only march greater distances but were also willing to continue despite painful blisters.[32] It goes without saying that a 'weapon' such as this was taken into use in the war. Since endurance and fighting spirit are also important factors in many branches of sport, neither is it surprising that here, too, it became widespread, particularly because the use of amphetamine was not banned.

While the drug continued to be valued and increasingly used in a military context – during the period 1966–69 the US military consumed 225 million amphetamine tablets which is more than the combined American and British use during World War II[33] – in about 1960 it increasingly began to be seen as a problem in sport. It was one thing for professional athletes to use the drug. It was quite another when 'proper' sportsmen, in other words amateurs, began to take it in direct contravention of the ethos of amateur sport. A burgeoning public interest in sport, fertilized by radio and TV transmissions along with dramatic episodes in which athletes collapsed through over-exertion, brought the drug into further disrepute. When in 1960 the Danish amateur cyclist, Knud Enemark Jensen, died during a 100 km team event at the Olympic Games in Rome, an unsubstantiated rumour circulated that he had taken amphetamines.[34] This set a process in motion that resulted in the introduction of doping controls, initially in 1965 for cycle sport and later, at the Olympics Games in Mexico in 1968, for sport as a whole.

In the 1950s concerns about athletes' use of medication had not yet found expression in an anti-doping policy. However, the British sports doctor, Adolpho Abrahams, had ascertained that a widespread belief was prevalent among amateur athletes that there existed medication that could increase endurance levels, and his impression was that they would not hesitate to take it if it was offered to them. This worried him for professional reasons, since suppressing the body's natural signals of fatigue could have fatal consequences. His concerns were, however, devoid of moral undertones, and he did not go out of his way to consider whether there were reasons to ban a substance that had performance-enhancing effects but no side-effects:

> ... 'for the sake of argument', a scenario featuring a drug 'capable of conferring enhanced athletic efficiency' that posed no medical hazard whatsoever and that was 'universally available', thereby eliminating the problem of limited access for a favoured few. 'What objection could be raised against its use?' he asks. 'Only that – to use the question-begging term – it would be unsporting to enable athletes to surpass records achieved by the giants of the past, who lacked that advantage. I do not think the conscience of the sporting world would or need be disturbed'.[35]

With this thought experiment in 1953, Abrahams floated the possibility of the future legalization of performance-enhancing medicine. Until now the viewpoint has not had much currency, partly because it could be countered by arguments pointing out the damage to health incurred by such drugs. Experiences with unregulated EPO doping in the 1990s, which tempted riders in professional cycling sport to push their hematocrit values to near-lethal levels, seem to show that, if the fight against doping were abandoned, endurance sports would go down the road leading to something resembling Russian roulette. Nevertheless, Abrahams' question becomes ever more insistent.

Scientific development does not cease. We have long since got used to the idea of women taking the pill. That women can use the pill to manipulate their menstrual cycle and so acquire an advantage over those women who – for ecological or religious reasons – refrain from using it is not an issue about which anti-doping authorities get upset. It would be deeply controversial to ban female athletes from taking contraceptive hormones. The pill has contributed to the sexual liberation of women and promoted their autonomy and self-determination. The reverse of the coin is that, due to the evident advantages of the pill, responsibility for contraception has been laid to a greater extent at the woman's door. A contraceptive pill for men would represent progress for sexual equality. For that reason it would also be possible to regard it as deeply controversial to ban male athletes from using contraceptive pills based on testosterone and progesterone, when they come on the market. Considering the medical puritanism that currently dominates sporting officialdom, it is probable that a contraceptive pill for men containing testosterone would immediately be banned. However, a discussion about gender discrimination would undoubtedly follow. Of course it can be argued that men have an alternative in the form of the condom, but so have women in the femidom, even though this has never become a hit. The pill is just one example of how research into medical technologies has ceased to focus exclusively on the treatment of disease. In all likelihood, therefore, anti-doping work has serious problems ahead of it.

At the US Army Aeromedical Research Laboratory, for example, research is being conducted into ways in which sleep deprivation affects performance. In one test, pilots were kept awake for two 24-hour periods interrupted by a single night's sleep. Measurements of their response speeds and precision skills showed that untreated sleep deprivation resulted in significant falls in performance. However, if the pilots were given the narcolepsy medication, Modafinil, they were only slightly affected by sleep deprivation and had significantly better test results.[36] This research into sleep does not, of course, open up possibilities only for the military. 'Scientists are exploring the prospect that people may be able to sustain a state of poised and productive alertness for days on end. Some have even raised the question of whether advances in bio-pharmacology will ultimately make regular sleep unnecessary'.[37] Although it is highly unlikely that we will ever reach the point at which medicine can replace sleep, there is not the shadow of a doubt that the future will see the development of a range of measures that will be able to reinforce human normality. Modafinil would seem to be an obvious choice to use in gruelling motor races such as Le Mans and the Dakar Rally. The revision of the doping list in 2004, in which caffeine and pseudoephedrine were removed, saw the prohibition of Modafinil. Neurochemistry is a wide-ranging potential, and the question is whether it will be just as easy to ban substances that will be able to improve memory and the ability to concentrate without having any side-effects. It is difficult to imagine that a drug able to increase humans' cognitive capacities will be able to be kept off the market. A decision to prohibit competitors such as chess players, cross-country runners or gymnasts studying for a degree from using the same measures as their fellow students in their hunt for a good job simply because those measures would be advantageous in their competitive lives would necessarily raise difficult ethical questions. The situation would, of course, be even worse if the intense research in gene technology at some point made possible a general increase in longevity by using genetic engineering to bring about a strengthening of the cardiovascular system. If this becomes something that parents have to decide for their children, just as they currently opt for or against giving them the MMR vaccination, it is likely that those who can afford it will opt for life-prolonging gene manipulation. After that, all talk of competition on a level playing field will be obsolete. In other words there are good grounds for supposing that developments in medical technology will in time cause the erosion of the ideals of cleanness in sport that are currently dominant.

In a thought-provoking advertising campaign, the sports clothing company, Puma, shows a future in which cyborgization has made a break-through.[38] Even though the idea may seem far-out, it has not appeared from nowhere. The interest of science – and especially of military science – in opportunities for optimizing the human organism does not allow any winding back of the clock. It is an integral part of a modern arms race.[39] As far as we can judge, therefore, we must gird ourselves for a future in which the ideals of equality in real physical sport will not be able to be upheld, but in which bodies in competition are in various ways adapted medically or technologically. On the other hand a virtual alternative is in the process of emerging.

Computer research attached to the American military has given us the internet, and this has now developed into one of the pillars of our social order. A significant portion of the wars of the future can, therefore, be expected to be played out in this arena. Furthermore, it is in line with historical development that sporting competitions should now also be established in this medium. Some of these, such as the popular game *Battlefield*, resemble war. Others, such as FIFA's football game, simulate real sports disciplines. Players who control their virtual teams can keep themselves alert with the aid of Coke, coffee or Modafinil, but the spectator's experience will be entirely clean. Computer sport can, therefore, come to appear as the ideal sport, devoid of any possibility for cheating, while players in reality are sitting behind their screens, perfecting new military skills.

Notes

1 John Hoberman, 'Sport and the Technological Image of Man', in William J. Morgan and Klaus V. Meyer, eds, *Philosophical Inquiry in Sport* (Champaign, IL: Human Kinetics, 1988), 202.
2 Ibid., 203.
3 Ibid.
4 Ibid.
5 See, for example, Allen Guttmann, *From Ritual to Record* (New York: Colombia University Press, 1978).
6 Cited in Stephen G. Miller, *Arete – Greek Sports from Ancient Sources* (Berkeley: University of California Press, 1991), 148.
7 Ibid., 149.
8 R.F. Willets 'Greek Physical Education', in J.G. Dixon et al., eds, *Landmarks in the History of Physical Education* (London: Routledge and Kegan Paul, 1957), 9.
9 Georges Vigarello, 'The Upright Training of the Body from the Age of Chivalry to Courtly Civility', in Michel Feher, Ramona Naddaff and Nadia Tazi, eds, *Fragments for a History of the Human Body: Part Two* (New York: Zone Books, 1989).
10 David G. McComb, *Sports in World History* (London: Routledge, 2004), 28.
11 Troels Lund, 'Legemsøvelser og dansk hofkultur – Ridderspil, dystridt, fægteskole og slagsmål i nyere tid', in *Idrætshistorisk Årbog 1991* (Odense: Odense University Press, 1900), 11.
12 McComb, *Sports in World History*, 12.
13 Eric Hobsbawm, *The Age of Capital 1848–1875* (London: Weidenfeld & Nicolson, 1975), 41.
14 See Mike Jenkins, 'Advanced materials and sporting performance', *Interdisciplinary Science Reviews*, 27, 1 (2002).
15 ntrs.nasa.gov/archive/nasa/casi.ntrs.nasa.gov/20020076122_2002119597.pdf.
16 N.J. Mills, 'Running shoe materials', in Mike Jenkins, ed., *Materials in Sports Equipment* (Cambridge: Woodhead Publishing, 2003).
17 Joakim Jacobsen, *Le Tour* (Copenhagen: Gyldendal, 2004), 65.
18 Christian W. Larsen, 'Tennisteknologi – et spørgsmål om sweet spot og stil' [Tennis technology – a question about sweet spot and style], in Jørn Ravn, *Sport og teknologi* [Sport and Technology] (Copenhagen: Teknologinævnet, 1994), 63 ff.
19 See John Bale, *Sports Geography* (London: Routledge, 2003), 139.
20 Ove Bøje, *Idrætsteori* (Odense: Forlaget Arnkrone, 1995), 153.
21 Ibid., 153 f.
22 Ibid., 154.
23 Ibid., 156.
24 Ibid., 157.
25 Terry Todd, 'Anabolic Steroids: The Gremlins of Sport', *Journal of Sport History*, 14, 1 (1987), 93.
26 Ibid.
27 John Hoberman, *Mortal Engines: The Science of Performance and the Dehumanization of Sport* (New York: Free Press, 1992), 221.
28 See, for example Giselher Spitzer, *Doping in der DDR: Ein historisher Überblick zu einer konspirativen Praxis* (Cologne: Bundesinstitut für Sportwissenschaft, 2000); and Steven Ungerleider, *Faust Gold Inside the East German Doping Machine* (New York: Thomas Dunne Books, 2001).
29 The quotation is taken from Todd, 'Anabolic Steroids', 88.
30 Ibid., 94.
31 www.iaaf.org/news/newsId=42896,printer.html.
32 See Leslie Iversen, *Speed, Ecstasy, Ritalin: The Science of Amphetamines* (New York: Oxford University Press, 2006).
33 Ibid., 72.
34 What we know is that he had taken the drug Roniacol, which has the opposite effect to amphetamine. This he had been given by his trainer, who thought (wrongly) that the vasodilative drug would

12 Entrepreneurship

Dilwyn Porter

Though it is something of a journalistic cliché to recall an age of innocence when amateur values predominated and the influence of money was absent, sport and business have an intimate and long-standing connection. Much that is recognizably 'modern' in their relationship dates from the late 19th and early 20th centuries. Yet, as Neil Tranter has noted of Britain, the commercialization of sport had a significant pre-history. Cricket, horse-racing, pedestrianism, prize-fighting and rowing all had 'a long history of mass spectating, profit-seeking promoters, paid performers, stake-money contests and gambling'.[1] Derek Birley notes a newspaper advertisement from 1700 notifying 'Gentlemen and others who delight in cricket-playing' of a match to be held on Clapham Common for £10 per head. There was, he observes, 'a distinct commercial message behind the polite language'. Later, in 1787, when Thomas Lord leased some land in London, built a high fence around it, and prepared a ground for cricket that could be hired by aristocratic patrons it was with the intention of making money. Lord's original enclosure staged pedestrian events, pigeon-shooting matches and even hopping contests as well as cricket.[2] Its entrepreneurial proprietor clearly regarded sport as a business opportunity.

Lord would probably have admired the enterprise of O.E. McGregor, owner of the Molineux Arms and Gardens in Wolverhampton, who cashed in on the enthusiasm for velocipedes that exploded in the late 1860s and early 1870s to create a venue – now more closely connected with soccer (football) than cycling – that became 'England's bicycle racing Mecca'. The races he promoted were 'most definitely a profit-making activity, in line with other leisure-time entertainments and amusements such as the music-hall or the theatre'.[3] By this time the connections between sport and industrialization were becoming apparent. English bicycle racing in the 1870s, driven forward by commercially minded promoters such as McGregor, 'gave a powerful economic and manufacturing stimulus to the young bicycle industry', not least in terms of design. With the emergence of urban mass markets business success or failure in the production of sports goods was related to a company's ability to exploit large-scale, machine-based production methods. Hence Dunlop and the North British Rubastic Company prospered as manufacturers of golf balls in the last years of the 19th century at the expense of the undercapitalized Anglo-French Golf Ball Manufacturing Company.[4]

Industrialization helped to create conditions in which organized sport and those who saw it as a potential source of profit could flourish. As Wray Vamplew has argued:

> The industrialisation of British sport can be charted as the working-out of supply and demand in the market-place. Favourable changes in demand parameters, particularly time and income, encouraged the injection of factors of production into the supply of sport and the application of modern technology.[5]

New construction techniques were especially important in this respect as they facilitated the construction of stadiums in which large crowds of paying spectators could be accommodated. In the USA industrialized production methods enabled A.G. Spalding, baseball star turned entrepreneur, to manufacture sports goods for the mass market. The Spalding Manufacturing Company was turning out over a million baseball bats a year at its factory in Hastings, Michigan, by 1887; a few years later the Reach plant in Philadelphia (a Spalding subsidiary from 1889) was making an estimated 18,000 baseballs daily. At the same time new distribution techniques helped him to sell what his factories produced across the USA. Department stores, such as Macy's in New York, and the ubiquitous Sears Roebuck mail-order catalogue, which in 1895 allocated 80 pages to sporting goods, were an integral part of the distribution chain.[6]

The growth of cities was also critical. Sport, as Steven A. Riess has observed, 'is not merely a recreational activity that happened to take place in cities, but is an institution that has been shaped, reshaped, and further molded by the interplay of the elements comprising the process of urbanization'.[7] Entrepreneurs in the USA and other urbanizing (and increasingly suburbanizing) societies were quick to seize the opportunities that presented themselves as the inhabitants of growing cities sought release from the constraints of the great indoors by engaging in sport as participants or as spectators. Either way, it was a welcome distraction from factory and office routine. Urbanization was especially important in relation to the development of spectator sports, especially when it was combined with economic changes that had the effect of increasing demand. 'What should be stressed', notes Vamplew, 'is that it was not until the economic benefits of industrialisation filtered down to the mass of the population that a large and regular paying clientele could be relied upon for sports events'.[8]

Towards the end of the 19th century urban consumers with some free time and disposable income to spend on entertainments were to be found in large numbers in cities across America and Europe. Sports entrepreneurship sprang from this urban context. Purveyors of commercialized sports in Toronto – where baseball, boxing, Caledonian Games, horse-racing, pedestrianism, skating, track and field and wrestling were among the distractions on offer – 'promoted athletic events and activities with no intent beyond a return on their investments'.[9] In France it seemed entirely appropriate that Clovis Clerc, director of the *Folies Bergères*, should have been one of the first to invest in *vélodromes*, cashing in on Parisian working-class enthusiasm for indoor cycling in the 1890s. For Clerc, as Richard Holt has explained, 'the attraction of cycling lay not so much in the racing itself as in the prospect of creating a new and lucrative form of public entertainment'.[10] Arthur Elvin, who risked £150,000 in 1927 to purchase the rapidly deteriorating Wembley Stadium and reversed its decline by introducing Londoners to the new entertainment of greyhound racing, was similarly motivated. 'Wembley', as Mike Cronin has noted, 'offered a night out at the dogs, but with all the facilities of a top night on the town'.[11]

It was during the 1880s that the gentlemen who had founded England's Football Association (FA) in 1863 and supervised soccer's development thereafter had first sensed that they were being supplanted by men 'who made a business of the game and consequently could no longer treat it as a sport'.[12] Paternalism made way for commercialism as soccer began to engage with the mass market. Arguably, what has happened over the course of the long 20th century is that sport's links with business have become progressively more systematic and more visible. For some time it was possible – and sometimes politically expedient – to keep commerce at a distance. 'There are those who hold that one side of our game, the professional branch, is a business on a purely commercial basis', observed FA secretary Sir Frederick Wall in 1935. 'They are welcome to their opinion', he continued, 'but apart from the honest desire to pay all just dues, the leading clubs, whether they engage professionals or not, have no desire to make money for the sake of money'.[13]

By the 1990s, certainly as far as England's Stock Exchange-listed Premiership clubs were concerned, this no longer applied. Major shareholders demanded profit-maximization *and* utility-maximization, dividends as well as trophies. The game's new business environment could be explored through *Soccer Analyst* and *Soccer Investor* as well as via dedicated coverage in *The Financial Times*.[14] In reality, the writing had been on the wall for some time. Manchester United fans hostile to Malcolm Glazer's takeover bid in 2005 were reminded that, while the owner of the Tampa Bay Buccaneers might not have been the people's choice, 'neither was the late Louis Edwards, who made his fortune from meat packaging before Matt Busby suggested that he might like to rebuild [the club] from the wreckage of the Munich crash'. Historically, it was the Edwards family, major shareholders from 1970 to 2002, who had 'succeeded in extracting the greatest financial benefit from the club'.[15] United, a club which enjoyed an unusually high profile after the 1958 tragedy, was in the vanguard of this process of transformation.

One outcome of the emerging new order, as historian James Walvin has argued, was a fundamental discursive shift as terrace talk gave way to the language of the financial markets. Soccer was now an 'entertainment product', famous old clubs were merely competing 'brands'; fans were 'captive customers' and their support a form of 'brand loyalty', the value of which could be measured in sales of season tickets and licensed merchandise. Celebrating a fourth English Premiership title in 1997, Manchester United plc's annual report commended the team's 'attractive style of play throughout the season [which] has further strengthened the popular support for Manchester United and considerably enhanced shareholder value'.[16] This is not to suggest that it is only in recent years that soccer clubs or other sporting institutions have defined themselves as businesses. Most professional soccer clubs in Britain, as Matthew Taylor has noted, have a long history as limited liability companies and they are not alone; sports organizations from golf clubs to race courses have followed the same route. This has methodological implications for sports historians not least because it means working with archival evidence which is 'similar to that of conventional firms'.[17]

What has changed is that there is now, especially for those engaged in sport at an elite level, a greater tendency than before to define themselves *primarily* as businesses. On occasions the transition has been sudden and dramatic, as in rugby union, a sport that adopted professionalism only in the mid-1990s. When multi-millionaire property developer Sir John Hall was persuaded to bankroll Newcastle Gosforth (rebranded as Newcastle Falcons) the whole ethos of the club changed. It was, one business writer observed, 'all part of the growth of sport as a major profession, as far removed from the old amateur ethic of dirty whites, damp socks and dingy changing-rooms on the edge of some God-forsaken field as one could imagine'.[18] The long-delayed commercialization of English rugby union simply replicated what had been happening elsewhere. 'Another sports battle was under way', noted Stephen Hardy with reference to the controversy surrounding the decision to move the Los Angeles Rams to St. Louis in 1995, 'but like most interesting contests of the 1980s and 1990s, the combatants wore pinstripe suits and carried briefcases, not footballs'.[19]

It is important to retain a sense of the wider picture. In Britain the hegemony of gentlemanly forms of capitalism endured until the second half of the 20th century. This meant that sport developed inside a patrician framework within which amateur values were privileged and rampant commercialization was discouraged. King George V, attending a Scotland–England rugby union international between the wars, was reported to have asked James Aikman Smith of the Scottish Rugby Football Union why Scotland's players wore no numbers. 'This is a game for gentlemen', Smith had explained, 'not a cattle market'.[20] Scottish rugby union is perhaps an extreme case but even in professional soccer the FA imposed restraints on the commercial exploitation of sport, notably by imposing a top limit on the annual dividends that clubs could pay to shareholders. It was only after 1960 that the amateur hegemony in British sport was eroded, thus opening the way for the systematic colonization of sport by business.[21]

Elsewhere, where the containing framework of amateurism was weaker or absent altogether, there was a greater readiness to admit to a connection between sport and money.[22] Steven Pope has argued that amateurism, rather against the odds, was embraced by most American sports as an ideal at the end of the 19th century.[23] It had, however, developed within the framework of American capitalism in the age of the 'robber barons'. In these circumstances amateur values, though often compromised, had their place, especially in the universities, while a 'win at all costs' mentality continued to prevail in sports such as baseball where commercialization was well established. Perhaps this helps to explain why Spalding was himself something of a robber baron in business, ruthlessly squeezing rival manufacturers and retailers. His involvement with the short-lived American Bicycle Company (ABC), a trust established with other manufacturers in 1899, is indicative of this aspect of his business practice. Though ostensibly interested in bicycle manufacture the company was in effect a vehicle that enabled Spalding and his collaborators to shift resources into the up-and-coming automobile industry at other people's expense. 'The sporting goods manufacturers who organized ABC were capitalists', it has been noted. 'They manipulated New Jersey corporation law and the financial system to their advantage, with no regard for stockholders or debenture-bond owners'.[24]

Yet, though variations in economic and social conditions may have dictated the speed at which business and sport have converged in different countries, the tendency to converge is not in doubt. Its ever-expanding parameters may be difficult to define but 'sportsbiz', like 'showbiz', has arrived. Indeed, as Sean Hamil argued in relation to English soccer in 1999, sport was 'being incorporated into the conventional "commercial" leisure sector'; stock-market quoted firms were listed under 'Leisure, Entertainment and Hotels'.[25] Recent developments in the trade press supply significant indicators with the fashionable elision of 'sport/s' and 'business' in *SportsBusiness Journal* (USA) and *SportBusiness International* (UK) underlining the realities of convergence. Though there are limits – sport has to retain a degree of autonomy if it is to retain credibility as a product – business has increasingly determined the nature of the spectacle. 'Modern formula one cars lined up on the starting grid', it was noted in 1975, 'project a bizarre array of products – from contraceptives to filter-tipped cigarettes – and the 308C, with the glamorous and articulate James Hunt at the wheel, looks like a highly marketable proposition'.[26] Sponsorship, which has developed massively since the 1970s, inevitably foregrounded the business of sport; television viewers of today's major sporting events can hardly ignore the sponsor's logo when it is projected onto the playing area.

'What was once sport, pure and simple, has become what I like to call Sportsbiz', claimed business journalist Stephen Aris in 1990, 'which is neither pure nor simple'. Arguably this was – and remains – something of an overreaction and Aris did recognize that the emergence of Sportsbiz may be 'simply an acceleration of a process that has been going on for as long as organised sport itself'.[27] Yet, as the relationship between sport and business intensifies, it also becomes more visible. Business activities that were once behind-the-scenes are increasingly integrated with the performance on offer to the public. According to Charles Korr, changes in contract status of American baseball players after 1976 and soccer players within the European Union after 1995 changed the way that the clubs did business and the way that professional sport was covered by the media. 'So-called back-room activities of clubs are now played out in the press, on television, and across the internet, sometimes before they are anything more than rumours'.[28] The televised pre-season auction of cricketing talent currently organized by the Indian Premier League is as much a part of the spectacle as the games which the 'overnight millionaires' will contest for Bangalore Royal Chall, Chennai Super Kings and Delhi Daredevils.[29]

Increasingly, too, sport and business appear to share a common lexicon. There is a tendency for those engaged in business to see themselves as engaged in some kind of competitive sport, or at least to describe business activities in sporting terms. 'Assuming similar backgrounds and capabilities', asked Mark McCormack, founder of the International Management Group (IMG), 'why do some people shoot straight to the top while others seem to languish forever in the morass of middle management?' The answer, he suggested, was that effective performers in the corporate sphere, like the best American footballers, grasped the importance of teamwork and understood the game they were playing, thus developing the capacity to achieve success in a position that they could make their own.[30] Given IMG's business interests in sports management and marketing it was not surprising that McCormack should have made this connection but the sporting analogy surfaces in other, less likely contexts. Leading British industrialist John Harvey-Jones, reflecting on his career at Imperial Chemical Industries (ICI), described himself as a practitioner of 'managerial judo' where 'the power of the opponent [was used] to defeat himself'. Faced with an industrial relations problem it was often best to do nothing, to let the clock run down, to play out time. 'The erosion of time itself', he observed, 'affects people's views and people's thinking … It is a good example of the passive judo approach'.[31] What this indicates is a belief that skills learned and strategies deployed in sport are applicable in competitive business and vice versa.

Thus it is no surprise to learn that a 28-minute motivational training film, *Second Effort*, featuring Vince Lombardi, legendary coach of the Green Bay Packers, was the largest-selling industrial film of all time. 'America's corporate executives', it has been argued, 'have been quite willing to believe that football experience equates with business experience'.[32] They are not alone. Britain's men in suits have proved equally susceptible. Former England rugby union captain, Will Carling, became an advocate of Total Quality Management (TQM), advising business clients on how to improve performance across the entire range of a company's activities. The secret was 'doing the right things better, and then improving all over again. It's a concept with which all players in all sports are deeply familiar. However good you are your PB [Personal Best] can always be improved'. Carling also made it clear that the link between sport and business worked both ways. Tracy Edwards and the crew of *Maiden*, the first all-female team to compete in the Whitbread Round-the-World Yacht Race, were praised for the relationships they established with sail-makers and other key suppliers. Edwards, it seems, 'was beginning to assemble the equivalent of the basic unit of modern management: a team of specialists, covering every need, who can also work together as a highly efficient unit'.[33] Perhaps, as Jack Rowell – Carling's former coach and also a director of the food group Dalgety –

once claimed, there really was 'very little difference between running the England rugby team and turning round Golden Wonder crisps'.[34]

Sports history and business history

Given this tendency for boundaries between sport and business to dissolve it may be useful to consider the relationship between sports history and business history. It is possible to regard them, like sport and business, as separate activities practised by historians drawing information from quite different types of source and equipped with quite different forms of expertise. Yet it is also important to recognize that they have much in common, Business history, as one practitioner has suggested, 'is essentially an eclectic activity which, while remaining firmly wedded to historical method, draws on several social science disciplines'.[35] The questions that business historians ask of their sources, the particular terms of their dialogue with the past, have been derived principally from economics, econometrics and management science. A description of sports history could be similarly constructed. Like business history it is essentially eclectic, drawing – among other disciplines – on psychology, sociology and sports science to inform the historical narrative. This similarity is underpinned in both instances by the institutional locations in which teaching and research takes place. It is relatively unusual for either business historians or sports historians to work in conventional history departments. Arguably both sub-disciplines have the kind of 'open architecture' that facilitates two-way exchanges with scholars in adjacent fields.[36]

There are other parallels, not least in the way that they have developed in recent years. The progress of business history, it has been ruefully observed, has been hampered by the perception that 'business historians are fact-mongers without theory, more concerned with the particular than the general and unable to dovetail with other, higher profile subjects'.[37] Sports history, similarly, has often struggled to attain full membership of the academy, not only because of the long-standing prejudice that sport was an essentially trivial pursuit but also because so many of its practitioners were seen as archive rats scurrying heads down to gather surviving traces of the past from which they constructed – or as Douglas Booth would say 'reconstructed' – their narratives of triumph and disaster. Indeed, Booth argues at the end of his recent critique of the field that 'sports history generally remains very firmly anchored to a bedrock of empiricism and to an unshakeable belief that historians can recover the past, its realities and truths'.[38]

Yet it should be recognized that both business history and sports history have refocused in recent years to take wider perspectives into account. 'A new agenda has emerged', it has been noted, 'where the emphasis is not simply on the firm itself but on the firm and the complex, multifaceted environment in which it operates'.[39] In particular, cultural history has helped to redefine the agenda of business history and there is now greater awareness that the decision-making process is deeply embedded in corporate and national cultures.[40] This means that while the firm and its archives remain at the heart of business history they are not necessarily over-privileged. A parallel movement in sports history has seen the emphasis shift from reconstructing the past via archival research to explaining what sport meant and why it mattered. As Martin Polley has observed, only by embedding the history of sport in a broader cultural context has it been possible to nail once and for all the idea that sport 'has nothing to do with anything else'.[41] Thus 'reconstructionists' are increasingly outnumbered by 'constructionists' and 'deconstructionists' as sports historians search for meaning rather than facts.[42]

Having drawn attention to these similarities and noted that the conventional boundaries that once separated disciplines are dissolving, it would seem appropriate to argue that sports historians might derive some benefit from a closer acquaintance with business history, or even just with the history of some other branches of the entertainment business. Criticism of the small businessmen who ran professional soccer in England for much of the 20th century was something of a cliché even before Len Shackleton, Sunderland and England's 'clown prince', notoriously devoted a blank page in his 1955 auto-biography to 'the average director's knowledge of football'.[43] Matthew Taylor's recent work offers a more nuanced assessment. The Football League's retain and transfer system, while clearly a restraint of trade as far as players were concerned, was probably no more oppressive than employment conditions in the music-hall business where proprietors often imposed contractual conditions on performers that restricted their rights to work elsewhere. Some, just like English and Scottish soccer clubs, even enforced a maximum wage limit. Similarly, the League's reluctance to allow radio match commentaries – regarded in the interwar period as a threat rather than as an opportunity to market the game – seems less perverse when set alongside efforts by theatres to prohibit live broadcasts.[44] It sometimes pays to look beyond sport.

Sports historians might also consider engaging more systematically with some of the conceptual thinking that has shaped business history. In tracing the growth of A.G. Spalding and Brothers, the commercial vehicle through which 'A.G.' capitalized on the fame he had achieved through his career in baseball, Peter Levine, writing in 1985, supplied a compelling account of the rapid growth of Spalding's business empire. This started with his first retail store, opened in Chicago in 1876, and eventually encompassed publishing and the manufacture of a wide range of sporting goods and clothing, not to mention bicycles. Crediting Spalding with 'creatively nurturing a new industry', Levine compares him to other dynamic business leaders of the period. 'Like them', he notes, '[Spalding] recognized the advantages of modern concepts of industrial organization, emphasized innovation and diversification, and took pride in his firm's ability to dominate its competitors'.[45] Spalding's various enterprises, it seems, were not untypical of those that flourished in an economic system moving rapidly towards what Alfred D. Chandler Jr called 'managerial capitalism', a process facilitated by the size and rapid growth of the relatively homogenous American market.[46] Growth was secured by a strategy of buying up rival firms, by adding to the range of Spalding sporting goods and by opening up new centres of distribution in towns and cities across the USA and elsewhere. Given that Levine's work predated Chandler's second magisterial volume, it might well be useful for sports historians to revisit A.G. Spalding and Brothers, the Spalding Manufacturing Company and the American Bicycle Company in the light of both *The Visible Hand* (1977) and *Scale and Scope* (1990). Chandler remains, after all, the 'avuncular giant' bestriding business history; 'whatever the reaction, Chandler is the starting point'.[47]

Yet, to date, sports historians have shown little inclination to revisit sports businesses with Chandler in mind. Stephen Hardy, in 1986, pointed to the emergence of baseball leagues in the USA as an example of market stratification shaped by a discernible business strategy, an intervention by the 'visible hand' that was designed to stabilize market conditions via enforced segmentation.[48] Pamela Cooper's imaginative work on the New York City Marathon, which appeared a few years later, focused on Fred Lebow, the entrepreneur who seized control of the event in the mid-1970s and enhanced its potential to attract corporate funding by opening up the event to non-elite participants, thus converting what had been a race into a festival. In so doing, she argues, Lebow 'changed the nature of the New York Road Runners club, which administers the New York City Marathon, from a volunteer organization serving the athletic interests of its members to a business enterprise with a staff of salaried managers'. This transformation – featuring 'a hierarchy of salaried executives' and 'distinct operating units' – illustrates management's strategic role as capitalism's 'invisible hand' in jointly co-ordinating the flow of goods and services.[49] Yet, among sports historians, the application of what business historians refer to as the 'Chandlerian paradigm' has rarely been followed through in any systematic fashion.

Studies of international rivalry, seeking to explain why some nations excel at sport generally or why they excel at particular sports, might find much of value in Michael Porter's *The Competitive Advantage of Nations*, regarded by business historians as of seminal importance. What sports historians may find useful here, for example, are arguments that supply a justification for their continuing interest in questions of identity and culture and in the relationship between the global and the local. Porter argues that 'history matters', in the sense that a nation's economic performance is to a large extent determined by its pre-existing base of industries, institutions and values. This is not far removed from the work of economists and econometric historians who have established a relationship between Gross Domestic Product (GDP) *per capita* or total GDP and the comparative performance of nations in the international sports arena.[50] Such factors, it might be suggested, should at least be considered by sports historians alongside the cultural advantages conferred by *jettinho*, the habit of individual improvisation, when explaining Brazil's success in world soccer.[51]

Porter has also argued that one discernible effect of intensified global competition has been that the local has become more rather than less important. 'National differences in character and culture', he observes, 'far from being threatened by global competition, prove integral to success in it'.[52] Some recent work on the development of soccer in Japan suggests the possibility of useful cross-fertilization here. The introduction of the 'J League' in 1993, it has been noted, led to 'the gradual diminishing of differences when compared to the global practice of soccer'. This was evident, for example, in the improved performance of the Japanese national team in international matches and in transfers of star players to leading European clubs. Yet, paradoxically, community support for J League clubs 'has begun to actuate local culture and highlight differences between regional cultures that have been suppressed for the last century and a half'.[53] This points to a research agenda that will enable sports historians to test theories regarding the homogeneity of the globalized sports product and the existence of what David L. Andrews has identified as 'an ubiquitous late capitalist "structure of [sporting] feeling" that goes beyond traditional sporting, and indeed national, boundaries'.[54] What goes on within those boundaries may still be important.

It is not, however, only at the macro level that useful common perspectives are to be found. Research at the micro level is equally important for both sports and business historians, not least because it is important to avoid the trap of writing only the history of winners and neglecting losers, thus perpetuating a rather skewed version of the past. 'Business historians', it has been observed, 'for the most part study successful enterprises'; the result is that they often assume 'that the enterprises they have been researching are superior in some robust way – that they are the outcomes of historical processes that have produced higher forms of business organization'.[55] In sport and in business – and in sports business – there are more losers than winners so it is important to redress this imbalance. Reviewing the state of sports history in 1998, Neil Tranter suggested shifting the focus of research 'away from its current preference for the best-known and most prestigious institutions, promoters and performers towards a greater concern for the less famous and obscure organizations and personalities'. There was, he continued, 'a history of the more mundane and obscure still waiting to be satisfactorily uncovered'.[56]

Archive-led business historians researching the history of family firms may sometimes attract criticism from those who look to the study of the past primarily to underpin expansive models and broad hypotheses but there may be some advantages in following their lead. In Britain, for example, little is known about the history of sports goods retailing, a sub-sector of the economy in which the small shopkeeper predominated for most of the 20th century. There were, James Jefferys noted in his pioneering study based on the 1938 Census of Distribution, 1,500 outlets selling a wide range of sports goods, a further 1,000–1,500 selling a medium range and 2,000–2,500 selling a limited range.[57] It appears to have been a highly unstable sector of retailing where price cutting was rife and failures were frequent. Yet, apart from a tantalizing reference in Richard Holt's *Sport and the British* to Mr Edwards, the amenable and ever-available proprietor of a sports goods shop in upmarket Tunbridge Wells, this aspect of the economic history of sport remains largely a mystery.[58] An acquaintance with micro-level business history could yield useful insights here. Moreover, in pursuing such a project it may be possible for historians to develop a more refined definition of the sports club, the most basic organizational unit in modern sport. To date sports historians have been inclined to concentrate almost entirely on its associational functions, yet all clubs have to buy or rent premises, attract members and find the funds to finance their activities. Considering these business-related aspects of club histories opens up new perspectives and permits a more holistic approach.

Sport: a 'triple commodity'

The principal difficulty confronting any historian seeking to explore the business history of sport is where to set the boundaries. 'Sport' might be used to describe a wide range of competitive and/or recreational activities which occur in both the market and the non-market sectors of the economy. To complicate matters further sports-related business often defies simple categorization, spilling over from one sector into another. It was difficult for Jefferys, for example, to calculate sales of sports goods because 'sportswear' was simply categorized as clothing and various indoor games as 'toys'. The problem remains. 'Sportswear', as *The Financial Times* explained helpfully in 1996, 'includes obviously common or garden sportswear (soccerwear, cricketwear, swimwear) but also aerobicswear, dancewear, beachwear, surfwear, sports fashionwear, fitnesswear, activewear, musclewear, bodywear, many types of leisurewear … and – for the cool – various types of streetwear'.[59] The problems of definition evident here have led some economists to assign track-suits and trainers, often worn simply as leisurewear, to a separate category designated 'trite goods'. Moreover, in recent years some specialist producers have followed the path of inter-industry diversification; thus Nike bought Cole Haan and Reebok bought Rockport, both manufacturers of non-sports footwear; while clothing retailer Benetton reversed the process, buying into the sports goods sector by acquiring Nordica (ski boots), Prince (rackets) and Rollerblade.[60] These developments in the retail sector suggest that sport and leisure, once categorized as separate sectors of the economy, are converging. The stadium, as John Bale has argued, is being replaced by the 'tradium', a commercialized space centred on sport where spending is a leisure activity.[61]

Thus the problems associated with defining precisely what is meant by 'sport' manifest themselves as imperfections in the available statistical data and are compounded by difficulties of categorization as boundaries between sport and other sectors are blurred. Yet sports goods – clothing and footwear, bats and balls – are at least tangible. In societies where people define themselves increasingly by what they consume rather than what they produce sport often presents itself in the form of an experiential commodity and here definitions are even more elusive. If Manchester United plays Liverpool at football in the Premier League just what kind of experience is being offered for sale? Is it a spectacle to be consumed by paying spectators at the stadium and armchair fans via television in their own homes? Or is the product a particular form of competition in which uncertainty of outcome is guaranteed to generate interest and excitement? Are 'football' (live and televised), 'Manchester United', 'Liverpool' and the 'Premier League' simply competing products and/or entertainment brands that consumers can be persuaded to buy? To what extent is the match itself an advertising vehicle for replica shirts and other sports-related fashionwear? Whether tangible or experiential, the sports product refuses to be pinned down.

Fortunately, Stephen Hardy has provided sports historians with some guidance should they seek to negotiate this difficult terrain by defining sport as a 'triple' or 'three-part commodity'. 'These parts', he explains, 'which can exist in isolation but which reach full expression in combination are … the activity or game form, the service and the goods'. A particular sporting activity, in its original form, is not necessarily a commodity per se, though it may subsequently be commodified if consumers are prepared to pay to play, watch or otherwise engage in it. Sports-related services of various kinds then grow to supply the miscellaneous needs generated by the commodified activity – players need agents to negotiate their salaries, clubs need stadiums and other facilities for spectators, punters require bookmakers to accept their wagers, sporting brands need the media to advertise their presence in the entertainment market. Sports goods, necessary requirements of the game form – basically any equipment or clothing required by the players or facilities such as running tracks or swimming pools without which the activity could not take place – form the third part of the composite sports product.[62] An article in the *Economist*, prompted by the revival of golf as Britain's consumers made the great leap forward into affluence in 1960, illustrates Hardy's tripartite structure and the dynamic relationship between its component parts:

> The golfer enters a busy world. He plays by excellent though lengthy rules made by the Royal and Ancient Club at St Andrews [*the game form*]; his 'pro' instructor belongs to the PGA [Professional Golfers Association], his club to the English, Welsh, Scottish, Irish or Ladies Golf Union. He can read *Golfing*, *Golf Illustrated*, *Golf Monthly*. He is sure of the latest book by one of the masters for his birthday and another for Christmas [*sports-related services*]. Unless he is unusually choosy, his equipment probably comes from one of a very few manufacturers. The balls he buys are almost certainly made by Dunlop. Slazenger (owned by Dunlop), Spalding, or Penfold, and all steel golf shafts are made by a single company. However, the major producers of finished clubs still share the market with a number of very small undertakings (including 200 professionals who still make their own wooden clubs) [*sports goods*].[63]

A more up-to-date version of the above would no doubt refer also to tournament golf [*game form*], extensive press and television coverage [*sport-related services*], golf courses, driving ranges, golf carts and golfwear [*sports goods*].

Hardy's idea that sport is a triple commodity remains influential though it has been subject to some modification. George H. Sage, for example, divides commercialized sport into three 'segments' characterized by 'performance', 'promotion' and 'production'.[64] These segments correspond broadly, but not precisely, to the three component elements of sports business as identified by Hardy. This modified categorization might be especially useful when discussing branded sports clothing that carries an endorsement from an athlete known to the public through 'performance', that is marketed via various forms of 'promotion' (including exposure to spectators and television viewers via athletes who are paid to wear the brand while performing), and is 'produced' in commercial quantities to meet the requirements of mass consumption. 'Being a realistic man', one sportswear entrepreneur has noted, 'I have never worried about admitting that my name is better known worldwide, not for winning Wimbledon three times, but because of Fred Perry shirts and sportswear'.[65] 'Fred Perry' shirts, with their distinctive laurel wreath emblem, were first manufactured and marketed in the late 1940s, pioneering the concept of a sports-derived 'designer' tag which appears to be both ubiquitous *and* exclusive.

The entrepreneur in sport

Having outlined his model Hardy went on to suggest an agenda for historical research into sports business that revolved largely around the role of entrepreneurs in creating the modern sports product. In pursuing this theme he developed a critique of earlier research into the history of 'leisure-time business' in the USA and, in particular, the idea that entrepreneurs, in their single-minded pursuit of profit, had developed sport as a commercialized entertainment for an increasingly urbanized consumer market at the expense of traditional, homespun and largely rural leisure activities. Hardy's spin on this well-worn tale was to suggest that the role of entrepreneurs had been both more subtle and more complex. The profit motive may have been important – 'it has surely nudged sport in certain directions' – but may not by itself have been a decisive influence. Moreover, risk-taking, another activity often associated with entrepreneurship, may not have been critical in a sector effectively subsidized by the state via high school athletics or by philanthropic agencies, such as the YMCA movement, which had their own non profit-driven reasons for encouraging participation in sport.[66] It may be useful to explore entrepreneurship a little further here, not least because it is a subject that facilitates bridge-building between the separate worlds of sport and business history.

It has to be recognized that entrepreneurs and the functions that they perform have often posed major methodological problems for economists. In the 18th and early 19th centuries Adam Smith and David Ricardo assigned primacy to markets in determining the allocation and use of resources, effectively downplaying the role of the individual. The impact of industrialization, however, and in particular the emergence of large-scale enterprises prompted economists to think again. 'From this period', Martin Ricketts has recently observed, 'derives the idea of the heroic entrepreneur, a transformer or founder of industries, an undertaker of massive feats of engineering, an opener of continents'.[67] Economists could hardly ignore these giants of enterprise and began to assign them a specific role in the development of capitalist economies.

The most decisive contribution in this respect was made by the J.A. Schumpeter in his ground-breaking *Theory of Economic Development* (1934) where he assigned specific functions to the entrepreneur. These encompassed revolutionizing production through exploiting invention, producing a new commodity, producing an old commodity in a new way, opening up new sources of supply or new outlets for production, and reorganizing production and distribution. Though economists still dispute some aspects of entrepreneurship – for example, whether risk-taking is a necessary function – the idea that entrepreneurs make an essential contribution to economic development is now widely accepted. Modern capitalism, according to J.S. Metcalfe, 'is strongly ordered but restless'. Entrepreneurial activity is what drives it forward; 'the entrepreneur is the crucial agent whose role it is to generate new economic knowledge and thus transform the structure of economic activity'.[68]

Problems of definition remain, not least because entrepreneurs come in all shapes and sizes and because, as enterprises grow, some of the functions of entrepreneurship may become the responsibility of managers, employees of the firm who are not required to risk their own capital. Arguably, Herbert Chapman, who transformed the fortunes of Arsenal Football Club both on and off the field between 1925 and 1934 behaved in an entrepreneurial fashion. Not only did he introduce new tactics but he also insisted that the nearest London underground station should carry the name of the club. Chapman, however, had no financial interest in Arsenal beyond his salary and remained throughout his tenure an employee of the club.[69] 'Entrepreneurship', as Ricketts observes, 'is not a concept that has a tightly agreed definition'.

No doubt this helps to explain why the label 'entrepreneur' is popularly applied to such a diverse range of individuals – small traders, self-employed businessmen, 'self-made men', 'middlemen', opportunists, innovators and improvers, as well as founders of major business empires.[70] Any one of these types might behave in ways that could be described as entrepreneurial, in particular through exercising judgement and applying knowledge to assess the level of risk and the likelihood of profit in any given market situation. This kind of behaviour is as likely to occur in relation to sports business as any other. 'Making matches occupies almost the whole of my thinking day', explained one British boxing promoter. 'In the bath, eating, looking at television, even when I'm talking, my mind is wondering what fight could top such-and-such a bill; what boy could be put in against so-and-so for a box-office draw somewhere else'.[71] This captures the quality of restlessness often associated with individual entrepreneurs and raises the issue of whether it may be possible to construct a psychological or sociological definition of entrepreneurship.

Business historians, however, have been less concerned with the individual entrepreneur than with entrepreneurship as an agent of economic change. The essence of entrepreneurship, according to Schumpeter, was the discovery of 'new combinations' that would act as forces of creative destruction, unsettling existing arrangements and generating change. While recognizing that this function may reside in individuals Chandler argued that, under modern conditions, it was more likely to be found within large enterprises that developed an organizational capacity that enabled them to behave in an entrepreneurial fashion.[72] These insights may be of value to the sports historian when used in conjunction with Hardy's idea of the tripartite sports product. Indeed, it might be argued that, as far as sport is concerned, entrepreneurial activity occurs when individuals or firms combine two or more parts of the sports product, or when they combine part or parts of the sports product with a non-sports product to create something new. This definition should be sufficiently flexible to encompass entrepreneurial activity on both a large and a small scale.

A.G. Spalding was unusual in that his business enterprise involved the systematic exploitation of all three parts of the sports product. This is best illustrated with reference to the best-selling *Spalding's Official Baseball Guide*, published annually from 1876 and claiming sales of 50,000 copies a year by the mid-1880s. In that it set out what appeared to be the definitive version of how baseball should be played the *Guide* allowed Spalding to exploit the *game form* itself. Along with publications such as the National League 'book', which Spalding marketed as if it were an official publication, it constituted an important *sports-related service* that could be sold both to players and to spectators. Finally, as the advertisements carried by these publications indicated, Spalding could supply the *sports goods* that were required to play the game according to the rules – from bats and balls to uniforms, gloves and chest protectors. Spalding's entrepreneurial function was to bring together this new combination of business activities. Moreover, as his empire grew, mainly by strategic mergers with manufacturing companies that could extend both the scale and scope of his sports goods business, it developed a capacity for corporate entrepreneurship that underwrote its primacy in the American domestic market and its expansion overseas. This is evident in the powers devolved on executives like Julian Curtiss, who introduced English golf equipment to the American market, and F.N. White, Spalding's hustler-in-chief.[73]

Cycling provides numerous examples of entrepreneurship involving the development of a new game form – or at least a variant of an original – alongside either a sports-related service or a new product. Entrepreneurial activity in relation to cycle racing was often simply opportunistic with manufacturers promoting a race over a particular course in order to advertise their particular brand of sports goods. Thus Michelin promoted a Paris to Clermont-Ferrand race in 1892 simply to prove that its tyres were superior to those produced by Dunlop.[74] Sponsorship of cyclists attempting to cross Australia by bicycle a few years later was similarly motivated. 'It affords me genuine pleasure to say, voluntarily, that the "Swift" No.1 Light Roadster, fitted with Dunlop Roadster tyres, ridden by me from Port Darwin, Northern Territory, to Melbourne, via Alice Springs and Adelaide, has given me complete satisfaction', was the testimony of Albert MacDonald after his heroic effort in 1897. Trans-continental cycling, not surprisingly, was 'a short-lived adventure sport whose ties to the bicycle industry troubled [amateur] purists'.[75] It supplies, nevertheless, an example of a kind of low-level entrepreneurial activity that has sometimes been linked to sport.

The *Tour de France*, however, established by Henri Desgrange of *L'Auto* in 1903, primarily to increase circulation at the expense of a rival cycling paper, was clearly a highly significant variation of the road-race form. With the race unfolding in daily stages readers could follow the progress of riders as if they were reading a serial. In its own way this was a 'new combination' of the kind to which Schumpeter had referred. The fortunes of the race and *L'Auto* were linked and it was a measure of Desgrange's success in bringing about this combination that *L'Auto's* circulation rose from 25,000 in 1903 to a peak of 854,000 during the 1933 *Tour*. Moreover, within a few years the *Tour* was effectively being subsidized by cycle manufacturers who seized on it as an opportunity to advertise their machines. 'Cycle racing', as Richard Holt has observed, did not have to rely purely on its own appeal as a spectacle … [it] became intrinsically bound up with the business of selling bicycles'.[76] Thus the *Tour* represents an entrepreneurial triumph, the creation of a unique sporting brand par excellence.

Initially, Desgrange's success involved bringing together two parts of the tripartite sports product: a staged race (the game form) and a related service (the sports press). Arguably, modification of game forms by establishing new forms of competition, such as leagues, while simultaneously providing a new service through building stadiums to accommodate paying spectators, constituted the most common form of sports-related entrepreneurial activity from the late 19th to the mid-20th century. It was a robust model, especially applicable to team sports such as baseball in the USA, where the National League was founded (1876), and soccer in the United Kingdom where leagues of professional clubs were established in England (1888) and Scotland (1890). Yet, though such developments did create conditions in which entrepreneurial activity was evident, it was subject to constraints.

Arguably, the English FA's ceiling on dividends, designed to keep profiteers at bay, may also have deterred entrepreneurs from seeking soccer club directorships, to the detriment of the game's interests in the longer term. It certainly modified entrepreneurial behaviour in some respects. Having bought the Stamford Bridge stadium, developed it and installed Chelsea Football Club there in 1905, H.A. Mears had to reap the rewards of entrepreneurship indirectly via the catering concession. More significantly, it seems likely that it encouraged club directors to become utility-maximizers, dovetailing neatly with the limited ambitions of businessmen motivated principally by the prestige to be derived from a connection with their home-town club.[77] It has sometimes been argued that this tendency has been stronger in Britain than in the USA but, even there, it should not be underestimated. 'Professional sports is not a business', observed Maurice Podoloff of the National Basketball Association (NBA) in 1957, recalling that he had seen many a team owner leave the arena on the verge of tears. 'He didn't moan and groan because he had lost money', Podoloff explained. 'He moaned and groaned because he had lost the game'.[78]

There is also the possibility that leagues themselves may inhibit entrepreneurship in various ways. Professional team sports leagues have been described as 'classic, even textbook, examples of business cartels'.[79] The nature of the game form is such that rival firms have to combine, first in order to stage a match, and then again in order to create the added value that is generated by locating that match within the framework of a league competition. A relatively high degree of co-operation is thus a basic function of what is sometimes referred to as the 'peculiar economics' of team sports, where it is necessary to ensure that rival firms stay in business so that they can help each other to create the competitive entertainment that is the essence of the sports product. This does not eliminate commercial competition altogether. 'The dynamic of league behaviour', as Braham Dabscheck has observed, 'is how to outwit or take advantage of rivals with whom one is having a continuing or interdependent relationship'.[80] It does, however, limit the potential scope for entrepreneurial activity.

As far as entrepreneurs are concerned problems arise when leagues impose restraints on member firms, usually with a view to ensuring that competition between teams on the field of play is balanced in a way that will create a degree of uncertainty as to the outcome of matches, thus making them more attractive to spectators and television viewers. Salary caps, cross-subsidization through revenue sharing, collective agreements to sell television rights, and the NFL's reverse-order draft are examples of this kind of arrangement. It has been argued with reference to National League baseball in the interwar years that team owners often '[worked] against their own cartel's government for short-term gain'.[81] This suggests a certain degree of entrepreneurial frustration whatever long-term advantages were derived from the game's exemption from federal anti-trust legislation in 1922. Until relatively recent times professional team sports have not offered the kind of competitive business environment in which entrepreneurship tends to thrive. It is not surprising that the free-wheeling Tex Rickard, who promoted five world championship fights that grossed over US$ 1 million at the gate in the 1920s, found boxing a more attractive proposition than baseball.[82]

Conclusion

Hardy's definition of sport as a tripartite product remains useful, especially in relation to the era of A.G. Spalding. It may, however, require some modification in relation to sport in the late 20th and early 21st centuries. The careers of two modern entrepreneurs, Mark McCormack and Rupert Murdoch, are instructive here. McCormack's business connection with sport began in 1960 when he became golfer Arnold Palmer's agent; within a few years McCormack's IMG was representing golf's 'big three' (Nicklaus, Palmer and Player) and developing sportswear and sports equipment franchises that capitalized on their fame. By the late 1960s IMG was developing a corporate style that Chandler would have recognized, notably by recruiting the expertise required to set up and manage a new television division, Trans World International (TWI). By the mid-1980s McCormack could boast that TWI was 'the world's leading independent producer of sports programming', though this comprised what now seems a very modest 200 hours annually.

Significantly, this output included various sporting contests, such as 'The Superstars', which manipulated existing game forms in the interests of good television. McCormack's corporation also developed the capacity to broker television rights deals for major tournaments such as the US Open, Wimbledon, the NBA and the NFL, while yet another division, Merchandising Consultants International (MCI) was started to advise companies who 'wanted to get into sports but had no idea how to do it'. In many respects McCormack prefigured later developments, but his entrepreneurial ambition acknowledged some limits. It is clear that he recognized certain defining boundaries between business and sport, which it would not be in IMG's interests to cross. Thus, for example, IMG resisted the temptation to change the structure of sports such as golf and tennis. 'Our long term interest', he explained, 'is in enhancing any sport in which we are involved'. He continued: 'This is not because we are "good sports", but because we are good businessmen'.[83]

Surveying the world of sport at the millennium it was clear that much had changed since IMG had branched out from the agency business into the media. At some point in the 1990s rapidly changing communications technology supplied business – and the media business in particular – with the capacity to make sport its own. As Ian Andrews has observed with reference to Australian football, 'the [Victorian Football] League has moved from an institution that is primarily bound up with culture ... to one that is primarily driven by the economic imperative to produce exchange value, often for external television and sponsorship interests'.[84] As sport gave way to 'mediasport' the product was redefined and relabelled, a process decisively initiated by media entrepreneur Rupert Murdoch's decision to use sport as part of a global expansion strategy. 'We will be doing in Asia what we intend to do elsewhere in the world', he explained to News Corporation's shareholders in 1996, 'that is, [using] sports as a battering ram and a lead offering in all our pay television operations'.[85]

It was a strategy that had already seen English Rugby League purchased for £87 million in 1995, thereby transforming a sport rooted in northern working-class culture into a corporate entity owned and controlled by BSkyB. In the radical restructuring that followed a European Super League was formed, old clubs were remarketed to create new brands ('Bradford Bulls', 'Wigan Warriors', 'Halifax Blue Sox'), and the playing season was switched from winter to summer. Murdoch was quite open about News Corporation becoming 'part of the sports establishment', a strategy that would allow it to protect its investment in the rights that it had bought.[86] This kind of intervention goes far beyond anything that McCormack would have contemplated a generation earlier.

The business history of sport has generated numerous entrepreneurs whose success has been based on their ability to negotiate a profitable relationship with the media. Pete Rozelle, NFL commissioner from 1960 to 1989, falls into this category. Having merged the NFL with the rival AFL in 1964, Rozelle successfully remarketed the World Championship Game as the 'Super Bowl' and, with Roone Arledge of ABC, helped to ensure that *Monday Night Football* became a national institution.[87] Yet sports historians have to recognize that the postmodern world of sport that Murdoch and those who would emulate him have called into existence is very different from the one in which Rozelle so recently operated. It comprises, as David Andrews has indicated:

> ... sports franchises and/or leagues commandeered by – or indeed turned into transnational corporations seeking to add multiple revenue streams derived from the all important entertainment economy; sports spectacles manipulated by commercial media outlets pursuing the audience demographic most palatable to their corporate advertisers; and, sports stars as *de facto* embodied advertisements acting on behalf of their coterie of endorsement affiliations.[88]

While sports entrepreneurs remain important, their significance in the era of mediasport is secondary to that of entrepreneurs whose primary interests lie in the media. Among these Rupert Murdoch, for better or worse, is by far the most important, his achievements comparable to those 19th-century entrepreneurs whose achievements Schumpeter deemed 'heroic'. His triumph encapsulates a reformulation of the sports product with game forms and sports goods now clustered around a media-dominated sports-related service sector.

Notes

1 Neil Tranter, *Sport, Economy and Society in Britain 1750–1914* (Cambridge: Cambridge University Press, 1998), 14–15.
2 Derek Birley, *A Social History of English Cricket* (London: Aurum Press, 1999), 14–15, 47, 54.
3 Andrew Ritchie, 'The Origins of Bicycle Racing in England: Technology, Entertainment, Sponsorship and Advertising in the Early History of Sport', *Journal of Sport History*, 23, 3 (1999), 489–518.
4 Ritchie, 'Origins of Bicycle Racing in England', 490; Tranter, *Sport, Economy and Society*, 76.
5 Wray Vamplew, *Pay Up and Play the Game: Professional Sport in Britain, 1875–1914* (Cambridge: Cambridge University Press, 1988), 281–83; an especially useful and succinct analysis of the relationship between industrialization and the emergence of modern sport. See also the elegant summary by Neil Tranter, 'The Patronage of Organised Sport in Central Scotland, 1820–1900', *Journal of Sport History*, 16, 3 (1989), 227.
6 George H. Sage, 'The Sporting Goods Industry: from Struggling Entrepreneurs to National Businesses to Transnational Corporations', in Trevor Slack, ed., *The Commercialisation of Sport* (London: Routledge, 2004), 33–36. See also Peter Levine, *A.G. Spalding and the Rise of Baseball: The Promise of American Sport* (New York: Oxford University Press, 1985), 71–95.
7 Steven A. Riess, *City Games: The Evolution of American Society and the Rise of Sports* (Urbana, IL: University of Illinois Press, 1991), 252–59.
8 Vamplew, *Pay Up and Play the Game*, 281.
9 C.A. Tony Joyce, 'Sport and the Cash Nexus in Nineteenth Century Toronto', *Sport History Review*, 30, 2 (1999), 140–68.
10 Richard Holt, *Sport and Society in Modern France* (Basingstoke: Palgrave, 1981), 86–88.
11 Mike Cronin, 'Arthur Elvin and the Dogs of Wembley', *The Sports Historian*, 22, 1 (2002), 100–14.
12 N.L. ('Pa') Jackson, *Sporting Days and Sporting Ways* (London: Hurst & Blackett, 1932), 101; see also Dilwyn Porter, 'Revenge of the Couch End Vampires: The AFA, the FA and English Football's "Great Split", 1907–14', *Sport in History*, 26, 3 (2006), 406–28.

13 Sir Frederick Wall, *Fifty Years of Football 1884–1934* (Cleethorpes: Soccer Books, 2006), 105–6; first edn 1935.

14 Stephen Morrow, *The New Business of Football: Accountability and Finance in Football* (Basingstoke: Macmillan, 1999), 1–2.

15 'United's New Order Banks on Business as Usual', *The Guardian*, 14 May 2005, Sport, 2–3.

16 James Walvin, *The Only Game: Football in Our Times* (Harlow: Longman, 2001), 200; Morrow, *New Business of Football*, 1. In the United Kingdom 'plc' indicates a 'public limited company'.

17 Matthew Taylor, 'Football Archives and the Historian', *Business Archives*, 78, (1999), 1–12.

18 Richard Evans, *David Lloyd: How to Succeed in Business While Really Trying* (London: Bloomsbury, 1996), 165. For the transformation of rugby union in this period see Adrian Smith, 'Civil War in England: the Clubs, the RFU, and the Impact of Professionalism on Rugby Union, 1995–99', in Adrian Smith and Dilwyn Porter, eds, *Amateurs and Professionals in Post-War British Sport* (London: Frank Cass, 2000), 146–88.

19 Stephen Hardy, 'Sport in Urbanizing America: a Historical Review', *Journal of Urban History*, 23, 6 (1997), 675–708.

20 Huw Richards, *A Game for Hooligans: The History of Rugby Union* (Edinburgh: Mainstream, 2006), 136–37.

21 See Dilwyn Porter, 'British Sport Transformed: Sport, Business and the Media since 1960', in Richard Coopey and Peter Lyth, eds, *Business in Britain in the Twentieth Century: Decline and Renaissance?* (Oxford: Oxford University Press, 2009), 330–55.

22 See the comments on A.G. Spalding's attitude to professionalism in Charles P. Korr, 'Two Paths to Player Power', *Sports Historian*, 22, 1 (2002), 60–78.

23 Steven W. Pope, 'Amateurism and American Sports Culture: the Invention of an Athletic Tradition in the United States, 1870–1900', *International Journal of the History of Sport*, 13, 3 (1996), 290–309.

24 Lawrence W. Fielding and Lori K. Miller, 'The ABC Trust: A Chapter in the History of Capitalism in the Sporting Goods Industry', *Sport History Review*, 29, 1 (1999), 44–58; see also Richard O. Davies, *Sports in American Life: A History* (London: Blackwell, 2006), 90–91.

25 Sean Hamil, 'A Whole New Ball Game? Why Football Needs a Regulator', in Sean Hamil, Jonathan Michie and Christine Oughton, eds, *A Game of Two Halves? The Business of Football* (Edinburgh: Mainstream, 1999), 23–37.

26 'Farewell Lap', *Economist*, 22 November 1975, 37.

27 Stephen Aris, *Sportsbiz: Inside the Sports Business* (London: Hutchinson, 1990), ix.

28 Korr, 'Two Paths to Player Power', 61.

29 'Overnight Millionaires Struggle to Focus on Current Field of Vision', *Guardian*, 7 February 2009, Sport, 14.

30 Mark H. McCormack, *What They Don't Teach You at Harvard Business School* (London: Collins, 1984), 71–72. Fred Biletnikoff of the Oakland Raiders is singled out as an example for business executives to emulate. 'Fred Biletnikoff was effective … He was a star at his position'.

31 John Harvey-Jones, *Making It Happen: Reflections on Leadership* (London: Collins, 1988), 141–44.

32 Steven J. Overman, '"Winning Isn't Everything. It's the Only Thing": The Origin, Attributions and Influence of a Famous Football Quote', *Football Studies*, 2, 2 (1999), 77–99.

33 Will Carling and Robert Heller, *The Way To Win: Strategies for Success in Business and Sport* (London: Little, Brown and Co., 1995), 35–36, 167–74.

34 Richard Evans, *David Lloyd*, 160.

35 Terry Gourvish, 'Business History: Cinderella, Prince Charming or Ugly Sister?', in Kurt Bayertz and Roy Porter, eds, *From Physico-Theology to Bio-Technology: Essays in the Social and Cultural History of Biosciences: a Festschrift for Mikulas Teich* (London: Clio Medica, 1995), 6–19.

36 Geoffrey Jones and Jonathan Zeitlin, 'Introduction', in Geoffrey Jones and Jonathan Zeitlin, eds, *The Oxford Handbook of Business History* (Oxford: Oxford University Press, 2007), 1–6.

37 Charles Harvey and John Wilson, 'Redefining *Business History*: An Editorial Statement', *Business History*, 49, 1 (2007), 1–7.

38 Douglas Booth, *The Field: Truth and Fiction in Sports History* (London: Routledge, 2005), 210–11.

39 Richard Coopey, Sean O'Connell and Dilwyn Porter, *Mail Order Retailing in Britain: A Business and Social History* (Oxford: Oxford University Press, 2004), 231.

40 For links between business history and other forms of history see Patrick Fridenson, 'Business History and History', in Jones and Zeitlin, eds, *Oxford Handbook of Business History*, 9–36.

41 Martin Polley, *Moving the Goalposts: A History of Sport and Society since 1945* (London: Routledge, 1998), 4–5.

42 For definitions see Booth, *The Field*, 8–13.

43 David Jack, ed., *Len Shackleton, Clown Prince of Soccer: His Autobiography* (London: Nicholas Kaye, 1955), 78.

44 Matthew Taylor, *The Leaguers: The Making of Professional Football in England, 1900–1939* (Liverpool: Liverpool University Press, 2005), 100–1, 116–17, 270–72.

45 Peter Levine, *A.G. Spalding and the Rise of Baseball: The Promise of American Sport* (New York: Oxford University Press, 1985), 71–95. See also Steven A. Riess, *Sport in Industrial America 1850–1920* (Wheeling, IL: Harlan Davidson, Inc, 1995), 37–39.

46 See Alfred D. Chandler Jr, *The Visible Hand: The Managerial Revolution in American Business* (Cambridge, MA: Harvard University Press, 1977), 498–500 on the USA as the 'seed-bed of managerial capitalism'; also *Scale and Scope: The Dynamics of Industrial Capitalism* (Cambridge, MA: Harvard University Press, 1990), 14–46.

47 Peter Lyth, review of Jones and Zeitlin, eds, *Oxford Handbook of Business History*, in *Business History News: The Newsletter of the Association of Business Historians*, 35 (Spring 2008), 14–17.

48 Stephen Hardy, 'Entrepreneurs, Organizations and the Sport Marketplace: Subjects in Search of Historians', *Journal of Sport History*, 13, 1 (1986), 27–28.

49 Pamela L. Cooper, 'The "Visible Hand" on the Footrace: Fred Lebow and the Marketing of the Marathon', *Journal of Sport History*, 19, 3 (1992), 244–56.

50 Michael E. Porter, *The Competitive Advantage of Nations; with a new introduction* (New York: The Free Press, 1998) 175; see also Wladimir Andreff, 'Comparative Advantage of Nations', in Wladimir Andref and Stefan Szymanski, eds, *Handbook on the Economics of Sport* (Cheltenham: Edward Elgar, 2006), 331–34.

51 For *jettinho* see Jonathan Wilson, *Inverting the Pyramid: A History of Football Tactics* (London: Orion, 2008), 103–5.

52 Porter, *Competitive Advantage of Nations*, 30. That globalization is a complex and multi-faceted process is largely acknowledged by sports historians working in this area. 'It has become accepted knowledge that simple theories like cultural imperialism, Americanisation, hybridisation or creolisation, mask the complications of cultural exchange and adaptation'. Paul Dimeo, 'The Local, National and Global in Indian Football: Issues of Power and Identity', *Football Studies*, 5, 2 (2002), 84.

53 Richard Light and Wataru Yasaki, 'Breaking the Mould: J League Soccer, Community and Education in Japan', *Football Studies*, 6, 1 (2003), 37–50; 'J League Soccer and the Rekindling of Regional Identity in Japan', *Sporting Traditions*, 18, 2 (2002), 31–46.

54 David L. Andrews, 'Dead and Alive? Sports History in the Late Capitalist Moment', *Sporting Traditions*, 16, 1 (1999), 73–83.

55 Naomi R. Lamoreaux, Daniel M.G. Raff and Peter Temin, 'Economic Theory and Business History', in Jones and Zeitlin, eds, *Oxford Handbook of Business History*, 38.

56 Tranter, *Sport, Economy and Society*, 96.

57 James B. Jefferys, *The Distribution of Consumer Goods: A Factual Study of Methods and Costs in the United Kingdom in 1938* (Cambridge: Cambridge University Press, 1950), 370–71. It is encouraging to see that some historians are at last making use of the Census of Distribution; see Mike Huggins and Jack Williams, *Sport and the English, 1918–1939* (London: Routledge, 2006), 70–73.

58 Richard Holt, *Sport and the British: A Modern History* (Oxford: Oxford University Press, 1989), 133.

59 Jefferys, *Distribution of Consumer Goods*, 370; 'There's No Business Like Sports Business', *The Financial Times*, 23 September 1996, 14.

60 Wladimir Andreff, 'The Sports Goods Industry', in Andreff and Szymanski, eds, *Handbook on the Economics of Sport*, 27–39.

61 John Bale, 'The Changing Place of Football: Stadiums and Communities', in Jon Garland, Dominic Malcolm and Michael Rowe, eds, *The Future of Football: Challenges for the Twenty-First Century* (London: Frank Cass, 2000), 93–101.

62 Stephen Hardy, 'Entrepreneurs, Organizations, and the Sport Marketplace', 14–33; 'Entrepreneurs, Organizations, and the Sport Marketplace', in Steven W. Pope, ed., *The New American Sport History: Recent Approaches and Perspectives* (Urbana: University of Illinois Press, 1996), 341–65.

63 'Tigers and Rabbits', *Economist*, 30 July 1960, 14–15.

64 George H. Sage, 'The Sporting Goods Industry: from Struggling Entrepreneurs to National Businesses to Transnational Corporations', in Trevor Slack, ed., *The Commercialisation of Sport* (London: Routledge, 2004), 29–51.

65 For the story of Fred Perry sportswear see Fred Perry, *An Autobiography* (London: Hutchinson, 1984), 148–59.

66 Hardy, 'Entrepreneurs, Organizations, and the Sport Marketplace', 20–24.

67 Martin Ricketts, 'Theories of Entrepreneurship: Historical Development and Critical Assessment', in Mark Casson, Bernard Yeung, Anuradha Basu and Nigel Wadeson, eds, *The Oxford Handbook of Entrepreneurship* (Oxford: Oxford University Press, 2006), 33–58; see also Geoffrey Jones and R. Daniel Wadhwani, 'Entrepreneurship', in Jones and Zeitlin, eds, *Oxford Handbook of Business History*, 501–28.

68 J. Stanley Metcalfe, 'Entrepreneurship: An Evolutionary Perspective', in Casson et al., *Oxford Handbook of Entrepreneurship*, 59–90.

69 For Chapman see Neil Carter, *The Football Manager: A History* (London: Routledge, 2006), 49–62.

70 Ricketts, 'Theories of Entrepreneurship', 34–38.

71 Mickey Duff (with Bob Mee), *Twenty and Out* (London: CollinsWillow, 1999), 106–7.

72 Jones and Wadhwani, 'Entrepreneurship', 502–5, 515–16.

73 See Levine, *Spalding*, 89–91.

74 Holt, *Sport and Society in Modern France*, 85–86.

75 John Weaver and Joan Tamorria Weaver, '"We've had no punctures whatsoever": Dunlop, Commerce and Cycling in *fin de siècle* Australia', *International Journal of the History of Sport*, 16, 3 (1999), 94–112.

76 Holt, *Sport and Society in Modern France*, 85–86, 96–101.

77 See Dave Russell, *Football and the English: a Social History of Association Football in England, 1863–1995* (Preston: Carnegie Publishing, 1997), 42–45; Matthew Taylor, *The Association Game: A History of British Football* (Harlow: Pearson Longman, 2008), 70–73.

78 Podoloff quoted in Donald Fisher, 'The Rochester Royals and the Transformation of Professional Basketball, 1945–57', *International Journal of the History of Sport*, 10, 1 (1993), 20–48. For profit versus utility-maximization see Vamplew, *Pay Up and Play the Game*, 77–80.

79 Rodney Fort and James Quirk, 'Cross-subsidization, Incentives and Outcomes in Professional Team Sport Leagues', *Journal of Economic Literature*, 33, 3 (1995), 1265–90. See also Stefan Szymanski, 'The Sporting Exception and the Legality of Restraints in the US', in Andreff and Szymanski, eds, *Handbook on the Economics of Sport*, 730–34; J.R. Shackleton, 'Football as a Business', *Football Studies*, 3, 1 (2000), 80–88.

80 Braham Dabscheck, 'The Unstable Oligopoles that are Professional Team Sports', *Sporting Traditions*, 15, 2 (1999), 93–100.

81 See Kent M. Krause, 'Regulating the Baseball Cartel: A Reassessment of the National Commission, Judge Landis and the Anti-Trust Exemption', *International Journal of the History of Sport*, 14, 1 (1997), 55–77.

82 For Rickard's career see Davies, *Sports in American Life*, 171–75.

83 McCormack, *What They Don't Teach you at Harvard Business School*, 161–72.

84 Ian Andrews, 'From a Club to a Corporate Game: the Changing Face of Australian Football, 1960–99', *International Journal of the History of Sport*, 17, 2/3 (2000), 225–54.

85 See John Horne, *Sport in Consumer Culture* (Basingstoke: Palgrave, 2006), 49–51.

86 See David L. Andrews, 'Sport in the Late Capitalist Moment', in Slack, ed., *The Commercialisation of Sport*, 10–16; for BSkyB and rugby league see Tony Collins, *Rugby League in Twentieth Century Britain* (London: Routledge, 2006), 181–84.

87 For Rozelle see Davies, *Sports in American Life*, 238–46.

88 Andrews, 'Dead and Alive? Sports History in the Late Capitalist Moment', 74–75.

13 Religion

William J. Baker

From the earliest glimmer of civilization to the most recent World Cup, religion and sport have been intimately connected. Not surprisingly, religious devotion and competitive sport share essential attitudes and modes of behaviour. They hold similarly polarized visions of good and evil, heaven and hell, winning and losing. Both require total commitment and discipline of adherents whose efforts contribute to communal values and beliefs. Rabid sports fans and religious fanatics drink from a common cup of true belief. Both religious and sporting events thrive on rituals, ceremonies and liturgies; each spawns self-defining creeds and mythologies. As religion and sport have interacted vigorously throughout history, the terms of their relationship have changed over time, but never has the one been far removed from the other.[1]

At the outset of the human saga, people imaginatively spun yarns to explain their origins, their fears and their hopes. Often as not, these narratives featured physically competitive activities. Victorious foot races, wrestling matches and ball games supposedly won the favour of the gods. Thus did Mayan and Aztec ball players, African village wrestlers and ancient Olympic track champions all compete not only for survival and personal esteem but also for the honour of pleasing their various tribal deities. For the most part, antiquity mixed cultic ceremonies and athletic rituals so thoroughly that it was difficult, if not impossible, to separate the two.[2]

At ancient athletic festivals around the rim of the Mediterranean, even the Greeks hedged their rational bets by devoting an inordinate amount of time, energy and rhetoric to their gods. For the original Olympic Games, a heavy dose of religious processions, chants, burnt offerings and prayers consumed fully half of a five-day programme of activities. Greek poets and philosophers often spoke critically of narrow athleticism, but assumed the interest of the gods in these matters. The poet Pindar lauded athletic 'high gifts shaped by the gods' that enabled the stellar runner, wrestler, or boxer to 'cast his anchor at the furthest shore of happiness, honored of heaven'.[3]

Medieval Christendom raised the ante by effectively providing time, place and encouragement to sport. After the worship hour on Sunday morning, labourers played and competed athletically, and all the more so on seasonal and liturgical holidays. Not by coincidence did some Italians schedule *palio* races on holy days honouring church saints; nor was it thought inappropriate for English Shrove Tuesday festivities to feature rugged games of peasant football. Apparently a competitive exercise of handball, a distant forerunner of tennis, originated in medieval French monasteries. The first simple set of rules for tennis fittingly came from the hands of a 16th-century Italian monk, Antonio Scaino de Salo.[4]

From other corners of religious life in 16th-century Europe, sport came under a barrage of criticism. In Geneva, John Calvin and his reform-minded friends chafed at the association of sport with old Catholic holidays. More specificallly, they denounced the gambling and the desecration of the Christian sabbath (Sunday) that often accompanied sport. Calvin's Dutch and English disciples mimed Geneva in banning a wide range of competitive physical activities. In England, these 'Puritans' sought to enforce their principles, but with limited success. In 1617 King James I issued a *Declaration on Lawful Sports*, declaring that his subjects should be allowed to engage freely in any 'harmless recreation' that did not cause an 'impediment or neglect of Divine Service'. This principle survived a Puritan victory in the civil war and a subsequent decade of Puritan rule largely because English country folk clung to a more casual, traditional way of life that featured festive, playful holidays.[5]

Negative Puritan attitudes toward sport flourished more in the North American colonies than in England. Especially in New England, early settlers prohibited cock-fighting, bowling, horse-races and all those other sportive activities that encouraged gambling and desecration of the Christian sabbath. What Puritan colonists took away with one hand, though, they gave back with the other. Their capitalist impulse produced sporting equipment and events more attuned to the Protestant ethic than to Puritan pulpit harangues. All the while, militia training sessions featured wrestling, foot races and competitive marksmanship, enterprises eagerly endorsed by undergraduates at Harvard, Yale and the College of New Jersey (Princeton), institutions created for the training of young Protestant divines.[6]

England, meanwhile, was undergoing a social upheaval that was to transform the entire sport-and-religion equation. As industrialism, urbanization and commercialism worked together to dissolve the ties that bound people to customary beliefs and behaviours, old informal, spasmodic patterns of play gave way to codified, organized sport. In the 18th century, rules and governing bodies emerged for cricket, the turf, golf and boxing, followed in the 19th century by football in modernized soccer and rugby variants. The early years of Victorian England witnessed the birth of a complex, controversial mentality called muscular Christianity.[7]

Derived from the public school commitment to chapel prayers as well as cricket and football fields of play, muscular Christianity was at first a term of derision associated with a liberal Anglican priest and novelist, Charles Kingsley. In good Victorian fashion, another popular novelist, Thomas Hughes, penned *Tom Brown's Schooldays* (1857) as a vivid, memorable depiction of the muscular Christian's zestful pugnacity and pious fair-play principles. A novel and a Bible: Tom Brown and King James quickly became cosy travel companions for soldiers, governors and emigrants making their way to the distant corners of the British Empire.[8]

The Young Men's Christian Association (YMCA), created in London several years prior to the publication of *Tom Brown's Schooldays*, became the organizational expression of muscular Christianity. An evangelical antidote to urban vice, the YMCA provided lodging, Bible study and prayer groups to young men newly come to the city. Amidst vigorous debate, health and physical exercise programmes soon became staple items on the YMCA menu. Competitive athletics stood in the wings, eager to join the party. However, not in Britain, where conservative leaders clung to an older evangelical ethos that remained largely hostile to modern sport. The North American YMCA took an altogether different route. In both Canada and the USA, by the 1870s large new gymnasia were being built in most major cities; by the 1880s, numerous local YMCAs sponsored track meets, tennis tournaments, and baseball, football and ice-hockey clubs.[9]

Out of this muscular Christian womb sprang a new team sport, basketball, which now nearly rivals soccer (football) in global appeal. Basketball is perhaps the only major team sport that was created instantaneously, without a long evolutionary history. Its conception occurred in mid-December 1891 and its birthplace was Springfield, Massachusetts, the home of a YMCA leadership-training college. James Naismith, the inventor of basketball, was a Canadian son of Scottish immigrants. A stocky muscular Christian incarnate, Naismith had studied for the Presbyterian ministry while playing rugby at anglophile McGill University. Upon graduation he decided that he could best serve God and the world by devoting his energies to the YMCA rather than to a parish ministry. For professional training, Naismith went south to the YMCA training college in Springfield.[10]

An imaginative mentor assigned a tough seminar project: a new indoor game for the winter snowy months, a game that would appeal to young men accustomed to highly competitive baseball and football (gridiron) games. Naismith's proposal entailed 13 rules typed by a school secretary and pinned to a bulletin board just before the class gathered. For goals that could be suspended on an elevated running track around the little Springfield gym, Naismith asked the janitor for wooden boxes. No boxes could be found – would peach baskets suffice? The name of Naismith's new game was obvious, the game itself instantly successful. Basketball's energetic but non-violent tempo recommended it to women as well as men; its relatively low cost made it a game favoured by church, school and university teams. The international character of the YMCA facilitated the global diffusion of the gospel of basketball throughout the world, especially in Asia and South America.[11]

However, not in the British Isles, where reasonably mild winters allowed year-round outdoor play. As the need for an indoor gym was not urgent, few were built. British males also initially ignored basketball because it was reminiscent of a popular schoolgirls' game, netball. Instead, soccer became the winter game much preferred by both Anglicans and nonconformists in Britain. By the 1880s churches and chapels sponsored nearly half of all the soccer clubs in the industrial North and Midlands. The sporting parson became a solid fixture in Victorian popular culture, though more often than not he was garbed as a cricketer. For a time, Anglican priests regularly led their teams toward Lancashire and Yorkshire county championships. Cricket references appeared frequently in the sermons of the day. 'Put your whole soul into the game and make it your very life', urged one vicar; 'hit clean and hard at every loose ball, for the least bit of work that helps anyone nearer God is blessed work and gladdens the Captain's heart'.[12]

This enthusiastic religious acceptance of sport can be easily dismissed as a manipulative, practical ploy to attract youth. Many religious folk used sport merely as a fish-hook to nab unsuspecting youths into the church and to hold them there. Others, though, endorsed sport as a healthy, moral adjunct to religious commitment. Anglo-American proponents of the social gospel especially carved out an important place for sport within their theological rationales and institutional programmes. In 1906 seven Anglican churches in Ottawa, Canada, organized an Amateur Athletic Association for the supervision of tennis matches, track meets, and baseball, softball, basketball and ice-hockey games. Toronto's Protestant churches linked energetic arms with local Catholic churches to supervise 128 ice-hockey squads competing in an interchurch league.[13]

The 'father' of the American social gospel, Washington Gladden, liberally declared wholesome recreation and sports to be 'means of grace' and 'helps to a godly life – just as truly as is the prayer meeting itself'. However, Gladden resisted the impulse to have churches actively sponsor athletic teams and leagues, ironically placing himself in the company of conservative southern churches the evangelical principles of which prompted them to denounce sport for all the usual puritanical reasons. While Gladden hesitated, other American advocates of the social gospel barged forward with revolutionary schemes of church-based recreational and sports activities. A notable example occurred at St George's Episcopal Church on New York City's lower east side, under the rectorship of the Reverend William Rainsford. When Rainsford arrived in 1882, St George's was in a bad way, struggling to survive the removal of its members away from the numerous German immigrants flooding into that area of the city. For theological as well as practical reasons, Rainsford demanded that the church be a place of play as well as prayer and preaching. He supervised the construction of a five-story parish house with an entire floor given to bowling alleys, gymnastics and billiards rooms, wrestling mats and a basketball court. Little wonder that St George's flourished under Rainsford's ministry.[14]

Wielding a baseball bat in one hand and a tennis racket in the other, Rainsford and his clerical kind provided clout to the public park-and-playground movement that thrived in the late 19th century. On behalf of their immigrant congregations, Protestant ministers, Catholic priests and Jewish rabbis lobbied city officials for both the physical space and trained supervision necessary for good playgrounds. Whereas only 41 American cities provided supervised playgrounds in 1906, no fewer than 500 did so by 1915. New York City's first commissioner of parks, Charles B. Stover, was a graduate of Union Theological Seminary. Like James Naismith and many other young men of that era, Stover initially planned to engage in a formal church ministry, but later pursued a larger commitment to social needs, a commitment that included recreation and sport. Playground enthusiasts thought their work valuable not merely for its provision of fresh air and physical exercise for city youths who would otherwise be confined to unhealthy ghettos, but also as a means of turning unlettered immigrants into responsible, patriotic citizens. On the playground, Irish, Italian and Eastern European newcomers learned to lay aside their alien ways, to 'play by the rules' like good citizens should. As the founder of the national Playground Association, Henry S. Curtis, put it, playground athletic contests gave 'large opportunities for social and moral culture'. Team games especially taught youths the virtue of unselfish co-operation. The mentality that inspired a boy to play baseball or basketball primarily for the team's success, insisted Curtis, was the same sense of loyalty that bred good citizenship and patriotism.[15]

For all its isolationist tendencies, the USA danced to a patriotic jig common to industrialized Western nations. As World War I approached, religion, sport and patriotism meshed to form a most formidable trinity. Eric Hobsbawm suggests a familiar metaphor: 'Nationalism became genuinely popular essentially when it was drunk as a cocktail. Its attraction was not just its own flavour, but its combination of some other component or components which, it was hoped, would slake the consumers' spiritual and material thirst'. Around the turn of the century, national anthems soared and flags waved as religion, sport and nationalism mixed to make a patriotic cocktail that citizens happily swallowed.[16]

This habit was deeply embedded in European history. Early in the 19th century, Friedrich Ludwig Jahn, a Lutheran minister's son, created German gymnastics groups to inspire patriotic resistance to foreign (Napoleonic) rule. Jahn's motto, '*frisch, frei, frolich, fromm*' (bold, free, joyous, pious) yoked religion and sport to a revolutionary nationalist ideology. Later in the 19th century, German gymnasts placed their athleticism and piety on a new altar: the chauvinistic policies of Bismarck's German Empire. By 1898, in public ceremonies as well as private gatherings, more than 6,000 gymnastics clubs proudly displayed the Kaiser's new black, white and red flags. Mass gymnastics performances served as a cultural glue bonding citizens of diverse religious, class and regional interests.

Before soccer became the rage, gymnastics flourished as Europe's international sport of choice. Like the Germans, Scandinavian gymnasts performed with the assurance that their efforts had a unifying effect on their nation. For most of western and central Europe, though, gymnastics mirrored both historic conflicts and deep cultural divisions. Czech nationalists, the Sokols, annually donned red shirts and caps for mass formations and gymnastic displays in Prague. Set to patriotic music, these demonstrations against Austro-Hungarian rule readily called to mind the 15th-century resistance (and martyrdom) of Jan Hus to Rome's dominance. Still beholden to Rome, gymnasts in Belgium and France stood at the centre of a complex mixture of religious and patriotic issues. Catholic church-sponsored gymnastics and sports networks emerged in opposition to liberal anti-clerical measures. Beginning in Belgium in 1892 and in France in 1903, they organized annual flag-waving gymnastics festivals with inspirational speeches and frequent renditions of the national anthem.[17]

Anti-semitism lurked in the back rooms of most gymnastics clubs, and in the 1890s a movement for muscular Judaism emerged as a minor but important part of the Zionist impulse for Jews to protect themselves by creating their own territorial state. At the very first Zionist Congress, at Basel in 1897, a prominent German neurologist and social critic, Max Nordau, announced that 'muscular Judaism' would determine the future of Jews. 'There are no people in the world for whom gymnastics could have so splendid a result as for us', he later explained. 'Gymnastics is destined to fortify us in the body and spirit. It will give us self-confidence'.[18]

Lacking a gymnastics tradition, Britain promoted outdoor sports, especially ball games of all shapes and sizes. For England, Ireland, Scotland and Wales, different games served distinct nationalistic purposes, blending always with age-old religious affiliations and rhetoric. This religion-tinged patriotism took its most dramatic sportive form on the Celtic fringe of the British Isles.

In Catholic Ireland, sport became a protest against both the cultural and political dominance of England. As the Catholic Archbishop of Cashel, Thomas William Croke, framed the issue, centuries of English rule in Ireland had rendered old Irish pastimes and native athletic games 'not only dead and buried but in several locations ... entirely forgotten and unknown'. Despite severe political disagreements, Croke in 1884 co-operated with an old Fenian, Michael Cusack, to create the Gaelic Athletic Association (GAA) with the intention of resurrecting ancient Irish games. Actually, the centrepiece of GAA inventiveness, Gaelic football, turned out to be a newly created game with the magical Gaelic reference in its name. Hurling was another story: an authentically ancient stick-and-ball game retrieved from the trash heap of medieval history. The hurley joined the harp as romantic symbols of Irishness. To Charles Stewart Parnell's stormy public meetings, GAA bodyguards came armed with hurley sticks. So many outstanding hurling players were arrested after the Easter Rebellion in 1916 that the final match of the Wolfe Tone Tournament had to be played in a prison camp in Wales. Lest the religious aspect of this patriotic athleticism be lost from view, the largest stadium for Gaelic games – Croke Park in Dublin – is named after the ecclesiastical patron of the Gaelic Athletic Association. In 1908 the editor of the GAA's annual report noted that the 'ideal Gael' was an athlete who loved 'his religion and his country with a deep and restless love'. A jigger each of religion, sport and patriotism made a heady cocktail for Irish consumption.[19]

In Scotland, too, religion and sport worked in tandem with nationalism. Having adopted 'fitba' shortly after England's Football Association was formed in 1863, fiercely proud Scotsmen liked nothing better than to beat their 'auld enemy' at their own game.

An annual international match, begun in 1872, provided salve for the Scottish wounds of ancient military debacle and more recent political and economic subservience. Soccer especially thrived in industrialized Glasgow. In 1893, construction began on a monstrous new stadium, Hampden Park, that would hold 150,000 spectators. Presbyterian patriarchs had reason to fear this new popular passion. To the presbytery of Dumbarton, the Saturday evening sporting paper that carried all the football scores seemed nothing less than 'the young man's Bible and sermon'.[20]

Catholics as well as Protestants apparently read that Bible. Ever since the potato famines of the 1840s, Irish immigrants had flooded into Scotland searching for jobs, food and shelter. As industrial Glasgow attracted both Ulster Protestant and Irish Catholic immigrants, soccer clubs emerged to represent each faction. The Rangers, founded in 1872, catered to Protestant players and fans. The Celtic originated in 1888 as a means of raising money to feed needy Irish Catholic families in the East End of Glasgow. Cheering the Celtic had the further benefit of keeping the Catholic community focused on Catholic heroes in an alien land. Little wonder that a Celtic–Rangers match around the turn of the century approximated a holy war.[21]

Less violently, but no less seriously, Welshmen combined amateur rugby with chapel sermons and gospel hymns as emblems of Welsh nationalism. From the smallest non-conformist community to sprawling industrial centres, religious revivals and rugby matches were the two constants for miners and mine owners alike. In 1905, when a Welsh team beat an undefeated All Blacks squad at Cardiff Arms Park, the game was ballyhooed for its implications of Welsh prowess. The victory 'kicked the last great religious revival into touch', says one scholar. 'Rugby', says another, 'took its place alongside chapel, choirs, self-education, and socialist unionism in the new canon of Welshness'.[22]

Cricket took a similar place of honour in the Victorian canon of Englishness. 'English cricket', says Richard Holt, 'came to have a special place in the Anglican heart beside the *King James Bible* and the *Book of Common Prayer*'. An 1891 edition of the *Encyclopedia Britannica* suggested that cricket's requirement of 'patience, calculation, and promptness of execution' made it 'the national game of Englishmen'. The structure of the game certainly brought sport and morality together in a combination most English. Cricket rewarded skill, not raw strength; courage and patience, not overt aggression or violence. At its highest level, it honoured age-old class distinctions by having Gentlemen (amateurs) and Players (professionals) come onto the field through different gates, then compete with gentlemanly zeal.[23]

At its late-Victorian and Edwardian zenith, cricket took on a hallowed reputation. Curates and parsons played the game alongside mechanics and aristocrats. Lord's, the appropriately named home of the premier Marylebone Cricket Club, became sacred ground trod with reverence by those who 'weighed and pondered and worshipped', as Kipling phrased it, 'and practiced day by day'. Mention of England's greatest cricket hero, W.G. Grace, often reminded journalists of a favourite old Protestant hymn: Amazing Grace, how sweet the sound of his mighty bat swatting the ball. Colonials especially worshipped at the cricket altar. On the eve of World War I, cricket was the unrivalled British Empire game, providing colonial rivalries as well as emulation of English ways. Before soccer became the global game and before the USA became the world's policeman, cricket was the only game on which the sun never set. If God was an Englishman, as English sporting patriots assumed, He seemed to smile most on a good game of cricket.[24]

Of all the turn-of-the-century sports scenes doused with the double potion of religious and patriotic passion, the modern Olympic Games heads the list. Its founder, Baron

Pierre de Coubertin, came of age in an era filled with preachments about racial pride, national vigour and physical prowess, issues that coloured all Coubertin's efforts towards a renewal of the Olympics. Equally important, though, was a set of religious assumptions stoking Coubertin's fire. Having spent his youth in a French Jesuit school studying for the priesthood, he replaced orthodox Catholic creeds with a fashionable humanistic philosophy, Comte's 'religion of humanity'. He came to view sports as a new kind of religion with its own dogma and rituals, 'but especially with religious feeling'. On behalf of his new-found faith, Coubertin poured money and energy towards the creation of a modern Olympics as means of achieving 'a ceaselessly reborn humanity'. Aggressively he preached his new gospel of sport: 'Have faith in it', he wrote to a friend, 'pour out your strength for it; make its hope your own'.[25]

A doctrinal renegade, Coubertin nonetheless linked religious terms and sensibilities to sport. He thought of athletes as 'new adepts', disciples of an emergent 'muscular religion'. He viewed spectators and coaches as 'the laity of sport'; as he constructed the International Olympic Committee, he envisaged 'a college of disinterested priests'. In creating Olympic festivals, Coubertin employed rites and ceremonies reminiscent of the liturgical traditions of his Catholic youth: sacred sites and oaths, invocations, hymns, holy processions, wreaths and crowns. Like worshippers of old, Olympic spectators would be exposed to a plethora of colourful sights and sounds that would, by quadrennial repetition, achieve the status of ritual.[26]

For all his use of traditional Christian symbols and rhetorical flourishes, Coubertin drew heavily from contemporary anthropology and classical scholarship to recover a pre-Christian 'human religion' and 'cult of humanity'. Pope Pius X rightly suspected the 'pagan-seeming' character of the scheme. Not until 1906, when some gymnasts gave a private exhibition at the Vatican, did the Pope give his blessing to the modern Olympics. In Coubertin's final public comment, a recorded message broadcast at the 1936 Berlin Games, he underscored the 'religious sense' at the heart of Olympism past and future. Though changed by time and circumstance, a religious spirit remained 'in essence the same as that which led the young Greeks, zealous for victory through the strength of their muscles, to the foot of the altar of Zeus'.[27]

The impulse to link religion, sport and patriotism reached its apex during World War I when Canadian and American YMCAs co-operated with their respective governments to furnish Allied troops with canteen items, reading material, spiritual and moral consultation, and recreational gear.

A Canadian, Fred J. Smith, worked so effectively at YMCAs in wartime Britain that King George V honoured him with the Order of the British Empire medal for distinguished service on behalf of the war effort. Once the USA entered the war, notable American college coaches and athletes volunteered to direct lively YMCA programmes of boxing, basketball, baseball and volleyball at American military bases in France.[28]

These YMCA wartime activities represented the last gasp of Protestant dominance on the religion-and-sport scene. Especially in the USA, Jewish and Catholic immigrants set new sportive directions. Both eagerly took to baseball as a means of acculturation, and even more to basketball, the origins of which coincided with their own arrival in the USA. The first Jewish basketball star, Barney Sedran, was born of immigrant parents in 1891, the same year James Naismith invented basketball. American Jews and the hoops game grew up together, the one supporting the other. Not by coincidence, the centre of basketball enthusiasm for more than half a century was New York City, where about a million Jews lived on the lower east side. In addition to basketball, professional boxing welcomed pugilists sporting the six-pointed Star of David. From 1920 to 1939, popular lightweight fighters Benny Leonard and Barney Ross headed a parade of 18 Jewish champions.[29]

Prior to the momentary dominance of Jewish boxers, a similar hunger for fortune and fame drove Irish Catholic fighters into the ring. America's first athletic superstar was a second-generation Irishman, heavyweight champion John L. Sullivan. By 1930 amateur boxing tournaments headed the sports menu of the new Catholic Youth Organization (CYO), founded in Chicago as a rival to the Protestant-biased YMCA. The CYO's larger purpose, as articulated by zealous patron Bishop Bernard Sheil, was to combat juvenile delinquency. A 'shiner and a bloody nose' in a CYO ring would be better than thievery and gang wars on the streets of Chicago, reasoned Sheil as he proudly sent three CYO boxing champions to represent the USA at the Berlin Olympics in 1936.[30]

In addition to boxing programmes, the CYO sponsored community centres, bowling tournaments, track and swim meets, and summer softball leagues. Except for boxing, though, basketball mattered most. Years before the CYO, basketball attracted Chicago's Catholic community. In 1923 Loyola University, Chicago's premier Catholic institution, initiated an annual National Catholic Basketball Tournament. By 1930 this all-Catholic event drew some 30 teams representing virtually every section of the city. For the first CYO boys' and girls' tournaments in 1931, no fewer than 140 teams registered; by the next year, 2,200 players competed on 182 teams. Nor could the CYO remain confined to Chicago; it quickly became a national organization. Through the Depression and World War II, the unlikely tandem of basketball and boxing provided abundant athletic outlets for Catholic youths.

Catholic colleges and universities also aggressively sponsored athletic programmes. From Boston College in New England to Santa Clara in California, Catholic campuses especially leapt into the gridiron game of American football, a game that had been adapted from British rugby by university students at Harvard, Yale and Princeton. In the 1920s a tiny unknown college, Notre Dame, emerged as a national powerhouse. Coached by Knute Rockne, a Norwegian immigrant and convert to Catholicism, Notre Dame quickly became a beacon of pride for American Catholics beleaguered by Ku Klux Klan bigotry. In a highly successful quest for national championships, the 'Ramblers' (the earliest popular nickname for the 'Fighting Irish') frequently travelled east to New York City and west to Los Angeles. Rockne adroitly integrated religious symbolism with athletic mythology to create a mystic blend of efficient superiority and inspiration. The famous line, 'Win one for the Gipper', supposedly came from the mouth of a dying All-American halfback, George Gipp, but was actually Rockne's invention that would be later embellished by Hollywood actor Ronald Reagan.[31]

One of the great American monuments to the blend of religion and sport is a colourful stained-glass bay window in the Episcopal cathedral church of St John the Divine on the upper west side of Manhattan. The idea originated with Bishop William Thomas Manning's vision for 'a visible and beautiful symbol' to inform visitors 'not only that the Church does not frown on sport but that the Church sympathizes with it, encourages it and rejoices in it'.[32] At the sports bay window's inception in 1925 (just one year after Eric Liddell's refusal to run on Sunday at the Paris Olympics), Bishop Manning was engaged in a heated public debate over the issue of Sunday amusements and sports contests. On one occasion, he declared that 'a well-played game of polo or of football or of any other game is, in its own place and in its own way, just as pleasing to God as a beautiful service of worship in a cathedral'.[33] In response to Bishop Manning's solicitations, American sports clubs, Olympic officials and individual athletes eagerly funded the construction of the sports bay window. Finally finished shortly after World War II, it graphically depicts in vivid reds and blues numerous athletic events ranging from baseball games and boxing matches, to horse-races and auto races.[34]

By the time the sports bay window was completed for public view, the relation of religion to sport in the USA had taken a dramatic turn to the right. Earlier religious enthusiasm for sport had come from liberal and moderate elements of religious opinion, with most evangelicals remaining hostile for reasons that reached all the way back to Puritan opposition to sport. In the wake of World War II, though, evangelicals turned to sport as an ally in the effort to defeat godless Communism and to win souls to Christ. The crusade began in the late 1940s with a fiery young revivalist, Billy Graham, inviting big-name athletes and coaches onto his podium (often in a massive football stadium) to tell of their religious conversion. Biographical blurbs invariably cited Graham's youthful play on southern baseball diamonds and his more recent enthusiasm for golf. The Billy Graham organization always referred to itself as a 'team'. In good ball-game fashion, they 'kept score' of every convert and publicized their numbers 'won to Christ'. Billy Graham's ideal American in the 1950s was not a salesman in a grey flannel suit, but rather a man in a baseball cap and football jersey, making a pitch for Jesus.[35]

Several new organizations emerged to represent this youthful American marriage of sport and evangelical religion. The first one, born in the midst of the Korean War, set its sights on winning Formosa (Taiwan) to Christ by means of evangelistic crusades wrapped around basketball exhibitions. The core purpose of this anti-Communist crusade remained firm; the group's name changed several times before finally settling on Sports Ambassadors. In 1966 it was superceded by Athletes in Action, a travelling squad of athletes offering track meets, wrestling matches and basketball games for both domestic and international consumption. After each event, the athletes provided homilies and spiritual consultation.

Similarly evangelical but largely confining itself to the American scene, the Fellowship of Christian Athletes (FCA), originated in 1954, was destined to become the largest and most influential of all these mergers of athleticism and evangelicalism. The brainchild of Oklahoman Don McClanen, the FCA initially thrived on the financial support of an old Methodist major league baseball magnate, Branch Rickey, who years earlier had brought Jackie Robinson onto the roster of the Brooklyn Dodgers. The FCA encouraged coaches and athletes at professional, college and schoolboy levels to form 'huddles' for Bible study, prayer and religious discussions. At summer camps in the Colorado Rockies, big-name coaches and athletes declared their faith and displayed their athletic skills to hundreds of eager participants. At its 50th anniversary in 2004, the FCA claimed weekly gatherings of some 7,000 student huddles and more than 14,000 members attending dozens of summer camps.

Behind this public merger of evangelical religion and sport lay a quiet revolution in professional locker rooms. A traditional bastion of bawdy behaviour and off-colour conversation, dressing rooms cleaned up their acts under the puritanical influence of born-again Christians. The change began in professional (NFL) football. As Sunday games made church attendance difficult, Protestant and Catholic enthusiasts arranged devotional services prior to each game in a room just off the central dressing room. Invariably simple, mostly fundamentalist and heavy on self-motivation, this 'chapel' ministry in the 1960s spread throughout the National Football League and then to major league baseball's locker rooms. By 1970, many club payrolls included chaplains.

The best organized of all the chapel ministries appropriately emerged in the National Association for Stock Car Auto Racing (NASCAR), the sport that has been most receptive to the evangelical ethos. The roots of NASCAR lie deep in the American South, the regional heart of fundamentalism. Moreover, the sport itself is incredibly dangerous, threatening sudden death for famous and unknown drivers alike. Little wonder that an organization called Motor Racing Outreach employs a full-time director and five chaplains to cover each of the 39 races on the gruelling Winston Cup circuit.

Prior to the races, chaplains lead Bible study for drivers and crews, provide child-care facilities for families, then pray an invocation to begin each race. The NASCAR speedway is littered with religious signs, pamphlets and tracts. Superstar Dale Earnhardt walked and drove with a devil-may-care swagger, but carefully taped Biblical verses on his dashboard – until his instant demise in 2001 when he crashed head-on into the wall on the final lap of the Daytona 500.

Largely because of this evangelical persuasion, televised American athletic contests are regularly punctuated with fingers pointed to the heavens and post-game credit offered to Jesus for decisive home runs, touchdowns, knock-outs and last-second baskets. British and Australian athletes occasionally do the same, but their infrequency proves the rule: that only in the USA is an evangelical ethos sufficiently strong to render these religious gestures acceptable, if not admirable, to a nationwide audience.

What is good for the Protestant evangelical goose is also good for the black Muslim gander. Until Americans went on a xenophobic binge of fear in the wake of the tragedy of 11 September 2001, Allah rivaled Jesus in the mantra of victorious African-American boxers, basketball players and track stars. Heavyweight champ Cassius Marcellus Clay led the way in the 1960s, changing both his religious point of view and his name (to Muhammad Ali). College and professional basketball giant Lew Alcindor soon followed. As Kareem Abdul-Jabbar, he marched at the head of an impressive parade of African-American athletes from all sectors of American sport trumpeting the rituals and moral code of the Islamic faith. A few enjoyed moments of sporting fame; most did not. Easily recognized by their newly adopted unfamiliar names, they joined a chorus of Protestant, Catholic and Mormon athletes demonstratively singing the praise of their various deities.[36]

This 'commingling' of American religion and sport prompts some commentators to view modern sports as a new religion of the masses: a 'natural', 'folk', or 'civil' religion with all the passion, ceremonial drama, moral mandates, sacred space and holy shrines customarily associated with age-old expressions of faith. Charles Prebish, a university professor of religious studies, sees 'a complete identity' between sport and religion in the USA. Rather than sport and religion exhibiting merely similar or parallel attractions, sport '*is* religion for growing numbers of Americans', says Prebish. For many Americans, this 'sport religion' is 'a more appropriate expression of personal religiosity than Christianity, Judaism, or any of the traditional religions'. With some quibbling over the nuances of this assertion, a similar point of view informs the perspective of Catholic theologian Michael Novak as well as the eclectic contributors to Joseph L. Price's provocative *From Season to Season: Sports as an American Religion*.[37]

Mircea Eliade's study of mythologies and 'the sacred in its entirety' stands behind much of this depiction of sport as a modern religion. As that view attracts believers from all quarters, Jack Higgs, a former grid athlete for the US Naval Academy and now a retired professor of literature, leads a small body of argument to the contrary. Loose references to '*sacred*' sites, holidays and national interests associated with modern sport, says Higgs, obscure the classic religious quest for '*the Holy*', a mysterious, inconceivable transcendence that is alien to the mass consumption of modern sport. Today's meshing of religion and sport makes for an 'unholy alliance': a marriage made on earth, not in heaven, 'a religion that is at once so strange, so new, and so very, very old'.[38]

Notes

1 Rudolph Brasch, *How Did Sports Begin? A Look at the Origins of Man at Play* (New York: McKay, 1970); Johan Huizinga, *Homo Ludens: A Study of the Play Element in Culture* (Boston: Beacon, 1950). For ancient and early-modern contours of this interaction culminating in Britain and the USA, see William J. Baker, *Playing with God: Religion and Modern Sport* (Cambridge, MA: Harvard University Press, 2007).

2 Vernon L. Scarborough and David R. Wilcox, eds, *The Mesoamerican Ballgame* (Tucson: University of Arizona Press, 1991) and Karl Taube, *Aztec and Maya Myths* (Austin: University of Texas Press, 1993).

3 Ludwig Drees, *Olympia: Gods, Artists and Athletes*, translated by Gerald Onn (New York: Praeger, 1968); M I. Finley and H.W. Pleket, *The Olympic Games: The First Thousand Years* (London: Chatto & Windus, 1976).

4 For a colourful but ill-researched account of medieval sport and religion, see Robert W. Henderson, *Ball, Bat, and Bishop: The Origins of Ball Games* (New York: Rockport, 1947); cf. John Marshall Carter, *Sports and Pastimes of the Middle Ages* (Columbus, GA: Brentwood University, 1984); John Armitage, *Man at Play: Nine Centuries of Pleasure Making* (London: Frederick Warne, 1977), 17–48; Thomas S. Hendricks, *Disputed Pleasures: Sport and Society in Preindustrial England* (New York: Greenwood, 1991), 13–68; William J. Baker, *Sports in the Western World* (Urbana: University of Illinois Press, 1988), 42–55.

5 Hendricks, *Disputed Pleasures*, 69–127; Dennis Brailsford, *Sport and Society: Elizabeth to Anne* (London: Routledge & Kegan Paul, 1969); Robert W. Malcolmson, *Popular Recreations in English Society, 1700–1850* (Cambridge: Cambridge University Press, 1973).

6 Bruce C. Daniels, *Puritans at Play: Leisure and Recreation in Colonial New England* (New York: St Martin's Press, 1995) and Nancy L. Struna, *People of Prowess: Sport, Leisure, and Labor in Early Anglo-America* (Urbana: University of Illinois Press, 1996).

7 For this cultural transformation, see Baker, *Sports in the Western World*, 85–114; J.H. Plumb, *The Commercialisation of Leisure* (Reading: University of Reading Press, 1973); Hugh Cunningham, *Leisure in the Industrial Revolution c. 1780–1880* (London: Croom Helm, 1980); Richard Holt, *Sport and the British: A Modern History* (Oxford: Clarendon Press, 1989); Allen Guttmann, *From Ritual to Record: The Nature of Modern Sport* (New York: Columbia University Press, 1978); Richard D. Mandell, *Sport: A Cultural History* (New York: Columbia University Press, 1984), 132–57.

8 See David Newsome, *Godliness and Good Learning: Four Studies on a Victorian Ideal* (London: John Murray, 1961); J.A. Mangan, *Athleticism in the Victorian and Edwardian Public School: The Emergence and Consolidation of an Educational Ideology* (Cambridge: Cambridge University Press, 1981); J.A. Mangan, *The Games Ethic and Imperialism: Aspects of the Diffusion of an Ideal* (London: Viking, 1986).

9 For the British roots of the YMCA, see Clyde Binfield, *George Williams and the YMCA: A Study in Victorian Social Attitudes* (London: Heinemann, 1973); for the American version of muscular Christianity, see Clifford Putney, *Muscular Christianity: Manhood and Sports in Protestant America, 1880–1920* (Cambridge, MA: Harvard University Press, 2001) and Tony Ladd and James A. Mathisen, *Muscular Christianity: Evangelical Protestants and the Development of American Sport* (Grand Rapids: Baker Books, 1999).

10 Bernice Larson Webb, *The Basketball Man: James Naismith* (Lawrence: University Press of Kansas, 1973).

11 For the basketball story as told by its creator, see James Naismith, *Basketball: Its Origin and Development* (New York: Association Press, 1941); for its global dissemination, see Elmer L. Johnson, *The History of YMCA Physical Education* (Chicago: Association Press, 1979).

12 For the soccer saga in Britain, see Tony Mason, *Association Football and English Society 1863–1915* (Sussex: Harvester Press, 1980) and James Walvin, *The People's Game: The Social History of British Football* (London: Allen Lane, 1975).

13 Canada's blend of sport and religion is evident in Alan Metcalfe, *Canada Learns to Play: The Emergence of Organized Sport, 1807–1914* (Toronto: McClellan and Stewart, 1987) and Gerald Redmond, *The Sporting Scots of Nineteenth-Century Canada* (East Brunswick, NJ: Associated University Presses, 1982).

14 See 'Sweetening the Gospel with Sport', in Baker, *Playing with God*, 64–84; for a regional contrast, see 'When Dixie Took a Different Stand', 85–107.

15 On the intersection of the social gospel, the playground movement and organized sport, see Dominick Cavallo, *Muscles and Morals: Organized Playgrounds and Urban Reform, 1880–1920* (Philadelphia: University of Pennsylvania Press, 1981) and Stephen Hardy, *How Boston Played: Sport, Recreation, and Community, 1865–1915* (Boston: Northeastern University Press, 1982).

16 S.W. Pope, *Patriotic Games: Sporting Traditions in the American Imagination, 1876–1926* (New York: Oxford University Press, 1997) is the best analysis of this concoction.

17 For Belgium gymnastics and religious patriotism, see Jan Tolleneer, 'Gymnastics and Religion in Belgium (1892–1914)', *International Journal of the History of Sport* 7 (1990), 335–47; and 'The Dual Meaning of "Fatherland" and Catholic Gymnasts in Belgium, 1892–1914', *International Journal of the History of Sport* 12 (1995), 94–107. Mandell, *Sport*, 158–74, provides a summary of the continental gymnastics movement. For France, see Richard Holt, *Sport and Society in Modern France* (London: Macmillan, 1981).

18 See Mandell, *Sport*, 174–77.

19 See Mike Cronin, *Sport and Nationalism in Ireland: Gaelic Games, Soccer, and Irish Identity since 1884* (Dublin: Four Courts Press, 1999); cf. W.F. Mandle, *The Gaelic Athletic Association and Irish Nationalist Politics, 1884–1924* (London: Christopher Helm/Gill and Macmillan, 1987); John Sugden and Alan Bairner, *Sport, Sectarianism and Society in a Divided Ireland* (Leicester: Leicester University Press, 1993).

20 Grant Jarvie and Graham Walker, eds, *Scottish Sport in the Making of the Nation: Ninety Minute Patriots?* (Leicester: Leicester University Press, 1994).

21 W.J. Murray, *The Old Firm: Sectarianism, Sport and Society in Scotland* (Glasgow: John Donald, 1984).

22 See Gareth Williams, 'How Amateur Was My Valley: Professional Sport and National Identity in Wales, 1890–1914', *British Journal of Sports History* 2 (December 1985), 248–69.

23 Sporting parsons and cricketers are sprinkled throughout Holt, *Sport and the British* (quotation p. 264), and H.A. Harris, *Sport in Britain* (London: Paul, 1975), but especially see Coral Lansbury, 'A Straight Bat and a Modest Mind', *Victorian Newsletter* 49 (Spring 1976), 9–18.

24 Kipling quoted in Coral Lansbury, 'A Straight Bat and a Modest Mind', *Victorian Newsletter* 49 (Spring 1976), 9–18. In addition to Mangan's *Games Ethic and Imperialism*, see Allen Guttmann, *Games and Empires: Modern Sports and Cultural Imperialism* (New York: Columbia University Press, 1994), 15–40. Gerald R. Gems, *The Athletic Crusade: Sport and American Cultural Imperialism* (Lincoln: University of Nebraska Press, 2006) documents the American version of this imperial tendency to wrap the flag around sport and religion.

25 The essential source is John J. MacAloon, *This Great Symbol: Pierre de Coubertin and the Origins of the Modern Olympics* (Chicago: University of Chicago Press, 1981).

26 On religious themes in modern Olympism, see Siegfried von Kortzfleisch, 'Religious Olympism', *Social Research: An International Quarterly of Political and Social Science* 37 (1970), 231–36 and John J. MacAloon, 'Religious Themes and Structures in the Olympic Movement and the Olympic Games', in Fernand Landry and William A.R. Orban, eds, *Philosophy, Theology, and History of Sport and Physical Activity* (Miami, FL: Symposia Specialists, 1978), 161–69.

27 Pierre de Coubertin, quoted in John MacAloon, *This Great Symbol: Pierre de Courbertin and the Origins of the Modern Olympic Games* (Chicago: University of Chicago Press, 1981), 141.

28 On the athletic efforts of the YMCA in World War I, see Nancy K. Bristow, *Making Men Moral: Social Engineering during the Great War* (New York: New York University Press, 1996) and Wanda Ellen Wakefield, *Playing to Win: Sports and the American Military, 1898–1945* (Albany: State University of New York Press, 1997).

29 For Jewish contributions to American sport, see Peter Levine, *From Ellis Island to Ebbets Field: Sport and the American Jewish Experience* (New York: Oxford University Press, 1992) and Steven A. Riess, ed., *Sports and the American Jew* (Syracuse: Syracuse University Press, 1998).

30 The standard source on the CYO, Roger L. Treat's *Bishop Sheil and the CYO* (New York: Julian Messner 1951), has now been superceded by Gerald R. Gems, 'Sport, Religion, and Americanization: Bishop Sheil and the Catholic Youth Organization', *International Journal of the History of Sport* (August 1993), 233–41. For the earlier great Irish-American boxer, John L. Sullivan, see Michael T. Isenberg, *John L. Sullivan and His America* (Urbana: University of Illinois Press, 1988).

31 Murray Sperber's *Shake Down the Thunder: The Creation of Notre Dame Football* (New York: Henry Holt, 1991) is a big book that copes admirably (critically) with the big task of doing justice to Notre Dame.

32 Bishop William Thomas Manning, 'The Church and Wholesome Play', *Playground* 20 (January 1927), 537.

33 Bishop William Thomas Manning, 'Manning Extols Value of Sport', *New York Times*, 31 December 1925.

34 Joe D. Willis and Richard D. Wettan, 'Religion and Sport in America: The Case for the Sports Bay in the Cathedral Church of St John the Divine', *Journal of Sport History* 4, 2 (1977), 189–207; cf. Baker, *Playing with God*, 168–70.

35 See 'Making a Pitch for Jesus', in Baker, *Playing with God*, 193–217. This story is largely embedded in daily American newspapers and popular periodicals, but see Brian W.W. Aitken, 'The Emergence of Born-Again Sport', *Studies in Religion* 13 (Autumn 1989), 391–405 and James A. Mathisen, 'From Muscular Christians to Jocks for Jesus', *Christian Century* 109 (1–8 January 1992), 12–13.

36 See Thomas Hauser, *Muhammad Ali: His Life and Times* (New York: Simon and Schuster, 1891) and David Remnick, *King of the World: Muhammad Ali and the Rise of an American Hero* (New York: Random House, 1998). For Mormons and sport, Richard Ian Kimball, *Sports in Zion: Mormon Recreation, 1890–1940* (Urbana: University of Illinois Press, 2003) is splendid.

37 Charles S. Prebish, *Religion and Sport: The Meeting of the Sacred and the Profane* (Westport, CT: Greenwood, 1993), 25–26; Michael Novak, *The Joy of Sports: End Zones, Bases, Baskets, Balls, and the Consecration of the American Spirit* (New York: Basic Books, 1976); Joseph L. Price, *From Season to Season: Sports as American Religion* (Macon, GA: Mercer University Press, 2001). Also, see Craig A. Forney, *The Holy Trinity of American Sports: Civil Religion in Football, Baseball, and Basketball* (Macon, GA: Mercer University Press, 2007) and Christopher H. Evans and William R. Herzog, II, *The Faith of Fifty Million: Baseball, Religion, and American Culture* (Louisville: John Knox Press, 2003).

38 Robert J. Higgs and Michael C. Braswell, *An Unholy Alliance: The Sacred and Modern Sports* (Macon, GA: Mercer University Press, 2004); cf. Robert J. Higgs, *God in the Stadium: Sports and Religion in America* (Louisville: University Press of Kentucky, 1995). See Tara Magdalinski and Timothy J.L.Chandler, eds, *With God on their Side: Sport in the Service of Religion* (London: Routledge, 2002).

14 Imperialism

S.W. Pope[1]

Early historians from Herodotus to Gibbon examined the rise and fall of empires as perhaps their underlying theme and produced what we would now refer to as 'imperial histories'.[2] Historians of the modern era continued this tradition of studying empires and the attendant processes of 'imperialism'. Indeed, as Stephen Howe writes, 'it could be said that *all* history is imperial – or colonial – history, if one takes a broad enough definition and goes far enough back'.[3] Although the dominant imperial systems have collapsed, their legacies persist throughout the world today as well as within the historiographical landscape wherein there is a thriving debate among scholars as to what has replaced the empires of old. For example, does the USA and its allies, transnational companies, financial and media institutions, or the forces of 'globalization' constitute a new imperial world order?[4] In the recent literature on empire, scholars have explored how European imperialism was a precursor to globalization.[5] One key work within this tradition is Niall Ferguson's *Empire: The Rise and Demise of the British World Order and the Lessons of Global Power* wherein he postulates that, for good or ill, the British Empire paved the way to an interconnected world and as such, remains the empire's most enduring and revolutionary legacy.[6]

The terms empire, imperialism, colonialism, globalization, neo-imperialism, neo-colonialism, cultural imperialism and post-colonialism are complex terms infused with ideological passions and thus with fiercely contested meanings. A review of this broader terminology and debate is beyond the scope of this chapter.[7] Although identifying something as 'imperial' or 'imperialistic' tends to have negative or derogatory association, historians have long debunked the idea that any empire – whether Western or Eastern, Christian or Muslim – can be viewed as either exclusively bad or exclusively good. Empires, like nations, as Grave Vuoto writes, 'are far too complicated, encompass too many time frames, and contain too many diverse occurrences to be reduced to simple characterizations – especially since former empires form the basis of much that our contemporary society has decided to preserve'.[8] This generalization is substantiated in the vast literature traversing virtually all academic fields in the humanities and social sciences wherein postmodern and post-structural theories have been intertwined, according to Howe:

> … sometimes productively, often explosively – with issues of nationalism, community, and ethnicity, class, and perhaps above all [with] those of 'race' … At every step, these enormously varied attempts to study, and sometimes to judge, the history of empires have posed questions of the relationships among knowledge, identity, and power.[9]

Early examples

Sport and imperialism are inextricably entangled phenomena. Empire has a long trajectory within not only world history, but also sports history. As Donald Kyle writes, '[e]very society has sport, but the nature of that sport is influenced by local conditions and culture – by historical contexts and not just race, national character, or zeitgeists'.[10] Complex societies, large cities or states and especially empires, with more people in hierarchical societies, with greater territories and military concerns, and with autocratic centralizations of political power, need more elaborate spectacular performances as forms of communication and rituals of power.

The spectacle model arose in the hydraulic civilizations of Mesopotamia and Egypt, and spread to the civilizations of the Late Bronze Age.[11] It entailed highly orchestrated performances associated with the royal court. Trained performers gave entertaining physical demonstrations and monarchs ritually and predictably achieved feats that communicated cosmic and social order and royal power. Also, to exert and affirm territorial and imperial control, empires fostered more violent spectacles: humans and animals suffered and often died in orchestrated combats and royal hunts.[12]

Sports historians have produced a voluminous literature on ancient sport – particularly that of the Greeks and Romans. Donald Kyle's chapter in this collection provides an incisive overview of this historiography. The literature is strongest on the use of mega-events and spectacles. While the ancient Greeks developed a less centralized regional empire (with Athens as its epicentre), the Olympic model – owing to its location, the rivalry between city states, colonization and aristocratic display – succeeded as a form of cultural imperialism spreading as it did to influence local and Panhellenic contests and traditions such as torch races, events and crowns, organization and rules. Such festivals became more elaborate and spectacular – notably the Panathenaia of Classical Athens. As Kyle writes, 'after Alexander assimilated the Near Eastern models of kinship and spectacles, and founded numerous cities that spread Greek athletic facilities and traditions over vast territories, the Hellenistic Era was a spectacular age of statecraft and stagecraft'. Indeed, according to Kyle, the monarchs of large Hellenistic states 'used sport hegemonically to control and manipulate the lower orders, and to reinforce their socio-political superiority'.[13]

The function of ancient sporting spectacles to legitimize and solidify imperial elites' power has been well documented by historians. Perhaps one of the most enduring generalizations of this history is the way in which Roman rulers used such spectacles as 'bread and circuses' to bond the empire at home and export imperial ideas to the provinces. In terms of the development of ancient sport, the imperial administration and the emperor cult, Kyle writes, 'provided institutionalization and regularity for both (traditionally) Greek and Roman entertainments' and thus, the 'local and imperial levels were mutually reinforcing networks that created opportunities for the advancement of performers, patrons, and partisans'.[14] This long Greco-Roman imperial sporting tradition dissipated as a result of the demise of the Roman Empire's political and military hegemony as well as the more general demise of urban centres in the West.

To date, sports history remains overwhelmingly dominated by an implicit or explicit 'western' storyline. I would venture to guess that most academics in North America and Europe who teach the broad-ranging 'global' history of sport (and there are much fewer such courses taught than 10 or 20 years ago) continue to organize them along the well established storyline of 'sport in Western culture'.[15] In this rendering, the next 'phase' in the development of sport after the ancients is the long, dry spell of more austere localized folk games and fair venues within 'Medieval Europe'. Within this narrative, there was a fundamental disconnect between the vibrant, imperial sporting tradition of ancient Greek and Roman cultures and the decentralized, largely rural world which prevailed in Europe between the fifth and 16th centuries. At the end of this imagined millennial period, the growth of cities in larger, stronger, richer nation-states of the 'pre-modern' era of the 17th and 18th centuries enabled mostly European folk sports to be set on the path toward evolving into 'modern' sporting spectacles. In this narrative, the next critical stage in the development of sports history was the rediscovery of the vibrant, physical tradition of the ancients (especially the Greeks) and a rupture of the supposed dominance of the Church's focus upon the heavenly (as opposed to earthly infatuations). In this incantation, those in southern Europe during the 'Renaissance' were more likely to break with the hegemonic strictures of the Church from the 'evils' of the physical than those in northern Europe who were forced to negotiate with an emergent, formidable force known as Protestantism or Puritanism which strictly forbade the pleasures of the 'flesh' (which included active participation in leisure and sporting activities).[16]

Fortunately for the field of sports history, this narrative has become problematical by virtue of not only recent historical scholarship in medieval and pre-modern Europe but a fledgling scholarship on sport outside the terra firma of the still dominant transatlantic historiography. Although it may be premature to suggest that a fundamental revision of this sturdy narrative is underway, there is abundant scholarship, published during the past decade, which suggests that a revisionist interpretation of the global history of sport is at hand. To date, only Allen Guttmann has attempted such a synthesis, which employs his formidable breadth of reading in non-English language sources and his authoritative grasp of the abundant, international secondary literature on the first 5,000 years of sports history (particularly regional developments in Asia and Latin America) which are relevant to better understanding the history of sport and imperialism.[17]

Modern sport and the British Empire

The key development in the relationship between sport and imperialism centres upon the great European imperial rivalries in carving up much of the globe among themselves between the 17th and 20th centuries. Far and away the best documented force or entity in this critical historical process has been the British Empire. It has become almost cliché to claim that 'the British taught the world to play', although this is a sturdy theme within the voluminous scholarship on sport and imperialism.

The British imperial role in the spread of modern sport was one of the most productive areas within the literature between the 1970s and early 1990s.[18] An important intervention within this scholarly debate was Allen Guttmann's 1994 book *Games and Empires* wherein he challenged (what had become orthodoxy) whether the diffusion of modern sports from Great Britain and the USA constituted 'cultural imperialism'. Guttmann begged to differ from this narrative trope and suggested that imperialism is not the most accurate term to characterize what happened in the process of ludic diffusion. Much to the surprise of neo-Marxist scholars (whose assumptions, terminology and theoretical frameworks had been the target of Guttmann's polemics for nearly two decades),[19] Guttmann selected a term – 'cultural hegemony' (a veritable buzzword among 'left' scholars during the 1980s–90s – which had been indelibly associated with the Italian Communist political theorist Antonio Gramsci) to supersede 'imperialism'. According to Guttmann, the general export process can be characterized as follows: a horizontal diffusion in which colonial officers (administrators, clergy, educators, military personnel) took cultural practices with them overseas and effectively 'sold' them to the indigenous whom they conscripted into their service. The indigenous – primarily cosmopolitan upper-class types presumably at one with their masters – were the early adopters of the foreign cultural form which typically followed trade and other capitalist routes of global entrepreneurialism. The vertical diffusion of the cultural formation followed later and was the result of lower-class appropriation. The vertical class diffusion 'at home' seemed to be reproduced abroad.[20] In short, by the mid-1990s, it had become consensual among 'imperial' historians – many of whom were influenced by Marxist or neo-Marxist theories of imperialism – that the leading critic of this theoretical tradition within sports historiography (Guttmann) had been evidently converted to their conceptual terminology.

Britain and the colonies

Semantics aside, the British model remains the quintessential case study in sporting imperial history. The dominant themes of British imperial history old and new include the uniting of the kingdom; slavery and merchant trade; settling the 'new worlds'; Britain in India; further global growth of the empire; ruling the empire; being ruled; gender and sexuality issues; imagined communities contesting the empire; and decolonization.[21] Imperial historians differentiate between what was essentially two British Empires – one, a formal one constituted by various commercial and political outposts; and another more informal one, comprising cultural relationships (involving the spread of sports such as football, cricket and rugby).

Within the vast literature on the British Empire, the emphasis has been largely upon the winning and subsequent loss of political control of imperial power in the colonies. Until quite recently, the historiography focused upon political, diplomatic and military aspects of the imperial process. The inherent assumption of this historiographical tradition is that the empire was established, succeeded and ultimately failed due in large measure to the formidability of Britain's 'hard power' (e.g. imperial administrative structure, economic resources, geopolitical considerations and military power). Historians paid scant attention to the ways in which British domination was maintained through cultural ('soft') power – the ideas, beliefs, values and conventions diffused throughout the empire by British administrators, military officers, educators, missionaries and the like. With the ascendancy of the 'new' social and cultural history between the 1960s and 1980s (along with debates within Marxist and post-structural theories which informed this historiography), historians began to analyse the importance of ideology, social processes and the ways in which banal aspects of everyday life influenced empire at both home and abroad. Within this broader revisionist trend, an increasing number of historians turned their attention to the dynamics of class, race, ethnicity, gender, popular culture and even sport for better understanding imperial and colonial histories.

During the mid-1980s, sports historians began gravitating to imperialism as a suitable topic for investigation. The pioneering work in this new foray was J.A. Mangan's 1987 edited collection, *The Games Ethic and Imperialism* which featured essays by scholars whose work had been influenced by Mangan's important 1981 book, *Athleticism in the Victorian and Edwardian Public School*. The other early contribution to this fledgling area of sports historiography was Brian Stoddart's 1988 article 'Sport, Cultural Imperialism, and Colonial Response in the British Empire' which built upon (and extended arguments from) his previous 1984 book, *Cricket and Empire*.[22] Mangan and Stoddart placed sporting imperialism on the agenda and elevated it as a critical area of research which had been sorely neglected by both sport and mainstream imperial historians alike prior to the mid-1980s. Stoddart demonstrated how the power of British imperialism existed outside mere bureaucratic and military force. Drawing upon the theoretical literature that emanated from Antonio Gramsci, Pierre Bourdieu and the Centre for Contemporary Cultural Studies, Stoddart posited 'cultural power' as a concept for understanding how ruling ideas and conventions became hegemonic throughout the empire and at home. 'The success of this cultural power', Stoddart wrote:

> ... rested with the ability of the imperial system to have its main social tenets accepted as appropriate forms of behaviour and ordering by the bulk of the client population, or at least by those important sections of that population upon whom the British relied for the mediation of their ruling practices, objectives and ideology.[23]

Sport was a powerful but largely informal social institution and practice in the arsenal of British imperial cultural power which bolstered the growth of the empire during the second half of the 19th century.[24] Mangan has done more than any other historian in documenting sport's place within British imperial culture. As he shrewdly delineated its historiographical importance, late Victorian, Edwardian and 'later imperialism now [become] a matter of English social history, and in turn the task within a historical, anthropological and sociological framework becomes that of developing hypotheses about imperialism in relation to cultural ideals and processes'.[25]

During the past decade in particular, scholars have increasingly focused their attention on the cultural (as opposed to the political and military) aspects of empire. Within the 'new' imperial history scholarship of the past decade or so, scholars have attempted to better understand how Britons experienced the empire at home. Catherine Hall and Sonya Rose note how 'the majority of Britons most of the time were probably neither "gung-ho" nor avid anti-imperialists, yet their everyday lives were infused with an imperial presence'. For most Britons, the empire was just there – it was ordinary and banal, merely out there somewhere – and imperialism was an example of the 'taken-for-granted' aspect of Britain's place in the world.[26] Hall and Rose maintain that the 'everyday-ness' of empire 'held within itself a potential for visibility and contestation that its ordinariness disguised'.[27] In British Studies, as Kathleen Wilson writes, much of the exciting new work:

> ... has been influenced by a rather remarkable re-discovery of the importance of empire in the British past, and a simultaneous interest in the methodologies of social and cultural history and criticism to address questions about identity and difference in imperial settings.

One of the central themes has focused upon the 'role of representation in enabling, mystifying, or contesting British imperial power'.[28] Although mainstream imperial historians have not explored how the role of sport has been used to contest British imperial power, sports historians have demonstrated this vital legacy of British imperialism in a variety of geographical and cultural contexts. The 19th-century British (and later, American) colonial expansion and military power was widely attributed to the moral strength of its leaders, developed through a games education – within such a context, the imperial powers viewed the absence of sport in colonies as a sign of cultural, racial and moral inferiority. The physical body's commodification as an object of social reform during the age of high imperialism was linked to the depiction of the globe as an understandable entity.

> More elaborate international communications technologies allowed nations to be defined and compared as if they were physical bodies. In a sense, bodily metaphors helped make the unification of the globe possible at an ideological and conceptual level if not always so in actual practice.[29]

John Nauright and Timothy Chandler's *Making Men* and Patrick McDevitt's *May the Best Man Win* are two of the most noteworthy book-length examples of the recent, fledgling literature that explores how imperialism shaped masculinity at home and conceptions of masculine 'others' in the colonies.[30]

To date, the bulk of the scholarly literature has focused upon the export and adoption of British sporting practices in the colonies. Mangan has argued that 'within imperial sport racism, sexism and imperialism were as valid a Trinity as athleticism, militarism and imperialism. To a considerable extreme imperial sport was a favoured means of creating, maintaining and ensuring the survival of dominant male elites'.[31] Cricket and soccer (football) were played by British expatriates around the world. At first, in most countries, it was prominent citizens' wealthy children (many of whom went to England to complete their education or were taught by British schoolmasters), who adopted football, which spread to a large degree because English gentlemen played the game with gentlemen in other countries who saw the sport as embodying the virtues of the nation and their class, and saw the spreading of their game as a kind of missionary work. During this period of football's international diffusion, Great Britain had both a formal empire (in places such as India, Australia, Canada, South Africa) and an informal empire (South American countries) where British commercial interests and even the British prime minister often transcended the nominally independent governments. As such, the spread of football was intimately tied to British imperial and commercial power at the end of the 19th century, the role of the English gentlemen amateurs[32] as well as to a 'muscular Christian' packaging upon which William Baker has elucidated.[33]

The islands of the Caribbean are one of the prime examples of British sporting imperialism. As anthropologist Sidney Mintz has suggested, the islands of the Caribbean constitute the world's first 'modern' societies – formations linked through trade to the centres of Europe and structured as commodity producers by overseas European capital. The Caribbean has been a zone of contest and interaction since the end of the 15th century as competing empires vied for the domination and exploitation of thee region, resulting in the creation of at least four linguistically and culturally distinct zones (Hispanic, Francophone, Anglophone and Dutch-speaking) wherein invaders established their own sporting traditions.[34] Cricket, the quintessentially English game, took root throughout the British West Indies during the late 19th century between colonial elites and accompanying military establishments. The game was promoted through clubs and ultimately became known to the masses through the employment of black West Indian bowlers. The introduction of the game was accompanied by a code and culture embodied in the phrase 'it's not cricket' – which, as Douglas Midgett writes, 'impose[d] the ethos of the colonial master through its internationalization by the colonial subject'. However, in the Caribbean, cricket developed into a street and beach game, played by the emerging, postemancipation proletariat, appropriated by them and bearing the stamp of their new cultural expression which contributed to West Indian nationalism.[35]

Postcolonial sports historians have demonstrated how the cricket match became a critical site for examining social and cultural phenomena within Caribbean life and social history – a point introduced by C.L.R. James in his 1963 treatise on cricket and West Indian social history, *Beyond a Boundary*. James posed a classical rhetorical question: 'what do they know of cricket who only cricket know?' This remains *the* most discerning evocation of the general imperial relationship within global sport. Whereas the English, James wrote, 'have a conception of themselves bred from birth which … constitutes a national tradition' under-developed countries 'have to go back centuries to rebuild one. We, of the West Indies, have none at all, none that we know of'.[36]

Although fully mindful of the power of imperial sporting traditions, James was also wary of overstating the power of the British Empire. James' book – published in the same year as E.P. Thompson's monumental *The Making of the English Working Class* – challenged historians to understand the dynamic power relationships between ruling elites and the subjects. Whereas Thompson broke important new ground in excavating the history of working-class resistance in England to the onset of the industrial revolution, James provided a view of the way in which colonials negotiated with their imperial 'masters' within a hallowed leisure 'pastime' (in this case, cricket). As imperial historian Stephen Howe writes, within spheres such as:

> … music, sport, popular fiction, even TV soap opera, the postcolonial story is not just one of Euro-American dominance, nor 'nativist' cultural resistance, but an immensely rich, complex nexus of appropriation, adaptation, indigenization – and of influences flowing from Kinshasa to Brussels, Bombay to London, Havana to New York.[37]

Sports historians have documented this process in the various colonial settings of the British Empire. Fan Hong shows how modern, competitive sport was not a native Asian phenomenon; rather, it hailed from the West, initially with missionaries and subsequently by way of Asian students returning from Britain and the USA. Western traders, soldiers and sailors played key roles but no group was ultimately as influential in spreading sport and modern sporting values as the YMCA, which organized and initiated the Far Eastern Championship Games (FECG) in 1913 – the culmination of Protestant missionaries' half century efforts to Christianize the Chinese – whose emphasis on physical fitness had an important impact on China, Japan and other Asian countries. The FECG were, as Hong writes, 'a product of Western cultural imperialism designed to replace traditional Eastern cultures with Western ethics, morality and masculinity'; but simultaneously, the Games (like other Western sporting exports) ultimately provided a platform for the colonial recipients to demonstrate their athletic prowess within the host societies as well as within competitions with rival neighbouring countries.[38]

As a colonial outpost, sporting practices brought by migrants in the second half of the 19th century in Australia represented a way to recreate some of the cultural trappings of the distant motherland. Although the colonials were initially in awe of the British touring athletes, they were quick students and began to compete closely in cricket, rowing and rugby. Although their sporting success provided colonial self-confidence and allayed negative attitudes about their convict past and rumblings about Antipodean inferiority, Australians' deep attachment to cricket, the most English of sports, affirmed their strong bond with the empire. As Doug Booth and Colin Tatz write 'Australians showed little desire to express themselves as a truly independent state in the comity of nations' – a tendency which generally prevailed until at least World War II.[39] Historians, such as Greg Gillespie, have examined the meaning and function of 19th-century sporting tours of lacrosse, rifle shooting and cricket by colonials to Britain (e.g. the way in which a prominent British cricketer used the travel literary genre in a 1872 MCC tour to document the way in which sport played a prominent role in constructing a loyal, favourable image of Canadian national identity as well as a favourable destination for Britons).[40]

The general contours of the British imperial diffusion process also inhere in India (and the subcontinent). The work on this critical context/process has been advanced inexorably in recent years by the work of Boria Majumdar.[41] For more on the historiography of the subcontinent, see Chris Valiotis's regional review chapter in this book.

Even beyond the formal empire, the British model had a sturdy legacy. Wojciech Liponski notes the way in which the British sporting influence preceded either German or Swedish gymnastics within the Slavic region of eastern Europe. 'Though it never played any role in national movements', British sport and recreations became evident in Russia and Poland in the late 18th century and to such an extent, according to Liponski, that a 'history of British influences on the Slavonic countries would be a large book'.[42]

Sport and American imperialism

Until very recently the relationship of the USA to Europe was rarely described in terms of 'imperialism' or 'empire'; rather, the relationship was characterized as 'empire by invitation', or 'empire by consensus' as the by-product of 'Americanization', or, a the cusp of the 21st century, in vague terms such as an effect of the 'American Century'.[43] Whereas empire has been a central topic for British sports historians during the past couple of decades, with a couple of noteworthy exceptions, American sports historians have hardly analysed their subject within a global context – much less have they demonstrated that sport has had a role in the development of the modern empire and imperial mentalities.[44] American reticence to acknowledge the existence of an empire or a well-established imperial mentality in their nation's past (and present) derives from the way in which Americans have imagined themselves to be fundamentally unique, special, or 'exceptional'. Historians (including sports historians) have been seduced by the interpretive talisman of *American exceptionalism* – a term, as Trevor B. McCrisken, explains, used to describe 'the belief that the United States is an extraordinary nation with a special role to play in human history; a nation that is not only unique but also superior'.[45]

In his rhapsody to the imperial tradition, Niall Ferguson maintains that 'the United States is an empire but that it has always been an empire'.[46] In this fundamental sense, the development of an American sporting tradition was, thus, incubated within a wider struggle against European colonialism as well as within a messianic sense of national destiny to transform the continent and conquer new territories. The North American context provided the first case study for the export of British sport to the colonies.[47] As Elliott Gorn and Warren Goldstein have written, 'settlers did not just transport English pastimes to the New World; they also brought their *ideas* about the role of play ... across the ocean'. As such, the American colonists 'were heirs to England's bifurcated leisure heritage' which as various historians have documented, vacillated between Puritanical strictures regarding excessive physical and worldly joys and fantasizing upon how 'an easy, plentiful life could be recreated in terms of the old ideal of a leisurely paradise'. English colonists carried both traditions to North America and would attempt to shape their lives with them.[48] During colonial and antebellum times, Americans imported various British sports and games, and subsequently transformed them with newly invented rules, conventions, traditions and meanings after the Civil War.

Sport's place within an early imperial imagination was abetted by an Anglo-American Protestant religious ideology. Gerald Gems has shown how, as early as the 1820s, American missionaries arrived in Hawaii and preached the virtues of Protestantism and capitalism as part of a fledgling effort to introduce the WASP values of time and work discipline, initially through residential boarding schools but later through sport. By the 1840s, the missionaries, according to Gems, 'enjoyed great influence as advisors to the monarchy, instituting judicial, commercial and capitalist systems unfamiliar to the native population'. Such *ad hoc* efforts on behalf of missionaries evolved into a more systematic effort of 'sweetening the gospel with sport' (to use William Baker's felicitous phrase) by the YMCA beginning in the 1850s and 1860s. Baker has demonstrated how the American YMCA movement 'created a principled but flexible institution run by highly motivated, well-trained personnel, an institution equipped to carry the gospel of sport all over the world'. The YMCA was the most visible and effective organization to promote a white, middle-class, Anglo-Saxon, Protestant ideology of 'muscular Christianity' within Britain, in the USA and throughout the world. Although the American YMCA embraced sport sooner and more zealously than its British counterpart, muscular Christians in the USA, according to Baker, 'faithfully reproduced a highly class-conscious attitude that was born and bred in Britain'. In short, the trans-Atlantic ideology of muscular Christianity provided a crucial moral justification for the institutionalization in the USA and Britain as well as a sense of mission for the export of American and British sporting practices abroad. Imbued with notions of 'manifest destiny', social Darwinism and cultural superiority, the YMCA-styled muscular Christianity informed American imperial ideas with regard to sport.[49]

The early American imperial mentality during the 19th century is dramatized in two other representative 19th-century examples. First, the manner by which native Indians were forced into a type of internal colonialism by the federal government; executed with the help of educators, the boarding school was designed to assimilate Indians into white-American society by obliterating tribal identities and cultural heritage. Athletic programmes at Indian boarding schools represented a prop to American imperial thinking at home while simultaneously offering a venue for resistance to empire for native colonials. As C. Richard King writes, '[u]nder the guise of the more benevolent perspective of the social gospel, [Anglo] conquerors took on the "white man's burden" of educating, Christianizing, and civilizing the conquered. In the USA the process of cultural assimilation began with the forced relocation of tribes to allotted lands or reservations, the imposition of agricultural or vocational lifestyles at the expense of nomadic or traditional ones, and institutionalized education'.[50] Second, moving beyond the continental US boundaries, there are few more-incisive examples of an emergent American imperial mentality toward sport than the way in which sports entrepreneur Albert Spalding sought to market baseball – reputedly a distinctly American national pastime – as a global game, as well as to extend his sporting goods empire abroad. In his recent book, Thomas Zeiler demonstrates how Spalding's 1888 'world' baseball tour revealed the roots of the American empire. Zeiler shows how the baseball tourists carried dominant nationalistic values as well as a more general cultural ordering of races and societies; they combined 'an entrepreneurial spirit with principles as well as imperial intentions' and were part of a larger project of 'reshaping the world in the coming century under American leadership'. By linking baseball to a growing US presence overseas and 'viewing the world as a market ripe for the infusion of American ideas, products, and energy, Zeiler maintains, Spalding's world tour 'packaged business, technology, culture, and a political representation into a weighty national identity that promised a future of imperial eminence'.[51]

Beginning with baseball (a game which derived from British rounders and cricket), and then gridiron football (which derived from rugby and soccer) between the mid- and late 19th century, Americans transformed various British exports into forms which supposedly equated with the national character. While only basketball and volleyball were truly American creations, sporting leaders and cultural commentators systematically built a patriotic, nationalistic sports culture – a history which was especially well documented and analysed by sports historians during the 1980s and 1990s.[52] By the turn of the century, Americans sought to export 'their' games and evangelize the attendant values abroad as part of a more systematic imperialist effort. Gems shows how American imperialists found many rational uses for sport in 'the cultural interplay that transpired in colonialism'. As he writes, 'sport forms and practices offered myriad responses in the negotiation of culture, ranging from acculturation to political and surrogate warfare. The only assurances that were dictated confirmed that both dominant and subordinate groups would be changed in the process'. American imperialists created 'comprehensive athletic programs in schools, parks, playgrounds, and settlement houses, often run in close alliance with the YMCA, and attempted to inculcate an ideology of whiteness with varying degrees of success'.[53]

Baseball arrived abroad (in Cuba and Japan) as a function of British-styled, Victorian-era imperialism, trumpeting 'American' ideals by solidifying notions of white pre-eminence in the global racial order.[54] As Alan Cobley documents, American sporting traditions spilled into the Caribbean basin especially in the islands of the northern Caribbean (Cuba, Puerto Rico, Dominican Republic) and in the countries of Central America that border the Caribbean (Costa Rica, Nicaragua, El Salvador and Panama) – in most of these places, baseball penetrated the popular culture to such extent that it eventually achieved the status of the national sport.[55] Thomas Carter argues that baseball became the national sport in Cuba not because of American imperialism or colonialism, but because *criollos* – 19th-century island elites – made deliberate efforts to equate the game with a nascent Cuban nationalism to differentiate themselves from the Spanish. As a distinctive practice, baseball provided a symbolic discourse for an independent Cuba.[56] Sport, thus, provided a venue to define and dramatize what was allegedly 'American' and delineate how that differed from other cultures and peoples. Americans learned and applied a wider, racialized view of the world from the long-established British practices of denigrating colonial groups' practices within popular discourse/culture. There is, however, a need for historians to link more explicitly the expansive literature on 'race' and 'racism' to notions of American empire and imperial thinking (although Gems has done some of this in his book, *The Athletic Crusade*).

World War I was an important watershed in American imperial thinking with regard to sport. Americans emerged from it with a newfound sense of confidence in their ability to exert cultural and political muscle with other European powers as well as within the nation's established spheres of influence in the Caribbean and the Far East. Nowhere was this cultural swagger any more apparent than in Americans' attempt to convert Europeans to American sport. The 1919 Inter-Allied Games is a prime example of the way in which US military and sports leaders optimistically assumed that their sporting traditions would make the globe more 'American'. One prominent sportswriter thanked 'the American doughboy, and his confreres, the marine and the blue jacket', for bringing 'to the world over' sport's 'greatest revival'. Noting that baseball had always 'followed the flag' to Latin America and the Far East, the writer surmised that it had taken 'the big war' to introduce the game throughout Europe and as such the growing popularity of American sport signalled 'a new era for sport'. Although baseball never took hold in Europe as the writer naively imagined, the Inter-Allied Games is illustrative of how Americans broadened their sense of imperial sporting destiny. Assuming that just as the nation had supplanted Britain as the emergent global power, they also, as Mark Dyreson writes, 'assume[d] that their sporting traditions would make the globe more American – precisely as the British had believed about British sports and a British world culture a generation earlier'.[57] The impact of this process upon local and regional sporting cultures during the first half of the 20th century remains to be more fully explored by sports historians.

Historians have characterized the 1920s as the 'golden age' of American sport due to the ways in which post-war developments in media technologies enabled the creation of a first generation of national sporting heroes within a national mass culture (recognized in most households). One of the ironies with the growing global influence of the USA during the 1920s–30s is that Americans were increasingly less successful at exporting their sports. Barbara Keys demonstrates how prior to World War II American influence expanded not by persuading other nations to play their games (one exception would be baseball in Japan), but rather, by 'imbuing sport with moral and technocratic impulses, and in expanding its connections to the worlds of entertainment and mass culture'.[58] The Davis Cup illustrates this type of American influence on international sport. The tennis competition began in 1900 as a challenge by the Americans to the British and contained elements of both an imperialist mentality alongside a much longer Anglo–American dynamic within sports history. The Cup competition is a prime example of the longer historical pattern of American imitation and absorption of British models and then the gradual reversal of the process to a later, more reciprocal interrelationship within popular culture.[59] The Davis Cup competition is an example of the way in which Americans indigenized a cultural sporting import, namely tennis; created a nationalistic, international sporting competition; and pioneered a marketing effort which connected the competition to the world of entertainment (especially during the 1920s–30s). The USA quickly eclipsed their British rivals in the early 20th century (who won their last Cup in 1936) and then the Americans were surpassed by another British colony, Australia, which dominated the competition between the 1950s and the 1960s.[60]

Post-World War II developments

The aftermath of World War II provides a final, convenient watershed in the history of sports and imperialism. The numerous colonial independences that materialized during the 1940s–50s signalled the end of the once significant British Empire throughout the globe (as well as the demise of other European empires). It also marked the emergence of a Cold War rivalry between the USA and Soviet Union – which has been characterized by historians as the beginning of 'the American century'. The nation's official opposition to imperialism and empire notwithstanding, the desire to see 'subjected' people granted independence and self-government (as articulated in the Truman Doctrine) became the ideological basis for the development of a capitalist, anti-communist empire (and explicit leadership of the so-called 'free world'). American leaders chose 'containment' strategies over anti-colonialism sympathies (and embraced some of the worst despots in the second and third worlds) and in so doing, the self-professed, anti-imperialist nation ultimately proved not to be so anti-imperial after all. David Caute characterizes it as a modern imperial struggle between 'the pax Americana and the pax sovietica' – the Cold War encompassed an 'ideological and cultural contest on a global scale and without historical precedent'. In the process, 'culture' became a vehicle though which – in the absence of more conventional forms and frequencies of military engagement – the competing communist and capitalist orders sought to assert their civil, ideological and moral ascendancy.[61]

During this period, of course, the Olympics assumed a critical venue for the competition between the American and Soviet empires.[62] With regard to the way in which this process played out within the Soviet Union, historian Alfred Senn shows how Soviet sports officials in Lithuania had remade their realm into a clone of Moscow. 'They had created a centralized, hierarchical structure that valued mass sports activity as producing better workers and soldiers', Senn writes. In so doing, the Lithuanians:

> … demonstrated pride in good performance by their athletes, but they had repeatedly emphasized their concern for developing a collective consciousness in place of individualistic, star mentality. They had not had time to develop any outstanding athletes, but they had made clear the price that the Lithuanian people would have to pay for Soviet-style athletic success.[63]

John Soares has recently explored international ice-hockey among the USA, Canada, the Soviet Union and Czechoslovakia between 1947 and 1980, which he argued provides important clues to the eventual outcome of the Cold War.[64]

As the USA, the dominant Western political power, wrestled with the Soviet Union during the Cold War, Britain experienced an unravelling of its empire. The history of the Commonwealth Games provides insight into this process. Envisaged by John Ashley Cooper in the early 1890s, the Empire Games were first staged in Hamilton, Ontario (Canada) in 1930. During the 1930s–40s in the 'oath of allegiance to the British monarch, the singing of the British national anthem and the releasing of doves at the opening ceremony', Matthew Taylor notes, 'there was a conscious effort to establish the Games as a symbol of imperial unity at a time when formal political control was weakening'. Adapting to the broader political developments, the event was renamed the British Empire and Commonwealth Games in 1952, and in 1966 and 1974 respectively, the words 'Empire' and 'British' were dropped, leaving only the Commonwealth Games.[65] Michael Dawson has explored the multiple and conflicting local meanings of the 1954 Commonwealth Games (held that year in Vancouver, British Columbia) and has introduced the concept of 'liquid imperialism' to highlight the complexity of Canada's imperial connection in the post-war era. Although the organizers employed the Games to reinforce imperial and Commonwealth solidarity among participants and audiences, this was rarely a dominant or hegemonic understanding of the Games' purpose and rationale. As Dawson argues, the:

> … ideals of Empire continued to inform Canadian political culture but in a less direct and less complete fashion than they had just a few decades earlier. Sympathy for a (re-imagined) Empire was now one current of political culture among many in a complex and increasingly crowded public sphere.[66]

Globalization

The so-called process of 'globalization' has fundamentally altered the terms and conditions for understanding empire and imperial modes of thinking. The old institutions and practices which were formerly known as 'British imperial sport' occupy an ambiguous place in the wider world. British sports such as cricket, rugby and football have outlived the empire and their practices transcend the boundaries of lands formerly controlled by the British. Whereas before World War II the locus of scrutiny focused on the actions and official policies of the nation-state (and national institutions), in recent decades, the imperialist torch has been carried by multinational and transnational corporations. As Michael Silk et al. explain, the locus of control 'in influencing the manner in which the nation and national identity are represented becomes exteriorized through, and internalized within, the promotional strategies of transnational corporations'. Simply put, the politico-cultural nation-state of the 19th and early 20th centuries has been 'replaced by the corporate-cultural nation' – a process that Silk and Andrews term *corporate nationalisms* (the way in which national cultures are 'corporatized, and reduced to a branded expression of global capitalism's commandeering of collective identity and memory') – processes that are qualitatively distinct from those that helped to constitute the symbolic boundaries of maturing nation-states during the nineteenth century'.[67] Whereas even a decade ago the debate about the globalization of sport focused on how this process threatened to marginalize, if not transcend the efforts of nation-states, in recent years a number of scholars have questioned such suppositions. One of the few American sports historians who has weighed into this debate (and one of the few who has attempted to integrate American sport within world sports history) is Mark Dyreson, who has argued that the 20th-century history of globalized sport has 'served to invigorate national cultures rather than to transform them into cosmopolitan partners in a new world system … [and in this sense, as] the language of sport has spread around the globe, it has functioned as an element in national discourses'.[68]

Since the end of the Cold War, most of the analysis has focused on the concept of 'soft power' (cultural imperialism or neo-imperialism as opposed to old-styled imperial administration) via globalization – whereby sport is subsumed within the broader exportation of popular culture, entertainment, fashion, music, fast food and the like.[69] Walter LaFeber, one of the most distinguished historians of American foreign policy, brought his well-established expertise on the expansion of American power to bear upon the transnational corporation Nike, in *Michael Jordan and the New Global Capitalism*. According to LaFeber, Nike is a prime example of how, in harnessing the communications and marketing technologies of the post-industrial age, transnational corporations (with virtually no governmental interference) transmit American-styled sports culture (via sports celebrities and sporting goods) so as to dominate the world in novel ways.[70] LaFaber's book provides insight into this recent phase which has witnessed what Keys documented in her study of the 1930s – namely, the triumph of American-styled corporate marketing on the global sports world. During this recent phase, American corporations have fundamentally shaped global sport, especially the manner in which it is organized, packaged and marketed.

As the dominant American sports played outside the USA, the National Basketball Association (NBA) and Major League Baseball (MLB) are currently in the vanguard of American 'soft power' (sporting-cultural imperialism). MLB has long pursued an imperial relationship with regard to the systematic cultivation of talent in the Caribbean (and

Latin America more generally) region and has developed the World Baseball Classic to further promote the game internationally, while the NBA has systematically established its brand image around the world, most recently within China.[71] John Kelly examines the processes of global capitalism and the legacies of colonization through the lens of the newly established World Baseball Classic. Organized by Major League Baseball as a way of promoting the further globalization of the sport, Kelly argues that the WBC is the vehicle by which US 'Organized Baseball' intends to take over international baseball, which provides a case study for the 'capacity of the formal symmetries and independence of nation-states to mask sustained real inequality'.[72] This is one of the relative handful of scholarly analyses of American sporting imperialism that simultaneously provide invaluable insight into the role of sport as a decolonization social practice in Latin America.

One final example illustrates the transition from early notions of imperialism within the realm of sport to the corporate soft-power style engendered by globalization. Between the 1920s and 1950s, MLB played a type of economic 'hard ball' as an 'imperialist neo-colonizer' – a history rife with class and racial implications. According to Robert Lewis, MLB's imperial pursuit of talent from the Caribbean region became systematic *after* the failure of its internal colonial practices within the USA, which began first with the recruitment of white rural players during the 1920s and 1930s, and then black players, for the Negro League, in the late 1940s. 'As a result of resistance from its colonies at home and abroad as well as greater market competition', he contends, 'MLB now plays a more cultural "soft ball" as a multinational corporation'. However 'soft' MLB's presence actually is within Latin America, currently all 30 major league teams operate minor league facilities and summer league teams in the Dominican Republic and 28 teams have facilities in Venezuela.[73]

While Americans celebrate the globalization of baseball as evidence of the nation's sporting influence outside North America, historians have given relatively scant attention to the ways in which the game was adapted and transformed abroad. Nowhere did the colonials better demonstrate their facility with the American 'national pastime' than in the Dominican Republic – a country that has produced more professional baseball players than any other, apart from the USA. It has represented the epicentre of Caribbean baseball since the mid-1950s, when Major League Baseball systematically engaged in deceptive practices to secure athletic talent (and were aided and abetted by the Dominican government). During the past several decades, MLB teams have co-opted locals in the recruitment and development process, which John Krich characterizes as a 'pimpocracy'.[74] In this case, MLB has acted as a typical multinational corporation in its pursuit of valued-added resources, namely labour power and, ultimately, profits. In his 1991 book, *Sugarball*, Alan Klein shows how Major League Baseball clubs have operated in a fashion similar to that of other powerful economic and political interests in promoting the presence of the USA throughout the Caribbean (by, for example, conveniently establishing baseball clubs near sugar refineries). Whereas most of the historical literature on the export of baseball has posited a top-down approach, Klein's work (which incorporates political economy, sociology and ethnography, as well as history) demonstrates the nuances between hegemony and resistance to imperialism by fans, the local media and the players themselves in an effort of the Dominicans to retain their hold on the game (despite the deleterious effects that the major leagues have had on the integrity and health of Dominican ball). As Klein writes, 'it is one thing to say that hegemonic influences are at work, and quite another to say that they are overriding. Nations that depend on the industrialized West are entirely capable of stemming foreign cultural domination' – a process Klein calls 'cultural resistance'. As he writes, the 'Dominican attitudes toward Americans, the curious mix of approach and avoidance, reflects the tension between hegemony and resistance' as Dominicans both ape North Americans and simultaneously express national pride by 'infus[ing] the game with their own raucous, melodramatic, highly individualistic' style of play; 'an easygoing attitude' on and off the field; and 'music and dancing, and crowds by turns temperamental and tranquil'.[75]

Notes

1 Some of the following material appeared earlier in S.W. Pope, 'Rethinking Sport, Empire and "American Exceptionalism"', *Sport History Review* 38 (November 2007), 92–120.

2 The most well-known pre-modern work in English on empire is Edward Gibbon's *Decline and Fall of the Roman Empire*. For a good recent synthesis of imperial history, see John Darwin, *After Tamerlane: The Global History of Empire* (London: Penguin, 2007). For an in-depth overview of this area of historical scholarship, see William Roger Louis, ed., *The Oxford History of the British Empire* (Oxford: Oxford University Press, 1999).

3 Stephen Howe, *Empire: A Very Short Introduction* (Oxford: Oxford University Press, 2002), 1. This theme underpins Eric Wolf's *Europe and the Peoples without History* (Berkeley: University of California Press, 1982). W.H. McNeill's *The Rise of the West* (Chicago: University of Chicago Press, 1964) remains one of the most ambitious attempts to write a history of the world in a single volume.

4 This question is posed by Howe, op. cit., 6. The spectrum of opinion on the meaning of the United States' superpower status in the contemporary world is captured by critics, such as Noam Chomsky, the most influential scholar on American imperialism – see, for example, his *Hegemony or Survival: America's Quest for Global Dominance* (New York: Henry Holt, 2003) – and apologists, such as the British historian Niall Ferguson whose book argues in favour of American global leadership. For reflections and theoretical ruminations of contemporary American imperialism within social science scholarship, see Harry Harootunian's *The Empire's New Clothes: Paradigm Lost and Regained* (Chicago: Prickly Paradigm Press, 2004).

5 See, for example: Nicholas B. Dirks, *The Scandal of Empire: India and the Creation of Imperial Britain* (Cambridge: Belknap Press, 2006); David Armitage, *The Ideological Origins of the British Empire* (Cambridge: Cambridge University Press, 2000); Sugata Bose, *A Hundred Horizons: The Indian Ocean in the Age of Global Empire* (Cambridge, MA: Harvard University Press, 2006); Andrew Thompson, *The Empire Strikes Back? The Impact of Imperialism on Britain from the Mid-Nineteenth Century* (Harlow: Pearson Longman, 2005); and Charles Maier, *Among Empires: American Ascendancy and Its Predecessors* (Cambridge, MA: Harvard University Press, 2006).

6 Niall Ferguson, *Empire: The Rise and Demise of the British World Order and the Lessons of Global Power* (New York: Basic Books, 2004).

7 For a brief, incisive overview of basic terminology, see Howe, op. cit., 9–34.

8 G. Vuoto, 'The Anglo-American Global Imperial Legacy: Is There a Better Way?', *Canadian Journal of History* 42 (2007), 262–63.

9 Howe, op. cit., 123.

10 Donald Kyle, *Sport and Spectacle in the Ancient World* (London: Blackwell, 2007), 340. Kyle's bibliography is as up-to-date as any available and readers are encouraged to consult it for key works. Given its broad, synthetic nature, I have relied upon it for some generalizations below out of convenience.

11 Wolfgang Decker, *Sports and Games of Ancient Egypt* (New Haven: Yale University Press, 1992). For an overview of ancient empires that compares them with more modern ones, see Susan E. Alcock, et al., *Empires* (Cambridge: Cambridge University Press, 2001).

12 Kyle, op. cit., 342.

13 Ibid., 343.

14 Ibid., 345. For a recent, sophisticated analysis of key texts illuminating athletic culture, see Jason Konig, *Athletics and Literature in the Roman Empire* (Cambridge: Cambridge University Press, 2005).

15 The model for this approach to the long history of sport (and still the best of the genre despite being written 25 years ago) is William J. Baker, *Sports in the Western World*, 2nd edn (Urbana: University of Illinois Press, 1988). Another competing text is Robert A. Mechikoff and Steven G.

Estes, *A History and Philosophy of Sport and Physical Education: From Ancient Civilization to the Modern World*, 3rd edn (New York: McGraw Hill, 2002).

16 For a narration of the key literature of medieval and pre-modern historical scholarship pertaining to empire and imperialism, see Darwin, op. cit., 558–62 for a concise bibliographical review.

17 Allen Guttmann, *Sport: The First Five Millennia* (Amherst: University of Massachusetts Press, 2004). Alas, Guttmann remains tied to a very traditional modernization framework which obstructs a new manner for considering this new scholarship. For Guttmann, the transformation of traditional (pre-modern) to modern sporting practice has tended to be unidirectional – modernization wins out and, as a result, traditional sports become over-determined by secularization, bureaucratization, scientization and so on. As Alan Ingham noted, overdetermination is not the only consequence of modernization: some traditional activities simply become extinct. For two critical assessments of Guttmann's *Games and Empires* and *Sports: The First Five Millennia*, see Ingham's review in the *Sociology of Sport Journal* 14 (1997), 304–9, and Pope, *Journal of Social History* 41 (2008), 783–85.

18 For two invaluable reviews of this historiography, see William J. Baker, 'The State of British Sport History', *Journal of Sport History* 10 (1983), 53–66 and Richard Holt, 'Sport and history: the state of the subject in Britain', *Twentieth Century British History* 7(2) (1996), 231–52. For the most current overview, see Martin Johnes's chapter in this book. Key works on sport and the British empire include J.A. Mangan, *The Games Ethic and Imperialism: Aspects of the Diffusion of an Ideal* (Harmondsworth: Viking, 1986); J.A. Mangan, *Pleasure, Profit and Proselytism: British Culture and Sport at Home and Abroad, 1700–1914* (London: Frank Cass, 1988). Other useful works include R. Holt, *Sport and the British: A Modern History* (Oxford: Clarendon/Oxford University Press, 1989); and J. Williams, *Cricket and Race* (Oxford: Berg, 2001).

19 Guttmann had waged a consistent and often strident polemical dismissal of Marxist and neo-Marxist theorists of sport since the publication of his immensely influential 1978 book *From Ritual to Record*.

20 Guttmann, *Games and Empires*, 11, 178. This concise characterization of Guttmann's thesis derives from Ingham, op. cit., 304.

21 These descriptive categories of the British imperial tradition come from Philippa Levine's *The British Empire: Sunrise to Sunset* (Harlow: Pearson/Longman, 2007). See the bibliographical essay in Victoria DeGrazia's *Irresistible Empire: America's Advance through Twentieth Century Europe* (Cambridge, MA: Harvard University Press, 2005) for an excellent overview of this scholarship. See also Piers Brendon's useful *The Decline and Fall of the British Empire, 1781–1997* (New York: Knopf, 2008).

22 B. Stoddart, 'Sport, Cultural Imperialism, and Colonial Response in the British Empire', *Comparative Studies of Society and History* 30 (1988), 649–73; and Ric Sissons and B. Stoddart, *Cricket and Empire* (London: Allen & Unwin, 1984).

23 Stoddart, 'Sport, Cultural Imperialism', 650, 652. For two excellent overviews of sport and critical social theory, see Grant Jarvie and Joseph Maguire, *Sport and Leisure in Social Thought* (London: Routledge, 1994) and Richard Giulianotti, ed., *Sport and Modern Social Theorists* (London: Palgrave, 2004).

24 For a succinct, albeit descriptive summary of sport and the British empire during the mid-to-late 19th century, see Mike Huggins, *The Victorians and Sport* (London: Hambledon, 2004), 219–47.

25 J.A. Mangan, *The Cultural Bond: Sport, Empire, Society* (London: Routledge, 1993), 3.

26 C. Hall and S. Rose, eds, *At Home with Empire: Metropolitan Culture and the Imperial World* (Cambridge: Cambridge University Press, 2006), 2. For an important perspective on the culture of nationalism which informed the 'new' cultural history, see Michael Billig, *Banal Nationalism* (London: Sage, 1995).

27 Hall and Rose, op. cit., 23.

28 K. Wilson, *A New Imperial History: Culture, Identity, and Modernity in Britain and the Empire, 1660–1840*, (Cambridge: Cambridge University Press), 2, 19.

29 Michael Anton Budd, *The Sculpture Machine: Physical Culture and Body Politics in the Age of Empire* (New York: New York University Press, 1997), 121. See also Donald Roden, 'Baseball and the Quest for National Dignity in Meiji Japan', *American Historical Review* 85 (1980), 511–34; and Richard Light's essay on Japan in this volume.

30 J. Nauright and T. Chandler, eds, *Making Men: Rugby and Masculine Identity* (London: Routledge, 1996); P. McDevitt, *May the Best Man Win: Sport, Masculinity, and Nationalism in Great Britain and the Empire, 1880–1935* (Basingstoke: Palgrave, 2004).

31 Mangan quoted in Patrick McDevitt, 'The King of Sports: Polo in late Victorian and Edwardian India', *International Journal of the History of Sport* 20(1) (2003), 22.

32 See Pierre Lafranchi and Matthew Taylor, *Moving with the Ball: The Migration of Professional Foot-ballers* (Oxford: Berg, 2001); S. Szymanski and A. Zimbalist, *National Pastime: How Americans Play Baseball and the Rest of the World Plays Soccer* (Washington, DC: Brookings Institution, 2005), 48–54.

33 William J. Baker, *Playing with God: Religion and Modern Sport* (Cambridge, MA: Harvard University Press, 2007), 22–42; on the YMCA at home and abroad, see Baker 2007, 42–84. Recent scholarship has avoided conflating muscular Christianity with the 'games ethic' and has challenged the presumption that muscular Christianity was merely a hyper-masculinized, chauvinistic and self-righteous expression of Victorian imperialism. See John J. MacAloon, ed., *Muscular Christianity in Colonial and Post-Colonial Worlds* (London: Routledge, 2007).

34 See Alan Cobley's chapter in this book.

35 Douglas Midgett, 'Cricket and Calypso: Cultural Representation and Social History in the West Indies', *Ethnicity, Sport, Identity*, 6, 2/3 (2003), 239–41; Cite Beckles, who asserts that West Indians have 'promote[d] cricket as an agent in the dismantlement of the imperial order and a symbol of liberation' (cited in Midgett, 258).

36 C.L.R. James, *Beyond a Boundary* (New York: Pantheon, 1963), 224–25. See also J. Williams, *Cricket and Race*.

37 Howe, op. cit., 121.

38 Fan Hong, 'Prologue: The Origin of the Asian Games: Power and Politics', *Sport in Society* 8(3) (2005), 392–403.

39 Booth and Tatz, *One-Eyed: A View of Australian Sport* (St Leonards: Allen & Unwin, 2000), 110. For two other excellent surveys of Australian sport, see Richard Cashman, *Paradise of Sport* (Melbourne: Oxford University Press, 1995); and Daryl Adair and Wray Vamplew, *Sport in Australian History* (Melbourne: Oxford University Press, 1997).

40 Greg Gillespie, 'Wickets in the West: Cricket, Culture, and Constructed Images of Nineteenth-Century Canada', *Journal of Sport History* 27 (2000), 51–66.

41 For a version of his doctoral thesis published as 'essays on Indian cricket', see the special issue featuring Majumdar's reseach in the *International Journal of the History of Sport* 23(6) (2006). See also Patrick McDevitt, 'The King of Sports: Polo in late Victorian and Edwardian India', *International Journal for the History of Sport* 20(1) (March 2003), 1–27. For a comparative study on these dynamics as they apply to football, see Paul Dimeo and James Mills, eds, *Soccer in South Asia: Empire, Nation, Disapora* (London: Frank Cass, 2001).

42 Wojciech Liponski, 'Sport in the Slavic World before Communism: Cultural Traditions and National Functions', *European Sports History Review*, J.A. Mangan, ed., vol. 1: Sport in Europe: Politics, Class, Gender (1999), 221.

43 For a thorough review of this historiographical tradition, see DeGrazia op. cit.

44 Notable exceptions to this scholarly inattention include: G.R. Gems, *The Athletic Crusade: Sport and American Cultural Imperialism* (Lincoln: University of Nebraska Press, 2006); B.J. Keys, *Globalizing Sport: National Rivalry and International Community in the 1930s* (Cambridge, MA: Harvard University Press, 2006); and T.W. Zeiler, *Ambassadors in Pinstripes: The Spalding World Baseball Tour and the Birth of the American Empire* (Lanham, MD: Rowman & Littlefield, 2006). For an introduction to Gems' larger book project, see his 'Sport, Colonialism, and United States Imperialism', *Journal of Sport History* 33 (2006), 3–25. Another valuable contribution to this emergent literature is M. Dyreson's 'Globalizing the Nation-Making Process: Modern Sport in World History', *International Journal of the History of Sport* 20 (2003), 91–106. To be sure, there were several articles and book chapters on the diffusion of American sport in the Far East and Latin America through the US military and YMCA, but these efforts scarcely contextualized sport within the longer tradition of American imperialism.

45 A recent exception to this is Mark Dyreson and J.A. Mangan, eds, *Sport and American Society: Exceptionalism, Insularity and 'Imperialism'* (London: Routledge, 2007) wherein the essays collectively indicate why American sport will most likely 'continue to promote the nation rather than the global community', xvii. For an extended analysis of this see S.W. Pope, 'Rethinking Sport, Empire and "American Exceptionalism"', *Sport History Review* 38 (November 2007), 92–120. For a review of recent writing within the broader American historiography on 'exceptionalism', see Winfried Fluck, 'Inside and Outside: What Kind of Knowledge Do We Need?', *American Quarterly* 59 (2007), 23–32.

46 N. Ferguson, *Colossus: The Rise and Fall of the American Empire* (New York: Penguin, 2005), 2. For a descriptive account of the growth of American empire/expansionism/imperial thinking by a

journalist, see Robert Kagan, *Dangerous Nation: America's Place in the World from Its Earliest Days to the Dawn of the Twentieth Century* (New York: Knopf, 2006); for a scholarly, transnational approach, see Nicholas Canny, 'Writing Atlantic History; or, Reconfiguring the History of Colonial British America', *Journal of American History* 86(3) (1999), 1,093–107.

47 The most succinct overview of this colonial interplay between the British and American colonials is Elliott J. Gorn, 'Sports through the Nineteenth Century', in S.W. Pope, ed., *The New American Sport History: Recent Approaches and Perspectives* (Urbana: University of Illinois, 1997), 3–46. For the most recent review of American sports historiography to date, see Mark Dyreson's chapter in this book.

48 Elliott J. Gorn and Warren J. Goldstein, *A Brief History of American Sports*, 2nd edn (Urbana: University of Illinois Press, 2004), 6, 16–17.

49 Gems, 'Sport, Colonialism, and United States Imperialism', a paper delivered to the Chicago Seminar on Sport History, copy in author's possession, 3. By 1890 foreigners owned 75 percent of the acreage, much of it in plantations, where baseball served as a social control mechanism for a multicultural labour force. For additional documentation of this, see Gems, *Athletic Crusade*, 66–81; W.J. Baker, *Playing with God: Religion and Modern Sport* (Cambridge, MA: Harvard University Press, 2007), 44.

50 C. Richard King, *Native Athletes in Sport and Society: A Reader* (Lincoln: University of Nebraska Press, 2005), 2. King and C. Springwood document how this colonial past lives on in the contemporary use of Indian mascots in intercollegiate and professional sport 'characterized as a ritual drama serving to reconcile a dominant pattern of violence that marks the history of white America in its relations with Native Americans', in King and Springwood, eds, *Beyond the Cheers: Race as Spectacle in College Sport* (Albany, NY: SUNY Press, 2001), 49, *passim*.

51 Zeiler, *Ambassadors in Pinstripes*, ix–x, 41, 191.

52 The literature on the development of an American sporting culture is voluminous. See for example S.W. Pope, *Patriotic Games: Sporting Traditions in the American Imagination, 1876–1926* (New York: Oxford University Press, 1997; 2nd edn published in 2007 by the University of Tennessee Press); Mark Dyreson, *Making the American Team: Sport, Culture, and the Olympic Experience* (Urbana: University of Illinois Press, 1998); and D. Mrozek, *Sport and American Mentality, 1880–1910* (Knoxville: University of Tennessee Press, 1982).

53 Gems, 'Sport, Colonialism, and United States Imperialism', 32–33. See also Gems, 'Puerto Rico: Sport and the Restoration of National Pride', *International Journal of Regional and Local Studies* Series 2, 1(1) (2005), 107–20; and 'Sports, War and Ideological Imperialism', *Peace Review* 11 (December 1999), 573–78.

54 See Zeiler, *Ambassadors in Pinstripes*, 88 and *passim*. Interestingly, as Zeiler recognizes, 'baseball took hold in places that the tour had not reached, such as Japan and the Caribbean, and it was ironic that these were nations of color rather than the white imperial outposts so lauded by the tourists' (188).

55 See Alan Cobley's chapter in this book.

56 Thomas F. Carter, 'The Manifesto of a Baseball-playing Country: Cuba, Baseball, and Poetry in the Late Nineteenth Century', *International Journal of the History of Sport* 22 (March 2005), 246–65.

57 For the sportswriter's comments see Edwin A. Goewey, 'Fewer Fans and More Athletes', *Leslie's Weekly* (1 February 1919), 168. M. Dyreson, 'Globalizing the Nation-Making Process', 102. Dyreson devotes more attention to this in his book *Making the American Team*. See also his recent book, *Crafting Patriotism for Global Dominance: America at the Olympics* (London: Routledge, 2007).

58 Keys, *Globalizing Sport*, 5.

59 'John Bull and Uncle Sam: Four Centuries of British–American Relations', Library of Congress exhibition, www.loc.gov/exhibits/british/brit-7.html.

60 See S.W. Pope, 'American, European and Commonwealth Rivalries in the Davis Cup', in David Wiggins and Pierre Rodgers, eds, *Sports Rivalries: Traditions of Meaning and Representation in American Culture* (Fayetteville: University of Arkansas Press, 2009).

61 For a benign interpretation of US involvement in its colonial settings see Roberta J. Park, '"Forget About that Pile of Papers": Second World War Sport, Recreation and the Military on the Island of Puerto Rico', *International Journal of the History of Sport* 20(1) (March 2003), 50–64.

62 This has been a surprisingly neglected area in the historiography which has been capably addressed by recent publication of S. Wagg and D. Andrews' edited collection, *East Plays West* (London: Routledge, 2007). For an incisive history of the Olympics which provides an analysis of Soviet

documents see Alfred Senn, *Power, Politics and the Olympic Games* (Champaign, IL: Human Kinetics, 1999). See also the fine essays in the journal *Olympika*, published since 1992 by the International Center for Olympic Studies at the University of Western Ontario.

63 Senn, 'The Sovietization of Lithuanian Sports, 1940–41', *Journal of Baltic Studies* 23 (Spring 1992), 79.

64 John Soares, 'Cold War, Hot Ice: International Ice Hockey, 1947–80', *Journal of Sport History* 34(2) (Summer 2007), 207–30. See Wagg and Andrews for the best available collection on Cold War sport published to date.

65 Matthew Taylor, 'Commonwealth Games', in Richard Cox et al., eds, *The Encyclopedia of British Sport* (Oxford: ABC-CLIO, 2000), 73. For a study of the origins of this competition, see K. Moore, 'The Pan-Britannic Festival: A Tangible but Forlorn Expression of Imperial Unity', in J.A. Mangan, ed., *Pleasure, Profit, Proselytism: British Culture and Sport at Home and Abroad, 1700–1914* (London: Frank Cass, 1988), 144–62.

66 Michael Dawson, 'Acting Global, Thinking Local: "Liquid Imperialism" and the Multiple Meanings of the 1954 British Empire & Commonwealth Games', *International Journal of the History of Sport* 23 (1) (2006), 20, 22.

67 M. Silk et al., *Sport and Corporate Nationalisms* (Oxford: Berg, 2005), 2, 4, 7.

68 M. Dyreson, 'Globalizing the Nation-Making Process', 93. M. Silk, D. Andrews, and C.L. Cole consider the ways in which globalization has brought about the 'changing', as opposed to the 'withering', of the nation: Silk, et al. 2005.

69 For an excellent survey of this general process of American cultural diffusion, see Penny M. von Eschen, 'Globalizing Popular in the "American Century" and Beyond', Organization of American Historians' *Magazine of History* (July 2006), 56–63.

70 W. LaFeber, *Michael Jordan and the New Global Capitalism* (New York: Norton, 1999). For broader analyses of sport and globalization, see Maarten van Bottenburg, *Global Games* (Urbana: University of Illinois Press, 2001); R. Giulianotti and R. Robertson, eds, *Globalization and Sport* (Oxford: Blackwell, 2007); and R. Giulianotti and R. Robertson, *Globalization and Football* (London: Sage, 2009).

71 See Grant Farred, *Phantom Calls: Race and the Globalization of the NBA* (Chicago: Prickly Paradigm Press, 2006).

72 John D. Kelly, *The American Game: Capitalism, Decolonization, World Domination, and Baseball* (Chicago: Prickly Paradigm Press, 2006), 5.

73 R. Lewis II, '"Soft Ball": MLB Shifts from Neocolonizer to Multinational Corporation', paper presented at the Cooperstown Symposium on Baseball and American Culture, June 2006. The term 'soft power' is attributed to J.S. Nye as delineated in his *Bound to Lead: The Changing Nature of American Foreign Policy* (New York: Free Press, 1990), and more recently, *Soft Power: The Means to Success in American Foreign Policy* (New York: Foreign Affairs, 2004).

74 See Lewis, 'Soft Ball', 10; J. Krich, *El Beisbol: Travels through the Pan-American Pastime* (New York: Prentice Hall, 1989), 111. Other key works on baseball in Latin America include Rob Ruck, *The Tropic of Baseball: Baseball in the Dominican Republic* (Westport, CT: Meckler, 1991); and P.C. Bjarkman, *Baseball with a Latin Beat: A History of the Latin American Game* (Jefferson, NC: McFarland, 1994).

75 A. Klein, *Sugarball: The American Game, The Dominican Dream* (New Haven, CT: Yale University Press, 1991), 6, 99, 47, 112.

15 International relations

Barbara Keys[1]

For a century presidents and foreign ministers have debated issues and formulated policy about sport. 'Mega-events' such as the Olympic Games and soccer's (football's) World Cup have long been highly sought-after platforms for countries to project messages to huge global audiences. The globe's biggest corporations use them as prime marketing tools, and television networks compete to pay hundreds of millions of dollars to broadcast them. International sports organizations claim more members than the United Nations and influence the international system in untold ways. Despite the long-standing and profound connections between sport and international affairs, the study of these ties was for decades a mere backwater in sports studies and in diplomatic history. In the 1970s, as social and cultural history flourished while diplomatic history stagnated, histories of sport overwhelmingly focused on sport's role in society – its relationships to class, ethnicity, race and gender, and its uses in constructing local and national identities.[2] Few sports historians tackled the international dimensions of sport, and the scholarship they produced before the 1990s tended to focus on decrying unwanted political 'intrusions' into sport.

Historians of international relations, for their part, showed no interest at all in sport until very recently. In textbooks, surveys and monographs on international history, sport's rare appearances took the form of perfunctory asides. A survey might mention President Jimmy Carter's boycott of the 1980 Moscow Olympic Games in a list of US responses to the Soviet invasion of Afghanistan, but sport's deeper significance went unnoticed. This neglect paralleled that of top diplomats and policymakers themselves, who saw sports issues come across their desks but rarely recognized them as anything other than peripheral to the main concerns of diplomacy. Henry Kissinger, for example, was a passionate soccer fan and dealt with a number of important issues relating to the Olympic Games, including the 1972 terrorist attack in Munich, during his tenure as National Security Adviser and Secretary of State. Yet aside from a discussion of the 'ping-pong diplomacy' that led to the opening to China, Kissinger mentions sport just twice, both times only in passing, in nearly 4,000 pages of detailed memoirs.[3] His thick account of the art and history of diplomacy contains no reference to sport.[4]

For realists like Kissinger, sport was irrelevant to the real sources of power in international affairs. Mere games could play no role in foreign policies that were shaped by hard, tangible national interests such as security and economics. The realist theory espoused by Kissinger reigned supreme in the academy during the Cold War. Its attendant neglect of sport was reinforced by an intellectual disdain for matters of the body, which in turn was rooted in a Western belief in the separation of the spheres of work and leisure.[5] The myth, deeply embedded in most Western democracies, that sport exists in the realm of play, free – at least in ideal terms – from political and economic 'taint', also contributed to a longstanding inclination to exclude sport from the study of 'real' politics.[6] The widely held assumption that sport is a 'natural' activity, rather than an historically contingent one, meant that scholars also failed to see global sport as the result of an astonishingly successful process of cultural transmission deserving of explanation and analysis.[7]

The end of the Cold War accelerated the rise of new forces in global affairs and, at the same time, challenged long-standing modes of thinking about international relations. As a result of these trends, the deep-seated mutual indifference between sports studies and diplomatic history began to dissolve, and in recent years the study of sport's international connections has undergone dramatic changes. Rising interest in globalization and the role played by non-state actors in global affairs is propelling new interest in sport's international dimensions. Increasing numbers of historians from other specializations are turning their attention to sport's economic and political ramifications, and sport's evident position as a central element of global culture has resulted in an explosion of studies on sport's connections to globalization. The paradigms that shaped Cold War-era interest in sport and foreign policy – sport boycotts, superpower rivalry, and the quest for recognition and prestige – are being supplanted by new avenues of research on the ways international sport shapes domestic politics, processes of 'internationalization' and the global community.

This chapter surveys developments in the historiography of sport and international relations since the 1960s, including its connections with fields outside history and treatment of the subject in the discipline as a whole. Any effort to delineate this historiography is necessarily artificial and imperfect, for determining where the 'national' ends and the 'international' begins is virtually impossible in the case of sport. Sport, after all, is almost everywhere a foreign import and is typically regulated by international bodies, and its powerful role in identity-formation is always at least implicitly shaped in an international context. As a result, much, if not all, work done on sport in any context has some relevance for foreign relations, and many of the other chapters in this volume are relevant to an understanding of sport's international dimensions. For the sake of coherence, however, this chapter covers only studies that focus explicitly on international affairs. It makes no attempt to survey all sports, all regions of the world, or all aspects of international relations; instead it chronologically charts major thematic shifts and historiographical trends, looking first at the predominant themes and assumptions of studies produced during the Cold War and then attempting to delineate the explosion of work in the post-Cold War era. Its purview is limited to the 20th century, when international events proliferated and became major factors in global society, even though sport had implications in the realm of foreign relations well before then.[8]

One of the observers at the first Olympic Games in Athens in 1896 was Charles Maurras, an extreme right-wing French nationalist and founder of the political movement *L'Action française*. He had opposed the efforts of his compatriot Pierre de Coubertin to create a modern Olympic Games, because Maurras believed the event would promote unhealthy 'mixing' of different nationalities. On his trip to Athens, however, he was delighted to find that the Olympic Games inflamed 'patriotic passion' and exacerbated national rivalries. 'In the past', he wrote, 'nations dealt with each other through ambassadors … Now peoples confront each other directly, insulting each other face to face'.[9]

Maurras's assessment was the first salvo in the intellectual debate over the meaning of international sport. His conclusions were echoed in George Orwell's famous remarks some six decades later. Orwell, a prominent British writer and intellectual at the other end of the political spectrum from Maurras, was dismayed by boorish and unruly behaviour by players and spectators during a Soviet soccer team's goodwill tour of Britain in 1945. Not inclined, as was Maurras, to celebrate displays of nationalism, Orwell wrote that international sport was 'an unfailing cause of ill-will' which led 'to orgies of hatred'. In words still often quoted, he continued: 'It is bound up with hatred, jealousy, boastfulness, and disregard of all rules and sadistic pleasure in witnessing violence; in other words it is war minus the shooting'.[10]

It would be another two decades before sustained scholarly analysis of international sport began, but when it did, it would be shaped by the debate launched by intellectuals like Maurras and Orwell. The key task would be defined as elucidating the relationship between sport's ostensibly contradictory roles as a vehicle for international understanding on the one hand, and nationalist rivalry on the other – what I call the 'peace or rivalry paradigm'. These studies typically took as their starting point the founding myth of the modern Olympic Games, one taken up (to lesser degrees) by other international sports bodies as a core element of their legitimizing strategy: the idea that international sport promotes peace and mutual understanding among nations. Some neo-Marxist philosophers and sociologists – Jean-Marie Brohm is perhaps the most notable – took the opposite tack, arguing that international contests such as the Olympic Games were inherently repressive and imperialist, but most of the historical work produced in the Cold War began from the premise that sport was a force for good (or could be, if only the politicians stopped meddling).[11]

Taking their cue from the most visibly politicized elements of international sport around them, Cold War-era scholars focused their attention on proving, often with breathless indignation, that the 'reality' departed from the 'ideal'. Their emphasis was on government use (almost invariably characterized as 'misuse') of international sport competitions for political ends. Studies focused on politically inspired sports boycotts, the use of sport as a vehicle of political propaganda, and the quest for national prestige and recognition through sport victories and the hosting of major sports events. Most of these approaches implicitly embraced the assumptions that sport itself was politically neutral, or an 'empty vessel' into which political messages could be poured, and that it was a 'tool' or 'mirror' of larger forces in the international system.

The first major treatment of sport and international politics was authored by British politicians Philip Goodhart and Christopher Chataway in 1968. Drawing largely on newspaper accounts, *War Without Weapons* was a journalistic exposé of political interference in sport. Devoting the bulk of their attention to sport in the Cold War, the authors covered issues such as South African apartheid, and Soviet and US uses of sport diplomacy. Echoing the kind of public criticisms that had become common since the 1920s, the authors deplored what they saw as a growing distance from the original Olympic ideals of amateurism and international amity. They described 'the Olympic Frankenstein' as 'one of the main manifestations' of nationalist chauvinism in the world and argued that sports contests 'mirror' political conflicts among nations. Despite the disapproving tone, in the end the authors put a positive spin on sport's 'politicization'. Drawing on ethologist Konrad Lorenz's theory that sport was a means of discharging aggression, Goodhart and Chataway argued that the Olympic Games and other major international sports contests served to promote peace by providing a safe outlet for tendencies that might otherwise be channelled into war *with* weapons.[12]

Preoccupation with the 'peace or rivalry paradigm' was reflected in most of the works produced in the next two decades. In his 1971 book on the 1936 Berlin Olympic Games, Richard Mandell wrote: 'I tried to determine whether the 1936 Games as an episode and the modern Olympics as a movement have been forces for peace'. His answer was a resounding no.[13] He wrote of athletes as victims and tools of 'abrasive patriotism' and urged a 'return' to celebration of individual achievement rather than national competition. He portrayed the 1936 Games as a stunning success for the Nazis, who efficiently staged a magnificent pageant that diverted the world's attention from their evil intentions and increased their legitimacy at home.[14]

The Nazi years were a major focus of sport research in Germany in the 1970s and 1980s. Germany had one of the oldest traditions of sports historiography and German scholars were then at the forefront of sports history. Initial scholarship shared the view that sport was fundamentally apolitical, and historians like Hajo Bernett condemned the 'misuse' and politicization of sport by the Nazis.[15] In 1972 Arnd Krüger, who would become a leading authority on European sport, published a detailed examination of international opinion on the 1936 Olympics that took a more sceptical view of the event's success than Mandell. Krüger concluded that at home the Games led Germans to believe they had gained international respect, but abroad the events had tended simply to reinforce pre-existing opinions.[16] East Germany's carefully constructed and ultimately successful quest to use international sporting success as a vehicle for gaining international recognition as an independent state also attracted attention.[17] In a 1980 study of sport competition between the two German states, political scientist Ulrich Pabst described sport as a tool in the competition for international recognition and as an element that created links between the two states.[18] In France the inter-war years and sport's use in building national prestige were the focus of what little attention was devoted to sport and foreign affairs.[19]

The socialist 'workers' sport' movement of the inter-war years attracted attention as a foil to Nazi sport and the growing commercialization of elite sport. Two international organizations had contended for leadership of workers' sports in the 1920s and 1930s: the socialist Lucerne Sport International and the communist Red Sport International run by the USSR. Each staged its own version of Workers' Olympiads; each regarded Coubertin's Olympic festival as an elitist, national chauvinist and militaristic spectacle that served the interests of the ruling classes. Scholarly interest in these groups was in part a logical outgrowth of the new labour and social history. Scholars tended to portray workers' sport in sympathetic terms, seeing it as a worthy international cultural movement and an admirable effort to promote international fraternity rather than national rivalry.[20]

Considerable scholarly attention was directed to sport boycotts over the issue of racism, reflecting the issue's prominence in public debates. Beginning in the 1950s, South Africa had been the subject of controversy because of apartheid, reflected in its refusal to field or play against racially mixed teams in international competition. Newly independent African states pressed international sports organizations and the United Nations to enforce bans on South African participation and in 1970 South Africa became the first country expelled from the Olympic Games. Richard Lapchick's 1975 study was the first of many to chronicle the history of such boycotts and exclusions. Lapchick showed that international pressure was a powerful influence in South Africa because of the country's strength of interest in sport and that international exclusion was perceived internally as condemnation of racism.[21] However, the conclusions of Lapchick and others were challenged in the 1990s by David R. Black and John Nauright who argued that the scholarship on sports boycotts and their efficacy placed too great an emphasis on the Olympics when the sport that really mattered to the target group of white South Africans was rugby union.[22]

Despite scholarly emphasis on sport's role in enhancing national prestige, relatively few studies examined the use of sport as a tool of nation-building by newly emerging states in the era of decolonization. Henning Eichberg's perceptive 1984 critique of Olympism as neo-colonialism was one of the few such works to appear in the Cold War.[23] Third World challenges to European dominance of the Olympic Games, such as the Games of the New Emerging Forces (GANEFO) set up by Indonesia in 1962 and the 1976 Olympic takeover bid mounted by the United Nations Educational, Scientific and Cultural Organization (UNESCO) and supported by many Asian and African nations, attracted little attention and to this day await thorough examination.[24]

The first survey of Olympic sport and international relations appeared in 1979. Focusing on the years 1944–76, Richard Espy's *The Politics of the Olympic Games* provided a competent account of the extended controversies over East German, Chinese and South African participation. Espy's framework was signalled in his first sentence: 'The modern Olympic Games symbolize the struggle between man's ideals and the reality in which he must live'. Concluding unhappily that sport has not encouraged peace but more often has promoted conflict, Espy's tale was one of the politicization of Coubertin's 'noble' ideals by governments intent on using the Games to advance national interests. Although Espy perceptively noted the importance of international sport organizations to the international system, his claim to see the Olympic Games as an actor in world politics was not substantiated in the book, which largely described Olympic politics as 'a mirror' or 'microcosm' of international forces, which merely used sport as a 'tool'.[25] Based largely on *The New York Times* and the papers of Avery Brundage, who had served as head of the International Olympic Committee (IOC) from 1952 to 1972, the study was also limited by its reliance on perspectives from within the IOC and the USA.

David Kanin's 1981 *Political History of the Olympic Games* offered a briefer and less factually reliable, but conceptually more sophisticated, analysis. The book sprang from a PhD dissertation on 'The Role of Sport in International Relations' completed at Tufts University's Fletcher School of Law and Diplomacy. A political scientist and analyst for the US Central Intelligence Agency, Kanin argued that the Olympics were not an empty vessel occasionally 'injected' with political content; rather, he asserted, 'political content … is a fundamental underpinning of the Olympic system'. As Kanin rightly saw, every international sports event is an inherently political event, and the common habit of lamenting 'the intrusion' of politics in sport was futile. The book debunked the 'Olympic mythology' of apolitical sport by showing the pervasive imbrication of politics and the modern Olympics since their founding in 1894.[26]

The Olympic boycotts of 1980 and 1984 attracted surprisingly little serious scholarly interest. Political scientist Derick Hulme, Jr, who would later go on to write on terrorism and the Israeli–Palestinian conflict, wrote one of the few academic books on the subject. The product, like Kanin's work, of a Fletcher School PhD dissertation, the book examined why the Games had become 'highly susceptible to political intrusions'. 'States, terrorists, and minority groups' now sought to use the Olympics as a political tool, Hulme lamented. Sport's politicization, he argued, was due to its similarity to the competitive international system – it provided a means of competition with low risks and costs – and because 'the ideal of sport [has] been impinged upon, and perverted, by wicked statesmen'.[27] Although Hulme argued that the Games were used for political purposes with little risk because of their 'politically peripheral nature', his evidence showed that the Carter Administration's failure to persuade most of its allies to join the boycott harmed America's self-confidence and global image.[28]

Brian Stoddart's seminal 1985 article on the politically fraught soccer match between England and Germany held in London in 1935 criticized superficial treatments of sport and international politics that depicted sport as 'symbolic' or peripheral to major political concerns. He argued that when studied in its cultural context, sport could be seen to influence political thinking – in this case, even 'help[ing] contribute' to British appeasement of Germany.[29] Stoddart's piece was a rare exception, however, both in its estimation of sport's autonomy and in using soccer to illuminate international relations. The Olympic Games garnered most of the attention devoted to sport's international ramifications, even as soccer became the premier global sport. As Bill Murray has noted, 'the serious study of soccer has almost been in inverse proportion to the game's popularity'.[30] Like the Olympic Games, however, soccer was entwined with international politics – in this case, almost in *direct* proportion to the devotion with which its proponents claimed otherwise. The international soccer federation (the Fédération Internationale de Football Association, or FIFA) has pushed ideas about sport as a factor for world peace with slightly less fervour than the IOC, but it has been equally devout in its adherence to the line that sport is apolitical. When the academic study of soccer began in the mid-1970s, however, it focused almost exclusively on local and national aspects of the game. It was not until the 1990s that significant scholarly attention was paid to soccer's international political and cultural dimensions (see below).

The true measure of the significance of sports studies must be its penetration of mainstream scholarship. Until the 1990s, sports studies remained ghettoized as a marginal sub-field within history and the social sciences. The dizzying expansion of sub-fields and specializations in the 1970s and 1980s was partly to blame; even generalists could no longer keep track of every topic. Sport, though, was marginalized to an unusual degree. Unlike other sub-fields, sport had virtually no advocates within the mainstream disciplines. Most of the scholarship on sport and international relations produced before the 1990s was written by scholars who specialized in sports studies, many of whom worked in sport institutes and physical education departments. They wrote primarily for each other, publishing articles in the proliferating journals devoted to sports history, where their work was easily ignored by outsiders.[31] Articles on sport and international relations very rarely appeared in mainstream scholarly journals, and scholars outside sports studies almost never felt compelled to engage with the literature on sport, which often lacked the conceptual sophistication and deep research base found in other fields.

The relatively narrow parameters of the studies that dealt with international sport before the 1990s can be explained in part by a preoccupation with the issues that were making the headlines. Boycotts, terrorism and superpower rivalry were matters of significant popular interest and deserved scholarly attention, but scholars in other fields could too easily dismiss these manifestations as merely showing that sport was a political 'tool'. The quest for national prestige was clearly an important element of international sport and one that garnered much attention, but scholars made little headway in showing that it had net effects on the international scene except in rare cases such as East Germany. Meanwhile, less visible manifestations of sport's power in global affairs were unduly neglected.

The dominant assumptions and conceptual underpinnings of many Cold War-era studies of sport and international politics helped to limit the subject's relevance and significance. The assumption that international sport could or should be apolitical led, as Trevor Taylor noted, to 'the role of politics in the Olympics frequently being resented rather than understood'.[32] As long as sport scholars maintained that sport was a 'mirror' or 'tool' of larger forces, scholars outside the field had little reason to attend to sport when they could study those larger forces directly: if sport was merely a reflection of international politics, why not simply study the thing itself? The peace or rivalry paradigm lent support to the idea that the key issues in the international arena were conflict and war, which again could be studied without reference to sport. The framework suggested that the test of sport's relevance was whether it averted or provoked war, which was surely too much to pin on a cultural activity, the 1969 El Salvador–Honduras 'soccer war' notwithstanding.[33] Sport scholars, moreover, had tended to discuss sport within a narrow frame of reference, often situating their work primarily in dialogue with other sport specialists rather than in the context of larger historiographical debates.

In 1997 the anthropologist and prominent Olympic scholar John MacAloon levied a sharp critique of scholarly preoccupation with 'the boring old curriculum of topics: fascist, socialist, and capitalist Olympics; government "interference" in sport; Cold War battles between "East" and "West"; terrorism, boycotts, and so on'. He called instead for attention to international sport's connection to other 'macro-political forces and trends', including new social movements and non-governmental organizations. Drawing on his own ethnographic fieldwork, he described the Olympic Games as an ideal venue for certain kinds of political activity. 'Nowhere else', he wrote:

> ... do such favorable conditions exist for otherwise difficult meetings – on an invisible, informal, and agenda-less basis – among such a total range of global political elites, including from nations at war or having no diplomatic relations with one another.... When diplomatic and national security historians and analysts put aside their cultural and scientific biases and explore this context, they will make some very interesting discoveries.[34]

Scholars were slow to heed MacAloon's call. After the Cold War, the old themes continued to dominate the agendas of many books, articles, conferences and symposia in sports history.[35] Scholars and journalists, writing exposés of new and deeper levels of corruption in international sport (bribery scandals, rampant commercialization), continued to adopt tones of ill-informed outrage at how far sport had strayed from its allegedly pure roots.[36] Gradually, though, the field has moved toward the position that international sports competitions and organizations are actors in their own right, which influence both international politics and domestic affairs, adding substance to the claim that sport is worthy of study in its own right. Scholars from other fields have taken up the subject of sport, bringing with them the central historiographical concerns of their primary fields – the role of consent in the German Democratic Republic, for example – and helping to place sport more clearly in the mainstream of historical debates.

The field's rigour and conceptual sophistication has grown along with its intellectual respectability. Newer studies of time-honoured topics, such as a recent collection of essays on the 1936 'Nazi Olympics', go further in illuminating the political contexts in various nations, showing how the Games affected politics and society.[37] Studies of sport diplomacy grew in number, delved further into the archives and took more nuanced views of sport's utility as a tool of foreign relations.[38] At the same time, diplomatic historians began to take up the subject of sport. In 1999, two diplomatic historians with distinguished records of publishing on traditional economic and political topics breached the long-standing intellectual barrier with books on sport: the British Peter Beck, with a book on British soccer and international diplomacy before World War II; and the American Walter LaFeber, with a study of basketball star Michael Jordan as symbol and agent of the 'new global capitalism'.[39]

Uta Balbier's recent work on inter-German relations is indicative of the new directions sports history is taking. Balbier sees sport not merely as a theatre of Cold War politics, but as a form of soft power that helped to shape national politics and identity. Expanding on previous studies of the German Democratic Republic's use of sport to attain international recognition and internal legitimacy, her account shows how the IOC and international sports federations were key actors in the political drama. Most interesting is her portrayal of the reaction within the Federal Republic of Germany. Although West Germany defined sport as 'non-political' in the 1950s, by the 1960s, as the GDR's success in international competitions drew increasing recognition, West Germany began to fashion its own strategy of sporting self-representation. By 1972, when Balbier's study ends, the West had largely embraced sport as a matter of state. Balbier's analysis moves beyond the formula of sport as an arena for nationalist competition to show elements of mutual influence and interdependence.[40]

Sandra Collins's 2003 dissertation exemplifies the ways the new international history of sport draws on exhaustive, multilingual archival research to provide fresh assessments of sport's importance at key historical junctures. Extending themes developed in earlier work on Fascist Italy and Germany, she carefully demonstrates that the 1940 Tokyo Olympic Games, though eventually cancelled due to war, were central to 'the production of ideology' in 1930s Japan. They were seen in Japan as a key opportunity both to shape public attachment to the expanding empire and to influence the world order by securing recognition of Japan as a legitimate world power.[41]

The either/or formulation of the 'peace or rivalry agenda' has been supplanted by a recognition that nationalism and internationalism are not mutually exclusive but mutually interdependent forces that operate in tandem. Guoqi Xu's superb book on China and international sport in the 20th century demonstrates that sport has been central to China's 'internationalization', which Xu defines as the ways countries 'engage in and are engaged by the international system, ideas, forces, and trends'. As Xu demonstrates, during a century when the Chinese were obsessed with their country's international standing, participating in sport competitions became a key means of joining the international community. His study is unusual in its success at tying together the ways sport acts jointly to construct national identity and to promote internationalization.[42] Along similar lines, my own recent study of international sports competitions in the 1930s argues that the growth of sport was fuelled by nationalist rivalry but simultaneously propelled internationalism. Nations attempted to use international sport for their own purposes, but found that participation also entailed acceptance of norms and values with domestic social and political consequences.[43]

Events of the late 1980s and 1990s lent support to those who saw sport as a factor of real consequence in international relations. The earlier consensus that sport was merely an ancillary factor gave way to an appreciation of sport as a potent political force (with some observers claiming the pendulum had shifted too far toward exaggerated claims of sport's influence).[44] The 1988 Seoul Olympic Games triggered interest in the question of international sport's potentially catalytic effect in spurring democratization. The political reforms in South Korea that followed on the heels of the Olympic Games provide potentially powerful evidence that international sport, far from being a mere 'mirror', can be a transformative influence. Political scientist Jarol Manheim, in an article exploring South Korea's use of the event as 'public diplomacy', was one of the first scholars to argue that the Seoul Games created 'overwhelming pressure' for political reform.[45] In similar fashion, the end of apartheid in South Africa in 1994 suggested that sports boycotts had helped undermine the racist system. Douglas Booth, Black and Nauright, and others concluded in the 1990s that although other factors were more important in ending apartheid, sport boycotts were an important cause of the deracialization of South African sport that began in the 1970s, which in turned helped undermine support for apartheid.[46]

Political scientists have also begun to turn their attention to sport. In 1986 Trevor Taylor characterized the relationship between sport and the field of international relations as one of 'mutual neglect', but new challenges to the realist paradigm have opened up space for an appreciation of sport's role in international relations.[47] Barrie Houlihan, a professor of sport policy, published a valuable overview of sport and international politics in 1994, which supported a pluralist approach to understanding international politics. Focusing on diplomacy, ideology, nation-building, access to international audiences, and commerce, Houlihan's careful analysis persuasively attributed greater significance to sport than had been commonly recognized.[48] A more recent collection offers primarily non-realist perspectives on sport's relationship to key issues in international relations, including gender, capitalism and international political economy.[49] In a case study of relations between South Africa and New Zealand, and the international anti-apartheid movement and those opposed to sporting boycotts, David Black and John Nauright argue for an understanding of the special circumstances in sport where otherwise-marginal societies can have a global impact in international relations, a fact widely overlooked in the international relations literature.[50]

As they suggest, single sports can make a difference in particular contexts. French international relations scholar Pascal Boniface has become perhaps the most vigorous advocate of the view that soccer is an important part of foreign affairs. The definition of statehood, he writes, used to include territory, government and population; now, he claims, a fourth category must be added: a national soccer team. Because of its power to shape a nation's popular image, soccer must rank as an important element of 'soft power'. Its influence should not be overrated, Boniface cautions; soccer will not produce peace or war, but it can promote or influence rapprochement or splits already underway.[51]

The 'cultural turn' in diplomatic history has, after a long lag, begun to provide a new agenda for the study of sport. Since the 1970s diplomatic historians have increasingly broadened their conception of the subject matter that falls under their purview. Once caricatured as the study of 'what one clerk said to another', diplomatic history now embraces subjects as diverse as environmental problems, human rights and gender. Horizons have widened so much that practitioners have moved to adopt a new name for the field: international history.[52] A key element driving the expansion of diplomatic history has been the introduction of culture alongside politics and economics as a significant area of international interaction. The pioneering scholar of cultural relations, Akira Iriye, offered the following definition:

> Cultural relations [are] interactions, both direct and indirect, among two or more cultures. Direct interactions include physical encounters with people and objects of another culture. Indirect relations are more subtle, involving such things as a person's ideas and prejudices about another people, or cross-national influences in philosophy, literature, music, art, and fashion.[53]

(One might add sport, too!) Since Iriye's pioneering call in 1978 to incorporate culture in diplomatic history, studies of cultural relations – tourism, World's Fairs, film, music – proliferated, and in recent years sport has finally made the list as well.[54]

Although culture's utility as an explanatory factor is not universally accepted by scholars of international history, cultural relations offers sports studies a promising alternative to the conceptually sterile framework that sees sport as a 'mirror'.[55] If 'culture is power', as culturalists assert, sport, too, is power. Sport is implicated in the three major categories culturalists have identified: language, identity and values. As diplomatic historian Andrew Rotter notes, '[h]ow a state sees itself affects the ways in which it relates to other states, how it defines national security and how it comes to understand its interests and objectives'.[56] Such perceptions, both of self and others, have been shaped significantly by sports contacts. Imagine, for example, where Brazil's international reputation would be without soccer, or the status of ideas about gender without the rise of women's sports in international competition.[57] Studies of government use of sport for national prestige, of course, always privileged matters of perception. However, a cultural-relations approach provides both a theoretical underpinning for showing how influence operates and allows us to move beyond governments as actors. Demonstrating how insights from cultural relations can productively be applied to sport, Sayuri Guthrie-Shimizu, for example, shows that baseball's diffusion in Meiji Japan created a transnational community of players, spectators and organizers that helped sustain 'an enduring undertow of affinity' between the USA and Japan despite the vicissitudes of war and conflict.[58]

The Cold War, long treated as a politico-ideological conflict, is now seen also as a cultural battleground. Walter Hixson and Yale Richmond have highlighted the significance of cultural exchange – ballet, art, music, film – in the competition between the superpowers, suggesting that cultural infiltration played a role in the Soviet collapse.[59] Sport, which provided the most sustained contact, was clearly a potentially significant vector for such cultural infiltration.[60] Yet, as Soviet historian Robert Edelman noted, despite the enormous resources and attention the Soviet regime devoted to sport, academics virtually ignored the subject until very recently.[61] It was only in 2004 that the first Russian-language, archive-based study of the politics of Soviet sport appeared, detailing the wide-ranging influence exerted by the Communist Party and the Soviet State on international sport contacts.[62] Edelman's pioneering study of Soviet spectator sport concluded that the sporting triumphs of the 'Big Red Machine' helped to conceal the Soviet system's weaknesses, an assessment that suggests the USSR's sport success may have played a role in Western overestimations of Soviet strength.[63]

Race is another issue where culture, domestic affairs and foreign policy overlapped with significant consequences.[64] In the Cold War in particular, racial issues were never purely domestic affairs; for the USA, racism at home became a major foreign-policy issue. Like Penny von Eschen's study of the ambivalent role African Americans played in US State Department-sponsored jazz tours in the Cold War, Damion Thomas's work shows that official goodwill sport tours, though intended to sell ideas about progress in race relations, had the unintended consequence of politicizing black athletes.[65] Amy Bass's excellent work on African American athletes, centring on the famous 'black power' salute by sprinters John Carlos and Tommie Smith on the podium at the 1968 Olympic Games, provides evidence for the effects global affairs had on the civil rights movement at home.[66]

Journalist Franklin Foer captured the fascination with sport's role in globalization in the delightfully hyperbolic title of his 2004 bestseller, *How Soccer Explains the World*.[67] The boom in globalization studies, more than any other development, has propelled a massive surge of scholarly interest in sport. Sociologists, media scholars and historians have investigated sport's powerful ties to global media – newspaper sports pages, magazines, literature, film, advertisements, radio and the internet. It is, of course, above all television that made sport into a global business of behemoth proportions. (Television rights to the 1960 Rome Olympics sold for about US$ 1.2 million. By 1988, NBC paid $300 million for the US rights to the Seoul Olympic Games.)[68] Christiane Eisenberg, a German historian of European social history who has written extensively on sport, has ably explored the tight inter-relationship between the growth of soccer and the rise of modern media over the last century.[69] Anthropologist and globalization theorist Arjun Appadurai has suggested that the media transmission of spectator sports such as cricket creates 'imagined worlds' along transnational lines. With attention to the role of corporate sponsors, the entertainment industry and journalists, he explores how cricket – implanted by the British as a tool of colonization – became indigenized in India as a nation-building, anti-colonial tool.[70] Globalization in general and television in particular can also retard the development of sport: in India, for example, the availability of cable and satellite broadcasts of European soccer matches has stifled the local game.[71]

Globalization significantly affects flows of people as well as information. Sport tourism (leisure-based travel to participate in or watch sports, or to sightsee at places of sport-related interest) is a rich topic with connections to economics, perceptions and cultural flows. It has been explored by scholars in tourism and sports management, but, except for studies of soccer hooliganism, has yet to receive sustained attention from historians.[72] Mostly unstudied, for example, are the ways that travel to international tournaments shapes new understandings of hosts and neighbours for tens of thousands of fans.[73] Migration and Diasporas offer another important new terrain of study: immigrants bring sporting traditions to their new countries and the growing international labour market in sport affects athletes, fans and their societies.[74]

Ties between sport and the globalization of commerce and media brought eminent historian of US foreign relations Walter LaFeber into the sports history fold with his 1999 book on basketball superstar Michael Jordan. In fact the book is less about sport than about commerce: the protagonist of LaFeber's book is not Jordan but US capitalism, in the guise of a sports shoes company, and LaFeber's driving interest, as in his earlier studies, remained the economically motivated expansion of US power. For LaFeber, the Nike Corporation epitomized a new and uniquely powerful agent of capitalism: the 'transnational corporation', which harnessed the technological developments of the post-industrial age (like satellites and cable television) to dominate world markets in novel ways. LaFeber charts how Nike, Ted Turner's Cable News Network (CNN), and clever manipulation of Michael Jordan's global celebrity combined to build 'the new global capitalism'.[75] Similar studies could be written about the powerful transnational links great soccer celebrities like Pelé and David Beckham have created around the world.[76]

Economic globalization is also the focus of Thomas Zeiler's excellent recent study of Albert Spalding's 1889 world baseball tour. Zeiler, the second established scholar of US diplomatic history to produce a book on sport, framed the significance of his subject along lines similar to LaFeber: the tour, according to Zeiler, contributed to the building of an American imperial identity. Viewing the baseball players and their entourage as 'tourists' who disseminated American culture abroad and brought global influences back home, he deftly sets the tour in the cultural and political context of the time.[77]

Scholars of cultural globalization have turned their attention to sport as a major element of global culture. Debates have raged over globalization's homogenizing and localizing effects. One sociologist has labelled the spread of Western sport and its supplanting of non-Western body cultures not merely cultural imperialism but 'cultural genocide'.[78] An alternative view suggests that sport resists globalizing processes and is 'deeply dependent on the production of difference'.[79] As yet, this debate has primarily involved sociologists, and historians have devoted little attention to empirical studies explicitly testing these theories. Allen Guttmann's 1994 *Games and Empires* remains the key historical treatment of 'ludic diffusion' and its relationship to cultural imperialism, one that concludes that the process has had largely beneficial effects.[80] Such views are probably shared by most sports historians. Bill Murray's pioneering books on soccer around the world, for example, though highlighting inequalities, emphasize soccer's importance as a vehicle for expressing local and national distinctiveness; he titles one chapter 'colonialism by consent'.[81]

The 'Americanization' of the world, especially the influence of American popular culture and media, has produced an explosion of scholarship, but Americanization has been less obvious in sport than in other forms of popular culture.[82] Although the major team sports in the USA are unusually parochial (with the exception, recently, of basketball), the political economy of global sport has been increasingly shaped by the US model. As Richard Cashman and Anthony Hughes caution in the case of Australia, however, popular myths of cultural dominance can be overstated. Michael Jordan was more famous than any Australian athlete in the 1990s, but the dominance of rugby, Australian rules football, and cricket mean that American sport has had only limited influence 'down under'.[83]

Historians, political scientists and sociologists have devoted considerable attention recently to the role of international non-governmental organizations (INGOs) in international affairs, and it is here that scholars have been most forthcoming in acknowledging sport's role. The IOC and international sports federations are highlighted as significant players in two major studies of INGOs.[84] Both the IOC and FIFA have more members than the United Nations, and membership in these organizations is recognized as a prerequisite to nationhood.[85] The important roles these bodies play in the international system is now widely recognized.

Interest in globalization and international organizations has also fuelled an explosion of studies on international sports contests as 'mega-events' and 'spectacles'.[86] Pushing beyond older obsessions with the propaganda value of the 'Nazi Olympics', some excellent recent work has focused on how countries use such events to shape global perceptions, combat stereotypes and recalibrate patriotism. Eric Zolov, a historian of Mexico, has argued that foreign stereotypes of Mexican underdevelopment shaped the way the Mexican government promoted the 1968 Mexico City Games.[87] Christopher Young and Uta Balbier have examined the 1972 Munich Olympic Games as an opportunity for West Germany to move beyond its recent past; in a particularly innovative study, Young unpacks the aesthetic dimensions of the Games and the 'interaction of ideology and spatial and visual design'.[88] In quite different ways, the 2006 soccer World Cup in Germany offered a platform for a new, unapologetic German nationalism.[89]

The study of international sport has, by now, moved far from the 'boring old curriculum' John MacAloon once deplored. The obvious point that sport is everywhere and always politicized needs no further affirmation. Sport's autonomy as an influence in its own right and not merely a 'mirror' of other forces is now well-established. Its imbrication in many of the areas of interest to intercultural historians suggests fruitful new avenues of study. Indeed the wide array of themes, directions and theoretical approaches available, combined with the legacy of decades-long neglect, mean that sport and foreign affairs offer a goldmine for scholars looking for fresh new topics. Many areas have only begun to be explored. The racial implications of international sport remain under-studied; to cite just one example, the career of famed US boxer Muhammad Ali, a prominent critic of the Vietnam War and a devout Muslim, is relevant for understanding global influences in race, religion and politics in ways that have been barely tapped.[90] The proliferation of studies on cultural and globalized aspects of sport has entailed neglect of some political topics. The use made of the Olympic Games by intelligence agencies remains virtually untouched, though it is nearly certain that intelligence agencies have been present at every Olympic Games since the Gestapo at the 1936 Olympics. During the Cold War the Olympics provided unusually good cover for a wide range of intelligence-related activities, including provocations, defections, propaganda and recruitment.[91] The study of the shaping of images, perceptions and cross-cultural transfer as well as the conduct of *sub rosa* diplomacy at international sports competitions could keep a gaggle of historians richly occupied for decades.

There are encouraging signs that sport is taking its proper place alongside other significant topics in the new international history. Increasing numbers of fully-fledged diplomatic historians have followed the lead of Walter LaFeber and Peter Beck by writing on sport.[92] Scholars of modern European history, both new and established, are also helping to bring sport and international relations into the mainstream.[93] More so than in other areas of international history, the study of sport entails fruitful cross-fertilization with other fields, notably political science and sociology (and to a lesser extent anthropology), the members of which are also writing about sport in greater numbers. Combined with rising interest in transnational issues among sport scholars, whose numbers and journals continue to grow, these trends promise a rapid increase in our understanding of sport's international dimensions.

As yet, however, the explosion of scholarship on sport's connections to international affairs has had little impact on international history or the discipline of international relations. In a recent textbook on 20th-century international history, sport appears only once, in a brief mention of the terrorist attacks at the 1972 Munich Olympic Games.[94] The various editions of William Keylor's widely used survey of 20th-century international history contain only incidental references to the Olympic Games.[95] In 2004 the eminent British political scientist Christopher Hill noted that international relations scholars continued to lag behind sociologists and historians in treating sport as a subject of academic inquiry.[96] However, there are a few signs of light. In a recent survey of the state of the art in international history, for example, the author of the entry on 'Non-Governmental Organizations and Non-State Actors' noted that athletic competition, 'though generally under-studied by historians, ... in the late nineteenth and early twentieth centuries contributed to the growth of international society through events and organizations free from direct state control'.[97] A key compilation of articles about diplomacy includes a chapter on sport diplomacy.[98] Given the increasing range, depth and vigour of studies on international sport, it is only a matter of time before such acknowledgments become standard, and ignoring sport becomes as intellectually disreputable as it was once intellectually acceptable.

Notes

1   I would like to thank Roy Hay and Bill Murray for useful comments on an early draft of this chapter; the rest of the Victorian chapter of the Australian Society for Sport History for helpful suggestions; and Carlos Aguirre for sharing his soccer bibliography.

2   Richard Cox's recent sport bibliography is suggestive of the state of the field: the table of contents has a handful of entries on general histories and on international competitions such as the Olympic

Games, but the rest consists of lists of individual sports and countries: *International Sport: A Bibliography, 1995–1999* (New York: Routledge, 2004).

3 For the references to sport, see Henry Kissinger, *White House Years* (Boston: Little, Brown & Company, 1979), 709–15, 1,299; idem, *Years of Upheaval* (London: Weidenfeld and Nicolson and Michael Joseph, 1982), 1,179–80. There are no references to sport in *Years of Renewal* (New York: Simon & Schuster, 1999). (I base my count on consultation of the books' indexes.)

4 Henry Kissinger, *Diplomacy* (New York: Simon & Schuster, 1994). Again, I am relying on the index.

5 On this point see also Steven Pope, 'Rethinking Sport, Empire, and American Exceptionalism', *Sport History Review* 38 (2007), 91–119; and John J. MacAloon, 'Politics and the Olympics: Some New Dimensions', Working Paper no. 128 (Institut de Ciències Polítiques i Socials, Barcelona, 1997), 5, available at www.icps.es/archivos/WorkingPapers/WP_I_128.pdf (accessed 12/01/07).

6 This belief is particularly entrenched in the USA, where sport is regarded as a 'private' affair and the government has long adopted a more hands-off approach than in many other democracies.

7 Barbara Keys, 'The Internationalization of Sport, 1890–1939', in Frank A. Ninkovich and Liping Bu, eds, *The Cultural Turn: Essays in the History of U.S. Foreign Relations* (Chicago: Imprint Publications, 2001), 201–20.

8 The emphasis is also on literature in English, though I have included references to key sources in other European languages.

9 Charles Maurras, 'Le Voyage d'Athènes', *La Gazette de France*, 19 April 1896, 1–2.

10 George Orwell, 'The Sporting Spirit', *Tribune* (London) (December 1945).

11 In English, see Jean-Marie Brohm, *Sport: A Prison of Measured Time; Essays*, translated by Ian Fraser (London: Ink Links, 1978).

12 Philip Goodhart and Christopher Chataway, *War Without Weapons* (London: W.H. Allen, 1968), 2, 17–19, 128, 140–48. Both Goodhart and Chataway were members of the Conservative Party; Chataway had competed in track at the Olympics and was an early opponent of competing against South Africa because of apartheid. Konrad Lorenz's *On Aggression* appeared in 1963. For similar views, see Norbert Elias and Eric Dunning, *Quest for Excitement: Sport and Leisure in the Civilizing Process* (New York: Basil Blackwell, 1986).

13 Richard Mandell, *The Nazi Olympics* (Urbana: University of Illinois Press, 1987; reprint of 1971 edn), xxvi–xxvii.

14 Ibid., xxvi, 288–89, xii–xxvi.

15 Hajo Bernett, *Sportpolitik im Dritten Reich* (Schorndorf bei Stuttgart: Karl Hoffmann, 1971); Arnd Krüger, 'Puzzle Solving: German Sport Historiography of the Eighties', *Journal of Sport History* 17 (Summer 1990), 261; Allen Guttmann, 'Sport, Politics and the Engaged Historian', *Journal of Contemporary History* 38, 3 (2003), 364.

16 Arnd Krüger, *Die Olympischen Spiele 1936 und die Weltmeinung: Ihre außenpolitische Bedeutung unter besonderer Berücksichtigung der USA* (Berlin: Bartels & Wernitz, 1972).

17 Andrew Strenk, 'Diplomats in Track Suits: The Role of Sports in the Foreign Policy of the German Democratic Republic', *Journal of Sport and Social Issues* 4 (1980), 34–45; Gunter Holzweißig, *Diplomatie im Trainingsanzug. Sport als politisches Instrument der DDR in der innerdeutschen und internationalen Beziehungen* (Munich: Oldenbourg, 1981).

18 Ulrich Pabst, *Sport – Medium der Politik? Der Neuaufbau des Sports in Deutschland nach dem 2. Weltkrieg und die innerdeutschen Sportbeziehungen bis 1961* (Berlin: Bartels and Wernitz, 1980).

19 See Maurice Spivak, 'Prestige national et sport: cheminement d'un concept, 1890–1936', *Relations internationales* 38 (1984), 175–91.

20 Heinz Timmermann, *Geschichte und Struktur der Arbeitersportbewegung, 1893–1933* (Ahrensburg: Czwalina, 1973); David Steinberg, 'Workers' Sport Internationals', *Journal of Contemporary History* 13 (1978), 233–51; Hans Joachim Teichler, ed., *Arbeiterkultur und Arbeitersport* (Clausthal-Zellergeld: DVS, 1985); Arnd Krüger and James Riordan, eds, *Der internationale Arbeitersport* (Cologne: Pahl-Rugenstein, 1985). For later studies, see Pierre Arnaud, ed., *Les Origines du sport ouvrier en Europe* (Paris: L'Harmattan, 1994); and Arnd Krüger and James Riordan, eds, *The Story of Worker Sport* (Champaign: University of Illinois Press, 1996).

21 Richard Edward Lapchick, *The Politics of Race and International Sport: The Case of South Africa* (Westport, CT: Greenwood Press, 1975). Lapchick noted that 'politics has become an integral and growing, if unwelcome, part of sports' (xxi). Richard Thompson's *Race and Sport* (Oxford: Oxford University Press) appeared in 1964 but dealt narrowly with South African sporting relations with

New Zealand. Thompson followed up with his 1975 study *Retreat From Apartheid*, while many others examined the issue of sporting boycotts and South Africa, most from an activist position prior to the 1990s.

22 David Black and John Nauright, *Rugby and the South African Nation* (Manchester: Manchester University Press, 1998), which builds on their work on this issue undertaken throughout the 1990s.

23 Henning Eichberg, 'Olympic Sport – Neocolonization and Alternatives', *International Review for the Sociology of Sport* 19 (1984), 97–106. See also James Riordan, 'State and Sport in Developing Societies', *International Review for the Sociology of Sport* 21 (1986), 287–309.

24 Swanpo Sie, 'Sport and Politics: The Case of the Asian Games and the GANEFO', in Benjamin Lowe, David B. Kanin and Andrew Strenk, eds, *Sport and International Relations* (Champaign, IL: Stites, 1978), 279–95; Ewa T. Pauker, *GANEFO: Sports and Politics in Djakarta* (Santa Monica: Rand Corporation, 1964). The latter is a mere 28 pages, but notable for being produced by Rand. On UNESCO see Barrie Houlihan, *Sport and International Politics* (New York: Harvester Wheatsheaf, 1994), 83–86.

25 Richard Espy, *The Politics of the Olympic Games* (Berkeley: University of California Press, 1979), vii–ix, 9, 168–71.

26 David B. Kanin, *Political History of the Olympic Games* (Boulder, CO: Westview Press, 1981), v, ix, 1, 152. See also the very uneven collection of essays in Lowe, et al., eds, *Sport and International Relations*.

27 Derick L. Hulme, Jr, *The Political Olympics: Moscow, Afghanistan, and the 1980 U.S. Boycott* (New York: Praeger, 1990), 7–8. See also Baruch Hazan, *Olympic Sports and Propaganda Games: Moscow 1980* (New Brunswick, NJ: Transaction Books, 1982); and for a thoughtful philosophical critique, John Hoberman, *The Olympic Crisis: Sport, Politics and the Moral Order* (New Rochelle: NY Aristide D. Caratzas, 1986).

28 Hulme, *Political Olympics*, 127–28.

29 Brian Stoddart, 'Sport, Cultural Politics and International Relations: England versus Germany, 1935', in Norbert Müller and Joachim Rühl, eds, *Olympic Scientific Congress, 1984, Official Report: Sport History* (Niedernhausen: Schors-Verlag, 1985), 385–411. See also the brief but suggestive article written by Didier Braun at about the same time: 'Le football international: symbols et réalités', *Relations internationales* 38 (1984), 245–50.

30 W.J. Murray, *The World's Game: A History of Soccer* (Urbana: University of Illinois Press, 1996), 201.

31 Journals that focused on history included: *The Canadian Journal of History of Sport and Physical Education*, beginning around 1969; the *Journal of Sport History* in 1974; *Stadion* in 1975; and the *British* (later the *International*) *Journal of History of Sport* in 1984. See Roy Hay, 'The World and Its Games: Researching and Writing Sport History', unpublished manuscript, which provides a useful survey of sports historiography primarily from a social history point of view. Outside of foreign affairs, a few historians did bridge the divide: on French sport, for example, Richard Holt and Eugen Weber were important bridge figures. On the situation in West Germany, see Krüger, 'Puzzle Solving', 265–66. It is worth noting that the evident partisanship of many sport scholars was regarded with undue suspicion outside the field. Scholars of human rights could be human-rights activists without undermining their credibility, but for a sport scholar to reveal a passion for sport was to impart a whiff of 'fan' literature to his or her work.

32 Trevor Taylor, 'Sport and International Relations: A Case of Mutual Neglect', in Lincoln Allison, ed., *The Politics of Sport* (Manchester: Manchester University Press, 1986), 28.

33 In later years, when historians began to study transnational dimensions of art, music and the like, none of them felt compelled to consider whether or not those cultural activities were forces for peace. On the so-called soccer war, see the brief account in Ryszard Kapuscinski, *The Soccer War* (London: Granta, 1990), 157–59.

34 John MacAloon, 'Politics and the Olympics', 4–5. For a similar point, see Houlihan, *Sport and International Politics*, 205.

35 See, for example, the traditional line-up of topics in James Riordan and Arnd Krüger, eds, *The International Politics of Sport in the Twentieth Century* (London: E & FN Spon, 1999); and Pierre Arnaud and James Riordan, eds, *Sport and International Politics: The Impact of Fascism and Communism on Sport* (London: E & FN Spon, 1998).

36 Christopher R. Hill, *Olympic Politics* (Manchester: Manchester University Press, 1992); Vyv Simson and Andrew Jennings, *The Lords of the Rings: Power, Money, and Drugs in the Modern Olympics* (New

York: Simon & Schuster, 1992). See also Bill Murray's useful review article, 'Higher, Further, Faster, Dearer: Ludus and Lucre at the Olympic Games', *Sporting Traditions* 9 (1992), 84–101.

37 Arnd Krüger and William J. Murray, eds, *The Nazi Olympics: Sport, Politics, and Appeasement in the 1930s* (Urbana: University of Illinois Press, 2003).

38 Per Olof Holmäng, *Idrott och utrikespolitik: den svenska idrottsrörelsens internationella förbindelser 1919–1945* (Gothenburg: Historiska institutionen, Goteborgs universitet, 1988); Hans-Joachim Teichler, *Internationale Sportpolitik im Dritten Reich* (Schorndorf: Karl Hofmann, 1991); idem, 'Sport und NS-Außenpolitik. Zur Rolle des deutschen Sports in der Macht-und Herrschaftspolitik des Dritten Reiches', in Wolfgang Buss, ed., *Die Entwicklung des Sports in Nordwestdeutschland 1945–1949* (Duderstadt: Mecke Druck & Verlag, 1991), 227–54; Pierre Arnaud and Alfred Wahl, eds, *Sports et relations internationals* (Metz: Centre de Recherche 'Histoire et Civilisation de l'Europe Occidentale', 1994); Pierre Arnaud, 'Des Jeux de la guerre aux jeux de la paix; sport et relations internationales, 1920–24', in Pierre Arnaud and Thierry Terret, eds, *Éducation et politique sportives* (Paris: Éditions du CTHS, 1995), 315–48; Kristina Exner-Carl, *Sport und Politik in den Beziehungen Finnlands zur Sowjetunion, 1940–1952* (Wiesbaden: Harrassowitz, 1997); and Harald Oelrich, *Sportgeltung, Weltgeltung: Sport im Spannungsfeld der Deutsch-italienischen Außenpolitik von 1918 bis 1945* (Munich: Lit, 2003). See also Sven Güldenpfenning's study of sport and the peace movement: *Frieden-Herausforderungen an der Sport* (Cologne: Pahl-Rugenstein, 1989).

39 Peter Beck, *Scoring for Britain: International Football and International Politics, 1900–1939* (London: Frank Cass, 1999); Walter LaFeber, *Michael Jordan and the New Global Capitalism* (New York: W.W. Norton, 1999). Beck was the first diplomatist writing in English to undertake serious study of sport; see his first article, 'England v Germany, 1938', *History Today* (June 1982), 29–34.

40 Uta Andrea Balbier, *Kalter Krieg auf der Aschenbahn: Der deutsch-deutsche Sport 1950–1972; Eine politische Geschichte* (Paderborn: Schöningh, 2007). See also the collection by Arié Malz, Stefan Rohdewald and Stefan Wiederkehr, eds, *Sport zwischen Ost und West* (Osnabrück: Fibre, 2007); and Tobias Blasius, *Olympische Bewegung, Kalter Krieg und Deutschlandpolitik: 1949–1972* (Frankfurt: Peter Lang, 2001).

41 Sandra Collins, 'Orienting the Olympics: Japan and the Games of 1940', PhD dissertation, University of Chicago, 2003. See also Exner-Carl's *Sport und Politik*, based on Finnish, German and Soviet sources; and Barbara Keys, *Globalizing Sport: National Rivalry and International Community in the 1930s* (Cambridge, MA: Harvard University Press, 2006), which is based on archival research in four countries and four languages.

42 Guoqi Xu, *Olympic Deams: China and Sports, 1895–2008* (Cambridge, MA: Harvard University Press, 2008).

43 Keys, *Globalizing Sport*, 3–4, 89, 188–89.

44 Lincoln Allison and Terry Mornington, 'Sport, Prestige, and International Relations', in Lincoln Allison, ed., *The Global Politics of Sport: The Role of Global Institutions in Sport* (London: Routledge, 2005), 5.

45 Jarol B. Manheim, 'Rites of Passage: The 1988 Seoul Olympics as Public Diplomacy', *Western Political Quarterly* 43 (June 1990), 279–95. See also David Black and Shona Bezanson, 'The Olympic Games, Human Rights, and Democratisation: Lessons from Seoul and Implications for Beijing', *Third World Quarterly* 25 (2004), 1,245–61; Jeffrey N. Wasserstrom, 'Using History To Think about the Beijing Olympics: The Use and Abuse of the Seoul 1988 Analogy', *Harvard International Journal of Press/Politics* 7, 1 (Winter 2002), 126–29; Richard Pound's fascinating memoir of the IOC's role in the negotiations between North and South Korea, *Five Rings over Korea* (Boston: Little, Brown, 1994); and MacAloon, 'Politics and the Olympics', which is in part an extended review of Pound's account.

46 Douglas Booth, 'Hitting Apartheid for Six? The Politics of the South African Sports Boycott', *Journal of Contemporary History* 38 (2003), 493; see also idem, *The Race Game: Sport and Politics in South Africa* (London: Frank Cass, 1998); Black and Nauright, *Rugby and the South African Nation*; John Nauright, *Sport, Cultures and Identities in South Africa* (London: Leicester University Press and Cape Town: David Phillip, 1997); idem, '"Like Fleas on a Dog": New Zealand and emerging protest against South African sport, 1965–74', *Sporting Traditions* 10, 1 (1993), 54–77.

47 Trevor Taylor, 'Sport and International Relations: A Case of Mutual Neglect', in Lincoln Allison, ed., *The Politics of Sport* (Manchester: Manchester University Press, 1986), 27–48.

48 Houlihan, *Sport and International Politics*.

49 Roger Levermore and Adrian Budd, eds, *Sport and International Relations: An Emerging Relationship* (London: Routledge, 2004). The editors' conclusions are somewhat timid: they argue that sport is

worth studying because it is part of the international system and that a deeper understanding of sport 'may foster greater understanding of the international environment', 9.

50 Black and Nauright, *Rugby and the South African Nation*.

51 Pascal Boniface, *La Terre est ronde comme un ballon: Géopolitique du football* (Paris: Seuil, 2002). See also idem, *Football et mondialisation* (Paris: Armand Colin, 2006). A conference on soccer and international relations resulted in the 1998 volume by Pascal Boniface, ed., *Géopolitique du football* (Brussels: Editions Complexe, 1998). For a survey of some of his key points in English, see Boniface, 'Football as a Factor (and a Reflection) of International Politics', *International Spectator* 33 (October–December 1998), 87–98.

52 See Patrick Finney, 'Introduction: What Is International History?', in Patrick Finney, ed., *Palgrave Advances in International History* (New York: Palgrave Macmillan, 2005), 1–35.

53 Akira Iriye, 'Cultural Relations and Policies', in Alexander DeConde et al., eds, *Encyclopedia of American Foreign Policy*, 2nd edn (New York: Scribner, 2002).

54 Akira Iriye, 'Culture and Power: International Relations as Intercultural Relations', *Diplomatic History* 3 (Winter 1978), 115–28.

55 For one critique of the cultural approach, see Robert Buzzanco, 'Where's the Beef? Culture without Power in the Study of U.S. Foreign Relations', *Diplomatic History* 24 (2000), 623–32.

56 Andrew Rotter, 'Culture', in Finney, ed., *Palgrave Advances in International History*, 269.

57 For a fascinating cross-national examination of public opinion and gender testing, see Stefan Wiederkehr, '"Unsere Mädchen sind alle Einwandfrei": Die Klobukoswka-Affäre in der zeitgenössischen Presse (Polen, BRD, Schweiz)', in Malz et al., eds, *Sport zwischen Ost und West*, 269–86. For further introduction to the literature on sport and gender, see this volume's entries on women's sports and masculinity.

58 Sayuri Guthrie-Shimizu, 'For Love of the Game: Baseball in Early U.S.-Japanese Encounters and the Rise of a Transnational Sporting Fraternity', *Diplomatic History* 28 (November 2004), 641.

59 Walter Hixson, *Parting the Curtain: Propaganda, Culture, and the Cold War, 1945–1961* (New York: St Martin's, 1997); Yale Richmond, *Cultural Exchange and the Cold War: Raising the Iron Curtain* (University Park: Pennsylvania State University Press, 2003).

60 For a suggestive treatment, see Barbara Keys, 'The Soviet Union, Cultural Exchange, and the 1956 Melbourne Olympic Games', in Malz et al., eds, *Sport zwischen Ost und West*, 131–45.

61 Robert Edelman, 'Foreword', in Stephen Wagg and David L. Andrews, eds, *East Plays West: Sport and the Cold War* (London: Routledge, 2007), xi. One exception is Victor Peppard and James Riordan, *Playing Politics: Soviet Sport Diplomacy to 1992* (Greenwich, CT: JAI Press, 1993).

62 M. Iu. Prozumenshchikov, *Bol'shoi sport, bol'shaia politika* (Moscow: Rosspen, 2004); see also Jenifer Parks, 'Verbal Gymnastics: Sports, Bureaucracy, and the Soviet Union's Entrance into the Olympic Games', in Wagg and Andrews, eds, *East Plays West*, 27–44. Soviet historians were careful to work on politically safe topics such as the Red Sport International and inter-war sports ties with workers' clubs in Europe. The few books produced on Cold War sport tended to be celebratory memoirs that carefully toed the party line.

63 Robert Edelman, *Serious Fun: A History of Spectator Sports in the U.S.S.R.* (New York: Oxford University Press, 1993), 151. On the cultural Cold War, see also Peter Beck, 'Britain and the Cultural Cold War's Olympics', *Contemporary British History* 19 (2005), 169–85.

64 On soccer see Michiko Hase, 'Race in Soccer as a Global Sport', in John Bloom and Michael Willard, eds, *Sports Matters: Race, Recreation and Culture* (New York: New York University Press, 2002), 299–319.

65 Penny von Eschen, *Satchmo Blows Up the World: Jazz Ambassadors Play the Cold War* (Cambridge, MA: Harvard University Press, 2004), 250–60; Damion Thomas, 'Playing the 'Race Card': U.S. Foreign Policy and the Integration of Sports', in Wagg and Andrews, eds, *East Plays West*, 207–21.

66 Amy Bass, *Not the Triumph But the Struggle: The 1968 Olympics and the Making of the Black Athlete* (Minneapolis: University of Minnesota Press, 2004).

67 Franklin Foer, *How Soccer Explains the World* (New York: HarperCollins, 2004). Foer offered a mixed picture: soccer, he concluded, maintained tribal loyalties even under the pressures of globalization, but could also offer – as in the case of Iran – a vision of secular nationalism that undermined religious fundamentalism. Simon Kuper wrote an earlier journalistic and anecdotal account along similar lines. Originally entitled *Football against the Enemy* (London: Orion, 1994), a subsequent US edition was given a catchy subtitle: 'How the World's Most Popular Sport Starts

and Fuels Revolutions and Keeps Dictators in Power'. For another notably extravagant title, see Richard Crepeau, 'Pearl Harbor: A Failure of Baseball?', *Journal of Popular Culture* 19 (1982), 67–74.

68 Robert K. Barney, Stephen R. Wenn, and Scott G. Martyn, *Selling the Five Rings: The International Olympic Committee and the Rise of Olympic Commercialism* (Salt Lake City: University of Utah Press, 2002), 51–58.

69 Christiane Eisenberg, 'Medienfußball: Entstehung und Entwicklung einer transnationalen Kultur', *Geschichte und Gesellschaft* 31 (2005), 586–609.

70 Arjun Appadurai, 'Playing with Modernity: The Decolonization of Indian Cricket', in *Modernity at Large: Cultural Dimensions of Globalization* (Minneapolis: University of Minnesota Press, 1997).

71 Boria Majumbar and Kausik Bandyopadhyah, *A Social History of Indian Football* (London: Routledge, 2006), 142–43.

72 For a recent set of essays from a management perspective, see Heather Gibson, *Sport Tourism: Concepts and Theories* (London: Routledge, 2006). On tourism and foreign relations, see Christopher Endy, *Cold War Holidays: American Tourism in France* (Chapel Hill: University of North Carolina Press, 2004).

73 For one intriguing recent analysis, see Roy Hay and Tony Joel, 'Football's World Cup and Its Fans', *Soccer and Society* 8 (January 2007), 1–32.

74 See, for example, Juan Javier Pescador, 'Vamos Taximaroa! Mexican/Chicano Soccer Associations and Transnational/Translocal Communities, 1967–2002', *Latino Studies* 2, 3 (December 2004), 352–76.

75 LaFeber, *Michael Jordan*.

76 Tony Mason, 'The Reign of Pelé', in *Passion of the People? Football in South America* (New York: Verso, 1995), 77–95.

77 Thomas W. Zeiler, *Ambassadors in Pinstripes: The Spalding World Baseball Tour and the Birth of the American Empire* (Lanham: Rowman & Littlefield, 2006).

78 Richard Giulanotti, 'Human Rights, Globalization and Sentimental Education: The Case of Sport', in Richard Giulanotti and David McArdle, eds, *Sports, Civil Liberties and Human Rights* (London: Routledge, 2006), 66.

79 David Rowe, 'Sport and the Repudiation of the Global', *International Review for the Sociology of Sport* 38 (2003), 281–94.

80 Allen Guttmann, *Games and Empires: Modern Sports and Cultural Imperialism* (New York: Columbia University Press, 1994), 171–88. See also J.A. Mangan, ed., *Europe, Sport, World* (London: Frank Cass, 2001), which covers the transplanting of German gymnastics to Brazil, athletics to Japan, soccer to the Palestinian Autonomous Areas, and African soccer players to Europe, among many other topics, as windows into cultural contact and diffusion.

81 Murray, *World's Game*, and Bill Murray, *Football: A History of the World Game* (Aldershot: Scolar, 1994), esp. 52. See also Wolfram Manzenreiter and John Horne, eds, *Football Goes East: Business, Culture, and the People's Game in China, Japan and South Korea* (New York: Routledge, 2004). On the effects of Western sport on Soviet cultural practice in the 1930s, see Barbara Keys, 'Soviet Sport and Transnational Mass Culture in the 1930s', *The Journal of Contemporary History* 38, 3 (July 2003), 413–34; on the incorporation of the Third World into the international sport system; see idem, 'The 1956 Melbourne Olympic Games and the Postwar International Order', in Carole Fink et al., eds, *1956: European and Global Perspectives* (Leipzig: Leipziger Universitätsverlag, 2006), 283–307.

82 For an argument about Americanization of the Olympic Games and American influences in amateur sport, see Barbara Keys, 'Spreading Peace, Democracy, and Coca-Cola: Sport and American Cultural Expansion in the 1930s', *Diplomatic History* 28, 2 (April 2004), 165–96; and idem, *Globalizing Sport*.

83 Richard Cashman and Anthony Hughes, 'Sport', in Philip Bell and Roger Bell, eds, *Americanization and Australia* (Sydney: University of New South Wales Press, 1998), 179–92.

84 Akira Iriye, *Global Community: The Role of International Organizations in the Making of the Contemporary World* (Berkeley: University of California Press, 2002); and John Boli and George M. Thomas, *Constructing World Culture: International Nongovernmental Organizations since 1875* (Stanford, CA: Stanford University Press, 1999).

85 For a useful brief history of FIFA, see Bill Murray, 'FIFA', in Riordan and Krüger, eds, *The International Politics of Sport in the 20th Century*, 28–47; and John Sugden and Alan Tomlinson, *FIFA and*

the Contest for World Football (Cambridge: Polity, 1998). On the IOC, see the good early study by Karl Adolf Schere, *Der Männerorden: Die Geschichte des Internationalen Olympischen Komitees* (Frankfurt: Limpert, 1974); its official history: *1894–1994: The International Olympic Committee – One Hundred Years*, 3 vols (Lausanne: International Olympic Committee, 1994); and Christiane Eisenberg, 'The Rise of Internationalism in Sport', in Martin Geyer and Johannes Paulmann, eds, *The Mechanics of Internationalism* (Oxford: Oxford University Press, 2001), 375–403. For an interesting call to place the IOC in comparative context, see John Hoberman, 'Toward a Theory of Olympic Internationalism', *Journal of Sport History* 22 (Spring 1995), 1–37.

86 John MacAloon, 'The Theory of Spectacle: Reviewing Olympic Ethnography', in Alan Tomlinson and Christopher Young, eds, *National Identity and Global Sports Events* (Albany: State University of New York Press, 2006), 15–39; Maurice Roche, *Mega-events and Modernity: Olympics and Expos in the Growth of Global Culture* (London: Routledge, 2001).

87 Eric Zolov, 'Showcasing the "Land of Tomorrow": Mexico and the 1968 Olympics', *The Americas* 61, 2 (October 2004), 159–88.

88 Uta Andrea Balbier, 'Der Welt das moderne Deutschland vorstellen: Die Eröffnungsfeier der Spiele der XX. Olympiade in München 1972', in Johannes Paulmann, ed., *Auswärtige Repräsentationen: Deutsche Kulturdiplomatie nach 1945* (Cologne: Böhlau, 2005), 105–19; Christopher Young, 'Munich 1972: Re-presenting the Nation', in Tomlinson and Young, eds, *National Identity* 9, 117–32.

89 Hay and Joel, 'Football's World Cup', 9.

90 For exceptions see Stephen Wenn and Jeffrey Wenn, 'Muhammad Ali and the Convergence of Olympic Sport and U.S. Diplomacy in 1980', *International Journal of Olympic Sport* 2 (1993), 45–66; Maureen Smith, '*Muhammad Speaks* and Muhammad Ali', in Tara Magdalinski and Timothy Chandler, eds, *With God on Their Side: Sport in the Service of Religion* (New York: Routledge, 2002), 189.

91 Philip Agee, *Inside the Company: CIA Diary* (New York: Bantam Books, 1975), 522. On the KGB's infiltration of the Olympics, see Prozumenshchikov, *Bol'shoi Sport*, 32–33, 58; Christopher Andrew and Vasili Mitrokhin, *The KGB and the Battle for the Third World* (New York: Basic Books, 2005), xxvii–xxviii (Mitrokhin was a member of the KGB escort to the 1956 Games); and memoirs of Western diplomats. On Britain's MI6, see Michael Smith, *The Spying Game* (London: Politico's, 2003), 183–84. For an interesting look at how Argentine fans sometimes turn to international conspiracy theories involving the CIA to explain losses by the national soccer team, see Jeffrey Tobin, 'Soccer Conspiracies: Maradona, the CIA, and Popular Critique', in Joseph Arbena and David LaFrance, eds, *Sport in Latin America and the Caribbean* (Lanham: Rowman & Littlefield, 2002), 51.

92 Historians include the author, Sayuri Guthrie-Shimizu, Nicholas Sarantakes, Thomas Zeiler and Guoqi Xu.

93 Historians include Martin Geyer, Uta Balbier, Molly Wilkinson Johnson, Jenifer Parks, Stefan Wiederkehr and Annette Vowinckel. Martin H. Geyer, 'Der Kampf um nationale Rapräsentation. Deutsch-deutsche Sportbeziehungen under die 'Hallstein-Doktrin', *Vierteljarshefte für Zeitgeschichte* 44 (1996), 55–86; Molly Wilkinson Johnson, 'The *Friedensfahrt*: International Sports and East German Socialism in the 1950s', *International History Review* 29 (March 2007), 57–82.

94 Anthony Best, Jussi M. Hanhimäki, Joseph A. Maiolo and Kirsten E. Schulze, *International History of the Twentieth Century* (London: Routledge, 2004), 416.

95 See, for example William Keylor, *The Twentieth-Century World: An International History*, 4th edn (New York: Oxford University Press, 2001), 390, where he notes that Carter 'organized a boycott of the Olympic Games held in Moscow in July 1980'. Keylor's *A World of Nations: The International Order since 1945* (New York: Oxford University Press, 2003) has similar coverage. Wayne C. McWilliams and Harry Piotrowski, *The World since 1945: A History of International Relations*, 5th edn (Boulder, CO: Lynne Rienner, 2001), mentions the Olympics more often but always as a peripheral issue, and has no index entries for sport or soccer.

96 Christopher Hill, 'Prologue', in Roger Levermore and Adrian Budd, eds, *Sport and International Relations: An Emerging Relationship* (London: Routledge, 2004), 1.

97 Finney, ed., *Palgrave Advances in International History*, 234; see also 235, 237–38.

98 H.E. Chehabi, 'Sport Diplomacy between the United States and Iran', in Christer Jönsson and Richard Langhorne, eds, *Diplomacy* (London: Sage, 2004), III: 238–52. Chehabi emphasizes the limits of sport diplomacy.

References

Balbier, Uta Andrea, *Kalter Krieg auf der Aschenbahn: Der deutsch-deutsche Sport 1950–1972; Eine politische Geschichte* (Paderborn: Schöningh, 2007).

Beck, Peter, *Scoring for Britain: International Football and International Politics, 1900–1939* (London: Frank Cass, 1999).

Boniface, Pascal, *La Terre est ronde comme un ballon: Géopolitique du football* (Paris: Seuil, 2002).

Booth, Douglas, *The Race Game: Sport and Politics in South Africa* (London: Frank Cass, 1998).

Espy, Richard, *The Politics of the Olympic Games* (Berkeley: University of California Press, 1979).

Houlihan, Barrie, *Sport and International Politics* (New York: Harvester Wheatsheaf, 1994).

Kanin, David B., *Political History of the Olympic Games* (Boulder: Westview Press, 1981).

Keys, Barbara, *Globalizing Sport: National Rivalry and International Community in the 1930s* (Cambridge: Harvard University Press, 2006).

LaFeber, Walter, *Michael Jordan and the New Global Capitalism* (New York: W.W. Norton, 1999).

Lowe, Benjamin, David B. Kanin and Andrew Strenk, eds, *Sport and International Relations* (Champaign, IL: Stites, 1978).

Murray, Bill, *Football: A History of the World Game* (Aldershot: Scolar, 1994).

Wagg, Stephen and David L. Andrews, eds, *East Plays West: Sport and the Cold War* (London: Routledge, 2007).

Xu, Guoqi, *Olympic Deams: China and Sports, 1895–2008* (Cambridge, MA: Harvard University Press, 2008).

Zeiler, Thomas W., *Ambassadors in Pinstripes: The Spalding World Baseball Tour and the Birth of the American Empire* (Lanham: Rowman & Littlefield, 2006).

16 Nationalism

Matti Goksøyr

'The imagined community of millions seems more real as a team of 11 named people.'[1]

To depict a national community as a football team points to some key positions regarding nationalism and sport. In paraphrasing Benedict Anderson, who entitled his most influential book on nationalism 'Imagined Communities', and by using the words 'more real' and 'team', Eric Hobsbawm delves into well-known images and challenges of nationalism and sport relationships. The quotation has been cited repeatedly in academic and popular writings on the subject.[2]

Various sports historians have found the subject of nationalism and national identities interesting and important. A substantial amount of the recent literature has confronted the relationship between nationalism and sport in a variety of ways on a wide range of empirical materials. This chapter will attempt to present an overview of the field, however ambitious and, therefore, imperfect, this may come out. The aim is not to cover every aspect, every example of interactions between sport and nationalism, but, rather, to present interesting cases that cover a broad scope of nationalism-related histories of sport. In addition, the chapter will have its own perspective, by trying to negotiate which kinds of nationalistic perspective can be found to be most rewarding for sports history and what their implications are. The following will also attempt to discuss what particular characteristics the field of sport contains that are relevant to the specific way in which the eventual 'sports nationalism' might have emerged and presented itself, as well as link the discussion to wider historiographical debates.

Since sport experienced a break-through as a modern phenomenon in the late 19th century, relationships between sport and nationalism have been visible and manifest. They can be found, if not all over the world, then certainly in numerous places on the globe. Naturally such a relationship became even more striking as modern sports and nationalism in many places had almost parallel development. However, similarity in time does not prove connections. So we have to ask the fundamental questions: What is the historical relationship between sports and nationalism? How has this relationship proved itself? When, or in which situations, has national identity been mobilized?

Most scholars would concur that sport can function as a marker for identities of many sorts. Even if this may not be the main reason for individuals to perform sport, there is a general agreement that from the perspectives of the spectators, the media, the large public sphere and, of course, the sports researchers, sports can function as an identity-constructor. This chapter will mostly take the general societal view and attempt to explore the functions and meanings of nationalism in sport and vice versa: sport's impact and interaction with nationalism.

Nationalism and national identity

The terminology associated with the word nationalism used to be dogged with pitfalls, as the political implications of being involved with the term and the ideology sometimes have been drastic. Modern studies have tried to lower some of these risks and have, in effect, made nationalism a more 'normal' field of research. Still, the term nationalism is bound up with various and sometimes contradictory meanings. Due to its historical context the meaning of nationalism has varied. It has connoted words such as independence and liberty, as well as aggression and the repression of others. This cleavage is also visible in the present use of the word, where parts of the world prefer to use the words nationality and national identity when connecting this to positive or non-controversial conditions, while nationalism, especially since World War II, has produced negative associations. This is not the case all over the world, though. Varying attitudes towards the term can be seen, for example in the English language where nationalism is not as burdened/laden as it is in some countries (Germany, Sweden), where it is almost synonymous with racism and variants of Nazism/Fascism. Quite contrary to this was the discourse around the new, independent African nations from the 1960s. Here nationalism was a word of credit and tribute and had only positive associations. The nationalist urge for new, independent nations to develop with their own political units could hardly be interpreted as anything other than democratization.

The historical stigma associated with the word nationalism had consequences for nationalism studies. The Finnish historian Aira Kemiläinen claimed that in the 1970s and 1980s researchers of nationalism had a cloud of suspicion hanging around them, and had to ensure and prove that they themselves were not nationalists.[3] Often, the less controversial term of national identity was preferred. Although related, the two are not synonymous. In the ongoing discourse nationalism usually implies the existence or construction of forms of national identity, while the latter does not presuppose the existence of the former. As sport is an international phenomenon, the terms nationalism and national identity describe currents that are in themselves international. The concept thrives on contests and rivalries. There is, perhaps, an historical irony in the fact that this concept, which points to the values of singularity, homogeneity and uniqueness, is such an international phenomenon.

What kind of historical phenomenon is nationalism? How has nationalism been studied and presented by nationalism scholars? Very few writers have suggested that it is an eternal phenomenon in human societies. Some would imply that nationalism can be intrinsic, waiting to be evoked; however, the majority of recent scholars maintain that nationalism is a historical phenomenon arising from modernization and the emergence of nation-states.

Writing on nations and nationalism mainly came up alongside the political development of nation-states and the idea that national communities should develop their own political units. The different approaches and perspectives to the phenomenon can be structured in different ways. Contributing to the unsettled state is that as the interest in nationalism has grown, so has the knowledge of an increasing number of different forms of nationalism. Inside one nation there can be many paths to a realization of national uniqueness.[4] However, even if the particular nationalism projects and their historical contexts vary, researchers are inclined to distinguish some common characteristics of how different nationalisms have come into existence.

One basic question that they all have to confront is when nationalism started. There will always be the occurrence of historical findings of expressions of identities claimed to be national before modern times. The Icelandic chronicler Snorri Sturluson, for example, writing around 1200, described a battle between Scandinavian Vikings taking place around 1000 BC and asserted that the battling men were able to distinguish between Danish, Swedish and Norwegian Vikings, based upon looks, language and ways of behaviour, and hence had a clear recognition of national identities (and thereby also what could be expected from them when it came to fighting abilities).[5] A majority of writers, though, have linked nationalism to a 'modern society', based upon nation-states, ideas of the French and American Revolutions, capitalism, mass communications and so on, at the same time emphasizing shifting aspects as crucial. Hence, it is fair to say that the 'modernist view' has dominated the nationalism studies scene. There is, though, reason to distinguish within the modernist group. An early stage of nationalism historiography sought to identify differences in perspectives. One of the first dichotomies to arise distinguished 'French' civic from 'German' ethnic nationalisms. Other elaborate distinctions have since then developed; modern research talks about modernists, primordialists (based upon land and territories), statists and political mythologists. Lately, anti-statist nationalisms also have been identified.[6]

The nation

One of the pioneers dealing with the question of what a nation was and is, was the French writer Ernest Renan. We shall give him some attention both because his writings have become a landmark in nationalism studies and because it is possible to trace his influence further, into sports. 'A nation is … a large-scale solidarity, constituted by the feeling of the sacrifices that one has made in the past and of those that one is prepared to make in the future', Renan wrote in 1882.[7] A national community is a 'kind of moral conscience' and a 'daily plebiscite'. This has since been taken as a signal of one of the main ways of understanding nationalism. Also known as the 'French', or 'civic' way, this emphasizes the individual, 'political' stand towards the national issue, in contrast to what is known as the 'German', or 'ethnic' way, which instead emphasizes characteristics such as 'blood' and 'race', or the ethnic dimension.

The Renan perspective can be said to be especially relevant for the question of nationalism and sport. The 'daily plebiscite' that Renan talked about constitutes itself in a pledge to the nation, the constitution, the flag and to other symbols conceived to be of importance to the nation. In principle, this means that a person's ethnic origin or heritage does not bear any significance. It is a voluntary, individual decision – taken every day – to be an American, or a Frenchman/woman. It is a conscious decision, not something a person is born into, as the ethnic version of nationalism emphasizes. The two versions must, of course, be considered principal or ideal types of nationalism. In real life many sorts exist, as well as mixtures of the two ideal types.

Benedict Anderson's description of national units as 'imagined communities' points to another dimension relevant for the nationalism and sport issue – the lived, experienced imagination of a community. This is related to Renan's statement about 'daily plebiscites', in emphasizing what goes on in the minds of people and not through their veins. Where Renan highlights the conscious statement, though, Anderson delves into the imagination.

How can a human feel (s)he has something in common with a person (s)he does not know, just because they share passports? This is where the imagined community comes in, according to Anderson. Shared nationality in some ways vouches for a mutual understanding on issues such as language, history, culture and other symbols. As we know, this is not always the case in a growing number of more or less multicultural and multi-lingual nations such as Switzerland, Belgium, Finland, Spain, the USA and others. Still, Anderson's 'imagined community' has long survived as a distinct observation on what constitutes national identities.[8]

Eric Hobsbawm maintains a Marxist-oriented view that nationalism is a conscious political strategy applied by elites or ruling classes to ensure stability and support. National identity re-socialized rootless individuals in times of turmoil and contributed to integration in a constructed community. The notion of nationality also contributed to historical continuity. He claims that 'the invention of tradition' was a means to achieve all this. This is where sport comes in, according to Hobsbawm. National celebrations and sports events channelled the energy of the masses into activities that did not undermine the existing power structures.[9] However, Hobsbawm did not entirely disregard other mechanisms that could be involved. He stressed that there had to be a popular resonance for an invention to become perceived as a tradition.[10] The constituents of a nation thereby have a way of influence regarding what is to be accepted as national symbols. This popular 'sounding board' could also be worth looking into as an entry to understanding how and why the relationship between sport and nationalism has come about in the different ways that it has. For the concept of national identity to have any consequence there should be some consensus, some community resonance around the national issues.

Delanty and Kumar summarized the nationalism debate and concluded that 'self-determination' is a key element in nationalism.[11] Transferred to the cultural dimension, this would emphasize a collective consciousness, while the political goal in some sense would be sovereignty. The commitment to commonality and cohesion is a common denominator and seems to account for the way in which a community can exist out there somewhere. A national community shares 'something'; this 'something' may not be original or exclusive, but enough or satisfactory to fill the need of symbols for communities. This 'something' could range from ideas and values (including beliefs in myths stressing the community's ethnic uniqueness), via languages, religions and history, to activities and territories.[12]

Much of this well-established scholarship relates well to sport without grave problems. However, we also have to bear in mind that these concepts and perspectives mostly are developed and used for other fields than sport. Therefore, without degrading the mentioned works, we should ask if the nationalism concepts applied within the wider historical discipline are applicable and relevant to sports history, or if sport is a special field that requires its own concepts? In other words, is there such a thing as sports nationalism?

There are specific challenges attached to the study of nationalism in sport. While political and mainstream cultural nationalism usually have no problem finding sources and spokespersons and can link their studies to preserved written or oral expressions of nationalism, sports as a research area presents challenges on these issues. Dealing with a physical and transitory phenomenon, historians of sport face the problem of sources/ historical evidence, and may have to focus on the ideological perspectives because of this. To connect sports to nationalism creates an extra problem, as the basis of nationalism is a claimed and imagined community. If we consider that a 'popular resonance' is a precondition for speaking about nationalisms as motive forces, we must then ask: who has been speaking on behalf of this community? The government or other state officials? The sports representatives? Or is it, in the end, the 'people' – at least the sports-interested part of the nation – who are the most rewarding keepers of genuine national sentiments?

To find historical evidence of popular attitudes is a general problem in history. However, popular culture and sports are arenas where it is possible to find utterances other than official, political statements. Verbal expressions from grandstands are often different to written statements from the responsible men and women in charge of society, to put it mildly. Sports seem to provide a potential for letting out attitudes that are not proper to display in other arenas. Whether we should attach great importance to such expressions is debatable, but in the sense that we here discuss repeated and customary ways of speaking and actions, such 'social practices' can become historically interesting as expressions of something that obviously has found a certain resonance in parts of the population.

The available sources from the 19th century derive mainly from the social classes that had the resources to have their attitudes and ideologies recorded for the future. Still, some questions remain, such as how are we to measure the strength of the nationalism?[13] Chroniclers of nationalism who have focused on the ideological side and the discourses around the phenomena have not paid so much attention to the methodological challenges involved in understanding and reproducing nationalism. We shall see that sports historians here are more inclined to delve into these matters. For example, Mike Cronin mentions how 'countless different forces … feed the creation of the imagined nation'. Sports historians, thereby, have made comments and contributions to the concept of 'banal nationalism'.[14]

The problem with immigration

A relatively young research area like the history of sports has from the start demonstrated what can be called a relative autonomy regarding on which perspectives to focus. However, from a beginning characterized by rather coarse studies, sports history has become more in tune with mainstream history. Hence, when the last decades have seen terms like nationalism, globalization and also regionalization being hailed as the forefront of interesting research subjects for social scientists and historians, the same concepts have raised interest also among sports historians. More particularly, nationalism as a concept and phenomenon over the last 20 years has received frequent attention in sports historical studies. How, then, can the sports historians' interest in nationalism and national identities provide new insights to the general historical area? The challenge of the sports historians will be to demonstrate that studies of sport and nationalism can go deeper than just showing that sports have played a role as one of many symbols necessary for the con-struction of a national identity, as many historians of nationalism have admitted. Recent historians interested in the field of sports have attempted to study how sports can present new views of societies, outlooks and analyses that would not be so easy to detect from other points of view. As a part of this, they would also study whether the nationalism involved in the discourse and practice around sport is of another character than 'normal', 'traditional' or 'ordinary' nationalism.[15] Could one say, with some degree of earnestness, that there exists such a thing as 'sports nationalism', and that this could be a fruitful and relevant term?

One of the first to encounter the challenges of the crossroads of modern sport and national identities and not least national sentiments, and to visualize what it (in his mind) was all about, was the notorious English conservative politician Norman Tebbitt who, in 1990, introduced a term which should be of interest for sports historians with a curiosity for nationalism. He called for a cricket test of immigrants to Britain. For people outside the British cultural sphere this could easily have been interpreted as a call for a test of immigrants' (lack of) practical skills in the arch-British game of cricket. This was, though, not the case. The test was not meant for immigrants from Europe or (North) America. The immigrants in question did not lack any interest in or knowledge of the game. Such expertise was taken for granted. The problem (for Tebbitt) was the immigrants' enthusiasm when following the game, especially when this enthusiasm came out 'wrong', i.e. when immigrants failed to support their new homeland and, instead, rooted for their country of origin when playing against England. For Tebbitt, this was hard to take and he, more or less earnestly, suggested that a 'cricket test' would prove a new citizen's loyalty. Cricket matches between England and, for example, Pakistan, India, Bangladesh, Sri Lanka or the West Indies, would efficiently decide the matter. Tebbitt was conspicuously ambiguous about the consequences of lack of support to the new homeland, but clearly it was not fortunate to demonstrate 'incorrect' loyalties. Tebbitt was inclined to interpret the whole thing as a test of will to become integrated. The idea led to a heated debate into which we shall not enter here.[16]

Tebbitt's infamous proposal demonstrates that sports can be an instrument for displaying and constructing various national sentiments. It also seems to constitute a special and maybe different arena when it comes to identities. The question to ask from the 'cricket test' is whether sport as a field of identities has other codes and relevancies than the ones to which politicians are accustomed. Perhaps the sports arena makes the 'us against them' dichotomy that Tebbitt envisaged even clearer. Then again, sports invite both serious and playful involvement with aspects like deep and complementary identities. Perhaps the field of sport illustrates the dilemma of many contemporary human beings, being rooted and uprooted, living in a multicultural existence where displaying complementary identities is not a huge problem. Actually, the development of an ever-more multicultural Europe makes the whole idea of a test stand out as an extremely interesting notion. Perhaps, at the end of the day, Tebbitt took the immigrants' 'disloyalty' too seriously, but there are other perspectives to the case of immigrants and national identity.

The question of loyalty to a new homeland versus the ability to express one's 'real' identity is demonstrated in the analyses of immigrants coming to the USA and Australia, respectively. Ever-renewing waves of European immigration to the USA brought thousands of soccer-playing males in the early 20th century, and soccer (football) for a while was a considerable sport in the immigrant communities at the east coast. However, according to John Sugden, as part of their effort to become Americans the newcomers chose to take up the sports of the hosts: baseball and American football.[17] This could also serve as a partial, though not comprehensive, explanation of why the global game of soccer never managed to get a decisive grip on the USA. The wave of European immigrants to Australia after World War II also brought soccer players, but to a different, smaller host population and in general on a lower scale. The history of Croatian soccer in Australia shows how immigrants, in spite of the host country's assimilation policy, chose to found their own 'Croatian' soccer clubs – not to contest their new Australian identity, but more as a celebration, perhaps, of an imagined community which before had been impossible, due to political constraints.[18] This possibly demonstrates that the weight of Australian assimilation was not as heavy as the American one. Australian post-World War II culture was very British and, therefore, had seen few problems in granting Irish and

Scottish representatives privileges when it came to identity representation. It was easier, then, for other immigrant groups such as Croatians or Greeks to claim equal treatment. It could be argued that as Australian identity was 'made in England',[19] a distinctive homegrown national identity had not yet been constructed and met with consensus, something that enabled other immigrant groups to establish their own imagined communities within the imagined community that was Australia.

It should perhaps be noted, though, that this habit of establishing ethnic, i.e. immigrant, sports clubs seems to have been well-known in many countries that were on the receiving end of immigration.[20] It was not accidental that this could be done in sports, rather safe from prosecution of any kind. As we shall see, sport constitutes an arena outside the ordinary.

Although sports, and particularly soccer in most of the world, can form 'a privileged space',[21] there can be limits also within the field of sport. Pierre Lanfranchi and Alfred Wahl discuss what they call 'the myth of the well-integrated immigrant'. The French soccer player Raymond Kopa was the big star of the French national team who won bronze medals at the soccer World Cup in 1958. Born of Polish parents with the family name Kopaszewski he was the classic example of a poor immigrant's son who climbed the social ladder and thus demonstrated the opportunities in a modern society. A national hero should not diverge too much, though. When he involved himself in a clash of professional footballers' rights, he was told by media on the other political wing to 'play up and shut up'.[22] Lanfranchi and Wahl provide a serious account of how immigrants 40 years before the celebrated champions of 1998 also could take on a hero role in a multicultural France.[23]

In summary, immigration introduces the ethnic factor in the nationalism discourse in a more direct and, for many, more challenging way, as Tebbitt's proposal of a cricket test showed – particularly when the immigrant does not wish to live up to the myth of a 'well-integrated immigrant'.[24] The question of immigration and nationalism is but one of many aspects of the challenges to a homogenous perception of the 'national'. The meeting of people across national boundaries has been one of sport's main functions. Nowhere has this task been so explicitly expressed as in the Olympic movement. What is more, the Olympics have provided some potential for nationalism to take the stage.

Nationalism at the Olympics

Even if new research on nationalism and sport did not take off until the late 1980s, there are numerous observations and reflections upon the historical encounters of the two modern phenomena 100 years earlier. The newly invented tradition of the Olympic Games invited reflection upon this, even though Olympism claimed an international foundation. For example, did the Frenchman Charles Maurras comment to his compatriot Pierre de Coubertin that his new invention, the Olympic Games, provided a form of nationalism with which he could sympathize? Maurras stated: 'I see that your internationalism … does not kill national spirit – it strengthens it'.[25] Even if this was not Coubertin's official idea, he did little to quell the nationalism that surrounded the Olympic Games from the very beginning. In stead he 'encouraged it, through symbols and actions'.[26]

After an initial phase marked by uncertainty regarding its organizational status, the Olympic Games after 1908 emerged as a suitable arena for political and nationalistic actions. Across the Atlantic rivalry between the English and expatriate Irish-Americans was evident. The controversy during the 1908 Games involved even President Roosevelt. On the European Continent antagonism between Germany and France was well-known and spilled over into the Olympic arena. Preparation for the Olympics very much resembled preparation for war, according to eager German sports officials who were building up for the Games in Berlin in 1916.[27] Some years earlier Scandinavia had seen its first political sports boycott when Norway refused to travel to the Nordic Games in Stockholm in 1905 because of Swedish allegedly intolerable attitudes in the ongoing struggle over the eventual upheaval of the union between the two countries. Swedish sports authorities responded by breaking up Scandinavian sports collaboration and by making the Olympic Games an arena for the settling of scores.

Another aspect arising from the growing importance of the Olympic Games was their utility in the creation of new nations. The International Olympic Committee (IOC) early on had claimed that the Olympics were a competition and meeting between individuals and not nations. Nevertheless, the IOC itself invited nationalistic fervour by stating that the individuals had to represent Olympic committees that were national by nature. The IOC also allowed symbols and rituals that added to the national feature of the Games, for example by operating its own official national points tables, until after World War I. Another unsolved challenge was that the IOC very early on had elected members from geographical areas with an unresolved political adherence. This raised the IOC dilemma of whether to distinguish between sports geography and political geography, or in other words between 'sports nations' and political nation-states.[28]

The fact that early modern sport in the Western world connoted amateur, upper-class activities and, in some cases, military and politically right-wing values, placed the issue of nationalism in a more open political context in some countries than in others. Finland, a very successful nation in Olympic history, provides some useful and interesting information. In track and field athletics, particularly in events like long-distance running and javelin throwing, the Finns dominated for large parts of the 20th century.[29] The Finnish example of how to utilize sports victories to gain national status was, undoubtedly, more successful in the cultural sphere than at the political. Finnish independence in 1917 relied on the break up of the tsarist empire and the Russian revolution. Sports victories played their part not in this, but in proving cultural force and what Eklund called 'national strength'.[30] This rather diffuse term pointing to ability to perform national endeavours and gain national prestige has been part of the early sports nationalism discourse. Coubertin himself was affected by this in his first writings on sport: to make France big again through sports, as physical education was a major objective for him initially.[31] Coubertin here connected with the English myth that the 'battle of Waterloo was won on the playing fields of Eton', which has proved to be a saying with rather low historical value, while the survival of the saying is an indicator of the belief in the relationship between sports, military power and national strength.[32] Sports were a means to call attention and respect to the existence of a small nation, to establish the small nation's place in the consciousness of the big world.

The case of the German Democratic Republic (GDR) has been described by several, particularly German, historians, both before and after the fall of the Berlin wall in 1989 and the collapse of the East German regime.[33] The political authorities of GDR put tremendous weight on sportive, Olympic success. Until 1989 there were no other nations that gave such priority to national self-assertion through Olympic medals than the GDR. The systematic cultivation of sports achievements – either by clever pharmaceutical support or elaborated training methods, or both – was meant to strengthen and build an East

German identity both for internal and external use. Sporting success only functioned as a shining varnish, however. Regardless of how many gold medals the cultivation of sport had brought, it was a thin basis on which to build a nation – thus effectively killing off any idea of correlation between national strength counted as Olympic gold and national strength in a political and socio-economic sense, as Arnd Krüger has pointed out.[34] Sporting success and the cultivation of national heroes failed to build a lasting identity in the GDR.

Many of the former colonies had borders that were not naturally demarcated, having been drawn at the conference table of the colonial powers. The new independent units contained ethnic groups that seldom constituted a natural community. To create a nation under these circumstances was a challenge that the new nations met. Nation building through uniting national heroes was launched as one prospect for creating national unity.[35] Certain East African countries, especially Kenya and Ethiopia, from the 1960s succeeded in producing impressive athletes, particularly in long-distance running. African gold medal-winning athletes did harvest international recognition. It has been debated, though, how deep the identity created through sports success has gone. They do not seem to have penetrated traditional ethnic or tribal thinking in Kenya, at least. Sports success as a form of enclave culture has also been discussed. Terje Tvedt asked if the export of national prestige had substantial local effects.[36]

Isolation, separatism or just resistance?

National sports heroes are clearly for internal use, as is most nationalistic behaviour, even political conflicts over disputed territories. Peter Waage has claimed that political nationalism can function as a refrigerator in reverse. On the inside it is warm and friendly, while on the outside it creates a cold and hostile atmosphere.[37] A parallel to this has existed in the sports field. In the extreme form it means shutting the door on the rest of the world and living a sporting life in splendid isolation. Such forms of isolationism seem to have been more dominant in earlier periods of the history of sports, before the international became really the overriding discourse in sport. However, as we shall see, remnants of this attitude still exist in some variants.

Conservatism disguised as nationalism has been a function especially where one nation has claimed a status of inventor of a sport. Such a status quite often has led to conservative positions when faced with expansion perspectives like internationalization and rule development. British attitudes to internationalization of soccer is a prime example. When ideas of an international football federation emerged around the turn of the 20th century, the British did not see a need for such a venture.[38] As inventors of the game, the British felt they had little to learn from the rest of the world.[39] Hence, when the Federation International de Football Association (FIFA) was founded in 1904 the British initially resisted, then finally joined in 1906, departed in 1920 and stayed away until 1946. In 1950 England for the first time took part in a World Championship and then had to face the reality that other parts of the world had learned to play, even the USA, which beat England in the first round. FIFA accepted the situation and has since confirmed the British prerogative by stating that today's ruling body (The International Football Association Board) still has four British members, while Ireland has been replaced by Northern Ireland; the modification is that the rest of the world also have four members.[40] The privilege of the British in the FIFA is confirmed by the fact that Britain can assemble four different national teams, contrary to all other nations, while the Olympics only allows one Great Britain team.[41]

A parallel to this has been the story of the Scandinavians and skiing. Particularly the Norwegian Skiing Association felt little need of international co-operation. In their eyes they had invented skiing as a modern sport and led a policy which was a mix of conservatism and nationalism, and which for a long period came out as isolationism. All proposals to change the rules of the sport in another direction than the Norwegian way were strongly opposed. However, internationalization of the sport and hence a growing influence by 'foreigners' could not be prevented. Reluctantly, the Norwegians had to go along with the launching of an International Skiing Federation (the FIS, *Federation Internationale du Ski*) in 1924. However, there was even more resistance to the proposal of organizing a separate Winter Olympic Games. The Olympics in their opinion meant sporting compromises and ideological degradation. The president of the Norwegian Ski Association warned against 'the continental view', which in his eyes meant 'record-mania, specialization and un-healthy idol-creation'.[42] As a powerhouse in the world of skiing, both in the hills and tracks and at the negotiating table, Norway together with Sweden could block proposals they did not like. As self-appointed protectors of the sport's 'real values', they often embraced conservative positions. Underneath was the opinion that the continental Europeans had not yet understood what genuine skiing was all about. They needed education and that would take time.[43]

Thus, the British authorities perceived national prerogatives in international football, just as the Scandinavians sensed privileges in skiing. The statutes of the FIS determined that the president and the general secretary must come from one of the three Nordic country members (Finland, Sweden or Norway). Nevertheless, the Norwegians seem to have gone through a period characterized by ideological defeats. Their ideal of versatile skiing did not catch on internationally. 'Nordic combined', though, secured a space in the programme and remained a 'Norwegian parade branch' for internal satisfaction. On other issues, however, despite their privileges, the Norwegians had to face that they had become a minority in their own sport. In addition to resistance to the Winter Olympics, they also initially opposed alpine skiing, women's cross-country and relay competitions. This resistance was not solely built upon ideological arguments; a more material reason for opposing the Winter Olympics was a growing fear that the national Holmenkollen races would lose their status as the most influential skiing contest, which could lead to a loss of income, prestige and, hence, power. In other words, the ideology presented could be 'nationalism with concealed incentives'.[44] As a national symbol, skis have survived, despite being made of a totally different, foreign material and even despite being made abroad. One can ask how many innovations such symbols take before they lose all original meaning. This is where sport's relationship to nationalism comes in. These symbols were a tool for activity and in the last century it has been the *activity* on skis that has defined the national meaning.[45]

The history of football in the Basque region of Spain throws light upon the social and political history of the Basque people and especially their relationship with Spain. Football and Basque nationalism seem to have evolved together over the last century.[46] Football, as well as Basque traditional sports, decorated with the *ikurriña*, the Basque flag, have become symbols for struggling national aspirations. However, here the form they have taken is rather exceptional. While not denying the British influence, the Basque regions have seen aspects of isolationism come to the surface as ethnic and political separatism. As sports clubs have become national symbols, they have been made into an extreme variant of the imagined community, by emphasizing their ethnic component. The Basque-only athletes recruiting policy practised by Basque football clubs and cycling teams during most of the 20th century is one example. Both the big football clubs, Athletic Bilbao and Real Sociedad, San Sebastián, chose this way of highlighting their national identity. In recent years, Real Sociedad has opened up to outsiders, while Athletic still swears by the Basque-only policy for its squad. This could have been a normal policy for a local amateur team, but for a highly professional club, operating in a Spanish league that has become ever-more commercialized, it has been considered as an extra handicap. However, to win with this extra handicap gives additional joy and motivation. Though struggling at times, Athletic has managed to hold a position as one of the league's top clubs, winning several trophies. Like certain other clubs in Spain, Athletic has been organized as a venture jointly owned by its members and not organized as a limited company. The fact that the supporters of the team also to some extent have been its owners opens up a particular form of identity in modern football. To celebrate victories in such a setting becomes perhaps distinctively strong. After Athletic won the Spanish league in 1984, the newspaper *El Correo Español* described the celebrations as 'the communion of a people with its team and, at root, the communion of a people with itself ... Athletic is ourselves'.[47]

Euphoria is a well-known element of sports nationalism in good times, and many nations and cultures would claim a particular capacity in this respect. The Basques, though, seem to be serious in their celebrations, and even more in their lack of celebration, or decision not to celebrate. The air of the streets of Bilbao – the otherwise football mad city in Spain – was definitely not in a celebratory mood after Spain won the Euro 2008.[48] Demonstratively indifferent attitudes to the first Spanish victory in the national sport of football sent out compelling signals of what matters and what does not matter. The message of both celebrations and non-celebrations was that Spain was irrelevant to the Basques, a nation by themselves.

If one wishes to put Basque football history into models, the difference between Athletic and Real Sociedad can be seen as ethnic vs. political nationalism. The former represents the 'blood that runs through the veins' to use the language of populist nationalists of any nation. The latter represents the community of a Basque club made up by players from different places, united in the understanding that they have something important in common: they represent a Basque football team. They constitute an imagined community which may have come together for temporary and rather un-idealistic reasons apparent in modern commercialized football. In this matter they would have less in common than a regular national team, who at least would have the same passport. The case of Real Sociedad illustrates that the imagined community is a wide concept, which can contain a community that does not need much imagination, as well as the opposite.

There are also other places where the sports nationalism is not so 'banal' (to use Billig's terminology). The Republic of Ireland has an unusual sports history, which, more importantly, has played an important role in the construction of Irishness. Both the revival/construction of Irish games such as hurling and Gaelic football, as well as soccer in the 20th century, played a vital role in this respect.[49] There is a vital difference between the two, though. The development of hurling and Gaelic football into symbols of Irishness was connected to an open political battle. Here, political and cultural nationalisms operated together. The founding of the Gaelic Athletics Association (GAA) in 1884 was a political act in the sense that it meant open cultural resistance to the British and their sports.[50] The GAA would not only prevent their members from playing soccer and other sports defined as British, but they would also prevent them from watching these sports. It followed as natural, then, that 'foreign' sports were banned from their grounds.

In today's divided Ireland, sport is a key to a broader understanding of political splits, but to understand politics and history it is also necessary to understand sports. According to Alan Bairner, the GAA in Northern Ireland 'has continued to play the counter-hegemonic role for which it first came into existence'. Northern nationalists were inclined to view the GAA and Gaelic games as a reminder of unfinished business, meaning the unification of the island. Such a view, it can be claimed, was supported by acts of the unionist ruling bodies in the North.[51]

Bairner summarizes Irish sports separatism like this: 'In other countries it was enough to beat the British at their own games. The Irish nationalists, however, were to go one step further'. They would engage in sporting activities that were exclusive to them. The purpose of this was to 'maintain their sense of having a separate and unique side'.[52] If one compares this to another distinct separatist nationalism, the result could be this: The Basques could play soccer precisely because it was British, not Spanish. The Irish of the GAA could not play soccer because it was British. For the Basques, the point was to beat the Spanish in a game none of them could claim was 'theirs'. One can add, as Lanfranchi and Wahl have done, that for colonialized people, if modern sport was seen as a legacy of cultural imperialism, their passion for the same sport could only be legitimized if it was interpreted as 'part of a struggle against colonialism using colonial methods'.[53]

Nationalism and media

Football and sport can still be standard bearers for hope, the hope of one ecstatic day when the unbelievable happens. The unbelievable being that a small frustrated football nation actually beats the bigger, unbeatable powerhouse. The radio reporter Bjørge Lillelien put this in words when he reported a rather unexpected Norwegian win over England in football in 1981. In his professional ecstasy he listed all the English heroes (as well as celebrities) he could find at the moment. His conclusion was: 'We have beaten them all! We have beaten all of them!' His full outburst is worth repeating:

> There he (the referee) blows. There he blows. Norway has beaten England 2–1 in soccer. It is absolutely unbelievable. We have beaten England – England, home of giants, Lord Nelson, Lord Beaverbrook, Sir Winston Churchill, Sir Anthony Eden, Clement Atlee, Henry Cooper, Lady Diana. We have beaten all of them. We have beaten all of them. Maggie Thatcher, can you hear me? Maggie Thatcher, I have a message to you, now in the middle of your election campaign. I have a message to you: We have knocked England out of the World Cup in soccer. Maggie Thatcher: As they say in your language, in the boxing bars around Madison Square Garden in New York: Your boys took a hell of a beating. Your boys took a hell of a beating. Maggie Thatcher. Norway has beaten England in soccer. We are the world's number one.[54]

The reporter's conclusion, then, was that not only 'eleven named people', but 'we', i.e. all Norwegians, had beaten 'all of them', i.e. not only their 'eleven named people' and not only every English person living, but also all the historical English heroes of varying qualities that the reporter managed to list. If we regard this outburst as exaggerated, one should take into consideration that this radio narrator was taken to the nation's heart, and that his outburst was seen as a wonderful example of national passion and euphoric happiness over a soccer game. The outburst, then, has become a national myth, enabling the memory of a rather lucky win over an England side that definitely was not the best in the world to live on, much longer than it otherwise would have done.

There is reason to stress the impact of modern media on nationalism and sport. Benedict Anderson stressed the importance of the printed word, books and newspapers, in paving the ground for modern nationalism. It can be argued, though, that the technological development of the 20th century, in the form of radio and television, has strengthened this significance of the imagined community, perhaps in the direction of a community with common experiences, even more. The radio, introduced to most of Europe after World War I, more than the press made possible simultaneous experiences. It created a new way of taking part in and experiencing sport that did not require a physical presence at the arena and hence enabled participation from larger parts of the nation. The radio then made sports events into events of national importance and radio listeners became integrated in a culture of simultaneous participation and insight. When such common experiences find resonance and a foothold in the collective memory, they can also contribute to the shaping of the national identity.[55]

The introduction of televised images from sports events has strengthened this development even further. Several media studies have emphasized aspects of the relationship between TV and sport; however, we must stick to the impact of TV on sports and nationalism. While the radio gave an impression of simultaneous experience communicated by a reporter who was present, TV gave the impression of actually being there and seeing the event with one's own eyes. Parallel to this, the feeling of authenticity grew and new methods of national involvement were made possible. TV viewers had become an ever-more important segment. In recent decades, the TV studio has become the place from which to reach out to the nation. Televised sports in many countries have become the most popular broadcasts. Politicians have discovered this and try to connect with the populace through the medium of sport.

A more subtle form of nation building is the making of national rituals through the TV screen. In probably most advanced TV nation in the world, the USA, Thanksgiving Football and the Super Bowl have become rituals that unite the population through the TV screen. As Steven Pope has suggested, they are also examples of rather recently invented traditions that enable Americans to feel good about themselves and link sports with other more established national customs like the Thanksgiving celebration.[56] In this way, sports influenced the transformation of the holiday from a religious occasion to a secular one. The TV shows constructed around these events make an effort to combine sports, popular culture, national symbols and quite often politics, at least politics defined as patriotism. In essence, the big TV shows on these occasions create a sense of what it means to be American.

The linking of national holidays to sports and eventually to TV, making new traditions connected to sports can be seen also in other parts of the world. The British Boxing Day soccer is mainly a tradition for going to the stadium; recently, however, they have also become TV affairs. The same could apply to a number of sports, as TV becomes an increasingly important transmitter of experiences, including sports experiences, to the degree that the 'real' sport, the one that people, i.e. the nation, talk about, is the sport that they have watched on TV. On the other hand, televised soccer in large parts of the world, particularly in the hyped, commercial form, through its unbinding character, seems custom built for a variant of sports nationalism to which we shall return: the so-called 90-minute nationalism.

Nationalism and masculinities/gender

As sports have been linked to masculine values, it should come as no surprise that the most celebrated national sports are particularly entangled with masculinity. The case of Basque football provided both self images and views from others of brave, courageous, tough, hard-working men.[57] In their own eyes they are inventors of the *furia*, later colonized by the Spanish, meaning the Spanish rage/furiousness.[58] Eduardo Archetti has studied the relationship between masculinity and national identity in Argentina on the basis of three physical and cultural activities: football, polo and tango.[59] Archetti particularly emphasizes how the 'essentialist' discourse has surrounded Argentine sport. Contemporary players were always evaluated as to how they lived up to ideals claimed to be established by former, golden-age generations which had established *how to play*, and also managed to establish some consensus around the conception that this was the Argentine way.[60]

Brazil's passion for soccer is a well-established story.[61] The obsession makes it natural that they would have a distinct term for playing style: the 'samba football' is meant to describe the Brazilian way of playing the game. This is, of course, as much an essentialist image as the one Archetti has described for Argentina. Even if samba is usually a dance performed by two persons of different sexes, Brazilian soccer, like the Argentine, has been always a male preserve. Hence, the playing style has been depicted as the way Brazilian men like to play and should play. The national style, then, is heavily based upon technical skill and keeping the ball low to the ground. Latino soccer also has sexual connotations. To be outplayed by a 'tunnel', i.e. to have a ball dribbled through a player's legs, according to Archetti, is a sexual insult and the top of individual humiliation on a soccer field.[62] As soccer machismo has been prevalent in Latin America, the soccer craze traditionally has had the effect of connecting national pride through sport to masculinity. In Brazil this has been the case of soccer players and Formula One motor racing drivers in the main. Recent decades, though, have seen female sports rising in attention. Even the arch-masculine soccer has seen world-class players being produced and exported to the USA and Europe. What this will do to the national image of ball-playing Brazilians – traditionally men – remains to be seen.

The American historian Robert Edelman has taken an interest in soccer in the Soviet era, as a special aspect of everyday life in Soviet times. Edelman in recent works has drawn upon studies by the Argentine social anthropologist Eduardo Archetti, who has written extensively on national identity and sport. While Archetti's speciality was Latin American, particularly Argentine, football, Edelman describes the southern Soviet republics (Armenia and Georgia). He does so using perspectives from Archetti. If not exactly the Latinos of the Soviet Union, then certainly Armenian and Georgian players through their playing styles represented identities which were to become ever-stronger symbols for growing nationalist sentiment. Spartak Moscow's Armenian coach, Abram Dangulov, was said to bring a 'Southern style' to Russian/Soviet football around 1950. Georgian and Armenian players were renowned for their technical skills and for their 'fiery Southern passion'.[63] The essentialist attitude of what constitutes national identity seems to have been prevalent also in post-World War II Soviet football.[64]

The way rugby football has been a part of the construction of several nationalist masculinities has been a frequent topic in sports history writing. As nationalism has many facets, so has masculinity. Rugby and Welsh masculinity, then, is a different story to that of rugby and South African masculinity. In both nations rugby has played a vital role in different nationalist narratives, but as the historical meaning of Welsh rugby can be connected to issues of class and Welsh mining communities, the South African game was played out in a context of extreme ethnic and racial divisions. The dominating public image of rugby was connected to rough Boer masculinity. In the Boer rhetoric rugby in a physical way demonstrated the values beneath white supremacy. The linking of rugby to nationalist sentiments in South Africa at that time, up to the 1990s was limited to a very select part of the nation: the white minority. Scholars such as Grundligh, Nauright, Booth and others have analysed how the game functioned, and especially what happened to the nationalist fervour around rugby after the apartheid system was abandoned in the early 1990s. The successful World Cup on home ground in 1995, when the formerly accused terrorist prisoner Nelson Mandela handed the cup to the team captain was a symbolic moment of hitherto unseen dimensions. Mandela was dressed in the Springbok jersey, with the captain's number on his back. The springbok symbol had been closely associated to Boer rugby. Hence, in the story of the new South Africa, Mandela had seized a symbol of white South Africa in a white sport and turned the victory into a sensational event for the whole, united South Africa. The immediate effect of this was euphoric. If this policy was successful it would give South African rugby a whole new meaning. The outcome of an historical action is often uncertain, and in the South Africa of the last decade this may be more true than in other places. However, the event is an example that history can be made also in our times. It also shows that the relationship between sports, nationalism and other cultural and political issues probably have been more dramatic in South Africa than in most other countries.[65]

National sports – national styles

Sports can mean varying things to different nations. Some nations like to present an image of being interested in sports in general. Australia is an example of a nation excelling in most water sports, like swimming, sailing, rowing and others, as well as having four professional leagues in four different footballing codes. On the other hand, there are sports that are of specific significance to a nation. So-called 'national sports' have been a repeated, but unqualified term in the less academic sports discourse.

In South Africa there is an obsession with rugby, whereas in the Caribbean, baseball is played with obsession in areas with a Spanish influence (Cuba, Dominican Republic), while cricket is a visible part of the English heritage in the West Indies. In Asia, and particularly China, table tennis holds a dominating position among the billions that perform sport. Indonesia has a love affair with martial arts and badminton. Canada 'is' ice-hockey, while the Scandinavian/Nordic countries adore skiing. Sometimes the explanation of these different preferences is taken to be based on natural causes: temperature, climate, nature, and then seen as an almost deterministic historical outcome. This is, though, too simplistic an explanation.

If one wishes to delve into the discourse of national sports, it could be argued that the concept itself consists of different approaches to the subject – the subject being that a nation or an imagined community conceives one particular sport as more important, more prestigious than any other sport. As earlier argued, the term 'national' involves some popular consensus, hence the national sport must be embraced with some kind of recognition. The forms of recognition may differ, however. The crucial question seems to be what, or who, defines the national sport? Then, how is this chosen sport to be portrayed?

Are there any common characteristics of all these 'national sports'? One interpretation representing what we might call an early phase of national identity is that every national sport seems to be a carrier of claimed implicit virtues highly regarded in the home country, and that they are symbols of uniqueness; the activity itself makes the identity. The sport or the game will, accordingly, symbolize the moral value or the character of a particular people better than most other phenomena. National sports all symbolize the same things: 'our greatness, our uniqueness', whether it is Gaelic, American or Indonesian. Only accidental cultural and natural differences make the symbolic sports themselves differ. More rewarding, perhaps, then is to look at the *functions* of the national sports? Is it possible to distinguish categories for interpreting the concept?

I argue that analytical categories, here in the form of *idealtypes*, as developed by Max Weber, can be useful as tools in historical research, though they may never have occurred empirically in their pure form.[66] Rather, it is a way of sorting out features that are considered important in the historical and cultural variations of the phenomenon.[67] By applying the idealtype approach we can gain an overview of how the 'national sport' concept has been used.

Different ways of applying the term, ranging from politically determined applications, to cultural preferences showing themselves through activity or spectator interest, can be distinguished. They illustrate various historical approaches to the cultural role of sport, and they indicate a concept still considered applicable in certain connections.

The first case in point may be discovered in the new nations that we have discussed briefly, which have been involved in nation building. This type could be defined by its political and administrative imperatives: national authorities officially have declared a certain sport or activity to be, or rather to become, the national sport of the country. The contemporary examples that spring immediately to mind are from so-called Third World countries eager to establish their own identity. Historically, though, the need to define uniting cultural symbols allegedly rooted in the 'national heritage' has been clearly visible in many states all over the globe in this phase of national development. In the new nation of Indonesia the *pencak silat*, a modern version of a traditional martial art, was declared the national sport not long after independence in 1948, clearly as a conscious political act to build a new Indonesian identity. However, in order to give the traditional martial art, which according to Andrew Weintraub had existed in at least 157 different types of either *pencak* or *silat*, a legitimate uniting function for the whole of the new nation-state, one had to acknowledge a standardized, national version with at least some consensus.[68] This is also an example of how identity building implies new innovations as well as struggles over history: was this martial art a genuine Indonesian innovation, or was it something with a common South-East Asian origin? To illustrate that the topic we are discussing is international and of relevance everywhere and in any epoch where cultural and national identity building is in question, how was the sport to be presented internationally, if it were presented at all? Was it correct to diffuse the sport, to organize world championships, or would this kind of sportization mean cultural debasement and even demise? What virtues would be promoted in the sportized version of *pencak silat*? What would this new version mean for Indonesian national identity? All these questions are, of course, not unfamiliar to other historical settings as well.

A second and not so official approach to the phenomenon of 'national sports' can be found in nation-states having moved further on in the process of nation building, but where there still exists a need or desire to elevate an element of the popular culture to something national and uniting. The US approach to baseball can be put into this category. According to baseball entrepreneurs, and some historians, baseball represented what they saw as typical American virtues. Albert G. Spalding actually set out to 'prove' that the game was a genuine American invention.[69] In such an interpretation, the game emphasizes central features in American culture. The game 'was too lively for any but Americans to play', according to Spalding.[70] Irrespective of such dubious statements, baseball in the USA is relevant to the idea of 'national sports' in various countries with an urge for a common identity. Allen Guttmann would perhaps suggest that Spalding – and many others – mistook the characteristics of modernity for the characteristics of the new nation. However, over the years a national consensus on the notion that baseball is 'America's game' did develop. One illustration of baseball's position is the amount of publications on baseball; in the early 1990s this rose to an average of more than 350 annually.[71]

A third ideal type for applying the concept has been to 'elect' national sports on the basis of how well the country has been doing in international sports. In other words, the national sport is the one in which the country has gained most international merit in recent decades. This does not seem very cultural, a rather more cynical way of inventing uniting symbols. It is not a way of building or representing deep identities. Nevertheless, it would be the consequence of a reduction of the nation – at least the sports-interested part of the nation – to sports consumers without any real loyalty. Such a strategy can, thus, be a means of buying short-term popularity. In times of modern consumerism, these kinds of loyalties have come to mean quite a lot, and it would not be a total anachronism to speak of 'our new national sport' as some media do whenever fortune has been good. To return to the Indonesian example, it has brought forward a debate on whether badminton instead of *pencak silat* should be considered as the true Indonesian sport.

A fourth way of detecting a country's national sport has been to study participation and simply state that what the people of the nation *do* must be the national sport or pastime. In other words, the sport with the largest number of active participants would be held up as the national sport of that country. Such an approach is made, from time to time, especially by countries where the sports organization historically has been built on popular movements with an inherent and explicit goal of mass sport, as in many northern European nations.[72] The 'proof of the pudding' would in these cases lie in the amount of participation, or in other words: identity through mass activity.

Finally, we can broaden the definition of a national sport even more, to a fifth idealtype, and investigate what the nation *engages* in, meaning also as spectators, be it on the arena or in front of the TV set. In this way, the sport that engages people the most – in the modern term of ratings – would be the national sport. From such a perspective sports would be regarded as part of the mass culture and the commercialized entertainment industry. The difference between the fourth and fifth definitions is cultural, dealing with opposing views on what is most important: the active participatory side, or the commercialized entertainment side. In this way, it illustrates that distinct definitions of cultural phenomena have to be applied to studies of different cultures.

Rivalries: war without weapons

Historically, rivalry has been a breeding ground for all sorts of nationalism. This is also the case for sports and nationalism. For the Scottish soccer player Dennis Law, 'anti-Englishness … was the proof of true Scottishness'.[73] However, where the rivalry is taken into the sports field, there is a chance of dealing with it in a more peaceful manner. Even if George Orwell's famous phrase of sport as 'war minus the shooting' in many cases seems to have been a relevant and well-coined depiction, it still was without the shooting.[74] Some sports encounters may have come close to Orwell's description, though. In general, did the Cold War provide for portrayals like this when the two superpowers, the USA and the Soviet Union met? One particular example of this was the semi-finals in the Olympic ice-hockey tournament in 1980 in Lake Placid, USA – a game that has been depicted in US movies and in writing, all portraying the story of rivalry, a war without weapons, stereotyping, all so important to nationalistic storytelling. Clearly, ice-hockey is a sport where the physical encounters are literate and expressive.

Other sports may have less potential for violence, but still have a meaning that could be just as prestigious in rivalry. Cricket is often portrayed as an arch-British game, displaying values and attitudes considered to be typically British – even if it is often contested what these values are.[75] However, there is also the image of cricket as the game of the British Empire. Hence, cricket has come to mean a lot to nations that have not much else in common, but their having been a part of the British Empire, either as a dominion or a colony: Australia, New Zealand and South Africa, the West Indies and the Indian sub-continent.[76] The nations stemming from the Jewel in the Crown – India, Pakistan, Bangladesh and Sri Lanka – may occupy a special place in cricket history, and India and Pakistan's cricket rivalry has long been filled with prestige. These meets have taken place in a context of grave political unrest and could, therefore, be an arena that could ignite sparks. Instead, encounters in the national sport of both countries so far have been chances for relatively peaceful gatherings, even for initiatives along a diplomatic channel.[77]

Rivalry in the sports ground has been perfect for reconstructing traditional stereotypes of 'the other'. Particularly when the issue was to challenge the arch rival, often perceived as the big brother in an uneven relationship, and in anthropological/sociological terms 'the relevant other' – the one time when it really mattered to win – interest grew. For historical reasons, one nation in Europe especially seems to have to play the role of nationalistic 'prügelknabe' in populist media. Germany, historically has been the arch rival of France and England. UK newspapers, in particular, have excelled in stereotypes, almost all stemming from World War II, when an important soccer match between the two countries has been played.[78] In modern soccer, they have also become the 'relevant other' for the Netherlands to beat. Having been invaded and occupied by Germany in two world wars, the political relationship between the Netherlands and Germany stabilized and returned to more friendly associations. The meets at the sports grounds eventually, but not immediately, as Simon Kuper points out, became more important as an arena of contest. Kuper's description of the relationship the Netherlands had with Germany after World War II fits well into the concept of the 'relevant other'. As the military side of the confrontation grew more distant, the importance of keeping up the performance at sports grounds allowed them to keep the images and stereotypes from the old days, but in a less dangerous way. According to Kuper, the match of Netherlands vs. Germany – 'the greatest grudge match in European football' – in 1988, which ended with a Dutch win, brought the largest ever congregation of people to the streets since peace was announced in 1945.[79] The enormous relief and reaction on the Dutch side was clearly related to the war; but on the other hand, it was not only related to the war. Kuper tried to show how sports, and soccer particularly, had emerged to be the field where a qualitatively different type of meeting could take place, and that a sporting rivalry is something apart from a political and military campaign.

Nationalism's dark sides: xenophobia and ethnic cleansing

While sport often presents potential for friendly rivalry, political nationalism at the outside can also radiate an 'us vs. them' climate, which exudes hostility and aggression.[80] The

Olympics of 1936 (The 'Nazi Olympics') are one well-known example.[81] The Balkan wars in the 1990s are an even more striking example where sports actually played an important role in the build up to the wars that ravaged this part of Europe only recently. Allen L. Sack and Zeljan Suster have investigated the relationship between soccer and Croatian nationalism and have found close interactions.[82] Two soccer matches were significant in 1990: one led to the worst sports-related riots in Yugoslavian history, while the other, according to Croat sources, led to the restoration of the Croatian national team. Both incidents were of vital symbolic meaning. Sack and Suster are, however, insisting that the importance of these games can only be seen in a historic and political perspective. The multicultural state of Yugoslavia had led a fairly successful unification policy until the late 1980s. People had married across the ethnic divide, the national teams of the state were broadly supported across boundaries. The decline of Communism worldwide and the death of head of state, Tito, meant that unifying forces were weakened. Traditional religious and national identifications began to reassert themselves. The election in April 1990 of Franjo Tudjman as President of Croatia raised nationalist passions 'to a level not seen since the Ustashe rule in World War II', according to Sack and Suster. Symbols like the new Croatian flag added to these passions. Two weeks after the election the two big clubs, Dynamo Zagreb and Red Star from Belgrade met, this time in the context of a Yugoslavia in crisis and rapidly intensifying nationalism. At the match, clearly politically motivated riots broke out. Both Croat and Serb media seem to agree that this traditionally prestigious clash was a decisive match. Not in a sporting sense, but taking the hostilities to another level. The game was on national TV. However, the riots that followed also involved a third factor, the Yugoslavian police, by the Croats perceived as the long arm of the Serbs. Sack and Suster claim that one event from the game was of particular symbolic importance: when the star and captain of Dynamo Zagreb, Zvonimir Boban, entered the stage to defend a Dinamo fan from a Yugoslav police officer. Boban ended up punching one officer and kicking another. Not just in a symbolic way, but with the physical force of one of Yugoslavia's most famous players, who was also a Croat, attacking an officer of the state, which was still the legitimate governing body where Boban lived and played soccer. 'Perhaps no single event during the riot better captures the nature of the strained political relations between Croats and Serbs in May 1990 than the attack of Dinamo's team captain, Zvonimir Boban, on a Yugoslav police officer'.[83] Boban received a temporary suspension, but within Croatia 'he became a national hero'.[84]

What Boban had done was symbolically to challenge the legitimacy of the entire Yugoslav Federation. A couple of months later another event took place. Croatia's 'national team' was about to play their first international game since World War II. They were playing against the USA in October 1990. The Yugoslav Federation was still a sovereign nation of six republics and Croatia was not a member of FIFA, but Croatia's new president, Tudjman, was striving for independence and full international recognition. In this respect, the game against the USA was a 'major public relations coup'.[85] Using the match to associate Croatian nationalist symbols, some of which had a dubious past, with symbols of freedom and democracy in the USA was deft political craftsmanship. By allowing the US soccer team to accept an invitation to play a Croatian all-star team that called itself the 'Croatian National Team', Sack and Suster claim, the USA was arguably extending informal diplomatic recognition to Croatia.[86] Only months later, war broke out between Croats and Croatian Serbs; the fighting lasted until 1995. In the intervening years, the ugly side of nationalism had operated. Armed campaigns 'cleansed' areas based upon ethnic identities. Such 'ethnic cleansing' was performed by both sides during the war, but when the Croats took full control of the formerly multicultural geographic area of Croatia in 1995, they had driven away around 250,000 Serbs.

The story of these events underlines one important issue: that sport does not solely mirror larger social and political events, but actually has the power to influence them. Croatian nationalists clearly used soccer for political purposes. The two soccer matches not only reflected the conflicts in Yugoslavia, but mobilized public support for the civil war that seemed inevitable.[87]

Recent trends in historical nationalism studies and their relevance to the history of sport

Nationalism over the last few decades has met new surroundings and new environments. The globalization of nationalism contributes to new and changing forms of the phenomenon which can still be labelled nationalism. The socio-political environment of today's nationalism is different from the conditions under which traditional nationalism was first invented.[88] The global context is different. The nation-state is in debate. Other forms of societal organizations exist. That nationalism is fluid and not static is, however, old wisdom.

Alan Bairner claims that globalization has not reduced the content and impact of national identity in sport. At the very least, it seems that identities revealed through sports are different from the more 'official' identities. In my opinion, Bairner could have taken this discussion further. In modern Europe there are numerous cases that could illustrate this. Another thing Bairner misses in a book about 'European perspectives' and globalization is a debate on the deliberate policy of the European Union to 'get rid' of nationalism, in sport as well as politics – a policy that, to say the least, has not proved successful so far. A consideration of this would have made Bairner's implicit discussion on the characteristics of 'sporting nationalism', and the field of sport as a special arena and instrument for displaying and constructing national sentiments, more explicit and, therefore, thorough. What is it that makes the relationship between sport and nationalism remain 'as strong as ever',[89] despite efforts by the European Union and the effects of the process of 'globalization'?

As we know, sport can function in many ways and 'modern' identity in sport seems to have found an arena where modernity's most flagrant characteristics can be displayed. Through sport, national identity can be connected both to exterior uniforms and to loyal adherence. Here we perhaps approach the characteristics of sports nationalism. Through sport, 'deep identity' can be displayed despite behaviour and use of symbols that are unbinding, but unbinding use of symbols is not synonymous with accidental use of symbols. (Unbinding does not have any bearings upon, for example political stands outside sport.) When symbols become popular it can be because they meet a popular resonance. According to Michael Billig, nationalism today has become normalized, taking 'banal forms'.

The movement of players and athletes in an ever-more commercialized, global sports world disentangles the ethnic dimension of sports nationalism. Generally, immigrants are more welcome in modern sport, and in a national team, than in other fields of modern society. Dauncey and Hare, who analyse the effects and the meaning of the French victory on home turf at the soccer World Cup in 1998, maybe overemphasized the unifying outcomes of the triumph.[90] However, the symbolic value of a team so diverse in ethnicity (black, beur and blancs – they constitute les bleus) to bring a World Cup to their common national home, can hardly be overrated. Worth noting also is that this home for many of the players was neither the land of their birth, nor their mother country, a point made by politicians with an anti-immigrant stance. In the national euphoria such criticism evaporated and the 'plebiscites' and imagined communities of that time left no doubt about who composed the nation: the 11 named people of the football team. As sports can present short glimpses of intense, but transitory happiness, the natural question deals with the longevity of this effect. Permanent changes can hardly be accomplished by sports alone, at least not by one win. Patrick Mignon calls victory celebrations 'symbols of a call for unity precisely because that unity is far from real'.[91]

A gradual upheaval of this difference would be desirable. That general historians take an interest in the subject of sports is, of course, welcome, and to a certain extent such a tendency can be found. At the same time, however, history is becoming ever-more specialized, there are always new sub-disciplines to the mother field. Sports history is, of course, one of them, as a result of a new research interest since the 1970s. It could be said that general history should always try to keep up with such traits. In that respect, sports history definitely deserves a place within modern history.

The quintessence of modern sports nationalism: is there such a thing?

If there is, it could be described like this: intense but superficial/shallow/apparent. Experiences that are powerful and compelling, but at the same time superficial? Communities that are intense and passionate, but momentary and short-lived? Can such experiences, with no guarantee of longevity, give or be applied to anything outside the moment or the 90 minutes in which they are lived? Fascination or passion, joint happiness or despair; these things can lead to thoughts of functions, and then to spheres like circus and theatre rather than suppression or deceiving. However, if modern sport is circus and theatre, it does not necessarily mean it leads to passivity.

This way of portraying sports nationalism – intense but shallow, deep but transitory – can be linked to recent trends in the historical studies of nationalism. For example, has 'banal nationalism' become a term pointing to the omnipresent, daily 'flagging' of national symbols and institutions, the Western, sedate form of nationalism? According to Michael Billig, this nationalism is always ready to be mobilized during drastic events, which might include a big sporting event, such as a match between national football teams.[92] If one wishes to relate sports nationalism to 'banal' nationalism, the sporting case would be the instance that demonstrates how ordinary, daily nationalism can present itself as vital, energetic stuff. John Hutchinson suggests two types of nationalism: the 'hot' and the 'banal', where the latter is what 'people consume as part of giving meaning to the experiences of everyday life'.[93] Hutchinson's concern and objective is how the 'masses' have come to identity with the nation, how a 'sense of rootedness' and a 'national repertoire' were adopted.[94] Part of this national repertoire was learning to take leisure and practise sports, and hence contribute to thicken 'the texture of national culture'.[95] However, are 'expressions of allegiances in international sporting contests' merely a banal form of nationalism – even if they contribute 'to form the identities of the mass nation'?[96]

International football provides an interesting case with two competing scenes, one controlled and dominated by the national associations and their international federations, emphasizing the national arena; the other, the club scene dominated by the big clubs in an ongoing threat to break free of the national and international organizations. The power struggle has so far been controlled by the national side, making the World Cup an attractive money-spinning event. The growing multiculturalism of the biggest clubs makes them an interesting subject when it comes to attractiveness and identity.

Maybe sport provides an arena for identities that may still exist, but are not approved in other fields? Identities, for example of the 90-minute variety, are very well-adapted to the modern world, equally strong, but not as lasting or binding in other areas. Sports can be experienced without obligation by the 90-minute tourists, or it can be intensive for the partisans. This possibility for collective identification has been a strength when the matter is to attract supporters, or in modern times, consumers. Nevertheless, it is striking that in modern society such belonging is strengthened through national symbols, which may show that not all collective identities have been dissolved. It may also show that the national issue – understood as a simultaneous community of destinies that is made visible during the 90 minutes of the game – still exists. The 90-minute nationalism, then, can be short and without obligation, and at the same time vigorous and powerful, and sometimes felicific, as long as our 'named people' are capable of bringing it to us.

Sports can function in many ways, and 'modern' identity in sport seems to have found an arena where modernity's most flagrant characteristics can be displayed. Through sport, national identity can be connected both to exterior uniforms and to loyal adherence. Here we perhaps approach the characteristics of sports nationalism. Through sport, 'deep identity' can be displayed despite behaviour and use of symbols that are unbinding. When symbols become popular it can be because they have a popular resonance.

Sports in the contemporary world, in other words, constitute complementary identities. Gymnasts could practise Swedish or German gymnastics without impairing their nationality. Politically conscious workers could be both internationally and nationally oriented. Such things were simpler in practice than in (revolutionary) theory. Maybe this is true also for modern debates on immigration? Perhaps it is possible to be English and support Sri Lanka at the same time? Norman Tebbitt's initial proposal is, in other words, hopelessly outdated; today, supporting Brazil in soccer is rather unimaginative and unbearably trendy in the whole Western world, yet no serious politician would take citizenship away from people who demonstrate such an identity. Still, Tebbitt in a probably unintentional way, pointed to the assumption that sport is not a traditional arena when it comes to displays of identity.

What happens in sports arenas invites thought about 90-minute nationalism (or evanescent nationalism, as Cronin prefers),[97] connected to strong emotions and loyalties. Just as the English politician Norman Tebbitt gave name to one test concerning nationalism and sport, a Scottish politician, Jim Sillars, introduced the term that proved that he also had little knowledge of the relationship between sports and nationalism. After having lost an election, he expressed his bitter disappointment at the thousands of spectators who fiercely supported Scotland at internationals at Hampden Park, but did not follow up by voting for his Nationalist Party when election time came.[98] Thence came the term '90-minute patriots'. What Sillars did not see, of course, was that the patriotism or nationalism expressed at soccer games or other sporting events is of a different character to political nationalism and, therefore, could quite well be called '90-minute nationalism', not as a frustrated negativism, but as a neat description of the national identity displayed through sports in modern times. Although lasting no more than 90 minutes, it reveals an underlying reality that still exists: the history of sports shows that short-lived moments can last for a long time in a nation's collective memory.

Key questions in general studies of nationalism are: when does nationalism become more important than any other category or distinction? In which situations will the 'national card' be played out? Sports provide no clear answers to these questions other than that the national card will be played when the situation demands it. As this chapter has tried to show, these situations can vary. Sports nationalism covers a whole variety of discourses and constellations. Sports, then, seem to constitute one of very few remaining reservations where open presentation and display of emotions and sentiments which are not quite proper elsewhere, can take place relatively freely.

Notes

1 Eric J. Hobsbawm, *Nations and Nationalism since 1780* (Cambridge: Cambridge University Press 1991), 143. E.J. Hobsbawm and Terence Ranger, eds, *The Invention of Tradition* (Cambridge: Cambridge University Press, 1983).

2 E. Hobsbawm is a historian who has written international historical overviews as well as more detailed studies of nationalism. Even though he does not pay much attention to sport in his general historical works, he, unlike many other nationalism researchers, certainly does so in his more specialized nationalism studies. Anderson, on the other hand, has presented a book, the title and main message of which have had a considerable impact on writings on the subject of nationalism and national identity. Even if the book contains very little, if anything, related to sport, its perspectives can still be linked to a debate around nationalism and sport – as Hobsbawm proved it could. Benedict Anderson, *Imagined Communities: Reflections of the Origins and Spread of Nationalism* (London and New York: Verso, 1993).

3 Aira Kemiläinen, 'The Idea of Nationalism', *Scandinavian Journal of History*, 9, 1 (1984), 39. Also, Eric Hobsbawm stresses that 'no serious historian of nations and nationalism can be a committed political nationalist ... Nationalism requires too much belief in what is patently not so'. Hobsbawm 1991, 12.

4 Based upon a major research project on Norway in the 19th century, Ø. Sørensen, for example, distinguished between 14 forms of nationalism, or what he called nationalism projects – some successful, but also many failures. Ø. Sørensen, ed., *Jakten på det norske* (Oslo: Ad Notam Gyldendal, 1998).

5 Snorri Sturluson, *Orig Overs* (Gustav Storm, 1897).

6 G. Delanty and K. Kumar, eds, *The SAGE Handbook of Nations and Nationalism* (London, Thousand Oaks, New Delhi: Sage, 2006).

7 Ernest Renan, 'What is a Nation?', in Geoff Eley and Ronald Grigor Suny, eds, *Becoming National: A Reader* (New York: Oxford University Press, 1996), 41–55.

8 Karl Deutsch defined nationality as a 'modern communication community' in *Nationalism and Social Communication* (Cambridge, MA: MIT Press, 1953). Ernest Gellner focused upon the consequences of industrial society, its need for a functional political unity built around an idea of cultural community, in other words a nation-state; Ernest Gellner, *Nations and Nationalism* (Oxford: Blackwell, 1983). The educational system would be an important channel for cultural and social homogenization. National identity would then express itself in behaviour and conduct. In other words it would have a cultural rather than a structural basis. Øyvind Østerud, *Hva er nasjonalisme?* (Oslo: Universitetsforlaget, 1994). See also works by Gellner, Anderson, Hroch, Hobsbawm, Østerud, Østergaard, Sørensen, Hylland Eriksen, Kedourie, Harris, Mimmi and so on. From classical contributors Ernest Renan, Max Weber, Norbert Elias and Jürgen Habermas, to modern nationalism researchers such as Ernest Gellner, Benedict Andersson, Anthony D. Smith, Miroslav Hroch and Eric Hobsbawm, and more recent writers, for example Elie Kedourie, Nigel Harris, Peter Alter, Ephraim Nimni, Uffe Østergaard, Thomas Hylland-Eriksen, Øyvind Østerud, Øystein Sørensen and Billy Ehn, they all have produced or at least related their work to nationalism theories and perspectives.

9 Eric J. Hobsbawm, *Nations and Nationalism since 1780* (Cambridge: University Press 1990). E.J. Hobsbawm and Terence Ranger, eds, *The Invention of Tradition* (Cambridge: University Press 1983). See Ephraim Nimni, *Marxism and Nationalism: Theoretical origins of a political crisis* (London, Boulder: Pluto Press, 1991), for alternative Marxist views.

10 Anthony D. Smith, *The Ethnic Origins of Nations* (Oxford: Blackwell, 1986). A.D. Smith, *National Identity* (Harmondsworth: Penguin, 1991). Anthony D. Smith introduced the ethnic component to the modernist view on nationalism. He claimed that nationalities cannot be mere inventions, created for particular purposes by national elites, and elaborated the need for popular resonance further. Smith gives history an essential role here. History gives identity through surviving myths and symbols. However, the myths that can be applied have to build on a basis of memories, traditions and symbols that people can recognize and to which they can feel related. These traditions Smith calls the ethnic origin of nations.

11 G. Delanty and K. Kumar, 'Introduction', in G. Delanty and K. Kumar, eds, *The SAGE Handbook of Nations and Nationalism* (London, Thousand Oaks, New Dehli: Sage, 2006).

12 Matti Goksøyr, 'Phases and Functions of Nationalism: Norway's Utilization of International Sport in the Late Nineteenth and Early Twentieth Centuries', in J.A. Mangan, ed., *Tribal Identities: Nationalism, Europe, Sport* (London: Frank Cass, 1999), 127.

13 Mike Cronin, *Sport and Nationalism in Ireland: Gaelic Games, Soccer and Irish Identity since 1884* (Dublin: Four Courts Press, 1999), 30. Matti Goksøyr, 'Phases and Functions of Nationalism: Norway's Utilization of International Sport in the Late Nineteenth and Early Twentieth Centuries', in: J.A. Mangan, ed., *Tribal Identities: Nationalism, Europe, Sport* (London: Frank Cass 1999), 125–28.

14 Cronin 1999, 32.

15 Cronin 1999. See also: Alan Bairner, *Sport, Nationalism and Globalisation* (New York: SUNY, 2001).

16 The discussion has recurred several times. See, for example *The Observer*, 25 November 2001. See also Bairner 2001, xi–xii, 169.

17 J. Sugden, 'USA and the World Cup: American Nativism and the Rejection of the People's Game', in J. Sugden and A. Tomlinson, eds, *Hosts and Champions: Soccer Cultures, National Identities and the USA World Cup* (Aldershot, UK: Arena, 1994), 219–52; Bairner 2001

18 Roy Hay, 'Croatia: Community, Conflict and Culture: The Role of Soccer Clubs in Migrant Identity', in Mike Cronin and David Mayall, eds, *Sporting Nationalisms: Identity, Ethnicity, Immigration and Assimilation* (London: Frank Class, 1998).

19 David Malouf, 'Made in England. Australia's British Inheritance' *Quarterly Essay*, 12 (2003).

20 For example, in the name 'Norwegian Turn Verein, Brooklyn, N.Y.', which took part in the Olympic Games of 1904, there was a mix of three different nationalities: Norwegian, German and American, relating to the origin of the participants, the activity and the location of the club; David R. Francis, *The Universal Exposition of 1904* (St Louis: Louisiana Purchase Exposition Company, 1913), 541.

21 Pierre Lanfranchi and Alfred Wahl, 'The Immigrant as Hero: Kopa, Mekloufi and French Foot-ball', in Richard Holt, J.A. Mangan and Pierre Lanfranchi, *European Heroes: Myth, Identity, Sport* (London: Frank Cass, 1996), 123.

22 Ibid., 123.

23 Ibid., 123.

24 Ibid., 119, 125.

25 Quoted in Allen Guttmann, *The Olympics: A History of the Modern Games* (Urbana and Chicago: University of Illinois Press, 1992), 19.

26 Arnd Krüger, 'Forgotten decision: The IOC on the Eve of World War I', in *Olympika: The International Journal of Olympic Studies* Vol. VI (1997), 89.

27 The 1916 Olympics were cancelled because of World War I. German sports officials Carl Diem and Martin Berner quoted in Arnd Krüger, '"Buying Victories is Positively Degrading": European Origins of Government Pursuit of National Prestige through Sport', in J.A. Mangan, ed., *Tribal Identities: Nationalism, Europe, Sport* (London: Frank Cass, 1996), 192.

28 Arnd Krüger, 'Forgotten decision: The IOC on the Eve of World War I', in *Olympika: The International Journal of Olympic Studies* Vol. VI (1997), 91.

29 Until 1980 the Finns won half of the available gold medals in 5,000 and 10,000 metres (IOC statistics). See Kjell Westö for a useful literary account of these issues: Kjell Westö: *Der vi engång gikk* (Helsingfors: Otava, 2006). Juhani Paasivirta, *Finland och de olympiska spelen i Stockholm: Diplomatin bakom kulisserna.* (Ekenäs, 1963). Jan Lindroth, 'Idrott och nationalism – några historiska exempel'. In: *SCIF årbok*, (1979). Matti Klinge, *Blick på Finlands historia* (Helsinki: Otava, 2000).

30 Artur Eklund, 'Idrotten som nationell kraftexponent' (1913), reprinted in A. Eklund, *Idrottens filosofi* (Helsingfors: Söderström & Co, 1917), 315–21.

31 John J. MacAloon, *This Great Symbol* (Chicago: University of Chicago Press, 1981).

32 The quote is usually attributed to the Duke of Wellington, but is probably apocryphal.

33 Jochen Teichler, Klaus Reinartz, et al., *Das Leistungssportsystem der DDR in den 80er Jahren und im Prozeß der Wende* (Schorndorf: Verlag Karl Hofmann, 1999). Gertrud Pfister, *Frauen und Sport in der DDR* (Cologne, 2002).

34 See Krüger 1996, 183.

35 William J. Baker and James A. Mangan, eds., *Sports in Africa: Essays in Social History* (New York: Africana, 1987).

36 Terje Tvedt, 'Sport in Africa', in *Norsk Idrettshistorisk Årbok 1989*, 186–87.

37 Peter Normann Waage, *Jeg, vi – og de andre. Om nasjoner og nasjonalisme i Europa* (Oslo: Cappelen, 1993).

38 Dave Russell, *Football and the English: A Social History of Association Football in England, 1863–1995* (Preston: Carnegie Publishing, 1997), 91.

39 Dave Russell, *Football and the English*. Richard Holt, *Sport and the British: A Modern History* (Oxford: Clarendon Press, 1990). Lis Crolley and David Hand, *Football and European Identity: Historical Narratives through the Press* (London and New York: Routledge, 2006). Mark Perryman, ed., *The Ingerland Factor: Home Truths from Football* (Edinburgh: Mainstream, 1999).

40 Pierre Lanfranchi, Christiane Eisenberg, Tony Mason and Alfred Wahl, *100 years of Football: The FIFA Centennial Book* (London: Weidenfeld and Nicolson, 2004).

41 H.F.Moorhouse, 'One State, Several Countries: Soccer and Nationality in a 'United' Kingdom', in J.A. Mangan, ed., *Tribal Identities. Nationalism. Europe. Sport* (London: Frank Cass, 1999).

42 Kristen Mo, 'Norsk motstand mot vinter-OL i 1928', in *Norsk Idrettshistorisk Årbok 1989* (Oslo, 1989), 57.

43 Ibid.

44 Jens Arup Seip, 'Nasjonalisme som vikarierende motiv', in Jens Arup Seip, *Fra embetsmannsstat til ettpartistat og andre essays* (Oslo: Universitetsforlaget, 1963).

45 Matti Goksøyr, 'Idretten og det norske: Aktivitet som identitet', in Ø. Sørensen, ed., Jakten på det norske (Oslo: Ad Notam Gyldendal, 1998).

46 Lis Crolley and David Hand, *Football and European Identity: Historical Narratives through the Press* (London and New York: Routledge, 2006), 127–28.

47 *El Correo Español*, 7 May 1984, quoted in MacClancy 1996, 189.

48 Personal observation by Dr Yngvar Ommundsen, Bilbao 29 June 2008.

49 Cronin 1999; Bairner 2001.

50 Even if Cronin and Bairner differ in their views on how directly political the GAA was in their first decades.

51 Bairner 2001, 80–81.

52 Bairner 2001, 72.

53 Pierre Lanfranchi and Alfred Wahl, 'The Immigrant as Hero: Kopa, Mekloufi and French Football', in Richard Holt, J.A. Mangan and Pierre Lanfranchi, *European Heroes: Myth, Identity, Sport* (London: Frank Cass, 1996), 121.

54 Bjørge Lillelien on NRK radio, September 1981. Original text (in Norwegian) in Matti Goksøyr and Finn Olstad, *Fotball: Norges Fotballforbund 100 år* (Oslo, 2002), 159.

55 Matti Goksøyr, 'Opplevde fellesskap og folkelig nasjonsbygging: Norge og idretten 1905–40', *Historisk Tidsskrift* 80, 3 (2000).

56 Steven Pope, *Patriotic Games: Sporting Traditions in the American Imagination, 1876–1926* (Oxford: Oxford University Press, 1997).

57 Lis Crolley and David Hand, *Football and European Identity: Historical Narratives through the Press*. (London and New York: Routledge, 2006): 133–34.

58 Jeremy MacClancy, 'Nationalism at Play: The Basques of Vizcaya and Athletic Club de Bilbao', in Jeremy MacClancy, ed., *Sport, Identity and Ethnicity* (Oxford: Berg, 1996), 190.

59 Eduardo Archetti, *Masculinities: Football, Polo and the Tango in Argentina* (Oxford, New York: Berg, 1999).

60 Eduardo Archetti: 'In search of National Identity: Argentinian Football and Europe', in J.A. Mangan, ed., *Tribal Identities. Nationalism. Europe. Sport* (London: Frank Cass, 1996), 201–02.

61 Alex Bellos, *Futebol: The Brazilian Way of Life* (London: Bloomsbury, 2003). Janet Lever, *Soccer Madness: Brazil's Passion for the World's Most Popular Sport* (Illinois: Waveland Press, 1995). Tony Mason, *Passion of the People? Football in South America* (London: Verso, 1995).

62 See also: Eduardo Archetti, 'Playing Football and Dancing Tango: Embodying Argentina in Movement, Style and Identity', in Noel Dyck and Eduardo Archetti, eds, *Sport, Dance and Embodied Identities* (Oxford, New York: Berg, 2003).

63 Robert Edelman, *Spartak Moscow: The People's Team in the Workers' State* (Ithaca and London: Cornell University Press, 2009), 170 ff.

64 Eduardo Archetti: 'In search of National Identity: Argentinian Football and Europe', in J.A. Mangan, ed., *Tribal Identities. Nationalism. Europe. Sport* (London: Frank Cass, 1996), 201f.

65 Albert Grundlingh, Andre Odendaal and Burridge Spies, *Beyond the Tryline: Rugby and South African Society* (Johannesburg: Ravan Press, 1995); John Nauright, *Sport, Cultures and Identities in South Africa* (London: Leicester University Press, 1997); Douglas Booth, *The Race Game: Sport and Politics in South Africa* (London: Frank Cass, 1998).

66 Matti Goksøyr, 'Our Games – our Virtues? "National Sports" as Symbols: A Discussion of Ideal-types', in Floris van der Merwe, ed., *Sport as Symbol, Symbols in Sport* (ISHPES Studies, vol.4, Academica Verlag, 1996), 363–71.

67 Max Weber, *The Theory of Social and Economic Organisation* (New York: Free Press, 1964), 330–32.

68 Andrew Weintraub, *The Politics of Sport: Pencak Silat and the Construction of Indonesian National Identity*, unpublished paper, UC Berkeley, Centre for South East Asian Studies, 1993. For another view see Henning Eichberg, 'Spielverhalten und Relationsgesellschaft in West Sumatra', *Stadion* No.1 (1975), also Eichberg, 'En anden sport end "verdenssporten"', *Centring* 3–4 (1981).

69 Allen Guttmann, *Games and Empires: Modern Sports and Cultural Imperialism* (Columbia University Press, 1994), 71–72.

70 Albert G. Spalding, *America's National Game* (New York, 1911), 10.

71 Melvin Adelman, *A Sporting Time: New York City and the Rise of Modern Athletics, 1820–1870* (Urbana: University of Illinois Press, 1986), 110f. Larry R. Gerlach, 'Not quite ready for Prime-Time: Baseball History, 1983–93', *Journal of Sport History* 2 (1994).

72 This would for Norway mean that football, not skiing was the national sport of Norway for most of the 20th century (from the 1930s). However, there is one catch to this: it deals with registered members in organized sport. If we also register people performing outside organized sport, more as a pastime or recreational exercise, the picture would be altered, though not by much (hiking, without and with skis, would surpass the other activities). Cfr M.Goksøyr, *The Role of Winter Sports in the Building of National Identity in Norway around the Turn of the 19th Century*, in Goksøyr and Mo Lippe, eds, Selected Papers from the 2nd International ISHPES Seminar: On the history of Winter Sports and Winter Olympic Games (forthcoming).

73 Richard Holt 1994, quoted in Bairner 2001, 65.

74 George Orwell, 'The Sporting Spirit', *The Tribune*, 14 December 1945, in Sonia Orwell and Ian Angus, eds, *The Collected Essays, Journalism and Letters of George Orwell, Vol. IV: In Front of your Nose 1945–1950* (New York: Harcourt, Brace and World, 1968), 42.

75 Richard Holt, *Sport and the British*.

76 See the West Indian political writer C.L.R. James for a personal account of the role of cricket in a West Indian setting: C.L.R. James, *Beyond a Boundary* (London: Stanley Paul, 1963/1986).

77 Arne Næss-Holm, *Batting for Peace: A Study of Cricket Diplomacy between India and Pakistan* (Saarbrücken: VDM Verlag, 2008).

78 Lis Crolley and David Hand, *Football and European Identity: Historical Narratives through the Press* (London and New York: Routledge, 2006), 73f.

79 Simon Kuper, *Football against the Enemy* (London: Phoenix, Orion, 1996), 8.

80 Waage 1993.

81 Arnd Krüger and Bill Murray, eds, *The Nazi Olympics* (Chicago: University of Illinois Press, 2003).

82 Allen L. Sack and Zeljan Suster, 'Soccer and Croatian Nationalism: A Prelude to War', *Journal of Sport & Social Issues* 24, 3 (August 2000), 305–20.

83 Ibid., 311.

84 Ibid., 312.

85 Ibid., 314.

86 Ibid., 315.

87 Ibid., 317.

88 Gerard Delanty and Krishan Kumar, 'Introduction', in G. Delanty and K. Kumar, eds, *The SAGE Handbook of Nations and Nationalism* (London: Sage / New Delhi: Thousand Oaks, 2006).

89 Alan Bairner, *Sport, Nationalism, and Globalization: European and North American Perspectives* (Albany: State University of New York Press, 2001), xi.

90 Hugh Dauncey and Geoff Hare, eds, *France and the 1998 World Cup: The National Impact of a World Sporting Event* (London: Cass, 1999).

91 Patrick Vignon, 'Fans and Heroes', in Hugh Dauncey and Geoff Hare, eds, *France and the 1998 World Cup: The National Impact of a World Sporting Event* (London: Cass, 1999), 96.

92 Michael Billig, *Banal Nationalism* (London: Sage, 1995).

93 John Hutchinson, 'Hot and Banal Nationalism: The Nationalization of "the Masses"', in G. Delanty and K. Kumar, eds, *The SAGE Handbook of Nations and Nationalism* (London: Sage / New Delhi: Thousand Oaks, 2006), 295.

94 Ibid., 299.

95 Ibid., 303.

96 Ibid., 305.

97 Cronin 1999, 131.

98 Bairner 2001, 47. Grant Jarvie and Graham Walker, eds, *Scottish Sport and the Making of the Nation: Ninety Minute Patriots?* (Leicester: Leicester University Press, 1994), 1–8.

17 Alternative sports

Robert E. Rinehart

Autumns the fields were deliberately burned by a fire so harmless children ran through it
making up a sort of game.
Women beat the flames with brooms and blankets, so the fires were said to be *under control*.
Carolyn Forché, 'The Angel of History'

Out on the open ground not far from the buildings
an abandoned newspaper has lain for months, full of events.
It grows old through nights and days in rain and sun,
on the way to becoming a plant, a cabbage-head,
on the way to being united with the earth.
Just as a memory is slowly transmuted into your own self.
Tomas Tranströmer,
'Graphing the Archipelagoes of History'

Carolyn Forché, in the above epigraph from her poem 'The Angel of History', writes of kinetic subjectivities (they are moving targets, really, differential ways of 'seeing'), while paying homage to Walter Benjamin's classic essay 'Theses on the Philosophy of History' (Benjamin 1969). She recollects how Benjamin described the image of the 'angel of history':

> A Klee painting named 'Angelus Novus' shows an angel looking as though he is about to move away from something he is fixedly contemplating. His eyes are staring, his mouth is open, his wings are spread. This is how one pictures the angel of history. His face is turned toward the past. Where we perceive a chain of events, he sees one single catastrophe which keeps piling wreckage upon wreckage and hurls it in front of his feet. The angel would like to stay, awaken the dead, and make whole what has been smashed. But a storm is blowing from Paradise; it has got caught in his wings with such violence that the angel can no longer close them. This storm irresistibly propels him into the future to which his back is turned, while the pile of debris before him grows skyward. This storm is what we call progress.
> (Benjamin 1969, 257–58)

Benjamin, it seems to me, is no more enthralled by a static view of history than the angel is; he demands a new reckoning of something that is unmappable, something that demands a fluidity of purpose and a recognition of the changing nature of history. He demands not accuracy, but rather verisimilitude, an account that includes effect and context, and one that merely approaches similitude.

Benjamin writes, '[t]he true picture of the past flits by. The past can be seized only as an image which flashes up at the instant when it can be recognized and is never seen again' (Benjamin 1969, 255). This moment of recognition, fleeting and transitory, fits in with other similar moments to form (for most historians) a contextualized whole fabric, and this series of mere 'flits' – that are conceived differentially, by different positionalities, stances, world views, and so forth – becomes a contested, vaguely-recalled memory. It becomes 'a', and then 'the', agreed-upon, consensualized history.

Similarly, in his poem 'About History', Tomas Tranströmer moves toward the sense of a co-enacted history, a history that breaks down over time, a history that both acts upon and acts with its object(s). Using organic images from nature (perhaps to imply the 'naturalness' of the patina-ed, erosive effect of time on memory), he, like Forché and Benjamin, see 'history' not as an emplanted and solid artifact, but rather as a co-produced, fluid, mutable and finally unarticulatable concept. History is organic and malleable, and there are no longer any capital 'T' truths – only power relations that insist upon their own truths.

I see such a view of history similarly, but I think the view of history as fluid and mutable can be utilized effectively to study certain groups, or times, or, in the case of this piece, recollections and broad accountings of historical movements. The pastiches of never-truly-recovered memories for alternative sport forms by sports historians in the late 20th and early 21st centuries are the cases I will use to examine these broad views of what I call a 'holographic' history.

Tying down the series of contentious, conflicted and commodified moments within a never-agreed-upon 'life' for extreme/ action/ lifestyle/ alternative sport forms has become a series of rather selective attempts to capture static, often decontextualized, snapshots of differing ethos, eras, players, argot, techniques and locations.[1] As Richardson reminds us, though it all is only 'partial, local, and historical knowledge[, it] is still knowing' (Richardson and Adams St Pierre 2005, 961). The very partiality of this kind of knowledge, though, must be represented not as a mapping of what *is* or *was*, but rather as a singular representation of one positionality. To do otherwise, for historians interested in studying 'extreme' sports, would be to replicate mistakes made previously in other kinds of histories, where grand theory replaces deep – and still partial – knowledge.

As I intend to appraise the extant scholarly literature on 'action'/ 'extreme' sports, I will use the metaphor of the historical holograph as an attempt to provide a sense of context. I will situate these 'lifestyle' sports within a wider discussion of the concept of holographic historiographical methodologies and themes, particularly looking at what these relatively new sport forms might mean to an ongoing project that is both fluid and dynamic, and is *potentially* transgressive and transformative.[2]

Baudrillard discusses the 'hologram' within an historical context that includes *trompe l'oeil*, which is a 'style of painting which gives the appearance of three-dimensional, or photographic realism' (ArtLex 2009). Though one of the intentions of *trompe l'oeil* is to pique interest in discussions of viewer/audience situatedness *vis-à-vis* art forms, one of the intentions of the hologram was, in Baudrillard's view, to attempt exactitude, a clear tracing of the original. This, Baudrillard tells us, is impossible, for:

> ... there is no escape from this race to the real and to realistic hallucination since, when an object is exactly like another, *it is not exactly like it, it is a bit more exact*. There is never similitude, any more than there is exactitude.
>
> (Baudrillard 1994, 107, emphasis in original)

Furthermore, '... everything escapes representations, escapes its own double and its resemblance' (p.107). Nothing is ever the same; nothing can be rendered exactly after the experience. The moment, the *now*, is what we experience.

I agree with Baudrillard's assessment of the inaccuracy of the hologram as a totalizing and accurate portrayer of *what happened*, but I still think it can be a closer approximation to the *sense* of what happened than, for example, a photograph (Benjamin 1969). Baudrillard points out that nothing is exactly similar to anything else due to temporal and spatial differences.

Looking at action sports research in context (holographically) may give us a better sense of what is going on, how these sport forms are enacted and lived into being, than simply looking at each individual piece of research independent of its context or of other researches (as a snapshot might). It may not approach *what happened*, but of course the paradox is that lived experience may never, in fact, be relived the same way.

Mainstream, dominant sport practices have been criticized for years by sport scholars as being heavily laden with a variety of problematics, including strict adherence to a 'sport ethic' (Coakley 2007), naturalized kinds of inequities (such as various forms of stratification), imbedded globalization practices, and assumed and naturalized capitalistic and competitive structures. On the other hand, alternative sport practices appeared to have great *potential* for political, gendered, racialized and class-based revolutionary egalitarianism.[3]

Some scholars – as well as some participants – were (and still are) attracted to alternative sport forms for this potential. To date, much of that potential has been co-opted by commodification practices, reduced to replications of dominant power (im)balances, and returned to new forms of consumers being duped by the *trappings* of counterculture and resistance. (Noticing this, however, still does not deny to 'differentness' of alternative sport from mainstream sport.) Unfortunately, historiographical research within the area of alternative sport, with a few exceptions, has tended toward a similar type of entropy – with some critical engagement, but also, using snapshot methodologies, with historical blinders.

In 2006 I suggested a new historiographical form,[4] one I termed an historical 'holograph,' which might approach a look at these sport forms in a fresh, contextualized, dynamic and fluid way (Rinehart 2006b). In musing over that 2006 piece, I see further connections with the whole of alternative sport, the potential for exciting new ways of 'seeing' sport forms, as they develop, as they are lived, as they fade away or morph into amalgams of themselves.[5]

Thus, with this description of historical method and of the slippery 'form' that comprises action/extreme/whiz/lifestyle/alternative sport as a *caveat*, this chapter will overview the extant research on alternative sport; continue to discuss historiographical method and intent, and historical/sociological/cultural research of alternative sport; and indicate possibilities for future research and directions within the study of alternative sport. In looking at historiographical research, such questions as the following may occur to the reader: how might these differing sport formations be influenced by or influence historiographical methodologies? What may or may not constitute 'differentiation' or 'difference' – in terms of values, ethos, world views of, for example, 'lifestyle' activities like fishing, hunting and tramping – as related to alternative sport? What might differentiate alternative sport from mainstream sport? How might 'alternative' sport be doomed to become 'mainstream' sport? What stories will evolve to become privileged by members of the 'lifestyle' or 'extreme' or 'action' sport communities? Might those stories run counter to mainstream stories of such beginnings/origins? How might alternative sport *embody* its practices differentially than mainstream sport? These thematic-related questions may anticipate future research projects within alternative sport.

This rather daunting task is meant to be an initial foray – in hopes that it may lead to rich discussion among a growing number of intellectuals concerned with alternative sport – rather than an exhaustive and proscriptive position statement. A discussion of action sports, however, must be initially grounded within an historical discussion of these and similar types of edgy, non-normative, non-mainstream, physically-based activities and lifestyles.

'We're different!': some characterizations of alternative sport

The explosive advent and popularity of 'alternative sport' requires some exploration. Also variously known by different constituencies as 'action sport'[6] or 'extreme' sport[7] or 'whiz' sport[8] or 'lifestyle' sport[9] in the late 20th century, alternative sport has received relatively short shrift within sport studies. The naming of these cultural artifacts matters, though. Who has control to name? What does that control imply? How do the connotations and denotations of naming work to shape what these activities become, who they attract (e.g., practitioners, media, consumers, scholars), how culturally 'hip' and cool they are perceived to be? For our purposes here, what do the names mean to shaping how we study these activities, what imbedded assumptions we bring to looking at such activities? In some ways, of course, the various names all have cultural cachet and salience – for varying groups, even for various scholars.

Might the salience of each type of name be contextually specific, for example? Might where we are housed – geographically, or even within our various university departmental structures and units – nudge us toward privileging one name over another? Might the ebbs and flows within different eras of cultural and symbolic capital influence how we name and what we study?

On what might we all agree? I reiterate: the most salient impulse for these activities, for all groups involved (that is, participants, corporate and media sponsors, audiences, scholars, disinterested folks) is their deliberate, intentional 'differentness' from mainstream sports – whether the differentness is exploited in the clothing and equipment and argot participants use, or in the values they bring to the endeavour, or in the rush and 'flow' of the activity, or in the oppositional nature (including a resistance to adult supervision and coaching), or even in the dedication and imbeddedness of the activities within an individual's life. This deliberate, overt, self-conscious 'differentness' is captured, I think, in the relatively bland name 'alternative' sport.

Though these specific activities – and other like activities – were of course participated in earlier, their impacts upon mainstream culture were largely insignificant (though revisionist histories sometimes work to remember them quite differently – see, e.g., M. Donnelly 2008). There have been discussions of the characteristics, values and counter-valences of the sports and sub-groupings within the sports themselves (for example, see P. Donnelly 2003); there have also been some interrogations into the complications of race, gender and class issues within the alternative sport scene (Beal 1995, 1996; Kay and Laberge 2003, 2004; Kusz 2001, 2003, 2006; Rinehart 1998a, 2005a; Wheaton 2000, 2003, 2004); scholars also have looked at the relationship(s) between alternative sports and other '(post)modernist' institutions, such as media, new electronic media (the use of YouTube, for example, for skateboarders to share their affective experiences with one another), popular music, and art (Wilson 2002; Atencio and Beal 2006).

The study of the historical advent of these sport forms, however – the mythological 'histories' of action sports as a class, including meanings brought to these activities in different eras – has itself been somewhat lacking. Popular culture 'stories' have generally provided the framework upon which academics build their cases – and, usually, uncritically.[10] Generally, most scholars will agree that these *types* of activities – or at least some of the impulses for similar activities – have existed within the world of sport for tens, if not hundreds, of years, but the actual nomenclature – and specific proliferation of sports – of 'extreme' or 'action' sports has been in existence for only about a dozen years, dating from the mid-1990s. This conflated problematic – of who gets to name, who has the power to claim, whose 'stories' will prevail – is entangled with the dearth of research on the meanings, inventions and innovations that have come to be known as and are attached to 'action' sports (Foner 2002). Throughout these discussions, though, celebrations of various forms of 'differentness' are highlighted and seen as salient to self-definition. For me, this reinforces the case for using 'alternative' as a descriptor.

There is evidence that the claiming wars are currently thriving: witness, for example, ESPN's (the USA-based Entertainment and Sports Programming Network) hyperbole that their X Games have become massified to the extent that they have 'reached worldwide appeal' (Wallace 2002, 9). The focus on extreme or action sports clearly cannot be easily separated from the globalization (in ESPN's case, Americanization) of alternative sport and of the way it is considered by media, various publics, insiders of the sports and sport scholars.

Thus, though specific historical changes in clothing, equipment, argot, mass appeal, events, branding and sponsorship are interesting and remarkable details, changes in values and affect toward the activities seem to be some of the defining criteria of participants' claim that their activities may be 'different'. The clothing, equipment and so on are markers, tangible indicators, of those types of differentness, but seeking to be and being 'alternative' to dominant values – or creating stories to celebrate 'differentness' – seems to be an attitude that runs through these sports and activities.

Alternative in what?: specific values of extreme and action sports' participants

Beneath the umbrella term of alternative sport – and its meaning – there exist many other specific values within these activities. The values may, in fact, push us to think at given points of an activity as 'extreme', 'lifestyle', 'whiz', or 'action' dominant. Movement among these groupings – and indeed, as I will argue in the conclusion, between 'alternative' and 'mainstream' – may also be highly fluid. What values do participants bring in these activities that may be 'alternative' to mainstream values? Certainly the overriding 'value' participants relish is that they see themselves as truly different, as truly oppositional or alternative in some ways – for example, by degree of commitment, or by the very fact that they see themselves as truly risking death. What research has looked into alternative sport values, except superficially, and what potential for historical research into values might there be?

Booth and Thorpe, speaking explicitly about *extreme* sport, point out that ' … disciples of extreme sports … commit … significant amounts of time and money to their activities … share a willingness to take risks, a social ideology of fun, and a tendency toward codifying and institutionalizing their interests' (Booth and Thorpe 2007, 181). These keys are all true of action sport enthusiasts, but they are also true of mainstream sport participants. The salience of each 'standpoint' may vary from era to era, from individual to individual, so that the fluidity of the investments of practitioners (and the historio-graphical noticing of such fluidity) may be an important key to deeper understanding of some of the [sub]cultures within action sports. These stances don't necessarily privilege the fact of participants' views that theirs is an 'alternative' activity or position.

For example, earlier practitioners of alternative sport may have been less interested in becoming commodified by and within their activity than current athletes are. Today, it is *de rigeur* for an aspiring pre-teen skateboarding phenomenon to be courted as a professional sponsor of various clothing, equipment and other action sport-related products. The influence of this 'professionalization' model upon very young participants is unprecedented in Western sport forms. In some cases, their orientations are more toward the market-place, less toward some sense of altruism. Again, historical periodization and contextual markers may provide a clue as to reasons why different generations may see something like commodification differentially. In the sense of commodification, then, some sports have moved, in less than 20 years, from 'alternative' to 'mainstream'.

Even seemingly-altruistic acts, like Tony Hawk's originally-praised visit to war-savaged Sierra Leone in 2004, become criticized by some as the epitome of American neo-liberal self-promotion (Norcross 2004). This is due to a heightened sense of a celebrity culture, it is true, but there is also a certain cynicism revolving around some commodified action sports which has replaced a generalized hope – perhaps even altruism – and selflessness that was present even as late as the mid-1990s (Eisenberg 2003; Rinehart 1998a). If cultures and individuals within them have become more cynical, how has this influenced the 'innocence' of alternative sport values and skewed the overt rejection of mainstream values?

Earlier extreme and action sport participants (pre-1996 or 1997) may have had a slightly more nuanced historical view and understanding of important *figures* within their own sport activities. Their 'sense of history' – or at least of their place in 'history' – may have influenced their own celebration of a constructed 'sport lineage' which linked them to foundational, authentic membership. They may have seen the development of their own activity as sport as an important and necessary building – but it is also possible that they may be currently exercising a form of elaborate nostalgia for their youth. Historical holographic research might provide better contextual clues for such questions.

In fact, several scholars have interrogated the place of 'pioneers' such as Stacy Peralta and Tony Alva in terms of the placement of origination myths and developmental stories of early alternative sport within Hollywood films like *Dogtown and Z Boys* and *Lords of Dogtown* (Rinehart 2005b). What is more, Kusz has examined 'codes of racial different-ness [which] disaffiliate the Z Boys from whiteness' (Kusz 2006, 148) within the rhetorics of *Dogtown and Z Boys*.

These codes specifically work to demonstrate 'that [the Z Boys] are economically unprivileged' (Kusz 2006, 147), while, of course, their privilege is relative to those who had even less opportunity. This facet of the origination myths aggrandizing Southern Californian skating worked to sanctify the Z Boys' placement within the historical memory of skateboarding, but it also promoted the attitude that the Z Boys were deserving of and justified in becoming commodified within the larger action sports culture. Their authenticity became unquestioned and their films were seen as cool and necessary items of cultural capital for aspiring skaters.

While the explicit 'alternativeness' of these activities is unquestionable, it may also be important to look briefly at some of the research that has been conducted on action and extreme sports participants' shared commitment of time and money, risk-taking behaviours, and commitment to fun (ludic spirit), as well as the moves toward institutionalization of some of these sports. Again, the *caveat* here is that the research reflects the specific action and extreme sport culture(s) it is examining: generalizability among action sports, as well as among action sport research, has only been attempted, in a few cases, by the recent trend towards an encyclopedic knowledge of the activities (Booth and Thorpe 2007). Finding generalities among these fluid, malleable, geographically-specific and -grounded activities remains a difficult task, and any characterization of the activities that is grand, of course, can be criticized on the grounds of its non-generalizability.

'Live the life': time and money commitment

There is an uneasy dynamic of making a living in order to participate in many action sports (the economic demographics of which range greatly). Witness, for example, the cost of a skateboard and the availability of places and times to skate versus the cost of practising windsurfing, snowboarding or skysurfing (Borden 2001) and finding time to commit to actual participation in these sports. Research in these areas has been documented in some action sports but not in others. Skysurfing, for example, seems an intuitive example: according to Brooker, the costs for sky surfing are prohibitive for many aspiring skysurfers (even in 1998):

> Skysurfboard: $500–$750. Camera helmet: $500. Jumpsuit: $250. PC7 camera: $2,500. Of course, you first need to be certified to skydive, which can take several weeks: $1,500. For training at the pro level, figure 12 jumps a day, six days a week. At $16 a jump, that's $1,152 per week for the skysurfer, another $1,152 if you want a camera flyer to record it all for posterity. Call Daddy.
>
> (Brooker 1998, 66)

Clearly, some types of action sports delineate by class and economics. Included in this grouping are many of the snow sports, which require transportation to and from often exotic locales (but certainly geographically remote slopes); sports that require the use of relatively expensive motorized vehicles (Skiddoo, waterskiing, wakeboarding, motocross) and the fuel and upkeep for them; other sports are deliberately or ostentatiously located away from city and population centres (Veblen 1979; Coakley 2007). For those who do not have the financial or temporal wherewithal, a new class of commoditized aspiring athlete has developed: the sponsored action or extreme sport athlete. Teams of skilled athletes, linked together within a rubric of corporate solidarity, have developed their own hierarchical structures.

The divide between some of these alternative sports and others – such as skateboarding, street-hockey (with in-line skates), or even BMX bike riding in its various incarnations – is analogous to the increasingly complex divide – and intersections – among and between, for example, horse polo and basketball. In fact, the appropriation of action (or extreme) sports by white suburban, middle-class youth is also a gesture towards this re-appropriation of physical and symbolic space, *seemingly* lost (at least in the USA), by privileged white youth (Kusz 2001, 2003, 2006, 2007).

Wheaton (2000, 2003) has also documented time and psychic – as well as monetary – commitment of windsurfers, many of whom travel from region to region pursuing good waves and near-ideal wind conditions. Surfers, skiers, snowboarders: many seasonal action sports enthusiasts have committed to 'following the season' for their sport, or becoming multiple action sports (snowboarding in winter, surfing in summer, for example) aficionados.

Kay and Laberge (2003) also identified resource needs by skiers who imperialistically toured various worldwide sites on behalf of Warren Miller films. Among other things, they found that these skiers, who were financed for their exploits, would have had to invest an incredible financial, psychic and personal commitment to pursuing snow year-round – including cost for travel, loss of work opportunities and loss of traditional forms of stability. The upsides, of course, may include the sense of freedom and the sense of entitlement that comes with such 'freedom'. (Being a part of a corporate 'team', with its own sets of rules, though, has proven to belie some of the initial sense of 'freedom' for a few of these sponsored individuals.)

It is clear that, just as in other leisure pursuits and sporting activities, there are differential time and money commitments for participants in different action sports. Across time, some of these commitments may have changed so that there is increased accessibility for surfers, for example, in surf villages along the coasts of the South Pacific, to 'crash' in order to be able to surf. Communities have also built up around snow culture, supporting the lifestyle that is nomadic in nature – thus, the cost of following snow around the world may have decreased since snowboard seekers first hit the slopes. The very massification of these activities has worked to create more and cheaper possibilities for individuals within the systems of these sports. The use of space – particularly the drifting nomadic nature of changing eras of time – for action sport enthusiasts has categorically changed over time, particularly in enclaves for whom the cycles of wind or weather work to create 'ideal' conditions.

Many of the questions that scholars must begin to answer deal with the relative salience – to participants – of time, psychic and money commitments to action or extreme sports. The demands of, relative merits of, and rewards for participants' commitments have, with several notable exceptions, also not been adequately explored.

'Safe danger': the oxymoron of risk-taking

There is a burgeoning literature on risk-taking, particularly risk-taking in the late capitalist-commodity moment. Mostly, the literature concentrates on one of two dovetailing facets of risk-taking: it is either framed as a hedonistic, self-centred approach focused on individuals, often as an outgrowth of the so-called freer decades of the 1960s; or it is, secondarily, sometimes seen – in contemporary society – as an antidote to or escape from the so-called tameness of contemporary life (Lyng 2005; Møller 2007; Laurendeau 2008; Fletcher 2008). Occasionally, these arguments fold over one another and the conditions of risk behaviour are conflated.

As it relates to alternative sport forms, the first body of literature relies heavily on the presupposition that action sports enthusiasts are unconstrained by such factors as gender, age, race, sexuality and class, and the accompanying reduction of agency and barriers (cultural, psychological, practical) of such positionalities. Much of this literature (mostly popular, but often psychology-based), in fact, finds unproblematic the 'origination myths' and self-articulated public bravados within the discourse within many action sports, often relying upon them to establish normative behaviours (notable exceptions, not psychologically-based, include Kusz 2001, 2003, 2006, 2007; Kay and Laberge

2003, 2004). Seeing risk-taking as a hedonistic, unproblematized pursuit of pleasure is, of course, particularly ensconced in a cultural-imperialist tradition. If the viewing of risk behaviour is seen simply, only through a psychological, singular lens, and not complexly, through more historicized and sociological sets of frameworks, then such 'discrete' and simplistic sets of variables are desirable.

Psychologists, in an effort to isolate behavioural factors from societal factors perhaps influencing behaviours (and utilizing a 'scientific' model of isolated variables) have written of a 'thrill-seeking' personality. Farley (1989), in particular, created a popular cultural buzz when he published an article in the popular US magazine *Psychology Today* detailing his theory about personalities – and individuals – who demonstrated along a continuum of thrill-seeking. He termed these individuals 'Type T personalities'. A relatively simplistic, 'elegant', biologically-based theory like this, naturally, caught on well with the public imagination. His later attempts to refine the theory have largely been ignored.

This kind of behaviourist approach also has been utilized by, for example, sport management academics to predict consumption patterns within the new niche market of extreme or action sport. If one assumes that a 'type' of 'adrenaline junky' exists, *sui generis*, then that individual may be more easily manipulated by a market economy. This capitalistic aim, of course, runs counter to the professed ethos of many so-called action sports, and the earlier ways that alternative sport participants characterized their activities. It is ironic that many of the originators of these activities, while simultaneously seeking vocations related to their action sport avocations, have thoughtfully attempted to reject a market-based economy – at least for a while (e.g., Rinehart 2007).

Kay and Laberge (2003) among others, however, have complicated the simple fictions of belief in a Type-T personality by drawing attention to both implicit and explicit class benefits, assumptions and desires in the ideological and imperialistic films of Warren Miller (e.g., *Ski Fantasy* 1953, *Around the World on Skis* 1962, *Any Snow, Any Mountain* 1971, *Endless Winter* 1995, *Children of Winter* 2008). Such pulpy fictions, with ever-improved footage and technical facility, and with the incessant message drummed home accompanied by current hip soundtracks, work to promote a sense of privilege, licence and *carte blanche* that erase critical thought. Kay and Laberge point out that Miller's use of the concept of freedom is, in fact, a *commoditized* freedom, that Miller's '1998 film *Freeriders* ... demonstrate[s] how a tenet of the extreme subculture, in this case freedom, can be co-opted and commodified to suggest and/or reify a sport's "extreme" status' (Kay and Laberge 2003, 382). In this case, freedom is hardly free, and free choice is not agency, but rather at least partially constrained by market demands.

The linkage between Miller's ethnocentric brand of 'freedom' and the Western ideal of the hedonistic pursuit of pleasure, ego-invested as it must be, as opposed to, for example, Eastern ethoi and world views, should be rather obvious (Rinehart 2007). The view of seeing risk-taking as a problem with a linear, logical solution, which has been seen as a subset of the hedonistic hypothesis, also figures within Lyng's ideas circulating around risk-taking, specifically his concept of 'edgework', which is the second major thread of the risk-taking literature.

Lyng's (2005) major distinction between what he sees as classical sociological theory surrounding risk-taking and his idea of 'edgework' lies in the voluntary nature of one's engagement in risk-taking behaviours. While the former kind of risk-taking can be seen (by 'risk sociologists') as 'an inevitable problem of modern industrial societies' (p.18), 'edgework' kinds of risk-taking rely on the voluntary entry aspect of risk. What draws people engaged in risk-taking behaviour? In this sense, and very closely aligned to the hedonistic concept of pleasure seeking, the individual who engages in 'edgework' has been seen to be ' ... increasingly alienated from rationalized production and consumption as means to self-realization' (p.30).

Commitment to risk can be seen as culturally and environmentally based, voluntarily entered into, as opposed to being genetically keyed into one's personality structure. Lyng's emphasis within the risk cultures is largely concerned with the 'nurture' dimension of the nature/nurture debate.

Perhaps because of the apparent emphasis on voluntary − and thus, it is implied, socially constructed − views on risk, it may be no surprise that some action sport (e.g., adventure racing) participants involved in the Discovery Channel Eco-Challenge adhere to naturalized and rather stereotypically gendered roles (Kay and Laberge 2004). While Joanne Kay was an active participant-observer in the 1999 Patagonia, Argentina-based Eco-Challenge, she and Laberge grouped participants − the females were characterized as so-called 'mandatory equipment' for the largely male teams − into three categories: elite, above-average and average/novice. 'The elite women participants aimed to improve their position in the field [of women participants; ... they therefore] censor emotion, carry heavy loads, take risks and push their bodies to capacity' (p.169).

The above-average participants tended to behaviours that were situational: that is to say, they sometimes acted more like elite women participants, sometimes like average/ novice adventure racers. The average/novice athletes 'tend to accept and reinforce their weakness relative to men, downplaying their competitiveness and "toughness", setting low expectations and emphasizing their emotionally supportive role on the team' (p.170).

As Kay and Laberge (2004) ably demonstrate, the very idea of risk and its acceptance may be affected by salient other factors, such as gender, race, age, recent injury, disability, perceptions of worthiness and so on. Acceptance or rejection from an adventure racing team, for example, might create a context where a participant chooses to push or back off. Entry into risk, while accepted, promoted and reinforced by a hegemonically-centred and -privileged male culture, has been demonstrated to be a 'proving ground' for masculinity, and normalized as such (Messner and Sabo 1990; Messner 1992; Albert 1999; Robinson 2004; Walk 2006).

There is obviously no definitive or singular *raison d'être* for the contemporary commitment to risk behaviours: for individuals and groups alike, propensity for risk varies along a complex, non-linear 'continuum' of fluid factors. These factors include, but are not limited to, environmental influences (e.g., parental behaviours and attitudes toward risk, previous experiences, readiness for high risk, sibling influences, permission from a variety of societal 'structures', encouragement processes) and genetic factors (e.g., propensity and/or capacity for vertiginous actions, physical prowess and body type). Other salient influences may include previous experiences, curiosity, sense of safety and exposure to mediated exemplars, and the complex interactions of all these types of mitigations. Many of these factors might be examined when scholars look at 'risk' as a motivating factor for involvement within alternative sport.

'Hedonism R Us': A commitment to fun
The best way to enjoy New Zealand's stunning scenery
is upside-down while bouncing on the end of a piece of elastic.

Bungy jumping, quite possibly the most pointless of all
adrenaline sports. Invented by a New Zealander
... naturally.

> Label on Steinlager beer bottle, 2008 (emphasis added)

Yet another characterization of these action, or extreme, sports is one advanced – and certainly exploited – by New Zealand Breweries, Limited: these sports are *adrenaline* sports. (This description blends in with many others: another facet of action sports, as currently imagined, is their institutionalization, including their commodification by transnational and multinational corporations, media sources and publics – in a variety of ways.) With this simple adjective, *adrenaline*, the beer company has successfully conflated the ideas of risk and what Caillois (1961) terms 'vertiginous' activity with the simple idea of hedonistic, pleasure-seeking fun. A need for a lifestyle is born, and the drinker of Steinlager will be simultaneously borne to a younger, freer age. If the very activity of participating in white water rafting, bungee jumping, snowboarding, or the leisure pursuits of shooting zip lines, running the bulls in Pamplona, testing high-ropes courses, rolling downhill in a Zorb, tandem skydiving, swinging on a Swoop,[11] whitewater rafting, or any of a variety of sports linked to recreational, outdoors-y activities becomes blended with an enjoyment of a disequibrillating endeavour, then action sports may be the 21st century panacea for 'fun fulfilment.'[12]

Closely aligned with the concept of 'risk', for some,[13] 'fun' is a simple concept, yet it is fraught with meaning. Does fun transfer transnationally, so that, like action films, everyone interprets enjoyment and pleasure simultaneously? When fun is strategically attached to something as apparently banal as action sports, often the innocence of nostalgic youth is recollected. As a marketing strategy, of course, 'fun' is intentionally linked to lifestyle, to need, to desire. 'Fun' is largely seen, likewise, in the public imagination, as a dominion of the young. The ageist ramifications of action sport have yet to be explored, satisfactorily, though a preliminary study of action sports films has looked into the way that these visual texts have worked to reify and privilege youth within the realms of action sports (Rinehart 2005; Sarkisian and Rinehart, unpublished).

As Booth and Thorpe point out, citing Loy and Coakley's essay on 'Sport' in the *Blackwell Encyclopedia of Sociology*:

> ... [there are] several theoretical concepts related to fun, including George Simmel's 'sociability,' Erving Goffman's 'euphoric interaction,' Norbert Elias and Eric Dunning's 'quest for excitement,' and Brian Sutton Smith's 'emotional dialectics'.
>
> (Booth and Thorpe 2007, 184)

While all of these theorists characterize facets of the concept of 'fun', its use in current action sport parlance is inclusive of all of these dispositions while remaining somewhat unique.

In action sports, 'fun' is *both* a pursuit and a process. Media – including advertising and popular culture concepts of action sports – have defined 'action' sports as, at core, enjoyable activities. If someone tries out snowboarding, for example, and finds the boots are too tight, the effort at cutting curves too stressful, falling down and getting wet too uncomfortable, the pre-conceived and -packaged ideal of 'fun' will be missed. On the other hand, an exhilarating run down a slope with a modicum of style and technique can feel quite accomplished, thrilling and 'fun'. The obvious subjectivity of both being within the activity and the review of that activity, post-activity, make 'fun' a bit of a learned, as well as an experienced, phenomenon.

Simultaneously, action sports are also seen as processual and 'fun' pursuits. That is to say, these activities, without pre-determined goals, can be enjoyable simply for the rush of air and the disorientating effects inherent in the activities. Looking good to others often matters less than intrinsically and sensually enjoying the *process* of the activity.

Enclosures: codes and institutionalization

While Booth and Thorpe discuss the concept of institutionalization in extreme sports in terms of 'a continuum of expressivity-instrumentality' (Booth and Thorpe 2007, 185), and this appears to be a helpful stratagem for studying how extreme sport forms have (d)evolved from grass-roots activities to highly-massified forms, there are other approaches that may prove fruitful when studying alternative sport. Indeed, the tension between grass-roots participation and highly commoditized and commercialized forms of activity is another simple way of describing such institutionalization – albeit a less broad categorization. In this commoditization, it is athletes, activities, lifestyles, attitudes, music, argot and world views themselves that become the commodities which can be appropriated, borrowed, tried on, bought and sold – for a price.

There is no simplistic binary, however, between these two discrete camps of alternative sport participants – the 'grass roots' and the 'highly-commoditized'. As Thorpe (forthcoming) points out, there exists a range of types of extreme sport participants – and imbedded within this variegated quilt of stances and standpoints is a wide range of fluid and dynamic participatory strategies. Though most studies have looked at 'participation' from an active, athlete stance, there are whole groups who likewise 'participate' in alternative sports and activities. Even grass-roots 'athletes' are touched by vendors selling equipment (e.g., shoes, boards, clothing, stickers, enhancement products), videos, niche market magazines and so forth, directly related to their particular 'action' or 'extreme' sport (Rinehart 1998b). There are also the products that tangentially affect a range of action-sport 'athletes': food, drink, travel, lifestyle-related products, all of which have been married to a particular (or general) sense of action sport.

Communities – also imagined communities (Andersen 1983; Agamben 1993) – get involved in discussing and authenticating these sport activities, in creating events, in satisfying their 'tribal' needs for communitas (Turner 1974), pleasure and variation. The acts of discussing such practices themselves are part of the enjoyment of the activities. Anticipation and replay of events sometimes involves a whole host of 'players' (Rinehart 1998b).

For example, Levinson describes the Pentacost Islanders' ritual of vine jumping as 'an agricultural ritual meant to ensure an abundant crop of yams' (Levinson 2007, 338). The islanders prepared for this event, with many individuals (not simply the 'jumpers') participating, measuring out the length of the vines, creating the softened earth landing, building the towers, cheering and clapping for the jumpers, and so on. This ritual 'has received considerable attention, such that in 1995 [ironically, the advent year of ESPN's the eXtreme Games] the government banned it because it had become too commercialized' (p.338). An agricultural ritual in the Pentacost Islands had become too commercialized!

Another interesting problematic may be a comparative look at how mainstream and alternative sports have become institutionalized (Pearson 1979). Do the compressions of temporality (that is, the shortened time spans of the sports' spread), for alternative sport, have any meaning that may make them distinct from mainstream sport institutionalization?

These 'extreme'/action sports and activities have only been in the dominant and/or mainstream public's view *as sport* since about 1995. They have, of course, been referred to as 'extreme' primarily by the electronic and print media, 'action' by many practitioners; 'extreme' characterizes what they *are*, 'action' what they *do*. The impulse to practise such embodied activities has been around for much of humankind.

Yet, with a few notable and somewhat isolated exceptions, such as the late 19th-century cycle contest manias (Thompson 2006), or bare-knuckled and open fighting competitions since ancient times (Poliakoff 1987; Roberts 1977), these extraordinary attempts to exceed others' efforts were generally not characterized as sport. They were, more notably, seen as survival techniques, entertainment, as some sort of sociological or anthropological oddity, or as an exploration (such as Tenzing Norgay and Edmund Hillary's climb up Mount Everest). By the 21st century, each of these examples has become sportified into, respectively, bicycle endurance races, open cage or Ultimate Fighting (Masucci 2007), and various forms of mountain climbing (P. Donnelly 2003). They are all seen, at the time of their doing, unquestionably as being sport. While they largely have been seen as 'alternative', they have not always been viewed as 'risky', 'edgy', 'extreme', or daring. (Ironically, and interestingly, it is this very embracing by the mainstream that may be reducing the case for some of these sport forms as being 'alternative'.)

Even skateboarding, practised by many youths in the 1960s, was, at that time, considered by the mainstream as a fringe activity akin to Hula-Hoop or Yo-Yos, a leisure pursuit, an artistic lifestyle choice, and/or a mode of transportation. Just as there are evolutionary advances in equipment over time,[14] so too have the ethos of alternative sports changed over time – and in different regions of the world. However, it is vitally clear that there has been an uneven, albeit accelerated, mainstream acceptance and naturalization of many alternative sports over the past 15+ years. Many of these activities have become non-remarkable. They are no longer *avant-garde* or cutting edge (if they ever were), so if being oppositional or trendy was a practitioner's primary aim, the action sports that have become mainstream are no longer the best alternative.

Yet, having said that, new forms are constantly being 'invented' and proposed: witness *parkour* (Normile 2009), which intertextually relates to so many action aspects of 21st century action films (for example, the extended chase scenes in *Casino Royale*, where both 'agonists' jump from buildings to other buildings and scale open beams of a construction site, is just one example of the Hollywoodization of the embodied form of parkour). The inventiveness and relatedness to one's environment in new and creative ways is certainly one of the aspects of these alternative sport forms, but the 'inventers' of them (in parkour's case, French teenager David Belle is generally given credit[15]) lose 'their' view of them as soon as others play with the forms. The fluidity, then, of the (d)evolution of alternative sport forms is foreshortened and largely uncontrollable by the individual.

Alternative sport developments (movements from local, grass-roots-based organizing groupings to regional, national and international organizational structures) tend to mirror the movements of many other massified, commodified and, now, mainstreamed, sport activities (see, e.g., Elias and Dunning 1986; Guttmann 1978). This process is not new, but its multiple incarnations might be: not only are they institutionalized rapidly (viewing them on YouTube is also a form of 'institutionalization'), but they are also modified, changed, re-formed in myriad new and actively creative ways.

That is, local ritualized and instrumental practices like those of the Pentacostal Islanders' form of bungy jumping develop as antecedents for current practices – with greatly different emphases and values attached. Then a capitalist entrepreneur like A.J.

Hackett, in New Zealand, 'discovers' the embodied movement and adapts it and its former sacred aspects to fit his own needs and desires. Is Hackett then the originator of 'bungy jumping'? Is 'bungy jumping' in its present Westernized, commodified and touristy form the same as that practised by the Pentacostal Islanders to insure a good agricultural season?

Like the much-studied and historically-placed movements and evolutions of British-based sport (Guttmann 2004), the 'developments' of alternative sport have been uneven, across a variety of sometimes disparate, sometimes similar action sports (bungy jumping and sky surfing, parkour and orienteering, surfing and mountain unicycling), the time-spans have been compressed and the values (of participants, administrators and audiences) remain fluid and contested.

The 'disciples' of such action sports have not been (necessarily) English or American white Christian missionaries or adventurous 'gentlemen' gainfully recording, absorbing, modifying and co-opting the mores and practices of native inhabitants (and *vice versa*), but rather have been 'core members' of their sport activity – surfers, boarders of every ilk, well-meaning postmodern-day missionaries of planned obsolescence, facile travellers and tramplers of inhabited territories, eager and, generally, uncritical proselytizers of capitalism, hedonism, democracy (Kay and Laberge 2003), and, throughout, competition. Their goals, then, like the British and American antecedents, have been instrumental – but consciously instrumental based on advancing their sport or activity, not based on proselytizing others to become 'civilized' or to become 'more British' or 'more Christian', for example.

While the developments of each form of alternative sport need to be assessed individually – teased out by sport, region and time period – generally, this sense of temporal compression may be one of the facets that distinguishes historiographical inquiry in action sports from similar inquiry into mainstream and dominant sports. There is a sense that within these sport forms and their adherents, views of them change almost *hysterically* from one moment to another. This compression of time is, of course, exacerbated by the use of electronic and other types of communication within post-structural and alternative sport life. For example, YouTube has changed the way we – and this is differentially salient for different age groups – apprehend what is currently 'cool' and what is not (Wilson 2002) and the way we join new social movements or choose to reject them (Wilson 2007; Thorpe and Rinehart, forthcoming).

In summary, the overriding value of 'differentness' appears to be one of the abidingly critical factors that differentiates these sport forms from mainstream sport forms, though of course there are continuums, degrees of salience between alternative and mainstream sport value orientations. In this section, I have identified several key values that may be researched historically and contextually, including the very idea of 'differentness' or 'alternativeness', the concept of authenticity, attitudinal differences (toward commodification, sponsorship, altruism, appreciation for history of their activity and of key individuals within their activity), commitment of time and money, risk-taking, the core concept of fun and the move toward institutionalization. These values may or may not distinguish specific alternative sports from mainstream sports, but they all, to some degree, remain key factors for research into alternative sport.

Conclusions: future research and directions

In this piece, I have proposed a possible methodology, which takes into account temporal, geographical and other spatial concerns. By studying alternative sport with traditional methods, we may miss the gist of what is important, of what is happening: concerns with different themes (such as, for example, authenticity, nostalgia, pleasure, affect, creation of meaning) may help to more effectively contextualize alternative sport. I have argued for a contextually-based holographic method, one which may more accurately near a sense of 'similitude' of differential, philosophical and embodied moments in alternative sport.

In other words, we are using methods well-suited for mainstream sport forms to study something potentially different. Why, then, do we not challenge our approaches and attempt new ways of seeing? Perhaps we can approach a 'history' that values floating, shifting, uncertain and unsteady socio-historical projects in a new way (Thorpe and Rinehart, forthcoming; Thrift 2008).

Utilizing the kinds of research I called for in this piece as historiographical method, however, will require transgressive, resistant and oppositional approaches, world views and attitudes within sports historiography and sports history research traditions. It will require a conscious effort on the part of alternative sport scholars to see the subject matter they study as ever-moving, as sometimes having a beginning (which is characterized by those characteristics that demonstrate beginning-ness), a middle (with middle-ness), and an end (with characteristics of end-ness), or, 'alternatively', as having no linear form whatsoever. This work will have to be seen in terms of itself, in terms of Williams's view of the 'emergent' forms, as well as his view of that which precedes the emergent, the 'pre-emergence, active and pressing but not yet fully articulated' (Williams 1977, 126).

What matters, finally, in understanding emergent culture, as distinct from both the dominant and the residual, is that it is never only a matter of immediate practice; indeed it depends crucially on finding new forms or adaptations of form (Williams 1977, 126). Williams's insight, then, is that emergence (and its precursor, pre-emergence) is never solid and trackable; rather, it is always moving, always fluid and malleable, always, by definition, one step ahead of that which seeks to describe it.

Beyond simply calling for a research that more accurately mirrors 'that which happened', I am also attempting to nuance that call. Thus, another way that historio-graphical method may be qualitatively different for these new sport forms (and the tools to apprehend them perhaps insufficient) is in discussion of the *overt* aims of those who manage to 'penetrate' new areas with action sport ethos and attitudes. If, in fact, the defining point of these sport forms that discriminates them from mainstream sports is their overt 'differentness', and they are constantly being absorbed into mainstream culture, an active, capitalist-based system is in operation to provide new, *avant-garde* approaches to sport experiences. Determining that system – that is analogous to the artistic *avant-garde* system of a modernist world view (for earlier discussions of the impact of the *avant-garde* model on sport, see Rinehart 1998b) – is the work of sociologists and historians, to evidence what is really happening.

Looking at the variety of competing 'histories' and the nuances involved in discover-ing who did what within any given action sport activity may, in fact, solve a few of the difficulties scholars have had with speaking of the sport activities. Though we approach these problematics from sometimes equally viable theoretical stances, we could all turn our focus to the developments of alternative sports.

For example, the assumed aims of skateboarders who lived in Dogtown during the mythologized settings of *Dogtown and Z Boys* and *Lords of Dogtown* have really not been examined in terms of competing genealogies of skating. What were the overt and covert aims of the members of the Zephyr skate team and their adult leaders, both then and now? How have their 'stories' become lived experiences, who do the stories privilege, how does the hierarchical privileging of some stories over others work to reify a partial history of skateboarding? How are sports historians and sociologists complicit in that reification through their own silences? Some of the recent admissions within sports historiography of the existence of multiple-situated 'truths' (or stories, or myths) co-existing simultaneously is perhaps a step towards understanding nuanced positionalities, without, one hopes, a sense of the hierarchical competitiveness that has characterized much of previous discussions (Foner 2002).

There is no unitary stance, no singular reason that people do what they do – that is, snowboard, skate, jump, climb, test themselves or challenge their own fears, sell products, market themselves, chase the 'endless summer', 'go for the rush', and so forth – particularly within action sport communities (Booth 2005). (Of course, there is no singular reason that a woman chooses to play rugby, or a male determines that he wants to be a cheerleader – there never was, but problematizing those stances makes for better historiography, better understanding.) Thus, it is essential that scholars working in the fields of alternative sport research come to terms with terminology and, to some degree at least, 'operationally define' (or at least reach agreed-upon mutual understandings of) what time period and place they are studying. Context, historians have found, is critical in understanding histories and the stories of history (Thorpe 2006) and is important in not simply reproducing uncritical and unreflexive flawed histories. Every history is made up of partial knowledge, but the overt recognition of this truth makes a great difference.

Thus, many alternative – both 'extreme' and action – sports in the 21st century appear and feel very different from how they were in 1995 at ESPN's first eXtreme Games. The inclusion of the fourth dimension of time by historians creates a closer approximation of what really happened and is happening. Looking at generational differences – in material culture like clothing and equipment; in aims and goals; in ethical stances; in philosophies and ethos – sites histories of 'extreme' sports differently than simply lumping them all into a unitary mass. For example, issues like differential media attention for female and male athletes, while still stunningly uneven and imbalanced, are no longer seen by many as elemental concerns within commodified action sports culture. These issues have been talked about, and third-wave feminists have found the issues much more complex than thought, even in the 1990s. The lens that researchers use – in this case, second-wave or third-wave feminism – may in fact colour the very issues that are seen as salient. Of course, these kinds of arguments can characterize any era, any study.

The point is, many of the normalized values of *mainstream* sport – misogyny, both overt and covert racism and sexism, classism, ageism, homophobia and heteronormativity, to name a few – have become naturalized within *action* sports sub-cultures within less than 20 years (Stedman 1997).[16] Alternative sports – 'alternative to what?', one might ask – are in many cases no longer alternative to mainstream values. Many of the extreme and action sports, though arguably qualitatively different in some interesting ways from mainstream sport – particularly value orientations (Booth and Thorpe 2007; Beal and Smith 2008; Rinehart 2007) – have been 'massified', commodified and mainstreamed. Just like 'major' sport, dominant sport, or 'power and performance' sport participants' principles (Coakley 2007), many action and extreme sport participants' values have become normalized so that, at least on the constructs of oppositionality or resistance, it is safe to say many of these forms are no longer 'alternative'. There are new forms, however, non-massified forms that are 'alternative'. These are the forms historians may want to study as they emerge, as they evolve.

The idea of generational differences in terms of alterity, then, is an important component within the historical hologram. I do not simply mean generational differences of those we study, though their differential attitudes and interpretations are vital to the process. I also mean that the generational differences of scholars need to be taken into account, particularly when looking at such a new cultural form as alternative sport.

For example, older Western scholars have been raised in cultures where, for the most part, sponsorship of school sports has been subsidized by local, regional and national governments. Younger scholars in the USA and some other Western countries, since the era of Reagan and Thatcher in the 1980s, have been raised in an environment where school sports have been not entirely subsidized by the state. This difference in environment – coupled with very complex attitudes about individualism, responsibility and debates regarding professionalism and amateurism – has worked to qualitatively colour different generations of alternative scholars' fundamental assumptions about commoditization and corporate sponsorship (Howell 1991).

The way parts of these sports are emphasized, broadcast and promoted may, in fact, vary from era to era, from class to class, from region to region, from imagined community to 'real' community to virtual community (see, e.g., Andersen 1983; Agamben 1993). Typical mass media forms such as slick niche market magazines, home-produced 'zines, and the use of the internet by such media multinationals; individual forms of media like YouTube, home videos, cell and mobile phones, Apple iPhones, Google Android phones, and other electronic modalities; word-of-mouth, very localized and seemingly primitive forms of 'media': all of these forms of emphasis, broadcast, or promotion are very different (in their tone, tenor, purpose, apprehension by audience and so forth) from former ways of dissemination of sport forms. Use of them may (or may not) vary by gender or race, age or ability, sexual orientation or class; mere observation of specific groups does not adequately answer these kinds of questions.

The very virtuality of the means of disseminating, observing, learning and spectating alternative sports makes for more covert forms of individual expression – thus, for example, misogyny may be more readily 'practised' in private, from cell phone to cell phone, within small pockets of individuals, than in more public spaces. The use of irony, misdirection, deliberate forms of insincerity on public spaces like Facebook – many of these guises that younger generations use demonstrate different generational senses of candour, playfulness and ethos. Observations of these groups' insider statuses only may point to the *possibilities* of misogynic practices. Historical analysis – in this case, looking at themes over time, with differing groups – may provide a more holistic picture (hologram) of the contextual specifics of how these practices became normalized, how new technologies may have changed the way such thematic practices have become changed within alternative sport as compared to mainstream sport.

There are exceptions that have taken into account historical context within the literature: as one recent example, Beal and Smith (2008), in discussing the California surf site of Mavericks, make it very clear that they are talking about Mavericks in the early 21st century – which would not compare in attitude, style, ethos, or values oriented toward consumption with a discussion of the right-break waves of Raglan, New Zealand as they were surfed during the late 1960s. While Beal and Smith's discussion is primarily about Mavericks, it is also about what Mavericks is *not*: this negative capability is, of course, critical for researchers to envision and make clear (either explicitly or implicitly) to the reader. Of course, this is an obvious example, but the point is that when a new area of research opens up, studies are occasionally conducted willy-nilly. There is no one assurance that the research is conducted in a careful, thoughtful, or even logical way. So research protocols must be carefully scripted within a working tradition in order for some semblance of coherence to occur.[17]

Among the action sports, at varying points in time, differential emphases may include an emphasis on aesthetics versus technique, or privileging of physical power over beauty, for example. As it is with most 'action' sport, conceptions of injury, risk, individuality, even of the 'sportiness' of the activity may have changed fairly extensively since the mid-1990s. In fact, Walk (2006) has clearly delineated how these action sports have become more aligned in their value orientations regarding risk, injury and celebration with 'power and performance' sports' ethos (Coakley 2007), while simultaneously aligning with the ethos of alternative, green or sustainable movements. The multiple meanings of action sports – the various complications between an adolescent misogyny and a growing appreciation for feminist values, for example – make the studies of these new sport forms interesting and vital. However, those who study them have to have clear eyes for cultural and historical nuance: Walk's work, in fact, is quite prescient, looking also at the usages action sport enthusiasts have made of recent technologies to advance their own 'imagined communities'.

In summary, it is important for sports historians to come to grips with an ever-evolving, malleable and spirited group of cultures within postmodern, post-structural, sporting practices. Capturing such unstable and quickly moving targets is difficult, to be sure, but capturing the *sense* of 'what happened' may be worth the effort.

Notes

1 Indeed, scholars cannot even agree on the terms we use to describe these activities. Again, such 'truth' claims mirror power struggles. I do not exclude my own work from this criticism.

2 The potential for transgressive or transformative types of movement forms such as action or extreme sports has been studied by various scholars (c.f., Beal 1995, 1996; Eisenberg 2003; Midol 1993; Midol and Broyer 1995; Rinehart 1998a, 1998b, 2005a; Rinehart and Grenfell 2002; Wheaton 2004; Wilson 2002, 2007). Since a recognition of this feature is something that most scholars agree upon when discussing these sports, I use the term 'alternative' (implying alternative to the mainstream as the salient value) generally for these sport forms.

3 Or so we like to think: see, for example, George Orwell's (1945) essay 'The Sporting Spirit', where he discusses the Russian Dynamo versus British Arsenal football match and the resultant 'ill-will existing in the world at this moment … ', for a contrasting view.

4 Are there ever any 'new forms'? Perhaps saying 'a return to a formerly unsuccessful, yet potentially satisfying, form' would be more accurate.

5 C.f., Williams (1977), particularly regarding his use of the concepts of dominant, residual and emergent. These concepts, it seems to me, fairly neatly encapsulate the post-structural sport scene nearly everywhere, and particularly describe the advent of alternative (emergent) sport forms.

6 'Action' sports are so named because of the perception of constant movement; whether this term owes its naming to corporate dazzle and hype, or has caught on because it is currently the least offensive of the labels to choose from is an interesting question, and beyond the scope of this paper. However, it must be pointed out that so-called dominant sport forms are filled with action as well. Perhaps the MTV style of broadcasting televisually these alternative sports, with little dead time and a perception of constant flow and action makes the term 'action' sports less objectionable to participants who resist being named and labelled.

7 'Extreme' sports is a term that sports cable giant ESPN applied to these activities; they changed their advertising and siting of the naming of their annual alternative sports Olympic-type event from 'The eXtreme Games' to the 'X Games' within the first year (1996), but still called the activities 'eXtreme' (cf., Rinehart 1998a).

8 'Whiz' sports is a term that French scholar Nancy Midol (1993; Midol and Broyer 1995) applied to sports the salient facets of which, to the practitioner, were speed and disorientation. This term aligned neatly with Caillois' notion of ilinx, or vertigo.

9 Belinda Wheaton has utilized the term 'lifestyle' sports to reference the potential and often very real deep personal involvement and commitment of participants within their activity. See, e.g., Wheaton 2004.

10 Why it matters that these origination stories are critically challenged and at least triangulated in verifying truth claims is that inequities become reified, stories become concretized and naturalized – resulting in more power invested in the originators of the stories, and less voice and power to those who may have also had a stake in instantiating such mythics. The uncritical reification of origination stories by scholars serves to create yet another barrier which works to bar groups and individuals from whole participation, and to instill covert and overt inequities among potential 'consumers'.

11 A 'Zorb' is a transparent plastic sphere (also known as 'sphering' or 'globe-riding'), inside which one to three riders sit while the sphere is rolled down a gentle slope. 'Swoop' is a free falling ride for one to three, where the riders sit in hang-glider harnesses and swing down and forward, reaching speeds of up to 130 km an hour (Rotorua, NZ Visitor Guide, 2008).

12 'Fun' is a widely discussed term, often linked to 'happiness', though, of course, not necessarily. It is beyond the scope of this chapter, but interested readers may want to explore the kingdom of Bhutan's concept of 'Gross National Happiness' as an index of philosophically based cultural difference in world view (Larmer 2008), particularly *vis-à-vis* 'The Other Final', which is a Dutch documentary about the football match between Bhutan (FIFA ranked #202) and Montserrat (FIFA ranked #203) (Kramer 2003). It must be noted, however, that 'fun' can be a sudden rush, an extended joy, a deep satisfaction, a sense of accomplishment, a creation of balance – all dimensions that keep getting reinvented in the 21st century in their specifics, but not in their object.

13 I am reminded of the continuum that Abraham Maslow (1968) envisioned between 'safety' and 'growth' of individuals, groups, societies. When one moves from an area of safety, one's capacity and potential for growth increases; similarly, when one moves from growth toward safety, one's capacity and potential for growth decreases.

14 For example, the development of the polyurethane-based wheel allowed skaters of all persuasions to glide over various terrain that made skating more accessible: until that development, metal wheels prevented mass access on everyday streets (see, e.g., Eisenberg 2003).

15 This assumed 'credit' is, again, a mythos of the origination of parkour, unremarked upon and, over time, uncontested until seen as 'truth'. Does it matter if David Belle and his friends began running as freely as possible in France in the 1990s and that they were the originators of this leisure/art/sport form? In historiographical terms, it does matter: the victors get to tell the story and that particular inequity has lead to myriad imbalances in perception and fact.

16 Indeed, as sport, they were never *not* reflective of the many the dominant cultural ethos and values, except in a hopeful way: foundational works in extreme sports have highlighted the dominant societies' perverse and pervasive value structures within these alternative sport forms. See, e.g., Becky Beal's originary works on skateboarding and imbalances in gendered behaviour (1995, 1996), Kyle Kusz's ground-breaking examinations of extreme/action sports and a white male backlash to a perceived non-white dominance in other sports (2003, 2007), and Belinda Wheaton's in-depth examinations of subcultures and class (2000, 2003) as examples of these discussions within action sport studies.

17 This is not a call for more surveillance of the field: it is merely an observation that research protocols in some areas (e.g., gender studies in sport) jump from 'hot topic' to 'hot topic'. I'm not sure this is the most efficacious way of studying areas of interest, and yet, efficacy is not always the major goal in research.

References

Agamben, Giorgio, *The Coming Community*, translation Michael Hardt (Minneaolis: University of Minnesota Press, 1993).

Albert, Edward, 'Dealing with Danger: The Normalization of Risk in Cycling', *International Review for the Sociology of Sport* 34 (2) (1999), 157–71.

Andersen, Benedict, *Imagined Communities: Reflections on the Origin and Spread of Nationalism* (London: Verso, 1983).

ArtLex, *Trompe l'oeil*, www.artlex.com/ArtLex/t/trompeloeil.html (accessed 23 February 2009).

Atencio, Matthew and Becky Beal, 'Consuming "Street Credibility": Skateboarding and the Art of Entrepreneurial "Cool"', paper presented at the North American Society for the Sociology of Sport annual meeting, Pittsburgh, PA (November 2006).

Baudrillard, Jean, *Simulacra and Simulation*, translated by Sheila Faria Glaser (Ann Arbor: University of Michigan Press, 1994 [1981]).

Beal, Becky, 'Disqualifying the Official: An Exploration of Social Resistance through the Subculture of Skateboarding', *Sociology of Sport Journal* 12 (3) (1995), 252–67.

—— 'Alternative Masculinity and its Effects on Gender Relations in the Subculture of Skateboarding', *Journal of Sport Behavior* 19 (3) (1996), 204–20.

Beal, Becky and Maureen Smith, 'Experiencing Mavericks: The Hybridity of Consumption', paper presented at the North American Society for the Sociology of Sport annual meeting, Denver, CO (2008).

Benjamin, Walter, *Illuminations: Essays and Reflections* (New York: Schocken Books, 1969 [1955]).

Booth, Douglas, *The Field: Truth and Fiction in Sport History* (London: Routledge, 2005).

Booth, Douglas and Holly Thorpe, 'The Meaning of Extreme', in Douglas Booth and Holly Thorpe, eds, *Berkshire Encyclopedia of Extreme Sports* (Great Barrington, MA: Berkshire Publishing Group LLC, 2007), 181–97.

Borden, Iain, *Skateboarding, Space and the City: Architecture and the Body* (Oxford: Berg, 2001).

Brooker, Kevin, *Way inside ESPN's X Games* (New York: Hyperion/ESPN Books, 1998).

Caillois, Roger, *Man, Play, and Games* (New York: Free Press, 1961).

Campbell, Martin (Director), *Casino Royale* (film, Metro Goldwyn-Mayer, 2006).

Coakley, Jay J., *Sports in Society: Issues and Controversies*, 9th edn (New York: McGraw Hill, 2007).

Crepeau, Richard C. and Rob Sheinkopf, 'The Eddie Scissons Syndrome: Life Imitating Art Imitating Life', *Aethlon* 8 (1) (1990), 175–84.

Donnelly, Michele K., 'Alternative and Mainstream: Revisiting the Sociological Analysis of Skateboarding', in Michael Atkinson and Kevin Young, eds, *Tribal Play: Subcultural Journeys through Sport* (Bingley, UK: Emerald JAI, 2008), 197–216.

Donnelly, Peter, 'The Great Divide: Sport Climbing vs. Adventure Climbing', in Robert E. Rinehart and Synthia S. Sydnor, eds, *To the Extreme: Alternative Sports, Inside and Out* (Albany: State University of New York Press, 2003), 291–304.

Donnelly, Michele, 'Studying Extreme Sports: Beyond the Core Participants', *Journal of Sport and Social Issues* 30 (2) (2006), 219–24.

Eisenberg, Arlo, 'Psychotic Rant', in Robert E. Rinehart and Synthia S. Sydnor, eds, *To the Extreme: Alternative Sports, Inside and Out* (Albany: State University of New York Press, 2003), 21–25.

Elias, Norbert and Eric Dunning, *Quest for Excitement: Sport and Leisure in the Civilizing Process* (Oxford: B. Blackwell, 1986).

Farley, Frank, 'The Big T in Personality: Thrill-seeking often Produces the Best Achievers But It Can Also Create the Worst Criminals', *Psychology Today* 20 (1989), 44–48.

Fletcher, Robert, 'Living on the Edge: The Appeal of Risk Sports for the Professional Middle Class', *Sociology of Sport Journal* 25 (3) (2008), 310–30.

Foner, Eric, *Who Owns History? Rethinking the Past in a Changing World* (New York: Hill & Wang, 2002).

Forché, Carolyn, 'The Angel of History', in *The Angel of History* (New York: HarperPerennial, 1994), 3–21.

Guttmann, Allen, *From Ritual to Record: The Nature of Modern Sports* (New York: Columbia University Press, 1978).

——*Sports: The First Five Millennia* (Amherst: University of Massachusetts Press, 2004).

Howell, Jeremy, '"A Revolution in Motion": Advertising and the Politics of Nostalgia', *Sociology of Sport Journal* 8 (3) (1991), 258–71.

Kay, Joanne and Suzanne Laberge, 'Oh Say Can You Ski?: Imperialistic construction of freedom in Warren Miller's *Freeriders*', in Robert E. Rinehart and Synthia S. Sydnor, eds, *To the Extreme: Alternative Sports, Inside and Out* (Albany: State University of New York Press, 2003), 381–98.

——'"Mandatory Equipment": Women in Adventure Racing', in Belinda Wheaton, *Understanding Lifestyle Sports: Consumption, Identity and Difference* (London: Routledge, 2004), 154–74.

Kramer, Johan (Director), *The Other Final* (film, KesselKramer, 2003).

Kusz, Kyle, '"I Want To Be the Minority": The Politics of Youthful White Masculinities in Sport and Popular Culture in 1990s America', *Journal of Sport and Social Issues* 25 (4) (2001), 390–416.

——'BMX, Extreme Sports, and the White Male Backlash', in Robert E. Rinehart and Synthia S. Sydnor, eds, *To the Extreme: Alternative Sports, Inside and Out* (Albany: State University of New York Press, 2003), 153–75.

——'Dogtown and Z Boys: White Particularity and the New, New Cultural Racism', in C. Richard King and David J. Leonard, eds, *Visual Economies of/in Motion: Sport and Film* (New York: Peter Lang, 2006), 135–63.

——*Revolt of the White Athlete: Race, Media and the Emergence of Extreme Athletes in America* (New York: Peter Lang, 2007).

Larmer, Brook, 'Bhutan's Enlightened Experiment', *National Geographic* 213 (3) (2008), 124–49.

Laurendeau, Jason, '"Gendered Risk Regimes": A Theoretical Consideration of Edgework and Gender', *Sociology of Sport Journal* 25 (3) (2008), 293–309.

Levinson, David, 'Vine Jumping', in Douglas Booth and Holly Thorpe, eds, *Berkshire Encyclopedia of Extreme Sports* (Great Barrington, MA: Berkshire Publishing Group LLC, 2007), 337–39.

Lyng, Stephen, 'Sociology at the Edge: Social Theory and Voluntary Risk Taking', in Stephen Lyng, ed., *Edgework: The Sociology of Risk-taking* (New York: Routledge, 2005), 17–49.

Maslow, Abraham, *Toward a Psychology of Being* (Princeton, NJ: Van Nostrand, 1968).

Masucci, Matthew A., 'Ultimate Fighting', in Douglas Booth and Holly Thorpe, eds, *Berkshire Encyclopedia of Extreme Sports* (Great Barrington, MA: Berkshire Publishing Group LLC, 2007), 329–32.

Messner, Michael, *Power at Play: Sports and the Problem of Masculinity* (Boston: Beacon Press, 1992).

Messner, Michael A. and Donald Sabo, eds, *Sport, Men, and the Gender Order: Critical Feminist Perspectives* (Champaign, IL: Human Kinetics, 1990).

Midol, Nancy, 'Cultural dissents and technical innovations in the "whiz" sports', *International Review for the Sociology of Sport* 28 (1) (1993), 23–32.

Midol, Nancy and G. Broyer, 'Toward an Anthropological Analysis of New Sport Cultures: The Case of Whiz Sports in France', *Sociology of Sport Journal* 12 (2) (1995), 204–12.

Møller, Verner, 'Walking the Edge', in Mike McNamee, ed., *Philosophy, Risk and Adventure Sports* (London: Routledge, 2007), 186–97.

Norcross, Don, 'It Opened My Eyes', *The San Diego Union-Tribune* (5 May 2004), signonsandiego.com/uniontrib/20040505/news_1s5hawk-jp.html (accessed 17 September 2008).

Normile, Dwight, 'Urban Gymnastics', *International Gymnast* 51 (1) (2009), 38–40 (retrieved 5 April 2009 from SPORTDiscus database).

Orwell, George, 'The Sporting Spirit', (1945), orwell.ru/library/articles/spirit/english/e_spirit (accessed 22 April 2009).

Pearson, Kent, 'The Institutionalization of Sport Forms', *International Review for the Sociology of Sport* 14 (1) (1979), 51–60.

Poliakoff, Michael B., *Combat Sports in the Ancient World: Competition, Violence, and Culture* (New Haven, CT: Yale University Press, 1987).

Richardson, Laurel and Elizabeth Adams St Pierre, 'Writing: A Method of Inquiry', in Norman K. Denzin and Yvonna S. Lincoln, eds, *The Sage Handbook of Qualitative Research*, 3rd edn (Thousand Oaks, CA: Sage Publications, Inc., 2005), 959–78.

Rinehart, Robert E., 'Inside of the Outside: Pecking Orders within Alternative Sport at ESPN's 1995 "The eXtreme Games"', *Journal of Sport and Social Issues* 22 (1998a), 398–414.

——*Players All: Performances in Contemporary Sport* (Bloomington: Indiana University Press, 1998b).

——'"Babes" and Boards: Opportunities in the New Millennium?', *Journal of Sport and Social Issues* 29 (3) (2005a), 233–55.

——'Ollies, Shredders, & Nostalgia: Re-inventing Ageism in Action Sports', paper presented at the International Sociology of Sport Association, Buenos Aires, Argentina, December 2005b.

——'The "Eddie Scissons Syndrome" and Fictionalized Public Confessionals: Embellishment, Storytelling, and Affecting Audience in Recall Narrative', *Qualitative Inquiry* 12 (6) (2006a), 1,045–66.

——'Beyond Traditional Sports Historiography: Toward a Historical "Holograph"', in Murray G. Phillips, ed., *Deconstructing Sport History: A Postmodern Analysis* (Albany, NY: SUNY Press, 2006b), 181–201.

——'The Performative Avant-garde and Action Sports: Vedic Philosophy in a Postmodern World', in Mike McNamee, ed., *Philosophy, Risk and Adventure Sports* (London: Routledge, 2007), 118–37.

Rinehart, Robert E. and Christopher Grenfell, 'BMX Spaces: Children's Grass Roots Courses and Corporate-Sponsored Tracks', *Sociology of Sport Journal* 19 (3) (2002), 302–14.

Roberts, Randy, 'Eighteenth Century Boxing', *Journal of Sport History* 4 (3) (1977), 246–59.

Robinson, Victoria, 'Taking Risks: Identity, Masculinities and Rock Climbing', in Belinda Wheaton, ed., *Understanding Lifestyle Sports: Consumption, Identity and Difference* (London: Routledge, 2004), 113–30.

Sheinkopf, Rob, 'The Eddie Scissons Syndrome: An Epidemic Out of Control', paper presented at the Sport Literature Association annual meeting, Johnson City, TN, June 2001.

Stedman, Leanne, 'From Gidget to Gonad Man: Surfers, Feminists and Postmodernisation', *The Australia & New Zealand Journal of Sociology* 33 (1) (1997), 75–90.

Thompson, Christopher S., *The Tour de France: A Cultural History* (Berkeley: University of California Press, 2006).

Thorpe, Holly, 'Beyond "Decorative Sociology": Contextualizing Female Surf, Skate, and Snow Boarding', *Sociology of Sport Journal* 23 (3) (2006), 205–28.

——'The Psychology of Extreme Sport', in Tatiana Ryba, Robert Schinke and Gershon Tenenbaum, eds, *The Cultural Turn in Sport and Exercise Psychology* (Fitness Information Technology, forthcoming).

Thorpe, Holly and Robert E. Rinehart, 'Alternative Sports and Affect: Non-representational Theory Examined', *Sport and Society* (Special Issue: Belinda Wheaton, Ed.) (forthcoming).

Thrift, Nigel, *Non-representational Theory: Space / Politics / Affect* (London: Routledge, 2008).

Tranströmer, Tomas, 'About History', in Robert Hass, ed., *Selected Poems 1954–1986* (New York: Ecco Press, 1987), 74–75.

Turner, Victor, *Dramas, Fields, and Metaphors: Symbolic Action in Human Society* (Ithaca, NY: Cornell University Press, 1974).

Veblen, Thorstein, *The Theory of the Leisure Class* (New York: Penguin Books, 1979 [1899]).

Walk, Stephen, 'Painography, Risk Voyeurism, and the Near-life Experience', presidential address, annual meeting of the North American Society for the Sociology of Sport, Vancouver, BC, November 2006.

Wallace, Tim, 'Reaching Global Extremes? Are Broadcasters' Claims for X Games' Worldwide Appeal Justified?', *Sportbusiness International* 72 (2002), 9.

Wheaton, Belinda, 'Just Do It: Consumption, Commitment, and Identity in the Windsurfing Subculture', *Sociology of Sport Journal* 17 (2000), 254–74.

——'Windsurfing: A Subculture of Commitment', in Robert E. Rinehart and Synthia S. Sydnor, eds, *To the Extreme: Alternative Sports, Inside and Out* (Albany: State University of New York Press, 2003), 75–101.

—— ed., *Understanding Lifestyle Sports: Consumption, Identity and Difference* (London: Routledge, 2004).

Williams, Raymond, *Marxism and literature* (Oxford: Oxford University Press, 1977).

Wilson, Brian, 'The "Anti-jock" Movement: Reconsidering Youth Resistance, Masculinity, and Sport Culture in the Age of the Internet', *Sociology of Sport Journal* 19 (2) (2002), 206–33.

——'New Media, Social Movements, and Global Sport Studies: A Revolutionary Moment and the Sociology of Sport', *Sociology of Sport Journal* 24 (4) (2007), 457–77.

18 Africa (sub-Saharan)

John Nauright

Sub-Saharan Africa has not received its due attention within histories of sport internationally, nor has the role of sport been given fair coverage in histories of Africa whether over the pre-colonial, colonial or post-colonial eras. It is not enough to merely assert that the Sudan was 'a land of Blacks ruled by Blues', in reference to the tendency of the British colonial service to prefer Oxbridge sportsmen as colonial officials. It is important to interrogate both sides of the racial divide in examining the place of sport in sub-Saharan Africa over the past several centuries and while there are several excellent studies of sport and body cultures in Africa, there is much still to do.

Historians of sport have made some progress in recent years, most notably in South Africa which has a well-developed literature among local academics and has also been well covered by foreign based researchers (though there is still much to be done there as well). A large proportion of the early critical work on South Africa revolved around the politics of apartheid and was generated by activists in the anti-apartheid movement.[1] Since the 1990s, however, a broader more contextualized literature has emerged out of the struggles for equality of opportunity in society and on the sports field that will be discussed below.[2] Other countries have had their share of coverage but in most cases we can count on one hand (sometimes one finger) the number of researchers who have published academic works on a particular country or region.[3]

It is difficult to discuss the history of sport in sub-Saharan Africa without reference to imperialism, colonialism, racism and then post-colonialism, topics covered in general elsewhere in this volume. The history of European interaction with Africa has been the central force behind the development of modern sporting competitions on the continent as well as shaping perceptions of traditional African physical contests and body cultures. Thus much of what we know about the history of African body cultures and physical activities have been read through the lens of European missionaries, anthropologists, officials, and later a wider array of journalists and academics, and, in listening to many of those voices (though there are occasional exceptions), we would be led to believe that Africa does not really have much of a sporting history.[4] Three vignettes about Africa and sport in the late 20th century will illustrate this point.

South African historian of sport Andre Odendaal relates that most white South Africans believe that black South Africans have only 'discovered' sport fairly recently. In 1977, the official *South African Yearbook* stated that 'it is only relatively recently that the Black peoples have shown a marked increase in what may be called modern sporting activities. For centuries they found their recreation in traditional activities, such as hunting and tribal dances'.[5] In 1980, former Springbok national rugby team captain and later member of Nelson Mandela's government of national unity, Dawie de Villiers exclaimed 'Don't Forget that Blacks have really known western sports only for the last ten years ... they have not reached the same standard [as whites]'.[6] As Odendaal, Nauright, Alegi, Callinicos and others have shown, this assessment could not be further from the truth and black South Africans have played modern sport for roughly the same amount of time as white South Africans.[7] Phyllis Martin further demonstrates that this was not unique to South Africa, Africans in colonial Brazzaville took to association football almost as soon as they were exposed to the game before 1920.[8]

As John Bale outlines at the outset of his study of the Tutsi physical activity *gusimbuka-urukiramende*, as recently as 1995 the London *Times* reported that British Prime Minister John Major supported a call to send 'sporting missionaries' to mine African talent. The accompanying photo meant to illustrate late 20th century African sporting talent was of *gusimbuka* and actually shot in 1907. Bale argues that the article 'implied the need for the more civilized Europe to rescue African athletes from their primitive conditions by giving them the gift of Western sports. In this way they could be taken to places where their skills would be appreciated and used'.[9]

Not long after Prime Minister Major wanted to send his athletic 'missionaries' to Africa, the results of efforts by the greatest 'missionary' group in global sport, the International Olympic Committee, with the support of the International Swimming Federation (FINA), to 'develop' some sports in areas where they had not formerly been popular, was clear for all to see at the Sydney 2000 Olympics. Eric Moussambani, a competitor in the 100-metre freestyle event, ended up swimming his heat solo after his fellow racers false started. Moussambani, hardly ready for the Olympic Games on qualifying time, barely made it to the finish. As Nauright and Magdalinski illustrate:

> The Moussambani spectacle was mediated by a number of discourses common to the portrayal of the 'exotic' African in Western culture, while at the same time the swimmer was praised as an exemplar of Olympic spirit and representative of Olympic inclusivity and universality.[10]

These three recent case studies illustrate the complexities of dealing with the history of African sport and that there is much work to be done both to recover African sporting histories and to move analysis beyond imperial and colonial influenced racial ones to view African sporting and physical cultures with respect and to understand the great complexities of sport in Africa. Having said that, it is clear that we cannot write histories of African sport without reference to colonialism and imperialism. Nor can we write histories of modern sports and their diffusion without such discussion. Otherwise, how can we explain the West African Arthur Wharton becoming a sporting success in late 19th century England, or Learie Constantine's experience in Lancashire League cricket in England, let alone the use of sport in nationalist independence movements or in the anti-apartheid movement? In this chapter I outline four major themes that have emerged in discussion of African sport: the experience of imperialism and colonialism; African body cultures and their representation; the particular case of South Africa in the contexts of segregation and apartheid; and finally, the lack of research on the history of sport in the post-colonial era.

Imperialism, colonialism and sport

While much of sub-Saharan Africa was too inhospitable to attract large scale European settlement, European settler colonies appeared in Southern and Central Africa and in the highlands of East Africa, particularly in Kenya. Great Britain and France were the most active colonial powers in Africa, particularly once German colonies were redistributed after World War I. The British had colonies from the Cape to Cairo and in West Africa, while the French were active mostly in West Africa, Cameroon and part of the Congo. The rest of the Congo was run as the major enterprise of Belgian colonialism while Portugal held settler colonies in Mozambique and Angola. Our understanding of the workings of colonialism and white settlement on African societies is most well documented in the case of South Africa, which had the largest settler population, at one stage as high as 20 percent of the total population. Other colonies such as the Rhodesias, now Zimbabwe and Zambia; Namibia, formerly South West Africa; Kenya; Mozambique and Angola had small but vibrant settler populations where many aspects of European culture were recreated.

It is widely known that European nations divided up Africa among themselves in the latter years of the 1800s. European imperial powers created artificial boundaries that disrupted the process of African state formation that was well under way by that time. Europeans actually ruled much of Africa with a surprisingly low number of officials on the ground, with the colonial system relying on a substantial number of Western-educated locals who largely emerged from schools set up by missionaries keen to spread Christianity and Western cultural values to Africa.

Western sport was introduced in many cases by missionaries eager to attract adherents as well as missionary and colonial officials concerned to control and order the lives of urbanizing Africans who they hoped to attract to 'civilization' and to help staff colonial and business offices. Where too many Africans were required, such as in the Witwatersrand gold mines in South Africa, a migrant labour system developed whereby African workers were to be in the city only temporarily to work while their families remained in the rural areas sometimes hundreds of miles away. There was a strong current within the British colonial service at least that viewed the African as a rural being and cities as being largely European creations and that it was the 'White Man's Burden' to bring the 'light' to the 'Dark Continent'. Many of the horrors of urban life in European societies they hoped would be avoided in the African context. Thus, paradoxically, colonial practice outwardly projected the bringing of a 'civilized' future to Africans while at the same time the 'British colonial practice seemed to pride itself on retarding rather than hastening change, drawing on the values of feudalism rather than those of capitalism'.[11] Collectivism was widely promoted by the 1920s and individualism discouraged. Individualism was thought by many officials to have 'corrupted' British society and was therefore to be discouraged in Africa as a way of 'protecting' the local populations from the excesses of modern capitalism and modern life which led to a paternalist system that stunted the growth of modern capitalism in much of Africa. As a result, social organizations were promoted by officials and missionaries alike – including sporting ones. Team sports such as soccer (football) were widely encouraged and where individual 'civilized' sports such as tennis were promoted they were firmly ensconced in social/sporting clubs such as the Bantu Men's Social Centre in Johannesburg. This led to, as Tim Couzens puts it, a strong imperative to 'moralize' the leisure time of Africans.[12]

All across Africa, football and other sporting clubs began to emerge in the latter part of the 19th century. John Iliffe, in a rare discussion by a historian of Africa, examines the role of football in colonial Tanganyika briefly in his magisterial history of the country. He states that the first recorded football match that had been promoted by missionaries took place there in 1884. By 1914 there were 38 registered clubs playing in Dar es

Salaam alone. Sadly he recounts, the history of soccer in this era was yet to be written.[13] Years later, this is still largely the case there as in many other African countries.

While Europeans actively promoted sports within their promotion of the virtues of 'civilization', African elites, many of whom were educated on mission stations, eagerly took to the vestiges of 'Western civilization' in setting themselves apart from the masses through adhering to an 'ideology of respectability'. In racially divided societies such as South Africa and colonial Zimbabwe (formerly Rhodesia) modern sports became part of a culture of respectability among African elites. By 1885 there were over 15,000 Africans being educated in mission schools in South Africa with sporting clubs appearing in the Eastern Cape region as early as the 1860s. By 1887 the African newspaper in the region, *Imvo Zabantsundu*, began a section devoted to sports.[14]

Though Europeans promoted football as a way to 'moralize' leisure time, very quickly football was taken up enthusiastically by a wide spectrum of African male society and football clubs often formed prototype groups for future political organizations and struggles. This connection has been mentioned in several studies of sport in Africa, yet remains under-explored. Iliffe shows that the African Association's development in Zanzibar was an outgrowth of the amalgamation of several local football clubs in 1933.[15] Colonial officials grasped this potential for football clubs to become outlets for subversive activity in colonial Brazzaville in the Congo. In an official letter the Lt Governor explained the dominant view to the Governor-General in 1932:

> ... requiring the native sports clubs to be affiliated with the official body will allow an additional means of surveillance, so that we can prevent undesirable elements who, under the cover of sport, get together for the purpose of political agitation and provoking disorder.[16]

Nauright points out that in South Africa, sports administration 'provided one of the few outlets, outside of work on joint councils or local advisory boards dominated by whites, for African men to practice leadership skills'.[17] In South Africa, many African National Congress leaders, such as Albert Luthuli, cut their political and leadership teeth in sporting club and association administration. Peter Alegi suggests that the success of Africans in sports administration led authorities to view 'football clubs and competitions as subversive because they challenged the local notion that blacks lacked the ability to manage their lives without white supervision'.[18]

In one way, sports administration promoted the very divisions in society that colonizers hoped to use in their 'divide and rule' strategies. In many sports clubs across Africa, English or another colonial language was used as the official lingua franca of sporting clubs and associations. In Durban, South Africa the Durban and District African Football Association formally adopted English as its official language in 1932 and delegates who wished to address meetings in Zulu had to receive special permission even though all the players in that area were Zulu speakers.[19] Similarly in Cape Town, 'Coloured' rugby players, nearly all of whom spoke Afrikaans as a first language, recorded all of their minute books and held formal discussions in English.[20] Though initially class and occupation based, the generation of a common language among sports officials assisted in communication between regions, the formation of national associations, the development of international contacts and eventual Pan-Africanist thinking.

Colonial officials were right to be wary. British colonial officials knew this all too well from their experience dealing with politics and revolutionary plotting in Ireland that often centred on Gaelic Athletic Association clubs. Stuart points out that football clubs were the focal points in generating support for mass strikes in colonial Zimbabwe in the 1940s. He states that '[i]t should be unsurprising that there was no boundary between political action and sport among urban black leaders'.[21]

The consensus in the histories written about sport in colonial Africa largely agree that modern sports were promoted by missionaries and colonial officials, particularly in British colonies, by the latter 1800s, that African elites used sport to establish their 'civilized' *bona fides* and to set themselves apart from the masses, that once organized in sporting clubs and wider networks of regional and national associations, sport provided a locus for nascent political activity that led to the formation of liberation movements by the 1940s and 1950s.[22] Examples from a range of locales speak to this general pattern, but our picture to date remains partial at best and many more studies are needed.

African body cultures

While African physical and sporting activity has a much longer history than African experience of modern (Western) sports, less attention has been paid to this area of research by sports historians. While some historians of Africa have touched on African body cultures, it largely has been tangential to their major concerns. Exceptions to this can be found in John Bale's study of Western portrayals of *gusimbuka-urukiramende* mentioned above; research on activities such as stick fighting in southern Africa;[23] anthropological work on wrestling in West Africa and traditional sports across Africa;[24] and recent analysis of African embodiment by Booth and Nauright, though this latter work does not concern itself as much with 'traditional' African physicality.

As discussed in brief in the chapter on race and sport, the athletic body has been central to thoughts about race in the modern world, whether that be the muscular black body in the image of Jack Johnson or concepts of comparative Asian or Jewish frailty. In Africa, the body was central to the imperial project though as much through the ways in which class was read onto the colonial body as race. Participation in modern sport was viewed as part of 'civilized' development and the 'civilizing' project which was centred on the adoption of Western styles of dress and bodily deportment. Those Africans who adopted Western dress, attitudes and sports were accepted as junior partners in the colonial hierarchy while those who remained uneducated or involved in 'traditional' activities were viewed differently. The colonial project hinged on the support of traditional hierarchies and class and cultural distinctions, though it could by no means control the outcome once sport was unleashed on the rapidly increasing urban masses in Johannesburg, Durban, Brazzaville, Leopoldville, Lusaka, Nairobi or Lagos.

Bale argues that the representation of African body cultures by Europeans was as significant as actual colonial rule in generating perceptions of 'Africa' both on the continent and globally. Bale refers to 'Africanism', drawing upon Edward Said's concept of 'Orientalism', to explain a Western style that makes statements about Africa: 'representing Africa in a style for dominating, restructuring, and, often, having authority over it'.[25] Bale argues further that while there are a number of works that discuss sport and empire, 'they are characterized by an unwillingness to attempt an excavation of colonial representations of pre-colonial movement cultures'.[26] The African body has been central to discussions of what 'Africa' is and means for at least 150 years if not longer. Z.S. Strother posits that '[t]he body became the signifier of the real, the authentic. Its choreographed presence validated the colonial imagination'.[27] In presenting a number of illustrations of *gusimbuka*, Bale states that these produced 'a variety of ways of seeing Africa and the African: as exotic, mysterious, powerful – and as athletic'.[28] However, Bale reminds us that within Rwanda itself, the result of representations of Tutsi body culture led to them being viewed as a super 'race' of athletic bodies shaped in European discourse, and, by implication, the Hutu were different or inferior as they did not have a similar body culture tradition. Here Bale touches on a crucial point that requires further analysis in the history of sport in Africa. We have to begin to unravel the impact of sport, colonialism and representation on groups within various locales in Africa as well as between 'African' and 'European'. As Phyllis Martin's work on colonial Brazzaville shows, football in particular was a sport of the streets with local teams generating intense loyalty that developed over decades. Rivalries emerged between different sections of the city as well as between groups from varied backgrounds. Alegi, Jeffries and Nauright demonstrate that similar circumstances existed in Johannesburg, Durban, Vereeniging and Cape Town in South Africa.[29]

Control of the African body, whether through representation, politics and policy work or leisure, was viewed by colonial officials, missionaries and other Europeans as essential to the success of the imperial project. In sport, Europeans attempted to shape African physical culture in their own image through control of sporting organizations, clubs and facilities. In this process a clash of cultures took place. As Martin argues:

> Africans, although serious about improving their skills, were in it [football] for fun and were unwilling to be regimented by whites in training sessions. Europeans, on the other hand, were interested in the inculcation of values such as 'team spirit', 'perseverance', and 'fair play'.[30]

In Cape Town, coloured cricketers in the Bo-Kaap area rejected the defensive style of play that was officially taught in favour of a more attacking style suited to the limited time in which matches could be completed. Additionally much cricket was played in the street and if one broke a window of a nearby house one was more than just 'out' in the game. Thus the straight drive was a stroke local players such as Basil d'Oliveira mastered.[31]

In South Africa rugby union cultures in black communities differed from white ones in acceptable use of the body and intimidatory tactics. In white rugby, tough, vigorous play was valorized, but in coloured rugby in Cape Town, getting away with transgressions and direct intimidation of the opposition were highly valued as masculine virtues.[32] Beyond this displays of the body in South African culture and sport were integral to both the politics of apartheid and the politics of resistance, yet little research to date has placed the body at the centre of analyses of sport in South Africa as Booth and Nauright point out in a now hard to find article on embodiment and sport in South Africa.[33]

The history of sport in a racially divided society: South Africa

While the imperial project impacted all regions of Africa, the case of South Africa was different in many respects to other African societies. In the early 1900s, whites made up nearly 20 percent of the population. Even in nearby Southern Rhodesia (Zimbabwe) whites never passed 5 percent of the total population. Additionally, South Africa underwent an industrial revolution and received substantial amounts of capital investment in secondary industry on a scale still not seen in other parts of the continent. The mainstay of the economy for much of the 20th century was gold and South Africa has for over a century been the world's leading producer. However, the mines produce very low grade ore and are labour intensive, meaning that a large workforce is needed at the lowest possible wage. This helped create the migrant labour system that sought to keep Africans in the rural areas except for the men required to work contracts on the mines. The cities were to be primarily for Europeans and the rural areas for Africans, though this was more a dream than a reality. As a result of settlement and development, South Africa developed its own university system well ahead of other areas of colonial Africa. Thus, research on sport has been more prevalent there than elsewhere in sub-Saharan Africa. The political divisions created by apartheid and campaigns to isolate the apartheid nation in international sport also meant that greater attention was paid to the history of South African sport. Thus international scholars as well as local ones have written about the history of sport in South Africa both in English and in Afrikaans.

While, as we have seen, all groups in South Africa participated in modern sport from its inception in South Africa, until the 1970s virtually all histories published focused on white South Africans and sport, though few have problematized that history in the context of imperialism and colonial connections.[34] Murray and Merrett point out in their history of cricket in South Africa that there was a long held belief (at least among whites in South Africa as well as abroad) that the history of cricket in the country was a 'white' one. They counter by demonstrating that:

> ... cricket is a sport that historically involves all the people of South Africa; it is the one major sport that has been widely played by each of the country's major population groups – African, coloured, Indian and white – Afrikaans as well as English-speaking. Yet until recently it has not served as a point of identification between all communities.[35]

Indeed cricket in post-apartheid South Africa was able to fill a temporary void caused by rugby being identified as 'white' and soccer as 'black' and became the sport that promoted unity best in the early 1990s.

The bulk of historical studies of South African sport emerged from the tradition of social history that sought to recover history 'from below' to understand the dynamics of sport within individual lives and among disadvantaged groups seeking to redress older institutional histories of white sport. Grundlingh, Morrell, Nauright, and Booth and Nauright have all sought to situate the social construction of masculinities particularly in work on rugby union.[36] Morrell, in an excellent history of rugby and schooling in colonial Natal, examines how rugby and other sports were used to shore up beliefs of superiority among a small settler population in colonial Natal;[37] while Grundlingh explores links between rugby, Afrikaner nationalism and masculinity that draws on British imperial sporting practices in rugby but recasts them as Afrikaner ones.[38]

Odendaal examines the history of black cricket and rugby in a series of studies as well as the ways in which tennis and cricket were used by African elites to distinguish themselves from the mass of 'tribal' and non-mission educated Africans.[39] Willan demonstrates that urbanizing elites in Kimberley such as Sol Plaatje were active in sports as a key social activity that marked them as 'civilized' or at least 'civilizing'.[40] Badenhorst and Cobley, as mentioned, follow this group of African 'elites' to Johannesburg as well as the response of the local state to African urbanization and needs for leisure facilities. Badenhorst follows the interaction between state officials, capitalist interests, black leaders and sports administrators in the middle decades of the 20th century.[41] Jeffrey's study of soccer in Sharpeville and Top Location outside Vereeniging examines patrons and their role in the maintenance of local footballing teams and leagues[42] which Nauright initially followed to a national level[43] and Alegi has taken to a full length study of the intricate social, political and economic history of soccer in South Africa as a whole.[44]

Oral history has been an important feature of social history in South Africa and has featured heavily in studies of sport in South Africa since the 1940s. Alegi, Booth, Nauright and Odendaal all utilize oral histories in recovering the past condition of sport in black communities. Fortunately, South Africa has preserved much of its historical record in newspaper collections, private collections and official archives. Murray and Merrett, and Merrett have made significant use of recently opened records from the Department of Sport and Recreation during the 1960s and 1970s that have confirmed and extended knowledge about sport and the apartheid state.[45]

A key feature of history of sport in South Africa, as I have touched upon, is the history of the internal and external struggle for equality of opportunity for all South Africans in sport. This has lured two generations of scholars on the left to analyses of sport and politics in South Africa. While many of the early studies were focused on a specific political outcome, they were certainly influential on future studies. The early 1980s work of Archer and Bouillon has proved to be remarkably resilient and useful,[46] while Booth's 1998 study of sport and politics in South Africa is seminal,[47] as is Black and Nauright's conterminous examination of rugby in the context of South Africa's strategies in international relations, particularly in its relationship with the other world rugby goliath, New Zealand.[48] In an earlier study, Jarvie effectively linked sport to the wider South African political economy of the 1970s and 1980s and demonstrates that sport was a crucial element of the South African state's international campaign against opposition as well as a key facet of the liberation struggle.[49]

While this emerging literature is welcomed in South Africa and in other countries of sub-Saharan Africa, many gaps remain. In 1997 I stated that virtually nothing had been written on women's sports history in South Africa even though the sport of netball was tied to the politics of Afrikaner nationalism in many of the same ways as rugby union. Hargreaves, Jones and Roberts have made a small start on this problem, but the history of women in sport in South Africa lags well behind similar histories in North America, Europe and Australasia.[50] Thankfully, a similar assertion about the dearth of good histories of black soccer, rugby and cricket has been redressed in significant ways, however, many other sports still require much greater examination both in South Africa and in other regions of the continent.

Conclusion: sport in post-colonial Africa

Despite most African countries gaining independence in the 1950s and 1960s, histories of African sport in the period since independence have been few and far between beyond those examining apartheid sport and resistance to it as South Africa and nearby countries in southern Africa were slower to gain full civil rights for all living there. Research on sports history in African universities remains isolated and sporadic. This picture is beginning to change with several historians trained by Mangan and others now beginning to publish histories of sport in the colonial and post-colonial periods such as Ndee's work on Tanzania or Hokkannen's work on Malawi.[51] The bulk of research is still being done by Westerners, however, with more work still be done on South Africa than the rest of sub-Saharan Africa combined.

While there have been significant advances in our knowledge of African sports history in the past generation, much of what we have learned has been focused on South Africa, particularly on the male dominated sports of association football, cricket and rugby union. We have also gained significant insight into how liberation movements used the colonial powers' assumptions that sport was apolitical to develop communication links that helped to form liberation movements. The ways in which Europeans have viewed the African body has also been explored in attempts to understand complexity of discourses of race and imperialism.

Much remains to be done even in South Africa, though we need to know much more about other areas as well. We know virtually nothing about the experience of women in African sport or how participation by men has affected women. While the quality of studies of African sports history can match those done on any other continent, the range of these studies has been limited and we know less about the history of sport in Africa than perhaps we do about any other region of the world. The groundwork has been done; however, there are many intriguing topics for researchers to pursue.

Notes

1 Examples of this include R. Archer and A. Bouillion, *The South African Game: Sport and Racism* (London: Zed Press, 1982); C. de Broglio, *South Africa: Racism in Sport* (London: International Defence and Aid Fund, 1970); R. Lapchick, *The Politics of Race and International Sport: The Case of South Africa* (Westport, CT: Greenwood Press, 1975); R. Thompson, *Race and Sport* (London: Oxford University Press, 1964); D. Woods, *Black and White* (Dublin: Ward River Press, 1981).

2 Of the more recent work, many studies have been produced by academics trained in history (for example, Peter Alegi, Alan Cobley, Albert Grundlingh, Bruce Murray, John Nauright, Andre Odendaal), geography (Cecile Badenhorst, John Bale) and political science (David R. Black, Douglas Booth), and several excellent historians of Africa have included sport in their broader works (John Iliffe and Phyllis Martin for example), though they remain a minority among historians of Africa. A smaller number of academics trained in physical education have also written sports history focused on Africa (Floris van der Merwe, Dean Allen).

3 Indeed, there are only a couple of collections specifically aimed at the broad history of sport in Africa, see W. Baker and J.A. Mangan, eds, *Sport in Africa* (New York: Africana, 1987). The bulk of this chapter refers to literature in the English language and also focuses more closely on countries that were colonies in the British Empire as the literature on sport, such as it is, is more developed in those contexts.

4 For example the American Board Missionary, Ray Phillips, spent much time working with urban Africans in Johannesburg in developing sport further during the 1930s. See R. Phillips, *The Bantu in the City: A Study of Cultural Adjustment on the Witwatersrand* (Lovedale: Lovedale Press, 1936). Also see a summary of much of the missionary involvement and other black sporting initiatives in A.G. Cobley, *The Rules of the Game: Struggles in Black Recreation and Social Welfare Policy in South Africa* (Westport, CT: Greenwood Press, 1997).

5 A. Odendaal, '"The Thing That is Not Round": The Untold Story of Black Rugby in South Africa', in A. Grundlingth, A. Odendaal and B. Spies, eds, *Beyond the Tryline: Rugby and South African Society* (Johannesburg: Ravan Press, 1995), 24.

6 Quoted in D. Black and J. Nauright, *Rugby and the South African Nation* (Manchester: Manchester University Press, 1998), 39.

7 For example, see Odendaal, 'The Thing That is Not Round' and 'South Africa's Black Victorians: Sport and Society in South Africa in the Nineteenth Century', in J.A. Mangan, ed., *Pleasure, Profit and Proselytism: British Culture and Sport at Home and Abroad, 1700–1914* (London: Frank Cass, 1988), 193–214; J. Nauright, *Sport, Cultures and Identities in South Africa* (London: Leicester University Press and Cape Town, David Philip, 1997); P. Alegi, *Laduma! Soccer, Politics and Society in South Africa* (Durban: University of KwaZulu-Natal Press, 2004); L. Callinicos, *Working Life 1886–1940, Vol. 2: Factories, Townships, and Popular Culture on the Rand* (Johannesburg: Ravan Press, 1987), 210.

8 P. Martin, *Leisure and Society in Colonial Brazzaville* (Cambridge: Cambridge University Press, 1995), 101–2.

9 J. Bale, *Imagined Olympians: Body Culture and Colonial Representation in Rwanda* (Minneapolis: University of Minnesota Press, 2002), xvii.

10 J. Nauright and T. Magdalinski, '"A Hapless Attempt at Swimming": Representations of Eric Moussambani', *Critical Arts*, 17, 1&2 (2003), 107.

11 A. Phillips, *The Enigma of Colonialism: British Policy in West Africa* (Bloomington: Indiana University Press, 1989), 3.

12 T. Couzens, '"Moralizing Leisure Time": The Transatlantic Connection and Leisure Activities on the Witwatersrand 1918–30', in S. Marks and R. Rathbone, eds, *Industrialisation and Social Change in South Africa 1870–1930* (London: Longman, 1982), 314–37.

13 J. Iliffe, *A Modern History of Tanganyika* (Cambridge: Cambridge University Press, 1979), 393.

14 D.R. Black and J. Nauright, *Rugby and the South African Nation* (Manchester: Manchester University Press, 1998), 42–3.

15 Iliffe, *A Modern History of Tanganyika*, 416.

16 Quoted in Martin, *Leisure and Society in Colonial Brazzaville*, 105.

17 Nauright, *Sport, Cultures and Identities in South Africa*, 107.

18 Alegi, *Laduma!*, 32.

19 Alegi, *Laduma!*, 33.

20 Nauright, *Sport, Cultures and Identities in South Africa*.

21 O. Stuart, 'Players, Workers, Protestors: Social Change and Soccer in Colonial Zimbabwe', in J. MacClancey, ed., *Sport, Identity, and Ethnicity* (Oxford: Berg, 1996), 177.

22 Key texts in this regard are Martin, *Leisure and Society in Colonial Brazzaville* (for the Congo); Alegi, Booth, Cobley, Nauright, Odendaal for South Africa; Iliffe, *A Modern History of Tanganyika*; Stuart, 'Players, Workers, Protestors'.

23 See P. La Hausse, '"The Cows of Nongaloza": Youth, Crime and Amalaita Gangs in Durban, 1900–936', *Journal of Southern African Studies*, 16, 1 (1990), 79–111.

24 E.L. Powe, *Combat Games of Northern Nigeria* (Madison: Dan Aiki Publications, 1994).

25 Bale, *Imagined Olympians*, xxi.

26 Bale, *Imagined Olympians*, xxvi.

27 Z.S. Strother, 'Display of the Body Hottentot', in B. Lindfors, ed., *Africans on Stage: Studies in Ethnological Show Business* (Bloomington: Indiana University Press, 1999), 37.

28 Bale, *Imagined Olympians*, 158.

29 Alegi, *Laduma!*; I. Jeffrey, 'Street Rivalry and Patron-Managers: Football in Sharpeville, 1943–85', *African Studies*, 51, 1 (1992), 69–94; J. Nauright '"Bhola Lethu": Football and Urban Popular Culture in South Africa', in G. Armstrong and R. Giulianotti, eds, *Football in the Making: Developments in the World Game* (London: Macmillan, 1999), 189–200.

30 Martin, *Leisure and Society in Colonial Brazzaville*, 108.

31 G. Emeran interviewed by J. Nauright, Bo-Kaap, Cape Town, 30 January 1995.

32 J. Nauright, 'Muscular Islam and "Coloured" rugby in Cape Town, South Africa', *International Journal of the History of Sport*, 14, 1 (1997), 184–90.

33 D. Booth and J. Nauright, 'Sport, Race and Embodiment in South Africa', *Contours: A Journal of the African Diaspora*, 1, 1 (2003), 16–36.

34 An exception for the pre-apartheid period is D. Allen, 'South African Cricket, Imperial Cricketers and Imperial Expansion, 1850–1910', *International Journal of the History of Sport*, 25, 4 (2008), 443–71.

35 B. Murray and C. Merrett, *Caught Behind: Race and Politics in Springbok Cricket* (Durban: University of Kwa-Zulu Natal Press and Johannesburg: University of Witwatersrand Press, 2004), 3.

36 See contributions by these authors in Nauright and Chandler, eds, *Making Men*; Booth and Nauright, 'Sport, Race and Embodiment in South Africa'.

37 R. Morrell, 'Forging a Ruling Race: Rugby and White Masculinity in Colonial Natal, c.1870–1910', in Nauright and Chandler, eds, *Making Men*.

38 A. Grundlingh, 'Playing for Power?: Rugby, Afrikaner Nationalism and Masculinity in South Africa, c.1900–1970', in Nauright and Chandler, eds, *Making Men*.

39 Odendaal, 'South Africa's Black Victorians', and 'The Thing That is not Round'; *Cricket in Isolation: The Politics of Race and Sport in South Africa* (Cape Town: The Author, 1977); *The Story of an African Game* (Cape Town: David Phillip, 2003).

40 B. Willan, *Sol Plaatje: South African Nationalist 1876–1932* (Berkeley: University of California Press, 1984).

41 C. Badenhorst, 'New traditions, old struggles: organized sport for Johannesburg's Africans, 1920–50', *Sport in Society*, 6, 2/3 (2003), 116–43.

42 I. Jeffrey, 'Street Rivalry and Patron-Managers: Football in Sharpeville, 1943–85, *African Studies*, 51, 1 (1992), 69–94.

43 Nauright, '"Bohla Lethu"'.

44 Alegi, *Laduma!*.

45 Murray and Merrett, *Caught Behind*; C. Merrett, 'In Nothing Else are the Deprivers so Deprived', *The International Journal of the History of Sport*, 13, 2 (1996), 146–65; C. Merrett, 'Sport, Racism and Urban Policy in South Africa, Pietermaritzburg: A Case Study', *Sporting Traditions*, 10, 2 (1994), 97–122.

46 Archer and Boullion, *The South African Game*.

47 D. Booth, *The Race Game: Sport and Politics in South Africa* (London: Frank Cass, 1998).

48 Black and Nauright, *Rugby and the South African Nation*.

49 G. Jarvie, *Class, Race and Sport in South Africa's Political Economy* (London: Routledge and Kegan Paul, 1985). Four scholars who have worked on the history and politics of South African sport (Badenhorst, Black, Jarvie and Nauright) all spent time between 1980 and 1992 at Queen's University in Canada, which has a strong tradition of critical sports analysis, of work on sport and politics generally, and of South African historical and geographical studies.

50 J. Hargreaves, *Heroines of Sport: The Politics of Difference and Identity* (London: Routledge, 2009), 14–45; D. Jones, 'In Pursuit of Empowerment: Sensei Nellie Kleinsmot, Race and Gender Challenges in South Africa', *International Journal of the History of Sport*, 18, 1 (2001), 219–36; C. Roberts, *Against the Grain: Women and Sport in South Africa* (Cape Town: Township Publishing Co-operative, 1992).

51 H. Ndee, 'Sport as a Political Tool: Tanzania and the Liberation of Africa', *International Journal of the History of Sport*, 22, 4 (2005), 671–88 and 'Modern Sport in Independent Tanzania: "Adapted" Sport and the Process of Modernization', *International Journal of the History of Sport*, 19, 4 (2002), 89–113; M. Hokkannen, 'Christ and the Imperial Games Fields in South-Central Africa – Sport and the Scottish Missionaries in Malawi, 1880–1914: Utilitarian Compromise', *International Journal of the History of Sport*, 22, 4 (2005), 745–69.

19 Australia

Daryl Adair

Despite the high profile of sport in Australian culture, the historical analysis of sport there has a low profile, whether in terms of academic research, media interest, or the reading public. Australian sport fans are eager to recount glorious performances by the nation's teams and athletes, and certainly indulge themselves in eulogistic books and magazines about sport. However, these enthusiasts have comparatively little knowledge about, or interest in, Australian history and the role of sport in shaping its evolution. This is, in large part, a reflection of inadequate education: in many schools history has been supplanted as a key area of study, with the Australian story conveyed as part of broad brush subjects such as 'social studies' or 'civics and citizenship'.[1] Moreover, at university level Australian history is typically taught with scant regard for the explanatory potential of sport and physical culture. Too often, sport has been relegated by Australian academics to the 'toy department' rather than the history department where, incidentally, there are few scholars for whom sport is a serious focus of research.[2] This is illogical, because sport can provide important insights into themes and issues that have been pivotal to the evolution of Australian history. Indeed, as this chapter indicates, sports historians have carved out areas of research that contribute ably to the study of Australia's past.

It should be acknowledged that two of the best known chroniclers of Australian history, Manning Clark and Geoffrey Blainey, both recognized the role of sport in community and nation building. Clark's epic six-volume collection *A History of Australia* (1963–87) includes numerous scattered references to major sports, such as cricket and Australian Rules football, as well as moments of high drama, such as the famous Anglo-Australian 'Bodyline' series.[3] It would be an exaggeration, though, to claim that sport was a key theme in Clark's narrative, despite his personal fondness for it and his passion for Carlton Football Club. Sport was simply not on the social history 'radar' when Clark was in his prime, and the fact that he actually gave it some profile was noteworthy in itself. Blainey, a long-time supporter of the Geelong Football Club, took a different route: his monographs of the Australian story barely mentioned sport, but he eventually produced *A Game of Our Own* (1990).[4]

From within the academy, a lesser known but far more influential contributor to sports history laid the intellectual groundwork from which the sub-discipline would slowly emerge. W.F. 'Bill' Mandle read history at Oxford University and later accepted academic appointments in New Zealand and Australia. He has been described, in retrospect, as a 'giant' figure upon whose shoulders fledgling early sports historians stood.[5] In particular, Mandle's emerging interests in nationalism and identity allowed him to bring the subject of sport firmly into new discussions of Australian history.[6] Fittingly, Mandle was a key contributor to the first academic conference on sports history in Australia –

'Sporting Traditions' – which was staged at Sydney in 1977. An edited book was a key outcome, and, four such conferences later, the Australian Society for Sport History was formed in 1983.[7] The following year ASSH's refereed journal, *Sporting Traditions*, was launched. By the mid-1980s, therefore, a small but enterprising group of academics had begun a collaborative approach to the historical study of Australian sport. Names such as Tatz, Stoddart, Vamplew, Cashman and O'Hara – to mention a few – had the audacity to make sport central, rather than peripheral to their research. Significantly these trendsetters were typically situated in Arts and Humanities or Social Science faculties; thus they were part of intellectual environments within which the study of history was valued.

However, by the early 21st century, as these early exponents of sports history moved on or retired from academia, they were not replaced by scholars with similar research or teaching interests. At the University of New South Wales, for example, Richard Cashman had successfully taught sports history for many years, and established the Australian Centre for Olympic Studies. When he retired in 2004, UNSW not only put an end to the sports history programme – which was popular with students – it also closed down ACOS, despite it having contributed significantly to research on the Sydney Olympic Games and their legacy. Cashman's swift transfer of ACOS to the Faculty of Business at University of Technology Sydney, and his appointment there as an Adjunct Professor, symbolized a wider trend for academic practitioners of sports history today. This current generation of academics resides almost solely in either Business or Human Movement faculties, and none has the title 'historian'. They lecture in sport management or the socio-cultural dimensions of human movement, and do their best to infuse historical perspective into these teaching programmes. They continue to pursue historical research into sport, but do so in working environments where colleagues typically focus on contemporary issues, such as sport marketing, sport pedagogy and the science of athletic performance. In short, intellectual environments within which history is generally not valued.

It is, therefore, a credit to academics, past and present, whatever their disciplinary background or location, that the subject of sports history has retained an identity as a discrete sub-discipline and, moreover, has contributed something tangible to the wider history of Australia. There have been noble efforts to produce synthesis studies of Australian sports history, with Cashman's *Paradise of Sport* (1995) the most comprehensive and Booth and Tatz's *One Eyed* the most argumentative.[8] No-one can claim, after a little over two decades of ASSH-led exploratory study, to be an authority on Australian sports history. There is simply too much yet to be researched, and too few academics putting their shoulder to the sports history wheel. So, as the following survey indicates, there has been welcome progress but significant gaps remain. Three pivotal historical areas will be surveyed: place, space, athleticism and self image; perceptions about class, status, gender and norms of physicality in Australian sport; and issues of indigeneity, 'race' and ethnicity in a white-dominated sports culture. Analysis of these key areas of sport and society will enable educators to add value and depth to existing approaches to Australian history.

Place, space, athleticism and self image

According to historian Geoffrey Blainey, Australia has been cursed by the 'tyranny of distance'.[9] As a British colonial outpost it was literally on the other side of the world, and, particularly before air travel and electronic communication, this meant separation from the so-called 'motherland'. Sport was one way in which Britain and its colonies, whether in Australia or elsewhere, could be connected. It was, as both Cashman and Daly have averred, part of the cultural baggage of migrants – particularly those who arrived as free settlers in the second half of the 19th century.[10] Efforts to establish race tracks, cricket fields and rugby pitches were part of the colonial drive to recreate – even if in the imagination – some of the cultural trappings of a distant 'homeland'. It was therefore of particular note when sports teams and competitors from Britain toured the colonies. The locals were initially in awe of visiting athletes, such as in cricket, where English sides toyed with their colonial counterparts. However, as historians have shown, from the 1860s onwards the tide slowly turned – most notably in cricket, rowing and rugby – with Antipodean teams and crews performing creditably in Anglo-Australian contests.[11] The importance of this sporting relationship was firmly established in 1882, when the legend of the 'Ashes' was born in the wake of a surprise Australian win over England at The Oval in London. That victory, together with other triumphs in sport, impacted positively on colonial self confidence: athletes and teams were eagerly representing 'Australia' abroad before the nation existed.[12] They were still fiercely pro-Empire, but anxious to overcome negative attitudes about a convict past and rumblings about Antipodean inferiority.[13] Sport, with its immutable scoreboard, was thus an important way of establishing a sense of Anglo–Australian parity – and ultimately rivalry.

Mandle sees in sport, though most notably in cricket, seeds of a colonial nationalism that went beyond culture into politics.[14] Australians were for many years lukewarm about the idea of Federation, and it took two referenda for that proposal to be passed – and eventually by only a small majority.[15] Mandle contends that inter-colonial and Anglo–Australian sport provided examples of effective administrative co-operation at the national level, which many had thought unlikely in an era when parochial colonies protected their local economies with tariffs and, by producing different sized railway gauges, effectively stymied regional trade and travel.[16] This rather 'reluctant' Commonwealth of 1901 provided a very hybrid sense of nationhood.[17] Australia remained a Dominion of the British Empire and would continue to prove its loyalty to Britain by military service in the Boer War and two world wars. Through 'Empire' sports such as cricket and rugby, together with active support for British troops in Europe, Australians developed a formidable reputation on both playing fields and battle fields. This combination of sport and wartime service has received attention by scholars interested in questions of identity, loyalty and gender norms.[18] However, the subject has not been treated exhaustively; surprisingly so given the depth of interest in military history in Australia and the elevation of the ANZACs to the status of legend.[19]

Use of space and response to climate are lynchpins of Australian history. With European annexation of land, many colonists looked to establish agricultural properties and mining operations in rural or remote areas. However, they proved exceptional; most whites resided in urban centres along the outer rim of a vast, largely dry, island continent. There they had ready access to the ocean and regular supplies of water from coastal river systems – both of which also provided opportunities for aquatic sports.[20] The city of Sydney, with its sunny weather, panoramic harbour and lengthy Parramatta River, provided regular opportunities for sailing and rowing regattas, which proved to be some of the most popular sporting spectacles of the 19th century.[21] Today, of course, some of the most iconic recreational spaces in Australia are beaches, with both surfers and surf lifesavers quintessential symbols of local aquatic culture.[22] Yet as historians have shown, during the colonial era there was conflict between picnickers and surf bathers, and efforts to proscribe swimming in public. For many moral conservatives, bathing at the beach in daylight hours was frowned upon as improper; exposing too much flesh at a time when modesty was acute.[23] Indeed, when public bathing eventually became more widely accepted, whether at the beach or in swimming pools, men and women were initially segregated.[24] Surf lifesaving – an Australian invention – dates from 1907, but until recent decades this was a male dominated institution. The timing and extent of gender reform is, however, still hotly debated by sports historians.[25]

As public space, the beach provides historians with a fascinating resource for tracking changing perceptions about the human body and norms of public behaviour. Surfing, for example, became part of a 1960s beachside 'counterculture' in which self expression and aesthetic movement in the surf were highly prized. New swimwear was intended to accentuate body display, and was soon commercialized as a fashion item.[26] Booth's research has revealed structural tensions at the modern beach. 'Surfies' preferred to stay aloof from formality and civic engagement, while surf lifesavers volunteered their time to clubs and the wider beach-going community. To the lifesavers the surfies appeared self indulgently radical; to surfies the lifeguards seemed subservient to authority and conformist. These were convenient stereotypes; both of these male-dominated groups could, in their own way, be a law unto themselves. Lifesaving clubs were ideal places to drink heavily; many were sponsored by alcohol companies or pubs. Surfers, meanwhile, were more likely to experiment with illicit drugs. None of these substances was conducive to optimum motor skills or water safety.[27] Today many of the best Australian surfers are part of a global professional circuit, with style being rewarded in cash.[28] Concurrently, surf lifesaving clubs have sought to curb excess drinking, make membership more gender inclusive, and actively recruit volunteers from culturally and linguistically diverse backgrounds. Indeed, a positive response to the infamous Cronulla Beach riots of 2005, which involved conflict between ultranationalist 'whites' and beachgoers of Middle Eastern background, has been surf lifesaving's 'On the Same Wave' programme, which has actively recruited volunteers from diverse ethnic and cultural backgrounds.[29]

While space, place and geography are pivotal to our understanding of Australian history, these subjects have yet to be developed extensively by sports historians. Indeed, although regional differences have been noted about sport around Australia,[30] there is no systematic geographically informed or comparative research – certainly nothing to rival the comprehensive work of John Bale in Britain.[31] Our notions about athleticism, identity and self image are therefore lacking a demonstrated awareness of similarities *and* differences about sport and history across what is, after all, a vast continent with varying terrains, climates, populations and cultures. As is now discussed, there were key norms and power relationships in society that established social boundaries within sport.

Class, status, gender and norms of physicality in Australian sport

The Australian colonies did not reproduce a class system based on nobility. There were self-styled migrant aristocrats from Britain, but in the Antipodes elevated status was shaped overwhelmingly by holding public office or 'making good' economically. Australians were not equal in wealth or power, though there was a commitment to opportunity; an achievement culture. Those who 'made it' were, however, frowned upon if they adopted 'airs and graces'. Hirst has described this as 'a democracy of manners'. He contends that 'it is the feel of Australian society that is markedly egalitarian, not its social structure'.[32] This hypothesis can also be usefully applied to Australian sport. Sociologists have done much to dispel widespread assumptions that sport is structurally egalitarian in contemporary society. Yet they also note the persistence of discourses that present sport as inherently 'open to all'.[33] Historians, meanwhile, have tried to put inequalities in context: class and status divides in sport were typically more pronounced in the 19th and 20th centuries than today, and some sports were more elitist than others.

In late Victorian England there was a serious divide between professional and amateur versions of sport. This schism soon impacted on Australia, particularly as rules for the amateur code tended to be drawn up in Britain.[34] In the colonies there evolved amateur and professional versions of sports such as rugby football,[35] athletics,[36] cycling,[37] and rowing.[38] A further sporting innovation from abroad was the Olympic Games, where amateur status was needed for eligibility to take part. Hence there was considerable surveillance of sports to which prize money and wagering were attached.[39] By and large, though, the amateur code was read and applied more stringently in Britain than in Australia. With rowing, for example, English clubs not only banned participants who had competed for a wager or prize money, they eventually imposed a test of status and privilege – anyone deemed working class was proscribed from membership of an amateur club.[40] In Australia, however, non-pecuniary amateur status was more important than class background; hence the introduction of a manual labour amateur classification at many rowing clubs.[41] In Australian sport the amateur code was open to different interpretations, and the penalties associated with transgressions varied: officials could be very harsh while some conveniently turned a blind eye. This was very much sport and politics.[42] It used to be thought that amateur and professional sport in Australia were entirely separate domains. Recent research, however, has thrown that easy assumption into disarray. In mid-19th-century rowing, for example, it was quite common to offer prizes to amateur victors and this did not compromise their amateur status. What was more, they often competed on the same programme (though generally in different events) as professional competitors.[43] Most startling of all, though, Stuart Ripley's PhD thesis has revealed that some of Australia's leading sport officials presided over both amateur and professional competitions during the late 19th and early 20th centuries.[44]

In terms of the evolution of amateur and professional modes of elite sport in Australia, much has changed since the advent of live television broadcasts from the 1970s. Significantly, neither tennis nor cricket offered long term professional careers within Australia until players sought, in effect, a slice of the TV revenue being earned by not-for-profit sporting bodies. However, while there has been much debate about the World Series Cricket 'revolution' that spawned the rise of full-time professional cricketers in Australia,[45] remarkably little has been written about the schism in Australian tennis, wherein some of the great players of the 1950s and 1960s turned professional at a time when the Majors were for amateurs only.[46] Golf provides another complex scenario: professionals in private clubs of the early 20th century were modestly paid coaches or lowly paid caddies appointed to serve the interests of members, with many of the latter coming from wealthy backgrounds. This 'master and servant' relationship has now evolved to the point where a club professional holds a position of considerable status, and the burgeoning prize money offered on Australian and overseas circuits has raised the income of the elite golfer and caddy into the upper echelons of athlete income.[47]

Tennis and golf are also interesting historically because they have long been sites of public access or private privilege. The fees associated with membership of a private club has always acted as an economic filter, but so too has social vetting of members by club boards. Curiously, though, too little is presently known about questions of inclusion and exclusion in two of Australia's largest participant sports.[48] Indeed, there is a general lack of systematic historical analysis into questions of class, status and privilege in a range of emergent elite sports such as sailing, motor racing and horse-racing, where wealth and social position impact on membership of private clubs and the capacity to own yachts, grand prix cars and thoroughbred horses.[49] The eminently popular Melbourne Cup is perhaps the quintessential example of Hirst's dictum about structural inequality and a 'democracy of manners' in Australia. This horse-race literally stops much of the nation for two minutes on the first Tuesday in November; to that extent it is a shared celebration. However, Flemington racecourse separates spectators according to their status as club members, horse owners and 'ordinary' punters. They might be at the same event, but the idea that all classes 'rub shoulders together' on Melbourne Cup Day – whether at the race course or over a champagne lunch – is one of the nation's most alluring myths.[50]

Australian schools have long been nurseries for major sports like rugby, Australian football, cricket and netball. Back in the 19th century there was a particular effort by denominational schools to instil in pupils the British-inspired athletic ideal of 'muscular Christianity', within which amateurism was a core value. This not only applied to Anglican and Protestant schools; amateurism was a hallmark of Irish sport too, hence its significance within Catholic education.[51] A major examination of sport, religion and ideology in Australian history none the less awaits.[52] Perhaps the biggest gap, though, is in our historical understanding of varying physical education and sport opportunities for children across the two educational systems: state-funded, secular schools and state-subsidized, private schools.[53] For example, in Sydney, a small elite clique known, from 1892, as the Athletic Association of the Great Public Schools of New South Wales (or Great Public Schools) have provided sport facilities and resources, such as rowing sheds, swimming pools and tennis courts, that are typically absent from the grounds of non-selective state schools and second-tier independent schools. One of the major events on the GPS sporting calendar is the exclusive 'Head of the River' regatta, which dates back to 1893 and is modelled on boat races among the elite public schools of England.[54] Sydney's GPS schools have been a traditional nursery for recruitment into New South Wales rugby union clubs; and, since the majority of these schools catered for boys rather than girls, the social construction of masculinity through body contact sport.[55] This is not to suggest that girls have had no place in school sport, either in the state or private systems; but it has been very much a secondary place. For example, not until 1996 did female students in New South Wales have their own Head of the River regatta.[56]

Gender identities and associated norms of physicality are indeed keys to investigate sport in Australian history. It has been largely a male domain, as elsewhere. Scholars have shown that for many young boys sport has been a significant rite of passage into manhood. This reflects longstanding cultural assumptions that boys are 'inherently' combative and aggressive, and that sport provides a focus for such overtly 'masculine' behaviours.[57] For young females the reverse has been true; until the late 20th century girls had fewer opportunities to participate in sport, and they were often encouraged to undertake 'female appropriate' activities, such as netball, that did not compromise traditional notions of femininity.[58] Even today, with important efforts to improve female access to a range of sports, the institution of sport itself remains a key to the gendering process; for not only are men and women typically separated in competitive physical activity, at the elite level females are celebrated as athletes of calibre on too few occasions, such as Olympic and Commonwealth Games, where they receive equal media coverage alongside men.[59] The history of women in Australian sport has been characterized, on the one hand, by radical feminist criticism of marginalization and oppression by males;[60] and on the other hand, by liberal feminist arguments that women have indeed been more active in sport than many (male) historians have bothered to notice.[61] There is, however, little debate about one point: as the work of Dennis Phillips has shown, Australian women have repeatedly outperformed their male counterparts in terms of procuring medals at the Olympic Games. His research offers an alternative way of recognizing and valuing female sport achievement.[62] Similarly, Rob Hess has examined the historical importance of women as sports fans; their contribution as supporters of Australian Rules football, in particular, is unsurpassed by any other code.[63] Today, though, the analysis of women in Australian sports history seems to have reached a hiatus; the 21st century has yet to produce much in the way of new research.[64]

The historical analysis of group identity, inclusion and exclusion in Australian sport must also engage with societal issues for Indigenous peoples, other non-whites and ethnic minorities generally. As the following discussion indicates, this means taking seriously endemic problems of racism and stereotyping 'others' on the basis of their skin colour or ancestry.

Aborigines, non-whites and ethnic minorities

Well before the arrival of Europeans and the subsequent British annexation of *Terra Australis*, a vast array of Aboriginal peoples were custodians of the land and sea. They were regionally disparate and spoke different languages, but had much in common. This included an ingenious capacity to observe, understand and respect the natural environment, and a constructive mutualism that enabled co-existence for at least 40,000 years. Aborigines were spatially aware and physically dexterous; they needed these attributes when fishing and hunting for food. It was here that play, games and sports provided input. Within Aboriginal communities there were games of strategy and play activities requiring athleticism and dexterity. Footraces promoted speed, ball games fostered agility, while spear and boomerang throwing contests demanded eye-to-hand co-ordination important for hunting.[65] However, Aboriginal societies were fragmented by white annexation of land, with many Aborigines confined subsequently to colonial reserves and missions. This dislocation meant that traditional Aboriginal sports and games began to lose their functional relevance, with the meaning and significance of such activities not passed on to later generations. A decline in these customs was part of a wider diminution of Aboriginal culture and identity under European colonization.[66]

Recently, there have been efforts to trace, record and revive traditional Indigenous games. Using the medium of oral history, Queensland academic Ken Edwards has spent many years talking with Aboriginal and Torres Strait Islander elders. Through this dialogue, as well as by reading early anthropological accounts, he has established a formidable record of customary Aboriginal recreation.[67] That knowledge now has applied significance because Edwards, with the assistance of the Australian Sports Commission, has produced a user friendly booklet for schools and community groups which explains the purpose of particular Indigenous games and how they may be played today.[68] This is a significant development: through sport and recreation non-Aboriginal Australians can be introduced to aspects of a living culture. Too often Indigenous history and customs are neglected as 'irrelevant' in discourses of modernity in Australia.

Histories of Aboriginal responses to colonialism, and the regime of controls exerted on Indigenous peoples by representatives of the British Crown, have developed significantly over the past 20 years.[69] So too stories of the various missions that institutionalized Aborigines and separated them from white settlers.[70] This confinement introduced Indigenous people to language, religion and customs from Britain. That process of colonial acculturation included sport – most notably the game of cricket – as a means of instilling in Aboriginal boys and men agreement on rules, respect for the decisions of those in authority, and a common goal of teamwork in a competitive setting. It seems remarkable, at first glance, that in 1868 the first 'Australian' cricket team which toured England consisted almost entirely of Aborigines. However, as historians have shown, this was an entrepreneurial initiative on the part of white sponsors and management, who saw an opportunity to draw big crowds and significant revenue for themselves from a series of exhibitions abroad – involving both cricket and displays of Aboriginal physical culture.[71] The Aboriginal cricketers performed ably, winning as many games as they lost. This did not establish Indigenous players in Australian cricket back home. Indeed, although there were some fine young Aboriginal cricketers in the late 19th and early 20th centuries, they faced significant obstacles to play at the elite level.[72] There were logistical problems owing to laws that constrained the movement to cities of Aborigines impounded on rural missions and reserves. What was more, as sports historians have shown, the few Indigenous players who did make it to first-class cricket had chequered experiences, such as outstanding bowlers Jack Marsh and Eddie Gilbert, both of whom had problems with cricket officials that negated their opportunity to play for Australia.[73]

Despite negative Aboriginal experiences in cricket, Newlin and Moran make the salient point that 'there have always been Aboriginal achievers in sport, but few people know this'.[74] Sports historians, led by Colin Tatz, have tried to rectify this lack of awareness, while also detailing ways in which Aborigines have been discriminated against in sport and society.[75] Indigenous athletes were most likely to appear in activities that offered the prospect of financial reward; amateurism was a white, middle-class philosophy of privilege that was not relevant to their circumstances. No surprise then that Aborigines featured in prize-money events, particularly pedestrianism (sprinting), boxing and as jockeys in horse-racing.[76] However, they were basically invisible in sports that required expensive equipment, such as sailing and rowing, or membership of a private club, such as golf and tennis.

When Australia was proclaimed a Commonwealth in 1901, the restrictive White Australia Policy (WAP) was enshrined in law. The focus of this federal legislation was non-English speaking immigrants and (de facto) people of 'colour' seeking to be residents of Australia. However, short-term visitors could, with the support of a local sponsor and the consent of immigration authorities, be provided with an 'exemption certificate' that temporarily overlooked their 'alien' or 'coloured' status.[77] Intriguingly, this loophole allowed occasional visits by non-white, 'foreign' athletes who performed publicly at Australian sport venues. Notwithstanding the racial separation implicit in the WAP, local sport fans typically appreciated the athletic skills and 'exotic' appearance of these 'coloured' competitors. However, there were also differences of opinion and reaction. African-American boxer Jack Johnson was admired for his boxing prowess, but hated by many for defeating a white title holder in Sydney in 1908.[78] Yet only two years earlier African-American cyclist Marshall 'Major' Taylor had beaten all comers in Sydney and was widely coveted by local sport fans.[79] In 1915, the man widely accredited with giving surfing a high profile, Hawaiian Duke Paoa Kahanamoku, was revered when he took to the waves in Australia.[80] Similarly, Alick Wickham, a Solomon Islander in Australia, became the most famous exponent of the 'crawl' stroke.[81] Athletes of Asian origin were less renowned in Australia but do not seem to have been excluded from local sporting culture.[82] Indeed, despite local fears of eventual invasion by the so-called 'yellow peril' from East Asia, swimmers from Japan and footballers from China were received very hospitably during the 1920s.[83] There is plenty of irony about athletes of non-white appearance being accorded such status; not only because of the WAP, but because in the first half of the 20th century Indigenous Australians had such a low profile in the nation's sporting culture.[84]

There were signs of change in the 1960s and 1970s. When Aboriginal boxer Lionel Rose claimed the world bantamweight title in Japan in 1968, he was mobbed by well wishers upon return to Australia. Not only was Rose the first Aborigine to win a world boxing title, he also became the first Indigenous person to be awarded the prestigious title of 'Australian of the Year'. A year later he reached the top of the music charts with a country and western song 'I Thank You'.[85] Along with tennis player Evonne Goolagong, who twice won the Wimbledon singles crown, Rose presented the image of an Aborigine who had 'made it' in white society. Like Cathy Freeman, who lit the cauldron at the opening of the 2000 Olympic Games, both Rose and Goolagong appealed to many white observers who, ordinarily, had little contact with or sympathy for Aboriginal dissidents, such as those who fashioned the Aboriginal Tent Embassy in Canberra in 1972;[86] or, for that matter, Aborigines who took their protests about land rights to the streets during the Commonwealth Games of 1982. In the latter case the Queensland government was so 'spooked' by this Aboriginal assertiveness that it declared a state of emergency in order to constrain such public demonstrations.[87]

During the 1980s and 1990s increased numbers of Aborigines participated at the elite level in the country's two largest football codes – Australian Rules and rugby league. By the early 21st century players from Aboriginal or Torres Strait Islander heritage constituted around 10 percent of all professional players in both the AFL and the NRL – a staggering proportion given that the Indigenous population of Australia is about two percent of the national total.[88] However, as scholars have shown, these footballers battled long and hard against racism on and off the field. Not until the late 1990s did football administrators have anti-vilification policies fully in place, and they were in effect pushed into doing so by outspoken and articulate players such as Essendon's Michael Long.[89] The profile, status and remuneration of professional Indigenous athletes has never been better,[90] but there remains more to be achieved – particularly in terms of career transition planning and retirement experiences of Aboriginal sportspeople.[91]

Issues of discrimination and stereotyping in sport have also been apparent among ethnic minority groups in Australia. While soccer (football), for example, was an important sport for the great flood of European migrants after World War II, the game was typecast as 'foreign' by comparison to the existing staples of the rugby codes and Australian Rules.[92] Soccer was commonly ridiculed as 'wogball' and a game for 'poofters'; this derision not only impacted upon so-called 'New Australians' playing soccer, but residents of Anglo-Celtic heritage with a passion for the sport.[93] Ethnicity has, of course, been part of Australian sport since the 19th century. Scots were particularly noticeable in golf and lawn bowls, Irish Catholics were prominent as bookmakers in the racing industry, while the English were especially zealous about cricket and fox hunting. These practices were basically extensions of migrant cultural baggage in the Antipodes.[94] It would be misleading, though, to speak of ethnic enclaves among the Australian population or within the sporting culture of the late 19th and early 20th centuries. Indeed, despite protracted Anglo–Irish tensions, most notably after the Easter Rising of 1916, which had local impacts upon Australian society, sport appears to have been less affected by sectarianism than education, party politics and the public service.[95] There have been suggestions that Irish-Catholic Test cricketers suffered discrimination at the hands of team mates and selectors, though there is debate among historians as to whether this was systematic persecution or merely a series of personality conflicts.[96]

In Australia, historical research into sport and ethnicity has focused principally on the second half of the 20th century.[97] It was given impetus as a subject for inquiry by the emergence of a federal government policy of multiculturalism, first adopted by Labour in 1973. Previously, 'New Australians' were expected to assimilate into a dominant English-speaking, Anglo-Celtic culture. Now there was an emphasis on respect for group differences within a society that, as a consequence of mass migration – not only from Europe but increasingly Asia – had become more culturally diverse and ethnically cosmopolitan.[98] In terms of sport, however, little seemed to change. For example, although a promising 19-year-old fast bowler, Len Durtanovich, played junior representative cricket for New South Wales, it was the pragmatically re-named Len Pascoe who played for Australia between 1977 and 1982. His parents' Yugoslavian origins were, however, still a source of derision for some cricket opponents.[99] Soccer, meanwhile, was still subject to discourses propounding it as a game for ethnic 'others' (minorities) and thus not 'true-blue' Australian.[100] Sport therefore remained a culturally conservative institution within which traditional forms and norms of physical activity dominated.

In the past two decades, however, there has been a greater emphasis on social inclusion and the engagement of various communities into sport – with a particular focus on attracting people from culturally and linguistically diverse backgrounds (CALD).[101] Yet this has coincided, ironically, with a move away from sports clubs dedicated to particular ethnic groups, and towards the 'cosmopolitanizing' of Australian sport culture – within which people of all ancestries and skin colours are assumed to have a place. On the one hand this has represented loss. For example, sports clubs organized by and for Jews have a long lineage in Australia.[102] This includes the Monash Golf Club in Sydney, named after Australia's renowned Jewish military commander of World War I. However, demographic and socio-economic changes have in effect transformed Monash into a 'cosmopolitan' golf club, albeit with a Jewish past.[103]

This theme of loss has also been noticeable among soccer clubs that were originally formed to cater for the fraternal needs of ethnic groups from non-English speaking backgrounds – Italians, Greeks, Serbs, Croats and so on.[104] The profile and status of such clubs has been denuded, since the mid-1990s, by a National Soccer League decision to in effect 'de-ethnicize' elite-level club competition in Australia.[105] A key expectation was that club names be revamped in an attempt to garner fan support from beyond an 'ethnic' base. Greek club West Adelaide Hellas, for example, changed its name to the West Adelaide Sharks. This was part of an explicit effort to reinvent soccer as a game intended to appeal to 'mainstream' Australia, not just the particular ethnic communities that many of the clubs appeared to represent.[106] At the elite level, club soccer faced protracted financial and administrative difficulties, as well as a perception (sometimes created by the media) that matches between Serbs and Croats, for example, were little more than occasions for historic, European-based inter-group hostilities to be played out in an Antipodean setting.[107] Intriguingly, NSL efforts to 'mainstream' soccer were a contrast to strategies by the AFL and the NRL, both of which actively courted players and supporters from CALD backgrounds and, though they did not put it this way, a more conspicuously 'cosmopolitan' following.[108]

However, no Australian sport has gone through more reform than soccer in recent decades; and, while this has involved loss it has also presented opportunity. The NSL has been supplanted by the A-League, which involves team franchises and single clubs representing cities or regions. It has received financial backing from Jewish-Australian property magnate Frank Lowy, while the long overdue involvement of the Socceroos in the World Cup (2006) gave the sport – renamed football in Australia – unprecedented profile and public following. Although it is early days, the 'mainstreaming' of football via the A-League and the expectation of the Socceroos participating regularly in the World Cup, appears to have put the game in a sounder financial position.[109] What is more, preliminary research indicates that CALD fans of the NSL have, for the most part, not been isolated by the A-League, and that a new generation of football fans – from all sorts of backgrounds – are attending matches.[110] As with the Monash Golf Club there is both loss and opportunity: erosion of ethnic traditions, but opportunity to engage a wider range of followers. It is an example of the emerging cosmopolitanization of Australian sport cultures. Of course sport and Australian nationalism persists, but for many people it is a hybrid sense of fan allegiance – Australian *and* Vietnamese, Australian *and* Serbian and so on. Rather than a site of monolithic parochialism and patriotism, Australian sport – both in local and global contexts – appears to be moving towards a postmodern, cosmopolitan phase.[111]

'Re-visioning' and revisiting Australian sports history

As explained at the outset, there are very few career opportunities in Australia for academics aspiring to work as sports historians, and the vast majority of current practitioners are located in Human Movement or Sports Studies environments within which historical analysis tends to have a low priority. That said, there have been some important contributions by Australians to the practice of sports history. Murray Phillips and Douglas Booth have been at the forefront of global initiatives to make the sub-discipline more receptive to innovations within social and cultural history generally. They have encouraged researchers to explicitly situate themselves within a theoretical paradigm; they have urged scholars to be more conscious of archives as sources of power, not simply evidence; they have prompted writers to reflect upon their research methods and their positions, as investigators, within that process; and they have emphasized the constructed and contingent nature of 'findings'.[112] Their counsel has so far received mixed responses: sports historians familiar with the 'cultural' or 'linguistic' turn in the discipline of History are well placed to benefit from both the Phillips and Booth recommendations, but those limited to conventional social history face something of a challenge from deconstructionism and postmodernism.[113] Concepts such as reflexivity and tropes, as well as methods of discourse analysis or semiotics are not grasped easily, in part because many who deploy them insist on highly specialized, even obtuse language. Thus the challenge for Phillips and Booth, world leaders in their own right, is to convey their arguments in a way that inspires others to follow.

While there has recently been important debate about a 're-visioning' of the craft of sports history, there are further priorities that need revisiting. First, remarkably little systematic research has been conducted into the economic history of Australian sport.[114] In Britain, by contrast, there is a wealth of knowledge about club ownership, profit and utility maximizing behaviours, player salaries and unions, and so on.[115] Second, while there has been sustained research into the impact of the media on Australian sport since the late 1970s, the era when television became crucial to professionalization and commercialization,[116] too little is presently known about the role and significance of the print media and radio in the formative years of Australian sport.[117] Such conventional forms of mass mediated sport are less significant in the age of digital television and the Internet, but they are surely of major historical import. Third, there are distinctive aspects of Australian sports history that are well known but poorly understood. Why is it that professional clubs in the football codes and cricket have typically been member-based rather than, as with soccer and baseball in Britain and the USA, either owned by individuals or shareholders?[118] What values and aspirations have been associated with club membership in Australian sports history?[119] Why, in addition, is there no tradition (other than in soccer) of Australian sport spectators being formally segregated in stadiums on the basis of team allegiance? What is more, given the passion typically associated with 'barracking' at Australian sport, why has the hard core 'hooligan' phenomenon been largely absent from the football codes 'down under'?[120] In sum, a key problem with the state of Australian sports history is not simply a lack of theoretical or methodological vision, but also a need to systematically revisit historical archives – documentary, visual and oral. Revisionism can emerge from reforms to the academic craft of sports history; equally they can arise from painstaking reading and interpretation of primary sources – many of which are as yet untouched by scholars of sport.

Notes

1 Recently, though, there have been important efforts to try to revive Australian History as a school subject. This has also involved heated debate between conservatives and progressives about the content and delivery of such a subject. Department of Education, Employment and Workplace Relations, 'Teaching Australian History', www.dest.gov.au/sectors/school _education/policy_initiatives_reviews/ key_issues/australian_history/default.htm (accessed 4 April 2008).
2 D. Booth, 'Sports History: What Can Be Done?', *Sport, Education and Society*, 2, 2 (1997), 191–204; D. Adair, 'Location, Location! Sports History and Academic Real Estate', *Australian Society for Sports History Bulletin*, 36 (August 2002), 11–14.
3 C.M.H. Clarke, *A History of Australia*, vols 1–6, (Melbourne: Melbourne University Press, 1963–87).
4 G. Blainey, *A Game of Our Own: The Origins of Australian Football* (Melbourne: Information Australia, 1990).
5 D. Booth, '"On the Shoulders of a Giant": W.F. Mandle and the Foundations of Sports History in Australia', *International Journal of the History of Sport*, 19, 1 (2002), 151–58.
6 W.F. Mandle, 'The Professional Cricketer in England in the Nineteenth Century', *Labour History*, 23 (1972), 1–16; 'Games People Played: Cricket and Football in England and Victoria in the late 19th century', *Historical Studies: Australia & New Zealand*, 15, 60 (1973), 511–35; 'Cricket and Australian Nationalism in the Nineteenth Century', *Journal of the Royal Australian Historical Society*, 59, 4 (1973), 225–46; and *Going it Alone: Australia's National Identity in the Twentieth Century* (Ringwood, Vic.: Allen Lane and Penguin, 1978).
7 R. Cashman and M. McKernan, eds, *Sport in History: The Making of Modern Sporting History* (St Lucia: University of Queensland Press, 1979).
8 R. Cashman, *Paradise of Sport: The Rise of Organised Sport in Australia* (Melbourne: Oxford University Press, 1995), and D. Booth and C. Tatz, *One-Eyed: A View of Australian Sport* (Sydney: Allen & Unwin, 2000). Another synthesis study, D. Adair and W. Vamplew's *Sport in Australian History* (Melbourne: Oxford University Press, 1997), offers a basic introduction for non-specialist readers. Studies that include both sociology and an element of history include B. Stoddart, *Saturday Afternoon Fever: Sport in the Australian Culture* (North Ryde, NSW: Angus & Robertson, 1986); and P. Kell, *Good Sports: Australian Sport and the Myth of the Fair Go* (Sydney: Pluto Press, 2000).
9 G. Blainey, *The Tyranny of Distance: How Distance Shaped Australia's History* (Melbourne: Sun Books, 1966).
10 Cashman, *Paradise of Sport*, and J.A. Daly, *Elysian Fields: Sport, Class and Community in Colonial South Australia, 1836–1890* (Adelaide: J.A. Daly, 1982).

11 D. Adair, M. Phillips and J. Nauright, 'Sporting Manhood in Australia: Test Cricket, Rugby Football, and the Imperial Connection, 1878–1918', *Sport History Review*, 28 (1997), 46–60; and D. Adair, 'Rowing and Sculling', in W. Vamplew and B. Stoddart, eds, *Sport in Australia: A Social History* (Melbourne: Cambridge University Press, 1994), 172–92.

12 R. Cashman, 'Symbols of Imperial Unity: Anglo-Australian Cricketers, 1877–1900', in J.A. Mangan, ed., *The Cultural Bond: Sport, Empire, Society* (Frank Cass: London, 1992), 129–41; and E. Nielsen, 'Australian Nationalism and Middle-Class Britishness: Understanding Australian Identity Through Amateur Sport', Paper presented to the 27th Annual Conference of the British Society for Sports History, 17–19 August 2009, University of Stirling 2009.

13 J.B. Hirst, *Convict Society and its Enemies: A History of Early New South Wales* (Sydney: Allen & Unwin, 1983); and R. Hughes, *The Fatal Shore: A History of the Transportation of Convicts to Australia, 1787–1868* (New York: Random House, 1987).

14 Mandle, 'Cricket and Australian Nationalism', 225–46.

15 See R. Norris, *The Emergent Commonwealth: Australian Federation, Expectations and Fulfilment 1889–1910* (Melbourne: Melbourne University Press, 1975).

16 Mandle, 'Cricket and Australian Nationalism', 225–46.

17 N. Meaney, 'Britishness and Australian Identity: The Problem of Nationalism in Australian History and Historiography', *Australian Historical Studies*, 32, 116 (2001), 76–90; and R. McGregor, 'The Necessity of Britishness: Ethno-cultural Roots of Australian Nationalism', *Nations and Nationalism*, 12, 3 (2006), 493–511.

18 M. McKernan, 'Sport, War and Society: Australia, 1914–18', in R. Cashman and M. McKernan, eds, *Sport in History: The Making of Modern Sporting History* (St Lucia: University of Queensland Press, 1979), 1–20; D.J. Blair, '"The Greater Game": Australian Football and the Army at Home and on the Front during World War I', *Sporting Traditions*, 11, 2 (May 1995), 91–102; E. Jaggard, 'Forgotten Heroes: The 1945 Australian Services Cricket Team', *Sporting Traditions*, 12, 2 (1996), 61–79; M.G. Phillips, 'Football, Class and War: The Rugby Codes in New South Wales, 1907–15', in J. Nauright and T.J.L. Chandler, eds, *Making Men: Rugby and Masculine Identity* (London: Frank Cass, 1996), 158–80; M.G. Phillips, 'Sport, War and Gender Images: The Australian Sportsmen's Battalions and the First World War', *International Journal of the History of Sport*, 14, 1 (1997), 78–96; G. Rodwell and J. Ramsland, 'Cecil Healy: A Soldier of the Surf', *Sporting Traditions*, 16, 2 (2000), 3–16; M. Crotty, *Making the Australian Male: Middle-Class Masculinity 1870–1920* (Melbourne: Melbourne University Publishing, 2001); J. Ramsland, 'A Remarkable Life: Roden Cutler as Sporting, Military and Local Hero', *Sporting Traditions*, 20, 2 (May 2004), 39–54; and P. Cohen, 'Behind Barbed Wire: Sport and Australian Prisoners of War', *Sporting Traditions*, 23, 1 (November 2006), 63–86.

19 G. Seal, *Inventing ANZAC: The Digger and National Mythology* (St Lucia: University of Queensland Press, 2004).

20 This concentration of people in cities persists: Australia remains one of the most urbanized countries in the world, with the vast majority of its population living near the coastline. See P. Drew, *The Coast Dwellers: Australians Living on the Edge* (Ringwood, Vic.: Penguin, 1994).

21 D. Adair, '"Two Dots in the Distance": Professional Sculling as a Mass Spectacle in New South Wales, 1876–1907', *Sporting Traditions*, 9, 1 (November 1992), 52–83; and R. Cashman and T. Hickie, 'The Divergent Sporting Cultures of Sydney and Melbourne', *Sporting Traditions*, 7, 1 (1987), 24–46.

22 K. Saunders, '"Specimens of Superb Manhood": The Lifesaver as National Icon', *Journal of Australian Studies*, 56 (1998), 96–105.

23 D. Booth, *Australian Beach Cultures: The History of Sun, Sand, and Surf* (London: Frank Cass, 2001); E. Jaggard, ed., *Between the Flags: One Hundred Summers of Australian Surf Lifesaving* (Sydney: UNSW Press, 2006); S. Brawley, *Vigilant and Victorious: A Community History of the Collaroy Surf Life Saving Club, 1911–1995* (Collaroy, NSW: Collaroy Surf Life Saving Club, 1995); and C. White, 'Picnicking, Surf-Bathing and Middle-Class Morality on the Beach in the Eastern Suburbs of Sydney, 1811–1912', *Journal of Australian Studies*, 80 (2004), 101–10.

24 M.G. Phillips, 'Public Sports History, History and Social Memory: (Re)presenting Swimming in Australia', *Sporting Traditions*, 15, 1 (1998), 93–102; and M.-L. McDermott, 'Changing Visions of Baths and Bathers: Desegregating Ocean Baths in Wollongong, Kiama and Gerringong', *Sporting Traditions*, 22, 1 (November 2005), 1–19.

25 D. Booth, 'Surf Lifesaving: The Development of an Australasian "Sport"', *International Journal of the History of Sport*, 17, 2 (2000), 166–87; E. Jaggard, 'Tempering The Testosterone: Masculinity,

Women and Australian Surf Lifesaving', *The International Journal of the History of Sport*, 18, 4 (2001), 16–36; D. Booth, 'The Dark Side of Surf Lifesaving', *Journal of Sport History*, 29, 1 (2002), 7–14; E. Jaggard, 'Writing Australian Surf Lifesaving's History', *Journal of Sport History*, 29, 1 (2002), 15–24; M.G. Phillips, 'A Critical Appraisal of Narrative in Sport History: Reading the Surf Lifesaving Debate', *Journal of Sport History*, 29, 1 (2002), 25–40; and D. Booth, 'A Tragic Plot? A Reply to Jaggard and Phillips', *Journal of Sport History*, 29, 1 (2002), 41–48.

26 D. Booth, 'From Bikinis to Boardshorts: Wahines and the Paradoxes of Surfing Culture', *Journal of Sport History*, 28, 1 (2001), 3–22. For some bathers, no swimwear was preferred. See C. Daley, 'From Bush to Beach: Nudism in Australasia', *Journal of Historical Geography*, 31, 1 (2005), 149–67.

27 D. Booth, '"War off the Water": The Australian Surf Lifesaving Association and the Beach', *Sporting Traditions*, 7, 2 (1991), 134–62; D. Booth, 'Surfing '60s: A Case Study in the History of Pleasure and Discipline', *Australian Historical Studies*, 26, 103 (1994), 262–79; and D. Booth, 'Swimming, Surfing and Surf-Lifesaving', in W. Vamplew and B. Stoddart, eds, *Sport in Australia: A Social History* (Melbourne: Cambridge University Press, 1994), 231–54.

28 D. Booth, 'Ambiguities in Pleasure and Discipline: The Development of Competitive Surfing', *Journal of Sport History*, 22 (1995), 189–206.

29 C. Giles and J. Fitzgerald, 'Embracing Cultural Diversity in SLSA: "On The Same Wave"', Paper Presented to the 12th National Conference on Volunteering, Gold Coast, Queensland, 3–5 September 2008, www.volunteeringaustralia.org/files/ICIATN1SJ9/bn08020_VA8_Chris%20Giles.pdf (accessed 10 November 2008).

30 C. Forster, 'Sport, Society and Space: The Changing Geography of Country Cricket in South Australia 1836–1914', *Sporting Traditions*, 2, 2 (May 1986), 23–47; Cashman and Hickie, 'The Divergent Sporting Cultures of Sydney and Melbourne', 24–46; S. Bennett, 'Regional Sentiment and Australian Sport', *Sporting Traditions*, 5, 1 (November 1988), 98–111; J. O'Hara, 'The Jockey Club and the Town in Colonial Australia', *Journal of Gambling Studies*, 7, 3 (1991), 207–15; J. O'Hara, *Big River Racing: A History of the Clarence River Jockey Club 1861–2001* (Sydney: UNSW Press, 2002); T. Magdalinksi, 'Cricket and Regional Development on the Sunshine Coast', *Sporting Traditions*, 18, 2 (2002), 15–29; D. Topp and J. Nauright, 'Rugby League, Community and Identity in the Lockyer Valley, Queensland', *Sporting Traditions*, 21, 1 (November 2004), 53–65; K. Atherley, 'Sport, Localism and Social Capital in Rural Western Australia', *Geographical Research*, 44, 4 (2006), 348–60; and P. Horton, 'Football, Identity, Place: The Emergence of Rugby Football in Brisbane', *International Journal of the History of Sport*, 23, 8 (2006), 1,341–68.

31 See J. Bale, *Landscapes of Modern Sport* (Leicester: Leicester University Press, 1994); and J. Bale, *Sports Geography* (London: Routledge, 2003).

32 J.B. Hirst, *Sense & Nonsense in Australian History* (Melbourne: Black, 2006), 30–31.

33 Stoddart, *Saturday Afternoon Fever*; G.A. Lawrence and D. Rowe, eds, *Power Play: Essays in the Sociology of Australian Sport* (Sydney: Hale & Ironmonger, 1986); D. Rowe and G. Lawrence, eds, *Sport and Leisure: Trends in Australian Popular Culture* (Sydney: Harcourt Brace Jovanovich, 1990); J. McKay, *No Pain, No Gain?: Sport and Australian Culture* (Sydney: Prentice Hall, 1991).

34 See Richard Holt's chapter 'Amateurism and the Victorians' in his *Sport and the British: A Modern History* (Oxford: Oxford University Press, 1989); and Richard Cashman's chapter 'Amateur versus Professional' in his *Paradise of Sport*.

35 C. Cunneen, 'The Rugby War: The Early History of Rugby League in New South Wales', in R. Cashman and M. McKernan, eds, *Sport in History: The Making of Modern Sport History* (St Lucia: University of Queensland Press, 1979), 293–306; P.A. Horton, 'Dominant Ideologies and their Role in the Establishment of Rugby Union Football in Victorian Queensland', *International Journal of the History of Sport*, 11, 1 (1994), 115–28; and C. Little, 'The "Hidden" History of the Birth of Rugby League in Australia: The Significance of "Local" Factors in Sydney's Rugby Split', *Sport in History*, 27, 3 (2007), 364–79.

36 J. Ross, 'Pedestrianism and Athletics in England and Australia in the Nineteenth Century: A Case Study in the Development of Sport', Bachelor of Human Movement Studies (Hons) thesis, University of Queensland, St Lucia, 1984; P. Mason, *Professional Athletics in Australia* (Adelaide: Rigby, 1985); J.A. Daly, 'Track and Field', in W. Vamplew and B. Stoddart, eds, *Sport in Australia: A Social History* (Melbourne: Cambridge University Press), 255–68.

37 R. Hess, 'A Mania for Bicycles: The Impact of Cycling on Australian Rules Football', *Sporting Traditions*, 14, 2 (1998), 3–24; J. Weaver and J.T. Weaver, '"We've had no Punctures Whatsoever": Dunlop, Commerce and Cycling in *Fin de Siècle* Australia', *International Journal of the History of Sport*,

16, 3 (1999), 94–112; and C.S. Simpson, ed., *Scorchers, Ramblers and Rovers: Australasian Cycling Histories*, ASSH Studies 21 (Melbourne: Australian Society for Sports History, 2006).

38 Adair, 'Two Dots in the Distance', 52–83.

39 I. Jobling, 'The Making of a Nation Through Sport: Australia and the Olympic Games from Athens to Berlin, 1898–1916', *Australian Journal of Politics & History*, 34, 2 (1988), 160–72.

40 E. Halladay, *Rowing in England: A Social History: The Amateur Debate* (Manchester: Manchester University Press, 1990).

41 Adair, 'Rowing and Sculling', 172–92; M. Crotty, '"Separate and Distinct"? The Manual Labour Question in Nineteenth-century Victorian Rowing', *International Journal of the History of Sport*, 15, 2 (1998), 152–63; and S. Ripley, 'The Golden Age of Australian Professional Sculling or Skullduggery?', *International Journal of the History of Sport*, 22, 5 (2005), 867–82.

42 K. Moore and M.G. Phillips, 'The Sporting Career of Harold Hardwick: One Example of the Irony of the Amateur–Professional Dichotomy', *Sporting Traditions*, 7, 1 (1990), 61–76; Cashman, *Paradise of Sport*, 54–71; Adair and Vamplew, *Sport in Australian History*, 37–40; M.G. Phillips, 'Diminishing Contrasts and Increasing Varieties: Globalisation Theory and "Reading" Amateurism in Australian Sport', *Sporting Traditions*, 18, 1 (2001), 19–32; J. Senyard, 'From Gentleman to the Manly: A Large Step for the Amateur', *Sporting Traditions*, 18, 2 (2002), 1–14; and E. Nielsen, '"Oh Error, Ill-conceived": The New South Wales Amateur Sports Federation, Rugby League and Amateur Athletics', Paper presented to The Centenary Conference of Rugby League in Australia, Powerhouse Museum, Sydney, 7–8 November 2008.

43 Senyard, 'From Gentleman to the Manly', 1–14; Adair, 'Two Dots in the Distance', 52–83; and Adair, 'Rowing and Sculling', 172–92.

44 See S. Ripley, 'A Social History of New South Wales Professional Sculling, 1876–1927', unpublished PhD thesis, School of Arts and Humanities, University of Western Sydney, 2003; and Ripley, 'The Golden Age of Australian Professional Sculling or Skullduggery?', 867–82.

45 As examples, see I. Harriss, 'Packer, Cricket and Postmodernism', in D. Rowe and G. Lawrence, eds, *Sport and Leisure: Trends in Australian Popular Culture* (Sydney: Harcourt Brace Jovanovich, 1990), 109–21; R.K. (Bob) Stewart, '"I Heard it on the Radio, I Saw it on the Television": The Commercial and Cultural Development of Australian First Class Cricket: 1946–85', unpublished PhD thesis, School of History, La Trobe University, Melbourne, 1995; and G. Haigh and R. Dundas, *The Cricket War: The Inside Story of Kerry Packer's World Series Cricket* (Melbourne: Text Publishing, 2001).

46 There are, of course, numerous non-academic eulogies of Australian professional tennis, but analytical studies are rare. Fewster looks at the impact on Australian team tennis of the many Americans joining professional circuits in the 1950s. See K. Fewster, 'Advantage Australia: Davis Cup Tennis 1950–59', *Sporting Traditions*, 2, 1 (November 1985), 47–68. There is also a rather cursory discussion of professional tennis in G. Kinross-Smith, 'Lawn Tennis', in W. Vamplew and B. Stoddart, eds, *Sport in Australia: A Social History* (Melbourne: Cambridge University Press, 1994), 133–52.

47 B. Stoddart, 'Golf', in W. Vamplew and B. Stoddart, eds, *Sport in Australia: A Social History* (Melbourne: Cambridge University Press, 1994), 77–92.

48 Key studies include G. Kinross-Smith, 'Privilege in Tennis and Lawn Tennis: The Geelong and Royal South Yarra Examples But Not Forgetting the Story of the Farmer's Wrist', *Sporting Traditions*, 3, 2 (May 1997), 189–216; B. Blashak, '"The Ignorant Labelled it a Ladies' Game": Masculinity in Australian Tennis in the Late Nineteenth and Early Twentieth Centuries', in I. Warren, ed., *Sport, Gender and Theory: The Formative Years of Tennis and Snowboarding*, ASSH Studies 16 (Melbourne: Australian Society for Sports History, 2004), 1–59; C. Tatz and B. Stoddart, *The Royal Sydney Golf Club: The First Hundred Years* (Sydney: Allen & Unwin, 1993); M.G. Phillips, 'Ethnicity and Class at the Brisbane Golf Club', *Sporting Traditions*, 4, 2 (May 1988), 201–13; and M.G. Phillips, 'Golf and Victorian Sporting Values', *Sporting Traditions*, 6, 2 (May 1990), 120–34.

49 Key studies include B. Griffen-Foley, 'Playing with Princes and Presidents: Sir Frank Packer and the 1962 Challenge for the America's Cup', *Australian Journal of Politics & History*, 46, 1 (2000), 51–66; C. Thompson, 'Boats, Bondy and the Boxing Kangaroo: The 1983 America's Cup', in I. Warren, ed., *Buoyant Nationalism: Australian Identity, Sport, and the World Stage 1982–1983*, ASSH Studies 14 (Balaclava, Vic.: Australian Society for Sports History, 2004), 60–117; J. O'Hara, 'Horse Racing and Trotting', in W. Vamplew and B. Stoddart, eds, *Sport in Australia: A Social History* (Melbourne: Cambridge University Press, 1994), 93–111; and J. O'Hara, 'Globalisation, Historical Consciousness and the Melbourne Cup', *Sporting Traditions*, 23, 2 (2007), 33–46.

50 Q. Beresford, 'The Melbourne Cup: Australia's First National Day', *Hemisphere*, 27 (November–December 1982), 180–84; K. Ahearne, 'The Myth Lives On: Cultural Significance of the Melbourne Cup', *Australian Society*, 6, 12 (December 1987), 52, 57–58; and R. White, 'National Days and the National Past in Australia', *Australian Cultural History*, 22 (2003), 55–72.

51 M. Cronin, 'Defenders of the Nation? The Gaelic Athletic Association and Irish Nationalist Identity', *Irish Political Studies*, 11, 1 (1996), 1–19; P.F. McDevitt, 'Muscular Catholicism: Nationalism, Masculinity and Gaelic Team Sports, 1884–1916', *Gender and History*, 9, 2 (1997), 262–84; I. D. Brice, 'Ethnic Masculinities in Australian Boys' Schools: Scots and Irish Secondary Schools in Late Nineteenth-century Australia', *Paedagogica Historica*, 37, 1 (2001), 139–52; and N.J. Watson et al., 'The Development of Muscular Christianity in Victorian Britain and Beyond', *Journal of Religion and Society*, 7 (2005), 1–21.

52 Key publications include R. Crawford, 'Athleticism, Gentlemen and Empire in Australian Public Schools: L.A. Adamson and Wesley College, Melbourne', in W Vamplew, ed., *Sport and Colonialism in 19th Century Australasia* ASSH Studies 1 (Bedford Park, SA: Australian Society for Sports History, 1986), 42–64; D.W. Brown, 'Muscular Christianity in the Antipodes: Some Observations on the Diffusion and Emergence of a Victorian Ideal in Australian Social Theory', *Sporting Traditions*, 3, 2 (1987), 173–87; M. Connellan, *The Ideology of Athleticism, its Antipodean Impact, and its Manifestation in Two Elite Catholic Schools*, ASSH Studies 5 (Bedford Park, SA: Australian Society for Sports History, 1988); B. Stewart, 'Athleticism Revisited: Sport, Character Building and Protestant School Education In Nineteenth Century Melbourne', *Sporting Traditions*, 9, 1 (November 1992), 35–50; and M. Crotty, 'Manly and Moral: The Making of Middle-class Men in the Australian Public School', *International Journal of the History of Sport*, 17, 2 (2000), 10–30.

53 B. Collins, M. Aitken and B. Cork, *One Hundred Years of Public School Sport in New South Wales 1889–1989* (Sydney: New South Wales Department of School Education, 1990); D. Kirk and K. Twigg, 'Civilising Australian Bodies: The Games Ethic and Sport in Victorian Government Schools, 1904–45', *Sporting Traditions*, 11, 2 (1995), 3–34; D. Kirk and K. Twigg, 'The Militarization of School Physical Training in Australia: The Rise and Demise of the Junior Cadet Training Scheme, 1911–31', *History of Education*, 22, 4 (1993), 391–414; D. Kirk, 'Foucault and the Limits of Corporeal Regulation: The Emergence, Consolidation and Decline of School Medical Inspection and Physical Training in Australia, 1909–30', *International Journal of the History of Sport*, 13, 2 (1996), 114–31; and I.R. Wilkinson, 'School Sport and the Amateur Ideal: The Formation of the Schools' Amateur Athletic Association of Victoria', *Sporting Traditions*, 15, 1 (1998), 51–70.

54 G. Sherington, 'Athleticism in the Antipodes: The Athletic Association of the Great Public Schools of New South Wales', *History of Education Review*, 12, 2 (1983), 16–28.

55 R. Light and D. Kirk, 'High School Rugby, the Body and the Reproduction of Hegemonic Masculinity', *Sport, Education and Society*, 5, 2 (2000), 163–76; and R. Light and D. Kirk, 'Australian Cultural Capital – Rugby's Social Meaning: Physical Assets, Social Advantage and Independent Schools', *Culture, Sport, Society*, 4, 3 (2001), 81–98.

56 R. Crawford, 'Sport for Young Ladies: The Victorian Independent Schools 1875–1925', *Sporting Traditions*, 1, 1 (1984), 61–82; B. Stewart, 'Athleticism Revisited: Sport, Character Building, and Protestant School Education in Nineteenth Century Melbourne', *Sporting Traditions*, 9, 1 (1992), 52–83; and D. Kirk, 'Gender Associations: Sport, State Schools and Australian Culture', *International Journal of the History of Sport*, 17, 2 (2000), 49–64.

57 J. Nauright and T.J.L. Chandler, eds, *Making Men: Rugby and Masculine Identity* (London: Frank Cass, 1996); Light and Kirk, 'High School Rugby, the Body and the Reproduction of Hegemonic Masculinity', 163–76; and C. Hickey, 'Physical Education, Sport and Hyper-masculinity in Schools', *Sport, Education and Society*, 13, 2 (2008), 147–61.

58 M. Treagus, 'Playing Like Ladies: Basketball, Netball and Feminine Restraint', *International Journal of the History of Sport*, 22, 1 (2005), 88–105; and T. Taylor, 'Gendering Sport: The Development of Netball in Australia', *Sporting Traditions*, 22, 1 (November 2005), 57–74.

59 M.G. Phillips, *An Illusory Image: A Report on the Media Coverage and Portrayal of Women's Sport in Australia 1996* (Canberra: Australian Sports Commission, 1997); Adair and Vamplew, *Sport in Australian History*, 48–62; and R. Payne, 'Rethinking the Status of Female Olympians in the Australian Press', *Media International Australia incorporating Culture and Policy*, 110 (February 2004), 120–31.

60 A classic example of this approach is L.M. Randall, *A Fair Go?: Women in Sport in South Australia, 1945–1965*, ASSH Studies 6 (Bedford Park, SA: Australian Society for Sports History, 1988).

61 The quintessential example of this approach is M.K. Stell, *Half the Race: A History of Australian Women in Sport* (North Ryde, NSW: Angus & Robertson, 1991).

62 D. Phillips, 'Australian Women at the Olympics: Achievement and Alienation', *Sporting Traditions*, 6, 2 (1990), 181–200; and *Australian Women at the Olympic Games* (Sydney: Kangaroo Press, 1996).

63 R. Hess, 'Women and Australian Rules Football in Colonial Melbourne', *International Journal of the History of Sport*, 13, 3 (1996), 356–72; '"Ladies are Specially Invited": Women in the Culture of Australian Rules Football', *International Journal of the History of Sport*, 17, 2 (2000), 111–41; and '"For the Love of Sensation": Case Studies in the Early Development of Women's Football in Victoria, 1921–81', *Football Studies*, 8, 2 (2005), 20–30.

64 Exceptions include A. Burroughs and J. Nauright, 'Women's Sports and Embodiment in Australia and New Zealand', in J.A. Mangan and J. Nauright, eds, *Sport in Australasian Society: Past and Present* (London: Frank Cass, 2000), 188–205; M. Haig-Muir, 'Many a Slip twixt Cup and the Lip: Equal Opportunity and Victorian Golf Clubs', *Sporting Traditions*, 17, 1 (2000), 19–38; T. Brabazon, 'Time For a Change or More of the Same? Les Mills and the Masculinisation of Aerobics', *Sporting Traditions*, 17,1 (2000), 97–112; Taylor, 'Gendering sport', 57–74; A. Burroughs, 'Women, Femininity and Sport: The Contribution of the "New Woman" to Nationhood', in R. Cashman, J. O'Hara and A. Honey, eds, *Sport, Federation, Nation* (Sydney: Walla Walla Press, 2001), 165–80; C. Little, '"What a Freak-show they Made!" Women's Rugby League in 1920s Sydney', *Football Studies*, 4, 2 (October 2001), 25–40; R. Riddell, 'Wild Women: Out of Their Corsets – A History of the Melbourne Women's Walking Club', *Australasian Parks and Leisure*, 4, 4 (December 2001), 19–20; M. Haig-Muir, 'Handicapped from Birth? Why Women Golfers Are Traditionally a Fairway Behind', *Sport History Review*, 35, 1 (May 2004), 64–82.

65 R.A. Howell and M.L. Howell, *The Genesis of Sport in Queensland* (St Lucia: University of Queensland Press, 1992), 7–16; and K. Edwards, *Choopadoo: Games from a Dreamtime* (Brisbane: Queensland University of Technology Press, 1999).

66 A. Smith, ed., 'Games From the Dreamtime', interview with Ken Edwards, *The Sports Factor*, ABC Radio National, 10 November 2000, fulltext.ausport.gov.au/fulltext/2000/sportsf/s210119.htm (accessed 4 April 2008).

67 Edwards, *Choopadoo*.

68 K. Edwards (with T. Meston), *Yulunga: Traditional Aboriginal Games* (Canberra: Australian Sports Commission, 2008).

69 See various books by Henry Reynolds, such as *Dispossession: Black Australians and White Invaders* (Sydney: Allen & Unwin, 1996); and *The Other Side of the Frontier: Aboriginal Resistance to the European Invasion of Australia* (Sydney: UNSW Press, 2006).

70 C. Stevens, *White Man's Dreaming: Killalpaninna Mission, 1866–1915* (Melbourne: Oxford University Press, 1994); and J. Mitchell, *Flesh, Dreams and Spirit: Life on Aboriginal Mission Stations, 1825–1850: A History of Cross-cultural Connections* (Canberra: Australian National University, 2005).

71 J. Mulvaney and R. Harcourt, *Cricket Walkabout: The Australian Aborigines in England* (South Melbourne: Macmillan, 1988); and D. Sampson, 'Strangers in a Strange Land: The 1868 Aborigines and other Indigenous Performers in Mid-Victorian Britain', PhD thesis, Faculty of Humanities and Social Sciences, University of Technology Sydney, 2000, Australian Digital Thesis Repository, hdl.handle.net/2100/314.

72 See various studies by Bernard Whimpress, such as 'Few and Far Between: Prejudice and Discrimination Among Aborigines in Australian First Class Cricket 1869–1988', *Journal of the Anthropological Society of South Australia*, 30, 1–2 (December 1992), 57–70; and *Passport to Nowhere: Aborigines in Australian Cricket, 1850–1939* (Sydney: Walla Walla Press, 1999).

73 B. Whimpress, 'The Marsh-Maclaren Dispute at Bathurst, 1902, and the Politics of Selection', *Sporting Traditions*, 10, 2 (May 1994), 45–58; M. Colman and K. Edwards, *Eddie Gilbert: The True Story of an Aboriginal Cricketing Legend* (Sydney: ABC Books, 2002); and M. Bonnell, *How Many More Are Coming? The Short Life of Jack Marsh* (Petersham, NSW: Walla Walla Press, 2003).

74 N. Newlin and C. Moran, 'Living Cultures', in R. Craven, *Teaching Aboriginal Studies* (Sydney: Allen & Unwin, 1999), 35.

75 See various publications by Tatz, such as: *Aborigines in Sport*, ASSH Studies 3 (Bedford Park SA: Australian Society for Sports History, 1987); and *Obstacle Race: Aborigines in Sport* (Kensington: UNSW Press, 1995).

76 G.C. Blades, 'Australian Aborigines, Cricket and Pedestrianism: Culture and Conflict, 1880–1910', Honours thesis, Bachelor of Human Movement Studies, University of Queensland, 1985;

R. Broome, 'Professional Aboriginal Boxers in Eastern Australia 1930–79', *Aboriginal History*, 4, 1–2 (June 1980), 49–71; R. Broome, 'Theatres of Power: Tent Boxing Circa 1910–70', *Aboriginal History*, 20 (1996), 1–23; and C. Mooney and J. Ramsland, 'Dave Sands as Local Hero and International Champion: Race, Family and Identity in an Industrial Working-class Suburb', *Sport in History*, 28, 2 (2008), 299–312.

77 A. Honey, 'Sport, Immigration Restriction and Race: The Operation of the White Australia Policy', in R. Cashman, J. O'Hara and A. Honey, eds, *Sport, Federation, Nation* (Sydney: Walla Walla Press, 2001), 26–46.

78 R. Broome, 'The Australian Reaction to Jack Johnson, Black Pugilist, 1907–9', in R. Cashman and M. McKernan, eds, Sport in History (St Lucia: University of Queensland Press, 1979), 343–63; and J. Wells, *Boxing Day: The Fight That Changed the World* (Sydney: Harper, 1998).

79 A. Ritchie, *Major Taylor: The Extraordinary Career of a Champion Bicycle Racer* (Baltimore, MA: Johns Hopkins University Press, 1996).

80 G. Osmond, M. Phillips and M. O'Neil, '"Putting up your Dukes": Statues, Social Memory and Duke Paoa Kahanamoku', *International Journal of the History of Sport*, 23, 1 (2006), 82–103.

81 G. Osmond and M.G. Phillips, 'The Bloke with a Stroke', *Journal of Pacific History*, 39, 3 (2004), 309–24; and G. Osmond and M.G. Phillips, '"Look at That Kid Crawling" – Race, Myth and the "Crawl" Stroke', *Australian Historical Studies*, 37, 127 (2006), 43–62.

82 G. Osmond and M.-L. McDermott, 'Mixing Race: The Kong Sing Brothers and Australian Sport', *Australian Historical Studies*, 39, 3 (2008), 338–55.

83 S. Brawley, '"They Came, They Saw, They Conquered": The Takaishi/Saito Tour of 1926/27 and Australian Perceptions of Japan', Paper presented to the Conference *Sport, Race and Ethnicity: Building a Global Understanding*, University of Technology Sydney, 30 November–2 December 2008; and N. Guoth, 'Kangaroos and Dragons: The 1923 Chinese Football Tour of Australia', Paper presented to *Sporting Traditions XVI*, the Biennial Conference of the Australian Society for Sports History, Canberra, 27–30 June 2007.

84 B. Whimpress, 'Absent Aborigines: The Impact of Federation on Indigenous Sport', in R. Cashman, J. O'Hara and A. Honey, eds, *Sport, Federation, Nation* (Sydney: Walla Walla Press, 2001), 47–54.

85 L. Rose and R. Humphries, *Lionel Rose Australian: The Life Story of a Champion* [as told to Humphries by Rose] (Sydney: Angus and Robertson, 1969).

86 E. Goolagong Cawley and P. Jarratt, *Home! The Evonne Goolagong Story* (East Roseville, NSW: Simon & Schuster, 1993); T. Bruce and C. Hallinan, 'Cathy Freeman: The Quest for Australian Identity', in D. Andrews and S. Jackson, eds, *Sports Stars: The Cultural Politics of Sporting Celebrity* (New York: Routledge, 2001), 257–70; and K. Lothian, 'Moving blackwards: Black Power and the Aboriginal Embassy', in I. MacFarlane and M. Hannah, eds, *Transgressions: Critical Australian Indigenous Histories*, Aboriginal History Monograph 16 (Canberra: ANU E-Press, 2007), 19–34.

87 C. Tatz, 'Aborigines and the Commonwealth Games', *Social Alternatives*, 3, 1 (1981), 48–51; 'Race, Politics and Sport', *Sporting Traditions*, 1, 1 (1984), 2–36; and N. Shannon, 'The Friendly Games? Politics, Protest and Aboriginal Rights at the XII Commonwealth Games, Brisbane 1982', in I. Warren, ed., *Buoyant Nationalism: Australian Identity, Sport and the World Stage, 1982–1983*, ASSH Studies 14 (Melbourne: Australian Society for Sports History, 2004), 1–59.

88 J.-U. Korff, 'Aboriginal Indigenous Sport', www.creativespirits.info/aboriginalculture/sport/ (accessed 7 January 2009).

89 G. Gardiner, 'Racial Abuse and Football: The Australian Football League's Racial Vilification Rule in Review', *Sporting Traditions*, 14, 1 (1997), 3–26; I. Warren, 'Racism and the Law in Australian Rules Football: A Critical Analysis', *Sporting Traditions*, 14, 1 (1997), 27–53; L. McNamara, 'Tackling Racial Hatred: Conciliation, Reconciliation and Football', *Australian Journal of Human Rights*, 6, 2 (2000), 5–31; and I. Warren, 'Combating Vilification: The AFL and NRL Anti-vilification Rules', *ANZSLA Commentator*, 9, 4 (2000), 13–15.

90 C. Tatz and P. Tatz, *Black Diamonds: The Aboriginal and Islander Sports Hall of Fame* (St Leonards, NSW: Allen and Unwin, 1996); and *Black Gold: The Aboriginal and Islander Sports Hall of Fame* (Canberra: Aboriginal Studies Press, 2000).

91 G. Stocks and A. East, *Lewie, Lewie: Chris Lewis – An Aboriginal Champion* (Perth: Specialist Sports Management, 2000); S. Gorman, *Brotherboys: The Story of Jim and Phillip Krakouer* (Crows Nest, NSW: Allen and Unwin, 2005); and M. Stronach and D. Adair, 'Retirement Experiences of Elite Indigenous Australian Athletes: Policies, Programs and Practices', Paper Presented to the

Conference *Sport, Race and Ethnicity: Building a Global Understanding*, University of Technology Sydney, 30 November–2 December 2008.

92 R. Hay, '"Our Wicked Foreign Game": Why has Association Football (Soccer) Not Become the Main Code of Football in Australia?', *Soccer and Society*, 7, 2 (2006), 165–86.

93 J. Warren, A. Harper and J. Whittington, *Sheilas, Wogs and Poofters: An Incomplete Biography of Johnny Warren and Soccer in Australia* (Sydney: Random House Australia, 2002).

94 D. Adair, 'Conformity, Diversity, and Difference in Antipodean Physical Culture: The Indelible Influence of Immigration, Ethnicity, and Race During the Formative Years of Organised Sport in Australia, *c.*1788–1918', in M. Cronin and D. Mayall, eds, *Sporting Nationalisms: Identity, Ethnicity, Immigration, and Assimilation* (London: Frank Cass, 1998), 14–48.

95 M.C. Hogan, *The Sectarian Strand: Religion in Australian History* (Ringwood, Vic.: Penguin Books, 1987); and J. Kildea, *Tearing the Fabric: Sectarianism in Australia 1910 to 1925* (Sydney: Citadel Books, 2002).

96 For a summary, see A. Bairner, 'Wearing the Baggie Green: The Irish and Australian Cricket', *Sport in Society*, 10, 3 (2007), 457–75.

97 P. Mosely, et al., *Sporting Immigrants: Sport and Ethnicity in Australia* (Sydney: Walla Walla Press, 1997).

98 J. Jupp, 'One Among Many: The Relative Success of Australian Multiculturalism', in D. Goodman, C. Wallace-Crabbe and D. O'Hearn, eds, *Multicultural Australia* (Newham, Vic.: Scribe, 1991), 119–33.

99 See G. Lawson, *Henry: The Geoff Lawson Story* (Randwick, NSW: Ironbark Press, 1993); and G. Haig, 'Pascoe Was Like a Bull at a Batsman', *Age*, 21 (February 2004).

100 J. Hughson, 'Australian Soccer: "Ethnic" or "Aussie". The Search for an Image', *Current Affairs Bulletin*, 68, 10 (1992), 12–16; and L.M. Danforth, 'Is the "World Game" an "Ethnic Game" or an "Aussie Game"? Narrating the Nation in Australian Soccer', *American Ethnologist*, 28, 2 (2001), 363–87.

101 T. Taylor and K. Toohey, 'Negotiating Cultural Diversity for Women in Sport: From Assimilation to Multiculturalism', *Race, Ethnicity and Education*, 1, 1 (1998), 75–90.

102 A. Hughes, 'Muscular Judaism and the Jewish Rugby League Competition in Sydney, 1924 to 1927', *Sporting Traditions*, 13, 1 (1996), 61–80; and A. Hughes, 'Sport in the Australian Jewish Community', *Journal of Sport History*, 26, 2 (1999), 376–91.

103 C. Tatz, *A Course of History: Monash Country Club 1931–2001* (Sydney: Allen and Unwin, 2002).

104 P. Mosely, *Ethnic Involvement in Australian Soccer: A History 1950–1990* (Canberra: National Sports Research Centre, 1995); and R. Hay, 'Croatia: Community, Conflict and Culture: The Role of Soccer Clubs in Migrant Identity', *Immigrants and Minorities*, 17 (1998), 49–66.

105 J. Hughson, 'Football, Folk Dancing and Fascism: Diversity and Difference in Multicultural Australia', *Journal of Sociology*, 33, 2 (1997), 167–86.

106 H. Westerbeek et al., 'De-ethnicization and Australian Soccer: The Strategic Management Dilemma', *International Journal of Sport Management*, 6, 3 (2005), 270–88.

107 J. Hughson, 'The Boys are Back in Town: Soccer Support and the Social Reproduction of Masculinity', *Journal of Sport and Social Issues*, 24, 1 (2000), 8–23; J. Hughson, '"The Wogs are at it Again": The Media Reportage of Australian Soccer "Riots"', *Football Studies*, 4, 1 (April 2001), 40–55; and R. Hay, '"Those Bloody Croatians": Croatian Soccer Teams, Ethnicity and Violence in Australia, 1950–99', in G. Armstrong and R. Giulianotti, eds, *Fear and Loathing in World Football* (Oxford: Berg, 2001), 77–90.

108 For a comparison of the football codes in Australia, see B. Stewart, ed., *The Games are not the Same: The Political Economy of Football in Australia* (Carlton, Vic.: Melbourne University Press, 2007).

109 J. Skinner, 'Coming in From the Margins: Ethnicity, Community Support and the Rebranding of Australian Soccer', *Soccer and Society*, 9, 3 (2008), 394–404; and B. Dabscheck, 'Moving Beyond Ethnicity: Soccer's Evolutionary Progress', in B. Stewart, ed., *The Games Are Not the Same: The Political Economy of Football in Australia* (Carlton, Vic.: Melbourne University Press, 2007), 198–235.

110 D. Lock, T. Taylor and S. Darcy, 'Soccer and Social Capital in Australia: Social Networks in Transition', in M. Nicholson and R. Hoye, eds, *Sport and Social Capital* (Oxford: Butterworth-Heinemann, 2008), 317–38; and D. Lock, 'Fan Perspectives of Change in the A-League', *Soccer and Society*, 10, 1 (2009), 109–23. For a dissenting view, see R. Hay, 'A Victory for the Fans? Melbourne's New Football Club in Recent Historical Perspective', *Soccer and Society*, 8, 2 (2007), 298–315.

111 B. Bowden, 'Nationalism and Cosmopolitanism: Irreconcilable Differences or Possible Bedfellows?', *National Identities*, 5, 3 (2003), 235–49.

112 M.G. Phillips, 'Public Sports History, History and Social Memory: (Re)presenting Swimming in Australia', *Sporting Traditions*, 15, 1 (1998), 93–102; 'Deconstructing Sport History: The Postmodern Challenge', *Journal of Sport History*, 28, 3 (2001), 327–44; M.G. Phillips, ed., *Deconstructing Sport History: A Postmodern Analysis* (New York: State University of New York Press, 2006); D. Booth, 'Escaping the Past? The Cultural Turn and Language in Sport History', *Rethinking History*, 8, 1 (2004), 103–25; 'Evidence Revisited: Interpreting Historical Materials in Sport History', *Rethinking History*, 9, 4 (2005), 459–83; *The Field: Truth and Fiction in Sport History* (London: Routledge, 2005); and 'Sites of Truth or Metaphors of Power? Refiguring the Archive', *Sport in History*, 26, 1 (2006), 91–109.

113 For a range of responses, see R. Hay, 'Approaches to Sports History: Theory and Practice', *Sporting Traditions*, 22, 2 (2006), 70–81; B. Stoddart, 'In Search of Meaning: Historians and Their Work', *Sporting Traditions*, 22, 2 (2006), 82–87; M. Johnes, 'Archives, Truths and the Historian at Work: A Reply to Douglas Booth's "Refiguring the Archive"', *Sport in History*, 27, 1 (2007), 127–35; and A. Guttmann, 'Review Essay: The Ludic and the Ludicrous', *International Journal of the History of Sport*, 25,1 (2008), 100–12.

114 Important exceptions include B. Stewart, 'The Economic Development of the Victorian Football League 1960–84', *Sporting Traditions*, 1, 2 (May 1985), 2–26; B. Dabscheck, 'The Professional Cricketers Association of Australia', *Sporting Traditions*, 8, 1 (November 1991), 2–27; and 'Early Attempts at Forming Soccer Player Unions in Australia', *Sporting Traditions*, 10, 2 (November 1994), 25–40; R. Booth, 'History of Player Recruitment, Transfer and Payment Rules in the Victorian and Australian Football League', *Australian Society for Sports History Bulletin*, 26 (1997), 13–33; B. Dabscheck, 'Australian Baseball's Second Unsuccessful Attempt to Establish a Players' Association', 14, 2 (May 1998), 87–90; B. Stewart, 'The Crisis of Confidence in Australian First-Class Cricket in the 1950s', *Sporting Traditions*, 20, 1 (November 2003), 43–62; R. Booth, 'The Economics of Achieving Competitive Balance in the Australian Football League, 1897–2004', *Economic Papers – Economic Society of Australia*, 23, 4 (2004), 325–44; and Stewart, *The Games Are Not the Same*.

115 Classic examples include W. Vamplew, *The Turf: A Social and Economic History of Horseracing* (London: Allen Lane, 1976); W. Vamplew, *Pay Up and Play the Game: Professional Sport in Britain, 1875–1914* (Cambridge: Cambridge University Press, 1988); and N. Tranter, *Sport, Economy, and Society in Britain, 1750–1914* (Cambridge: Cambridge University Press, 1998).

116 Key studies include D. Rowe, *Sport, Culture and the Media* (Buckingham: Open University Press, 1999); Lawrence and Rowe, *Power Play*; B. Hutchins and M.G. Phillips, 'Selling Permissible Violence: The Commodification of Australian Rugby League 1970–95', *International Review for the Sociology of Sport*, 32, 2 (1997), 161–76; and M.G. Phillips and B. Hutchins, 'Losing Control of the Ball: The Political Economy of Football and the Media in Australia', *Journal of Sport and Social Issues*, 27, 3 (2003), 215–32.

117 Exceptions include C. Cunneen, 'Elevating and Recording the People's Pastimes: Sydney Sporting Journalism 1886–1939', in R. Cashman and M. McKernan, eds, *Sport: Money, Morality, and the Media* (Sydney: UNSW Press, 1981), 162–76; R. Grow, 'Nineteenth Century Football and the Melbourne Press', *Sporting Traditions*, 3, 1 (November 1986), 23–37; S.R. Wenn, 'Lights, Camera, Little Action: Television, Avery Brundage and the 1956 Melbourne Olympics', *Sporting Traditions*, 10, 1 (1993), 38–53; P. Brown, 'Gender, the Press and History: Coverage of Women's Sport in the *Newcastle Herald*, 1890–1990', *Media Information Australia*, 75 (1995), 24–34; and B. Stewart, 'Radio's Changing Relationship with Australian Cricket: 1932–50', *Sporting Traditions*, 19, 1 (2002), 49–64.

118 J. Nauright and M. Phillips, 'A Fair Go For the Fans?: Super Leagues, Sports Ownership and Fans in Australia', *Social Alternatives*, 15, 4 (1996), 43–45; M.G. Phillips and J. Nauright, 'Sports Fan Movements to Save Suburban-based Football Teams Threatened With Amalgamation in Different Football Codes in Australia', *International Sports Studies*, 21, 1 (1999), 16–38; J. Nauright and M. Phillips, 'Us and Them: Australian Professional Sport and Resistance to North American Ownership and Marketing Models', *Sport Marketing Quarterly*, 6, 1 (1997), 33–39.

119 Significant academic studies thus far include, R. Stremski, *Kill for Collingwood* (Sydney: Allen and Unwin, 1986); A. Moore, *The Mighty Bears!: A Social History of North Sydney Rugby League* (Sydney: Macmillan, 1996); M.G. Phillips, 'Rugby League and Club Loyalty', in D. Headon and L. Marinos, eds, *League of a Nation* (Melbourne: ABC Books, 1996), 106–11; and Lock, Taylor and Darcy, 'Sport and Social Capital'.

120 I. Warren, *Football, Crowds and Cultures: Comparing English and Australian Law and Enforcement Trends*, ASSH Studies 13 (Canberra: Australian Society for Sports History, 2003).

20 Belgium and the Netherlands

Ruud Stokvis

Introduction

According to Norbert Elias, the establishment of an academic discipline involves three closely related developments: a) the recognition of the relative autonomy of a certain field of science in relation with other fields of science; b) the development of a relatively autonomous body of theory concerning this field of science; and c) the development of specialized academic departments and professional groups devoted to the scientific study of the field.[1] The trouble with history writing is that it was practised for a very long time outside the university; it was practised even before the rise of universities – think of Herodotus, Thucydides, Josephus, Tacitus and later Gibbon. People who made history sometimes also wrote it: Julius Caesar and Sir Winston Churchill are eminent examples. For a very long time the past has been recognized as a field of study. The formulation of special theories and the establishment of academic departments are, compared with the long standing interest in the study of the past, only relatively recent developments. This is also the case with the history of sports. Even if one limits oneself to modern sports, the competitive pastimes that became organized and standardized on local, national and international levels during the 19th and 20th centuries, one can recognize a long tradition of non-academic history writing. The other phases in the establishment of an academic discipline of sports history are much more recent.

In the Low Countries, since the end of the 19th century, veteran sport practitioners, journalists and other amateurs produced many histories of sports. Most of these histories were published as jubilee books or as memorial books for special occasions. From the viewpoint of academic professional historians this sort of book may have many shortcomings. In some cases they are nearly useless, especially when the history of a sport is just considered as a succession of matches or races, without attention to the backgrounds and motives of the athletes and the officials and organizations that facilitated these competitions. However, many of these publications do contain these elements. A good example for the English-speaking world is *The History of the Football Association*,[2] which was published in 1953 on the occasion of the coronation of Queen Elizabeth II. Especially for historians from other countries, who do not have easy access to the archives of the Football Association, it gives a wonderful overview of early English soccer (football) history. In the first part of this chapter, I will deal with this non-academic tradition of sports historiography in the Low Countries. I discuss it until the 1960s, though that does not mean that it does not exist in more recent times. However in the second part, for the period after the 1960s, I concentrate on the academic tradition of sports history writing.

Jubilee books and other 'special occasion' publications

One of the most important promoters of modern sports in the Low Countries was Pim Mulier (1865–1954).[3] During the 1890s, when sports had become a limited but established practice in the Low Countries, he wrote three books in which he looked back at the sports of his youth. In *Wintersport, Athletiek en Voetbal* (Athletics and Soccer) and *Cricket*, next to descriptions of famous matches and athletes and advice for training and materials, he described the history of these sports, the way they were organized in England, how they came to the Low Countries and his own role in the introduction of these sports in the Netherlands. These books have contributed to the image of Mulier as the 'Father of Dutch Sports', an image that is not completely beyond historic reality, though in the light of more recent historical research his centrality in the development of Dutch sports has been reduced somewhat.[4]

In 1900, on the occasion of the new century, the well-known aristocratic sports writer and journalist Jan Feith published *Het boek der sporten* (The Book of Sports), in which a popular amateur in each branch of sport contributed an essay, with the history of his sport in the Netherlands having a central place in the text.[5] So we have essays on the early history of sport in the Netherlands for 20 branches of sport. At that time, sports had a somewhat wider meaning than the way they are considered in the 21st century. It is now more debatable than a century ago if hunting, fishing and dog shows should be considered sports. But the 17 others in the book all are popular sports in our time. The essays differ in quality. In some of them the enumerations of match results are not very interesting, neither are the expressions of enthusiasm of the contributors for their sports. However, in most essays one learns a lot about the way the sport was introduced, the social milieu in which this happened, the typical motives of the first participants, the rise and actions of its organizations and the conditions that contributed to the success or lack of success of these sports. The essay on cycle racing shows convincingly how during the 1880s the sport (track racing) became popular among young men of the upper-middle class and how with the rise of professionalism the people of this category deserted the sport. This meant that track racing lost many supporters from the higher social classes. Their support for the sport was not replaced by visitors to the professional races. As a consequence, cycle racing in the Netherlands became a professional sport for lower-class men in which not much money was earned. The most talented cyclists went to Paris and London. This is the first analysis of a more general phenomenon, where sports are deserted by members of the higher classes when people from the lower classes begin to enter in significant numbers. During the 1920s and 1930s this process was described by Miermans for soccer (see below).

During the 1970s it happened in lawn tennis and since the 1990s in golf. For the well-documented essay on horse-racing and trotting, there has not been written anything better about the subject since then. This essay shows the unequal development of horse-racing, a sport that had been imported from England, and trotting, a form of racing that has its roots deep in Dutch social history. We see that horse-racing suffered while it was not supported by a large social category of aristocrats or other group of the very rich. In the Netherlands, the aristocracy was too small and the rich bourgeois kept their distance from the aristocratic pastimes. Since the end of the Middle Ages trotting has been popular among farmers and villagers. It remains until today the most popular form of racing with horses in the Netherlands.

In the essay on soccer the author was already convinced of the position of Mulier as the 'Father' of the sport. In this essay we can see the process of myth-making at work.

The author used Mulier as his main source for the early history of soccer in the Netherlands. Jan Feith wrote in 1941 one of the few monographs on sports history after the work of Mulier. His *Sport in Indië*[6] (The Dutch East Indies, present day Indonesia) contains descriptions of many traditional Indonesian competitive pastimes. In the second half of this small book of 89 pages, Feith describes how modern Western sports were introduced and how they diffused throughout the archipelago. One finds in the book a short description of the performance of the Dutch-Indian team during the world championships in France in 1938.

Probably the most professional work from the category of early histories by amateurs is *Een halve eeuw wielersport 1867–1917* (A Half Century of Cycling Sport 1867–1917) by George J. M. Hogenkamp.[7] In his introduction the author declares he planned originally just to write down the history of cycling in the Netherlands. However, after he began, he discovered something that many historians after him would also discover: you cannot write down the history of a sport in one country without taking into account the development of the sport on the international level. The best cyclists of one country try to meet the champions of other countries to see who really is best. We have to praise Hogenkamp that he did not avoid the challenge this international character of cycling meant for the historian. Each year he begins with the situation of cycling in the Netherlands and after a few pages he shows how the situation in that country was connected with the developments in other countries, and with the international level of organization and competition. Thanks to Hogenkamp, in the Low Countries we are very well informed on the early history of race cycling in the Netherlands and in Europe. His book is illustrated with many photos, which together with the text contribute to our knowledge of cycle racing in the past.

A very rich source of sports histories are the jubilee books of local sports clubs and national sports associations. It is impossible to describe all these histories, often based on intensive archival studies. The jubilee books of the national associations offer information on the development of a branch of sport on the national level; often they have to deal with international issues, too. Alongside these books of the national associations we have a large number of jubilee books of local clubs. Some of the larger and older clubs publish a new jubilee book every 25 years, with the history of the previous 25 years. Further to this, there are the sports history books published in connection with the Olympic Games, such as the *Nationaal Sport Gedenkboek*[8] (National Sport Memorial Book) of 1928 and *Honderd Jaar Sport*[9] by the sports journalist M.J. Adriani Engels (1960). Like *Het boek der sporten* from 1900 we find in the *Nationaal Sport Gedenkboek* histories of 15 branches of sport, now with an additional 28 years more of their past.

The books that were produced after the first quarter of a century or after the first half century of the existence of a club or association, in particular, give detailed information and interesting images of the early stages of Dutch sports. For historical-sociologists who try, if possible, to avoid the archives, these jubilee books offer most of the data they need. I will limit myself to a short description of just four examples from this rich source of historical information on sports. *Driekwart eeuw zwemmen 1870–25 juni 1945* (Three Quarters of a Century of Swimming 1870–25 June 1945) by J.P.A. Luirink,[10] in 1945 the treasurer of the Amsterdam Swimming Club AZ 1870, is a very informative book on the origins of organized swimming in Amsterdam. He describes the foundation of the first swimming pools, the relationship between the sexes in swimming, the involvement of the town board and the relationship of social class to the sport. This latter issue enters history because the gentlemen of the clubs took the responsibility for offering swimming courses for people of the lower classes. These courses were deemed important to them because it made them more employable as seamen and it could prevent them from drowning in the Amsterdam channels. In the book one gets a sense that swimming was a sport that could develop in a competitive fashion, as well as in the form of non-competitive physical education. Interesting also is the differentiation in the sport: the development of platform diving and water polo.

In 1932 the Dutch Ice Skating Union published its jubilee book: *Koninklijke Nederlandschen Schaatsenrijdersbond 1882–1932*.[11] It is the history of the national association for skating. Local clubs had been founded already in the 1840s and some of these clubs also had their own jubilee books. One of the best is that of the Amsterdam Ice Club,[12] which already had published by 1914 a well-researched book about its 50-year history. In the book of the national skating union, one of the central themes is the struggle between the representatives of native short-track racing competitions for money prizes and the supporters of long-track racing, imported from England along with its amateur rules. During the first decades of the 20th century, short-track racing was reduced into a folkloristic sport, with its main base in the Northern provinces of the Netherlands. Long-track racing became dominant. One could ask what more could be studied besides what has been done already in these jubilee books. With regard to skating, what one really misses is the development of the social base of skating and of the social meaning of this sport in Dutch society. Without further study, the extreme enthusiasm of Dutch fans for the performances of the Dutch skaters in international championships remains a mystery.

Of course, soccer – by far the most popular sport in the Low Countries – is the subject of a large number of very well-documented jubilee books. For the early history of the sport in the Netherlands one of the best is *Het N.V.B.-Boek: Gedenkboek bij het 40-jarig bestaan van den Nederlandschen voetbalbond 1889–8 december 1929* (The NVB Book: Memorial Book on the Occasion of the 40-year Existence of the Dutch National Soccer Association 1889–8 December 1929).[13] The association had not yet acquired the right to use the adjective 'Koninklijke' (Royal); this happened 10 years later, when NVB became KNVB. The book was collected and for the large part written by a prominent journalist, D. Hans, who was among other fields active in sports journalism. This book was written with a sharp historical-sociological perspective. The main subject is how the national association acquired and kept its power over all developments in Dutch soccer. Clubs and regional associations wanted to keep as much autonomy as possible, but for the national association this was not workable. It suppressed effectually the attempts of women to start a competition. It fought against tendencies in the direction of pro-fessionalism and against tendencies among the traditional high-class clubs to organize a competition of their own when the number of lower-class clubs undermined their tra-ditional dominance in the sport. More than the book of the skating association, this book informs us about the social position and meaning of soccer in Dutch society.

In 1945 the Belgian soccer association published its wonderful book on the occasion of its 50-year jubilee: *Geschiedenis van de voetbalsport in België en in de Belgische Kongo* (History of the Sport of Soccer in Belgium and the Belgian Kongo),[14] largely written by Victor Boin. It is as detailed and informative as its Dutch equivalents. The detailed history of the association (317–438) has the form of a chronicle in which for each year the most import events are summarized. This simple form of history writing is strongly related to the major sources for these association histories, which were the minutes of the board meetings and the annual reports of the Chairman of the Board. One needs a certain amount of experience in history writing to take the analysis of the sources one step further and to present the data in a thematic, chronological setting, as did Hans in his NVB book. In the book on the Belgian association, the first 300 pages deal with all kinds of separate thematic issues, which could have been more integrated in the historical narrative if the data had been presented in a thematic, chronological order. The last chapter of the book gives detailed information about the development of soccer in the Belgian Congo. During the 1930s it was already a very popular sport in the Congo. The teams of Europeans had a separate competition to the teams of natives. The native teams were divided into those playing with shoes and those playing barefoot. The quality of African national soccer teams at that time does not come as a surprise when one realizes the relatively early development of the sport on that continent.

To finish this all-too-brief overview of pre-academic sports history writing in the Low Countries, I would like to point to the theoretical contribution of the most important of the Dutch historians: Johan Huizinga. In his book *Homo Ludens* (1938)[15] he discussed the concept of 'play'. He defined play as: 'a voluntary action, performed within spatial and temporary limits according to voluntarily accepted binding rules with its purpose in the action itself, accompanied by a mood of tension and joy and the realization that one is involved in something different from the normal course of life'. Huizinga argued that the culture of a society originated from playing. According to him, sport originated from playing, but already in his time, with the professionalization and bureaucratization of sport's organization, it had lost its character as a form of play. Therefore, it had lost its connection with the culture of societies and had become something outside culture: an institution by itself. This concept of play has become very useful for analysing all kinds of developments in sports. One does not have to agree with Huizinga's critical and somewhat prejudiced view on modern sports to analyse their development from the perspective that this very useful concept offers.

The academic tradition

After a number of PhD dissertations, especially in the Netherlands, during the 1990s, we see the beginnings of the establishment of an academic discipline in the field of sports history in the Netherlands, as well as in Belgium. In Belgium the discipline became rooted more firmly than in the Netherlands.

The first dissertation on sport in the Netherlands was C. Mierman's study *Voetbal in Nederland: Maatschappelijke en sportieve aspecten* (Soccer in the Netherlands: Social and Sportive Aspects),[16] in 1955. In a sense, one might characterize it as a superior kind of jubilee book on the development of soccer in the Netherlands. It deals with the origins of soccer, the foundation of the first clubs in an elite milieu and the increase in the number of players owing to the participation of the lower classes, the development of its organization on a national level, and in a third section it offers all kinds of interesting statistics on the number of clubs, players and visitors. It is in a sociological-historical sense superior to most jubilee books, because Miermans discusses more fully the consequences of Dutch class and religious differences in the development of soccer. The book was finished in the year that the soccer association (KNVB) was forced to allow the introduction of professional soccer at the highest level of the competition. Miermans clearly did not like this development. This dissertation on a subject from the field of sport remained unique for 23 years.

In 1979 my own dissertation was published: *Strijd over sport: Organisatorische en ideologische ontwikkelingen* (Disputes on Sport: Organizational and Ideological Developments).[17] The inspiration for this book came from the debates during the 1970s about amateurism and professionalism, top sports and recreational sports, and the relationship between politics and sport. I tried to go back to the origins of these debates and to relate the development of the debates to the development of the power relations between the different parties involved in these debates on the national (Netherlands) and international levels. In the Netherlands, this dissertation was one of the first that used the figurational and process perspectives introduced by Norbert Elias. With the use of this perspective, the development of sport organizations and ideologies in the Netherlands was firmly placed in the international development of sport. A few other dissertations also have these characteristics of a process and figurational approach and, consequently, a sharp eye for the development of sport on the international level. Impressive and successful was Maarten van Bottenburg's dissertation from 1994: *Verborgen Competitie. Over de uiteenlopende populariteit van sporten* (Hidden Competition: On the Differences in Popularity of Sports),[18] in which he introduced the concept of a world sport system and studied the development of that system. He demonstrated that differences in popularity of sports in various countries can be accounted for on the basis of the international power relations between countries and the specific class relations within each country. The sports of the most powerful nations in a certain era tend to diffuse most to other countries within their sphere of influence. Exclusive sports in the powerful nations remain exclusive in other nations if there is an exclusive category to adopt these sports with all their signs of exclusivity. Van Bottenburg's book is the only Dutch historical-sociological book on sport that has been translated into English; the title of the English translation of 2001 was 'Global Games'.[19] A third dissertation in this process tradition of sports history writing is Ruurd Kunnen's study, *Schaken in stijl: De ontwikkeling van schaakstijlen al een proces van sportification* (Chess in Style: The Development of Chess Styles as a Process of Sportification), published in 2002.[20] On the basis of a statistical analysis of the opening moves of all known chess games in tournaments and other important matches between 1851 and 1975, Kunnen demonstrated that indeed there has been a succession of different styles. The purpose of his study was to find a satisfying explanation for the direction of these style changes. His major point is that one can't explain these changes only in terms of their increasing effectiveness; one also has to take into account the changes over time in the nature of the figurations of professional players, amateurs, and their clubs and associations, financers, media and the public.

Several other dissertations have been written outside the process sociology tradition. These studies remained limited to sport in the Dutch context. In these studies one sees how all kinds of characteristics of Dutch society are coming back in sport too. The 'pillarization' of Dutch society, the tendency to organize politics and social life according to religious and political conviction (Catholics, Protestants, socialists and liberals) during the first six decades of the 20th century, left its traces on the field of sport and, as a consequence, in sports history writing. Within each section of society, the elite tried to keep the lower classes within the confines of their 'pillar'. The elite themselves had a somewhat broader outlook. As a consequence, mainly in sports in which the youth of the lower classes participated, we see the foundation of stratified sports organizations. In 1981 Hans Dona published his dissertation on *Sport en Socialisme: De geschiedenis van de Nederlandse Arbeiderssportbond 1926–1941* (Sport and Socialism: The History of the Dutch Workers' Sport Association 1926–1941).[21] In 1990 the combined masters theses of Marjet Derks and Marc Budel appeared as *Sportief en Katholiek: Geschiedenis van de katholieke sportbeweging in Nederland in de twintigste eeuw* (Sportsmanlike and Catholic: History of the Catholic Sport Movement in the Netherlands During the 20th Century).[22] We are still waiting for the appearance of a study from the Protestant point of view. In fact, the liberals did not form a real pillar; however, because everybody else was part of a pillar, the liberal – without aspiring to it – automatically formed a pillar, too. Common to these pillarized associations, which never attracted more than about 20 percent of all sports participants, there was a strong pedagogic ideology. Sports should have an educational purpose and elite, spectator-focused sports did not fit into that perspective. The Catholics, in particular, had a lot of trouble with the possible allure of female athletes, based on their sports clothing, while the Protestants tried to avoid sports on Sundays.

Another important theme of Dutch sports history is the position of sports during the German occupation of World War II. It was the subject of the dissertation of André Swijtink (1992): *In de Pas: Sport en lichamelijke opvoeding tijdens de Tweede Wereldoorlog* (In Step: Sport and Physical Education in the Netherlands During the Second World War).[23] As can be said for the whole Dutch population, the behaviour of Dutch sports officials and practitioners vacillated between accommodation and collaboration with the occupying forces. There was not much solidarity with the Jewish athletes and officials. The number of participants in most sports associations increased strongly during the war. The theme of women's emancipation in Dutch sports is dealt with in J. Steendijk-Kuypers' book, *Vrouwen-Beweging: Medische en culturel aspecten van vrouwen in de sport, gezien in het kader van de sporthistorie, 1880–1928* (Women's Movement: Medical and Cultural Aspects of Women in Sport, Seen in the Light of the History of Sport, 1880–1928).[24] For a relatively long period, sports participation remained restricted to women of the higher social classes. Catholic and Protestant pedagogical authorities tried to restrict the participation of women. The involvement of the Dutch Government in the development of sport has been chronicled in the dissertation of Dolf Pouw: *50 jaar national sportbeleid* (50 Years of National Sport Policy).[25] In 2004 Gerrit Valk presented his dissertation, *AZ is de naam. Geschiedenis van het betaald voetbal in Alkmaar* (The name is AZ: History of Professional Soccer in Alkmaar).[26] Valk describes the remarkable success of a professional soccer team in a small, provincial town in the west of the Netherlands. In periods when the club lacks rich sponsors, deep downfalls of the club show the disadvantage of its narrow basis of support. As I wrote of Miermans for the national level of soccer, this book can be seen as a sophisticated jubilee book of a local club.

A monograph from outside the university sphere that is worthy of attention is J.J. Kalma (1972), *Kaatsen in Friesland: Het spel met de kleine bal door de eeuwen heen* (Bouncing Ball in Friesland: the Game with the Small Ball through the Ages).[27] In a class of his own in terms of the quality of his research and of his style and composition, are the two books on the Tour de France by Benjo Maso: *Het zweet der Goden'* (1990) (The Sweat of the Gods) is an historical-sociological study of the development of the Tour de France between its origins and the 1980s. In *Wij waren allemaal goden: De Tour van 1948* (We all Were Gods: The Tour of 1948) (2003), Maso analyses the competition between the Italian stars Fausto Coppi and Gino Bartali and the significance of this for the Italians and Italian politics.[28]

In Belgium, the harvest of dissertations and monographs on sport is smaller and it has a different nature. One sees a dominance of physical education rather than an historical or historical-sociological perspective on sports, which means that there are substantial numbers of academic historical studies in the field of physical education, while similar studies in the field of sport are all but absent. It also results in a perspective on sport that is limited to the Belgian context. We have the dissertation of Jan Tolleneer, *De Belgische*

Katholieke Turnbond 1892–1992 (The Belgian Catholic Gymnastics Association), from 1992.[29] This dissertation has many characteristics of a good-quality jubilee book. Another dissertation that belongs more to the field of physical education than the field of sports is Pascal Delheye's *De opkomst van de bewegingscultuur in Belgie en haar wetenschappelijke legitimering en institutionalisering (1830–1914)* (The Rise of Movement Culture in Belgium and its Scientific Legitimation and Institutionalization (1830–1914)), published in 2004.[30] Another consequence of the dominance in Belgium of a physical culture perspective on sport is that one is less interested in competitive top sports and more interested in the recreational sporting activities of people: the elite and the lower classes. Luc Celis' dissertation, *Arbeiderssport als tegencultuur?* (Worker Sport as Counter Culture?),[31] published in 1998, is an example of this interest. One sees it, too, in the very well-researched dissertation of Marijke den Hollander: *Sport in 't stad: Sociaal-historische analyse van de sport in Antwerpen 1830–1914* (Sport in Town: Social-historical Analysis of Sport in Antwerp, 1830–1914) (2002).[32] In this dissertation den Hollander gives, among other interesting information, a network analysis of the town elite as expressed in their membership of sports clubs.[33] The Belgians do not often position their sports in a wider context than their national state, as can be seen in Renson's study: *De herboren Spelen: De VIIe Oympiade Antwerpen 1920* (The Reborn Games: The VIIth Olympiad of Antwerp 1920), published in 1995.[34] In the Netherlands, a similar study was *Amsterdam 1928: Het verhaal van de IXe Olympiade* (Amsterdam 1928: The Story of the IXth Olympiad) by Paul Arnoldussen (1994).[35] Knowing the interest of the Belgians and especially perhaps the Flemish people in cycle racing, it is surprising that there are no dissertations or quality monographs on this subject. It would not be difficult to devote an article to the rich history of Belgian, and especially Flemish, cycling, as written down by sports journalists and other amateurs of the sport. However, for serious academic studies of the subject one has to look into the field of masters theses (*licentiaatsverhandelingen*), which are generally unpublished. In the bibliography of Bert Moeyaert's thesis, *Van Wielerbaan tot ... Velodroom: De geschiedenis van het baanwielrennen in Belgie van 1890 tot 2003* (From Cycling Course to ... Velodrome: The History of Track Racing in Belgium from 1890 to 2003),[36] we see other theses that deal with subjects such as cycle racing during World War II, female cycle racing and several other general histories of the sport.

From a historiographical point of view, the most important development in the 1990s was the foundation of historical sport magazines in the Low Countries. *Sportimonium*[37] is both the name of the Flemish museum for sports, and its journal. In its modern form under the name *Sportimonium*, this journal has been published since 1992. Owing to the close relationship between academic sports historians and the editors of the journal, *Sportimonium* could be considered the academic sports history journal of Belgium. Originally, since 1980, the museum, as well as its journal, was focused on the traditional competitive pastimes in Belgium and in other parts of the world. These are the pastimes that were pushed into the folkloristic corner after the advent of the modern British, German and American sports. The journal still bears the stamp of this policy. It gives much space to the study of traditional sport forms and the attempts to revive them. Related to this interest in traditional pastimes is the attention that is being paid to national developments in the history of physical education and gymnastics. However, it also has become the place in which many interesting articles on the history of the modern sports have been published. In one of its first issues one finds an excerpt of a masters thesis on the history of the *soigneur* (caretaker) in cycle racing. The lack of academic studies on the history of cycling is compensated for by the many serious articles about the subject in this journal.

In 1995 the journal began a series on the history of soccer in Belgium, which brought the history of the sport up to date since 1945, when the jubilee book of the KBVB was published. To this series were added many more articles on soccer in later issues. Short national histories are to be found in this journal on other sports like netball, swimming, fencing (sports with overlaps in the field of physical education), athletics and especially weight lifting and body building.

In 1994 in the Netherlands, history students founded the *Study Group Sport History*. A year later this name was changed to *De Sportwereld* (*The World of Sport*). In 1997 this foundation started a newsletter, also called *De Sportwereld*,[38] which evolved from a double-folded A4 page into a simple, but interesting magazine. It is hard to summarize its contents: it differs from its Belgian counterpart in that it is mainly interested in the history of modern sports. Some of the contributors go back far into the past, earlier than the 19th century, to find the origins of these sports. Many of these contributions are serious articles based on intensive archival research by history students. Over three issues one could follow the research on the question of to what level Pim Mulier should be considered the founding father of Dutch sports. Did he overestimate his role in the books that are named in the first part of this contribution and has he been mythologized by others who did not do careful research? The conclusion seems to be that he should be seen as one of a wider group of people who introduced modern sports in the Nether-lands, and not as its sole founding father. A major step in the development of sports history studies in the Netherlands was the publication of what was called a 'biblio-graphical apparatus'[39] for Dutch sports history. In this book one finds all the publications relevant to Dutch sports history (7,656 titles), sorted in the most relevant and efficient categories for the sports historian, and an inventory of the places where one can find these publications and the major archives. Owing to this book, together with the two magazines and the sports history dissertations, in Eliasian terms, we have squarely reached the second stage of the development of sports history as a discipline. In Belgium and in the Netherlands the first academic Chairs for this discipline have been founded, so we are on the threshold of entering the third stage, though much remains to be done.

Notes

1   Norbert Elias, *Was ist Soziologie?* (Munchen: JuventaVerlag, 1970), 62.
2   Geoffrey Green, *The History of the Football Association* (London: The Naldrett Press, 1953).
3   W. Mulier, *Wintersport* (Haarlem, 1893); *Athletiek en voetbal* (Haarlem: Loosjes, 1894); *Cricket* (Haarlem: De erven Loosjes, 1897).
4   Nico van Horn, '125 jaar voetbal in Nederland?', *De Sportwereld* 35 (December 2004), 8–14.
5   Jan Feith, *Het boek der sporten* (Amsterdam: Van Holkema en Warendorf, 1900).
6   Jan Feith, *Sport in Indie* (Deventer: W. van Hoeve, 1941).
7   George J.M. Hogenkamp, *Een halve eeuw wielersport* (Amsterdam, 1916).
8   H.A. Meerum Terwogt, ed., *Nationaal Sport Gedenkboek* (Amsterdam: Koloniale boekcentrale, 1927).
9   M.J. Adriaans Engels, *Honderd jaar sport: Een historische documentatie over de sport gedurende een eeuw* (Amsterdam: Strenghold, 1960).
10 J.P.A. Luirink, *Driekwart eeuw zwemmen 1870–25 juni 1945: Ter gelegenheid van het 75-jarig bestaan der Amsterdamsche Zwemclub AZ 1870* (Amsterdam, 1945).
11 G.W.A. van Laer Czn., *Gedenkboek van den Koninklijken Nederlandschen Schaatsenrijdersbond bij het vijftig jarig bestaan 1882–1932* (Amsterdam: v/h Ellerman, Hans & Co., 1932).
12 J.F.L. Balbian Venster, *De Amsterdamsche IJsclub 1864–1914: Gedenkschrift bij het 50-jarig bestaan* (Amsterdam: Roeloffsen-Hubner en Van Santen, 1915).
13 D. Hans, ed., *Het N.V.B.-Boek: Gedenkboek bij het 40-jarig bestaan van den Nederlandschen Voetbalbond 1889–8 december 1929* (n.p.: n.p., 1929).

14 Victor Boin, *Geschiedenis van de voetbalsport in België en de Belgische Kongo: Het gulden boek van de KBVB 1895–1945* (Brussels: Les Editions Leclerq & De Haas, 1945).

15 J. Huizinga, *Homo Ludens: Proeve eener bepaling van het spel-element der cultuur* (Groningen: H.D. Tjeenk Willink, 1938).

16 Cees Miermans, *Voetbal in Nederland: Een onderzoek naar de maatschappelijke en sportieve aspecten* (Assen: Van Gorcum & Com, 1955).

17 R. Stokvis, *Strijd over sport: Ideologische en maatschappelijke ontwikkelingen* (Deventer: Van Loghum Slaterus, 1979).

18 Maarten van Bottenburg, *Verborgen competitie: Over de uiteenlopende populariteit van sporten* (Amsterdam: Bert Bakker, 1994).

19 Maarten van Bottenburg, *Global Games* (Urbana and Chicago: University of Illinois Press, 2001).

20 Ruud Kunnen, *Schaken in stijl: De ontwikkeling van schaakstijlen als een proces van sportificatie* (Zoetermeer: Swob de Kade, 2002).

21 Hans Dona, *Sport en Socialisme: De geschiedenis van de Nederlandse Arbeiderssportbond 1926–1941* (Amsterdam: Van Gennip, 1981).

22 Marjet Derks and Marc Budel, *Sportief en katholiek: Geschiedenis van de katholieke sportbeweging in de twintigste eeuw* (Nijmegen: Katholiek documentatiecentrum, 1990).

23 André Swijtink, *In de pas: Sport en lichamelijke opvoeding in Nederland tijdens de Tweede Wereldoorlog* (Haarlem: De Vrieseborch, 1992).

24 J. Steendijk-Kuipers, *Vrouwen-beweging: Medische en culturele aspecten van vrouwen in de sport, gezien in het kader van de sporthistorie (1880–1928)* (Rotterdam: Erasmus Publishing, 1999).

25 Dolf Pouw, *50 jaar nationaal sportbeleid: Van vorming buiten schoolverband tot breedtesport* (Tilburg: Tilburg University Press, 1999).

26 Gerrit Valk, *AZ is de naam: Geschiedenis van het betaald voetbal in Alkmaar* (Amsterdam: Veen, 2004).

27 Jaap J. Kalma. *Kaatsen in Friesland: Het spel met de kleine bal door de eeuwen heen* (Franeker: Wever, 1972).

28 Benjo Maso, *Het zweet der goden: Legende van de wielersport* (Amsterdam: Veen, 1990); *Wij waren allemaal goden* (Amsterdam: Atlas, 2003).

29 Jan Tolleneer, *De Belgische Katholieke Turnbond 1892–1992* (Brussels, 1992).

30 Pascal Delheye, *De opkomst van de bewegingscultuur in België en haar wetenschappelijke legitimering en institutionalisering (1830–1914)* (Leuven, 2005).

31 L. Celis, *Arbeiderssport als tegencultuur? Een Durkheimiaanse ritueeltheorie geïllustreerd aan de hand van de historiografie van de Belgische socialistische arbeiderssportbeweging vanaf haar ontstaan tot aan de vooravond van de Tweede Wereldoorlog* (Brussels: VUB onuitgegeven doctoraatsverhandeling, 1998).

32 Marijke den Hollander, *Sport in 't stad: Sociaal-historische analyse van de sport in Antwerpen 1830–1914* (Leuven, 2002).

33 Marijke den Hollander, 'Sport in't stad', *Sportimonium* 2 (2002), 21–31.

34 Ronald Renson, *De herboren Spelen: De VIIe Olympiade Antwerpen 1920* (n.p., 1995).

35 Paul Arnoldussen, *Amsterdam 1928: Het verhaal van de IXe Olympiade* (Amsterdam: Thomas Rap, 1994).

36 Bert Moeyaert, *Van Wielerbaan tot … Velodroom: De geschiedenis van het baanwielrennen in België van 1890 tot 2003* (Leuven, 2003).

37 *Sportimonium: Verderzetting Nieuwsbrief van de Vlaamse Volkssportcentrale*; www.sportimonium.be.

38 *De Sportwereld: Magazine voor geschiedenis en achtergronden van de sport*; www.desportwereld.nl.

39 Wilfred van Buren (mmv Peter Los and Nico van Horn), *Bibliografisch apparaat voor de Nederlandse sportgeschiedenis* (Nieuwegein: Arko Sports Media /Stichting de Sportwereld, 2006).

21 Canada

Amanda N. Schweinbenz

Introduction

Sport is an important part of life for many Canadian men and women. It can evoke emotions of passion, excitement, invigorate the imagination in incredible ways, and can promote unity, nationalism and competitiveness.[1] Frank G. Menke indicates that '[n]o country in the world is more devoted to sports than Canada'.[2] Canadians play for fun, fantasy, excitement and even for exercise: 'Play allows us to be totally frivolous about important things in our work-centred lives or to be completely serious about things that are trivial'.[3] As individuals and as a collective nation, we revel in the success of Canadian teams and athletes at international competitions and celebrate these successes as if they are intricate parts of our lives. Many Canadians over the age of 40 can remember the exact moment Paul Henderson scored the winning goal that secured victory over the Soviet Union for Team Canada in the 1972 Summit Series, or for those a little younger, the day that hockey legend Wayne Gretzky was traded to an American team or when he announced his retirement. Many remember celebrating Donovan Bailey's gold medal performances at the 1996 Olympic Games in Atlanta and Mike Weir's final shot when he won the 2003 Masters. Undoubtedly, Canadians remember watching and celebrating the gold medal performances of both the men's and women's Olympic hockey teams at the 2002 Olympic Winter Games in Salt Lake City:

> It is impossible to account for the whereabouts of every Canadian yesterday afternoon, but it is safe to assume one thing: If there wasn't a television in the room, chances are nobody was there … cities in the rest of the country were downright spooky. Busy streets and typically bustling shopping malls looked like ghost towns as people spent the afternoon inside and in front of the TV. However, when the final seconds ticked away and Canada won the gold medal, joyous fans streamed down bustling Yonge Street in downtown Toronto, many draped in flags and clad in red and white. Some leaned precariously out of car windows as they leaned on their car horns. One fan was seen sprinting down the street, clad in nothing but a Canadian flag. 'It's the greatest thing I've ever seen in my life', said Sue Murray from Flin Flon, Man. 'I'm a happy, happy person today. I cried. We all cried. Fifty years without a gold medal. We deserve it'. 'That was better than losing my virginity!' screamed one fan in the frenzied moments after Canada won gold.[4]

These examples attest to the important place sport occupies in Canadian society. While sport and sport participation can unite people and evoke feelings of cohesion, it can also clearly provide indications of contradiction and divisions. As a social activity, sport is instructive, explaining how people interact with one another, men to men, women to men, and women to women through gendered and class-influenced discourses. Through an understanding of the social restrictions placed upon the body and its involvement in sport and play, we gain insight into the accepted discourses of society. For example, Victorian notions of female frailty rendered middle-class women incapable of participation in physical activity. Women were encouraged to be passive and supportive spectators of men's sport, all the while preserving their vital energy for matrimony and motherhood. Conversely, middle-class men were encouraged to participate in vigorous sport and physical activity that promoted and developed masculinity. Sport has and continues to reinforce and/or celebrate discourses of masculinity and femininity. An understanding of these discourses provides some of the tools necessary to understand society more broadly. Throughout the history of Canadian sport, men and women have adhered to particular codes of masculinity and femininity, which have differed according to social class, ethnicity and religion; sport participation has been designed to specifically and intentionally distinguish between men and women in a way that is meaningful and instructive for us as historians.[5]

Despite the cultural importance of sport, historians have often neglected examining it and its relevance to society.[6] Historical works have traditionally considered wars, government, religion and trade, however:

> The historian … is apt to forget that sport in some form or other is the main object of most lives, that most men work in order to play, and that games which bulk so largely in the life of the individual cannot be neglected in studying the life of the nation.[7]

It was not until recently that sports history was added to academia. Sport and physical activity were originally considered insignificant areas of study, however, since the 1960s, historians and sociologists have come to realize that forms of popular culture can be utilized to examine and understand society. Academics have thus looked to previously perceived un-intellectual or irrelevant forms of popular culture, including mass media, film and sport, to interpret and understand the development of society. As Bruce Kidd argues, '[i]t is impossible to describe modern life accurately without some account of sports'.[8] Thus, through the examination of sport, one can identify that sport involvement is structured in ways that privilege certain people and '[o]ne of the most impacting of these structuring mechanisms is gender'.[9]

Arguably sports history has traditionally been gendered as the majority of academic research has focused on masculinity and men's history. Traditional historiography has largely excluded women from the 'universal' history in which men have documented the history of participation in sport. With the rise of gender as a category of analysis in the humanities and social sciences, feminist sports historians sought to include gender as a broad and powerful category for analysis of sport for both women and men. Over the past few decades, research on the gendered nature of sport represents one of the fastest growing areas of sport studies and Canadian academics have played an important role in the emergence of this scholarship. This is not to negate the emergence of other areas of focus such as region, space and place, other forms of identity, and the impact of globalization and continentalization on Canadian sport, all of which have been appearing in recent scholarship, however, gender has emerged as a central organizing theme in Canadian sports history.[10]

Within the feminist paradigm, gender is considered a key dimension of overall identity and a determinant of behaviour. Gender stereotypes are scrutinized and their influences on socialization are evaluated. The ties between sex inequality and other institutional processes are diligently studied. Sex-based status differences and patriarchal values are discerned and described, and their significance for social control and culture maintenance is explored. Feminism is yielding new interpretations of social history and of the nature of social scientific knowledge itself. Sport, among the most masculine of social institutions, has not been immune to these sorts of feminist challenges. This chapter examines the literature related to Canadian sport with particular emphasis on the examination of gender as a central theme in the analysis of Canadian sport throughout history, though there is so much new work appearing all the time that it is impossible to claim to be all-inclusive.

The early beginnings of Canadian sports history

The growing interest in the examination of the history of sport in Canada parallels the study of sport in other Western societies. Like many others eager to document the history of sport and sport participation, early Canadian sports historians largely documented the chronological development of specific sports, teams, leagues, as well as detailed biographies of famous sports personalities from the past. These documents provided considerable insight into the specific 'facts' of sport, including changes in rules or styles of play, or the history of leagues, teams, clubs and individuals.

The earliest forms of Canadian sports history came from three primary sources: *From Rattlesnake Hunt to Hockey: The Story of Sports and Sportsmen of the County of Peel*, 'A History of Sports and Games in Eastern Canada Prior to World War I', and a number of historical books published by journalist Henry Roxborough. *From Rattlesnake Hunt to Hockey*, published in 1934 by self-proclaimed sports enthusiast William Perkins Bull, chronicles the history of sport in the county of Peel, now a part of the Greater Toronto area. Perkins Bull outlined the importance of sport and play in the development of this small community between 1798 and 1934.[11] Some 17 years later, Steward Davidson, an American, produced the first academic dissertation related to Canadian sports history entitled, 'A History of Sports and Games in Eastern Canada Prior to World War I'.[12] While these previous documents marked significant developments in the documentation of Canada's sporting history, it was Roxborough who provided material accessible to the masses. During the late 1950s and through the 1960s, Roxborough contributed four detailed Canadian sports history chronicles: *Great Days in Canadian Sport*; *Canada at the Olympics*; *The Stanley Cup Story*; and *One Hundred – Not Out – The Story of Nineteenth Century Canadian Sport*.[13] In these four texts, Roxborough presented the origins and growth of sport in the nation and recounted major accomplishments of Canada's sporting history. Roxborough is among the most notable journalists who penned books on Canadian sport, others, including W.A. Hewitt, Scott Young, Eric Whitehead, Brian McFarlane and William Houston, also contributed to the documentation of the nation's sporting history, primarily related to the game of (ice) hockey.[14]

These authors contributed by documenting the history of specific sports, primarily hockey and sport participation in local areas, and provide interesting anecdotes for readers. However, their texts are also limited. Few of the documents have specific references, which makes it difficult to verify any statements of fact made by the authors, an issue many historical texts on popular culture share. As such, readers cannot be certain as to the sources and reliability of the data described. Furthermore, these descriptive chronologies give little insight into the broader relationship between sport and Canadian society as sport is disassociated from Canadian culture. For example, these works predominantly describe the history of middle-class, white men's participation in sport without acknowledging issues of race, class and gender; women are conspicuously absent from these histories. The history of sport in Canada, according to these authors, followed a 'modernization' framework, which presented what has occurred in Canadian sport as desirable and inevitable. As such, the teams, clubs, leagues and people who did not conform to the pattern of modernization are marginalized. Their history is perceived as a failure for not adapting with the development of sport across the nation.

It is not surprising that these sports writers did not acknowledge the importance of sport in wider society. Sport was simply perceived as an opportunity to be physically active or serve as a social release valve, not a reproduction or construction of social norms or gender relations. Even former International Olympic Committee President Avery Brundage vehemently believed that sport was a separate entity unaffected by politics. This naïve argument that sport is separate from issues of race, class, gender, religion, or politics avoided any form of critical analysis. Emphasis was placed on documentation rather than analysis. What mattered was who won and who lost and what each player scored in particular games. Any debate that emerged was limited to comparisons between teams and players rather than in-depth social or political debate. Although void of critical examination, these early chronicles marked an important beginning in the writing of Canadian sports history.

While it was early sports journalists and sports writers who initiated the documentation of sports history, the breadth of scholarly work on Canadian sport and Canadian sports history has been largely written in university faculties of physical education, kinesiology and human kinetics. What is interesting is that many of those who are considered to be the founders or pioneers of Canadian sports history were not native Canadians. Canadian sports history scholarship was initiated primarily by Australian-born Maxwell Howell and his colleagues and graduate students at the University of Alberta during the 1960s. Like many of the sports writers before them, the work produced by the 'Alberta school' compiled detailed chronologies of Canadian sports histories, or what Howell referred to as 'first order studies'.[15] Howell's intent was to 'compile, sport by sport and era by era, a Canadian history of sport'.[16] Methodologically, the 'Alberta school' drew heavily on primary data collected from newspapers, through which they documented the major developments of a number of sports and institutions across the country. Arguably, one of Howell's most significant contributions to Canadian sports history is *Sports and Games in Canadian Life: 1700 to the Present*. Written in collaboration with his then wife Nancy, *Sports and Games in Canadian Life* is a general survey of the nation's sporting history. Howell and Howell noted that the book was not a complete history of one sport, or even one region of Canada, rather it was an attempt to tell how sports and games have related to Canadian life.[17] In the introduction, the authors articulated that they had hoped that their book would 'stimulate detailed and definitive studies of various periods and of specific sports and games'.[18]

Following in their mentor's footsteps, graduate students from the University of Alberta wrote extensive histories of sport, games and physical activity. Among those who were part of Canada's initial academic sports history work were: Frank Cosentino, Keith Langsley and Don Morrow. Cosentino recorded the development of Canadian football during the 20th century; Langsley chronicled the changing definitions of amateur eligibility in the Amateur Athletic Union of Canada; and Morrow documented the history of Canada's first athletic federation the Montreal Amateur Athletic Association.[19] These graduate students documented aspects of sport that had largely been forgotten and have provided important references – names, dates, rule changes and sources – that are still utilized by scholars today.

While the research produced by the 'Alberta school' has provided an important entry point into academic documentation of Canada's sporting histories, this research also largely ignored themes such as class, gender and ethnicity, and suggested that sport was an egalitarian pastime. Ann Hall, a former graduate student of Howell, has suggested that '[w]e were all amateur historians in those days, coming to our subject with little previous training in historiography, but with a consuming passion for sport, mostly because we were athletes or physical educators or both'.[20] The early sports historians who emerged from the 'Alberta school' suggest that everyone everywhere played sport together on equal grounds. These initial reconstructionist histories sought to resolve historical issues and tell the 'truth' about history through the objective investigation of unique events. Reconstructionist history, as Douglas Booth has argued, is evidence based, non-philosophical and non-theoretical.[21] These researchers intend to discover the past as it actually happened, where facts precede interpretation because history occurs independently of the historian. Those who were part of the 'Alberta school' produced histories that followed a trademark formula that Kidd has argued begin with:

> ... a description of the 'social background' of the relevant period, then proceed to discuss sporting developments with scarcely a mention of those circumstances, let alone an analysis of how they might have influenced or been influenced by what happened in sports.[22]

Sport was depicted as a linear evolution towards its contemporary form that was influenced solely by industrialization and urbanization; however, these influences were not examined in depth. Relationships of power were pushed aside or overlooked despite the obvious importance they have had in Canadian sport throughout history. As in all areas of social life, power relations and social struggles have played a key role in the development of the meaning, organization and practices of sport and others were interested to examine and articulate these relationships.[23]

While the initial academic documentation of Canadian sports history was primarily chronologies, this began to change during the 1970s. Scholarly developments in universities promoted critical examination of sport and faculties of physical education began to change the focus of study from teaching and leadership to theoretical knowledge. While physical and biological sciences were widely accepted as logical additions to the curriculum, many departments also began to offer courses in the social sciences. These courses provided students with a 'less idealistic, more sociological understanding of sports'.[24] Scholars were forced to reconsider the place of sport within society and 'the extent to which they were "socially specific" or "socially constructed"'.[25]

This field of academic interest expanded across Canada and scholars began to examine sport and associated themes such as nationalism, colonialism, race, ethnicity, the body and gender. Theory developed as an important part of the critical analysis of Canadian sport. Among the first to use theory, or even some system of analysis to examine Canadian sports history, were Alan Metcalfe, one of the 'Alberta school's' most vocal critics, and Jean Duperreault.[26] Their objective was to move beyond the status quo of research which documented 'one damn fact after another' and challenge the notions of the 'democracy of sport'.[27] These scholars intended to write thematic-descriptive history rather than descriptive-narrative. They stressed the need for 'high quality, credible evidence and that the road to this type of historical evidence is sign posted with terms such as "objectivity", "subjectivity", "bias", "probability", "plausibility" and "error"'.[28] They formulated questions of sports relationships to social control and hegemony soon arose: 'Did sports serve to enhance class and gender power, either by excluding others from participation or by incorporating them in ways which would keep them at a disadvantage?'[29] They analysed these questions based on relevant theoretical frameworks. These scholars added to previous chronological research and all have 'challenged the notions of the "democracy of sport" and the social autonomy of sporting development'.[30] They have shown that sport in Canada is complex, stratified, affected by economic and social structures, and often contradictory.

In his earliest work, Metcalfe showed that sport in Canada was highly stratified during its formative years of the late 19th century. Metcalfe has examined the social and ideological roots of the leaders of and participants in sport in Montréal during the late 19th century and has shown that they were largely upper middle-class British men who drew upon their managerial and commercial backgrounds to create sporting clubs, their constitutions, leagues and schedules.[31] Furthermore, the leadership of recreational sports clubs during the 19th century was limited to the professional, commercial and military elite in the urban community who focused on social rather than competitive sport.[32] These men were able to define who was permitted to participate and on what terms. As such, definitions of amateurism were of vital importance. Sporting leaders were eager to separate themselves and their fellow club members from the working-class 'professionals'. The distinction between amateur and professional athletes was in a large part an attempt to exclude working-class participants. Those with money did not wish to participate alongside or even against working-class participants, because they were considered to be socially inferior and they did not want to lose to anyone who was inferior. While there were instances in which private clubs hosted 'open' events and contact between social classes in athletic contests symbolized the 'equalization' of participants, class distinctions were implicitly recognized by the provision of trophies for 'gentlemen' and cash prizes for others, following closely the traditions being established in British sport.

Following Metcalfe's lead, class relationships became an important part of sport studies. Beyond the work of sports historians, sport sociologists have contributed considerably to the breadth of knowledge of sport in Canada and Richard Gruneau has undoubtedly played a key role in the historiography of Canadian sport. Considered by many a master Marxist scholar, Gruneau's early work primarily examined the role of class divisions and class conflict in shaping institutional and cultural arrangements.[33] He focused on class relationships to argue that 'the whole issue of opportunities for *participation* is much less important than the question of opportunities for *control*'.[34] Jay Coakley and Peter Donnelly have suggested that 'money and power fund and promote sport forms that fit their own interests and foster ideas supportive of economic arrangements that work to their advantage'.[35] Referencing Pierre Bourdieu, Donnelly and Jean Harvey argue that 'different sports mean different things to individuals according to their social class background'.[36] Yet, these definitions of amateur and professional omitted any mention of women, thus providing an indication that their participation was irrelevant. The absence of women from the analysis of these histories marginalizes their sporting experiences and overlooks the obvious gender implications of their absence.

Within sport studies, a multidisciplinary approach had been initiated and by the 1970s relationships between sport and racism, class inequality, nationalism, violence, drug use and other social issues were central to analysis; however, the relationship of gender and sport had yet to be fully developed. Academics had somehow overlooked or ignored the fact that throughout history sport has largely been an 'exclusive arena of *male* experience and *male* relations'.[37] Sport in contemporary Western culture has been viewed as a 'masculinizing project', a cultural activity in which boys develop into men and form bonds of masculine solidarity. It appeared 'natural' that women were absent from the investigation of sport because the majority of available data documented men's participation. Yet this omission of women from scholarly research provided clear evidence that sport was a male activity, not a female one. As Michael Messner and Donald Sabo have indicated, '[t]his blind sport concerning the fundamental relationship between sport and the social construction of gender resulted in a very incomplete – sometimes distorted – analysis of the historical and contemporary importance and meaning of sport'.[38] Some male scholars began to include gender in their analysis, notably Bruce Kidd. His use of a Gramscian application of hegemony in his extensive examination of Canadian sports history, in *The Struggle for Canadian Sport*, does acknowledge the presence of gendered power structures that impacted women's sport participation. Yet Kidd's work is only a glimpse into the gendered nature of sport and it has been other feminist scholars who have taken upon the task of a more extensive analysis.[39]

The gendered nature of Canadian sport and physical activity

As a consequence of the groundwork laid by leading feminist historians, feminists in academia began to critique sport 'as a fundamentally sexist institution that is male dominated and masculine in orientation' and part of the fundamental dividing line between groups of people in society.[40] In one of the most extensive texts specifically directed at documenting the history of Canadian women's involvement in sport and physical activity, M. Ann Hall indicated that:

> The history of modern sport is a history of cultural struggle. Privileged groups in our society – seemingly by consent – are able to establish their own cultural practices as the most valued and legitimate, whereas subordinate groups (like women) have to fight to gain and maintain control over their own experience and at the same time have their alternative practices and activities recognized as legitimate by the dominant culture.[41]

Female athletes have always struggled to prove their value and legitimacy in an arena that has been built and controlled by men.

Nancy Struna, one of the first North Americans to examine women's sports history, questioned the restrictive assumption that contemporary sport could be uncritically characterized as male.[42] Feminist scholars argued that Canadian sport has been, and remains, an area dominated by heterosexual males and as such, the way in which sport is experienced by boys and girls, women and men, straight and gays has been vastly different. Hidden histories of female athleticism were uncovered and through the examination of sex differences in patterns of athletic socialization, feminists demonstrated how the dominant institutional forms of sport have naturalized men's power and privilege over women.[43] Scholars demonstrated that the marginalization and trivialization of female athletes reproduced 'the structural and ideological domination of women by men'.[44]

A 'deeper analysis of the ways in which sport has historically perpetuated male dominance and female oppression' was called for by many feminist scholars, including Helen Lenskyj.[45] Lenskyj was among the first to examine the power relationships that have constructed women's participation in sport and physical activity and how men have claimed control over women's bodies. Central to her analysis of the study of women and sport in Canada since the late 19th century is the 'political institution of compulsory heterosexuality'.[46] In the introduction to *Out of Bounds: Women, Sport and Sexuality*, Lenskyj indicates:

> It is to be hoped that by understanding women's sporting heritage and by becoming alert to the ways in which sport has been, and continues to be, co-opted for the purpose of male control over female sexuality and the female reproductive function, women will be strengthened in the struggle for autonomy in sport.[47]

Lenskyj argued that it is the long-standing hegemonic control that men have claimed over women's bodies that has impacted and often prevented female participation in sport and physical activity throughout history. She poignantly discussed the dominating influence of the medical establishment, the media, modern psychiatry and psychology upon women's bodies and thus their sporting lives.

In his portrait of Canadian ice-skating icon Barbara Ann Scott, Don Morrow, moving beyond his 'Alberta School' roots, indicated that the media has historically focused on the physical appearance and heterosexuality of female athletes rather than their athletic abilities. Through the examination of *Time* magazine's descriptions of the 1948 Olympic women's figure skating champion, Morrow showed precisely how the media served as a vehicle to promote traditional heterosexual femininity at the expense of competitive athletic performance: 'She weighs a trim, girlish 107 pounds, neither as full-bosomed as a Hollywood starlet, nor as wide-hipped as most skaters. She looks, in fact, like a doll which is to be looked at but not touched'.[48]

Not surprisingly, this preoccupation with women's heterosexual feminine bodies was not new. Patricia Vertinsky has illustrated clearly how biological determinism reproduced gender divisions not only in sport, but in society more broadly, throughout North America as well as in Britain. In *The Eternally Wounded Woman: Women, Doctors and Exercise in the Late Nineteenth Century*, Vertinsky showed how the medical profession was instrumental in upholding Victorian stereotypes about women's health and exercise.[49]

Feminist historiography 'has disabused us of the notion that the history of women is the same as the history of men and that significant turning points in history have the same impact for one sex as for the other'.[50] Feminist historians have encouraged scholars to not simply add women to the dominant history, but rather rewrite history according to the major turning points affecting women, such as childbirth, sexuality and family structure.[51] While women's history is different from men's, the two are in fact relational, neither exists in isolation:

> When women are excluded from the benefits of economic, political and cultural advances made in certain periods, a situation which gives women a different historical experience from men, it is to those 'advances' we must look to find the reasons for the separation of the sexes.[52]

Feminist social research embarked upon the goal of telling better stories of gendered social realities that acknowledge women as knowers or agents of knowledge. Furthermore, the intent was also to address the absence of diversity in women's sports histories. Feminist sports historians came to realize that there was no universal woman, nor a singular 'woman's history'. Some sports historians have forged new understandings of the historical relationship between sport and the social construction of gender for women from different demographics than have previously been examined. Emphasis is laid on the histories of women and minority groups, the experiences of immigrants, homosexuals and people of colour.

Some of those who have been repeatedly overlooked include First Nations women. Like others, gender is embedded in sport participation for First Nations people. In 'Doing Race, Doing Gender: First Nations, "Sport", and Gender Relations', Victoria Paraschak argues that 'race embedded within gender relations, examines the reproduction of Native racial identity in gendered sport practices under Native control'. When Native athletes participate in Native sport, they (re)produce gender relations that are specific to their culture, and when Native athletes participate in non-Native sport, they encounter racism and sometimes adopt 'civilized' (non-Native) gendered practices.[53] Race, gender and class relations that exist are complex and extend beyond First Nations peoples. Yet these important histories are rarely told because they often highlight the inequalities that exist within Canadian society. While second-wave feminists negotiated to gain access to the playing fields that their fathers and brothers so enjoyed, other women are struggling to simply (re)gain their health.

Groundbreaking work has been conducted by Wendy Frisby, Colleen Reid and Pamela Ponic on physical inactivity and social isolation of a diverse group of low-income women including single mothers, older women, recent immigrant women and women with disabilities.[54] They have shown that Canadian social policies have done little to improve the gendered disparities of income and health issues that exist across the country. They have argued that municipal recreational department 'programming is delivered in a top-down fashion without substantial community input'.[55] As such, community-based organizations, including Women Organizing Activities for Women (WOAW), have been initiated to address the needs of low-income women to improve their sense of social isolation and overall health by involving community members in service delivery decisions. This has proved to be mutually beneficial for citizens and their communities, and has helped empower women living below the poverty line.[56]

Yet gendered historiography has broadened beyond solely examining women's sporting history and the way in which gendered discourses have influenced women's experiences. During the 1980s, the focus of women-centred investigations and analyses of sex roles in sport shifted to an examination of gender roles which involved both women and men. Previously documented traditional histories of events and processes were being revisited from a gender perspective. Vertinsky has noted that 'gender offered a good way of thinking about sport and sport history'.[57] Academics began to challenge accepted methodology, epistemology and historical writings, and argued that they were inextricably associated to gender relations and more specifically to discourses of masculinity and femininity. It was not only women that needed to be examined, but 'men and the construction of dominant masculinity/ies [that] had to be understood and explored'.[58] Gender was a system of power relationships in which masculinities and femininities were constructed, contested and continually changed. These masculinities and femininities became fundamental to the analysis of sport.

Sports historians also began to look at the reciprocal nature of gender and society and how this related to sport. While sport had been recognized as a predominantly male domain, it was also acknowledged as a gendered domain. Jim McKay, Michael Messner and Donald Sabo were among the first male scholars to utilize feminist analysis to highlight the gendered nature of Canadian men's sport and to lead a new and more comprehensive understanding of the traditional relationship between men and sport. It was recognized that sport legitimized and celebrated violence as a sign of true masculinity.

Varda Burstyn added to the breadth of literature with her exploration of the relationship between masculinism and capitalism and this relationship is 'practiced, modelled, and animated through the culture of sport'.[59] In *The Rites of Men: Manhood, Politics, and the Culture of Sport*, Burstyn approaches sport as a complex and powerful paradigm of 'hypermasculinity' in which destructive warrior ideology is promoted, unnecessary violence is celebrated, sexual and racial hierarchies are perpetuated, and capitalist and imperialist interests are supported. Her analysis begins with the late 19th-century development of sport in relation to the rise of industrial capitalism. Like many before, Burstyn highlights the importance of control over sport, typically held by white, middle-class men. However, Burstyn added that sport became an essential activity to reinforce masculinity in spite of the predominant feminine culture they were growing up in. With:

> ... the emerging urban classes in the domesticated nuclear middle- and working-class families of the nineteenth century, working fathers became absent figures ... Without a father and older brothers or uncles working at or near the domestic site, young boys were ... left with their mothers, sisters and nannies (if middle-class) until puberty.[60]

While this argument has been utilized by others, her significant contribution comes with the criticism of modern sport as constituting 'the unnamed masculinist movement', a mass movement she parallels to the post-Civil War feminist movement.[61]

Discourses about masculinity must also be examined with relation to homosexuality. The traditional discourses associated with appropriate femininity and masculinity in sport have been linked closely with heterosexuality. Heterosexuality is accepted and celebrated as the norm and those who differ are castigated. Brian Pronger has also stepped beyond the current literature on men, sport and masculinity, and examined these with relation to gay men. One of his objectives in *The Arena of Masculinity: Sports, Homosexuality, and the Meaning of Sex*, is to abolish the gender myths of what is considered masculine and/or feminine.[62] He has contended that gender is not culturally created and has argued that this can be readily proved by observing that what is deemed masculine and feminine varies from culture to culture. Masculinity and femininity are not singular concepts but rather, there are ranges of masculinities and femininities that are continually being constructed and challenged.

Others in Canada have also examined gender and its relationship to sport to expand on previously examined areas. For instance Patricia Vertinsky's recent work on the space and place of sport, 'drawing attention to the importance of context and social relations in analyzing places designed for sport and physical culture'.[63] Feminist scholars have argued that built landscapes have been designed to 'confine, control and exclude women' and thus, deliberately express stereotyped gender roles in their spatial arrangements.[64] The value and importance of a space, for example a gymnasium or hockey arena, can only be explained by examining the 'social relations subject to a variety of influences within the context of the time'.[65]

Given the nation's obsession with the sport of hockey and the Olympic Games, it is not surprising that both have been central in the analysis of the gendered nature of sport and Canadian culture. In *Hockey Night in Canada: Sport, Identities and Cultural Politics*, Richard Gruneau and David Whitson use Roland Barthes' definition of myths to explore the mythical unification of Canadian identity and the sport of hockey.[66] Hockey in Canada is accepted as quintessential Canadian-ness because of its history of class and cultural struggle. The romanticized myths of commonality, belonging and Canadian identity are often manipulated and contrived. The myth that ALL Canadian men play or watch hockey is only a partial truth that embodies fundamental cultural values that are deeply rooted in emotions and are marketed for financial gain. This mythology is further challenged in *Artificial Ice: Hockey, Culture, and Commerce* where the contributors examine the political economy of the sport as well as the racial and gendered nature of hockey.[67] It is also acknowledged that the celebration of this contact sport as a bastion of hegemonic masculinity is challenged with the increasing participation of women in hockey.[68] Historically 'the association of girls and women with the game tended to be defined only through the participation of the men in their lives', however, this has drastically changed over the last two decades especially with the success of the Canadian women's Olympic hockey teams.[69] However, Julie Stevens maintains that the additional opportunities that have come about for female hockey players has signalled women's acceptance of the game as designed by men, rather than challenging the established norms.[70]

Some of the recent scholarly research on the Olympic Games has addressed this very issue. Kevin B. Wamsley has been central in the critical examination of the Olympic Movement and its gender inequalities in the addition and removal of events for women to the Olympic programme.[71] He has argued that in many instances female sport administrators have traded control over sport to gain access to the Olympic Games. This has resulted in men defining women's participation levels according to traditionally accepted heterosexual norms of femininity. Wamsley and the graduate students of The International Centre for Olympic Studies at The University of Western Ontario have repeatedly argued that the Olympic Movement has maintained its racist, sexist and class-based structure since its inception in 1894.[72] They have also challenged the legitimacy of hosting the Olympic Games as Vancouver is embarking upon this multi-billion dollar two-week sporting extravaganza.[73] The attempt by the Vancouver Organizing Committee to highlight Canadian culture has led to working relationships with First Nations People. Yet, historically this embracing of Aboriginal heritage can be interpreted as overtly racist. As Janice Forsyth has noted in 'Teepees and Tomahawks: Aboriginal Cultural Representation at the 1976 Olympic Games', organizers of the Montreal Olympic Games in 1976 painted Caucasian dancers as Indians to dance in the closing ceremonies.[74]

Conclusion

The history of both women's and men's sports in Canada is still fragmented. Scholars have traditionally documented the history of certain sports, for example ice-hockey, involving certain individuals, mostly middle-class, white men. However, the burgeoning scholarship in sports history and gender relations aims at much more than simply writing women into sports history. It seeks to forge new understandings of the historical relationship between sport and the social construction of gender by examining gender as a dynamic, relational process through which unequal power relations between women and men have been continually constructed and contested. The inclusion within sports history of a focus upon gender has pressed an increasing number of sports historians to pay attention to a much wider and deeper version of the history of sport and physical activity.

The challenge has thus become to acknowledge diversity and 'look at sport and gender issues in terms of the lives of different types of Canadians'.[75] One cannot simply argue that there is one history of sport for all Canadians. Rather, the relationships of gender and sport differ among Anglophones, Francophones, those from different regions, religions, ethnicities, sexual orientations and social classes. The meanings and identities associated with sport are multifaceted and they are constantly being constructed and contested. As sports historians we must acknowledge the ever changing nature of sport and recognize that our analysis, while based on theory, is only one analysis.

Finally, sports historians have also cautioned that the focus of gender can also obscure, marginalize, or even erase women from history.[76] Since the history of sport could be said to be centrally a history of masculinity, this focus on gender could ignore women completely. Additionally, while the attention to theories of gender have offered important ways to examine sport and its power relationships throughout history, it also threatens to alienate women of colour, ethnicity, working women, aging women and those with disabilities. The stories of these women have been hidden from sports historiography and they are the people whose voices must be heard.

Notes

1 Don Morrow and Kevin B. Wamsley, *Sport in Canada: A History* (Don Mills, ON: Oxford University Press, 2005), 1.
2 Frank G. Menke, *The New Encyclopedia of Sports* (New York: A. S. Barnes, 1947), 314.
3 Richard Gruneau, *Class, Sports, and Social Development* (Champaign, IL: Human Kinetics 1999), 2.
4 James McCarton, 'A Coast-to-coast Celebration: Canada Comes Together to Share in Olympic Hockey Triumph', www.canada.com/sports/olympics/news/story.html (found in Morrow and Wamsley, 200, accessed 10 December 2008).
5 Morrow and Wamsley, *Sport in Canada*.
6 Bruce Kidd, 'Improvers, Feminists, Capitalists and Socialists: Shaping Canadian Sport in the 1920s and 1930s', unpublished PhD thesis, York University 1990, 10.
7 A. Lunn, *A History of Skiing* (London: Oxford University Press, 1927), 3, found in Nancy Howell and Max Howell, *Sports and Games in Canadian Life: 1700 to Present* (Toronto: Macmillan of Canada, 1969).
8 Bruce Kidd, *The Struggle for Canadian Sport* (Toronto: University of Toronto Press, 1996), 5.
9 Kevin Young and Philip White, 'Preface', *Sport and Gender in Canada* (Don Mills, ON: Oxford University Press, 2007), xiv.
10 See for example the work of Colin Howell, *Northern Sandlots: A Social History of Maritime Baseball* (Toronto: University of Toronto Press, 1995); *Blood, Sweat, and Cheers: Sport and the Making of Modern Canada* (Toronto: University of Toronto Press, 2001); and Chapter 8 in this volume. Several historians, sociologists and sports marketing scholars have examined the loss of Canadian professional sports teams and the impacts they have had on local and regional communities and identities; for example, see Richard Gruneau and David Whitson, *Hockey Night in Canada: Sport, Identities and Cultural Politics* (Toronto: Garamond, 1993); David Whitson and Richard Gruneau, eds, *Artificial Ice: Hockey, Culture, and Commerce* (Toronto: Garamond, 2006); Philip White, Peter Donnelly and John Nauright, 'Citizens, cities and sports teams', *Policy Options*, 18, 3 (1997), 9–12; reprinted in Peter Donnelly, ed., *Taking Sport Seriously: Social Issues in Canadian Sport*, 2nd edn (Toronto: Thompson Educational Publishing, 2000); John Nauright and Philip White, 'Professional Sport, Nostalgia, Community and Nation in Canada', *AVANTE*, 2, 4 (1996), 24–41; Jim Silver, *Thin Ice: Money, Politics, and the Demise of an NHL Franchise* (Halifax: Fernwood Press, 1996). Most of these authors discuss the significance of gender in modern Canadian sports history, but it is not the principal organizing theme of their work.
11 William Perkins Bull, *From Rattlesnake Hunt to Hockey: The Story of Sports and Sportsmen of the County of Peel* (Toronto: George J. McLeod Ltd, 1934).

12 S.A. Davidson, 'A History of Sports and Games in Eastern Canada Prior to World War I', unpublished EdD dissertation, Columbia University, 1951.

13 H.H. Roxborough, *Great Days in Canadian Sport* (Toronto: The Ryerson Press, 1957); *Canada at the Olympics* (Toronto: The Ryerson Press, 1963); *The Stanley Cup Story* (Toronto: The Ryerson Press, 1964); *One Hundred – Not Out: The Story of Nineteenth Century Canadian Sport* (Toronto: The Ryerson Press, 1966).

14 W.A. Hewitt, *Down the Stretch: Recollections of a Pioneer Sportsman and Journalist* (Toronto: The Ryerson Press, 1958); Scott Young, *War on Ice: Canada in International Hockey* (Toronto: McClelland and Stewart 1976) and *Hello Canada: The Life and Times of Foster Hewitt* (Toronto: McClelland and Stewart-Bantam, 1985); Eric Whitehead, *Cyclone Taylor: A Hockey Legend* (Toronto: Doubleday Canada, 1977), and *The Patricks: Hockey's Royal Family* (Toronto: Formac Publishing 1983); Brian McFarlane, *Fifty Years of Hockey 1917–1967: A History of the National Hockey League* (Toronto: Pagurian Press, 1967); William Houston, *Inside Maple Leaf Gardens: The Rise and Fall of the Toronto Maple Leafs* (Toronto: McGraw-Hill Ryerson, 1989) and *Maple Leaf Blues: Harold Ballard and the Life and Times of the Maple Leafs* (Toronto: McClelland & Stewart, 1990).

15 Kidd, *The Struggle for Canadian Sport*, 9.

16 M. Ann Hall, *The Girl and the Game: A History of Women's Sport in Canada* (Peterborough, ON: Broadview Press, 2002), ix.

17 Nancy Howell and Max Howell, *Sports and Games in Canadian Life: 1700 to Present* (Toronto: Macmillan of Canada, 1969).

18 Ibid., 1.

19 Frank Cosentino, *Canadian Football* (Toronto: Musson, 1969); Keith Langsley, 'The Amateur Athletic Union of Canada and Changing Concepts of Amateurism', unpublished PhD thesis, University of Alberta, 1971; Don Morrow, *A Sporting Evolution* (Montreal: MAAA, 1982).

20 Hall, *The Girl and the Game*, ix.

21 Murray Phillips, 'Introduction', in *Deconstruction Sport History: A Postmodern Analysis* (New York: State University of New York Press, 2005), 3. Also see Douglas Booth, *The Field: Truth and Fiction in Sport History* (London: Routledge, 2005).

22 Bruce Kidd, 'Improvers, Feminists, Capitalists and Socialists', 33.

23 Jean Harvey and Hart Cantelon, 'Part One: The Historical Determinants of Contemporary Sport', in Jean Harvey and Hart Cantelon, eds, *Not Just a Game: Essays in Canadian Sport Sociology* (Ottawa: University of Ottawa Press, 1988), 5–8.

24 Kidd, 'Improvers, Feminist, Capitalists and Socialists', 13.

25 Ibid., 23.

26 Don Morrow, 'Canadian Sport History: A Critical Essay', *Journal of Sport History*, 10, 1 (Spring 1983), 71.

27 Ibid., 71.

28 Robert Day and Peter Lindsay, eds, *Sport History: Research Methodology* (Calgary: University of Alberta, 1980), 189.

29 Kidd, 'Improvers, Feminists, Capitalists and Socialists', 35.

30 Kidd, *The Struggle for Canadian Sport*, 10.

31 Alan Metcalfe, 'Organized Sport and Social Stratification in Montreal 1840–1901', in Richard Gruneau and John Albison, eds, *Canadian Sport Sociological Perspectives* (Don Mills, ON: Addison-Wesley, 1976), 77–101.

32 Ibid.

33 Allen Guttmann, 'Review, *Class, Sports, and Social Development*', *Journal of Sport History*, 11, 1 (Spring 1984), 97–99.

34 Richard Gruneau, *Class, Sports, and Social Development* (Champaign, IL: Human Kinetics, 1993), 129.

35 Jay Coakley and Peter Donnelly, *Sports in Society: Issues and Controversies*, 1st Canadian edn (Toronto: McGraw-Hill Ryerson, 2004), 322.

36 Peter Donnelly and Jean Harvey, 'Class and Gender: Intersections in Sport and Physical Activity', in Kevin Young and Philop White, eds, *Sport and Gender in Canada*, 2nd edn (Don Mills, ON: Oxford University Press, 2007), 102.

37 Michael Messner and Donald Sabo, 'Preface', in Messner and Sabo, eds, *Sport, Men, and the Gender Order: Critical Feminist Perspectives* (Champaign, IL: Human Kinetics, 1990), v.

38 Ibid.

39 Bruce Kidd, *The Struggle for Canadian Sport* (Toronto: University of Toronto Press, 1996).

40 Nancy Theberge, 'A Critique of Critiques: Radical and Feminist Writings on Sport', *Social Forces* 60, 2 (1981), 342.

41 M. Ann Hall, *The Girl and the Game: A History of Women's Sport in Canada* (Peterborough, ON: Broadview Press, 2002), 1.

42 Nancy Struna, 'Beyond Mapping Experience: The Need for Understanding the History of American Sporting Women', *Journal of Sport History*, 11, 1 (1984), 120–33.

43 Messner and Sabo, 'Toward a Critical Feminist Reappraisal of Sport, Men, and the Gender Order', in *Sport, Men, and the Gender Order*, 2.

44 Ibid.

45 Patricia Vertinsky, 'Gender Relations, Women's History and Sport History: A Decade of Changing Enquiry, 1983–93', *Journal of Sport History*, 12, 1 (Spring 1994), 10.

46 Helen Lenskyj, *Out of Bounds: Women, Sport and Sexuality* (Toronto: Women's Press, 1986), 14.

47 Ibid.

48 Don Morrow, 'Sweetheart Sport: Barbara Ann Scott and the Post World War II Image of the Female Athlete in Canada,' *Canadian Journal of History of Sport*, 18, 1 (1987), 78.

49 Patricia Vertinsky, *The Eternally Wounded Woman: Women, Doctors and Exercise in the Late Nineteenth Century* (Manchester: Manchester University Press, 1987).

50 Joan Kelly-Gadol, 'The Social Relation of the Sexes: Methodological Implications of Women's History', *Journal of Women in Culture and Society*, 1, 4 (1976), 812.

51 Ibid.

52 Ibid., 813.

53 Victoria Paraschak, 'Doing Race, Doing Gender: First Nations, "Sport", and Gender Relations', in Kevin Young and Philip White, eds, *Sport and Gender in Canada* (Don Mills, ON: Oxford University Press, 2007), 149.

54 Wendy Frisby, Colleen Reid and Pamela Ponic, 'Levelling the Playing Field: Promoting the Health of Poor Women Through a Community Development Approach to Recreation', in *Sport and Gender in Canada*, 121.

55 Pamela Ponic and Wendy Frisby, 'Feminist Organizing as Community Development: A Strategy for Delivering Accessible Recreation to Women Living in Poverty', paper presented at the 11th Canadian Congress on Leisure Research, Malaspina University-College, Nanaimo, BC, 2005.

56 Wendy Frisby and Larena Hoeber, 'Factors Affecting the Uptake of Community Recreation for Women on Low Incomes', *Canadian Journal of Public Health* 93, 2 (March–April 2002), 129–33.

57 Patricia Vertinsky, 'Time Gentlemen Please: The Space and Place of Gender in Sport History', in Murray G. Phillips, ed., *Deconstructing Sport History: A Postmodern Analysis* (Albany: State University of New York Press, 2005), 232.

58 Ibid.

59 Varda Burstyn, *The Rites of Men: Manhood, Politics, and the Culture of Sport* (Toronto: University of Toronto Press, 1999), 4.

60 Ibid., 51.

61 Ibid., 59.

62 Brian Pronger, *The Arena of Masculinity: Sports, Homosexuality and the Meaning of Sex* (New York: St. Martin's Press, 1990).

63 John Bale and Patricia Vertinsky, 'Introduction', in Patricia Vertinsky and John Bale, eds, *Sites of Sport: Space, Place, Experience* (London: Routledge, 2004), 2.

64 Ibid., 2.

65 Patricia Vertinsky, 'Locating a "Sense of Place": Space, Place and Gender in the Gymnasium', in *Sites of Sport*, 9.

66 Richard Gruneau and David Whitson, *Hockey Night in Canada: Sport, Identities and Cultural Politics* (Toronto: Garamond Press, 1993).

67 David Whitson and Richard Gruneau, eds, *Artificial Ice: Hockey, Culture, and Commerce* (Toronto: Broadview/Garamond Press, 2006).

68 David Whitson, 'The Embodiment of Gender: Discipline, Domination, and Empowerment', in Susan Birrell and Candice Cole, eds, *Women, Sport, and Culture* (Champaign, IL: Human Kinetics, 1994).

69 Whitson and Gruneau, 2.

70 Julie Stevens, 'Women's Hockey in Canada: After the "Gold Rush"', in *Artificial Ice*, 85–100.

71 Kevin B. Wamsley and Guy Schultz, 'Rouges and Bedfellows: The IOC and the Incorporation of the FSFI', in Robert Barney, Kevin Wamsley, Scott Martyn and Gordon MacDonald, eds, *Bridging*

Three Centuries: Intellectual Crossroads and the Modern Olympic Movement (London, ON: The University of Western Ontario, International Centre for Olympic Studies, September 2000), 113–18.

72 See Christine M. O'Bonsawin, 'The Conundrum of "Ilanaaq" – First Nations Representation and the 2010 Vancouver Winter Olympics', in Nigel B. Crowther, Robert K. Barney and Michael K. Heine, eds, *Cultural Imperialism in Action Critiques in the Global Olympic Trust: Eighth International Symposium for Olympic Research* (London, ON: The University of Western Ontario, International Centre for Olympic Studies, October 2006), 287–94; Gordon MacDonald, 'Going Downhill: Relations between the IOC and Fédération Internationale de Ski in the late 1930s', in *Bridging Three Centuries*, 105–12; and Carly Adams, 'Fighting for Acceptance: Sigfrid Estrom and Avery Brundidge: Their Efforts to Shape and Control Women's Participation in the Olympic Games', in Kevin B. Walmsey, Robert K. Barney and Scott G. Martyn, eds, *The Global Nexus Engaged: Past, Present, Future Interdisciplinary Olympic Studies* (London, ON: The University of Western Ontario, International Centre for Olympic Studies, October 2002), 143–48.

73 Kevin B. Wamsley and Michael K. Heine, 'Tradition, Modernity, and the Construction of Civic Identity: The Calgary Olympics', *OLYMPIKA: The International Journal of Olympic Studies*, 5 (1996), 81–90.

74 Janice Forsyth, 'Teepees and Tomahawks: Aboriginal Cultural Representation at the 1976 Olympic Games', in *The Global Nexus Engaged*, 71–76.

75 Kevin Young and Philip White, 'Afterword', in Kevin Young and Philip White, eds, *Sport and Gender in Canada* (Don Mills, ON: Oxford University Press, 2007), 329.

76 Vertinsky, 'Time Gentlemen Please'.

22 The Caribbean

Alan Gregor Cobley

'So there we are, all tangled up together'.[1]

Introduction: sport – a Caribbean success story

Since the middle of the 20th century the Caribbean has consistently produced world-class players in several major sports, including cricket, track athletics (particularly those events requiring speed and power – the 100, 200 and 400 metres), baseball and soccer (football). It has also produced world-beaters, albeit with less consistency, in an eclectic range of other sports, such as boxing, netball, body-building and horse-racing.[2]

In cricket, the West Indies announced themselves as one of the top three or four cricket playing nations in the world by defeating England at the home of cricket, Lords, in 1950. According to Keith Sandiford:

> For about fifty years after World War II, the West Indies were consistently the most exciting team on the international stage. They provided the sport with some of its finest batsmen and the majority of its fastest bowlers. West Indian dominance reached a peak during the period 1975–95. Indeed, in one golden streak from 1980 to 1995, the islanders played unbeaten for 29 test series, winning 59 out of 115 matches, losing only 15, and dominating the majority of the 41 left drawn (often because of the weather).[3]

Two out of the top five 'Cricketers of the Century' selected by *Wisden Cricketers' Almanac* in 2000 were West Indians: Sir Garfield Sobers (No. 2) and Sir Vivian Richards (No. 5).[4] Another West Indian Batsman, Brian Lara, holds the world record for the number of runs scored in a test innings (400).

On the track, the Caribbean is second only to the USA in its catalogue of world record holders, world champions and Olympic medallists in the sprint events. The Jamaicans lead the way: the dominating performances of the Jamaican Sprinters at the Beijing Olympics in 2008, headed by Usain Bolt's world record shattering gold medal runs in the 100 and 200 metres, were merely the most dramatic in a long history of outstanding performances. Most famous among the men, apart from Bolt, are Arthur Wint, Herb McKenley, Dennis Johnson, Donald Quarrie, Bert Cameron and Asafa Powell: on the female side, there is Marilyn Fay Neufville, Merlene Ottey, Grace Jackson, Juliet Cuthbert, Deon Hemmings, Veronica Campbell-Brown and Shelly-Ann Fraser. To these may be added such names as Hasely Crawford, Ato Bolden and Richard Thompson from

Trinidad and Tobago, Kim Collins from St Kitts-Nevis, and Obadele Thompson from Barbados, as well as a powerful cohort of Bahamian sprinters. Bahamian women especially have proved to be perennial threats in the sprint relays at major championships over the past 20 years – led by such names as Debbie Ferguson, Chandra Stirrup, Pauline Davis-Thompson and Tonique Williams-Darling. Numerous sprinters with Caribbean origins have also represented other countries successfully: prime examples include Ben Johnson and Donovan Bailey (Jamaica), Mark McCoy (Guyana) and Bruny Surin (Haiti) for Canada; McDonald Bailey (Trinidad) and Linford Christie (Jamaica) for England; Sandra Farmer-Patrick (Jamaica) for the USA; and Marie Jose Perec and Christine Arron (Guadeloupe) for France. Meanwhile, Cuba has been recognized as a leading force in Olympic and World championship events in track and field ever since Alberto Juanterena – known as 'White Lightning' – won Olympic Gold in the 400 and 800 metres at Montreal in 1976. The significance of Cuba as a sporting nation is such that it will be dealt with as a special case below.

In the Hispanic Caribbean, despite the presence of other sports, 'baseball is king'.[5] Baseball was introduced into Cuba by university students returning from the USA in the 1860s, where it quickly became part of the social milieu of the Havana elite. Subsequently, it became intertwined in broader Cuban national consciousness as part of the struggle for independence from Spain, to the extent that the game was banned for a time by the Spanish authorities.[6] By the early 20th century, in the wake of the defeat of Spain by the USA, it had become an integral part of Cuban identity – and more particularly, according to Thomas Carter, a vehicle for the expression of Cuban masculinity.[7] For example, the future revolutionary leader, Fidel Castro, was voted the 'Number One' High School athlete in Cuba in 1943 based on his prowess as a baseball pitcher, basketball player and 400-metre runner. However, Castro never went on to a career in the Major Leagues in the USA as some of his compatriots did. After the Revolution in 1959, the supply of Cuban baseball talent to the USA all but dried up, although a trickle of defectors continued. After that date, it was the Dominican Republic that emerged as the leading supplier in the Caribbean of professional baseball players to the USA. Over 350 Dominicans have played in the Major Leagues since 1956. The success of players from that country in North America led to the establishment of baseball academies there by several Major League baseball clubs in the late 1970s and early 1980s. They included the Toronto Blue Jays, the Los Angeles Dodgers, the San Francisco Giants and the Pittsburgh Pirates. According to Alan Klein, partly as a result of this system, there were 43 Dominicans playing in the Major Leagues by 1989, with a further 300 in the minor leagues.[8] Among the many stars in Major League baseball to have emerged from the ranks of players in the Caribbean are Roberto Alomar and Roberto Clemente (Puerto Rico), Jose Conseco and Orlando Hernández (Cuba), Juan Marichal and Sammy Sosa (Dominican Republic).

Finally, there is soccer. A recent survey of Jamaican footballers playing overseas identified 23 currently playing professional soccer in England and 10 in the USA. Several Caribbean-born players, including Luther Blissett (Jamaica), John Barnes (Jamaica) and Cyrille Regis (French Guiana) have played for England, as have dozens born in England of Afro-Caribbean parentage.[9] Elsewhere, several players from the former Dutch Caribbean territory of Suriname have starred for the Netherlands national team over the past 20 years, including Stanley Menzo, Edgar Davids, Clarence Seedorf, Aron Winter and Jimmy Floyd Hasselbaink. Others of Surinamese extraction to have played for the national side include Frank Rijkaard, Patrick Kluivert and Ruud Gullit. Similarly, the French national team has drawn on the services of several players from the French West Indies or of French West Indian descent in recent years, including Thierry Henry, William Gallas, Lilian Thuram, Sylvain Wiltord, Pascal Chimbonda and Louis Saha (Guadeloupe), Éric Abidal and Nicolas Anelka (Martinique) and Florent Malouda (French Guiana).

The great flowering of sporting talent among Caribbean people, and people of Caribbean origin, has been one of the more remarkable features of world sport over the past half century. Current research in sport and exercise science is looking at genetic, nutritional and sociological factors to try to understand why 'certain populations experience disproportionate success in particular sporting events', but much of this work is still at an early stage.[10] This chapter seeks to identify some of the historical factors responsible for this phenomenon in the Caribbean.

Historical origins of Caribbean sport

In historical terms, the Caribbean islands and the territories bounding the Caribbean Sea have never been constituted as a single space politically, economically or culturally. The reason for this is simple. For more than five hundred years, since the intrusion of European invaders at the end of the 15th century, it has been a zone of interaction and conflict, as competing empires have vied for the domination and exploitation of the region. The result of this complex and dynamic history has been the creation of (at least) four linguistically and culturally distinctive zones, which may be labelled for convenience, the Hispanic, the Francophone, the Anglophone and the Dutch-speaking Caribbean. In each of these zones the invaders established their own traditions, including – by the end of the 19th century – their own sporting traditions.

Cricket was the quintessentially English game that took root throughout the British West Indies during the 19th century, while another game with British roots, football (soccer) was established in all four of the European colonial zones in the Caribbean during the same time period. Although both began within the colonial elites and their accompanying military establishments, these sports quickly attracted a popular following in the societies where they were played.

The first references to an organized cricket match in the West Indies press were in Barbados in 1806 and 1807 and involved the St Ann's Garrison Cricket Club.[11] By that time it seems the game was already well on the way to becoming an exemplar of high culture among the white colonial elite. They went on to form a number of socially and racially exclusive clubs across the West Indies by the mid–late 19th century. Paradoxically, according to Hilary Beckles:

> The desire of the coloured and black communities to play cricket their own way seemed to have grown in direct proportion to the white elite's determination to establish it as the exclusive sport of propertied, the educated, and the 'well-bred'. By the mid-century, versions of the game were being played and celebrated at all levels of colonial society.[12]

In Beckles' view, cricket provided 'a framework of oppositional behaviour'[13] within which the excluded majority could challenge the basis for their social exclusion. As a result cricket grew rapidly in the British West Indies in the post-Emancipation era, ranging from the formal contests played on carefully manicured grounds by the white and (increasingly) the brown elite to informal games played by members of the black working class using improvised equipment on cart roads or clearings in the cane fields. By the end of the 19th century a network of new clubs was beginning to emerge that embraced brown and black players, as well as white, so that the game 'had been transformed from a minority elite "English" sport into the region's first expression of popular mass culture'.[14]

Although association football developed first as an organized sport among the elite, it quickly established itself as the leading 'working-class' game in large parts of Europe during the second half of the 19th century. As James Walvin explains:

> It was simple to play, easy to grasp and could be played on any surface under any conditions, by indeterminate numbers of men. It needed no equipment but a ball, and could last from dawn to dusk. Football could be played by anyone, regardless of size, skill, or strength.[15]

In the Caribbean, football developed most rapidly in the French- and Dutch-speaking territories, such as Haiti and Suriname. In the English-speaking islands, it did not rival cricket in popularity throughout the colonial era, while baseball, similarly, occupied pride of place in the Spanish-speaking islands. Nevertheless, football put down roots in almost every corner of the Caribbean, and was played almost everywhere by the early 20th century.

Unlike cricket and football, some sports introduced during the colonial period remained firmly associated with the white colonial elite and retained a high degree of exclusivity, at least until post-colonial times; these included tennis, yachting, shooting, game fishing, golf and polo.[16] A major reason for this exclusivity was cost: these sports required special playing areas, specialized equipment and other forms of support that were not available to the common folk. This aura of exclusivity explains why these sports enjoyed a renaissance in the post-colonial Caribbean, where they were developed largely as attractions for up-market tourists from Europe and North America.[17]

One sport that has managed consistently to bring the elite and the working class together in the Caribbean, as elsewhere in the world, is horse-racing. While the ownership of racehorses was confined to the military and to a tiny wealthy elite throughout the colonial period, and remains in the post-colonial Caribbean the purview of the moneyed classes, racing has been embraced in popular culture in many Caribbean countries, partly as a spectacle, and partly because of the opportunities for gambling associated with the sport. This appeal across social classes has led to notable success in the sport internationally: (white) Barbadian Sir Michael Stoute has been champion trainer in Britain nine times, while (black) Barbadian jockey Pat Husbands has been the champion jockey in Canada five times in the last nine years. Both began their careers in horse-racing at the Garrison Savannah in Bridgetown, where horse-racing has been staged regularly since 1845. John Mitrano and Robbin Smith go so far as to argue that the huge popularity of horse-racing in St Croix provided a vehicle for community solidarity and played a therapeutic role for the island's population in the wake of the devastation of Hurricane Hugo in 1989.[18]

Despite the many imposed political, social and economic divisions in the colonial Caribbean, there have also been counter-veiling commonalities. These influenced Caribbean people in their attitudes to each other, and to the wider world, during the colonial period, and have helped to break down – or at least mitigate – many of the divisions since the end of colonial rule. Foremost among these is a sense of shared history and heritage, in as much as the majority of people in the Caribbean are the product of one transcendent historical episode: the transatlantic slave trade from Africa to the Americas, and one transcendent system: plantation slavery. Traces of this shared history and heritage are found in common patterns of thought, common modes of expression, common religious beliefs and practices, which were carried over into the new Caribbean environment in the holds of countless slave ships during the 350-year history of transatlantic slavery, and which continue to underpin Caribbean culture and identity today. This commonality was not erased by the subdivision of the region into competing colonial zones by the European powers and provided an important mass-based counter culture, which has helped to mediate, and, on occasion, to challenge the hegemonic influence of the West in Caribbean societies. Thus, although colonial elites across the Caribbean were largely composed of people of European descent, who continued to identify closely with European cultural mores, creolized Caribbean versions of Spanish, French and English, for example, reproduced African patterns of speech, and even incorporated African words and phrases to some extent. A similar process can be seen at work in Caribbean music and religion. Much smaller diasporas of indentured workers from India and China – as well as from Europe – brought their own unique patterns to add to the wider Caribbean tapestry, but always in relation to (or sometimes as a commentary on) the insistent presence of the African majority.

Of course, modern sport, as understood today, is largely the product of a conjunction of forces associated with the rise of industrial capitalist societies in Western Europe and the formal separation of 'work' and 'recreation' undertaken as part of the creation of a new social, cultural and moral order in the West during the second half of the 19th century. However, most modern sports evolved from pastimes that were part of pre-modern societies, particularly those that are essentially contests of physical strength, dexterity and skill. Contests such as wrestling, 'stick-licking', 'pitch-and-toss', as well as games such as Warri, which were common in West African societies during the era of the transatlantic slave trade, migrated along the transatlantic trade routes with the enslaved Africans to become part of life in the Caribbean. It has been argued by at least one writer that the great West Indian batting tradition in cricket owes something to the much older sport of 'stick-licking' – or 'batonniers' as it was known in Trinidad,[19] while the vast popularity of games of dominoes and of draughts ('checkers' in North American parlance) in rum shops, and other liming spots throughout the Caribbean islands, may also have connections to these older African traditions.[20] The various sporting traditions introduced into the Caribbean from Europe in the 19th and early 20th centuries were, therefore, to some extent grafted onto pre-existing traditions. This may explain why some sporting imports flourished, while others did not.

Further complexity was introduced into Caribbean sport by the intrusion of American imperialism into the region from the mid-19th century onwards, a movement in which the Spanish-American War of 1898 was a watershed. This brought American sporting traditions – and above all, baseball – spilling into the Caribbean basin. A steady trickle of interest in American sports became a flood as American commercial interests grew in the region during the first half of the 20th century, accompanied in places by the extended sojourns of American troops. The impact was especially marked in the islands of the Northern Caribbean (Cuba, Puerto Rico, the Dominican Republic) and in the countries of Central America that border the Caribbean (Costa Rica, Nicaragua, El Salvador, Panama). In most of these places, baseball penetrated the popular culture to such an extent that it eventually achieved the status of the national sport.

As suggested above in the case of Cuba, part of the initial appeal of baseball in these countries was that it exemplified a 'New World' culture and consciousness that challenged the 'old world' hegemony of Spain in the Americas. A 'home run' could be seen, in an almost literal sense, as a blow against colonialism and for nascent nationalisms in the Hispanic Caribbean. The role of the USA at the end of the 19th century as champion of these new nationalisms in the Americas helped to embed the sport in popular culture in several Caribbean societies: by the time heavy-handed interventions into the region by the USA began to provoke less favourable assessments of American influence in the region by mid-century, the processes of creolization had ensured that baseball would survive by taking on its own robust local identity.

Sport, ethnicity and identity

As we have seen, the mode of introduction of organized sport into Caribbean societies as imports from the imperial metropoles tended at first to underline and even intensify pre-existing economic, social and cultural divisions. Since the elites in the Caribbean remained mostly white well into the 20th century, participation in formal sporting activity tended at first to be ethnically, as well as socially, determined. Some of the oldest established sporting clubs in the Caribbean operated colour bars until relatively recent times: examples include The Georgetown Cricket Club (1858) in Guyana, the Kingston Club (1863) in Jamaica, Wanderers Club (1877) and Pickwick Club (1882) in Barbados, the Queen's Park Club (1891) in Trinidad, and the Habana Baseball Club (1878) in Cuba.[21] Ideologically, exclusion of the masses from participation in formal sporting activities was a means by which the colonial elite sought to demonstrate and perpetuate its exclusivity.

Yet, already by the end of the 19th century challengers to this exclusive system were beginning to emerge. In the case of cricket, the mainly brown-skinned or mulatto middle class that had emerged in West Indian societies during the 19th century were the first to challenge the white monopoly by forming their own clubs. In Barbados the first such club was Spartan, formed in 1894, the membership of which was composed of lawyers, doctors, senior civil servants, schoolmasters from the leading schools and businessmen. Its President was Barbados' first brown-skinned Chief Justice, Conrad Reeves.[22] The first black club, Empire, was formed 20 years later in 1914, catering to the hitherto excluded black lower middle class.[23] The black working class did not get the opportunity to participate fully in Barbadian cricket until the formation of the Barbados Cricket League by J.M. 'Mitchie' Hewitt in 1936 as a rival to the more elitist Barbados Cricket Association.[24] A similar ethnic sub division was evident in cricket in Trinidad, where the elite, almost exclusively white, represented by the Queen's Park and Shamrock clubs, competed with Maple, 'the club of the brown-skinned middle class', Shannon, 'the club of the Black lower middle class', and Stingo, 'totally black and no social status whatever'.[25] C.L.R. James describes agonizing as a young man over which club to join – Shannon or Maple – and how he eventually opted for Maple on the basis of his hopes for future career advancement. Yet even in retrospect, James did not condemn these racialist and class-based divisions, regarding them as 'a natural response to local social conditions, [which] did little harm and sharpened up the game':[26]

> I haven't the slightest doubt that the clash of race, caste and class did not retard but stimulated West Indian cricket. I am equally certain that in those years social and political passions, denied normal outlets, expressed themselves so fiercely in cricket (and other games) precisely because they were games.[27]

Although the racial division of cricketers into ethnically distinctive clubs neatly reflected the racial stratification of West Indian society under colonialism, it seemed less logical when the islands began to play representative matches, whether playing each other in 'inter-colonial' contests, or pitting themselves against visiting teams from England and elsewhere. In fact a few brown and black players had already been selected to play for 'white' teams by the end of the century, having been hired initially as 'groundsmen' or employed as bowlers for net practice.[28] Their obvious talent, together with the success of the growing number of 'non-white' clubs in local competition, challenged the racial stereotypes that had previously refused to see black and brown players as equals – at least within the confines of the game. As Hilary Beckles has shown, it was Sir Pelham 'Plum' Warner, a white Creole born in Trinidad, the son of the Attorney General, but later captain of England and the MCC, who led the campaign to 'democratize' cricket in the West Indies, and 'to throw open the gates of West Indian cricket to all men of talent and social quality irrespective of their race, colour or class'. He strongly supported the inclusion of black players in the West Indies teams that toured England in 1900 and 1906, on the grounds that the team would be impoverished without them, and later agitated for the awarding of test status to the multiracial West Indies team – a feat that was not achieved until 1928: 'In the West Indies he was hailed as a supporter of cricket's democratic impulse, a promoter of popular participation at all levels, and an advocate of its finest, humanist values'.[29]

C.L.R. James, who grew up in Trinidad in this era as a young black West Indian intellectual under colonialism, found in his passion for cricket both a means to critique the nature of British colonialism, and ultimately a vehicle to challenge it. This is the essential theme of his ground-breaking work, *Beyond a Boundary*, which offers a socio-cultural analysis of cricket's place in colonial West Indian society, and by this means exposes the ethnic and class prejudices at its core.[30]

If Warner represented the effort to accommodate the democratization of West Indian cricket within the confines of colonialism, James represents the effort to use cricket as a means to democratize society and so break down the vestiges of colonialism. This is most apparent in the latter half of James's book, in which he recounts the successful campaign during the late 1950s to have Frank Worrell appointed as the first black captain to lead the West Indies in a test series. This was finally achieved in 1960. The honour had been unjustly denied to Learie Constantine a generation earlier, and had scandalously been withheld from Worrell for a decade. The popular campaign to make Worrell captain, of which James was part, was symbolic of the internal struggle against the entrenched power of the white colonial elite within the West Indies, embodied in this instance by the exclusively white membership of the West Indies Board of Cricket Control, and of the wider struggle of West Indian nationalists during the 1950s towards the achievement of full independence from Britain.

The rearguard action fought by the white cricket establishment against this campaign utilized racist assumptions about the capacities of black West Indian cricketers that went back to the early history of the sport in the Caribbean in the 19th century. As Maurice St Pierre notes, black West Indian cricketers were often described during the late colonial era – and even after it – as 'impetuous', 'entertaining', 'inconsistent'. These were, he suggests:

> … catch words for the inability to delay gratification and the tendency to wilt under pressure, which were part of the hidden transcript of domination that emphasized inferiority, [and] were utilized to convey, implicitly, the idea that non-white West

Indians, in particular, were incapable of achieving greatness, especially in cricket. In other words, the character building that the British associated with the game had escaped the grasp of the typical West Indian player.[31]

These arguments flew in the face of the steadily accumulating evidence of performances by black players in the test arena after 1928, but were used to justify the selection of lesser players who were white as captains and batsmen for the West Indies until the end of the 1950s. The appointment of Worrell as captain of the West Indies in 1960 was therefore a seminal moment, not only in the history of West Indian cricket but of black sport as a whole. The subsequent success of the team finally put paid to the notion in the West Indies that black people were incapable of effective leadership, although, regrettably, it did not bring to an end the resort to racist stereotypes in the former imperial metropoles, where they continued to be used to describe and belittle the achievements of black sportsmen and women in popular culture and the media. Some of the crudest examples of this continuing racism could be heard in comments from some white coaches, especially in football.[32] Even when the West Indies cricket team was carrying all before them in the 1970s and 1980s, commentators characterized them more or less disparagingly as 'calypso cricketers' – as though technique and peerless professionalism had nothing to do with their success. When the team began to lose in the 1990s, it was characterized glibly by some white commentators as a reversion to type.

It is interesting to reflect that there were many parallels between cricket and baseball in the Caribbean in these years, in that social and ethnic divisions also marked the development of baseball. In Cuba, for example, the first national Baseball League begun in 1878 was composed initially of exclusively white clubs. However, the road to racial integration in Cuban baseball began when the League was won by the first all-black baseball team, San Francisco, in 1900. In the Dominican Republic, meanwhile, the struggle for black self-determination in cricket influenced the future development of baseball in a remarkable way. Thousands of black West Indian labourers from neighbouring British islands migrated to the Dominican Republic in the early 20th century. They were attracted by a sharp increase in demand for labour in the sugar growing areas around San Pedro, fuelled by American investment and markets for Dominican sugar; this was occurring at the same time as the sugar industry in the British West Indies was in sharp decline, undermined by competition in Europe from beet sugar. Racially and culturally distinctive, and regarded in the Dominican Republic as a social underclass, the 'Cocolos' as they were called, used cricket as a vehicle for promoting community solidarity and pride. Gradually their children and grandchildren took up baseball, but they infused it within the same 'British' values of pride, discipline and hard work with which they had previously approached cricket. This is what made Dominican baseball unique.[33]

Independence, national identity and sport

In the second half of the 20th century, many Caribbean societies emerged from colonial rule and established themselves as independent countries.[34] This movement was marked by struggles with the spectre of neo-colonialism on the one hand and highly self-conscious efforts at 'nation-building' on the other. Here too, sport often played a role. Individual Caribbean sportsmen and women who excelled in international competition were objects of national pride and were held up as role models, feted as national heroes and showered with honours. Successful national teams took national pride to another level, becoming catalysts for a heightened national consciousness – especially when their success included triumph over the country's former colonial masters.

The full flowering of the West Indies cricket team as world-beaters under Worrell, Sobers, Lloyd and Richards in the 1960s, 1970s and 1980s, provided the backdrop to the rolling back of British colonialism in the Anglophone Caribbean and the emergence of ten independent black-led states, from Guyana in the South to the Bahamas in the North. In the process the more genteel intellectual nationalism of the Worrell generation ultimately gave way to the black-power fuelled assertiveness of Lloyd's fearsome four-pronged pace attack and Richards' 'intimidatory batting'.[35] As Keith Sandiford explains:

> The Caribbean people basked in the reflected glory of their cricketers who gave them a stronger sense of pride and identity than they had ever known before. It strengthened their faith in themselves and vindicated their claims to self-determination.[36]

Even in the early 1990s, when West Indian cricket supremacy seemed to be faltering, Calypsonian David Rudder could still call on West Indians to affirm their loyalty to the team and 'Rally Round the West Indies', a song that has become an enduring cricket anthem. In the same period, Gary Sobers became the first West Indian cricketer to be named an official 'National Hero' in his home island of Barbados. This was another way of embracing cricket as an exemplar of national pride. It is clear that for West Indians, cricket has always been more than a game, and that, by the time of independence, it had become intimately intertwined with national identity. But it was in Cuba after the socialist revolution that sport was most overtly politicized in the Caribbean as a vehicle to promote national independence, pride and achievement. As Sugden, Tomlinson and McCartan show, Cuba transformed itself from a country before the revolution in which sporting success was limited to professional baseball and boxing, to become one of the top ten sporting nations in the world by the mid-1970s. The transformation was largely the work of the National Institute of Sport, Physical Education, and Recreation (INDER) established in 1961.[37] Initially drawing on the best examples and technical expertise from the Soviet bloc in Eastern Europe, INDER co-ordinated government policy and marshalled resources to create a comprehensive national policy on sport that provided opportunities for all Cubans to participate in physical education 'from the cradle to the grave'. It included the incorporation of physical education as a core subject in the curriculum at all levels of the education system from pre-school to tertiary level, as well as provision for physical activity for the over-60s through local polyclinics. Students who showed a particular talent for sport were sent to special schools called 'Escuelas de Iniciación Deportiva Escolar' (EIDE – 'Schools for the Initiation of Scholastic Sport') at the age of 11 or 12 – or even younger (eight or nine) in some sports. The best prospects then went on to provincial sport schools, and eventually to the National Training Centre in Havana or to Universities affiliated to it. Those not destined for a state-supported career in competitive sport were trained to become PE teachers. One result of this system was that by 1990 Cuba had 28,000 specialist PE teachers – one for every 360 people in the population.[38] By that date Cuba had also established one of the highest rates of popular participation in sport in the world (at around 10 percent of the population), and had dramatically increased participation in sport by women. Although INDER's emphasis from the mid-1980s was on 'massification' in sport – a socialist variant on the European 'Sport for All' policy – Cuba's elite athletes continued to perform well, and reached a new peak of achievement in the early 1990s. When Cuba hosted the Pan

American Games in Havana in 1991, many observers believed the recent collapse of the Soviet Eastern Bloc and the deepening economic crisis that had resulted from Cuba's growing isolation would lead to public demonstrations against Castro in the full glare of the international media.[39] In the event, however, the Games were a triumph for Castro and for Cuban national pride: Cuba won 140 gold medals in the Games, compared to 130 won by its arch rival, the USA (though total medals favoured the USA over Cuba by 352 to 265).[40] For a country of only eleven million people this was a phenomenal achievement. In the following year, at the Olympics in Barcelona, Cuba achieved its greatest ever result, winning 31 medals. The country was fifth in the number of gold medals won, and sixth overall in the international medal table. Another indicator of the strength of Cuba's sporting programme by this date was that nine other teams competing at Barcelona – mostly developing countries with links to Cuba through the Non-Aligned Movement – employed Cuban boxing coaches.[41] While international observers and Cuban exiles continued to predict economic collapse and the implosion of the Cuban sporting programme throughout the 1990s, Cuba's international sporting success continued.[42] At the Atlanta Games in 1996, Cuba was seventh in gold medals and ninth in total medals won, while at the Sydney Games in 2000, Cuba placed eighth in total medals and ninth in gold medals (this was better than the United Kingdom and all other western hemisphere countries except the USA). At the last Olympiad in Athens in 2004, Cuba still managed to win nine golds and 27 medals overall, placing eleventh in the international medal table. It will be interesting to see how the country fares at Beijing in 2008.

Cuba's international success in sport since the 1970s is chiefly a reflection of the country's success in creating a remarkable infrastructure for the propagation of sport in Cuban society. One motivation for this was to demonstrate the success of Castro's revolution, both to his own people and to the international community. However, there is little doubt that since the collapse of Cuba's communist allies, and in the face of continuing economic sanctions, 'Cubans see their prowess at sports as a means of equalizing their relationship with the United States'.[43] The fact that the three leading sports in Cuba – baseball, basketball and boxing – are also leading sports in the USA has added piquancy to the contest. Ultimately sport in Cuba has become a vehicle to promote nationalist pride and consciousness in the face of adversity rather than being simply a continuing argument for socialism. At the same time, whatever the political and ideological reasons for Cuba's continuing heavy investment in sports, it cannot be doubted that it has had enormously beneficial effects on the health and well-being of the Cuban people.

Globalization, commodification and migration in Caribbean sport

The post-colonial and post-Cold War Caribbean has seen shifting fortunes in sport over the last two decades. This had been a reflection of the changing economic and social conditions facing Caribbean sportsmen and women. Politically and ideologically, the role of sport has become both more complex and more ambiguous in Caribbean societies than a generation ago. As Toby Miller et al. argue:

> … sport is so central to our contemporary moment's blend of transnational cultural industrialization and textualization that it does more than reflect the global – sport is big enough in its effects to modify our very use of the term 'globalization'. As sports professionalize and internationalize, their commodification and bureaucratization become fundamental if we are to understand profound changes in national culture.[44]

In cricket, the 1990s was a decade of decline for the once all-conquering West Indies team, despite the presence of Brian Lara, one of the greatest batsmen in the history of the game. Such was the perplexing nature of this decline to many West Indians that cricket historian Hilary Beckles devoted the whole of the second volume of his two volume history of West Indies Cricket published in 1998, entitled 'The Age of Globalisation', to an attempt to explain this phenomenon. Beckles' thesis is that the 'nationalist paradigm', within which West Indies cricket grew to maturity and achieved dominance under Lloyd and Richards, is in retreat in the face of 'globalizing transformations in the social order'. The 'crisis' in West Indies cricket is therefore a reflection of a wider crisis in West Indian society engendered by the post-colonial (and postmodern) forces of globalization – evidence of which is seen throughout the region in 'talk of intellectual emptiness, mass unemployment, youth lawlessness and indiscipline, and increasing criminalisation of the poor'.[45]

According to Keith Sandiford, the 'prolonged and devastating slump [in West Indies Cricket] has done untold damage to the regional psyche' of Caribbean people.[46] He attributes it to a wide range of factors, some of which are the natural by-product of rapid social and economic development, such as the 'spectacular explosion' of the black and brown middle class, many of whom no longer count sport among their priorities; urbanization; co-education (accompanied by a falling number of trained cricket coaches in schools); and the diversification of Caribbean sports at the expense of cricket. However, he agrees with Beckles that some factors contributing to the decline of West Indies cricket are a direct result of the impact of globalization in the region, such as a burgeoning drug culture, the rampant 'Americanization' of Caribbean society – especially through the influence of satellite TV, and the emergence of 'a very powerful spirit of individualism ... especially among the younger cricketers'.[47] The latter shift is hardly surprising since the forces associated with globalization have led to the commodification of professional sport and the ubiquity of sport in the electronic media the world over; cricket, in common with other sports, is now big business, so that the most pertinent characteristic of the contemporary cricketer is not his 'team spirit' but his marketability. One result is that in common with other major sports, cricket in recent years has been blighted by periodic disputes about competing sponsorship deals, corporate logos and the 'branding' of teams and players.[48]

For Beckles, Brian Lara – a cricketer lauded by the West Indian public throughout his career as batting superstar, but simultaneously berated for alleged 'selfishness' and lack of team spirit – is 'the first hero of the new paradigm', a paradigm in which the old loyalty to West Indian nationhood has been displaced by logos and designer shades. In his book, Beckles sets out a vision for a 'third rising' of West Indies cricket, which would recognize and embrace the new realties of global sport, but which would also overcome the current fragmentation of team loyalty and spirit in the West Indies by promoting a new, much broader and more integrated Caribbean regional identity – a kind of supra-Caribbean nationalism engineered for the age of globalization. In keeping with the spirit of the age, it would require the co-ordinated intervention of regional governments to put in place the changes required in the management of the game.[49] Unfortunately, ten years later, the prospects of achieving this 'third rising' still do not look good.

The staging of the International Cricket Council (ICC) Cricket World Cup in the West Indies in 2007 was sold to the region as a potential vehicle for the renaissance of West Indies cricket culture. In the aftermath of the event, it was hailed by Chief Executive Officer, Chris Dehring, as 'the most profitable Cricket World Cup to date'.[50]

However, as numerous commentators pointed out, the success of the event could not be measured only in terms of the revenue generated through the sale of advertising, tourist packages and global television rights. The competition failed to excite the interest of the West Indian public due to unprecedented regulation of crowd behaviour for security reasons (musical instruments, for example, were banned), excessive ticket prices and the continuing failure of the home team, while local businesses complained that they failed to receive the expected financial spin-offs. Most of the matches were played before low-keyed crowds in half-empty stadiums, so that even the international media complained that there was little that was recognizably 'Caribbean' about the event.[51] Far from re-igniting local interest in cricket, for many the World Cup was another signpost on the road to decline of the game in the West Indies.

Two aspects of the post-colonial condition in Caribbean life that continue to have a negative impact on competitive sport in the region are insularity and ethnicity.[52] The results of the underlying tendency towards fragmentation of West Indian identity are obvious. Football is a case in point. Despite the wealth of football talent in the Caribbean and its Diaspora, Caribbean teams have reached the final stage of the FIFA World Cup on only a handful of occasions. These include Cuba in 1938, Haiti in 1974, Jamaica in 1998 and Trinidad and Tobago in 2006. Costa Rica, El Salvador and Honduras have also made occasional appearances as representatives of the Central American zone. The historic cup run of Jamaica's 'Reggae Boyz' under Brazilian coach Rene Simoes that led to their qualification for the World Cup in France in 1998 evoked pride among Caribbean people everywhere. As the authors of one commemorative book put it:

> Out of Africa in 1994 had come Cameroon, challenging the first world professionals. Now, out of the Caribbean, a team from an island known mainly for its music, its beaches, a failing economy and a terrifying crime rate, had stepped onto the world stage, one of the players barely 19, to attest to the raw talent and indomitable will of the Jamaican people.[53]

Similarly, when Trinidad and Tobago qualified for the Finals in Germany in 2006, flags supporting the 'Soca Warriors' could be seen flying on cars throughout the English-speaking Caribbean. A hard fought group stage match in Germany against the old colonial master, England, brought the region to a virtual standstill, though it ended in honourable defeat for the Soca Warriors. The achievements in reaching the finals in 1998 and 2006 gave a strong boost in popularity to football across the Caribbean, and even gave currency to an argument that the islands should emulate cricket and field a combined football team to compete in major competitions. After the initial euphoria, however, the idea quickly faded away as the enduring difficulties of practising unified sport in the highly fragmented Caribbean environment reasserted themselves. A united team was never a serious possibility.

As already suggested, the forces associated with globalization and the ubiquity of sport in the electronic media have engineered a shift in the popular consciousness of Caribbean youth over the past 25 years. Nowhere has this been more apparent that in the spectacular rise in the popularity of another American import in the region, which had previously been confined to the Hispanic Caribbean: basketball. From the ubiquity of brand-named sneakers and shirts emblazoned with the names of NBA teams and marquee players, to the naming of local teams after NBA franchises, the influence of American basketball on popular culture among Caribbean youth has been profound. Yet, as Mandel and Mandel show, the failure of basketball to transcend the constraints of insularity in the region has held up the development of the game by starving it of money and quality of competition.[54] It has become to a large extent the preferred game of the poor and marginalized youth; but the only hope for the most talented individual players (mostly forlorn) is that they will be 'spotted' and given a chance to make the grade in collegiate or professional ball in the USA.

Migration is, of course, a time honoured route to a better life economically and socially for Caribbean people. One baleful legacy of intensive and highly coercive capitalist exploitation of the region by various imperial powers over several centuries was that, long after the formal end of slavery during the 19th century, the shadow of the plantation continued to stifle personal freedom, social progress and economic innovation in many parts of the Caribbean. This is turn would spark a common pattern across the Caribbean of extensive outward migration in search of economic opportunity, beginning in the second half of the 19th century, but intensifying dramatically in the first half of the 20th century. At first, much of the movement was 'intra-Caribbean' – from South to North – but increasingly the search for a better life took Caribbean people to Europe and North America. Some of these Caribbean migrants or their descendants were able to use the common language of sport as a route to acceptance and success in the host societies.[55]

In the late 20th century, 'sports migration' has become one of the features of globalization in sport, and the Caribbean – as in colonial times – has proved to be a reservoir of sporting talent that the more powerful sporting nations to the North can draw on.[56] In addition to the training camps for several North American baseball teams (aptly termed 'franchises') established in the Dominican Republic which were discussed earlier, talent scouts from other professional sports teams in North America, as well as the agents for numerous North American College sports programmes have been active in the Caribbean for at least 30 years. Local talent is recruited with sports scholarships and the promise of potentially lucrative future careers in professional sport in the USA or Canada. While no comparable system of collegiate sport functions in Europe, recruiters for professional sports teams in various European countries also visit the region regularly to identify likely prospects, especially in football. In some cases, local sports associations provide financial support for promising local prospects to go abroad for training and more challenging competition, or for trials with professional teams.

Conclusion

As the end of the first decade of the 21st century approaches there seems to be no immediate prospect that the well of sporting talent in the Caribbean will run dry. The pressing issue for the developing societies of the Caribbean as a whole is whether they will continue to allow this resource to be consumed willy-nilly – primarily by, or in the interests of, the developed world – or whether they can summon the will to ensure that national and regional policies are put in place to put that talent to work in the service of Caribbean people. Of course, this is the same question that Caribbean societies must confront in the new global environment in all other areas of their economic, social and cultural life.

Against this background, it is possible that the success of the Jamaican Sprinters in the Beijing Olympics in 2008 may lead to something of a sea change in regional attitudes to sport and the management of sport. Although in the immediate aftermath of the gold medal winning performances in Beijing, Jamaicans gleefully attributed the success of Bolt and his team mates to the consumption of good Jamaican yams, it quickly emerged that there were other reasons for their success. Whereas in previous decades, the raw talent nurtured through the schools system and put on display each year at the Annual School Championships (or simply 'Champs' as it is called locally)[57] had been snapped up by scouts from the USA, who spirited them away to join the US collegiate circuit, Bolt and several of his team mates were part of a cohort who had been persuaded to remain in Jamaica to participate in the athletics programme at the University of Technology in Kingston. They benefited from world-class coaching at home in Jamaica, adapted to local conditions, and with its foundations in local knowledge. This world-beating combination of indigenous sporting talent and indigenous knowledge has shown Caribbean governments and people that there are opportunities to be exploited, as well as challenges to face, in the new global environment.

Notes

1 C.L.R. James, *Beyond a Boundary* with an Introduction by Robert Lipsyte (London: Serpent's Tail, 1994), 252.
2 In body-building, Earl Maynard of Barbados was 'Mr Universe' three times in the 1960s – a title later held by Arnold Schwarzenegger. In netball, 11 of the 34 members of the International Federation of Netball Associations were from the Caribbean by 1994. Trinidad and Tobago won a share of the world championship title in 1983: Anthony Clarke, *Calypso Netball in the Caribbean* (Port of Spain: Anthony Clarke, 1994), 73–74.
3 Keith Sandiford, 'Cricket and a crisis of identity in the Anglophone Caribbean', in Adrian Smith and Dilwyn Porter, eds, *Sport and National Identity in the Post-War World* (London: Routledge, 2004), chapter 7, 128–44.
4 The third West Indian in the top 10 was Frank Worrell, voted equal sixth: *Wisden Cricketers' Almanac 2000*.
5 From the 'Introduction' to Joseph L. Arbena and David LaFrance, eds, *Sport in Latin America and the Caribbean*, Jaguar Books on Latin America, No. 23 (Wilmington, DE: Scholarly Resources, 2002), xiv.
6 Thomas Carter, 'Baseball Arguments: Aficionismo and Masculinity at the Core of *Cubanidad*', in J.A. Mangan and Lamartine DaCosta, eds, *Sport in Latin American Society Past and Present* (London: Frank Cass, 2002), chapter 5, 119–22.
7 Carter, 'Baseball Arguments', 118.
8 Alan M. Klein, 'Headcase, Headstrong and the Head-of-the-Class: Resocialization and Labeling in Dominican Baseball', in Michael A. Malec, ed., *The Social Roles of Sport in Caribbean Societies* (Langhorne, PA: Gordon and Breach Publishers, 1995), chapter 6, 125–26, 131–32.
9 A record nine black players were used in a football game for England against Australia in February 2003: at least six were of West Indian heritage, including Rio Ferdinand (St Lucia), Ledley King (Antigua), Ashley Cole (Barbados), Sol Campbell, Darius Vassell and David James (Jamaica). The origins of the others have not been identified.
10 The quotation comes from the website for the Sport and Exercise Science programme at the University of Glasgow, which lists the University of the West Indies as one of its collaborating institutions: www.gla.ac.uk/departments/integrativesystemsbiology/exerciseandsportsscience/ (accessed 17 October 2008).
11 Hilary McD. Beckles, *The Development of West Indies Cricket, Vol.1 The Age of Nationalism* (Kingston: The University of the West Indies/London: Pluto Press, 1998), 5–6.
12 Hilary McD. Beckles, 'The Origins and Development of West Indies Cricket Culture in the Nineteenth Century: Jamaica and Barbados', in Hilary Beckles and Brian Stoddart, eds, *Liberation Cricket: West Indies Cricket Culture* (Kingston, Jamaica: Ian Randle Publishers, 1995), chapter 2, 35.
13 Beckles, 'The Origins and Development of West Indies Cricket Culture', 35.
14 Beckles, 'The Origins and Development of West Indies Cricket Culture', 42.
15 James Walvin, *The People's Game: The Social History of British Football* (London: Allen Lane, 1975), 45.
16 In Barbados a working-class version of tennis, called road tennis, has evolved. The 'Professional Road Tennis Association' was formed in 2000. According to its website the game was first played

in the 1930s and was known as 'poor man's tennis': 'In the early days two players used pieces of wood as racquets and in extreme cases hard back books. Courts were marked out in roads with marlstones and a piece of wood represented a net ... The table tennis scoring system was used. As the game evolved the fur from the lawn tennis ball was removed. This process is known as 'skinning'. Racquets made out of plywood soon replaced pieces of wood and the road tennis courts were painted'. The website also claims that road tennis 'has become the most exciting version of tennis': www.proroadtennis.com/history.html.

17 In some parts of the Caribbean the golf courses and polo fields have been laid out as the centrepieces for the creation of exclusive golf and polo 'villages', which have been marketed internationally.

18 John Mitrano and Robbin Smith, 'And They're Off: Sport and the Maintenance of Community in St Croix', in Malec, ed., *The Social Roles of Sport in Caribbean Societies*, chapter 11, 229–51.

19 Richard D.E. Burton, 'Cricket, Carnival and Street Culture in the Caribbean', in Grant Jarvie, ed., *Sport Racism and Ethnicity* (London: The Falmer Press, 1991), chapter 1, 14–15.

20 The current 'World Champion' in checkers is Barbadian Ronald 'Suki' King, who has won 11 world titles since 1991 and was the 2008 'Sports Personality of the Year' in Barbados.

21 Maurice St Pierre, 'West Indian Cricket as Cultural Resistance', in Michael A. Malec, ed., *The Social Roles of Sport in Caribbean Societies*, chapter 3, esp. 56–57; H. Beckles, 'The origins and development of West Indies Cricket culture', 5–12.

22 Brian Stoddart, 'Cricket, Social Formation and Cultural Continuity in Barbados: A Preliminary Ethnohistory', in H. Beckles and B. Stoddart, eds, *Liberation Cricket*, chapter 4, 69.

23 Stoddart, 'Cricket, Social Formation and Cultural Continuity in Barbados', 69–70; Trevor Marshall, 'Ethnicity, Class, and the Democratization of West Indies Cricket', in Hilary McD. Beckles, ed., *An Area of Conquest: Popular Democracy and West Indies Cricket Supremacy* (Kingston, Jamaica: Ian Randle Publishers, 1994), chapter 3, 21.

24 Stoddart, 'Cricket, Social Formation and Cultural Continuity in Barbados', 68.

25 C.L.R. James, *Beyond a Boundary*, 49–50.

26 James, *Beyond a Boundary*, 58.

27 James, *Beyond a Boundary*, 66.

28 Kevin A. Yelvington, 'Cricket, Colonialism and the Culture of Caribbean Politics', in Malec, ed., *The Social Roles of Sport in Caribbean Societies*, chapter 2, 17–18.

29 Beckles, *The Development of West Indies Cricket: Volume 1*, 35.

30 For a discussion of the significance of *Beyond a Boundary*, see Yelvington, 'Cricket, Colonialism and the Culture of Caribbean Politics', 170.

31 St Pierre, 'West Indian Cricket as Cultural Resistance', 63.

32 In the 1970s it was common to hear the view expressed that black players had the flair and flamboyance to make good attackers, but did not have the character to apply themselves as mid-fielders or defenders. See Ernest Cashmore, *Black Sportsmen* (London: Routledge and Kegan Paul, 1982).

33 Rob Ruck, 'Three Kings Day in Consuelo: Cricket, Baseball and the Cocolos in San Pedro de Macorís', in Malec, ed., *The Social Roles of Sport in Caribbean Societies*, chapter 5, 75–88. In recent years, a fascinating reversal of this process has occurred. The emergence of a community several thousand-strong of migrants from the Dominican Republic in Antigua has led to the establishment of baseball as a popular minority sport in that cricket-mad country, with cricket grounds being pressed into service for baseball games: see Stanley H. Griffin, 'Antiguan Baseball: Re/Shaping Cricket Grounds, Re/Defining the Nation', unpublished seminar paper, presented at the University of the West Indies, Cave Hill Campus, Barbados, 17 December 2007.

34 Some important exceptions to the broader movement towards sovereign independence include Puerto Rico and the US Virgin Islands, which retain links to the United States; Martinique and Guadeloupe, which are 'Départements d'Outre Mer' of France; the Dutch Antilles (St Martin, Curacao, Bonaire and Saba); and a scattering of small British Dependencies, including Montserrat, the British Virgin Islands, Anguilla and the Cayman Islands.

35 The phrase was coined by cricket commentator John Arlott. For a discussion of 'Richards' Mission' see Beckles, *The Development of West Indies Cricket: Volume 1*, 83–95.

36 Sandiford, 'Cricket and a Crisis of Identity in the Anglophone Caribbean', 132.

37 John Sugden, Alan Tomlinson and Eamon McCartan, 'The Making and Remaking of White Lightning in Cuba: Politics, Sport, and Physical Education Thirty Years After the Revolution', in Malec, ed., *The Social Roles of Sport in Caribbean Societies*, chapter 10, esp. 215–20.

38 Sugden et al., 'The Making and Remaking of White Lightning', 215.

39 Paula J. Pettavino and Geralyn A. Pye, 'Sport in Cuba: Castro's Last Stand', in Arbena and LaFrance, eds, *Sport in Latin America and the Caribbean*, chapter 9.

40 'Introduction' to Arbena and LaFrance, eds, *Sport in Latin America and the Caribbean*, xx.

41 Pettavino and Pye, 'Sport in Cuba', 150.

42 See for example Pettavino and Pye, 'Sport in Cuba'.

43 Sugden et al., 'The Making and Remaking of White Lightning', 222.

44 Toby Miller, Geoffrey Lawrence, Jim McKay and David Rowe, *Globalization and Sport: Playing the World* (London: Sage Publications, 2001), 1.

45 Hilary Beckles, *The Development of West Indies Cricket: Volume 2 The Age of Globalization* (Kingston: University of the West Indies Press/London: Pluto Press, 1998), 1.

46 Sandiford, 'Cricket and a Crisis of Identity in the Anglophone Caribbean', 136.

47 Sandiford, 'Cricket and a Crisis of Identity in the Anglophone Caribbean', 138.

48 Toby Miller et al., *Globalization and Sport*, relate an incident involving the American Basketball 'Dream Team' at the Barcelona Olympics in 1992 in which the loyalty of players such as Michael Jordan and Charles Barkley to their personal sponsor, Nike, led them to refuse to wear the logo of Olympic sponsor, Reebok, at the gold medal ceremony. As Barkley explained: 'Us Nike guys are loyal to Nike because they pay us a lot of money. I have two million reasons not to wear Reebok' (126).

49 Beckles, *The Development of West Indies Cricket: Volume 2*, chapter 6 – 'The Post-Lara Generation'.

50 Dehring told a summit of CARICOM Heads of Government in Barbados: 'In the context of a Caribbean Single Market, this should serve as a model for the future and an example of what can be achieved through unity': reported on the West Indies Cricket Board website (www.windiescricket.org) under the headline, 'Prime Ministers satisfied with delivery of World Cup' (accessed 7 July 2007).

51 See for example the comments of Simon Barnes, 'Sun will never truly go down on West Indies' everlasting gift', *The Times* (London), 13 March 2007. Several stadiums were purpose built or completely renovated to dramatically increase their capacity for the World Cup. Since the ending of the World Cup, there has been a growing debate in some countries about what to do with these expensive white elephants, which far exceed the capacity needed for most local and regional sporting events.

52 Sandiford, 'Cricket and a Crisis of Identity in the Anglophone Caribbean', 134–35.

53 Earl Bailey and Nazma Miller, *Jamaica's Reggae Boys World Cup 1998* (Kingston, Jamaica: Ian Randle Publishers and Creative Communications, 1998), 7.

54 Jay R. Mandel and Joan D. Mandel, *Caribbean Hoops: The Development of West Indian Basketball* (Langhorne, PA: Gordon and Breach, 1994), esp. chapter 7, 'Constraints and Potential in Basketball's Future'.

55 Cashmore, *Black Sportsmen*.

56 John Bale and Joseph Maguire, eds, *The Global Sports Arena: Athletic Talent Migration in an Interdependent World* (London: Frank Cass, 1994), esp. Part Three.

57 'Champs' has a long tradition in Jamaica and holds an important place in Jamaican popular culture. For example, Norman Manley, Chief Minister (and latterly Premier) of Jamaica from 1955 to 1962, Jamaican national hero and father of Michael Manley, was the winner of the Annual School Championships in 1910 and 1911.

23 Central and Eastern Europe

Marek Waic and Stefan Zwicker

This chapter deals with sport in Central and Eastern Europe, where there has been a tension between politics, nationalities and sport that has been of a different dimension from Western and Western Central Europe. Within the borders of this area's states (which changed frequently during the 20th century) different nationalities and ethnic groups lived together and alongside in a situation of concurrence, which has been characterized by the term *Konfliktgemeinschaft* (community of conflict).[1] Under these circumstances physical education and sports were of special importance, as a means to show a nation's will to struggle for emancipation and as a way for people to represent themselves as an ethnic-national collective.

State of research

We are in no way planning to postulate the theory of *Kulturgefälle* (incline of culture), which allegedly becomes more and more severe the farther you get from Western Europe, but this is certain: sports as a subject of (historical) research have, at least concerning synthetic studies, not (yet) found the same consideration in Central and Eastern Europe that they have within the Anglo-American cultural area.[2] We can say with confidence, though, that the state of research undoubtedly has been enriched during recent years, in the German-speaking parts of Europe as well as in the region we attend to here, Central Eastern Europe: the former Czechoslovakia (i.e. the historic Czech lands – belonging to Austria until 1918 – which are geographically more or less identical to today's Czech Republic and Slovakia), Poland and Hungary. A summarizing, synthetic depiction of sports in Eastern Europe does not yet exist; however, a series of anthologies has been published recently as a result of international co-operation, which has given us a much better understanding of the relationship between sports and society in Central and Eastern Europe.[3]

Minorities

The *Vielvölkerreich* (empire consisting of many nations and ethnic groups) of the Habsburg monarchy disintegrated at the end of World War I. The successor states of Czechoslovakia, Poland and Hungary before World War II were definitely multi-ethnic. A large Jewish community lived in each of the three states, most of their members later victims of the Holocaust. Jewish sportsmen and -women were active and successful in clubs together with members of the non-Jewish majority, as well as in Zionist orientated sports organizations, by that means disproving the anti-Semitic stereotype of the 'unathletic Jew'.[4]

A strong minority of ethnic Germans lived within the borders of the Czechoslovak Republic (ČSR); in 1930 they formed about 25 percent of the population, and in the Czech lands about one-third of the inhabitants spoke German as their mother tongue. These Sudeten Germans were active in football and winter sports, their *Turnbewegung* was equivalent to the Slavic *Sokol* ('Falcon') movement, into which we will go more in detail later.[5] This was led – at least officially – by the *Führer* of *Deutscher Turnverband* (DTV), Konrad Henlein. The *Sudetendeutsche Partei* (SdP), newly founded at the beginning of the 1930s, was to become the strongest German political party in the country. The SdP increasingly just followed orders from Adolf Hitler's government in Berlin and argued for the 'homecoming' of the *Sudetenland* to the *Third Reich* (the slogan was *Heim ins Reich!*). This came into being as a result of the Munich Agreement in 1938. When almost the entire German-speaking population was expelled from the Czech lands after World War II – similarly in Poland (including the former German Provinces of Pomerania, Silesia and East Prussia, that became part of Poland) – the history of German sports in Eastern Central Europe ended.[6]

Czech lands and Czechoslovakia

Although the Czechs entered the elite club of sporting nations rather late, at the end of the 19th century, their entrance was all the more powerful mainly owing to the Sokol movement, which was founded by Miroslav Tyrš in 1862 shortly after Austria became a constitutional monarchy. Until World War II, the Czech lands were not solely 'Czech' in nationality, as we can see in the development of the German Turner movement (*Turnvereine*), which was much stronger in numbers in this region than in Austria.

Sokol, to become a symbol of both Slavonic ability to fight and Czech self-consciousness, was created according to a German model by founders of ethnic German origin (Tyrš as well as his closest comrade, Jindřich Fügner), who had both 'converted' to the Czech nation. They had a lot in common with Friedrich Ludwig Jahn's *Turnbewegung*, not only physical training and paramilitary attitudes, but also glorification of the nation's collective past. The *sokolovny* (gymnastic halls) were decorated with busts and portraits of Hussite military leaders and training of the body was declared not to be an end in itself or something for the individual athlete's sake; its purpose was to serve country and nation.[7] Similarly to German *Turnen*, Miroslav Tyrš offered 'his' organization up fully for the cause of national emancipation. Nevertheless, he kept Sokol away from the political parties, fearing a possible ban by Austrian authority. This idea of non-party organization proved to be a far-sighted decision, as it helped Sokol to become the biggest Czech association and personification of Czech nationalism from the 1880s onward. Sokol instructors and Czech Sokol inspired other countries to found similar organizations. Without exaggeration, it is possible to say that Sokols were at the birth of modern physical education and culture for all Slavic nations – the Poles, Bulgarians, Croatians and Slovenes. The Sokols, moreover, assisted as teachers of physical education and instructors in the formation of Russian physical education. Sokol units also started to spring up among the Czech minority in Vienna and emigrants in Western Europe and the USA, where the first Sokol unit was founded in 1865. With their achievements in gymnastics on the international field (in 1889, for example, they won in the competition organized by the French Gymnastics Union for foreign athletes in Paris), Sokol contributed to the fact that the Czechs were considered a developed country in sports by the European public.

From the end of the 1860s, Czech and German sports clubs started to emerge in the Czech lands. Czech and German athletes joined in the struggle for emancipation, but at the same time the phenomenon of club identity started to appear. As early as the 1880s, a distinctive 'sporting space', which was provided by economic means and transport possibilities, emerged spontaneously. The language of communication was German, which was also the language of all the sporting competitions and national sports meetings of athletes from Vienna, Prague and Budapest, with occasional participation of athletes from Berlin. Whereas Hungarian athletes could rely on their autonomy, the Czechs could rely only on the performance of their athletes. A great triumph of the struggle for national emancipation was the autonomous Czech representation in the International Olympic Movement and autonomous participation in the Olympic Games. A Czech, Jiří Guth Jarkovsk, was even one of the founding members of the International Olympic Committee (IOC). This was possible because of rules, valid until 1914, that National Olympic Committees could also be founded by members of a nation that did not have a state of its own. However, the Czech presence as an autonomous nation at the Olympic Games was greatly disliked by Austrian officials for reasons of state and, therefore, limited at the 1912 Games at Stockholm.[8]

Nationality conflicts, virulent between Czechs and Germans since the middle of the 19th century, were present in the sphere of sports clubs as well, especially in football. While the relationship between the Prague sides *DFC* (*Deutscher Fußball-Club*) *Prag* and *Slavia* were hostile until the 1920s, other Czech and German clubs cultivitated excellent relationships. These conflicts between the clubs were not necessarily a result of national antagonism, but rather partly an expression of financially motivated club interests.[9]

The Slovaks in the Hungarian part of the monarchy were in a more inferior position than the Czechs in Cisleithania and their national politics were rather weak. It was for these reasons that there were only scarce attempts to form 'national' physical education and sports in Slovakia before World War I. A good number of sports clubs existed on Slovak soil before 1918, but those had been Hungarian clubs. However, after the foundation of Czechoslovakia in October 1918, the sporting fate of Czechs and Slovaks united. Most of the gymnastics and sports clubs turned into Czechoslovakian organizations dominated by the Czechs, despite considerable development of Slovak physical education and sport, just as the Magyar (Hungarian) or Magyarized upper classes had dominated before 1918.

At the coup d'état in Prague in October 1918, which preceded the foundation of the new state, Sokol functionaries took part in leading positions and after that Sokol units, for a short but very important time, took over the role of the army in this new state.[10] Between the two world wars, physical culture in Czechoslovakia created a colourful spectrum of gymnastics, sports, tourist and Scout organizations. Sokol and the German Turner association in Czechoslovakia dominated among the gymnastics organizations. Examples of these organizations remind us that physical education played a significant role in the political life of Czechoslovakia. For a few weeks after Czechoslovak independence, the Sokols served as a provisional army; *Turnen*, on the other hand, contributed to the disintegration of Czechoslovakia in 1938. The paths of Czech and German physical education parted after the German invasion of Czechoslovakia on 15 March 1939. During the Protectorate of Bohemia and Moravia, the majority of organizations were prohibited and their members joined the resistance groups. Members of Sokols also participated in the assassination attempt on the leading local Nazi functionary, Reinhard Heydrich.

The first Czechoslovak republic was, according to its own official self-definition, a very modern state, in which great attention was given to sports and physical education. This was reflected in leading politicians' attitudes towards sports, which emphasized how important sports were for the development of the youth. Founder of the state, President Tomáš Garrigue Masaryk, said on the eve of the state's 10th jubilee in October 1928 in front of 25,000 pupils:

> Take care, that your bodies are clean, don't fear the water, enjoy washing, go bathing, swimming, move in fresh air and let the sun shine on you … Train and exercise the body with games and do sports in a sensible way.[11]

Having been born in 1850, Masaryk regretted that he had never participated in sports in the more modern sense (although he practised swimming and horse-riding), but he pointed out that even in old age he observed the Sokol training every day.[12] In the case of Masaryk's secretary of state for many years and then successor as president in 1935, Edvard Beneš, the press as well as official depictions referred to his football activities during his early years, which had allegedly already shown his qualities later proven in politics.[13] Other politicians used sports for their own purposes as well. Nationalist politician and newspaper editor Jiří Stříbrn, who had been a minister in the government several times, was for five years president of *Sparta* Prague, the most successful Czech football club besides local rival *Slavia*.[14]

In gymnastics and sports organizations based on national, religious or political ideas of Sokol, Deutscher Turnverband, Catholic *Orel* (eagle) or socialist organizations, training of the body took place for the sake of a certain ideology. The sport that attracted most spectators, just as in Poland, Hungary and in almost the whole of Europe, was soccer (football). Although crowds in the professional league, introduced in 1925, were not very large at the beginning,[15] up to 50,000 spectators flooded the Prague grounds when international matches (between national squads or clubs, e.g. in the *Mitropa* – Central European – Cup, a forerunner of the European Cup challenges) were played. Players such as Karel Pešek-Káďa or Josef Bican enjoyed the status of stars as popular as those of the movies. When in January 1927 young national squad member Jaroslav Poláček, who had suddenly died at the age of 21, was taken to the cemetery in his hometown of Pilsen (Plzeň), the press reported that there had never before in the town's history been a similar funeral with so many mourners.[16] Within first republic literature and film, football found its place as well. Two of the most-read authors of this era, Eduard Bass and Karel Poláček, wrote successful novels about this sport, which were quickly adapted for cinema.[17]

After the liberation of Czechoslovakia in 1945, the Communist party immensely strengthened its political power. It also directed its attention to sport and sought to create a unified sports organization that could be controlled, succeeding in its efforts soon after the coup of February 1948, when it usurped power in Czechoslovakia. In 1952, the Communist party disbanded Sokol and remained in control of sports up to 1989, using various forms of organization for enforcing its dictates. During the years when Communist despotism was extremely harsh, prominent sportsmen could suddenly become victims of the system: a large number of the national ice-hockey squad, one of the best teams in the world, was arrested in 1950 just before leaving for the world championships in London, due to an alleged conspiracy, and players were sentenced in a show trial to long sentences and forced labour.[18]

Similarly to other Communist countries, physical education and sports were part of the preferred areas of control, as they were valuable for military training and for propaganda.

The extent of subjection to the ideology and particular intentions of the Communist regime oscillated in accordance with the changes in the political situation in Czechoslovakia and in the Communist bloc. Except in the late 1960s, Czechoslovakia was one of the reliable allies of the Soviet Union even in sports.

The fall of Communism and return to individual freedom and parliamentary democracy brought changes to the world of physical education and sports. Some of the historical organizations, headed by Sokol, revived their activities and the Olympic Committee and sports associations transformed into independent entities. After the dissolution of Czechoslovakia into the Czech Republic and Slovakia, the National Olympic Committee was also dissolved into two independent bodies. The same thing occurred in virtually all organizations of physical culture.

By World War I, the Sokol organization had already been in existence for 50 years. At that time, it enjoyed great popularity and influence in Czech society and it possessed considerable financial potential. Alongside physical training, the Sokol management also paid a lot of attention to the education of its members. All of these circumstances facilitated the early emergence of a Czech historiography of sport, even if it only produced works of a descriptive character. Many of those that were produced up to the 1950s were rich in facts. These included the more than 800-page work by Karel Petrů.[19]

After the coup of February 1948, the dictate of Communist ideology fundamentally affected social sciences, including the choice of research topics and interpretation of research results. The history of sport was considered marginal in comparison with the history of politics, economics and culture, but despite this, authors were unable to escape the attention of Communist ideologists. When the normalization of the 1970s replaced the liberalization of social life which came after the Soviet Army occupation of Czechoslovakia in August 1968, authors also could not escape self-censorship. The extent of this was obviously not the same for all of authors, but the works with no self-censorship could not be published. No research topic was prohibited *de jure*, but some, which the sports historians tried to avoid, were impossible to carry out without the strong distortion of interpretation caused by the influence of Communist ideology.

The founding father of modern Czechoslovak historiography is František Krátk, co-founder of the *Internationales Komitee für Leibeserziehung und Sport* (International Committee of Physical Education and Sport). Among his students was also Jiří Kössl, internationally recognized historian of the Olympic movement, who laid the foundations of Czech and Czechoslovak Olympic movement history, mainly in his book *History of the Czechoslovak Olympic Movement*.[20] His work has been carried on by his co-worker and successor František Kolář, for example, in *Who Was Who – Our Olympians*.[21] Another contemporary of František Krátk was Jaromír Perútka, an important Slovak historian of sport, who was later succeeded by his co-worker Ján Grexa. Both individually and together, they focused their research on the history of sports in Slovakia.[22] After the fall of Communism in 1989, the ideological pressure was completely relieved and some topics could be returned to without any interpretative taboos.[23] Since the dissolution of Czechoslovakia in 1993, Czech and Slovak historiography has separated; however, the Czech and Slovak historians of sports still work closely together. Since the 1990s, they also co-operate with German historians. The result of this co-operation is, for example, *German Physical Education and Sport Clubs in Czech Countries and Czechoslovakia*. Moreover, the interest of many international authors shows evidence of the international importance of the Sokol movement, for example, C.E. Nolte's *The Sokol in the Czech Lands to 1914: Training for the Nation*.[24]

Football in Poland and Hungary, as well as practically everywhere in Western and Western Central Europe, is the most popular sport, while in the Czech and Slovak Republics, as in Sweden and Finland, ice-hockey attracts the largest number of spectators.[25] Anti-Soviet protests and riots in several towns after a Czechoslovak win against the Soviet Union, which may have been supported or even organized by *agents provocateurs* belonging to the Communist secret service, served for the regime in the beginning of 1969 as a pretext to force 'normalization' (i.e. liquidation of the 'Prague Spring' reform process).[26] When the Czech ice-hockey squad led by coach Ivan Hlinka won the Gold medal at the Olympic Games in Japan at Nagano in 1998, collective enthusiasm overwhelmed Bohemia and Moravia, and similarly in Slovakia when the country's team won the World Championship in 2002. When Ivan Hlinka, one of the most popular people in public life, died in a car crash in 2004, the Czech Republic as a nation was stunned.

Poland

While the Czech lands were one of the more developed countries of the Danube monarchy, where political representatives strived for autonomy similar to that of the Hungarians in 1867, the territory of Poland was divided between Prussia, or more precisely Germany, Russia and Austria, up to World War I. The development of Polish modern physical education and sports was, therefore, influenced by different levels of economy and culture and by the extent of national oppression in the individual partitions of the formerly powerful Polish state. Nevertheless, the sense of national identity and the intensity of the struggle for national emancipation, both acknowledged by the Polish intelligentsia, were not less important than in the Czech lands and Hungary. As in other Slavic countries, the Polish sports movement served in the struggle for national emancipation, which lead to the union of Poles and rediscovery of a 'great' Poland.

Miroslav Tyrš' idea of physical education as a means of unification of the nation and strengthening of its physical and moral health suited the needs of the Polish national movement. The public performances of Tyrš' gymnastics system, which was similar to that of the German Turner movement, strengthened the national self-confidence and served also as military training. At the turn of the year 1867, a gymnastics club was founded in Lemberg (today Lvov) in Galicia, which took on the name Sokol in 1869. The members of the democratic intelligentsia, coming mainly from the academic youth, were behind the birth of this club. Some of the prominent representatives of Lvov Sokol took gymnastics courses and introduced Tyrš' system into Polish physical education. Among them was, for example, Edward Madeyskis who became, in 1893, the Chairman of the Association of Sokol Gymnastics Societies of the Danube monarchy. In 1913, the federation had 30,000 members from 250 clubs in the whole of Galicia.

In the 1890s, the Sokol movement spread to other Polish partitions. In the Prussian part, Sokol units were founded in Inowrocław (German Hohensalza), Bydgoszcz (Bromberg) and Poznań (Posen). In 1893, these individual units were united in the Association of the Greater Poland Sokol Societies. Sokol units sprang up also in other then-German cities with Polish inhabitants, such as Gdansk (Danzig) and Wrocław (Breslau). The Sokol movement became a means of connection and communication between the Poles living in Prussia, Pomerania, Silesia, etc. In the Russian section, the first Sokol unit was founded in 1905. A year later, other units appeared in Warsaw, Lodz and other cities. After the suppression of the revolutionary movement in 1905, the tsarist authority broke up many of the Sokol units and made other units change their name. Nevertheless, until World

War I, the Polish Sokol movement was completely comparable with the Czech one in numbers and importance for the national emancipation movement.

After World War I and the foundation of independent states, the membership of the Czech Sokol Organization augmented immensely. The Polish Sokol, on the other hand, did not experience the same increase in numbers. This suggests that Sokol was not as significant in the social life of Poland as in Czechoslovakia; however, it remained the most important gymnastics organization. In 1919, Polish Sokols founded the Union of Gymnastics Societies 'Sokoł'. In between the world wars, the number of members exceeded 60,000. While the Czechoslovak Sokol movement retained its liberal and anticlerical character in the inter-war era, the Polish Sokol was overrun by conservative Catholicism. In the same year, the Polish Olympic Committee was created. In inter-war Poland, state organs headed by the Ministry of Defence became involved in the organization of physical culture and sports for the reasons of military training and, in 1927, a State Bureau of Physical Education and Military Training came into existence.

After Germany and the Soviet Union had divided Poland at the beginning of World War II as a result of the Hitler-Stalin Pact, the mere physical survival of the Polish nation was endangered. Sports activities were forbidden for Poles by the Nazi occupants, even under threat of capital punishment. Numerous Polish sportsmen and -women joined the resistance movement and many lost their lives.[27]

During World War II and the occupation of Poland, Sokol was prohibited. After the liberation, the activity of the Sokol organization was restored in some places, but the accession of new totality brought about its complete dissolution. In the time of temporary and partial liberalization of the Communist regime in 1956 and 1980–81, the struggle for the restoration of Sokol intensified but the process was completed only after the fall of Communism in the 1990s. Contrary to the Czech Republic, where Sokol belongs among the more important organizations, Polish Sokol, with 4,000 members in 1997, does not hold a significant position in the system of Polish sports.

Between 1948 and 1956, Polish sports came under the influence of the Soviet Union. In January 1947, the Communist party (Polish United Worker's Party) won in the falsified elections and by the end of the year liquidated the democratic opposition. In the first half of the 1950s, Polish sports were then directed in accordance with the Soviet model by various state organs that followed the instructions of the Communist party. The working unions also entered sporting life and sports, including competitions, started to be organized within the manufacturing branches. Top athletes in Poland as well as in Czechoslovakia were, again after the Soviet model, concentrated in Army Clubs. In February 1956, Nikita Khrushchev denounced Stalin's crimes in his Secret Speech at the Soviet Communist Congress. Two months later the Cominform was dissolved. This was a signal for the Soviet satellites that, in the future, Big Brother would not have to be unconditionally copied. Consequently in 1956–57, the ineffective system of direct state control was, in some European Communist countries including Czechoslovakia and Poland, replaced by a more liberal model of voluntary social organizations; these were, though, still under the control of the Communist party.

As in other parts of society – the most well-known example is the position of the Polish Catholic church and its religious freedom – the state attitude to sports from the 1960s was more liberal in the Polish People's Republic than in most other socialist countries, which also meant greater possibilities to travel for athletes. After the year of transformation in 1989, Poland, as in other Central European countries, saw great changes occurring in sports.[28]

The community of sports historians in Poland is much larger than in the Czech Republic, which corresponds to the size of Poland and the number of academic and other workplaces that are concerned with the history of sports. While it is not possible here to cover all the themes and important representatives of Polish sports historiography, we will mention the two most significant themes studied by Polish sports historians:

- Physical education in relation to national emancipation and sport of the national minorities. Herein, a work by one of the most significant Polish historians of sports, Bernard Woltman's *Polish Physical Culture in the German Eastern Poland*,[29] and a work by one of his students Tomasz Jurek's *Physical Culture of the German Minority in Poland in the Years 1918–1939* should be mentioned.[30]
- The Sokol movement. Herein, a work by Andrzej Bogucki, *Gymnastic Fraternity 'Falcon' 1893–1934*[31] could be mentioned. The Sokol movement of the Polish minority in German lands was also the focus of a German historian, Diethelm Blecking's *History of Polish National Physical Educational Organizations 'Falcon' in the German Empire*.[32] We should also mention a study about a Polish immigrants' sports movement in the USA.[33]

Hungary

Contrary to the Czech and Polish lands, the birth of modern Hungarian physical culture was linked with activities that can be specified as sport activities and which started to appear in Budapest in the 1830s. These were, for example, swimming, shooting and fencing (allegedly, even a performance of skiers took place at the Pest market in January 1837). In Hungary, there was no 'national' Turner movement to the extent it existed in Germany and the Slavonic countries; neither was there a great rivalry between those who practised 'English sports' (football or rugby) and gymnasts.[34]

Unlike in Prague, the Budapest revolution of 1848 turned into regular war between Hungary and the Austrian power, which ended in the defeat of the Hungarians. Consequently, the revolution started off the tradition of strong aversion to Austria in Hungarian society and was equally projected in the sports movement that was shaping at that time.

The Hungarian opposition towards Austria succeeded in 1867 in the Austro-Hungarian Compromise. In the following period, gymnastics and sports societies emerged in which 'spirit of revolution' prevailed. The most important society was the National Gymnastics Club, founded in 1867. In 1880, the Hungarian Gymnastics Clubs Association came into existence but, unlike the Sokol organization, it was only an open association of individual gymnastics clubs. Since the 1870s, sporting life in Hungary started to be concentrated in sports clubs. In 1875, for example, the Hungarian Athletics Club was founded by Earl Esterhazy Miksa.

The development of Hungarian sport and its growing popularity with the wider public was facilitated by various competitions organized on the occasion of the celebration of the Hungarian millennium in 1896, which was also visited by Austrian Emperor and Hungarian King Francis Joseph I. Some of the competitions had international attendance (140 competitors from Italy, France and Germany took part in the fencing tournament organized by the Hungarian Athletics Club), while some ended in failure. Nevertheless, through the participation in the celebration of the Hungarian arrival to the Carpathian Basin, the athletes acquired certain political influence which was later projected in the formation of a National Council for Sports in 1913. Its main objectives were an ambitious project of reforms in physical education at schools and in military training, the construction of the National Stadium and the foundation of the University of Sport.

At the turn of the 20th century, Hungarian sports gained prestige not only in the Danube monarchy, but throughout the whole European sporting public. Ferenc Kemeny, who studied at the Sorbonne where he met Pierre de Coubertin, became one of the founding members of the IOC. He was also a co-founder of the Hungarian National Olympic Committee. Nevertheless, he got into an argument with the Hungarian Athletics Association and was forced to resign from his posts both on the International and National Committees, the main reason for the disagreement with the representatives of Hungarian sport and political circles actually being his social class origins. Contrary to the Czech lands, where sports became the domain of middle-class young men, Hungarian sport remained controlled by aristocrats. The Hungarians did not play a secondary role in the IOC; quite the contrary. In 1896 and 1939, for example, Budapest entered the competition for hosting the Olympic Games. Moreover, Hungarian athletes participated in all Olympic Games, except in 1920 (when they were excluded because Hungary, too, had lost in World War I) and 1984 (when they were forced to do so by Communist group discipline).

Jewish sportsmen and -women, and functionaries in Hungary used to play an even more important role than in the countries described before. Several athletes of Jewish origin won Olympic Gold in fencing, a sport in which Hungary traditionally had always been very strong. Some clubs, such as the football club *MTK Budapest*, for example, were regarded as 'Jewish', although Christians were among the members and fans as well.[35]

In the inter-war era, Hungary remained among the important sporting countries. The field of physical education and sport enjoyed the support of the state, which resulted in the foundation of the University of Sport in 1925. It was Earl Kuno Klebelsberg, the Minister under whose department sport belonged, who is given the credit for its foundation. Unlike in Czechoslovakia and Poland, which acquired the independence they hoped for, Hungary belonged among the defeated countries. The feeling of injustice and bitterness for territorial and other losses, which changed Hungary into one of the smaller countries of Central Europe, led to state interventions in numerous areas including sport. These interventions attempted to revive the Hungarian nation and strengthen its defence capability.

Similarly to other countries in Central and South-Eastern Europe, Hungary was, after World War II, seized by Communist power. This process of subjugation was completed in 1948. The accession of Communism in Hungary introduced direct state control of sporting life. In March 1948, the State Sports Bureau was established. The events of 1956, when the national revolution was bloodily suppressed by the Soviet army, delayed the foundation of the Hungarian Association of Physical Education. Contrary to contemporary Czechoslovakia, the state remained in direct control of sport activities. In 1973, Hungary adopted 'state regulation of physical education and sport'. In the 1980s, sport was controlled by the State Bureau for Physical Education and Sport. After the fall of Communism, Hungarian sports started their journey back to their traditional structure and have been trying for success on the international scene.

In football, Hungary had been one of the strongest countries in Europe from the beginnings of the game until the 1960s, just as Czechoslovakia had been; they twice reached the World Cup final, but lost both times. Fame has faded since then and mainly one associates Hungarian football with their sensational defeat at the 1954 World Cup in Switzerland, although their team was then regarded as the strongest national squad in football history. This 1950s 'Golden Team' led by legendary striker Ferenc Puskás, pampered by the Communist regime as 'ambassadors of socialism', had not lost a single match since 1950 and twice defeated England. However, the clear favourites sensationally lost the most important match, the final at Bern, against the outsiders from the Federal Republic of (West) Germany. Some theories even create a connection between this match and the anti-Communist national uprising in 1956, because football-crazy Hungarians' immense disappointment had mixed with dissatisfaction over the political situation. The year 1956 meant the end for the 'Golden Team', because most players emigrated to Western Europe.[36]

Doyen of the Hungarian historiography of sport was Dr Mező Ferenc, whose book *History of the Olympic Games*[37] was awarded at the Olympic Games in Amsterdam in 1928. Hungarian historiography of sports reflects the richness and diversity of its history. In this limited space, it is again problematic to choose from among the important themes and authors. We would, therefore, like to mention a synthetic work of Hungarian historiography by Éva Foldes, Kun László and Kutassi László: *History of Hungarian Physical Education and Sport*[38] and an analytical monograph by Katalina Szikora: *Physical Education and Sport in the Time of the Consolidation Politics of Bethlems Government*.[39] In conclusion, we would also like to point out a work by István Kertész, an expert on Classical Greek sport, mainly in the Hellenic period.[40]

Common ground in sports history of the Eastern Central European states

Despite all the differences we have outlined, the three Central European states of Czechoslovakia, Poland and Hungary had, concerning sports and politics, one thing in common after 1945–48: being part of the Eastern bloc, they were also a part of the competition between East and West, between socialist and capitalist systems of sports and their ways of promotion, carried out at the Olympic Games and other great tournaments such as the football World Cup. On the other side, towards the 'Big Brother' Soviet Union in contrast to official propaganda of friendship, not only rivalry but even secret enmity was felt. This was traditionally the case in Poland, but in the other countries it existed since the Hungarian uprising of 1956 and the subsequent suppression of the 'Prague Spring' in 1968. At great sporting events these tensions were sometimes very well visible. During the Olympic Games at Melbourne in November/December 1956, taking place shortly after Soviet troops had brutally liquidated the Hungarian uprising, demonstrations for the freedom of Hungary occurred. About 40 Hungarian and Romanian athletes did not return, but decided to emigrate. The tensions reached their climax during this tournament at a water polo match between the Soviet Union and Hungary. Players carried out this match in a manner described as a kind of substitute to war, although in contrast to fighting in Hungarian cities, nobody was killed.[41] At the Games in Moscow in 1980, at a time when people in Poland feared a Soviet invasion because of the activities of the oppositional trade union movement, the Polish could enjoy a national triumph when one of their athletes won a Gold medal in pole vault. The jumper did not let himself be intimidated by the very hostile attitude of the Russian attendants.[42] We have also already mentioned the explosive duels in ice-hockey between Czechoslovakia and the Soviet Union.

Several waves of emigration after 1945 had a negative effect on sports, as well as on the cultural life in the countries described here. The first ones were when the Communists had gained power, when many people emigrated from Hungary in 1956, from Czechoslovakia after 1968, and from Poland throughout the 1970s and 1980s. In questions of sports politics, they had to obey the commands from the Soviet Union, as when they had to join the boycott of the Olympic Games at Los Angeles 1984 (which also was 'revenge' for the absence of the USA and many of their Western allies at the Moscow Games four years before). Similarly, there were the changes and challenges that popular as well as competitive sports had to face in the now four states (the Czech and Slovak Republics separated at the end of 1992) after 1989. Here, one could mention the end of 'state amateurism' (although state-run institutions such as the army still play an important role as employers of athletes, just as they do in Western Europe), the introduction of 'capitalist' structures in competitive sports, the change of structure in popular sports, the question of restitution of once 'nationalized' property, as was the case with the Czech *Sokol* and many others.

Perspectives for research on sports in Central Eastern Europe

The prospects for development in the history of sports in the post-Communist countries of Central Europe are naturally influenced by different material and personal resources of historiography in individual countries, and by specific research interests. In the European context, the position of sports historiography is getting better, mainly due to new topics of research and also owing to the gradual weakening of the 'hegemony' of traditional historiography, which has always focused mainly on the 'grand' political, economic and cultural themes. Such a trend is apparent also in the post-Communist countries of Central Europe. Sports historians have numerous possibilities for future success in historical research, mainly owing to the fact that physical education and sports played a special role in the national emancipation, politics and culture of the Central European countries in the 19th and 20th centuries. Moreover, a considerable space is opening up for sports historians from the Czech Republic, Slovakia, Poland and Hungary to co-operate and compare the historical development of this phenomenon, which contributed to the formation of modern European society. That is mainly in these areas:

- The formation of Central European sports space, primarily within the Austro-Hungarian monarchy and within the parts of the German empire at the end of the 19th century and at the outbreak of World War I. During this period, the sense of national identity often clashed with the newly born sense of club identity. Sports became a political matter, but at the same time lived their own life in natural regions where form was often dictated by specific sports interests, which cross over the national and state boundaries. Such a phenomenon is very interesting, among others also from the perspective of present vision of multicultural Europe with natural regions.
- The relationship of sport and the majority and minority in newly established countries of the Versailles arrangement, which brought about new national antagonisms in all mentioned countries, but, surprisingly, also moments of good and correct co-operation, for example, in sports representation of these countries.
- Naturally, a great opportunity for collective historical research rests in the comparison of sports development after the establishment of Communist dictatorship, when the sports were politicized and subordinated to totalitarian ideology and simultaneously became the preferred part of life in the Communist countries.

Similar possibilities rest in the comparison of the transformation of sports in newly established democracies after the fall of the Communist regimes in the 1980s. While we have a better picture of the history of sports in spaces occupied by the Czech and Slovak Republics, Hungary and Poland than in many other areas of the world, there is much research still to be done.

Notes

1 That is the title of Czech historian Jan Křen's standard study about nationality conflicts within the Czech lands. *Die Konfliktgemeinschaft: Tschechen und Deutsche 1780–1918* (München: Oldenbourg, 1996). Much has been written about the so-called national *Gemengelage* (state of mixture) in Eastern Central Europe, into which for obvious reasons we cannot go in more detail.

2 Just to mention one example: in Zdeněk Karník's extensive study (comprising three volumes and almost 2,000 pages) about the First Republic – *České země v eře první republiky* [The Czech lands in the era of the First Republic] (Prague: Libri, 2002–03) – only about nine pages are dedicated to sports and physical education. In an ambitious companion, where scholars and experts from both countries deal with the relationship between Germans and Czechs (which has not been always positive but very close throughout the centuries) – Walter Koschmal, Marek Nekula, Joachim Rogall, eds, *Deutsche und Tschechen: Geschichte – Kultur – Politik* (München: Beck, 2001), a Czech version was published simultaneously – there is not a single article on the subject of sports. A similar anthology about Germans and Poles – Andreas Lawaty and Hubert Orłowski, eds, *Deutsche und Polen: Geschichte – Kultur – Politik* (München: Beck, 2006) – includes such an essay: Robert Rduch and Stefan Zwicker, *Sport*, 465–76; in the Polish version: *Polacy i Niemcy: Historia – kultura – polityka* (Poznań: Wydawnictwo Poznańskie, 2003), 529–44.

3 Gertrud Pfister et al., eds, *Sport und Sozialer Wandel. Sports and Social Changes. Sport et Changements Sociaux. Proceedings of the ISHPES Congress 1998* (St Augustin: Academia, 2001); Marek Waic, ed., *Češi a Němci ve světě tělovýchovy a sportu: Die Deutschen und Tschechen in der Welt des Turnens und des Sports* (Prague: Karolinum, 2004); Dittmar Dahlmann, Anke Hilbrenner and Britta Lenz, eds, *Überall ist der Ball rund: Geschichte und Gegenwart des Fußballs in Ost-und Südosteuropa* (Essen: Klartext, 2006); Stephen Wagg and David L. Andrews, eds, *East Plays West. Sport and the Cold War* (London: Routledge, 2006); Arié Malz, Stefan Rohdewald and Stefan Wiederkehr, eds, *Sport zwischen Ost und West: Beiträge zur Sportgeschichte Osteuropas im 19. und 20. Jahrhundert* (Osnabrück: Fibre, 2007); Diethelm Blecking and Marek Waic, eds, *Sport-Ethnie-Nation: Zur Geschichte und Soziologie des Sports in Nationalitätenkonflikten und bei Minoritäten* (Hohengehren: Schneider, 2008).

4 Cf. Michael Brenner and Gideon Reuveni, eds, *Emanzipation durch Muskelkraft: Juden und Sport in Europa* (Göttingen: Vandenhoeck & Ruprecht, 2006), especially the contributions on Poland and Hungary; about Jewish sports in the Czech lands, see Kateřina Čapková, *Češi, Němci, Žide? Narodní identita Židů v Čechach 1918–1938* [Czechs, Germans, Jews? Jewish National Identity in Bohemia 1918–1938] (Prague, Litomyšl: Paseka, 2005), 246–59.

5 Monographs have been published recently on the German sports movement in Slovakia as well as in Poland: Miroslav Bobrík, *Nemecká menšina na Slovensku a jej telovýchovné a športové aktivity 1918–1945* [The German Minority in Slovakia and their Activities in Physical Education and Sports 1918–1945] (Bratislava: STU, 2006); Tomasz Jurek, *Kultura fizyczna mniejszości niemieckiej w Polsce w latach 1918–1939* [Physical Culture of the German Minority in Poland in the Years 1918–1938] (Gorzów Wielkopolski: Polskie Towarzystwo Naukowe Kultury Fizycznej, 2002). An entire depiction of Sudeten Germans' sporting activities does not exist, but see on the *Turnvereine* (Turner) movement see Andreas Luh, *Der deutsche Turnverband in der Ersten Tschechoslowakischen Republik: Vom völkischen Vereinsbetrieb zur volkspolitischen Bewegung* (München: Oldenbourg, 1988); on football, see Lubomír Král, *Historie německé kopané v Čechách* [A History of German Football in Bohemia] (Prague: MJF, 2006), a book full of information, facts and pictures, but without a scientific approach. Král has found very interesting material, for example, on the subject of conflicts between German and Czech football clubs in Prague before 1914. He suggests they were not so much due to 'national' reasons, but rather economic ones.

6 For a survey of German sports in these regions see Horst Ueberhorst, *Vergangen, nicht vergessen: Sportkultur im deutschen Osten und im Sudetenland* (Düsseldorf: Droste, 1992).

7 Claire E. Nolte, *The Sokol in the Czech Lands to 1914: Training for the Nation* (Basingstoke: Palgrave, 2003), 96, 56.

8 See František Kolář et al., *Kdo byl Kdo – Naši olympionici* [Who Was Who – Our Olympic Athletes] (Prague: Libri, 1999), 12–16.

9 See Král, *Historie německé kopané*, 12–21; Marek Waic and Stefan Zwicker, 'Der Wandel der deutsch-tschechischen Beziehungen den Fußball betreffend in den böhmischen Ländern und der Tschechoslowakei', in Marek Waic, ed., *Deutsche Turn-, Sport-, Touristik-und Pfadfinderorganisationen in den böhmischen Ländern und der Tschechoslowakei – Entstehung und Entwicklung bis zum Jahre 1938* (Prague: Karolinum, 2008); as well as contributions in Dahlmann, Hilbrenner, Lenz, *Überall ist der Ball rund*.

10 Karník 2002–03, I, 34, 49.

11 Quoted in Harry Klepetař, *Seit 1918 ... Eine Geschichte der tschechoslowakischen Republik* (Mährisch-Ostrau: Julius Kittls Nachfahren, 1937), 264.

12 K.Č. [Karel Čapek], *Hovory s. T.G. Masarykem* [Talking to T.G. Masaryk] (Prague: Fr. Borov – Čin, 1946, first published 1928–35), 52.

13 One can often find hints of this in the sports press of the 1930s, where hope was expressed that Beneš would promote sports and improve possibilities for sportsmen because of his own experiences. A publication published after World War II – *Sport a tělovchova v pohraničí: Sportovní almanach* [Sports and Physical Education in the Border Regions: A Sports Almanac] (Liberec: Talík, 1946) – praised him as 'a great friend and Anhänger of sports and physical education, a former competitive sportman and gymnast' (5).

14 Josef Pondělík, *Století fotbalu: Z dějin československé kopané* [The Century of Football: About Czechoslovak football history] (Prague: Olympia, 1986), 69 f.

15 Radovan Jelínek, Miloslav Jenšík et al., *Atlas českého fotbalu od roku 1890* [Atlas of Czech Football Since the Year 1890] (Prague: Infokart, 2005), 84–87.

16 Czech sports magazine, *STAR* No. 45 (1927), 2.

17 Stefan Zwicker, 'Fußball in der deutschen und tschechischen Gesellschaft, Literatur und Publizistik: Ansätze zu einer vergleichenden Studie', in Brücken, *Germanistisches Jahrbuch Tschechien und Slowakei* (2000), 247–86, here 263–66.

18 See Vilém Hejl, *Zpráva o organizovaném násilí* [A Report on Organized Violence] (Prague: Univerzum, 1990), 204; Kolář et al. 1999, 164f., 208f.

19 Karel Petrů, *Dějiny československé kopané* [History of Czechoslovak Football] (Prague: Národní nakladatelství A. Pokorn, 1946).

20 Jiří Kössl, *Dějiny československého olympijského hnutí* [History of the Czechoslovak Olympic Movement] (Prague: Olympia, 1977).

21 Kolář et al. 1999.

22 For example, *Dějiny tělesnej kultury na Slovensku* [History of Physical Culture in Slovakia] (Bratislava: Šport, 1995).

23 For example, M. Waic et al., *Sokol v české společnosti* [Falcon in the Czech Society] (Prague: Univerzita Karlova Fakulta tělesné vchovy a sportu, 1996); or M. Bobrík, *Německá menšina na Slovensku a jej tělochovné a športové aktivity 1918–1945* [German Minority in Slovakia and its Physical Education and Sport Activities 1918–1945] (Bratislava: Slovenská technická univerzita, 2006).

24 Marek Waic et al., *Německé tělovchovné a sportovní spolky v českh zemích a Československu* [German Physical Education and Sport Clubs in Czech Countries and Czechoslovakia] (Prague: Univeryita Karlova, 2008). C.E. Nolte, *The Sokol in the Czech Lands to 1914: Training for the Nation* (Basingstoke: Palgrave, 2003)

25 For statistics and a detailed map of football and ice-hockey strongholds in the Czech Republic, see Jelínek, Jenšík et al. 2005, 84f. Of course, while football, at least in organized clubs, is played more than ice-hockey, the attraction of the game on ice to the spectators, especially matches shown on TV, is greater.

26 On these incidents see Jörg Ganzenmüller, 'Bruderzwist im Kalten Krieg. Sowjetisch-tschechoslowakische Länderspiele im Umfeld des "Prager Frühlings"', in Malz, Rohdewald and Wiederkehr 2007, 113–30.

27 Cf. Rduch/Zwicker, *Sport*, 469. For an entire depiction of sports in Poland, see Stefan Sienarski, *Sport w Polsce* [Sport in Poland] (Warsaw: Interpress, 1976); Dariusz Matyja, ed., *Sport* (Warsaw: Wydawnictwo Naukowe PWN, 2000).

28 Cf. the articles by Tomasz Jurek and Bernard Woltmann, 'Wirtschaftliche Veränderungen in Polen nach der Wende 1989 und ihre Auswirkungen auf die Entwicklungen des Leistungssports: Der Einfluß der Gesellschaftstransformation auf die Organisation des Sports in Polen', in Pfister et al. 2001, 103–05, 125–31.

29 Bernard Woltman, *Polska kultura fizyczna na wschodnim pograniczu niemieckim 1919 – 1939* [Polish Physical Culture in the German Eastern Poland] (Poznań: AWF, 1980).

30 Tomasz Jurek, *Kultura Fizyczna Mniejszosci Niemieckiej W Polsce W Latach 1918–1939* [Physical Culture of the German Minority in Poland in the Years 1918–1939] (Gorzów Wielkopolski: Polskie Towarzystwo Naukowe Kultury Fizycznej, 2002).

31 Andrzej Bogucki, *Towarzystwo Gimnastyczne 'Sokol' na Pomorzu 1893–1934* [Gymnastic Fraternity 'Falcon' 1893–1934] (Bydgoszcz: Centrum Informaciji Naukowej Sokolstwa Polskiego, 1997).

32 Diethelm Blecking, *Die Geschichte der nationalpolnischen Turnorganisation 'Sokół' im Deutschen Reich 1884–1939* [History of Polish National Physical Educational Organizations 'Falcon' in the German Empire] (Münster: Lit Verlag, 1990).

33 Donald E. Pienkos, *One Hundred Years Young: A History of the Polish Falcons of America, 1887–1987* (Boulder, CO: EEM / New York: Cambridge University Press, 1987).

34 Cf. Hardy Grüne, 'Ungarn: Das lange Warten auf das nächste Wunder', in Hardy Grüne, *Weltfußballenzyklopädie: Europa und Asien* (Göttingen 2007: Verlag die Werkstatt), 273–79, here 273.

35 Cf. Viktor Karady and Miklós Hadas, 'Fußball und Antisemitismus in Ungarn', in Brenner and Reuveni 2006, 216–37.

36 Cf. Andrew Handler, *From Goals to Guns: The Golden Age of Soccer in Hungary* (New York, 1994), xxx; Peter Kasza, *1954 – Fußball spielt Geschichte* (Berlin: be.bra Verlag, 2004).

37 Mezö Ferenc, *Az olympiai játékok története* [History of the Olympic Games] (Budapest, 1928).

38 Éva Fóldes, László Kun and László Kutassi, *A magyar testnevele?s e?s sport to?rte?nete* [History of Hungarian Physical Education and Sport] (Budapest, 1977).

39 Katalin Szikora, *Testnevelés és sport a Bethlem kormány konszolidációs politikájának szolgálatában* [Physical Education and Sport in the Time of the Consolidation Politics of Bethlem's Government] (Budapest, 1987).

40 István Kertész, *A görög sport világa* [The Greek World of Sport] (Budapest, 2001).

41 Barbara Keys, 'The 1956 Olympic Games and the Postwar International Order', in Carole Fink, Frank Hadler and Tomasz Schramm, eds, *1956: European and Global Perspectives* (Leipzig: Leipziger Universitätsverlag, 2006), 283–307, here 288–90.

42 Cf. Rduch and Zwicker, *Sport*, 470.

24 China

Fan Hong

In both the East and the West, the study of the history of sport has become an academic discipline since the 1980s. Experts are emerging in a steady stream and publications are impressively increasing. Sports historians can claim these accomplishments with pride. Although the sports historians speak different languages, have different focuses and have different methodologies, their fundamental approach remains the same. It consists of (1) documenting large structural changes between society and sport; (2) explaining the evolution of culture and sport; (3) constructing a coherent analysis of social relationships in and through sport; (4) reconstructing the experience of athletes and ordinary people's sporting lives; and (5) establishing a unique empire in the field of social science. This chapter will focus on the development of the study of sports history in China. It will examine the development of sports history studies in China and the West and provide the readers with an overview.

Sports history studies in China

The evolution of the study of Chinese sports history could be divided into three periods: Feudal China, pre-1911; the Republic of China, 1911–49; the People's Republic of China, 1949–2009. Each period, like sport, has seen changes of ideology, culture, politics and society.

Feudal China, pre-1911

Over 5,000 years of written history has left China with a large number of history books. The Chinese have been very proud of their tradition of historical research and historical records. However, there are few records on the history of sport, for example, some articles on *Cuju* (ancient Chinese football) in the Han Dynasty (221 BC–AD 24) and *Jiaoli ji* (The Records of Wrestling) in the Tang Dynasty (AD 960).[1] Most historical records of physical education, sport and leisure activities are scattered in the history of literature, arts, education, religion, philosophy, medicine and politics.

Although sport played an important role in feudal China it was never regarded as an independent discipline. Academics were not interested in writing history about sport. In addition, players and entertainers were regarded as manual labourers and had no social status in society. Therefore, their activities were not worth recording.[2] Consequently, there was no comprehensive study of the history of sport in ancient China.

The Republic of China, 1911–49

The 1911 Revolution overthrew the Qing government and ended the feudal social system which had dominated China for thousands of years. The Nationalists established the Republic of China after the Revolution. China began to change from a feudal to a modern social system. In order to create a new culture for the new society, in 1915 some intellectuals embraced anarchy, nationalism or socialism and started a campaign called the 'New Culture Movement' (Xinwenhua yundong). Western concepts, especially 'science' and 'democracy', became weapons with which they attacked China's still influential feudal culture – Confucianism, which, in their eyes, was the major obstacle on the road to modernity. They saw the weakness of traditional Chinese culture and wanted it reformed through westernization. By studying Western philosophical works and observing European and American societies, they came to the conclusion that the vigour which had accounted for the advance of the Western powers resided in the strong individual development of mind and body. Physical exercise, physical education and sport, they argued, should be strongly emphasized in schools and society.

The Republic government responded to the progressives' call for reformation of the physical education system. On 1 November 1922, the Ministry of Education issued 'The Decree of the Reformation of the School System'. This new school system emphasized that education must suit the needs of social evolution and pay attention to developing individualism in pupils. In 1923 the new curriculum was issued and published in the *Education Journal* (*Jiaoyu zazhi*). Physical education and sport was a part of the curriculum, including Western sports such as ball games, athletics, gymnastics and Western academic courses such as physiology and hygiene.[3]

This period also saw the beginning of sports history studies. Guo Xifen, a young physical educationalist, began his teaching post in Shanghai Patriotic Girls School and East Asian Sports School and felt the need for a text book for his course on sports history. He wrote a book called the *History of Sport in China* and published it in 1919. In his book Guo Xifen searched through Chinese historical records and divided Chinese sports into eight categories: gymnastics, wrestling, boxing, fencing, archery, dancing, swimming and entertainment. He also traced the development of Chinese sports from ancient to modern times.[4]

In 1926, Hao Gengshen, a Chinese YMCA physical educationist, published *On Chinese Physical Education and Sport*, which was an extension of his graduate thesis at Springfield College in the USA. He discussed the development of Chinese sport in the early 20th century including the influence of the modern Western physical education and sport in Chinese education system and society.[5]

In the 1930s and 1940s, along with the development of modern physical education in schools and China's participation in the Olympic Games, books on the history of Western sports and Olympics were increasing, including Zhang Jiwu's *The Brief History of Sport in the World* (1932); Ruan Weichun's *The History of Athletics* (1933); Wu Wenzhong's *The History of the Olympics* (1941); Xie Shiyan's *Olympic History* (1944); Cheng Dengke's *The Brief History of World Sport* (1946); and Wu Wenzhong's *Sports History* (1946).

In the meantime, twelve sports newspapers and nine sports journals and magazines were published in China.[6] Some sports history articles appeared in these journals and newspapers. Most of them were introductions to, or descriptions of, physical education and sport in the West, including ancient Greek and Roman sports, modern physical education systems in Europe and America, and the ancient and modern Olympic Games.

The publications reflected the transformation of the Chinese physical education and sports system from traditional to modern, which originated largely under influences from the West. Modern sport came to China as an element of Western culture and was accompanied by military force, which directly challenged Chinese traditional culture and patriotism. This provoked conflict and confrontation between radicals and conservatives in Chinese society in the Republic era. Consequently, an important debate occurred in the 1930s.[7] The focus of the debate was on whether China should reject or accept Western sport – an alien culture. Many politicians, educationists and physical educationists took part in the debate, which brought the direct consequence that modern sport became a major part of modern Chinese culture and a new physical culture embracing both the traditional and contemporary was born. The debate also stimulated research in China about Chinese and Western sports history.

The study in the Republic era of sports history marked the beginning of sports historical studies in China. This period found China engaged in various civil wars and the eight-year war of resistance against Japanese invasion, which impeded further progress of sports history research. Nevertheless, it was a beginning.

The People's Republic of China, 1949–2009

In 1949 the Communists won the civil war and controlled all China except Taiwan, to which the Nationalist government had fled. The Communists established the People's Republic of China (PRC) in October 1949. They established the All-China Sports Federation (Zhonghua quanguo tiyu zonghui) in June 1952 to be the governing body in charge of all sporting affairs in China. Later, learned from the system of the Soviet Union, in November 1952, the Ministry of Sport was founded to replace the All-China Sports Federation as the governing body. It had status equal to the Ministry of Education and was directly supervised by the State Council.

Sport in the PRC, from its beginning, was promoted as an extremely useful tool in politics, diplomacy, economics, military defence and national unity. Sports historical studies were part of a wider strategy of historical investigation and the promotion of sport under Communism.

In 1956 the Sports Technology Committee was established in the Sports Ministry in Beijing. The Head was Professor Dong Shouyi, who was also a member of the International Olympic Committee. The major responsibility of the Sports Technology Committee was to conduct research into Chinese sports history. In April 1958 the Committee via the Sports Ministry sent a request to regional and local sports commissions and asked them to assist in the collection of sports history material. From 1957 to 1961, led by Professor Tang Hao, nine volumes (one million words) of *Chinese Sports History Research Material* were edited by the Committee and published by the People's Sports Press in Beijing.[8] The achievement was profound. It was an icebreaker. The volumes contained invaluable sources of ancient sports events material and first-hand material of the development of modern sports history before 1949. The Committee held a national conference in 1957 to discuss the promotion of sports history studies nationally and decided to publish a comprehensive book on Chinese sports history in five years. However, due to the failure of the Great Leap Forward in 1960 the budget was cut and the Committee dispersed.

Therefore, research on sports history became a responsibility of physical education institutes. In March 1960 the Sports Ministry held a conference in Beijing to discuss issues of research and teaching in Chinese sports history in the physical education institutes. Following the conference the first sports history research centre was set up in Chengdu Physical Education Institute in 1962. Three professors, one doctorate (who obtained his doctorate in sports history in the USA in the 1940s) and some young graduates from the Institute started systematic research into Chinese sports history. After four years' concentrated work the Research Centre published *The Ancient Chinese Sports Material* (three volumes); drafted the book called *Modern Chinese Sports History*; and translated four books on world sports history from English and Japanese.[9] In the same period sports history courses were taught both in Chengdu and Beijing Physical Education Institutes.[10]

The Cultural Revolution, which began in 1966, interrupted the progress of sports history studies. The goal of the Cultural Revolution was to re-establish the ideological purity of Communism threatened by the revisionists and capitalists over the previous 18 years and to recreate unpolluted Mao Zedong Thought. It was believed that by using mass political action and revolutionary ideology the Maoists could achieve their revolutionary goal and further socio-economic development. In fact, the consequence was a chaotic and violent political upheaval accompanied by ferocious ideological debate, which engulfed the whole country. Clarity of debate was often marred by the intensity of the power struggle that influenced and shaped the issues under discussion. This occurred everywhere, including the Sport History Research Centre in Chengdu Physical Education Institute. The Centre was seen as a nest of elite intellectuals and a place to produce feudal and bourgeois rubbish. It was disbanded.

It was only in the 1980s that the spring of the study of sports history came to China. In 1982 the Sports History Working Committee (hereafter Committee), led by Professor Bi Shiming, was established in the Sports Ministry in Beijing. It soon formed an umbrella network with the sports history offices in 31 provincial and 64 local sports commissions, and more than 30 physical education departments and institutes. The aim of the Committee was to promote a systematic study of sports history in general and Chinese sports history in particular. An annual working conference was held between 1982 and 1990 to examine progress.[11]

The Chinese Society for the History of Physical Education and Sport (hereafter Society) was established in 1984. Its headquarters were in the Committee. The Executive Board of the Society consisted of representatives from major physical education institutes and departments of universities. Its membership increased rapidly and by 1990 it had more than 600 members.[12]

From 1984 to 1998, the Society and the Committee organized 16 national conferences and published 16 conference proceedings. The Society also held international conferences twice: the International Conference on Oriental Sports in 1992 and the ISHPES Conference in 1997. It is a board member of ISHPES and the East Asian Sports History Society, which holds annual conferences in China, Taiwan, Japan and South Korea in turn. The Society has established an exchange programme with Japan and South Korea. It sent a delegation to the annual conferences of the Japanese and South Korean sports history societies, and vice versa.[13] Meanwhile, at home, the regional and local sports commissions organized more than 100 conferences between 1984 and 1998.[14] The major themes of those conferences have been regional and local sports history, the lives of local sports heroes and heroines, and the experiences of ordinary people.

From 1981 to 2008 more than 100 books on sports history were published, the most influential including: Li Jifang's *Ancient Chinese Sports History* (1984); Yan Shaolu and Fan Hong's *From the Ancient Olympics to Modern Sports* (1984); Rong Gaotang's

Contemporary Chinese Sport (1984); Chinese Society for the History of Physical Education and Sport (hereafter CSHPES)'s *Modern Chinese Sports History* (1989); Yan Shaolu and Zhou Xikuan's *Sports History in the World* (1989); Zheng Zhengkun's *The History of Ancient Chinese Sports Philosophy* (1989); Gu Shiquan and Lin Boyuan's *Ancient Chinese Sports History* (1989); Bi Shiming's *Ancient Chinese Sports History* (1990); Hu Xiaoming's *Sports History of the Chinese Ethnic Minorities* (1990); Wang Zengming's *The History of Red Sports in the Communist Area before 1949* (1990); Su Jingcheng's *The History of Physical Education in China* (1994); Wu Shaozhu and Xiong Xiaozheng's *Sports History of the People's Republic of China* (1999); and Luo Shiming's *The History of China's Participation in the Olympic Games* (2005).

In addition, a series of the history of sports events books were jointly edited and published by the Committee and the sports associations. It included 22 books on major sports events, for example: *The History of Fencing in China* (1992); *The History of Chinese Football* (1993); *The History of Mountain Climbing in China* (1993); and *The History of Chinese Athletics* (1997).

Local and regional sports history research centres based in the sports commissions concentrated on local and regional sports historical research and also published books on regional and local sports history, for example: *Anhui Historical Records of Sports in Anhui Province* (16 volumes); *Historical Material of Sports in Sichuan Province* (12 volumes); and *Beijing Sports History Material* (five volumes).

Physical education institutes also published 24 volumes of sports history material, including original literature, documents, autobiography, biography, memoirs and interviews throughout ancient, modern and contemporary China. Five sports history text books were produced to meet the needs of teaching in the universities and colleges. The most updated text books were Hao Qin's *Sports History* (2006) and Tan Hua's *Sport History* (2007).

Some 26 local and regional sports history journals appeared between 1984 and 1998. The national academic publication – *Journal of Sports History and Culture* (bimonthly) – was issued in 1983. It is compulsory reading for academics, coaches and sports administrators in China. By 2005 more than 4,000 articles on sports history had been published in the journal.

The distinguished Sport History Research Centre in Chengdu was restored in 1980. From 1983 to 1988 the Centre, in conjunction with the Chinese Sports History Society, organized sports history teaching training classes on three occasions. More than 200 lecturers from universities in China attended the classes. They became a major force to promote sports history study and teaching in China. It again became the centre of sports history studies. By 1990 sports history was taught in all 15 physical education institutes and 159 physical education departments of universities and colleges in China.

At the beginning of the 1990s three new research centres emerged in Zejiang University in Hangzhou, South China Normal University in Guangzhou and Beijing Sports University (previously the Beijing Physical Education Institute). They all offer MA and PhD degrees in sports history.

Sports history in China has become an academic discipline. Within this discipline there are specialized research areas including ancient Chinese sports history; modern Chinese sports history; contemporary Chinese sports history; Red sports history (sports in the Communist areas before 1949); sports events history; Chinese traditional sports history including Wushu (martial arts) history; minority sports history; women's sports history; and world sports history.[15]

At the end of the 20th century and the beginning of the 21st when China put in a bid for the hosting of the Olympic Games there was a new fever of study of Olympic history in China which was promoted both by the government and by sports historians.

The Olympic Research Centre at Beijing Sports University was the first Olympic research centre established in China. It was the research centre for sports history in the early 1980s. However, in response to Beijing's bid for the Olympics in 1993 it changed its name to the Centre for Olympic Studies in the early 1990s. Professor Hai Ren is a leading scholar in the centre. Over the years it has published the following books: *The Olympic Movement* (1993); *Olympic Studies* (1994); *The Olympic Movement Encyclopaedia* (2000); *Olympic Studies Series* (2001); *The Olympic Gallery* (2002); *Humanistic Olympics* (2005); *The Olympic Movement Reader* (2005).[16]

After Beijing's successful bid for the Olympics in 2000, two more research centres were established in Beijing: the Humanistic Olympic Studies Centre at Renmin University and the Olympic Culture Research Centre at Beijing Union University. Each of the three major Olympic research centres belonged to each hosting university. They received funds from various government bodies, such as the Ministry of Education and the Beijing Olympic Organizing Committee and from commissioned research.

The Humanistic Olympic Studies Centre (HOSC) at Renmin University was founded in October 2000 after Beijing's successful bid for the 2008 Games. Its aim was to improve, strengthen and co-ordinate academic efforts for the Beijing Olympics. HOSC operates as an independent research centre under the supervision of Renmin University of China. In September 2004, the HOSC was appointed by the Beijing Philosophical Social Programming Committee and the Beijing Municipal Commission of Education as the official Beijing Humanistic Olympic Studies Base. It received funding to conduct research on the history and culture of the Olympic Games.

In order to evaluate the social, environmental, cultural and economic impact of the Olympic Games on the host city and the wider world, the International Olympic Committee has established the Olympic Games Global Impact (OGGI) project. Each host city is required to undertake this study. The Centre was awarded responsibility for this project.

The Olympic Culture Research Centre in Beijing Union University also played an important role in the field of the history and culture of Olympic Studies. It was founded in October 2000. There were three sections in the research centre: Olympic History and Culture, Beijing Humanistic Olympics and Sports News. It undertook projects including Olympic cultural history, the history of Chinese traditional sports culture and foreign sports culture in Beijing. In addition, sports historians throughout the country all gathered under the banner of Olympic Studies. They received funding from the Olympic Research Projects Fund based in the State General Administration of Sport and from the National Planning Office of Philosophy and Social Science. These two government bodies provided research funding annually for researchers from universities, sport research centres and provincial and regional sports commissions to conduct designated research in order to meet the needs of the development of sport in China. Therefore, between 2005 and 2008, the majority of funds were provided to research projects relating to Olympic Studies.[17]

Sports historians also actively participated in the national Olympic Education Programme sponsored by the Beijing government, the Beijing Olympic Organizing Committee, the Education Ministry and local governments. Its aim was to spread the Olympic idea, principle and history throughout China. They produced text books, which were used nation-wide. They also published a large number of academic, and non-academic / populist books which focus on Olympic history and current issues.[18] Furthermore, a wide range of multimedia teaching materials such as TV programmes, videos, internet flash cartoons and tapes have also been made to meet the needs of Olympic Education. Sports historians in China suddenly appeared on all the media to talk about Olympic history.

From 2002 to 2008, universities in China staged a wide range of international and domestic academic conferences focused on the Olympics. The history of the Olympic Games, China's relationship with the Olympic movement and Beijing's contribution to the Olympic Games were topics discussed enthusiastically at the conferences.

Reasons for the development of Chinese sports history studies

Why have sports history studies developed rapidly in China in the past two decades? One explanation is traditional Chinese culture, which has encouraged the study of history. The Chinese believe that history can inform the present and predict the future. The old saying is: 'Do not forget history, history is always your teacher.' When the country is prosperous the mission of the historians is to write down what has happened in society to provide models for future generations. From the beginning of the 1980s when China began its journey of dramatic transformation, historians, in general, were very excited. They felt it was the right time and right place for them to perform, since they had been muted for so long. Just like art historians who wrote about art histories and political historians who rewrote the history of the People's Republic of China, sports historians simply took on the responsibility of writing the history of sport.[19]

The other explanation is that the systematic production of sports history is a reflection of the power of the government. Indeed, the state has played a very important part and government bodies – the Sports History Working Committee and The Chinese Society for History of Sport and Physical Education in the 1980s and 1990s and the Education Ministry and Beijing Olympic Organizing Committee at the beginning of the 21st century – deserve much credit.[20]

However, despite traditional culture and promotion by the government the emergence of sports history studies since the 1980s is an innovative intellectual movement. Its growth has paralleled the major transformation of society – ideological, political, economic, social and cultural. After the death of Chairman Mao in 1976 the Cultural Revolution came to its end. The country had embarked on a new course of accelerated economic development: the Four Modernizations in industry, agriculture, science and technology and national defence. The Party declared the Four Modernizations a sufficient basis for transforming China. It made a new effort to combine 'capitalism' with 'people's democracy' in order to ensure the success of modernization. The intellectuals were encouraged to free their minds from orthodox Maoist principles, and to 'seek truth from facts' and 'make practise the sole criterion of truth'. The slogan 'Let hundreds of flowers bloom and hundreds of birds sing', which appeared in 1958 and put thousands of intellectuals in jail, appeared again in a new form. Dozens of signs pointed to a new cultural thaw, among which open criticism of Mao Zedong's class struggle principle became acceptable; the 'literature of the wounded' stimulated debate and reflection about China's past and future prospects; the study of the long-taboo subjects of comparative religion, such as Buddhism, Daoism, Islam and Christianity, was tolerated. So too was history.

History studies had lost integrity as far back as the 19th century. Different parties with different ideologies used history to serve their different purposes. In the 1980s the need for a serious study of history became important. 'A nation without honest history has no future' became the slogan and touched most historians' hearts. Historians started to re-examine and re-write Chinese history in order to 'return to the real face of history'. This movement had a strong impact on sports history studies. A large number of able, energetic intellectuals from history, literature, arts and sports studies entered the sports history field. They shared in the excitement of enlarging the vision of sports history. They were not happy to be bookkeepers of athletic records. They wanted to take sports history studies with them to join the exciting social and cultural changes. They not only inherited traditional historical methods and subjects, but also created a new field, which has profoundly affected historical consciousness by broadening both the subject matter and methods of history.

They sought to uncover the sporting lives of inarticulate people and embarked on an unprecedented effort to rewrite history from the bottom up. This approach was motivated by a real need to uncover the concerns of cultural continuity that had hitherto been neglected. The interest in new sources of evidence is also a reflection of the pronounced populist bias of the new sports history, the feeling that ordinary people in the past 5,000 years also had their own sports experience. The new sports history, on the one hand, addressed large questions, such as national character, social systems, economic impact and political ideology. On the other hand, it shifted the locus of this enquiry to the unknown masses and busied itself in widening knowledge of the sporting lives of ordinary Chinese in feudal China and Nationalist China. For the first time those people found their voice in the historical sports record.

They established the status of sports history as a science, a perspective achieved by integrating it in the field of social science. This new scientific status was different from the past, even different from history itself. The sports historians borrowed methods and terminology from the wide range of social science to analyse and examine sports in society. This enlarged the vision of sports history. Publication of the first issue of the *Journal of Sports History and Culture* in 1983 was the landmark of this intellectual exchange between history and social science.

Despite successes Chinese sports historians need to overcome their weaknesses if they want to continue to progress. Sports history is not a political tool, or political propaganda. Writing history needs courage. Writing an honest history needs extra-courage. The mission of sports history should not encourage the study of such generalized constructs as 'the superiority of the Chinese Communist sports system'.

Chinese sports historians have available a lot of first-hand material. They have now transcended the fragmentation which characterized a generation of descriptive work and now attempt a higher level of analysis. They have produced some high quality analytic sports history books and articles in both Chinese and English. However due to the language barrier most sports historians in China have not fully engaged with the international sports history community to make their own contribution to it.

For historical reasons, most Chinese scholars who were born in the 1950s are unable to speak and write in fluent English. In the 1950s Russian was the only foreign language taught at the universities. From 1962 to 1965, when China broke away from the USSR, universities started to teach English. However during the Cultural Revolution (1966–76) English was seen as a poison of capitalism and revisionism. A pupil in Beijing who refused to learn English became a national heroine. The famous slogan was 'Our revolution does not need to learn ABC'. Therefore, English courses were discontinued in schools and universities. Thus most sports historians who grew up in this period did not have necessary knowledge of foreign languages. However, the situation began to change when a younger generation – who were born in the late 1970s and the 1980s – received uninterrupted education in China and abroad. Having first-hand knowledge of Chinese history and culture, they also speak and write in fluent Chinese and English. They are the new force in the field of Chinese sports history studies.

In the meantime, Taiwan scholars have published more than 20 books on sports history between the 1950s and the 1990s, including Tang Minxing's *The History of the Basketball Team of the Republic of China's Participation in International Competition* (1952); Wu Wenzhong's *One Hundred Years' History of Chinese Sports* (1956); Lin Boyuan's *Ancient Chinese Sports History* (1979); Cai Zengxiong's *The History of Physical Education in Schools during the Japanese Occupation* (1995); and Xu Yixiong and Xu Yuanmin's *The Sports History of Modern Chinese Schools* (1999). From the mid 1980s, collaboration on research projects on sports history between the mainland and Taiwan began. From 1990, the exchange of students and scholars began between universities in Taiwan and the mainland.

The future of Chinese sports history studies in China

The past two decades have witnessed great developments in the field of Chinese sports history studies. At the national level, sports research leadership has been established. The Sports History Working Committee in the Sports Ministry and the Chinese Society for the History of PE and Sport have formed an umbrella system and a network to promote sports history studies in the sports commissions and sports institutes. Its journal, the *Journal of Sports History and Culture*, became a leader in its field. In addition, *The Journal of the Chengdu Physical Education Institute* and *Sports Studies Journal*, published by the South China Normal University, is regarded as among the leading university journals.

At university level, research centres have been established at institutes and universities. Researchers have been actively engaged in their research. Sports history is taught in universities and institutes as a compulsory or optional course. Books on sports history have been published. Conferences on sports history take place every year nationally and regionally.

However, sports historians have predicted that there will be a decline of the study of sports history in China in the 21st century, especially after the 2008 Beijing Olympic Games.[21] The major reason is that the new and emerging movement of sports history is closely linked to current political, economic and social developments in terms of funding application and resource support. When China becomes more and more commercialized the areas of business, economy and management will receive more funding than history. The new teaching and research areas, such as sports management, sports media and sports industry have attracted more students and researchers. Some universities have already taken the course of sports history off their curricula and added the course of sports management and sports media instead.[22]

Nevertheless, sports history studies will continue to grow, but in a more structured form. The fever of Olympic Studies will cool down because of the exhaustion of all the resources in the past eight years. The following areas will begin to attract more critical and analytic research: comparative studies between Chinese traditional sports and Western sports; the YMCA/YWCS' and Christian missionaries' influence on, and contribution to, modern Chinese physical education and sports; influential sports and physical education personalities in the Nationalist and Communist era; the history of ethnic minority sports;

the history of traditional sports including Wushu; the change of sports policy, system and practice in the PRC era; and sport and international relations in the PRC era.[23]

Chinese history studies in the West

Before the 1990s, for most sports historians in the West, Chinese sports history was virtually non-existent. It is not surprising. William T. Rowe has pointed out that for most Western historians Chinese history 'remains essentially lower case – it describes not so much a methodological movement as simply an orientation to addressing problems of society and social change'.[24] For many sports historians in the West there remains considerable doubt regarding what this much heralded 'sports history' achievement by the Chinese in China is all about. In the West there are only a handful of pioneer works on Chinese sports history, for example, before 1990 there was only one book: Jonathan Kolatch's *Sports, Policies and Ideology in China* (1971).

Since 1990 books on Chinese sports and sports history in English have been published. The first was H.G. Knuttgan, Ma Qiwei and Wu Zhongyuan's edited collection *Sports in China* (1990). It is an introduction to Chinese sports systems and organizations. Susan Brownell's *Training the Body for China: Sport in the Moral Order of the People's Republic* (1995) was the first book that attempted to examine the relationship between sport, ideology, the body and gender relations in China.

Fan Hong's *Footbinding, Feminism and Freedom: the Liberation of Women's Bodies in Modern China* (1997) concentrates on women in China and the emancipation of their bodies between 1840 and 1949. The author argues that the dramatic and brutal patriarchal tradition of physical repression of the female body in Chinese history makes the physical emancipation of Chinese women an issue of special significance in the history of the liberation of the modern female body. Dong Jinxia's *Women, Sport and Society in Modern China: Holding Up More than Half the Sky* (2002) could be regarded as a sequel to Fan Hong's book. It takes up the story of Chinese women and sport from 1949 to the 1980s and explores the rise of the Chinese super-sportswomen in the People's Republic and their relationship with politics, culture and society before and during the Cultural Revolution and through China's transition to a market economy. Andrew D. Morris's *Marrow of the Nation: A History of Sport and Physical Culture in Republican China* (2004) is a clearly written and well documented work on the origins and development of modern Chinese sport. It explains the relationship between sport, nationalism and politics in modern China.

Grant Jarvie, Hwang Dong-jhy and Mel Brennan's *Sport, Revolution and the Beijing Olympics* (2008) is a cultural history of sport in China. The most interesting part is its analysis of sport, politics and diplomacy between Taiwan and Beijing. Susan Brownell's second book on Chinese sport focuses on *Beijing's Games: What the Olympics Mean to China* (2008). With her passion for China and her understanding of the importance of the Beijing Olympic Games and the feelings of Chinese people she tries to provide a balanced view of Beijing's effort to host the Olympic Games. Paul Close, David Askew and Xu Xin's book *The Beijing Olympiad: The Political Economy of a Sporting Mega-Event* (2008) is not a history book but has an historical element. It provides readers with an in-depth analysis of the relationship between sport, national identity and international relations.

Fan Hong, Duncan Mackay and Karen Christensen's *China Gold: China's Quest for Global Power and Olympic Glory* (2008) was written by Chinese experts in close collaboration with US and European historians and sports writers and enhanced by full-colour photos and illustrations. It offers the readers a fascinating story of China's relationship with the

International Olympic Movement. It explains, in simple and clear language, how and why China has become, since rejoining the international community only 25 years ago, a sporting giant and major player on the world political and economic stages.

Xu Guqin's *Olympic Dreams: China and Sports, 1895–2008* (2008) is one of the most accomplished books on Chinese sports history published in English. With his understanding of Chinese society and first-hand material the author traces the development of modern sport in China. It provides readers with a comprehensive coverage of the complexity of the period. After his thorough examination of the function of sport in China's political, social and cultural lives the author argues that sport has brought major political, cultural and social changes in the past, and will continue to play its role in the future. It is not only a book of sports history, but also a political and cultural history.

Meanwhile, well-known Western scholars such as Allen Guttmann, J.A. Mangan, John Hoberman, Ian Henry, James Riordan, Grant Jarvie, Roberta J. Park, William W. Kelly, John Kelly, Julia Lovell, Thierry Terret, Mark Dyreson, Peter Horton, Victor Cha and others have written journal articles and book chapters on China, Chinese sports history and its relationship with Europe, America and Australia.

Their articles have appeared in mainstream history journals, such as the *China Quarterly* and the *Journal of Modern Chinese History*; and sports studies journals, such as *The Journal of Sport History, Sport in History, Journal of Olympic History, Sport History Review, The Sociology of Sport Journal, International Review for the Sociology of Sport, European Sport Management Quarterly* and *The International Journal for the History of Sport*, which has played an important role in facilitating sports studies in China since the 1990s. It began to publish its Asia–Northeast regional issue from 2007 which has devoted large space to China.

In general, Western scholars have overcome their language and cultural barriers and produced some appraisable high-quality research on Chinese sports in the historical and social context. However, some scholars may still face the problem of access to archival sources. They may have access to materials without official sanction, but they may have drawbacks such as unsystematic supply and unconfirmed authenticity. The information about sport, about people who practise it, and about the change of sports structure and culture, may be misleading, whether it comes from official or non-official sources. The simple lack of information might hinder a better understanding of Chinese sports in the past, present and future.

This raises another issue of evidence and interpretation. Of all the elements that affect the quality of an historical work, none is more important than thoroughness in the search for evidence. Academics take issue with those who argue that details are subordinate to interpretation, not because they celebrate facts for their own sake, but because the quality of an historical interpretation is critically dependent on the accuracy of the evidence. Time and again the interpretation of major historical events, sometimes of whole areas, has been transformed by factual correction. There is a difference between a profound historical study and a casual journalistic survey. If we want to give readers, especially students, accurate information about, and intelligent comment on, China, we must be sure of our facts and informed in our judgements. We should pay sufficient attention to the search for accurate Chinese evidence and avoid inexcusable, blatant and lazy historical mistakes, such as the year, the name and details of events.

Western scholars also face disciplinary problems. Generally speaking, the methodology, models and techniques developed by Western historians and sports historians have rarely been applied to the study of China, and even more rarely applied with ingenuity. They equally have had no effect on the Chinese. In addition, the ignorance of body culture in feudal China did not encourage the Chinese to develop their own sports history tradition. When this tradition did arise, in the 1920s, it was dominated from the start by politicization that has continued to handicap the field. Demands for orthodoxy by Chinese Nationalist and Communist ideologues, and the radical anti-intellectualism of the Great Proletarian Cultural Revolution, all took a considerable toll. In addition, with regard to the study of Communist sport, the overt nature of the political and ideological content remained a serious obstacle to contemporary studies in Communist China. Nevertheless, Western scholars normally over-emphasize the impact of politics and ideology and overlook the other social, cultural and economic factors.

The most serious problem is attitudes and values. It is important that Western sports historians do not allow their own values to distort their perceptions of Chinese sports culture and history. This in no way implies that they must discard their values in their assessment of that culture and history. However, if Western scholars want to write satisfactory Chinese sports history, they should be aware of Chinese informed perspectives; employ meticulous scholarship; have appropriate language skills; and have a satisfactory understanding of Chinese culture and history. They should avoid adopting a double standard (with its patronising overtones) toward Chinese sport, since their position as Western scholars in regard to both Western and Chinese sports studies depends on their integrity as outside observers. Above all, they should remain conscious of their own identities and not claim to speak on behalf of the whole or of any section of the Chinese people.

Conclusion

The emergence of sports history studies since the 1980s in China is an innovative intellectual movement. Its growth paralleled the major transformation of society – ideological, political, social and cultural. The new field benefited from an unprecedented number of able and energetic intellectuals who shared in the excitement of enlarging the vision of sports history. They creatively used, and use, it to take part in a large structural social change. This new field has profoundly affected historical consciousness by broadening both the subject matter and methods of history. In short, history is change, and so is sports history. Sports historians should now begin to free themselves from historical tradition, and use the vast accumulation of social science description to generate their own theories and to build sound explanatory frameworks. Sports history should not come to dominate history, but should have a much stronger impact on all aspects of history.

In the most general sense, however, the 1990s have indeed seen an advance of Chinese sports history studies in the West. Some satisfying results have emerged, most especially in the areas of gender, politics, ideology and Olympic Studies. They have produced a burgeoning interest in the West. They also have opened up a new field for Western scholars. This new field is a challenge. It requires language skills, cultural understanding and creative imagination, and, most of all, analytical academic capacity, to cultivate future success. It is time for the West and East to come together in the historical study of sport in society, to record the past, analyse the present and influence the future.

Notes

1 Zhou Xikuan et al., *Zhongguo gudai tiyu shi* [The Physical Education and Sports History of Ancient China] (Chengdu: Sichuan guji chubanshe, 1986); Gu Shiquan and Lin Boyuan, *Zhongguo tiyu shi* [The Chinese History of Physical Education and Sport] (Beijing: Beijing tiyu xueyuan chubanshe [Beijing Physical Education Institute], 1989).

2 Zheng Zhilin and Zhao Shanxing, 'Sports History Studies in the Past 80 Years', *The Guide of Sport Culture* 3 (2008), 22–28.

3 Fan Hong and Tan Hua, 'Sport in China: Conflict between Tradition and Modernity, 1840 to 1930s', in J.A. Mangan and Fan Hong, eds, *Sport in Asian Society: Past and Present (Sport in the Global Society)* (London: Frank Cass, 2002), 189–212; CSHPES (Chinese Society for the History of Physical Education and Sport), ed., *Zhongguo jindai tiyu shi* [Modern Chinese Sports History] (Beijing: Beijing tiyu xueyuan chubanshe [Beijing Physical Education Institute Press], 1989); Chengdu tiyu xueyaun tiyushi yanjiushuo [Chengdu Institute of Sports History Studies], ed., *Zhongguo jindai tiyushi zhiliao* [Historical Archives of Modern Chinese Sports History] (Chengdu: Sichuan jiaoyu chubanshe, 1989).

4 Guo Xifen, *Zhongguo Tityushi* [History of Sport in China] (Beijing: China Shangwu Press, 1919).

5 Hao Gengsheng, *On Chinese Physical Education and Sport* (1926).

6 Sao Shanxin and Zhen Zhilin, 'Jin xian dai tiyu baozi gaikuang' [Overview of Sports Newspapers in the Nationalist Period], *Tiyu wenshi* (1989), 74–75; Cui Lequan, 'A Review of Sports History Studies in China', *The Guide of Sport Culture* 1 (2002), 39–41.

7 Fan Hong and Tan Hua, 'Sport in China: Conflict between Tradition and Modernity, 1840 to 1930s', in J.A. Mangan and Fan Hong, eds, *Sport in Asian Society*, 189–213; CSHPES, ed., *Zhongguo jindai tiyu shi*; Chengdu tiyu xueyaun tiyushi yanjiushuo, ed., *Zhongguo jindai tiyushi zhiliao*.

8 Cui Lequan, 'A Review of Sports History Studies in China'; Gu Shiquan, 'Review of Sports History Studies in China', *The Guide of Sport Culture* 11 (2003), 58–61; Zheng Zhilin and Zhao Shanxing, 'Sports History Studies in the Past 80 Years'.

9 Ibid.

10 Ibid.

11 Hu Hong, 'A Review and Prospect Study on the History of Modern Sport in China', *Journal of Chengdu Sport University* 27, 1 (2001), 17–19; Gu Shiquan 'Review of Sports History Studies in China'; Tan Hua, 'Research on Sports History in China Over the Last Two Decades', *Journal of Chengdu Physical Education Institute* 23 (1997), 1–5; Wang Junqi, 'Re-Dissertation the Current State and the Future of Sports History', *Journal of Physical Education* 14, 6 (2007), 48–51.

12 Cui Lequan, 'A Review of Sports History Studies in China'; Gu Shiquan, 'Review of Sports History Studies in China'.

13 Luo Shiming, 'From Memory to the Future Reality – the Revival of Sports History', *The Guide of Sport Culture* 5 (2007), 19–22; Sun Yue, 'Review and Prospective in the Research of Chinese Sports History', *Journal of TUS* 23, 1 (2008), 15–20.

14 Cui Lequan, 'A Review of Sports History Studies in China'; Gu Shiquan, 'Review of Sports History Studies in China'; Hu Hong, 'A Review and Prospect Study on the History of Modern Sport in China'.

15 Yi Jian-dong and Xiong Dong-ping, 'Review and Prospect of the Researches of Sports History in China Since 2000', *Journal of Shandong Institute of Physical Education* 65, 5 (2004), 5–7; Zhou Chaoqun, He Minghui and Gu Zurong, 'New Materials for Sports History Studies – Construction of the New System of Sports History Research in Contemporary China', *Journal of Shandong Institute of Physical Education and Sports* 23, 5 (2007), 20–21.

16 Fan Hong, Ian Henry and Lu Zhouxiang, *The Contribution of the Chinese Further and Higher Education Sectors to the Staging and Delivery of the 2008 Beijing Olympic Games*, Report to PODIUM, the Further and Higher Education Unit for the 2012 London Olympic Games, 2008.

17 Ibid.

18 Ibid.

19 Hao Qin, 'Problems, Opportunities and Solutions for the Discipline of Sports History', *Journal of Chengdu Sport University* 34, 7 (2008), 1–3; Wang Junqi, 'Re-Dissertation the Current State and the Future of Sports History'; Zheng Zhilin and Zhao Shanxing, 'Sports History Studies in the Past 80 Years'.

20 Gu Shiquan, 'Review of Sports History Studies in China'; Cui Lequan, 'A Review of Sports History Studies in China'; Fan Hong, Ian Henry and Lu Zhouxiang, 2008.

21 Sun Yue, 'Review and Prospective in the Research of Chinese Sports History'; Hao Qin, 'Problems, Opportunities and Solutions for the Discipline of Sports History'; Lang Jing and Meng Zhongjie, 'Ershi Shiji Zhongguo Tiyushi Yanjiu De Zai Fansi' [Sports History Studies in the 20th Century], *The Guide of Sport Culture* 2 (2005), 33–35.

22 Luo Shiming, 'From Memory to the Future Reality'; Cao Shouhe, 'Tiyu Shixueke Xianzhuang Zhi Gaijin Sanyi' [Research on Sports History Studies in China], *Journal of Chengdu Physical Education Institute* 34 (2008), 4–5.
23 Cui Lequan, 'A Review of Sports History Studies in China'; Cui Lequan, 'Dangdai Tiyushixue Yanjiu Zhongdian Fenxi' [The Focus of Sports History in the 21st Century], *The Guide of Sport Culture* 2 (2002), 28–29; Hu Hong, 'A Review and Prospect Study on the History of Modern Sport in China'; Lang Jing and Meng Zhongjie, 'Sports History Studies in the Twentieth Century'; Sun Yue, 'Review and Prospective in the Research of Chinese Sports History'; Yi Jian-dong and Xiong Dong-ping, 'Review and Prospect of the Researches of Sports History in China Since 2000'; Zhou Chaoqun, He Minghui and Gu Zurong, 'New Materials for Sports History Studies'.
24 William T. Rowe, 'Approaches to Modern Chinese Social History', in Olivier Zunz, ed., *Reliving the Past: The Worlds of Social History* (Chapel Hill: University of North Carolina Press, 1985), 236–96.

References

Anhui tiyu wenshi weiyuanhui [Committee of Anhui for the History of Sports], *Anhui tiyushi zhiliao* [Historical Records of Sports in Anhui Province] (16 vols, 1984–94).

Beijing tiyu wenshi weiyuanhui [The Committee of Beijing for the History of Sports], *Beijing tiyu wenshi* [Beijing Sports History Material], (5 vols, 1984–90).

Brownell, Susan, *Training the Body for China: Sport in the Moral Order of the People's Republic* (Chicago: University of Chicago Press, 1995).

——*Beijing's Games: What the Olympics Mean to China* (Lanham: Rowman & Littlefield Publishers, Inc, 2008).

Cai Zengxiong, *The History of Physical Education in Schools during the Japanese Occupation* (Taiwan: Normal University Press, 1995).

Chen, Changyi, 'Lun Tangdai funu de cuju' [On Women's Ball Games in the Tang Dynasty], *Tiyu wenshi* [The Journal of Sports Culture and History] 3 (1985),18–20.

Cheng, Yuanhui, ed., *Laojiefangqu jiaoyu zhiliao* [Educational Archives of Soviets and Liberated Areas] (Beijing: Jiaoyu kexue chubanshe, 1981)

Close, Paul, David Askew and Xu Xin, *The Beijing Olympiad: The Political Economy of a Sporting Mega-Event* (London: Routledge, 2007).

CSHSPE, ed., *90 yayunhui* [1990 Asian Games] (Wuhan: Wuhan chubanshe, 1990).

——*Zhongguo jindai tiyu wenxuan* [Historical Material on Modern Chinese Physical Education and Sport] (Beijing: Renming tiyu chubanshe, 1992).

Dong Jinxia, *Women, Sport and Society in Modern China: Holding Up More than Half the Sky* (London: Routledge, 2002).

Fan Hong, *Footbinding, Feminism and Freedom: The Liberation of Women's Bodies in Modern China (Sport in the Global Society)* (London: Frank Cass, 1997).

——'Which Road to China? An Evaluation of Two Different Approaches' *The International Journal of the History of Sport* vol. 18 (2001),148–67.

Fan Hong, Duncan Mackay and Karen Christensen, eds, *China Gold: China's Quest for Global Power and Olympic Glory* (Great Barrington: Berkshire Publishing, 2008).

Fan, Wenlan, *Zhongguo tongshi* [The History of China] (Beijing: Renmin chubanshe [People's Press], 1952, 4 vols).

Guangdong tiyu wenshi weiyuanhui [The Committee of Guangdong for the History of Sports], *Guangdong tiyu shiliao* [Historical Material on Sports in Guangdong Province] (16 vols, 1984–94).

Guojia tiwei weishi gongzhuo weiyuanhui [Working Committee of Sports History, Ministry of Sport], *Tiyu wenshi* [Journal of Sports Culture and History], Beijing, (1984–2000).

Guojia tiwei zhenche yanjiushi [Department of Sports Policy Study, Ministry of Sport], *Tiyu luntan* [Journal of Sports Theory], Beijing, (1985–89).

Guttmann, Allen, *Sports: The First Five Millennia* (Massachusetts: University of Massachusetts Press, 2004).

Hao Qin, *Tiyushi* [Sports History] (Beijing: Renmin tiyu chubanshe [People's Sports Press], 2006).

Jarvie, Grant, Hwang Dong-jhy and Mel Brennan, *Sport, Revolution and the Beijing Olympics* (Oxford: Berg Publishers, 2008).

Jiangxi renmin chubanshe [Jiangxi People's Press], *Suqu jiaoyu ziliao xuanbia* [Selected Archives of Education in the Soviet Areas] (Nanchang, 1981).

Jilin tiyu wenshi bangongshi [The Department of Jilin for Sports History], *Jilin tiyu shiliao* [Historical Records of Jilin Province] (15 vols, 1985–94).

Liu Xuesong, 'Research on Sports History in China Over the Past 30 Years', *Journal of Chengdu Physical Education Institute* 34 (2008), 6–7.

Ministry of Sport Department of Policy Research, *Tiyu yundong wenjian xuanbian 1949–1981* [Selected Sport and Physical Culture Documents 1949–1981] (Renmin tiyu chubanshe, Beijing, 1982).

Morris, Andrew D., *Marrow of the Nation: A History of Sport and Physical Culture in Republican China* (Berkeley: University of California Press, 2004).

Qiao Keqin and Guan Wenmin, *Zhongguo tiyu sixiang shi* [The History of Chinese Sorts Philosophy and Ethics] (Lanzhou: Gansu minzu chubanshe [Gansu Minorities Press], 1993).

Renming chubanshe, *Shan Gan-ning geming genjudi shiliao xuanji* [The Historical Material of Sha-Gan-Ning Border Area] (Renming chubanshe, Beijing, 1958).

Shanxi tiyu wenshi weiyuanhui [The Committee of Shanxi for the History of Sports], *Shanxi tiyu shiliao* [Historical Material of Sport in Shanxi Province] (15 vols, 1984–94).

Shiming, Luo, *The History of China's Participation in the Olympic Games* (Beijing: Qinghua daxue chubanshe, 2005).

Sichuan tiyu wenshi weiyuanhui [The Committee of Sichuan for the History of Sports], *Sichuan tiyu shiliao* [Historical Material on Sports History in Sichuan Province] (12 vols, 1985–94).

Tan Hua, ed., *Tiyushi* [Sports History] (Beijing: Renmin jiaoyu chubanshe [People's Education Press], 2007).

Tang Minxing, *The History of the Basketball Team of the Republic of China's Participation in the International Competition* (Taiwan: Basketball Association of the Republic of China, 1952).

Tang, Hao, ed., *Zhongguo tiyu chankao zhiliao ji* [Chinese Sports History Record] (8 vols, Renmin tiyu chubanshe, Beijing, 1958–65).

Wang Daping and Fan Hong, *Tiyu shihua* [Sports History] (Beijing: Kexue puji chubanshe [Chinese Science Press], 1990).

Wu Wenzhong, *One Hundred-Year History of Chinese Sports* (Taiwan: Taiwan Shangwu Press, 1956).

Xie Yanlong et al., eds, *Aulinpike yanjiu* [Olympics Studies] (Beijing: Beijing tiyu daxue chubanshe, 1994).

Xu Guqin, *Olympic Dreams: China and Sports, 1895–2008* (Harvard University Press, 2008).

Xu Yixiong and Xu Yuanmin, *The Sports History of Modern Chinese Schools* (Taiwan: Normal University Press, 1999).

Yong Gaotang, et al., eds, *Tiyu baike quanshu* [The Encyclopedia of Chinese Sport] (Beijing: Zhongguo baike quanshu chubanshe [Chinese Encyclopedia Press], 1980).

Zhang Xiping and Peng Qiong, 'Changes in the Research Thought of Contemporary Chinese Sports History', *Journal of Shenyang Physical Education Institute* 25 (5) (2006), 24–25.

Zhejiang tiyu wenshi bangongshi [Department of Zhejiang for History of Sports], *Zhejiang Tiyu Shiliao* [Historical Material of Sports History in Zhejiang Province] (16 vols, 1984–93).

Zhongguo tiyushi xuehui [Chinese Society for History of Sport and Physical Education], *Tiyushi lunwei ji* [Selected Works of Sports Culture and History] (9 vols, Beijing, 1984–2000).

25 France

Thierry Terret

Introduction

The history of sport and physical education was relatively unknown in France before the second half of the 1960s.[1] Over the past 40 years, the production of knowledge has considerably increased and contributed to the exploration of the issue in various perspectives. Yet English-speaking scholars have tended to ignore these works, despite a couple of historiographical statements made in international journals by Allen Guttmann in 1983, André Gounot in 2001 and Thierry Terret in 2007,[2] completed by more thematic papers published by Richard Holt on French sports history and sociability in 1989, Thierry Terret on French sports history and gender in 2000 and Evelyne Combeau-Mari on French colonial sports history in 2007.[3] Furthermore, French scholars rarely submit their research in international publications, with about 50 papers published in the four dominant journals of the field, the *Journal of Sport History,* the *International Journal of the History of Sport, Stadion* and *Sport History Review* during the last 30 years. As a consequence, a number of English-speaking sports historians are familiar with French sports history mainly through Richard Holt's *Sport and Society in Modern France,* which dates back to 1981 and thus hardly reflects the historiographical changes of the last 20 years.

The emergence of a field in France

For years, French historians were unlikely to study sports because of the risk of being discredited as frivolous and of being accused of having chosen a socially disqualified topic. The starting point of French sports historiography can be seen in Jacques Ulmann's dissertation in 1964, published the following year by a prestigious Parisian publisher specializing in philosophy under the title, *De la gymnastique aux sports modernes.*[4] This voluminous analysis of main discourses in physical education and sport since Antiquity remained a reference source for two decades, but it was completed by several works in the early 1970s, thanks to three major changes in the French context.

Sport itself became more popular and more visible in French society at the end of the 1960s. In 1967, 39% of the population claimed to practise a sport, while the figure was not higher than 10% 15 years earlier. At the same time, television was becoming widespread, in almost one out of two households, with sport events such as the Olympic Games (held in France in the winter 1968), the five nations tournament in rugby and the national football championships attracting still more spectators. This change led to the publication of journalist-based or hagiographic books,[5] but it also provoked new interest by scholars from various different social sciences.

This interest benefited from the consequences of the university revolution in France, which occurred in the aftermath of May 1968. From now on, new subjects for investigation emerged at the fringes of traditional ones. The recognition of a new 'leisure society' created a need to better understand these activities named as games, recreation or sport. The latter was still not accepted by most historians, because the structural-economic models proposed by Fernand Braudel and Camille-Ernest Labrousse hardly lent themselves to it. However, following the pioneering book of Roger Caillois,[6] it became discussed in psychological, psychosocial, anthropological and philosophical works, all of them often having a complementary focus on history.[7] These early books were directly influenced by the structuralism of Levi-Strauss and the phenomenology of Merleau-Ponty, two efforts to go beyond the Marxist models that had hitherto dominated much of French intellectual life. Such studies sought to position French sports history research, which concentrated more on continuities than ruptures, and more on the 'longue durée' than on the event.

Finally, a third change was undergone in French physical education during the 1960s, when this school subject, which had been dominated by Swedish gymnastics since the end of the 19th century, radically changed its content of sport activities. This rupture created an unexpected professional identity crisis for many PE teachers, some of whom sought recognition and response in the history of their discipline and profession. The intellectually more active part of this socially dominated group began preparing theses at university, focusing mainly on the history of physical education. From 1965 to 1978, about 20 dissertations were written in France on the subject, resulting, though, in a certain lack of history of sport institutions in the historiography.[8] An exception to this narrow focus on school sports was Jean-Marie Brohm, also a PE teacher, who chose in 1966 to work on a neo-Marxist and socio-historical critique of sports.[9]

Thus, the historians of physical education dominated the field from the mid-1970s to the end of the 1980s. When Paris hosted the congress of the International Association for the History of Physical Education and Sport (HISPA) twice in 1972 and 1978, it was they who handled the organization and also had the most prominent place in the scientific programme. Soon afterwards they took advantage of the integration of sport sciences and physical education at the university with the creation of a new section: the so-called Sciences and Techniques of Physical Activities and Sport (STAPS). More and more students were attracted to these courses where the history of sport and PE became widely taught, thanks to the course's compulsory position within the annual state competition to become a PE teacher. The book market increased considerably[10] and the earlier group of PE teachers who had done research in the 1970s – most of them with positions at university in the 1980s – expanded their centre of interest in the direction of sports history and not only toward the history of physical education. Their theoretical background remained social history, as it was the historiographical current close to the *Annales* tradition, which dominated the field in the 1970s. Therefore, as pointed out by Marcel Spivak,[11] many works focused on a particular social group: Jacques Thibault on bourgeois sport, Bernard Deletang, Yvon Léziart and Christophe Lamoureux on the worker's sport … [12] Further-more, and for the same reasons, the research was often restricted to a limited area, with a number of regional monographs, which contributed to strongly nuancing the knowledge one had on a national level.[13] More generally, these studies focusing on the social and ideological differences became widely developed throughout the 1980s. As a example, the special issue on sports history of the journal *Recherche* (1980) started with a intro-ductive paper by American historian Eugen Weber on 'Gymnastique et sports en France à la fin du XIXème siècle: opium des classes?' and several papers on the same topic.[14]

However, three other historiographical trends emerged in the same time, which were more disconnected from the PE background of the previous group of authors and rooted in different theoretical traditions. From 1981 to 1987, four out of 10 authors did not belong to the PE and sports studies fields.[15]

In the departments of history, a new generation of social historians began to develop an interest in the history of sport, taking a high risk in their own careers within a circle where the topic was still not considered respectable. However, the new awareness of the body, the emergence of the history of mentalities and the first steps in cultural history announced the so-called 'nouvelle histoire'[16] and paved the way for such innovative works. Here, the first privileged entry was the history of the Olympic Games[17] and studies of France's most popular sports: cycling, rugby and soccer.[18] Other sports appeared only rarely, for example with Dominique Lejeune's PhD on the social history of the French Alpine Club.[19]

The second privileged entry was the place of sports in the social history of politics. Marianne Amar tackled the relationship between sport, the state and the workers' movement in the years after World War II;[20] Marcel Spivak examined the relationship between sport, physical education and the army;[21] and Albert Bourzak researched the paramilitary school battalions of the late 19th century.[22] Finally, marginal entries focused on mixed approaches where history was associated with literature in Pierre Charreton's pioneering dissertation, with anthropology in Alain Ehrenberg's dissertation, and with social geography in Jean-Pierre Augustin's studies.[23]

Following Pierre Bourdieu's opening lecture at the HISPA conference in Paris in 1978,[24] new research appeared in France, based on the main concepts of structuralist sociology. Sport was seen as the result of a balance between a demand and an offer, a relatively autonomous 'field' in which social actors with 'habitus' tried to impose a legitimate form of practice. In France, this approach was adopted more by sports sociologists than by sports historians. Between the two, historical sociologists such as Jacques Defrance followed Bourdieu's programmatic perspectives. Defrance's dissertation supervised by Bourdieu in 1978 became the basis for many later works in the 1980s,[25] many published by the team at the French National Institute for Sports and Physical Education (INSEP).[26]

Finally, the last historiographical tradition in sports history in France is linked to the particular influence of Michel Foucault and of his disturbing analyses on the body.[27] Indeed, the Foucaldian anthropological theoretical project was not long to seduce a small group of PE teachers who were seeking critical models to deconstruct both the school and sport dominant institutions. Many such as Jean-Marie Brohm, Georges Vigarello and Daniel Denis organized themselves around a philosopher of the body, Michel Bernard, founder of the journal *Quel corps?*[28] They began to publish highly stimulating and provoca-tive essays on the political and social uses of the body,[29] influencing other scholars outside their circle such as Jacques Thibault and André Rauch on their attempt to deconstruct the pedagogical use of the body.[30] Some of these works integrated the history of sport into their perspectives, although Foucault himself was not interested in the history of sport, as he admitted in several interviews.[31]

Conditions of historical production and institutional renewal

The social history of physical education, political history of sport and sporting events, socio-historical history of sport and anthropological history of the body all reflected the main characteristics of the field in the mid 1980s. However, the situation remained difficult, not only because of the diversity of the approaches, but also because of the size of scientific production and the attitude of mainstream historians. Thus, following the model of Great Britain in 1982, a French Society of Sport History was created in 1987 with Gilbert Andrieu as president, and the journal *Sport-Histoire* was launched one year later with Pierre Arnaud as editor. Despite the enthusiasm of the members, neither the society nor the journal survived. A later attempt by the journal *Sport et Histoire* in 1992 was no more successful.

It was precisely the conditions of the production of knowledge, the size of the market and the increased recognition of the field which progressively changed this situation after 1992. A new generation of sports historians began to reach institutional positions from where they could diffuse their works. Several thousand books, chapters and articles were published over the past 15 years, for a national market of 40,000–50,000 students in sports studies, which made the publications less risky for publishing companies. Major editors agreed to publish syntheses.[32] However, the best example of this new trend is L'Harmattan (Paris), which launched a special collection ('Espaces et temps du sport') devoted to sports history in 1994. It has since become the largest series of essays in the field in France, with almost 100 books published.[33]

This change also reflects a stronger connection between mainstream history and sports historians, although most social and cultural historians entering the field of sports are unaware of the studies produced earlier by sports historians at either the national or the international level. Nevertheless, a good indicator of the transformation within the field is the increasing number of conferences, linking people from various fields. The Comité des Travaux Historiques et Scientifiques – CTHS [Committee of Historical and Scientific Work], created in 1834, organized annually a congress on diverse topics, on top of a regular conference on the French Revolution. More than one and a half centuries later, the president of the CTHS approached the leading sports historian, Pierre Arnaud, to suggest a conference on the history of sport within the 116th congress of the CTHS in 1991. The initiative made sense precisely at that time, because France was the host country of the Winter Olympic Games in 1992, and the congress was held in Chambéry, a city neighbouring Albertville. The success of this conference[34] led to an agreement for the next four years, creating a regular meeting point for all sports historians in France (Clermond-Ferrand in 1992, Pau in 1993, Amiens in 1994 and Aix-en-Provence in 1995), as well as the publication of the proceedings, a valuable source, which served as a bridge between sports historians and mainstream historians.[35]

The resulting dynamic was strong enough to ensure a certain perenity of the process. Despite the end of the agreement with the CTHS, the community of sports historians decided to maintain an annual or biennial conference, which has been organized since then in various places and on topics that are decided democratically by the participants at the previous event. Leading historians are often invited to give keynote lectures, giving these congresses good visibility and solid credibility. The proceedings, published in the collection 'Espace et temps du sport', constitute the most prominent collection of work in sports history in France, reflecting all the variations of the field.[36] It also created a new basis for the revival of the French society of sports history, in 2003, and a new journal, *Sport et sciences sociales*, in 2008.

These new conditions caused at the very least a major change in the topic that, for years, had dominated the field: the history of physical education. Not only have these numerous analyses[37] remained specific in comparison with the way they are written in other countries, as pointed out by Flemish-speaking Belgian Jan Tolleneer,[38] but they have more recently embraced new areas totally ignored by the previous generation of historians, such as, for example, the role of leisure activities within the curriculum, the influence of the PE teachers' unions on teaching, the role of politics in the definition of PE, the specificity of physical education for girls and the gender issue in PE, and the influence of other countries on the political and pedagogical decisions made in France.[39]

Social and political analysis of sport institutions

The new generation of researchers has been less focused on the quest for identity in physical education and more interested in the history of sports. It has also been more influenced by the international community of sports historians, yet retaining some specific areas.

The birth, early development and transformation of clubs and federations in France have been particularly studied using a social and, more often, a political approach. Thanks to France's political centralism and the recurrent opposition between Paris and the provinces, the role of the state was especially explored in gymnastics at the end of the 19th century. This activity developed in France in close association with the political power and its relays (school, the army …), thus becoming a vehicle for nationalistic ideology in a way that, as pointed out by Richard Holt, was clearly distinctive from what happened in Great Britain at the same time.[40] The best studies on the political history of gymnastics were published by Pierre Arnaud.[41] Although sport developed as a private matter, the French Government became progressively conscious of its potential for foreign policy as well as for internal social mass regulation. This process was studied with a special focus on the inter-war period (with the Popular Front in 1936), and on the 1960s, during the De Gaulle period.[42] Less attention was given to local powers and, at the other extreme, to international relations. Exceptions concerned some stimulating comparative monographs[43] and the analysis of particular events such as the inter-allied games of 1919.[44]

During the 1990s and early 2000s, the traditional social divisions of the sport field were less explored than some particular social groups, which had the benefit of little previous attention or which required deeper analysis. This was the case for workers' sports, the national study of which was renewed for two reasons. On the one hand, a more comparative and international approach created a totally new understanding of the issue, especially from the works of Andre Gounot and Pierre Arnaud.[45] On the other hand, detailed local monographs completed the scope,[46] showing that the three levels – the local, the national and the international – followed partly distinct roads.

Another example of this concern for specific sport institutions and social groups is the focus on the history of Catholic sport. For sure, the relationship between sport and religion as a whole still needs some work, especially when considering the nearly total absence of powerful analysis of the French history of Jewish sport or Muslim sport. However, a new focus was forged in France's dominant religion, owing to two complementary dissertations, which studied the policy of the national federation – the Fédération Gymnastique et Sportive des Patronages de France – and the activity of local Catholic sports clubs throughout France.[47] Such studies are to be expected in a country where the separation of state and religion has been written into law since 1905, a division that is obviously reflected in sport.

The last strong renewal of French sports historiography in terms of specific groups concerns women in sports history. Although the issue became more important in Anglo-Saxon historiography during the 1980s,[48] and despite the suggestive essays written by

French sport sociologists,[49] little was done by French sports historians before the mid-1990s on this subject. The resistance within the field and, more generally, in French history[50] began to lessen with a congress organized on this issue in Lyon in 1994, followed by the publication of proceedings in two volumes.[51] However, one had to wait until 2001 to see the first dissertation on the topic,[52] again at the University of Lyon, which had become a leader in this area. Over 10 years, what had been mainly a history of women in sport had become a set of gender studies where the questions of domination, homophobia, masculinity, homosexuality and all other issues developed within the international community are considered, as shown by a successful congress in 2004, followed by the publication of four key volumes.[53]

Finally, race studies and the issue of minorities are just beginning. Only one PhD has been written on the black/white question[54] and the analyses on ethnicity are mainly confined to the study of colonial sport, an area that has grown tremendously over the last 10 years, following Bernadette Deville-Danthu's superb dissertation on sports history in French colonial Africa.[55] As I have already mentioned elsewhere, 'in a country that sees itself as a land of welcome and where integrating individuals into a "single indivisible Republic" is fundamental to the national Constitution, investigations into the historical role of sports in the relationships among communities were rejected for long in the collective unconscious'.[56]

Cultural history of sports

In the context of the extension of the topics attached to cultural history, sports history could no longer remain outside the mainstream transformations of history. In academic studies, these new approaches concerned especially the history of sports and sport events, which were convincingly developed with a focus on cycling, football and rugby, and major events such as the Olympic Games, throughout the 1980s. This sub-field continued to grow in the 1990s and 2000s, but three trends should be highlighted.

The first one is an extension of the previous studies, completing the level – from local to international – as well as the interpretations. Football, for instance, benefited from many new studies, going from the role of North African migrants in French football to a political history of the football world cups, via the role of the sport in local identity.[57] French scholars played a large role in the success of the book published to celebrate the 100-year anniversary of Fédération Internationale de Football Association (FIFA), in 2004.[58] Both the history of cycling and of the Tour de France were revisited with new perspectives, where gender, space, politics, social groups and economy were all used to challenge previous knowledge.[59] Particular attention should be given to Alex Poyer's extensive dissertation on the early development of cycling clubs in France, where the author used archival material from each of the 90 regional archives of the country.[60] Finally, new histories of rugby were written in the context of France organizing the World Cup in 2007.[61] The history of the Olympic Games and Olympism, not yet very active, remains, nevertheless, important in the form of political history of the Games,[62] the study of particular Olympic events or,[63] with the discovery of new archives on Coubertin by Patrick Clastres, history, which sees the renovator of modern Olympism as a way to analyse French society and the role of the elite during France's third republic.[64]

The second trend is an extension of these works toward other sports. In 15 years a considerable amount of cultural history has emerged, focusing on the specificity of every sport in the sports system and assuming the idea that each developed with a distinct permeability to the main forces of society. Radically different from the journalistic and hagiographic histories written to glorify events and athletes in various sports, these histories use what Bourdieu called a 'relative autonomy'[65] in order to investigate the social construction and meaning, internal and external conflict, and major influences that crossed a given sport. Based on large sets of sport archives as well as other archives and materials, surprising and stimulating studies have explored the cases of track and field, boxing, swimming, judo, rowing, tennis, mountain climbing, winter sports and caving, to name only the major ones.

The third trend is the emergence of a social and cultural history of sporting techniques. Here, the community is indebted to Georges Vigarello, who published a general frame for such investigations in 1988. In contrast to positivist histories that marvel at the 'progress' of techniques, Vigarello invited one to problematize the evolution of technical thought and the social, institutional and sexual conditions for the transformation of movement in sport.[66] His perspectives were particularly deep in the cases of football, swimming and water-polo,[67] and led to unexpected works on the diffusion of technical cultures from one country to another, or from one social group to another, as demonstrated in Anne Roger's dissertation on the history of training in track and field, or in Joris Vincent's dissertation on the reappropriation of British rugby culture in France.[68]

Apart from these new tendencies and extensions of previous works, the main traditions of the 1970s and 1980s seem to be no longer dominant in current French sports history. A good example here is the near disappearance of the history of the body linked to the history of sport, despite the fascinating three volumes recently edited by Alain Corbin, Jean-Jacques Courtine and Georges Vigarello, which included, for instance a chapter on sports history by the British Richard Holt.[69] However, more generally, this issue has become little visible. This observation might be linked to the rejection of Michel Foucault by French historians, who have never forgiven him for the way he wrote his most 'historical' book, *Surveiller et punir [Discipline and Punish]* in 1975. Criticism was especially strong in Michelle Perrot's collection, *The Impossible Prison* (1980),[70] where famous social historians demonstrated that Foucault had clearly deviated from the rules of historical method. Since the historians of the body were mainly influenced by Foucault's theoretical frame, it became for them more difficult to keep going on the same approach. Most of them turned to new topics, with the exception of Jacques Gleyse, at the crossroads of the history of ideas and epistemology, and Christian Vivier and Jean-François Loudcher.[71] More generally, French historians and sports historians remain wary of deconstruction and philosophical speculation in the writing of history.[72] Paradoxically, they make little use of the clues theorized by their postmodernist citizen fellows such as Jacques Derrida, Jean Baudrillard, Michel de Certeau, Paul Ricoeur or Jean-François Lyotard.

Despite the theoretical limits of the history of mentalities denounced by American Peter Burke and Frenchman Roger Chartier,[73] the concept of sociability developed in the 1970s by famous French historian Maurice Agulhon sturdily influenced sports historians. Although the concept was developed initially for 19th-century middle-class groups, it was taken up by sports historians to designate 'the organization set up by people wishing to practice a sport, and the ties that develop within these movements, groups, and associations'.[74] Pierre Arnaud's 1986 studies of the pre-World War I rise of the sports movement and gymnastics associations opened the path to the use of the concept,[75] and he was soon followed by a whole generation of researchers on a range of activities and periods. Thus, in the late 1980s and 1990s, a fairly large number of studies focused on the relational forms, affinities and identity that characterized specific groups or sports institutions. To take one example, Christian Vivier's nearly 1,000-page dissertation described how the gradual transition between 1865 and 1930 of one of the sport associations in the town of Besançon from boating to rowing was accompanied by a transformation of the interpersonal relationships among its members.[76]

Conclusion

French sports historiography has grown mainly on the fringe of the international community and more under the influence of mainstream social and cultural history as it developed in France. On the other side, the dense French production in the field has remained little known outside the French-speaking countries.[77] This situation has provoked some unexpected tendencies in terms of topics and approaches, with some reluctance to integrate other disciplines such as sociology or philosophy, and to take up the postmodern challenge.[78]

The field is, though, relatively dynamic and the community has grown significantly over the last 15 years. Around a dozen new PhD dissertations are completed and as many new books are written every year, on top of a large number of less academically based publications. New insights on the sources and material to investigate are on the agenda.[79] Finally, the rise of comparative studies, as exemplified by the recent book on the politics of stadiums by André Gounot, Denis Jallat and Benoit Caritey,[80] could lead to more prominent interaction between French sports historians and the international community.

Notes

1 Exceptions are, for instance: H.-R. D'Allemagne, *Sports et jeux d'adresse* (Paris: 1880); J.-J. Jusserand, *Les sports et jeux d'exercices dans l'Ancienne France* (Paris: Plon, 1901); B. Gillet, *Histoire du sport* (Paris: PUF, 1948); J. Le Floch'Hmoan, *La genèse des sports* (Paris: Payot, 1962); F. Legrand and J. Ladegaillerie, *L'éducation physique au XIXème et au XXème siècles, tome 1: en France* (Paris: Colin-Bourrelier, 1970).

2 A. Guttmann, 'Recent Work in European Sport History', *Journal Sport History* 10 (1983), 35–52; A. Gounot, 'Le sport en France de 1870 à 1940. Intentions et interventions', special issue of *Stadion* XXVII (2001), especially the paper of J.F. Loudcher, A. Gounot and C. Vivier, 'French Sports Historiography Institutional Aspects, *Stadion* XXVII (2001); T. Terret, 'French Sport Historiography', *The International Journal of the History of Sport* 24, 12 (2007).

3 R. Holt, 'Ideology and Sociability: A Review of New French Research into the History of Sport (1870–1914)', *The International Journal of the History of Sport* 6 (1989); T. Terret, 'Femmes, sport, identité et acculturation: Eléments d'historiographie française', *Stadion* XXVI (2000), 41–53; E. Combeau-Mari, 'Sport in the French Colonies (1880–1962): A Case Study', *Journal of Sport History* 33, 1, (2006), 27–57. Interestingly enough, the last two topics (gender and colonialism) remain marginal in French sports historiography.

4 J. Ulmann, *De la gymnastique aux sports modernes* (Paris: Vrin, 1965).

5 Examples of such uncritical and event-oriented books are M.T. Eyquem, *Pierre de Coubertin et l'épopée olympique* (Paris: Calman-Levy, 1966); P. Y. Boulongne, *La vie et l'œuvre pédagogique de Pierre de Coubertin: 1863–1967* (Ottawa: Leméac, 1975); G. Lagorce and R. Parienté, *La Fabuleuse Histoire des Jeux Olympiques: Eté-Hiver* (Paris: ODIL, 1972).

6 R. Caillois, *Les jeux et les hommes* (Paris: Gallimard, 1958); translated as *Man, Play, and Games* (New York: Free Press of Glencoe, 1961).

7 For instance: M. Bouet, *Signification du sport* (Paris: Editions universitaires, 1968); B. Jeu, *Le sport, la mort, la violence* (Paris: Editions universitaires, 1972); B. Jeu, *Le sport, l'émotion, l'espace* (Paris: Vigot, 1977).

8 Among them: G. Andrieu, *La dimension esthétique de l'éducation physique (1848–1972)* (ENSEPS Thesis: Paris, 1972); J. Thibault, *Sports et éducation physique, 1870–1970* (Paris: Vrin, 1972). C.

Pociello, *Une tentative de rationalisation scientifique de l'éducation physique: Demeny, Marey* (ENSEPS Thesis: Paris, 1972); P. Arnaud, *Le corps a sa raison ou des finalités de l'éducation physique*, PhD dissertation, University of Lyon II, 1978 (published under the title *Les savoirs du corps* (Lyon: Presses universitaires de Lyon, 1982)).

9 Especially with the special issue of the journal *Partisan* in 1966, and through a series of articles and books, including: J. M. Brohm, *Sociologie politique du sport* (Paris: J.P. Delarge, 1976); *Les Jeux Olympiques de Berlin* (Paris: Complexe, 1978); *Le mythe olympique* (Paris: Christian Bourgeois, 1981).

10 On top of Thibault's 1972 book, the best sales in the early 1980s were for P. Arnaud (ed.), *Le corps en mouvement, précurseurs et pionniers de l'éducation physique* (Toulouse: Privat, 1981), and B. During, *La crise des pédagogies corporelles* (Paris: Scarabée, 1981).

11 M. Spivak, 'L'historiographie de l'éducation physique et des sports à la croisée des chemins', *Travaux et recherches en EPS* 6 (1980), 16–19. See also B. During, 'Tendances du développement de l'historiographie du sport en France', *Sciences et motricité* 2 (1987), 35–43.

12 J. Thibault, 'Du dandysme au sport', *revue EPS* 134 (1975), 64–66; B. Deletang, *Sport, histoire, éducation: Le mouvement sportif ouvrier: une tentative de domestication de l'histoire* (PhD dissertation, University of Paris-VIII, 1980); Y. Léziart, *Création et diffusion du modèle sportif dans les différentes classes sociales en France* (PhD dissertation, University of Paris-V, 1984) (published under the title *Sport et dynamique sociale* (Joinville-le-Pont: Actio, 1990)); C. Lamoureux, *Le sport dans la culture ouvrière. Sportifs d'hier, sports d'aujourd'hui dans une commune de Basse-Loire* (PhD dissertation, University of Nantes, 1987). The focus on worker's sport rather than on the social group who dominated sport at the end of the 19th century in France was probably a consequence of the Marxist political convictions of the authors.

13 For instance J. L. Gay-Lescot, *Le développement du mouvement associatif sportif et de l'éducation physique en Ile-et-Vilaine de 1870 à 1939* (PhD dissertation, University of Rennes, 1985), and the numerous essays of Pierre Arnaud on the region of Lyon (the second largest city on France), which were synthetized in a masterpiece of history: P. Arnaud, *Le sportsman, l'Ecolier et le Gymnaste; la mise en forme scolaire de la culture physique (1869 – 1914)* (PhD dissertation, University of Lyon-II, 1986).

14 A. Ehrenberg, *Aimez-vous les stades?*, special issue of *Recherches* 43 (1980). Good examples of these orientations are also: P. Arnaud and J. Camy, eds, *La naissance du mouvement sportif associatif en France* (Lyon: Presses universitaires de Lyon, 1986); P. Arnaud, ed., *Les Athlètes de la République, gymnastique, sport et idéologie républicaine, 1870–1914* (Toulouse: Privat, 1987).

15 P. Arnaud, 'Histoire du sport: Bilan 1981–87', in *Sciences sociales et sports: Etats et perspectives*, Strasbourg: *Proceedings of the symposium of Strasbourg 13–14 November 1987*.

16 J. Le Goff, ed., *La nouvelle histoire* (Paris: Retz-CEPL, 1978); F. Dosse, *L'histoire en miette: Des 'Annales' à la 'Nouvelle histoire'* (Paris: La Découverte, 1987).

17 D. Braun, *La politique du sport de la France entre les deux guerres* (PhD dissertation, University of Paris, 1977); L. Callebat, *Pierre de Coubertin* (Paris: Fayard, 1988).

18 P. Gaboriau, *La classe ouvrière et le vélo* (PhD dissertation, University of Nantes, 1980); C. Pociello, *Le rugby ou la guerre des styles* (Paris: A.M. Metaillé, 1983); J.P. Bodis, *Rugby, politique et société dans le monde des origines à nos jours (1972): Etude comparée* (PhD dissertation, University of Toulouse-II, 1986); A. Wahl, *Les archives du football. Sport et société en France 1880–1980* (Paris: Gallimard-Julliard, 1989); A. Wahl, *La balle au pied, Histoire du football* (Paris: Gallimard-Découvertes, 1990); A. Wahl, 'Le football, un nouveau territoire de l'historien', *Vingtième siècle* 26 (1990), 127–31.

19 D. Lejeune, *Les alpinistes en France à la fin XIXè siècle et au début du XXè siècle* (PhD dissertation, University of Montpellier, 1975) (published in Paris: CTHS, 1988).

20 M. Amar, *Nés pour courir: Sports, pouvoirs et rebellions, 1944–1958* (Grenoble: Presses universitaires de Grenoble, 1987).

21 Spivak, *Les origines militaires de l'éducation physique française: Education physique, sport et nationalisme en France, du Second Empire au Front Populaire* (PhD dissertation, University of Paris-Sorbonne, 1983).

22 A. Bourzac, *Les bataillons scolaires: Histoire et idéologie* (PhD dissertation, University of Lyon-II, 1982) (published by l'Harmattan, 2004).

23 P. Charreton, *Le thème du sport dans la littérature française contemporaine* (PhD dissertation, University of Lyon, 1981); A. Ehrenberg, *Archanges, guerriers, militaires et sportifs: Essai sur l'éducation de l'homme fort* (PhD dissertation, Ecole des Hautes Etudes en Sciences Sociales, 1978) (partly published in A. Ehrenberg, *Le corps militaire: Politique et pédagogie en démocratie* (Paris: Aubier-Montaigne, 1983); J.P. Augustin, 'Espaces et histoire des sports collectifs: Rugby, football, basket – L'exemple des Landes (1890–1983)', *Travaux et recherches en EPS* 8 (1985), 84–94.

24 Later published as P. Bourdieu, 'Comment peut-on être sportif?', in P. Bourdieu, *Questions de sociologie* (Paris: éditions de Minuit, 1980), 173–95.

25 J. Defrance, *La fortification des corps. Essai d'histoire sociale des pratiques d'exercices corporels* (PhD dissertation, Ecole des hautes Etudes en Sciences Sociales, 1978), published under the title: *L'excellence corporelle: La formation des activités physiques et sportives modernes (1770–1914)* (Rennes: Presses Universitaires de Rennes & éditions revue STAPS, 1987).

26 *Travaux et Recherches en EPS* 6 (Paris: INSEP, 1980) and 8 (Paris: INSEP, 1985).

27 The works that puzzled the majority of PE teachers were M. Foucault, *Histoire de la folie à l'âge classique* (Paris: Plon, 1961); *La naissance de la clinique* (Paris: Plon, 1963); *Les mots et les choses* (Paris: Gallimard, 1966); *L'archéologie du savoir* (Paris: Gallimard, 1969), and *Surveiller et punir: Naissance de la prison* (Paris: Gallimard, 1975).

28 J. Gleyse, 'La mystique de la revue *Quel corps?* et l'éducation physique. 1975–97', in T. Terret, ed., *Education physique, sport et loisir: 1970–2000* (Marseille: AFRAPS, 2000), 143–62.

29 The most prominent examples are J.M. Brohm, *Corps et politique* (Paris: Jean-Pierre Delarge, 1975), and G. Vigarello, *Le corps redressé* (Paris: Jean-Pierre Delarge, 1978).

30 J. Thibault, *Les aventures du corps dans la pédagogie française* (PhD dissertation, 1976), published under the following year (Paris: Vrin, 1977); A. Rauch, *Le corps en éducation physique* (Paris: Presses universitaires de France, 1982); A. Rauch, *Le souci du corps* (Paris: Presses universitaires de France, 1983).

31 *Quel corps?* 2 (1975).

32 R. Hubscher, J. Durry and B. Jeu, *L'histoire en mouvements* (Paris: Armand Colin, 1992); N. Bancel and J.M. Gayman, *Du guerrier à l'athlète: Eléments d'histoire des pratiques corporelles* (Paris: Presses universitaires de France, 2002); P. Dietchy and P. Clastres, *Sport, culture et société en France du XIXe siècle à nos jours* (Paris: Hachette, 2006); T. Terret, *Histoire du sport* (Paris: Presses universitaires de France, 2007).

33 The collection was initiated by Pierre Arnaud, before being taken over by Jean Saint-Martin and Thierry Terret.

34 P. Arnaud and G. Garrier, eds, *Jeux et sports dans l'histoire*, two vols (Paris: CTHS, 1992).

35 P. Arnaud and T. Terret, eds, *Education et politique sportives: XIXè–XXè siècles* (Paris: CTHS, 1995); P. Arnaud and T. Terret, eds, *Education physique, Sports et Arts: XIXè–XXè siècles* (Paris: CTHS, 1996); P. Arnaud and T. Terret, eds, *Le sport et ses espaces: XIXème–XXème siècles* (Paris: CTHS, 1998).

36 C. Vivier and J.F. Loudcher, eds, *Le sport dans la ville* (Paris: L'Harmattan, 1998); J.M. Delaplace, ed., *L'histoire du sport, L'histoire des sportifs: Le sportif, l'entraîneur, le dirigeant. 19è et 20è siècles* (Paris: L'Harmattan, 1999); S. Fauché, J.L. Gay-Lescot, J.P. Laplagne and J.P. Callède, eds, *Sport et identité* (Paris, L'Harmattan, 2000); P. Arnaud, T. Terret, P. Gros and J.P. Saint-Martin, eds, *Le sport et les Français pendant l'Occupation*, two vols (Paris: L'Harmattan, 2002); P.A. Lebecq, ed., *Sports, éducation physique et mouvements affinitaires*, two vols (Paris: L'Harmattan, 2004); T. Terret et al., eds, *Sport et genre*, four vols (Paris: L'Harmattan, 2005); L. Munoz, ed., *L'eau et les pratiques corporelles* (Paris: L'Harmattan, 2007).

37 T. Terret, 'Anciens et nouveaux objets d'étude dans l'histoire de l'éducation physique en France', *Spirales* 13–14 (1998), 363–81.

38 I. Tolleneer, 'Historical Perspectives in recent Physical Education Journals (1993–96)', *International Journal of Physical Education* 2 (1996), 52–64.

39 Among many examples, see especially: J.L. Martin, *La politique de l'éducation physique sous la Ve République: 1958–1969* (Paris, Presses universitaires de France, 1999); T. Terret, *Education physique, sport et loisir* (Paris: Ed. AFRAPS, 2000); M. Attali, *Le syndicalisme des enseignants d'éducation physique* (Paris: L'Harmattan, 2004); M. Attali and J. Saint-Martin, *L'Education physique de 1945 à nos jours: Les étapes d'une démocratisation* (Paris: Armand Colin, 2004); J. Saint-Martin, *L'éducation physique et la nation* (Paris: Vuibert), J. Saint-Martin and T. Terret, *Sport et genre, vol. 3: Apprentissage du genre et institutions éducatives* (Paris: L'Harmattan, 2005).

40 R. Holt, 'Contrasting Nationalisms: Sport, Militarism and the Unitary State in Britain and France', *The International Journal of the History of Sport* 12 (1995), 39–54.

41 One good example is P. Arnaud, *Le militaire, l'écolier, le gymnaste* (Lyon: PUL, 1991).

42 See P. Arnaud and T. Terret, eds, *Education et politique sportives: XIXè–XXè siècles* (Paris: CTHS, 1995); J.P. Callède, *Les politiques sportives en France: Eléments de sociologie historique* (Paris: Economica, 2000).

43 For the local level, see: B. Michon and T. Terret, eds, *Pratiques sportives et identités locales* (Paris: L'Harmattan, 2004). For the international level, see: P. Arnaud and A. Wahl, eds, *Sports et relations internationales* (Metz: Actes du Colloque de Metz-Verdun, Centre de recherche histoire et civilisation, 1994); P. Arnaud and J. Riordan, eds, *Sports et relations internationales, les démocraties face aux régimes autoritaires* (Paris: L'Harmattan, 1998).

44 T. Terret, *Les Jeux interalliés de 1919, sport, guerre et relations internationales* (Paris: L'Harmattan, 2002).

45 P. Arnaud, ed., *Les origines du sport ouvrier en Europe* (Paris: L'Harmattan, 1994); A. Gounot, 'Sport or Political Organization? Structures and Characteristics of the Red Sport International, 1921–37', *Journal of Sport History* 28 (2001), 23–39.

46 K. Bretin, *Histoire du mouvement sportif ouvrier en Bourgogne: un autre regard sur les organisations sportives travaillistes (fin des années 1930 – fin des années 1970)* (PhD dissertation, University of Bourgogne, 2004).

47 Both were published. See L. Munoz, *Une histoire du sport catholique: La fédération sportive et culturelle de France; 1898–2000* (Paris: L'Harmattan, 2003); F. Grœninger, *Sport, religion et nation: La Fédération des patronages d'une guerre mondiale à l'autre* (Paris: L'Harmattan, 2004).

48 P. Vertinsky, 'Gender Relations, Women's History and Sport History: A Decade of changing enquiry, 1983–93', *Journal of Sport History* 21 (1994), 1–58.

49 A. Davisse and C. Louveau, *Sport, école, société: La part des femmes* (Paris: Actio, 1991).

50 M. Riot-Sarcey, 'The Difficulties of Gender in France: Reflections on a Concept', *Gender & History* 11 (1999), 489–98.

51 P. Arnaud and T. Terret, eds, *Histoire du sport féminin* (Paris: L'Harmattan, 1996).

52 Published two years later: L. Prudhomme-Poncet, *Histoire du football féminine* (Paris: L'Harmattan, 2003).

53 The congress was organized in Lyon and attracted several hundred historians. The best papers were published in T. Terret (ed.) et al., *Sport et genre* (Paris, L'Harmattan, 2005). For a synthesis on the French historiography of sport and gender, see T. Terret, 'Le genre dans l'histoire du sport', *Clio: Femmes, histoire, société* 23 (mai 2006), 211–40.

54 Published as T. Jobert, *Champions noirs, racisme blanc: La métropole et les sportifs noirs en contexte colonial (1901–1944)* (Grenoble: PUG, 2006).

55 B. Deville-Danthu, *Le sport en noir et blanc: Du sport colonial au sport africain dans les anciens territoires français d'Afrique Occidentale (1920–1965)* (Paris: L'Harmattan, 1997). Among prominent works in this area are E. Combeau-Mari, *Sport et décolonisation à la Réunion* (Paris: L'Harmattan, 1998), and N. Bancel, D. Denis and Y. Fates, eds, *De l'Indochine à l'Algérie: La jeunesse en mouvements des deux côtés du miroir colonial, 1940–1962* (Paris: La découverte, 2003).

56 T. Terret, 'French sport historiography', *The International Journal of the History of Sport* 24, 12 (2007).

57 *Migrations société* 19, 110, (mars/avril 2007); P. Dietschy, Y. Gastaut and S. Mourlane, Histoire politique des Coupes du monde de football (Paris: Vuibert, 2006); Y. Gastaut and S. Mourlane, eds, *Le Football dans nos sociétés: Une culture populaire, 1914–1998* (Paris: Autrement, 2006).

58 C. Eisenberg, P. Lanfranchi, T. Mason and A. Wahl, *FIFA 1904–2004: Le siècle du football* (Paris: Le cherche midi, 2004).

59 Among many examples: P. Gaboriau, *Le Tour de France et le vélo: Histoire sociale d'une épopée contemporaine* (Paris: L'Harmattan, 1994); P. Boury, *La France du Tour, le Tour de France, un espace à géométrie variable* (Paris: L'Harmattan, 1997); P. Porte and D. Vila, eds, *Maillot jaune: Regards croisés sur le Centenaire du Tour de France* (Biarritz: Atlantica, 2003).

60 Published in A. Poyer, *Les premiers temps des véloces-clubs: Apparition et diffusion du cyclisme associatif français entre 1867 et 1914* (Paris: L'Harmattan, 2003).

61 See for instance, J.Y. Guillain and P. Porte, eds, *La planète est rugby: Regards croisés sur l'Ovalie*, two vols (Biarritz: Atlantica, 2007).

62 *Relations internationales* 111 (autumn 2002) and 112 (winter 2002), special issue *Olympisme et relations internationales*. See also F. Carpentier, *Le comité international olympique en crises: La présidence de Henri Baillet-Latour, 1925–1940* (Paris: L'Harmattan, 2004).

63 P. Arnaud and T. Terret, *Le rêve blanc: Olympisme et sport d'hiver* (Bordeaux, PUB, 1993); M. Berlioux, *Des jeux et des crimes: 1936, le piège blanc olympique*, two vols (Biarritz: Atlantica, 2007).

64 P. Clastres, P. Dietschy and S. Laget, *France Olympisme* (Paris, Association pour la diffusion de la pensée française (ADPF), Ministère des affaires étrangères, 2004).

65 The application of this model to sports history was presented in France in T. Terret, *Histoire des sports* (Paris: L'Harmattan, 1996).

66 G. Vigarello, *Techniques d'hier et d'aujourd'hui: Une histoire culturelle du sport* (Paris: R. Laffont et Revue EPS, 1988).

67 A. Wahl, *La balle au pied*, op. cit.; T. Terret, *Naissance et diffusion de la natation sportive* (Paris: L'Harmattan, 1994); P. Charroin and T. Terret, *L'eau et la balle: Une histoire du water-polo* (Paris: L'Harmattan, 1998).

68 A. Roger, *L'entraînement en athlétisme en France (1919–1973): une histoire de théoriciens?* (PhD dissertation, University of Lyon, 2003); J. Vincent, *Le crochet, la passe et la mêlée: Une histoire des techniques en rugby de 1845 à 1957* (PhD dissertation, University of Lyon, 2003).

69 A. Corbin, J.J. Courtine and G. Vigarello, eds, *Histoire du corps* (Paris: Seuil, 2005).

70 M. Perrot, *L'impossible prison* (Paris: Seuil, 1980).

71 J. Gleyse, *L'instrumentation du corps* (Paris: L'Harmattan, 1997); J.F. Loudcher, *Histoire de la savate, du chausson, et de la boxe française. 1797–1978*; J.F. Loudcher, C. Vivier and M. Herr, 'Michel Foucault et la recherche en histoire de l'éducation physique et du sport', *STAPS* 38 (1995), 7–18.

72 A. Prost, *Douze leçons sur l'histoire* (Paris: Seuil, 1996); R. Chartier, 'Histoire intellectuelle et histoire des mentalités', in R. Chartier, *Au bord de la falaise* (Paris: Albin Michel, 1998).

73 P. Burke, 'Strengths and Weakness of the History of Mentalities', *History of European Ideas* VII (1986); R. Chartier, 'Intellectual History or Sociocultural History? The French Trajectories', in D. Lacapra and S. Kaplan, eds, *Modern European Intellectual History* (Ithaca and London: Cornell University Press, 1982).

74 Entretien avec Maurice Agulhon, in *Sport et Histoire* 1 (1988).

75 P. Arnaud, *Le sportsman, l'Ecolier et le Gymnaste; la mise en forme scolaire de la culture physique (1869–1914)* (PhD dissertation, University of Lyon, 1986); P. Arnaud, *Les Athlètes de la République, gymnastique, sport et idéologie républicaine, 1870–1914*, op. cit.

76 Published in C. Vivier, *La sociabilité canotière* (Paris: L'Harmattan, 1999).

77 With rare, but notable, exceptions such as British specialist in French cultural studies Phil Dine, who wrote a splendid book on French rugby; see P. Dine, *French Rugby Football: A Cultural History* (Oxford and New York: Berg, 2001).

78 M. Phillips, 'Deconstructing Sport History: The Postmodern Challenge', *Journal of Sport History* 28 (2001), 327–44.

79 F. Bosman, P. Clastres and P. Dietschy, *Le sport de l'archive à l'histoire* (Besançon: Presses universitaires de Besançon, 2006).

80 A. Gounot, D. Jallat and B. Caritey, *Les politiques du stade: Etudes comparées des manifestations sportives du XIXe au XXe siècle* (Rennes: Presses universitaires de Rennes, 2007).

26 Germany

Arnd Krüger

When Ernst Curtius, then professor of classics at Göttingen, made his famous speech in Berlin in 1852 on behalf of excavating ancient Olympia, he hit a respondent chord, since there was a general interest in the historiography of ancient 'sport' at this time.[1] Some of the better known historians of antiquity have maintained this interest in physical culture up to the present. It is no wonder, then, that the international journal on sports history of ancient times, *Nikephoros: Zeitschrift für Sport und Kultur im Altertum* (1988–present), has been published in Germany and that *Stadion: Internationale Zeitschrift für Geschichte des Sports* (1975–present), the other German-based international journal, has also been strong on ancient sports. There are also *SportZeiten* (1987–present, sometimes under different names) and *Beiträge zur Sportgeschichte* (1995–present), two German sports history journals, as well as the *Jahrbuch der Niedersächsischen Sportgeschichte* (1988–present) and the *Turn-und Sportgeschichte in Westfalen und Lippe: Zeitschrift des Westfälisch-Lippischen Instituts für Turn-und Sportgeschichte* (1996–present) two regional sports history yearbooks. 'When one turns to Germany there has been so much good history written one hardly knows where to begin a discussion', Allen Guttmann wrote.[2]

Friedrich Ludwig Jahn (1778–1852), the 'father' of German gymnastics (*Turnvater*), based his new physical culture on his studies of the past and recommended the study of history.[3] Therefore, it is not surprising that the courses to prepare *gymnastics (Turner)* teachers included classes on the history of physical exercise and the role of exercise in the preparation of the nation. Soon it developed its own historiography, *Turngeschichte*, the history of national gymnastics. Some of the better known historians of *Turnen*, like Euler,[4] Hirth,[5] Angerstein[6] and Wassmannsdorff, provided a solid foundation of texts, source material and awareness during the 19th century on which future generations could build.

This link between PE teachers' training and the history of *Turnen* and sport was even more evident later on. When university departments for PE were formed in the 1920s, there was a need for qualified personnel holding any doctorate degree. Given the strong emphasis on *Turnen* and little on Swedish Gymnastics, this field was generally not medicine but history. The separation between *Turnen* and the medical profession took place in the *Barrenstreit* of the 1860s; since then, physiotherapy is part of the medical school while *Turnen* was attached to character building and national education, i.e. the faculties of letters and science.[7] History departments were accepting doctoral work dealing with the history of physical exercise, and sports historians came to dominate chairmen (no chairwomen before 1967) positions of the PE departments in Germany.

The basis of this was introduced already in the 19th century and has been a distinguishing feature of German high school teaching ever since: a high school teacher has been and still is a teacher of (at least) two subjects. This means that up to a Masters degree or the equivalent teaching credential, the future teacher has to carry a double major. With PE and history as majors, he or she has had a good basis for a PhD in sports history. Even today, Germany is among the few European countries that have maintained this tradition of a double major.

The PE students needed textbooks to prepare for exams. The most widely used text was that of Cotta (1902),[8] which went through eight editions before being revised by Saurbier and Stahr (1931),[9] and then by Saurbier (1939).[10] It is not surprising that Bohus (1986) based his book also largely on Cotta.[11] Relatively little has been changed in and out of the Nazi era. Apart from these brief attempts to write an approved history for PE instruction, there are also longer texts that aim at a complete sports history. Bogeng (1926) compiled the first cultural history of sport, including prominent authors from all fields of science (783pp).[12] Neuendorff (1930–34) put together over 2,000 pages on the development of *Turnen* and PE in Germany to show that all of German history, and particularly that of *Turnen,* culminated in the Third Reich.[13] After the war, Carl Diem (1960)[14] profited from all of the previous works and Euler's *Handbook*[15] for his own world history of sport (1,223 pp). Horst Ueberhorst's monumental task of compiling a genuine world history, which includes six volumes of global coverage (1972–89) and 3,667 pages, also falls within this tradition.[16] More than 100 scholars from all over the world have participated in this impressive project. For some countries in Africa, Asia, or Latin America, this was the first time that the history of their sport had ever been written, while for such other areas as Germany (vol. 3, 1,144pp) it was the most up-to-date account. Michael Krüger's three-volume history of physical education and sport (currently 721pp) is in the same tradition, with a strong emphasis on *Turnen.*[17]

Of course, it is questionable whether many of the early physical activities can be considered 'sports', but there is a German tradition to show this lengthy continuity in the history of exercise. When A. Krüger and McClelland took issue with Guttmann[18] that 'sport' as we know it really started in Britain in the second half of the 19th century, there was plenty of German research to show otherwise.[19]

During the Nazi period (1933–45) there was little room for such 'useless' activities as innovative sports historical research. The sports historians continued their work, however. If you look at ancient sports history, they simply worked on Sparta instead of Athens, the use of sport for military preparedness rather than sport at the cradle of democracy.[20]

For the historiography of sport in East Germany (German Democratic Republic, GDR) the immediate post-war years were a peak period. Skorning,[21] Schröder,[22] Schuster,[23] Eichel,[24] Wonneberger[25] and Lukas[26] rewrote German sports history from a Marxist-Leninist standpoint. They also attempted to outdo Diem and Neuendorff with their own *Geschichte der Köperkultur in Deutschland* (1,288pp). It was later revised with a large illustrated edition (1983, 524pp) demonstrating that GDR sports were in the best German tradition.

From the late 1960s onward, West German sports historiography started to catch up again. It is here that Guttmann's quote seems to be correct. Why were the 1970s the most productive era? It was a time when the university departments expanded. PE departments were just being granted the right to award their own doctoral degrees, so they needed qualified personnel who had earned doctorates elsewhere. It was basically the same situation as in the 1920s. History departments were more inclined to accept an 'exotic' subject like sport than most others. The solid methodological preparation for doing modern political history, the definite interest in sports and the motivation to embark upon an academic career in sport then made possible the extraordinary development of German sports historiography. However, it hindered progress from the 1980s onward. Now a PhD thesis can be written in most PE departments. This seems to serve as a 'better' qualification for the job market than an exterior qualification, but leaves out a solid methodological basis in fields such as sports history. At the height of development, there had been 20 university professors for sports history in Germany; now there are only six active ones left – and most of their positions will be cut when they retire.

There used to be very little research of sports history outside PE departments in the 20th century, with the notable exception of ancient sports history, with Aigner[27] and Weiler,[28] and medieval history.[29] This is also reflected in the professional organization of sports historians, their main publication outlets and their sources for outside funding. Sports historians have organized themselves as a section of the sport science association *(Deutsche Vereinigung für Sportwissenschaft)*, along with all of the other employees of the PE departments, and not with the historians nor independently. In 2008 the German organization of historians *(Historikertag)* organized a section on sports history for the very first time, indicating that sports history is now as much present in the mainstream as among pure sports historians.[30] As for outside funding, university research has been supported by the *Deutsche Forschungsgemeinschaft* on a competitive basis with peer evaluation of the research projects since 1949. It does not include 'sport', as sport research is financially supported by the *Bundesinstitut für Sportwissenschaft*. As this federal institute is mainly responsible for elite sport, areas like sports history have a hard time getting funded at all. As long as the history peers were reluctant to deal with such exotic topics as sport, it was difficult to have sports history topics funded.

Workers' sport

In a number of areas one can see that the history of sport has been integrated into general history. The *Journal of Contemporary History* (1978) has included much work already done in Germany and there has been a lot since with a rich interchange with labour historians on this field.[31] This started with the early works of Wonneberger,[32] Ueberhorst,[33] Timmermann,[34] and was taken up by Teichler,[35] Krüger and Riordan,[36] and Nitsch.[37] The workers' sports movement, sports in close connection with the socialist trade union movement, which was very strong in Germany during the period 1893–1933 before it was suppressed by the Nazis, has always fascinated academic youth as a possible alternative to 'bourgeois sport', However, it is quite a challenge to do archival work on the workers' sports movement and its clubs, as they were outlawed in 1933 and it was dangerous to keep worker sport material during the Nazi era. So much of the workers tradition remains strong in the hearts of the members, but not in the archives. This applies especially to the role of women in workers' sport. Sigrid Block (1987) and other modern sports feminists have looked into this part of the past and hoped to find a better sports culture for women there. Yet despite all of its progressive elements, a strong polarization of the sexes could be found there as well. Women accepted the principle of 'separate but equal', with all its limitations, in workers' sport even more readily than in 'bourgeois sport'.[38]

Two detailed local studies have shown a trend up to present times: Viola Denecke tries to show the 'brotherly' spirit prevailing in the workers' sports clubs in the city of Brunswick. This is an extremely difficult task, since it requires showing the difference in attitude between workers in a workers' sports club and workers in bourgeois clubs, where they might represent a large part of the membership. Such studies in the history of 'mentalities' and everyday life require oral history methods along with those of social and political history.[39] Dierker has written a political study of the largest German workers' sport club, *Fichte* Berlin. This was an important club where the quarrels between communists and social democrats took place within the club rather than between clubs. At one time or another, the major personalities of the Communist Red Sport International and the Social Democratic Socialist Workers' Sports International were members of *Fichte* Berlin.[40]

Such detailed studies were also provided by Stiller and Wetterich on the workers' sport youth.[41] After a conference on the occasion of the 100th anniversary of its foundation in Leipzig,[42] far less was published. One of the remaining riddles of workers' sport could only be resolved after the opening of Soviet archives: Gounot looked at the communist workers' sport by using Moscow-based material. Not even the workers' sports historians of the former GDR had had access to this.[43] The Soviet domination could now be proven from archival material rather than just by supposition. Fasbender compared the situation of the workers in company-owned 'yellow' workers' clubs and 'red' trade union clubs in the Ruhr area. It was not really predictable who would choose one and who the other. To find out, local, if not biographical studies are necessary.[44] Soccer is an interesting case as far more workers were playing in 'normal' clubs with middle-class management than in ideologically founded clubs. Making a decent *Deutschmark* for playing (amateur) football in front of a large number of spectators seemed far more important for many workers than the ideological purity in a trade union-dominated club with fewer spectators and less money.[45]

If you look at the most recent development you can see that Fankhauser's[46] doctoral dissertation looked at workers' sport in Switzerland in a traditional way. As the laws were far more liberal, it is a field in which a much earlier (1874) form of workers' culture than in Germany (1893) can be studied, and Andrea Bruns interprets the signs and symbols of Coubertin's Olympics and the Workers' Olympics of the 1920s, showing that the cultural turn has reached the very political field of workers' sports.[47]

Nazi sport

The cultural turn took place quite early in German sports history, in that there has always been a tradition of taking the history of sport as something different from the political field. As the chairmen of the 1950s and 1960s had been active in the Nazi period, it took until 1966 for the first book to be published on Nazi sports (Bernett 1966; enlarged second edition 2008).[48] Bernett soon became the most prominent author for this period.[49] Bernett was remarkably reluctant to deal with the problem of continuity of people after 1945, taking issue only with Guido von Mengden,[50] who was yet sufficiently active to publish a full-length rebuttal (Mengden 1980) questioning the methodological competence of Bernett, as he had not used oral sources and had not looked at the alternatives people had in the Nazi period.[51] Additional early publications were added by Joch[52] on the Nazi ideology in PE, A. Krüger on the 1936 Olympics,[53] Buss on university education[54] and Teichler on the international politics of the Nazis.[55]

Most of the early publications were remarkable in that they found a lot of material where Diem and others had claimed that everything was gone, making the Nazi period by far the best-researched era of German sports history. As the works were either concerned with the body cult, with propaganda or Nazi symbolism, they fit into the mainstream of historical thought.[56] They also duplicated historical thinking in the way they dealt with collective or individual 'guilt'. For Bernett anything Nazi was evil *per se*, while Krüger differentiated already between the categories of postwar denazification, accepting, for example, *fellow travellers*. A. Krüger took this up in the context of continuity of personnel and the insecurity of the situation in early 1933,[57] Theodor Lewald, the president of the organizing committee of the 1936 Games and Hans Fritsch, the flag bearer of the 1936 Olympics.[58] The question of an educated value judgement plays, of course, a large role in the literature dealing with sports under Nazi occupation. Should you play football with the enemy?[59]

While in the sprit of 1968 everything was political, the question of an *Eigenwelt* [a sphere of its own] of sports was later taken up by many more authors in detail.[60] Where are the borders of acceptable opportunism and where does it start to become unethical? For Heimerzheim this is a key question when looking at Ritter von Halt, IOC member and (honorary) president of the German Track and Field Association before and after the war, and the only prominent sports person who was considered a war criminal by the Nuremberg courts.[61]

There is a substantial amount of literature concerned with the Nazi school system, which includes the PE that was so prominent on the Nazi agenda. Sports history is here fully integrated into the history of education. This emphasis started with Ueberhorst and the Nazi elite schools (of which he was a pupil himself),[62] while Schäfer discusses also the consequences of such elite education, and Kliem emphasizes the systematic problems of school education during the Nazi period with its emphasis on extracurricular activities such as the Hitler Youth.[63] Peiffer emphasizes the preparation for war in boys' schools.[64] The situation in Austria was somewhat different in that it had its own Fascist organizations which were closer to the Italian than the German model.[65] As Karl Gaulhofer, one of the most prominent Austrian physical educators and the only one who created a widely used system, became a prominent Nazi, Austrians have been quite reluctant to discuss the Nazi past in PE.[66] This is of course not much different from Carl Diem in Germany, for whom a supposedly neutral biography is in progress (Frank Becker). While Diem has been defended by his disciples or accused by his rivals, some cities decided to rename roads and sports grounds which had carried his name when it became known that during the final days of war-torn Berlin he encouraged 15-year-olds to march towards Soviet tanks almost empty handed.[67] Appell, one of the Hitler Youth who listened to his pep talks, later became a prominent journalist and wrote about it in his memoirs, ruining much of the Diem legacy and again putting sports history in the midst of political discussion.[68]

Body politics were discussed in the context of Nazi sports by Alkemeyer and Wildmann,[69] who followed the lead of French sociologist Jean-Marie Brohm who became well known in Germany after a symposium on the occasion of the 50th anniversary of the Olympic Games of 1936.[70] Recently there have been quite a number of publications dealing with body image particularly in the Nazi era.[71] While these publications of the cultural and visual type were mainly concerned with the interpretation of images of the Nazi period, there is also an element of body history referring particularly to dance.[72] As the German nudists became a sport organization in 1933 to overcome the Nazi threat of abolishment, studies of nudism have played a role in the history of the body and of gender.[73] Wedemeyer-Kolwe has shown that the history of physical culture and body building can also be seen as one of the predecessors of Nazis. The notion that 'weakness is a crime' was ever present in physical culture and in Nazism.[74]

While most scholars assumed that Nazi sports had German roots, A. Krüger and Oelrich looked at the other sources from which the Nazis took many ideas, particularly in the formative years. Much was copied from the Italian Fascists at first, while later on the Italian Fascists learned from the Germans.[75]

Jewish sports

While some of the interest in Jewish sports resulted in its destruction during the Nazi period, it soon became evident that one had to look at the roots of Jewish sports in Germany and the involvement of men and women of Jewish faith in other sport organizations to fully understand the loss to German culture.[76] 'German' is here taken in a wide sense, as Jewish sports were also strong in Austria[77] and Switzerland.[78] Schulze-Marmeling identified Jewish football players and described their distinctive careers.[79] Tönnihsen followed the life of an individual Jewish athlete in full book length, while most biographies were only papers or book chapters.[80] It is, of course, difficult to identify Jewish persons without falling into the Nazi trap. Who is a Jew? Is it legitimate to look only for people of Jewish faith, when people were persecuted in Germany because of their Jewish decent? Should you look only for the members of Jewish sports clubs? Mayer as well as Körner and Patka took a very wide approach, fully aware of the problem, in their encyclopaedias of Jewish athletes.[81]

A. Krüger and Sanders looked at the first Jewish sports club in the Netherlands and found the differences between the three basic forms of Jewish clubs: Maccabi (i.e. Zionist), national-Jewish (Diaspora oriented), and neutral. As the national traditions were completely destroyed by the Nazis and only the Zionist Maccabi survived, national-Jewish sport clubs are completely forgotten[82] and have hardly had a chance to remain in the collective memory.[83]

Football and national identity

Although there are endless books dealing with the history of a particular football (soccer) club or about football in particular, only in more recent years have these books achieved an acceptable quality. Only on the anniversary of the German victory in the football World Cup was the question of football and national identity widely discussed.[84] Winning the World Cup 1954 under a coach who had been in charge of the national team during the Nazi era created national enthusiasm for the first time after the lost war and seemed to show that Germany was back on the international stage. Winning as an underdog against the seemingly invincible Hungarians increased the feeling of 'we are back'. The Federal Republic of Germany might have been founded in 1949, but the population started to identify itself with the new state only after winning the World Cup in 1954. Mainstream historians started to take sport seriously, as it provided more sense of coherence than politics or the economy.[85]

At the same time Havemann published his apologetic history of the collaboration between German football and the Nazis. This is still a topic under discussion, as it has become evident that many battles fought in general history about the role of ordinary citizens within the Nazi era have now reached sports and, in particular, football.[86]

Gender

Much of the best history of women's sports has been written by German scholars.[87] The situation in Germany was different to the Anglo-Saxon world. As the German

Government became involved early (1914) in financing elite sport for the purpose of national representation and desired medals, gender did not matter: women's sports were receiving similar privileges to men's sport. Basically, there are two main streams of thought in gender history: the achievements of women and the demand for equal access to leadership positions in sports governing bodies (Gertrud Pfister); and the wider participation of women,[88] their access to elite sports, and public visibility as a means to acquire an acceptable role.[89] Despite legal equality, women have been discouraged to go in for sports by the medical profession. This dilemma can best be seen in the Nazi era when the official propaganda wanted child-bearing women for the war effort, while the propaganda minister wanted medals no matter whether they were won by men or women.[90] As sport is one of the places in which gender roles have their place, it became a standard theme in German gender studies, whether historical or sociological.

Cold War and sports in the German Democratic Republic (GDR)

Research about the post-war era should be divided into the time before and after German unification. Before unification much of the writing was done in the spirit of the Cold War. Normally, archival sources are closed for 30 years, but when the Berlin Wall fell, the archives of the former GDR (including the files of the secret police, the *Stasi*) were opened wide. As sport had been one of the few areas in which the GDR had dominated the West, sport-related research was high on the agenda and provided the possibility for sports historians to have a lively interchange with other contemporary historians studying the GDR and inner German relations. Methodologically, the question came up again: to what extent can or should people separate themselves from a political system? Can or should sports historians of the former GDR be included in research projects about their own past? The working groups of Teichler and Spitzer in Potsdam said 'no' to this latter question,[91] while the Göttingen group with Buss and Becker said 'yes'.[92] Spitzer specialized, then, in doping and other issues, which could only be documented using the *Stasi* files,[93] while Buss and Becker excelled in everyday history of the GDR, where they could rely on oral history sources.

Olympic history

Ever since Carl Diem brought some of the Coubertin papers to Berlin (and later Cologne), Germany has been a stronghold of Olympic history. *The Journal of Olympic History* (1992–present) is now published in Germany and the three-volume collected papers of Coubertin are also published there.[94] This covers a wide field from international comparisons,[95] to detailed studies of single Olympic Games,[96] Coubertin's involvement in Nazism,[97] or the connection between Coubertin and the USA.[98] The work is stronger on the side of political history and is accepted by historians of culture. There is, of course, also much Olympic ideology, but the quality of work on the Olympic Games has been improving.

Conclusion

German sports historiography has a very long tradition in the field. It has accumulated an enormous amount of material that can be used for political, cultural and intellectual history. Although sport sociologists have been part of sociology organizations, they have been more concerned with the present day than with historical research. Sport is seldom put into the context of the history of science.[99] Due to a strong tradition of amateurism, economic data on sports are limited, so only recently have sports data been used in economic research.[100] Postmodern thinking has scarcely touched sports history.[101] However, mainstream historians have started to use sports history material, so the chances are that the long tradition that had its base in the PE departments will gradually shift to the history departments.

Notes

1 Ernst Curtius, 'Olympia, Vortrag im Wissenschaftlichen Verein zu Berlin: Berlin 1852', in Georg Hirth, ed., *Das gesamte Turnwesen*, Vol. 1 (Hof: Rudolf Lion, 1893), 46–61.

2 Allen Guttmann, 'Recent Works in European Sport History', *Journal of Sport History* 10 (1983), 35–53, quote 41.

3 Friedrich Ludwig Jahn, *Deutsches Volkstum* (Lübeck: Niemann & Comp., 1810).

4 Carl Euler, *Geschichte des Turnunterrichts* (Gotha: Thienemann, 1881).

5 Georg Hirth, ed., *Das gesamte Turnwesen: Ein Lesebuch für deutsche Turner* (Hof: Lion, 1865, 3 vols).

6 Eduard F. Angerstein, *Geschichte der Leibesübungen in den Grundzügen*, 2nd edn (Vienna: Pichler, 1897), 6th edn revised by Otto Kurth 1926.

7 Arnd Krüger, 'Geschichte der Bewegungstherapie', in *Präventivmedizin* (Heidelberg: Springer Loseblatt Sammlung, 1999), 07.06, 1–22.

8 Carl Cotta, *Leitfaden für den Unterricht in der Turngeschichte* (Leipzig: R. Voigtländer, 1902).

9 Bruno Saurbier and Ernst Stahr, *Geschichte der Leibesübungen: Eine kurzgefaßte Darstellung* (Leipzig Voigtländer, 1939).

10 Bruno Saurbier, *Geschichte der Leibesübungen*, 9th edn (Frankfurt/M: Limpert, 1976).

11 Julius Bohus, *Sportgeschichte: Gesellschaft und Sport von Mykene bis heute* (München: BLV, 1986).

12 Gustav Adolf Erich Bogeng, *Geschichte des Sports aller Völker und Zeiten* (Leipzig: Seemann, 1926).

13 Edmund Neuendorff, *Geschichte der neueren deutschen Leibesübung vom Beginn des 18. Jahrhunderts bis zur Gegenwart* (Dresden: Limpert 1930–34, 4 vols).

14 Carl Diem, *Weltgeschichte des Sports* (Stuttgart: Cotta, 1960).

15 Carl Euler, ed., *Encyklopädisches Handbuch des gesamten Turnwesens und der verwandten Gebiete* (Leipzig: Pichler, 1894–96, 3 vols).

16 Horst Ueberhorst, ed., *Geschichte der Leibesübungen* (Berlin: Bartels & Wernitz 1972–89, 6 vols).

17 Michael Krüger, ed., *Einführung in die Geschichte der Leibeserziehung und des Sports Sport und Sportunterricht* (Schorndorf: Hofmann, 1993ff, 3 vols).

18 Allen Guttmann, *From Ritual to Record: The Nature of Modern Sports* (New York: Columbia, 1978).

19 Arnd Krüger and John McClelland, eds, *Die Anfänge des modernen Sports in der Renaissance* (London: Arena, 1984); John M. Carter and Arnd Krüger, eds, *Ritual and Record: Sport in Pre-Industrial Societies* (Westport, CT: Greenwood, 1990). Other German works that also showed 'sports' in earlier period are by J.K. Rühl (Middle Ages) and Wolfgang Decker (ancient Egypt).

20 Arnd Krüger and Dietrich Ramba, 'Sparta or Athens? The Reception of Greek Antiquity in Nazi Germany', in Roland Renson, Manfred Lämmer and James Riordan, eds, *The Olympic Games Through the Ages: Greek Antiquity and its Impact on Modern Sport* (Athens: Hellenic Sports Research Institute, 1991), 345–56.

21 Lothar Skorning, 'Uber die Schwerpunkte bei der Forschungsarbeit in der Geschichte der Körperkultur', *Theorie und Praxis der Körperkultur* 1 (1952), 59–65; Lothar Skorning, ed., *Kurzer Abriss einer Geschichte der Körperkultur in Deutschland seit 1800* (Berlin: Sportverlag 1952).

22 Willi Schröder, *Burschenturner im Kampf um Einheit und Freiheit* (Berlin: Sportverlag 1967).

23 Hans Schuster, *Arbeitersportler im Kampf um die Jugend: Zur Geschichte des revolutionären Arbeitersports 1893–1914* (Berlin: Sportverlag, 1962).

24 Wolfgang Eichel, ed., *Geschichte der Körperkultur in Deutschland* (Berlin: Sportverlag, 1964–67, 4 vols); Wolfgang Eichel, ed., *Illustrierte Geschichte der Körperkultur* (Berlin: Sportverlag, 1983, 2 vols).

25 Günter Wonneberger, *Arbeitersportler gegen Faschisten und Militaristen, 1929–1933: Zur historischen Bedeutung des revolutionären Arbeitersports* (Berlin: Sportverlag, 1959); Günter Wonneberger, ed., *Geschichte der Körperkultur in Deutschland 1945–1961*, Vol. 4 (Berlin: Sportverlag 1967).

26 Gerhard Lukas, *Die Körperkultur in den frühen Epochen der Menschheitsentwicklung* (Berlin: Sportverlag, 1969).

27 Heribert Aigner, *Ausgewählte Schriften* (Graz: Grazer Univ.-Verl., 2008).

28 Ingomar Weiler, *Der Agon im Mythos: Die Einstellung der Griechen zum Wettkampf* (Darmstadt: Wiss. Buchges., 1974); Ingomar Weiler, *Der Sport bei den Völkern der alten Welt*, 2nd edn (Darmstadt: Wiss. Buchges., 1988); Ingomar Weiler, ed., *Olympia – Sport und Spektakel* (Hildesheim: Weidmann, 1998). The worldwide expert on sport in ancient Egypt was, however, working in the Cologne Sport University, see Wolfgang Decker, *Pharao und Sport* (Mainz: von Zabern, 2006).

29 Josef Fleckenstein, ed., *Das ritterliche Turnier im Mittelalter* (Göttingen: Vandenhoeck & Ruprecht, 1985); the most comprehensive work is, though, not by a German but by John McClelland, *Body and Mind: Sport in Europe from the Roman Empire to the Renaissance* (London: Routledge, 2007).

30 Donata von Neree, 'Warum die allgemeine Geschichte die Sportgeschichte nicht zur Kenntnis nimmt', in Arnd Krüger and J.K. Rühl, eds, *Aus lokaler Sportgeschichte lernen* (Hamburg, 2001), 19–26.

31 Robert F. Wheeler, 'Organized Sport and Organized Labour: The Workers' Sports Movement', *Journal of Contemporary History* 13 (1978), 191–210.

32 Günter Wonneberger, *Arbeitersportler gegen Faschisten und Militaristen, 1929–1933: Zur historischen Bedeutung des revolutionären Arbeitersports* (Berlin: Sportverlag, 1959).

33 Horst Ueberhorst, *Frisch, frei, stark und treu: die Arbeitersportbewegung in Deutschland 1893–1933* (Düsseldorf: Droste, 1973).

34 Heinz Timmermann, *Geschichte und Struktur der Arbeitersportbewegung 1893–1933* (Ahrensburg: Czwalina, 1973).

35 Hans Joachim Teichler, *Arbeiterkultur und Arbeitersport* (Clausthal-Zellerfeld: DVS, 1985); Hans Joachim Teichler, ed., *Illustrierte Geschichte des Arbeitersports* (Bonn: Dietz, 1987).

36 Arnd Krüger and James Riordan, eds, *Der internationale Arbeitersport: der Schlüssel zum Arbeitersport in 10 Ländern* (Köln: Pahl-Rugenstein, 1985); Arnd Krüger and James Riordan, eds, *The Story of Worker Sport* (Champaign, IL: Human Kinetics, 1996).

37 Franz Nitsch, ed., *90 Jahre Arbeitersport* (Münster: Lit, 1985).

38 Sigrid Block, *Frauen und Mädchen in der Arbeitersportbewegung* (Münster: Lit, 1987).

39 Viola Denecke, *Die Arbeitersportgemeinschaft: Eine kulturhistorische Studie über die Arbeitersportbewegung in den zwanziger Jahren* (Duderstadt: Mecke, 1990).

40 Herbert Dierker, *Arbeitersport im Spannungsfeld der Zwanziger Jahre: Sportpolitik und Alltagserfahrungen auf internationaler, deutscher und Berliner Ebene* (Essen: Klartext, 1990).

41 Eike Stiller, *Jugend im Arbeitersport: Lebenswelten im Spannungsfeld von Verbandskultur und Sozialmilieu von 1893–1933* (Münster: Lit, 1991); Jörg Wetterich, *Bewegungskultur und Körpererziehung in der sozialistischen Jugendarbeit 1893 bis 1933: Lebensstile und Bewegungskonzepte im Schnittpunkt von Arbeitersportbewegung und Jugendbewegung* (Münster: Lit, 1993).

42 Franz Nitsch, ed., *Die roten Turnbrüder: 100 Jahre Arbeitersport* (Marburg: Schüren, 1995).

43 André Gounot, *Die Rote Sportinternationale, 1921–1937: kommunistische Massenpolitik im europäischen Arbeitersport* (Münster: Lit, 2002).

44 Sebastian Fasbender, *Zwischen Arbeitersport und Arbeitssport: Werksport an Rhein und Ruhr 1921–1938* (Göttingen: Cuvillier, 1997).

45 Eike Stiller, *Karl Bühren, Arbeitersportler und Sportfunktionär: vor Hitler geflohen – unter Stalin getötet* (Berlin: Nora, 2007).

46 Dominique Marcel Fankhauser, 'Die Arbeitersportbewegung in der Schweiz. 1874–1947', PhD dissertation, University of Göttingen, 2008.

47 Andrea Bruns, 'Sport und Ideologie in der Zeit zwischen I. und II. Weltkrieg – Zwischen Gesellschaftskritik und sozialreformatorischen Bestrebungen', PhD dissertation, University of Göttingen, 2009.

48 Hajo Bernett, *Nationalsozialistische Leibeserziehung: eine Dokumentation ihrer Theorie und Organisation* (Schorndorf: Hofmann, 1966), 2nd edn revised by Hansjoachim Teichler 2008.

49 Hajo Bernett, *Sportpolitik im Dritten Reich: aus den Akten der Reichskanzlei* (Schorndorf: Hofmann, 1971); Hajo Bernett, *Untersuchungen zur Zeitgeschichte des Sports* (Schorndorf: Hofmann, 1973); Hajo Bernett, *Der jüdische Sport im nationalsozialistischen Deutschland 1933–1938* (Schorndorf: Hofmann, 1978); Hajo Bernett, *Der Weg des Sports in die nationalsozialistische Diktatur: die Entstehung des Deutschen (Nationalsozialistischen) Reichsbundes für Leibesübungen* (Schorndorf: Hofmann, 1983).

50 Hajo Bernett, *Guido von Mengden: 'Generalstabschef' des deutschen Sports* (Berlin: Bartels & Wernitz, 1976).

51 Guido von Mengden, *Umgang mit der Geschichte und mit Menschen: ein Beitrag zur Geschichte der Machtübernahme im deutschen Sport durch die NSDAP* (Berlin: Bartels & Wernitz, 1980).

52 Winfried Joch, *Theorie einer politischen Pädagogik* (Bern: Lang, 1971); Winfried Joch, *Politische Leibeserziehung und ihre Theorie im nationalsozialistischen Deutschland* (Bern: Lang, 1976).

53 Arnd Krüger, *Die Olympischen Spiele 1936 und die Weltmeinung: Ihre außenpolitische Bedeutung unter besonderer Berücksichtigung der USA* (Berlin: Bartels & Wernitz, 1972).

54 Wolfgang Buss, *Die Entwicklung des deutschen Hochschulsports vom Beginn der Weimarer Republik bis zum Ende des NS-Staates: Umbruch und Neuanfang oder Kontinuität?* (Göttingen: GAU, 1975).

55 Hans Joachim Teichler, *Internationale Sportpolitik im Dritten Reich* (Schorndorf: Hofmann, 1991).

56 Henning Eichberg, *Massenspiele: NS-Thingspiel, Arbeiterweihespiel und olympisches Zeremoniell* (Bad Cannstatt: Frommann-Holzboog, 1977); Frank Becker, 'Massengesellschaft – Massensport – Massenritual', *Sportwissenschaft* 37 (2007), 363–80.

57 Arnd Krüger, *Sport und Politik, Vom Turnvater Jahn zum Staatsamateur* (Hannover: Fackelträger, 1975); Arnd Krüger, '"Heute gehört uns Deutschland und morgen … ?" Das Ringen um den Sinn der Gleichschaltung im Sport in der ersten Jahreshälfte 1933', in Wolfgang Buss and Arnd Krüger, eds, *Sportgeschichte: Traditionspflege und Wertewandel* (Duderstadt: Mecke, 1985), 175–96.

58 Arnd Krüger, *Dr. Theodor Lewald: Sportführer ins Dritte Reich* (Berlin: Bartels & Wernitz, 1975); Rolf Pfeiffer and Arnd Krüger, 'Theodor Lewald: Eine Karriere im Dienste des Vaterlands oder die vergebliche Suche nach der jüdischen Identität eines "Halbjuden"', *Menora* 6 (1995), 233–65; Arnd Krüger, 'Der Fahnenträger: Hans Fritsch (1911–1987)', in Arnd Krüger and Bernd Wedemeyer, eds, *Aus Biographien Sportgeschichte lernen* (Hoya: NISH, 2000), 252–71.

59 Hans Bonde, *Football with the Foe: Danish Sport under the Swastika* (Odense: Southern Denmark University Press, 2008).

60 Christiane Eisenberg, *'English sports' und deutsche Bürge: eine Gesellschaftsgeschichte 1800–1939* (Paderborn: Schöningh, 1999).

61 Peter Heimerzheim, *Karl Ritter von Halt – Leben zwischen Sport und Politik* (Sankt Augustin: Academia, 1999).

62 Horst Ueberhorst, *Elite für die Diktatur: die nationalpolitischen Erziehungsanstalten 1933–1945* (Düsseldorf: Droste, 1969).

63 Harald Schäfer, *Napola: die letzten vier Jahre der Nationalpolitischen Erziehungsanstalt Oranienstein bei Diez an der Lahn 1941–1945* (Frankfurt/M: Fischer, 1997); Konstantin Kliem, *Sport in der Zeit des Nationalsozialismus: Entwicklung und Zielsetzung im Höheren Schulwesen und in der Hitlerjugend* (Saarbrücken: Müller, 2007).

64 Lorenz Peiffer, *Turnunterricht im Dritten Reich – Erziehung für den Krieg? Der schulische Alltag des Turnunterrichts an den höheren Jungenschulen der Provinz Westfalen vor dem Hintergrund seiner politisch-ideologischen und administrativen Funktionalisierung* (Köln: Pahl-Rugenstein, 1987).

65 Rudolf Müllner, *Die Mobilisierung der Körper: der Schul-und Hochschulsport im nationalsozialistischen Österreich* (Vienna: WUV, 1993).

66 Wolfgang Rechberger, *Karl Gaulhofer: historisch-biographische Untersuchungen zu Leben und Werk des österreichischen Schulturnreformers* (Salzburg: IfS, 1999). Recently, Austrian works on Nazi history have included political and cultural dimensions, see Matthias Marschik, *Sportdiktatur: Bewegungskulturen im nationalsozialistischen Österreich* (Vienna: Turia & Kant, 2008).

67 Achim Laude, *Der Sport-Führer: die Legende um Carl Diem* (Göttingen: Die Werkstatt, 2000).

68 Reinhard Appel, *Es wird nicht mehr zurückgeschossen … Erinnerungen an das Kriegsende 1945* (Bergisch Gladbach: Lingen, 1995), see 19–22.

69 Thomas Alkemeyer, *Körper, Kult und Politik: von der 'Muskelreligion' Pierre de Coubertins zur Inszenierung von Macht in den Olympischen Spielen von 1936* (Frankfurt/Main: Campus, 1996); Daniel Wildmann, *Begehrte Körper: Konstruktion und Inszenierung des 'arischen' Männerkörpers im 'Dritten Reich'* (Würzburg: Königshausen & Neumann, 1998).

70 Jean-Marie Brohm, *Sport, A Prison of Measured Time: Essays* (London: Links, 1978); Jean-Marie Brohm, 'Zum Verhältnis von Olympismus und Nationalsozialismus', in Gunther Gebauer, ed., *Olympia-Berlin: Gewalt und Mythos in den Olympischen Spielen von Berlin 1936* (Berlin: FUB, 1986), 190–205.

71 Stefanie Grote, '"Objekt" Mensch: Körper als Ikon und Ideologem in den cineastischen Werken Leni Riefenstahls: ästhetisierter Despotismus oder die Reziprozität von Auftragskunst und Politik im Dritten Reich', PhD dissertation, University of Frankfurt (Oder), 2004; Paula Diehl, ed., *Körper im Nationalsozialismus: Bilder und Praxen* (Paderborn: Schöningh, 2006); Adrian Schmidtke,

Körperformationen: Fotoanalysen zur Formierung und Disziplinierung des Körpers in der Erziehung des Nationalsozialismus (Münster: Waxmann, 2007); Elena Pavlova, *KörperBilder-BildKörper: Annäherungen an Elfriede Jelineks Theater unter besonderer Berücksichtigung seiner kritischen Dekonstruktion des faschistischen Körper-Diskurses* (Saarbrücken: VDM, 2007).

72 Harald Justin, *'Tanz mir den Hitler': Kunstgeschichte und (faschistische) Herrschaft: die Entfaltung einer Idee, exemplarisch verdeutlicht an Theorie und Praxis prominenter Kunsthistoriker unter dem Nationalsozialismus* (Münster: SZD, 1982); Lilian Karina, *Tanz unterm Hakenkreuz: eine Dokumentation* (Berlin: Henschel, 1996).

73 Arnd Krüger, 'Zwischen Sex und Zuchtwahl: Nudismus und Naturismus in Deutschland und Amerika', in Norbert Finzsch and Hermann Wellenreuther, eds, *Liberalitas: Eine Festschrift für Erich Angermann* (Stuttgart: Steiner, 1992), 343–65.

74 Bernd Wedemeyer-Kolwe, *'Der neue Mensch': Körperkultur im Kaiserreich und in der Weimarer Republik* (Würzburg: Königshausen & Neumann, 2004).

75 Arnd Krüger, 'Sport im faschistischen Italien (1922–1933)', in Giselher Spitzer and Dieter Schmidt, eds, *Sport zwischen Eigenständigkeit und Fremdbestimmung* (Bonn: P. Wegener, 1986), 213–26; Arnd Krüger, 'Strength through Joy: The Culture of Consent under Fascism, Nazism and Francoism', in James Riordan and Arnd Krüger, eds, *The International Politics of Sport in the 20th Century* (London: Spon, 1999), 67–89; Harald Oelrich, *'Sportgeltung – Weltgeltung': Sport im Spannungsfeld der deutsch-italienischen Außenpolitik von 1918 bis 1945* (Münster: Lit, 2003).

76 Hajo Bernett, *Der jüdische Sport im nationalsozialistischen Deutschland 1933–1938* (Schorndorf: Hofmann, 1978); Arnd Krüger, '"Wenn die Olympiade vorbei, schlagen wir die Juden zu Brei": Das Verhältnis der Juden zu den Olympischen Spielen von 1936', *Menora* 5 (1994), 331–48.

77 John Bunzl, *Hoppauf Hakoah: jüdischer Sport in Österreich; von den Anfängen bis in die Gegenwart* (Vienna: Junius, 1987); Felix Simmenauer and Kurt Schilde, *Die Goldmedaille: Erinnerungen an die Bar Kochba-Makkabi Turn-und Sportbewegung 1898–1938* (Berlin: Hentrich, 1989).

78 Walter Hochreiter, *Sport unter dem Davidstern: die Geschichte des jüdischen Sports in der Schweiz* (Basel: Reinhardt, 1998).

79 Dietrich Schulze-Marmeling, ed., *Davidstern und Lederball: Die Geschichte der Juden im deutschen und internationalen Fußball* (Göttingen: Werkstatt, 2003).

80 Gereon Tönnihsen, *Julius Hirsch: ein deutscher Fußballnationalspieler jüdischer Herkunft aus Karlsruhe* (Karlsruhe: INFO, 2008).

81 Paul Yogi Mayer, *Jüdische Olympiasieger: Sport – ein Sprungbrett für Minoritäten* (Kassel: Agon, 2000); Ignaz Hermann Körner and Marcus G. Patka, eds, *Lexikon jüdischer Sportler in Wien: 1900–1938* (Vienna: Mandelbaum, 2008). Lorenz Pfeiffer and Moshe Zimmermann (Hebrew University) are currently studying all of the Jewish sports clubs in pre-war Lower Saxony in a major research project.

82 Arnd Krüger and Astrid Sanders, 'Jewish Sports in the Netherlands and the Problems of Selective Memory', *Journal of Sport History* 26 (1999), 271–86.

83 Paul Connerton, 'Seven Types of Forgetting', *Memory Studies* 1 (2008), 59–71.

84 Wolfram Pyta, 'German Football: A cultural history', in Alan Tomlinson and Christopher Young, eds, *German Football* (London: Routledge, 2006), 1–22; Franz Josef Brüggemeier, *Zurück auf dem Platz: Deutschland und die Fußballweltmeisterschaft 1954* (München: DVA 2004).

85 Wolfram Pyta, ed., *Der lange Weg zur Bundesliga: zum Siegeszug des Fußballs in Deutschland* (Münster: Lit, 2004).

86 Nils Havemann, *Fußball unterm Hakenkreuz: der DFB zwischen Sport, Politik und Kommerz* (Frankfurt am Main: Campus, 2005).

87 Gertrud Pfister and Annette Hofmann are part of a very active international working group on women's sport, for one of the most recent publications see Susan J. Bandy, Annette Hoffman and Arnd Krüger, eds, *Gender, Body and Sport in Historical and Transnational Perspectives* (Hamburg: Kovač, 2007).

88 Most of the German-language literature on this topic is by Gertrud Pfister, for her work see Annette R. Hofmann and Else Trangbaek, eds, *International Perspectives on Sporting Women in Past and Present: A Festschrift for Gertrud Pfister* (Copenhagen: Copenhagen University, 2005).

89 Antje Fenner, *Das erste deutsche Fräuleinwunder: Die Entwicklung der Frauenathletik in Deutschland von ihren Anfängen bis 1945* (Königstein: Helmer, 2001).

90 Michaela Czech, *Frauen und Sport im nationalsozialistischen Deutschland* (Berlin: Tischler, 1994).

91 Hans Joachim Teichler, ed., *Sport in der DDR: Eigensinn, Konflikte, Trends* (Köln: Sport und Buch Strauss, 2003); Giselher Spitzer, ed., *Schlüsseldokumente zum DDR-Sport: ein sporthistorischer Überblick*

in Originalquellen (Aachen: Meyer & Meyer, 1998); Giselher Spitzer, ed., *Sicherungsvorgang Sport: das Ministerium für Staatssicherheit und der DDR-Spitzensport* (Schorndorf: Hofmann, 2005).

92 Wolfgang Buss, ed., *Der Sport in der SBZ und frühen DDR: Genese – Strukturen – Bedingungen* (Schorndorf: Hofmann, 2001); Wolfgang Buss and Christian Becker, eds, *Aktionsfelder des DDR-Sports in der Frühzeit 1945–1965* (Köln: Sport und Buch Strauß, 2001).

93 Giselher Spitzer, *Wunden und Verwundungen: Sportler als Opfer des DDR-Dopingsystems; eine Dokumentation* (Köln: Sportverl. Strauß, 2007).

94 Norbert Müller, ed., *Édition de textes choisis de Pierre de Coubertin* (Zürich: Weidmann, 1986).

95 Arnd Krüger and William Murray, eds, *The Nazi Olympics: Sport, Politics and Appeasement in the 1930s* (Champaign, IL: University of Illinois Press, 2003).

96 Karl Lennartz, ed., *II. Olympische Spiele 1900 in Paris: Darstellung und Quellen* (Kassel: Agon, 1995).

97 Hans Joachim Teichler, 'Coubertin und das Dritte Reich', *Sportwissenschaft* 12 (1982), 18–55.

98 Stephan Wassong, *Pierre de Coubertins US-amerikanische Studien und ihre Bedeutung für die Analyse seiner frühen Erziehungskampagne* (Würzburg: Ergon, 2002).

99 Angelika Uhlmann, *'Der Sport ist der praktische Arzt am Krankenlager des deutschen Volkes': Wolfgang Kohlrausch (1888–1980) und die Geschichte der deutschen Sportmedizin* (Frankfurt am Main: Mabuse-Verl., 2005).

100 Matthias Marschik, ed., *Das Stadion: Geschichte, Architektur, Politik, Ökonomie* (Vienna: Turia & Kant, 2005).

101 Arnd Krüger, '"What's the Difference between Propaganda for Tourism and for a Political Regime?" Was the 1936 Olympics the first Postmodern Spectacle?', in John Bale and Mette Krogh Christensen, eds, *Post-Olympism? Questioning Sport in the Twenty-first Century* (Oxford: Berg, 2004), 33–50.

27 Great Britain

Martin Johnes

In 1940 the journalist Bernard Darwin, writing a pamphlet for a series on British life and thought, claimed:

> Sport, to use the term in its widest sense, is an older thing here than elsewhere with a more settled custom and more generally accepted place in the national life … In fact sport is one of the most obvious features in the general background of life, and of all interests it is perhaps the one which is common to the greatest number of people of all classes.[1]

Aficionados of the cinema might dispute whether sport was really Britain's most popular pastime, but the importance of sport in British culture and the importance of Britain in global sporting culture has meant that the United Kingdom is home to one of the older and more vibrant historiographies of sport.

If that field of writing has a founding father in the UK, Peter McIntosh probably comes closest to fitting the bill. Rather than just provide a traditional descriptive narrative of the development of sport, he employed ideas like 'social control' and high-lighted the influence of the public-school ideology of muscular Christianity.[2] Since his work lacked footnotes it did not make the impact on history that it did on physical education, but it did influence J. A. Mangan, whose study of athleticism in Victorian and Edwardian public schools argued that sport was central to middle-class constructions of manliness, and McIntosh's themes later became cornerstones of considerations of sport's history.[3] Perhaps the most significant early academic study of British sport, though, was one more interested in the workers than the elite. Tony Mason's *Association Football and English Society, 1863–1915* emerged out of the social history movement, which saw working-class experiences brought into the mainstream of historical writing. It was not the first history of football, even by an academic, but it did, in its depth, breadth of research and subtle treatment of class, set new standards. Mason crossed the contemporary arguments that leisure was either about class control or class expression and showed that both were at play. Administrators tried to use football to encourage moral improvement, fair and reputable behaviour, but fans and players often imposed their own ideas of partisanship and aggression on the game.[4]

Building on these early pioneering works, the academic history of sport in the UK grew through the 1980s. The British Society of Sports History (BSSH) was founded in 1982 and a *British Journal of Sports History* was launched in 1984.[5] By 1989 there was enough work for Richard Holt to publish a masterly synthesis of British sports history that has yet to be superseded.[6] Seven years later he claimed that, 'sports history can lay claim to being a sub-discipline – if such a category or status is meaningful'.[7] Today sports history in the UK has perhaps developed too much into a self-contained sub-discipline. In the very first issue of the *British Journal of Sports History* Walvin argued that if the journal was to succeed it needed 'to make an impact beyond the pale of the specialism itself. And its greatest task will be to overcome that deep and abiding intellectual suspicion which is commonly manifested towards the very concept of sports history'. He also warned that specialism can create 'a form of intellectual "tunnel vision" which shuts out the broader perspective'.[8] The suspicion of studying sport is not dead, but it has faded, perhaps more because academia itself has moved on than because of the impact of anything sports historians themselves have written. However, Walvin's warning of tunnel vision has not always been heeded. Sports history's vibrancy has made it easier to only talk, in print and at conferences, to other sports historians and the subject has become distanced from mainstream history. The pages of its journals may be full, but few historians read them who are not already involved in working on sport.

This is a shame because the history of sport has much to contribute to wider under-standings of the past. Sport was part of the fabric of the lives of so many people and places. It was intertwined with the identities of place, class, ethnicity and gender. There were other pastimes that were more popular, but none that drew so many together in a single place all at once.[9] Moreover, through its place in the landscape and its depictions in the press, in the newsreels and on television and radio, it was inescapable. Its history should thus make a significant contribution to an understanding of everyday life: what people did for fun, how they behaved, what mattered to them, and how they thought of their lives and the world they lived in. It is when the historiography has addressed such issues that it has taken on its biggest significance. In recognition of this, in 2003 BSSH changed the title of its journal from *The Sports Historian* to *Sport in History*. What should matter in the historiography is not so much sport's own history but sport's place in wider history.

A number of key themes have emerged within writing about the history of sport in Britain. The first and most persuasive is class.[10] The influence of the social history movement, which tried to examine history 'from below', was key to establishing class as the dominant analytical paradigm in sports history. Historians' concern with class was more than intellectual fashion, however. Britain was a class-based society and class shaped people's experiences and perceptions of sport. This is best illustrated by Rugby league, which not only became known as a working-class game, but whose whole existence was bound up with ideas of the working class and the industrial north of England. The sport was created when northern clubs broke away from the Rugby Football Union in 1895 over arguments of whether working men should be compensated for the time they missed from their normal jobs when playing. This and its geographical concentration in the industrial north created a popular association between the sport and working-class identity, something which only strengthened as the 20th century continued and media coverage of the sport played upon the image. Furthermore, players' attitudes to their work and their bosses were shaped by the physicality and resistance to authority that characterized working-class industrial labour. Rugby league was, thus, as Collins put it, 'a proletariat at play' and its class-based identity was 'part of a generalised working-class outlook that saw the world as divided between "us and them"'.[11]

Rugby's great split is illustrative of how arguments over professionalism hung heavy over the development of sport in the late 19th and early 20th centuries. The concept of amateurism emerged in middle-class culture in response to people being paid to play sports such as athletics, boxing, horse-racing, cycling, football and rugby. It was about more than money: it was an ideology; a code of conduct; an outlook on sport and life. Combining 19th-century middle-class ideas and older upper-class sporting ideals, amateurism involved playing the game for its own sake rather than winning, a disdain for gambling and an adherence to fair play, disciplinary codes and winning with grace but losing without candour. Above all, amateurism was about social position. To be an amateur in late Victorian and Edwardian Britain was to not need to be paid to play. Thus enforcing amateur regulations was about displaying status, avoiding too much mixing with the masses and preventing the challenges to the older hierarchies that were beginning to emerge in the realms of work and politics. In cricket, for example, where amateurs and professionals often played in the same team, social distinction was preserved through the use of different changing rooms, different ways of displaying names on scorecards and initially requiring professionals to labour with bowling and even menial tasks such as cleaning the kit. Thus, quite deliberately, it created both a physical and moral space between the workers and middle classes.[12]

The whole concept of amateurism became a battleground over the meaning and ownership of sports, but it was not a black-and-white matter. Despite the snobbery that underpinned amateurism, there was a general reluctance in most sports to impose explicit class-based restrictions on participation, though rowing and athletics were 19th-century exceptions.[13] In most amateur sports, exclusion was enforced more subtly, through relying on economic realities to ensure working men could not afford time off work to play with their social betters. The class basis of amateurism was further complicated by the middle class itself being divided over the wrongs of professionalism. Arguments over professionalism in both rugby league and football revealed a schism between a southern, public school-educated middle class and a more commercially orientated northern middle class.[14] Even gentlemanly conduct, with all its connotations of fair play, taking part and chivalry, was more image than reality and Tony Collins has shown how the middle classes often played with a good deal of gamesmanship and even violence in their determination to win.[15] Nor was the amateur ideal adhered to strictly and historians of cricket in particular have clearly shown the financial demands of amateur players.[16]

Thus the rhetoric of amateurism was an expression of one particular set of middle-class values, even if they were not always adhered to or universal across that class. Similarly, sport also became a loose expression of working-class values, as people played and watched in ways shaped by their wider culture. The physicality and partisanship of working-class sport was the product of the harsh conditions of working-class communities, which were happy to take up sports encouraged by the middle classes but who wanted to play and watch in their own ways. Thus a belief in hardness, co-operation and effort, but also luck and a resigned fatalism ran through both sport and wider working-class culture. The communal festivity of sport is also evidence that working-class life was far more than the drudgery, exploitation and political struggle that has characterized much labour history.[17]

Historians have tended to be both more interested in and sympathetic to these working-class sporting values than they have to the middle class. This is partly the result of the influence of social and labour history on sports history, but it also perhaps rooted in the politics and backgrounds of many of the writers themselves. Lowerson's *Sport and the English Middle Classes* was a notable exception that showed the importance sport also had in middle-class social networks.[18] The upper classes continue to be the least studied, although their role as patrons and fanatics of horse-racing has been charted by Huggins, as has the late 18th- and early 19th-century fashion for archery amongst the aristocracy and landed gentry. Such work has shown that the importance of sport as an expression of cultural values ran far beyond the masses.[19]

Nonetheless, it is in considering sport's political relationship with ideas of working-class identity and culture that sports historians have made some of their most important contributions to wider understandings of society. The most Marxist view of sport's working-class history came from John Hargreaves, who suggested that sport divided, distracted and manipulated the masses and was part of a project to create a middle-class hegemony. While not all accepted such a reductionist view of the past as a battle between the classes, it did create an agenda to be supported or refuted.[20] In a less Marxist vein, Jack Williams argued that cricket 'strengthened cultural and social harmony in England', but while he is convincing on cricket reflecting wider harmony (and tensions) he does not expand on precisely how it might have strengthened and thus added to that harmony.[21] In contrast, Collins sees rugby league as providing 'a supplementary narrative' of class tensions 'rather than a diversion from, those offered by the labour and trade union movement'.[22] With perhaps less certainty, Dave Russell has argued of football that it 'is inconceivable that something which drew the time, energy and money of so many people did not have ideological repercussions for some of them'. He thus suggests that football had:

> ... some impact on attitudes and behaviour, even if only in the sense of legitimising and reinforcing existing values. Indeed, the football ground has been an important arena within which individuals can learn lessons about social and political roles and identities which are then carried 'back' into other aspects of daily life.

He does not elaborate on what those lessons were, but he does maintain that football, as one of those things that working men did, helped to generate 'a consciousness of class rather than class consciousness'.[23]

More mainstream historians have also considered the impact sport and mass leisure had on politicizing identities. Eric Hobsbawm goes further perhaps than any sports historian in arguing that commercial leisure forms created a mass culture, which in turn fed class consciousness, enabling the rise of the Labour Party.[24] In other words, leisure gave working men similar lives and thus helped them feel similar, thus underpinning the growth of a politicized class consciousness. In contrast, Gareth Stedman Jones has argued that working men were largely non-political and that commercial leisure was beyond their control. It did, though, create 'a culture of consolation' that compensated for the hardships workers endured and contributed to their lack of radicalism.[25] Ross McKibbin, meanwhile, has acknowledged the agency workers had over their free time, leisure and hobbies, but has argued that leisure did detract from political activism by absorbing working-class time and energy.[26]

Despite such arguments, sport's impact on the politics of class was never straightforward because class itself was never a straightforward framework. People saw their lives in complex and contradictory ways and postmodern historians argue that class was just one identity that people possessed amongst many.[27] Class structured people's daily lives and opportunities but they only thought of themselves as working class in certain contexts. For example, at work a miner might think of himself as working class and feel distinctly different to the mine owner and manager, but at a football match class could take a backseat and he might first of all think of himself as local man like the middle-class fans at the game. Thus, if we simply interpret the football match as political because it joined together the classes, then we are reading too much into it and distorting how people saw the game at the time. To the working-class supporters, an ordinary football match might have had nothing to do with class or the divisions that existed between people at work or in wider society. Class was not a lens through which people looked at every aspect of life and thus it can not be used as the yardstick to analyse every aspect of the past.[28]

Nonetheless, Russell and others are surely right that sport was so important in some people's lives that it must have had some political impact, whether contemporaries recognized it or not. Beyond localized arguments over wages and admission prices, sport was rarely a direct form of working-class resistance and revolt, but it might, perhaps, encourage resistance or political fatalism in other spheres of life. Defining the impact of this in any precise manner is impossible since it was a highly individualized process that was dependent on individuals' own experiences of the three spheres at the core of working-class life: work, home and leisure. Leisure was never the only lens through which the working class saw the world and thus any conciliatory or challenging role sport played in the wider political and social hegemony cannot be disentangled from other influences, making it complex and ambiguous.[29] Proving any direct correlation or relationship between the experience of everyday pleasures and contemporary political attitudes is thus simply impossible. The historian can only infer, interpret and guess, but it is in doing this that the history of sport can become an area that is of wide and genuine significance.[30]

The importance of class has also focused minds on the importance of the wider economic structure in shaping social and political experiences, and economics has emerged as a second integral theme within the history of sport. Some of this work has concentrated on the economics of sport itself. In a capitalist society, money inevitably mattered and spectator sport was clearly organized on a commercial basis, but a pioneering study by Vamplew demonstrated how sports organizations sought to utilize profits rather than maximize them.[31] This was clear in football where the Football Association limited the dividends payable to shareholders and clubs made few attempts to diversify their income. Similarly, the Football League operated as a cartel, limiting price competition and ensuring equality between teams.[32] Williams, meanwhile, argues that cricket was inherently uncommercial, with no county clubs and only one league club registered as a limited liability company between the wars. Little profit was made and the clubs were reliant on fundraising, subscriptions and gate receipts. He concludes that cricket represented a pastoral and traditional view of England that was at odds with a commercial world.[33] Investors in football, rugby and cricket thus made little money and were driven by other motives, and Vamplew has spoken of the 'psychic capital' drawn from the local prestige of sitting on the board.[34] In contrast, athletic grounds were built by Victorian and Edwardian entrepreneurs seeking to capitalize on the growing public taste for sporting spectacles. Some sports themselves were also industries of sorts that were clearly profit driven. Greyhound racing was imported from the USA in the 1920s and became a successful commercial venture, even propping up the finances of Wembley stadium.[35] Professional boxing was another sport where money clearly mattered and was the key motive of both fighters and promoters.

Highlighting the lack of profits in the major sports also underplays the extent to which commercial concerns were inescapable because playing, providing and watching sport was expensive. Even playing a team game in a local league required money for membership, equipment and somewhere to play. Indeed, some sports associated with the working class were actually very expensive to take part in, meaning they relied on people being willing to make sacrifices.[36] Watching professional soccer before World War II was beyond the regular means of the urban poor and those for whom poverty was never far away in a climate of irregular income. Crowds were thus dominated by the skilled workers who enjoyed some disposable income.[37] Indeed, professional spectator sports could not have developed at all in the late 19th century had it not been for the contemporary rise in real wages. Similarly, a collapse in the local economy could have a significant impact on the fortunes of local professional clubs. A number of northern and Welsh teams lost their Football League status in the inter-war depression and Welsh rugby haemorrhaged talent to the more secure employment environments of rugby league.[38] Andrew Davies' study of leisure in Salford and Manchester has argued that watching professional sport did not feature in the lives of the urban poor, but this underestimates the interest that people took from afar, via the media, how their talk could be sport-dominated and how they could make sacrifices to watch the occasional game.[39] What such arguments have shown is that the history of depressed and poor communities cannot simply be examined through a lens of gloom and deprivation. Indeed, sport could be very resistant to local economic problems. Rugby league was able to survive the economic problems of Lancashire and Yorkshire and although average gates in the Football League fell by about a quarter during the depressed years of 1927–33, success could keep the paying public coming, partly by attracting hitherto passive or latent fans.[40] The impact of economic conditions on sport was perhaps clearest in the late 1940s and early 1950s. Full employment and a desire to forget the horrors of war created a high demand for entertainment, but material shortages and the government's need to export manufactured goods meant there was little on which people could actually spend their money. Spectator sport, though, was both cheap and easily accessible, and attendances thus reached an all-time high in this period.[41]

Money also mattered because gambling was integral to many sports and the poor, who had the most to gain from a small win, were often amongst the most regular placers of bets.[42] Without gambling, horse-racing would not have been viable or as remotely exciting.[43] Gambling was not so integral to most other sports, but there were few that were not bet on, whether through a friendly wager or a large organized venture like the football pools, which was bet on by over 16 times as many people as actually watched football.[44] The pools were an example of the profit-driven subsidiary industries that grew around sport, supplying the goods and services that it required to function. The sports equipment industry still awaits its own historian, but it was integral to sport and an important industry in its own right.

The third theme that has dominated much British sports history writing is the identities of place. Sport helped give meaning to people's lives, but it also helped give meaning to the overlapping communities that they lived in. This is clear in the work of Metcalfe on the mining villages of East Northumberland. He argues that:

> … sport was not just a momentary diversion from the harshness of life; it also served as a visible symbol of the community both within the mining villages and also in terms of their position relative to the outside world. Sport was one of the few activities that brought all segments of the community together; albeit in situations that served to reinforce the relationships which flowed from the mine.[45]

The mining villages were built and created by mining companies, but sport allowed miners to stamp something of their own identity on the places they lived. Football developed inter-village rivalries thus strengthening local identity, but through support for Newcastle United it also helped unite the different villages and create a sense of regional identity amongst the miners.[46] It was professional clubs like Newcastle that were the most powerful articulators of civic identity. Richard Holt has argued that by 'supporting a club and assembling with thousands of others like himself a man could assert a kind of membership of the city, the heart of which was physically and emotionally his for the afternoon'.[47] This was perhaps all the more important given that 19th-century urbanization and industrialization had brought greater homogeneity to urban life. Communications, newspapers, mass schooling and the cinema all encouraged standardization in urban life but supporting town teams reinvigorated the distinctiveness of town identities. This was especially true in towns with few other public symbols.[48]

At no time was the role of sport in civic identity clearer than at times of success, when a city's club could unite not just its own inhabitants but the wider region, too, demonstrating how different identities were multi-layered and contextual. When professional clubs, notably in football and rugby league, won something there were civic celebrations for the team when they returned home. This was a ritualized form of street theatre. These were 'official', with links to the local authority, and the press coverage and scale of the celebrations made them difficult to avoid, even for those who did not like sport. Yet when doing badly a team's role as symbol of civic identity could decline or come to mean something different, such as an emblem of a wider decline in the town. Sport was promoted because of its ability to paper over tensions; it created what Hill has called an 'idealised community', one that obscured the normal divides of class, gender, ethnicity and religion.[49] The ability of success to unite a region subsided in the 1960s, however. Local rivalries became more felt, ritualized and profound as smaller clubs tried to impose their own identity in response to television and better travel attracting local supporters away to more glamorous teams.[50]

Localized studies of sport have made up an important part of British sports historiography. Jack Williams has suggested that:

> An added justification for undertaking localised studies of recreational sport is that they seem likely to be a way of evaluating in microcosm the impact of sport upon class and gender divisions, sociability and the creation of community. Sport provides a means of penetrating the seemingly closed world of male working-class culture.[51]

They also allow a consideration of cultural variation within nations. People's individual tastes for what they did in their spare time varied and there were regional phenomena such as baseball in south-east Wales or rounders in Lancashire. The patterns that did develop in the distribution of specific sports were often seemingly random, but were actually shaped by local spatial, economic and social conditions and the influence of specific individuals.[52] However, the geographic balance of local casestudies has not been even and little has been said about London, much of Scotland or the south of England.[53] There have been profitable examinations of how sport contributed to a distinct sense of northern identity, but other regional identities, such as those in the Midlands, East Anglia and north Wales, could also be profitably mined if we are to understand to what extent there were national cultures in either Britain or its constituent nations.[54] Despite sport's role in articulating regional identities and the variations in personal sporting tastes and which sports were popular where, the essential structures and meanings of sport appear much the same across Britain. Mason has thus concluded that England was an example of 'variations on a single culture', while McKibbin maintains there was 'no common culture, rather a set of overlapping cultures'.[55]

Sport rarely features in most surveys of national identity in the UK. For example, Kumar's otherwise masterful study of English identity relegates football to a footnote, while Day's seminal study of Wales and McCrone's of Scotland almost ignore sport completely.[56] Yet, from the names of its teams to the songs of its supporters, sport is loaded with national symbolism and resonance, making it one of the most common forms of what Billig has called 'banal nationalism'.[57] Although often overlooked by the mainstream literature on nationalism, there is a significant set of historical work exploring sport's links with national identity within the British Isles. It argues that sport actively contributed to how people thought about their and others' nationhood, although perhaps in an effort to emphasize its own significance this work can be guilty of reading the expressions of national identity too literally. In historical terms there is more work on sport and national identity in Scotland and Wales than there is for England. Sport was a central tenet in inventing, maintaining and projecting the idea of a single Welsh national identity in and outside her blurred borders. Rugby and football helped gloss over the different meanings that the people of Wales attached to their nationality, enabling them to assert their Welshness in the face of internal division and the political, social and cultural shadow of England.[58] Much the same was true of Scotland where football, in particular, was a vehicle for a popular patriotism, although one that perhaps over-emphasized working-class industrial culture within Scottish identity. Beneath this veneer of unity were religious divides that football helped sustain and fears that sport was acting as substitute for political nationalism.[59]

While cricket's role as a symbol of a pastoral and cohesive England has been explored, little has been said about other sporting discourses of Englishness. The lack of a study of the impact of the English national football team is a particularly surprising gap in the literature, although Porter and others have offered important beginnings.[60] Similarly, Britishness remains to be adequately probed in a sporting context, either in terms of the construction of a shared identity based on how sport should be played, or in terms of what sport says about Britain's alleged post-1945 decline. Rugby union's British and Irish Lions and the Olympics, two of the few major sporting arenas where the UK played as a single team, are two potential casestudies that could build on claims from studies of Welsh sport that Britishness mattered.[61]

A final space where sport clearly mattered was the British Empire. Sport played a significant role in the lives of British people serving in the Empire and at times it was even encouraged amongst colonized peoples as a means of transposing British values. Influenced, if rather loosely, by postcolonialism, the reactions of the 'colonies' to the 'motherland' have been explored and sport appears to have occasionally subverted ideas of Empire by allowing nations to show their status and equality with Britain. However, there remains much to be said from the British perspective about how important sport was in the maintenance of Empire and, especially, about what sport suggests in terms of whether most people actually thought the Empire was important at all.[62]

If class, economics and the identities of place are three themes that have run through much writing about the history of sports in Britain, there are others of which more should have been made. Indeed, the whole range of sports analysed is rather narrow and in some ways is more reflective of current interests than past concerns.[63] Football, rugby and cricket dominate the literature, although Huggins has advanced the case of horse-racing to be the national sport, showing its popularity amongst all the classes.[64] Football hooliganism was something of an historical obsession in the 1980s, further showing how the present has shaped the questions asked about the past.[65] Boxing, a sport the popularity of which is in long-term decline, is woefully understudied given its past popularity, and athletics, fishing and motor racing are other sports that deserve far more attention.[66]

The biography of either the famous or the ordinary has not had the hold on academic writing about the history of sport that it has on more popular sports writing.[67] The beginnings of academic work in this area has not employed the terminology of the linguistic turn but, in the repeated emphasis on what heroes meant rather than just who they were, there is evidence of how wider historiographical trends have impacted on academic sports history.[68] To develop an understanding of how and why heroes were made, Holt has suggested that 'Historians need to take aesthetics and style seriously and try to make connections between the image of a performer and the wider audience'.[69] That call has not yet been met and academic interest in British sports history has remained firmly focused on placing sport within its wider contexts rather than studying what happens on the actual field of play.

The laissez-faire ideology that pervaded political attitudes to sport, in theory at least, has meant that the long-term relationship between the state and British sport also awaits its historian. Beck has shown that the increasing inter-war politicization of sport on the continent, not least in the Fascist states, meant that the British Government felt it could not always follow its instinct and leave sport to its own devices. The interventions were periodic rather than systematic, but they need further consideration, not least in terms of the use of sport to influence physical health within Britain. As the work of Beck and others show, there is a wealth of information in the National Archives to which historians of sport should pay closer attention.[70]

Historians should also not neglect the cultural sphere, where politics are a more complex, less institutional or categorized phenomenon.[71] In many historical studies, the consideration of this has dwelled upon gender and race but neither category are as prominent in British sports historiography as they are in wider writings about the British past.[72] Women remain on the fringes of the subject, both in terms of who is writing and about whom it is being written. There are, though, some significant studies that show that sport did play a part in the life of some women. For middle-class women in the 19th and early 20th centuries, pursuits like croquet, tennis or archery were rare opportunities to take part in physical exercise without compromising their feminine poise and respectability. Such arenas were also places for men and women to meet, court and flirt with their social equals, again demonstrating the importance of sociability in understanding sport's appeal.[73] However, many sporting opportunities remained closed to working-class women, as much through lack of time and money as through any overt prejudice.[74] Working-class females were, after all, used to physical labour such as factory or housework. Indeed, during World War 1 they were positively encouraged to take up factory work and football was promoted as a means of pushing young women away from the pub and other potentially immoral activities.[75] The boom this created in women's football was shortlived and is probably overly emphasized by historians, but women's wider involvement in male sports was more long lasting. Wives, mothers and friends played an important role in many male recreational sports, helping organize the clubs, making the tea, doing the washing, running fundraising events and offering their support. Their presence helped ensure that clubs were something of a community institution. Many of these female functions were traditional ones and thus sport was reinforcing wider social norms, not challenging them. Young women also watched professional football in the inter-war years. Occasionally they were the subject of some resentment amongst male fans, but more often they were treated with respect, although there was some humour at their enthusiasm and even bad behaviour.[76] They were in the minority, though, and for most working-class women, the comfort and escapism of the cinema was a far more attractive pastime than sport.

Although men dominate the historiography of sport, there is very little attention paid in sports history to masculinity and its meanings beyond Mangan's explorations of how sport was promoted for its manly virtues and was seen as a way of turning boys into the right sort of men. To what extent such ideas were adopted by the working classes is less clear, but they were probably not very influential amongst the masses despite being preached in church, school and groups like the Boy Scouts.[77] Tosh has argued that masculinity was forged by a mixture of home, work and male associational culture, and sport interacted with all three spheres, although there remains much to be done in investigating precisely how.[78] Sport was shaped by the shared physical and social values of the workplace, but it also compensated for them by offering some men the status and self-respect they were denied in their subservient work. It took men out of the domestic sphere in their freetime (with or without family blessing), but sport could also be constrained by domestic duties and expectations. The sociability of sport's associational culture was certainly a key part of many men's masculinity. Team sports, on and off the pitch, were obvious manifestations of the value working-class culture placed upon male bonding. Clubs and governing bodies were social organizations with social activities beyond playing. Watching sport, too, was an intensely social and shared activity, while the links between sport and pubs furthered the social base of sport.[79] Men's reaffirmation of their manhood by associating with one-another probably had an added importance because of the uncertainty of home and work as bases of masculine identification.[80] Reconciling the different demands and expectations of work, home and sociability was not always easy. How men did this defined what kind of man they were and for many sport was part of that complicated equation.[81]

Oral history offers much potential for investigating how the skills and physical rewards of playing sport interacted with what they derived from their working and family lives. However, it remains surprisingly underused as a source despite its potential to access the emotional economy of sport and its dynamics in working-class communities.[82] Historians of sport have been far more comfortable using newspapers as their main primary source. This is understandable given that local and national newspapers provide a rich vein of information and that most people's experience of sport was, at least partially, mediated. The press thus contributed to, rather than just reported, local perceptions and understandings of sporting culture.[83] The press has typically been supplemented by sources created by sporting organizations, such as financial records and minutes, but historians are becoming more adventurous and beginning to turn their attention to literary and visual sources and, in doing so, starting to tackle the vexed question of audience reception.[84]

Problems of sources mean that few historians have tackled pre-industrial sports, although Griffin's recent study of the 18th century has shown that there was a vibrant sporting culture before the industrial revolution, while Harvey has pointed to its commercial basis.[85] Understanding pre-industrial sport is fraught with difficulties, given that many historians argue that before industrialization work and leisure were not separate spheres.[86] Others question the extent to which the industrial revolution changed the nature of leisure.[87] As Borsay argues, there is a danger of applying modern concepts to pre-modern societies, and there were certainly some fundamental continuities, such as the symbolism of leisure and its involvement of play and the carnival, between industrial and pre-industrial communities.[88]

Turning to other periods, the late 19th century and Edwardian era have received far more attention than the inter-war and post-1945 years. This is because historians have viewed this as the period of a sporting revolution, when there was 'a notable transformation in the scale and nature of Britain's sporting culture'.[89] Much research has concentrated on mapping that transformation and analysing its causes and effects. The unevenness of coverage is beginning to change as people look for new topics, but we still know too little about sport's more recent past.[90] Immigration, the growth of a mass media, the decline of traditional working-class culture and ideas of national decline are the themes that have dominated mainstream post-war British history and they all have echoes in and impacts on sport. Important overviews by Polley, Holt and Mason have offered a starting place, but there remains huge scope for the detailed empirical accounts that characterize writing about the history of sport for earlier periods.[91]

Thus, from one perspective there are many gaps to be plugged in the coverage of the history of sport. Yet, from another the field has grown so much in the UK and beyond that it is in danger of becoming too discreet and losing perspective on its relationship with wider historical inquiry. Tony Collins has argued, 'for the historian, sport has wider significance (it seems to me at least) only when it acquires a wider importance than the mere playing of a game'.[92] This is, perhaps, going too far: the simple importance of sport in many people's lives surely gives its own internal dynamics some historical importance. However, too much research does concentrate on the history of sport at the expense of what the history of sport says about wider trends, themes and processes. It is consequently only of interest to other sports historians. It is not enough to look at how sport has been shaped by wider social, cultural and economic trends; historians need to pay more attention to how sport contributed to those wider trends. The work that has been done here displays the influence of the cultural turn and Clifford Geertz's idea of 'deep play', where cultural practices and texts structure and shape meanings rather than just mirror outside influences.[93] Along this vein Jeff Hill has argued that the texts and practices of sport and leisure:

> ... exist not simply as something shaped by other forces, but as cultural agencies with a power to work on their participants and consumers ideologically. In other words, they are processes from which we derive *meaning*. In their manifold activities are inscribed and structured habits of thought and behaviour which contribute to our ways of seeing ourselves and others, to a making sense of our social relationships, and to the piecing together of some notion of what we call 'society'.[94]

Historians have clearly shown that sport was an active rather than passive agent in social and cultural life, not least in the study of identities: of who people thought they were, to whom or what they belonged, and what all that meant. However, a note of caution is needed here, too. Arguing that sport contributed to rather than just reflected the mental horizons of the past might become a self-serving way of justifying the historical study of sport and Collins has warned that historians sometimes 'impute too much meaning to a sporting activity or event'.[95]

The development of sports history has also led to an over-emphasis on sport as a monolithic cultural experience or entity. There are surely only limited structures and experiences that unite, say, snooker and soccer. Collins again perceptively observes that different sports often have little in common and thus it makes 'more sense to study them in their own particular social contexts, as activities and manifestations of meaning for particular social groups, rather than as part of the continuum of sport'.[96] Furthermore, there is surely no emotion, motive or pleasure involved in sport that could not also be found in other pastimes. Sports offered physical recreation, but so too did taking a stroll, dancing, gardening and even sex. Sports were competitive, but so too was dancing, gardening, music and even baking. Sports could be social or solitary, but so too was every form of leisure. Nor does its organization and structure suggest that sport is unique. Sports were regulated, governed and organized, but then the whole British tradition of associational activity was based on clubs with regulations and rules.

In many ways it thus makes more sense to study the concept of leisure rather than sport.[97] Without comparing and contrasting sports with other leisure forms historians will struggle to fully understand the historical significance of sport. They will fail to see both the extent to which the people who played and watched sports also took part in other pastimes, and how sports were interrelated with other aspects of people's lives. Good sports history, like any kind of history, requires an understanding of structure and agency, of the experience of the individual and its relationship with wider structures. This interplay between personal choice and the restrictions imposed by the economic, political, social and cultural structure is what governed people's lives, whether they recognized it or not. The history of sports has helped show what that meant for individuals and groups in Britain, but it must not lose sight of the fact that life for those same individuals and groups was far more diverse than sport alone.

Notes

1   Bernard Darwin, *British Sport and Games* (Longmans Green: London, 1940), 11.
2   Peter McIntosh, *Physical Education in England since 1800* (London: G. Bell, 1952), and *Sport in Society* (London: C. A Watts, 1963).
3   Mike Huggins, 'Walking in the Footsteps of a Pioneer: Peter McIntosh – Trail-Blazer in the History of Sport', *International Journal of the History of Sport* 18, 2 (2001), 136–47. J. A. Mangan, *Athleticism in the Victorian and Edwardian Public School: The Emergence and Consolidation of an Educational Ideology* (Cambridge: Cambridge University Press, 1981).
4   Tony Mason, *Association Football and English Society, 1863–1915* (Brighton: Harvester, 1980). For an appreciation of the book see Richard Holt, '"No ideas but in things": Tony Mason's *Association Football and English Society*', *The Sports Historian* 22, 1 (2002), 1–15. For the first history of English football by an academic see James Walvin, *The People's Game* (London: Allen Lane, 1975).
5   The *British Journal of Sports History* was renamed the *International Journal of the History of Sport* in 1987 and an internal schism within the field led to the journal losing its links with BSSH.
6   Richard Holt, *Sport and the British: A Modern History* (Oxford: Oxford University Press, 1989). Other overviews include Derek Birley, *Sport and the Making of Modern Britain* (Manchester, 1993), *Land of Sport and Glory: Sport and British Society, 1887–1910* (Manchester: Manchester University Press, 1995), and *Playing the Game: Sport and British Society, 1910–45* (Manchester: Manchester University Press, 1996); Neil Wigglesworth, *The Evolution of English Sport* (London: Frank Cass, 1996); Tony Mason (ed.), *Sport in Britain: A Social History* (Cambridge: Cambridge University Press, 1989).
7   Richard Holt, 'Sport and history: the state of the subject in Britain', *Twentieth Century British History* 7, 2 (1996), 231–52, quote 233.
8   James Walvin, 'Sport, Social History and the Historian', *British Journal of Sports History* 1, 1 (1984), 5–13.
9   Jack Williams, '"One Could Literally Have Walked on the Heads of the People Congregated There": Sport, the Town and Identity', in Keith Laybourn, ed., *Social Conditions, Status and Community, 1860–c. 1920* (Stroud: Sutton, 1997), 123–38.

10 For an overview of the early writing on class and sport see Steven Reiss, 'From Pitch to Putt: Sport and Class in Anglo-American Sport', *Journal of Sport History* 21, 2 (1994).

11 Tony Collins, *Rugby League in Twentieth-Century Britain* (London: Routledge, 2006). Tony Collins, *Rugby's Great Split: Class, Culture and the Origins of Rugby League Football* (London: Frank Cass, 1998). Jack Williams, '"Up and Under": Eddie Waring, Television and the Image of Rugby League', *The Sports Historian* 22, 1 (2002).

12 For an overview of amateurism see Mike Huggins, *The Victorians and Sport* (London: Hambledon, 2004), chapter 3.

13 See Neil Wigglesworth, *The Social History of English Rowing* (London: Frank Cass, 1992).

14 Mason, *Association Football*; Collins, *Rugby's Great Split*.

15 Tony Collins, 'Violence, Gamesmanship and the Amateur Ideal in Victorian Middle-class Rugby', in Mike Huggins and J. A. Mangan, eds, *Disreputable Pleasures: Less Virtuous Victorians at Play* (London: Frank Cass, 2004), 172–84.

16 Derek Birley, *Willow Wand* (London: Sportspages, 1989); Keith Sandiford, *Cricket and the Victorians* (Aldershot: Scolar Press, 1994); Wray Vamplew, *Pay Up and Play the Game: Professional Sport in Britain, 1875–1914* (Cambridge: Cambridge University Press, 1988). W.G. Grace is the best-known example of shamateurism in cricket. For a biography of this sporting giant see Simon Rae, *W. G. Grace* (London: Faber & Faber, 1998). On the post-1945 decline of amateurism in a number of sports see Adrian Smith and Dilwyn Porter, eds, *Amateurs and Professionals in Post-War British Sport* (London: Frank Cass, 2000).

17 These themes run through the historiography of football, rugby league and cricket, but also see Richard Holt, ed., *Sport and the Working Class in Modern Britain* (Manchester: Manchester University Press, 1990), and Jeff Hill and Jack Williams, eds, *Sport and Identity in the North of England* (Keele: Keele University Press, 1996).

18 John Lowerson, *Sport and the English Middle Classes, 1870–1914* (Manchester: Manchester University Press, 1993). Also see Mike Huggins, 'Second-class Citizens? English Middle-class Culture and Sport, 1850–1910: A Reconsideration', *International Journal of the History of Sport* 17, 1 (2000), 1–35.

19 Mike Huggins, *Flat Racing and British Society, 1790–1914: A Social and Economic History* (London: Frank Cass, 2000). Martin Johnes, 'Archery, Romance and Elite Culture in England and Wales, c.1780–1840', *History* 89, 2 (2004), 193–208. Mike Huggins, ed., 'The British Upper Classes and Sport', special issue of *Sport in History* 28, 3 (2008).

20 John Hargreaves, *Sport, Power and Culture: A Social and Historical Analysis of Popular Sports in Britain* (Oxford: Polity Press, 1986). Another Marxist-influenced view is Stephen Jones, *Sport, Politics and the Working Class: Organised Labour and Sport in Interwar Britain* (Manchester: Manchester University Press, 1988).

21 Jack Williams, *Cricket and England: A Cultural and Social History of the Inter-War Years* (London: Frank Cass, 1999), 191.

22 Collins, *Rugby League*, 188.

23 Dave Russell, *Football and the English* (Preston: Carnegie Publishing, 1997), 114, 72, 237.

24 Eric Hobsbawm, *Worlds of Labour* (London: Weidenfeld & Nicolson, 1984).

25 Gareth Stedman Jones, *Languages of Class* (Cambridge University Press, Cambridge, 1983).

26 Ross McKibbin, *The Ideologies of Class: Social Relations in Britain 1880–1950* (Oxford University Press, Oxford, 1991).

27 For example, Patrick Joyce, *Visions of the People: Industrial England and the Question of Class, 1840–1914* (Cambridge: Cambridge University Press, 1991).

28 This argument is developed in Martin Johnes, *Soccer and Society: South Wales, 1900–39* (Cardiff: University of Wales Press, 2002).

29 See Martin Johnes, 'Pigeon racing and working-class culture in Britain, c.1850–1950', *Cultural and Social History* 4, 3 (2007), 361–83.

30 John H. Arnold calls the 'art of good guessing' the third virtue (after being critical and suspicious) of the modern historian. John H. Arnold, *History: A Very Short Introduction* (Oxford: Oxford University Press, 2000), 25.

31 Wray Vamplew, *Pay Up and Play the Game*.

32 Matthew Taylor, *The Leaguers: The Making of Professional Football in England, 1900–1939* (Liverpool: Liverpool University Press, 2005).

33 Jack Williams, *Cricket and England: A Cultural and Social History of the Inter-War Years* (London: Frank Cass, 1999).

34 Vamplew, *Pay Up and Play the Game.*

35 Mike Huggins, '"Everybody's Going to the Dogs?" The Middle Classes and Greyhound Racing in Britain Between the Wars', *Journal of Sport History* 34, 1 (2007), 96–120. Michael Cronin, 'Arthur Elvin and the Dogs of Wembley', *The Sports Historian* 22, 1 (2002), 100–14.

36 For example, see Johnes, *Soccer and Society*, chapter 3, and Johnes, 'Pigeon racing'.

37 For example see Mason, *Association Football*, and Nicholas Fishwick, *English Football and Society, 1910–1950* (Manchester: Manchester University Press, 1989).

38 Gareth Williams, 'The Road to Wigan Pier Revisited: The Migration of Welsh Rugby Talent since 1918', in John Bale and Joseph Maguire, eds, *The Global Sports Arena: Athletic Migration in an Interdependent World* (London: Frank Cass, 1994), 25–38. Johnes, *Soccer and Society*, chapter 2. Martin Johnes, 'Mushrooms, Scandal and Bankruptcy: The Short Life of Mid Rhondda Football Club', *The Local Historian* 32, 1 (February 2002), 41–53. Dave Russell, 'Football and Society in the North-West, 1919–39', *North West Labour History* 24 (1999–2000), 3–14. Gareth Williams, 'From Grand Slam to Great Slump: Economy, Society and Rugby Football During the Depression', *Welsh History Review* 9 (1983), 338–57.

39 Andrew Davies, *Leisure, Gender, and Poverty: Working-class Culture in Salford and Manchester, 1900–1939* (Buckingham: Open University Press, 1992).

40 Russell, 'Football and Society'. Collins, *Rugby League*, chapter 2.

41 Richard Holt and Tony Mason, *Sport in Britain, 1945–2000* (Oxford: Blackwells, 2000), chapter 1. Matthew Taylor, *The Association Game: A History of British Football* (Harlow: Peason, 2007), chapter 4.

42 R. McKibbin, 'Working-Class Gambling in Britain, 1880–1939', *Past and Present* 82 (1979); Mark Clapson, *A Bit of a Flutter: Popular Gambling and English Society, c. 1823–1961* (Manchester, 1992). Roger Munting, *An Economic and Social History of Gambling in Britain and the USA* (Manchester: Manchester University Press, 1996). Mike Huggins, 'Betting, Sport and the British 1918–39', *Journal of Social History* 30 (2007), 283–306.

43 Mike Huggins, *Flat Racing and British Society 1790–1914: A Social and Economic History* (London: Frank Cass, 2000); Mike Huggins, *Horse Racing and British Society 1919–1939* (Manchester: Manchester University Press, 2003); Wray Vamplew, *The Turf: A Social and Economic History of Horse Racing* (London: Allen Lane, 1976); Roger Munting, *Hedges and Hurdles: A Social and Economic History of National Hunt Racing* (London: J.A. Allen, 1987).

44 Walvin, *The People's Game*, 119.

45 Alan Metcalfe, 'Sport & Community: A Case Study of the Mining Villages of East Northumberland, 1800–1914', in J. Hill and J. Williams, eds, *Sport and Identity in the North of England* (Keele: Keele University Press, 1996), 14. Cf Alan Metcalfe, *Leisure and Recreation in a Victorian Mining Community: The Social Economy of Leisure in North-East England, 1820–1914* (London: Routledge, 2006).

46 On north-eastern identity in England see also Mike Huggins, 'Sport and the Social Construction of Identity in North-east England, 1800–1914', in Neville Kirk, ed., *Northern Identities: Historical Interpretations of the North and Northernness* (Aldershot: Ashgate, 2000).

47 Richard Holt, 'Football and the Urban Way of Life in Nineteenth-century Britain', in J. A. Mangan, ed., *Pleasure, Profit, Proselytism: British Culture and Sport at Home and Abroad, 1700–1914* (London: Frank Cass, 1988), 67–85, quote 81.

48 Williams, 'One Could Literally Have Walked', 126. N. A. Phelps, 'Professional Football and Local Identity in the "Golden Age": Portsmouth in the Mid-twentieth Century', *Urban History* 32, 3 (2005), 459–80.

49 Tony Collins, 'Wembley, The Rugby League Cup Final and Northern English Identity', *International Journal of Regional and Local Studies* 1, 1 (2005); Jeff Hill, 'Rites of Spring: Cup Finals and Community in the North of England', in Jeff Hill and Jack Williams, *Sport and Identity in the North of England*; Johnes, *Soccer and Society*; Williams, 'One Could Literally Have Walked'.

50 Gavin Mellor, 'The Social and Geographical Make-Up of Football Crowds in the North West of England, 1948–62, "Super-Clubs", Local Loyalty and Regional Identities', *The Sports Historian* 19, 2 (1999), 25–42. Gavin Mellor, 'The Genesis of Manchester United as a National and International "Super-Club", 1958–68', *Soccer and Society* 1, 2 (2000), 151–66.

51 Jack Williams, 'Recreational Cricket in the Bolton Area between the Wars', in Richard Holt, ed., *Sport and the Working Class in Modern Britain* (Manchester: Manchester University Press, 1990).

52 Martin Johnes, 'Poor Man's Cricket: Baseball, Class and Community in South Wales, c.1880–1950', *International Journal of the History of Sport* 17, 4 (2000), 153–66. Liz Oliver, '"No Hard-brimmed Hats or Hat-pins Please": Bolton Women Cotton-workers and the Game of Rounders, 1911–39', *Oral*

History 25, 1 (1997), 40–45. Sarah Cowell, 'Working Class Women and Rounders in Interwar Bolton', *North West Labour History* 24 (1999/2000), 15–29. Dave Russell, '"Sporadic and Curious": The Emergence of Rugby and Soccer Zones in Yorkshire and Lancashire, c.1860–1914', *International Journal of the History of Sport* 5, 2 (1988), 185–205. Neil Tranter, 'The Chronology of Organised Sport in Nineteenth Century Scotland: A Regional Study. I. Patterns', *International Journal of the History of Sport* 7, 2 (1990) 188–203, and 'The Chronology of Organised Sport in Nineteenth Century Scotland: A Regional Study. II. Causes', *International Journal of the History of Sport* 7, 3 (1990), 365–87.

53 For a study of a professional London football club and its community see Charles Korr, *West Ham United: The Making of a Football Club* (London: Duckworth, 1986). For examples of local Scottish studies see John Hutchinson, 'Sport, Education and Philanthropy in Nineteenth-century Edinburgh: The Emergence of Modern Forms of Football', *Sport in History* 28, 4 (2008), 547–65; W. H. Murray, *The Old Firm: Sectarianism, Sport and Society in Scotland* (Edinburgh: John Donald, 1984); and Neil Tranter, 'The Patronage of Organised Sport in Central Scotland, 1820–1900', *Journal of Sport History* 16, 3 (1989), 227–47.

54 Hill and Williams, *Sport and Identity in the North of England*. On southern English identity see Nicholas Phelps, 'The Southern Football Hero and the Shaping of Local and Regional Identity in the South of England', *Soccer and Society* 2, 3 (2001), 44–57. This is a study which underplays the extent to which class united different regional experiences. There is some work on Cornwall, an English county with a unique identity, see Andy Seward, 'Cornish Rugby and Cultural Identity: A Socio-historical Perspective', *Sports Historian* 18, 2 (1998), 78–94. For a beginning on north Wales see Martin Johnes and Ian Garland, '"The New Craze": Football and Society in North-east Wales, c.1870–90', *Welsh History Review* 22, 2 (2004), 278–304.

55 Tony Mason, 'Football, Sport of the North', in Jeff Hill and Jack Williams, eds, *Sport and Identity in the North of England* (Keele: Keele University Press, 1996), 41–52, 49. Ross McKibbin, *Classes and Cultures: England 1918–1951* (Oxford: Oxford University Press, 1998), 527.

56 Krishan Kumar, *The Making of English National Identity* (Cambridge University Press, 2003). Graham Day, *Making Sense of Wales: A Sociological Perspective* (Cardiff: University of Wales Press, 2002). David McCrone, *Understanding Scotland: The Sociology of a Stateless Nation* (London: Routledge, 1992).

57 Michael Billig, *Banal Nationalism* (London: Sage, 1995). For an introduction to work on sport and national identity see Alan Bairner, *Sport, Nationalism, and Globalization: European and North American Perspectives* (Albany: State University of New York Press, 2001).

58 Martin Johnes, *History of Sport in Wales* (Cardiff: University of Wales Press, 2005). Johnes, *Soccer and Society*. Johnes, 'A Prince, a King and a Referendum: Rugby, Politics and Nationhood in Wales, 1969–79', *Journal of British Studies* 47, 1 (2008), 129–48. Gareth Williams, *1905 and All That: Essays on Rugby Football, Sport and Welsh Society* (Llandysul: Gomer, 1991). David Smith and Gareth Williams, *Fields of Praise: The Official History of the Welsh Rugby Union 1881–1981* (Cardiff: University of Wales Press, 1980).

59 Grant Jarvie, ed., *Sport in the Making of Celtic Cultures* (Leicester, Leicester University Press, 1999). Grant Jarvie and John Burnett, eds, *Sport, Scotland and the Scots* (Phantassie: Tuckwell Press, 2000). Grant Jarvie and Irene A. Reid, 'Sport, Nationalism and Culture in Scotland', *The Sports Historian* 19, 1 (1997), 97–124. Grant Jarvie and Irene A. Reid, 'Scottish Sport, Nationalist Politics and Culture', *Culture, Sport and Society* 2, 2 (2002), 22–43. Grant Jarvie and Graham Walker, eds, *Scottish Sport and the Making of the Nation: Ninety Minute Patriots?* (Leicester: Leicester University Press, 1994). H.F. Moorhouse, 'Scotland against England: Football and Popular Culture', *International Journal of the History of Sport* 4, 2, (1987), 189–202. H.F. Moorhouse, 'Shooting stars: footballers and working-class culture in twentieth-century Scotland', in Richard Holt, ed., *Sport and the Working Class in Modern Britain* (Manchester: Manchester University Press, 1990). Grant Jarvie, *The Highland Games: The Making of the Myth* (Edinburgh: Edinburgh University Press, 1991).

60 Dilwyn Porter, '"Your Boys Took One Hell of a Beating!" English Football and British Declines, c.1950–80', in Adrian Smith and Dilwyn Porter, eds, *Sport and National Identity in the Post-War World* (London: Routledge, 2004), 31–51. Also see Martin Polley, 'Sport and National Identity in Contemporary England', in Adrian Smith and Dilwyn Porter, eds, *Sport and National Identity in the Post-War World* (London: Routledge, 2004), 10–30. There have been studies of specific matches and moments. Tony Mason, 'England 1966: Traditional and Modern?', in Alan Tomlinson and Christopher Young, eds, *National Identity and Global Sporting Events: Culture, Politics, and Spectacle in the Olympics and the Football World Cup* (New York: State University of New York Press, 2006),

83–98. Special issue on England vs. Hungary, 1953: *Sport in History* 23, 2 (2003/4). Peter Beck, *Scoring for Britain: International Football and International Politics, 1900–1939* (London: Frank Cass, 1999), which looks at some of the political ramifications of international contests.

61 On the Olympics and Britain see George R. Matthews, 'Controversial Olympic Games of 1908 As Viewed by the *New York Times* and the *Times* of London', *Journal of Sport History* 7, 2 (1980), 40–53. On Britishness in Wales see Johnes, *Soccer and Society*, and Johnes, *History of Sport in Wales*.

62 J.A. Mangan, ed., *The Cultural Bond: Sport, Empire and Society* (London: Frank Cass, 1992). Brian Stoddart and Keith A. P. Sandiford, eds, *The Imperial Game: Cricket, Culture and Society* (Manchester: Manchester University Press, 1998). J.A. Mangan, ed., *The Games Ethic and Imperialism: Aspects of the Diffusion of an Ideal* (Harmondsworth: Viking, 1986). J.A. Mangan, ed., *Pleasure, Profit, Proselytism: British Culture and Sport at Home and Abroad, 1700–1914* (London: Frank Cass, 1988). Harold Perkin, 'Teaching the nations how to play: sport and society in the British Empire and Commonwealth', *International Journal of the History of Sport* 6, 2 (1989), 145–55. Patrick McDevitt, *May the Best Man Win: Sport, Masculinity, and Nationalism in Great Britain and the Empire, 1880–1935* (Basingstoke: Palgrave Macmillan, 2004).

63 For an analysis of different sports featured in *The Sports Historian* journal see Martin Johnes, 'Putting the History into Sport: On Sports History and Sports Studies in the UK', *Journal of Sport History* 31, 2, (2004), 145–60.

64 Mike Huggins, *Flat Racing and British Society 1790–1914: A Social and Economic History* (London: Frank Cass, 2000); Mike Huggins, *Horse Racing and British Society 1919–1939* (Manchester: Manchester University Press, 2003).

65 For important examples of works on hooliganism see Eric Dunning, Patrick Murphy and John Williams, *The Roots of Football Hooliganism: An Historical and Sociological Study* (London: Routledge, 1988). R.W. Lewis, 'Football Hooliganism in England before 1914: A Critique of the Dunning Thesis', *International Journal of the History of Sport* 13, 3 (1996), 310–39. Martin Johnes, 'Hooligans and Barrackers: Crowd Disorder and Soccer in South Wales, 1906–39', *Soccer and Society* 1, 2 (2000), 19–35.

66 For a start on boxing see John Welshman, 'Boxing and the Historians', *International Journal of the History of Sport* 14, 1 (1997), 195–203; and Kasia Boddy, *Boxing: A Cultural History* (London: Reaktion, 2008).

67 An example of the best non-academic sports history biographies is John Harding, *Football Wizard: The Billy Meredith Story* (London: Robson, 1998).

68 Richard Holt, J.A. Mangan and Pierre Lanfranchi, eds, *European Heroes: Myth Sport and Identity* (London: Frank Cass, 1996).

69 Richard Holt, 'Sport and History', 244.

70 Beck, *Scoring for Britain*. Also see Richard Holt, 'Great Britain: The Amateur Tradition', in Arnd Krüger and William J. Murray, eds, *The Nazi Olympics: Sport, Politics and Appeasement in the 1930s* (Urbana and Chicago: University of Illinois Press, 2003), 70–86; and Martin Polley, '"No Business of Ours"?: The Foreign Office and the Olympic Games, 1896–1914', *International Journal of the History of Sport* 13, 2 (1996), 96–113.

71 Jeff Hill, 'Introduction: Sport and Politics', *Journal of Contemporary History* 38, 3 (2003), 355–61.

72 On race see Jack Williams, *Cricket and Race* (Oxford: Berg, 2001); and Phil Vasili, 'Walter Daniel Tull, 1888–1918: Soldier, Footballer, Black', *Race & Class* 38:2 (1996), 51–69.

73 Kathleen E. McCrone, *Sport and the Physical Emancipation of English Women* (London: Croom Helm, 1988). Jennifer Hargreaves, *Sporting Females: Critical Issues in the History and Sociology of Women's Sports* (London: Routledge, 1993). J.A. Mangan and Roberta J. Park, eds, *From Fair Sex to Feminism: Sport and the Socialization of Women in the Industrial and Post-industrial Eras* (London: Frank Cass, 1987); Jon Sterngass, 'Cheating, Gender Roles, and the Nineteenth-century Croquet Craze', *Journal of Sport History* 25, 3 (1998), 398–418. Lowerson, *Sport and the English Middle Classes*. Johnes, 'Archery'.

74 Catriona M. Parratt, *More than Mere Amusement: Working-class Women's Leisure in England, 1750–1914* (Boston: Northeastern University Press, 2002). Claire Langhamer, *Women's Leisure in England 1920–1960* (Manchester University Press: Manchester University Press, 2000).

75 For a beginning on the history of women's football see Jean Williams, *A Game for Rough Girls?: A History of Women's Football in Britain* (London: Routledge, 2002).

76 Fishwick, *English Football*. Johnes, *Soccer and Society*.

77 Mangan, *Athleticism*. For an argument that such ideas influenced teachers see J.A. Mangan, 'Missing Men: Schoolmasters and the Early Years of Association Football', *Soccer and Society* 9, 2 (2008), 170–88.

78 John Tosh, 'What Should Historians Do with Masculinity? Reflections on Nineteenth-century Britain', *History Workshop Journal* 38, 1 (1994), 179–202.

79 Tony Collins and Wray Vamplew, *Mud, Sweat and Beers: A Cultural History of Sport and Alcohol* (Oxford: Berg, 2002). Holt, *Sport and the British*, is one of the many accounts that stresses the sociability of the sport. For a useful casestudy of masculinity in sport see Tony Collins, *A Social History of English Rugby Union* (London: Routledge, 2009), chapter 4.

80 Tosh, 'What Should Historians Do with Masculinity?'.

81 Johnes, 'Pigeon racing'.

82 For a vivid collection of oral sources see Rogan Taylor and Andrew Ward, *Kicking and Screaming: An Oral History of Football and England* (London: Robson, 1995).

83 On the press as a source see Jeff Hill, 'Anecdotal Evidence: Sport, the Newspaper Press and History', in Murray Phillips, ed., *Deconstructing Sport History: A Postmodern Analysis* (Albany: SUNY Press, 2006), 117–29.

84 Mike Huggins, 'Cartoons and Comic Periodicals 1841–1901: A Satirical Sociology of Victorian Sporting Life', in Mike Huggins and J.A. Mangan, *Disreputable Pleasures: Less Virtuous Victorians at Play* (London: Routledge, 2004), 124–52. Jeff Hill, *Sport and the Literary Imagination: Essays in History, Literature and Sport* (Bern: Peter Lange, 2006). Martin Johnes, 'Texts, Audiences and Postmodernism: The Novel as Source in Sport History', *Journal of Sport History* 34, 1 (2007).

85 Emma Griffin, *England's Revelry: A History of Popular Sports and Pastimes 1660–1830* (Oxford: Oxford University Press, 2005). Adrian Harvey, *The Beginnings of a Commercial Sporting Culture in Britain, 1793–1850* (Aldershot: Ashgate, 2004). Also see Dennis Brailsford, *A Taste for Diversions: Sport in Georgian England* (Cambridge: Lutterworth, 1999).

86 Peter Bailey, *Leisure and Class in Victorian England: Rational Recreation and the Contest for Control, 1830–1885* (London: Routledge, 2004), 4.

87 For a review of the literature see Emma Griffin, 'Popular Culture in Industrializing England', *The Historical Journal* 54, 3 (2002), 619–35.

88 Peter Borsay, *History of Leisure: The British Experience Since 1500* (Basingstoke: Palgrave Macmillan, 2006), 8–12.

89 Neil Tranter, *Sport, Economy and Society in Britain, 1750–1914* (Cambridge: Cambridge University Press, 1998), 13.

90 For an overview of the inter-war years see Mike Huggins and Jack Williams, *Sport and the English, 1918–1939* (London: Routledge, 2006).

91 Martin Polley, *Moving the Goalposts: A History of Sport and Society since 1945* (London: Routledge, 1998). Richard Holt and Tony Mason, *Sport in Britain, 1945–2000* (Oxford: Blackwells, 2000).

92 Tony Collins, 'Work, Rest and Play: Recent Trends in the History of Sport and Leisure', *Journal of Contemporary History* 42, 2 (2007), 397–410.

93 Clifford Geertz, 'Deep Play: Notes on the Balinese Cockfight' *Daedalus* 101 (1972).

94 Jeff Hill, *Sport, Leisure and Culture in Twentieth-Century Britain* (Basingstoke: Palgrave, 2002), 2.

95 Tony Collins, 'Work, Rest and Play', 400–01.

96 Ibid., 399.

97 For an example of an ambitious and wide-ranging history of leisure that incorporates sport see Borsay, *History of Leisure*.

28 Ireland

David Hassan and Philip O'Kane

Introduction

The Irish, many would argue, are a sport-obsessed race. There are few other countries where sport plays such an integral part in the cultural life of a nation or is as closely linked to questions of identity.[1] In fact, the study of the role played by sport in Ireland has offered a valuable insight into the changing trends in Irish culture and identity throughout the 20th century. However, there is a distinction to be drawn between events of the past, on the one hand, and a description and analysis of these same events, on the other. In the latter case, historians may choose to bring their own views, opinions and agendas to the fore. Moreover, the fact that historical works reflect not only the outlook of the author but also those of the values and norms of society at that time has led to the rise in the study of historiography or the process by which historical knowledge is obtained and examined.[2] Historians explore myths about the nation's heritage and in many cases redefine the past so as to have repercussions for the development of identity in the present.

The study of historiography is more analytical in its approach in comparison with the writing of traditional history. The discipline arose in the early 20th century when, in an attempt to keep the study of history and society more relevant and topical, historians began to examine the past within the context of contemporary society. These 'progressive' historians argued that the study of history should be relevant to the present and explain how society has developed. This led to alternative ways of looking at history. For example, the 'New Left' historians of the 1960s brought a Marxist interpretation to the field stressing social factors more readily than had previously been the case. This process of evolution has continued through to the postmodernist historians of the current era, who combine the study of conventional history with fresh perspectives and new skills reflecting particular cultural and ideological interests. In all cases this study of history as collective memory allows people to develop a sense of their own social and national identity.[3]

Traditionally certain Irish historical works, including *A History of Ireland* (1936) by Edmund Curtis, *The Making of Modern Ireland* (1966) by J.C. Beckett and *Ireland since the Famine* (1973) by F.S.L. Lyons had adopted a broadly conventional approach to the study of Irish history, with an emphasis being placed on political events rather than social or cultural aspects of society.[4] It was argued by new Irish 'Revisionist' historians that this stringent approach resulted in such works being much too narrowly focused and prevented a complete analysis of Irish history and the development of Irish society from unfolding. As such, the works of these so-called 'Revisionist' historians such as T.W. Moody, Robert Dudley Edwards, Roy Foster and Ciaran Brady offered a revolutionary approach to the study of Irish history and society.[5] Their particular style attempted to alter the way in which the past in Ireland had been written about and indeed succeeded in adapting the way in which it was presented to contemporary Irish society.[6] Their position argued that a more scholarly approach to Irish history was needed to replace a somewhat romantic and simplistic view, which had defined the field up until that point. This led to a new way of interpreting Irish history with a re-evaluation of controversial areas and significant events such as The Great Famine and the development of Irish Republicanism. Ultimately, it involved drawing a distinction between history and myth and led to many long-held beliefs based on such myths being debunked. This helped broaden the parameters within which the study of Irish history, culture and society took place.

T.W. Moody and Robert Dudley Edwards are regarded as being the fathers of the Irish Revisionist movement. They founded the Irish Historical Society in 1936 and its journal, *Irish Historical Studies*, first published in 1938, afforded aspiring Revisionist historians the opportunity to develop their ideas about the study of history and thereby affect the course of this history in the years ahead. As this new Revisionist approach made its mark, more influential works were published, including T.W. Moody and F.X. Martin's collection of essays entitled *The Course of Irish History* (1967), Francis Shaw's *The Canon of Irish History* (1972), *Natives and Newcomers: The Making of Irish Colonial Society* (1986) edited by Brady and Gillespie, and Steven Ellis's *Nationalist Historiography and the English and Gaelic Worlds* (1989).[7] That said, the two key Revisionist works on Irish history remain Roy Foster's *Modern Ireland 1600–1972* (1990) and *Ireland 1912–1985: Politics and Society* (1990) by Joseph Lee.[8] These books offered much more in-depth analysis than had previously been available whilst still stressing the overall importance of politics in Irish history. However, both authors argued that the analysis of the development of Irish society must be understood within the broader context of economic, social and cultural issues.

Within the field of Irish Historical Revisionism new areas of study, such as the influence and role played by gender, became more important, as did broader cultural themes such as music, language and, significantly, the study of the role and impact that sport has exercised on the development of Irish cultural life. These historians recognized the study of popular culture to be of crucial importance in providing an insight into the development of a particular society. Indeed it has been consistently argued that sport in Ireland is inextricably linked to the construction of various forms of identity.[9] In its most rudimentary guise, sport provides a social and cultural bond between people of different ages, social classes and genders. Together these factors help to shape a section of society that shares a similar outlook, experiences a mutual sense of attachment and expresses a common identity. Cultural historians argue, therefore, that the study of the role and impact of sport in Ireland is a crucial aspect in understanding Irish national identity more generally.[10]

Over the past few decades historians, sociologists and political scientists have come to realize that the vast resource of popular culture represented by sport can be used to interpret and understand the development of society. Ireland has a more varied sporting culture than many other nations due to the mix of traditional Gaelic Irish sports, colonial sports and sports introduced by economic migrants.[11] Importantly, each of the sports and their associated activities are closely bound to a range of ideas about what it means to be Irish.[12] It is ironic, then, that at the same time it aids this process of identity formation, sport also retains the potential to divide people, opinions and communities in a manner seemingly unmatched by most other aspects of civil society. Thus an examination of sport in Ireland against the backdrop of a range of associated themes such as nationalism, colonialism, gender and sectarianism, has provided fertile ground for the study and evaluation of Irish culture and identity more generally.[13]

As a result of all of this it is perhaps surprising that no single recognizable history of sport in Ireland currently exists. It seems a remarkable omission when one considers the important role sport has played in the founding, projection and evolution of the Irish nation. In the absence of this there exists a body of work charting the history of individual sports, national governing bodies, leading performers and athletic clubs.[14] The majority of this material is written from a somewhat sympathetic standpoint, is overwhelmingly narrative in nature and aimed at a broad readership. Nevertheless, there has been some excellent academic work detailing sport in Irish society over recent times and, indeed, what follows offers a critical review of much of this scholarship. That said, there is a need to set much of this work, both 'academic' and 'non-academic', in an appropriate context. It seems that those writing about sport, especially from an historical standpoint, have been reluctant to fully embrace the opportunity it presents when undertaking a critical inspection of wider society.

While those advocating the study of 'low' culture have been correct in drawing attention to its ongoing neglect within Irish political and literary scholarship, equally they have made only limited inroads into the study of sport themselves. This level of under-research is all the more remarkable when one considers that the field of sports studies is often ahead of its time when reflecting a full, nuanced and unrestrained cultural and political synopsis of a particular society. Whereas the political process, for example, is adept at presenting an image of broad acquiescence on the part of those exposed to its outworking, no such opportunity exists in the field of sport, where individuals voluntarily constitute a collective and may convey personal views and aspirations regarding a host of social issues. It is timely, therefore, that this essay continues by engaging in a critical retrospection of the historical development of sport in Ireland, the way it has been written and the meanings attached to it. The dominant theme throughout is its close association with Irish nationalism, and so the latter part of this essay undertakes a review of the changes that have taken place in a range of sports settings in Ireland, beginning with the Gaelic Athletic Association (GAA), and asks how certain developments in sport may indicate a wider process of change unfolding within Irish life as a whole.

A history of sport in Ireland

Traditionally, historical texts dealing with Irish sport, including *Story of the GAA* (1916) by Thomas O'Sullivan, *The Story of Irish Rugby* (1999) by Edmund van Esbeck and *100 Years of Irish Football* (1990) by Malcolm Brodie, adopted a standard approach to relaying their subject matter.[15] The accent was very much on detailing the chronological development of the sport in question rather than examining any wider relevance it may have had within everyday life. In some respects this was understandable as those sympathetic to certain codes innocently believed that sport had no part to play in wider society beyond the opportunity to engage in physical activity and provide a release from the pressures of everyday life. In their view, then, sport should remain separate from issues like politics and religion. That said, in reality it is perhaps more accurate to record the fact that such authors chose to underplay the extent to which sport was actually implicated in this process.

Unsurprisingly, it was felt by those involved in subsequent analyses of the role of sport in Irish society that such an approach failed to relay the full extent of its importance in the lives of everyday people. As such, the work of W.F. Mandle's *The Gaelic Athletic Association and Irish Nationalist Politics, 1884–1924* (1987), *The Politics of Irish Athletics* (1990) by Padraig Griffin, and Kennedy's (1989) *The Belfast Celtic Story* brought a more sophisticated, indeed realistic portrayal of sport in Ireland, one that acknowledged the full extent of its broader role within society.[16] Their argument, that any portrayal of sport in Ireland that neglected its broader historical, sociological or political importance remained incomplete, added to an ever-growing list of publications detailing the precise role that various sports, clubs and individuals performed in Irish life. Such an approach helped push back the academic boundaries within which the study of Irish sport had traditionally taken place.

It is evident from even a cursory examination of sports history in Ireland that the affairs of the GAA dominate the field.[17] Formed in 1884 as a cultural adjunct to a wider political strategy designed to secure an independent and sovereign Ireland, the association has been accused of adopting an overtly political agenda at various stages throughout its existence. On occasions such criticisms have proven to be entirely justified, yet to label the entire organization as such is equally unfair and simply inaccurate. In this regard, the dearth of alternative approaches to the study of sports history in Ireland has cast a particular spotlight upon the affairs of the GAA. It is a hugely popular sporting body, Ireland's largest by some considerable way, but it is symptomatic of an outdated view of its role within Irish life to 'confine the GAA to a near ghetto of politicized leisure'.[18] Garnham (2004) is correct in his assertion that those writing about sport in Ireland have been guilty of overemphasizing its political dimension to the detriment of most other available avenues of study.[19] Nevertheless, Ireland remains a heavily politicized island, whilst Northern Ireland was the site of an ethno-sectarian conflict that lasted almost three decades, from 1969 to 1998. Yet it appears few academics can refute an accusation that, on occasions, they have resorted to unnecessarily pessimistic interpretations of the dispute which, whilst perfectly legitimate under the circumstances, left little room for alternative approaches to develop.

John Sugden and Alan Bairner, regarded as the leading authorities on sport in a divided Ireland, have offered insightful and informed commentary on the Irish 'question' for almost 25 years. Their seminal text, *Sport, Sectarianism and Society in a Divided Ireland* (1993) detailed, for the first time, the broader political and social historiography of sport in Ireland.[20] That said, their focus was primarily on Northern Ireland and their approach a combination of political science and sociological thought. Whilst their text is still relevant for academics to this day, some of their early analysis perhaps lacked the nuanced approach typical of their more recent work, which captured the relationship between sport and politics in Northern Ireland very accurately indeed. Nevertheless, the broad body of literature produced by Sugden and Bairner in the late 1980s and early 1990s helped to offer considerably more light and shade to the role of sport in Ireland than had been the case up until that point. Indeed, as will become apparent, Bairner's work during the interim period dealing with sport and identity politics is universally regarded as amongst the most informed understanding of these issues available within any academic setting.[21]

As this new approach to the study of sport in Ireland grew in prominence, further works were published. These included Mike Cronin's *Sport and Nationalism in Ireland* (1999), Coyle's *Paradise Lost and Found: The Story of Belfast Celtic* (1999) and the second edition of Marcus De Burca's seminal work *The GAA: A History* (1999).[22] These books reflected issues of national identity, sectarianism and post-colonialism, which remained the primary themes in the study of Irish sport during the latter part of the 20th century.

Over the same period the focus of Bairner's scholarship began to broaden and included collaborations on football, sectarianism and masculinity, football hooliganism and the role of the state in divided societies.[23] In a similar vein Cronin's academic pursuits, which have rarely dealt with the issue of Northern Ireland directly, expanded to include further work on the iconography of sport in Ireland and a series of articles on the Aonach Tailteann Games. He also penned a critically acclaimed piece on the politics of boxing in Ireland, a sport that, on the face of it, appears to have remained mercifully free from the spectre of identity politics in Northern Ireland.[24] Indeed, Cronin's (1999) text forced those involved with sport scholarship in Ireland to reflect upon the changing nature of the social and political landscape in which they operated. The emergence of a 'new Ireland' created alternative avenues for people to demonstrate different forms of identity and reflect an evolving political consciousness, which included a more mature attitude towards their relationship with Great Britain.

Within the field of sport studies in Ireland new areas of investigation, such as the influence and role of the Irish Diaspora, grew in importance during this time, as did broader themes like gender, community reconciliation and post-nationalism. This was inevitable as up until this point the main focus had been on Irish nationalism and the plight of Catholics in Northern Ireland. There was clearly a failure to adequately record the role sport played in the lives of the Ulster Unionist community in that country or indeed any sustained analysis of a position beyond that dealing with the cause of Irish nationalists. Now, due largely to the detailed scholarship of Neil Garnham, a lot more began to be known about the British in Ireland, especially within the sports of association football and rugby union. Again, though the focus has largely been on politics, including Garnham's (2003) own piece on rugby in pre-World War I Ireland, which revealed how attitudes to sports confirmed significant levels of division between Irish men on political grounds. Interestingly, Barnard's (2004) subsequent study of Protestant material culture during the 18th century also makes reference to the prestige attached to certain sports in Ireland. In a further attempt to redress the apparent imbalance against coverage of the Unionist voice, Jonathan Magee began to uncover issues surrounding Protestant fragmentation in Northern Ireland soccer, whilst Bairner again offered a sophisticated analysis of the sense of Irishness experienced through sport by those of an Unionist persuasion.[25] His musings are expressed alongside those of others in Bairner's edited collection, *Sport and the Irish: Histories, Identities and Issues* (2005), which has since received critical acclaim.

Since the publication of this collection Darby and Hassan (2008) have completed a compendium detailing the role of sport in the lives of the Irish Diaspora, which includes work by Joseph Bradley on Gaelic sport, soccer and Irishness in Scotland and Marcus Free's latest analysis entitled 'Tales from the Fifth Green Field: The Psychodynamics of Migration, Masculinity and National Identity amongst Republic of Ireland soccer supporters in England.'[26] Hassan's work, reflecting the changing dynamics of Ireland's leading sports governing bodies, emerges from a background in political science. In contrast, his piece on the history of ice-hockey in Belfast throughout the 20th century perhaps suggests a departure from expressly linking sport to politics in the Irish context.[27] In a similar vein, Katie Liston's expanding body of work on gender relations within Irish sport is a welcome addition to what, up until comparatively recently, has been a narrow focus of investigation.[28] Indeed, the history of sport in Ireland appears relatively under-researched on a whole number of levels. The overemphasis on a small number of male team sports has meant little is known about a host of other activities. Garnham (2004) correctly points out that virtually nothing has been published on folk games and traditions prior to the official codification of sport, whilst he is equally valid in his criticism of those who choose to overlook sports like cricket in the lives of the Irish, albeit this specific oversight has begun to receive academic attention in recent times. Indeed Garnham's (2007) latest piece detailing the survival of blood sports in Victorian Ulster is an equally welcome attempt to address shortcomings in this area of study.[29] In summary, the field of sports history in Ireland is showing signs of development and this will continue to be the case as the memories of troubled times in the country diminish. In light of these changing trends, it is perhaps appropriate to examine how the pre-eminent relationship between sport and politics, which is a consistent thread of Irish sports history, closely reflects the nature of this evolving process.

The wider significance of sports history in Ireland

It is clear that contested issues surrounding nationalism, identity politics and community reconciliation have dominated much of the work detailing the history of sport in Ireland. This continues to be true despite the most recent phase of violence in the country drawing to a close with the signing of the Belfast-Good Friday Agreement on 10 April 1998. That said, the nationalist and republican constituencies in Northern Ireland, whilst unquestionably supportive of an end to inter-ethnic violence, are left to reflect upon the extent to which their aspirations of an end to British rule in Ireland have been achieved. A devolved assembly (from Westminster), a Unionist first minister of the Legislative Assembly, Northern Ireland's status within the United Kingdom secured, the dropping of Articles 2 and 3 from the Constitution of the Republic of Ireland and a failure of Sinn Fein to make any form of electoral impact there, questions the relevancy of a classic form of Irish nationalism within modern Ireland.[30] It is this idealistic form of Irish nationalism around which organizations like the GAA built their success and, indeed, this vision of a free and independent Ireland clearly resonated with a whole host of other sports clubs and athletes as well. Instead of this, however, the nature of Irish nationalism has evolved considerably so that it exercises a quite different influence today than it did over the course of the last 125 years. It is perhaps equally interesting that sports trends, the development of new interests and the eradication of long-standing diktats within Irish sport provide a very useful insight into the full extent of these changes for the nationalist community.

Since Cronin (1999) penned his views on sport and nationalism in Ireland the rate of change within Irish sport has been remarkable. For example, the decision taken by the GAA on 17 November 2001 to remove Rule 21 was universally acclaimed as a magnanimous gesture on the part of an organization that had performed a central role in Irish cultural life. Indeed certain political leaders expressly linked this move, which permitted serving police officers in Northern Ireland and members of the British Army to play Gaelic sports, to the fledging peace process. Yet, with the exception of County Down, this decision was opposed en masse by GAA followers in Northern Ireland. Clearly the GAA's rank and file considered this development at best premature and at worst inconsistent with the aims of the association. After nearly 115 years of conservative administration, those in charge of the GAA perhaps felt the need to make up for lost time when on 16 April 2005 it again moved to offer a temporary suspension of Rule 42, which had prevented the playing of non-indigenous or so-called 'foreign' games at GAA grounds. The association, which up until 1971 had banned its members from playing a range of sports, including association football, rugby union and other Anglicized games, was now willing to sanction the playing of such sports at Croke Park, its foremost stadium.[31]

Thus, the repeal of Rule 21 and the ongoing suspension of Rule 42 suggest a changed attitude within the GAA towards its role as a touchstone for Irish nationalism. Such decisions have also served to highlight broader societal changes within both parts of Ireland and have seen the relevancy of the GAA in certain regions throughout Ireland diminish. Of course this argument is made all the more salient when one reflects upon that which has filled the ideological void created by the GAA's new found sense of liberalism. The growth of association football in the Republic of Ireland, inspired by the success of the country's international team over the last two decades, has been exceptional. The continued acceptance of rugby union, essentially a British game, by Irish people is similarly noteworthy.

Indeed, the extent to which sport can be used to illustrate changing trends in Irish identity is evidenced by the rise in the popularity of cricket on the island following the Irish cricket team's performances at the 2007 International Cricket Council (ICC) World Cup, staged in the West Indies. Here the side defeated the much fancied Pakistani team to qualify for the latter stages of the tournament, the so-called 'Super 8s'. As a result of this achievement, cricket has enjoyed renewed popularity in schools and clubs and captured a degree of interest for the wider community that was not always there. For many years in Ireland, cricket was interpreted as the most quintessential of English sports and synonymous with British rule in Ireland. For this reason it was shunned by the Catholic community in particular, albeit interesting exceptions to this are to be found in parts of the north-west of Ireland. The fact that cricket is now making significant gains in popularity illustrates the extent to which Irish culture and society has moved away from the old, somewhat dated view of Irish identity. Indeed, the extent to which the sport has been successful in doing so marks it out as worthy of further study. Irish society arguably no longer looks to the past for solace but instead looks ahead to the future as an independent nation capable of a confident and mature cultural relationship with England, one that is no different to that of any other European nation state.

In light of such developments, then, the question as to what the popularity of these sports tells us about the changing nature of Irish society becomes ever-more relevant. If, as is argued here, it suggests that Irish society is becoming increasingly liberal in its outlook and is undergoing something of a sporting transformation in which the politicization of such activities has diminished, then a study of the history of sport in Ireland assumes even greater importance. In other words any analysis of Irish history that precludes the study of culture, including sport, offers a very narrow definition of history indeed.

Such observations become even more relevant when one considers an issue like immigration in Ireland. Whilst the impact Irish emigrants have made on sport throughout many parts of the world has received considerable academic coverage, little is known about the impact overseas immigrants have made on sport in Ireland. The Republic of Ireland has been the destination of choice for a great many migrants over the last decade, but their engagement in mainstream sport has, on the face of it, been limited. Attitudes to unprecedented levels of immigration in Ireland have varied, with examples of resistance on the part of certain indigenous communities not uncommon. By the same token it is possible that the recent success of the Republic of Ireland soccer team in international competition and its universal acclaim within that country is indicative of a maturing attitude on the part of the Irish to the question of identity. Many of Ireland's best known soccer players were not born in Ireland and in that way remained more representative of the wide Irish Diaspora than the nation state. Now, as Ireland is recognized as an attractive location for economic migrants from Eastern Europe and elsewhere, so sport may well play a role in negotiating Ireland's acceptance of its expanding boundaries and those contained within them.

Thus, recent Irish historians have attempted to replace the old traditional view of Irish history with a less sentimental and simplified account, which makes reference to all the dynamics at work in Irish society.[32] This continued trend will surely result in the parameters of the study of sport being further broadened to take into account new themes of investigation. It is likely that where some works have concentrated on sectarian issues in the past they may focus more on ethnic issues in the future. As has been suggested, the success of foreign sports stars in Ireland could be used to evaluate and promote the positive nature of migration, as was identified in a report published in 2005 by the East of England Development Agency. If migrants continue to play a more influential role in sport in Ireland then this could possibly change attitudes towards the 'new' Irish by those who have been resident there for generations.[33] Of course, it is worth keeping in mind that sports migration is a multi-directional process, as illustrated through the recent trend of young Gaelic footballers going to Australia to play Australian Rules football. Indeed, this potentially is a development that may have a long-term impact on the appeal of Gaelic Football in Ireland.

It is clear, then, that several important themes on the study of Irish society have emerged over the past few decades in terms of the study of sport in Ireland. This period has been amongst the most turbulent in Irish history and yet has witnessed many notable developments, from the 'Troubles' in the North to the economic boom of the 'Celtic Tiger' in the South, the subsequent peace process in Northern Ireland and the radical changes that this has brought to Irish society as a whole. Sport reflects these changes and the cultural study of sport parallels the historical and political analysis of the time bringing academic study and popular culture together during an important period in Irish history. The rapid modernization of Irish society during the latter half of the 20th century has led to a great many social and economic changes and the creation of a more affluent and multi-cultural Irish society. As a result of this process of modernization Irish society has moved on at a tremendous rate, leaving behind the mythical and romantic Ireland portrayed in past historical works. Nonetheless, due to these changes, the concept of 'Irishness' and what it means to be Irish has become more problematic and difficult to define.[34] Of course, many traditional historians would still argue that this inter-disciplinary approach to academic history and popular culture undermines the integrity of history itself. In contrast, other historians feel that it opens up new possibilities for the study of history as they are obliged to address topics of relevance within modern society. These historians view the field as being a hybrid discipline that straddles both the humanities and the social sciences, which only adds to its complexity.[35]

The message of contemporary cultural historians is, then, not to dwell in the past but to look to the future and accept the changes that have taken place in this pragmatic new Irish society. As Ireland faces the challenges of the 21st century it may be necessary to accept that the old romantic image of Ireland is dead, if in fact it ever really existed. The recent transformation of Irish society means that historians must continue to broaden their horizons in order to understand and interpret these changes. The romantic mythical Ireland may be largely irrelevant, but historians must now examine what has filled this void in Irish culture and national identity.[36] Historians must continue to study society and re-evaluate history in order to fully address this dilemma. The Italian historian Franco Venturi was once asked what, for him, defined the 20th century. He replied, 'historians can't answer this question, for me the 20th century is only the ever renewed effort to understand it'.[37] This, then, is the aim of the cultural historian when studying the history and development of sport, particularly in the context of 20th-century Ireland.

Conclusion

We have discussed how the role of sport in Irish society has been addressed by academics in order to help interpret Irish history and identity. Indeed, the constantly changing nature of sporting culture means that new avenues of study will continue to develop. In recent years in Ireland the role of sport in society has continued to evolve with increased media coverage leading to an enhanced profile for the country's leading athletes. Sport has become big business in Ireland with rugby union turning professional in the mid-1990s and the GAA, a staunchly amateur organization, threatening to pursue a similar strategy amid an often difficult debate with some of its leading performers. The continued expansion of the historiography of Irish sport to take into account these changing factors will result in renewed scope for the academic study of the social significance of sport in Ireland from both historical and social science perspectives.[38]

The important impact that the presentation of history, both in an academic sense and in terms of popular culture, has on the construction of identity is clear. The study of the changing presentation and view of Irish history in successive decades tells the cultural historian a great deal about the development of concepts of identity in Ireland. This study of identity brings history closer to the social sciences and somewhat further from the field of humanities. A study of what lessons society can take from history rather than the study of history for its own sake is a key theme of the historiographical works on Irish history and popular culture. This approach to history helps the historian to evaluate changing trends in society and the causes and nature of these changes. The academic study of the impact and influence of sport in Ireland has played a key role in this process. As such, the examination of different aspects of popular culture, including sport, gives the historian an overview of the way in which various myths and traditions in society have been re-evaluated and represented by successive generations. The works of academics dealing with sport in Ireland have attempted to analyse the changing nature of Irish society and Irish identity and make this identity more applicable to contemporary society. As the 21st century progresses these scholars will no doubt continue to expand and develop the study of sport in order to analyse and deconstruct Irish society in the years ahead.

Notes

1 A. Bairner, ed., *Sport and the Irish: Histories, Identities, Issues* (Dublin: UCD Press, 2005); M. Cronin, *Sport and Nationalism in Ireland: Gaelic Games, Soccer and Irish Identity since 1884* (Dublin: Four Courts Press, 1999).

2 R. Spalding and C. Parker, *Historiography* (Manchester:Manchester University Press, 2007).

3 J. Tosh, *The Pursuit of History: Aims, Methods and New Directions in the Study of Modern History* (London: Longman, 1991).

4 E. Curtis, *A History of Ireland* (London: Methuen, 1936); J.C. Beckett, *The Making of Modern Ireland* (London: Faber, 1966); F.S.L. Lyons, *Ireland since the Famine* (London: Fontana, 1973).

5 T.W. Moody and F.X. Martin, eds, *The Course of Irish History* (Cork: The Mercier Press, 1967); R. F. Foster, *Luck and the Irish: A Brief History of Change, c. 1970–2000* (London: Allen Press, 2007); R.F. Foster, *Modern Ireland 1600–1972* (Harmondsworth: Penguin, 1989); C. Brady, ed., *Interpreting Irish History: The Debate on Historical Revisionism, 1938–1994* (Blackrock: Irish Academic Press, 1994).

6 Brady, *Interpreting Irish History.*

7 Moody and Martin, eds, *The Course of Irish History*; F. Shaw, *The Canon of Irish History* (Dublin, 1972); C. Brady and R. Gillespie, eds, *Natives and Newcomers: Essays on the Making of Irish Colonial Society, 1534–1641* (Dublin: Irish Academic Press, 1986); S. Ellis, *Nationalist Historiography and the English and Gaelic Worlds* (Dublin, 1989).

8 R.F. Foster, *Modern Ireland 1600–1972* (London: Penguin, 1990); J.J. Lee, *Ireland 1912–85: Politics and Society* (Cambridge: Cambridge University Press, 1990).

9 M. Cronin, *Sport and Nationalism in Ireland*.

10 A.D. Smith, *National Identity* (London: Penguin Books, 1991).

11 J. Sugden and A. Bairner, *Sport, Sectarianism and Society in a Divided Ireland* (Leicester: Leicester University Press, 1993).

12 A. Bairner, ed., *Sport and the Irish*; M. Cronin, *Sport and Nationalism in Ireland*.

13 Beyond the work already referred to, examples include: A. Bairner 'Up to their Knees? Football, Sectarianism, Masculinity and Protestant Working Class Identity', in P. Shirlow and M. McGovern, eds, *Who are 'The People?' Unionism, Protestantism and Loyalism in Northern Ireland* (London: Pluto, 1997), 95–113; M. Cronin, 'Enshrined in Blood: The Naming of Gaelic Athletic Association Grounds and Clubs', *The Sports Historian* 18 (1998), 90–104; R. Davis. 'Irish Cricket and Nationalism', *Sporting Traditions* 10 (1994), 77–96; D. Fahy, *How the GAA survived the Troubles* (Dublin: Wolfhound Press, 2001).

14 One example of a plethora of similar work includes C. Short, P. Murray and J. Smyth, *Ard Macha 1884–1984: A Century of GAA Progress* (Armagh, Ireland: Armagh GAA, 1985).

15 T. O'Sullivan, *Story of the GAA* (Dublin, 1916); E. van Esbeck, *Irish Rugby 1874–1999: A History* (Dublin: Gill and Macmillan, 1999); M. Brodie, *100 Years of Irish Football* (Belfast: Blackstaff, 1980).

16 W.F. Mandle, *The Gaelic Athletic Association and Irish Nationalist Politics, 1884–1924* (London: Croom Helm, 1987); P. Griffin, *The Politics of Irish Athletics 1850–1990* (Ballinamore, Co. Leitrim: Marathon Publications, 1990); J. Kennedy, *Belfast Celtic* (Belfast: Pretani, 1989).

17 W.F. Mandle, *The Gaelic Athletic Association and Irish Nationalist Politics*; M. De Burca, *The GAA: A History*, 2nd edn (Dublin: Gill and Macmillan, 1999); J. Sugden and A. Bairner, *Sport, Sectarianism and Society in a Divided Ireland*.

18 N. Garnham 'Sport History: The Cases of Britain and Ireland Stated', *Journal of Sport History* 31, 4 (2004), 140.

19 Ibid.

20 J. Sugden and A. Bairner, *Sport, Sectarianism and Society in a Divided Ireland*.

21 A. Bairner, 'Up to their Knees? Football, Sectarianism, Masculinity and Protestant Working Class Identity'; A. Bairner, 'Soccer, Masculinity and Violence in Northern Ireland: Between Hooliganism and Terrorism', *Men and Masculinities* 1, 2 (1999), 284–301; A. Bairner, *Sport, Nationalism and Globalisation: European and North American Perspectives* (Albany, NY: State University of New York Press, 2001); A. Bairner, ed., *Sport and the Irish*; A. Bairner, 'Sport, Irishness and Ulster Unionism', in A. Bairner, ed., *Sport and the Irish*, 157–71.

22 M. Cronin, *Sport and Nationalism in Ireland*; P.Coyle, *Paradise Lost and Found: The Story of Belfast Celtic* (Edinburgh, Mainstream and Belfast: Blackstaff, 1999); M. De Burca, *The GAA: A History*.

23 See Bairner works listed in note 21.

24 M. Cronin, 'Which Nation, Which Flag? Boxing and National Identities in Ireland', *International Review for the Sociology of Sport* 32, 2 (1997), 131–46.

25 N. Garnham, 'Rugby and Empire in Ireland: Irish Reactions to Colonial Rugby Tours before 1914', *Sport in History* 23 (2003), 107–14; N. Garnham, 'Football and National Identity in pre-Great War Ireland', *Irish Economic and Social History* 28 (2001), 13–31; N. Garnham, 'Sport History: The Cases of Britain and Ireland Stated'; N. Garnham 'The Survival of Illegal Blood Sports in Victorian Ulster', *Proceedings of the Royal Irish Academy*, Series C. CV11 (2007), 107–26; T. Barnard, *Making the Grand Figure: Lives and Possessions in Ireland, 1641–1770* (London: Yale University Press, 2004); J. Magee, 'Football Supporters, Rivalry and Protestant Fragmentation in Northern Ireland', in A. Bairner, ed., *Sport and the Irish*, 172–90; A. Bairner, 'Sport, Irishness and Ulster Unionism', in A. Bairner, ed., *Sport and the Irish*, 157–71.

26 M. Free, 'Tales from the Fifth Green Field: The Psychodynamics of Migration, Masculinity and National Identity amongst Republic of Ireland Soccer Supporters in England', in P. Darby and D. Hassan, *Emigrants at Play: Sport and the Irish Diaspora* (London: Taylor and Francis, 2008).

27 D. Hassan, 'From Kings to Giants: A History of Ice Hockey in Belfast, 1930–2002', *Sport in History* 24 (2004), 77–93.

28 Examples of this scholarship include K. Liston 'The Gendered Field of Irish sport', in M. Corcoran and M. Peillon, eds, *Ireland Unbound: A Turn of the Century Chronicle* (Dublin: Institute of Public Administration).

29 N. Garnham, 'The Survival of Illegal Blood Sports in Victorian Ulster'.

30 Articles 2 and 3 of the Constitution of the Republic of Ireland laid claim to Northern Ireland until the declaration was removed as part of the Belfast-Good Friday Agreement, signed on 10 April 1998.

31 Croke Park is the GAA's largest stadium in Ireland, with the capacity for 82,500 spectators. For many GAA members the stadium has particular resonance as a site of Irish nationalist expression, hence the considerable opposition from certain quarters to the playing of association football and rugby union (by virtue of the temporary repeal of Rule 42) at the ground.

32 D. Kiberd, *Inventing Ireland* (Cambridge, MA: Harvard University Press, 1997).

33 Some interesting early findings in this field of scholarship can be found by accessing T. Carter, H. Donnan, S. Ogle and H. Wardle, *Global Migrants: The Impact of Migrants Working in Sport in Northern Ireland* (Belfast: Sports Council for Northern Ireland, 2003).

34 Kiberd, *Inventing Ireland*.

35 J. Tosh, *The Pursuit of History*.

36 R. F. Foster, *Luck and the Irish*.

37 E.J. Hobsbawm, *Age of Extremes: The Short Twentieth Century, 1914–1991* (London: Michael Joseph, 1994).

38 Bairner, *Sport and the Irish*.

29 Japan

Richard L. Light

Introduction

This chapter examines the history of sport in Japan by locating its development within significant periods of social, cultural and economic change over the following four periods: Pre-Meiji (before 1868), Meiji Era to the Pacific War (1868–1939), the post-war period (1945–93) and the contemporary period (1993–2008). In it I work with an interpretation of sport as a rationalized practice originating in the massive economic and social changes associated with industrialization in Great Britain, as suggested by sociologists and historians (Bourdieu 1978; Mangan 1981). While there are links between sport and the folk games of pre-industrial Europe, the unregulated folk games from which sport, as we now know it, developed cannot be considered as sport. From this perspective neither the plethora of court games of the nobility nor the aggressive games and contests of the peasant classes in Japan in the pre-Meiji Era (1868–1912) can be considered as sport. Some Japanese scholars make a similar distinction between the 'sport-like' activities of pre-Meiji Japan and 'modern sport' as that which originated from Western sports (for example, see Kusaka 2006). Working with this view of sport highlights the importance of the Meiji Era for its development in Japan. The Meiji Era was a period of immense change in Japan arising from the opening up of the country to the outside world after a long period of enforced isolation during the Tokugawa period (1603–1868). Like industrialization in 18th-century England, it brought about massive social, cultural and economic change tied into an opening up to the West that facilitated the development of sport. After two and a half centuries of isolation Japan's rush to catch up with Western powers involved the introduction of Western sports and their dissemination through the new system of mass education.

The development of sport in Japan was not limited to the importation of Western sport. Resulting from a backlash against the wholesale adoption of Western ideas and culture in the late 19th century, the military practices of the samurai classes were reconstituted into sporting forms in a process through which they were 'sportified' (Abe, Kiyohara and Nakajima 1990) beginning with judo and now referred to as martial arts (*budo*). The Meiji Restoration created the social, economic and cultural conditions from which sport emerged as a medium for the dissemination of a hegemonic culture politically promoted to ensure social cohesion during a period of dramatic social change as Japan shifted from an agrarian, feudal society to a modern, industrialized society over a remarkably short period (Light 2000a). The one explicit exception to this view of sport as being visible only from the Meiji Era is sumo. Sumo has a very long history in Japan, beginning in Japanese mythology and has been practised in many different forms for over 2,000 years. The rationalized, regulated and commercialized sporting practice that it is today has changed little from the late 18th century. Indeed, its contemporary practice, cultural meanings and its attendant rituals are identifiable from the 17th century when its was reinvented as a quasi-religious practice (Light and Kinnaird 2002). For this reason sumo dominates the first section on sport in the pre-Meiji Era, which begins with a very brief outline of some significant court games and peasant contests.

The pre-Meiji era

Some historians, both Japanese and non-Japanese, have taken a view of what constitutes sport in Japan's history that includes consideration of 'sport' from as far back as pre-historic times in Japan. For example, the transformation of traditional sport into modern sport in Japan through a process of modernization forms the main thrust of one of the major treatments of sport in Japan published in English (Guttman and Thompson 2001). However, from the perspective outlined in the introduction the folk games, court games and peasant contests of pre-Meiji Japan cannot be seen as being sport. This section, then, offers only a brief outline of some of the more significant court games and rural contests of the pre-Meiji Era before moving on to focus on the development of sumo from the 17th century when it could be considered to be a sport.

Kemari

This is a game involving keeping a ball in the air for as long as possible through kicking. Similar games can be traced as far back as 644 with a set of rules established in the 13th century. Throughout the history of *kemari* it has been played primarily as a court game of the nobility with some evidence that it was played at times by the lower classes and was mostly a secular activity (Guttman and Thompson 2001). Played by eight players using four trees as the corners of the court it was typically a non-competitive leisure activity, but Guttman and Thompson suggest that it was at times made competitive, that records were sometimes kept and that it was popular, with local variations across Japan, during the Edo period. It was, though, essentially a non-competitive court game restricted to the city and the nobility, with no links to modern sport.

Dakyuu

Dakyuu was a game that was similar to Western polo deriving from the same Persian game via China. It was recorded as early as 727 but died out soon after and did not reappear until the 18th century in a different form. The 18th century form of *dakyuu* involved using a net on the end of a long pole used to scoop up the ball instead of a hammer used to strike it. The 18th-century form of *dakyuu* involved the riders scooping up the ball to carry it and throw it, which is very much like the contemporary Australian game of polocrosse (a blend of polo and lacrosse). *Dakyuu* had a martial connection and was used to develop riding skills for the military classes but now, as Guttman and Thompson suggest, remains only as a cultural relic.

Gitchou

Gitchou was an activity practised by the peasant classes, resembling the sport of ice-hockey in that it involved players on foot striking a flat object like a puck with a stick and was contested between two teams. Bearing some similarity to folk football in pre-industrial Great Britain, one version of the game described by Guttman and Thompson (2001) involved two large teams starting in the middle of town. Players struck the 'puck' as far as possible aiming to drive the opposition team backwards and, eventually, out of the town or village.

Chikaraishi

Chikaraishi was a competitive test of strength favoured by the peasant classes, which involved variations on lifting and carrying large boulders, popular from the 17th century to the 19th century. Some contests involved lifting large boulders while others involved lifting and carrying boulders of up to 245kg (Guttman and Thompson 2001).

Sumo

Sumo is a highly complex cultural practice embodying significant cultural meaning tied into its close association with Japan's indigenous religion of *Shinto* (Light and Kinnaird 2002). It is likely Japan's most culturally distinctive sport and has played a significant role in the development and reproduction of a particular Japanese culture since the Meiji Restoration. It does, though, have a far longer history, with sumo featuring in contemporary accounts of the mythological origins of Japan. According to the Records of Ancient matters, 712 AD (*Kojiki*), a bout between two gods was staged to determine who would gain control of the Japanese islands, with the victory by Takemi-Kazuchi enabling the sun goddess Amaterasu to produce an imperial line that is claimed to remain unbroken to today (Hikoyama 1940; Anzu 1986). It was commonly performed as an agricultural ritual used to gain favour from the gods from the Yayoi and Kofun periods (200 BC–552 AD) (Kuhaulua 1973). There was also a common form of sumo called *kusa-zumo* (grass sumo) used as a test of strength between village strongmen. Sumo was also practised as a court activity, but with the replacement of imperial power by military power this court sumo disappeared to see a military form, *buke-zumo* (warrior sumo) developed as part of samurai training. This form of sumo included techniques that can be found in contemporary judo and jui-jitsu (Kuhaulua). During the Kamakura period (1185–1333) sumo also emerged as a form of entertainment and during the Muromachi period (1336–1573) it was used to raise funds for religious purposes through the donations made by the crowds attracted to the contest. These donations were shared with the wrestlers and masterless samurai (*ronin*) wandering the country sought to take part in these contests of *kanjin-zumo* as a means of survival. The introduction of military technology by the Portuguese that led to the decreased importance of hand-to-hand combat in the military stimulated growth in this form of sumo (Cuyler 1985). Other samurai took part in a rougher form of sumo, *tsuji-zumo* (street corner sumo), where they fought for money as a form of entertainment in the growing entertainment quarters of towns and cities. Both forms of sumo were violent, with *tsuji-zumo* commonly becoming a fight to the death. Owing to concern with the violence of both forms of sumo and its impact upon civil order the government banned sumo in 1648.

Although there have been innumerable forms of sumo practised over Japanese history, they tended to fall into two forms of sumo up until the 18th century. Sumo as religious ritual and sumo as a rough and brutal form of combat practised by the peasant classes existed side by side over hundreds of years of Japanese history. Sumo as it is practised today finds its origins in the late 17th-century renewal of interest in native Japanese cultural traditions and ancient literature. Growing nationalist sentiments saw the rejection of foreign practices and ideas including Chinese thought and ideology and the imported religion of Buddhism. Japan's native religion Shinto grew in popularity among the ruling classes and was seen to be an expression of 'true Japanese spirit' (Light and Kinnaird 2002). The ban on sumo was lifted in 1684 as a result of promoters' efforts to reduce the levels of violence of the rougher form of sumo as entertainment for the peasant classes and to link it with Shinto (Cuyler 1985). The restructured version of *kanjin-zumo* with its Shinto rituals marked the beginning of the professional sumo performed today. By 1791 the highly ritualistic form of sumo seen today was put in place by promoters seeking to gain favour with the ruling classes. One promoter in particular, Yoshida Oikaze, is credited with the creation of sumo as it is performed in contemporary Japan. Yoshida legitimated sumo through further strengthening of its links with Shinto at a time of growing nationalist sentiment, within which the native religion of Shinto was strongly favoured by the aristocracy (Light and Kinnaird 2002). Yoshida linked sumo more closely with eighth-century court sumo and Shinto through the introduction of more Shinto rituals and the invention of others to make it appealing to the ruling classes, while maintaining its appeal to the peasant classes as an aggressive physical contest. It is a development of the more brutal form of sumo practised as a form of entertainment for the lower classes made acceptable to the aristocracy by the invention of links with Shinto.

The Meiji era (1868–1912) to the Pacific war

After unifying Japan through military conquest over a long period of war the first Shogun, Tokugawa Ieyasu, attempted to consolidate his rule and deal with concerns over growing Western influence by closing Japan off from the rest of the world. Fears of Western influence led to restrictions in trade with the West from 1612 followed by the slaughter of thousands of Japanese Christians in 1622 and the systematic expulsion of foreigners beginning with the Spanish in 1624. By the Closed Country Edict of 1635, the country was shut off from the outside world. This isolation, although never complete, was maintained by generations of Tokugawan rulers until the Meiji 'revolution' in 1868. The Meiji Revolution was validated by the restoration of the Emperor (the Meiji Restoration) and given a sense of urgency by the colonization of China and other parts of Asia by Western powers during the 19th century. During this period Japan's vulnerability to external threat from the West was highlighted when the American Admiral Perry forced open the ports of Shimada and Hakodate to American trade by bombarding Shimada in 1853 in a show of force. Followed by similar agreements within months with England and then other Western powers, this led to the development of flourishing Western settlements in designated port cities around Japan, such as Kobe and Yokohama.

In these settlements the Americans and the British brought with them the games ideology, playing sports at social and recreational clubs of which some still exist today such as the Kobe Recreation and Athletics Club and the Yokohama Athletics Club. The 19th-century British colonial expansion and military power was widely attributed to the moral strength of its leaders developed through a games education and by the late 19th century the vigour of team games had come to function as a symbol of national strength and health in England. Within this context, the colonial powers such as Great Britain and the USA viewed the absence of sport in Japan as a sign of cultural, racial and moral inferiority (Roden 1980). The government's drive to modernize and strengthen its military saw a range of sports such as horse-riding, rifle shooting, fencing and skiing introduced along with gymnastics. Horse-racing was introduced as early as 1862, with the Kobe Jockey Club formed in 1870 (Guttman and Thompson 2001). Westerners initially played team sports in communities that grew around port cities such as Yokohama and Kobe where sports such as baseball, football and rugby were regularly played. Typically, teams of Westerners living in Japan would field teams against teams fielded by visiting naval ships. Much like British colonies such as Australia, cricket was also played as early as 1864 between garrison members and crew of a visiting naval ship. In 1869 British residents of Kobe and a team from the HMS Ocean played and the Yokohama Cricket and Athletics Club was formed in the same year. Cricket, though, did not excite the Japanese and was never taken up by them to any extent (Guttman and Thompson 2001).

Team sports were introduced during this period of rapid transformation from a feudal to a modern society, which accelerated following the dismantling of the feudal system in 1871. In a rush to close the gap between Japan and the Western powers, educational reform ranked as one of the key mechanisms used in the remarkably rapid transformation of Japan into a modern, unified state (Passin 1980). Initiated in 1872, the system of mass schooling not only provided a skilled workforce, but also formed a central mechanism for the development of a unified state during a period of radical change and unrest (Passin 1980). Education was seen by the Meiji leaders as a central means through which they could bridge the technological, industrial, political and economic gap between Japan and the Western powers (Passin). In the rush to catch up with the West the Japanese single-minded commitment to education meant that many students undertook no physical exercise at all. The British in Japan thus saw Japanese students as being effeminate and morally inferior, with Western teachers in Japanese universities voicing concern over their lack of virility (Roden 1980). Japanese teachers also expressed concern with students' preoccupation with study, their lack of strength and their poor health. In response, gymnastics was introduced into schools with the National Institute of Gymnastics established in 1879.

Universities were exempt from compulsory gymnastics, but criticism of under-exercised and physically weak students led to the adoption of team games in these institutions serving the social elite. Baseball was introduced in 1872 and football in 1873. These were followed by more team sports, such as rugby, which was introduced at Keio University in 1899 to keep baseball players fit over the winter (Ikeguchi 1981). While individual sport such as athletics were also introduced, Roden (1980) suggests that team games such as baseball were more appealing to Meiji leaders concerned with the effects of Western individualism and the need to maintain a cohesive society and build a sense of national identity. Educationalists thus promoted the propensity of team games to contribute toward national strength and the development of the *esprit de corps* needed for a modernizing nation, with team sports spreading from the university system to schools from the end of the 19th century. Football did not initially attract much attention from the Japanese with the first recorded game between two Japanese teams not played until 1907. On the other hand, baseball proved an immediate hit, with rugby also very becoming popular in universities at the turn of the 20th century across Japan and later spreading to schools.

After 20 years of uncritical fascination with all things Western, the 1890s saw a backlash against this wholesale adoption of anything from the West. For two decades Japan had systematically identified the best the West had to offer in industry, the military and social institutions and set out to emulate it in Japan. The efficiency with which this was achieved is evident in the speed with which Japan developed its navy to the extent that it was able to defeat the Russian navy in 1905. From the close of the 19th century the Japanese continued to emulate Western technology, but the Meiji leaders increasingly rejected Western culture and, from the 1890s, promoted the adoption of Western technology combined with the strength of 'traditional' Japanese culture. This assertion of Japanese culture was formalized in 1890 with the 'Imperial Rescript on Education', which promoted reverence of the Emperor and Japanese culture. In 1872 the Minister for Education, Mori Arinori, was so enamoured with the West that he suggested the adoption of English as the national language of Japan. In 1889, in a climate of growing nationalism, he was assassinated (Passin 1980).

Stimulated by a rise in nationalism, Japan's rapidly expanding military might and its dominance in the region, team games in universities flourished during the 1890s. The collective nature of team games made sports such as baseball, football and rugby attractive as vehicles for the promotion of a hegemonic culture based on the values of the pre-Meiji samurai classes with their emphasis on loyalty, respect and the preservation of order. In his examination of baseball in Meiji Japan, Roden (1980) argues that team sports formed a central element in the education system and played a significant role in the development of national identity. As many other historians have argued (for example, see Passin 1980), the social cohesion required at a time of such radical change was achieved through the dissemination of the culture of the samurai classes as the culture of all Japanese through mass education. From its inception, mass education formed hotly contested terrain with social and political groups fighting for control in a struggle characterized by tension between liberal Western ideals and 'traditional' culture and ideals derived from the values of the pre-Meiji samurai classes (Light 2000a). Within this context, team sports formed important vehicles for the reproduction of a dominant form of culture derived from the samurai classes emphasizing cultural homogeneity and the values promoted as those of the Japanese (Light 2000a). Conservative team sports such as baseball and rugby continue to reproduce this cultural hegemony to some extent (Light 1999a, 2003; Moeran 1986).

This period also saw the emergence of the martial arts as a reformulation of pre-Meiji military practices into sporting forms. Roden (1980) suggests that the sentiments of this period led educators to locate the games ideology within traditional samurai culture and the fusion of values of the samurai with Victorian values of manliness in the practice of team games. Concerns with the negative effects of Western liberalism on Japanese society from the 1890s saw a more selective adoption of Western technology, which rejected Western cultural ideals captured in the catch cry, *Wakon yosei* (Japanese culture, Western technology). This saw the increasing transformation of the practice and meaning of imported sport and the development of the military arts of the samurai into what we now refer to as martial arts. The sentiment at the end of the 19th century that encouraged the regeneration of 'traditional' Japanese culture also gave rise to the reconstitution of the military combat techniques of the samurai (*bujitsu*) into forms of practice modelled on Western sport as *budo*. The techniques of war practised by pre-Meiji samurai were resurrected through the transformation of *bujitsu* (martial techniques) into modern sporting forms (*budo*) led by the reconstruction of *jiujitsu* into judo by its founder, Kano Jigoro. This process involved the reconstruction of the techniques of warfare used by the pre-Meiji samurai into modern sporting forms shaped by the model of Western sport, yet maintaining strong links with the culture and values of the samurai classes.

As Inoue (1997) suggests, the development of *budo* made a strong contribution toward a cohesive, national cultural identity and the connection with what were promoted as the traditional values of all Japanese in times of immense social and economic change. Although *budo* such as judo and kendo embodied the values of the samurai, they were individual in nature and were not seen as being as effective as team games in promoting the collective ideals promoted as a means of maintaining social cohesion (Light 2000a). They have, though, formed important practices for the reproduction of what is now seen as traditional Japanese culture – the culture of the pre-Meiji samurai classes. All secondary schools in Japan still offer a range of martial arts, with judo and kendo the most common. In fact, *budo* is a compulsory part of all boys' education in Japanese schools.

From liberalism to militarism (1912–45)

The first two decades of the 20th century saw the expansion of team games in universities and their spread to schools, with their practice shaped by the ideals of Victorian manliness intermeshed with the military values of *bushido*. In 1911 the founder of Judo, Jigoro Kano, established the National Association of Sport/Physical Education. This organization was set up with the express aim of enabling Japan to compete in the Olympic Games (Kusaka 2006). The 1920s saw the establishment of national governing bodies for major team sports such as rugby (1926) and football (1921) and in 1929 Japan was admitted to the Fédération Internationale de Football Association (FIFA). In 1935 the Japanese (Amateur) Association of Sport was established to govern all sport at a national level (Kusaka 2006). Fees were first charged to watch baseball games from 1907, and from 1908 professional teams from the USA toured Japan playing against amateur teams made up primarily of university students. Over 1913 and 1922 teams of American baseball stars toured Japan to play games and conduct clinics. In 1920 two Japanese professional teams were established and toured the newly acquired Japanese colonies of Manchuria and Korea to promote baseball, with baseball also acting as a means of promoting Japanese culture. However, professional baseball did not develop until over a decade later. By the 1930s the popularity of intercollegiate baseball had grown rapidly enough to create government concern with crowd behaviour, leading the Ministry of Education to introduce the 'Baseball Control Act' that prohibited amateurs playing with professionals (Hirai 2001). This created a problem for the *Yomiuri Shinbun* (newspaper), as it had organized a professional US All-Stars team to play in Japan, which it solved by establishing a fully professional All Japan team in 1934. The Greater Japan Tokyo Baseball Club (later to become the Yomiuri Giants) was joined by the Osaka Baseball Club (later to become the Hanshin Tigers) in 1935 and by five new clubs in 1936, to form the Japanese Baseball League. Over this period a number of Americans played professional baseball in Japan with famous names such as Babe Ruth and Lou Gehrig playing exhibition games (Hirai 2005).

Responses to the famous victory of the *Ichiko* baseball team (comprising students) over a team of Americans from the Yokohama Athletic Club in 1896 with a stirring 29–4 victory reflected the strong links made between sport and war, as is evident in the yearly report of the club claiming that, '[t]he aggressive character of our national spirit is a well-established fact, demonstrated first in the Sino-Japanese War and now by our great victories in baseball' (Roden 1980, 530). Encouraged by military victories over China (1895), Russia (1905) and the annexation of Korea in 1910 the ideals of *bushido* came to be manifested in nationalistic and militaristic approaches to the practice of sport in schools and universities. Under these conditions sport enjoyed growth throughout schools and universities, with the national football team earning a shock win over

Sweden in its first Olympics (Nogawa and Maeda 1999). A short period of prosperity following the end of World War I saw a shift toward Western liberalism reflected in liberal approaches to education such as that of American educational philosopher, John Dewey. During this period athleticism in Japan 'reached its zenith' (Abe et al. 1990).

Japan's desire for colonies and the resources that could provide for an expanding economy and an increasingly aggressive militarism from the late 1920s, led to the development of anti-Western sentiment. This saw English terms in sport replaced by Japanese terms and the practice of all sports increasingly guided by the practices and values of the martial arts in a process of the 'Japanization' of Western team sports (Inoue 1997). From the late 1920s military values promoted through the martial arts shaped increasingly demanding training in team sports with martial arts incorporated into the national school curriculum. Within schools the teaching of team sports was modelled on *budo* so that they could better embody 'Japanese spirit'. Over this period, Western team sports suffered a decline in popularity and were radically transformed to promote what were seen as the unique qualities of the Japanese spirit, captured in the notion of *Yamato damashi*. Team sports such as baseball and rugby in universities and schools were characterized by the promotion of a 'traditional' militaristic form of masculinity manifested in severe hierarchical disciplinary practices, hazing and extreme training regimes that often resulted in death (Rholen 1983).

From the 1930s, as Japan headed toward war, the practice and meaning of team sport was radically changed to promote what were seen as the unique qualities of the Japanese that would allow them to overcome the military and industrial might of America (Roden 1980). Central to this was the promotion of cultural imperatives associated with the pre-Meiji samurai classes such as *Yamato damashi* and the cultural concept of *seishin ryoku* (spiritual strength) seen to be developed through the rigours of hard training, in sports such as baseball and rugby in particular, which transformed their practice and meaning. The practice and meaning of sport changed radically as it became a vehicle for the promotion of traditional Japanese military values. The similarities of rugby with warfare made it particularly appealing to the militarists (Light 2000a). During this period the practice of team sports was modelled upon the martial arts (*budo*) (Abe et al. 1990). The practice of *budo* rose to prominence as a means of instilling a martial spirit and of promoting a belief in the unique qualities of the Japanese that would enable them to overcome the industrial and military superiority of the USA and its allies. In 1943 English terms were banned in baseball and as the war intensified all sport was abandoned (Hirai 2001).

The post-Pacific War period (1945–93)

The practice of sport was severely curtailed by defeat in the Pacific War, the destruction of Japan and the decimation of its population of young men. There was, though, recognition by the occupation forces of the need to rebuild Japan within the context of increasing concern with Russian power in the region. Rebuilding the education system included paying critical attention to the practice of sport in schools and universities. The ways in which the notion of *seishin ryoku* had been used in school sport by the militarists leading up to war, led to a restructuring of the ways in which sport was organized and practised in schools. Based upon the US club system this was aimed at fostering democratic ideals (Passin 1980; Rholen 1983). The Supreme Commander for Allied Powers' (SCAP) revision of education initially forbade the teaching of *budo* as it was seen to develop militaristic 'martial spirit' and determined that physical training of any kind, including sport, should not be associated with the idea of *seishin kyoiku* (Passin 1980). Sports such as baseball (1946) and rugby (1945) were recommenced soon after the finish of the war, but the teaching of martial arts in schools was banned by the occupation forces until 1948.

Inoue (1997) argues that the post-war period saw the reversing of the relationship between *budo* and the practice of sport that developed over the decades leading up to the Pacific War. In response to growing concern with the ways in which Western culture contradicted valued Japanese culture at the end of the 18th century the Meiji leaders strove to embed adopted Western technology and institutional models with Japanese values. Within this context the samurai arts of war and the code of *bushido* were restructured into martial arts (*budo*) as we know them today. From its introduction into schools, *budo* and the traditional values it embodied came to increasingly shape the practice and cultural meanings of imported Western sport. Following defeat in the Pacific War and beginning with the restructuring of sport in schools the practice of *budo* was shaped by the model of competitive sport (Kusaka 2006). Although still linked to the idea of traditional samurai values, the practice of *budo* and sport in post-war Japan sought to remove the severe training driven by the notion of *seishin kyoiku* of pre-war Japan.

Baseball had a professional league from 1936, recommenced from 1946, and grew rapidly enough during the post-war period for it to be split into two separate national leagues. In 1950 the Japan Baseball League was divided into the Central League and the Pacific League, with head-to-head games between the winners of both leagues. With the exception of baseball, team sports had traditionally been restricted to schools and universities. In the post-war period other team sports began to move beyond the confines of the education system when, in 1945, Kobe Steel formed the first company rugby team in Japan (JRFA 1998). Using rugby as a form of exercise for promoting the health of employees and developing identity with the company, other companies followed suit and set up company rugby teams, leading to the staging of the inaugural national championships in 1949, only four years after the end of the war. The publicity provided by media coverage of rugby matches and the symbolism attached to success in rugby games made fielding rugby teams an even more attractive proposition for Japanese companies (Light 2000a).

Despite the growth in company rugby during the post-war period, university rugby has always attracted more attention from the general public and the media. Much of this is due to patterns of identification with sports teams in Japan. Up until the introduction of the J. League (football) in 1993, all Japanese sports teams had been based on educational institutions or on companies and not on location or region. Fans of sports teams were thus either students or had graduated from the school or university, or were employees of the company. As Nakane (1970) explains in her seminal book on Japanese society, the Japanese have traditionally identified more strongly with their schools and companies than with their local region. The large numbers of people who pass through schools and universities over time means that the pool of rugby fans for university teams is far bigger than that for company teams and university games have historically drawn bigger crowds. In addition to this larger pool of fans, university rugby is linked more closely with the historical ideal of sport as a means of developing, expressing and confirming particular valued cultural ideals (Light 1999a). Matches between famous universities such as Waseda, Meiji and Keio are saturated with cultural meaning and traditionally drew enormous crowds. The biggest crowd of the year in Japanese rugby is for the annual match held between traditional rivals, Meiji and Waseda within days of the annual Oxford and

Cambridge match in England. Attendances of 60,000 (a full house) surpass figures for any company game or game between the national team and international opposition. Indeed, international matches involving the national team tend not to draw large crowds. The interest shown in the traditional Meiji and Waseda match extends beyond regular followers of rugby to those who know little about rugby yet recognize the cultural symbolism attached to the contests. The interest in high school sport means that events such as the national baseball championships at Koushien, in particular, are highlights of the annual sporting calendar in Japan; the national high school rugby championships at Hanazono and the national schools football championships also attract considerable attention (Moeran 1986; Light 2000b).

The 1964 Olympic Games was the biggest and most significant sporting event held in Japan between 1945 and 1993, marking its sporting progress and growing competitiveness at an international level and its emergence as a growing economic power. Japan was granted the right to host the 1940 summer Olympics by the International Olympic Committee (IOC), but lost it when it invaded Manchuria, with the honour of hosting the games being passed onto Helsinki. Japan was awarded the rights to host the 1964 Olympics in 1959, which were the first to be held in a non-Western nation. Japan had great success in the Tokyo Games, placing third in the medal count behind the USA and the Soviet Union, and stimulating great public pride in the efforts of Japanese athletes. As popular sports in Japan, judo and volleyball were introduced as medal sports with Japan winning three gold medals in judo. Although it had previously been a sport in the games during the early 20th century, Japan's national sport of baseball was introduced as a demonstration sport that became a medal event in the 1992 Barcelona Games. The Games played a very important role in the development of sport in Japan during a period over which it began its development as a powerful economy.

Sport in contemporary Japan (1993–2008)

Over the post-Pacific War period the practice of sport moved beyond the confines of schools and universities into the corporate sector, but up until the early 1990s access to sport was restricted to educational and corporate institutions. The launch of the professional football league, the J. League, in 1993 marked what could be argued was profound change in the practice, organization and meaning of sport in Japan. The introduction and subsequent success of the J. League provided a new model for sport in Japan arising from the economic, cultural and social impact of the globalization of sport in Japan. The conditions that facilitated the coming of the J. League and its success heralded significant changes in Japanese sport that are visible in other sports such as sumo, swimming, tennis and rugby (Horne 1998; Light and Yasaki 2002; Light, Hirai and Ebishima 2008). One year after the national football team's impressive performance at the 1964 Tokyo Olympics, the Japan Soccer League (JSL) was introduced and, as the first amateur sports league in Japan, provided a model for other amateur sports, including volleyball, basketball and ice-hockey (Nogawa and Maeda 1999). The national team won a bronze medal at the 1968 Mexico Olympics, leading to a period of popularity for football, but by the mid-1980s public interest was waning with average crowd numbers of only 7,000 (Nogawa and Maeda 1999). In 1989 the JSL sought to reinvigorate the organization by setting up an action committee that included representation from four major advertising companies. In the following year the Japan Football Association (JFA) accepted its recommendations to set up a fully professional league. Although the JSL had been an innovation in 1965, it still followed the established pattern of having clubs based in, funded by and bearing the names of large corporations. With baseball easily *the* national sport in Japan and so dominant, the JFA faced a difficult task in establishing football as a major sport. After extensive research, the JFA decided to use the German model to make a radical change in direction in the organization and promotion of sport in Japan. This involved setting up clubs based upon location and the targeting of regions outside the major urban centres such as Tokyo and Osaka (Light and Yasaki 2002). The JFA used the JSL teams as the basis for the J. League, seeking to maintain the financial support of the parent companies but removing the company name from the name of the team. This was not readily accepted by most companies and has been a source of ongoing tension between the JFA and some clubs.

The JFA also sought the support of local governments and local businesses, not only for financing teams but also as part of its strategy of building strong local identity with teams, and this was particularly well received in regional centres outside the major cities. For example, the Sumitomo JSL team based in Kashima, the regional capital of Ibaraki prefecture, was renamed the Kashima Antlers (see Light and Yasaki 2004 for a detailed case study on this club). The J. League has been an outstanding success, with massive growth in crowds over its first few years. As early as 1994 popular teams were attracting unheard-of crowds for football games with Verdy Kawasaki (now known as Tokyo Verdy 1969) enjoying average attendances of 30,000, and the J. League looked like challenging baseball as Japan's major sport. Light and Yasaki (2003) demonstrate through an analysis of how different J. League clubs have fared in terms of attendances after dropping the parent company name and promoting local identity, how developing local or regional identity has been central to the success of the J. League. While baseball is still the major sport in Japan, football offers an alternative and is far more popular with younger Japanese. Baseball in Japan is a traditional, conservative sport but football is promoted and marketed as a fresh new sport or, as Watts (1998) suggests, as *shinhatsubai,* a trendy new product. Indeed, contemporary football is organized and practised more like a commercial commodity rather than a vehicle for education and the reproduction of hegemonic culture. These changes extend down to youth sport and have significant implications for the practice of youth sport in general. Up until 1993 young people and children could only play football at school, but the JFA's promotion of J. League teams within local regions and communities has extended to setting up junior and youth leagues. Indeed, its mission clearly states its goal of addressing the exclusive nature of sport confined to schools by providing access to football (and other sports) to all children and young people with a focus on the 'golden age' of 7–12 years of age (Light and Yasaki 2003). Coaching knowledge developed within the senior teams is used to develop the younger leagues, each of which competes in competitions up to national level with school and non-school competitions running in parallel.

The success of the national team and the joint hosting of the 2002 FIFA World Cup by Japan and South Korea have assisted the growth of football in Japan as a spectator sport. Japan now has a well-regarded and successful sports team competing in the most popular game in the world and has generated a sense of national pride and identity with it that other sports have not been able to achieve. This has assisted Japanese football in 'opening up' Japanese sport to 'outside' ideas on aspects of sport, ranging from coaching methods to its marketing and professionalization, which have an impact down to 'grass roots' sport for children and youth. While this radical new model of sport provided by the J. League is the most successful and visible sport to adopt this approach, it forms part of a broader change in sport in Japan and the growing impact of globalization on it. Indeed, the tension between historical traditions of sport in Japan and the forces of sport's globalization have attracted considerable interest over the past decade (for example, see Chiba, Ebihama and Morino 2001; Hirai 2005; Maguire and Nakayama 2006). These changes are occurring at both the elite level and in youth sport, and are contextualized within major economic and social change. The adoption of what can be seen as 'global' practices in coaching, developing the game and ways of playing, challenge the traditional model of sport in schools and its role as a vehicle for social, cultural and moral education. Over the past 15 years the Ministry of Education, Culture, Sports, Science and Technology (*Mobushou*) and powerful elements of the Japanese corporate community have pushed for sport to move beyond schools in order to produce more champions on the world stage and develop the commercial aspects of sport in Japan. This is also one of the objectives of the J. League as outlined in its mission statement. Bodies governing school sport have rigorously opposed this, but change is taking place with growth in community-based and commercial clubs in sports such as swimming providing tangible results in terms of Japan's international performance. As Horne (1998) has noted in regard to the J. League, this has occurred within a climate of economic change from a production-based economy to a consumption-based economy and change in the role of sport to one of assisting in the accumulation of capital through corporate sport.

Over the past 15 years or so, sport's globalization has impacted upon the practice, organization and promotion of sports beyond football, but few have profited from it as has football. Indeed, the effect of globalization in sport has generally been problematic for sport that has developed in relative isolation from the rest of the world. Rugby has been one of the 'casualties' of football's rise in Japan, with numbers of participants in schools decreasing over the past decade. Despite being the powerhouse of Asian rugby, the national team is uncompetitive at an international level and does not generate significant interest at home. The Japan Rugby Football Association (JRFA) has responded to this crisis much like the JFA did, by reorganizing rugby in a new format designed to revitalize it, but with far less success. It also had to accommodate the professionalization of rugby from 1995 within the context of a sport that championed amateurism and did not produce its first professional contract until 2001 (Light, Hirai and Ebishima 2008). This restructuring of the company league into the Top 14 has been superficial and relatively ineffective with attendances at Top 14 games averaging only 5,000. Foreign players and coaches have increasingly featured in *shakaijin* (company) rugby and university rugby and have even had some impact upon high school rugby. This opening up of Japanese rugby has upset the traditional rituals and historic rivalries of post-war Japanese rugby, yet has failed to either significantly raise the international standing of the national team or to produce an exciting commercial product like the J. League (Light, Hirai and Ebishima 2008). Although it is also a very conservative sport, baseball has fared much better than rugby due to its ability to rest upon a long history as the unchallenged national sport. The success of the J. League did, though, contribute toward financial hardship in baseball and to some significant changes it is organization. The success of the J. League reduced average attendances at baseball games and led to some teams attempting to emulate the strategies of the J. League by de-emphasizing corporate ownership and, in some cases, by relocating teams from urban centres to regional Japan. A decline in profits caused by the popularity of the J. League led to baseball's first strike for 70 years in 2004. The brief two-day strike by players was in response to plans to merge two teams to increase profits. Negotiations between management and the players led to a decision not to go ahead with the merger and to initiate a range of strategies aimed at making baseball more appealing and entertaining.

Global forces in sport have increased the flow of athletes across increasingly porous national borders and this is having a very significant impact upon sport in Japan (Hirai 2005; Chiba et. al 2001). Recent movement of Japanese baseball stars to the Major League in the USA has created some problems for domestic baseball. In post-war Japan there has been a continual stream of ball players from the USA playing in Japan (for example, see Whiting 1990). However, it has only been over the past decade or so that the best Japanese players have succeeded in the US Major League, beginning with pitcher Hideo Nomo transferring from the Kintetsu Buffaloes to the L.A. Dodgers in 1995 (for a detailed account, see Hirai 2001). Nomo was Rookie of the Year in 1995, retired in 2008, and his success led to a wave of Japanese players moving to the Major League, with Daisuke Matsuzuka earning a US$ 52 million six-year contract with the Boston Red Sox in 2006 and the Red Sox paying a $51.1 million transfer fee to the Seibu Lions. The growing number of Japanese players being signed up by Major League teams brings great pride to Japanese baseball fans, but it has had a negative effect on the domestic leagues by robbing them of their most marketable players. This led to declining interest by Japanese viewers in the domestic product and increased interest in the performances of Japanese stars and their teams in the Major League. Conversely, sumo has suffered a downturn in popularity due to the rising numbers of foreign wrestlers in a sport that has traditionally been seen to embody the unique spirit of the Japanese. This has been exacerbated by a recent series of scandals involving sumo wrestlers (*sumodori*), such the failure of Mongolian Grand Champion Aashoryu to declare the equivalent of $1 million (Australian) in pre-tax earnings in 2007.

Conclusion

With the exception of sumo, the rationalized and regulated practice of sport as we know it today finds its beginnings in Japan in the late 19th century, a period of immense social, cultural and economic change. During this period sport played a significant role in the rapid development of modern Japan as an important aspect of the new mass education system required for Japan to catch up to the West. Due to concern with social cohesion and stability during a period of such massive change, the Meiji leaders promoted a hegemonic common culture as *the* culture of all Japanese with sport offering an ideal vehicle for its dissemination throughout the education system. With baseball the exception, sport had been restricted to educational institutions from the late 19th century to the post-Pacific War period. In these settings its practice and cultural meanings were shaped by larger changing social and political conditions involving ongoing tension between imported Western ideals and culture embedded in the practice of sport (and team games in particular) and 'traditional' Japanese values as embedded in the practice of *budo* martial arts.

During the post-Pacific War period sport moved beyond educational institutions to be taken up in the corporate sector. Initially it was used to improve employee health and promote identification with the company while maintaining its role as a vehicle for social and cultural education. Later, larger companies with successful sports teams increasingly used it as a valuable means of advertising, though baseball had performed this function from the mid 1930s. This added a commercial dimension to the use of sport in Japan alongside its historical function as an educational medium for the reproduction of dominant culture that developed slowly as Japan's economic might grew from the 1960s.

Despite Japan's growing engagement in international sport from its hosting of the 1964 Olympics in Tokyo, it remained relatively isolated from the influence of international developments. Indeed, despite its industrial and economic development over the past half century, Japan has maintained a relatively culturally insulated approach that can be linked historically to its two centuries of self-imposed isolation in the early 17th century. To a degree, this has insulated Japanese sport from many global developments, but the initiation of the J. League in 1993 constitutes a major change in direction for sport in Japan, heralding changes in all sports played at all levels from youth sport to sport at the most elite international level.

The period from 1993 onward marks the beginning of a period of significant change in the practice, organization, meaning and promotion of sport in Japan at the end of over a century of relative isolation from the outside world of sport. This has significant implications for all sports practised in Japan, from those that make up physical education lessons in primary schools to high-profile professional sports such as baseball, football, sumo, swimming, and track and field. With an economy that has flattened out over the past two decades and the rising economic and military might of the People's Republic of China in a rapidly globalizing world, Japan is faced with a range of challenges to which it must respond. Within these conditions the practice and meaning of all sports in Japan will likely continue to undergo significant change.

References

Abe, I.Y. Kiyohara and K. Nakajima, 'Sport and Physical Education under Fascistization in Japan', *Bulletin for Health and Sport Sciences*, Tsukuba University, 13, 1990, 28.

Anzu, M., *Shinto to Nihonjin* [Shinto and the Japanese] (Tokyo: Kodansha International, 1986).

Bourdieu, P., 'Sport and Social Class', *Social Science Information* 12 (6), 1978, 819–40.

Chiba, M., D. Ebihama and S. Morino, 'Globalization, Naturalization and Identity', *International Review for the Sociology of Sport* 36 (2), 2001, 203–21.

Cuyler, P.L., *Sumo: From Rite to Sport* (Tokyo: John Wetherhill, 1985).

Guttman, A. and L. Thompson, *Japanese Sports* (Honolulu: University of Hawaii Press, 2001).

Hikoyama, K., *Sumo, Japanese Wrestling*, Vol. 34 (Japan Tourist Bureau, 1940), 12.

Hirai, H., 'Globalising Sports', in S. Alomes, ed., *Islands in the Stream: Australia and Japan Face Globalisation* (Melbourne: Maribymong Press, 2005), 79–90.

——'Hideo Nomu: Pioneer or Defector?', in D. L. Andrews and S. J. Jackson, eds, *Sport Stars: The Cultural Politics of Sporting Celebrity* (London and New York: Routledge, 2001), 187–200.

Horne, J., 'The Politics of Sport and Leisure in Japan', *International Review for the Sociology of Sport* 33 (2), 1998, 171–82.

Ikeguchi, Y., *Kindai no rugubi hyaku nen kan* [A Hundred Years of Modern Rugby] (Tokyo: Baseball Magazine Company, 1981).

Inoue, 'Sports and the Martial Arts in the Making of Modern Japan', paper presented to the *International Conference for the Sociology of Sport*, Japan Society for the Sociology of Sport, Kyoto, 27–29 March 1997, 2.

Japan Rugby Football Association (JRFA), *Dai 50 kai zenkoku shakaijin ragubi futoboru taikai* [50th National Corporate Rugby Championships] (1998).

Kojiki, *Records of Ancient Matters*, 712 AD.

——*Nihon shoki nihonji*, Chronicles of Japan, 720 AD.

——*Manyoshu*, anthology of poetry, eighth century.

Kuhaulua, J., *Takamiyama – The World of Sumo* (Tokyo: Kodansha International, 1973).

Kusaka, Y., 'The Emergence and Development of School Sport', in J.A. Maguire and M. Nakayama, eds, *Japan, Sport and Society: Tradition and Changes in a Globalizing World* (London and New York: Routledge, 2006), 19–34.

Light, R., 'Sport and the Construction of Masculinity in the Japanese Education System', in K. Louie and M. Low, eds, *Asian Masculinities* (London: Routledge Curzon, 2003), 100–17.

Light, R., 'A Century of Japanese Rugby and Masculinity: Continuity and Change', *Sporting Traditions* 16 (2), 2000a, 87–104.

——'From the Profane to the Sacred: Culture and Pre-game Ritual in Japanese High School Rugby', *International Review for the Sociology of Sport* 35 (4), 2000b, 451–65.

——'Learning to Be a "Rugger Man": High School Rugby and Media Constructions of Masculinity in Japan', *Football Studies* 2 (1), 1999a, 74–89.

——'Regimes of Training and the Construction of Masculinity in Japanese University Rugby', *International Sports Studies* 21 (2), 1999b, 39–54.

Light, R., H. Hirai and H. Ebishima, 'Professionalism and Tensions in Japanese Rugby', in G. Ryan, ed., *The Changing Face of Rugby: The Union Game and Professionalism since 1995* (Cambridge, UK: Cambridge Scholars Press, 2008), 147–64.

Light, R and L. Kinnaird, 'Appeasing the Gods: Sumo, Shinto and "True" Japanese Spirit', in T. Magdalinski and T. Chandler, eds, *With God on Their Side: Sport in the Service of Religion* (London: Routledge, 2002), 39–159.

Light, R. and W. Yasaki, 'Winds of Change for Youth and Children's Sport in Japan? A Case Study of the Kashima Antler's Soccer Development Program', *Asian Journal of Exercise and Sport Science* 1 (1), 2004, 63–74.

——'Breaking the Mould: Community, Education and the Development of Professional Soccer in Japan', *Football Studies* 6 (1), 2003, 37–50.

——'J. League Soccer and the Rekindling of Regional Identity in Japan', *Sporting Traditions* 18 (2), 2002, 31–45.

Maguire, J. A. and M. Nakayama, eds, *Japan, Sport and Society: Tradition and Change in a Globalizing World* (London and New York: Routledge, 2006).

Mangan, J. A., *Athleticism in the Victorian and Edwardian Public School* (Cambridge: Cambridge University Press, 1981).

Manzenreiter, W. and J. Horne, *Football Goes East: Business, Culture and the People's Game in China, Japan and Korea* (London: Routledge, 2004).

McDonald, B. and C. Hallinan, 'Seishin Habitus: Spiritual Capital and Japanese Rowing', *International Review for the Sociology of Sport* 40 (2), 2005, 187–200.

Moeran, B., 'Individual, Group and Seishin: Japan's Internal Cultural Debate', in T. Lebra and W. Lebra, eds, *Japanese Culture and Behavior* (Honolulu: University of Hawaii Press, 1986), 62–79.

Nakane, C., *Japanese Society* (Tokyo: Tuttle, 1970).

Nogawa, H. and H. Maeda, 'The Japanese Dream: Soccer Culture towards the New Millennium', in R. Giulianotti and G. Arstrong, eds, *Football Cultures and Identities* (London: Macmillan, 1999), 223–33.

Passin, H., *Society and Education in Japan* (Tokyo: Kodansha, 1980).

Rholen, T., *Japanese High Schools* (Berkley, CA: University of California Press, 1983).

Roden, D., 'Baseball and the Quest for National Identity in Meiji Japan', *The American Historical Review* 85:1, 1980, 511–24.

Sansom, G.B., *The Western World and Japan* (London: Knopf, 1962).

Sydney Morning Herald, 'Big Trouble', *Sydney Morning Herald*, 28 August 2007, 37.

Watts, J., 'Soccer Shihatsubai: What Are the Japanese Consumers Making of the J. League?', in D.P. Martinez, ed., *The Worlds of Japanese Popular Culture: Gender, Shifting Boundaries and Global Cultures* (Cambridge: Cambridge University Press, 1998), 181–201.

Whiting, R., *You Gotta Have Wa* (New York: Vintage Books, 1990).

30 Mexico and Central America

Richard V. McGehee

The area described in this chapter encompasses the nations between the USA to the north and Colombia to the south. Mexico is by far the largest and most populous of these countries. It is bounded to the north by the USA and to the south by the narrow band of Central America, from Guatemala and Belize, through Honduras and El Salvador, Nicaragua, Costa Rica and Panama. The entire region was home to a variety of indigenous people when Spanish conquerors arrived in the early 16th century, first in Mexico and then extending their dominion southward over the remainder of the region. The modern nations were created when they became independent of Spain in 1821. Guatemala, El Salvador, Honduras, Nicaragua and Costa Rica were the original Central American republics. Panama was first part of Colombia, only obtaining its independence in 1903, and Belize was a British territory (called British Honduras) between the late 17th century and its independence in 1981, although it was claimed by Guatemala (as one of the political subdivisions of the nation, with the name Belice) during that period. Foreign interference, especially by the USA (and also France and Mexico), in the internal affairs of most of these nations has been common. US and European business interests, residence of foreign business representatives in each nation, and attendance by Mexicans and Central Americans in overseas schools and colleges, have been prominent factors in the social and cultural development of these countries, especially as regards early modern sport activities.

The principal 'racial' categories existing in the region in the past and still present today include indigenous people; *mestizos* (those who are a mixture of Spanish and indigenous, and all their subsequent combinations); those considering themselves to be of pure European stock (*criollos blancos*); and those of African origin, who emigrated long ago from the Caribbean islands. A distinct group, identifiable mainly in Belize and the Caribbean coastal areas of Guatemala, Honduras and Nicaragua, are the *Garífunas*, a mixture of African and indigenous Caribs, who also migrated from Caribbean islands to the mainland and Honduras' offshore islands.

Indigenous people of the region were variously exterminated, worked to death, isolated, or incorporated in one form or other into the life established by the Spanish conquerors. Some of them retained languages, religions and customs of their ancestors (especially in Mexico and Guatemala). At the other extreme, they became mixed with the Spaniards, creating a 'new race' referred to as *mestizo*, forming the most numerous class of society, speaking Spanish and adopting modern cultural elements such as sport. Indigenous people of Mexico and Guatemala tend to consider themselves independent from the modern nations where they live.

With the exception of studies of indigenous sport by anthropologists, there has been very little sports history research completed related to Mexico and Central America. There are a few articles on special topics specific to Mexico, Guatemala, Nicaragua and

Costa Rica, and some books and articles on sport in Latin America in general contain material about Mexico and Central America. Authors of research on sport in the region are mainly foreigners; within the region sports historians tend to be journalists rather than academics, and their work largely involves descriptions of athletes, coaches and matches, rather than sociological and political aspects of sport. Much of their writing is largely anecdotal and rarely includes references that can aid an academic researcher. Most existing historical studies have focused on descriptions of general development of sport in a country, sport's relation with society, government and nationalism, or the birth and development of a particular series of competitions. Two bibliographies compiled by Joseph Arbena for sport in Latin America reference many materials related to Mexico and Central America, arranged by period and by country of interest.[1]

Very little exists in the way of secondary sources for sports history in Mexico and Central America. Primary sources of historical information in the region are mainly newspapers. *Hemerotecas* (periodical collections) and libraries in Mexico and Central America contain newspapers dating from the late 19th century, with collections being less complete with increasing age. Older newspapers are in relatively good condition in Mexico, Guatemala and Costa Rica, but in Nicaragua they have been exposed to humidity and high temperatures and many have decomposed to the point of being unusable. The principal newspapers in Mexico City included *El Universal*, *Excélsior* and *El Demócrata*. In Guatemala City it was *Diario de Centro-America*; in Managua there were *El Comercio* and several others. Sport-related items appeared in newspapers in the late 1890s and greatly increased in number and volume in the early 20th century. At first, there was no separate section for sport news; sport could be found in any part of the paper, including the front page. Sport illustrations began to appear around 1919 in *El Diario de Centro-America*, first in the form of drawings. At about the same time photographs began to be used; they generally showed athletes, teams and spectators, rather than play action.

By the mid-20th century *El Universal* and *Excélsior* were still the dominant newspapers in Mexico, but in Guatemala *El Imparcial* was the leader, and in Managua it was *La Prensa*. Additionally, during the second half of the century specialized sport dailies (*La Afición*, *Esto* and *Ovaciones*) existed in Mexico.

As early as the late 1890s, some specialized sport magazines existed, and magazines of more general content carried some sport-related articles and photographs. The general magazines were aimed at the upper levels of society. Magazines and newspapers are held by libraries in separate collections, the *hemerotecas*. In Managua, Nicaragua's *Hemeroteca Nacional* has its own building, located away from the national library. The principal *hemerotecas* in Mexico City are located at the National Library, on the campus of the Universidad Nacional Autónoma de México, the Biblioteca de México and the Biblioteca Miguel Lerdo de Tejada.

The Archivo General de la Nación in Mexico City contains early documents related to sport and sport personages. Other specialized or private archives, such as those of the Ministry of Education and the Archivos Plutarco Elías Calles y Fernando Torreblanca in Mexico City, and the Archivo General de Centroamérica and the Biblioteca César Brañas in Guatemala City also contain some sport- and physical education-related items. The national Olympic committees of Guatemala and Mexico hold some historical materials.

Indigenous and colonial sport

The best-known athletic activity of the indigenous people of the region (although some people question its status as 'sport') is the Mesoamerican ball game. Ball courts have been found from central Mexico to El Salvador and western Honduras (Copán), and an extensive literature exists relative to this 'game'. Running was another indigenous activity, although known examples generally had religious overtones (the *Tarahumara* kickball race of northern Mexico), or involved work (such as bringing fresh fish from the Gulf of Mexico for dinner tables of the Aztec nobility in *Tenochtitlán*). The ball game known as *pelota mixteca*, from the state of Oaxaca, Mexico – and still played there – resembles a European medieval sport considered to be a precursor of tennis. Indigenous people of Mexico performed a variety of acrobatic feats, which still existed at the time of the Spanish conquest. Mexicans also played 'board games', such as *patolli*, which involved casting dice, beans, or stones. In another Mexican game players tried to climb a greased pole to win the prizes located on top of the pole. This activity still existed in patron saint festivals of 20th-century Nicaragua. In the Mexican indigenous game of *los voladores* (the flyers), four participants climbed to the top of a tall pole; tied to ropes coiled around the pole, they leaped from the top and spun around the pole, flying outward from it, until touching the ground.[2]

Mexico's Federación Mexicana de Juegos y Deportes Autóctonos y Tradicionales (Federation of Indigenous and Traditional Games and Sports) seeks to investigate and preserve early aspects of the nation's sports history. Currently, a Mexican graduate student in the doctoral programme in history of physical education and sport in the University of Tsukuba (Japan) is investigating Mexican indigenous sport as well as the present geographic distribution of Mexico's indigenous populations and their traditional games.[3]

The earliest form of ball game (*juego de la pelota*) existed in the Gulf Coast and inland areas of south-central Mexico at least 2,300 years ago. It involved striking a rubber ball with hands and perhaps hips and arms. Decapitation of losing players was a feature of the game, which gradually took on religious significance. Modifications of the game with time and geography included using balls of other materials, kicking the ball and striking it with sticks, and variations in the playing area, which finally took on the shape of a capital letter I and used position markers as well as large vertical circular goals in some courts. Information about the game comes from ceramic figures, low-relief sculptures, wall paintings, and remnants of markers, rings and the courts themselves.

Colonial sporting activity included bullfighting, cockfighting and horse-races. All of these activities continue to the present time in Mexico, but are not as widespread in Central America. The *Plaza México* in Mexico City is the largest bullfighting arena in the world. Many of the *toreros* (bullfighters) are, and were in the past, Spanish, but Mexico and some other Latin American countries also produce bullfighters. Cockfighting is common at state fairs in Mexico. Bullfighting in Nicaragua is very different from the traditional form of the activity. It features a rider on the bull and multiple *toreros*, and the bull is not injured.

In Mexico, *charro* activities (*charrería* or *jaripeo*) existed since the earliest colonial period. They have prospered to the present and now include horsemanship by men and women (the women's skilled and elegant riding event is called *escaramuza*) and men's roping, wild horse riding, and upending bulls from horseback by jerking their tails sideways. Mexico City's Museum of Charrería contains exhibits and text illustrating *charro* history from the early 1500s, when the skills were developed for practical ranch work, through the disappearance of the great *haciendas* after the Mexican Revolution, and the emergence of *charrería* as sport.[4]

Another activity of the entire region that extended from the colonies into the 20th century, is the *carrera de cintas* (ribbon race). It bears considerable resemblance to tilting at rings and involves men on horseback (or bicycles or motorcycles) riding fast toward a transverse rope from which are suspended small rings. The rider tries to insert a small rod or stick into a ring and tear it away from its supporting ribbon. After multiple passes, the winner is the rider who has speared the most rings. Each rider receives a handmade sash from the young woman whose name is found in the ring, and the overall winner gets to select the queen for the evening ball that follows the *carrera de cintas*.

Beginnings of modern sport: late 19th and early 20th centuries

Modern sport began to develop in Mexico and Central America in the mid-to-late 19th century. The first practitioners were mainly socially elite Hispanics and foreigners, especially from the USA and Great Britain. Elite sport and social clubs, such as the Reforma Athletic Club (1894), *Deportivo Chapultepec*, *Club Deportivo Internacional* and *Real España* in Mexico; the Guarda Viejo Tennis Club (1895), *Club Deportivo y Social Hércules* (1909) and Guatemala Lawn Tennis Club (1916) of Guatemala City; the *Club Atlético de Managua* (Nicaragua); and the *Sociedad Gimnástica Española* of San José, Costa Rica, were the sites of most athletic activity, and early competitions tended to be within and between clubs of similar social prestige. Mexico City's Country Club building was inaugurated in 1907; the Country Club was a leader in golf and offered polo and other elite sport activities.

By the second and third decades of the 20th century, many sports had spread to a much wider spectrum of social levels and, eventually, competition became indiscriminate among the different categories of clubs and social status of individuals. The *Asociación Cristiana de Jóvenes* (YMCA) was a force in the introduction and promotion of sport, especially in Mexico, where several of its athletic directors had attended the association's college in Springfield, MA. The YMCA's new building in Mexico City was inaugurated in 1910. Sport activity also became more available for women, with basketball being the most widespread team sport. Women also played tennis and golf, and even gymnastics and track (the latter two accomplished at first while wearing corsets and long skirts).[5]

20th-century developments

Development of Western sports in Mexico and Central America

For Mexico and most of Central America, soccer (football) has been the most important participatory and spectator sport for many years. The first soccer club in Mexico was established by British miners in Pachuca in 1900, while other Britons introduced the sport in Orizaba, Mexico City and other locations soon afterwards, and foreigners dominated the sport until 1912. Later, Mexicans participated fully and the first professional teams and their youth 'farm' teams were established. Boys attending private schools and the elite National Preparatory School in Mexico City were introduced to soccer and a variety of other imported spots in the 1910s and 1920s.

Most countries of the region developed amateur and professional soccer leagues in the early years of the century and also played internationally. Young Guatemalans who had discovered soccer while studying in England introduced the sport in their country in 1902. Several clubs were established over the next few years and championships (one called the Central American Cup) were soon being contested. Guatemala's first national selection was formed in 1921 to compete in the first Central American Games. Costa

Rica also had soccer clubs as early as 1904, with the Catholic Church being a supporter of the sport. *Club Sport La Libertad* was founded in San José in 1905 and produced many great teams, which won national and international tournaments. Today, boys all over the region grow up playing soccer on any available space in cities and countryside, and amateur play continues well into middle age for many men. Immigrants from the region have carried their interest in the sport into their cities of residence in the USA. However, the sport is still not played widely by women.[6]

In contrast with the rest of the region, baseball is by far the dominant sport in Nicaragua. It was introduced into the country in the early 1890s by young men who had studied in the USA, and it sprung into prominence about the same time on the Caribbean coast and in the cities of the west, such as Managua, Granada, Masaya and León. Baseball is also very important in Mexico and Panama. Mexico has supported professional baseball leagues, generally playing winter ball but at times competing with Major League Baseball in the summertime. Mexico, Nicaragua and Panama have all supplied players to the US major leagues, outstanding examples being pitchers Fernando Valenzuela (Mexico) and Denis Martínez (Nicaragua). Baseball already existed in Mexico in the 1890s and during the early years of the 20th century, baseball was Mexico's 'king of sports'. Along with jai alai, for a while it was the only professional sport. Around 1902 both baseball and cricket were being played in Costa Rica's Caribbean port town of Limón by foreigners including West Indian blacks; it was probably introduced in the western cities about the same time by young men who had studied in the USA.[7]

Although some schools (for example, in Costa Rica) were playing basketball as early as 1906, the sport did not take hold in the region until the early 1920s, and in some areas it was first played mainly by women. Some men (for example, in Nicaragua) thought the sport to be too feminine for them. In Mexico the YMCA was a promoter of basketball, but it was also played by men and women in schools and sport clubs. Managua and other Nicaraguan cities had teams consisting of girls from the highest social circles. Guatemala and El Salvador also had women's teams early in the decade.[8]

The Mexican YMCA was an early promoter of track and field meets, and throughout the region track and field events were prominent in school and club competitions and formed the mainstay of early national and international multi-sport festivals. Events included most of those practised internationally.

Mexico was the leader in early motor sports, with races held for automobiles, buses and motorcycles. The first auto race in Mexico City was held on the Peralvillo horse racetrack in 1903, and in 1909–11 road races were organized between Mexico City and Puebla. By 1914 the Condesa horse racetrack was being used for Mexico City's car races, and in the early 1920s the Chapultepec course was built specifically for motor vehicles. In 1923 women drivers raced cars in Mexico City, each with a man as co-pilot. Newspaper reports showed one driver's wrecked vehicle and a photo of her co-pilot lying in his hospital bed (he later died). Another Mexico City race featured buses carrying the driver and a helper, who had to leap out of the bus and load a bag of sand onboard once each lap. Cycling was popular in many parts of the region as a recreational activity and competitive sport since the 1890s. High society cyclists and their competitions were featured in magazines (such as Jorge Ubico, future long-term dictator of Guatemala, after he won a race as an adolescent). Road races were available to almost any competitor with a bicycle. In Costa Rica long-distance races were held, from the capital city to the Pacific coast. At the turn of the 20th century, Mexico City's horse racetracks (and in the 1920s, the automobile track) were available at times for cycling contests, and Mexican cyclists participated in long road races, for example between Mexico City and Toluca (64 km) and even Guadalajara to Mexico City (596 km).

A variety of other sports already existed in the region in the early years of the 20th century. Sailing, rowing, polo, fencing, golf and tennis were played in all areas, but generally were limited to wealthy social elites. Some clubs were formed around single sports, such as the Guatemala Polo Club, Guatemala Lawn Tennis Club, Guatemala's *Club de Caza, Tiro y Pesca* (hunting, shooting and fishing), and Mexico's Club de Regatas Alemán (German Rowing Club). Equipment and access to facilities for these sports were too expensive for most people. The only facilities for golf and tennis in Mexico and Central America are still private clubs, with the exception of some schools and universities that have tennis courts for the use of their students and faculty members. Shooting was another sport limited to social elites. Shooting competitions, especially pistols and trap/skeet were particularly popular in Mexico and Guatemala, and shooters were among the first international competitors from these two countries.

Competitive swimming and diving appeared in the 1920s. Swimming pools existed in Mexico before 1925; for example there were indoor and outdoor pools at the Mexico City YMCA. Mexico City's Pane swimming pool had a high diving platform and featured competitions in swimming and water polo. In other areas, such as Guatemala and Nicaragua, lakes were used for the first swimming competitions. More recently Mexico has had excellent divers, such as Joaquín Capilla, who won Olympic silver in 1952, and gold and bronze in 1956; Costa Rican swimmers Sylvia and Claudia Poll won Olympic medals (silver and gold, respectively) in 1988 and 1996.

Volleyball was promoted early by the YMCA, and it is played competitively by men and women throughout the region.[9] Badminton has little following but has been included in international multi-sport festivals involving nations of the region. Softball is widely played, with leagues of all competitive levels, for both men and women. Women's softball is the most outstanding high-level sport in Belize. Wrestling and gymnastics activities existed in early 20th century Mexico, but international competition in these sports developed much more recently in the region. Guatemala and El Salvador have had success in men's and women's competitive gymnastics. Although, its classification as sport is suspect, Mexican professional wrestling has been an extremely popular spectacle (both live attendance and on TV) for many years. Men and women participated in roller skating in Mexico, some clubs being all male and others for men and women. In the early years of the 20th century, skating clubs staged artistic exhibitions as well as men's competitive matches of hockey on skates.[10]

Amateur and professional boxing have existed in the region since the early 20th century. Mexicans were enthusiastic supporters of the professional sport as early as the 1910s. Jack Johnson resided in Mexico City in 1919, and his exploits were frequently featured in the newspapers. Other famous foreign boxers, such as Sam Langford, resided in Mexico City or visited around that time, and the arrival of heavyweight champion Jack Dempsey for exhibition matches in 1926 was possibly the most exciting sporting event of the decade. Mexican boxers attracted spectators, and matches of world figures such as Dempsey, Carpentier, Gene Tunney, Luis Angel Firpo and Harry Wills were extensively reported in newspapers and shown in films.[11] More recently, Mexican boxers have been important figures in the lighter weight classes, and Julio César Chávez had an exceptional record of wins, with titles in three weight divisions. Central American countries also produced amateur and professional boxers early in the 20th century, some of the professionals travelling to other countries of the region for fights. Nicaragua was perhaps the leader in Central American boxing and even featured women boxers in a 1926 match in Managua.

Jai Alai is played almost entirely as a Mexico City professional sport, existing as a vehicle for betting. Most of the professional players are Spanish. However, there are other, amateur, forms of *pelota vasca* played by Mexicans. All employ courts resembling jai alai *frontones*, but of different dimensions and utilizing hands, paddles (*pelota vasca con palas*), and racquets (*frontenis*). As the courts are expensive to build, they are mainly found in private clubs.

American football found a place in a few sport clubs in Mexico and Guatemala in the 1930s, and it is played competitively today by a few Mexico City high schools, the Universidad Nacional Autónoma de México and the Instituto Politécnico Nacional (both in Mexico City), the Instituto Politécnico de Monterrey (Mexico), and the Universidad de las Américas (in Cholula, a suburb of Puebla, Mexico). The Dallas Cowboys are especially popular in Mexico, and there is enough spectator interest that a few National Football League (NFL) games have been played in Mexico City's great soccer stadium (the *Estadio Azteca*) and are shown on Mexican television.

International sport

International competition between clubs began around 1920 and soon after, national teams began to be established for international multi-sport competitions and single-sport championships. A few baseball games were held between teams of northern Mexican and Texas cities as early as the late 1800s. Mexican athletes travelled to Guatemala in 1923 for soccer, basketball and tennis matches, and Mexicans representing the Mexico City YMCA played a series of basketball games in Texas and Louisiana that year. Salvadorans came to Guatemala City in 1920 for tennis matches, and clubs from El Salvador and Guatemala played a home-and-home basketball series in 1926. Also in 1926, Salvadoran and Nicaraguan boxers and a Belizean soccer team competed in Guatemala, a Mexican professional soccer team played matches in Cuba and Mexico hosted games against a professional Cuban soccer club, while Costa Rica's national team also competed against the visiting Cuban soccer professionals. In the 1920s Costa Rican soccer teams played in Nicaragua, Guatemala and Jamaica, and Costa Rica hosted soccer teams from Peru, Ecuador, Colombia and Jamaica, as well as a baseball team from Panama. Cubans also played baseball in Panama.

The First Central American Games were held in Guatemala City in 1921 as part of the Central American independence centennial celebration. All five of the traditional Central American republics sent athletic representatives; the sport programme included baseball, soccer, tennis, swimming, tug-of-war, and 18 track and field events. Some attempts were made to continue this festival, but only one lightly attended repetition occurred (in San José, Costa Rica in 1924–25). After 48 years, in 1973 in Guatemala City a new series of Central American Games was begun and has continued to the present day.[12]

In 1926 Mexico City hosted a regional competition recognized by the International Olympic Committee (IOC) and also called the 'First Central American Games'. Some 14 countries, from Mexico, south to Colombia and Venezuela, along with some Caribbean countries, were invited, but only Mexico, Cuba and Guatemala participated. Competition was held in fencing, pistol shooting, basketball, baseball, tennis, swimming, and track and field, and exhibition events included rifle shooting and a 100-km race by Tarahumara Indians, from Pachuca to Mexico City. Much of the competition featured only Mexicans and Cubans, as only a very small delegation came from Guatemala. This sport festival did prosper and expand and has continued to the present, being known since 1938 as the Central American and Caribbean Games. It was held in El Salvador (1935), Panama (1938), Guatemala (1950), and Mexico (1954 and 1990). The competition has been dominated for many years by Cuba, but Mexico is always a strong contender. Central American countries have had relatively little athletic success in the Central American and Caribbean Games.[13]

Mexico and the Central American nations (not all present for the initial Games) have participated in the Pan American Games since their inception in Buenos Aires in 1951.[14] Mexico hosted the Pan American Games in 1955 and 1975. Commemorative volumes (*memorias*) produced for many of these sport festivals contain information about the events and give results of the athletic competitions.

Mexico sent its first Olympic team to Paris in 1924, and was the first (and to date, the only) Latin American nation to host an Olympics, in 1968. Some Mexicans saw their first Olympic participation, as well as hosting the Central American Games of 1926, as vehicles for producing feelings of national unity and diminishing undesirable images of the country overseas after years of revolutionary activity. Central American countries began Olympic participation at various times and generally with relatively small delegations. For example, Panama sent one athlete to the 1928 Olympics, and Guatemala had its first Olympic participation in 1952. Mexico City's 1968 Olympics was the first for British Honduras, El Salvador and Nicaragua. Costa Rican swimmers, sisters Sylvia (silver 1988) and Claudia (gold 1996) Poll, were the first women from their nation to win Olympic medals, and Claudia's medal was the first Olympic gold ever for a Central American woman.[15]

Mexico, Costa Rica, El Salvador and Guatemala have Olympic Academies that provide information and history of the Olympic Movement, including educational programmes for children and youth. Mexico and Costa Rica also have Olympic Museums.[16]

Mexico City's Olympics were noteworthy from various standpoints, including controversies over competition at high altitude and questions of admission of a South African delegation and related threatened boycotts by several African nations, outstanding performances such as the men's long jump, and expressions of protest of racial discrimination in the USA by some US African-American athletes. Mexico was represented by more than 300 athletes and won an all-time high nine medals. New construction for these Olympics added beauty and sporting opportunities within the city. The Tlatelolco massacre and other disruptions to life in the city, sometimes cited as having links to the Games, had more to do with student complaints about academic rules and protests against the Echeverría government, than with questions related to the Mexico City Olympics.[17]

The International Olympic Committee has had members from the region since the early 20th century. In the 1920s IOC members included Miguel de Beistegui (member, 1901–31), Marquis de Guadalupe (1922–24), Jorge Gómez de Parada (1924–27), and Moisés Sáenz (1928–32, elected after directing the 1926 Central American Games), all from Mexico, and Pedro J. de Matheu (El Salvador, 1920–40). Guatemalan Miguel Ydígoras Fuentes (1948–52) was an IOC member at the time Guatemala held the sixth Central American and Caribbean Games, and Mexico's José de Jesús Clark Flores became an IOC member in 1952 and was vice-president of the organization from 1966 to 1970. His countryman, Marte R. Gómez, was a member 1934–73, and Mexico's Mario Vásquez Raña (1991–) is a member of the IOC Executive Board and president of the Association of National Olympic Committees (ANOC) and the IOC Solidarity Commission. Vásquez Raña has been president of the Pan American Games Organization since 1975, when he organized the Games for Mexico City after they were switched there at the last minute. He has been president of the Mexican Olympic Committee since 1974, held other important sport positions, and received the IOC's Olympic Order in Gold in 1988. Panama had IOC members Agustín A. Sosa (1952–67), Virgilio de León (elected in 1969), and Melitón Sánchez Rivas (elected in 1998). Mexican Pedro Ramírez Vázquez was elected in 1972 and Eduardo Hay in 1974. Guatemala's Willi Kaltschmitt has been a member since 1988 and was president of the Organizing Committee for the 119th IOC Session held in July 2007 in Guatemala City.

Mexico and Central America entering the 21st century

Since the 1990s Mexico and Central America have continued to expand sport activity in many disciplines, with construction of new facilities and hosting major international events. Honduras is playing a larger role than ever before in the region, although it, along with Nicaragua and Belize, continues to make less of a sporting mark than the other Central American nations and Mexico. Honduras constructed major new sport facilities in connection with hosting the 1990 Central American Games in Tegucigalpa and the 1997 edition of the games in San Pedro Sula. The 1994 Central American Games were held in San Salvador, and subsequent Central American Games in Guatemala City (2001 and 2005).

Mexico has fine practice and competition sites, including their Olympic developmental centre, a world-renowned velodrome, stadiums, gymnasia and pools used in the 1968 Olympics and other international competitions. Mexico, Honduras and Costa Rica have presented strong national teams in professional soccer, but have not advanced very far in World Cup competitions. Mexico hosted the World Cup in 1970. The 119th IOC Session was held in Guatemala City for the first time in July 2007, and Guatemala City was in the preliminary group of cities being considered for the site of the 2010 Summer Youth Olympics.

Future directions for sports history research in Mexico and Central America

Research in autochthonous and traditional sport and games continues in Mexico, but more can be done there, and this area is especially open to more work in Central America. Traditional activities of many indigenous groups, for example, the Garífunas de Nicaragua and Honduras, are almost entirely unknown. While basic groundwork has been done on the topic of early development of modern sport in Mexico, Guatemala, Nicaragua and Costa Rica, studies of this type are still needed for Honduras, El Salvador, Panama and Belize. Of special interest would be investigations into how sport spread from the socially elite sport clubs of the late 19th and early 20th centuries, to working class people and their clubs; women's participation in sport; government, community and church support of recreational and competitive sport; and the continuing role of organizations such as the YMCA, physical education departments in universities and Mexico's specialized colleges for training physical education teachers and coaches.

Notes

1 Joseph L. Arbena, *An Annotated Bibliography of Latin American Sport: Pre-Conquest to the Present* (Westport, CT: Greenwood Press, 1989). Joseph L. Arbena, *Latin American Sport: An Annotated Bibliography, 1988–1998* (Westport, CT: Greenwood Press, 1999).

2 Richard V. McGehee, 'On the Road: Endurance Running by Indigenous People of the Americas', *Proceedings, 38th World Congress of ICHPER•SD* (1995), 139–41. Armando de María y Campos, *Las Peleas de Gallos en México* (México, DF: Editorial Diana, 1994). Gustavo Casasola, *Seis Siglos de Historia Gráfica de México* (Mexico City: Editorial Gustavo Casasola, 1989). Carl Lumholtz, *Unknown Mexico* (New York: Scribner's Sons, 1902). Román Piña Chan, 'Juegos y Deportes en el México Antiguo', in *Olimpia y sus Juegos* (México: UTEHA, 1968). Jorge R. Acosta and Hugo Moedano K., 'Los Juegos de Pelota', in *México Prehispánico* (México, DF, 1946). Vernon L. Scarborough and David R. Wilcox, eds, *The Mesoamerican Ballgame* (Tucson, AZ: University of Arizona Press, 1991). Walter Krickeberg, *El Juego de Pelota Mesoamericano y su Simbolismo Religioso* (México: Traducciones Mesoamericanistas/Sociedad Mexicana de Antropología, 1966). Heiner Gillmeister, *Tennis: A Cultural History* (London: Leicester University Press, 1997). María Berrios Mayorga, *Juegos Nicaragüenses* (León, 1960).

3 Lourdes Alvarez, personal communication. The website for the Federation carries descriptive text and photographs illustrating many traditional games, www.codeme.org.mx/autoctonoytradicional.

4 Mary Lou LeCompte, 'Hispanic Roots of American Rodeo', *Studies in Latin American Popular Culture* 13 (1994), 57–75. Kathleen M. Sands, *Charrería: An Equestrian Folk Tradition* (Tucson: University of Arizona Press, 1993). José Alvarez de Villar, *Men and Horses of Mexico* (Mexico City: Ediciones Lara, 1979). Enrique Guarner, *Historia del Toreo en México* (Mexico City: Editorial Diana, 1979). James Norman Schmidt, *Charro: Mexican Horseman* (New York: G.P. Putnam's Sons, 1969). Leovigildo Islas Escárega, 'Historical Synthesis of Charrería', *Artes de Mexico* 99 (1968), 19–21. Carlos Rincón Gallardo, *El Charro Mexicano* (Mexico City: Librería de Porrua Hnos., 1939). Nicolás Rangel, *Historia del Toreo en México: Epoca Colonial, 1529–1821* (Mexico City: Imp. Manuel León Sánchez, 1924). Octavio Chávez, *La Charrería: Tradición Mexicana* (Mexico City: Instituto Mexiquense de Cultura, 1991).

5 William Beezley, *Judas at the Jockey Club and Other Episodes of Porfirian Mexico* (Lincoln: University of Nebraska Press, 1987). Joseph L. Arbena, 'Sport, Development, and Mexican Nationalism, 1920–70', *Journal of Sport History* 18 (1991), 350–64. Richard V. McGehee, 'Sports and Recreational Activities in Guatemala and Mexico, Late 1800s to 1926', *Studies in Latin American Popular Culture* 13 (1994), 7–32. Richard V. McGehee, 'Early Development of Modern Sport in Costa Rica, 1890s to 1926', *Journal of ICHPER•SD* 41 (2005), 57–63. Richard V. McGehee, 'Sport in Nicaragua, 1889–1926', in Joseph L. Arbena and David G. LaFrance, eds, *Sport in Latin America and the Caribbean* (Wilmington, DE: Scholarly Resources, 2002), 175–205. Richard V. McGehee, 'The Impact of Imported Sports on the Popular Culture of Nineteenth- and Early Twentieth-Century Mexico and Central America', in Ingrid E. Fey and Karen Racine, eds, *Strange Pilgrimages: Exile, Travel, and National Identity in Latin America, 1800–1990s* (Wilmington, DE: Scholarly Resources, 2000), 95–111. Richard V. McGehee, 'Carreras, Patrias y Caudillos: Sport/Spectacle in Mexico and Guatemala, 1926–43', *South Eastern Latin Americanist* 41 (1998), 19–32. Richard V. McGehee, 'The Rise of Modern Sport in Guatemala and the First Central American Games', *International Journal of the History of Sport* 9 (1992), 132–40. Richard V. McGehee, 'Nacimiento y Desarrollo Inicial del Deporte Moderno', in Jorge Luján, ed., *Historia General de Guatemala* 5 (1996), 349–58. Richard V. McGehee, 'Mexico', in David Levinson and Karen Christensen, eds, *Berkshire Encyclopedia of World Sport*, vol. 3 (Great Barrington, MA: Berkshire Pub. Group, 2005), 1,005–10. Richard V. McGehee, 'Honduras', in David Levinson and Karen Christensen, eds, *Berkshire Encyclopedia of World Sport*, vol. 2 (Great Barrington, MA: Berkshire Pub. Group, 2005), 756–58. Joseph L. Arbena, 'Sport, Development, and Mexican Nationalism, 1920–70', *Journal of Sport History* 18 (1991), 350–64. Gilbert M. Joseph, 'Forging the Regional Pastime: Baseball and Class in Yucatan', in *Sport and Society in Latin America: Diffusion, Dependency, and the Rise of Mass Culture* (Westport, CT: Greenwood Press, 1988). Eric A. Wagner, 'Sport in Revolutionary Societies: Cuba and Nicaragua', in *Sport and Society in Latin America: Diffusion, Dependency, and the Rise of Mass Culture* (Westport, CT: Greenwood Press, 1988). Keith Brewster, Patriotic Pastimes: 'The Role of Sport in Post-Revolutionary Mexico', *International Journal of the History of Sport*, 22 (2005), 139–57. Agustín Salas, *Historia del Deporte en Costa Rica* (San José: Imprenta Universal, 1951).

6 J. A. Guzmán, ed., *Guatemala deportiva: Historia del futbol nacional en sus bodas de oro* (Guatemala: Tipografía Nacional, 1953). Fernando Mejía Barquera, *Futbol Mexicano: Glorias y Tragedias, 1929–1992* (México, DF: El Nacional, 1993). Luis Mojica Sánchez, *Una Historia de Gol y Pasión: Los Setenta y Ocho Años del Club Diriangén* (Diriamba, Nicaragua, 1995). Javier Bañuelos Rentería, 'Balón a Tierra', in Fernando García Ramírez, ed., *Crónica del Futbol Mexicano* (México, DF: Editorial Clio,

1998). Chester Urbina Gaitán, 'The Catholic Church and the Origins of Soccer in Costa Rica in the Early 1900s', in Joseph L. Arbena and David G. LaFrance, eds, *Sport in Latin America and the Caribbean* (Wilmington, DE: Scholarly Resources, 2002), 1–8.

7 Richard V. McGehee, 'Baseball, Latin America', in David Levinson and Karen Christensen, eds, *Encyclopedia of World Sport* (Santa Barbara, CA: ABC-CLIO, 1996), 84–91. Carlos J. García, *Reseña de Cien Años de Béisbol en Nicaragua* (Managua, 1991). Ramón G. Pérez Medina, *Historia del Baseball Panameño* (Panama: Dutigrafía, 1992). Alan M. Klein, 'Baseball Wars: The Mexican Baseball League and Nationalism in 1946', *Studies in Latin American Popular Culture* 13 (1994), 33–56. *Enciclopedia del Béisbol Mexicano* (Mexico City: Una Publicación de Revistas Deportivas, 1992). David G. LaFrance, 'Labor, the State, and Professional Baseball in Mexico in the 1980s', in Joseph L. Arbena and David G. LaFrance, eds, *Sport in Latin America and the Caribbean* (Wilmington, DE: Scholarly Resources, 2002), 89–115. Edgard Tijerino, *Doble Play* (Managua: Editorial Vanguardia, 1989).

8 Tiburcio Blanco Pedrero, *Historia del Basquetbol en Chiapas* (Tuxtla Gutiérrez, Chiapas: Impresora Gutiérrez, 1985). Carlos F. Vallejo, *Guía y Reglas del Basket Ball en la América Latina: Dedicada a Nicaragua, C.A. con la Historia de la X Serie Mundial de Base Ball* (Monterrey, Mexico, 1948).

9 Richard V. McGehee, 'Volleyball – The Latin American Connection', *Journal of ICHPER•SD* 33 (1997), 31–35. Edeltraud Minar, *Historia de la Natación Hondureña* (Tegucigalpa: Solidaridad Olímpica and Comité Olímpico Hondureño, 1996).

10 William H. Beezley, 'Bicycles, Modernization, and Mexico', in *Sport and Society in Latin America: Diffusion, Dependency, and the Rise of Mass Culture* (Westport, CT: Greenwood Press, 1988).

11 Richard V. McGehee, 'The Dandy and the Mauler in Mexico: Johnson, Dempsey, et al, and the Mexico City Press, 1919–27', *Journal of Sport History* 23 (1996), 20–33. Ricardo Arredondo and Guillermo Murray, *Quince Rounds* (México: Editorial Diógenes, 1973). Rafael Barradas Ossorio, *El Box Fuera del Ring: Lo Blanco y lo Negro del Boxeo Profesional de México* (México, 1989). Armando Zenteno, *Julio César Chávez, Nuestro Campeón* (México: Editorial Pax México, 1990). Raúl Talán, *En el 3er. Round* (México, DF, 1952).

12 Richard V. McGehee, 'Sport in Small Nations: Origins and Early Years of the Central American Games', *ICHPERSD World Congress Proceedings* (2005), 296–300. Richard V. McGehee, 'The Rise of Modern Sport in Guatemala and the First Central American Games', *International Journal of the History of Sport* 9 (1992), 132–40.

13 Enrique Montesinos and Sigfredo Barros, *Centroamericanos y del Caribe: Los Más Antiguos Juegos Deportivos Regionales del Mundo* (La Habana: Editorial Científico-Técnica, 1984). Abraham Ferreiro Toledano, *Centroamérica y el Caribe a Través de sus Juegos* (Mexico City: privately published, 1986). Richard V. McGehee, 'Revolution, Democracy, and Sport: The Guatemalan "Olympics" of 1950', *Olympika* 3 (1994), 49–81. Richard V. McGehee, 'The Origins of Olympism in Mexico: The Central American Games of 1926', *International Journal of the History of Sport* 10 (1993), 313–32. José Beracasa, 'From 1926 to 1976: Twelve Central American and Caribbean Games', *Olympic Review* 109/110 (1976), 626–29, 659.

14 Richard V. McGehee, 'Pan American Games', in David Levinson and Karen Christensen, eds, *Berkshire Encyclopedia of World Sport*, vol. 3 (Great Barrington, MA: Berkshire Pub. Group, 2005), 1,142–47. Abraham Ferreiro Toledano, *Historia de los Juegos Panamericanos 1951–1991* (Mexico City: Pro Excelencia del Deporte, 1992).

15 Richard V. McGehee, 'Latin America and the Caribbean in the Modern Olympic Movement', *Journal of ICHPER•SD* 32 (1996), 12–15. Antonio Lavín U., *México en los Juegos Olímpicos* (Mexico City, 1968).

16 Richard V. McGehee, 'Olympic Education in Mexico, Central America and South America', *Journal of the International Council for Health, Physical Education, Recreation, Sport, and Dance* 37 (2001), 56–58.

17 Keith Brewster and Claire Brewster, 'Mexico City 1968: Sombreros and Skyscrapers', in Alan Tomlinson and Christopher Young, eds, *National Identity and Global Sports Events: Culture, Politics, and Spectacle in the Olympics and Football World Cup* (New York: State University of New York Press, 2006), 99–116. Joseph L. Arbena, 'Hosting the Summer Olympic Games: Mexico City, 1968', in Joseph L. Arbena and David G. LaFrance, eds, *Sport in Latin America and the Caribbean* (Wilmington, DE: Scholarly Resources, 2002), 133–43. John E. Findling and Kimberly D. Pelle, eds, *Historical Dictionary of the Modern Olympic Movement* (Greenwood Pub. Group, 1996).

31 The Middle East and North Africa

Mahfoud Amara

The complexity of questioning modern sports in the Arab (and Islamic) context, in 'late modernity'

In examining sport in the history of the Arab World contradictions often arise, particularly between the question of modernity (progress) and the past (authenticity), which is yet to be resolved there.[1] One of the major consequences of the colonial project in de-legitimizing the pre-colonial history (and geography) of colonized societies, including the Arab region, is the establishment of a schizophrenic relation with the past. This has led to the (over) glorification of the (Islamic and pre-colonial) past in claiming an historical legitimacy (as a substitute to political illegitimacy) and in mobilizing national communities around the post-independence project of the party (and monarchy) states. The other consequence is that of denial or trauma.[2] The past here, at least in the way it was institutionalized by the formal history (selective memory), is perceived as archaic, traditional, non-secular and even anti-revolutionary, thus an obstacle to the party-state's (secular) project for development.[3] This burden of the (colonial) past in newly independent countries in general is well articulated by Berque:

> Having long identified themselves with a world and a tradition appropriated by the west, the colonised had had to battle against the external and psychological worlds that the West had penetrated equally. Hence being curious about himself and about the Other, the colonised found himself in a predicament that posed not only 'sociological' questions but also 'psychoanalytic' ones (an ontological search for self-hood, the internalised contradictions of identity created the Western Other, the internalised absence of historical time). However, since the Other's (The European's) civilisation had so deeply entered the colonised society, this technological civilisation could not be rejected because 'in refusing the Other, they [were] refusing themselves'.[4]

Furthermore, in studying the significance of sport (which is yet to be included) in contemporary histories of the Arab World, we are challenged by the imposing debate of (Western) modernity (as a break with past), which claims its uniqueness (as a master signifier) in defining the meaning and, therefore, the history (also territoriality) of modern sport. Here, Venn Couze's concept of Occidentalism is applicable to the domain of sport, too. In Cuze's terms:

> Occidentalism thus directs attention to the becoming-modern of the world and becoming-West of Europe such that Western modernity gradually became

established as privileged, if not hegemonic, form of sociality, tied to a universalizing and totalizing ambition. Occidentalism indicates a genealogy of the present which reconstructs a particular trajectory of modernity, inflected by the fact of colonialism and capitalism.[5]

Hence, the analysis of modernity in the Arab World is not meaningful without an analysis of the historical context of dominance/dependence/interconnectedness between the West/non-West. As Edward Said has noted:

> ... we cannot discuss the non-Western world as distinct from developments in the West. The ravages of colonial wars, the protracted conflicts between insurgent nationalism and anomalous imperialist control, the disputations new fundamentalist and nativist movements nourished by despair and anger, the extension of the world system over the developing world – these circumstances are directly connected to actualities in the West.[6]

While the Arab World is yet to overcome its crisis of authenticity (and modernity), the West is going through its own crisis of modernity.[7] Commentators such as Nilüfer Göle[8] point out that there is a need to rethink the concept of modernity; to move from seeing this as a uniform, homogeneous phenomenon, to one which has local occidental and non-occidental manifestations – examples of what Göle refers to as 'local modernity'. Compared with Western modernity based on 'assimilation' and an occidental tradition of social analysis, privileged by indigenous 'Western' intellectuals, the local modernity approach seeks a more exclusive and pluralist reflection towards modernity. It involves a movement from a universalist conceptualization to that of particularistic conceptualization, using a new type of 'intellectual sensibility', which focuses upon the rereading of modernity according to the historical practice of non-occidental countries. This return towards local modernity can be viewed as an attempt to de-connect both theoretically and intellectually from the occident – what Lyotard defines as a process of de-universalization of Western meta-narratives.[9]

Many sociologists, historians and philosophers are preaching the end of an era (modernity) and the beginning of a new era (postmodernity). One of their arguments put forward is that modernity as a philosophy and value system has reached its saturation stage and has showed its failure to achieve progress for humanity. Instead, postmodern sociology or at least sociology of postmodernism is regarded as the substitute to this failure. This also applies to the 'Rest', the periphery, or the so-called developing countries, where (imposed) post-colonial projects of developmentalism (Thirdworldism, Baatism, Pan-Arabism, Nassirism ...), have known their limits and, as a result, other political ideologies based on Islamism or 'Islamized' modernity as well as local regionalist (ethnic and cultural) identities, have emerged to challenge the secular nationalism of the party-state.

In the same vein, Ziaudine Sardar and Ahmed Akbar[10] attempted to redefine post-modernism according to non-occidental or non-Western histories and traditions. For Sardar, adopting strategies for cultural authenticity and cultural autonomy are the *conditions* for surviving postmodernism. As for Akbar, it is the return to Islamic values. Both authors claim their attachment to some features of Western modernity (nation-state, technology, etc.), but reject Western hegemony and appropriation of knowledge, progress or human rights, even in the name of postmodernism, which has been presented by Western postmodernists, according to Sardar, as a new (Western) theory of liberation that promotes pluralism, but which in fact is another Western project. Its real aim is to transform other cultures into perpetual consumers of its (own) products, 'by isolating and further marginalising other cultures by irony and ridicule'.[11] Sardar and Akbar emphasize in their works the power of the media and image in the postmodern era. Because of 'its capacity to subvert reality, to simplify issues dangerously and influence events',[12] the media (the central feature of dominant global civilization) is being transformed into a potential source of disruption to traditional life. Therefore, non-Western cultures need to understand and acknowledge the threats (and benefits) in order to face/resist their challenging messages and images. Sardar points out that a serious effort has to be made to replace the global (meaningless, violent and perverted) free market and profit-making TV and cinema programmes by *indigenous* cultural products and the making of local television programmes.

Based on the above discussion, there is a need today for new tools of analysis and methodological frameworks to be applied in order to break free from the thoughts of globalist Western 'visions' about the rest of the world, including the Arab (and Muslim) domain, and the localist-provincial, including Arab (and Muslim), 'essentialist' critics of the West. Distinction should be made here between globalization and globalism, where the former is used in the sense of global and local cultural exchanges and the latter to refer to the claim for 'the end of history'. We differentiate, also, between the local application and interpretation of modernity in the sense of intellectual and scientific striving for the progress of humanity, and localism which reduces the resistance to global trends to mere anti-Western polemics. Similarly, there is a need today in the Arab World to deconstruct and demystify the overpoliticized and ideological discourses about sport, literature, cinema, music, religion, education, history and so on, or what Aron portrayed as 'the over-politicization of the social order which confounds administration and government, state and society'.[13] This politicization of the societal domain has occurred as a reaction, or in opposition, to colonial history and the phenomenon of the over-secularization of Western societies. That said, we cannot understand the significance of the modernization concept (and in this case modern sport) independently from the histories and discourses of modernity in Arabo-Islamic contexts. In other words, it cannot be done outside the remit of the 'late modernity' debate or the crisis of modernity in the West on the one hand, and the failure of nationalist projects of development in Arabo-Islamic countries, on the other.

Sport and pan-Arab nationalism

Among the first Arab nationalist thinkers was Al-Tahtaoui. His conception of nationalism, *Watan*, was different from predominant Western notions. In comparison with Western nationalism, which preaches individualism and secularism (or *laïcité*), Al-Tahtaoui insists on the formation of political authority within the tradition of Islamic values that take the Prophet and his companions as a model. He also emphasizes the importance of *Shari'aa* (Islamic legislation), which was described as being similar to the rationalist and natural law of modern Europe. With Al-Tahtaoui, the new era (known as *El-Nahda* or the renaissance) in Islamic and Arab World history began. The leaders (like El-Afghani and Abdou) of this movement aimed to impose Islam as a path and project for society, by enriching it with discoveries of rational European science (at least that which is not contradictory to Islamic values). During this period Islam became a basis for the anti-colonial movement, which called for political actions against imperial (British and

French) Europe, in addition to the adaptation of progressive elements of European civilization that might strengthen Islamic universalism and maintain Islam as an important part of national education.

In addition to the reformist movement, which sees Islam as the foundation of nationality for Muslims, superior to any other form of association or any national commitment, another movement or Arab nationalist mode of thinking was part of the modern Arab history of nationalism. It developed as a consequence of Western acculturation or depersonalization of Arab societies, in the form of a cultural bourgeois movement or literary renaissance that sought at the beginning (under Ottoman rule) an independent Arab cultural nation without a state, promoting both religious toleration and separation of religion from politics, and the adoption of a liberal model of freedom and bourgeois democracy based on Western lines, partly Francophile and partly Anglophile. However, after World War I and due to colonization by French and British troops (the early supporters of Arab separatist movements in the Ottoman Empire), Arab nationalism took a different form. There was a shift from the cultural bourgeois form to that of a political (populist and separatist) movement and, subsequently, with the influence of Al-Husri, a form of Pan-Arab nationalism. Al-Husri's ideas of Arab national liberalism were based principally on two schools of thought: the traditional German concept of nationalism and Ibn Khaldoun's philosophy. From Al-Husri's perspective and the German interpretation of nationalism, if a nation is able to keep its language alive under foreign rule, it has been able to survive. While language is the soul of the nation, its history, which is defined as the common memory of the people, should be seen as its consciousness. Based on these conditions in relation to language and history, Al-Husri claims that all Arab people, though living in a number of states (with borders designated by the colonial power), actually belong to a single all-Arab nation, which could form a macro Pan-Arab state, united by a single language and common historical memory.

Second, the social and historical philosophy of Ibn Khaldoun, particularly the issue regarding the concept of *assabia*, which has been variously interpreted by modern sociologists as 'group feeling', 'solidarity', 'nationalism' and 'nationality' is also key to Al-Husri's thinking. According to Ibn Khaldoun, group feeling is at its strongest in the early phase of civilization (which he designates the nomadic stage), but as the process of civilization continues, its intensity decreases. As a consequence of this decline in group feeling or solidarity, the civilization unravels and its place is taken by other groups (civilizations or dynasties), the group feeling of which is younger and thus stronger. This was described as the cyclical theory of civilizing process consisting of two main stages: the growth stage characterized by urbanization, specialization and ideology (e.g. religious values), and demographic development; and the decline or regression stage characterized by the decline of group feeling, growth of internal conflicts and susceptibility to external invasion.

After World War II a new stage in the historical development of Arab nationalism began. It was based on a nationalism that presents its opposition to the West entirely in terms of Western imperialism. Its main goal, particularly in the 1950s and 1960s, was to combine Pan-Arabism or Pan-Arab national considerations with those of local identities, ensuring the separate independence of the Arab states, while at the same time keeping the doors open for gradual measures of co-operation, integration and unification.[14] The establishment of the League of Arab States was a formalization of this compromise. It was composed at the beginning mainly of Arab states situated in the Middle East, which were under the protectorate of the British Empire and gained their independence earlier than the states of the Maghreb Union in North Africa.

This hostility towards Western values, however, did not last. It lost its strength (in varying degrees) for a number of reasons. The new world system, globalization, multinational diversification and division of labour, and the generalization of the Western model of the nation-state, in combination created contradictory imperatives for 'Third World' countries, particularly for Arab nations, resulting in disillusionment with a previous era of nationalism that had not realized its 'populist hopes'.[15] The new geopolitical and economic situation has had an impact on the fragmentation and localization of Arab nationalism politically, ideologically and economically. The division of Arab nations between Maghreb and Gulf unions, and Middle East co-operation, the 'Islamization' of Sudan, 'Africanization' of Libya, the crisis between the western Sahara and Morocco, the political division of the Arab League during the Gulf wars and at various points in the Palestinian–Israeli conflict, these are all evidence of the heterogenization of Pan-Arab nationalism. As a result, new protest movements developed seeking the reconstruction of Arab society's lost identity and integrity, which was seen as under threat as a consequence of the failure of Pan-Arab modernism. The ideology of this movement could be described as being neo-reformist, proclaiming (like the early reformist movements) a return to pre-national values of religion and Islamic solidarity (the re-Islamization of Arab society). Tahar Ben Jelloun states that today Arab ideology or *'la pensée Arabe'* is confronted by universalist challenges (global politics, economy and culture, in addition to Pan-Islamism) and internal conflicts, which were underestimated or ignored in the past when populist unitary values held sway. In the name of unity, these internal problems have been used as a veil by political regimes in the Arab World to resist the principles and conditions of democracy (a recognition of diversity), introduced by the new world system.[16]

The Pan-Arab games

The Pan-Arab Games were established by the League of Arab States in 1953 as a means of expressing cultural unity between Arab peoples across nation-state boundaries. They provide a useful lens through which to identify the contradictions of Arab nationalism and pan-Arabism. The crisis of modernity in the Arab states, resulting from the decline of the so-called progressiste and secular ideologies (e.g. one-party state, socialism, pan-Arabism, pan-Africanism, etc.), and the imposed definition of nationalism in the sense of 'imagined community', have also been felt in the sporting fields. After being used as a tool – sometimes as a privileged instrument – for nation-state building and the gathering of masses around states' ideologies and its essentialist definition of national unity, sport is becoming today the object for all forms of regionalist and nationalist antagonism.

The Arab countries located in the Mediterranean throughout the history of the games have been dominant in terms of sporting performance. This is in part a reflection of early acceptance of sport culture in their societies as a result of (imposed or negotiated) urbanization and modernization compared with other Arab states. Furthermore, the secularization process favoured the participation of both genders, which consequently gives those countries a significant advantage in the final table of medals. Even though some countries in the Arabian Peninsula, like Saudi Arabia, hold a higher position in the Pan-Arab Games Association, and play an important role in financing the Games (for example, in the case of the Lebanon Games in 1997),[17] these countries have yet to host the event. This could be argued as due to ideological and cultural barriers, particularly in relation to female participation, which is limited to some events such as the chess and the shooting competitions.

As a consequence of the global diffusion of the Western model of the nation state and (Western) sport systems based on nationalist values, national identities and national political and economical interests have taken the place of single all-Arab nation considerations of unity and co-operation. The Pan-Arab Games, supposedly based on non-nationalist feelings that reject the borders drawn by colonial powers, has become through its history another arena for ideological struggles and regional conflicts, which may lead to more fragmentation based on regional solidarity rather than unity (e.g. the Maghreb Union, Gulf Council of Co-operation, the West Asian partnership). The same sense of 'regionaliza-tion' expressed at a political level is also present in the sporting arena. Sport, which was put in the colonial and postcolonial era at the service of Pan-Arab solidarities (demonstrated in the staging of regional games such as the Pan-Arab Games, aimed at strengthening unity between nation-states that share the same history and culture), has become a space for ultra-nationalist sentiment and popular chauvinism. In some cases it has become the direct cause of conflict between Arab nations. As a result, this has transformed the sense of unity expressed in political speeches, in Arab League circles, to an illusory objective, hard to achieve even in the field of sport. The further challenges for the games, which merit a critical review, are related to both external and internal factors: the place and the need of Pan-Arabism in the global political, economic and cultural order; the fragmentation and regionalization of Pan-Arab ideology, due to sub-national political and economic interests; and the emergence of 'Islamist' ideology (calling for Islamic unity or universalism), which is perceived as a threat to (secular) Pan-Arab nationalism.

Soccer in colonial and post-colonial Algeria

The account of the historical development of Algerian football that follows seeks to describe the complexity and richness of the Algerian context and the role that sport in general and football in particular have played in the articulation of different (ideological, political and cultural) struggles within Algerian society.

The colonial era

The diffusion of modern sport described as *l'héritage de l'occupant* started just after coloniza-tion and the arrival of the first groups of (European) immigrants. The creation of the first 'school of swimming' goes back to 1844 in Algiers and the first sports clubs founded were *Le Sport Nautique d'Alger* in 1867 and the Regional Association of the Algerian Gymnastics Society in 1891. Physical education, particularly gymnastics, first appeared in the colonial school as a form of military education, and later became part of the national curriculum for education (by a decree from the Ministry of Public Instruction in 1882). However, it should be mentioned that physical activities were part of Algerian culture centuries before colonization. Fates goes a step further by stating that Algerians were not 'inculte' or 'physically illiterate', since Algeria had its own cultural life and traditional physical activities.[18] The most evident example of colonial sport we can cite is football, which according to Alfred Wahl developed in a spectacular manner in France and outre-mer after World War I. When it was first introduced, teams were organized in Algeria by ultra-nationalists and European groups (Spanish, Italian, Maltese and Jewish), reflecting the Mediterranean representation in, and cultural richness of, Algerian society under the rule of the French Republic. The local indigenous population was excluded from this colonial sporting culture and hostility was expressed by European settlers regarding the local indigenous population's participation in or access to sport. Participation in sport was strictly reserved for European citizens, Algerian indigenous people were not considered as citizens, but 'subjects' and, therefore, they did not have the same rights as European settlers and state officials. According to civil law, which was constructed on the values of the French Revolution, citizens' rights of freedom of thought, of speech and other media, of assembly and the right to found associations, did not exist for non-citizens. Because the majority of non-citizens were in the indigenous category, they were effectively excluded from creating their own associations or having access to organized sport activities. Meanwhile, as a result of a rapid increase in the level of competitions and profit during the 1940s and 1950s, some clubs, which until then had been composed mainly of European players, were forced to recruit talented indigenous players regardless of their ethnic origins. Some of these players were very successful and not only played as professionals in French teams, but were also selected to play international matches with the French national team.

However, despite the colonial administration's efforts at 'reconciliation' between different ethnic groups, there was clear determination by Algerian 'indigenous Muslims' to found their own Muslim sports associations, sometimes without the consent of the colonial authorities. The majority of the names of such indigenous clubs began with the words '*club Musulman*', or '*Union sportive Musulmane*'. Islam was thus a fundamental element and symbol of differentiation between Muslim and non-Muslim clubs. In addition, a considerable number of Muslim football clubs expressed their nationalist identity by adopting as their team colours the colours of the unofficial Algerian national flag, which were green, white and red. Starting from 1954, football had an important place in the National Liberation Front (FLN) strategy for the armed liberation struggle. For example, the final details of the armed revolution were planned by representatives of the FLN in Switzerland during the latter stages of the 1954 World Cup. The FLN ordered 'Muslim clubs' in 1956 to stop all sports activities and to join the National Liberation Army (ALN) troops in the fight against the colonial power. Those orders did not relate to Algerian professional players playing in France, but by 1958 the FLN understood the role that sport and particularly football (as the most popular game in the world) could play in the internationalization of the Algerian cause, and decided to create a national revolutionary team. They gave orders to all Algerian professional players, playing in various teams in the French league, to join the Algerian national team of 'fighters'. Ten players, among them Mekhloufi, Zitouni, Bentifour and Maouche, who were internationals and were certain to be selected by France for the 1958 World Cup in Sweden, responded positively.[19]

The post-colonial era

The appropriation of the dominant model of sport, despite its colonial origin, was seen as a necessity, given the multiple uses of sport as an element for political, social and cultural recognition. The adoption of this universal language (sport) was accomplished by the integration of newly independent countries, during the 1960s, into the homogeneous and pre-established sporting and administrative structure, rules and regulations of the international sports federations (particularly the Fédération Internationale de Football Association—FIFA and the International Olympic Committee—IOC). Sport came to be regarded as an effective arena for future international treaties and conventions between north and south, east and west. Hence a considerable financial investment, funded from oil and gas revenues, was made by Algeria in the development of mass sport, in the organization of physical education and in the training of new PE teachers and specialist sports workers. Investment was also made in the maintenance of sports facilities inherited from the colonial era and in the development of massive new Olympic sport infrastructures, such as the 5 July Stadium in Algiers. The aim of government was to host major events at national and international level, such as the African, Arab and Mediterranean games, which, according to Finn and Giulianotti, served to legitimize a specific state model of political administration (internally and externally).[20] Other facilities were also built throughout the country (particularly in big cities), in an effort to combat centralism and regionalism. In ideological terms, the ideals of international socialism, strengthening friendship and co-operation, promoting understanding and supporting the struggle for peace and democracy and eliminating Western influence, were expressed in operational terms in Algerian sports policy. Algeria and other African and Arab (socialist) countries developed a strong sporting relationship with the USSR and other socialist regimes from the Eastern bloc (which ostensibly shared the same ideals). These relations took the form of receiving Soviet specialists, experts, coaches, doctors and sports administrators, sending students and athletes to physical education institutes and joint training programmes, providing financial aid and sports equipment and exchanging sports delegations.

As a consequence of the national economic crisis resulting from the reduction in oil revenue, and the failure of the Algerian development programme due to over-centralization and external economic dependence, the 1980s were marked by a profound revolution in Algerian society. To face the economic crisis the government first started encouraging management autonomy for the large national corporations (which were part of the heritage of the political gigantism of the socialist era). These corporations were divided into autonomous regional entities, and became responsible for their own profitability and for finding their own supplies, sales and financing. After 20 years of socialism and public ownership, the governmental project was reoriented towards encouraging 'controlled' liberalization, privatization and increasing foreign investment. This involved the transition from a system of economic and social regulation administered by the state to a new system driven by market forces. The failure of the Algerian economic reforms and of the transition towards a market economy was due mostly to its mode of regulation, which was described by Safir as centralized regulation in an economy with problematic performance, strongly linked to the price of oil in the world market.[21] As a result, the transition towards a market economy, instead of being a source of democratization in Algerian society, became the cause of rivalries and conflict, creating a situation of multidimensional crisis and triple deficits: economic, social and cultural. The reigning atmosphere of insecurity and terror, particularly between 1993 and 1997, resulted in the decline in the level of activity of the football leagues and instability in the organization of competitions, principally at a regional level, where weekly travel for competition became perilous for staff, players and supporters. It should be mentioned, though, that despite all the violence, the Algerian Football Federation did not stop running the football league and supporters did not abandon the stadiums. The same could be said for the media (newspapers and television), which continued covering the games. In these circumstances football had become for some a symbol of resistance against political and ideological radicalism, and for others a source of distraction from the hard realities through which the country had been going.

Sport in the Gulf region: the 'commodifcation' of tradition

The Gulf countries, despite the apparent economic boom due to the phenomenal rise of oil prices after the second Gulf War (2003–), are facing a multitude of challenges to maintain their model of social order: the devastating consequences of the Gulf wars; the Iraqi crisis; the question of minorities (religious and ethnic); maintaining the religious and historical legitimacy of the ruling families; regulation of migration flows (talks about the control of migration flows and the nationalizing or 'Saudization', 'Omanization', 'Kuwitization', etc. of public sectors); the socio-economic condition of foreign workers; the issue of the civil rights of the migrant population (access to education, employment and housing, particularly for second-generation migrants whose claim to citizenship status is still denied); the increase in internal and external pressures for political reforms; and, last but not least, the problem of women's condition.

In order to tackle some of these problems and in an effort to diversify state revenues by developing and promoting other industries such as hospitality and tourism, real estate, the retail sector, technology, communication and finance,[22] a new controlled policy of economic reforms and structural readjustments is under way. This is taking place both at the level of the Gulf Cooperation Council (GCC)[23] and individual states.[24] For some analysts these manoeuvres are just another strategy by the 'royal families' to maintain their control over state affairs, in order to divert popular political energies into projects that actually sustain the very basis of the regime.[25] For others, it is a real sign of progress and the openness of Gulf societies to 'modernization' and a concrete sign of integration to the norms of global (consumerist) culture and economy. Huge investments are made today in the staging and sponsorship of international conferences, and trade and art exhibitions.[26] The aim is to market the new 'open' and 'liberal' Arabian Peninsula as the must-visit destination for tourists and businessmen. The fruit of these intense marketing and public relations strategies are starting to show.

The aim of the subsequent section is to discuss the internal dynamics of the Gulf region in the so called 'global', 'transnational' or 'translocal' era. Sport is used here as a lens through which to examine the global-local nexus in the region. It can be argued that sport, in its multiple forms, is becoming a tool for leaders in the Gulf to reposition their countries on the world map. This contemporary utilization of modern sport can be explained in relation to modernization debates as a way to build a new identity as an emerging model of (liberal) monarchy-states that have succeeded in finding the right balance between on the one hand Western 'efficiency' and on the other the 'authenticity' of Arab culture.

The 'sportification' of the Gulf region

Cities in the Gulf have been very active in shaping their image as destinations for business and pleasure and have shown tremendous investment in infrastructure. Following the first Gulf War (1990–91), sports became an important field of business activity linked to city re-branding, and the following section addresses the contextual background in which global (international sport organizations and multinationals) and local (local elite – business and political) forces shape city brands and finances. The study shows ways in which sports-related urban regeneration investment projects affect the regional economy as well as the reverse injection of local capital into global markets. According to Fox et al., in conveying the spectacular (e.g. Ski Dubai), the exotic ('cosmopolitan life' with 'Arabian charm'), and the chic (e.g. luxury hotels) the Emirates and other Gulf cities now reflect postmodern place making:

> The city spaces are rich mosaics of master-planned communities; neighbourhoods of luxurious villas with Arabian, Georgian, Italian designs; and themed shopping malls.

Wide boulevards are lined by flowers during all seasons (and cared for by legions of South Asian workers) and bright lights from the higher rise building; flood light beams of coloured rays about embellished architectural designs, creating a rich cavalcade of colour to contrast with the stark desert sands outside the cities in a kind of iridescent visual ecology. The lightly populated desert interiors starkly hold sway at the city limits, which have become tourist playgrounds for activities such as desert safaris and 'dune bashing' [...] They market visual consumption, that is, the acquiring of images and experience of exotic and the distinctive places that hold a certain stature in the consumers' imagination. Then, the Gulf cities become the place to be or to have visited among globe-trotting clientele.[27]

Large investments are being poured into Gulf countries in the staging and sponsorship of the world's leading sports events and clubs and the building of sporting infrastructures. The aim is to open the Arabian Peninsula to the world of business and finance and to establish the global reputation of a leading destination for international sporting events. The other endeavour is to promote sport among the young population in the Gulf and increase the level of national elite performance in international competitions, translated by the construction of massive sports infrastructures and elite sports centres, as well as the endorsement of professional sports. This has reached an unprecedented level with Qatar staging the Asian Games (the second biggest international sporting event after the Olympic Games),[28] and bidding to stage the 2016 Olympic Games. Examples of mega-sporting events and projects taking place in the Gulf region include:

- Gulf Air Bahrain Grand Prix
- Dubai Motor City project, Sport City project and Formula One Theme Park
- Manchester United Academy in Dubai
- The Dubai World Cup of horse-racing
- The International Grand Prix of Doha Qatar Cycling Tour
- The Qatar International Athletics Championship
- ASPIRE academy in Doha, Qatar

The other interesting phenomenon is that of media sport broadcasting. If we look at the Arab World, the number of Arab state-run, private free-to-air, and pay-per-view TV sports channels has significantly increased over the last 10 years, owing to satellite broadcasting technology. TV broadcasting offers diverse sports programmes, debates, documentaries, and national, regional and international sports competitions, ranging from traditional sports such as camel- and horse-racing, to extreme sports such as the Offshore Powerboat Championships. The dramatic rise in sports channels has also brought increased competition in the advertising market, valued according to industry estimates at US$ 300 million. Private sports channels, dominated by Arab Radio and Television (ART), are challenging the old concept of locality, particularly state sovereignty, and demonstrating that the power over media and communications no longer lies solely within nation-state borders.[29]

Alongside this, more efforts are being put into maintaining, under the patronage of royal families, a tradition of 'authentic' sport culture – for example, horse- and camel-racing, or falconry, which symbolize the royal families' affection for the 'authentic' Arab identity. Traditional sports such as camel-racing (*sibaqat al-hejin*) and falconry are becoming increasingly lucrative, with camel races being broadcasted live on both satellite and land channels. Falcon racing tournaments and hunting championships are being organized 'to reinforce the younger generation's interest in the traditional sport'.[30]

Conclusion

The Arab and Muslim world is torn between its fascination with Western modernity – represented by the nation-state system, industrial advance and information technology – and its struggle against Western colonial and neo-colonial dominance. The world of sport has this same conflict. The Arab and Muslim World has, on the one hand, accepted modern sport as a symbol of modernization in society (e.g. urban regeneration and re-imagining of the city) and as a privileged (propaganda) tool for nation-state building through the assertion of national unity beyond class/ethnic divides, integration of international sports organizations, and participation in, and organization of (or bidding for) mega-sports events. On the other hand, though, many Arabs – particularly representatives of Islamist movements – are wary of modern sport as a symbol of secularism and a deviation from the 'authentic' societal concerns of the *Ummah* (the nation of Muslim believers).

Sport arenas are also being used by the Arab population as a site for social and political contestations and expressions of all forms of frustration with their present condition. As argued by Al-Jabri, the actual deficit in contemporary Arab thought is located in the thinking about the present time:

> How to regain the greatness of our civilization? How do we resuscitate our tradition? These two questions closely overlap and in their interference, make up one of the three major axes around which revolves the problematic of modern and contemporary Arab thought. The dialogue surrounding this axis and the dialectic order that it implies are set between the past and the future. As for the present, it is not present, not only because we refuse it, but also because the past is very much present to the point that it infringes upon the future and absorbs it. Acting as the present, the past is conceived as a means to affirm and to rehabilitate one's identity.[31]

Notes

1 M. Bennabi, *Le problème des idées dans le monde musulman* (Le Caire: Dar El Fikr, 1970).
2 The trauma of the colonial experience as well as the trauma of decolonization and beyond. P.M.E. Lorcin, *Algeria and France 1800–2000: Identity, Memory, Nostalgia* (New York: Syracuse University Press, 2006).
3 This explains also the abandonment in most of the Arab world of traditional sporting practices, pushed into the domain of folkloric celebrations.
4 J.D. Le Sueur, 'Jaques Berque: The Other, The Orient, and the College de France—The Politics of Othering', in *Uncivil War, Intellectuals and Identity Politics During the Decolonization of Algeria* (Philadelphia: University of Pensylvania Press, 2001), 217–24.
5 V. Couze, *The Postcolonial Challenge: Towards Alternative Worlds*, published in association with *Theory, Culture & Society* (London: Sage Publications, 2006), 19.
6 E.W. Said, *Reflections on Exile and Other Essays* (Cambridge, MA: Harvard edition, 2001).
7 Unfulfilled modernity: Habermas and Derrida in G. Barradori, *Philosophy in a Time of Terror, Dialogue with Jürgen Habermas and Jacques Derrida* (Chicago, IL: University of Chicago Press, 2003); crisis of meanings: M. Arkoun, 'Present-Day Islam between its Tradition and Globalisation', in F. Daftary, ed., *Intellectual Traditions in Islam* (London: I. B. Tauris, 2001); demodernization: A. Touraine, *Un nouveau Paradigme pour Comprendre le Monde d'Aujourd'hui* (Paris: Fayard, 2005).
8 N. Göle, 'Modernité Locale', in M. Khelladi, ed., *Postcolonialisme: Décentrement, Déplacement, Dissemination* (Paris: revue Dédale 5 & 6, 1997).

9 J.F. Lyotard, *The Postmodern Condition: A Report on Knowledge* (Manchester University Press, 1984).

10 Z. Sardar, *Postmodernism and Other: The New Imperialism of Western Culture* (London: Pluto Press, 1998). A.S. Akbar, *Postmodernism and Islam: Predicament and Promise* (London: Routledge, 1992).

11 Sardar 1998, 291.

12 Akbar 1992, 224.

13 R. Aron, *Les désillusions du progrès: Essai sur la dialectique de la modernité* (Paris: Callmann-Levy, 1969).

14 S.E. Ibrahim, 'Discussion paper series 10, Management and Mismanagement of Diversity: The Case of Ethnic Conflict and State Building in the Arab world', MOST, 1996, www.unesco.org/most/ibraeng.htm (accessed August 2009).

15 F. Buell, ed., *National Culture and the New Global System* (London: Johns Hopkins University Press, 1994).

16 T. Ben Jalloun, 'La Mémoire deroutée', in M. Khelladi, ed., *Postcolonialisme: Décentrement, Déplacement, Dissemination* (Paris: revue Dédale 5 & 6, 1997).

17 Lebanon received US$ 28 million from Saudi Arabia and Kuwait to help in the construction of sports facilities destroyed during the civil war (*Jordan Times*, 8 April 1999).

18 Y. Fates, *Sport et Tiers Monde: Pratiques corporelle* (Paris: Presses University of France, 1994).

19 Simon Roger, 'Quand le FLN recrutait des footballeurs', *Le Monde*, 12 April 2008.

20 R. Giulianotti and R.G. Finn, eds, *Football Culture: Local Contests, Global Visions* (London: Frank Cass, 2000).

21 J. Safir, 'Origines et dimensions international de la crise', in G. Manceron, ed., *Algerie, comprendre la crise* (Brussels: Interventions, 1996), 139.

22 Major projects include Dubai International Exhibition Centre, Dubailand, Dubai Festival City, Saddiyat Island in Abu Dhabi, King Abdullah City in Saudi Arabia, Amwaj Island project and The Durrat resort in Bahrain, the Bahrain World Trade Centre, the Bahrain Financial Harbour, The Wave project and Blue City Oman, The Pearl island in Qatar, the Buobyan Island and the new Subiya City in Kuwait.

23 Established officially in May 1981, the GCC's role is to co-ordinate the industrial policies of its members by preparing them for the post-oil period. There is a project to extend membership to Iraq and Yemen.

24 A. Garesh and D. Vidal, *The New A–Z of the Middle East* (London: I.B. Tauris, 2004).

25 M. Karava, 'No-democratic States and Political Liberalisation in the Middle East: A Structural Analysis', *Third World Quarterly* 19, 1 (1998), 63–85.

26 In exchange for a sum said to be between US$ 800 million and $1 billion, France will lend the name, art treasures and expertise of the Louvre to a new museum to be built in Abu Dhabi. It is one of five museums planned for a multibillion-dollar tourist development on Saadiyat Island off Abu Dhabi, www.iht.com/articles/2007/01/12/features/louvre.php. For more information about Saadiyat Island, see www.saadiyat.ae.

27 W.J. Fox, N.M. Sabbah and M. al-Mutawa, *Globalisation and the Gulf* (London: Routledge, 2006), 6–7.

28 With a budget of US$ 2.8 billion, it is the biggest event after the Olympic Games in terms of the number of countries represented (45), sporting events (39), volunteers (45,000), viewers (cumulative audience of 1.5 billion), and broadcasting (2,000 hours of television coverage).

29 ART paid US$ 220 million for the exclusive rights to broadcast the 2006, 2010 and 2014 FIFA soccer World Cups to North Africa and the Middle East. M. Amara, 'When the Arab World Was Mobilised around the FIFA 2006 World Cup', *The Journal of North African Studies*, 12, 4 (2007), 417–38.

30 Fazza Falcon Hunting Championship, Department of Tourism and Commerce Marketing, the Government of Dubai, dubaitourism.co.ae/News/default.asp?ID = 1030.

31 A.M. Al-Jabri, *Arab-Islamic Philosophy: A Contemporary Critique* (Austin, TX: Centre of Middle Eastern Studies, University of Texas at Austin, 1999), www.aljabriabed.net/arabphimosophy.htm.

32 New Zealand (Aotearoa)

Malcolm MacLean

Like much of the rest of the English-speaking world, Aotearoa New Zealand sees itself as a place that is uniquely or particularly sporting.[1] Popular writing about sport consumes public spaces and discourses, while scholarly analyses concurrently produce, reproduce and critique dominant socio-cultural discourses. Most notably, Aotearoa New Zealand's sports history, like much other scholarly writing about Aotearoa New Zealand's history, is built within and builds a nationalist frame (as reproduced by this *Companion*). Despite a sense that the study of sport has been marginalized in academic history, New Zealand's sporting past has been addressed in a number of mainstream scholarly sources. Belich's two-volume general history and *The New Zealand Journal of History*, as well as encyclopaedia and reference books, including Else's history of women's organizations and McLintock's *Encyclopaedia*, have given considerable attention to a national sporting past.[2] New Zealand's sports history has also been explored in Douglas Booth's continuing development of a frame for sports historiography grounded in genre and explanatory paradigms, the first derived from work by Alun Munslow and Keith Jenkins, the second from David Hackett Fisher.[3] Booth's work will be considered in the final section of this chapter, and provides a framework against which this chapter may be read.

In writing sports history for Aotearoa New Zealand, scholars have accentuated three interwoven themes. In the first, there is a propensity to construct a history that is nationally distinctive. In the second, paradoxical given the first, there is a lack of comparative historical analysis. The third principle tendency is a focus on masculinist games – especially rugby union. This approach draws on a deep popular tradition of sports writing that until the 1960s addressed a wider range of body culture practices, including wrestling, wood chopping, cycling and equestrianism, than has been seen in more recent writing.[4]

National distinctiveness

New Zealand as a scholarly pursuit, like New Zealand itself, is relatively recent. Until at the earliest the late 1950s, Aotearoa New Zealand's history was seen as an element of (British) Imperial history, which is not to deny much earlier publication of nationally focused histories.[5] Nationally focused they may be, but these were not powerfully nationalist texts. It is only after the early 1960s that Aotearoa New Zealand's historians began to develop not only nationally focused, but nationalist texts and a nationalist, historical discourse. This emerging national history coincided with the growth of social history. The historiographical birth of the nation, despite some strong political inflections, then, took two primary forms: a focus on the colonial wars throughout the 19th century, and attention to the emerging distinctive social characteristics of the new nation. It also set conditions that allowed for an unreflexive nationalism in New Zealand history, leading Gibbons to note that 'New Zealand' and 'New Zealand national identity' are terms used 'without any sense of strain or difficulty', producing a sense of 'New Zealandicity' grounded in 'literary and historical antecedents'. While Gibbons notes that 'national identity' can be 'historiographically, a very valuable heuristic device', he calls on 'New Zealand historians to become less parochial and insular and to decentre or even dissolve "New Zealand" as a subject'.[6] There is limited but heartening evidence that sports history or the history of New Zealand sport is beginning to move beyond this national specificity or subjectivity.

Dominant 20th-century conceptions and constructions of New Zealand tended to a colonialist framework where a one-nation New Zealand incorporated European colonizers, overwhelmingly British, and indigenous Maori into a single socio-cultural entity within an imperial setting. New Zealand was constructed and proclaimed as Britain in the South Pacific, populated by a group of better Britons, some of whom were also Brown Britons.[7] This discourse saw New Zealand's History construct New Zealand as a nation within a context of Britishness – the settler population was overwhelmingly British and the 'natives' were claimed as almost as good as British. Second, its markers of distinctiveness took on two concurrently competing and complementary traits where indigeneity provided a source of New Zealandness, and a world standing was constructed that stemmed from martial practice – including Maori military prowess. These marks of distinctiveness are grounded in colonial nationalism. As a result, two events have been popularly held up as marking New Zealand's emergence as a maturing nation – the slaughter at Gallipoli during the attempted invasion of Turkey in 1915 and the tour of Britain by the national rugby union team in 1905, during which they acquired their team name, the All Blacks.

The sport at the centre of this 20th-century popular nationalism was rugby union. Much of the writing of Aotearoa New Zealand's sports history reflects and reinforces this centrality. Two of the most widely cited discussions of sport in Aotearoa New Zealand's history, J.O.C. Phillips's *A Man's Country?* and Keith Sinclair's *A Destiny Apart*, deal mainly but not exclusively with rugby union, in the context of the development of a specifically New Zealand and Pakeha (European settler) masculinity, and a sense of national distinctiveness: both stress the roles of the 1905 tour and the invasion of the Gallipoli peninsular as intimately interlinked moments in an assertion of nation.[8] The seriousness with which these two titles took sport as an historical factor marked a significant shift in writing about sport in Aotearoa New Zealand. Since the mid-1990s, some of the more serious popular sports writing has actively engaged with the debates within and around Phillips's and Sinclair's work.[9] That both Phillips and Sinclair focus on rugby union should not be surprising: it has great cultural capital and is 'a key formulator of Pakeha ethnicity and agent of interracial integration'.[10] Other footballs barely register alongside rugby union: there has been a small amount of historical work dealing with the rugby league in Aotearoa/New Zealand, but association football is notable by its near complete absence, the notable exception being Keane's insightful analysis of the brief boost in soccer's status during the 1982 World Cup and in the wake of the tumultuous 1981 South African rugby tour of New Zealand.[11]

These volumes by Phillips and Sinclair shifted sports history away from its status as a 'subaltern past'. This shift came about because sport was presented as an essential component of dominant forms of masculinity and nationhood, and as such exposed and drew into mainstream scholarly analysis 'life-worlds [that had been] subordinated by the major narratives of the dominant institutions'.[12] The effect was, then, in keeping with the agenda associated with social history as it emerged in its programmatic form through the 1970s, and with the emergence of New Zealand's national, and nationalist, history from the later 1950s.[13]

Sinclair and Phillips laid the foundation for Aotearoa New Zealand's sports history since the mid-1980s. This history is national-masculinist, is located in relations with 'Home' and assertions of Better Britonism, and 'suits a particular type of cultural nationalism and nationalistic history writing'.[14] Whereas both should have become sacrificial texts – analyses that subsequent scholars critique to develop a more sophisticated and richer understanding of a range of historical pasts – the tendency among analysts has been to accept both as if they were close to the definitive statements on rugby union's role in the manufacture of nationhood and masculinity. For instance, many of the contributors to the textbook *Sport in Aotearoa/New Zealand Society* cite Sinclair and Phillips to endorse the analysis of the 1905 rugby union tour to Great Britain as a key moment in New Zealand's nation building, but most who did so failed to note Daley's critique of the tour as invented tradition.[15] This tendency to literalism has been greater in respect of Phillips, where it is even more concerning given that Phillips set out to unpack, to deconstruct and expose, the myths of New Zealand's Pakeha masculinities.

The responses to Phillips's argument and to its use have been two-fold. In the first, some analysts have sought to develop a more nuanced view of gender and to represent more fully the range of gender forms, of which the 'hard man' Pakeha bloke associated with rugby union is only one. Daley, while explicitly excluding 'sport' from her analysis, explores the early 20th-century physical culture movement through a close reading of a tour of New Zealand by Eugene Sandow in 1902, and Sandow-inspired influences in the physical culture movement until the end of the 1930s.[16] Daley's nuanced depiction of a range of New Zealand's gender forms is extended when she moves from the discussion of Sandow to investigate New Zealand naturism/nudism from the 1920s through the 1950s, swimming and play spaces. Her treatment of the Sandow phenomenon, of physical culture and of naturism suggests a much more diverse set of ways of gendering New Zealand.

The second principal response has centred on the empirical rebuttal of Phillips's underpinning evidence, and is best seen in a series of analyses by Ryan.[17] The central plank in Ryan's appraisal has been an attempt to rupture the assumed link between rugby and rurality that is a central motif of the myths Phillips analyses. There can be little doubt that the myths of mateship Phillips is exploring draw on and accentuate idealized images of the pioneering rural male as adaptable, inventive and independent, or that there is a popular invented tradition that constructs rugby as the embodiment of that idealized rural masculinity. Ryan's approach to this topic is based in a concern that Phillips does not sufficiently critique or debunk the rural-rugby myth itself. The value of Ryan's critique is his methodical and rigorous rebuttal of the evidential basis for the rural-rugby myth; the key weakness is that his case presumes that this rebuttal is sufficient to debunk the myth, when it fails to unpack rural rugby as mythic trope: in debunking its reality, he fails to consider its realism – its paradigmatic presentation of iconic New Zealand manhood.[18] Ryan's critique points to the value of local studies and suggests the importance of moving beyond a focus on the national elite in myth slaying. A more successful critique of the rugby as national myth may be seen in Obel's discussion of the construction of provincial rugby audiences that successfully challenges the notion that the potency and power of rugby's support and appeal lay in the profile and success of the 1905 All Blacks.[19]

Comparison

The mythic status of rugby union and, to a lesser extent, cricket and netball, as markers of New Zealand's assertion of national prowess is weakened by two principal characteristics. The first is that they have limited presence outside the former British Empire where they are dominated, for the most part, by teams from only four or five nations (French rugby union is the obvious exception). The second is a major gap in scholarly analysis where there is very little comparative work exploring either the socio-cultural characteristics of these sports in New Zealand alongside other contexts, or considering how those or other sports negotiate the national-imperial dynamic in which they have developed: a gap that suggests a weak base for a case based on national distinctiveness. Despite the significance of netball as a national marker, there is, as is the case in the rest of the world, almost nothing in the scholarly socio-cultural literature that deals with netball-as/in-history, or indeed with netball at all, beyond the initial work done by Nauright and Broomhall in the 1990s.[20] As is the case in much other sports history, there is a tendency to take for granted that a social history of a sport elsewhere that explores a particular social characteristic, such as 'class' or 'masculinity' or 'nation', may be meaningfully compared with a similarly labelled social trait in Aotearoa New Zealand. For instance, rugby union is widely seen in many of the places it is played as a carrier and marker of dominant or socially significant forms of masculinity. Yet, a closer reading reveals class masculinities in England, Scotland and Australia, national masculinities in New Zealand, South Africa, and regional or sub-national masculinities in France and Wales.[21]

Even in relation to the closest and easiest to explore potential comparator the gaps are glaring. In Mangan and Nauright's edited collection *Sport in Australasian Society*, only three of the 14 essays deal with both Australia and New Zealand, with only two of those being in any significant sense comparative. As Adair notes, 'although there are *assumed* similarities between Australia and New Zealand in the book, historical differences between the two countries are not given serious and sustained thought'.[22] Adair points to a key problem in the nationalist frame through which much of New Zealand history, not just its sports history, is constructed – the assumption of similarities and differences tends to produce a case for distinctiveness that is not demonstrated. There are few sport-based analyses that break this mould, and one of the most useful recent ones, significantly, is the product of a non-New Zealand domicile. Adrian Smith's exploration of Australia–New Zealand sporting rivalry focuses on the later years of the 20th century and draws on a convincing range of trans-Tasman sources to reveal patterns of linkage and rivalry not just on the fields of play, but in policy, professional leadership and sports management.[23] Useful as this paper is, though, it barely scratches the comparative surface, the potential of which is also revealed in Booth's and Joyce's explorations of 'Australian surf life-saving in New Zealand'.[24]

A key reason for this lack of comparison is New Zealand's historiographical colonial nationalism. New Zealand's construction of itself as a mature nation is grounded in events in the early 20th century, where the major motifs are the 1905 rugby tour of the British Isles and participation in the South African War (1899–1903) and more especially World War I (1914–18). This is a national history shaped by an epistemic duality;[25] there are two specific events at the core of this system of thought – the 'disputed' Deans try against Wales in 1905 and failure to hold the hill known as Chunuk Bair on the Gallipoli Peninsula in 1915. Both these notable failures are constructed as examples of the limits imposed on New Zealanders' prowess – a bad refereeing decision and Welsh skulduggery in 1905, and a series of inept British military commands in 1915 – neither of which can be demonstrated compellingly. This version of New Zealand's national history holds that these 'Better Britons' came to self-awareness as a nation in itself, although not a nation for itself, in the context of an Edwardian Empire that allowed for 'the assertiveness of local autonomy and interest, the sense of cultural identity and of environment, [as well as] the desire for self rule and self-respect within a changing set of connections to the empire'.[26] The ambiguity of national-yet-imperial is often recognized but seldom unpacked in New Zealand history, let alone its sports history.

Given a tendency to unreflexive colonial nationalism, noting that the dominant sports are all a residue of British Imperial expansion suggests a number of options for further exploration. The notion that Maori are 'Brown Britons' pervades the national oeuvre, where sport has been seen as a marker of national unity and unification. There have been some challenges to this sense of sport as a mechanism of colonial reconciliation. Vincent et al. consider the complex relationship between Maori indigenous body cultures and the colonizers' sports in the latter years of the 19th century.[27] Ryan reveals the Maori-based discontent over the 1937 Springbok rugby tour of New Zealand that has been unrecognized in analyses of the politics of sporting contact with South Africa.[28] In an analysis influenced by new cultural history, MacLean explores the ways that Maori rugby players were recognized as legitimately involved in the game and nation because they were held to embody approved forms of warrior-masculinity.[29] Analyses such as these that recognize the distinctiveness of Maori engagement with colonial sport and body cultures are rare, though there are hints of a rich subaltern history of sport by Maori in a recent institutional history of Maori tennis, a history of the Otaki Maori Racing Club and a popular account of recent elite Maori rugby union.[30] Historians of New Zealand sport would do well to look at Hokowhitu's Foucault-inspired socio-historical analysis of Maori sport as a mechanism to discipline Maori bodies, and to develop a more anthropologically sensitive outlook to attempt to see ways that Maori engaged with the sports brought and developed by the colonizers.[31]

The identities asserted by these Imperial sports in a historiography shaped by the ambiguities of colonial nationalism should not be seen as simply nationalist or solely colonial/imperial. A more productive and relatively under-explored approach would see them as Janus-faced – looking to both the colonial and the national status, to the colony and to 'home'.[32] Rugby union, for instance, may be seen as asserting a set of residual imperial and colonial relations – as rugby it is firmly grounded in Britishness, or perhaps Englishness, but New Zealand rugby is often held to display a distinctive style. Ryan notes that during the Natives' tour of 1888–89 British observers were surprised at the 'Britishness' of the predominantly Maori team, in a manner that reflected Seeley's 1883 notion of the colonies of settlement as a part of Greater England, while during the 1905 tour the New Zealand team was both praised and criticized as stylistically innovative.[33] In an analysis of the 1908–09 (Australian) Wallabies rugby tour of Great Britain, Ryan shows the usefulness of comparative analyses, but limits it to a focus on British constructions of colonial difference.[34] A more promising development of this approach may be seen in his analysis of Anglo-New Zealand cricket in the mid-20th century.[35]

Given rugby's limited spread beyond the white Commonwealth, the profile of and attachment to rugby union in New Zealand reveals a certain form of Britishness. The Britishness of rugby union is not a direct relocation – class masculinity has been replaced by national masculinity and since the first tour of Great Britain by a representative New

Zealand rugby team the game has demonstrated a tendency to Polynesianization.[36] The focus on rugby union is problematic: as Falcous notes, rugby league disrupts the formation of a specific form of Britishness-through-sport through an implied critique of the claims to meritocracy and the myth of classlessness that is powerful in New Zealand's popular self image.[37] It may be that this challenge is also to dominant national masculinity projected through rugby union, although the issue of the other rugby code's links to this national masculinity remains relatively under-explored.[38]

The historiography of New Zealand-in-the-world reveals that New Zealand's international relations and cultural associations are not only with Great Britain.[39] Smith's exploration of Australia–New Zealand sports rivalry opens space for the development of comparative, trans-Tasman history, while Ryan's history of New Zealand cricket locates its development in part in the context of relations with both Australia and Great Britain.[40] Ryan's excellent monograph history of New Zealand cricket before World War I indicates the potential richness of New Zealand sports history beyond the rugby codes that draws on a comparative approach, but that also radically contextualizes the game in the specific social and spatial circumstances of colonial New Zealand.[41] Recent British Imperial history, especially if influenced by post-colonial approaches, suggests a more complex network of cultural relations. Ballantyne's exploration of Aryanism in the British Empire exposes links between New Zealand, Tahiti and India through the 19th century, while Boehmer reveals a network of cultural exchange including India, Ireland, South Africa and anti-colonial activists in Great Britain both before and after World War I.[42] A similar approach to cultural history in Aotearoa New Zealand has seen Williams identify three nationalisms in addition to the colonial kind – post-settler nationalism, Maori nationalism and bicultural nationalism.[43] While not explicitly located in this tradition, Watson's analysis of a series of inter-war Indian hockey tours of New Zealand should stimulate further analysis.[44] Rupturing the British-centred network, the colonies of settlement that became the white Commonwealth could open further areas of analysis – such as the netball networks incorporating, among others, New Zealand, Jamaica, and Trinidad and Tobago in the 1970s.

Beyond boys and balls

This potential for the investigation of a more subtle set of imperial relations would, following Gibbons, decentre New Zealand and New Zealand 'nationalism' as the dominant tropes of New Zealand's sports history. Given the interweaving of nation and masculinity in these discourses, such a move should reinforce attempts by some scholars to move beyond the boys and their balls school of sports history. Two challenges to this school may be seen in recent analyses of physical culture that, to many observers, would stretch the definition of 'sport' – Macdonald's exploration of competitive marching, Ross's discussion of tramping and Wevers's investigation of the pleasures of walking.[45]

Ross's and Wevers's papers connect to recent trends exploring the cultural and spatial dynamics of settlement, colonization and social relations. Wevers grounds the development of tourist walking tracks at the outset of the 20th century in walking as a means of claiming authority over newly 'settled' space, as well as the 19th-century English Romantic cultures of walking. Her analysis of tourist narratives of walking the Milford Track teases out and disrupts any discrete and rigidly binarized reading of Daley's distinction between unsanctioned pleasure and sanctioned leisure in both classed and gendered terms.[46] Although the paper may be fruitfully read in the light of Wevers's larger literary project concerning New Zealand travel writing, it also lends itself to being read as addressing an element on a continuum of outdoor leisure activities, suggesting largely unexplored links between tourism, physical activity and sport.[47] A similar anti-commercialism to that associated with the rejection of organized tours of the Track may be seen in tramping (hiking) clubs during the 1920s and 1930s. Ross exposes elements of the same continuum as Wevers in her discussion of tramping clubs that presented themselves as preservers of the environment and facilitators of access to life beyond the 'artificial' world of the cinema and dance hall. This organized recreational walking may also be seen in the context of New Zealand's popular engagement with science and ethnology.[48] Ross's analysis suggests two relatively unexplored aspects of New Zealand's sports history: scholarly analyses of mountaineering, which is odd given the popular interest in climbing and climbers as well as the iconic national profile of Sir Edmund Hillary, and scholarly analyses of clubs, though in the latter New Zealand's lacuna is hardly distinctive.[49] These papers by Wevers and Ross hint at a wider history of sport than that currently constructed within a nationalist paradigm shaped by a concern to explain the dominant and hegemonic, and an English public school-based conceptualization of sport as games.

In a paper that extends her tantalizing collaborative essay about the New Zealand Marching Association, Macdonald unravels the contradictory place of women's competitive marching in Cold War New Zealand culture.[50] Women's competitive marching was a uniquely New Zealand pastime that emerged from wartime experience that built on marching as display in the 1920s and 1930s, and in its post-war manifestation differed markedly from the pre-war display in being distinctly and explicitly competitive and sportized. For Macdonald, marching was paradoxical – it sportized martial space, it relied on disciplined movement and disciplined bodies clad in archaic military-style tunics and hats and short skirts that she characterizes as bringing together 'military preparedness and a decorative (almost flirtatious) femininity'.[51] More importantly, she identifies the discipline of (feminine) marching as a counterpoint to the disorder of the (masculine) rugby field, which was widely seen as means to channel and release men's excess social and sexual energy, all in the context of a much more complex and subtle reading of post-war gender relations as contested and contestable, and pointing to participants' experiences of marching as potentially disruptive. In making this case and drawing an image of gender and nation that is ambiguous, paradoxical and relational, Macdonald opens up challenging new areas for a New Zealand sports history in decentring men and the nation.

Along with Joyce's analysis of surf lifesaving, a much more explicit challenge to an assumed unproblematic contiguity between sport, men, nation and national identity may be seen in Daley's work on women's endurance swimming in the 1930s.[52] Central to her discussion is Katerina Nehua, a Maori (Nga Puhi) woman living in Sydney. Nehua decentres the nation – as a Maori woman she was marginalized by the dominant one-nation masculinist view of the colonial nation. Furthermore, she was spatially dislocated through living in Sydney, and participating in an event that failed to fit the received view of sport – the focus was more on endurance (staying in the water) than swimming. Daley's analysis also considers New Zealand women's swims of the English Channel, and English female endurance swimmers' visits to and celebrity in New Zealand. In doing so, she constructs an argument that radically decentres the nation, sport and masculinity. It is an analysis that explicates networks and webs of significance that disrupt the symbolic construction of colony, nation and empire, which provides a rich model for enhanced collaborative and comparative work. Along with Ballantyne's *Orientalism and Race*, it presents a significant challenge to the received analytical frameworks deployed in much New Zealand history.

On more conventional historiographical ground, Simpson's analyses of women's cycling consider the sport within a continuum of women's physical activity linked to broader social change in women's status. In making her case, she implies connections between British, North American, Australian and New Zealand 'first wave' feminism, and while recovering a history of women's physicality, also challenges much of the received wisdom about the late 19th-century gender order.[53] Working in a similarly safe epistemological space is Vincent's regional sports history, which is shaped by and responds to Fairburn's model of colonial settler society as atomized with only limited and weak community and communitarian links.[54] This smaller body of work exposes the power of the games motif in New Zealand's scholarly sports histories that exclude activities such as swimming, though Joyce's and Booth's works on surf lifesaving indicate the potential for challenges, as does Pearson's more sociological analysis of surfing subcultures.[55]

Histories that move beyond the boys and their balls school of sports history point to a rich sporting past to be uncovered, explored, constructed and interpreted, depending on the historian's epistemological stance. Hints of the richness of that past may be seen, for instance, in Davis's investigation of the manufacturer, merchant and trader J.S.M. Thompson in Australia and New Zealand.[56] Davis also points to the importance of racing clubs in New Zealand's upper-class society, the earliest of which were formed in the 1840s. Horse-racing was nationally organized during the early 1880s, and trotting in the 1890s. By the middle of the 1960s, 71 racing clubs, 17 hunt clubs and 295 days per year were allocated to racing, with a further 121 days allocated to trotting.[57] Despite this profile and the widespread popularity of racing and trotting, the sports and their supporting industries have attracted little scholarly interest, though there is an extensive serious popular literature.[58] These gaps suggest a reason for a sense in much New Zealand sports history that a recovery exercise is underway, though, as Booth has argued, genre and paradigms invoked by New Zealand's sports historians move well, if cautiously, beyond those often associated with salvage history.[59]

Sport in history

The move beyond salvage history means a move away from treating sport as an object of subaltern history. Such a shift lies at the heart of and at the same time makes unfair Watson's argument that there has been a failure to develop a 'comprehensive study of the role of sport in New Zealand history'.[60] Although sports history has been marginal in New Zealand history, the earlier discussions of the 1905 rugby union tour of Great Britain suggest that sport has not been insignificant. That tour has played a major role in popular perceptions of New Zealand nationalism and New Zealand's national status, even if it has been an invented tradition.[61] Watson's critique may be further challenged if we consider the struggle against sporting contact with apartheid-era South Africa.

Disquiet over New Zealand's sporting contact with South Africa had been expressed through most of the 20th century, though before 1939 it was for the most part restricted to Maori and, as a result, for the most part unrecognized or unobserved in (colonial) New Zealand.[62] Until 1960 this disquiet centred on the exclusion of Maori from teams touring South Africa – the 1956 South African tour to New Zealand passed without expression of discontent.[63] Public protest in 1960, when New Zealand toured South Africa, accentuated the sense that the exclusion of Maori from touring teams 'imported apartheid' to New Zealand and was an affront to New Zealand's claimed 'exemplary race relations'.[64] Although the 1960 campaign included protest marches involving several thousand people, the issue remained historically marginal and, despite militant protest in 1970, did so until 1973, when the government cancelled a proposed tour of New Zealand. By this stage the focus of the campaign had shifted from 'protection' of Maori to become a boycott-based anti-apartheid campaign. As a result, between 1975 and 1981 sporting contact with South Africa became a central issue in New Zealand politics. Sporting contact was a vital issue in the 1975 election campaign, New Zealand's tour of South Africa in 1976 led directly to the boycott of the Montréal Olympic Games and to the Commonwealth's increasingly forceful stand against apartheid, and there was mass disruption and intense political turmoil associated with the campaign against the 1981 tour of New Zealand.[65]

The significance of the campaign in 1981 has been obscured by the subsequent neo-liberal revolution and changes in Maori-state relations, while the Whiggish politics of the studies of New Zealand's recent history require the erasure of contentious events to create new myths as 'a necessary basis for identity'.[66] Its political significance is notable – it was the most intense of a series of high-profile and militant protests between 1969–70 and 1985, it mounted a direct challenge to the state, and it drew together many groups in a cross-class, multi-cultural, multi-gendered campaign that focused on two of New Zealand's foundational myths: rugby union as a marker of a dominant form of masculinity and New Zealand's exemplary race relations. The sheer breadth of the movement caused significant problems, in that it drew together people who were not used to political work together, and for many Pakeha was probably one of the first times they had engaged in active political campaigning with Maori.

A key analytical strand has not seen a focus on these colonial relations, but on gender. Thompson set the terms of the debate with her argument that the anti-tour campaign exposed to many women rugby union's role in the patriarchal order in New Zealand and challenged their adherence to the sport.[67] This analysis has held considerable sway over thinking about these events, in part because the heightened gender politics of the campaign resonated with activist-analysts. More recently, though, this view of gender as the central analytical trope for the anti-tour campaign has come into question: Hughes has revealed gender divisions in the anti-tour movement that critique Thompson's analysis. Hughes argues that feminist advocacy is understandable given the high profile of the women's movement at the time, but that in failing to explore masculinities' relationships with rugby union, the gender-analyses to date are inadequate.[68] Hughes's case reveals the anti-tour campaign as now coming within historians' purview, and the value of rigorous oral histories and source scepticism in sports history.

The gender-focused analysis has been challenged through an emphasis on the foundational 'race relations' myth. Although analysts of the Maori-based protest movements of the 1970s and 1980s regularly noted the 1981 campaign as significant in those movements, it often appears as if a footnote. MacLean's analyses of the campaign exploring, amongst other things, its interpretation in the context of specific local inflections of New Zealand's history, and the complex relationship between Maori and anti-tour movement, suggest that the events of 1981 may cast greater light on the cultural politics of the era than the gender analyses advanced by Thompson and the footnote to Maori activism perspectives may allow.[69] Daley's unpacking of the significance of 1905 in New Zealand's national mythology and Hughes's and MacLean's revisionist analyses of the New Zealand–South Africa sports nexus, while indicating the validity of Watson's claim, point to pathways beyond the situation he identifies.

Conclusion: writing history

This discussion has thus far provided a conventional historiographical lens through which to analyse Aotearoa New Zealand sports history. Scholarly writing about Aotearoa New Zealand sport has been the subject of historiographical interpretation by Booth, while Daley's distinction between unsanctioned pleasure and sanctioned leisure provides a further analytical frame. Booth's use of Munslow's historiographical frame to explore sports history has been the focus of considerable debate among sports historians.[70] Munslow's model proposes three epistemologies of history – reconstructionist, rooted in the belief that the past is knowable through 'the single statement of justified belief[... and] inference and the accurate demonstration of the historical agent's actions'; constructionist, which he sees as 'a highly complex conceptual and theory-laden ... approach[... that] means hypothesising about the causes of regularities in the past and explaining them'; and deconstructionist, wherein 'past events are explained and acquire their meaning as much by their representation as by their "knowable actuality"'.[71] Booth's analysis combines this typology of genre with a series of explanatory paradigms derived from Fischer's philosophy of history to argue that most New Zealand sports historians adopt reconstructionist and constructionist approaches, although some – he cites Macdonald's work on women's marching and MacLean's on the 1981 tour – are willing to 'accommodate epistemologically non-threatening forms of deconstructionism'.[72]

The difficulty with Booth's approach lies not in his use of Munslow, but with the suitability of Munslow's conceptualization of history in post-colonizing Aotearoa New Zealand. Munslow and his collaborator Keith Jenkins define history in narrow terms as a post-Enlightenment practice, which in strict disciplinary terms may be valid, except that it excludes large bodies of thought that explore ways of thinking and doing the past and the present.[73] It is conventional to cite Herodotus and the Venerable Bede as precursors to modern history, and they certainly demonstrate aspects of the modern historian's craft in their work. A more serious omission from this narrowly defined sense of history – a definition that has led Jenkins to claim that no-one had an historical consciousness before the 19th century[74] – is the development of historical practice outside the European peninsular, the most notable example of which is the Islamic scholar Ibn Khaldoun and, to a lesser extent, the 'travelling philosopher' Ibn Battutah.[75] Ibn Khaldoun's pre-Enlightenment *Muqaddimah* is a modern history exhibiting both 'reconstructionist' and 'constructionist' traits, even though, according to the Christian calendar, the author lived between 1332 and 1406. The jurist Ibn Battutah (writing between 1324 and 1352 AD) can be read through modern disciplinary lenses as jurist, travel writer, historian, sociologist and anthropologist.

The paradox of such a rigid definition of history is that it denigrates the position of reader so central to deconstructionist epistemologies: many Maori readers of the biographies that make up over half the Aotearoa Maori Tennis Association's history or of Bull's history of the Otaki Maori Racing Club, although both texts are reconstructionist, will understand those histories and biographies in a different way than Pakeha readers and construct different histories, almost certainly based in a genealogically framed world view.[76] Munslow's epistemologically narrow definition of history makes it useful to analyse, as Booth does, academic writing – but its usefulness in a post-colonizing setting where epistemologies draw on both (post-)Enlightenment thought and structures of knowledge beyond the tradition of which the European Enlightenment is a part remains, for the most part, unconsidered. As useful, then, as Booth's historiographical analyses are, they remain about New Zealand and not yet about Aotearoa.

Daley's less epistemologically rigid distinction between unsanctioned pleasure and sanctioned leisure may provide a more productive, though less philosophically demanding distinction in thinking about sports history in practice.[77] Whereas the Munslow-inspired approach invoked by Booth is useful in helping historians think about how we do what we do (although it has a lot to say about what we write, it has almost nothing to say about the process of getting the words on the page – how we write), Daley's distinction is helpful in encouraging historians to think about what the people we write about, and the people who write, do. A key way that it does this is by encouraging us to look differently and with greater subtlety at our subaltern historical subject and subjects. A crucial distinction underpinning this differentiation between the sanctioned and unsanctioned is the 'modernizing' tendency to distinguish between the irrational (pleasure) and the rational (leisure). Daley's approach allows researchers to do more than focus on the sanctioned and unsanctioned, rational and irrational, legitimate and subversive; it allows us to ground sport and leisure activities in a broader set of capitalist social relations, and the mundane world of control, of discipline and of social struggle. That is, it encourages us to find the people in our sports history and to locate them in the specific socio-cultural relations that are colonizing, colonial and post-colonizing Aotearoa New Zealand.

Scholarly sports history in Aotearoa New Zealand is not all that distinctive. It is written and read through a national(ist) frame, its principal subjects are men who are in many cases equated with that nation, its principal topics are activities pursued primarily or in an approved manner by men. It treats Aotearoa New Zealand's indigenous people as incorporated into the sporting life worlds of the dominant national formation (there is little recognition that Maori sport might be or is different), and as providing distinctive local colour and style. The paradox of this sports history is that it misses the very things that make it distinctive: in failing to be comparative it claims distinctiveness without testing the claim; the sports practices it explores are, for the most part, those of the old imperial 'home', yet there is little attention given to these sports practices as both and concurrently unifying through that British connection and distinguishing it as of Aotearoa New Zealand. If sports history as a branch of cultural history is to realize its potential then its practitioners need to respond to Gibbons' call 'to become less parochial and insular and to decentre or even dissolve "New Zealand" as a subject',[78] and to move beyond the boys-and-their-balls-as-nationalist-discourse school of history to raise questions about imperial and colonial sporting networks, to break from the sport-as-games mould, and to throw off its nationalist shackles.

Notes

1   This chapter uses the term Aotearoa New Zealand to refer to the cluster of islands in the southwest Pacific commonly known as New Zealand, Aotearoa to refer to Maori life worlds in those islands, and New Zealand to refer to the colonial space and cultural political entity. Some critics have noted that the use of Aotearoa incorrectly implies the existence of uniform or common Maori cultural space, and while I recognize that potential, note also that using New Zealand as a marker of cultural space might be seen to construct the classed, gendered, ethnically configured colonizer's life worlds in a similarly uniform and incorrect manner. Both Aotearoa and New Zealand are imagined and imaginary spaces, although their denizens are not free to imagine them as they choose. There is little doubt that whatever the labels used, a notion or actuality of a distinct Maori life world is absent from almost all sports history in Aotearoa New Zealand.

2   J. Belich, *Paradise Reforged: A History of the New Zealanders From the 1880s to the Year 2000* (Auckland: Allen Lane, 2001), 368–88; A. Else, ed., *Women Together: A History of Women's Organisations in New Zealand Nga Ropu Wahine o te Motu* (Wellington: Historical Branch/Daphne Brassell

Associates, 1993), 405–44; A. H. McLintock, ed., *An Encyclopaedia of New Zealand*, 3 vols (Wellington: R. E. Owen, Government Printer, 1966).

3 D. Booth, *The Field: Truth and Fiction in Sport History* (London: Routledge, 2005); D. Booth, 'Searching for the Past: Sport Historiography in New Zealand', *Sporting Traditions* 21(2) (2005), 1–28; D. Booth, 'Sport Historiography in Aotearoa New Zealand: Playing with the Past', in C. Collins and S. Jackson, eds, *Sport in Aotearoa New Zealand Society*, 2nd edn (Auckland: Thomson, 2007), 51–77.

4 M. Smith, *Champion Blokes: 44 Great New Zealand Sportsmen Then and Now* (Christchurch: Whitcombe & Tombs, 1964); W. Ingram, *Legends in Their Lifetime* (Wellington: A. W. & A. H. Reed, 1962). Ingram included one woman, equestrian Maggie Briggs, among his *Legends*.

5 W. P. Reeves, *The Long White Cloud Ao Tea Roa* (Auckland: Viking, 1987 [1898]); J. C. Beaglehole, *New Zealand: A Short History* (London: George Allen and Unwin, 1936); A. H. Reed, *The Story of New Zealand* (Wellington: A. H. and A. W. Reed, 1945 and subsequent edns).

6 P. Gibbons, 'The Far Side of the Search for Identity', *New Zealand Journal of History*, 37(1) (2003), 38–49.

7 J. Belich, *Making Peoples: A History of the New Zealanders From Polynesian Settlement to the End of the Nineteenth Century* (Auckland: Allen Lane, 1996); Belich, *Paradise Reforged*; W. B. Sutch, *The Quest for Security in New Zealand, 1840–1966* (Oxford: Oxford University Press, 1966).

8 J. Phillips, *A Man's Country? The Image of the Pakeha Male – A History*, revised edn (Auckland: Penguin Books, 1996); K. Sinclair, *A Destiny Apart: New Zealand's Search for National Identity* (Wellington: Port Nicholson Press/Allen and Unwin, 1986). Phillips, in this book, extends and develops arguments also advanced in different forms in 'Rugby, War and the Mythology of the New Zealand Male', *New Zealand Journal of History* 18(2) (1984), 83–103, and 'Of Verandahs and Fish and Chips and Footie on Saturday Afternoon', *New Zealand Journal of History* 24(2) (1990), 118–34.

9 S. Zavos, *The Gold and the Black: The Rugby Battles for the Bledisloe Cup, New Zealand vs. Australia 1903–94* (Sydney: Allen and Unwin, 1995); S. Zavos, *Ka Mate! Ka Mate! New Zealand's Conquest of British Rugby* (Auckland: Viking, 1998); S. Zavos, *Winters of Revenge: The Bitter Rivalry Between the All Blacks and the Springboks* (Auckland: Penguin, 1997); H. Richards, *Dragons and All Blacks: Wales v New Zealand – 1953 and a Century of Rivalry* (Edinburgh: Mainstream, 2004).

10 G. Watson, 'Sport and Ethnicity in New Zealand', *History Compass* 5 (3) (2007), 780.

11 C. Little, 'The Forgotten Game? A Reassessment of the Place of Soccer within New Zealand Society, Sport and Historiography', *Soccer and Society* 3 (2) (2002), 38–50; W. Keane, '"Ex-pats" and "Poofters" Rebuild the Nation: 1982, Kiwi Culture and the All Whites on the Road to Spain', in B. Patterson, ed., *Sport, Culture and Society in New Zealand* (Wellington: Stout Research Centre, 1999), 49–60.

12 D. Charabarty, *Provincializing Europe: Postcolonial Thought and Historical Difference* (Princeton: Princeton University Press, 2000), 101.

13 K. Sinclair, *A History of New Zealand* (Harmondsworth: Penguin, 1959).

14 C. Daley, 'Women Endurance Swimmers: Dissolving Grease Suits and Decentring New Zealand History', *Sporting Traditions* 21(2) (2005), 31.

15 Collins & Jackson, *Sport in Aotearoa New Zealand Society*; C. Daley, 'The Invention of 1905', in G. Ryan, ed., *Tackling Rugby Myths: Rugby and New Zealand Society 1854–2004* (Dunedin: Otago University Press, 2005), 69–87.

16 C. Daley, *Leisure and Pleasure: Reshaping and Revealing the New Zealand Body 1900–1960* (Auckland: Auckland University Press, 2003) (the exclusion of sport is noted on p. 10); C. Daley, 'Selling Sandow: Modernity and Leisure in Early Twentieth-Century New Zealand', *New Zealand Journal of History* 34(2) (2000), 241–61.

17 Several of these pieces are included in Ryan's edited collection *Tackling Rugby Myths: Rugby and New Zealand Society 1854–2004* (Dunedin: Otago University Press, 2005), including 'Rural Myth and Urban Actuality: The Anatomy of All Black and New Zealand Rugby 1884–1938', 33–54 (originally *NZJH* 35(1), 45–69), and 'The End of an Aura: All Black Rugby and Rural Nostalgia in the Professional Era', 151–72.

18 L. Coupe, *Myth* (London: Routledge, 1997).

19 C. Obel, 'Amateur Rugby's Spectator Success: Cultivating Inter-Provincial Rugby Publics in New Zealand, 1902–95', *Sporting Traditions* 21(2) (2005), 97–117.

20 The notable exceptions here are J. Nauright and J. Broomhill, 'A Woman's Game: The Development of Netball and a Female Sporting Culture in New Zealand, 1906–70', *International Journal of the*

History of Sport 11 (3) (1994), 387–407; J. Nauright, 'Netball, Media Representations of Women and Crises of Male Hegemony', in J. Nauright, ed., *Sport, Power and Society in New Zealand: Historical and Contemporary Perspectives* (Sydney: Australian Society for Sports History, 1995), 47–65.

21 J. Nauright and T.J.L. Chandler attempted to bridge this gap in their edited collections, *Making Men: Rugby and Masculine Identity* (London: Routledge, 1996) and the sequel volume, *Making the Rugby World: Race, Gender, Commerce* (London: Routledge, 1999); however, their work examines individual case studies which infer comparisons, other than the chapters by Nauright which examine New Zealand and South Africa in comparative context.

22 J.A. Mangan and J. Nauright, eds, *Sport in Australasian Society: Past and Present* (London: Routledge, 2000); D. Adair, 'Sports History in The "Antipodes" and "Australasia"', *Sporting Traditions* 19 (1) (2002), 65–74; my emphasis.

23 A. Smith, 'Black against Gold: New Zealand-Australia Sporting Rivalry in the Modern Era', in A. Smith and D. Porter, eds, *Sport and National Identity in the Post-War World* (London: Routledge, 2004), 168–93.

24 D. Booth, 'Healthy, Economic, Disciplined Bodies: Surfbathing and Surf Lifesaving in Australia and New Zealand, 1890–1950', *New Zealand Journal of History* 32(1) (1998), 43–58; E. Joyce, '"Fraternal Greetings to Kindred Clubs in Australia and New Zealand": Australian Surf Lifesaving on the New Zealand Beach', *Sporting Traditions* 24(1/2) (2007), 57–76.

25 Morris defines an epistemic singularity as 'one thing therefore one origin'. M. Morris, *Too Soon Too Late: History in Popular Culture* (Indiana: Indiana University Press, 1998), 97–100.

26 J. Eddy and D. Schreuder, 'Introduction', in J. Eddy and D. Schreuder, eds, *The Rise of Colonial Nationalism: Australia, New Zealand, Canada and South Africa First Assert Their Nationalities, 1880–1914* (Sydney: Allen and Unwin, 1988), 7.

27 G. Vincent, C. E. Timms and T. Harfield, 'Running, Jumping and Rowing to Marginalisation: The Maori Experience of Sport in Canterbury, 1850–80', *Sporting Traditions* 21 (2) (2005), 57–74. Important rebuttals to the tendency to sportization of pre-colonial body and movement cultures may be found in B. Hokowhitu, 'Maori Sport: Pre-Colonisation to Today', in Collins and Jackson, *Sport in Aotearoa New Zealand Society*, especially 79–83; F. Palmer, 'Treaty Principles and Maori Sport: Contemporary Issues', in Collins and Jackson, *Sport In Aotearoa New Zealand Society*, 317–34; and noting its place as a text of salvage ethnography, E. Best, *Games and Pastimes of the Maori* (Wellington: Dominion Museum Bulletin No. 8, 1925).

28 G. Ryan, 'Anthropological Football: Maori and the 1937 Springbok Rugby Tour of New Zealand', *New Zealand Journal of History* 34 (1) (2000), 60–79, reprinted in a modified form in *Tackling Rugby Myths*, 105–22.

29 M. MacLean, 'Of Warriors and Blokes: The Problem of Maori Rugby for Pakeha Masculinity in New Zealand', in T. Chandler and J. Nauright, eds, *Making The Rugby World: Race, Gender, Commerce* (London: Frank Cass, 1999), 1–26.

30 Aotearoa Maori Tennis Association, *A History of Maori Tennis: He Hitori o te Tenehi Maori* (Manukau City: Aotearoa Maori Tennis Association, 2006); A. Bull, *The Otaki-Maori Racing Club: A History 1886–1990* (Otaki: Otaki-Maori Racing Club, 1990); M. Te Pou with M. McIlraith, *Against the Odds: Matt Te Pou and Maori Rugby* (Wellington: Huia Books, 2006).

31 B. Hokowhitu, 'Rugby and Tino Rangatiratanga: Early Maori Rugby and the Formation of "Traditional" Maori Masculinity', *Sporting Traditions* 21 (2) (2005), 75–95; B. Hokowhitu, 'Tackling Maori Masculinity: A Colonial Genealogy of Savagery and Sport', *The Contemporary Pacific* 16 (2) (2004), 259–84; B. Hokowhitu, 'Race Tactics: The Racialised Athletic Body', *Junctures: the Journal for Thematic Dialogue* 1 (2003), 21–34.

32 This approach is explored in M. MacLean, 'Ambiguity Within the Boundary: Re-reading CLR James' *Beyond a Boundary*', *Journal of Sport History*, forthcoming.

33 G. Ryan, *Forerunners of the All Blacks: The 1888–89 New Zealand Native Football Team in Britain* (Christchurch: Canterbury University Press, 1993), 51–55; G. Ryan, *The Contest for Rugby Supremacy: Accounting for the Success of the 1905 All Blacks* (Christchurch: Canterbury University Press, 2005); J. Nauright, 'Sport, Manhood and Empire: British Responses to the New Zealand Rugby Tour of 1905, *International Journal of the History of Sport* 8:2 (1991), 239–55; G. R. Seeley, *The Expansion of England* (London: Macmillan, 1883), cited in C. Hall, 'Introduction: Thinking the Postcolonial, Thinking the Empire', in C. Hall, ed., *Cultures of Empire: A Reader* (Manchester: Manchester University Press, 2000), 1–2.

34 G. Ryan, '"A Lack of Esprit De Corps": The 1908–9 Wallabies and the Legacy of the 1905 All Blacks', *Sporting Traditions* 17 (1) (2000), 39–55.

35 G. Ryan, '"Britishers Anxious to Appear on the Cricket Map": Anglo-New Zealand Cricket in the Imperial Context 1927–58', *International Journal of the History of Sport* 25 (1) (2008), 18–40.

36 Ryan, *Forerunners of the All Blacks*.

37 M. Falcous, 'Rugby League in the Imaginary of New Zealand Aotearoa', *Sport in History* 27 (3) (2007), 423–46.

38 Other analyses of rugby league challenge the harmonious nationalism of New Zealand sport. See, for instance, C. Little, 'More Green Than Red: Sectarianism and Rugby League in Otago, 1924–35', *Sporting Traditions* 21 (1) (2004), 33–51; G. Vincent and T. Harfield, 'Repression and Reform: Responses within New Zealand Rugby to the Arrival of the "Northern Game", 1907–8', *New Zealand Journal of History* 31 (2) (1997), 234–50.

39 See, for instance, E. Fry, ed., *Common Cause: Essays in Australian and New Zealand Labour History* (Wellington: Allen and Unwin/Port Nicholson Press, 1986); J. Phillips, ed., *New Worlds? The Comparative History of New Zealand and the United States* (Wellington: Stout Research Centre, 1989); M. McKinnon, ed., *The American Connection: Essays from the Stout Centre Conference* (Wellington: Allen and Unwin/Port Nicholson Press, 1988); M. McKinnon, *Independence and Foreign Policy: New Zealand in the World Since 1935* (Auckland: Auckland University Press, 1993); D. Hamer, *New Towns in the New World: Images and Perceptions of the Nineteenth-century Urban Frontier* (New York: Columbia University Press, 1990).

40 Smith, 'Black against Gold: New Zealand-Australia Sporting Rivalry in the Modern Era'; G. Ryan, '"Extravagance of Thought and Feeling": New Zealand Reactions to the 1932/33 Bodyline Controversy', *Sporting Traditions* 13 (2) (1997), 41–58; G. Ryan, *The Making of New Zealand Cricket, 1832–1914* (London: Frank Cass, 2004).

41 Ryan is almost alone in his scholarly work on New Zealand cricket, aside from a frustratingly brief foray into women's cricket by A. Simpson, 'New Zealand's Wicket Women', in Patterson, *Sport, Culture and Society*, 61–72.

42 T. Ballantyne, *Orientalism and Race: Aryanism in the British Empire* (Basingstoke: Palgrave, 2002); E. Boehmer, *Empire, the National, and the Postcolonial, 1890–1920* (Oxford: Oxford University Press, 2002).

43 M. Williams, 'Crippled by Geography? New Zealand Nationalisms', in S. Murray, ed., *Not on Any Map: Essays on Postcoloniality and Cultural Nationalism* (Exeter: University of Exeter Press, 1997), 19–42.

44 G. Watson, 'Affirming Indian Identities? An Analysis of Imperial Rhetoric and Orientalism in the Tours of Indian Hockey Teams to New Zealand in 1926, 1935 and 1938', *Sporting Traditions* 21 (2) (2005), 119–40.

45 C. Macdonald, 'Putting Bodies on the Line: Marching Space in Cold War Culture', in J. Bale and P. Vertinsky, eds, *Sites of Sport: Space, Place, Experience* (London: Routledge, 2004), 83–100; K. Ross, 'Schooled by Nature: Pakeha Tramping Between the Wars', *New Zealand Journal of History* 36 (1) (2002), 51–65; L. Wevers, 'The Pleasure of Walking', *New Zealand Journal of History* 38 (1) (2004), 39–51.

46 Daley, *Leisure and Pleasure*, 6.

47 L. Wevers, 'Fishing for Empire; Sport and Travel in New Zealand from the 1870s to the 1930s', in Patterson, *Sport, Culture and Society*, 165–78; L. Wevers, *Country of Writing: Travel Writing in New Zealand, 1809–1900* (Auckland: Auckland University Press, 2002).

48 A. Dreaver, *An Eye for the Country: The Life and Work of Leslie Adkin* (Wellington: Victoria University Press, 1997).

49 On clubs, see S. Szymanski, 'A Theory of the Evolution of Modern Sport', S. A. Reiss, 'Associativity and the Evolution of Modern Sport', A. Krüger, 'Which associativity? A German Answer to Szymanski's Theory of the Evolution of Modern Sport', M. MacLean, 'Evolving Modern Sport', and S. Szymanski, 'Responses to Comments', all in *Journal of Sports History* 35 (1) (2008), 1–64; J. Hill, *Sport, Leisure and Culture in Twentieth Century Britain* (Basingstoke: Palgrave, 2002), 130–46; Else, *Women Together* contains a number of entries dealing with women's sports organizations.

50 J. Williams, V. Browning and C. Macdonald, 'New Zealand Marching Association 1945–', in Else, *Women Together*, 437–39.

51 Macdonald, 'Putting Bodies on the Line', 95.

52 Daley, 'Women Endurance Swimmers'.

53 C. Simpson, 'Atlanta Cycling Club 1892–c.1898', in Else, *Women Together*, 418–19; C. Simpson, 'The Development of Women's Cycling in Late Nineteenth Century New Zealand', in Nauright,

Sport, Power and Society, 21–45; C. Simpson, 'Nineteenth-Century Women on Bicycles Redefine Respectability', in Patterson, *Sport, Culture and Society*, 147–56; C. Simpson, 'Managing Public Impressions: Strategies of Nineteenth-Century Women Cyclists', *Sporting Traditions* 19 (2) (2003), 1–15; C. Simpson, 'Sights from the Saddle: Early Cycle Touring in New Zealand', *Sporting Traditions* 21 (2) (2005), 141–60.

54 G. Vincent, 'Sport, Class and Community in Canterbury, 1850–80: The Evidence of Rowing', in Patterson, *Sport, Culture and Society*, 157–64; M. Fairburn, *The Ideal Society and Its Enemies: The Foundations of Modern New Zealand Society* (Auckland: Auckland University Press, 1989).

55 K. Pearson, *Surfing Subcultures of Australia and New Zealand* (St Lucia: University of Queensland Press, 1979).

56 R. Davis, 'Softgoods, Engineering and Sport: J.S.M. Thompson in New Zealand and Victoria, 1868–1910', *Sporting Traditions* 20 (1) (2003), 1–16.

57 McLintock, *An Encyclopaedia of New Zealand*, vol. 3, 13–30.

58 J. Costello and P. Finnegan, *Tapestry of Turf: The History of New Zealand Racing* (Auckland: Moa Publications, 1988); D. Grant, *On A Roll: A History of Gambling and Lotteries in New Zealand* (Wellington: Victoria University Press, 1994); D. Grant, 'Clashes of Culture and Class: The Jockey's Strike of 1920', in Patterson, *Sport, Culture and Society*, 123–34; M. Redwood, *Proud Silk: A New Zealand Racing History* (Wellington: Reed, 1979); Bull, *Otaki-Maori Racing Club*.

59 Booth 'Searching for the Past'; Booth 'Sport Historiography'.

60 Watson, 'Sport and Ethnicity in New Zealand', 780.

61 Daley, 'The Invention of 1905'.

62 Ryan, 'Anthropological Football'.

63 M. Pearson, 'Heads in the Sand: The 1956 Springbok Tour to New Zealand in Perspective', in R. Cashman and K. McKernan, eds, *Sport in History: The Making of Modern Sporting History* (Brisbane: University of Queensland Press, 1979), 272–93; F. Andrewes, 'Demonstrable Virility: Images of Masculinity in the 1956 Springbok Tour of New Zealand', in Ryan, *Tackling Rugby Myths*, 123–36.

64 R. Thompson, *Retreat from Apartheid: New Zealand's Sporting Contacts with South Africa* (Wellington: Oxford University Press, 1975), 18–26.

65 These events have been the focus of a number of scholarly analyses, including M. MacLean, 'Football as Social Critique: Protest Movements, Rugby and History in Aotearoa New Zealand', *International Journal for the History of Sport* 17(2/3) (2000), 255–77; J. Nauright and D. Black, 'New Zealand and International Sport: The Case of All Black-Springbok Rugby, Sanctions and Protest Against Apartheid 1959–92', in Nauright, *Sport, Power and Society*, 67–93; J. Nauright, '"Like Fleas on a Dog": Emerging National and International Conflict over New Zealand Rugby Ties with South Africa, 1965–74', *Sporting Traditions* 10 (1) (1993), 54–77; T. Richards, *Dancing On Our Bones: New Zealand, South Africa, Rugby and Racism* (Wellington: Bridget Williams Books, 1999); M. Templeton, *Human Rights and Sporting Contacts: New Zealand's Attitudes to Race Relations in South Africa 1921–94* (Auckland: Auckland University Press, 1998). There is also a large body of serious popular analysis.

66 J. Black, 'Contesting the Past', *History* 93 (310) (2008), 225.

67 S. Thompson, 'Challenging the Hegemony: New Zealand Women's Opposition to Rugby', *International Review for the Sociology of Sport* 23 (3) (1998), 205–12; S. Thompson, 'Legacy of the "The Tour": A Continued Analysis of Women's Relationship to Sport', in Patterson, *Sport, Society and Culture*, 79–91.

68 C. Hughes, 'Moira's Lament? Feminist Advocacy and the 1981 Springbok Tour of New Zealand', in Ryan, *Tackling Rugby Myths*, 137–50.

69 M. MacLean, 'Making Strange the Country and Making Strange the Countryside: Spatialized Clashes in the Affective Economies of Aotearoa New Zealand during the 1981 Springbok Rugby Tour', in J. Bale and M. Cronin, eds, *Sport and Postcolonialism* (Oxford: Berg, 2003), 57–72; M. MacLean, '"Almost the same, but not quite … Almost the same, but not white": Maori and Aotearoa New Zealand's 1981 Springbok Tour', *Kunapipi: Journal of Postcolonial Writing* 23 (1) (2001), 69–82; M. MacLean, 'Confronting Foundational Myths: Apartheid, Rugby and the Post-Colonising of Aotearoa New Zealand', unpublished PhD thesis, University of Queensland, 2004.

70 A. Guttmann, 'Review Essay: The Ludic and the Ludicrous', *International Journal of the History of Sport* 25 (1) (2008), 100–12.

71 A. Munslow, *Narrative and History* (Basingstoke: Palgrave, 2007), 11–14.

72 D. Fischer, *Historian's Fallacies: Toward a Logic of Historical Thought* (New York: Harper Collins, 1970); Booth, 'Searching for the Past', 21.

73 See C. Dietze, 'Toward a History on Equal Terms: A Discussion of *Provincializing Europe*', *History and Theory* 47 (2008), 69–84; D. Chakrabarty, 'In Defense of *Provincializing Europe*: A Response to Carola Dietze', *History and Theory* 47 (2008), 85–96.

74 He made this claim in the context of a debate about memory at the 'New Manifestoes for History' workshop, Birkbeck Institute for the Humanities, University of London, 26 January 2008.

75 Ibn Khaldun, *The Muqaddimah: An Introduction to History*, translated by F. Rosenthal, abridged and edited by B. Lawrence (Princeton: Princeton University Press, 2005); Ibn Battutah, *The Travels of Ibn Battutah*, translated by H. Gibb and C. F. Beckingham, abridged and edited by T. Mackintosh-Smith (London: Picador, 2002). I am grateful to Sariya Contractor for the 'travelling philosopher' label for Ibn Battutah.

76 Aotearoa Maori Tennis Association, *A History of Maori Tennis*; Bull, *The Otaki-Maori Racing Club*.

77 Daley, *Leisure and Pleasure*, 6.

78 Gibbons, 'The Far Side of the Search for Identity'.

33 Nordic countries

Niels Kayser Nielsen

The main argument of this chapter is that the histories of Nordic countries in the 19th and 20th centuries – as a hybrid – are located within two European traditions; that sport has made a valuable contribution to this hybrid; and that sport as a wordless activity exacerbates a non-martial nationalism which must be distinguished from ordinary 'hot' nationalism, so often criticized.

On the one hand stands the tradition that a classical European main road goes from reason to civilization, namely, that the critical intelligentsia in France and England, provoked by absolutism, advanced a series of Enlightenment ideas that, by means of educational and Enlightenment activities, spread down to the arsenal of ideas of the rest of the social classes and spawned the French Revolution with its promises of freedom, equality and fraternity; principles that later – with variations – achieved universal validity in Western Europe.

On the other hand stands the history of Germany and Eastern Europe, which since the 1800s testifies to an entirely different sequence of historical development than that outlined above. Here it is not just a question of a lack of liberalism, but rather direct terror and tyranny, with dictatorships being the rule rather than the exception. German historians have thus operated with the concept of the German *Sonderweg* to designate this other tradition in Europe. Fundamentally, it is dominated by an anti-rationalistic current that was first expressed in soulful romanticism with its sense of the irrational and that which was not rationally justified. This tradition cultivated a radical revolt against the clear light of reason and instead celebrated the phenomenon of *Dämmerung*,[1] which designates a nostalgic longing for holistic communities in which controlled equality in the shape of *communitas,* rather than unimpeded freedom, is in focus in Germany. As has been said about Germany in the 19th century, nowhere in Western Europe was the population regarded so much as subjects and so little as citizens.[2] Particularism rather than universalism was the focal point in Germany, inasmuch as the organization of society was still rooted in the feudal estate society. In Germany it was not the universalistic *liberté, égalité, fraternité* of civilization that was at a premium, but rather the ability of the state to create *machtgeschützte Innerlichkeit*, that is, the individual's intense desire to realize his or her subjective core potential.[3]

While the most important political actor of the French tradition of Enlightenment was the *citoyen,* who enjoyed general voting and civil rights, the German tradition is incarnated in the phenomenon of the *Bürger,* who stood more for particularism and local interests.[4]

The Nordic third way

Nordic historians have recently begun taking an interest in a third way of Nordic political culture as a mixture of universalistic Western European ideas and particularistic German and Eastern European ideas, epitomized in the Prussian motto 'Jedem das seine'. This kind of research achieved increasing importance among especially Swedish and Finnish historians through the 1990s and was most recently and clearly discussed in the anthology *The Cultural Construction of Norden*,[5] the various contributions each outlining a facet of this Scandinavian *Sonderweg*.

This research is characterized by basically returning to the question of the relation between the culture of local society with its concrete agents and national-central political objectives. In this connection, studies of the historical channels and arenas for communication between the local perspective and the perspective of the central powers all the way back to the 17th and 18th centuries have played a large role. From these it appears that the state has both encouraged hierarchies and promoted communities, involving pressure from above as well as opposition from below.[6] This mediation is not outlined in an idealizing, nostalgic light, heroizing happy communities and gracious *communitas* of the past. Power and struggle are often underscored. It is not a matter of nostalgia for consensus, for they examine in particular conflicts and kinds of conflict resolution.

Along with unorthodox organizations, local administrations formed the background of Swedish civil society, which in the course of the 19th century was expressed in associations and voluntary associations such as temperance societies, health insurance societies and trade unions.[7] The increasing individualization and demands of personal freedom and independence which also reached the Nordic countries in the 18th and 19th centuries were supplemented with egalitarian associations as a counterpart to the dissociation.

This process begins in all the Nordic countries in the 19th century – albeit with considerable differences – and continues in the first half of the 20th century; with a growing emphasis of the relation between freedom, equality and nationalism. This is what generally characterizes the Nordic *Sonderweg*. The citizen of this *Sonderweg* distinguishes itself as a concept from both the *citoyen* and the *Bürger* by asserting a universalistic individualism of equality as well as particular private interests. He (in the 19th century it was chiefly a male project) emphasized the rights of the individual and protestant duties, but also holistic collectivism, and at the same time coalesced, first in associations and later in mass organizations. The individual duty to one's calling in life was linked up with the shared management of tasks.

Association activities and general education

These associations are characterized by their respect of the individual's right to be an individual: entering associations is voluntary and personal, and one participates in the activities without taking into consideration ancestry, occupation and confession. The principle of organization is precisely a balanced relationship between freedom and equality.[8] Here people meet in the middle: in grassroots organizations with individual membership, where people adapted to each other and thus established a characteristic conformity. At first this conformity is not unlike the universality characterizing the standardized classical Western European transition from modernity, but it still radically differentiates itself from this by being practical and concrete rather than fundamental. As a result, it is only with considerable unwillingness that partial cultures and private interests are entrusted with responsibility; normally this happens only in so far that they at the same time praise the principle that the consensus of discussion, debate and dialogue should be allowed to penetrate all the pores of society, characterized as it is by the universal common sense of everyday life.[9] Society should be governed in the same way as an annual meeting, where everyone has the right to express themselves if only they are reasonable, pragmatic and want the best for everyone. In practice it is not just the principle of voluntariness, but also consensus that characterizes the Nordic kind of association.[10]

This homogenization in the Scandinavian countries is rooted in the Lutheran-Evangelistic propaganda efforts. Christian universalism was introduced earlier than the political and legal assertion of human rights and natural rights. In the 19th century, when schooling became systematized in the shape of the state school systems, this homogenization and universalization was further strengthened by virtue of nationalism's necessarily inclusive view of citizens, everyone in the nation in principle being alike and equal.[11] With alphabetization and conscription, the Nordic tendency to conformism was dramatically reinforced.

This conformity is most clearly expressed in the view of education. Education in Scandinavia is neither a purely technical enterprise nor a question of brilliant and classically educated *Bildungsbürgertum*. Until the educational revolution in about 1960, education in Norden has always entered into a hybrid with a conception of civic education that was neither purely Greek nor German, but rather linked to an element of popular education.[12] It is rather a question of communicative self-education and of pragmatic help with self-help, which could be further developed in the various communicative fora on a local level such as councils and associations.

The Grundtvigian reading clubs, free churches, parish councils and so forth carried on the Western European universalistic Enlightenment project and may be considered as having accomplished this.[13] However, as Øystein Sørensen and Bo Stråth put it, these organizations always smell a bit of manure and cowshed, in the sense that the pragmatic and sly considerations prevail over the idealistic and utopian characteristic. Nordic Enlightenment rationalism is a trade-off. The particularistic side of the matter has continuously played a key role. It is not without reason that Ludvig Schrøder, the Danish principal of Askov Folk High School, who usually was good for a long, idealistic lecture, wanted a liquid-manure barrel for his silver wedding anniversary.

It can thus hardly be doubted that what we have here is a special Nordic *Sonderweg*, with three essential characteristics: a balance between freedom and equality, pragmatism as an organizational principle, and conformity as an organizational form; but there is a one more facet – alongside Christianity, school and conscription – that belongs in this picture. This facet is sport; sport as an embodiment of the combination of freedom, egalitarianism and nationalism.

The contribution of sport to the Nordic third way

It seems strange that the role played by sport and physical education in the development of the distinctive political culture and cultural politics of the Nordic countries has been largely overlooked. In general, Nordic education and self-education were from the start tied to sport and organized physical activity.[14] Precisely because sport – in principle if not in practice – is based on the possibility of being the best on equal terms, it has been tied to the balancing of freedom and equality that seems to be so typically Nordic that one can rightly speak of a special Nordic way. The idea that it is not just consciousness, but also the body that should be qualified and developed – and that physical activities contributed decisively to the modernization of Nordic societies – is characteristic of Norden.[15]

Physical exercises also have a pragmatic aim: from the beginning there was talk of a combination of educational idealism and matter-of-fact useful aims when the Danish estate owners and brothers J.L. and C.D. Reventlow introduced physical exercises for the children of farmers on their respective farms. Physical qualifications were the precondition for 'industrious' farmers, who, as enterprising citizens, could manage every single pound for the best of the community. One should learn to be civilized in a physical sense also. Earth, consciousness and the body should be cultivated.

At the same time, sport is characterized by a certain 'democratic' physical conformity: stomachs growl regardless of the social class to which people belong, and at physical competitions the prerequisites of farmers and workers are just as good as those of the middle classes. Just like the Grundtvigians in Denmark, at the beginning of the 20th century the most visionary labour leaders in all the Nordic countries realized that sport could become an excellent means of demonstrating what the lower classes could achieve when it was not birthright, intellect and education that constituted the authoritative basis. The democratic legitimacy of the body is an essential part of the Nordic *Sonderweg*.

This may be where one finds the reason for the strong Grundtvigian tradition of letting physical activities (sport, folk dancing, gymnastics exhibitions) be part of general education. These physical activities have had the ability to create communities to an extent that other kinds of general education do not manage, creating the possibility of letting the participants not only feel integrated, but also feel like co-creators. The integration takes place in the very act that one helps create. It is something quite different from general education 'from above'. Songs, parades, folk dancing and gymnastics carry meaning and create subjectivity themselves – regardless of how rigid and commando-like their elaboration may have been. Again: it is a question of letting the subject realize his inner potential – in the framework of the conformity and consensus of the community – not of obstinately insisting on one's own individual rights. In the body's strong, silent knowledge and enunciative force one finds the background for the colossal power of attraction.

We must return to sport – for the partial histories do not just reflect the history of society, but also contribute to creating it, while at the same time having their own institutionalized history and their own significance: both style and institutionalization have the right to their own specific of area of historical treatment, for they have their own peculiarities, their own meanings and their own logic characterized by inertia.[16] In Hvide Sande at the Jutland west coast you could, as the winner of a cup tie, have a big smoked salmon instead of a cup as prize.[17]

Considering this idea of the central importance of sport and the culture of the body in Nordic political culture, it is no coincidence, for example, that the game of handball, with its synthesis of the individual and the collective, was invented in Denmark; that Danish exhibition gymnasts in the inter-war period won so many triumphs all over the world, especially in Germany, Japan and South Africa; that Finland, after the USA, was the country with the most world records in 1934, and that sport, outdoor life and Bertil Gustafsson Ugglas's morning radio gymnastics in Sweden in the 1930s contributed to diminishing the demarcation between the private and the public, between the sexes and the classes,[18] where not only society left its mark on the body, but where the body also came to leave its mark on society and the material environment.

Without taking into consideration the physical side of the European modernistic Enlightenment project, one has difficulty completely understanding the special Nordic *Sonderweg*. The Scandinavian nationalistic Enlightenment project has to a great extent been characterized by the fact that the structure of society, general education and the culture of the body were an integrated whole. This was true in the 1790s with their echo of patriotism, in the bombastic general education of national romanticism in the 19th century, and in the struggle between welfare-oriented, democratic social-nationalism and fascistic-corporative, national-socialism in the 20th century.

Yet, it would imply reductionism to only see the culture of the body as forming part of the construction of society and nationalism in general; gymnastics and athletics are also more narrowly part of the construction of a special kind of nationalism: welfare-oriented, social-liberal nationalism. Or, in other words, athletics and the culture of the body are integral in determining the formation of this kind of nation-state.

The role of sport in the construction of Nordic society – in the sign of nationalism – can be demonstrated in different ways, as will be seen. The Scandinavian nationalistic project has largely been characterized by the construction of society, general education and the culture of the body being an integrated whole. This was true in the 1790s with their echo of patriotism, in the general education of the bombastic national romanticism of the 19th century, and in the struggle between welfare-oriented, democratic social-nationalism and the fascistic-corporative 20th century.

Norway's *sonderweg*

Turning to the Nordic countries in the 1930s, you may, as has the Norwegian folklorist Ørnulf Hodne and his fellow countryman Rune Slagstad, ask how it came about that Norwegian sport in the 1930s overcame its ideological and organizational divisions and instead assembled around a national educational function under the auspices of social democracy.[19]

A central position in this question is occupied by the history of working-class sport in inter-war Norway. This is a history of grandeur and collapse. At the end of the 1930s, Norwegian working-class sport was in a serious crisis. It was primarily a consequence of a hesitant attitude on the part of the Labour Party, which, like its counterparts in Denmark and Sweden, was prepared to sacrifice the class-struggle perspective in favour of a policy for 'the whole of Norway'. It also arose because of internal divisions between the politically aware leaders in working-class sport – who wanted to use sport (especially skiing, football and athletics) as part of the class struggle – and those members with little interest in party politics – who wanted to devote their spare time to either sports or dancing. The 'power moralists' were opposed here to the 'liberals', but the tendency to break the social barrier and enrich life with new and exiting experiences was important for the seemingly apolitical parts of working-class sport.

Here Hodne and Slagstad are thinking along the same lines as Jonas Frykman in his studies of the history of sport and outdoor life in Sweden in the 1930s.[20] Working-class sport, in other words, was part of a national-modernist project and a social democratic welfare project at the same time, and this is probably the real reason for the gradual cessation of working-class sport: that the Nordic social-liberal social democratism – with its alliance between workers and farmers and its alliance between the people and the state – did not leave any room for a narrow working-class organization.

Social democratic cultural policy in the 1930s showed itself, first in Sweden and Denmark, later in Norway too, to be a nationally oriented 'open air' policy. This applies to Denmark in particular, where, compared with Sweden and Norway, there was a special effort to achieve broad popular enlightenment, and where social democratic cultural policy, because of the work of the Grundtvigians, had difficulty in finding a place in the spiritual sun.

A popular Danish song in these years was called 'Comrade of the Sun', and it may serve as an emblem of this social democratic perception of their goal at the time: that everyone – as comrades and equals – should be able to enjoy life in the open air, where all could be equal thanks to the same bodily capacity. A book entitled 'Sport' (*Idrætten*), published by the Danish social democrats in 1934, described bodily exercise and fresh air as two of the most beneficial properties of sport.[21] In Finland, where the right-wing home-guard movement seized on sport and open-air life in the inter-war years for the purposes of national legitimation and sentiment,[22] the situation was politically different, but the interest in outdoor life was scarcely any less.[23]

Hodne and Slagstad deserve praise for showing how the race between nationalism and social democratism, as the two main isms of the 20th century, is flanked by bodily elements on a distinctive Nordic palette of values, where the things about which there was general agreement far outweighed the differences. Yet they simultaneously show how the labour movement, the youth movement and the sports movement, in their use of similar forms such as festivals, walks, tournaments, banners, courses and study circles, established pluralism and relativism as regards values, combining both 'Western' values such as freedom and equality, and 'German' values like *communitas*, rallying and *Stimmung*. Sport made a crucial contribution to the Nordic political culture with its hybrid of democracy and nationalism, but this very sport was characterized by its own hybridization of equal possibilities and local circumstances with distinct references to the local community and the need for internal cohesion.

The special case of Finland

In Finland the situation was partly different. Here, too, the people had to fight for national independence throughout the 19th century, but whereas the Norwegians for national reasons could hardly adopt the Ling gymnastics from Sweden, the situation was different in Finland, as Ling gymnastics represented what had been lost when Finland was swallowed up by Russia. However, this picture was confused by one specific factor: namely, that the struggle for national independence in Finland was linked to the struggle for the Finnish language. The Finns put it like this: 'We cannot be Swedes, we do not want to be Russians – let us therefore be Finns'.

To put it another way, from about 1860 Finnish national sentiment became 'Fenno-mania', in that it was also opposed to the Swedish-speaking upper class. Like Danish Grundtvigianism, it lacked a formal organization and rather had the character of an élitist movement which derived its legitimacy by professing to act on behalf of the people. A number of Swedish-speaking families, in solidarity with the aspirations of the young Fennomaniacs, changed their names from Swedish to Finnish (for example, from Forsman to Koskinen, from Gallén to Gallén-Kallela), and the composer Sibelius, who came from a family of Swedish-speaking officials, endeavoured to create a national Finnish musical iconography. Finnish was regarded as the heart of the nation, whereas Swedish was perceived as its stiffening shell.[24] This Fennomania made it difficult to automatically adopt the Swedish Ling gymnastics as a national representation. As in Norway, they had to go their own way, and it was competitive sport that triumphed.[25]

Here we should bear in mind, however, that the nation-building of the independent Finland in the 20th century had a very different character from Norwegian nation-building. First, it began later than in Norway, at a time when sport had made its breakthrough, at least in the cities. Second, it was of a much more dramatic character, in that Finland was the only Nordic country to be torn apart by a civil war. Third, all through the inter-war years there was the real or imagined threat of the Communist and collectivist Soviet Union to the east. This created a rather different agenda for the demands for a national bodily representation in the 20th century than in the other Nordic countries.

At the same time, one must bear in mind the geographical conditions. It could easily have happened that the Finns, like the Norwegians, chose skiing as their national symbol, but the period in which the new independent nation had to build an identity now had other options in the form of modern sport. At the same time, ideological considerations could have influenced the choice between individual sports and team sports. The fact that the Soviet '*kolkhoz* mentality' was regarded as one of the main enemies was not without significance; it was partly for political reasons that individual sports were valued more highly in the politically inflammable inter-war period, like the athletics training we see depicted in a novel by Väinö Linna about the right-wing-oriented Civil Guards. It might be appropriate here to quote the editor of the newsletter of the Danish Gymnastics Association (DDG), A. Pedersen Dømmestrup, whose statement in 1930 testifies to the affinity between the Grundtvigian gymnastics tradition in Denmark and the physical culture of the Fennomaniac heritage:

> The young people of Finland engage in athletics as the youth of Denmark indulge in gymnastics. Young Finns, especially in the countryside, practise athletics in the evenings and in their spare time, not in a stadium, since the distances are too great, but outside the farm, where they have their daily work.[26]

Other aspects of human geography are seen here, including the fact that there was still very little urbanization in Finland in the inter-war period. The urban population concentration in the towns was small, and even in the countryside the form of settlement in most of Finland comprised isolated farms rather than true villages of the kind found in Denmark and southern Sweden. If one wanted to compete with others, one had to travel – sometimes long distances. This, once again, favoured individual sports in which one could compete against oneself.

If we consider the late date of independent nation-building in Finland, at a time when sport was catching on, the factors all point in the direction of athletics; in other words, the great individual sport of the 20th century. It is characteristic that Finland's most splendid international sporting triumphs have been in athletics, especially in events that are suited to personal training, such as long-distance running and the javelin. If we look at world athletics in 1934, for example, we see that the records for races from 5 km upwards and for the discus (for both hands) and the javelin were held by Finns. Measured in terms of world records, Finland that year was the second-best athletics nation in the world, after the USA.

Collectivist Danish sports

The fact that athletics has found it much more difficult to catch on in Norway as the preferred individual sport can be explained to some extent by the close link between sport and nationalism which favoured skiing, as we saw above, but also by geographical conditions: both the human geography, as Norway is also a country of isolated farms and relatively little urbanization, and the physical geography, with the long winters inviting people to go skiing and skating.

It is trickier to understand why athletics has always found it difficult to gain a firm foothold in Denmark. Even back in 1909 the first composite work on Danish sport declared that Danish athletes appear to form the rear guard in the 'international athletic army'.[27] Otherwise, the climatic conditions should be good enough, with the mild weather and short winters, so that there is practically no competition from winter sports. However, climate alone is not decisive; other factors are involved.

We must bear in mind that athletics from the very beginning found it hard to secure a position as a consequence of the competition from Grundtvigian gymnastics. This competition did not affect football as much as track and field, because football was a collective game promoting team spirit. Nevertheless, the Grundtvigians disliked football because of the beer drinking in the football clubs. There was, in other words, a certain need for a more 'civilized' collective game that could combine modernity, team spirit and national ideas.

This need was exacerbated by the fact that many young people, not just in the towns but also in the countryside, were simply beginning to find gymnastics too boring. In many places Niels Bukh's jumping gymnastics had not caught on, and the stiff and static 'Swedish' gymnastics found it difficult to attract enough people. Besides, it was restricted to the winter half of the year, so there were no summer activities, and clubs in general perhaps had too many admonishing lecturers and pig-headed drill instructors.[28] The solution for the Grundtvigians became team handball. Known as a Danish invention dating back to 1897, it could satisfy the need for an indigenous game and at the same time could bring town and countryside closer to each other in national harmony.

Here we also may have part of the explanation for the breakthrough of sports in the countryside in the place of gymnastics. Sport was more dynamic and more in keeping with the urban culture that was beginning to attract many young rural people in the inter-war years, with the radio in the living room, buses to the nearest market town, and cinemas in the station town. The peasantry had been modernized in a distinctively Danish way a generation previously, partly owing to the village halls and mission houses, so that we are justified in speaking of a special Danish agrarian modernity, but this was now replaced by state initiatives in the direction of a shared national culture (in the form of the radio) and by private capitalist entertainment initiatives such as cinemas and weekly magazines. Sport fitted into this picture perfectly, with its speed and flair, it competition and performance.

Another important factor was that sport was able to bring the sexes together in the summer half of the year. In the heyday of gymnastics the rule had generally been for young people to wait for each other outside the village hall in the snow and slush until the gymnastics was over, so that a lad could walk his girl home. With the coming of sport, the picture changed. Now the long summer evenings could be used to the full and there were activities for both boys and girls, which meant that they could watch each other in full bodily vigour. As a rule, handball practice for girls and football practice for boys was held on the same evening, for practical reasons, and some boys played handball too, so that boys and girls had a shared interest. This was different from peeping through the keyhole of the village hall when the girls were doing gymnastics.[29] Light now shone over the country.

In addition, there came a new phenomenon, the 'sporting festival', held on free Sundays when a team competed with a team from another village to win badges to be pinned on the club flag. Whether the team played at home or went to a neighbouring village to play, it meant a broadening of experience in relation to the closed world of gymnastics. Not only were there the actual sporting activities, which could give rise to all kinds of comparison, but there were also the dances – to the music of a live band in the village hall – that followed the matches. The 'sweetheart market' was thus considerably expanded and boys and girls could mix more easily.

In 1938 there were already about 28,000 active handball players, twice the number of athletes; five years later, in the middle of World War II, there were 59,000 handball players in organized clubs.[30]

Sweden: in the middle

It is striking how the Swedes in the inter-war years, as part of a new modernizing welfare nationalism, took a delight in being able to 'do' and 'show' what had previously been concealed.[31] The watchwords of the time were discovery and experimentation. This resulted in a multitude of lightly clad bodies enjoying summer in the country, beside a lake or in a cottage in the woods. They turned their backs on the mawkish, pampered city life while pluckily conquering what was closest to them: their own bodies, in the embrace of nature.

This acquisition strategy with a simple way of life was in turn associated with national overtones, but of a different kind from before. The decadent upper-class patriotism of the turn of the century had to give way to an uncomplicated and 'natural' way of being Swedish. The new, healthy breed did what the bourgeois had previously talked about, and with their new habits they showed what modern Sweden was about. Not because they really knew what modernization was: it was rather the case that, with their new discoveries and inquisitive habits, they incarnated modernity. They sought something new – owing to the opportunities now afforded by statutory holidays and weekends – and new concepts such as hardening, pluck and sexuality began to appear, when words were needed for the new experiences one had enjoyed. The national Sweden – in its modernist variant – was primarily acquired wordlessly as a process, as action, as experience. Many of these experiences were had, for example, in the school dining hall.[32] Here one got the modern Sweden under one's skin. Then came the significant year, 1938, with the new law giving two weeks' paid holiday to all those in permanent employment,[33] and with the foundation of the National Institute of Public Health; in the same year the Swedish Advertising Association arranged a conference on the theme of public health and advertising.

Two years later, in 1940, the Stockholm Co-operative Occupational Sports Association, with its biggest clubs being those of the tram workers, the fire brigade and the police, organized the first Vasa Relay Race on skis, in collaboration with the daily newspaper *Dagens Nyheter* and Skansen. The race went from Brunnsviken to the birthplace of King Gustav Vasa at Lindholmen in Uppland and back to Skansen.[34] In 1945 the social democratic chairman of the Stockholm City Council, Carl Albert Andersson, took the initiative to found a national organization for inter-company sports; regional organizations had already been formed in Stockholm in 1918 and in Malmö in the 1920s. In other words, he was active in the co-operative movement, the labour movement and sports.

The new social-liberal acquisition of 'the people's home' thus took place from below, just as the modernization of Sweden also received its boost from below through wordless acts, in the form of tacit bodily knowledge. Gradually, however, codified templates appeared, and Arne Mattsson's famous film *Hon dansade en sommar* (One Summer of Happiness, 1951), as a cinematic representation of welfare-state Sweden,[35] merely put the dot on the i, but what a dot that was! There was evidently a great need for such a demonstration of the simultaneously 'genuine', 'natural', and 'modern' Sweden: 2.8 million Swedes saw the film. In Örnsköldsvik (in Lapland), 8,827 tickets to the film were sold, although the town only had a population of 7,356.[36]

Despite the shock she provoked, the girl who enjoyed one summer of happiness had numerous predecessors. The 20th-century cult of youth as a concept, with respect for doing more than saying, had an early spokesperson in Sweden in the author Ellen Key.[37] On the organizational level, people likewise devoted themselves to the wordless experience of the body and outdoor life, not just in sports but also in an otherwise so scarcely revolutionary form as the 4H activities in the agrarian movement and the Scout movement recommended by the national romantic poet Heidenstam.[38] All this was an integral part of the nation-building and modernization of Sweden.

This combination of hardening and endurance, this bodily democratic and presentative more than re-presentative demonstration of Swedishness, could hardly be materialized in a more obvious and concrete form than in Vasaloppet. Admittedly this ski race is not alone: you can also cycle all the way around Sweden's biggest lake, Vänern, do the Vansbro swimming marathon, enter the women's mini-marathon and so on, but Vasaloppet is something special. It combines the lofty, patriotic nationalism of the age of Oscar II, Artur Hazelius and Nils Andersson with the keep-fit nationalism of the welfare state, all in the name of King Gustav Vasa – according to the myth, he founded Sweden by escaping on skis from the pursuing Danes. In a seemingly uncomplicated interplay between the cult of tradition and permanent change, the competitors still race towards the goal in Mora, an arch bearing an inscription in Gothic lettering: 'In the trail of the fathers for future victories'. The race starts in Sälen on the first Sunday of March, as custom has ruled since 1922. Everything is the same from year to year – and yet different: in the 1930s, 94 percent of the skiers who finished the race came from Norrland or the provinces of Dalarna and Värmland, and only six percent from the southern half of Sweden. In 1970 the figures were almost reversed, 26 percent and 69 percent, respectively (the rest were foreigners).[39]

Vasaloppet has increasingly become an all-Sweden event, and hence a shared Swedish concern in which, paradoxically, they are so sure of the Swedish dimension of the race that international competitors, for example, from France and Italy, are accepted with no great problem. The time is long gone when the skiers were mainly taciturn loggers. Today it is the white-collar workers of urban Sweden who have themselves enrolled in Swedishness by *doing* something Swedish, by sacrificing themselves. It is not that the skiers start in Sälen with a blue-and-yellow consciousness and a desire to show themselves as genuine Swedes, but the bilberry soup they consume along the course is so Swedish that it cannot be avoided. Although it is true, as the Uppsala historian Harald Runblom has pointed out in a comparison of national political rhetoric in Europe and America, where history is constantly invoked as legitimation, that while a Swedish politician would never think of quoting Gustav Vasa's farewell speech to the Swedish Estates,[40] many thousands of Swedes, nevertheless, refer each year to Gustav Vasa through their bodies.

At the same time, Swedish nationalism has changed character. As Sweden became social democratic, the old militaristic patriotism of the 19th century was succeeded by a modern 'welfare nationalism', based not so much on the obedient as on the collaborating individual. Correspondingly, young people no longer perceived themselves as the ideological storm troopers of nationalism, but simply as young people. The puritanical bent was replaced by modern mass culture. The large youth movements became focal points for social activities – places where young people could meet and have fun.

In organizational terms, too, Sweden differed from Denmark, which, besides DIF, the body responsible for sport, had two other organizations which together were almost as big as DIF, and which took charge of gymnastics. In Sweden they had RF as the only significant organization for sport.

The pronounced public interest in sport and outdoor life in Sweden in the inter-war period also favoured the construction of sports facilities. The most up-to-date technological advances could be utilized in the form of cinder tracks, in which sand and gravel were mixed with granulated carbon or brick. This gave a much harder surface, thus ensuring a better foothold. The Swedish cinder tracks in the 1940s and 1950s had the reputation of being the best in the world; in other words, the fastest.[41] It was not least these technical factors that allowed the Swedes Gunder Hägg and Arne Andersson to set one world record after another in the war years; although, of course, there was less competition during these years from the war-torn world outside neutral Sweden.

Binding the threats

In his sophisticated collection of essays, *Solskensolympiaden* (The Sunshine Olympics), the Swedish literary scholar Per Rydén asks the delicate question: can one run one's way into a language?[42] That question is in many ways a suitable conclusion to this chapter, in that it indirectly touches on the question around which we have been circulating above: How is national identity experienced?

The book, with its title referring to the Olympic Games in Stockholm in 1912, is primarily about the way the Olympics were passed on to young people in the country-side. They identified with the Games. They ran, as the athletes had done in 1912, thanks to the matrices provided for them by the yellowing pages of old books about the Stockholm Olympics. Here they could read about Swedish heroes, yet the admiration for them did not result in passive reverence; instead it led to activity. They ran and ran, and this running made them Swedish. The Swedish people had come into movement after the Stockholm Olympics. Sport created a popular movement, and with their running Rydén and his childhood friends helped to incarnate the new Sweden which – together with the other Nordic countries – prided itself in being a new, modern society.

The question of whether one can run one's way into a language is not answered explicitly in the book. The answer is shown. Rydén demonstrates how the rural youths behaved like Swedes without being able to put words on what they were doing. What on earth could a 16 year-old say about being a Swede? There were no words for things. They scarcely knew what Sweden was, except that it was where they lived: the lake, the road, the new filling station. Nationalism came later. First you do things, then comes the interpretation. As an adult, Rydén ran the Stockholm marathon, which led him to describe his experience in the following words:

> Finally I am inside the Stadium for the first time. It is like coming home. Ever since the Sunshine Olympics this had been the goal of my daydreams. I had been there a thousand times in the sports newspaper *Idrottsbladet* and on the radio. I could have attested my presence by quoting details. The flag was hoisted on the bell-tower, just as on the diplomas. The whole of this Nordic dream in stone seemed to be floating. And now I am there, as in the dream, and my steps just will not bear me as fast as they do in the dream. But I manage to put on a spurt. Over the finishing line. Well ran![43]

Through his run, Rydén creates a Nordic/Swedish continuity in his life. He makes this biographical incarnation visible by accomplishing it in bodily activity, by running. In doing so he is not just enrolled in a Nordic community; he runs his way into it. This is where he belongs, as he experiences through his run. Word and thing can be united.

What was the ideal presented at the Sunshine Olympics of 1912 in Stockholm, that had inspired him to run? First and foremost it was a demonstration of the combination of sport as an emotional community and a relatively rigid system of rules and fixed areas. Secondly it was the first Olympics held in a stadium built as an ultramodern palace and a 'home'. The architect Torben Grut had had in mind both medieval Swedish town walls of red bricks and a monument of the new sports culture. The result was a specialized sports arena as well as a multifunctional place to be used not only for sports, but also as the home ground for festivals, parades, choir rallies, festivals, plays, etc. The best seats were, of course, reserved for the royal family, but in fact the stands in the curves where the common people were seated had the best view.[44] Was it an historical presage, referring to the impending Social Democratism of Sweden and the other Nordic countries?

Among the Young Conservatives in Sweden there was a lot of talking in those years about Sweden as a 'People's Home'. This slogan was around 10 years later adopted by the social democrat and later prime minister Per Albin Hansson in a speech at Stortorget in Gamla Stan in Stockholm, and became the overall ideal of not only Sweden, but all Nordic countries for the next three or four generations. Stockholm Stadium and the Sunshine Olympics worked as a tacit demonstration of what was to become the explicit societal norm in the Nordic social-liberal countries.

Putting it all into perspective

Benedict Anderson shares the credit for deconstructing the concept of nationalism, as he has shown how nationalism is a construction, an 'imagined community' in which one does not know all the others but still feels like them.[45] In other words, the sense of community is an idea more than the essence and the substantiality in which traditional apologists of nationalism have portrayed it. This praiseworthy debunking, however, has had a certain tendency to skip the important question: how was it possible for this imagined community to become a reality when the members did not know each other, when the community, in Rydén's terms, was based on words rather than things?

The weakness of Benedict Anderson's otherwise-inspiring view of nationalism as a construction and an airy idea is that it tends to ignore the fact that nationalism is also a lived idea, an experience, and that nationalism is not one and the same through all time and in all places. Otherwise, it would scarcely have survived as by far the strongest ideology in the world for more than 200 years, as the only 'metahistory' that has not yet been dismantled.

The fact is that the spiritual community of nationalism has always needed an incarnation, and it has been able to find one. In Norway the president of the constitutional assembly, Colonel Diderich Hegermann, in the struggle for national independence in the 19th century, wanted to make it a constitutional duty for the ecclesiastical, civil and military authorities to ensure that the young sons of the country went skiing in the winter.[46] In Sweden the utilization of skiing as a distinctive national feature got under way in earnest in the 1880s, after Nordenskiöld's expedition to Greenland in 1883, and skiing was part of the Swedish nation-building around the turn of the century owing to this and to books such as Elsa Beskow's children's story *Olles skidfärd* (Olle's Skiing Tour) and Carl

Grimberg's history, *Svenska folkets underbara öden* (The Wonderful Fortunes of the Swedish People), with its cult of Gustav Vasa.[47]

National identity is not just a demonstration of a pre-existing entity. Danish, Swedish, Norwegian and Finnish is not primarily something one is, it is something one becomes. National identity is not an identity, a culture that one enters, but rather an articulation process, a creation. Following Eric Hobsbawm's idea that not just nationalism but also national identity must be presented (that is, simultaneously created, confirmed and ventilated) again and again, Homi Bhabha calls it 'cultural elaboration'.[48] This means that national identity is constantly on the way to itself; it is created again and again through action. National identity is not something that arises after the event. Its meaning and significance is found *in media res*. Otherwise, people would probably have tired of the idea long ago. Acquiring nationalism, in fact, means having a reflexive attitude to what one does, to one's actions and physical behaviour.

This everyday side of nationalism is essential if we want to understand why nationalism is not constantly crystallized in war. Here we may return to the ideas put forward by Yi-fu Tuan that nationalism in comparison with universalism (but not cosmopolitanism) also contains what he – probably with an indirect reference to Ernst Bloch – call a 'warm glow':[49] it consists of habits, of a place to be in the world, of a way of life rather than of principles and ideas. This non-doctrinaire nationalism is probably much more predominant than is generally believed, and it seems to be important when one seeks to explain that we have, nevertheless, had more years of peace than of war in a century that has been ravaged by nationalism. People do not become murderers by using a sauna, by picking berries in the mountains, or by skiing; not even by eating Danish ryebread.

Notes

1 Ø. Sørensen and B. Stråth, eds, *The Cultural Construction of Norden* (Oslo: Scandinavian University Press, 1997), 3.
2 S. Berger, M. Donovan and K. Passmore, 'Apologias for the Nation-state in Western Europe since 1800', in S. Berger, M. Donovan and K. Passmore, eds, *Writing National Histories: Western Europe since 1800* (London and New York: Routledge, 1999), 7.
3 Ibid., 10.
4 B. Stråth, *Folkhemmet mot Europa: Ett historiskt perspektiv på 90-talet* (Stockholm: Tiden, 1992), 113.
5 Sørensen and Stråth 1997.
6 H. Gustafsson, 'Vad var staten? Den tidigmoderna svenska staten: sex synpunkter och en model', *Svensk Historisk Tidsskrift* 2 (1994).
7 B. Lindroth, *Sverige och odjuret: En essä om den goda svenska traditionen* (Stockholm: Moderna tider, 1994).
8 H. Stenius, *Frivilligt, jämlikt, samfällt: Föreningsväsendets utveckling i Finland fram til 1900-talets början med speciellt hänsyn till massorganisationsprincipens genombrott* (Helsingfors: Svenska litteratursällskapet, 1987), 43.
9 H. Stenius, 'Konformitetsideal blev universalitetsideal', in Göran Bexell and Henrik Stenius, eds, *Värdetraditioner i nordiskt perspektiv* (Lund: Lund University Press, 1997a), 85.
10 K.L. Goldschmidt Salomon, 'I grunden er vi enige: En ekskursion i skandinavisk foreningsliv', *Antropologi* 25 (1992).
11 B. Hettne, S. Sörlin and U. Østergård, *Den globala nationalismen: Nationalstatens historia och framtid* (Stockholm: SNS Förlag, 2006), 132.
12 O. Korsgaard and L. Løvlie, 'Indledning', in R. Slagstad, O. Korsgaard and L. Løvlie, eds, *Dannelsens forvandlinger* (Oslo: Pax, 2003); S. Högnäs, 'The Concept of *Bildung* and the Education of the Citizen – Traits and Developments in the Nordic Countries 1870–2000', S. Ahonen and J. Rantala, eds, *Nordic Lights: Education for Nation and Civic Society in the Nordic Countries, 1850–2000* (Helsinki: Finnish Literature Society, 2001).

13 N. Kayser Nielsen, *Krop og oplysning: Om kropskultur i Danmark 1780–1900* (Odense: Odense Universitetsforlag, 1993).

14 N. Kayser Nielsen, 'Kroppens dannelse og dannelsens krop', in R. Slagstad, O. Korsgaard and L. Løvlie 2003.

15 R. Slagstad, *(Sporten): En idehistorisk studie* (Oslo: Pax, 2008); N. Kayser Nielsen, 'Idræt og nationsdannelse i de nordiske lande: Forskelle og fællestræk', in B. Stoklund, ed., *Kulturens nationalisering: Et etnologisk perspektiv på det nationale* (Copenhagen: Museum Tusculanum, 1999).

16 R. Chartier, 'Geistesgeschichte oder histoire des mentalités?', in D. LaCapra and S.L. Kaplan, eds, *Geschichte denken: Neubestimmung und Perspektiven moderner europäischer Geistesgeschicte* (Frankfurt am Main: Fischer, 1988), 36.

17 N. Kayser Nielsen, 'Topografi, krop og idræt – eller noget om at få en røget fisk som tak for kampen', at www. idrottsforum.org/articles/nielsen, 2007.

18 J. Frykman, 'Nationella ord och handlingar', in B. Ehn, J. Frykman and O. Löfgren, eds, *Försvenskningen av Sverige: Det nationellas förvandlingar* (Stockholm: Natur och kultur, 1993), 167, 180.

19 R. Slagstad 2008; Ø. Hodne, *Idrett og fritid: En mellomkrigsstudie i norsk idrettskultur* (Oslo: Novus, 1995).

20 J. Frykman 'I rörelse: Kropp och modernitet i mellankrigstidens Sverige', *Kulturella perspektiv* 1 (1992).

21 A. Borgbjærg, 'Sportens betydning', in Seier Larsen, ed., *Idrætten* (Copenhagen, 1934), 12.

22 E. Vasara, 'För fred och kristen tro: Skyddskårsrörelsens upplysningsverksamhet', *Historisk Tidsskrift för Finland* vol. 80, no. 2 (1995), 178.

23 L. Laine, 'Ruumiinharjoitusten monet muodot', in Teijo Pyykkönen, ed., *Suomi uskoi urheiluun: Suomen urheilun ja liikunnan historia* (Helsinki: Liikuntatieteellinen seura, 1992), 183.

24 S. Högnäs, *Kustens och skogarnas folk – Om synen på svenskt och finskt lynne* (Stockholm: Atlantis, 1995).

25 L. Laine, 'Urheilu valtaa mielet', in Teijo Pyykkönen, ed., *Suomi uskoi urheiluun: Suomen urheilun ja liikunnan historia* (Helsinki: Liikuntatieteellisen seura, 1992).

26 A. Pedersen Dømmestrup, '1930: Idræt!', *Dansk Ungdom og Idræt* no. 28 (1930).

27 H. Grønfeldt, 'Løb, Spring, Kast m. m', in A.C. Meyer, ed., *Idrætsbogen*, vol. 2. (Copenhagen: Chr. Erichsens forlag, 1909), 27.

28 N. Kayser Nielsen, 'Sport og bondekultur – om foreningsliv i provinsen i mellemkrigstiden', *Fortid og Nutid: Tidsskrift for kulturhistorie og lokalhistorie* No. 1 (1995).

29 H. Gjøde Nielsen, *Gymnastik og idrætshistorie fra Viborg Amt* (Viborg: Gymnastik-og idrætshistorisk samling, 1994), 112.

30 N. Kayser Nielsen, 'Håndbold og folkelig idræt i 1930'erne', in N. Kayser Nielsen, ed., *Håndbold i 100 år – et overblik* (Copenhagen: DHF, 1997), 77.

31 J. Frykman, 'In Motion: Body and Modernity in Sweden between the World Wars', *Ethnologia Scandinavia* 1992.

32 E. Palmblad and B.E. Eriksson, *Kropp och politik: Hälsoupplysning som samhällsspegel* (Stockholm: Carlsson, 1995).

33 H. Hellström, *Kultur, arbete, tid* (Stockholm: Carlsson, 1994), 63.

34 R. Eriksson, *Arv att förvalta – Friskt framåt* (Stockholm: Svenska Korporationsidrottsförbundet, 1985), 48.

35 P. Forsman, *Det kluvna samhället: Perspektiv på samhällets omvandling* (Stockholm: Carlsson, 1995), 232.

36 I. Norlén, *Förbannade Ekström* (Stockholm: Carlsson, 1993), 59.

37 H. Berggren, *Seklets ungdom: Retorik, politik och modernitet 1900–1939* (Stockholm: Tiden, 1995).

38 K. Sandell and S. Sörlin, 'Naturen som fostrare: Friluftsliv och ideologi i svenskt 1900-tal', *Historisk Tidskrift* No. 1 (1994).

39 A. Lundberg, 'Vasaloppet och vi', *Svenska Turistföreningens årsskrift*, Dalarna, 1972, 299.

40 H. Runblom, *Majoritet och minoritet i Östersjöområdet: Ett historiskt perspektiv* (Stockholm: Natur och Kultur, 1995), 23.

41 O. Moen, *Från bollplan til sportcentrum: Idrottsanläggningar i samhällsbyggande under 100 år* (Stockholm: Byggforskningsrådet, 1992), 15.

42 P. Rydén, *Solskensolympiaden: Essäer* (Lund: Ellerström, 1994), 15.

43 Ibid., 68.

44 Slagstad 2008, 486.

34 Russia/The Soviet Union

James Riordan

Introduction

Anyone wishing to understand Russian and Soviet sport soon runs into two intractable problems: the paucity of information in any language, including Russian, and the tendentious attempt to glorify or denigrate the subject matter in much of the writing. The same applies to China. In the West, articles and monographs have often focused on coercive facets of the 'Big Red Sports Machine'. This is the case with the American author Henry Morton whose pioneering study, *Soviet Sport* (Morton 1963), offered the first extensive sociological analysis of sport as an integral aspect of Soviet ideology. Published at the height of the Cold War, Morton's book reinforced the already popularly held Western myth of the Soviet sports machine. An example of how difficult it was to publish a serious study of Soviet sport may be gauged from my own experience: during the US-led campaign to boycott the Moscow 1980 Olympic Games, the British government under Margaret Thatcher slapped a 'D-Notice' on my book *Soviet Sport: Background to the Olympics* (Riordan 1980), in an attempt to prevent newspapers and magazines printing reviews of the book – which the government obviously thought too pro-Soviet.

On the other side, Soviet historiography laboured under the Stalinist censorship of the 'dark spots' in Soviet sport, such as the security service sponsorship and financing of the dominant *Dinamo* Sports Club (also imposed on all other countries that came within Soviet political orbit), political interference, ethnic tension at sports events, the purges of top sports officials, the state preparation and dispensing of performance-enhancing drugs, etc. Ironically, in an interview with the then Sports Minister, Sergei Pavlov, in 1980, I was shown my own book on the history of Soviet sport, *Sport in Soviet Society* (Riordan 1977), translated into Russian, but for 'a restricted readership'. There was no other source for Soviet people to learn about Soviet sport and its roots in pre-revolutionary Russian society.

Surprisingly, the Russian people are not much better served today. Although Communism passed away at the end of 1991, no substantial book on Russian and Soviet sports history has been published in Russia. Instead, propagandist and sensationalist texts continue to appear, often written by the same sports bureaucrats who dominated sports history in Soviet times. See, for example, Vladimir Rodichenko, *Olimpiyskaya ideya dlya Rossii* [The Olympic Idea for Russia] (Rodichenko 1998). The author is Vice-President of the Russian Olympic Committee and, in Soviet times, was Deputy Sports Minister. At the same time, the new capitalist market contains a number of biographies of sports personalities (including of the football star, Eduard Streltsov, contentiously sentenced for rape in the late 1950s) and sensationalist exposures of the sinister side of Soviet sporting activities, such as Mikhail Prozumenshchikov's book, *Bolshoi sport i bolshaya politika* [Big-Time Sport and Big-Time Politics] (Prozumenshchikov 2004).

An impassable barrier for most Western students of sport is language. Very few Western sports scholars speak Russian (most speak only their native language). Western historians who do speak foreign languages have tended to regard sport as a non-serious area of research (as my old university professor used to say, 'Sports research is something to do in your spare time, like wine-making'!). Happily, times are changing. Those sports historians who have devoted their research to Russian sport, working inside Russian society and in the archives, have discovered a rich heritage that, importantly, provides unique contributions to wider historical debates.

For example, the American Robert Edelman has written of the novel role played by mass spectator sport in a totalitarian society, thereby exposing the issues and debates surrounding the politics of popular culture. In his ground-breaking book, *Serious Fun: A History of Spectator Sports in the USSR* (Edelman 1993), he concentrates on the Soviet public's consumption of sporting spectacles, what Soviet people chose to watch, not what the government tried to promote. In a more recent book, Mike O'Mahony, *Sport in the USSR: Physical Culture – Visual Culture* (Mahony 2006), examined Soviet sport as represented in the visual arts (mainly painting and sculpture), looking at the complex relationship between sport as an officially approved social practice and as a subject for cultural production. This emphasis on sport with these media highlights a significant departure from Western conventional practices.

The major thrust of my own research has been sociological and political, emphasizing the importance of sport for nation-building in modernizing societies. As I write in my preface to *Soviet Sport: Background to the Olympics*:

> Western commercialised sports on the one hand and the gentlemanly dictum "sport for sport's sake" on the other are often looked upon as entirely unsuitable (in modernising societies). Sport in … the Soviet Union is a serious business, with serious functions to perform: it is associated with health, hygiene, defence, patriotism, integration, productivity, international recognition, even nation-building. The Soviet experience of sports development may have more relevance to cultural revolutions in the emergent nations of Africa, Asia and Latin America than does our own.

The brief history of post-Communist Russian sport is examined in a few publications, such as Stephen Wagg and David Andrews's *East Plays West: Sport and the Cold War* (Wagg and Andrews 2007), and James Riordan and Arnd Kruger's, *European Cultures in Sport: Examining the Nations and Regions* (Riordan and Kruger 2003). However, the post-Cold War period has not brought a rich harvest in sports historiography as regards Russia. Perhaps that is understandable: it remains to be seen what of the immediate post-Communist society is transient or what provides a more permanent vista of Russia's future.

Sport in pre-revolutionary Russia

Russian sport and physical education have their roots deep in Russian history, in the people's traditions, the climate, fears about internal and external foes (in a land with borders with 12 foreign states), the organized sports pioneered largely by Great Britain, the gymnastics schools of Germany (Jahn), Scandinavia (Ling and Nachtegall) and the Czech lands (Tyrs), as well as in Prussian military training. The pattern of Russian sport has been shaped as much by these factors as it has by political ideals and the commercial market.

   As an industrial society developed in 19th-century Russia, liberal noblemen and native industrialists, along with foreigners resident in Russia, began to set up private sports clubs in the major cities. These embraced sports such as yachting (the Imperial Yacht Club, dating from 1846), tennis (the Neva Lawn-Tennis Circle, from 1860), ice-skating (the Amateur Skating Society, from 1864), fencing (the Officers' Fencing Gymnasium, from 1857), gymnastics (the Palma Gymnastics Society, from 1863) and cricket (the Saint Petersburg Tennis and Cricket Club, from 1868). Commercial promoters were also providing, for spectators and gamblers, such professional sports as horse-racing (the Saint Petersburg Horse-Racing Society, 1826), boxing (Baron Kister's English Boxing Arena, 1895), cycling (the Tsarskoye Selo Cycling Circle, 1880) and football (the Victoria Football Club, being the first established football club, in 1894). Various displays of strength were popular in circuses, featuring such world-famous performers as the Estonian Georgy Hakkenschmidt and the Russian Ivan Poddubny and his wrestling wife, Masha Poddubnaya.

   At the turn of the century, there were several Russian sports associations and, on the eve of World War I, as many as 1,266 Russian sports clubs existed with an average membership of 60 people. Although many of these clubs were located in the main Russian cities, the industrializing provinces also accounted for a growing number. For example, the Ukraine had 196 sports clubs with 8,000 members, and Belorussia had 1,000 members in its Sanitas, Sokol, Bogatyr and the Jewish Maccabee sports clubs (Jews being barred from entry to many Russian clubs).

   In 1917, when the Bolsheviks came to power through a coup, the new leadership inherited from tsarist Russia an incipient sports movement that differed in a number of ways from that which had developed in the West. In Great Britain particularly, individual enthusiasts from among the leisured class had pioneered the development of certain organized sports, given them their rules and conventions and often made them exclusive to their social, racial and sexual group. There were thus established single-sport clubs (for tennis, golf, football, etc.), governing bodies for individual sports separate from one another and from government, based for purposes of control and largely finance on their members.

   In Russia, on the other hand, as in the economy, the tsarist state had to some extent discouraged individual enterprise; it had established some control over the organization of sport – in schools, the armed forces, the national federations and the Olympic Committee (Russia being a founder member of the International Olympic Committee— IOC). It had set up the Office of the Chief Supervisor of Sport headed by an army officer, General Voyeikov, to co-ordinate the sports movement. Moreover, most Russian clubs became multi-sport centres, in so far as the organization of Russian sport developed in close association with the Olympic model; and these sports complexes were linked to local and central government. This enabled the regime to maintain close supervision over the development of organized sport and to prevent it being used for anti-monarchist, liberal or revolutionary purposes (as the Turner movement in Germany and the Sokol movement in the Czech lands had been; and the *dikie* ('outlaw') clubs were within Russia itself.

The Russian revolution of 1917 and its aftermath

The new Soviet government in 1917 was, therefore, able to take over a ready-made state organization of sport without having to dismantle a wide-ranging structure of autonomous sports clubs and federations, or to counter any firmly-rooted amateur values. What is more, with the sweeping away of a leisure class, there was no coherent group left in Russian society to develop sport for its own disport.

The first steps to be taken after the Bolsheviks came to power were by no means clear, for there was no pattern to follow. The change-over from criticism of tsarist sport to action in an 80-percent peasant, illiterate country in the throes of a world and civil war presented considerable problems. One source to turn to was the ideological legacy inherited not only from Western social thinkers like Marx, Engels and Rousseau, but from progressive Russian social reformers like the philosophers Chernyshevsky and Dobrolyubov, the writer Lev Tolstoy, the scientist Ivan Pavlov, and the physical educationist Lesgaft. It has to be remembered that in much 19th-century social thought metaphysics was in the grip of a dualism that separated mind from matter and, under the influence of Christian theology, often exaggerated a distinction into an antagonism. In such a world view, body and soul were seen as warring parties, with the body cast as villain.

The progressive social thinkers rejected this dualist philosophy and stressed that not only was there an intimate relationship between matter and mind, but that the former largely determined the latter. This had major implications for Soviet attitudes to the broad concept of 'physical culture', embracing sport, physical education, health and hygiene education, civil defence and exercise. First, sport with its broad relevance to education, health, culture and politics, and its capacity to mobilize people (predispose them towards change) could, it was felt, uniquely serve the purpose of nation-building and help foster national integration. This was of significance in a relatively backward society with a multinational population only half of whom were Russians. The Bolsheviks believed that sport was uniquely suited to this role in that it extended to and united wider sections of the population than probably any other social activity; it was easily understood and enjoyed, cutting across social, economic, educational, ethnic and language barriers; it permitted emotional release reasonably safely and was easily adapted to support educational, health and social welfare objectives.

Second, physical culture was regarded as equally important with mental culture in education and had to be treated as such for the all-round, harmonious development of the child and, ultimately, for the health of society. In as much as mental was on a par with physical culture in human development, it followed that talent in physical activities should be treated no differently from talent in such mental activities as art, music and science. In other words, a budding gymnast, say, should be regarded no differently from a promising ballet dancer, and should be given every opportunity to develop her or his gifts, both for self-fulfilment and for the enjoyment of the community. This was a different philosophy to that dominant in many Western societies where the early cultivation of talent in sport had long been hampered by prejudice against early specialization of children in sport.

Both the above-mentioned tsarist and ideological legacy naturally became entangled with the political, military and economic needs of the young Soviet state. In fact, the 'revolutionary imperative' of the first four years of the new state's existence led to mass nationalization not only of industry, but of sport, too, so that by the end of the 'War Communism' and Civil War period in 1921, not a single private, non-state sports club remained. Nor was the New Economic Policy (NEP) period (1921–28) to resurrect any. From 1917, therefore, Soviet sport was entirely state-run for utilitarian purposes and employed as an agent of social change, with such functions as raising physical and social health standards, socializing people into the new system of values, encouraging a population in rapid transition from country to town to identify themselves with wider communities (including the 'Soviet nation') and, after World War II, facilitating international recognition and prestige. This was a pattern of sport that was to predominate in many other modernizing societies.

Debates and influences on sport during the 1920s

During the 1920s, the crucial question being debated was, however, not what form sport should take, but whether competitive sport should exist at all in the new workers' state. After all, some revolutionaries argued, sports such as athletics, football, rowing, tennis and gymnastics were invented by the industrial bourgeoisie for their own diversion and character training for future careers as captains of industry and empire. It was thought perfectly natural by some after the Russian Revolution that an entirely new pattern of recreation would emerge that reflected the dominant values and needs of the new socialist state.

The two major groups that regarded competitive sport as debasing workers' physical culture and inculcating non-socialist habits were known as the Hygienists and the Proletkultists (from 'proletarian culture'). To the Hygienists, sport implied competition, games that were potentially injurious to mental and physical health. These included especially boxing, weightlifting, wrestling and gymnastics, which were said to encourage individualist rather than collectivist attitudes. The Hygienists condemned the emphasis on record-breaking and the professionalism of Western sport, and they favoured non-commercial forms of recreation that dispensed with grandstands and spectators. Sport, they said, diverted attention from providing recreation for all. Their list of 'approved' sports included athletics, swimming and rowing (all against oneself or the clock, rather than an opponent). Since the Hygienists had virtual control over the government body for sport (the Supreme Council of Physical Culture), the sporting press, the Ministry of Health and the physical education colleges, they were extremely powerful.

To the Proletkultists, sports that derived from bourgeois society were remnants of the decadent past and part of degenerate bourgeois culture. A fresh start had to be made through labour exercises and mass displays, pageants and folk games. In the decade after the Revolution, many factory yards and farm meadows could be seen full of muscular men and women rhythmically swinging hammers and sickles, simulating work movements in time to music. The Proletkultists went much further than the Hygienists in condemning all manner of games, sports and gymnastics 'tainted' by class society. They invented new games for children and organized mass sports activities portraying scenes of world revolution.

Essentially, however, sport during the first few years came to be geared to the needs of the war effort. All the old clubs and their equipment were commandeered for the Universal Military Training Board (*Vsevobuch*), the main aim of which was to supply the Red Army with contingents of trained conscripts as quickly as possible. A second major consideration was health. Regular participation in physical exercise was to be a means of improving health standards rapidly and of educating people in hygiene, nutrition and exercise. This could only succeed, in the opinion of Nikolai Podvoisky, head of *Vsevobuch*, if the emotional attraction of competitive sport were fully exploited.

Competitive sports began to be arranged from the lowest level upwards, culminating in the All-Russia Pre-Olympiads and the First Central Asian Olympics of 1920. Sports were taken from town to country, from the European metropolis to the Asiatic interior, as an explicit means of involving as many people as possible in organized sport and exercise. A third function of sport was integration. The significance of the First Central Asian Olympics, held in Tashkent over 10 days in early October 1920, may be judged from the fact that this was the first time that Uzbeks, Kirgiz, Kazakhs and other Turkic peoples, as well as Russians and other Europeans, had competed in any sporting event together.

Sports activity during the 1920s and 1930s

Throughout the 1920s, the actual amount of sports activity increased substantially. By 1929, sports club membership had risen 15-fold since 1913 (from 0.04 to 0.5 percent of the population). Furthermore, many sports had their national championships by 1929, including 14 women's sports. The big sports tournament of the decade was the First Workers' Spartakiad of 1928, with some 4,000 participants, including 600 foreign athletes (mainly Communists) from 12 countries. In view of the fact that the USSR had few contacts with international sports federations and none with the Olympic movement, this Spartakiad was intended to be a universal workers' Olympics – in opposition to the 'bourgeois' Olympics held that year in Amsterdam with roughly the same programme. Although Soviet sports performance was understandably below top world standards, in some events the USSR did have world-class athletes. Yakov Melnik (1896–1960), for example, had won the 5,000-metre speed-skating event at the Stockholm world championships in 1923.

During the 1920s the Communist Party made clear its own views on physical culture and took sport completely under government (as opposed to trade union and Young Communist) control. A resolution of 1925 emphasized that physical culture must be an inseparable part of political and cultural education and of public health. This, then, was the definitive statement on the enhanced role of sport in society to which all subsequent policy statements were to refer. Sport had been given the revolutionary role of being an agent of wide-ranging social change. As a means of inculcating standards of hygiene and regular exercise in a predominantly backward peasant country, its therapeutic role was, for example, widely advertised in the three-day anti-tuberculosis campaigns of the late 1920s. Sport was also expected to combat antisocial behaviour: the Ukrainian Party Central Committee issued a resolution in 1926 expressing the hope that 'physical culture would become the vehicle of the new life ... a means of isolating young people from the evil effects of prostitution, home-made alcohol and the street'. The role given to sport in the countryside was even more ambitious: it was to 'play a big part in the campaign against drunkenness and uncivilised behaviour by attracting village youth to more cultured activities ... In efforts to transform the village, physical culture is to be a vehicle of the new way of life – in the fight against religion and natural calamities'. Participation in sport, therefore, might develop healthy minds in healthy bodies. Sport stood for 'clean living', progress, good health and rationality, and was regarded by the Party as one of the most effective (and cheapest) instruments in implementing its social policies.

The implications for the sports movement of the economic and political processes (rapid industrialization, collectivization of agriculture and political dictatorship) of the late 1920s and early 1930s were extremely important, for it was then that the organized pattern of Soviet sport was formed – with the nationwide sports societies, sports schools, national fitness programme and the uniform rankings system for individual sports. The new society saw the flourishing of all manner of competitive sports with spectator appeal, of leagues, cups, championships, popularity polls and cults of sporting heroes. All were designed to provide recreation and diversion for the fast-growing urban populace. The big city and security forces (*Dinamo*) teams, with their substantial resources, dominated competition in all sports. Thus, out of its 26 clubs, the top football league of 1938 included nine Moscow and six *Dinamo* teams from the cities of Moscow, Leningrad, Kiev, Tbilisi, Odessa and Rostov.

In 1935, the government created voluntary sports societies based on the trade unions: *Spartak* for white-collar workers, *Lokomotiv* for railway workers, *Torpedo* for car workers, etc. Together with the clubs of the armed forces and security forces, they formed full-time professional 'teams of masters' to compete in the nationwide cup and league tournaments instituted in 1936. One of the principal tasks of the sports societies was to act as a catalyst in raising standards through rational organization and competition, to act as 'transmission belts' for talented athletes. Once these were discovered, it was then necessary to categorize them according to level of ability and to give them an incentive and special amenities to realize their potential. For this purpose, a uniform rankings system was introduced in 1937, with rankings decided by times, distances or weights recorded in a particular event and/or success in competition. Once an athlete had risen through the three adult rankings and reached the 'Master of Sport' level, he or she could apply him/ herself full time to sport, unencumbered by a job of work outside the sporting vocation.

The many sports parades and pageants which constituted a background to the sports contests were intended to create 'togetherness' and patriotic feeling. Significantly, sports rallies often began to accompany major political events and festivals (May Day, Anniversary of the Revolution, Constitution Day), thereby linking members of the public, through sport, with politics, the Party and, of course, with the nation's leader, Iosif Stalin.

A relatively close tie was re-established in the 1930s between sport and the military, stemming from the conviction that a state surrounded by unfriendly powers (especially with the rise of fascism in Italy and Germany) must be militarily strong. Sport openly became a means of providing pre-military training and achieving a relatively high standard of national fitness and defence. The two largest and most successful sports clubs were those run by the armed forces and the security forces: the Central House of the Red Army (later to become the Central Sports Club of the Army, *TsSKA*) and *Dinamo*, respectively. After 1931, moreover, the national fitness programme, the *GTO*, was expressly intended to train people, through sport, for military preparedness and work – the Russian abbreviation *GTO (Gotov k trudu i oborone)* standing for 'Prepared for Labour and Defence'.

Effects of the war and post-war sports competition with the West

The war years obviously retarded the sports movement, yet had certain far-reaching effects. The war convinced the authorities that they had been right to 'functionalize' sport and make nationwide physical fitness a prime target. It also reinforced a belief in a military bias in physical training and sport.

With the conclusion of the war and the setting of a new national target – to catch up and overtake the most advanced industrial powers in sport as in all else – the Soviet leaders felt it possible to demonstrate the pre-eminence of sport in Soviet socialist society. Given the limited opportunities elsewhere, sport seemed to offer a suitable medium for pursuing this goal as an area in which the USSR did not have to take second place to capitalist states. This aim presupposed a level of skill in a wide range of sports superior to that existing in the leading Western states.

This trend towards proficiency was strengthened after the war by mobilization of the total, if limited, resources of the entire sports system, by creating full-time, well-remunerated athletes and teams, and by giving them considerable backing (including, after 1960, some 40 sports boarding schools). Sport was seen as 'one of the best and most comprehensible means of explaining to people all over the world the advantages of the socialist system over capitalism'.

Prior to World War II, almost all sports competition was conducted within the USSR. With the conclusion of the war and the decision to join international sports federations and the IOC (in May 1951), the appearance had to be given that Soviet athletes complied with the definition of an 'amateur'. It transpired that proficient athletes would be classified either as a student or as a commissioned serviceman under the sponsorship of a sports society or club. In the case of the country's two best endowed societies, *Dinamo* and the Central Army Sports Club, the athlete would hold a commission, but not be expected to undergo any form of military service.

On the eve of war, Soviet sport was evidently approaching international standards in several sports; in some, it had actually reached it, as demonstrated by the four-match unbeaten tour of Great Britain by the Moscow *Dinamo* football team in the autumn of 1945. It was not long before the Soviet Union was to become the most successful and versatile nation in the history of sport, particularly at the Olympic Games.

While the Soviet Union dominated the summer and winter Olympics from its Helsinki debut in 1952, as well as some non-Olympic sports, like chess, it never seriously challenged the world's leading football teams; Soviet football failed to gain a place among the world's leading nations or clubs. The same might be said of professional basketball and cycling, though not ice-hockey, where the Soviet national team took on and beat the leading National Hockey League clubs in the 1970s and 1980s.

The pinnacle of sporting glory for the Soviet Union came in 1980 when it became the first Communist country to stage the summer Olympic Games. The IOC had selected Moscow as the 1980 host at its 75th session on 23 October 1974 in Vienna. Moscow won the vote comfortably over its sole rival, Los Angeles. At the time, many felt the USSR worthy of the honour: not only was it the most successful nation in Olympic history in terms of sporting performance, but it was considered to have done much in Olympic forums to enhance the pre-eminent role of sport and the Olympic movement. It was a popular choice with both Eastern European states (but not all Communist nations – the People's Republic of China and Albania turning down their invitations to go to Moscow) and many Third World countries, the political and sporting causes of which had gained Soviet support in such matters as, for example, the banning of racist South Africa from the Olympic movement, the training of coaches, construction of sports facilities and free attendance of athletes at Soviet sports institutes.

As for Western governments, despite their distaste for Communism and the Soviet human rights record, it was generally thought that the appointment of Moscow as Olympic host might somehow make a contribution to the process of détente then underway. At the very least, it might encourage some liberalization within the country or, at worst, expose it to the world as a cynical violator of the Helsinki Accords on human rights. Despite the subsequent US-led boycott (ostensibly in retaliation for the Soviet invasion of Afghanistan in December 1979 – ignoring the hosting of the Winter Olympics in the USA after the US invasion of Vietnam), the IOC announced on 27 May 1980 that 85 countries had accepted invitations to compete in Moscow. The Games went off without a hitch and represented one of the most successful and eye-catching sporting spectacles of our time.

Yet … at the very moment of reaching the pinnacle of sporting glory, the Soviet Union precipitously (and, to most people, unexpectedly) began to fall apart. Two years after the Games, the Soviet President, Leonid Brezhnev, died; three years and two presidents later, Mikhail Gorbachev came to power with radically new policies. Four years later, the Communist edifice crumbled throughout the eight nations of Eastern and Central Europe. The Soviet Union followed suit and ceased to exist as a unitary state in late 1991. It would be a mite extravagant to blame the Moscow Olympics for the demise of Communism. Yet for many citizens of Communist states, the 1980 Olympics brought tensions to a head, especially as the public was able to see those tensions in its own backyard. It is noteworthy that when the revolutions swept across Eastern Europe in late 1989, there was an intense debate about sport. Far from being at the periphery of politics, sport was right at the core.

The break-up of the Soviet Union

During the 1980s, radical changes had begun to appear in Soviet sport, breaking the mould of its functionalized and bureaucratic (plan-fulfilment) structure. Until then, not only had the state-controlled, utilitarian system hampered a true appraisal of realities that lay beneath the 'universal' statistics and 'idealized' veneer, it had prevented concessions to particular groups in the population – the 'we know what's best for you' syndrome whereby the fit tell the disabled that sport is not for them; men tell women what sports they should play; the old tell the young they can play only on their (old) terms, in their clubs, using their facilities; the leaders, mindful of international prestige, decide that competitive Olympic sports were the only civilized forms of culture. It also entailed Moscow (via the Warsaw Pact organization) telling other European Communist countries that they were to boycott the Los Angeles Olympics of 1984 (though Yugoslavia and Romania demurred).

What no one could say openly before, including during the 1980 Olympics, owing to strict censorship, was that *Dinamo* was the sports club sponsored by the security forces, that athletes of Master of Sport ranking and above devoted themselves full time to sport and were paid accordingly, that athletes received bonuses for winning (including scarce dollars), that the Soviet National Olympic Committee was a government-run institution and that its Chairman had to be a member of the Communist Party, that the Soviet state manufactured, tested and administered performance-enhancing drugs to its athletes, and so on.

Down the years the Soviet leadership had produced regiments of statistics to show that millions were regular, active participants in sport; that the vast majority of school and college students gained a national fitness badge (the *GTO*); that rising millions (one-third of the population) took part in the quadrennial spartakiads; and that the bulk of workers did their daily dozen – 'production gymnastics' – at the workplace. Just a few years after the Moscow Olympics, however, the new leaders declared that these figures were all fraudulent, a show to impress people above and below, and to meet pre-set targets. It was now admitted that no more than eight percent of men and two percent of women engaged in sport regularly.

Once people started to see journalists writing about the past and exposing the realities of elite sport, they started to question the very morality of sport, the price that society should pay for talent. Many expressed their distaste at what they felt was a race for false glory, the cultivation of irrational loyalties, the unreasonable prominence given to the winning of victories, the setting of records and the collecting of trophies – an obsessive fetishism of sport. This was the very criticism made of 'sport' by opposition groups back in the 1920s, particularly the Hygienists and the Proletkultists.

This is, of course, an issue not unknown in other societies, especially those of scarcity; but for a population that had been waiting years for housing, phones and cars, that saw their economy collapsing, and that felt that sporting victories were being attained for political values they did not share – i.e. that sports 'heroes' were not *theirs*; they were somehow accomplices in gilding the lily of the Communist Party – the vast sums being lavished on ensuring a grand Olympic show represented the straw that broke the camel's back.

Having allowed the nation to bare its soul, the leaders in the post-Gorbachev era radically changed their scale of priorities. They no longer saw the need to demonstrate the advantages of socialism, as they were trying to distance themselves from the command economy that had failed so badly and the totalitarian political system that had accompanied the imposition of Communism from above. Once the curtain came down on Communism, the international challenge was diluted through lack of state support; the free trade union sports societies, as well as the ubiquitous *Dinamo* and armed forces clubs, mostly gave way to private sports and recreation clubs; women's wrestling and boxing extracted more profit than women's chess and volleyball; the various nationalities preferred their own independent teams to combined effort and success. So *Dinamo* Kiev opted to compete in a Ukrainian league, Tbilisi *Dinamo* in a Georgian league, and Russian clubs in the Russian Football League set up in 1991.

The failed Communist coup of 19–21 August 1991 accelerated the shift from state control of and support for sport towards private, commercial sport, and a massive 'brain' and 'muscle' drain of top athletes, coaches, sports medics and scientists to the richest overseas buyer. The international market for sports talent enabled stars from one-time Communist states to offer themselves for sale to promoters around the world. All these developments weakened Russian interest in the Olympic movement and led to the removal of the sinecures of an army commission and 'eternal' studenthood for all top athletes, and to the dismantling of the 42 sports boarding schools. During the Gorbachev era, up to 1990, there had arisen a multiplicity of grass roots sports organizations for disabled sports people, women (in rugby, boxing and wrestling, as well as football), small-scale private swimming and tennis clubs, and senior fitness associations. They were soon to be steamrollered by a 'revolution' as far-reaching as anything in the past: exposure to the 'free' market and selling out to the global economy.

Sport in contemporary Russia

In the wake of the crumbling Communist edifice, a deadly struggle commenced for the control of sport. As the ostentatiously rich 'New Russians' went about acquiring symbols of wealth, sport became a convenient place to invest their vast riches. Like the primitive capitalism that underlay their power, the methods they used to exploit sport were often primitive in the extreme, including the fixing of results, the bribing and intimidation of officials, and even the 'hit' killings of those who stood in their way or tried to expose their nefarious operations. In many ways, the 1990s and early 2000s in Russia were reminiscent of mafia-dominated Chicago in the 1920s, with football taking the place of baseball.

The new Russian elite had, by the turn of the century, accumulated so much wealth that they had to seek ways of both investing and hiding it from the tax authorities. Sport seemed to be a convenient veil/shroud to cover their less sporting activities, an enjoyable plaything that brought them popular acclaim and prestige, and a means to launder their vast wealth. Initially, these 'oligarchs', as they are known, treated sports clubs like any other 'turf' that had to be won and retained. They took control, by fair means or foul, of the major sports clubs and tried to 'buy success' in domestic and international tournaments.

No wonder that some of the older generation began to hark back to the 'good old days' of Soviet 'high culture' and relative security. There were no 'hit' killings, no drain of talent, no takeovers by oligarchs, no American-style culture. All the same, sport continues to play a role among the Russian public of considerable social significance. In a society of cataclysmic change and authoritarian dictatorship, sport has always had a unique meaning for ordinary people in terms of emotional escape, the chance to belong to an apolitical institution. This is all the more important today to Russians who, for the first time, have moved from being citizens of a multi-ethnic state (the USSR) to Russian nationals in 'Mother Rus'. For the first time in their history, Russians have the country mostly to themselves.

Nonetheless, the sporting diaspora of Russian athletes and the nefarious activities of the oligarchs who own sports clubs have caused the same kind of nationalistic ire against multinational juggernauts and billionaire owners as it has caused elsewhere in the world. It has also had the effect of forcing fans to turn away from sport altogether. Football is one example: it has long been the most popular spectator sport during Russia's summer months (ice-hockey and, increasingly, five-a-side indoor football take over in winter). In Soviet times, during the 1970s and 1980s, the major grounds were packed to capacity, with an average of 35,000 fans at premiership matches. Today, the six major Moscow teams average just over 7,000 spectators a game between them – a pitiful figure by any European standards.

The oligarchs have brought a radical break with the past not only in Russian sport, but in sport the world over, particularly football. For the first time, the clubs they own in and outside Russia can buy players from all over the world, no matter what the price or the wages demanded. Money matters not a tittle in seeking success. In Russia the oligarchs are widely loathed. The great bulk of Russians believe the oligarchs stole the people's assets and left the Russian population worse off today than they were during the last 30 years of Communism. Like all businesses, however, it could change at any moment (e.g. by Russian presidential fiat), with the oligarchs walking out of the clubs they presently sponsor, leaving behind chaos and vast debts. Sport is not exactly their thing.

The radical shift in sports policy generally has obscured many of the positive features of Communist sport. The old system was generally open to the talents in all sports, probably more so than in the West. It provided opportunities for women to play and succeed, if not on equal terms with men, at least on a higher plane than Western women. It gave an opportunity to the many ethnic minorities and relatively small states within the USSR to do well internationally and to help promote that pride and dignity that sports success in the glare of world publicity can bring. Nowhere in the world was there, since the early 1950s, such reverence for Olympism, for Olympic ritual and decorum. One practical embodiment of that was the contribution to Olympic solidarity with modernizing nations: the training of Third World athletes, coaches, sports officials, medical officers and scholars at colleges and training camps. Much of this aid was free.

None of it was disinterested; but it also went to those who were clearly exploited, as was the case with the Soviet-led campaign against apartheid in sport.

Russia today is a society in transition, including its sport. Fixing the economy, cleaning up corruption, stopping the outflow of Russia's wealth and restoring a sense of pride and community would certainly contribute to a healthier society and sports system. It remains to be seen what sort of society will emerge from the present situation and the role that sport might play in the transition to a brighter future.

References

Edelman, Robert, *Serious Fun: A History of Spectator Sports in the USSR* (Oxford: Oxford University Press, 1993).

Morton, Henry, *Soviet Sport* (London: Collier-Macmillan, 1963).

O'Mahony, Mike, *Sport in the USSR: Physical Culture – Visual Culture* (London: Reaktion Books, 2006).

Prozumenshchikov, Mikhail, *Bolshoi sport i bolshaya politika* [Big-Time Sport and Big-Time Politics] (Moscow: Rosspen, 2004).

Riordan, James, *Sport in Soviet Society* (London: Cambridge University Press, 1977).

——*Soviet Sport: Background to the Olympics* (Oxford: Blackwell, 1980).

Riordan, James and Arnd Kruger, eds, *European Cultures in Sport. Examining the nations and regions* (Bristol: Intellect, 2003).

Rodichenko, Vladimir, *Olimpiyskaya ideya dlya Rossii* [The Olympic Idea for Russia] (Moscow: Sovietsky sport, 1998, reprinted 2004).

Wagg, Stephen and David Andrews, eds, *East Plays West: Sport and the Cold War* (London: Routledge, 2007).

35 South America

Cesar R. Torres

South America is typically referred to as the solid landmass located to the south of the Western Hemisphere. With a rough triangular shape, which markedly narrows down from north to south, it covers almost seven million square miles. South America is generally divided in the Andean region (Northern, Central and Southern), the lowland tropical rainforests, and the coastal regions (Atlantic and Pacific). It is believed that the first inhabitants of the Western Hemisphere entered from Asia during the late Pleistocene through what is known today as the Bering Strait. These groups of nomads moved south through North America and reached the Andes. The adoption of a settled lifestyle, among other factors, eventually led to the emergence and development of rich and diverse indigenous cultures throughout South America, of which the Huari, Tiwanaku and Inca empires in the Andes are among the better known. Many of these indigenous cultures flourished until the Iberian (Spanish and Portuguese) conquest of the 15th and 16th centuries. Yet, in spite of centuries of extermination, oppression and abandonment, many of them still struggle for survival, recognition and justice.[1]

This chapter is organized along the patterns of the traditional periodization of South American history. It outlines the historiography of 'sport' in South America starting with the indigenous cultures, continues with the Iberian conquest and colonization, then focuses on the subsequent struggles for independence and the establishment of the modern South American nations, and finalizes by analysing contemporary South America. While doing so, the chapter investigates the status, contributions and omissions of 'sport' history in wider historiographical debates in the region. Finally, the chapter discusses the role that the sub-discipline should or could play in the study of 'sport' in the region. Due to the growing status of the sub-discipline in these nations and, therefore, a more developed literature, Argentina and Brazil constitute the locus of the chapter.

The use of the term 'sport' in this chapter merits a brief reflection and clarification. As sport philosophers have argued, sports are artificial tests established by rules that not only prescribe the use of less efficient means to achieve the goal stipulated, but also require the implementation of physical skills to do so. The rationale behind sports is a 'gratuitous logic' that highlights the radical interdependency between the goal stipulated and the means proscribed and permitted to accomplish it.[2] To use Bernard Suits's terminology, in sports, the rules are accepted because they make possible the activity. This is captured by his notion of the 'lusory attitude'.[3]

Following this analysis of sport, some of what is labelled as such in 'sport' history, particularly in pre-modern times, turns out not to be so. Consider, for example, Allen Guttmann's categorization of sport in pre-modern or traditional and modern.[4] If the rules of the former were accepted primarily to satisfy the gods or to invoke their benevolence – that is, for sacred reasons – and not to partake in the artificial test, it is somewhat problematic to identify them as sport. If these comments are sound, the Mesoamerican ball game, for example, although an important element in the physical culture of the Mayans, cockfighting, or board games cannot legitimately be called sports. This does not mean that Guttmann's modernization-inspired thesis is fundamentally flawed. The set of characteristics that distinguish pre-modern or traditional physical cultures – including *some* sports – from modern ones seems to be correct and useful. Space limitations do not allow for a thorough elaboration of this issue, though; the point to highlight is that metaphysical analyses of sport cast doubt as to whether some of the physical undertakings labelled as sport in the sub-discipline can be legitimately labelled so. In this chapter, then, the term 'sport' is reserved for physical activities in which 'the sole reason for accepting such limitation [the rules] is to make possible such activity'.[5] Otherwise, the reference is to 'physical activities or exercises' and 'physical cultures' that are less related to productive or survival endeavours and more to enjoyment, recreation and leisure.[6] Rather than using 'sport' as an inclusive but porous term for all kinds of physical performativity, a more precise analytical framework is preferred. This, it is hoped, helps illuminate the complexity of the history of 'sport' in South America.

When the Iberians arrived in South America, they witnessed a variety of activities performed by indigenous peoples that were physical in nature, such as boxing, dancing, running, swimming and wrestling. They also found team physical exercises. Several of these practices resembled modern sports. The first chronicles of these activities came from Spanish missionaries. Later on, geographers, naturalists and travellers from Spain as well as other European nations, enthused by the rarity and excitement of what they considered the 'new world', also left accounts of South American indigenous physical cultures. Most of these accounts both describe the physical activities of the indigenous people and make sense of them in contrast with the chronicler's own background. In this sense, there is an ideological construction of the indigenous physical cultures and, consequently, an axiological interpretation that tends to portray them as secondary to their European counterparts.

José Sánchez Labrador, a Spanish Jesuit missionary, writing in the 18th century, explained that the Mocobíes, Vilelas and Guaicurúes of Argentina and Paraguay engaged in boxing, running and swimming. Sánchez Labrador said that boxing was reserved for men in these communities.[7] Florián Baucke, another Jesuit missionary, also provided reports of similar physical activities among the Mocobíes.[8] In his history of the Company of Jesus in Paraguay, Jesuit Nicolás del Techo noticed different kinds of indigenous physical exertion for recreational purposes.[9] Martin Dobrizhoffer, also a Jesuit missionary, gave an account of the equestrian abilities of Paraguay's Abipones.[10]

More than 1,000 km South of Paraguay, the Onas of Argentina and Chile were very fond of foot races. Throughout the 19th and early 20th centuries, explorers and researchers, both South American and European, such as Lucas Bridge, Antonio Coiazzi, Roberto Dabbene, Carlos R. Gallardo and Ramón Serrano Montaner, among others, recounted the running habits and competitions of the Onas, detailing their characteristics and conditions. There were sprints as well as long-distance races. According to Martin Gusinde, foot races were activities pursued for their own sake but also as a way to settle disputes and occasionally to celebrate the meeting of friendly groups. Observers did not find evidence of prizes and the foot races appeared to have been a practice reserved for males.[11]

This indigenous group also practised individual and group wrestling. If the former was a way to primarily measure individual strength and prowess, the latter was chiefly intended to settle disagreements.[12] Other favourite activities of the Onas included archery and several ball games. One of the ball games consisted simply in throwing a ball to each other as far as possible while another required several people to form a circle and hit the ball into the air alternatively without letting it get to the ground. Both boys and girls partook in the ball games. Children also engaged in a variety of games at the beach and in others involving snow.[13]

Geographically close to the Onas, Mapuches in Argentina and Chile practised a game called *palín* or *viñu*, similar to modern field hockey. It was organized in an area roughly 100 metres long by 50 metres wide. Teams consisted of around 10 men. The objective was to carry the ball into the opposing goal, marked at the end of the field with barks and bushes, hitting it with sticks made of *molle* or *coihue*, two types of wood. According to Augusto Guinnard, who spent few years in captivity in the 19th century among the Patagones, the game excited the players as much as the community.[14] This ball game and others practised by the Mapuches have been thoroughly researched by Carlos López von Vriessen.[15] More generally, scholars Emilio A. Breda, José Eduardo A. Machicote, Raúl Martinez Crovetto and Mario Moreno, among others, have studied the indigenous games and sports of Argentina, Chile and Paraguay.[16]

Nowadays, there is a growing trend in the region to revive and preserve regional indigenous physical cultures. Attempts have been made to include some indigenous physical activities and sports in regional school curricula. Events such as the *Juegos de la Araucaria* in Argentina and Chile, and the *Jogos dos Povos Indígenas*, also known as *Jogos Nacionais Indígenas*, in Brazil work towards preserving indigenous physical activities. The 1988 Brazilian constitution declared that it is the responsibility of the state to safeguard and promote the physical traditions of the indigenous populations.

Much like in the rest of South America, missionaries, explorers and travellers, generally European, were the first to recount the indigenous physical games, traditions and sports of Brazil. Unsurprisingly, these descriptions did not account for the rich and complex meanings that these activities had for the indigenous people who practised them. It was only in the early 20th century that more serious and systematic studies of the traditions of the Brazilian indigenous physical cultures took place. Both Brazilian and international researchers were part of this trend. In a book published early in the 1900s Stuart Culin made reference to some physical traditions of various Brazilian indigenous people and a few years later Telêmaco Borba studied the games of the Kaingàng tribe (Southern Brazil).[17] Around the middle of the 20th century an increasing number of Brazilian researches paid attention to the role that different types of games played in the lives of indigenous people. Among them were Eduardo Galvão, Carmen Junqueira and Darcy Ribeiro.[18]

The contemporary indigenous scenario in Brazil is very complex. There are more than 200 Indian tribes in Brazil, with a population exceeding 350,000 natives. Perhaps it is important to remember that before the Portuguese colonial occupiers arrived in the 16th century, the indigenous population was estimated at six million. Given the ethnic, cultural and geographic complexity of the Brazilian indigenous peoples, it is difficult to formulate a unifying account of their physical cultures. Among the more studied Indian tribes are the Xingu (central Brazil), Guarani (southern Brazil) and Canela (north-eastern Brazil). Different types of *zerabatana* (blowpipe), running, canoeing, archery, arrow throwing and wrestling, among other physical pursuits, were and are part of the cultural traditions of many tribes.

One of the better-known activities is the *corrida de tora*, a race in which two groups transport heavy logs over a set distance, anywhere from a few hundred metres to several kilometres. There are several different variations of the activity. It could be done as a form of diversion or include ritualistic connotations. Today the Xavante and Xerente (central Brazil), and Timbira groups (north-eastern Brazil) practise the activity. Another well-known activity is the *xikunahity*, or head football, cultivated by the Pareci indigenous people (central Brazil). This game, practised by adult males, involves two teams separated by a line. The aim is to hit a rubber ball into the opposing field so that it cannot be returned. The ball is allowed to be hit only with the head. Since the 1980s, these and other aspects of the vast Brazilian indigenous physical cultures have been the object of more research.[19]

The rest of the pre-columbian South American physical cultures have not received much attention, although there are signs that interest in them is growing. In September 2000, the Colombian Congress declared *tejo*, a modern version of the ancient game *turmequé*, a national sport. Some reports affirm that *turmequé* has been practised for more than five centuries. The modern version of the game consists of tossing stones or metallic disks underhand into a receptacle placed at a measured distance to explode blasting caps. Some of the physical activities performed by indigenous people in Peru, such as wrestling, have been studied by Denis Roberge, Emilia Romero and Máximo Cama Ttito.[20] The indigenous games and physical traditions of Colombia, Venezuela and Bolivia can be found in the work of Anna Curtenius Roosevelt and A.W. Miracle.[21]

In spite of the rich physical cultures they encountered upon arrival in South America, the Iberians did not become immersed in them. For the most part, indigenous physical activities were repressed. The Iberians imported their own games and physical pastimes. One of the most prominent activities was Spanish bullfighting, introduced to the region in the 16th century. Although practised throughout South America during colonial times, bullfighting did not enjoy much prominence in the Southern Cone. The *corridas* served many purposes, from celebrating the colonial order to transmitting the values of the metropolis. In the Viceroyalty of the Río de la Plata, bullfighting never reached the importance and splendour it had in the Viceroyalty of Peru, where the *corridas* rivalled those organized in Spain. Bullfighting continued to be practised in northern South America (Ecuador, Peru, Colombia and Venezuela) after independence and its meanings were reinterpreted. In those nations, bullfighting is still a widespread festival, predominantly for men. Distance from the main colonial urban centres as well as progressive cultural and economic ties with Europe and North America throughout the 19th century and the persistent association of bullfighting with the ancien régime help explain why bullfighting was eventually discontinued in southern South America. The history of bullfighting in the region, which was temporarily banned in different nations because of cruelty and links to Spain, has been explored by South American as well as European researchers.[22]

There were many other physical games and pastimes in Spanish American colonial society. Angel López Cantos has examined the festivals and games of the rulers and affluent inhabitants, as well as those of the middle and lower classes during this period. The Spanish colonizers brought the first horses to South America, which prompted the evolution of a rich equestrian culture that eventually became central to the life of the *gauchos* in Argentina, the *gaúchos* in Brazil, the *huasos* in Chile, the *llaneros* in Venezuela and Colombia, the *chalanes* in Peru, and the *morochucos* in Bolivia. These groups developed amazing degrees of horsemanship and put them to use not only in the necessities of rural tasks, but also in a variety of games, contests and diversions. The Argentine *gauchos*, for example, engaged in different kinds of horse-riding and horse-racing, including *doma*, a kind of rodeo, and *cuadreras* and *carrera de sortija*, two varieties of horse-racing.

During the 19th century the *gaucho* life was constructed as the manifestation of courage, freedom and independence. The epic poem *Martín Fierro* by José Hernández in Argentina and the novel *Doña Bárbara* by Rómulo Gallegos in Venezuela portrayed and praised horsemen. Years later, *gauchos*, *llaneros* and their traditions were seen as a hindrance to progress and modernity. Ironically, these traditions were revived in the 20th century as folkloristic activities, typical of a *criollo* lifestyle.[23]

One *gaucho* activity that traversed this intricate path is the game of *pato*, which goes back to the 17th century. The traditional game used a live duck (*pato*) inside a basket. The two teams of horsemen tried to snatch the basket from each other and when one succeeded, he galloped away trying to reach a predetermined ranch. The game was banned on several occasions from colonial times up to the 20th century. Religious, civic and economic reasons were used to justify the bans. In spite of the condemnation, former Argentine President Bartolomé Mitre and Argentine writer Rafael Obligado extolled the game during the 19th century. In the late 1930s, the last ordinance banning the game was lifted and the game developed to its present form, which unsurprisingly does not include a live duck. The modernization and institutionalization of the game transformed it from a folk activity into an elite one. *Pato* gained definitive recognition when former President Juan Domingo Perón declared it the national sport of Argentina in 1953. Much like polo, another equestrian sport, *pato* is controlled by the Argentine upper classes. The importation and adoption of 'civilized' polo by the upper classes was also an attempt to expunge vestiges of the pernicious *gaucho* traditions. Nevertheless, both *pato* and polo were constructed as sports with rural origins and identified with an Argentine *criollo* tradition. Throughout the first decades of the 20th century polo solidified in Argentina as a practice that recreated European values and exemplified the elite's political and economic project, yet rooted in an agricultural past. In the process, Argentina became known as a key site for the sport in the world.[24]

During the consolidation period of the modern South American states, Basque immigrants brought jai-alai and other ball games such as different variations of *pelota a paleta* to the region. These games are played with special racquets in a ball court and seem to have roots in the Middle Ages game of *jeu de paume*, from which court tennis developed. These games took on in the Southern Cone, especially in Buenos Aires and the Pampa region of Argentina, as well as in Uruguay and Chile, where there are vibrant communities of practitioners. In the last decades of the 19th century, *pelota a paleta* drew attention in political circles. For instance, former Argentine President Domingo F. Sarmiento attended the inauguration of a ball court in Buenos Aires, an early expression of a politician taking advantage of the promotional opportunities offered by sport activities. Although the basic structure of the different variations of the sport have been standardized, characteristics typical of pre-modern or traditional modes of sport have survived, as ball courts differ in size and, sometimes, even in shape.[25]

The Portuguese did not bring to Brazil any one given physical activity with the distinction and prominence that bullfighting had in Spanish America during colonial times. At least in urban centres, such as Rio de Janeiro, there were no frequent public displays of physical activities until the mid-19th century. Since muscular labour was restricted to the lower classes, physical activity did not find much favour in the middle and upper classes. Indeed, the paternalistic Brazilian colonial society was disinclined to physical activity.[26] The situation was somewhat different in the lower classes. *Capoeira*, a combat activity combining highly stylized movements with music and dance, was started by African slaves. Its origins are not entirely clear, but the roots of *capoeira* can be traced back to colonial times and involved the culture of the African Yorubas. Once slavery was abolished in Brazil in May 1888, *capoeira* migrated to the cities. However, due to its prohibition from the 18th century until 1940, the practice of *capoeira* was confined to a limited number of people. With the lift of the prohibition, it has gained much recognition both in Brazil and, increasingly, abroad, and it is a physical activity no longer restricted to oppressed groups. Although there are several forms, at its core *capoeira* continues to express the desire for freedom. The move of *capoeira* to mainstream society has also transformed it as a legitimate subject of study. Since the 1960s, it has occupied a more visible place in academia.[27]

Also, during colonial times, and in similar fashion to what happened in the rest of South America, equestrian competitions and diversions were common features of Brazilian rural life. *Vaquejada*, consisting of riding wild bulls and horses, is a rural practice in existence since the 16th century.

By the middle of the 19th century, a period in which the modern South American states were consolidating themselves, British investors, predominantly English, brought along with their capital a set of physical practices to the region that were seducing people from all over the world: modern sports. Sometimes these physical activities were imported by South American expatriates returning to their homelands. Although modern sports did not immediately capture the South American imagination and were, at times, resisted, by the turn of the 20th century they were a frequent sight in urban areas. Following the British model, sport clubs for the elite as well as the masses were steadily created. From football to boxing, car racing, cycling, field hockey, golf, rugby, swimming, track and field, and yachting, among others, modern sports became associated with a European progressive world view that would put South America on the road to progress and Western civilization. Modern sports also became associated with an ethic of discipline, organization, leadership, competition and healthy living, all necessary characteristics, the elite argued, to earn the respect of the civilized world.

By the 1930s, South American sport, motorized by a growing mass media and literacy in urban centres, was not only widespread but well organized. National sport structures and bureaucracies flourished, and became affiliated with the nascent world sport system. Around this time, efforts were made to organize multinational regional sport events and South American nations increasingly participated in the Olympic Games as well as other international sport tournaments. The popularization of modern sport in South America was also helped by the massive school systems, which progressively included physical education and sports in their curricula. Replicating global trends, South American women were slowly being accepted on sport fields, and as regional societies were transformed, especially in urban settings, they also enjoyed and benefited from the practice of sports. Although other forms of physical culture such as German and other northern European gymnastics systems were also imported to South America, they did not seriously rival the physical activities imported by the British. Only at the dawn of the 20th century did these gymnastic systems gain popularity among critics of British modern sports. Although the criticism did not entirely disappear, it was not powerful enough to question the essence of British modern sports, nor did they obtain significant endorsement in society.

While British modern sport consolidated in South America, another tide of modern sport was also imported to the region, this time from the USA. Mainly through the work of the national chapters of the Young Men's Christian Association (YMCA), modern sports developed in the USA, such as basketball and volleyball, became known in South America. Their recognition spread rapidly. If British modern sports took about 50 or 60 years, roughly from the 1860s to the 1920s, to take root in the South America, the adoption of US modern sports was on a fast track. Of course, familiar with British modern sports, South American societies were already prepared for the new sports developed in the USA, but equally important was the fact that this nation was also perceived as the ever-more dominating world power of the 20th century. Its capital dominated foreign investment in the region, and its political, economic and cultural ways were seen as conducive to democracy and economic wealth, especially after World War II.

By the 1950s, the sporting scene in South America had taken its contemporary shape. British and US modern sports were not only fully embraced, but also subjected to a complex process of cultural adaptation in which the locals infused them with new connotations, meanings and imageries. In an important sense, modern sports became social practices able to carry on national aspirations and to represent the perceived or imagined uniqueness of each South American nation. In this context, different nations constructed different ways of living and playing modern sports. The adoption and appropriation of modern sports in South America meant almost a total departure from indigenous as well as colonial physical cultures, although, as seen above, there are now efforts to recuperate and revitalize them. Only a few activities with a relatively large following such as *pato* in Argentina, *capoeira* in Brazil, and other equestrian events in countries throughout South American have roots in the colonial past and the period of national independence.

The first accounts of modern sports in South American were written by sport administrators, journalists, sportspeople and observers interested in telling the story of how modern sports initially developed in the region. Argentines Ernesto Escobar Bavio, Eduardo A. Olivera, Eugenio Pini and César Viale, and Brazilians Americo R. Netto and Roberto Trompowsky, Jr are among these first chroniclers of South American modern sports. Physical education pioneers such as Argentine Enrique Romero Brest also ruminated about the history of modern sport and physical education in their nations.[28] These accounts were very limited in scope as they were mainly preoccupied with describing 'what occurred when' and 'who was involved in the events'. In spite of their limitations, their value resides in the attempt to document and establish a chronology of modern sport in the region. As in many cases these chronicles were witnesses or even protagonists of what they described, perhaps their narratives constitute what could be seen as an embryonic regional sport memory – a valuable tool in itself for sports historians.

As sport, most specifically football, grew to consume people's attention and came to be associated with modernization and nationalism throughout the 20th century, journalists continued to produce accounts of this growth and its protagonists in the different South American nations. Their work was most visible in the popular press, notably through the expanding professional specialization known as sport journalism. Héctor Alberto Chaponick, Félix Frascara and Ricardo Lorenzo in Argentina, the brothers Mário and Nélson Rodrigues Filho, and José Lins do Rego in Brazil, and Diego Lucero in Uruguay are good examples.[29] Much like the accounts of the early chroniclers of South American modern sports, most of the work of these journalists was descriptive in nature and lack argument by way of theoretical frameworks, thus weakening their explanatory force. At best, these narratives could be portrayed as 'analytical history', primarily focusing on chronology rather than on interpretation. The exception to this trend was the aforementioned Brazilian journalists, who attempted to incorporate anthropological notions to their analyses of the development of football in their nation. In this sense, Mário Rodrigues Filho's 1947 *O negro no futebol brasileiro* and the reflections of Nélson Rodrigues Filho published in *À sombra das chuteiras imortais: Crônicas de futebol* and *A pátria em chuteiras: Novas crônicas de futebol* opened new vistas and interpretations of the significance of football in Brazil.[30]

During the latter part of the 20th century, the history of sport in the region was not a concern of professional historians. The lack of interest in modern sport was not confined to history, but rather to the social sciences *in toto*. The 'popular' or 'frivolous' status typically assigned to modern sport and its concomitant immediacy to personal experiences, which are constitutive of different forms of personal and group identities, influenced this academic bias. Traversed by their sporting experiences and affected by the articulation of sports as 'mere games', scholars were either unable or unwilling to distance themselves from their sporting tales to critically analyse modern sport, or ignored it academically altogether.[31] Nevertheless, starting around the early 1980s, modern sport slowly began to capture the interest of regional academicians, including historians. This trend was influenced by international tendencies that could no longer ignore the arresting transnational spectacle of modern sport and its evident connections to larger political, economic, social and cultural forces as much as by the democratization of South American societies in the 1980s, which extended to academia. In the discipline of history, this democratization meant the embrace of what became known as 'cultural history'. Thus, there was an increasing preoccupation with cultural phenomena enjoyed by people from all walks of life, a growing emphasis on themes such as gender, social class, race and multiculturalism, and the emergence of the history of sport, music, food, cinema and the medical professions to name a few areas of new concerns.[32]

In South America, historians, and social scientists in general, were first interested in the regional consuming passion for football. Although it did not cause a flurry of production, the trend was, nevertheless, visible. Inspired by the tradition pioneered by the anthropologist Clifford Geertz, historians paid attention to the role that football played in the nation-making process, in the construction of solidarities and personal identities, and in the expression of regional and local cultural characteristics. That is, at the core was the exploration of how football allowed people to image who they were and wanted to become. These cultural analyses draw largely on historical content. The 1982 collection of essays, *O universo do futebol: esporte e sociedade brasileira* edited by Brazilian Roberto Da Matta is considered the marker of the new critical engagement with football. Inspired by Da Matta's pioneering work, Argentine Eduardo P. Archetti expanded the possibility to study football in South America. During the 1980s and 1990s, Archetti wrote several influential articles, which culminated in the publication in 1999 of his celebrated *Masculinities: Football, Polo and Tango in Argentina*, a book that analyses how these seemingly peripheral social practices assist in the identity-making process on multiple levels. Implementing an ethnography that combined extensive field work with a careful reading of different forms of cultural texts, Archetti not only discussed how identities are forged through these social practices – putting the performativity of the human body at the centre of the analysis – but also demonstrated how Argentines historically conceived their identities. In the process, Archetti made clear the political nature of football and polo and their relationship to the nation.[33]

Da Matta and Archetti's legitimization of the study of football, and more broadly sport, as a fertile terrain to understand the historical creation of national consciousness and identities opened up novel disciplinary spaces. Others soon followed. The works of Pablo Alabarces, Julio Frydenberg, Pablo A. Ramírez and Amílcar G. Romero in Argentina, Ronaldo George Helal, José Sérgio Leite Lopes and Antônio Jorge G. Soares in Brazil, Eduardo A. Santa Cruz in Chile, Edgar Rey Sinning in Colombia, Fernando

Carrión in Ecuador, and Aldo Panfichi in Peru are worth mentioning, as they furthered the cultural and historical understanding of the development and meaning of football in the region. Although their works cover different historical periods, all attempt to discuss, in one way or another and with different degrees of success, the complexity of imagining nations, identities and subjectivities through football.[34] Similar to Da Matta and Archetti's production, these scholars have largely limited their studies to hegemonic modern sports and ideals, mainstream groups and urban settings. Identifying these limitations is not an indictment of their stimulating work, but rather discloses fascinating terrain for future research.

International scholars such as Janet Lever, Robert M. Levine, Steve J. Stein and Tony Mason, among others, have also contributed to the historical research of football in South America. Lever's 1983 *Soccer Madness: Brazil's Passion for the World's Most Popular Sport* is an early exploration of how football in Brazil is central to the nation's social structure and the reflection of its national character. Published more than a decade later, Mason's *Passion of the People? Football in South America* details the British role in the diffusion of the game in the region.[35] Despite its title, Mason mainly focused on Argentina, Brazil and Uruguay. A weakness of his book, and the work of other English-speaking scholars in this area, is the reliance on English sources, which prevents a more thorough contextualization of their narratives – including, most notably, the local perspective on events.

Both international and South American scholars studying football and, more broadly, sport and physical education, approached it through different theoretical lenses. In general, they have either explicitly or implicitly conceptualized their work along the better established paradigms in the sub-discipline: cultural diffusion, imperialism, dependency theory, modernization, Marxism and nationalism. When the focus is on the process of emergence and diffusion – that is the globalization – of football in the region, the tendency is to rely more on sociological (imperialism, modernization) and economic (Marxism) approaches; when it is on football's national expression and what is does in and for the life of people, the main approach is anthropological (cultural diffusion, nationalism). However, more and more, interdisciplinary theoretical frameworks are being utilized as complex realities, requiring equally complex approaches to make sense of them.

The interest in South American football expanded to other modern sports, at least for South American scholars, journalists and observers. For example, Archetti, Víctor Raffo, Jorge A. Demárcico and Héctor Pastrian have provided accounts of track and field, boxing, cricket and baseball, among other modern sports, in Argentina.[36] While Edgardo Marín and Pilar Modiano did so in Chile, Fernando de Azevedo and Manoel José Gomes Tubino, and Luis Gálvez Chipoco did so in Brazil and Peru, respectively.[37] Some journalists such as Ezequiel Fernandez Moore and Ariel Scher in Argentina, and Franklin Morales in Uruguay continued writing on the history of sports in their nations. Liliana Morelli paid attention to the history of women's sport participation in Argentina and Abelardo Sánchez-León reflected on Peruvian women's volleyball.[38] Eloy Altuve studied the development of sport in Venezuela, a nation in which baseball is more popular than football. Javier González, among others, wrote about the Venezuelan passion for *béisbol*.[39] Sports with wider followings are more represented in these scholars' and writers' narratives than those with a less popular status. The quality of these contributions is uneven. The chief limitation of many of these studies is that their authors do not use the sophisticated methodology and interpretative framework implemented by Archetti or other theoretical paradigms to frame them. Although these histories tend to be more linear and less nuanced, they are valuable not only because they focus on the spread of individual sports in the region, but also because they, too, disclose fascinating terrain for future research.

Brazilian sports historians saw these opportunities early on and established the most developed disciplinary tradition in South America. Following Lamartine Pereira DaCosta's pioneer work, Patrícia Falco Genovez, Silvana Vilodre Goellner and Victor Andrade de Melo, among many others, have produced important accounts of the diffusion of modern sports in Brazil from diverse methodological and theoretical approaches.[40] Pereira DaCosta has written more than 30 books and 100 articles on sport issues, many discussing the historical underpinnings of Brazilian and South American sport and its relevance for understanding society at large.[41] The work of these scholars has been useful in problematizing and challenging assumptions, received views and the 'mythologization' of sports history in Brazil. A case in point is the arrival of football in Brazil. Whereas Englishman Charles Miller is typically credited as the 'founder' of Brazilian football, Melo has shown that Jesuits introduced the game in the nation two decades before Miller.[42] These scholars have also directed their attention to previously neglected topics and groups. Goellner's and Argentine María Graciela Rodríguez's analyses of the place of women in Brazilian and Argentine football are good examples.[43] In spite of the growth of sports history in Brazil and the region, DaCosta has acknowledged the merits and demerits of both the regional and international disciplinary scholarship, and has pointed that these 'shortcomings should be dealt with in appropriate concern for the accumulation of careful and accurate research'.[44]

A growing body of research is also taking shape surrounding the South American involvement with the Olympic movement. Argentine Cesar R. Torres and Brazilians Márcia De Franceschi Neto, Otávio Tavares da Silva and Alberto Reppold Filho, among others, have studied the spread of Olympism in their nations as well as in the whole region, and its impact on national and regional sport bureaucracies.[45] They have also explored the complex reactions to the intention of the local elite to plant their nations on the Olympic map. Their studies reveal that the regional entry into the Olympic Games was another avenue to image the nation and that this process was affected by powerful national and transnational forces. Although these scholars subordinated their studies to the political, economic, social and cultural aspects of the Olympic Games' expansion into South America, their works also reveal the need to bring new vistas to the study of the Olympic experience in the region to understand more fully its complexity. For example, the voice of women and other under-represented groups are still waiting to be heard in relation to the Olympic process. The tension between amateur and professional ideals of sport – a conspicuous point of contention in Olympic circles – and how they affected the region is still to be studied. Similarly, whether other forms of physical activity resisted the 'Olympization' wave of the 1920s or not remains to be discussed. These lacunae reveal that regional sports historians have been fascinated by sport, and most precisely elite sport, leaving largely unattended the history of the wider physical culture.

However, the history of physical education in South America, always related in intricate ways with modern sport, has been increasingly analysed by Argentines Ángela Aisenstein, Lilia Ana Bertoni, Jorge Saraví Riviere and Pablo Scharagrodsky, as well as by Brazilians Amarílio Ferreira Neto, Lino Castellani Filho, Ademir Gebara and Carmen Lucia Soares. José Pedro Barrán and Raumar Rodríguez Giménez did the same in Uruguay.[46] Earlier in the 20th century Bolivian Rodrigo Saturnino, Brazilian Inezil

Penna Marinho, Chilean Luis Bisquertt Susarte, and Uruguayans Raúl V. Blanco and Julio J. Rodríguez also studied the development of physical education systems in their nations.[47] The newer scholarship analyses the political, economic, social and cultural forces behind the drive to build massive physical education systems and how it was intimately interweaved with the construction of the modern nation-states in the region. In doing so, it not only focused on the political nature of physical education, but also on the construction of the social body and the attempts to discipline and align the populace to particular political projects. Although more inclusive than other areas of South American sports history, there still is plenty of room in the historical analyses of physical education to explore its connections and effect on local communities and their construction of or resistance to the mandates of national education officials. Likewise, it might be interesting to fully know what sense different immigrant populations made of physical education. The same goes for the indigenous population and other dispossessed groups.

Admittedly, this chapter's inventory of the authors and scholars that have contributed and are contributing to the study and development of sports history in South America is far from exhaustive. The same goes for the works cited. Nevertheless, the authors and scholars mentioned, as well as the works discussed, are representative of the trajectory that the sub-discipline has traversed in the region. While the latter provide a clear picture of what topics, themes and theoretical frameworks have been and are of interest in the literature, their successes, weaknesses and omissions point to multiple directions that future researchers in the field might want, or need to pursue. The heterogeneity of South America and its diverse and rich physical cultures demand an effort to pursue these directions. While some nations (i.e., Argentina and Brazil) and some aspects of their physical cultures (i.e., football) and societies (i.e., dominant groups or urban settings) have received wide scholarly attention, other nations, groups and expressions of their physical cultures have been marginally studied or even neglected.

Despite its limitations, the study of sports history in South America has greatly matured in the last three decades. There is a solid and growing body of specialized literature in Portuguese, Spanish and English. Any student of South American sport can start exploring this literature by consulting Arbena's 1989 *An Annotated Bibliography of Latin American Sport: Pre-Conquest to the Present* and its 1999 update *Latin American Sport: An Annotated Bibliography, 1988–1998*.[48] Another point of entry, in this case specific to Brazil, is Falco and Melo's 1998 *Bibliografia brasileira sobre história da educação física e do esporte*.[49] Although a decade old, these bibliographies remain excellent resources. More current scholarship can be found in the recently launched peer-reviewed *Recorde: Revista de História do Esporte*, the first disciplinary journal in South America, which accepts manuscripts in Portuguese, Spanish, English and French. The peer-reviewed *Revista Brasileira de Ciências do Esporte* has regularly published articles on the history of sport. Occasionally, history journals have also printed sports history articles. The Argentine peer-reviewed journal *Entrepasados* is a case in point. Also, the Argentine-based *Todo es historia*, a publication that promotes the study of history beyond academic circles, and the electronic magazine *Lecturas: educación física y deportes* have paid attention to issues in regional and national sports history.

The growth of the study of sports history in the region is also manifested in its institutionalization, which has been noticeably slower than the disciplinary written production. Brazil is at the forefront, by quite a wide margin. Since the 1990s, scholars of sports history in Brazil have regularly gathered to share and discuss their work at the *Congresso*

Brasileiro de História do Esporte, Lazer e Educação Física. Although institutions of higher education in other South American nations have occasionally organized forums or accepted presentations at congresses on sport, physical education and leisure, the specificity, stability and level of participation of the Brazilian *congressos* of sports history is unique. Similarly, some Brazilian universities have embraced the historical study of sport as a legitimate area of study. For example, the *Universidade Gama Filho* in Rio de Janeiro has a line of research in '*produção histórica na educação física, esporte e lazer*' and grants masters and doctoral degrees accordingly. Unfortunately, this trend has not caught on in other areas of the region, although some university departments of history have accepted theses and dissertations analysing different themes in the history of sport or physical education. On the other hand, most undergraduate programmes in physical education, sport and leisure have a required course on the history of sport and physical education.

Reviewing Arbena's 1988 edited collection on sport and society in Latin America, Alan M. Klein observed in 1991 that Arbena's previous work 'may have been limited by the absence of sophisticated works on the subject'.[50] That does not seem to be the case any longer. Some 10 years after Klein's observation, DaCosta wrote that, 'Happily, it may be stated that in the light of recent developments associated with the study of the history of sport on this continent, historians of sport no longer occupy "marginal" but increasingly "mainstream" status in academia'.[51]

There is little doubt that sport as a subject of study and sports history as an academic sub-discipline have increased both their epistemological status and institutional legitimacy in South America. Nevertheless, DaCosta's optimism should be tempered in light of the uneven development of the sub-discipline across the region. Possibly, that optimism could be interpreted as a sign of disciplinary accomplishment and at the same time as a call to be ambitious and transform the marginal status that sports history is still assigned in several corners of South America. That is, sports history awaits full democratization in the region; efforts to do so could, in turn, by virtue of the required research, teaching and communication with the larger public, assist the democratic process in South America.

Thinking about South America as a whole and considering the development of the literature, one wonders if it is time for a comprehensive or unified account of the history of sport in the region; but then one questions whether such a history is possible, given the heterogeneous character of South America. Similarly, one wonders if sport is the more appropriate term to capture the heterogeneity of the physical cultures of the South American people. These two issues manifestly invite sports historians to do 'sports history', for much needs to be done to keep constructing and testing overarching explanations of the history of sport in the region. Two decades ago Levine claimed that 'the next generation of analysts of Latin American sport must dig deeper into untouched archives and other sources'.[52] South American sports historians have certainly been visiting the archives and it is there that they should continue to head. When they do so, as proven in the last three decades, they further the understanding of the intricacy, nuance, meaning and role that 'sport' has played in the recent and past history of South America.

Notes

1 See Richard L. Bruger, 'South America: Pre-Colombian History', in Barbara A. Tenenbaum, ed., *Encyclopedia of Latin American History and Culture*, vol. 5 (New York: C. Scribner's Sons; London: Simon & Schuster, Prentice Hall International, 1996), 154–59; and Simon Collier,

Thomas E. Skidmore and Harold Blakemore, eds, *The Cambridge Encyclopedia of Latin America and the Caribbean* (Cambridge and New York: Cambridge University Press, 1992), 128.

2 See R. Scott Kretchmar, 'From Test to Contest: An Analysis of Two Kinds of Counterpoint in Sport', in William J. Morgan and Klaus V. Meier, eds, *Philosophic Inquiry in Sport*, 2nd edn (Champaign, IL: Human Kinetics, 1995), 36–41; Klaus V. Meier, 'Triad Trickery: Playing with Sport and Games', in William J. Morgan and Klaus V. Meier, eds, *Philosophic Inquiry in Sport*, 2nd edn (Champaign, IL: Human Kinetics, 1995), 23–35; William J. Morgan, *Leftist Theories of Sport: A Critique and Reconstruction* (Urbana, IL: University of Illinois Press, 1994); Bernard Suits, *The Grasshopper: Games, Life and Utopia* (Toronto: University of Toronto Press, 1978); and Bernard Suits, 'What Is a Game?', in Ellen W. Gerber, ed., *Sport and the Body: A Philosophical Symposium* (Philadelphia: Lea & Febiger, 1972), 16–22.

3 Suits, *The Grasshopper: Games, Life and Utopia*, 22–41, 142–53.

4 Allen Guttmann, *From Ritual to Record: The Nature of Modern Sports* (New York: Columbia University Press, 1978).

5 Suits, 'What Is a Game?', 16.

6 This chapter follows the concept of 'physical culture' as developed by David Kirk. See, for example, his articles 'Gender Associations: Sport, State Schools and Australian Culture', in J.A. Mangan and John Nauright, eds, *Sport in Australasian Society: Past and Present* (London: Frank Cass, 2002), 49–64; 'Physical Culture, Physical Education and Relational Analysis', *Sport, Education and Society* 4, 1 (1999), 63–73; and 'Educational Reform, Physical Culture and the Crisis of Legitimation in Physical Education', *Discourse: Studies in the Cultural Politics of Education* 19, 1 (1998), 101–12.

7 José Sánchez Labrador and Guillermo Fúrlong Cárdiff, *Los indios pampas, puelches, patagones, según Joseph Sánchez Labrador, S.J.; monografía inédita* (Buenos Aires: Viau y Zona, 1936); and José Sánchez Labrador and Samuel A. Lafone Quevedo, *El Paraguay católico, homenaje de la Universidad nacional de La Plata al XVII Congreso internacional de los americanistas en su reunión de Buenos Aires, en mayo 16 á 21 de 1910* (Buenos Aires: Imprenta de Coni hermanos, 1910–17).

8 Florián Baucke and Edmundo Wernicke, *Hacia allá y para acá (una estada entre los indios mocobíes, 1749–1767)* (Tucumán and Buenos Aires: Universidad nacional de Tucumán, 1942); Johann Auweiler, *Memorias del P. Florián Paucke: misionero de la Compañía de Jesús, 1748 a 1767* (Buenos Aires: L. Mirau, 1900); and Florián Baucke and Guillermo Fúrlong Cárdiff, *Iconografía colonial rioplatense, 1749–1767; costumbres y trajes españoles, criollos e indios*, 2nd edn (Buenos Aires: Elche, 1973).

9 Nicolás del Techo, *Historia de la Provincia del Paraguay de la Compañía de Jesús* (Madrid: A. de Uribe, 1897).

10 Martin Dobrizhoffer, *An Account of the Abipones, an Equestrian People of Paraguay* (New York: Johnson Reprint Corp., 1970 [1822]); Martín Dobrizhoffer, Domingo Muriel, José Brigniel, Joaquín Camaño, José Jolís, Pedro Juan Andreu, José Cardiel and Vicente Olcina, *Entre los abipones del Chaco; según noticias de los misioneros jesuitas* (Buenos Aires: Talleres gráficos San Pablo, 1938).

11 Esteban Lucas Bridges, *Uttermost Parts of the Earth* (London: Hodder & Stoughton, 1948); Antonio Coiazzi, *Los indios del archipelago fueguino …* (Santiago de Chile: Imprenta universitaria, 1914); Roberto Dabbene, *Viaje á la Tierra del Fuego y á la Isla de los Estados* (Buenos Aires: Instituto Geográfico Argentino, 1903); Roberto Dabbene, *Los indigenas de la Tierra del Fuego: Contribución a la etnografía y antropología de los Fueguiros* (Buenos Aires: La Buenos Aires, 1911); Carlos R. Gallardo, *Tierra del Fuego: Los Onas* (Buenos Aires: Cabaut, 1910); Martin Gusinde, *Die Feuerland Indianer; Ergebnisse meiner vier Forschungsreisen in den Jahren 1918 bis 1924* (Mödling bei Wien: Verlag der Internationalen Zeitschrift Anthropos, 1931); and Ramón Serrano Montaner, *Noticias sobre el canal Trinidad i sus adyacentes* (Santiago de Chile: Imprenta nacional, 1881).

12 See the works by Coiazzi, Dabbene, Gallardo and Gusinde cited in note 11. See also S.K. Lothrop, *The Indians of Tierra del Fuego* (New York: Museum of the American Indian, Heye Foundation, 1928); and José Maria Beauvoir, *Los shelknam, indígenas de la Tierra del Fuego: sus tradiciones, costumbres y lengua por los misioneros salesianos* (Buenos Aires: Talleres gráficos de la compañía general de Fósforos, 1915).

13 Roberto Jorge Payró, *La Australia Argentina* (Buenos Aires: M. Rodriguez Giles, 1908).

14 Augusto Guinnard, *Tres años de cautividad entre los patagones* (Buenos Aires: Eudeba, 1961).

15 See, for example, Carlos López von Vriessen, 'Juegos Aborígenes de Chile: Contribución a una alternativa didáctica en la Educación Física Latinoamericana', *Revista Perspectiva Educacional* 26 (1996), 35–44; Carlos López von Vriessen, 'Tres juegos tradicionales Mapuches (Araucanos): El Inao o Linao o juego de pelota con las manos de los Mapuche-Huilliches', *Quinta Imagen: Revista de*

Educación y Cultura 2, 61 (1992), 12–13; Carlos López von Vriessen, 'Das Hockeyspiel der Mapuche-Indianer in Chile', Stadion 17 (1991), 278–291; and Carlos López von Vriessen, 'Das Hockeyspiel (Palin oder Chueca) der Mapuche-Indianer in Chile: ein Beitrag zur Ethnologie des Sports', PhD dissertation, Deutsche Sporthochschule, 1989. See also Leotardo Matus Zapata, 'El Linao: Rugby', *Revista Zig Zag* 223 (1909); Leotardo Matus Zapata, 'Juegos y ejercicios de los antiguos araucanos', *Boletín del Museo Nacional de Chile* (1920), 193–95; Ricardo Torres, *El palín: una cosmovisión trascendente* (Temuco: Universidad de la Frontera, 1995); and Agustín Alvarez Villablanca, 'El Linao', *Revista Chilena de Educación Física* 20, 81 (1954), 771, 778.

16 Emilio Alberto Breda, *La caza entre los indios del virreinato del Río de la Plata* (Buenos Aires: Casa Pardo, 1964); Emilio Alberto Breda, *Juegos y deportes entre los indios del Río de la Plata* (Buenos Aires: Ediciones Teoría, 1962); José Eduardo A. Machicote, *Actividades, juegos y deportes indígenas: Historia e introducción a la Educación Física en el contexto cultural argentino* (Rosario: Asociación Profesional de la Educación Física de Rosario, 1994); Raúl Martínez Crovetto, *Deportes y juegos de los indios ona de Tierra del Fuego* (Ushuaia: Cabo de Hornos Ediciones, 1987); Raúl Martínez Crovetto, *Algunos juegos de los Indios Vilelas* (Corrientes: Universidad Nacional del Nordeste, Facultad de Agronomía y Veterinaria, 1968); Raúl Martínez Crovetto, *Estudios sobre juegos Araucano-Pampas* (Corrientes: Universidad Nacional del Nordeste, Facultad de Agronomía y Veterinaria, 1968); Raúl Martínez Crovetto, *Juegos y deportes de los Indios Guaraníes de misiones (República Argentina)* (Corrientes: Universidad Nacional del Nordeste, Facultad de Agronomía y Veterinaria, 1968); Raúl Martínez Crovetto, *Viejos juegos de los Indios Mocovíes* (Corrientes: Universidad Nacional del Nordeste, Facultad de Agronomía y Veterinaria, 1968); and Mario I. Moreno, *Juegos aborígenes del sur del mundo* [Aborigine games from the south of the world] (Punta Arenas: Impresos Ateli y Cía, 2004).

17 Stuart Culin, *American Indian Games* (Chicago: n.p., 1903); Telêmaco Borba, *Actualidade indígena* (Curitiba: Impressora Paranaense, 1908).

18 Eduardo Galvão, 'O cavalo na América Indígena: nota prévia a um estudo de mudança cultural', *Revista do Museu Paulista* 14 (1963), 222–32; Carmen Junqueira, *Antropologia Indígena: uma introdução, história dos povos indígenas no Brasil* (São Paulo: Editora da PUC-SP, 1991); Carmen Junqueira, *Os índios de Ipavu: Um estudo sobre a vida do grupo Kamaiurá* (São Paulo: Editora Ática, 1975); Darcy Ribeiro, As Américas e a Civilização. Processo de Formação e Causas do Desenvolvimento Cultural Desigual dos Povos Americanos (Rio de Janeiro: Editora Civilização Brasileira, 1970); and Darcy Ribeiro, *Os Índios e a Civilização: A Integração das Populações Indígenas no Brasil Moderno* (Rio de Janeiro: Editora Civilização Brasileira, 1970). See also Curt Nimuendajú and Robert Harry Lowie, *The Eastern Timbira* (Berkeley and Los Angeles: University of California Press, 1946).

19 See José R. Mendonça Fassheber and Maria Beatriz Rocha Ferreira, 'A Eficácia Social do Futebol entre os Kaingàng', *Anais da 23 Reunião Brasileira de Antropologia* (2002) Gramado/RS, 1–9; Jacob Mehringer and Jürgen Dieckert, 'Running to Keep the World Going. The Log Race Performed by Brazilian Canela Indians Seen from an "emic" Point of View', *Journal of Comparative Physical Education and Sport* 19, 2 (1997), 85–95; Julio Cezar Mellati, 'Corrida de Toras', *Revista de Atualidade Indígena* 1, 1 (1976), 38–45; Maria Beatriz Rocha Ferreira, *Cultura corporal indígena* (Guarapuava: UNICENTRO, 2003); Maria Beatriz Rocha Ferreira, 'Jogos tradicionais e esporte em terras indígenas', in *Cultura e Contemporaneidade na Educação Física e no Desporto. E Agora? Livro de Resumos* (São Luis: Associação Prata da Casa, 2002), 231–31; Aracy Lopes da Silva, Ana Vera Lopes da Silva Macedo and Ângela Nunes, eds, *Crianças indígenas: ensaios antropológicos* (São Paulo: Global, 2002); and Veerle van Mele and Roland Renson, *Traditional Games in South America* (Schorndorf: Hofmann, 1992). Several doctoral dissertations and masters theses have been recently written on the Brazilian indigenous physical cultures. See, for example, Yumi Gosso, 'Pexe oxemoarai: brincadeiras infantis entre os índios Parakanã', PhD dissertation, Universidade de São Paulo, 2005; José R. Mendonça Fassheber, 'Corpo e etnodesporto indígena: contribuições da antropologia social a partir da experiência entre os Kaingàng', PhD dissertation, Universidade Estadual de Campinas, 2006; and Fernando Fedola de Luiz Brito Vianna, 'A bola, os "brancos" e as toras: futebol para índios Xavante', Masters thesis, Universidade de São Paulo, 2002.

20 Denis Roberge, 'Games of the Inca Empire', Masters thesis, University of Alberta, 1988; Emilia Romero, *Juegos del antiguo Perú, contribución a una historia del juego en el Perú* (México: Ediciones Llama, 1943); and Máximo Cama Ttito, *Ritos de competición en los Andes: luchas y contiendas en el Cuzco* (Cercado de Lima, Perú: Pontificia Universidad Católica del Perú, 2003).

21 Anna Curtenius Roosevelt, *Amazonian Indians from Prehistory to the Present: Anthropological Perspectives* (Tucson: University of Arizona Press, 1994); and Andrew W. Miracle, Jr, 'Some Functions of

Aymara Games and Play', in Phillip Stevens, Jr, ed., *Studies in the Anthropology of Play: Papers in Memory of B. Allan Tindall* (West Point, NY: Leisure Press, 1977), 98–105.

22 Alessandra Canessa, *Los toros en el Perú* (Lima: Aguilar, 2001); Carlos F. Díaz, *La história de los toros en Ecuador* (Quito: Dino Producciones, 1990); Cristina Escobar, 'Bullfighting Fiestas, Clientelism and Political Identities in Northern Colombia', in Luis Roniger and Tamar Herzog, eds, *The Collective and the Public in Latin America: Cultural Identities and Political Order* (Brighton and Portland, OR: Sussex Academic Press, 2000), 174–91; Fernando Jurado Noboa, *Quito, una ciudad de casta taurina: historia del toro y la fiesta brava entre el siglo XVI y principios del siglo XX* (Quito: Delta, 1996); Alberto Lopera, *Colombia, tierra de toros* (Madrid: Espasa-Calpe, 1989); Francisco López Izquierdo, *Los toros del nuevo mundo (1492–1992)* (Madrid: Espasa-Calpe, 1992); Gori Muñoz, *Toros y toreros en el Río de la Plata* (Buenos Aires: Schapire, 1970); Carlos Salas, *La fiesta brava en Caracas: cuatro siglos de historia*, 2nd edn (Caracas: Concejo Municipal del Distrito Federal, 1978); Carlos Salas, *Los toros en Venezuela* (Caracas: Imprenta Nacional, 1980); Adrian Shubert, *A las cinco de la tarde: una historia social del toreo* (Madrid: Turner, 2002); and Camilo Pardo Umaña, *Los toros en Bogotá: Historia y crítica de las corridas* (Bogotá: Editorial Kelly, 1946).

23 Ángel López Cantos, *Juegos, fiestas y diversiones en la América española* (Madrid: Editorial Mapfre, 1992). See also Antonio Garrido Aranda, *El mundo festivo en España y América* (Córdoba: Servicio de Publicaciones, Universidad de Córdoba, 2005); Edward Larocque Tinker, 'The Horsemen of the Americas', *The Hispanic American Historical Review* 42, 2 (1962), 191–98; and Jean Milne, *Fiesta Time in Latin America* (Los Angeles: W. Ritchie Press, 1965); Eugenio Pereira Salas, *Juegos y alegrías coloniales en Chile* (Santiago de Chile: Zig-zag, 1947); Richard W. Slatta, *Cowboys of the Americas* (New Haven: Yale University Press, 1990); and Richard W. Slatta, *Gauchos and the Vanishing Frontier* (Lincoln: University of Nebraska Press, 1983).

24 See Bartolomé Mitre, *Armonías de la Pampa* (Buenos Aires: La Cultura Argentina, 1916); and Rafael Obligado, *Santos Vega* (Buenos Aires: Colihue, 1987). See also Eduardo P. Archetti, *Masculinities: Football, Polo and Tango in Argentina* (London: Berg, 1999); and Richard W. Slatta, 'The Demise of the Gaucho and the Rise of Equestrian Sport in Argentina', *Journal of Sport History* 13, 2 (1986), 97–110. On 16 September 1953, Perón signed Decree No. 17.468 declaring *pato* the national sport of Argentina.

25 See Jorge Larroca, *San Cristóbal: El barrio olvidado (Apuntes para su historia)* (Buenos Aires: Editorial Freeland, 1969); Ricardo M. Llanes, *Canchas de pelotas y reñideros de antaño* (Buenos Aires: Municipalidad de la Ciudad de Buenos Aires, 1981); Ricardo M. Llanes, *El barrio de almagro* (Buenos Aires: Dirección de Bibliotecas Públicas y de Publicaciones Municipales, 1968); Alberto Sarramone, *Los abuelos vascos en el Río de la Plata* (Buenos Aires: Editorial Biblos Azul, 1995); and Carmelo Urza, *Historia de la pelota vasca en las Americas* (Donostia: Elkar, 1994).

26 Gilmar Mascarenhas de Jesus, 'Do espaço colonial ao espaço da modernidade: os esportes na vida urbana do Rio de Janeiro', *Scripta Nova: Revista Electrónica de Geografía y Ciencias Sociales* 45, 7 (1999).

27 Luiz Sergio Dias, *Quem tem medo da capoeira?: Rio de Janeiro, 1890–1904* (Rio de Janeiro: Prefeitura da Cidade do Rio de Janeiro, 2001); Luiz Edmundo da Costa, *O Rio de Janerio no tempo dos vice-reis (1763–1808)* (Rio de Janeiro: Imprensa Nacional, 1932); Carlos Eugênio Líbano Soares, *A capoeira escrava e outras tradições rebeldes no Rio de Janeiro, 1808–1850* (Campinas: Editora UNICAMP, 2002); Francisco Sérgio Mota Soares, Henriette Ferreira Gomes and Jeane dos Reis Passos, *Documentação jurídica sobre o negro no Brasil, 1800–1888: índice analítico* (Salvador: Secretaria da Cultura, 1988); Matthias Röhrig Assunção, *Capoeira: A History of an Afro-Brazilian Martial Art* (London and New York: Routledge, 2005); and Luiz Renato Vieira, *O jogo da capoeira: corpo e cultura popular no Brasil* (Rio de Janeiro: Sprint, 1995).

28 Ernesto Escobar Bavio, *Alumni: cuna de campeones y escuela de hidalguía* (Montevideo: Editorial Difusión, 1953); Eduardo A. Olivera, *Orígenes de los deportes británicos en el Río de la Plata* (Buenos Aires: L. J. Rosso, 1932); Eugenio Pini, *Historia de la esgrima argentina en la X Olimpíada de Los Angeles* (Buenos Aires: Gadola, 1932); Enrique Romero Brest, *El sentido espiritual de la educación física: evolución de una escuela argentina* (Buenos Aires: Librería del colegio, 1938); Enrique Romero Brest, *Bases de la educación física en la Argentina* (Buenos Aires: Librería del colegio, 1939); Americo R. Netto, *Jogos Olympicos de hontem, de hoje e de amanhã: estudo histórico, technico e social* (São Paulo: SPES, 1937); and Roberto Trompowsky, Jr, 'Desportos', in Instituto Histórico e Geográphico Brasileiro, ed., *Diccionario Histórico, Geográphico e Ethnográphico do Brasil*, vol. 1 (Rio de Janeiro: Impresa Nacional, 1922), 412–14; César Viale, *Cincuenta años atrás* (Buenos Aires: Piatti, 1950); and César Viale, *El deporte argentino* (Buenos Aires: Librería de A. García Santos, 1922).

29 Héctor Chaponick, *Historia del fútbol argentino* (Buenos Aires: Eiffel, 1955); Ricardo Lorenzo, *25 años en el deporte: fútbol, remo, ciclismo, golf, motociclismo, basket, automovilismo, box* (Buenos Aires: Editorial Atlántida, 1946); Diego Lucero, *Siento ruido de pelota: crónicas de medio siglo* (Buenos Aires: Freeland, 1975). A small number of the more than 1,500 football articles that José Lins do Rego wrote in Rio de Janeiro's *Journal dos Sports* from 1945 to 1957 were published in *Flamengo e puro amor* (Rio de Janeiro: José Olympio, 2002). Frascara and Lorenzo wrote for the Argentine sport magazine *El Gráfico.*

30 Mário Rodrigues Filho, *O negro no futebol brasileiro* (Rio de Janeiro: Civilização Brasileira, 1947); Nélson Rodrigues Filho, *À sombra das chuteiras imortais: Crônicas de futebol* (São Paulo: Companhia das Letras, 1994); and Nélson Rodrigues Filho, *A pátria em chuteiras: Novas crônicas de futebol* (São Paulo: Companhia das Letras, 1996).

31 See Pablo Alabarces, 'El último de los clásicos', *Primera Revista Latinoamericana de Libros* 1, 1 (2007), 14–16; and Cesar R. Torres, 'Introducción', in Cesar R. Torres and Daniel G. Campos, eds, *¡La pelota no dobla? Ensayos filosóficos en torno al fútbol* (Buenos Aires: Libros del Zorzal, 2006), 18–19.

32 See Peter Burke, *What is Cultural History?* (Cambridge: Polity Press, 2004).

33 Archetti, *Masculinities: Football, Polo and Tango in Argentina*; and Roberto Da Matta, ed., *O universo do futebol: esporte e sociedade brasileira* (Rio de Janeiro: Edições Pinakotheke, 1982). Another early work is Joel Rufino Santos, *História política do futebol brasileiro* (São Paulo: Brasiliense, 1981).

34 See, for example, Pablo Alabarces, *Fútbol y patria: El fútbol y las narrativas de la nación en Argentina* (Buenos Aires: Prometeo, 2002); Julio Frydenberg, 'Boca Juniors en Europa: el diario *Crítica* y el primer nacionalismo deportivo argentina', *História: Questões & Debates* 39 (2003), 91–120; Julio Frydenberg, 'Prácticas y valores en el proceso de popularización del fútbol: Buenos Aires 1900–1910', *Entrepasados* 12 (1997), 7–31; Pablo A. Ramírez, *Disparate e inmoralidad en el fútbol* (Buenos Aires: Corregidor, 1996); Amílcar G. Romero, *Deporte, violencia y política: crónica negra, 1958–1983* (Buenos Aires: Centro Editor de América Latina, 1985). See also Cesar Gordon and Ronaldo George Helal, 'The Crisis of Brazilian Football: Perspectives for the Twenty-First Century', in J.A. Mangan and Lamartine Pereira DaCosta, eds, *Sport in Latin American Society: Past and Present* (London and Portland: Frank Cass, 2002), 139–58; Ronaldo George Helal, Antônio Jorge G. Soares and Hugo Lovisolo, eds, *A Invenção do País do Futebol: mídia, raça e idolatria* (Rio de Janeiro: Mauad, 2001); José Sérgio Leite Lopes, 'Transformations in National Identity through Football in Brazil: Lessons from Two Historical Defeats', in Rory M. Millar and Liz Crolley, eds, *Football in the Americas: Fútbol, Futebol, Soccer* (London: Institute for the Studies of the Americas, 2007), 75–93; José Sérgio Leite Lopes, 'The Brazilian Style of Football and Its Dilemas', in Gary Amstrong and Richard Giulianotti, eds, *Football Cultures and Identities* (London: Macmillan, 1999), 86–98; Antônio Jorge G. Soares, *Futebol, malandragem e identidade* (Vitória: Secretaria de Produção e Difusão Cultural, 1994); Eduardo Santa Cruz and Luis Eduardo Santa Cruz, *Las escuelas de la identidad: la cultura y el deporte en el Chile desarrollista* (Santiago de Chile: LOM Ediciones, 2005); Eduardo Santa Cruz, *Origen y futuro de una pasión: fútbol, cultura y modernidad* (Santiago de Chile: LOM Ediciones, 1996); Edgar Rey Sinning, *Cultura popular costeña: del carnaval al fútbol* (Cartagena: Universidad de Cartagena, 1990); Fernando Carrión, *Quema de tiempo y área chica: fútbol e historia* (Quito: FLACSO Ecuador, 2006); and Aldo Panfichi, ed., *Fútbol: identidad, violencia y racionalidad* (Lima: Facultad de Ciencias Sociales, Pontificia Universidad Católica del Perú, 1994). During the 1990s, there was a visible increase in literary works on football. Two instructive cases are Uruguayan writer Eduardo H. Galeano's *El fútbol a sol y sombra* (Madrid: Siglo Veintiuno, 1995) and Argentine writer Osvaldo Bayer's, *Fútbol argentino: pasión y gloria de nuestro deporte más popular* (Buenos Aires: Sudamericana, 1990).

35 Janet Lever, *Soccer Madness: Brazil's Passion for the World's Most Popular Sport* (Chicago: University of Chicago Press, 1983); Robert M. Levine, 'Sport and Society: The Case of Brazilian *Futebol*', *Luso-Brazilian Review* 17, 2 (1980), 233–52; Steve J. Stein, 'The Case of Soccer in Early Twentieth-century Lima', in Joseph L. Arbena, ed., *Sport and Society in Latin America: Diffusion, Dependency, and the Rise of Mass Culture* (New York: Greenwood Press, 1988), 63–84; Tony Mason, *Passion of the People? Football in South America* (London: Verso, 1995).

36 Eduardo P. Archetti, *El potrero, la pista y el ring: Las patrias del deporte argentino* (Buenos Aires: Fondo de Cultura Económica, 2001); Víctor D. Raffo, *El origen británico del deporte argentino* (Buenos Aires: n.p., 2004); Jorge A. Demárcico, *Historia del boxeo aficionado en la Argentina* (Buenos Aires: Federación Argentina de Box, 1997); Héctor Pastrian, *Béisbol: Reseña histórica internacional y argentina* (Buenos Aires: Federación Argentina de Béisbol, 1977).

37 Pilar Modiano, *Historia del deporte chileno: Orígenes y transformaciones, 1850–1950* (Santiago de Chile: Dirección General de Deportes y Recreación, 1997); Edgardo Marín, ed., *Historia del deporte chileno: entre la ilusión y la pasión* (Santiago de Chile: Comisión Bicentenario Presidencia de la República, 2007); Fernando de Azevedo, *Da educação física: o que ela é, o que tem sido e o que deveria ser; Seguido de Antinous: estudo de cultura atlética; A evolução do esporte no Brasil e outros estudos* (São Paulo: Edições Melhoramentos, 1960); Fernando de Azevedo, *A evolução do esporte no Brasil* (São Paulo: Companhia Melhoramentos de São Paulo, 1930); Manoel José Gomes Tubino, *O esporte no Brasil: do período colonial aos nossos dias* (São Paulo: Editora Ibrasa, 1997); and Luis Gálvez Chipoco, *Historia del atletismo sudamericano* (Lima: Confederación Sudamericana de Atletismo, 1983).

38 Ezequiel Fernandez Moore, *Díganme Ringo* (Buenos Aires: Planeta, 1992); Ariel Scher, *La patria deportista* (Buenos Aires: Planeta, 1996); Ariel Scher and Héctor Palomino, *Fútbol: pasión de multitudes y de elites* (Buenos Aires: CISEA, 1988); Franklin Morales, *Maracaná: los laberintos del carácter* (Montevideo: Editorial Santillana, 2005); Franklin Morales, *Andrade: el rey negro de París* (Montevideo: Editorial Fin de Siglo, 2002); Liliana Morelli, *Mujeres deportistas* (Buenos Aires: Planeta, 1990); Franklin Morales, *Fútbol: mito y realidad* (Montevideo: Editorial Nuestra Tierra, 1969); Abelardo Sánchez-León, 'The history of Peruvian women's volleyball', in Joseph L. Arbena and David G. LaFrance, eds, *Sport in Latin America and the Caribbean* (Wilmington, DE: Scholarly Resources, 2002), 207–17.

39 Eloy Altuve, *Juego, historia, deporte y sociedad en América Latina* (Maracaibo: Universidad del Zulia, 1997); Eloy Altuve, *Educación física y juegos tradicionales* (Maracaibo: Astro Data, 1992); Javier González, *El béisbol en Venezuela: un siglo de pasión* (Caracas: Fundación Bigott, 2003); Milton H. Jamail, *Venezuelan Bust, Baseball Boom: Andrés Reiner and Scouting on the New Frontier* (Lincoln, NE: University of Nebraska Press, 2008); and Eleazar Díaz Rangel and Guillermo Becerra Mijares, *El béisbol en Caracas: 1895–1966* (Caracas: Círculo de Periodistas Deportivos, 1985).

40 Patrícia Falco Genovez, 'Os desafios de Clio: o esporte como objeto de estudo da história', *Revista Eletrônica de História do Brasil* 2, 1 (1998); Silvana Vilodre Goellner, 'As mulheres fortes são aquelas que fazem uma raça forte: esporte, eugenia e nacionalismo no Brasil do início do século XX', *Recorde: Revista de História do Esporte* 1 (2008); Silvana Vilodre Goellner and Angelita Alice Jaeger, *Garimpando memórias: esporte, educação física, lazer e dança* (Porto Alegre: UFRGS Editora, 2007); Silvana Vilodre Goellner, 'Feminismos, mulheres e esportes: questões epistemológicas sobre o fazer historiográfico', *Movimento* 13 (2007), 171–96; Victor Andrade de Melo, *Dicionário do esporte no Brasil: do século XIX ao início do século XX* (Campinas: Editora Autores Associados / Rio de Janeiro: Decania do Centro de Ciências da Saúde da UFRJ, 2007); Victor Andrade de Melo, *Cidade sportiva: primórdios do esporte no Rio de Janeiro* (Rio de Janeiro: Relume Dumará, 2001); Victor Andrade de Melo, *História da educação física e do esporte no Brasil: panorama e perspectiva* (São Paulo: IBRASA, 1999).

41 One of DaCosta's latest projects is the ambitious *Atlas do esporte no Brasil* [Atlas of Sport in Brazil] (Rio de Janeiro: Shape Editora, 2005).

42 See Lamartine Pereira DaCosta, 'Epilogue', in J.A. Mangan and Lamartine Pereira DaCosta, eds, *Sport in Latin American Society: Past and Present*, 192–93.

43 See, for example, Silvana Vilodre Goellner, 'Mulheres e futebol no Brasil: entre sombras e visibilidades', *Revista Brasileira de Educação Física e Esporte* 19, 2 (2005), 143–51; Silvana Vilodre Goellner, 'Pode a mulher praticar o futebol?', in Paulo Cesar R. Carrano, ed., *Futebol: paixão e política* (Rio de Janeiro: DP&A Editora, 2000), 79–93; and María Graciela Rodríguez, 'The Place of Women in Argentinian Football', *The International Journal of the History of Sport* 22, 2 (2005), 231–45.

44 DaCosta, 'Epilogue', 193–194. International scholars such as Joseph L. Arbena, Allen Guttmann and J.A. Mangan have written about the history of South American sport. See, Allen Guttmann, *Sports: The First Five Millennia* (Amherst, MA: University of Massachusetts Press, 2004); and Allen Guttmann, *Games and Empires: Modern Sports and Cultural Imperialism* (New York: Columbia University Press, 1994). See also the articles by Joseph L. Arbena and J.A. Mangan in J.A. Mangan and Lamartine Pereira DaCosta, eds, *Sport in Latin American Society: Past and Present.*

45 See, for example, see Cesar R. Torres, 'The Latin American "Olympic Explosion" of the 1920s: Causes and Consequences', *The International Journal of the History of Sport* 23, 7 (2006), 1,088–111; Cesar R. Torres, 'Ideas encontradas: la educación física y el deporte en el debate parlamentario sobre la participación argentina en los Juegos Olímpicos de 1908,' *Olympika: The International Journal of Olympic Studies* 11 (2002), 117–42; Cesar R. Torres, 'Tribulations and Achievements: The Early History of Olympism in Argentina', *The International Journal of the History of Sport* 18, 3

(2001), 59–92; Marcia de Franceschi Neto, 'A Participação no Brasil no Movimento Olímpico Internacional no Período de 1896 a 1925', PhD dissertation, Universidade Gama Filho, 1999; Otávio Tavares da Silva and Lamartine Pereira DaCosta, eds, *Estudos Olímpicos* (Rio de Janeiro: Editora Gama Filho, 1999); Katia Rubio, Alberto Reppold Filho, Nelson S. Todt and Roberto M. Mesquita, eds, *Ética e compromisso social nos estudos Olímpicos* (Porto Alegre: EDIPUCRS, 2007); and Alberto Reppold Filho and Nelson S. Todd, eds, *O Movimento Olímpico em face do novo milênio* (Rio de Janeiro: Universidade Gama Filho, 2002). See also Lamartine Pereira DaCosta, *Olympic Studies: Current Intellectual Crossroads* (Rio de Janeiro: Editora Gama Filho, 2002).

46 Ángela Aisenstein and Pablo Scharagrodsky, *Tras las huellas de la educación física escolar argentina: cuerpo, género y pedagogía, 1880–1950* (Buenos Aires: Prometeo, 2006); Ángela Aisenstein, 'El deporte en el discurso pedagógico: Argentina, 1880–1940', in Adrián Ascolani, ed., *El sistema educativo en Argentina: Estudios de Historia* (Rosario: Laborde Editor, 2004); Lilia Ana Bertoni, *Patriotas, cosmopolitas y nacionalistas: la construcción de la nacionalidad argentina a fines del siglo XIX* (Buenos Aires: Fondo de Cultura Económica, 2001); Jorge Saraví Riviere, *Aportes para una historia de la educación física 1900 a 1945* (Buenos Aires: IEF No. 1 'Dr Enrique Romero Brest', 1998); Pablo Scharagrodsky, 'Cuerpo, género y poder en la escuela: El caso de la Educación Física Escolar Argentina (1880–1930)', *Estudos Ibero-Americanos* 27, 2 (2001), 121–51; Amarílio Ferreira Neto, *A pedagogia no exército e na escola: a educação física brasileira, 1880–1950* (Aracruz: Faculdade de Ciências Humanas de Aracruz-FACHA, 1999); Amarílio Ferreira Neto, *Pesquisa histórica na educação física* (Vitória: UFES/Centro de Educação Física e Desportos, 1997); Lino Castellani Filho, *Educação física no Brasil: a história que não se conta* (Campinas: Papirus, 1988); Ademir Gebara and Luiz Alberto Pilatti, eds, *Ensaios sobre História e Sociologia nos Esportes* (Jundiaí: Fontoura, 2006); Carmen Lucia Soares, *Imagens da educação do corpo: estudo a partir da ginástica francesa no século XIX* (Campinas: Editora Autores Associados, 1998); and Carmen Lucia Soares, *Educação física: raízes européias e Brasil* (Campinas: Editora Autores Associados, 1994). See also José Pedro Barrán, *Medicina y sociedad en el Uruguay del Novecientos: La invención del cuerpo* (Montevideo: Ediciones de la Banda Oriental, 1995), and Raumar Rodríguez Jiménez, 'Escenas del cuerpo militarizado en el Uruguay de la dictadura (1973–1985)', in Rodolfo Rozengardt, ed., *Apuntes de Historia para profesores de Educación Física* (Buenos Aires: Miño y Dávila Editores, 2006).

47 Rodrigo Saturnino, *La reforma de la educación física en Bolivia* (La Paz, Imp. Renacimiento, 1932); Inezil Penna Marinho, *Introdução ao estudo da evolução desportiva no Brasil (colônia e império)* (Rio de Janeiro: Ministério da Educação e Cultura, Biblioteca Nacional, 1959); Inezil Penna Marinho, *História da educação física e dos desportos no Brasil: Brasil colônia, Brasil império, Brasil república: documentário e bibliografia* (Rio de Janeiro: n.p., 1952–54); Luis Bisquertt Susarte, *El Instituto de Educación Física y Técnica en su medio siglo (1906–1956)* (Santiago de Chile: Universidad de Chile, 1956); Luis Bisquertt Susarte, *Valor de la historia de la educación física* (Santiago de Chile: n.p., 1949); Raúl V. Blanco, *Educación física, un panorama de su historia* (Montevideo: Impresora Adroher, 1948); and Julio J. Rodríguez, *La educación física en el Uruguay* (Montevideo: Imprenta artística de Dornaleche hermanos, 1930).

48 Joseph L. Arbena, ed., *An Annotated Bibliography of Latin American Sport: Pre-Conquest to the Present* (New York: Greenwood Press, 1989); and Joseph L. Arbena, ed., *Latin American Sport: An Annotated Bibliography, 1988–1998* (Westport, CT: Greenwood Press, 1999).

49 Patrícia Falco Genovez and Victor Andrade de Melo, *Bibliografia brasileira sobre história da educação física e do esporte* (Rio de Janeiro: Editorial Central da Universidade Gama Filho, 1998).

50 Alan M. Klein, 'Sport and Colonialism in Latin America and the Caribbean', *Studies in Latin American Popular Culture* 10 (1991), 258.

51 DaCosta, 'Epilogue', 194.

52 Robert M. Levine, 'Sport as Dramaturgy for Society: A Concluding Chapter', in Joseph L. Arbena, ed., *Sport and Society in Latin America: Diffusion, Dependency, and the Rise of Mass Culture*, 145.

36 South Asia

Chris Valiotis

Historical writing on sport in the nations of South Asia is constantly developing. Currently, there is a predominant focus on cricket, particularly in post-independence India. Indeed, writings on the history of Indian sport dwarf those of the other South Asian nations of Pakistan, Sri Lanka and Bangladesh. There has, though, been a recent attempt made by scholars in the field to address this imbalance. To date, the major focus of this revisionist writing has been India and involves the study of sports development in regions that have been mostly overlooked. Bengal was one such region of notable omission. In the last decade its profile has been raised by scholars keen to emphasize that cricket and football development in the region aided in the push for Indian nationalism during colonization and in the emergence of a vigorous and thriving Indian national sports milieu post independence.

This chapter outlines the reasons for the recent reorientation of focus away from Bombay (Mumbai) and north India by scholars arguing for stronger recognition to be given to Bengal and other regions of India. It will look at the rise of writing on football – of that mostly played in Bengal, but also in other regions – and arguments claiming that the sport compares rather favourably to that of cricket in the national imagination. There will also be mention of developing areas of sports history in India, which include sports other than cricket and football, women's sports, and the role of traditional sport as an alternative discourse to modernist constructs deemed anathema to tradition. The chapter will conclude with an examination of Pakistani and Sri Lankan sports history to date. There is relatively little writing on either and what there is tends to relate to cricket as a vehicle for national cohesion in light of domestic political divisions, particularly among Pakistanis and Pakistani Diaspora communities in the United Kingdom.

Indian sports history: the early years

The writing of academic tracts on sports history took some time to develop in South Asia – much as it did elsewhere in the world. Dipesh Chakrabarty eloquently describes how early attempts to marry sports history to social history met with difficulty and, at times, outright hostility. History departments in the 1970s were averse to viewing sport as a social medium for 'cultural battles or as arenas in which modern disciplinary techniques could be instilled' into people for various socio-political reasons. There was little appreciation of the role of sport – or sporting clubs – as 'sites of "subject production" or class and ideological struggles' worthy of those that had been forged in homes, schools and parliaments, or that took place in public spaces and factory floors, argues Chakrabarty.[1] What has changed since the 1970s is 'the mediatization of sports', which has opened up myriad possibilities for the study of sport among many other cultural pastimes and industries. It is now far more recognized by scholars that the study of sport is crucial to an understanding of forces that relate to global capitalism, markets, cultures and identity formations the world over. This realization has led to an expanding corpus of acclaimed socio-historical and political studies of sport since the 1970s. Much of this has been the work of Western scholars and deals with sports histories that capture the significance of sport to Western audiences and national economies. In South Asia such studies have been fewer: a combination of continued departmental prejudices against the study of sport and lack of funding.[2]

With this in mind, the earliest historians of sport in South Asia have provided the crucial and necessary groundwork for current scholars in the field – and they did so at a time when their efforts were likely to have acquired little acknowledgement from peers. Such pioneering endeavours have led to vigorous debate and a burgeoning concern for the role of sport in constructions of South Asian nationalism. For the purposes of this chapter, scholarly publications between the late 1970s and the end of the 20th century will be deemed the work of the earliest writers of South Asian sports history.[3] Publications since 2000 will be the focus of subsequent sections, including that on Bengal's contribution to the history of Indian sport. The division of scholarly tracts before and after 2000 may be somewhat arbitrary, but it is not without relevance.

The earliest writers examined reasons for the spread of British sport and its development and popularization among South Asians.[4] They looked mostly at cricket, particularly in areas partitioned to India in both the colonial and postcolonial periods, but more so on Bombay and its much-lauded colonial communal tournament and post-independence commercial cricket scene. They also captured the significance of institutions – like public schools and the military – and institutional representatives and other dignitaries – teachers, army personnel, politicians and indigenous princes – on the growth of the game. What they uncovered was a symbiosis of creative input stemming from both British and local sources. In other words, their written appraisals defined institutional co-operation and geography – urban locales and military cantonments – as crucial symptoms for the game's development; but they did not close off the possibility for a broader range of insights to be arrived at – such as those that now appear in the work of the current generation of scholars in the field (post-2000).

The earliest writings were replete with critical discernment and debate. A lively discussion developed over a range of issues relating to the manner in which the game was introduced to Indians and how it was received by them during the colonial period. Scholars generally recognized that various Indian communities and political figures used cricket as a vehicle to promote their own socio-economic and cultural objectives within the framework of an indigenous setting. This included scope for power and prestige among the indigenous nobility, who became patrons of the game. It also provided a means for a few local players to escape the lower levels of the Indian caste structure. This all took place even while a few British educators and officials adhered to muscular Christian ideals and the need to institutionally 'civilize' sections of Indian society.

Despite the central role given to the Bombay tournament, British educators and officials, and to princely patrons, the earliest writers were fully aware of cricket's development elsewhere in colonial India. If they stand accused of underplaying the quality and strength of cricket elsewhere, it is only because of archival limitations and the problems encountered when first defining a new area of historical inquiry. Ramachandra Guha, for instance, argues that the success of the Bombay tournament encouraged the development of replica, though substantially subordinate and ancillary, competitions in other parts of India. Colonial officials outside Bombay were just as prone to believing that competitive sport would enhance indigenous morale and character and promote a sturdy and reliable satellite class of native collaborators fit to serve British interests and power. News of the Bombay tournament reached other Indians by bush telegraph and from the accounts of cricket teams and recruits, bureaucrats, business personnel and others from Bombay, or visiting, who were constantly on the move. By the early 1930s radio provided a further means of disseminating cricket news and scores.[5] Undeniably, Guha's account is Bombay-driven, but it does point to cricket developments beyond the city's environs.

Richard Cashman's earliest writing on Indian cricket reflects the success of other communal tournaments in colonial India, like those that were staged in Madras (Chennai), Karachi and Lahore. Interestingly, the latter two offer a genealogy for Pakistani cricket that has been little explored to date. Communal cricket in Karachi, for instance, did not begin until 1916 when the Parsees beat the Hindus in the final. Other teams in the first Sind Quadrangular Tournament included the Muslims and the Europeans. The tournament later became a Pentangular with the addition of the 'Rest' which comprised Christians and Jews. Colonel C.B. Rubie, who served in the British Army in Mesopotamia during World War I, was instrumental in the establishment of the Sind communal cricket tournament. He and other war veterans figured prominently in the cricket matches and administration of Karachi.[6]

Early writers were also concerned with the nature of communalism in cricket. The structure of communal tournaments reflected the official British disposition to classify local populations along religious lines irrespective of numerous historical traditions that ran counter to imperial logic.[7] While the British implemented a domestic cricket structure steeped in the rhetoric and policies of their communal beliefs, many Indian administrators and players still behaved in a manner befitting traditional practices of cross-cultural tolerance and interaction. More recently, Guha argues that indigenous collaborating elites, from both Hindu and Muslim merchant families, arranged and managed communal teams in Bombay because the British had deemed communal cricket an appropriate socio-cultural structure under the circumstances and realities of colonization. The indigenous elites worked with this structure not because of any inherent belief in it, but because it was just one more path for success and acceptance in a closely-knit community of Bombay businessmen.[8] Likewise, the players behaved accordingly. Convivial relations between them flourished as communal gymkhanas were located alongside one another and membership was not restricted to individuals from designated religious groups.[9]

Arjun Appadurai's description of the demise of communal cricket in colonial India highlights the prominence of local initiative in the design of cricket tradition. Indian national team representation and calls for international competition against other cricket-playing nations developed independent of nationalist forces at the political level. However, by the 1940s communal tensions at the political level began to penetrate into other historically shared traditions; cricket itself was not immune from these developments. Thus, a game that had never prefigured or played a part in the demands of local nationalists suddenly began to be noticed by them.[10] Guha endorses a similar view and comments on Congress Party denunciations of communal cricket during the 1930s and 1940s.[11] Aghast at the repercussions of a growing pastime openly canvassing a framework for communal segregation, nationalists like Mohandas Karamchand (Mahatma) Gandhi began to extol the merits of the Ranji Trophy, the National Cricket Championship of India, as an appropriate and suitable domestic competition for a population on the cusp of nationhood.

The nature of princely patronage also came under critical examination by the earliest writers. The Maharajas and Nawabs of India provided an alternative domestic approach to cricket organization and popularization. While a collaborating class loyal to the British, their patronage of the game did give to Indian cricket the spectacle and panache of an indigenous princely pageant. At the same time, it also emphasized traditional patterns of socio-cultural interaction and inter-community involvement that the British neglected.[12] One unique interpretation of princely patronage is that offered by Ashis Nandy. Nandy argues that cricket was adopted by the princes because as *khashatriya* (members of the warrior class) they found the game 'attractive for (its) defiance of fate, emphasis on style and sense of honour'.[13] This is in accordance with the overall premise of his book, which sees cricket as containing a deep and meaningful socio-cultural dialectic that informs Indians of who they are, particularly in a rapidly modernizing post-colonial world. In other words, cricket's origins may lay elsewhere, but its principles and spirit of play are inextricably linked with Indian spiritual asceticism and self-restraint, as well as warrior honour, defiance and courage in moments of adversity and tragedy. Thus, cricket does not only appeal to *khashatriya* castes, it also finds adherents amongst a host of *brahmin* (members of the priestly caste), who can relate to 'the posture of moral superiority and self-control of the gentleman cricketer'.[14]

While Nandy's argument offers an insight into why cricket may have appealed to a certain sector of Indian society – Hindu upper castes – it leaves little room for an analysis of the input and interest shown for the game by some of India's other communities and lower socio-economic classes, particularly in the post-independence period when public school graduates began taking up positions in industry and other professions that were expanding at the time, leaving little time for playing cricket. However, Nandy was first and foremost concerned with understanding why India's post-independence 'intellectual and media' elite were 'running breathlessly' to develop a 'modern nation-state', when this entailed processes of 'deculturation and homelessness' for millions of other Indians.[15] Cricket in post-independence India has its own paradox according to Nandy: it is a basis by which to measure India's growing industrial strength through test match victories against developed nations,[16] but it also represents 'the rhythm of a lost lifestyle [...] invoking an imaginary, idyllic homeland in the past that [...] serves [...] as the blueprint of an alternative future' to the modern industrial age.[17] It was in the quest to resolve the paradox that Nandy came up with the idea of cricket's appeal to upper-caste Hindus. In the process of arriving at this unique interpretation of the game's appeal to India's intellectual and media elite, he phrased a line reminiscent of C. L. R. James's, 'what do they know of cricket, who only cricket know'.[18] In opening his own treatise on cricket, Nandy suggests that it 'is an Indian game accidentally discovered by the English'.[19]

Bengal's contribution: cricket and football in the east

Since 2000, new writers have emerged with their own critical revision of earlier histories of Indian sport. These writers are concerned with the opening up of wider vistas of intellectual inquiry that aim to broaden the political, cultural and geographical parameters of Indian sports history. Of significant concern to them has been the minor role given to Bengal's own sporting traditions by earlier writers. The previous section looked at the predominant focus on cricket in Bombay and north India in earlier histories. These studies downplayed the contributions of other regions in constructions of Indian cricket nationalism that took place during the colonial period. Unintentionally, they may have suggested that regions like Bengal played a less than significant role in the push for Indian sporting nationalism in the lead up to partition. The new writers have sought to raise Bengal from the margins of Indian sports history. They have emphasized the rich and vibrant nature of Bengali sporting fields and spectatorship. This has entailed a revision of colonial Indian cricket history, with a more prominent position given to Bengal in constructions of cricket nationalism than was the case previously. It has also seen the rise of studies of Indian football, where Bengal has undeniably played a leading role.

The motivation for the rise of scholarly literature on Bengal has been to legitimize its historical legacy to India's current sporting success. Thereby the origins of this success are traceable to Bengal's active and vigorous colonial sporting traditions. According to the new writers, scant regard shown to these traditions prior to 2000 stemmed from defamatory depictions of Bengal's middle class as civil servants bereft of virility and disinterested in physical activity. To date, the leading proponent of the new literature is Boria Majumdar. He has endeavoured to overturn discriminative colonial characterizations of Bengalis that bore no resemblance to events that were occurring in local sporting arenas. He has also questioned the incessant emphasis on Bombay's contribution at the expense of regions like Bengal that have their own stories to tell.

In a review article, Majumdar argues that Bombay was the most recognizable playing region for cricket and the principal centre of the British organized domestic game.[20] The city game had enormous commercial appeal that was crucial to the development of Indian cricket traditions. However, he does not consider this as a reason to ignore the study of significant cricket cultures that were simultaneously developing, albeit with far less intensity, in other parts of India. When critiquing Guha's *A Corner of a Foreign Field* for its failure to grasp the importance of Bengal to the development of the colonial game, Majumdar writes: 'Bengal, it needs to be stated, had an equally rich cricketing tradition as Bombay, one that remains confined to the dusty shelves of archives'.[21]

Majumdar writes of frequent college cricket matches between teams from west and east Bengal that took place from the mid-1880s, including that between Dacca College and Presidency College (Calcutta/Kolkata) at the Eden Gardens in 1890. He also points out that inter-school cricket tournaments in India first began in Calcutta in 1887 (the Harrison Shield), and not in Bombay (with the Harris Shield of 1893) as is widely believed by many scholars and cricket aficionados.[22] Indeed, Bengali cricketers like Saradaranjan Ray and Bidhu Mukherjee,[23] and international fixtures against a Sri Lankan team and between the Presidency College of Calcutta and the Australians, both in 1884, are proof of the vibrant state of cricket in Bengal at the time.[24] Furthermore, Majumdar points to an administrative rivalry between the cricket regions of Bombay and Bengal in the 1930s. The rivalry centred on the omission of Bengali cricketers from India's national team. The princely ruler of Santosh and journalists from Bengal rejected Bombay's dominance and protested vehemently against selection policies deemed inimical to cricketers from Bengal and other minority provinces.[25]

Majumdar turns to vernacular sources from Bengal to attest to the development of the game in the region. The Bengali *bhadralok* (urban educated classes) were keen to promote cricket and other sports in Bengal and Tamil Nadu.[26] Their efforts did not go astray. They set up numerous sports clubs and competitions with cricket at the forefront of these developments. The primary motivation for Bengal's cricket growth – and that of other sports – in the second half of the 19th century lay in pejorative and prejudicial European depictions of the Bengali character. Adjudged to be effeminate by the British, prominent Bengali educators and public figures called for the introduction of European sport to inculcate a 'sense of pride and purpose' in 'young Bengali boys'.[27] Bengalis were even instructed that they would 'be nearer to God through football than through the Bhagwad Gita' by 'the religious and social reformer', Swami Vivekananda.[28] All this, writes Majumdar, 'was geared towards the fashioning of a new identity and individuality for the Bengali male'.[29]

Majumdar is keen to impress on readers the conscious role of the Bengali *bhadralok* in the dissemination of British sport to the masses. Initially indisposed to British games and 'indigenous sports like wrestling [that] were confined to the lower classes', the *bhadralok* raised awareness of British sport through printed vernacular sources. Sports writing became one way to counter allegations of effeminacy levelled mostly at Bengal's middle class by the end of the 19th century.[30] Coverage of the Mohun Bagan victory over the East Yorkshire regiment in the 1911 Indian Football Association (IFA) shield final demonstrates the resilience of the Bengali vernacular press during the period. Vernacular reports of the victory acquired nationalist overtones. The claims of Kamalendu Sarkar offer but one example: he described the occasion as 'a symbol of Black resurgence against the repressive White regime' and an 'Indian revival' and recompense for the 'ignominy of defeat on the fields of Plassey in 1757'.[31] In contrast, the reports of the British press marked the occasion as vindication of the colonial bond between colonizer and colonized and the success of the former's 'civilizing mission'.[32] The discrepancy in reports irked the *bhadralok*. Majumdar argues that this then compelled them 'to establish Bengali sports journalism on a firm footing from the 1930s'.[33]

Majumdar and other Bengali scholars have recently turned the focus on to football as a way to explain Bengal's sporting legacy. Their accounts offer the strongest evidence yet of Bengal's contribution to South Asian sporting nationalism. The earliest scholarly tracts on football in Bengal came from Western sources, however. J.A. Mangan views football as following the familiar imperialist trajectory that cricket undertook under the watchful guidance of muscular Christian educators and military officials. Its purpose was to turn indigenous schoolboys and soldiers into gentlemen servants for the British Empire, imbued with Western ideals and manners.[34] Tony Mason also emphasizes the crucial role of schools and the military in the development of the game, particularly the emergence of regimental teams and their input in the establishment of early local leagues. In addition, Mason argues that indigenous schoolboys continued their interest in the game by establishing football clubs in Calcutta after graduating.[35] Thereby, his study provides some indication of active local participation and promotion of Indian football in the colonial period that was absent from Mangan's account.

Since then, Paul Dimeo has also weighed in with his own considerations.[36] He has argued that football in Bengal perpetuated colonial, nationalist and communal ideals. First, it served to both include and exclude the local population from active participation with and against the colonial authorities. On the one hand, the authorities encouraged the colonial bond for reasons of loyalty; and this meant that football became an imperial tool for British power and local stability. On the other hand, the exclusion of Indian players from British teams and competitions encouraged resistance among locals. Second, resistance led to calls for nationalism through the playing of football in a period of growing nationalist agitation in Bengal. The peak for such calls occurred during the Mohun Bagan victory of 1911. Thousands of Indian spectators attended the match and rejoiced at the outcome of an indigenous team of barefooted players outscoring the best of the British on the local scene. In a manner reminiscent of the media depictions of the colonial authorities at the time, Dimeo views the victory as a triumph for British cultural imperialism over local calls for self-government. In other words, the match is recognition of local support for and acceptance of the merits of British culture and not a symbol for the disapproval and rejection of the British. Third, the success of the Mohammedan Sporting team and its legion of fans across India can be explained by growing nationalist divisions during the 1930s. The team became an emblem for Muslim unity and heightened communal tensions that began appearing at the political level.[37]

Majumdar and Kausik Bandyopadhyay are two Bengali scholars who refute the arguments of Dimeo and writers that preceded him. The Bengali literati view is that football was more than a game inherited from the British.[38] Over the colonial period it became an instrument for local resistance and empowerment. It is this conviction that informs the many writings of Majumdar in particular. Majumdar has outlined three areas of critical importance to the development of football in Bengal and India: the Mohun Bagan victory as a coming of age story of national (Bengali) significance; the socio-political importance of traditional rivalries between local football teams such as Mohun Bagan and East Bengal; and, the rise of a national governing body to oversee the management of the domestic game that emerged out of the bitter rivalries of regional administrators in the 1930s.

First, Majumdar and Bandyopadhyay describe the 1911 victory as a defining moment of national significance to Bengalis. Vernacular sources attest to unanimous support from the local population irrespective of 'class, caste or community' ties.[39] Beating the British 'at their own game' was a panacea for the repression and humiliation suffered at their hands over the years. For a brief while Mohun Bagan became synonymous with 'India's battle against the imperialists'. The 'national victory on the sports field' is thus deemed to have 'converged with the broader stream of Indian nationalism'.[40] In fact, the victory was a cultural awakening for Bengalis, transforming football into a popular pastime infused with 'socio-political meanings'.[41]

Second, traditional football rivalries bear testimony to the game's growing popularity and socio-political relevance in Bengal. Majumdar argues that the Mohun Bagan and East Bengal rivalry pre-dates independence. The East Bengal club was formed in Calcutta in 1920 for aggrieved East Bengalis – mostly from Dacca – who had made their way to the city to play football. Having experienced discrimination from club managers and team mates over selection policy and other issues, they found refuge at the new club.[42] Majumdar maintains that the rivalry was not based on ethnicity, as writers like Dimeo have stated, but sub-regionalism. Both were Hindu-Bengali clubs that shared a 'common language, religion and cultural past'. What separated them was class and place of origin. Mohun Bagan drew its support from Calcutta's *bhadralok* community; hence its ascription as *Ghati* – the 'settlers' club. East Bengal was known as *Bangal* because it was the 'immigrants' club – for those whose origins were from East Bengal.[43] The rivalry intensified after the foundation of the East Bengal club. Prior to its founding, East Bengali players had encountered success even as members of Mohun Bagan, and despite discrimination: 'eight of the eleven players of the victorious Mohun Bagan team in 1911 originally came from East Bengal'.[44] In fact, over time the rivalry came to represent more the politics and cultural identities of respective groups of supporters and administrators, and not the players at all. The latter were just as likely to appear for one club as for the other.

Partition added another episode to the drama. As part of the transfer of populations that accompanied the dismemberment of India at independence, East Bengali Hindus who made the journey to Calcutta gradually began to identify with the East Bengal club.

The club did not disappoint. It won a series of 'national level tournaments' that served to somewhat appease the agony of displacement and the reality of socio-economic hardship that immigrants were exposed to in their new surroundings.[45] The situation almost repeated itself in 1971, when more immigrants flowed into Calcutta after the independence of Bangladesh was recognized. Majumdar concludes his analysis of the Mohun Bagan and East Bengal rivalry with the view that commercialization altered the basis for fandom in the more modern game. Professionalism in the 1990s began eating into the traditional basis for identity at both clubs, creating a rivalry based on image and corporate success – not unlike those of football giants in South America and Europe. Increasingly, sub-regionalism became less meaningful to supporters 'as memories of Partition and the old homeland itself grew weaker'.[46]

Third, Bengal maintained its stronghold over the management of the domestic game in India up until 1937, largely through the support given to it by the British Football Association. Under the banner of the Indian Football Association (IFA), Bengal claimed to represent the interests of all India's regions. This claim was resented by the western and northern Indian states, in particular, and they formed the All-India Football Association (AIFA) to wrest the leadership away from Bengal. The AIFA was unsuccessful in its bid to remove the IFA, however, because the British continued to side with the latter. Eventually a compromise was agreed to, despite the IFA's stalling tactics. From 1937 the All-India Football Federation (AIFF) came into existence as the national governing body for the game. It provided the impetus for greater regional co-operation in the management of the national game, despite the ascendancy of Bengali football at the time.[47]

Increasing commercialism and professionalism changed the complexion of Bengali football in the 1990s, and this has necessitated some recent attention. Majumdar has explored the impact that growing corporate sponsorship has had on supporters of Mohun Bagan and East Bengal; but a very recent article looks at commercialism and its effect on club playing rosters in Calcutta.[48] Projit Bihari Mukharji argues that the decline of local talent brought about by the loss of 'appeal and audience to the ever-increasing popularity of cricket' by the 1990s meant that club managers and talent scouts turned to foreign players. Recruitment policies began to reflect a bias in the selection of footballers from West African countries. Such footballers, it was believed, possessed 'superior build and stamina to literally bulldoze through the defenses before unleashing a powerful shot to the back of the net'.[49] Thus, the game in Bengal came to be based on power and 'individual ball control'. The South Asian monsoons contributed to this process, having always made conditions unsuitable for an expansive passing game. Herein lie further reasons for the gradual diminution of local players of slender build.[50]

Mukharji's article provides a good social study of migration into Calcutta from West Africa. During the 1980s, West Africans on student visas were recruited by local clubs. When news of their success made its way to West Africa, other potential players followed suit: often arriving in Calcutta to become football players and not partake in educational studies at all. Not all were able to fulfil their potential as footballers and this gave rise to stories of hardship and tragedy for several unsuccessful players. Other methods of recruitment included recommendations from existing West African players already in Calcutta, and the sons of West African businessmen who accompanied their fathers on business trips in the hope of acquiring a contract.[51] Instrumental in all of this was the belief, hope and desire of unearthing talented footballers from West Africa to satiate local demand for a game experiencing change brought about by global forces and exchanges.

Other recent developments in Indian sports historiography

There are a few recent insights on sport beyond Bombay, north India and Bengal. Such writing is in its infancy and lacks substantial critical review. However, despite the scattered nature of material presented in this section in terms of themes and sports covered, the literature does contribute to the growth in sports studies of recent years. It also broadens the range of Indian sports that have come to the attention of academics. There are four areas of recent scholarship on Indian sport that will briefly be outlined below: football in Goa and Tibet; women's participation in sport, particularly football; boxing and tennis; and traditional Indian pastimes like wrestling and yoga.

James Mills's examination of football in Goa offers an interesting contrast to the game's development in British India.[52] The game was introduced to locals by Catholic missionaries in the 19th century. The Goan Catholic Church had by this time become 'fully indigenized' and the game found roots among the local population. Schools soon further popularized the game and its appeal increased when Goans entered British India for work. While there, football offered a means to maintain Goan Diaspora identities. It also provided a link to the homeland, particularly when Diaspora Goan football teams toured Goa. Mills argues that Goan football identity was perceived to be strong enough for the Portuguese to have Benfica tour the colony in the late 1950s 'as a populist effort at maintaining their hold on the area'.[53]

For a short while football took hold in Tibet, courtesy of British officials and Indian soldiers. Alex McKay claims that diplomacy between colonial India and Tibet extended to the football field in an effort to prevent Russia from extending its influence in the region.[54] The study points to the role of India as 'a point of transmission' for football. It was felt that football was one means of fostering a national consciousness among local Tibetans, thereby removing Russia's potential threat on the outskirts of the Indian colony.[55] It cannot be deduced to what extent the experiment of taking football to Tibet paralleled with its arrival in India; nor can it be ascertained that Indian soldiers were cognizant of, let alone active in, the propagation of potential local nationalist aspirations through football. Official support for the game was shortlived. By the 1920s, the Buddhist clergy had banned the playing of football on the basis that it was imbued with 'corrosive foreign' influences.[56]

The study of women's sport in India is much neglected. The compendium of articles edited by Majumdar and Mangan on sport in South Asian society offers an introduction to the sporting lives and experiences of Indian women as players of kabadi,[57] supporters of cricket,[58] and as members of minority sporting communities.[59] These tracts are some of the earliest academic appraisals of women's sport. However, the current restricted range and incipient nature of study in the field does not prevent some common concerns. These have been articulated by Majumdar in relation to women's football. The sport is frowned upon by the middle classes who deem it unworthy for women to play football. Middle-class discrimination has mostly restricted the game to the lower classes. The game lacks funding and commercial support; and it is not uncommon 'to see women footballers starving after retirement, often rescued from their plight by welfare organizations and sports enthusiasts'.[60] Majumdar also argues that the women's movement has yet to launch an attack against patriarchal prejudices preventing women from embracing sport to a far greater extent.[61] Undoubtedly, the women's movement considers numerous other political, cultural and socio-economic issues far more vexing and in need of redress before it can turn its attention to sport.

The volume of edited articles by Majumdar and Mangan addresses two other sports: boxing and tennis. Indian journalists Shamya Dasgupta[62] and Suvam Pal[63] provide historical narratives of the two sports. Dasgupta's study on boxing mostly takes in the colonial period. It assesses the role of the military and the Young Men's Christian Association (YMCA) (particularly in Bengal) in the emergence of recognized amateur and professional Indian boxers from the 1930s. It also briefly captures the prominent indigenous boxing personalities of the period before partition, such as P.L. Roy, Santosh Dey, Ateen Sur, Robin Sarkar, Aaron Joshua, Baby Aratoon and Robin Bhatta, among a host of others. Pal's account of tennis looks at the development of regional tennis organizations in Lahore and Calcutta in the late 19th century before the arrival of the All-India Lawn Tennis Championships in 1910 and the All-India Lawn Tennis Association, a decade later. Its post-independence focus is on the Wimbledon junior achievements of Rita Davar (Girls' 1952 runner-up), Ramanathan Krishnan (Boys' champion 1954), Ramesh Krishnan (Boys' champion 1979), and Leander Paes (Boys' champion 1990); the 1960s open circuit success of Ramanathan Krishnan; and the good form of Indian players like Paes during the 1990s.

There has been a recent concern to relate traditional cultural pastimes to constructions of nationalism. Joseph Alter examines the attraction that wrestling and yoga have for sections of modern Indian society.[64] Wrestling, referred to as *Bharatiya kushti* or *Pahalwani*, is an anti-modern discourse that aims to reinvigorate the 'national character'. Groups of young men turn to celibacy and ritual as methods of discipline. Ritual involves meticulous attention to detail in matters pertaining to physical preparation. It includes precise and proper conduct regarding '(d)efecation, bathing, teeth-brushing, tongue-scraping, eating and sleeping'. Preparations are administered by the guru, who must not be disobeyed – for the guru 'is greater than God'; and the student 'is regarded as a blank slate'.[65] In addition, Alter examines literature – like the magazine *Bharatiya Kushti*, founded in 1963 – and its relevance for wrestling aficionados. Clearly, the literature points to traditional wrestling's marginal position in post-independence India as the outcome of 'corrupting influences' brought about by modernity. Such corrupting influences include sports like cricket, football, and hockey, which many Indians follow, as well as the usual smorgasbord of Western vices, from music, film and fashion, to soft drinks, diet and sexual impropriety.[66] In one issue of *Bharatiya Kushti* it was stated that:

> These days the strength of society, not only in the villages, but everywhere, is being spent on intoxicants of all kinds. Our energy should be spent building strength and wisdom. In this way we can prevent the wastage of our national health. The health of the nation will increase. The character of the nation will grow.[67]

Yoga also has come to embody cries for spiritual and national regeneration in the face of excessive modernity and Western material ideals. Alter argues that the Bharatiya Yog Sansthan (BYS, which was founded in 1967) sought to disseminate Hindu nationalism through the peaceful practice of yoga. The organization accepted 'the broader agenda' of the Rashtriya Swayamsevak Sangh (RSS), but not its militancy.[68] Emphasis was placed on arriving at truth and enlightenment through 'the practice of physical postures ... breathing exercises', and meditation. These were designed to self-discipline groups of individuals and cure them of the 'malaise of modernity' – both physically and spiritually. The BYS founders organized daily morning yoga practice in Delhi. The hour-long sessions were devoted to yoga routines; discussion of philosophy was left out entirely. The founders felt that yoga performance alone would win the BYS adherents and rejuvenate Hinduism among followers. It was their expressed desire to expand throughout India. By the time of publication, Alter estimated that over 300 BYS units were in existence in India.[69]

The work cited in this section is but a brief look at Indian sports largely unexplored by scholars at the present. There are other preliminary accounts of hockey[70] and sport among Indian Diaspora communities[71] that have been written. Undoubtedly, these offer scope for the development of Indian sports history in the years to come, further adding to the rich texture and variety of studies of Indian social systems and political constructions. An example of Diaspora concerns and national ties will feature in the following section of this paper and will relate to reasons for additional Pakistani national discourses taking place outside of Pakistan.

The marginal sports histories of Pakistan and Sri Lanka

Sports histories of Pakistan and Sri Lanka are few. The reasons for this relate to insufficient archival resources, political instability, and disruptions and limits to development of sports infrastructure and governance. Pakistan and Sri Lanka's sports cultures were underdeveloped at the time both countries acquired independence. In Pakistan's case, its few sporting traditions had come under the organizational umbrella of colonial India. For instance, Pakistani cricket, with its roots in colonial India, 'found itself stranded in a new separate, imagined community' after partition. Those who became Pakistani cricketers in the early post-independence period had assumed before partition that 'the unity of the subcontinent was a given that would continue however the conflict between the British and the nationalists played itself out'.[72] Cricket in Pakistan required a new governing body. The Board of Control for Cricket in India (BCCI), which was founded in 1928, was no longer responsible for the game in areas partitioned to Pakistan, but rather took leadership of cricket in post-independence India. Furthermore, Pakistani cricket had to develop traditions of its own in a new nation that lacked a history of political and cultural unity. Many colonial cricketers and influential organizers of the game were lost to it after independence. This included Hindus and Sikhs in Lahore, and Hindus and Parsees in Karachi. To offset these losses, Pakistan acquired Muslim cricketers from the United Provinces, East Punjab, Gujerat and elsewhere who had little affinity for the new nation upon arrival.

In 1997 and 1998, to celebrate 50 years of Pakistani independence, Oxford University Press released its Jubilee Series on Pakistan. This entailed a number of publications, three of which dealt with sport. The books of Sydney Friskin,[73] Omar Noman[74] and Dicky Rutnagur[75] describe the achievements and failures of Pakistani hockey, cricket and squash, respectively, both domestically and on the international stage from the time of partition. They capture in detail the background and rise to prominence of Pakistani athletes from various locales, who have graced sporting arenas far and wide. There is also some recognition of the significance of World Cup, World Championship and Olympic Games triumphs to a young nation like Pakistan in search of relevance and acceptance in world affairs. This involves an explanation for political intervention in sporting contests and organizations and the emergence of local vernacular media advertising for sports and athletes.

My own research on Pakistan looks at how cricket has generated and harnessed greater levels of national integration than have Pakistani politicians over the years. Leadership of

Pakistan has, for the most part, been authoritarian and it has stymied the growth of popular political representation. In its official discourse, Pakistan continues to assert the 'two-nation' theory with the Indian Union now functioning as the enemy 'Hindu nation'. Historically, national leaders have upheld this discourse and sought to impose it on citizens to the exclusion of other variables of identity that have traditionally characterized the politics of Pakistan's regions. In turn, regional leaders have often vigorously asserted visions of identity in opposition to the official national narrative.[76]

Cricket's popularization in Pakistan was gradual. Socio-economic and technological changes from the 1970s saw the game find roots in wider society. Industrialization and urbanization meant that the educated classes took up lucrative positions in the commercial sector that removed them from traditional areas of employment, like the army. The lower classes, themselves displaced by the restructuring of the economy, were then recruited into the army to take the place of the educated classes. These new recruits mostly lacked formal education, spoke regional dialects and had no prior association with the military. Cricketers of the period had much in common with the new army recruits. They, too, came from similar surroundings and began to replace college players whose numbers were diminishing due to the downgrading of sport in educational institutions.

Conceptions of Pakistani nationalism in sport began to resonate among disenfranchised sections of society in ways its political variant could not. Rural and lower-class urban communities, previously lacking exposure to the game, grew more in touch with cricket rules and customs once networks of communication expanded to include them in constructions of supra-community and national belonging. Superimposed radio and television broadcasts of cricket onto traditional community and market spaces was a crucial factor behind the game's dissemination. In addition, the appearance of test cricketers from such communities, the introduction of a universal cricket parlance, and the ancillary use of Urdu in broadcasts perpetuated salient but transient notions of national unity within a global sports context and cultural milieu that could not be replicated at the political level.

Because of cricket's success in uniting disparate cultural groups, by the early 1970s national leaders – like Zulfiqar Ali Bhutto and Muhammad Zia ul-Haq to begin with – appropriated the game to procure political legitimacy at home and abroad. However, while the organization of cricket at the formal level became associated with the official national discourse, numerous other variations to the official game sprang up. Alternative responses to government control of cricket, particularly street cricket tournaments organized by local communities, emerged in poorer urban neighbourhoods and outlying regions – like the North-West Frontier Province where Afghan refugee children took to the game. These responses captured the myriad constructions and flexible nature of cricket identities in Pakistan. Players moved with ease between formal and informal cricket settings and upheld their own class and regional identities even within the official circles of the Pakistan Cricket Board (PCB).

A further avenue of inquiry relating to Pakistani cricket is its appeal to Pakistani Diaspora communities in England. I have argued that British Pakistanis saw themselves as English even while they were constructing cricket and other cultural identities that symbolized the values of Pakistani nationalism in South Asia. British Pakistanis did this to counter the institutional discrimination of white English society. They appropriated the 'two-nation' theory and used it specifically within the context of race relations in England. In the process, they constructed identities that empowered them but differed from one another depending on where they were located. In West Yorkshire, a fully-fledged alternative competition, the Quaid-e-Azam Trophy, was organized. This was the most pronounced response to social alienation and discrimination in English cricket, but it was specific to cricket relations in West Yorkshire and not to those found elsewhere in the country. The Quaid-e-Azam Trophy was a call for inclusion not exclusion. British Pakistanis organized this competition to offset their perceived exclusion from league and county cricket. They saw it as a vehicle for their improvement as cricketers and a preparation for their eventual acceptance by the Yorkshire County Cricket Club.[77]

Sri Lankan sport has attracted the scholarly interest of Mike Marqusee and Michael Roberts. They have examined the development of cricket on the island and regard the colonial legacy as important for an understanding of the post-independence game. Marqusee comments on the significance of school cricket, particularly the annual contest between Royal College and St Thomas's. The game between the two schools extends back to 1879, but it now attracts 15,000–20,000 spectators. While up-and-coming players diligently ply their trade out in the middle; off the field the atmosphere is conducive to a carnival. Old boys 'drink themselves silly' to the accompaniment of music, dancing and wild applause.[78] Out of these contests have emerged numerous test cricketers for Sri Lanka. With the introduction of the schools' league in 1987, school rivalries have become far more 'intense' and global. Players often emulate the behaviour of international cricketers by incorporating 'high fives' in their celebrations of a dismissal.[79]

Roberts assesses the demographic pull of Colombo from the 1870s onwards. The city became the island's commercial centre very early on. It was also the heart of all cricket activity. Indeed, when cricketers began to emerge from 'the seaside towns of Matara, Galle, Ambalangoda' and others, they quite often made their way to Colombo to further their career prospects as players.[80] Roberts also examines the ethnic composition of cricketers in the history of the game in Sri Lanka. While most have been of Sinhalese origin, cricket has been receptive to other communities over the years. From the 1860s this has included immigrants domiciled in Colombo like the descendants of Malay soldiers who 'had served in the Dutch armies', and Burghers (Europeans who served the Dutch and British East India Companies).[81] One community that has been lost to cricket has been the Tamils. Few of them had become international cricketers before the mid-1970s when the 'political gulf between Sri Lankan Tamils and the rest of the island widened'. Since then, Muttiah Muralitharan has acquired international fame as a player; but, argues Roberts, his roots are Malaiyaha Tamil ('Indian Tamil'), and his education at St Anthony's College in Kandy was courtesy of his father's small business earnings.[82] One final development that is an outcome of the civil conflict on the island is Tamil support for India in cricket matches against Sri Lanka. For many Tamils, such support also extends to any cricket nation competing against Sri Lanka.[83]

Conclusion

This chapter began with a look at studies of cricket's entry into India and has ended with observations of cricket as an agency for Tamil pride and nationalism: Muralitharan's success set against the backdrop of Sinhalese political authority. In between there were mentioned other more recent accounts of sports history in South Asia and their significance to nationalism in the region. From the beginning of this century, scholarly scrutiny has fallen on Bengal and its sporting traditions. Cricket and football histories about the province are historiographical revisions of earlier studies that tended to ignore the development of sport beyond Bombay and north India. The revision of sports history has not done away with conjecture over the relevance of regional sporting traditions and their contribution to the rise of nationalism during the colonial period. It has, though, shown that sport had penetrated far deeper into Indian society than it was thought to have done by many early writers. In addition to this revision, there has been some attempt to enlarge the focus on South Asian sports history. The histories of football elsewhere in India – including neighbouring regions like Tibet, women's sport, boxing, tennis, and the modern significance of traditional pastimes like wrestling and yoga are briefly told. Just as brief have been the critical narratives of sport – mostly cricket – in Pakistan and Sri Lanka. A greater acceptance of sports history by university departments in the region and abroad will allow these histories – and others like them – to prosper, thereby providing an additional heuristic lens through which the richness of South Asian communities and cultural identities can further be explained.

Notes

1 Dipesh Chakrabarty, 'The Fall and Rise of Indian Sports History', in Boria Majumdar and J.A. Mangan, eds, *Sport in South Asian Society: Past and Present* (London and New York: Routledge, 2005), 3.
2 Kausik Bandyopadhyay, 'Sports History in India: Prospects and Problems', *International Journal of the History of Sport* 22, 4 (July 2005), 712. Bandyopadhyay argues that historians of Indian sport are faced with the challenge of establishing 'the credibility of this new domain of research by overcoming odds that commonly accompany an under-researched field, but also because they have to confront a conscious, sophisticated exploitation of this under developed state of research by some not-too-learned academic or non-academic writers'.
3 Although the writing of Ramachandra Guha extends beyond 2000, he will still be considered among the earliest writers because of his strong focus on the pivotal role of Bombay in the development of Indian cricket.
4 I refer to the works of: Edward Docker, *History of Indian Cricket* (Delhi: Macmillan, 1977); Richard Cashman, *Patrons, Players and the Crowd: The Phenomenon of Indian Cricket* (Delhi: Orient Longman, 1980); Ashis Nandy, *The Tao of Cricket: On Games of Destiny and the Destiny of Games* (New York: Oxford University Press, 1989); Mihir Bose, *A History of Indian Cricket* (London: Deutsch, 1990); Ramachandra Guha, *Wickets in the East: An Anecdotal History* (Delhi: Oxford University Press, 1992); and Arjun Appadurai, 'Playing with Modernity: The Decolonization of Indian Cricket', in *Modernity at Large: Cultural Dimensions of Globalization* (Minneapolis: University of Minnesota Press, 1995).
5 Ramachandra Guha, 'Cricket and Politics in Colonial India', *Past and Present* 161 (November 1998), 175–76.
6 Cashman, 19.
7 G. Pandey, *The Construction of Communalism in Colonial North India* (Delhi: Oxford University Press, 1994, second impression), 10. Gyanendra Pandey writes that the British developed a system they thought best conceptualized the 'basic feature of Indian society – its religious bigotry and its fundamentally irrational character'. He views communalism as akin to tribalism and factionalism in that they are terms that are constructed by an outside group – in most instances a technologically and economically more advanced one – and applied without any empirical justification on another group, often perceived as backward and dysfunctional.
8 Ramachandra Guha, *A Corner of a Foreign Field: The Indian History of a British Sport* (London: Picador, 2002), 60–61.
9 Ibid.
10 Appadurai, 99.
11 Guha 1998, 181–82.
12 This included the selection of players for princely and All-India teams irrespective of religious affiliation.
13 Nandy, 7.
14 Ibid.
15 Ibid., preface to the Oxford University Press edn, 2002, xi.
16 Ibid.; in the original preface to the book, Nandy had proposed its writing as a 'warning' to his wife, 'who wants Indians to always win in cricket'.

17 Ibid., preface to the Oxford University Press edn, 2002, xi

18 C.L.R. James, *Beyond a Boundary* (London: Hutchinson & Co. Ltd, 1963).

19 Nandy, 1.

20 B. Majumdar, 'Cricket: The Indian History of a British Sport', review article, *The International Journal of the History of Sport* 20, 1 (March 2003), 168.

21 Ibid.

22 Ibid.

23 Ibid. Ray introduced the game to Aligarh College and is referred to as 'the father of Bengali cricket'; Mukherjee, 'one of the best batsmen' of the period, was selected for the 1911 All-India tour to England, but did not go.

24 Ibid.

25 B. Majumdar, *Twenty-Two Yards to Freedom: A Social History of Indian Cricket* (New Delhi: Penguin, 2004), 133–70.

26 Ibid., 142.

27 Ibid., 149.

28 Ibid.

29 Ibid., 151.

30 Boria Majumdar, 'The Vernacular in Sports History', *International Journal of the History of Sport* 20, 1 (2003), 108–12. Majumdar states that 'in the popular colonial imagination the word *babu* was used with a slight savour of disparagement, as characterizing a superficially cultivated but too often effeminate Bengali' (111).

31 Ibid., 118.

32 Ibid., 117.

33 Ibid., 119.

34 J. A. Mangan, *The Games Ethic and Imperialism: Aspects of the Diffusion of an Ideal* (Harmondsworth: Viking, 1985).

35 Tony Mason, 'Football on the Maidan: Cultural Imperialism in Calcutta' *International Journal of the History of Sport* 12, 1 (1990), 87.

36 Paul Dimeo, 'Football and Politics in Bengal', in Paul Dimeo and James Mills, eds, *Soccer in South Asia: Empire, Nation, Diaspora* (London: Frank Cass, 2001).

37 James Mills, 'A Historiography of South Asian Sport', *Contemporary South Asia* 10, 2 (2001), 213–14.

38 Boria Majumdar and Kausik Bandyopadhyay, *Goalless: The Story of a Unique Footballing Nation* (London: Penguin, 2006).

39 Ibid., 36.

40 Ibid.

41 Ibid., 50.

42 Boria Majumdar, '*Ghati-Bangal* on the Maidan: Subregionalism, Club Rivalry and Fan Culture in Indian Football', *Soccer & Society* 9, 2 (April 2008), 289.

43 Ibid., 287.

44 Ibid., 289.

45 Ibid., 292.

46 Ibid., 294–95.

47 Boria Majumdar, 'The Politics of Soccer in Colonial India, 1930–1937: The Years of Turmoil', *Soccer & Society* 3, 1 (Spring 2002), 22–36.

48 Projit Bihari Mukharji, '"Feeble Bengalis" and "Big Africans": African Players in Bengali Club Football', *Soccer & Society* 9, 2 (April 2008), 273–85.

49 Ibid., 275.

50 Ibid.

51 Ibid., 277–79.

52 James Mills, 'Football in Goa: Sport, Politics and the Portuguese in India', in Paul Dimeo and James Mills, *Soccer in South Asia: Empire, Nation, Diaspora* (London: Frank Cass, 2001).

53 Mills, *A Historiography of South Asian Sport*, 215.

54 Alex McKay, 'Kicking the Buddha's Head: India, Tibet and Footballing Communalism', in Paul Dimeo and James Mills, *Soccer in South Asia: Empire, Nation, Diaspora* (London: Frank Cass, 2001).

55 Mills, *A Historiography of South Asian Sport*, 215.

56 Ibid., 216.

57 Soma Basu, 'Bengali Girls in Sport: A Socio-economic Study of Kabadi', in Boria Majumdar and J.A. Mangan, eds, *Sport in South Asian Society: Past and Present* (Abingdon: Routledge, 2005).

58 Sudeshna Banerjee, 'Fleshing Out Mandira: Hemming in the Women's Constituency in Cricket', in Boria Majumdar and J.A. Mangan, eds, *Sport in South Asian Society: Past and Present* (Abingdon: Routledge, 2005).

59 Suparna Bhattacharya, 'Women in Sport: The Parsis and Jews in Twentieth-Century India', in Boria Majumdar and J.A. Mangan, eds, *Sport in South Asian Society: Past and Present* (Abingdon: Routledge, 2005).

60 Boria Majumdar, 'Forward and Backward: Women's Soccer in Twentieth-Century India', *Comparative Studies of South Asia, Africa and the Middle East* 25, 1 (2005), 205.

61 Ibid.

62 Shamya Dasgupta, '"An Inheritance from the British": The Indian Boxing Story', in Boria Majumdar and J.A. Mangan, eds, *Sport in South Asian Society*.

63 Suvam Pal, '"Legacies, Halcyon Days and Thereafter": A Brief History of Indian Tennis', in Boria Majumdar and J.A. Mangan, eds, *Sport in South Asian Society*.

64 Joseph Alter, *The Wrestler's Body: Identity and Ideology in North India* (Berkeley: University of California Press, 1992); Joseph Alter, 'Body, Text, Nation: Writing the Physically Fit Body in Post-Colonial India', in James Mills and Satadru Sen, eds, *Confronting the Body* (London: Anthem Press, 2004); and Joseph Alter, 'Yoga at the Fin de Siecle: Muscular Christianity with a "Hindu" Twist', *International Journal of the History of Sport* 23, 5 (2006), 759–76.

65 Alter 2004, 21–23.

66 Ibid., 24.

67 S. Atreya, 'Saccha Pahalwan Devta Hota Hai', *Bharatiya Kushti* 10 (1973), 7–9, 21–24, cited in Alter 2004, 25.

68 Alter 2004, 29

69 Ibid., 30–31. These were 'estimates drawn from the organization's self-perception'.

70 Boria Majumdar, 'When North-South Fight, the Nation is Out of Sight: The Politics of Olympic Sport in Postcolonial India', *International Journal of the History of Sport* 23, 7 (November 2006), 1,217–31.

71 Mike Marqusee, *Anyone but England: Cricket, Race, and Class* (London: Two Heads Publishers, 1998); Chris Searle, *Pitch of Life* (Manchester: The Parrs Wood Press, 2001); Jack Williams, *Cricket and Race* (Oxford and New York: Berg, 2001). These books look at Indian, Pakistani and West Indian Diaspora cricket communities in England.

72 Chris Valiotis, 'Cricket in "a Nation Imperfectly Imagined": Identity and Tradition in Postcolonial Pakistan', in Stephen Wagg, ed., *Cricket and National Identity in the Postcolonial Age: Following On* (London and New York: Routledge), 110.

73 Sydney Friskin, *Going for Gold: Pakistan at Hockey* (Karachi and Oxford: Oxford University Press, 1998).

74 Omar Noman, *Pride and Passion: An Exhilarating Half Century of Cricket in Pakistan* (Karachi and Oxford: Oxford University Press, 1998).

75 Dicky Rutnagur, *Khans Unlimited: A History of Squash in Pakistan* (Karachi and Oxford: Oxford University Press, 1998).

76 Chris Valiotis, *Sporting Nations of the Imagination: Cricket and Identity in Pakistan and Anglo-Pakistan*, PhD dissertation submitted at the School of History at the University of New South Wales, 2006; publication forthcoming, Routledge, 2009–10.

77 Once more, the studies of Marqusee and Searle cited above also assess the nature of Pakistani Diaspora cricket in England. In addition, Pnina Werbner has written on the subject: '"Our Blood is Green": Cricket, Identity and Social Empowerment Among British Pakistanis', in J. McClancy, ed., *Sport, Identity and Ethnicity* (Oxford: UK Berg, 1996); *Imagined Diasporas Among Manchester Muslims: The Public Performance of Pakistani Traditional Identity Politics* (Oxford: James Currey, 2002).

78 Mike Marqusee, *War Minus the Shooting: A Journey through South Asia during Cricket's World Cup* (London: Heineman, 1996), 172.

79 Ibid., 174.

80 Michael Roberts, 'Sri Lanka: The Power of Cricket and the Power in Cricket', in Stephen Wagg, ed., *Cricket and National Identity in the Postcolonial Age: Following On* (London and New York: Routledge, 2005), 132.

81 Ibid., 137.

82 Ibid., 135. The Malaiyaha Tamils were initially plantation foremen who then turned to small business.

83 Ibid., 135–36.

37 South-East Asia

Charles Little

Alongside perhaps the Middle East, South-East Asia stands out as one of the most marginalized and neglected regions within sports history. Only a handful of scholars have addressed issues of sport within any of the region's 11 nations: Brunei, Myanmar (Burma), Cambodia, East Timor, Indonesia, Laos, Malaysia, the Philippines, Singapore, Thailand and Vietnam. This neglect is reflected by the low number of articles relating to the region that have appeared in the leading sports history journals. At the time of writing, the *Journal of Sports History* had never featured an article and the *International Journal of the History of Sport* only 12 (four of which were included in the same special issue devoted to sport in Asia).

The paucity of coverage is highlighted even further when reflected against the size of the region. South-East Asia is home to almost 10 percent of the world's population. Indonesia, with over 230 million people, is the world's fourth most populous nation, with the Philippines, Vietnam and Thailand all placed within the top 20. Geographically, the region sits on a vital and vibrant global crossroads and is increasingly prosperous. Why, then, has it been so overlooked by sports historians?

It is not only sports historians that have been negligent in this regard. Regional historians have been equally unsuccessful integrating sport into their work. Sport is totally overlooked in works like Osborne's standard historical text on the region, the four-volume Cambridge history, and the recent three-volume encyclopedia of the region, whilst the prestigious *Journal of Southeast Asian Studies* has only ever published one article on sport. The picture is similarly bleak with regard to histories of the individual regional nations, with the inclusion of a chapter on sport in a recent history of Singapore a rare exception to this trend.[1]

Sport in South-East Asia

Part of the reason for this lack of attention is likely to be the fact that the region has never been a sporting powerhouse and, indeed, has returned unremarkable results in international competitions. The Olympic Games provides a case study of this. The Philippines were the first regional representatives[2] at the games in 1924, and won a bronze medal at the 1928 Amsterdam Olympiad. Since then, however, the 11 nations have won only 50 further medals between them, and only Indonesia (which won the region's first gold in 1992) and Thailand have even recorded gold (five each). Myanmar, Brunei, Cambodia, East Timor and Laos have won no medals, Singapore and Vietnam boast only a solitary silver each, Malaysia one silver and two bronze, and the Philippines two silver and seven bronze. Given the population of these states, these returns are relatively meagre.

A similar pattern has been played out in association football. Only one regional side, the Dutch East Indies (now Indonesia) in 1938, has competed in the World Cup, and they gained their place as the only team from Asia to enter the qualifying process.[3] Since then no team has come close to qualifying for either the men's or women's World Cup, and in the most recent Fédération Internationale de Football Association (FIFA) rankings only Thailand (ranked 96th) is in the world's top 100 nations.[4] Even within Asian football, only Myanmar, where football was introduced in around 1879,[5] has been a strong force. They were runners-up in the 1968 Asian Cup (the only team from the region to reach the final of this tournament), winning the gold medal at the Asian games in 1966 and 1970, and participating at the 1972 Olympics (where they obtained respectable results but failed to qualify for the group stages). John Cody, one of the few historians to touch on Myanmar sport, notes that 'proficiency in soccer football [sic] became a significant mark of Burmese identity and prestige'.[6]

The region has achieved a large measure of success in one sport, badminton, but this is a sport that has been overlooked by both sports historians and the Western media.[7] In fact, teams from South-East Asia have dominated the Thomas Cup (the international men's team championship). Malaya (comprising players from what is now Singapore and Malaysia) won the inaugural title in 1949 and the two subsequent cups, whilst the next eight titles were shared between Indonesia and Malaysia. It was only in 1982 that the People's Republic of China broke this regional stranglehold, but Indonesia (six titles) and Malaysia (one title) have won seven of the subsequent 12 championships. The introduction of badminton to the Olympic programme in 1992 has also provided five of the region's 10 Olympic gold medals (and all five for Indonesia). Interestingly, the region has achieved far more modest levels of success in the Uber Cup, the female teams event, winning just three (all by Indonesia) out of 21 tournaments, suggesting issues of gender inequality worthy of further consideration.

Is there a South-East Asian sporting culture?

Despite the geographical linkages within the region, it is difficult to talk about sport at a pan-South-East Asian level. Although some traditional sports had a popularity that transcended national boundaries (details of which will be addressed later), there were relatively few sporting linkages between the regional states until the late 20th century. This was in a large part due to the pattern of European colonization within the region, which saw it divided up between five European powers. Great Britain controlled Myanmar and what are now Malaysia, Singapore and Brunei; Indochina (comprising the current states of Cambodia, Laos and Vietnam) was under French rule; the Dutch colonized Indonesia; and the Portuguese colonized East Timor. The Philippines were under Spanish control until 1899, but passed to American rule after the Spanish-American War, whilst Thailand was the only nation to maintain its independence.

As well as this colonization, the recent history of the Indochinese states of Cambodia, Laos and Vietnam was also profoundly shaped by Soviet-inspired Communism. It was political ties, for instance, that kept these nations out of the South-East Asian Games from the mid-1970s until a regional rapprochement in the late 1980s.[8] These states appear to have followed a very different approach to sport than the rest of the Communist world, in that sport never seems to have played a significant role in state policy, but this is surprisingly overlooked in the key texts on Communism and sport.[9]

This pattern of colonization profoundly influenced the face of sport in the region. Aside from association football, which became popular across the region (with perhaps the exception of the Philippines[10]), each colonizing power brought their own sports and games. For the British cricket featured predominantly, with the central geographical positions of the main cricket grounds in Singapore and Kuala Lumpur, the Padang and the Selangor Club Padang (now Merdeka Square), standing as vivid testimony of the centrality of sport within the British colonial project.[11] The Spanish took the Basque sport of Pelota to the Philippines, where it became a popular basis for gambling until being banned in the 1980s. It was the subsequent period of American colonization, however, that had the greatest impact on sport in the Philippines, though, as Reeves notes, it was basketball, rather than the perhaps more obvious candidate of baseball, which most caught the local sporting imagination.[12]

Such legacies still shape regional sport. If asked to guess, for instance, which is the only international multi-sport festival in which the French sport of petanque is contested, most would probably opt for the Jeux de la Francophonie (Francophone Games), but it is actually the South-East Asian Games, where the sport has been contested since 2001. This is a legacy of French rule in Indochina, where the sport remains popular.

Perhaps even more importantly than the sports that were introduced, this pattern of colonization shaped the direction in which local states searched for sporting contacts. For the cricketers of the Straits Settlements (Singapore and Malaya) this was to be towards Hong Kong and Shanghai in the form of the Intersport series that began in 1890. Frequent ties were also maintained to Ceylon (now Sri Lanka) and to a lesser extent Myanmar, but efforts to establish links with clubs in Batavia (the present-day Jakarta, Indonesia) and Bangkok quickly floundered.[13] For the footballers of the Dutch East Indies, following incoming tours by Australia in 1928 and 1931, it was a visit to Europe, with the highlight being a match against a Dutch national selection, that marked their first overseas expedition.[14] The Philippines also looked beyond South-East Asia for sporting contacts, favouring contacts with Japan and China, principally through the Far East Championship Games. These Games, now recognized as an important precursor to the Asian Games, began in 1913, and featured only the Philippines, China and Japan, until India made an appearance in 1930 and the Dutch East Indies and Vietnam joined for their final instalment in 1934.[15]

Equally as important as patterns of colonization were patterns of migration, particularly the millions from China who settled across South-East Asia. Many of these saw themselves as sojourners, temporary economic migrants, rather than permanent settlers, and China continued to hold their cultural, national and sporting affiliations. Thus Morris notes that the martial arts practised by the Pure Martial Athletic Association (*Jingwu Tryuhui*) gained huge popularity with the Chinese Diaspora across South-East Asia. From the 1920s onwards, Chinese athletes from across the region also began to participate in the Chinese National Games, which by 1948 featured teams from Indonesia, the Philippines, Malaya (including Singapore), Vietnam and Thailand, as well as Hawaii and Toronto. Aplin notes that, until the 1950s, 'the Chinese-born in Singapore felt more closely associated with the sporting system in Shanghai or Nanking than they did to the colonial system in Singapore', exemplified by the fact that of the five Singaporean athletes at the 1948 London Olympics, four went as representatives of China.[16]

Even the history of the event that now provides the closest sporting binds between the various nations, the biennial South-East Asian Games (also called the SEA Games), reflects the lack of overall regional sporting unity. The Games were formed in 1959 as the South-East Asian Peninsular (SEAP) Games, featuring Thailand, Myanmar, Malaysia, Singapore, South Vietnam and Laos, but specifically excluding Indonesia and the Philippines. Cambodia joined in 1961, but withdrew from the Federation in 1967, and repeated calls by Singapore and Malaysia to expand the scope of the Games to cover all of South-East Asia were rejected until 1977. It was concerns over population rather than politics that had seen Indonesia and the Philippines being rejected, and it was only when the politically-inspired withdrawal of Vietnam and Laos threatened the viability of the event that these were overcome. It would not be until the 1995 Games that all 10 regional countries would send teams to the same Games, reflecting the lack of overall cohesion in regional sport.[17]

Historiography

In light of these divergent sporting cultures within the region, it is little surprise that there have been no pan-regional studies of South-East Asian sport. As a consequence, anyone seeking to develop an understanding of sport in the region needs to turn to studies of each particular country. There is a great deal of unevenness of quantity in the historiography of sport among each nation, as the following analysis makes clear.

Singapore is the only country for which it is possible to claim that there exists a relatively comprehensive treatment, although the overall number of publications remains small. Led by the efforts of Nick Aplin and Peter Horton, there exists a relatively broad span of coverage, with Aplin primarily addressing the colonial era and Horton the post-independence period.[18] Aplin has also conducted research into pioneering female athletes, producing the only full-length monograph on women's sport within South-East Asia.[19]

By contrast, neighbouring Malaysia, although sharing a common British colonial heritage and many sporting connections with Singapore, has been less extensively researched. Although Douglas has produced an engaging overview of sport in the nation, there are numerous significant gaps in the analysis of the country. For example, apart from some anecdotal coverage in Shennan's study of the British in Malaya, the diffusion of sport in the 19th century in largely untreated. Much more is known about the inter-war period, with Brownfoot examining the racial and sexual dynamics of sport in this era.[20] However, the independence and post-independence eras are again largely untreated. Geographically, most work also focuses on the Malayan Peninsular (including Singapore), with only limited attention to the situation in East Malaysia (Sabah and Sarawak on the island of Borneo). Malaysia has recently gained prominence in sport through the hosting of mega-events, and the 1998 Commonwealth Games in Kuala Lumpur have been the subject of no fewer than four articles analysing the cultural and political implications of this engagement.[21]

Coverage of the Philippines is similarly mixed. Aside from a short introductory history and a more anecdotal history of physical education, most attention has concentrated on particular eras. Thus, while traditional sports are well covered in Lopez's comprehensive study (running to 590 pages) of folk games, there has been almost no attention paid to the Spanish era. It is the period of American colonization that has captured most attention, with a number of studies by Beran and Gems investigating sport during the period of American rule. By contrast, sport in the post-independence era has been largely overlooked.[22]

After long being ignored, Indonesia is now beginning to produce a vibrant body of sports history. Although not yet on a par with the current boom in Indian sports history, both domestic and international scholars are beginning to give the nation the attention it deserves. Whereas writing on the Philippines has concentrated on the colonial era, only Colombijn's analysis of football in West Sumatra has investigated sport under the Dutch. The rest of the new Indonesian sports history has focused on the post-independence era, such as Brown's work on ethnicity and identity in international badminton and at the Indonesian National Games, and on re-evaluations of the landmark Games of the Newly Emerging Forces (GANEFO) sporting concept (which will be addressed later in this chapter).[23]

By contrast, Thailand has been particularly poorly covered. Despite being one of the largest countries in the region, and possessing a uniquely vibrant traditional sporting culture bequeathed through the absence of European colonization, few historians have investigated local sport. Aside from Anderson's short introductory history from 1989, only one journal article has subsequently been published specifically on Thai sport. In this, Karnjanakit and Samahito describe Thailand's key role as a host for the Asian Games, but give little attention to Thai domestic sport, while Allison makes some brief references to Thailand in his analysis of sport and civil society.[24]

Of the rest of the region, the lack of any specific attention to tiny Brunei is not unexpected, and it can be safely assumed that sport in the nation has taken a similar path to neighbouring Malaysia, with which it maintains strong links.[25] It is far more surprising to find that Myanmar has been overlooked, given its size, and especially as it would appear to present a number of unique case studies worthy of further research, especially regarding anti-colonialism (see later). Sport in the region's newest nation, East Timor, has also yet to be fully chronicled. There are, though, some studies of sport in other Portuguese enclaves in Asia that can serve as a useful point of comparison, while the story of the country's participation in the 2000 Sydney Olympics has been detailed by an insider account from the team's manager.[26]

At first glance the biggest historiographical gap in regional sport appears to be Indochina (Vietnam, Laos and Cambodia). There appears to have been very little historical writing about sport in the region, and this is certainly the case in terms of sports history journals and publications. Further research reveals, however, that there is a vibrant body of literature that has been produced by historians working within the field of French colonialism. Much of this work has focused on the period during and immediately after World War II, when Indochina was under the control of the quasi-Fascist Vichy regime, which was particularly active in using sport for a range of domestic political agendas. Much of this work is in French, but there are a small number of English-language sources. One particularly interesting aspect of this research is that sport is generally considered alongside other youth movements, notably Scouting, rather than independently, offering an intriguing historiographical perspective that has not been widely considered within 'mainstream' sports history.[27]

Traditional sports

Both within this existing literature and in currently unexplored areas there are a number of key themes that dominate South-East Asian sport. The first of these is the wide diversity of traditional sports within the region, with an Association of South East Asian Nations (ASEAN)-commissioned study identifying 165 different games from just six of the region's nations (Brunei, Indonesia, Malaysia, the Philippines, Singapore and Thailand). These pastimes cover a wide diversity of forms from children's games through to combat sports, with animal sports (ranging from blood sports through to dove-cooing contests) relatively popular. Many of these games remain important elements of contemporary sporting cultures across the region, particularly Sepak Takraw and combat sports like Muay Thai, Silat and Arnis.[28]

This is also one area in which it is possible to talk of a shared South-East Asian sporting culture, as many of these indigenous sporting traditions cross national boundaries. Games like top-spinning and kite-flying are popular across the entire region, while others like pirogue (traditional canoe)-racing are equally significant in the national cultures of both Cambodia and Laos. Such similarities can also cause conflict, which has been manifested most bitterly in a dispute between Cambodia and Thailand over the origins of what is now known as Muay Thai. Cambodia claims that it is the true home of this form of kickboxing (which they refer to as Pradal Serey) and that that the sport has been unfairly appropriated by Thailand, going so far as to boycott Muay Thai events at the South-East Asian Games in protest over their utilization of the Thai name for the sport.[29]

In terms of global impact, Muay Thai and Sepak Takraw stand out as the most significant regional sports and have both developed an international standing. Both are interesting as their current forms actually represent amalgamations of traditional games and Western sporting practices. Sepak Takraw, for instance, took its current form in the 1920s, with the addition of a net adopted from volleyball to the traditional pastime of kicking a rattan ball (known as a sepak), whilst Muay Thai adopted the ring, system of rounds, gloves and weight divisions after concerns about high levels of death and injuries during the 1920s.[30]

A final point worthy of note is that, while historians have been slow to engage with sport in South-East Asia, it has proved to be a fertile field of investigation for anthropologists. Perhaps the most famous work in this vein is Geertz's landmark study of the Balinese cockfight. Thailand, so poorly served by sports historians, has proven to be a particularly fertile ground for anthropologists. Hjorleifur Jonsson has produced a number of works exploring sport and ethnic identities amongst the nation's minority Mien people, while others have explored children's games.[31]

Similarly, while Osborne notes that historians have tended to treat Laos as 'little more than a footnote' to the wider history of Indochina, and a similar gap exists in the understanding of sport in the country, Archaimbault's French-language anthropological study of pirogue-racing on the Mekong provides the only attention given to Lao sport. This study investigated the cultural dynamics of these races at Luang Prabang, Vientiane and Champassac, emphasizing their role in representing local mythologies above their sporting context, as well as highlighting the ways in which they embody symbolic representations of sexuality and the relationships between the Lao and Kha peoples.[32]

Post-colonialism

While the role of colonialism in shaping South-East Asian sport has already been noted, it is also important to acknowledge that sport has played a role as an agent of anti-colonial resistance. There has been less written about this in the South-East Asian context than in other parts of the world (particularly South Asia), but there are examples. Colombijn's work on Indonesian football has touched on the role of football clubs in the nationalist movement and Raffin's work on Indochina also extends into the revolutionary period.

It was the Games of the Newly Emerging Forces (GANEFO), though, that still remain the most audacious challenge to sporting colonialism. GANEFO prompted some initial interest from Western scholars, notably Pauker's Rand Corporation-sponsored work, although Douglas suggests that this '[partook] somewhat of the prevailing Western tendency to regard Sukarno as demented'.[33] With the passing of time, however, this truly radical attempt to reform, or perhaps more accurately transform, the structure of global sport appears to be slipping into obscurity. The emergence of new perspectives on the Games, analysing the motivations of Indonesia and their Chinese sponsors, will hopefully reverse this trend and this development to the prominence it deserves. It may also prompt Western historians to revisit the issue, especially now that much relevant archival material has passed into the public domain, while there is a pressing need to analyse the impact of GANEFO on the wider South-East Asian region.[34]

Beyond GANEFO, there also appear to be a number of cases worthy of further attention. Of all the nations in the region, it is perhaps Myanmar that appears to offer some of the most intriguing links between sport and resistance. As in other parts of the Empire, notably in India, there is also some evidence of the British initially attempting to utilize sport to engage with the indigenous elite. Ashley-Cooper records, for instance, that King Thibaw, the last Myanmar king, and his brothers had been introduced to cricket while attending a Mission school in Rangoon.[35]

Howeer, as happened in India, sport could also be used as a form of subtle resistance to colonialism. George Orwell, recalling his time in Myanmar in the 1920s, noted that:

> as a police officer I was an obvious target and was baited whenever it seemed safe to do so. When a nimble Burman tripped me up on the football field and the referee (another Burman) looked the other way, the crowd yelled with hideous laughter. This happened more than once. In the end the sneering yellow faces of young men that met me everywhere, the insults hooted after me when I was at a safe distance, got badly on my nerves.[36]

Another link between Myanmar sport and resistance to colonial rule was the Young Men's Buddhist Association (YMBA). The YMBA was originally established in Ceylon in 1899 and was explicitly modelled on the Young Men's Christian Association (YMCA). It was first established in Myanmar in 1902, and had grown to over 50 branches by 1917. It also took on an important political dimension, serving as both a pressure group for Myanmar rights and an important training ground for Myanmar's future nationalist leaders. Unfortunately histories of the movement have been silent on the extent to which it mirrored the YMCA's promotion of sporting activities, and to how important a role sport played in attracting young men into the organization.[37]

The post-independence history of Myanmar sport would appear to offer further intriguing opportunities for sports historians, especially those interested in anti-colonialism and post-colonialism. The fate of cricket, for instance, poses striking questions. Although a Burmese Cricket Federation was established in 1947, the game virtually disappeared, and Myanmar appears unique as the only former British colony in Asia where the game failed to maintain a presence.[38] While the sport may simply have suffered a natural decline, there is evidence to suggest that it was deliberately rejected by Myanmar as a colonial relic. Anti-colonial sentiment remained strong in post-independence Myanmar, as evidenced by its refusal to join the British Commonwealth,[39] and cricket (along with other British team sports like rugby union and hockey) appears to have been tarred with the colonialist brush. When the game was re-established in the country in the early 2000s the government-backed *Myanmar Times* noted that 'the government had resisted previous efforts to promote the sport, which for many people smacks of elitism and the Myanmar's colonial past', and that 'many here still associate it with the invaders'.[40] Further investigation needs to be undertaken to confirm these suggestions, but it suggests a fruitful vein for investigation.[41]

Cambodia also offers some intriguing possibilities for further research. Cambodia gained its independence from France in 1953, under the leadership of King Norodom

Sihanouk. Sihanouk had been a keen disciple of the Vichy sports programme, and had launched a youth movement known as Yuvan on these principles. He would remain closely linked to Cambodian sport until the early 1970s, and also accompanied the Cambodian team on its first Olympic sojourn. This took place at the unlikely setting of the 1956 equestrian events in Stockholm, Sweden, and the notion of an underdeveloped nation, led by its flamboyant playboy King, making its Olympic debut in the largely aristocratic pastime of show jumping poses interesting, but hitherto unexplored, questions about the significance of social class, privilege and patronage in South-East Asian sport.[42]

It was in the 1960s, though, that Sihanouk's use of sport is most interesting and worthy of wider attention. As Head of State he took Cambodia into the non-aligned camp, rejecting previous links with both the USA and neighbouring nations in the process. Sihanouk used the opening of the country's impressive new National Sports Complex in 1964 to proclaim:

> [b]y our achievements and progress in all fields and by the dynamics of national unity, we have certainly shown to the world that we are not a bastard nation deprived of intelligence, courage and energy – as the enemies of our country and people have often pretended. Despite the criticism and slander of some of our neighbours and their imperialist masters, we have proved our capacity to transform our ancient kingdom into a modern nation.[43]

This new direction was reflected in sport by a wholehearted embrace of the GANEFO concept, even though this resulted in the cancellation of the 1963 SEAP Games that had been scheduled for Phnom Penh. Although other nations drew back from GANEFO after the inaugural meeting, Cambodia remained committed to the movement. It summarily withdrew from the SEAP Games Federation, stating that 'Khmer athletes [need to] devote themselves to the preparation of the very many games in which they are engaged', which can be translated as meaning GANEFO. This included staging the second and final GANEFO event, under the banner of the Asian GANEFO. Although the history of the original 1962 GANEFO is well known, this 1966 event has been largely overlooked. Significantly, the only published information about Sihanouk's motives for staging the event is contained in a history of Cambodian architecture (Vann Molymann's National Sports Complex is regarded as one of the foremost examples of what became known as 'New Khmer Architecture'), reflecting the chronic underdevelopment of sports history in the region.[44]

Notes

1 M. Osborne, *Southeast Asia: An Introductory History* (Crow's Nest: Allen & Unwin, 2000); N. Tarling, ed., *The Cambridge History of Southeast Asia*, four vols (Cambridge: Cambridge University Press, 1999); O. Gin, ed., *Southeast Asia: A Historical Encyclopedia from Angkor Wat to East Timor* (Santa Barbara: ABC-Clio, 2004); A. Pereira, 'It's Us Against Them: Sports in Singapore', in C. Bun and T. Kiong, eds, *Past Times: A Social History of Singapore* (Singapore: Times Editions, 2003).

2 Burma and Singapore first appeared in 1948, Indonesia, Thailand and the Republic of Vietnam (South Vietnam) in 1952, Malaya and North Borneo (competing separately, although they would compete together as Malaysia from the 1964 Games onwards) and Cambodia (only in the equestrian events at Stockholm) in 1956, Laos in 1980, and Brunei in 1996 (although one official had been present at the 1988 Seoul Games). Four athletes from East Timor competed under the designation of 'Individual Olympic Athletes' in 2000, with the nation making its first official appearance at the 2004 Games.

3 The side's only match in the tournament was a 6–0 loss to eventual finalists Hungary, in the first round.

4 Of the other regional sides, Vietnam are 116th, Singapore 128th, Indonesia 131st, Myanmar 163rd, Malaysia 169th, Cambodia 186th, Laos 187th, the Philippines 189th, Brunei 190th, and East Timor joint last at 200th. The best ever placing since the rankings began in 1993 was Thailand's 43rd in September 1998. FIFA, 'FIFA/Coca Cola World Ranking April 2008', FIFA online, 2008, www.fifa.com/worldfootball/ranking/index.html (accessed 11 May 2008).

5 Andrew Marshall's *The Trouser People* is a travelogue of the author's visits to contemporary Myanmar, but, despite its subtitle, gives little coverage to football. Moreover, Marshall's claim that 'the golden age of Burmese football died along with democracy after the 1962 military coup' is incorrect, with the nation's greatest international successes occurring in the late 1960s and early 1970s. A. Marshall, *The Trouser People: The Quest for the Victorian Footballer Who Made Burma Play the Empire's Game* (London: Viking, 2002), 112.

6 J. Cody, *The United States and Burma* (Cambridge, MA: Harvard University Press, 1976), 270.

7 The sport has never been the feature of an article in the *Journal of Sports History* and the only academic article published on the topic appears to be Brown's recent publication in an Indonesian history journal, C. Brown, 'Playing the Game: Ethnicity and Politics in Indonesian Badminton', *Indonesia* 81 (April 2006), 71–93.

8 South Vietnam and Laos had been founder members of the South-East Asian Peninsular Games in 1959, and Cambodia joined in 1961. Political changes saw them withdraw in 1975. Cambodia (competing under the banner of the People's Republic of Kampuchea) returned in 1983 (but was again absent from 1989 to 1995), and Laos and Vietnam rejoined in 1989.

9 North Vietnam never appears to have sought recognition from the International Olympic Committee, so there was no parallel of the two Germanys and two Chinas issues that dogged the IOC during the Cold War. Nor did it become a member of FIFA, and it played only 24 soccer internationals, almost all of which were part of the GANEFO festival or against Communist-bloc allies. Riordan notes that it did join the Soviet-aligned Sports Committee of Friendly Armies (SCFA) in 1958, but seems to have played no active part within the organization. Riordan's *Sport Under Communism* makes no references to North Vietnam, Laos or Cambodia, while his later *Sport, Politics and Communism* simply notes that 'poorer communist nations recovering from ruinous wars in Indochina and Afghanistan have more immediate priorities than sport and, unlike other developing nations – such as Ethiopia, Mongolia and North Korea, have never attempted to promote an elite sports infrastructure'. J. Riordan, *Sport Under Communism: The USSR, Czechoslovakia, the GDR, China, Cuba* (London: C. Hurst and Co., 1981); J. Riordan, *Sport, Politics and Communism* (Manchester: Manchester University Press, 1991), 5, 136.

10 V. Santos, X. Zhu and M. Gerlinger, 'Closing the Gap: A Model for the Assessment of Football Development in Asia including a Case Study of the Philippines', in *International Studies in Sport: Selected Essays 2001/2002* (Neuchatel, Switzerland: Editions CES, 2004).

11 Singapore's Padang has been home to the Singapore Cricket Club since 1852. It is located in the heart of the city and directly borders both the financial and administrative districts.

12 M. de Borja, *Basques in the Philippines* (Reno: University of Nevada Press, 1995), xv, 75; J. Reeves, *Taking in a Game: A History of Baseball in Asia* (Lincoln: University of Nebraska Press, 2002), 88–112.

13 I. Sharp, *Singapore Cricket Club* (Singapore: The Club, 1993), 43–45, 60, 227–28.

14 B. Murray, 'Cultural Revolution? Football in the Societies of Asia and the Pacific', in S. Wagg, ed., *Giving the Game Away: Football, Politics and Culture on Five Continents* (London: Leicester University Press, 1995), 144; F. Colombijn, 'View from the Periphery: Football in Indonesia', in G. Armstrong and R. Giulianotti, eds, *Football Cultures and Identities* (Basingstoke: Palgrave, 1999), 130.

15 F. Hong, 'Prologue: The Origin of the Asian Games: Power and Politics', in F. Hong, ed., *Sport, Nationalism and Orientalism: The Asian Games* (London: Routledge, 2007), 392–403.

16 The Chinese Olympic team at the 1936 Berlin Games included athletes who lived and had been born in Singapore, Malaya and the Dutch East Indies, and was very much seen as an All-China squad, and Chinese teams at the Far Eastern Championship Games also drew heavily on the Chinese Diaspora. A. Morris, 'Native Songs and Dances: Southeast Asia in a Greater Chinese Sporting Community, 1920–48', *Journal of Southeast Asians Studies* 31.1 (March 2000), 48–69; N. Aplin, 'Chinese Affiliations and the Olympics: The Paradox of Singapore', *Cultural Relations Old and New: The Transitory Olympic Ethos*, proceedings of the Seventh International Symposium for Olympic Research, October 2004, 185–97.

17 Brunei joined Indonesia and the Philippines in 1977, Cambodia (competing as the People's Republic of Kampuchea) rejoined in 1983 but was again absent between 1989 and 1995, while

Laos and Vietnam returned in 1989. East Timor became the 11th member of the Federation in 2001 after securing its independence from Indonesia. Anonymous, *Moments in Southeast Asian Sport* (Bangkok: Seiko, 1985), 8, 40, 48, 63, 70, 79; P. Seneviratne, *Golden Moments: The S. E. A. Games 1959–1991* (Singapore: Dominie Press, 1993).

18 P. Horton, '"Padang or Paddock"? A Comparative View of Colonial Sport in Two Imperial Territories', *International Journal of the History of Sport* 14.1 (April 1997); P. Horton, 'Complex Creolization: The Evolution of Modern Sport in Singapore', in J. Mangan, ed., *Europe, Sport, World: Shaping Global Societies* (London: Frank Cass, 2001), 77–104; P. Horton, 'Shackling the Lion: Sport in Independent Singapore', in J. Mangan and F. Hong, eds, *Sport in Asian Society: Past and Present* (London: Frank Cass, 2002), 243–74; N. Aplin and Q. Jong, 'Celestials in Touch: Sport and the Chinese in Colonial Singapore', in J. Mangan and F. Hong, eds, *Sport in Asian Society: Past and Present* (London: Frank Cass, 2002), 67–98; S. Yam, 'Singapore: Towards a Sporting Nation for All', in L. DaCosta and A. Miragaya, eds, *Worldwide Experiences and Trends in Sport for All* (Oxford: Meyer and Meyer, 2002), 193–205; M. McNeill, J. Sproule and P. Horton, 'The Changing Face of Sport and Physical Education in Post-Colonial Singapore', *Sport, Education, Society* 8.1 (January 2003), 35–56; A. Pereira, 'It's Us Against Them: Sports in Singapore', in C. Bun and T. Kiong, eds, *Past Times: A Social History of Singapore* (Singapore: Times Editions, 2003).

19 N. Aplin, 'Beyond the Boundaries of Propriety: Singapore's Pioneer Women Olympians', *Olympika* IX (2000), 91–114; N. Aplin, *To the Finishing Line: Champions of Singapore* (Singapore: SNP Editions, 2002).

20 S. Douglas, 'Sport in Malaysia', in E. Wagner, ed., *Sport in Africa and Asia: A Comparative Handbook* (Westport: Greenwood Press, 1989); M. Shennan, *Out in the Midday Sun: The British in Malaya 1880–1960* (London: John Murray, 2000), 35, 58–60, 121–26; J. Brownfoot, 'Emancipation, Exercise and Imperialism: Girls and the Games Ethic in Colonial Malaya', *International Journal of the History of Sport* 7.1 (1990), 61–84; J. Brownfoot, 'Emancipation, Exercise and Imperialism: Girls and the Games Ethic in Colonial Malaya', in J. Mangan, ed., *The Cultural Bond: Sport, Empire, Society* (London: Frank Cass, 1992), 84–107; J. Brownfoot, '"Healthy Bodies, Healthy Minds": Sport and Society in Colonial Malaya', in J. Mangan and F. Hong, eds, *Sport in Asian Society: Past and Present* (London: Frank Cass, 2002), 129–56; S. Singh and S. Khoo, 'Malaysia: Sport for All in Cultural Diversity', in L. DaCosta and A. Miragaya, eds, *Worldwide Experiences and Trends in Sport for All* (Oxford: Meyer and Meyer, 2002), 75–88.

21 M. Muda, 'The Significance of the Commonwealth Games in Malaysia's Foreign Policy', *Round Table* 87.346 (April 1998), 211–26; M. Silk, 'Together We're One? The "Place" of the Nation in Media Representations of the 1998 Kuala Lumpur Commonwealth Games', *Sociology of Sport Journal* 18 (2001), 227–301; M. Silk, '"Bangsa Malaysia": Global Sport, the City and the Mediated Refurbishment of Local Identities', *Media, Culture & Society* 24 (2002), 775–94; J. van der Westhuizen, 'Marketing Malaysia as a model modern Muslim state: the significance of the 16th Commonwealth Games', *Third World Quarterly* 25.7 (January 2004), 1,227–91.

22 J. Beran, 'Physical Education and Sport in the Philippines', in E. Wagner, ed., *Sport in Asia and Africa: A Comparative Handbook* (Westport: Greenwood Press, 1989); C. Bocobo-Olivor, *History of Physical Education in the Philippines* (Quezon City: University of Philippines Press, 1972); M. Lopez, *A Study of Philippine Games* (Quezon City: University of Philippines Press, 2001); J. Beran, 'Americans in the Philippines: Imperialism or Progress through Sport?', *International Journal of the History of Sport* 6.1 (May 1989), 62–87; G. Gems, 'The Athletic Crusade: Sport and Colonialism in the Philippines', *International Journal of the History of Sport* 21.1 (January 2004), 1–15; G. Gems, *The Athletic Crusade: Sport and American Cultural Imperialism* (Lincoln: University of Nebraska Press, 2006).

23 Colombijn, 'View from the Periphery', 126–38; C. Brown, 'Sport, Politics and Ethnicity: Playing Badminton for Indonesia', *Proceedings of the 15th Biennial Conference of the Asian Studies Association of Australia*, Canberra, 2004; C. Brown, 'The Indonesian National Games of 1951 and 1953: Identity, Ethnicity and Gender', *Proceedings of the 16th Biennial Conference of the Asian Studies Association of Australia*, Wollongong, 2006; I. Adams, 'Pancasila: Sport and the Building of Indonesia – Ambitions and Obstacles', in J. Mangan and F. Hong, eds, *Sport in Asian Society: Past and Present* (London: Frank Cass, 2002), 295–318; R. Lutan, 'Indonesia and the Asian Games: Sport, Nationalism and the "New Order"', *Sport in Society* 8.3 (September 2005), 414–24; K. Kenta, 'From Colonial to Reflection: A Local History of Indonesian Football' (Japanese-language article), *Asian and African Area Studies* 6.1 (2006), 44–76; C. Brown, 'Playing the Game: Ethnicity and Politics in Indonesian Badminton', *Indonesia* 81 (April 2006), 71–93.

24 W. Anderson, 'Sport in Thailand', in E. Wagner, ed., *Sport in Asia and Africa: A Comparative Handbook* (Westport: Greenwood Press, 1989); S. Karnjanakit and S. Samahito, 'Thailand and the Asian Games: Coping with Crisis', in F. Hong, ed., *Sport, Nationalism and Orientalism: The Asian Games* (London: Routledge, 2007); L. Allison, 'Sport and Civil Society', *Political Studies* 45.4 (September 1998), 719–21.

25 Brunei is geographically surrounded by the Malaysian state of Sarawak. It declined the opportunity to join with the other British states on Borneo as part of the new Republic of Malaysia in 1963, preferring to remain a protectorate of Great Britain (before finally becoming independent in 1984). Despite rejecting political union with Malaysia it maintained strong sporting links, continuing to field a team in the Malaysian soccer league and participating in the SUKMA Games (a national multi-sports event contested by the states and territories of Malaysia).

26 For comparisons with other Portuguese territories in Asia, see J. Mills, 'Football in Goa: Sport, Politics and the Portuguese in India', *Soccer and Society* 2.2 (Summer 2002), 75–88. The story of the 2000 Olympics team is told in F. Fowlie and P. Moss, *Prayer Road* (Frederick, MD: PublishAmerica, 2006).

27 The author is indebted to Philip Dine for advice and information on sources related to Indochina. Works in English include: E. Jennings, *Vichy in the Tropics: Petain's National Revolution in Madagascar, Guadeloupe and Indochina, 1940–1944* (Stanford: Stanford University Press, 2001); A. Raffin, 'Easternisation Meets Westernisation: Patriotic Youth Organisations in French Indochina during World War II', *French Politics, Culture and Society* 20.2 (2000), 121–40; A. Ruffin, *Youth Mobilization in Vichy Indochina and its Legacies, 1940 to 1970* (Langham: Lexington Books, 2005). Amongst the French-language sources are A. Larcher-Goscha, 'Volonté de puissance coloniale et puissance de volonté nationaliste: Aux origines de la création de l'Ecole d'Education Physique d'Hanoi (1913–1922)', in E. Combeau-Marie, ed., *Sports et loisirs aux colonies*, 2004, 35–49; A. Larcher-Goscha, 'Sports, colonialisme et identités nationales: premières approches du corps à corps colonial en Indochine (1918–1945)', in N. Bancel, D. Denis and Y. Fates, eds, *De l'Indochine à l'Algérie: La jeunesse en mouvements des deux côtés du miroir colonial 1940–1962* (Paris: Editions de la Découverte, 2003); A. Larcher-Goscha and D. Denis, 'Une adolescence indochinoise, entretien avec Pierre Brocheux', in N. Bancel, D. Denis and Y. Fates, eds, *De l'Indochine à l'Algérie: La jeunesse en mouvements des deux côtés du miroir colonial 1940–1962* (Paris: Editions de la Découverte, 2003); H. Dao, 'La constitution du scoutisme indochinois', in N. Bancel, D. Denis and Y. Fates, eds, *De l'Indochine à l'Algérie: La jeunesse en mouvements des deux côtés du miroir colonial 1940–1962* (Paris: Editions de la Découverte, 2003); J. Gomane, 'La jeunesse indochinoise française et indigène sous l'administration Decoux', in N. Bancel, D. Denis and Y. Fates, eds, *De l'Indochine à l'Algérie: La jeunesse en mouvements des deux côtés du miroir colonial 1940–1962* (Paris: Editions de la Découverte, 2003).

28 I. Rahman, *Inventory of ASEAN Traditional Games and Sports*, ASEAN Committee on Culture and Development, Malaysia, 1998; M. Wiley, 'Martial Arts, Philippines', in D. Levinson and K. Christensen, eds, *Encyclopedia of World Sport: From Ancient Times to the Present* (Oxford: ABC-Clio, 1996), 410–11.

29 M. Grimburg, *Some Games of Asia* (Singapore: Asia Pacific Press, 1974), 46–49; C. Archaimbault, *La Course de Pirogues au Laos: Un Complexe Culturel* (Ascona: Artibus Asia, 1972); P. Vail, 'Thailand's Khmer as "Invisible Minority": Language, Ethnicity and Cultural Politics in North-eastern Thailand', *Asian Ethnicity* 8.2 (June 2007), 111–30.

30 W. Anderson, 'Sport in Thailand', in E. Wagner, ed., *Sport in Asia and Africa: A Comparative Handbook* (Westport: Greenwood Press, 1989), 24; A. Trevithick, 'Takraw', in D. Levinson and K. Christensen, eds, *Encyclopedia of World Sport: From Ancient Times to the Present* (Oxford: ABC-Clio, 1996), 389–91.

31 C. Geertz, 'Deep Play: Notes on the Balinese cockfight', in C. Geertz, ed., *The Interpretation of Cultures* (New York: Basic Books, 1972); H. Jonsson, 'Traditional Tribal What? Sports, Culture and the State in the Northern Hills of Thailand', in J. Michaud and J. Ovesen, eds, *Turbulent Times and Enduring People: Mountain Minorities in the South East Asian Massif* (London: Routledge, 2000), 219–46; H. Jonsson, 'Serious Fun: Minority Cultural Dynamics and National Integration in Thailand', *American Ethnologist* 28.1 (February 2001), 151–78; H. Jonsson, 'Mien through Sports and Culture: Mobilizing Minority Identity in Thailand', *Ethnos* 68.3 (September 2003), 317–40; J. Hanks, 'Children's Play and Games in Rural Thailand: A Study in Acculturation and Socialization', *The Journal of Asian Studies* 44.4 (August 1985), 881–82; W. Anderson, *Children's Play and Games in Rural Thailand: A Study in Enculturation and Socialization* (Bangkok: Chulalongkorn University Social Research Institute, 1980).

32 Osborne, *Southeast Asia*, 176. Archaimbault, *La Course de Pirogues au Laos*: details of the contents of this book are drawn from A. Dessaint, 'Review of *La Course de Pirogues au Laos: Un Complexe Culturel*', *American Anthropologist* 77.4 (December 1975), 942–43, and H. Woodward, 'Review of *La Course de Pirogues au Laos: Un Complexe Culturel*', *The Journal of Asian Studies* 34.4 (August 1975), 1,079–80.

33 E. Pauker, 'GANEFO I: Sport and Politics in Jakarta', *Asian Survey* 5.1 (April 1965), 171–85; S. Douglas, 'Sport in Malaysia', in E. Wagner, ed., *Sport in Africa and Asia: A Comparative Handbook* (Westport: Greenwood Press, 1989), 182.

34 F. Hong and X. Xiaozheng, 'Communist China: Sport, Politics and Diplomacy', *International Journal of the History of Sport* 19. 2/3 (July 2002), 319–42; I. Adams, 'Pancasila: Sport and the Building of Indonesia – Ambitions and Obstacles', in J. Mangan and F. Hong, eds, *Sport in Asian Society: Past and Present* (London: Frank Cass, 2002), 295–318; R. Lutan, 'Indonesia and the Asian Games: Sport, Nationalism and the "New Order"', *Sport in Society* 8.3 (September 2005), 414–24.

35 F. Ashley-Cooper, *Cricket Highways and Byways* (London: Allen and Unwin, 1927), cited in D. Allen, 'Burma', in E. Swanton, ed., *Barclay's World of Cricket: The Game from A-Z* (London: Willow Books, 1986).

36 G. Orwell, *Shooting an Elephant and Other Essays* (London: Secker and Warburg, 1950), 3–12.

37 E. Sarkisyanz, *Buddhist Backgrounds of the Burmese Revolution* (The Hague: Martins Nijhoff, 1965), 128; H. James, 'Young Men's Buddhist Association (YMBA) (1906)', in O. Gin, ed., *Southeast Asia: A Historical Encyclopedia from Angkor Wat to East Timor* (Santa Barbara: ABC-Clio, 2004), 1,435–37.

38 The sport has thrived in India, Pakistan, Sri Lanka and Bangladesh, where it remained the most popular sport after independence and all four nations are amongst the 10 elite international Test Match-playing nations. The game also maintained a strong foothold in Malaysia, Singapore, Brunei and Hong Kong. By contrast, Myanmar fails to appear in any records of international cricket during the late 20th century. Significantly, the nation was absent from the membership of the International Cricket Council (ICC) after it opened its membership to non-Test nations in 1965. The game has recently been re-established in the country and it gained associate membership of the ICC in 2006. Myanmar's first international competition came at the Asian Cricket Council trophy later that year, where it suffered a serious of heavy defeats, including scores of just 20 and 10 runs (the latter a record low score in international cricket) against fellow minnows Hong Kong and Nepal. D. Allen, 'Burma', in E. Swanton, ed., *Barclay's World of Cricket: The Game from A-Z* (London: Willow Books, 1986); Asian Cricket Council, 'Results', in ACC Trophy 2006 (online), www.asiancricket.org/acctrophy06/results.htm.

39 J. Cody, *A History of Modern Burma* (Ithaca: Cornell University Press, 1960), 555–57.

40 Myanmar Times, 'Former Film Star takes a Swing at Cricket', in *Myanmar Times and Weekly Review* (online), 12–18 September 2005, www.myanmar.gov.mm/myanmartimes/no283/Myanmar Times15-283/t007.htm.

41 One possible approach would be to look at parallels with Ireland's Gaelic Athletic Association, which had also deliberately rejected British sports like cricket because of the game's perceived link with British imperialism.

42 Jennings, *Vichy in the Tropics*, 190; *The Official Report of the Organising Committee for the Equestrian Games of the XVIth Olympiad*, The Organisers, Stockholm, 1956, 15, 23, 55, 213, 250.

43 H. Ross and D. Collins, *Building Cambodia: 'New Khmer Architecture', 1953–1970* (Bangkok: Key Publisher Co., 2006), 12, 207, 212–14.

44 Anonymous, *Moments in Southeast Asian Sport* (Bangkok: Seiko, 1985), 79; H. Ross and D. Collins, *Building Cambodia: 'New Khmer Architecture', 1953–1970* (Bangkok: Key Publisher Co., 2006), 10–11, 163, 207, 212–14, 229.

38 The United States of America

Mark Dyreson

Though few Americans have read the work of West Indian historian and political reformer C.L.R. James, many share his passionate faith that sport serves as a scalpel for peeling back social veneers and uncovering fundamental truths about the inner workings of human cultures. In his magisterial *Beyond a Boundary* James neatly performed that very trick, exposing the beating heart of the British Empire in his meditations on the game of cricket. To his critics, academic and otherwise, James complained, '[i]f this is not social history what is?'[1] James's challenge reverberates in contemporary American popular and academic cultures. Histories related to sport abound in American culture. Libraries burst with thousands of academic tomes devoted to various historical aspects of sport in American culture.[2] Popular tomes litter the shelves of major bookstores and appear on bestseller lists.[3] These chronicles are transformed into major television documentaries or become Hollywood blockbusters.[4] Indeed, film critics have recently complained that every sports movie produced in the USA ham-handedly seeks to teach audiences a 'Disneyfied' lesson in the history of American race relations.[5]

James, who was born in 1901 and passed away in 1989, would no doubt see the proliferation that began in the 1970s of historical treatments of sport as a sea change in American culture. When he challenged his academic colleagues in 1963 to take sport seriously, he followed his bold assertion that sport should be at the centre of social histories with a mournful lamentation. Sport, he wailed, 'finds no place in the history of the people because the historians do not begin from what people seem to want but from what they think the people ought to want'.[6]

James' lament described historical treatments of American sports from their origins in the 19th century through the 1970s. Approximately a decade after James published *Beyond a Boundary*, American historians seized on sport as a crucial dimension of the 'the new social history'.[7] Surveying American sports historiography nearly a half century after James's original burst of genius, in a culture suffused by 'serious' studies of sport, his critique seems simultaneously prescient and antiquated. Americans have become thoroughly – though mostly unknowingly – Jamesian in their outlook.

Even before James generated the spark that ignited a scholarly revolution, some Americans took sport seriously. American knowledge of the role of sport in the nation's history springs from three distinct sources. Popular culture, especially books and films, from Hebert Warren Wind's epic *The Story of American Golf* (1947), to the Marx Brothers' comic epic *Horse Feathers* (1932), to David Maraniss' ponderous gridiron drama *When Pride Still Mattered* (1999), to Disney's even more ponderous gridiron drama *Remember the Titans* (2000) take sport quite seriously.[8] A historiography of histories of sports in popular culture, however, will have to wait for a different forum. This essay will limit its chronicles to the remaining two sources, both scholarly in origin. Academic historians have produced historical studies of sports. Academics in fields related to human movement in varied disciplines with many names, from physical education to physiology to exercise and sport science to kinesiology, have also produced historical studies of sports. From these latter two, scholarly springs flowed at the beginning of the 20th century a trickle and, by the beginning of the 21st century, a torrent of tomes devoted to sports history and to the history of sports. The terms 'sports history' and 'history of sports' are often used interchangeably to describe analyses of the historical dimensions of particular human practices. However, they reveal two different foci and two different pasts. They also share a co-mingled present and an uncertain future. The distinctions between the two are not merely semantic. Understanding the peculiarities of sports history and the history of sports is critical to grasping the present condition of the field and to chart paths to a robust future.[9]

The chronicles of sports history and the history of sports reveal two very different lineages. Academic interest in the history of sports dates to the 1917 publication by Frederic L. Paxson of an article entitled 'The Rise of Sport', in what was then the *Mississippi Valley Historical Review*, now re-christened the *Journal of American History*. Paxson was a distinguished disciple of the leading theorist of *fin de siècle* American history, the frontier thesis-spouting Frederick Jackson Turner who codified the idea of American exceptionalism for US academics. Turner made the frontier into the prime mover of every important US social institution and, bewilderingly, at the very same moment pronounced the American frontier as extinct. Turner's students made careers out of announcing that they had discovered 'new frontiers' to reanimate American civilization. Paxson famously discovered in sport a new frontier to keep America 'young', conveniently ignoring that modern sport had been born in 'old' Europe. Paxson's parochial grasp of world, or at least Western, history aside, he does deserve recognition for identifying sport as a major agent of American social change. Paxson credited sport with sparking the era of progressive reform in government and business, with making Americans more temperate in their consumption of alcohol, more committed to the quest for 'equal rights for all', and even with the 'real emancipation' of women. Sport, Paxson grandly concluded, would 'inspire a new Americanism for a new century'.[10]

Setting aside, for the moment, the credibility of Paxson's extravagant claims for sport as a progressive agent of social change, Paxson is the first professional American historian to make the study of sport essential to the understanding of American history. He proclaimed that 'no one can probe national character, personal conduct, public opinion' nor any other important dimension of modern American civilization without taking into account the 'rise of sport'.[11]

Academic historians, with few exceptions, promptly ignored Paxson's clarion call for the study of sport for the next 60 years. Among the handful who heard Paxson's pre-Jamesian chant about sport as the key to interpreting cultures was a quartet of scholars trained at Columbia University, one of the nation's leading academic factories for producing historians during the 20th century. As a young scholar, John Allen Krout published in 1929 his *Annals of American Sport*. Krout went on to churn out numerous volumes on American political and diplomatic history. Shortly after Krout's history of sports appeared, his fellow Columbia schoolmate Jennie Holliman followed the lead of Paxson and put the frontier thesis at the centre of her 1931 volume, *American Sports, 1785–1835*, a work that pushed back the history of sport chronology from the post-Civil War industrial and urban expansion era to the earliest days of the American republic.[12]

Holliman's book began as her doctoral thesis, as did the next history of American sport crafted by another Columbia-trained historian. Foster Rhea Dulles sought to confirm Paxson's and Holliman's claims about the links between sport, the frontier and American exceptionalism in his dissertation, which was published in 1940 as *America Learns to Play*. Dulles, who came from a politically well-connected family (during the Administration of President Dwight David Eisenhower his brother was a director of the Central Intelligence Agency and his cousin served as Secretary of State), quickly left the history of sports and enjoyed a long and distinguished career as a historian of American foreign policy, who also helped found the contemporary field of labour history.[13]

In 1951 Columbia graduate student John Rickards Betts followed Holliman and Dulles in choosing American sports as a history dissertation topic. Though he did publish some journal articles on the subject during his career in the professoriate, the book version of his thesis, *America's Sporting Heritage, 1850–1950*, did not appear until 1974, three years after his death in 1971.[14] Betts, along with Krout, Holliman and Dulles, did pioneering work on the history of American sports at one of the most prestigious graduate history programmes in the USA, but they earned little acclaim for the forays into athletics in American life. Although they all published their work, they made their names in political, diplomatic and social history – not in the history of sports. Through the early 1960s, only two other scholars who earned doctorates in history departments followed the Columbia 'school' into the realm of sport. Significantly, both Harold Seymour and David Quentin Voigt produced dissertations and books on baseball – a venue that has served as the most prominent arena for popular sports histories as well.[15] No one else followed their lead and developed sport as a field under the broad umbrella of American history until their work had passed into oblivion.

Not until the 1970s did scholars in history or related departments such as American studies produce explorations of sport in substantial numbers. When they did, they harkened back to Paxson's grand claims about the power of sport in reforming American life, as they explained to their colleagues in the plaintive apologia introducing their sporting tomes why they were studying matters most members of their profession dismissed as trivial and career-killing topics. From the 'founders' of the new American history of sports such as Allen Guttmann, Jules Tygiel, Randy Roberts, Steven Riess, Richard Crepeau, Benjamin Rader and Elliott Gorn in the 1970s and the 1980s, to their intellectual progeny who sprouted in the last decade of the 20th century and the early years of the 21st century, sermons decrying the neglect of sport and thundering its far-reaching significance tempered by mournful pleas not to banish historians of sports from the temple of academic history were required introductions to the burgeoning numbers of volumes produced.[16]

Meanwhile, in a very different realm, the field of sports history evolved. Indeed, academic sports history predates the history of sports. More than 30 years before Frederic Paxson discovered sports in American history, one of the founders of the academic discipline of human movement studies, Edward M. Hartwell, published a pioneering historical volume entitled *Physical Education in American Colleges and Universities* (1886).[17] Hartwell held an MD and a PhD in physiology. He developed a seminal programme in the study of human movement at Johns Hopkins University and later supervised physical education for the Boston public school system.[18] In 1885, a year before he published his original history of physical education in the USA, he helped to found the American Association for the Advancement of Physical Education (AAAPE).[19] The physical educators organized just a year after the founding of the American Historical Association (AHA).[20] The two professional clans sprang to life in the great age of rationalizing, bureaucratizing and nationalizing 'knowledge work' in American culture. The AAAPE and the AHA sought, with their fellow guilds, to control their domains, win the favour of governments and the public, and convince the nation that they could foster progress and increase the general welfare.[21]

Hartwell, a sport, or more accurately, a physical education historian, understood how this new game worked. Hartwell's history had a concrete and clear political purpose. He used his histories to promote his field and garner public and governmental support. He employed the history of American fitness to proclaim that the nation had neglected the scientific study and rational education of the body. That negligence, he warned, put the republic in peril.[22] His essays identified the failure to build institutions to train American bodies as a long-standing social problem. He wrote his histories to win public support for physical education, to carve out a place in school curricula for the field, and to win government support for training the body. In the social construction of the new knowledge domain of physical education, Hartwell and his followers used history to justify the need for a 'scientific' approach to the problems of building a fitter, healthier nation.[23]

Hartwell's histories reveal much about the social construction of knowledge in the new science of human movement. These works championed the importance of physical vigour in human societies, claimed places for physical education in school and college curricula and urged public support of physical education programmes. By connecting physical education and sport to the histories of other 'model' societies, especially to ancient Greece, these annals conferred legitimacy on modern practices.[24] Borrowing voraciously, if not always accurately, from Greek antiquity, physical educators have invariably linked physical fitness to social and moral wellbeing.[25] In this effort, dubbed in the 1920s as the 'new physical education', history has always played a prominent role.[26]

Sports and physical education histories also served as a basic component in the training of teachers – a common practice in American pedagogy training programmes. The histories generated by physical educators detailed the origins and development of the basic canon, the fundamental research methods and problems, and the reigning paradigms in the new field.[27] Institutional histories of early physical education, sport and recreation programmes also served to foster a sense of pride and place for students of the new discipline.[28] Like the scholars trained in history departments, some of the sports historians produced during the mid-20th century sweeping epics charting the growth of American sport, most prominently Frederick W. Cozens and Florence Scovil Stumpf's *Sports in American Life* (1953).[29]

Sport in American Life measured up to the handful of contemporary works produced during the middle of the 20th century by academic historians such as Krout, Holliman and Dulles. Much of the rest of the work produced in the physical education domain, however, was rather pedestrian. As the historian of sports S.W. Pope has observed, 'most of the academic interest in the subject inhered in physical education departments, whose practitioners' lackluster efforts failed to attract the attention of historians, American studies scholars, or social scientists'.[30] A survey of the leading research journal in physical education, the *Research Quarterly*, confirms Pope's contention. From the 1940s through the early 1960s *Research Quarterly* published mainly uncritical histories that generally advocated rather the analysed the role of sport in American culture, many of which were narrative chronicles of the development of the field of human movement studies.[31] In fairness, if the physical educators offered rather shallow studies, the historians generally did not even bother to explore sport, a lapse Pope has also chronicled.[32]

One exception, however, to the lack of methodological sophistication and analytical rigour was in the adoption of anthropological theories by Florence Stumpf and Frederick Cozens to conduct cross-cultural historical studies,[33] an innovation that predated the later fascination of American historians of sports with anthropology, especially with the ideas of Clifford Geertz.[34] Another exception occurred in the segregated shadows of American higher education, at Howard University in Washington, DC, where the pioneering African-American physical educator Edward Bancroft Henderson was producing as early as 1939 important but ignored work on race and American sport – a topic that would after the 1970s become one of the most important domains in the field.[35]

In an ironic twist, the physical educators also presaged the later postmodern command for politically-engaged scholarship. They produced a host of advocacy histories during World War II and the Cold War that promoted their field as the key to national vigour under martial conditions. The wars produced a popular demand for healthy bodies to combat the nation's enemies. School and college sports and physical education programmes became battlegrounds in new campaigns for military preparedness. Fears that American schools did not properly cultivate the body led to new physical education requirements and new certification rules for teachers. More federal and state money flowed into physical education programmes.[36] Histories of the social impact of war, the military necessity of physical education, the role of sport in martial prowess, and wartime changes in the nation's educational system appeared regularly.[37]

Sports history underwent a paradigm revolution during the 1960s and 1970s, a shift that actually preceded, albeit slightly, the revolution that would transform the history of sports in the more traditional homelands of historical research. Rarely had the histories written by physical educators that appeared in the pages of *Research Quarterly* from 1930 to 1960 been informed by the methods, themes, concerns and questions of mainstream professional history. While historians of sports such as Betts, Seymour and Voigt worked in exile from the margins of the mother discipline, the impetus for a much more rigorous scholarship developed in the realm of exercise and sport science. These changes sprang from both internal and external pressures. Within the study of human movement a call for more attention to history produced new organizational structures. Seward Staley, a leading physical educator at the University of Illinois, had argued since the 1930s that history should be central to the training of teachers and scholars in human movement studies.[38] In the early 1960s Staley and his students pushed the College Physical Education Association to recognize a 'History of Sport' section. At the same time, from outside of the field, came a direct challenge to the rigour and validity of studies of human movement. In 1963 James Conant, the president of Harvard University, lambasted physical education as unworthy of academic recognition. Conant's dismissal of the field led to a major reformation of physical education.[39]

With greater organizational support within the field but under attack for a lack of intellectual rigour from without, a new group of scholars began to publish sports histories that were clearly informed by the methodologies and philosophies of traditional historical research. While the older, relatively narrow biographies of founders, chronicles of recreations, or studies of institutions still appeared,[40] the *Research Quarterly* began to publish a new style of history that drew from the strength and breadth of mainstream history. The sports histories crafted during the 1960s by Marvin Eyler and his students, all of whom were trained in physical education departments,[41] revealed greater familiarity with trends and controversies in academic history.[42] Sports history, as practised by physical educators, began to relocate itself in the scholarship of mainstream history.

The move toward mainstream history was in part a direct response to President Conant's attack on the academic quality of physical education research. It was also part of a conscious effort to invigorate sport and physical education scholarship by looking toward mainstream history for new techniques and ideas. The effort to reach out actually began before Harvard's chief executive even issued his challenge to the legitimacy of physical education.[43] The outreach effort enjoyed felicitous timing. As scholars in physical education departments began to look more closely at history departments, American history itself was transformed by new ideologies and practices that pushed historians toward more thorough explorations of the social practices and cultural traditions of the masses. In that climate sport came suddenly into view as a legitimate and fruitful subject of historical contemplation.[44]

This 'new social history', as it was labelled, opened the floodgates for academics with PhDs in history to study sport. Finding a small but determined group of like-minded scholars in exercise and sport science departments, an unlikely but still flourishing marriage was consummated between the historians and the physical educators with the creation of the North American Society for Sport History (NASSH), founded in 1973, and its academic voice, the *Journal of Sport History* (*JSH*), inaugurated in 1974. The emergence of NASSH and the *JSH*, originally created by physical educators who welcomed curious historians with open arms, heralded the beginning of a boom of both sports history and the history of sports. The number of publication outlets among publishers of books and refereed journals has expanded astronomically since the 1970s.[45]

During the 1970s scholars began to argue that sport could reveal the essential structures of American society. Sport, they argued, clearly belonged to the common folk, the formerly unheralded and unknown masses who had made American civilization and whom the new social historians were dedicated to bringing to the centre of historical analyses. Sport brought to light racial dynamics, ethnic conflicts and religious differences. Sport showcased the fault lines of class and gender. Sport betrayed fundamental beliefs about social justice and cultural equity. Sport had deep connections to politics and economics. Indeed, they insisted, sport not only reflected social patterns but had the capacity to reinforce or transform them. Sport could function as an agent of social resistance or a tool for social coercion.

The new scholarly fascination with sport grew out of the intellectual ferment that produced the new social history, particularly from the *Annales* school in Continental Europe and the British neo-Marxist tradition, as well as from the influences of the comprehensive sociologies and philosophies of a diverse group of thinkers that stretched from Max Weber and Thomas Kuhn, to Norbert Elias and Michel Foucault.[46]

Particularly critical to the development of this new wave of sport scholarship were the works of a West Indian historian and an American anthropologist. Some of these new historians of sports and sports historians gravitated to C.L.R. James's autobiographical reflections on the meaning of sport in his life and in the cultural and social structures of the British imperial universe.[47] Originally published in 1963 by an obscure West Indian press, the book migrated to American shores and found a major US publisher in 1983.[48] James read through sport the complexities of West Indian history and social relations, from race and slavery to civil rights and black nationalism, from colonial mentalities and cultural assimilation to political liberation and postcolonial commemoration. In 1973, a decade after James's crucial interpretation appeared, the anthropologist Clifford Geertz published his ground-breaking essay about reading cultures through their sporting practices. Geertz's work complemented and amplified James's theories.[49]

Cross-pollinated by the field-shaping emergence of NASSH, both American historians of sports and American sports historians began in the 1970s to follow the trails blazed by James and Geertz and to borrow the tools developed by the new social history. In that process they revolutionized the academic study of sport in American society. A trickle of early works presaged a torrent that flooded the field after the appearance of Allen Guttmann's enormously influential *From Ritual to Record* (1978).[50] Emboldened by the development of the new social history, sports historians and historians of sport produced a legion of ground-breaking studies in the decade between 1978 and 1988. That period was book-ended by two landmark works by Guttmann. The aforementioned *From Ritual to Record* made modernization the reigning paradigm in the field. His lesser-recognized *A Whole New Ball Game* provided a Geertzian reading of sporting 'texts' in American culture.[51] Following Guttmann's lead, scholars from history, American studies and human movement studies backgrounds churned out between 1978 and 1988 volume after volume that 'read' sport as a text that revealed the basic parameters of American civilization.[52]

Those readings frequently occurred at NASSH meetings and established profitable connections between historians of sport and sports historians, blurring the historic distinctions between the two traditions.[53] The organization founded by sports historians opened its arms to historians of sport. NASSH united, at least temporarily in once-a-year professor-fests, faculty from physical education and kinesiology programmes with scholars from traditional history departments, as well as researchers from other domains such as American studies, sociology, anthropology, philosophy and even the curious new realm of 'sport studies'. NASSH created a commonwealth in which the historians of sport and the sports historians shared methods and theories, monographs and journals. Sports historians trained in kinesiology and exercise science departments since the 1970s have, as one of their leading scholars, David K. Wiggins revealed, increasingly taken large numbers of graduate courses in history, building a common educational background between the two tribes and forging a close alliance between them on both theoretical and practical issues.[54]

From the late 1970s through the 2000s, historians of sport and sports historians alike tackled the major themes set out by the new social history, especially race, ethnicity, gender and class. Following the lead of C.L.R. James and trends in mainstream American history, scholars found the racial dynamics of American civilization an especially fertile ground. *Baseball's Great Experiment*, Jules Tygiel's splendid history of the integration of professional baseball and American society, perhaps the best book ever written in the field, provided a lighthouse that drew a host of scholars to the complex shoreline of sport and race in American society.[55] Most of these studies have focused on African-American experiences and challenges on American playing fields, charting the parameters of segregation and the long struggle for integration, offering biographies of both famous and obscure black athletes, and seeking to amplify the histories of the 'American dilemma' in the national chronicles.[56]

Other racial groups have also provided rich subject material for American sport scholars, especially Native Americans and Hispanics.[57] European ethnicity, immigration and social class have been equal to race in recent American sporting sagas. A host of excellent works have analysed the role of sport in assimilation and resistance, the power of sport in the promotion of particular class ideologies and construction of alternative social spaces, and in the dynamics of sport in the emerging modern mass society produced by the industrial and urban revolutions.[58] In these many volumes the works of Stephen Riess, Randy Roberts, Stephen Hardy, Melvin Adelman and Elliott Gorn stand out.[59]

Religion, as well as ethnicity and social class, has provided sylvan territory for historical interpretations of the social and cultural dynamics of American sport.[60] In a move beyond the cultural and social boundaries that James charted, the new American studies of sport have also focused extensively on gender. Numerous studies have chronicled how sport has both reinforced and transcended gender stereotypes, examined the pervasive patterns of gender discrimination in modern sports, and uncovered the stories of pioneering women athletes.[61]

The sporting analyses of race, ethnicity, religion, class and gender uncovered the social dynamism of American culture in much the same fashion that James's reminiscences about choosing a cricket club in his native Trinidad revealed the social fabric of West Indian culture. American scholars borrowed more than just an insightful sensitivity to the racial and social boundaries that sport generated from James. They have also shared James's fascination with the ways in which sport could reveal and build local, national and even international cultures, those complex webs of ideas and institutions that knit together modern communities, modern nations and the modern globe. James understood that the culture-producing and community-forging power of sport worked through the modern mass media, that newspaper articles and books as well as radio broadcasts and television programmes made the most popular dramatic art of the age of the common folk.[62]

Indeed, James's ideas fit neatly with Clifford Geertz's notion of using sport as a 'text' for reading cultural patterns. In tandem, these ideas have had a great influence on the field, especially when combined with considerations of the role of the media in enhancing these cultural productions and reproductions. The prominent cultural historian Warren I. Susman produced some crucial early work on sport and national culture.[63] American historians of sport and sports historians have begun to follow James, Geertz and Susman in exploring how sports and the media have shaped local, regional and national cultures in the USA. One of the leaders in this area, Michael Oriard, has through several volumes on American football and American sports literature considerably broadened the horizons of the discipline.[64]

Several others have followed in Oriard's wake in seeking to unravel sport's role in the making of American national culture. Sport and nationalism have been a special focus of works by Donald Mrozek, S.W. Pope, Wanda Wakefield and Mark Dyreson.[65] In a path-breaking move away from the standard focus on the nation, Pamela Grundy has offered an insightful history of sport in shaping regional identity in her history of basketball, race, class and gender in North Carolina.[66] From another vantage point, the political theorist Robert Putnam has raised questions about the role of sport in producing 'social capital', the glue that he and others identify as the binding force in modern democratic societies such as the USA.[67] The studies on sport and American regional and national identities have been enhanced by a slew of good works on the role of the media – print, radio and television – in staging sporting spectacles for the masses and circulating the social capital of sport through every nook and cranny of American society.[68]

Scholars have also sought to put American regional and national sporting cultures into a global perspective by concentrating on international competitions with a strong US presence and by exploring efforts to export American culture through sport to global markets.[69] This development has marked the return of foreign policy historians to the subject of sport, a turn that Foster Rhea Dulles made in the 1940s.[70] In framing American sport in a global perspective, American historians are following the lead of James, who devoted significant sections of *Beyond a Boundary* to analysing the role of cricket in the history of the British Empire. James viewed cricket as the national pastime for the Empire's many national units, and insisted that national pastimes provided crucial clues for understanding national narratives. American historians have followed that lead as well, focusing on the American national pastime – baseball, in most reckonings – and on its many rivals for national passion in the USA.[71]

While historians of sport and sports historians have over the last three decades made remarkable strides, certain areas of American have been neglected. Relatively little work has been done on sport during the Cold War or the cultural tumults of the 1960s, though David Zang's *SportsWars* stands as notable exception to this trend.[72] The 'built environments' of American sport, stadiums, gymnasiums and other sporting sites, have also received very little attention.[73] The devotion to modernization and urbanization in American sporting sagas has produced, unsurprisingly, a general neglect of rural and traditional topics.[74] Finally, though hundreds of books devoted to American sports have appeared since 1970s, only Nancy Struna in her superb study *People of Prowess* has followed the route Jennie Holiman blazed in the 1930s and pushed back the chronology of American sport into the 17th and 18th centuries.[75]

While certain gaps in the literature remain in both sports history and in the history of sport, the climate for research has never been more favourable. University presses in the USA have started 'sport and society' lists grounded in historical approaches.[76] The number of journals devoted to sports history and to the history of sport have multiplied, while more general historical journals routinely publish sport-related articles.[77] The avalanche of new publications has spurred the development of new courses devoted to the history of American sport. Solid textbooks have sprung up to serve the new market.[78] Several anthologies have sprouted to supplement the texts.[79]

Indeed, one sign of the robust health of historical scholarship in sport has been the emergence since the mid-1990s of a robust debate on the need for new paradigms and new methodologies.[80] While some of these calls have taken on the alarmist tones of academic prophets, in sum they represent, not the end of sports history, nor the demise of the history of sport, but the maturation of the two fields. As early as 1990 Stephen Hardy argued that scholars needed to reconsider how they analysed time, memory and meaning in their endeavours.[81] While few scholars have followed Hardy's initial clarion, his ideas and those of others who have advocated new paradigms has begun to yield some very interesting fruit, including new perspectives of sport as a key tool in crafting collective memory – a major theme in the development of mainstream history as well.[82] Daniel A. Nathan's fascinating history of the shifting memories of baseball's 'Black Sox' scandal over the course of the 20th-century, *Saying It's So*, offers new vistas to those who seek fresh approaches.[83]

A close reading of Nathan's work reveals along with much that is fresh a continuing influence of the ideas of James and Geertz as well as a continuing debt to the new social and new cultural histories born decades earlier on the domain of sport. While new paradigms promise new insights, the older paradigms are hardly exhausted. The current state of American historical scholarship on sport seems healthier than it has ever been – and certainly far more vigorous than it was for the first three-quarters of the 20th century.

Still, just below the surface of this beneficent environment lurk some troubling signs. History departments have not yet begun to hire faculty for 'history of sport' positions, nor does it appear that they are moving in that direction.[84] Kinesiology, exercise science and physical education departments have, for a variety of reasons, not been as friendly in the last decade to those who investigate the history of sport and related social and cultural approaches to the study of human movement.[85] Both the history of American sport and American sports history face significant challenges.

These obstacles will in all probability produce a schism between the two provinces. For the last 40 years sports history and the history of sport have seemed indistinguishable. In fact, some of the differences between these two domains are now merely semantic, representing pride in ties to graduate training or to particular patches of academic turf. Since the 1970s, sports history and the history of sport have adopted the same methodologies, subjects, sources, tools, audiences and even canons. The contemporary divergence between the two domains resides in how they perceive their contributions to the larger academic discourses that swirl through expert and lay communities. Ultimately, the differences in ends rather than means will lead to some separation between the history of sport and sports history, breaking the seemingly seamless merger between the two that now exists.

Historians of sport seek to explain how American sport illuminates larger issues in the nation's development, from the nature and practice of political and social reform to the role of class, race and gender in shaping culture. Sports historians, on the other hand, are in some ways commanded to do the opposite. Their particular audience is far more interested in the nature of sport and other forms of physical activity in human societies than they are in the particularities of historical experience. They are neither familiar with, nor interested in the nuances of particular historiographies. For instance, the students and colleagues to whom sports historians write are little engaged with complexities of the Progressive Era in American history, though they are keenly interested in the 1891 invention of basketball. In contrast, the students and colleagues to whom historians of sport speak possess an inverted perspective, eager to speculate on how the invention of basketball illumines the patterns of progressivism.[86]

For historians of sport, history itself is the contextual shroud with which they seek to envelop their enterprises. Their work flows out of the broader intellectual projects of the historical profession and seeks to return home to animate and amplify scholarship in history. Sports historians serve different interests. Human movement rather than history represents their home turf. They must connect with different paradigms and different audiences.

Semantic differences litter this divide, but the divergence is not merely semantic.[87] Not only the term 'history' but the name 'sport' represented contested areas in these arenas. In fact, in human movement studies departments sport has fallen from favour while the broad but obtuse concept of physical activity has taken hold. Sports history faces pressure to broaden its views to incorporate this shift away from sport in order to connect to students and colleagues in the many disciplines that find homes in such departments, from exercise physiology to sport psychology to biomechanics to motor control. In such a climate, a much greater grasp of the histories of science, medicine and the body will become crucial. Under the banner of sports history and the history of sport, a literature on the subject has already begun to develop.[88] Much, though certainly not all, of the best work in this nascent area of 'physical activity' history focused on bodies, science and health has been done by scholars with training in and connections to kinesiology departments, especially Jack Berryman and Roberta J. Park.[89]

Historians of sport, on the other hand, will likely find the history of physical activity too vague for their sentiments. Additionally, the history of medicine and the history of science represent well-established sub-disciplines in mainstream historical studies that generally have not been connected to the history of sport. These arrangements may well lead sports historians away from sport and toward new partners in the mother discipline. If the meeting ground provided by sport erodes over the next few decades sports history may well became a semantic misnomer. Certainly historians in human movement science departments are already feeling the pressure to de-emphasize sport.[90]

Sport, though, shows no signs of fading quickly from the scene in spite of the hopes of certain American kinesiologists. Sport remains a fascinating topic for both academics and the public. The insights of C.L.R. James remain powerful in American considerations of the role of sport in their civilization. Consider the essay in *Sports Illustrated* by Alexandar Wolff, 'The Audacity of Hoops', which credits the 2008 election of Barack Obama to the presidency of the USA to the candidate's long love-affair with playing basketball.[91] Wolff's vision of Obama's immersion in high school basketball and then in pick-up hoops as the catalyst for propelling the new president into a historic role as the leader in a new American journey beyond boundaries profoundly echoes James's vision as Frank Worrell, the first black to captain a West Indian cricket side during the famous 1961 test against Australia, as the embodiment of the promise of a multi-racial West Indian democracy. While Wolff did not actually revise James's famous opening riddle, the *Sports Illustrated* scribe might as well have asked the Americans: 'What do they know of basketball, who only basketball know?' Wolff's answer, like James's response in *Beyond a Boundary*, is that those who only know basketball but do not grasp its power in the greater world beyond the court know little of value. Wolff asserts that the idea of sport has profoundly transformed American history.[92] Obama and basketball, Wolff argues, have made possible, to cite the words of the original historian of American sport, Frederick Paxson, 'a new Americanism for a new century'. For the past century American historians of sport and sports historians have been asserting such claims. Certainly that trend will continue for the next century.

Notes

1 C.L.R. James, *Beyond a Boundary* (Durham, NC: Duke University Press, 1993 [1963]), 184–85. [Editors' note: Both editors confess to having read the book and agree that more American sports historians should too].

2 The Ronald A. Smith Collection at Pennsvylania State University's library contains 2,890 titles, and it is not the sole location of sports history books, as thousands more inhabit the general stacks under a variety of call numbers, but especially in the GV section of the Library of Congress cataloguing system, cat.libraries.psu.edu/uhtbin/cgisirsi/TMmgG7CWCU/UP-PAT/94290319/123 (accessed 10 January 2009).

3 Indeed, in online search catalogues 'Baseball/History' is its own separate section, with hundreds of listings, www.allbookstores.com/Sports_and_Recreation.html (accessed 10 January 2009). *Sports Illustrated* produced a list of the one hundred leading sports books of all time: Pete McEntgart, L. Jon Wertheim, Gene Menez and Mark Bechtel, 'The Top 100 Sports Books of All Time', *Sports Illustrated* (16 December 2002), 85–95.

4 *Hoop Dreams* (Fineline Pictures, 1994); *Seabiscuit* (Universal Pictures, 2003); *Cinderella Man* (Universal Pictures, 2005); *Unforgivable Blackness: The Rise and Fall of Jack Johnson* (WETA, 2005); *Glory Road* (Buena Vista, 2006).

5 James Dixon, 'The Death of the Sports Movie', *Texas Monthly* 32 (January 2009), 45–8.

6 James, *Beyond a Boundary*, 184–85.

7 Standard interpretations of American historiography see the rise of the 'new social history' as a revolutionary event. See, for instance, Eric Foner, *Who Owns History?: Rethinking the Past in a Changing World* (New York: Hill and Wang, 2002).

8 Hebert Warren Wind, *The Story of American Golf, Its Champions and Its Championships* (New York: Farrar, Straus, 1948); *Horse Feathers* (Paramount, 1932); David Maraniss, *When Pride Still Mattered: A Life of Vince Lombardi* (New York: Simon & Schuster, 1999); *Remember the Titans* (Walt Disney Pictures, 2000).

9 As the historiographer Douglas Booth has uncovered in his explorations of this subject, some scholars have in fact argued for a focus on 'sports history' rather than on the 'history of sports'. Booth identifies historian Stephen Hardy, sociologist Maurice Roche and philosopher William Morgan as promoters of the notion that sports histories should engage and illuminate sports contexts rather than relentlessly seeking broader connections to other forms of histories. Douglas Booth, *The Field: Truth and Fiction in Sport History* (London: Routledge, 2006), 184–85. See also, Stephen Hardy, 'Entrepreneurs, Organizations, and the Sport Marketplace: Subjects in Search of Historians', *Journal of Sport History* 13 (spring 1996), 14–33; Jack Berryman, 'Sport History as Social History', *Quest* 20 (June 1973), 65–72; Maurice Roche, *Mega-Events and Modernity: Olympics and Expos in the Growth of Global Culture* (London: Routledge, 2000); William J. Morgan, *Leftist Theories of Sport: A Critique and Reconstruction* (Urbana: University of Illinois Press, 1994).

10 Frederic L. Paxson, 'The Rise of Sport', *Mississippi Valley Historical Review* 4 (September 1917), 143–68; quotation from 168.

11 Ibid., 167.

12 John Allen Krout, *Annals of American Sport* (New Haven, CT: Yale University Press, 1929); Jennie Holliman, *American Sports, 1785–1835* (Durham, NC: Seeman, 1931). American Sports began as Holliman's PhD dissertation at Columbia. Krout wrote a Columbia dissertation on the crusade against alcohol in the USA, published in book form as *The Origins of Prohibition* (New York: A.A. Knopf, 1925). Krout then turned from social and cultural topics to become a major figure in American political history and foreign policy, publishing more than 50 books. His extensive bibliography can be found on WorldCat: www.worldcat.org/search?q=John+A.+Krout&fq=ap%3A%22krout%2C+john+allen%22&se = yr&sd = desc&start = 11&qt = next_page (accessed 10 January 2009).

13 Foster Rhea Dulles, *America Learns to Play: A History of Popular Recreation, 1607–1940* (New York: D. Appleton-Century, 1940). Dulles wrote *America Learns to Play* as his Columbia dissertation, which he completed in 1940. Among his many important works published both before and after he earned his doctorate, are *The Old China Trade* (Boston: Houghton Mifflin, 1930); *Eastward Ho!: The First English Adventures to the Orient* (Boston: Houghton Mifflin, 1931); *America in the Pacific: A Century of Expansion* (Boston: Houghton Mifflin, 1932); *Lowered Boats: A Chronicle of American Whaling* (New York, Harcourt, Brace, 1933); *Forty Years of American-Japanese Relations* (New York: D. Appleton-Century, 1937); *The Road to Teheran: The Story of Russia and America, 1781–1943* (Princeton, NJ: Princeton University Press, 1944); *Twentieth Century America* (Boston: Houghton Mifflin, 1945); *China and America: The Story of Their Relations since 1784* (Princeton, NJ: Princeton University Press, 1946); *Labor in America: A History* (New York: Crowell, 1949); *The American Red Cross: A History* (New York: Harper, 1950); *America's Rise to World Power, 1898–1954* (New York, Harper, 1955); *The Imperial Years* (New York: Crowell, 1956); *The United States since 1865* (Ann Arbor: University of Michigan Press, 1959); *Yankees and Samurai: America's Role in the Emergence of Modern Japan, 1791–1900* (New York: Harper & Row, 1965); *Prelude to World Power: American Diplomatic History, 1860–1900* (New York: Macmillan, 1965); *Labor in America: A History* (New York: Crowell, 1966); *American Policy Toward Communist China, 1949–1969* (New York: Crowell, 1972).

14 Betts's 1951 dissertation, written for Columbia University's history department, 'Organized Sports in Industrial America', did not appear in book form until the 1970s. John Rickards Betts, *America's Sporting Heritage, 1850–1950* (Reading, MA: Addison-Wesley, 1974). Betts wrote several articles in major historical journals, including: 'Sporting Journalism in Nineteenth-Century America', *American Quarterly* 5 (Spring 1953), 39–56; 'Agricultural Fairs and the Rise of Harness Racing', *Agricultural History* 27 (April 1953), 71–75; 'The Technological Revolution and the Rise of Sport, 1850–1950', *Mississippi Valley Historical Review* 40 (September 1953), 231–56; 'Mind and Body in Early American Thought', *Journal of American History* 54 (March 1968), 787–805; 'American Medical Thought on Exercise as the Road to Health, 1820–1860', *Bulletin of the History of Medicine* 45 (1971).

15 Harold Seymour, 'The Rise of Major League Baseball to 1891', Thesis (PhD), Cornell University, 1956; Harold Seymour, *Baseball: The Early Years* (New York: Oxford University Press, 1960);

David Quentin Voigt, 'Cash and Glory: The Commercialization of Major League Baseball as a Sports Spectacular, 1865–1892', Thesis (PhD), Syracuse University, 1962; David Quentin Voigt, *Baseball: From Gentlemen's Sport to the Comissioner System* (Norman: University of Oklahoma Press, 1966).

16 My own overly-grand lamentation is typical: 'Still, even though sport has become the most important institution through which many Americans deliberate political, racial, ethical, and social questions, scholars too rarely take sport seriously', I wail on the very first page of my own intro-duction. 'That failure to consider sport seriously has hampered historical understandings of the United States, for the grand experiment in forging a working republic in the nation has become permeated with the cultural practices of modern athletics in myriad ways: politicians persistently frame their messages in athletic rhetoric; African-American Olympians protest their exclusion from republican promises with black-gloved protests against racism; judges hear frequent cases about the constitutional rights of athletes, teams, and sporting leagues; and Olympic basketball and hockey contests serve as defining moments in American foreign policy'. Mark Dyreson, *Making the American Team: Sport, Culture and the Olympic Experience* (Urbana: University of Illinois Press, 1998), 1.

17 Edward M. Hartwell, *Physical Training in American Colleges and Universities*, Circulars of Information of the Bureau of Education, No. 5, 1885 (Washington: Government Printing Office, 1886).

18 Roberta J. Park, 'The *Research Quarterly* and Its Antecedents', *Research Quarterly of Exercise and Sport Science* 51 (March 1980), 1–22; Nancy Struna, 'Sport History', in John D. Massengale and Richard A. Swanson, eds, *The History of Exercise and Sport Science* (Champaign, IL: Human Kinetics, 1997), 143–79. See also, Melvin Adelman, 'Academicians and American Athletics: A Decade of Progress', *Journal of Sport History* 10 (Spring 1983), 80–106; Roberta J. Park, 'Research and Scholarship in the History of Physical Education and Sport: The Current State of Affairs', *Research Quarterly of Exercise and Sport Science* 54 (June 1983), 93–103; Steven A. Riess, 'The New Sport History', *Reviews in American History* 18 (September 1990), 311–25; S.W. Pope, 'American Sport History – Toward a New Paradigm', in S.W. Pope, ed., *The New American Sport History: Recent Approaches and Perspectives* (Urbana: University of Illinois Press, 1997), 1–30.

19 Originally the Association for the Advancement of Physical Education, the society renamed itself the American Association for the Advancement of Physical Education in 1886. The organization has gone through seven name changes: Association for the Advancement of Physical Education (1885); American Association for the Advancement of Physical Education (1886–1902); American Physical Education Association (1903–37); American Association for Health and Physical Education (1937–38); American Association for Health, Physical Education and Recreation (1938–74); American Alliance for Health, Physical Education, and Recreation (1974–79); American Alliance for Health, Physical Education, Recreation, and Dance (1979 to the present). Park, '*Research Quarterly* and Its Antecedents', 1.

20 Wendy Gamber, Michael Grossberg and Hendrik Hartog, eds, *American Public Life and the Historical Imagination* (Notre Dame, IN: University of Notre Dame Press, 2003).

21 Robert H. Wiebe, *The Search for Order, 1877–1920* (New York: Hill and Wang, 1967); Burton J. Bledstein, *The Culture of Professionalism: The Middle Class and the Development of Higher Education in America* (New York: Norton, 1976); Paul Starr, *The Social Transformation of American Medicine* (New York: Basic Books, 1982); John R. Thelin, *A History of American Higher Education* (Baltimore: Johns Hopkins University Press, 2004).

22 See, for instance, Edward M. Hartwell, 'The Conditions and Prospects of Physical Education in the United States', *Proceedings of the American Association for the Advancement of Physical Education* (1892), 13–40.

23 On the history of sports and physical education as tools for building a healthy American republic see Melvin Adelman, *A Sporting Time: New York City and the Rise of Modern Athletics, 1820–1870* (Urbana: University of Illinois Press, 1978); George B. Kirsch, *The Creation of American Team Sports: Baseball and Cricket, 1838–1872* (Urbana: University of Illinois Press, 1979); Peter Levine, 'The Promise of Sport in Antebellum America', *Journal of American Culture* 2 (Winter 1980), 623–34; Dominick Cavallo, *Muscles and Morals: Organized Playgrounds and Urban Reform, 1880–1920* (Philadelphia: University of Pennsylvania Press, 1981); Stephen Hardy, *How Boston Played: Sport, Recreation and Community, 1865–1915* (Boston: Northeastern University Press, 1982); Donald Mrozek, *Sport and American Mentality, 1880–1910* (Knoxville: University of Tennessee Press, 1983); Roy Rosenzweig, *Eight Hours for What We Will: Workers and Leisure in an Industrial City, 1870–1920* (Cambridge: Cambridge University Press, 1983); Harvey Green, *Fit for America: Health, Fitness, Sport, and*

American Society (New York: Pantheon Books, 1986); Warren Goldstein, *Playing for Keeps: A History of Early Baseball* (Ithaca, NY: Cornell University Press, 1989); Steven A. Riess, *City Games: The Evolution of American Urban Society and the Rise of Sports* (Urbana: University of Illinois Press, 1989); Michael Oriard, *Reading Football: How the Popular Press Created an American Spectacle* (Chapel Hill: University of North Carolina Press, 1993); S.W. Pope, *Patriotic Games: Sport and the American Imagination, 1876–1926* (New York: Oxford University Press, 1997); Dyreson, *Making the American Team*.

24 Richard Hofstader, *The Progressive Historians: Turner, Beard, Parrington* (New York: Knopf, 1968).

25 David C. Young, *The Olympic Myth of Greek Amateur Athletics* (Chicago: Ares, 1984); Donald G. Kyle, *Athletics in Ancient Athens* (Leiden: E. J. Brill, 1987); Mark Golden, *Sport and Society in Ancient Greece* (New York: Cambridge University Press, 1998).

26 The foundational statement of this position can be found in Jesse F. Williams, *The Principles of Physical Education* (Philadelphia: W.B. Saunders, 1927).

27 Thomas S. Kuhn, *The Structure of Scientific Revolutions*, 3rd edn (Chicago: University of Chicago Press, 1996); John V. Pickstone, *Ways of Knowing: A New History of Science, Technology and Medicine* (Chicago: University of Chicago Press, 2001).

28 For a classic example see James G. Thompson, '*Logos Protreptikos*: Building Pride in the Profession', *Canadian Journal of Sport History* 15 (December 1984), 1–4. For the quest for 'unity through diversity' see Park, '*Research Quarterly* and Its Antecedents', 16–21. See also, John D. Massengale and Richard A. Swanson, 'Exercise and Sport Science in 20th-Century America', in Massengale and Swanson, eds, *The History of Exercise and Sport Science*, 1–14.

Following Hartwell's lead, in its first few decades the AAAPE published a smattering of historical studies in the antecedents of the *Research Quarterly* – the *Proceedings of the American Association for the Advancement of Physical Education* (1885–95) and the *American Physical Education Review* (1896–1929). Fred E. Leonard's historical series, which ran in the *American Physical Education Review* from 1899 to 1907, expanded on Hartwell's template: Fred E. Leonard, 'The Period of Philanthropism', *American Physical Education Review* 4 (March 1899), 1–18; 'Jahn's Life Up to Publication of *Die Deutsche Turnkunst* (1816)', *American Physical Education Review* 5 (March 1900), 18–39; 'A Select Bibliography of the History of Physical Training', *American Physical Education Review* 7 (March 1902), 39–48; 'The Beginnings of Modern Physical Training in Europe', *American Physical Education Review* 9 (June 1904), 89–110; 'Friederich Ludwig Jahn and the Development of Popular Gymnastics in Germany', *American Physical Education Review* 10 (March 1905), 1–19; 'The Transition from Medieval to Modern Times', *American Physical Education Review* 10 (September 1905), 189–202; 'The "New Gymnastics" of Dio Lewis', *American Physical Education Review* 11 (June 1906), 83–95, (September 1906), 187–98; 'Chapters from the History of Physical Training in Ancient and Medieval Europe', *American Physical Education Review* 12 (September 1907), 225–40, (December 1907), 289–302. Leonard and his followers produced a small but steady stream of essays chronicling the institutional development of American physical education. Struna, 'Sport History', 150–52.

By the late 1920s, the leadership of the organization, rechristened the American Association of Health, Physical Education, and Recreation (AAHPER), responded to the unceasing battles between various areas of interest in the profession by deciding to split the organization's publications into a more 'applied' periodical dubbed the *Journal of Health and Physical Education* and a more 'theoretical' journal christened the *Research Quarterly of the American Physical Education Association*. History had by then established a foothold, albeit a small one, in the multi-disciplinary study of human movement. History's cubbyhole would survive the schism. Park, '*Research Quarterly* and Its Antecedents', 2–5; George H. Sage, Mark Dyreson and R. Scott Kretchmar, 'Sociology, History, and Philosophy in *The Research Quarterly*', *Research Quarterly of Exercise and Sport Science* (Special 75th Anniversary Issue) 76 (June 2005 Supplement), S88–S107.

29 Frederick W. Cozens and Florence Scovil Stumpf, *Sports in American Life* (Chicago: University of Chicago Press, 1953). Cozens had an interesting career in which he developed both his historical scholarship and a solid reputation in more traditional domains. His other major books included such basic texts as Neils Peter Neilson and Frederick W. Cozens, *Achievement Scales in Physical Activities Education for Boys and Girls in Elementary and Junior High Schools* (New York: A.S. Barnes, 1934); John F. Bovard and Frederick W. Cozens, *Tests and Measurements in Physical Education* (Philadelphia: W.B. Saunders, 1938); Eugene White Nixon and Frederick Warren Cozens, *An Introduction to Physical Education* (Philadelphia: W.B. Saunders, 1941).

30 Pope, 'American Sport History – Toward a New Paradigm', 2–3.

31 See, for instance, Genevieve L. Braun, 'Kinesiology: From Aristotle to the Twentieth Century', *Research Quarterly* 12 (May 1941), 163–75; William Skarstrom, 'Life and Work of Amy Morris Homans: Pioneer and Leader in the Field of Hygiene and Physical Education', *Supplement to the Research Quarterly*, 'University of Iowa Studies in Physical Education', 12 (October 1941), 615–27; Clarence B. van Wyck, 'The Harvard Summer School of Physical Education, 1887–1932', *Research Quarterly* 13 (December 1942), 403–31; Helen M. Barton, 'A Study of the Development Textbooks in Physiology and Hygiene in the United States', *Research Quarterly* 14 (March 1943), 37–45; Ruth White Fink, 'Recreational Pursuits in the Old South', *Research Quarterly* 23 (March 1952), 28–37; Norma D. Young, 'Did Greeks and the Romans Play Football?' *Research Quarterly* 15 (December 1944), 310–16; Bruce L. Bennett, 'Contributions of Dudley A. Sargent to Physical Education', *Research Quarterly* 19 (May 1948), 77–92; Ralph E. Billett, 'Evidence of Play and Exercise in Early Pestalozzian and Lancasterian Elementary Schools in the United States, 1809–1845', *Research Quarterly* 23 (May 1952), 127–35; Franklin M. Henry, 'A Note on Physiological Limits and the History of the Mile Run', *Research Quarterly* 25 (December 1954), 483–84; Paul A. Hunsicker and Richard J. Donnelly, 'Instruments to Measure Strength', *Research Quarterly* 26 (December 1955), 408–20; Adelaide Hunter, 'Contributions of R. Tait McKenzie to Modern Concepts of Physical Education', *Research Quarterly* 30 (May 1959), 160.

32 Pope, 'American Sport History – Toward a New Paradigm', 1–6.

33 These anthropological histories of recreations among the world's few remaining non-modern peoples and reports on the centrality of games in ancient non-Western cultures made the case that the devotion to and the cultivation of sport was a universal human behaviour that bred healthy societies – in much the same manner as the invocations of the ancient Greeks had served. Stumpf and Cozens' work on sports in South Pacific cultures provided new data to support the old contention that sound bodies were necessary for the cultivation of sound minds. Florence Stumpf and Frederick W. Cozens, 'Some Aspects of the Role of Games, Sports, and Recreational Activities in the Culture of Modern Primitive Peoples: The New Zealand Maoris', *Research Quarterly* 18 (October 1947), 198–218; Florence Stumpf and Frederick W. Cozens, 'Some Aspects of the Role of Games, Sports, and Recreational Activities in the Culture of Modern Primitive Peoples: II. The Fijians', *Research Quarterly* 20 (March 1949), 2–20. See also, Helen L. Dunlap, 'Games, Sports, Dancing and Other Vigorous Recreational Activities and Their Function in Samoan Culture', *Research Quarterly* 22 (October 1951), 298–311; William A. Goellner, 'The Court Ball Game of the Aboriginal Mayas', *Research Quarterly* 24 (May 1953), 147–68.

34 In several places in his recent *The Field*, Douglas Booth implies that the theories of Clifford Geertz have not been consistently 'appropriated or applied' in regards to '"Western" sports'. Booth, *The Field*, 161, 199–201. More historians of sports than Booth recognizes have employed Geertz, in greater and lesser doses. I will return to this argument later in the essay.

35 Edwin Bancroft Henderson, *The Negro in Sports* (Washington, DC: Associated Publishers, 1939); *The Black Athlete: Emergence and Arrival* (New York: Publishers Co., 1969). For a fascinating biography of Henderson see also, David Wiggins, 'Edwin Bancroft Henderson, African American Athletes, and the Writing of Sport History', in *Glory Bound: Black Athletes in a White America* (Syracuse, NY: Syracuse University Press, 1997), 221–40.

36 Betty Spears and Richard A. Swanson, *History of Sport and Physical Education in the United States*, 3rd edn (Dubuque, IA: William C. Brown, 1988).

37 Lloyd M. Jones, 'Recent Changes in the Requirement and Conduct of Required Health and Physical Education for Men in Land Grant College and Universities', *Research Quarterly* 13 (October 1942), 364–72; Lawrence Rarick, 'College and University Physical Education Programs After One Year of War', *Research Quarterly* 14 (May 1943), 167–74; Louise S. Cobb and Verne S. Landreth, 'War Emergency Teacher Certification in Physical Education in the United States', *Research Quarterly* 14 (December 1943), 342–55; Ralph H. Johnson, 'Military Athletics at the University of Illinois', *Research Quarterly* 14 (December 1943), 378–84; A. Gwendolyn Drew, 'A History of the Concern of the Federal Government to the Physical Fitness of Non-Age Youth with Reference to the Schools, 1790–1941', 16 (October 1945), 196–205; T. Erwin Blesh, 'An Analysis of Prewar Certification Requirements for Teachers of Health and Physical Education in the 48 States', *Research Quarterly* 18 (March 1947), 54–61; Gladyce H. Bradly, 'The History of School Health Education in West Virginia, 1863–1945', *Research Quarterly* 18 (May 1947), 144–57; Laurence E. Moorehouse and Alex D. Aloia, 'Change in Certification Requirements of Physical Education Teachers in 13 States since 1942', *Research Quarterly* 19 (December 1948), 276–81.

38 Struna, 'Sport History', 152–57.

39 Massengale and Swanson, 'Exercise and Sport Science in 20th-Century America', 1–14; Struna, 'Sport History', 155–58.

40 See, for instance, the unintentionally humourous article, Barbara J. Hoepner, 'The Correct Spelling of Mrs. Beecher's Name: "Catharine" or "Catherine"', *Research Quarterly* 40 (March 1969), 235–36.

41 During the early 1960s his three most important doctoral students were Guy Lewis, John Lucas and Sharon Hale. Struna, 'Sport History', 152–57; Alan Metcalfe, 'Marvin Eyler: A Personal Tribute', *Journal of Sport History* 32 (Spring 2005), 71–5; John A. Lucas, 'Marvin Howard Eyler, A Consummate Educator', *Journal of Sport History* 32 (Spring 2005), 67–70; David K. Wiggins, 'Marvin Eyler and His Students: A Legacy of Scholarship in Sport History, *Journal of Sport History* 32 (Spring 2005), 77–90.

42 Marvin H. Eyler, 'Origins of Contemporary Sports', *Research Quarterly* 32 (December 1961), 480–89; Guy M. Lewis, 'America's First Intercollegiate Sport: The Regattas from 1852 to 1875', *Research Quarterly* 38 (December 1967), 637–48; John A. Lucas, 'Pedestrianism and the Struggle for the Sir John Astley Belt', *Research Quarterly* 39 (October 1968), 587–94; Maxwell L. Howell, 'Seal Stones of the Minoan Period in the Ashmolean Museum, Depicting Physical Activities', *Research Quarterly* 40 (October 1969), 509–17; Sharon McCarthy Hale, 'Possible Pythagorean Influences on Plato's Views of Physical Education in *The Republic*', *Research Quarterly* 40 (December 1969), 692–99; Guy M. Lewis, 'Theodore Roosevelt's Role in the 1905 Football Controversy', *Research Quarterly* 40 (December 1969), 717–24.

43 Struna, 'Sport History', 155–56.

44 Eric Foner, ed., *The New American History*, rev. edn (Philadelphia: Temple University Press, 1997).

45 Struna, 'Sport History', 155–60. In its first year NASSH captured 163 individual and eight institutional members, in the form of libraries, historical societies and other such entities. At its individual high point in 1997, NASSH had 418 individual members. The institutional high point was 1993 when 496 organizations joined. In the most recent data set for membership (2006), NASSH had 377 individual members and 452 institutional members. NASSH is currently in a very healthy position as a scholarly society. Annual conferences have drawn approximately 150 presenters for the last decade and the society enjoys a sound financial foundation. Ronald A. Smith, Secretary-Treasurer's Report for the Thirty-Fifth Annual Convention, May 25–28, 2007, Texas Tech University, Lubbock, TX.

46 Pope, 'American Sport History: Toward a New Paradigm', 3–6.

47 Two who did and took it to heart rank among the very top of American historians of sports, Elliott J. Gorn and Michael Oriard. They labelled James's book as 'the most profound and moving book ever written about sports'. Elliott J. Gorn and Michael Oriad, 'Taking Sports Seriously', *Chronicle of Higher Education*, (24 March 1995), A52.

48 C.L.R. James, *Beyond a Boundary* (Kingston, Jamaica: Sangster's Book Stores in association with Hutchinson, 1963); C.L.R. James, *Beyond a Boundary* (New York: Pantheon Books, 1983).

49 Curiously, in several places in his recent *The Field*, Douglas Booth implies that the theories of Clifford Geertz have not been consistently 'appropriated or applied' in regards to 'Western sports'. Booth, *The Field*, 161, 199–201. In fact, Geertz's ruminations on the methods and philosophies of cultural interpretation have had an enormous impact, particularly his *The Interpretation of Cultures* (New York: Basic Books, 1973); and *Local Knowledge: Further Essays in Interpretive Anthropology* (New York: Basic Books, 1984). Geertz's 'Deep Play: Notes on a Balinese Cockfight' in *Interpretation of Cultures* has greatly influenced recent American scholarship on sport, especially the work of such insightful historians as Elliott J. Gorn and Michael Oriard, who also tout the work of James. See the usages of prize fighting as cultural texts offered by Elliott J. Gorn, *The Manly Art, Bare-Knuckle Prize Fighting in America* (Ithaca, NY: Cornell University Press, 1986); and Elliot J. Gorn, ed., *Muhammad Ali: The People's Champ* (Urbana: University of Illinois Press, 1995). See also the masterful studies of American football as as a cultural text, Michael Oriard, *Reading Football: How the Popular Press Created an American Spectacle* (Chapel Hill: University of North Carolina Press, 1993), and *King Football: Sport and Spectacle in the Golden Age of Radio and Newsreels, Movies and Magazines, the Weekly & the Daily Press* (Chapel Hill: University of North Carolina Press, 2001). In fact, I have been applying Geertz to American sports for nearly two decades with a fervour that some colleagues have claimed borders on obsession. Mark Dyreson, *Making the American Team: Sport, Culture and the Olympic Experience* (Urbana: University of Illinois Press, 1998), and *Crafting Patriotism for Global Domination: America at the Olympics* (London: Routledge, 2008).

50 Gerald Redmond, *The Caledonian Games in Nineteenth-Century America* (Rutherford, NJ: Fairleigh Dickinson University Press, 1971); Dale A. Somers, *The Rise of Sports in New Orleans, 1850–1900* (Baton Rouge: Louisiana State University Press, 1972); Robert Creamer, *Babe: The Legend Comes to Life* (New York: Simon and Schuster, 1974); Leverett T. Smith, *The American Dream and the National Game* (Bowling Green, OH: Bowling Green University Popular Press, 1975).

51 Allen Guttmann, *From Ritual to Record: The Nature of Modern Sports* (New York: Columbia University Press, 1978), and *A Whole New Ball Game: An Interpretation of American Sports* (Chapel Hill: University of North Carolina Press, 1988).

52 The following list offers a semi-comprehensive, chronological list of these works: Allen Guttmann, *From Ritual to Record: The Nature of Modern Sports* (New York: Columbia University Press, 1978); Randy Roberts, *Jack Dempsey: The Manassa Mauler* (Baton Rouge: Louisiana State University Press, 1979); Cary Goodman, *Choosing Sides: Playground and Street Life on the Lower East Side* (New York: Schocken Books, 1979); John A. Lucas, *The Modern Olympic Games* (New York: A.S. Barnes, 1980); Steven A. Riess, *Touching Base: Professional Baseball and American Culture in the Progressive Era* (Westport, CT: Greenwood Press, 1980); Richard C. Crepeau, *Baseball: America's Diamond Mind: 19191941* (Orlando: University Presses of Florida, 1980); Leo Lowenfish, *The Imperfect Diamond: The Story of Baseball's Reserve System and the Men Who Fought to Change It* (New York: Stein and Day, 1980); Ted Vincent, *The Rise and Fall of American Sport: Mudville's Revenge* (New York: Seaview Books, 1981); Kendall Blanchard, *The Mississippi Choctaws at Play: The Serious Side of Leisure* (Urbana: University of Illinois Press, 1981); Dominick Cavallo, *Muscles and Morals: Organized Playgrounds and Urban Reform, 1880–1920* (Philadelphia: University of Pennsylvania Press, 1981); Michael Oriard, *Dreaming of Heroes: American Sports Fiction, 1868–1980* (Chicago, Nelson-Hall, 1982); Stephen Hardy, *How Boston Played: Sport, Recreation, and Community, 1865–1915* (Boston: Northeastern University Press, 1982); James C. Whorton, *Crusaders for Fitness: The History of American Health Reformers* (Princeton, NJ: Princeton University Press, 1982); Eugene C. Murdock, *Ban Johnson: Czar of Baseball* (Westport, CT: Greenwood, 1982); Jules Tygiel, *Baseball's Great Experiment: Jackie Robinson and His Legacy* (New York: Oxford University Press, 1983); Roy Rosenzweig, *Eight Hours for What We Will: Workers and Leisure in an Industrial City, 1870–1910* (Cambridge: Cambridge University Press, 1983); Donald Mrozek, *Sport and American Mentality, 1880–1910* (Knoxville: University of Tennessee Press, 1983); Randy Roberts, *Papa Jack: Jack Johnson and the Era of White Hope* (New York: The Free Press, 1983); Donn Rogosin, *Invisible Men: Life in Baseball's Negro Leagues* (New York: Atheneum, 1983); Allen Guttmann, *The Games Must Go On: Avery Brundage and the Olympic Movement* (New York, Columbia University Press, 1984); Benjamin G. Rader, *In Its Own Image: How Television Has Transformed Sports* (New York, Free Press, 1984); Charles C. Alexander, *Ty Cobb* (New York: Oxford University Press, 1984); Chris Mead, *Champion–Joe Louis: Black Hero in White America* (New York: Charles Scribner's Sons, 1985); Peter Levine, *A.G. Spalding and the Rise of Baseball: The Promise of American Sport* (New York: Oxford University Press, 1985); David Nasaw, *Children of the City: At Work and at Play* (Garden City, NY: AnchorPress/Doubleday, 1985); Melvin L. Adelman, *A Sporting Time: New York City and the Rise of Modern Athletics, 182070* (Urbana, University of Illinois Press, 1986); Elliott J. Gorn, *The Manly Art: Bare-Knuckle Prize Fighting in America* (Ithaca, NY: Cornell University Press, 1986); William J. Baker, *Jesse Owens: An American Life* (New York: Free Press, 1986); Harvey Green, *Fit for America: Health, Fitness, Sport, and American Society* (New York: Pantheon Books, 1986); Rob Ruck, *Sandlot Seasons: Sport in Black Pittsburgh* (Urbana: University of Illinois Press, 1987); Neil J. Sullivan, *The Dodgers Move West* (New York: Oxford University Press, 1987); Jeffrey Sammons, *Beyond the Ring: The Role of Boxing in American Society* (Urbana: University of Illinois Press, 1988); Larry Englemann, *The Goddess and the American Girl* (New York: Oxford University Press, 1988); Joan Chandler, *Television and National Sport: The United States and Britain* (Urbana: University of Illinois Press, 1988); Martha Verbrugge, *Able Bodied Womanhood: Personal Health and Social Change in Late Nineteenth-Century Boston* (New York: Oxford University Press, 1988); Charles C. Alexander, *John J. McGraw* (New York: Viking, 1988); Michael Isenberg, *John L. Sullivan and His America* (Urbana: University of Illinois Press, 1988); Ronald A. Smith, *Sports and Freedom: The Rise of Big-Time College Athletics* (New York: Oxford University Press, 1988); Allen Guttmann, *A Whole New Ball Game: An Interpretation of American Sports* (Chapel Hill: University of North Carolina Press, 1988).

53 Some of these path-breaking studies by scholars trained in history departments or American studies programmes such as Riess, *Touching Base* (1980); Crepeau, *Baseball* (1980); Oriard, *Dreaming of*

Heroes (1982); Whorton, *Crusaders for Fitness* (1982); Tygiel, *Baseball's Great Experiment* (1983); Mrozek, *Sport and American Mentality*; Roberts, *Papa Jack* (1983); Levine, *A.G. Spalding and the Rise of Baseball* (1985); Gorn, *The Manly Art* (1986); Adelman, *A Sporting Time* (1986); and Baker, *Jesse Owens* (1986). Scholars trained in human movement studies programmes also turned out first-rate studies, including Hardy's *How Boston Played* (1982); and Smith's *Sports and Freedom* (1988). Each of these scholars were major contributors to NASSH.

54 Wiggins, 'Marvin Eyler and His Students', 77–90.

55 Jules Tygiel, *Baseball's Great Experiment: Jackie Robinson and His Legacy* (New York: Oxford University Press, 1983), rev. edn (New York: Oxford University Press, 1997).

56 Some of these studies predated or appeared simultaneously with Tygiel's work, including Robert W. Peterson, *Only the Ball Was White: A History of Legendary Black Players and All-Black Professional Teams* (Englewood Cliffs, NJ: Prentice-Hall, 1970); William Brashler, *Josh Gibson: A Life in the Negro Leagues* (New York: Harper & Row, 1978); Roberts, *Papa Jack*, 1983; Rogosin, *Invisible Men*, 1983. Others followed in Tygiel's impressive wake, including Chris Mead, *Champion–Joe Louis: Black Hero in White America* (New York: C. Scribner's Sons, 1985); Baker, *Jesse Owen*, 1986; Robert Pennington, *Breaking the Ice: The Racial Integration of Southwest Conference Football* (Jefferson, NC: McFarland, 1987); Rob Ruck, *Sandlot Seasons: Sport in Black Pittsburgh* (Urbana: University of Illinois Press, 1987); Jeffrey Sammons, *Beyond the Ring: The Role of Boxing in American Society* (Urbana: University of Illinois Press, 1988); Andrew Ritchie, *Major Taylor: The Extraordinary Career of a Champion Bicycle Racer* (San Francisco: Bicycle Books, 1988); Martin Duberman, *Paul Robeson* (New York: Knopf, 1988); John Carroll, *Fritz Pollard: Pioneer in Racial Advancement* (Urbana: University of Illinois Press, 1992); Mark Ribowsky, *'Don't Look Back: Satchel Paige in the Shadows of Baseball* (New York: Simon and Schuster, 1994); David Zang, *Moses Fleetwood Walker's Divided Heart: The Life of Baseball's First Black Major Leaguer* (Lincoln: University of Nebraska Press, 1995); John M. Hoberman, *Darwin's Athletes: How Sport has Damaged Black America and Preserved the Myth of Race* (Boston: Houghton Mifflin, 1997); David Kenneth Wiggins, *Glory Bound: Black Athletes in a White America* (Syracuse, NY: Syracuse University Press, 1997); Sam Lacy and Moses J. Newson, *Fighting for Fairness: The Life Story of Hall of Fame Sportswriter* (Centreville, MD: Tidewater Publishers, 1998); Charles Kenyatta Ross, *Outside the Lines: African Americans and the Integration of the National Football League* (New York: New York University Press, 1999); Randy Roberts, *'But They Can't Beat Us': Oscar Robertson and the Crispus Attucks Tigers* (Champaign, IL: Sports Publishing, Inc., 1999); Mike Marqusee, *Redemption Song: Muhammad Ali and the Spirit of the Sixties* (New York: Verso, 2000); Pamela Grundy, *Learning to Win: Sports, Education, and Social Change in Twentieth-Century North Carolina* (Chapel Hill: University of North Carolina Press, 2001); Robert C. Cottrell, *The Best Pitcher in Baseball: The Life of Rube Foster, Negro League Giant* (New York: New York University Press, 2001); Richard Edward Lapchick, *Smashing Barriers: Race and Sport in the New Millennium* (Lanham, MD: Madison Books, 2001); Ron Thomas, *They Cleared the Lane* (Lincoln: University of Nebraska Press, 2002); Jules Tygiel, *Extra Bases: Reflections on Jackie Robinson, Race, and Baseball History* (Lincoln: University of Nebraska Press, 2002); Amy Bass, *Not the Triumph but the Struggle: The 1968 Olympics and the Making of the Black Athlete* (Minneapolis: University of Minnesota Press, 2002); Douglas Hartmann, *Race, Culture, and the Revolt of the Black Athlete: The 1968 Olympic Protests and their Aftermath* (Chicago: University of Chicago Press, 2003); David K. Wiggins and Patrick Miller, *The Unlevel Playing Field: A Documentary History of the African American Experience in Sport* (Urbana: University of Illinois Press, 2003); Michael E. Lomax, *Black Baseball Entrepreneurs, 1860–1901: Operating by Any Means Necessary* (Syracuse, NY: Syracuse University Press, 2003); Andrew M. Kaye, *The Pussycat of Prizefighting: Tiger Flowers and the Politics of Black Celebrity* (Athens: University of Georgia Press, 2004); Patrick B. Miller and David Kenneth Wiggins, *Sport and the Color Line: Black Athletes and Race Relations in 20th Century America* (New York: Routledge, 2004); Bill Kirwin, *Out of the Shadows: African American Baseball from the Cuban Giants to Jackie Robinson* (Lincoln: University of Nebraska Press, 2005); Amy Bass, *In the Game: Race, Identity, and Sports in the Twentieth Century* (New York, NY: Palgrave Macmillan, 2005); David Kenneth Wiggins, ed., *Out of the Shadows: A Biographical History of African American Athletes* (Fayetteville: University of Arkansas Press, 2006); David Margolick, *Beyond Glory: Joe Louis vs. Max Schmeling, and a World on the Brink* (London: Bloomsbury, 2006); Patrick Myler, *Ring of Hate: The Brown Bomber and Hitler's Hero, Joe Louis v. Max Schmeling and the Bitter Propaganda War* (Edinburgh: Mainstream, 2006); Jeffrey Lane, *Under the Boards: The Cultural Revolution in Basketball* (Lincoln: University of Nebraska Press, 2007); Milton S. Katz, *Breaking Through: John B. McLendon: Basketball*

Legend and Civil Rights Pioneer (Fayetteville: University of Arkansas Press, 2007); David C. Ogden and Joel Nathan Rosen, eds, *Reconstructing Fame: Sport, Race, and Evolving Reputations* (Jackson: University Press of Mississippi, 2008); Gena Caponi-Tabery, *Jump for Joy: Jazz, Basketball, and Black Culture in 1930s* (Amherst: University of Massachusetts Press, 2008); Katherine E. Lopez, *Cougars of Any Color: The Integration of University of Houston Athletics, 1964–1968* (Jefferson, NC: McFarland & Co., 2008); Michael E. Lomax , *Sports and the Racial Divide: African American and Latino Experience in an Era of Change* (Jackson: University Press of Mississippi, 2008); James W. Johnson, *The Dandy Dons: Bill Russell, K.C. Jones, Phil Woolpert, and One of College Basketball's Greatest and Most Innovative Teams* (Lincoln: University of Nebraska Press, 2009); Bob Luke, *The Baltimore Elite Giants: Sport and Society in the Age of Negro League Baseball* (Baltimore: The Johns Hopkins University Press, 2009).

57 On Native American sport see Kendall Blanchard, *The Mississippi Choctaws at Play: The Serious Side of Leisure* (Urbana: University of Illinois Press, 1981); John Bloom, *To Show What an Indian Can Do: Sports at Native American Boarding Schools* (Minneapolis: University of Minnesota Press, 2000); Jeffrey P. Powers-Beck, *The American Indian Integration of Baseball* (Lincoln: University of Nebraska Press, 2004); C. Richard King, ed., *Native Athletes in Sport & Society: A Reader* (Lincoln: University of Nebraska Press, 2005); C. Richard King, ed., *Native Americans and Sport in North America: Other Peoples' Games* (London: Routledge, 2007); and Linda S. Peavy and Ursula Smith, *Full-Court Quest: The Girls from Fort Shaw Indian School, Basketball Champions of the World* (Norman: University of Oklahoma Press, 2008). On Hispanics see Samuel O. Regalado, *Viva Baseball! Latin Major Leaguers and Their Special Hunger* (Urbana: University of Illinois Press, 1998); Adrian Burgos, *Playing America's Game: Baseball, Latinos, and the Color Line* (Berkeley: University of California Press, 2007); Jorge Iber and Samuel O. Regalado, *Mexican Americans and Sports: A Reader on Athletics and Barrio Life* (College Station: Texas A&M University Press, 2007).

58 Ethnicity, social class and modernization have been at the core of some of the finest works in the field, including Steven A. Riess, *Touching Base: Professional Baseball and American Culture in the Progressive Era* (Westport, CT: Greenwood Press, 1980); John Dizikes, *Sportsmen and Gamesmen* (Boston: Houghton Mifflin, 1981); Donald Mrozek, *Sport and American Mentality, 1880–1910* (Knoxville: University of Tennessee Press, 1983); Peter Levine, *A.G. Spalding and the Rise of Baseball: The Promise of American Sport* (New York: Oxford University Press, 1985); Elliott J. Gorn, *The Manly Art: Bare-Knuckle Prize Fighting in America* (Ithaca, NY: Cornell University Press, 1986); Warren J. Goldstein, *Playing For Keeps: A History of Early Baseball* (Ithaca, NY: Cornell University Press, 1989); George B. Kirsch, *The Creation of American Team Sports: Baseball and Cricket, 1838–72* (Urbana, University of Illinois Press, 1989); Steven A. Riess, *Sport in Industrial America, 1850–1920* (Wheeling, IL: Harlan Davidson, 1995); John M. Carroll, *Red Grange and the Rise of Modern Football* (Urbana: University of Illinois Press, 1999).

Many of the studies of these issues have been framed through the lens of urban history, one of the most dynamic components of the new social history. Sport has provided an especially important arena for urban histories. See particularly, Dale A. Somers, *The Rise of Sports in New Orleans, 1850–1900* (Baton Rouge: Louisiana State University Press, 1972); Cary Goodman, *Choosing Sides: Playground and Street Life on the Lower East Side* (New York: Schocken Books, 1979); Dominick Cavallo, *Muscles and Morals: Organized Playgrounds and Urban Reform, 1880–1920* (Philadelphia: University of Pennsylvania Press, 1981); Stephen Hardy, *How Boston Played: Sport, Recreation, and Community, 1865–1915* (Boston: Northeastern University Press, 1982); Roy Rosenzweig, *Eight Hours for What We Will: Workers and Leisure in an Industrial City, 1870–1910* (Cambridge: Cambridge University Press, 1983); David Nasaw, *Children of the City: At Work and at Play* (Garden City, NY: Anchor-Press/Doubleday, 1985); Melvin L. Adelman, *A Sporting Time: New York City and the Rise of Modern Athletics, 1820–70* (Urbana, University of Illinois Press, 1986); Steven A. Riess, *City Games: The Evolution of American Urban Society and the Rise of Sports* (Urbana: University of Illinois Press, 1989); Roy Rosenzweig and Elizabeth Blackmar, *The Park and the People: A History of Central Park* (Ithaca, NY: Cornell University Press, 1992); David Nasaw, *Going Out: The Rise and Fall of Public Amusements* (New York: BasicBooks, 1993); Gerald R. Gems, *Windy City Wars: Labor, Leisure, and Sport in the Making of Chicago* (Lanham, MD: Scarecrow Press, 1997).

An additional productive area includes histories of working-class and middle-class attitudes toward sport, leisure and labour. See especially, Ted Vincent, *The Rise and Fall of American Sport: Mudville's Revenge* (New York: Seaview Books, 1981); Richard Butsch, ed., *For Fun and Profit: The Transformation of Leisure into Consumption* (Philadelphia: Temple University Press, 1990); E. Digby

Baltzell, *Sporting Gentlemen: Men's Tennis from the Age of Honor to the Cult of Superstar* (New York: Free Press, 1995); Cindy Aron, *Working At Play: A History of Vacations in the United States* (New York: Oxford University Press, 1999).

59 Riess, *Touching Base* (1980); Roberts, *Papa Jack* (1983); Hardy, *How Boston Played* (1982); Adelman, *A Sporting Time* (1986); Gorn, *The Manly Art* (1986).

60 On sport and Judaism see Peter Levine, *Ellis Island to Ebbets Field: Sport and the American Jewish Experience* (New York: Oxford University Press, 1992); Steven A. Riess, ed., *Sports and the American Jew* (Syracuse, NY: Syracuse University Press, 1998); Jeffrey S. Gurock, *Judaism's Encounter with American Sports* (Bloomington: Indiana University Press, 2005). On Christianity and sport see Tony Ladd and James A. Mathisen, *Muscular Christianity: Evangelical Protestants and the Development of American Sport* (Grand Rapids, MI: Baker Books, 1999); Clifford Putney, *Muscular Christianity: Manhood and Sports in Protestant America, 1880–1920* (Cambridge, MA: Harvard University Press, 2003); Timothy B. Neary, *Taking It to the Streets: Catholic Liberalism, Race and Sport in Twentieth-Century Urban America* (Notre Dame, IN: Cushwa Center for the Study of American Catholicism, University of Notre Dame, 2004); and William J. Baker, *Playing with God: Religion and Modern Sport* (Cambridge, MA: Harvard University Press, 2007). On Mormonism and sport see Richard Ian Kimball, *Sports in Zion: Mormon Recreation, 1890–1940* (Urbana: University of Illinois Press, 2003).

61 On the gendered dimensions of American sport see especially, J.A. Mangan and Roberta Park, eds, *From 'Fair Sex' to Feminism: Sport and the Socialization of Women in Industrial and Post-Industrial Eras* (London: Frank Cass, 1987); Larry Englemann, *The Goddess and the American Girl* (New York: Oxford University Press, 1988); Patricia Marks, *Bicycles, Bangs, and Bloomers: The New Woman in the Popular Press* (Lexington: University of Kentucky Press, 1990); Allen Guttmann, *Women's Sports: A History* (New York: Columbia University Press, 1991); Barbara Gregorich, *Women at Play: The Story of Women in Baseball* (San Diego: Harcourt Brace & Co., 1993); Susan K. Cahn, *Coming on Strong: Gender and Sexuality in Twentieth-Century Women's Sport* (New York: Free Press, 1994); Susan Cayleff, *Babe: The Life and Legend of Babe Didrikson Zaharias* (Urbana: University of Illinois Press, 1995); Pamela Grundy and Susan Shackelford, *Shattering the Glass: The Remarkable History of Women's Basketball* (New York: New Press, 2005); Patricia Campbell Warner, *When the Girls Came out to Play: The Birth of American Sportswear* (Amherst: University of Massachusetts Press, 2006); Ralph Melnick, *Senda Berenson: The Unlikely Founder of Women's Basketball* (Amherst: University of Massachusetts Press, 2007); J.A. Mangan and Patricia Vertinsky, *Gender, Sport, Science: Selected Writings of Roberta J. Park* (London: Routledge, 2007).

Several excellent studies on Title IX and women sports have appeared in the last few years. See Ying WuShanley, *Playing Nice and Losing: The Struggle for Control of Women's Intercollegiate Athletics, 1960–2000* (Syracuse, NY: Syracuse University Press, 2004); Sarah K. Fields, *Female Gladiators: Gender, Law, and Contact Sport in America* (Urbana: University of Illinois Press, 2005); Welch Suggs, *A Place on the Team: The Triumph and Tragedy of Title IX* (Princeton, NJ: Princeton University Press, 2005); Nancy Hogshead-Makar and Andrew S. Zimbalist, *Equal Play: Title IX and Social Change* (Philadelphia: Temple University Press, 2007).

62 See particularly James's chapter, 'What Is Art?' in *Beyond a Boundary*, 191–211.

63 Warren I. Susman, 'Culture and Civilization: The Nineteen-Twenties', and 'Culture Heroes: Ford, Barton, Ruth', in *Culture as History: The Transformation of American Society in the Twentieth Century* (New York: Pantheon, 1984), 10524 and 12249.

64 Michael Oriard, *Dreaming of Heroes: American Sports Fiction, 1868–1980* (Chicago, Nelson-Hall, 1982); *Sporting with the Gods: The Rhetoric of Play and Game in American Culture* (Cambridge: Cambridge University Press, 1991); *Reading Football: How the Popular Press Created an American Spectacle* (Chapel Hill: University of North Carolina Press, 1993); *King Football: Sport and Spectacle in the Golden Age of Radio and Newsreels, Movies and Magazines, the Weekly & the Daily Press* (Chapel Hill: University of North Carolina Press, 2001); *Brand NFL: Making and Selling America's Favorite Sport* (Chapel Hill: University of North Carolina Press, 2007).

65 Mrozek, *Sport and American Mentality* (1983); Steven W. Pope, 'Negotiating the 'Folk Highway' of the Nation: Sport, Public Culture and American Identity, 1870–1940', *Journal of Social History* 27 (1993), 327–40; S.W. Pope, *Patriotic Games: Sporting Traditions in the American Imagination, 1876–1926* (New York: Oxford University Press, 1997), and rev. edn (Knoxville: University of Tennessee Press, 2007); Wanda E. Wakefield, *Playing to Win: Sports and the American Military, 1898–1945* (Albany: State University of New York Press, 1997); Steven R. Bullock, *Playing for Their Nation:*

Baseball and the American Military during World War II (Lincoln: University of Nebraska Press, 2004); Mark Dyreson, *Making the American Team: Sport, Culture, and the Olympic Experience* (Urbana: University of Illinois Press, 1998); Mark Dyreson, *Crafting Patriotism for Global Domination: America at the Olympics* (London: Routledge, 2008).

66 Pamela Grundy, *Learning to Win: Sports, Education, and Social Change in Twentieth-Century North Carolina* (Chapel Hill: University of North Carolina Press, 2001).

67 Arguments regarding the power of sport to produce social capital have been raised in particular by the political theorist Robert Putnam in his provocative and popular works on the subject. Robert D. Putnam, 'Bowling Alone: America's Declining Social Capital', *Journal of Democracy* 6 (1995), 65–78; Robert Putnam, *Bowling Alone: The Collapse and Revival of American Community* (New York: Simon & Schuster, 2000). For a critique of Putnam's thesis see Mark Dyreson, 'Maybe It's Better to Bowl Alone: Sport, Community, and Democracy in American Thought', *Culture, Society, Sport* 4 (2001), 19–30.

68 For a precursor to the studies of media and sport see Norris Wilson Yates, *William T. Porter and the Spirit of the Times: A Study of the Big Bear School of Humor* (Baton Rouge: Louisiana State University Press, 1957). Since the 1980s a plethora of excellent analyses of sport media have appeared. See in particular, Benjamin G. Rader, *In Its Own Image: How Television Has Transformed Sports* (New York, Free Press, 1984); Joan Chandler, *Television and National Sport: The United States and Britain* (Urbana: University of Illinois Press, 1988); Charles Fountain, *Sportswriter: The Life and Times of Grantland Rice* (New York: Oxford University Press, 1993); Mark Inabinett, *Grantland Rice and His Heroes* (Knoxville: University of Tennessee Press, 1994); Bruce J. Evensen, *When Dempsey Fought Tunney: Heroes, Hokum and Storytelling in the Jazz Age* (Knoxville: University of Tennessee Press, 1996); William A. Harper, *How You Played the Game: The Life of Grantland Rice* (Columbia: University of Missouri Press, 1999); Ronald A. Smith, *Play-by-Play: Radio, Television, and Big-Time College Sport* (Baltimore, MD: The Johns Hopkins University Press, 2001); Leonard Koppett, *The Rise and Fall of the Press Box* (Toronto: Sport Classic Books, 2003); Irwin Silber and Lester Rodney, *Press Box Red: The Story of Lester Rodney, The Communist Who Helped Break the Color Line in American* (Philadelphia: Temple University Press, 2003); Guy Reel, *The National Police Gazette and the Making of the Modern American Man, 1879–1906* (New York: Palgrave Macmillan, 2006).

69 Allen Guttmann, *The Games Must Go On: Avery Brundage and the Olympic Movement* (New York, Columbia University Press, 1984); Allen Guttmann, *Games and Empires: Modern Sports and Cultural Imperialism* (New York: Columbia University Press, 1994); Walter LaFeber, *Michael Jordan and the New Global Capitalism* (New York: Norton, 1999); David L. Andrews, *Michael Jordan, Inc.: Corporate Sport, Media Culture, and Late Modern America* (Albany: State University of New York Press, 2001); Amy Bass, *Not the Triumph but the Struggle: The 1968 Olympics and the Making of the Black Athlete* (Minneapolis: University of Minnesota Press, 2002); Douglas Hartmann, *Race, Culture, and the Revolt of the Black Athlete: The 1968 Olympic Protests and their Aftermath* (Chicago: University of Chicago Press, 2003); Larry R. Gerlach, ed., *The Winter Olympics: From Chamonix to Salt Lake City* (Salt Lake City: University of Utah Press, 2004); Barbara J. Keys, *Globalizing Sport: National Rivalry and International Community in the 1930s* (Cambridge, MA: Harvard University Press, 2006); Gerald R. Gems, *The Athletic Crusade: Sport and American Cultural Imperialism* (Lincoln: University of Nebraska Press, 2006); Susan Brownell, ed., *The 1904 Anthropology Days and Olympic Games: Sport, Race, and American Imperialism* (Lincoln: University of Nebraska Press, 2008); Mark Dyreson, *Crafting Patriotism for Global Domination: America at the Olympics* (London: Routledge, 2008).

70 The locus of this new trend has moved from Columbia University to Harvard University, as both faculty and graduate students have delved into international sport. LaFeber, *Michael Jordan and the New Global Capitalism* (1999); Keys, *Globalizing Sport* (2006).

71 The two historians of sport who began to work on baseball during the 1960s eventually published three-volume histories of the national pastime. Harold Seymour, *Baseball*, 3 volumes: I. *The Early Years*, II. *The Golden Age*, III. *The People's Game* (New York, Oxford University Press, 1960–76); David Q. Voight, *American Baseball*, 3 volumes: I. *From Gentleman's Sport to the Commissioner System*, II. *From the Commissioners to Continental Expansion*, III. *From Postwar Expansion to the Electronic Age* (University Park: Penn State University Press, 1983). A fine single-volume history of baseball has also appeared: Benjamin G. Rader, *Baseball: A History of America's Game* (Urbana: University of Illinois Press, 1992).

Monographs on specific baseball subjects have proliferated as well. Richard C. Crepeau, *Baseball: America's Diamond Mind: 1919–1941* (Orlando: University Presses of Florida, 1980); Leo Lowenfish,

The Imperfect Diamond: The Story of Baseball's Reserve System and the Men Who Fought to Change It (New York: Stein and Day, 1980); Eugene C. Murdock, *Ban Johnson: Czar of Baseball* (Westport, CT: Greenwood, 1982); Charles C. Alexander, *Ty Cobb* (New York: Oxford University Press, 1984); Neil J. Sullivan, *The Dodgers Move West* (New York: Oxford University Press, 1987); Charles C. Alexander, *John J. McGraw* (New York: Viking, 1988); Charles C. Alexander, *Our Game: An American Baseball History* (New York: Henry Holt, 1991); Andrew Zimbalist, *Baseball and Billions: A Probing Look Inside the Big Business of Our National Pastime* (New York: Basic Books, 1992); Michael Gershman, *Diamonds: The Evolution of the Ballpark* (Boston: Houghton Mifflin, 1993); Neil Lanctot, *Fair Dealing and Clean Playing: The Hilldale Club and the Development of Professional Baseball, 1910–1932* (Jefferson, NC: McFarland, 1994); Charles C. Alexander, *Rogers Hornsby: A Biography* (New York: Henry Holt, 1995); Patrick J. Harrigan, *The Detroit Tigers: Club and Community, 1945–1995* (Toronto: University of Toronto Press, 1997); Steven R. Bullock, *Playing for Their Nation: Baseball and the American Military during World War II* (Lincoln: University of Nebraska Press, 2004).

Next to baseball, boxing has enjoyed the most scholarly attention. Randy Roberts, *Jack Dempsey: The Manassa Mauler* (Baton Rouge: Louisiana State University Press, 1979); Randy Roberts, *Papa Jack: Jack Johnson and the Era of White Hope* (New York: The Free Press, 1983); Michael Isenberg, *John L. Sullivan and His America* (Urbana: University of Illinois Press, 1988); Jeffrey Sammons, *Beyond the Ring: The Role of Boxing in American Society* (Urbana: University of Illinois Press, 1988); Gerald Early, *The Culture of Bruising: Essays on Prizefighting, Literature and Modern American Culture* (Hopewell, NJ: Ecco Press, 1994); Elliott J. Gorn, ed., *Muhammad Ali: The People's Champ* (Urbana: University of Illinois Press, 1995); Andrew M. Kaye, *The Pussycat of Prizefighting: Tiger Flowers and the Politics of Black Celebrity* (Athens: University of Georgia Press, 2004).

American football, in particular the college version, has begun to receive a great deal of attention. On college and other brands of football and on college sports in general see, in addition to Michael Oriard's many works, Ronald A. Smith, *Sports and Freedom: The Rise of Big-Time College Athletics* (New York: Oxford University Press, 1988); Murray Sperber, *College Sports, Inc.: The Athletic Department vs. the University* (New York: Henry Holt, 1990); Murray Sperber, *Shake Down the Thunder: The Creation of Notre Dame Football* (New York: Henry Holt, 1993); John Thelin, *Games Colleges Play: Scandal and Reform in College Athletics* (Baltimore, MD: The Johns Hopkins Press, 1994); Robin Lester, *Stagg's University: The Rise, Decline, and Fall of Big-Time Football at Chicago* (Urbana, University of Illinois Press, 1995); Murray Sperber, *Onward to Victory: The Crises That Shaped College Sport* (New York: Henry Holt, 1998); Murray Sperber, *Beer and Circuses: How Big-Time College Sports Is Crippling Undergraduate Education* (New York: Henry Holt, 2000); John Watterson, *College Football: History, Spectacle, Controversy* (Baltimore, MD: The Johns Hopkins University Press, 2000); Gerald R. Gems, *For Pride, Profit, and Patriarchy: Football and the Incorporation of American Cultural Values* (Lanham, MD: Scarecrow Press, 2000); Ronald A. Smith, *Play-by-Play: Radio, Television, and Big-Time College Sport* (Baltimore, MD: The Johns Hopkins University Press, 2001); Richard Whittingham, *Rites of Autumn: The Story of College Football* (New York: Free Press, 2001); Raymond Schmidt, *Shaping College Football: The Transformation of an American Sport, 1919–1930* (Syracuse, NY: Syracuse University Press, 2007).

On basketball see Robert W. Peterson, *Cages to Jump Shots: Pro Basketball's Early Years* (New York: Oxford University Press, 1990); Randy Roberts, *'But They Can't Beat Us': Oscar Robertson and the Crispus Attucks Tigers* (Champaign, IL: Sports Publishing Inc., 1999); Murry R. Nelson, *The Originals: The New York Celtics Invent Modern Basketball* (Bowling Green, OH: Bowling Green State University Popular Press, 1999); Ron Thomas, *They Cleared the Lane* (Lincoln: University of Nebraska Press, 2002); Adolph H. Grundman, *The Golden Age of Amateur Basketball: The AAU Tournament, 1921–1968* (Lincoln: University of Nebraska Press, 2004); Jeffrey Lane, *Under the Boards: The Cultural Revolution in Basketball* (Lincoln: University of Nebraska Press, 2007); Milton S. Katz, *Breaking Through: John B. McLendon: Basketball Legend and Civil Rights Pioneer* (Fayetteville: University of Arkansas Press, 2007).

For other sports see Pamela Cooper, *The American Marathon* (Syracuse, NY: Syracuse University Press, 1998); Donald M. Fisher, *Lacrosse: A History of the Game* (Baltimore: Johns Hopkins University Press, 2002); Alan S. Katchen, *Abel Kiviat, National Champion: Twentieth-Century Track & Field and the Melting Pot* (Syracuse, NY: Syracuse University Press, 2009).

72 David Zang, *SportsWars: Athletes in the Age of Aquarius* (Fayetteville: University of Arkansas Press, 2001). For other exceptions see Randy Roberts and James Olson, *Winning Is the Only Thing: Sports in American Society since 1945* (Baltimore: Johns Hopkins University Press, 1989); Richard O.

Davies, *America's Obsession: Sports and Society since 1945* (Fort Worth: Harcourt Brace College Publishers, 1994); Mike Marqusee, *Redemption Song: Muhammad Ali and the Spirit of the Sixties* (New York: Verso, 2000); Kathryn Jay, *More than Just a Game: Sports in American Life since 1945* (New York: Columbia University Press, 2004); Tod Papageorge, *American Sports, 1970: Or How We Spent the War in Vietnam* (New York: Aperture, 2007); Kurt Edward Kemper, *College Football and American Culture in the Cold War Era* (Urbana: University of Illinois Press, 2009); James W. Johnson, *The Dandy Dons: Bill Russell, K.C. Jones, Phil Woolpert, and One of College Basketball's Greatest and Most Innovative Teams* (Lincoln: University of Nebraska Press, 2009).

73 For notable exceptions see Bruce Kuklick, *To Everything a Season: Shibe Park and Urban Philadelphia, 1909–1976* (Princeton, NJ: Princeton University Press, 1991); Peter Richmond, *Ballpark: Camden Yards and the Building of an American Dream* (New York: Simon & Schuster, 1993); Robert C. Trumpbour, *The New Cathedrals: Politics and Media in the History of Stadium Construction* (Syracuse, NY: Syracuse University Press, 2007); Mark Dyreson and Robert Trumpbour, eds, *The Rise of Modern Stadiums in the United States: Cathedrals of Sport* (London: Routledge, 2009).

74 A few good studies on those subjects have appeared. See, Gerald Redmond, *The Caledonian Games in Nineteenth-Century America* (Rutherford, NJ: Fairleigh Dickinson University Press, 1971); Mary Lou LeCompte, *Cowgirls of the Rodeo: Pioneer Professional Athletes* (Urbana: University of Illinois Press, 1993); Scott C. Martin, *Killing Time: Leisure and Culture in Southwestern Pennsylvania, 1800–1850* (Pittsburgh: University of Pittsburgh Press, 1995).

75 Nancy Struna, *People of Prowess: Sport, Leisure and Labor in Early Anglo-American* (Urbana: University of Illinois Press, 1996).

76 A by no means inclusive list of sport and society series would begin with the seminal series begun in the early 1980s at the University of Illinois Press and include the Sport in Global Society book series at Routledge Press, and series at the Syracuse University Press, University of Nebraska Press, the University of Tennessee Press, the University of Arkansas Press, the University of Mississippi Press, the State University of New York Press and Johns Hopkins University Press. Most university presses publish at least occasional volumes on the history of sport, including the University of North Carolina Press, Oxford University Press, Columbia University Press, Cornell University Press, Harvard University Press, University of Minnesota Press, New York University Press, University of Texas Press, Texas A&M University Press, University of California Press, Duke University Press, Yale University Press, Princeton University Press, University of Georgia Press, University of Oklahoma Press, Pennsylvania State University Press and Cambridge University Press.

77 The list of English-language journals focused on the historical approaches to sport is quite large, and includes the *Journal of Sport History*, the *International Journal of the History of Sport*, *Sport History Review Sport History Review*, *Sport in History*, *Sport and Society*, *Sporting Traditions*, *Journal of Olympic History*, *Olympika: The International Journal of Olympic Studies*, *Journal of Comparative Physical Education and Sport*, *Stadion*, *Nine* and *Football Studies*.

78 Among the earliest texts were those produced by scholars with homes in physical education: Betty Mary Spears, Richard A. Swanson and Elaine T. Smith, *History of Sport and Physical Activity in the United States* (Dubuque, IA: William C. Brown Co., 1978); John A. Lucas and Ronald A. Smith, *Saga of American Sport* (Philadelphia: Lea & Febiger, 1978); Paula D. Welch and Harold A. Lerch, *History of American Physical Education and Sport* (Springfield, IL: C.C. Thomas, 1981). Very quickly, those in history departments followed suit: Harry Jebsen, *Sports: A Microcosm of Twentieth-Century America* (St Louis, MO: Forum Press, 1978); William J. Baker, *Sports in the Western World* (Totowa, NJ: Rowman and Littlefield, 1982); Benjamin G. Rader, *American Sports: From the Age of Folk Games to the Age of Spectators* (Englewood Cliffs, NJ: Prentice-Hall, 1983). Rader's text become the seminal undergraduate reader in the field and is now in a sixth edition. Benjamin G. Rader, *American Sports: From the Age of Folk Games to the Age of Spectators*, sixth edn (Englewood Cliffs, NJ: Prentice-Hall, 2009). Following Rader were several other solid texts by both historians of sport and sports historians, including Elliott Gorn and Warren Goldstein, *A Brief History of American Sports* (New York: Hill and Wang, 1993); Richard O. Davies, *Sports in American Life: A History* (Malden, MA: Blackwell, 2007); Dave Zirin, *A People's History of Sports in the United States: 250 Years of Politics, Protest, People, and Play* (New York: New Press, 2008); Gerald R. Gems, Linda J. Borish and Gertrud Pfister, *Sports in American History: From Colonization to Globalization* (Champaign, IL: Human Kinetics, 2008).

79 The best, a solid collection of primary and secondary sources, is Steven A. Riess, ed., *Major Problems in American Sport History* (Boston: Houghton Mifflin, 1997). Other strong collections of secondary

sources include David K. Wiggins, *Sport in America: From Wicked Amusement to National Obsession* (Champaign, IL: Human Kinetics, 1994); S.W. Pope, ed., *The New American Sport History: Recent Approaches and Perspectives* (Urbana, IL: University of Illinois Press, 1997); Steven Wieting, ed., *Sport and Memory in North America* (London: Routledge, 2001); Mark Dyreson and J.A. Mangan, eds, *Sport and American Society: Insularity, Exceptionalism and 'Imperialism'* (London: Routledge, 2007); Benjamin Eastman, Sean Brown and Michael Ralph, eds, *America's Game(s): A Critical Anthropology of Sport* (London: Routledge, 2007); Alan Klein, *American Sports: An Anthropological Approach* (London: Routledge, 2008); Donald Kyle and Robert R. Fairbanks, eds, *Baseball in America and America in Baseball* (College Station: Texas A&M University Press, 2008).

80 In addition to Booth, *The Field*, and Pope, 'American Sport History – Toward a New Paradigm', there are several other excellent calls for moving beyond existing methodologies. See Stephen Hardy, 'Entrepreneurs, Structures, and the Sportgeist: Old Tensions in a Modern Industry', in Donald G. Kyle and Gary Stark, eds, *Essays in Sport History and Sport Mythology* (College Station: Texas A&M University Press, 1990), 45–82; Jeffery Hill, 'Reading the Stars: A Post-Modernist Approach to Sports History', *The Sports Historian* 14 (1994), 45–55; Jeffery Hill, 'British Sports History: A Post-modern Future?', *Journal of Sport History* 23 (Spring 1996), 1–19; Catriona Parratt, 'Reflecting on Sport History in the 1990s', *Sport History Review* 29 (May 1998), 4–17; Jeffery Hill, 'Cocks, Cats, Caps and Cups: A Semiotic Approach to Sport and National Identity', *Culture, Sport, Society* 2 (Summer 1999), 1–21; Synthia Sydnor, 'A History of Synchronized Swimming', *Journal of Sport History* 25 (Summer 1998), 252–67; Murray Phillips, 'Deconstructing Sport History: The Postmodern Challenge', *Journal of Sport History* 28 (Fall 2001), 327–43; Murray Phillips, ed., *Deconstructing Sport History: A Postmodern Analysis* (Albany, NY: State University of New York Press, 2006); Colin Howell, 'Assessing Sport History and the Cultural and Linguistic Turn', *Journal of Sport History* 34 (Fall 2007), 459–65.

In addition, see the issue of *Sporting Traditions* 16 (November 1999), 1–108, the Australian journal of the history of sport, devoted to the question, 'the end of sports history?' The issue includes very interesting essays by Douglas Booth and Annemarie Jutel, John Nauright, Colin Tatz, Joseph Arbena, Amanda Smith, Joan Chandler, Murray Phillips, J.A. Mangan, David L. Andrews, Stephen Hardy and Charlotte Macdonald.

81 I concur with S.W. Pope's assessment of the innovative challenge Hardy made to historians of sport and sports historians. Pope, 'American Sport History – Toward a New Paradigm', 6; Hardy, 'Entrepreneurs, Structures, and the Sportgeist', 45–82.

82 For an early effort at refocusing on memory and cycles instead of replicating the standard linear approaches of the modernization school see Stephen R. Fox, *Big Leagues: Professional Baseball, Football, and Basketball in National Memory* (New York: William Morrow, 1994). For an example of the trend in broader American historical discourse see Michael Kammen, *Mystic Chords of Memory: The Transformation of American Culture* (New York: Knopf, 1991).

83 Daniel A. Nathan, *Saying It's So: A Cultural History of the Black Sox Scandal* (Urbana: University of Illinois Press, 2003); also see John Nauright, 'Nostalgia, Culture and Modern Sport', in V. Møller and J. Nauright, eds, *The Essence of Sport* (Odense: University Press of Southern Denmark, 2003), 35–50.

84 Electronic searches of the *Chronicle of Higher Education* and *Perspectives*, the job-listing newsletter of the American Historical Association, reveal *nary a job advertised since 1988 in history departments that included sport as a desired sub-field*. Indeed, among the 126 specializations and 352 specific fields listed, including 'maritime' and 'chemistry', in the American Historical Association's History Doctoral Program Directory, the history of sport appears only in Kansas State University's entry, www.historians.org/projects/cge/PhD/Specializations.cfm (accessed 12 October 2007).

85 For an overview of the current state of kinesiology see Karl Newell, 'Kinesiology Challenges of Multiple Agendas', *Quest* 59 (February 2007), 5–24; Jerry R. Thomas, Jane E. Clark, Deborah L. Feltz, R. Scott Kretchmar, James R. Morrow, Jr, T. Gilmour Reeve and Michael G. Wade, 'The Academy Promotes, Unifies and Evaluates Doctoral Education in Kinesiology', *Quest* 59 (February 2007), 174–94; Roberta Rikli, 'Kinesiology: A "Homeless" Field: Addressing Organization and Leadership Needs', Quest 58 (August 2006), 287–309.

86 Dyreson, *Making the American Team*.

87 I stand between the two provinces in my own career both as a historian of sport and a sports historian. I earned a PhD in history (as well as an MA and a BS – in anthropology also) and taught in history departments for a decade before taking a position in one of the leading kinesiology departments in the USA. I regularly sneak my historian's training into my classes, pushing students to consider

how racial dynamics on playing fields illuminate the larger history of race relations in the USA and other nations. At the same time, since I am housed in a science-driven kinesiology department, my students need me to serve them as a sports historian, especially a sport science historian, and to ask them to reconsider notions that race is a scientific fact written in human biology that represents a causal force in the human physical abilities – a perspective that still shapes some of the science they learn. Confusing social data, such as the percentages of African-Americans in the National Basketball Association or National Football League, or the number of Olympic medals won by ethnicity or race, with genetic data remains an all too common problem in studies of race and sport, as Jon Entine's *Taboo: Why Black Athletes Dominate Sports and Why We Are Afraid To Talk About It* (New York: Public Affairs, 2000), illustrates. For histories that illuminate this particular intersection of science and culture see Hoberman, *Darwin's Athletes*; David K. Wiggins, '"Great Speed But Little Stamina": The Historical Debate Over Black Athletic Superiority', *Journal of Sport History* 16 (summer 1989), 158–85; Patrick B. Miller, 'The Anatomy of Scientific Racism: Racialist Responses to Black Athletic Achievement', *Journal of Sport History* 25 (Spring 1998), 119–51; Mark Dyreson, 'American Ideas About Race and Olympic Races from the 1890s to the 1950s: Shattering Myths or Reinforcing Scientific Racism?', *Journal of Sport History* 28 (summer 2001), 173–215. See also, Jeffrey T. Sammons, 'A Proportional and Measured Response to the Provocation That is *Darwin's Athletes*', *Journal of Sport History* 24 (Fall 1997), 378–88; and John Hoberman, 'How Not to Misread *Darwin's Athletes*: A Response to Jeffrey Sammons', *Journal of Sport History* 24 (Fall 1997), 389–96.

88 James C. Whorton, *Crusaders for Fitness: The History of American Health Reformers* (Princeton, NJ: Princeton University Press, 1982); Harvey Green, *Fit for America: Health, Fitness, Sport, and American Society* (New York: Pantheon Books, 1986); Martha Verbrugge, *Able Bodied Womanhood: Personal Health and Social Change in Late Nineteenth-Century Boston* (New York: Oxford University Press, 1988); David L. Chapman, *Sandow the Magnificent: Eugen Sandow and the Beginnings of Body Building* (Urbana: University of Illinois Press, 1994); Jan Todd, *Physical Culture and the Body Beautiful: Purposive Exercise in the Lives of American Women, 1800–1870* (Macon, GA: Mercer University Press, 1998); John D. Fair, *Muscletown USA: Bob Hoffman and the Manly Culture of York Barbell* (University Park: Pennsylvania State University Press, 1999).

89 Jack W. Berryman and Roberta J. Park, eds, *Sport and Exercise Science: Essays in the History of Sports Medicine* (Urbana: University of Illinois Press, 1992); Jack W. Berryman, *Out of Many, One: A History of the American College of Sports Medicine* (Champaign, IL: Human Kinetics, 1995); J.A. Mangan and Patricia Vertinsky, *Gender, Sport, Science: Selected Writings of Roberta J. Park* (London: Routledge, 2007).

Park's historical essays in the *Research Quarterly*, a key journal in human movement studies, illuminate her long concern with these subjects. Roberta J. Park, 'Concern for Health and Exercise as Expressed in the Writings of 18th Century Physicians and Informed Laymen (England, France, Switzerland)', *Research Quarterly of Exercise and Sport Science* 47 (December 1976), 756–67; 'Strong Bodies, Healthful Regimens, and Playful Recreations as Viewed by Utopian Authors of the 16th and 17th Centuries', *Research Quarterly of Exercise and Sport Science* 49 (December 1978), 498–511; 'Research Quarterly and Its Antecedents: History of the Research Quarterly', *Research Quarterly of Exercise and Sport Science* 51 (March 1980), 1–22; 'Research and Scholarship in the History of Physical Education and Sport: The Current State of Affairs', *Research Quarterly of Exercise and Sport Science* 54 (June 1983), 93–103; '1989 C.H. McCloy Research Lecture: Health, Exercise, and the Biomedical Impulse, 1870–1914', *Research Quarterly of Exercise and Sport Science* 61 (June 1990), 126–40; 'The Rise and Demise of Harvard's B.S. Program in Anatomy, Physiology, and Physical Training: A Case of Conflicts of Interest and Scarce Resources', *Research Quarterly of Exercise and Sport Science* 63 (September 1992), 246–60; 'A Long and Productive Career: Franklin M. Henry – Scientist, Mentor, Pioneer', *Research Quarterly of Exercise and Sport Science* 65 (December 1994), 295–307; 'G. Lawrence Rarick: Gentleman, Scholar, and Consummate Professional', *Research Quarterly of Exercise and Sport Science* 68 (September 1997), 182–94; Roberta J. Park, '"Time Given Freely to Worthwhile Causes", Anna S. Espenschade's Contributions to Physical Education', *Research Quarterly of Exercise and Sport Science* 71 (June 2000), 99–115.

90 That is certainly my experience in the Department of Kinesiology at Penn State.

91 Alexander Wolff, 'The Audacity of Hoops', *Sports Illustrated* (19 January 2009), 57–63.

92 James wrote in his brief preface, 'This book is neither cricket reminiscences nor autobiography. It poses the question *What do they know of cricket who only cricket know?* To answer involves ideas as well as facts'. *Beyond a Boundary*, xxi.

Select Bibliography

Note: Only books included.

Adair, A. and Vamplew, W. *Sport in Australian History* (Melbourne: Oxford University Press, 1997).

Adelman, M. *A Sporting Time: New York City and the Rise of Modern Athletics, 1820–1870* (Urbana: University of Illinois Press, 1986).

Alabarces, P. *Fútbol y patria: El fútbol y las narrativas de la nación en Argentina* (Buenos Aires: Prometeo, 2002).

Alegi, P. *Laduma! Soccer, Politics and Society in South Africa* (Durban: University of KwaZulu-Natal Press, 2004).

Allison, L. ed., *The Global Politics of Sport: The Role of Global Institutions in Sport* (London: Routledge, 2005).

Altuve, E. *Juego, historia, deporte y sociedad en América Latina* (Maracaibo: Universidad del Zulia, 1997).

Arbena, J. and LaFrance, D. eds, *Sport in Latin America and the Caribbean* (Lanham: Rowman & Littlefield, 2002).

Archetti, E. *Masculinities: Football, Polo and Tango in Argentina* (London: Berg, 1999).

——*El potrero, la pista y el ring: Las patrias del deporte argentino* (Buenos Aires: Fondo de Cultura Económica, 2001).

Arnaud, P. and Garrier, G. eds, *Jeux et sports dans l'histoire*, two vols (Paris: CTHS, 1992).

Arnaud, P. and Terret, T. eds, *Education et politique sportives: XIXè–XXè siècles* (Paris: CTHS, 1995).

Arnaud, P. and Terret, T. *Histoire du sport féminin* (Paris: L'Harmattan, 1996).

Bailey, P. *Leisure and Class in Victorian England: Rational Recreation and the Contest for Control, 1830–1885* (London: Routledge, 2004).

Bairner, A. *Sport, Nationalism and Globalisation: European and North American Perspectives* (New York: SUNY, 2001).

Baker, W. and Mangan, J.A. eds., *Sports in Africa: Essays in Social History* (New York: Africana, 1987).

Baker, W. *Jesse Owens: An American Life* (New York: Free Press, 1986).

——*Sports in the Western World* (Urbana: University of Illinois Press, 1988).

——*Playing with God: Religion and Modern Sport* (Cambridge, MA: Harvard University Press, 2007).

Balbier, U. *Kalter Krieg auf der Aschenbahn: Der deutsch-deutsche Sport 1950–1972; Eine politische Geschichte* (Paderborn: Schöningh, 2007).

Bale, J. and Cronin, M. eds, *Sport and Postcolonialism* (Oxford: Berg, 2003)

Bale, J. *Imagined Olympians: Body Culture and Colonial Representation in Rwanda* (Minneapolis: University of Minnesota Press, 2002).

Bandy, S., Hoffman, A. and Krüger, A. eds, *Gender, Body and Sport in Historical and Transnational Perspectives* (Hamburg: Kovač, 2007).

Barney, R., Wenn, S. and Martyn, S. *Selling the Five Rings: The International Olympic Committee and the Rise of Olympic Commercialism* (Salt Lake City: University of Utah Press, 2002).

Bass, A. ed., *In the Game: Race, Identity, and Sports in the Twentieth Century* (New York: Palgrave Macmillan, 2005).

Bass, A. *Not the Triumph But the Struggle: The 1968 Olympics and the Making of the Black Athlete* (Minneapolis: University of Minnesota Press, 2004).

Bayer, O. *Fútbol argentino: pasión y gloria de nuestro deporte más popular* (Buenos Aires: Sudamericana, 1990).

Beck, P. *Scoring for Britain: International Football and International Politics, 1900–1939* (London: Frank Cass, 1999).

Beckles, H. *The Development of West Indies Cricket, Vol. 1 The Age of Nationalism* (Kingston: The University of the West Indies/London: Pluto Press, 1998).

Betts, J. *America's Sporting Heritage, 1850–1950* (Reading, MA: Addison-Wesley, 1974).

Birley, D. *Sport and the Making of Modern Britain* (Manchester, 1993).

Black, D. and Nauright, J. *Rugby and the South African Nation* (Manchester: Manchester University Press, 1998).

Blanchard, K. *The Mississippi Choctaws at Play: The Serious Side of Leisure* (Urbana: University of Illinois Press, 1981).

Blecking, D. and Waic, M. eds, *Sport-Ethnie-Nation: Zur Geschichte und Soziologie des Sports in Nationalitäten-konflikten und bei Minoritäten* (Hohengehren: Schneider, 2008).

Bonde, H. *Mandighed og Sport* (Odense: Universitetsforlag, 1991).

Bonnell, V. and Hunt, L. eds, *Beyond the Cultural Turn: New Directions in the Study of Society and Culture* (Berkeley: University of California Press, 1999).

Booth, D. and Tatz, C. *One-Eyed: A View of Australian Sport* (Sydney: Allen & Unwin, 2000).

Booth, D. *Australian Beach Cultures: The History of Sun, Sand, and Surf* (London: Frank Cass, 2001).

——*The Field: Truth and Fiction in Sport History* (London: Routledge, 2005).

——*The Race Game* (London: Frank Cass, 1998).

Bouchier, N. *For the Love of the Game and the Honour of the Town: Amateur Sport and Middle Class Culture in Nineteenth Century Ontario Towns, 1838–1895* (Montreal: McGill-Queen's University Press, 2003).

Brabazon, T. *Playing on the Periphery: Sport, Identity, and Memory* (New York: Routledge, 2006), 2.

Brailsford, D. *A Taste for Diversions: Sport in Georgian England* (Cambridge: Lutterworth, 1999).

——*Sport and Society: Elizabeth to Anne* (London: Routledge & Kegan Paul, 1969).

Brenner, M. and Reuveni, G. eds, *Emanzipation durch Muskelkraft: Juden und Sport in Europa* (Göttingen: Vandenhoeck & Ruprecht, 2006).

Brohm, J.M. *Sociologie politique du sport* (Paris: J.P. Delarge, 1976).

Brownell, S. ed., *The 1904 Anthropology Days and Olympic Games: Sport, Race and American Imperialism* (University of Nebraska Press, 2008).

Brownell, S. *Training the Body for China: Sports in the Moral Order of the People's Republic* (Chicago, IL: University of Chicago Press, 1995).

Budd, M. *The Sculpture Machine: Physical Culture and Body Politics in the Age of Empire* (New York: New York University Press, 1997).

Burgos, A. *Playing America's Game: Baseball, Latinos, and the Color Line* (Berkeley: University of California Press, 2007).

Burstyn, V. *The Rites of Men: Manhood, Politics, and the Culture of Sport* (Toronto: University of Toronto Press, 1999).

Buss, W. ed., *Der Sport in der SBZ und frühen DDR: Genese – Strukturen – Bedingungen* (Schorndorf: Hofmann, 2001).

Cahn, S. *Coming on Strong: Gender and Sexuality in Twentieth Century Women's Sport* (London: Harvard University Press, 1994).

Caillois, R. *Les jeux et les hommes* (Paris: Gallimard, 1958); translated as *Man, Play, and Games* (New York: Free Press of Glencoe, 1961).

Caponi-Tabery, G. *Jump for Joy: Jazz, Basketball, and Black Culture in 1930s* (Amherst: University of Massachusetts Press, 2008).

Carrington, B. and McDonald, I. eds, *"Race," Sport and British Society* (London: Routledge, 2004).

——*Marxism, Cultural Studies and Sport* (London and New York: Routledge, 2009).

Carter, J. *Sports and Pastimes of the Middle Ages* (Lanham, MD: University Press of America, 1988).

Cashman, R. and McKernan, M. (eds), *Sport in History: The Making of Modern Sporting History* (St Lucia, Qld: University of Queensland Press, 1979).

Cashman, R. *Paradise of Sport: The Rise of Organised Sport in Australia* (Melbourne: Oxford University Press, 1995).

——*Patrons, Players and the Crowd: The Phenomenon of Indian Cricket* (Delhi: Orient Longman, 1980).

Caudwell, J. ed., *Sport, Sexualities and Queer/Theory* (New York: Routledge, 2006).

Cavallo, D. *Muscles and Morals: Organized Playgrounds and Urban Reform, 1880–1920* (Philadelphia: University of Pennsylvania Press, 1981).

Chandler, J. *Television and National Sport: The United States and Britain* (Urbana: University of Illinois Press, 1988).

Chandler, T. and Nauright, J. eds, *Making the Rugby World: Race, Gender, Commerce* (London: Frank Cass, 1999).

Coakley, J. and Dunning, E. eds, *Handbook of Sports Studies* (London: Sage, 2000).

Cobley, A. *The Rules of the Game: Struggles in Black Recreation and Social Welfare Policy in South Africa* (Westport, CT: Greenwood Press, 1997).

Collins, T. *Rugby League in Twentieth-Century Britain* (London: Routledge, 2006).

——*Rugby's Great Split: Class, Culture and the Origins of Rugby League Football* (London: Frank Cass, 1998).

Costa, D.M. and Guthrie, S.R. eds, *Women and Sport: Interdisciplinary Perspectives* (Champaign, IL: Human Kinetics, 1994).

Cox, R., G. Jarvie and W. Vamplew, eds, *Encyclopedia of British Sport* (Oxford: ABC-Clio, 2000).

Cronin, M. *Sport and Nationalism in Ireland: Gaelic Games, Soccer, and Irish Identity since 1884* (Dublin: Four Courts Press, 1999).

Daley, C. *Leisure and Pleasure: Reshaping and Revealing the New Zealand Body 1900–1960* (Auckland: Auckland University Press, 2003).

Darby, P. and Hassan, D. *Emigrants at Play: Sport and the Irish Diaspora* (London: Taylor and Francis, 2008).

Decker, W. and Jean-Paul Thuillier, *Le sport dans l'Antiquité: Égypte, Grèce et Rome* (Paris: Picard, 2004).

Decker, W. *Sports and Games of Ancient Egypt* (New York: Yale University Press, 1992).

Diem, C. *Weltgeschichte des Sports* (Stuttgart: Cotta, 1960).

Dine, P. *French Rugby Football: A Cultural History* (Oxford and New York: Berg, 2001).

Dong, J. *Women, Sport and Society in Modern China: Holding Up More than Half the Sky* (London: Frank Cass, 2003).

Dulles, F. *A History of Recreation: America Learns to Play* (New York: Appleton-Century-Crofts, 1965).

Dunning, E. and Sheard, K. *Barbarians, Gentlemen and Players: A Sociological Study of the Development of Rugby Football* (Oxford: Martin Robertson, 1979 / London: Routledge, 2005).

Dunning, E., P. Murphy and J. Williams, *The Roots of Football Hooliganism: An Historical and Sociological Study* (London: Routledge, 1988).

Dunning, E., Malcolm, D. and Waddington, I. eds, *Sport Histories: Figurational Studies of the Development of Modern Sports* (London: Routledge, 2004).

Dyreson, M. and Trumpbour, R. eds, *The Rise of Modern Stadiums in the United States: Cathedrals of Sport* (London: Routledge, 2009).

Dyreson, M. *Making the American Team: Sport, Culture, and the Olympic Experience* (Urbana: University of Illinois Press, 1998).

——*Crafting Patriotism for Global Domination: America at the Olympics* (London: Routledge, 2008).

Echevarria, R. *The Pride of Havana: A History of Cuban Baseball* (New York: Oxford University Press, 1999).

Edelman, R. *Serious Fun: A History of Spectator Sports in the U.S.S.R.* (New York: Oxford University Press, 1993).

——*Spartak Moscow: The People's Team in the Workers' State* (Ithaca and London: Cornell University Press, 2009).

Edwards, H. *The Revolt of the Black Athlete* (New York: Macmillan, 1969).

Eichberg, H. *Body Cultures: Essays on Sport, Space and Identity* (London: Routledge, 1998).

——*Die Veranderung des Sports ist gesellschaftlich* (Munster: lit, 1986).

——*The People of Democracy: Understanding Self-Determination on the Basis of Body and Movement* (Århus: Klim, 2004).

Elias, N. and Dunning, E. *Quest for Excitement: Sport and Leisure in the Civilizing Process* (Oxford: Blackwell, 1986).

Finley, M.I. and Pleket, H.W. *The Olympic Games: The First Thousand Years* (London: Chatto & Windus, 1976).

Fisher, D. *Lacrosse: A History of the Game* (Baltimore: Johns Hopkins University Press, 2002).

Foer, F. *How Soccer Explains the World: An Unlikely Theory of Globalization* (London: HarperCollins, 2005).

Fox, S. *Big Leagues: Professional Baseball, Football, and Basketball in National Memory* (New York: William Morrow, 1994).

Galeano, E. *El fútbol a sol y sombra* (Madrid: Siglo Veintiuno, 1995).

Gebara, A. and Pilatti, L. eds, *Ensaios sobre História e Sociologia nos Esportes* (Jundiaí: Fontoura, 2006).

Gems, G. *For Pride, Profit, and Patriarchy: Football and the Incorporation of American Cultural Values* (Lanham, MD: Scarecrow Press, 2000).

——*The Athletic Crusade: Sport and American Cultural Imperialism* (Lincoln: University of Nebraska Press, 2006).

Gems, G., Borish, L. and Pfister, G. *Sports in American History: From Colonization to Globalization* (Champaign, IL: Human Kinetics, 2008).

Gerber, E.W. *The American Woman in Sport* (London: Addison-Wesley, 1974).

Gillmeister, H. *Tennis: A Cultural History* (London: Leicester University Press, 1997).

Giulianotti, R. and Robertson, R. eds, *Globalization and Sport* (Oxford: Blackwell, 2007).

Giulianotti, R. ed., *Sport and Modern Social Theorists* (Harlow: Palgrave, 2004).

Golden, M. *Sport and Society in Ancient Greece* (New York: Cambridge University Press, 1998).

Goldstein, W. *Playing for Keeps: A History of Early Baseball* (Ithaca, NY: Cornell University Press, 1989).

Gori, G. ed., *Sport and Gender Matters in Western Countries: Old Borders and New Challenges* (Sankt Augustin: Academia Verlag, 2008).

Gori, G. *Female Bodies, Sport, Italian Fascism: Submissive Women and Strong Mothers* (London: Frank Cass, 2004).

Gorn, E. and Goldstein, W. *A Brief History of American Sports*, 2nd ed. (Urbana: University of Illinois Press, 2004).

Gorn, E. *The Manly Art: Bare-Knuckle Prize Fighting in America* (Ithaca: Cornell University Press, 1986).

Gounot, A., Jallat. D. and Caritey, B. *Les politiques du stade: Etudes comparées des manifestations sportives du XIXe au XXe siècle* (Rennes, Presses universitaires de Rennes, 2007).

Griffin, E. *England's Revelry: A History of Popular Sports and Pastimes 1660–1830* (Oxford: Oxford University Press, 2005).

Grundlingth, A., Odendaal, A. and Spies, B. eds, *Beyond the Tryline: Rugby and South African Society* (Johannesburg: Ravan Press, 1995).

Grundy, P. and Shackelford, S. *Shattering the Glass: The Remarkable History of Women's Basketball* (New York: New Press, 2005).

Grundy, P. *Learning to Win: Sports, Education, and Social Change in Twentieth-Century North Carolina* (Chapel Hill: University of North Carolina Press, 2001).

Gruneau, R. and Whitson, D. *Hockey Night in Canada: Sport, Identities and Cultural Politics* (Toronto: Garamond, 1993).

Gruneau, R. *Class, Sports, and Social Development*, 2d ed. (Champaign, Human Kinetics, 1999).

Guay, D. *La Conquete du Sport: Le sport et la societe quebecoise au XIXe siècle* (Outremont: Lanctot, 1997).

Guha, R. *A Corner of a Foreign Field: The Indian History of a British Sport* (London: Picador, 2002).

Guttmann, A. *From Ritual to Record: The Nature of Modern Sports* (New York: Columbia University Press, 1978).

——*The Games Must Go On: Avery Brundage and the Olympic Movement* (New York, Columbia University Press, 1984).

——*Women's Sports: A History* (New York: Columbia University Press, 1991).

——*The Olympics: A History of the Modern Games* (Urbana and Chicago: University of Illinois Press, 1992).

——*Games and Empires: Modern Sports and Cultural Imperialism* (New York: Columbia University Press, 1994).

——*Sports: The First Five Millennia* (Amherst: University of Massachusetts Press, 2004).

Hall, M. A. *Feminism and Sporting Bodies: Essays on Theory and Practice* (Champaign, IL: Human Kinetics, 1996).

——*The Girl and the Game: A History of Women's Sport in Canada* (Peterborough, ON: Broadview Press, 2002).

Hardy, S. *How Boston Played: Sport, Recreation, and Community, 1865–1915* (Boston: Northeastern University Press, 1982)

Hargreaves, J. ed., *Sport, Culture and Ideology* (Boston: Routledge & Kegan Paul, 1982).

Hargreaves, J. *Sport, Power and Culture: A Social and Historical Analysis of Popular Sports in Britain* (Cambridge: Polity Press, 1986).

——*Sporting Females: Critical Issues in the History and Sociology of Women's Sports* (London: Routledge, 1994).

Harris, H.A. *Greek Athletes and Athletics* (London: Hutchinson, 1964).

Hartmann, D. *Race, Culture, and the Revolt of the Black Athlete: The 1968 Olympic Protests and Their Aftermath* (Chicago: University of Chicago Press, 2003).

Harvey, A. *The Beginnings of a Commercial Sporting Culture in Britain, 1793–1850* (Aldershot: Ashgate, 2004).

Henderson, R. *Ball, Bat, and Bishop: The Origins of Ball Games* (New York: Rockport, 1947).

Heywood, L. and Dworkin, S.L. *Built to Win: The Female Athlete as Cultural Icon* (Minneapolis: University of Minnesota Press, 2003).

Higgs, R. *God in the Stadium: Sports and Religion in America* (Louisville: University Press of Kentucky, 1995).

Hill, J. *Sport and the Literary Imagination: Essays in History, Literature, and Sport* (New York: Peter Lang, 2007)

——*Sport, Leisure and Culture in Twentieth-Century Britain* (Basingstoke: Palgrave, 2002).

Hoberman, J. *Darwin's Athletes: How Sport Has Damaged Black America and Preserved the Myth of Race* (New York: Mariner Books, 1997).

——*Mortal Engines: The Science of Performance and the Dehumanization of Sport* (New York: The Free Press, 1992).

——*Sport and Political Ideology* (Austin: University of Texas Press, 1984).

——*Testosterone Dreams – Rejuvenation, Aphrodisia, Doping* (Berkeley: University of California Press, 2005).

——*The Olympic Crisis: Sport, Politics and the Moral Order* (New Rochelle: NY Aristide D. Caratzas, 1986).

Hollander, M. *Sport in 't stad: Sociaal-historische analyse van de sport in Antwerpen 1830–1914* (Leuven, 2002).

Holt, R. ed., *Sport and the Working Class in Modern Britain* (Manchester: Manchester University Press, 1990).

Holt, R. *Sport and Society in Modern France* (Basingstoke: Palgrave, 1981).

——*Sport and the British: A Modern History* (Oxford: Clarendon Press, 1989).

Hong, F. ed., *Sport, Nationalism and Orientalism: The Asian Games* (London: Routledge, 2007).

Hong, F. *Footbinding, Feminism and Freedom: The Liberation of Women's Bodies in Modern China* (London: Frank Cass, 1997).

Howell, C. *Northern Sandlots: A Social History of Maritime Baseball* (Toronto: Univesity of Toronto Press, 1995)

——*Blood, Sweat, and Cheers: Sport and the Making of Modern Canada* (Toronto: University of Toronto Press, 2001).

Huggins, M. *The Victorians and Sport* (London: Hambledon, 2004).

Huizinga, J. *Homo Ludens: A Study of the Play Element in Culture* (Boston: Beacon, 1950).

Iber, J. and Regalado, S. *Mexican Americans and Sports: A Reader on Athletics and Barrio Life* (College Station: Texas A&M University Press, 2007).

Ingham, A. and Loy, J. eds, *Sport in Social Development: Traditions, Transitions and Transformations* (Champaign, IL: Human Kinetics, 1993).

Jamail, M. *Venezuelan Bust, Baseball Boom: Andrés Reiner and Scouting on the New Frontier* (Lincoln, NE: University of Nebraska Press, 2008).

James, C.L.R. *Beyond a Boundary* (London: Stanley Paul, 1963).

Janson, G. *Emparons-nous du Sport: Les Canadiens francais et le sport au XIX siècle* (Montreal: Guerin, 1995).

Jarvie, G. and Maguire, J. *Sport and Leisure in Social Thought* (London: Routledge, 1994) and Richard Giulianotti, ed., *Sport and Modern Social Theorists* (London: Palgrave, 2004).

Jarvie, G. and Walker, G. eds, *Scottish Sport in the Making of the Nation* (Leicester: Leicester University Press, 1994).

Jarvie, G. *Highland Games: The Making of the Myth* (Edinburgh: Edinburgh University Press, 1991).

Jobert, T. *Champions noirs, racisme blanc: La métropole et les sportifs noirs en contexte colonial (1901–1944)* (Grenoble: PUG, 2006).

Johnes, M. *Soccer and Society: South Wales, 1900–1939* (Cardiff: University of Wales Press, 2002).

——*History of Sport in Wales* (Cardiff: University of Wales Press, 2005).

Jones, S. *Sport, Politics and the Working Class: Organised Labour and Sport in Inter-War Britain* (Manchester: Manchester University Press, 1988).

Kemper, K. *College Football and American Culture in the Cold War Era* (Urbana: University of Illinois Press, 2009).

Keys, B. *Globalizing Sport: National Rivalry and International Community in the 1930s* (Cambridge, MA: Harvard University Press, 2006).

Kidd, K. *The Struggle for Canadian Sport* (Toronto: University of Toronto Press, 1996).

Kimball, R. *Sports in Zion: Mormon Recreation, 1890–1940* (Urbana: University of Illinois Press, 2003).

King, C. Richard, ed., *Native Americans and Sport in North America: Other Peoples' Games* (London: Routledge, 2007).

Kirsch, G. *The Creation of American Team Sports: Baseball and Cricket, 1838–1872* (Urbana: University of Illinois Press, 1979).

Klein, A. *Sugarball: The American Game, the Dominican Dream* (New Haven, CT: Yale University Press, 1991).

Konig, J. *Athletics and Literature in the Roman Empire* (Cambridge: Cambridge University Press, 2005).

Krüger, A. and McClelland, J. eds, *Die Anfänge des modernen Sports in der Renaissance* (London: Arena, 1984).

Krüger, A. and Murray, W. eds, *The Nazi Olympics: Sport, Politics, and Appeasement in the 1930s* (Urbana: University of Illinois Press, 2003).

Krüger, A. and Riordan, J., eds. *The Story of Worker Sport* (Champaign: Human Kinetics, 1996).

Kuper, S. *Football against the Enemy* (London: Phoenix, Orion, 1996).

Kyle, D. *Athletics in Ancient Athens* (Leiden: Brill, 1987).

——*Spectacles of Death in Ancient Rome* (London: Routledge, 1998).

——*Sport and Spectacle in the Ancient World* (London: Blackwell, 2007).

LaFeber, W. *Michael Jordan and the New Global Capitalism* (New York: Norton, 1999).

Lafranchi, P. and Taylor, M. *Moving with the Ball: The Migration of Professional Footballers* (Oxford: Berg, 2001).

Lanctot, N. *Negro League Baseball: The Rise and Ruin of A Black Institution* (Philadelphia: University of Pennsylvania Press, 2004).

Langhamer, C. *Women's Leisure in England 1920–1960* (Manchester University Press: Manchester University Press, 2000).

Lapchick, R. *The Politics of Race and International Sport: The Case of South Africa* (Westport, CT: Greenwood Press, 1975).

Lenskyj, H. *Out of Bounds: Women, Sport and Sexuality* (Toronto: Women's Press, 1986).

Lever, J. *Soccer Madness: Brazil's Passion for the World's Most Popular Sport* (Chicago: University of Chicago Press, 1983).

Levine, L. *From Ellis Island to Ebbets Field: Sport and the American Jewish Experience* (New York: Oxford University Press, 1992).

Levine, P. *A.G. Spalding and the Rise of Baseball: The Promise of American Sport* (New York: Oxford University Press, 1985).

Lomax, M. *Black Baseball Entrepreneurs: Operating by Any Means Necessary, 1860–1901* (Syracuse, NY: Syracuse University Press, 2003).

Lowerson, J. *Sport and the English Middle Classes, 1870–1914* (Manchester: Manchester University Press, 1993).

MacAloon, J. ed., *Muscular Christianity in Colonial and Post-Colonial Worlds* (London: Routledge, 2007).

MacAloon, J. *This Great Symbol: Pierre De Coubertin and the Origins of the Modern Olympic Games* (Chicago, IL: University of Chicago Press, 1981).

Magdalinski, T. and Chandler, T. eds, *With God on their Side: Sport in the Service of Religion* (London: Routledge, 2002).

Majumdar, B. *Twenty-Two Yards to Freedom: A Social History of Indian Cricket* (New Delhi: Penguin, 2004).

Majumdar, B. and Bandyopadhyah, K. *A Social History of Indian Football* (London: Routledge, 2006).

Majumdar, B. and Mangan, J.A. eds, *Sport in South Asian Society: Past and Present* (London and New York: Routledge, 2005).

Malcolmson, R. *Popular Recreations in English Society 1700–1850* (Cambridge: Cambridge University Press, 1973).

Malz, A., Rohdewald, S. and Wiederkehr, S. eds, *Sport zwischen Ost und West* (Osnabrück: Fibre, 2007).

Mandel, J. and Mandel, J. *Caribbean Hoops: The Development of West Indian Basketball* (Langhorne, PA: Gordon and Breach, 1994).

Mandell, R. *Sport: A Cultural History* (New York: Columbia University Press, 1984).

——*The Nazi Olympics* (Urbana: University of Illinois Press, 1987; reprint of 1971 edn).

Mangan, J. A. ed., *Pleasure, Profit, Proselytism: British Culture and Sport at Home and Abroad, 1700–1914* (London: Frank Cass, 1988).

——*The Cultural Bond: Sport, Empire, Society* (London: Frank Cass, 1992).

Mangan, J.A. and Hong, F. ed., *Sport, Nationalism and Orientalism: The Asian Games* (London: Routledge, 2007).

Mangan, J.A. and Nauright, J. eds, *Sport in Australasian Society: Past and Present* (London: Frank Cass, 2000).

Mangan, J.A. and Park, R. eds, *From 'Fair Sex' to Feminism: Sport and the Socialization of Women in Industrial and Post-Industrial Eras* (London: Frank Cass, 1987).

Mangan, J.A. and Vertinsky, P., eds. *Gender, Sport, Science: Selected Writings of Roberta J. Park* (London: Routledge, 2007).

Mangan, J.A. *Athleticism in the Victorian and Edwardian Public School: The Emergence and Consolidation of an Educational Ideology* (Cambridge: Cambridge University Press, 1981)

——*The Games Ethic and Imperialism: Aspects of Diffusion of an Ideal* (Harmondsworth: Viking, 1987).

Markula, P. ed., *Feminist Sport Studies: Sharing Experiences of Joy and Pain* (Albany: State University of New York Press, 2005).

Marqusee, M. *War Minus the Shooting: A Journey through South Asia during Cricket's World Cup* (London: Heineman, 1996).

——*Redemption Song: Muhammad Ali and the Spirit of the Sixties* (New York: Verso, 2000).

Mason, T. (ed.), *Sport in Britain: A Social History* (Cambridge: Cambridge University Press, 1989).

Mason, T. *Association Football and English Society, 1863–1915* (Brighton: Harvester, 1980).

——*Passion of the People? Football in South America* (London: Verso, 1995).

McClelland, J. *Body and Soul: Sport in Europe from the Roman Empire to the Renaissance* (London: Routledge, 2007).

McCrone, K. *Sport and the Physical Emancipation of Women, 1870–1914* (London: Routledge, 1988).

McDevitt, P. *May the Best Man Win: Sport, Masculinity, and Nationalism in Great Britain and the Empire, 1880–1935* (New York: Palgrave Macmillan, 2004).

McIntosh, P. *Sport in Society* (London: C. A Watts, 1963).

McKay, J. et al., eds, *Masculinities, Gender Relations, and Sport* (Thousand Oaks, CA: Sage Publications, 2000).

McKay, J. *No Pain, No Gain? Sport and Australian Culture* (Sydney: Prentice Hall, 1991).

Messner, M.A. *Power at Play: Sports and the Problem of Masculinity* (Boston: Beacon Press, 1992).

Metcalfe, A. *Canada Learns to Play: The Emergence of Organized Sport, 1807–1914* (Toronto: McClelland and Stewart, 1987)

Millar, R. and Crolley, L. eds, *Football in the Americas: Fútbol, Futebol, Soccer* (London: Institute for the Studies of the Americas, 2007).

Miller, P. and Wiggins, D., eds. *Sport and the Color Line: Black Athletes and Race Relations in 20th Century America* (New York: Routledge, 2004).

Miller, S. *Ancient Greek Athletics* (New Haven, CT: Yale University Press, 2004).

Miller, T., Lawrence, G., McKay, J. and Rowe, D. *Globalization and Sport: Playing the World* (London: Sage Publications, 2001).

Morrow, D. and Wamsley, K. *Sport in Canada: A History* (Don Mills, ON: Oxford University Press, 2005).

Mrozek, D. *Sport and American Mentality, 1880–1910* (Knoxville: University of Tennessee Press, 1982).

Murray, W. *The Old Firm: Sectarianism, Sport and Society in Scotland* (Glasgow: John Donald, 1984).

——*The World's Game: A History of Soccer* (Urbana: University of Illinois Press, 1996).

Nandy, A. *The Tao of Cricket: On Games of Destiny and the Destiny of Games* (New York: Oxford University Press, 1989).

Nathan, D. *Saying It's So: A Cultural History of the Black Sox Scandal* (Urbana: University of Illinois Press, 2003).

Nauright, J. and Chandler, T. eds, *Making Men: Rugby and Masculine Identity* (London: Frank Cass, 1996).

Nauright, J. ed., *Sport, Power and Society in New Zealand: Historical and Contemporary Perspectives* (Sydney: Australian Society for Sports History, 1995).

Nauright, J. *Sport, Cultures and Identities in South Africa* (London: Leicester University Press, 1997).

Newby, Z. *Greek Athletics in the Roman World: Victory and Virtue* (Oxford: Oxford University Press, 2005).

Nielsen, N. *Body, Sport and Society in Norden – Essays in Cultural History* (Århus: Århus University Press, 2005).

Novak, M. *The Joy of Sports: End Zones, Bases, Baskets, Balls, and the Consecration of the American Spirit* (New York: Basic Books, 1976).

Oglesby, C.A. ed., *Women and Sport: From Myth to Reality* (Philadelphia: Lea & Febiger, 1978).

Oriard, M. *Reading Football: How the Popular Press Created an American Spectacle* (Chapel Hill: University of North Carolina Press, 1993).

——*King Football: Sport and Spectacle in the Golden Age of Radio and Newsreels, Movies and Magazines, the Weekly & the Daily Press* (Chapel Hill: University of North Carolina Press, 2001).

——*Brand NFL: Making and Selling America's Favorite Sport* (Chapel Hill: University of North Carolina Press, 2007).

Parratt, C. *More than Mere Amusement: Working-class Women's Leisure in England, 1750–1914* (Boston: Northeastern University Press, 2002).

Peterson, R. *Cages to Jump Shots: Pro Basketball's Early Years* (New York: Oxford University Press, 1990).

——*Only the Ball Was White* (New York: Oxford University Press, 1992).

Pfister, G. *Frauensport in der DDR* (Cologne: Strauss, 2002).

Phillips, M. ed., *Deconstructing Sport History: A Postmodern Analysis* (Albany: SUNY Press, 2006).

Poliakoff, M. *Combat Sports in the Ancient World* (New Haven, CT: Yale University Press, 1987).

Polley, M. *Moving the Goalposts: A History of Sport and Society Since 1945* (London: Routledge, 1998).

Pope, S.W. ed., *The New American Sport History: Recent Approaches and Perspectives* (Urbana: University of Illinois Press, 1997)

Pope, S.W. *Patriotic Games: Sporting Traditions in the American Imagination, 1876–1926* (New York: Oxford University Press, 1997; 2nd edn published in 2007 by the University of Tennessee Press).

Pronger, B. *The Arena of Masculinity: Sports, Homosexuality, and the Meaning of Sex* (New York: St Martin's Press, 1990).

Putney, C. *Muscular Christianity: Manhood and Sports in Protestant America, 1880–1920* (Cambridge, MA: Harvard University Press, 2001).

Rader, B. *American Sports: From the Age of Folk Games to the Age of Television* (Englewood Cliffs: Prentice Hall, 1983).

——*Baseball: A History of America's Game* (Urbana: University of Illinois Press, 1992).

Reeves, J. *Taking in a Game: A History of Baseball in Asia* (Lincoln: University of Nebraska Press, 2002).

Regalado, S. *Viva Baseball: Latin Major Leaguers and their Special Hunger* (Urbana: University of Illinois Press, 1998).

Remnick, D. *King of the World: Muhammad Ali and the Rise of an American Hero* (New York: Random House, 1998).

Riess, S. *Touching Base: Professional Baseball and American Culture in the Progressive Era* (Westport, CT: Greenwood Press, 1980).

——*City Games: The Evolution of American Urban Society and the Rise of Sports* (Urbana: University of Illinois Press, 1989).

Riess, S. ed., *Sports and the American Jew* (Syracuse: Syracuse University Press, 1998).

Rigauer, B. *Sport and Work* (New York: Columbia University Press, 1981).

Riordan, J. and Krüger, A. eds, *The International Politics of Sport in the Twentieth Century* (London: E & FN Spon, 1999).

Roberts, R. *Papa Jack: Jack Johnson and the Era of White Hopes* (New York: The Free Press, 1985).

Rosensweig, D. *Retro Ball Parks: Instant History, Baseball, and the New American City* (Knoxville: University of Tennessee Press, 2005).

Ruck, R. *Sandlot Seasons: Sport in Black Pittsburgh* (Urbana: University of Illinois Press, 1987).

Russell, D. *Football and the English: A Social History of Association Football in England, 1863–1995* (Preston: Carnegie Publishing, 1997).

Ryan, G. ed., *Tackling Rugby Myths: Rugby and New Zealand Society 1854–2004* (Dunedin: Otago University Press, 2005).

Sammons, J. *Beyond the Ring: The Role of Boxing in American Society* (Urbana: University of Illinois Press, 1988).

Sansone, D. *Greek Athletics and the Genesis of Sport* (Berkeley: University of California Press, 1988).

Scanlon, T. *Eros and Greek Athletics* (Oxford: Oxford University Press, 2002).

Senn, A. *Power, Politics and the Olympic Games* (Champaign, IL: Human Kinetics, 1999).

Seymour, H. *Baseball,* 3 volumes: I. *The Early Years,* II. *The Golden Age,* III. *The People's Game* (New York, Oxford University Press, 1960–76).

Silk, M. et al., *Sport and Corporate Nationalisms* (Oxford: Berg, 2005).

Simson, V. and Jennings, A. *The Lords of the Rings: Power, Money, and Drugs in the Modern Olympics* (New York: Simon & Schuster, 1992).

Smith, A. and Porter, D. eds, *Amateurs and Professionals in Post-War British Sport* (London: Frank Cass, 2000).

Smith, R. *Sports and Freedom: The Rise of Big-Time College Athletics* (New York: Oxford University Press, 1988).

Somers, D. *The Rise of Sports in New Orleans, 1850–1900* (Baton Rouge: Louisiana State University Press, 1972).

Sperber, M. *Shake Down the Thunder: The Creation of Notre Dame Football* (New York: Henry Holt, 1993).

Springwood, C. *Cooperstown to Dyersville: A Geography of Baseball Nostalgia* (Boulder, CO: Westview Press, 1996) for an ethnographic account of an athletic pilgrimage.

Steendijk-Kuipers, J. *Vrouwen-beweging: Medische en culturele aspecten van vrouwen in de sport, gezien in het kader van de sporthistorie* (1880–1928) (Rotterdam: Erasmus Publishing, 1999).

Stoddart, B. and Sandiford, K. eds, *The Imperial Game: Cricket and Cultural Power* (Manchester: Manchester University Press, 1998).

Stoddart, B. *Saturday Afternoon Fever: Sport in the Australian Culture* (North Ryde, NSW: Angus & Robertson, 1986).

Stokvis, R. *Strijd over sport: Ideologische en maatschappelijke ontwikkelingen* (Deventer: Van Loghum Slaterus, 1979).

Struna, N. *People of Prowess: Sport, Leisure, and Labor in Early Anglo-America* (Urbana: University of Illinois Press, 1996).

Sugden, J. and Bairner, A. *Sport, Sectarianism and Society in a Divided Ireland* (Leicester: Leicester University Press, 1993).

Szymanski, S. and Zimbalist, A. *National Pastime: How Americans Play Baseball and the Rest of the World Plays Soccer* (Washington, DC: Brookings Institution, 2005).

Taylor, M. *The Leaguers: The Making of Professional Football in England, 1900–1939* (Liverpool: Liverpool University Press, 2005).

——*The Association Game: A History of British Football, 1863–2000* (London: Longman, 2007).

Teichler, J. et al., *Das Leistungssportsystem der DDR in den 80er Jahren und im Prozeß der Wende* (Schorndorf: Verlag Karl Hofmann, 1999).

Terret, T. *Histoire des sports* (Paris: L'Harmattan, 1996).

——*Les Jeux interalliés de 1919, sport, guerre et relations internationales* (Paris: L'Harmattan, 2002).

Thuillier, J.P. *Les Jeux athlétique dans la civilization Étrusque* (Rome: École française de Rome, 1985).

Tomlinson, A. and Young, C. eds, *National Identity and Global Sports Events* (Albany: State University of New York Press, 2006).

Trangbæk, E. and Krüger, A. eds, *Gender & Sport from European Perspectives* (Copenhagen: Institute of Exercise and Sport Sciences, 1999).

Tranter, N. *Sport, Economy and Society in Britain 1750–1914* (Cambridge: Cambridge University Press, 1998).

Tygiel, J. *Baseball's Great Experiment: Jackie Robinson and His Legacy* (New York: Oxford University Press, 1983 and 25th anniversary edn, 2008).

Ueberhorst, H. *Vergangen, nicht vergessen: Sportkultur im deutschen Osten und im Sudetenland* (Düsseldorf: Droste, 1992).

Vamplew, W. and Stoddart, B. eds, *Sport in Australia: A Social History* (Melbourne: Cambridge University Press, 1994).

Vamplew, W. *Pay Up and Play the Game: Professional Sport in Britain, 1875–1914* (Cambridge: Cambridge University Press, 1988).

Van Bottenburg, M. *Global Games* (Urbana: University of Illinois Press, 2001).

Vertinsky, P. and Bale, J. eds, *Sites of Sport: Space, Place and Experience* (London: Routledge, 2004).

Vertinsky, P. and McKay, S., eds. *Disciplining Bodies in the Gymnasium: Memory, Monument, Modernism* (London: Routledge, 2004).

Vertinsky, P. *The Eternally Wounded Woman: Women, Doctors, and Exercise in the Late Nineteenth Century* (Urbana: University of Illinois Press, 1994).

Vincent, T. *The Rise and Fall of American Sport: Mudville's Revenge* (New York: Seaview Books, 1981).

Voigt, D. *American Baseball*, 3 volumes: I. *From Gentleman's Sport to the Commissioner System*, II. *From the Commissioners to Continental Expansion*, III. *From Postwar Expansion to the Electronic Age* (University Park: Penn State University Press, 1983).

Wagg, S. and Andrews, D., eds. *East Plays West: Sport and the Cold War* (London: Routledge, 2007).

Wagg, S. ed., *Cricket and National Identity in the Postcolonial Age: Following On* (London and New York: Routledge, 2005).

Waic, M. ed., *Češi a Němci ve světě tělovchovy a sportu: Die Deutschen und Tschechen in der Welt des Turnens und des Sports* (Prague: Karolinum, 2004).

Wakefield, W. *Playing to Win: Sports and the American Military, 1898–1945* (Albany: State University of New York Press, 1997).

Walvin, J. *The.People's Game: A Social History of British Football* (London: Allen Lane, 1975).

Wassong, S. *Pierre de Coubertins US-amerikanische Studien und ihre Bedeutung für die Analyse seiner frühen Erziehungskampagne* (Würzburg: Ergon, 2002).

Wells, C.W., et al, *Women, Sport and Performance* (Champaign, IL: Human Kinetics Publishers, 1985).

Wheaton, B. ed., *Understanding Lifestyle Sports: Consumption, Identity and Difference* (London: Routledge, 2004).

White, H. *Metahistory: The Historical Imagination in Nineteenth-Century Europe* (Baltimore, MD: The Johns Hopkins University Press, 1973).

White, P. and Young, K. eds, *Sport and Gender in Canada* (Oxford: Oxford University Press, 1999).

Whitson, D. and Gruneau, R. eds, *Artificial Ice: Hockey, Culture, and Commerce* (Toronto: Garamond, 2006).

Wiggins, D. and Miller, P. *The Unlevel Playing Field: A Documentary History of the African American Experience in Sport* (Urbana: University of Illinois Press 2004).

Wiggins, D. ed., *Out of the Shadows: A Biographical History of African American Athletes* (Fayetteville: University of Arkansas Press, 2006).

Wiggins, D. *Glory Bound: Black Athletes in a White World* (Syracuse: Syracuse University Press, 1997).

Williams, J. *Cricket and Race* (Oxford: Berg, 2001).

——A Game for Rough Girls?: A History of Women's Football in Britain (London: Routledge, 2002).

WuShanley, Y. *Playing Nice and Losing: The Struggle for Control of Women's Intercollegiate Athletics, 1960–2000* (Syracuse, NY: Syracuse University Press, 2004).

Xu, G. *Olympic Deams: China and Sports, 1895–2008* (Cambridge, MA: Harvard University Press, 2008).

Young, D. *The Olympic Myth of Greek Amateur Athletics* (Chicago, IL: Ares, 1984).

Zang, D. *SportsWars: Sport in the Age of Aquarius* (Fayetteville: The University of Arkansas Press, 2001).

Zeiler, T. *Ambassadors in Pinstripes: The Spalding World Baseball Tour and the Birth of the American Empire* (Lanham: Rowman & Littlefield, 2006).

Index